A HISTORY OF THE CRUSADES

Kenneth M. Setton, GENERAL EDITOR

A HISTORY OF THE CRUSADES

Kenneth M. Setton, GENERAL EDITOR

Volume VI

THE IMPACT OF THE CRUSADES ON EUROPE

Mehmed II, "the Conqueror." Portrait by Gentile Bellini. National Gallery, London

A HISTORY OF

THE

CRUSADES

KENNETH M. SETTON

GENERAL EDITOR

Volume VI

THE IMPACT OF THE CRUSADES ON EUROPE

EDITED BY

HARRY W. HAZARD

AND

NORMAN P. ZACOUR

THE UNIVERSITY OF WISCONSIN PRESS

Published 1989

The University of Wisconsin Press
114 North Murray Street
Madison, Wisconsin 53715

3 Henrietta Street
London WC2E 8LU, England

First printing

Printed in the United States of America

For LC CIP information see the colophon

ISBN 0-299-10740-X

Justissimum bellum

CONTENTS

xi

MAPS

*Maps compiled by Harry W. Hazard and executed by the
Cartographic Laboratory of the University of Wisconsin, Madison*

FOREWORD

As I observed in the Foreword to the preceding volume, it has been a long, hard journey. There were times when I wondered whether we should ever reach the end but now, after many years, we have finally done so. From time to time we have had to institute changes in our initial plans. At least some of these changes have been for the better. In some cases, to be sure, we have been forced to yield to practicality or to one circumstance or another. Also we have unfortunately lost along the way several of our contributors and two of our fellow editors, Marshall W. Baldwin and Robert Lee Wolff, who labored with a steadfast devotion to the first and second volumes of this *History of the Crusades*. I am saddened by the thought that they will not hold this last volume in their hands. It is a pleasure, however, to express my indebtedness to Dr. Harry W. Hazard and to Professor Norman P. Zacour, who have made possible the appearance of these volumes. With the courage and determination of a true crusader Dr. Hazard has borne a heavy load. Furthermore, we are most grateful to Mary Hazard for her valiant help. I am glad at last to be able to express in print my thanks to Professor Hans Eberhard Mayer, who, despite his numerous responsibilities, agreed *amicitiae gratia* to prepare a bibliography for all six volumes. We are pleased to welcome into our midst one of the outstanding crusading historians of our time.

We are grateful to Dr. Susan Babbitt, who is now with the American Philosophical Society in Philadelphia, for her help with this volume as well as with Volume V. I am also pleased at long last to acknowledge our indebtedness to Mrs. Elizabeth A. Steinberg, assistant director of the University of Wisconsin Press, whose conscientious attention to detail has been of endless assistance to us. It is now more than thirty years ago (in 1955) that I sketched in the Foreword to Volume I what I might call the historical background to this work. There I dwelt upon the interest taken in it and the impetus given to it by Dana C. Munro, August C. Krey, Frederick Duncalf, and John L. LaMonte before any plans had really been made or a single word had been written. Without the enthusiasm of these scholars, however, all of whom left us many years ago, this work would never have come into being. Therefore my fellow editors and I want once more to recall them to our readers and again to render thanks to all four of them.

KENNETH M. SETTON

The Institute for Advanced Study
Princeton, New Jersey
March 21, 1988

It is now some days ago that the sad news came of the death of Dr. Harry W. Hazard. He left us on 5 February (1989). My comrade-in-arms for almost forty years, as we wended our way through the long history of the Crusades, he will be sorely missed. His death led me to reread the Foreword to the first edition of Volume I of this *History of the Crusades* (1955) outlining the part played so many years ago by Munro, LaMonte, Duncalf, and Krey in planning a work that was initially to be in three volumes but, as time went on, became four, then five, and finally six. As one after another the volumes have appeared, they seem to bear almost no relation to the original planning. Year after year changes had to be made. We would have second thoughts. Contributors died, withdrew from the project, or failed to write their chapters. "Hap" Hazard was more patient than I as the almost endless changes had to be made.

Despite months of illness, Hap Hazard spent much time on this last volume, but it would not have been finished within the current year except for the assistance of his wife, Mary Hazard. She has retyped the Bibliography and the Gazetteer, added all the page references to the index cards from which the printers set the type, and shared with us the proofreading of the entire volume. But now I fear we must agree with our old friend Shakespeare that "Hector is dead: there is no more to say!"

K. M. S.

Princeton
February 12, 1989

PREFACE

This is the last volume of *A History of the Crusades*. It marks an end neither to the conflict with Islam nor to the very idea of crusade as a mass movement divinely sanctioned. The crusading impulse remained a vital force in the West whether directed towards a holy war to win Jerusalem or, later, a defensive struggle against Turkish aggression. Bede had long since taught the West about Ishmael, the father of Islam, whose hand was raised against all men, and against whom the hands of all men were raised in turn. Islam, then, remained an enemy with whom peace was unthinkable, war a duty. The duty would be all the more pressing in coming centuries when, as the Turkish threat grew, the very future of Christian Europe seemed to hang in the balance. Like so much else in medieval Europe, the crusade demanded both legal definition and theological justification, to say nothing of financial and military organization, constant preaching, and propaganda. Three centuries of crusading fervor accompanied by incredible hardships, massive sacrifices, legends of heroism, and propaganda of hatred, left for the future a heritage of profound consequence impossible to measure.

How sad that our colleague, Harry Hazard, was not allowed to hold this finished volume in his hands. But he was determined to see it through its final preparation. Hardly a page has not felt his touch. He was one of many who inspired the entire *History* and for whom in turn it has become something of a monument. It was with some prescience that, just before his death, he recalled the comments of Bil Gilbert: "By caring about and being moved by the persons and deeds of our ancestors, we give assurance—and are assured—of a sort of immortality."[1]

Norman P. Zacour

Centre for Medieval Studies
University of Toronto
Toronto, Canada
August 15, 1989

1. *Sports Illustrated*, XLIV (June 21, 1976), 76.

A NOTE
ON TRANSLITERATION
AND NOMENCLATURE

One of the obvious problems to be solved by the editors of such a work as this, intended both for general readers and for scholars in many different disciplines, is how to render the names of persons and places, and a few other terms, originating in languages and scripts unfamiliar to the English-speaking reader and, indeed, to most readers whose native languages are European. In the present volume, as in most of the entire work, these comprise principally Arabic, Turkish, Persian, and Armenian, none of which was normally written in our Latin alphabet until its adoption by Turkey in 1928. The analogous problem of Byzantine Greek names and terms has been handled by using the familiar Latin equivalents, Anglicized Greek, or occasionally, Greek type, as has seemed appropriate in each instance, but a broader approach is desirable for the other languages under consideration.

The somewhat contradictory criteria applied are ease of recognition and readability on the one hand and scientific accuracy and consistency on the other. It has proved possible to reconcile these, and to standardize the great variety of forms in which identical names have been submitted to us by different contributors, through constant consultation with specialists in each language, research in the sources, and adherence to systems conforming to the requirements of each language.

Of these, Arabic presents the fewest difficulties, since the script in which it is written is admirably suited to the classical language. The basic system used, with minor variants, by all English-speaking scholars was restudied and found entirely satisfactory, with the slight modifications noted. The chief alternative system, in which every Arabic consonant is represented by a single Latin character (ṯ for th, ḫ for kh, ḏ for dh, š for sh, ġ for gh) was rejected for several reasons, needless proliferation of diacritical marks to bother the eye and multiply occasions for error, absence of strong countervailing arguments, and, most decisively, the natural tendency of non-specialists to adopt these spellings but omit the diacritical marks. The use of single letters in this manner leads to undesirable results, but the spellings adopted for the present work may be thus treated with confidence by any writer not requiring the discriminations which the remaining diacritical marks indicate.

The letters used for Arabic consonants, in the order of the Arabic alphabet, are these; ', b, t, th, j, ḥ, kh, d, dh, r, z, s, sh, ṣ, ḍ, ṭ, ẓ, ', gh, f, q, k, l, m, n, h, w, y. The vowels are a, i, u, lengthened as ā, ī, ū, with the *alif bi-ṣurati-l-yā'* distinguished as â; initial ' is omitted, but terminal macrons are retained. Diphthongs are *au* and *ai,* not *aw* and *ay,* as being both philologically preferable and visually less misleading. The same considerations lead to the omission of *l* of *al-* before a duplicated consonant (Nūr-ad-Dīn rather than Nūr-al-Dīn). As in this example, hyphens are used to link words composing a single name (as also 'Abd-Allāh), with weak initial vowels elided (as Abū-l-Ḥasan). Normally *al-* (meaning "the") is not capitalized; *ibn-* is not when it means literally "son of," but is otherwise (as Ibn-Khaldūn).

Some readers may be disconcerted to find the prophet called "Mohammed" and his followers "Moslems," but this can readily be justified. These spellings are valid English proper names, derived from Arabic originals which would be correctly transliterated "Muḥammad" and "Muslimūn" or "Muslimīn." The best criterion for deciding whether to use the Anglicized spellings or the accurate transliterations is the treatment accorded the third of this cluster of names, that of the religion "Islam." Where this is transliterated "Islām," with a macron over the *a,* it should be accompanied by "Muslim" and "Muḥammad," but where the macron is omitted, consistency and common sense require "Moslem" and "Mohammed," and it is the latter triad which have been considered appropriate in this work. All namesakes of the prophet, however, have had their names duly transliterated "Muḥammad," to correspond with names of other Arabs who are not individually so familiar to westerners as to be better recognized in Anglicized forms.

All names of other Arabs, and of non-Arabs with Arabic names, have been systematically transliterated, with the single exception of Ṣalāḥ-ad-Dīn, whom it would have been pedantic to call that rather than Saladin. For places held, in the crusading era or now, by Arabs, the Arabic names appear either in the text or in the gazetteer, where some additional ones are also included to broaden the usefulness of this feature.

Large numbers of names of persons and groups, however, customarily found in Arabicized spellings because they were written in Arabic script, have been restored to their underlying identity whenever this is ascertainable. For example, Arabic "Saljūq" misrepresents four of the six component phonemes: *s* is correct, *a* replaces Turkish *e,* for which Arabic script provides no equivalent, *l* is correct, *j* replaces the non-Arabic *ch,* *ū* substitutes a non-Turkish long *u* for the original *ü,* and *q* as distinguished from *k* is non-existent in Turkish; this quadruple rectification yields "Selchük" as the name of the eponymous leader, and "Selchükid" — on the model of 'Abbāsid and Timurid — for the dynasty and the people.

It might be thought that as Turkish is now written in a well-conceived modified Latin alphabet, there would be no reason to alter this, and this presumption is substantially valid. For the same reasons as apply to Arabic, *ch* has been preferred above *ç,* *sh* above *ş,* and *gh* above *ğ,* with *kh* in a few instances given as a preferred alternate of *h,* from which it is not distinguished in modern Turkish. No long vowels have been indicated, as being functionless survivals. Two other changes have been made in the interest of the English-speaking reader, and should be remembered by those using map sheets and standard reference works: *c* (pronounced dj) has been changed to *j,* so that one is not visually led to imagine that the Turkish name for Tigris — Dijle/Dicle — rhymes with "tickle," and what the eminent lexicographer H. C. Hony terms "that abomination the undotted ı" has, after the model of *The Encyclopaedia of Islām,* been written î.

Spellings, modified as above indicated, have usually been founded on those of the Turkish edition, *İslâm Ansiklopedisi,* hampered by occasional inconsistencies within that work. All names of Turks appear thus emended, the Turkish equivalents of almost all places within or near modern Turkey appear in the gazetteer.

In addition to *kh,* Middle Turkish utilized a few other phonemes not common in modern Turkish: *zh* (modern *j*) *dh, ng,* and *ä* (modern *e*); the first three of these will be used as needed, while the last-mentioned may be assumed to underlie every medieval Turkish name now spelled with *e.* Plaintive eyebrows may be raised at our exclusion of *q,* but this was in Middle Turkish only the alternate spelling used when the sound *k* was combined with back instead of front vowels, and its elimination by the Turks is commendable.

Persian names have been transliterated like Arabic with certain modifications, chiefly use of the additional vowels *e* and *o* and replacing *ḍ* and *dh* with *ẓ* and *ẕ,* so that Arabic "Ādharbaijān" becomes Persian "Āẕerbaijān," more accurate as well as more recognizable. Omission of the definite article from personal names was considered but eventually disapproved.

Armenian presented great difficulties: the absence of an authoritative reference source for spelling names, the lack of agreement on transliteration, and the sound-shift by which classical and eastern Armenian *b, d, g* became western Armenian *p, t, k* and — incredible as it may seem to the unwary — *vice versa;* similar reciprocal interchanges involved *ts* and *dz,* and *ch* and *j.* The following alphabet represents western Armenian letters, with eastern variants in parentheses: a, p (b), k (g), t (d), e, z, ē, i̇, ṭ, zh, i, l, kh, dz (ts), g (k), h, ts (dz), gh, j (ch), m, y, n, sh, o, c̲h̲, b (p), ch (j), r̲, s, v̲, d (t), r, t̲s̲, u or v, ṗ, ḳ, ō, f. Many spellings are based on the Armenian texts in the *Recueil des historiens des croisades.*

In standardizing names of groups, the correct root forms in the respective languages have been identified, with the ending "-id" for dynasties and their peoples but "-ite" for sects, and with plural either identical with singular (as Kirghiz) or plus "-s" (Khazars) or "-es" (Uzes). In cases where this sounded hopelessly awkward, it was abandoned (Muwaḥḥids, not Muwaḥḥidids or Muwaḥḥidites, and certainly not Almohads, which is, however, cross-referenced).

The use of place names is explained in the note preceding the gazetteer, but may be summarized by saying that in general the most familiar correct form is used in the text and maps, normally an English version of the name by which the place was known to Europeans during the crusades. Variant forms are given and identified in the gazetteer.

HARRY W. HAZARD

[Princeton, New Jersey, 1962]

Reprinted from Volume I, with minor modifications.

ABBREVIATIONS

AFP   Archivum fratrum praedicatorum (Istituto storico Santa Sabina; Rome, 1930–).

ANS, NNM   American Numismatic Society, Numismatic Notes and Monographs (New York, 1920–).

AOL   Archives de l'Orient latin (Société de l'Orient latin; 2 vols., Paris, 1881–1884; repr. Brussels, 1964).

AR, *BSH*   Académie roumaine, *Bulletin de la section historique.*

BAR International Series   British Archaeological Reports International Series (Oxford, 1974–).

BOF   Biblioteca bio-bibliographica della Terra Santa e dell' Oriente francescano, ed. Girolamo Golubovich *et al.* (9 vols., Quaracchi, 1906–1927).

CSHB   Corpus scriptorum historiae byzantinae, ed. Barthold G. Niebuhr, Immanuel Bekker, *et al.* (50 vols., Bonn, 1828–1897).

CURC   Columbia University Records of Civilization: Sources and Studies (New York, 1915–).

EETS, ES   Early English Text Society, Extra Series (126 vols., London, 1867–1935).

IFD, BO   Institut français de Damas, Bibliothèque orientale.

Mansi, *Concilia   Sacrorum conciliorum . . . collectio,* ed. Giovanni Mansi, rev. ed. by Jean P. Martin and Louis Petit (53 vols., Paris, Arnhem, and Leipzig, 1901–1927; repr. Paris, 1960–1962).

MGH   Monumenta Germaniae historica . . . :

Epistolae saeculi XIII   Epistolae saeculi XIII e regestis pontificum romanorum selectae, ed. Georg H. Pertz and Carl Rodenberg (3 vols., Berlin, 1883–1894).

Epistolae selectae   Epistolae selectae . . . , ed. Michael Tangl, Erich Caspar, *et al.* (5 vols., Berlin, 1916–1952; repr.).

Legum   Leges, sect. IV: *Constitutiones et acta publica imperatorum et regum,* ed. Ludwig Weiland (8 vols., Hanover, 1896–).

Mer.   Leges, sect. V: *Formulae merovingici et karoli aevi,* 2 pts., 1882–1886).

SS   Scriptores, ed. Georg H. Pertz, Theodor Mommsen, *et al.* (Reichsinstitut für ältere deutsche Geschichtskunde; 32 vols., Hanover and elsewhere, 1826–1934).

Numis. Chr.   Numismatic Chronicle (Royal Numismatic Society, British Museum, London, 1839–).

PAN   Polska Akademia Nauk (Warsaw).

PC, Fontes   Pontificia commissio ad redigendum codicem iuris canonici orientalis: Fontes (Vatican City, 1944–).

PG   Patrologiae cursus completus: Series graeco-latina, ed. Jacques P. Migne (161 vols. in 166, Paris, 1857–1866).

PL   *Patrologiae cursus completus: Series latina,* ed. Jacques P. Migne (221 vols., Paris, 1844–1864).

PPTS   *Palestine Pilgrims' Text Society* (13 vols. and index, London, 1890–1897).

P.R.O.   Public Record Office (London).

RHC   *Recueil des historiens des croisades* (Académie des inscriptions et belles-lettres; Paris, 16 vols. in fol., 1841–1906).

    Arm.   *Documents arméniens* (2 vols., 1869–1906).

    Lois   *Les Assises de Jérusalem* (2 vols., 1841–1843).

    Occ.   *Historiens occidentaux* (5 vols., 1841–1895).

    Or.   *Historiens orientaux: Arabes* (5 vols., 1872–1906).

Rev. numis.   *Revue numismatique* (Paris, 1836–   ).

RHDFE   *Revue historique de droit français et étranger* (Paris, 1855–   ).

RHGF   *Recueil des historiens des Gaules et de la France,* ed. Martin Bouquet *et al.;* rev. ed. (24 vols. in fol., Paris, 1840–1904).

RISS   *Rerum italicarum scriptores . . . ,* ed. Lodovico A. Muratori (25 vols. in 28, Milan, 1723–1751); new ed. by Giosuè Carducci and Vittorio Fiorini (34 vols. in 109 fasc., Città di Castello and Bologna, 1900–1935).

ROL   *Revue de l'Orient latin* (Société de l'Orient latin; 12 vols., Paris, 1893–1911; repr. Brussels, 1964).

Rolls Series   *Rerum brittanicarum medii aevi scriptores: The Chronicles and Memorials of Great Britain and Ireland during the Middle Ages* (251 vols., London, 1858–1896).

SOL, *SH*   Société de l'Orient latin, *Série historique* (5 vols., Geneva, 1877–1887).

TKS   Topkapi Sarayi, Istanbul (archives).

ZDMG   *Zeitschrift der Deutschen Morgenländischen Gesellschaft* (Leipzig and elsewhere, 1846–   ).

Volume VI

THE IMPACT OF THE CRUSADES ON EUROPE

I

THE LEGAL AND
POLITICAL THEORY
OF THE CRUSADE

The basic legal theory of the crusade is the moral theology of the just war. The crusade was the perfect example of the just war, *justissimum bellum,* and the idea of a just war was inevitably developed and refined in the course of the crusading period. Before the crusades the just war was best defined by its opposite, though a number of the fundamental concepts already existed in church decretals. At all times, the notion was closely bound up with that of martyrdom and of Christian ascesis. On many points the Christian system as a whole approximated to the Moslem teaching on *jihād*. The only explicit war aim was the "recovery" of the holy places and of Christian land.

The status of a man who is fighting against "the enemies of God" is the crux of crusading law. If, even when he is killed, he is not a martyr, he must be engaged simply in a good work, and the crusade became the highest and most efficacious of good works, and so of penances. Penance has always been important in canon law, and under the pressure of the crusade the related theology of indulgences developed even faster than the theory of the just war.

A. Origins of the Concept of "Holy War"

The idea of holy war in the west takes shape early with the conversion of the Arian Franks, and Merovingian history, at least as Gregory of Tours relates it, reflects the idea that Catholic faith is rewarded by military and political victory. The definition of martyrdom, inherited from the age before Constantine, was much more precise. True martyrdom, like baptism, wipes out sin. The martyr knows no pains, no purgatory, needs no penance, but his act must be nothing more than a refusal to deny the Christian faith. He must not seek death or incur it rashly. For much of the crusading period the situation of the individual crusader was more exactly defined than the crusade itself.[1]

When the Arabs began to colonize the Spanish and Italian mainlands and Sicily, they were not thought of as unique, and the war against them was not "signed with the cross" more than war against any other invader. In this situation, however, pope Leo IV (847–855) asserted that Christians who die for the truth of their faith, the safety of their country, and the defense of Christians are sure of a heavenly reward.[2] This, of course, means no more than is self-evident in Christian terms, that death incurred in the course of these good and praiseworthy acts is particularly meritorious. "The repose of eternal life shall embrace those who fall in the conflict of war, from duty to the Catholic religion and struggling vigorously against pagans and infidels," wrote pope John VIII in 879, at a time of continual wars against the Arab colonizers of Italy.[3] Death for the "Christian faith and commonwealth", then, was a penance, and in pronouncing absolution, John made it conditional on penitence, foreshadowing theological development in a later period. He did so also in his many diatribes and exhortations against alliances of Christians with Moslems, requiring, for example, that prince Waiferius of Salerno "withdraw everyone from the fellowship of the pagans". He exhorted bishops Ayo of Benevento and Landulph of Capua to secure the dissolution of these ungodly alliances (*foedera impia*) or unnatural alliance (*infandum*). The Neapolitan duke Sergius II, warned to withdraw from an alliance, was threatened with attack by the temporal defenders of the church, but was promised, if he obeyed, both papal favors and "great heavenly rewards".[4] Thus an influential man, merely for not helping the Moslems, was offered almost as much as those who might be killed. Archbishop Athanasius of Naples was finally excommunicated for his treaty arrangements with Moslems (881), in rather more sober language.[5] John's aim is clear—the elimination of Moslem invaders from Italy. The justification is stated in another of his letters, more emotional in tone: he denounced the Mos-

---

1. Bruno Krusch and Wilhelm Levison, eds., *Gregorii episcopi Turonensis libri historiarum X* (*MGH, Mer.*, I, i; Hanover, 1951), e.g., II, 37 (pp. 85–88), and III, preface (pp. 96–97).
    2. *PL,* 115, col. 657 (ep. 1, *ad exercitum Francorum*).
    3. *PL,* 126, col. 816 (ep. 186, *ad episcopos in regno Ludovici constitutos*).
    4. *Ibid.,* cols. 708, 717–718, 723, 726 (ep. 55, *ad Guaiferium*; 63, *ad Landulphum*; 70, *ad Sergium*; 72, *ad Ajonem*).
    5. *Ibid.,* cols. 930–931 (ep. 321, *ad diversos episcopos*).

lems as "the sons of fornication" (though this may represent one of the usual propaganda criticisms of Islamic sexual moral law), together with those who, "under the name of Christians", kill "the sheep of the Lord", some by the sword, some by famine, while carrying others off as booty into captivity.[6] John did little more than support a policy of expelling the invaders with the strongest religious reasons he could think of. The alternative fates that he referred to, death and captivity (devastation was a by-product), reflect some part of the Islamic law of *jihād,* as applied to conquered Christians. He did not mention that the Christians were also offered conversion to Islam, though this, of course, can be assumed to have happened. Whether only those who refused conversion were enslaved we do not know; the slave-labor market seems to have flourished.

This period was formative of later law but produced nothing clear or unambiguous. The same is true of the years immediately preceding Urban II's 1095 initiative, when the reconquest of Sicily was already complete and the war in Spain reasonably successful; a tradition had grown up which gave ecclesiastical encouragement to any effort to recover European territory. Churches in Spain and Sicily were already described as "recovered" or "restored".[7] Europe was the last region to have come (in part) under Arab domination, and it was taken for granted that it should be recovered first, until the idea of the crusade supervened.[8] In Sicily and Spain the Christians fought campaigns blessed by the church, but not dominated by religious purpose. Harald Hardråde, count Roger of Hauteville, and Rodrigo Díaz of Vivar were probably all believing Christians in their different ways, but none was a crusader. Europe approached the proclamation of the First Crusade with some idea of holy war but also with a papal diplomatic tradition which would be suspended by, but would survive, the crusades. Even when the idea of a Levantine crusade was in the air, Gregory VII expected to have a working relationship with the Ḥammādid an-Nāṣir (1062–1088), to whom he wrote about the surviving local Latin hierarchy in North Africa, wishing him honor in this world and life in the next, in the bosom of Abraham. This was a wish which, though it may have been inspired by an acquaintance with Jewish belief, was equally appropriate for Moslems. He urged the Christian population to

---

6. *Ibid.,* col. 721 (ep. 67, *ad Wigbodum*); col. 716 (ep. 62, *ad episcopos in regno Caroli imp. constitutos*).

7. Erich Caspar, ed., *Das Register Gregors VII.* (*MGH, Epistolae selectae,* II; Berlin, 1920–1923), IV, 28 (pp. 343–347); and see note 12 below.

8. Denys Hay, *Europe, the Emergence of an Idea,* 2nd ed. (Edinburgh, 1968).

accept trials with patience and to set a good example to non-Christians around them.[9]

Urban II introduced a clearer legal and political situation. Whatever the confusion about Urban's exact words, all writers (some of whom were themselves among the new "crucesignati") recognized that the crusade proper was a new initiative. The initiative in crusading always remained with the papacy. Whenever initiative appeared elsewhere (as later it would do in the case of Frederick II), the papacy fought to regain it. The political theory therefore began as, and remained, a characteristically clerical concept of Christendom, and the theory common to all accounts of Urban's preaching is that of a defensive war by the Christian commonwealth. This is part of the history of propaganda, but it has major political and legal implications. From this date forward, the crusade was justified by long accounts of Arab aggression against Asia, Africa, and Europe in turn; the European reaction was now literally oriented to the "recovery" of the Holy Land. This was clerical lore. The wars of the Old Testament were thought to give further legal justification, in addition to their propaganda value. Politically, all crusades would continue to be regarded as defensive; legally, they were justified first as undertaken in defense of Christendom. The papacy purported to act on behalf of the Christian commonwealth.

The political concept amounted roughly to what would now be called "cultural imperialism". It is not only that Urban was believed to have appealed to a national sense, and especially to the French.[10] As soon as the "pilgrims" left the Latin world, and long before they met a Moslem, they came into conflict with cultures different from their own, and an inflexible "Latin" cultural intolerance remained with most of them throughout the crusading period.[11] Rejection of all but the Latin culture — and in Spain even the Latin, though not Roman, Mozarab rite was largely replaced — ensured that the crusade would never look like more than an alien colonization to Arab Christians as well as to Moslems. From the beginning, it was implicit in Urban's decision to preach the crusade at all, in his choice of Clermont, and in the way he was understood in the west, that the crusade in the east should be an expansion of western European society.

The key to both legal and political theory was the idea of "recovery". Guibert of Nogent says that Urban expected God, through the

9. Caspar, *Das Register Gregors VII.*, III, 20 (pp. 286–287), 21 (pp. 287–288); cf. I, 22 (pp. 36–39), and IV, 28 (pp. 343–347).

10. Robert of Rheims, *Historia Hierosolymitana*, I, 1–2 (*RHC, Occ.*, III, 728–730).

11. See Henry L. Savage, "Pilgrimages and Pilgrim Shrines in Palestine and Syria after 1095," in volume IV of the present work, pp. 60–68.

crusades, to "restore *lost* Jerusalem". In Robert of Rheims' account Urban called on the Franks to "repel aggression". In the Latin liturgy for the *recovery* of the Holy Sepulcher, as reported by John of Würzburg, the *Secreta* refers to "the city of Jerusalem, plucked out of the hand of the pagans".[12] It is necessary to labor this point in order to understand that from the beginning the notion that the Holy Land belonged of right to Christians underlay the legal concept of holy war. Palestine, which had been Arab for centuries, was conceived of as being as much Christian as were Spain and Sicily. The political fact that Spain, even more than Sicily, had a strong Latinate population on which to build effective reconquest had no reflection in political theory. That cultural (and ethnographic) realities meant nothing is admirably illustrated in a Genoese account of the capture of Caesarea during the First Crusade. According to this, two Arabs came out of the besieged city and argued with the legate and the patriarch, asking why the Christians want to kill people who are made in the form of the Christian God, and take the Arabs' land, when this is contrary to the Christian religion (or "law" — *lex*). The patriarch answered that the city belonged to St. Peter, not to the Arabs who lived in it and whose ancestors ejected St. Peter; furthermore, whoever strives against the law of God ought to be killed; to kill him is not contrary to the law of God, who said "Vengeance is mine." Therefore, if the Arabs will give up the land of St. Peter, they may safely depart with their goods, but if they refuse, "the Lord will strike you with his sword and you will be justly slain."[13] This "right" of killing in the crusade was important, and in due course would be elaborated scholastically.

It brings us back directly to the problem of the just war, at this date only a compendious phrase to cover a group of associated concepts: "defensive" war, war "for God" or against the "enemies of God", a "good" war as distinct from ordinary bad wars, war as penance, and war as a form of Christian ascetic life and a means of salvation particularly suited to anyone capable of fighting. The Latin for the crusade is, after all, "bellum sacrum". At this early stage the idea of the crusade as directing bad instincts to good ends was important. Fulcher's classic account describes the public crimes which the bishops and other authorities had failed to repress, such as the capturing and

12. Guibert of Nogent, *Gesta dei per Francos*, II, 4 (*RHC, Occ.,* IV, 137–140); Robert of Rheims, *Historia,* I, 1 (*RHC, Occ.,* III, 728); John of Würzburg, *Descriptio Terrae Sanctae*, cap. 13 (*PL,* 155, col. 1089). Emphasis added.

13. Caffaro di Caschifellone, *Cafari Genuensis de liberatione civitatum orientis,* XV (*RHC, Occ.,* V, 62–63); Romans 12:19; Deut. 32:35. The legate Adhémar was already dead, and no patriarch had yet been elected.

plundering of monks and clerics and nuns and their servants, and of pilgrims and merchants; his account condemns kidnappers, burners of houses, and all who consent to their crimes, but claims that private wars and lawlessness will be brought to an end by unity in fighting the Turkish and Arab invaders of the east: "May those who used to fight against their brothers and their families now justly (*rite*) war against the barbarians." In practice this would not end savagery, but as well turn it against the external enemy. "Let hatreds cease among you" meant "hate the enemy"; the theme was prominent in what came to be accepted as Urban's argument, as tendered, for example, by William of Malmesbury and, in due course, by William of Tyre, and the best clerical tradition in the crusading state.[14] In Monte Cassino the monks held that Urban enabled the lords to do penance by crusading, without having to admit publicly that they were doing so. The idea of the crusade as a penance naturally follows from its being a good work, literally a pilgrimage. We can illustrate the originality of this complex of attitudes by the fact that, once the idea of the crusade was enunciated, it was extended to older areas of conflict. The privileges (and often the opportunities for legal penance) were extended to the war in Spain, though not uninterruptedly or as fully as in the war in the east. As of 1100, we can define the just war as a defense, a restoration of rights, a resistance to aggression and cruelty, a substitute for wicked internecine warfare, a penance for rapine and lawlessness, and finally, a Christian way of life.

Urban brought existing ideas together; they were not yet precisely defined, but all the ideas of the crusade that developed later were present in some form or other.

B. *Indulgences and the Holy War*

The systematization of canon law relating to the different aspects of holy war, including indulgences, is best studied in its final form in the decretal collections. We may glance in passing at Bernard of Clair-

---

14. *Fulcheri Carnotensis historia Hierosolymitana*, ed. Heinrich Hagenmeyer (Heidelberg, 1913), I, 1 (pp. 119–123); William of Malmesbury, *De gestis regum*, ed. William Stubbs (Rolls Series, 90), II, 393 ff.; William of Tyre, *Historia rerum in partibus transmarinis gestarum*, I, 15 (*RHC, Occ.*, I, 39–42); cf. *ibid.*, I, 7 (pp. 21–25).

vaux, whose surviving crusade sermons, and whose treatise on the
knights of the Temple, naturally emphasize the "way of Christian life"
but, as concerns the law, stress two points. He is careful to define the
conditions of the papal offer of indulgence exactly, at a lower rhetorical level than usual—taking the cross and making contrite confession.
He contributed, as did many who never went to the east, to the conception of irreconcilability and the attempt to separate two civiliza-
tions by a barrier of canon law. Christ is considered glorified in the
death of the Moslem; the Christian in death is led into his reward. Again,
"the profit of the death which (the soldier of Christ) inflicts is Christ,
the profit of that which he receives is his own." Even Bernard thought
that this needed a bit of explaining. "Not that even the Moslems (*pagani*) ought to be destroyed, if by any other means they could be held
back from excessive aggression and violence against the faithful." Elsewhere, however, when he absolutely forbids any understanding with
Moslems (no allegiance, no money payments, no tribute), Bernard
sounds no less uncompromising than Cato, and writes, "either the religion or the people must be destroyed."[15]

A survey of the canons and papal bulls throughout the main period
of the crusades reveals no specific justification of war, although this
should have been the basic legal problem for church lawyers. The official documents that proclaim or support or enforce the crusade take
for granted that such justification as Urban, and particularly the idea
of "recovery", had lent the war was fully sufficient. The Moslems who
are the targets of the warfare continue to be referred to as "attackers".
Early in this period the crusade became a normal penance; for example, the Second Lateran Council (1139) decreed a year's service in Jerusalem or Spain for arson. The legal concept of holy war developed
most quickly in terms not only of penance, but of the indulgences
which the papal documents concede, and which became so popular
at this time.[16]

Indulgences evolved from the old system of penitentiaries, with their
tariffed penance, which, together with a process of redemptions, lasted
into the eleventh century. Indulgences in consideration of some good
or pious work first developed clearly in the course of this century, and
did so more definitely in the twelfth. The ordinary indulgence substi-

---

15. *De laude novae militiae,* III (*PL,* 182, cols. 924-925); *ibid.,* I (col. 922), and *Epistolae,*
col. 652 (ep. 457, *ad universos fideles*) and col. 653 (ep. 458, *ad Wladislaum*).

16. Karl J. von Hefele, tr. Henri M. Leclercq, *Histoire des conciles* (12 vols., Paris, 1907-1952),
V-1, p. 731.

tuted a stated good work for so many "day" units of purgatorial pains which would previously have been remitted by penance.[17] Throughout the crusading period, the plenary indulgence was confined to the crusade proper, and the first known unambiguous plenary indulgence (for all the pains of all sins committed, if confessed and repented) appears to have been that offered by Urban II himself at Clermont in 1095. Canon 2, as reported, conceded remission of all penance to whoever made the pilgrimage, not from pride and avarice but out of piety and in order to liberate the tomb of Christ.[18] Indulgences were inextricably associated with social motivation, especially the purpose of fighting. Their use should not be seen as the act of private devotion that it subsequently became. They were essential to the law of the crusade, and constitute a useful legal and political criterion.

Examples illustrate the development of this practice and its underlying theory. The Second Lateran decree was by later standards as imprecise as Urban had been at Clermont (it actually uses as a definition the phrase "as decreed by our lord pope Urban"): "To those who set out for Jerusalem, to defend the Christian nation and war against the tyranny of the unbelievers, we concede remission of their sins."[19] Much later, in 1181, it is interesting to see Alexander III associating the notions of defense and attack with the remission of sin. Thus in a bull to the master of the Temple, Arnold of Toroge, he writes of the duty of Templars to lay down their lives for their friends (John 15:13), adding "and you do not at all fear to protect them from the attacks of the pagans". He charges them "for the remission of sins, by the authority of God and the blessed Peter, prince of the apostles," to defend the church by attacking its enemies, and to rescue it where it is "under the tyranny of the pagans".[20] 1181 was the year of Reginald of Châtillon's brutal breach of the truce; Arab power was growing, but crusading aggression against Egypt was still fresh in the memories of men. In a few years' time Jerusalem would fall, and Gregory VIII would call all Christians to penance, good works, and the (armed) pilgrimage to the Holy Land, the "labor" of its recovery, "to look not for profit or worldly glory, but for the will of God". He granted the indulgence, which is of course "plenary", to those who undertake the "journey" with a contrite heart and humble spirit, "and to those who depart in repentance for sins and in a true faith, we promise full in-

---

17. *Dictionnaire de théologie catholique* (16 vols., Paris, 1923–1950), *s.v.* "indulgences".

18. Hefele, tr. Leclercq, *Histoire des conciles,* V-1, p. 401.

19. *Ibid.,* p. 634.

20. Aloysius Tomassetti, ed., *Bullarium diplomatum et privilegiorum . . . editio* (Turin, 1857–1872), Alexander III, II, 830 (no. 111).

dulgence of their offenses (*criminum*) and eternal life. They shall know that whether they survive or die, they shall have relaxation of the penance imposed, for all their sins of which they shall have made true confession. . . ."[21]

After the comparative failure of the Third Crusade, Celestine III wrote in stronger terms. We shall see how, stage by stage, failure made the papacy increasingly intransigent. Celestine preferred the threat of excommunication to the inducement of the indulgence. He reverted to Urban's old themes, while bringing them up to date and using the more legalistic phraseology of his own day. In condemning sin, he singled out private enmities and tournaments. By implication, the crusade offered meritorious enmity and a profitable tournament. Celestine did not claim that Jerusalem was Christian because Christians had been ruling it for nearly a century, but spoke of "the filthiness of the pagans in the taking of the Holy Land, *which is the inheritance of the Lord*"; he also said that they came "ruinously" and "violently". Later he referred to "that tiny piece of the portion of the land of the Lord which is still held under the power of the Christians". When, as so often in recruiting propaganda, the church is identified with the people of ancient Israel, it has in fact both a political and a legal implication. Politically, the church, (Latin) Christian society under papal guidance, has claimed the right to the "inheritance of the Lord" in the same way as the chosen people had a right to the promised land; and when Celestine approvingly quoted how one man overthrew a thousand, and "slaughtered something like an infinite multitude", he was coming close to a justification of the slaughter of infinite multitudes in any situation, because any situation may be seen as reproducing events of the Old Testament.[22] This gave the war its legality.

It was at the end of Innocent III's pontificate and during that of Honorius III that the definition of the "Holy Land" was extended to include Egypt; thus the legal concept of holy war and indulgence was stretched to cover what was originally no more than a strategic concept recommended by Richard I of England and actually attempted by the Fifth Crusade.[23] At the same time we reach the fullest expression of indulgence, but no more precise definition of holy war. For Innocent III it was still otiose to define closely the justification of the war. For example, he spoke of the "ungrateful slaves" and "disloyal

21. *Ibid.,* Gregory VIII, III, 52 (no. 2: 1187).

22. *Ibid.,* Celestine III, p. 88 (no. 12: 1193).

23. *Ibid.,* Honorius III, p. 332 (no. 16: 1217); *Chronique d'Ernoul et de Bernard le Trésorier,* cap. 31, ed. Louis de Mas Latrie (Paris, 1871), p. 338, if this is not hindsight. Cf. volume II of the present work, chapter XI.

servants" who refuse, "when the Lord of heaven and earth implores their help in recovering his own patrimony, which has been lost, not by his fault, but by theirs." Like his predecessors, he preferred to hover over the intermediate ground between political and legal theology. He argued from a familiar feudal situation: "Certainly, if some king in this world was thrown out of his kingdom by his enemies, and if his vassals did not venture their persons as well as their property for him, would he not, when he recovered his lost kingdom, condemn them as disloyal, and conceive unthought-of torments for them . . . ?" This unattractive picture of a worldly king became less attractive still when the pope drove home the comparison with the King of kings "as if ejected from the kingdom which he provided at the price of his blood". This is merely another variation on the theme of defense, but the picture of the enemy as a criminal or rebel was becoming clearer and acquiring a more obviously legal force. In the same bull, dated 1214, Innocent argued that the divine command to love one's neighbor requires men to fight to free their fellow-Christians "held among the unfaithful Moslems in the slave-yard of a fearful prison"; there are many thousands detained in "slavery or prison", he said.[24] This is a variation on the theme of persecution, and it is still as much an exhortation as an attempt at legal justification. Even in this great age of canon law, the legal basis remained uncertain. The key ideas were still the "recovery" of land rightfully possessed, and the "defense" against the "attack" (possession of the Holy Land); and these were determined on theological grounds.

The classic form of the plenary crusading indulgence is to be found in Innocent's decree calling for a new crusade, promulgated during the Fourth Lateran Council. The indulgence is based on the power of binding and loosing which was conferred on the pope by God's mercy and by the authority of the blessed apostles Peter and Paul. What was granted was "full pardon (*plena venia*) of their sins", if "truly confessed with a contrite heart and mouth". It was granted to those who undertook this labor (the crusade) in their own persons and at their own expense; but the same "full pardon" was conceded to those who paid someone else's expenses, or who went at the expense of someone else. As had long now become the custom, the property of crusaders was to be under the protection of the church during their absence.[25] In the same bull, he revoked the "remissions and indulgences" granted

---

24. Tomassetti, *op. cit.*, Innocent III, III, 223–224 (no. 62: 1208), and 274–278 (no. 92: 1214).

25. *Ibid.*, III, 300–304 (no. 107); Hefele, tr. Leclercq, *Histoire des conciles*, V-1, pp. 1390 ff.

for fighting against the Moors in Spain or against Albigensians in Languedoc, as only temporary. Subsequently it was enough that the indulgences should be announced "according to the statute of the [Fourth Lateran] general council".[26]

These problems of public war and private forgiveness are really quite simple, even in terms contemporary with the crusade. They were reduced to a few clear phrases by Thomas Aquinas, who had to deal with the objection that "he therefore who takes the cross according to the form of the papal letter, suffers no pain for his sins, and thus soars immediately aloft, having achieved the full remission of sins." Thomas had reservations: "Although indulgences are very valuable for the remission of pains, yet other works of satisfaction are more meritorious with regard to the essential reward, which is infinitely better than the discharging of temporal pains."[27] Crusading presupposes death in the course of a good work, in Aquinas's thought here as much as in the preaching of Urban. The good confession, the contrite heart, the "good work" of a just war, these were the reasons to hope for the forgiveness of sin, and the indulgence was a pious reward for those who feared the penalties of sin rather than sin itself. The indulgence is here seen to depend wholly on the identification of the war as just. For this, Aquinas required proper authority, the just cause, and the right intention. It does not surprise us that these conditions were believed without difficulty to be satisfied in the crusade; it was precisely these points that were supposed to characterize the crusade.

The evidence is insufficient, but it seems that the teaching was widely yet only superficially understood. The *Chanson de Roland*, even though there is a large clerical element in its composition, was certainly not written by a theologian, and it is essentially a work for a lay and courtly, but war-minded, public. In the *Chanson*, the warriors do not actually make a good confession before battle, but they are absolved by Turpin on their knees, and are given fighting itself as a penance.[28] It is true that this passage promises that they will be holy martyrs if they die, but the absolution and penance, however lightly or uncertainly conceived, make it clear that "martyr" here has only a popular sense. True martyrdom was not claimed. Long before, an eighth-century pilgrim to the Holy Land from Wessex had spoken of being "martyred" for smuggling. This may have been a joke; but it was no joke in the cru-

---

26. Gregory IX, in Tomassetti, *op. cit.*, III, 492–493 (no. 48: 1236).

27. *Quaestiones quodlibetales*, II, viii, 2; *Summa theologica*, III, *Supp.*, 25:2.

28. *La Chanson de Roland*, ed. Joseph Bédier (Paris, 1937; often reprinted), lines 1132–1141.

sading period. The *Gesta Francorum* ordinarily speaks of anyone who died on the crusade, for example of hunger, as martyred, but Albert of Aachen had heard that the clergy prayed for the souls of those who died at Dorylaeum.[29] There is not enough evidence for us to be sure how far the complex theology of martyrdom and indulgence penetrated to the soldiers and camp-followers, or even, later, to the residents of the Latin states, or how far, indeed, they were really interested. The suggestion underlies many chronicles that death in a holy war had the popular sense of "martyrdom" that we find in *Roland.* Later chansons provide even less evidence. The farther we recede from the theologians and canonists, the less we find any clear theological concept at all.

For two centuries from the first preaching of the crusade to the growing realization that it was no longer practical politics, the system determined a part of public life, and to the extent that law affects the ordinary public crusading did so; indeed, its influence continued till very much later. The old, disused system of tariffed penance would not have been enough for effective recruitment; indulgences reached far more people, and provided a legal basis for propaganda; persuasion was based on a theology that must reach everyone. There was some scope for legal compulsion. Once a man had taken the cross, he must be forced to put his vows into effect. The First Lateran Council (1123) imposed an interdict on the lands of all those who did not put their vows into effect between the next Easter and the Easter following, and forbade them to attend church; later, excommunication was the normal form of sanction.[30] William Marshal spent three years in the Holy Land in order to make good the crusade vow the young prince Henry —son of Henry II—had sworn before his death in 1183.[31] From knights or sergeants to monarchs, laymen benefitted in their different degrees from a tax levied to pay for soldiers. It was logical to extend the indulgence to those who financed other men's personal service, but such subventions soon opened the door to abuses which ultimately extended to the whole system of indulgences. The councils from Fourth Lateran in the early thirteenth century to Vienne a century later recognized the need for control, but established no effective method.[32]

A good canonist or an experienced preacher could see the problem

29. *Vita Willibardi, or Hodoeporicon,* in Titus Tobler, ed., *Descriptiones Terrae Sanctae* (Leipzig, 1874), pp. 56–76; *Gesta Francorum,* ed. and tr. Louis Bréhier under the title *Histoire anonyme de la première croisade* (Paris, 1924), pp. 42, 10, 92; Albert of Aachen, *Historia Hierosolymitana,* II, 43 (*RHC, Occ.,* IV, 332–333).

30. Hefele, tr. Leclercq, *Histoire des conciles,* V-1, p. 635; V-2, pp. 1390 ff.

31. *Histoire de Guillaume le Maréchal,* ed. Paul Meyer (Paris, 1901), lines 7277–7279.

32. Hefele, tr. Leclercq, *Histoire des conciles,* V-2, pp. 1390 ff.; VI-2, pp. 643 ff.

clearly, but could suggest no remedy beyond conscience, always the weakness of canon law. Gilbert of Tournai was only reviving condemnations of an earlier century when he attacked the financing of the crusade by exploiting the poor, but it was the whole public that was exploited; he also discussed the real legal abuse, which was the severity of sentences in the condemnation of those who, often for a good reason, failed to fulfil the crusading vow, when severity was used only to extort higher redemption money.[33] These abuses, by common consent, made the whole business unpopular. In fact it was a business, an often capricious system of tax collection which gave increasing prominence to redemption. Cash payments necessitated a return to the custom of partial indulgences ("proportionate" plenary indulgence), and there was no adequate means of assessment. In a study of legal theory one can do little more than emphasize the feebleness of the law which wholly failed to regulate the trade in indulgences or the scale of redemption.

Innocent's declaration at the Fourth Lateran Council of a new crusade illustrates the law at its height. After giving instructions for the "passage" (*passagium* = "crossing" or "crusade"), it announces miscellaneous provisions almost haphazardly. Clerks may retain the profit of their benefices while they are away. Those people who have taken the cross will be excommunicated if they do not go. All prelates and others responsible for the cure of souls must preach the crusade. Those who cannot go should pay a soldier to go for three years. Those who supply ships or contribute to their construction receive an indulgence. All clerks are to give a twentieth of their ecclesiastical revenues for three years, the pope and the cardinals a tenth. While crusaders are away they will be exempt from taxation and from payments of interest. Pirates who pillage pilgrims are excommunicated. The usual prohibition of contraband (arms, iron, and so forth) is repeated in slightly strengthened form. No ship is to go to the east for four years, lest the enemy benefit; on the contrary, it should remain in the Christian reserve. Tournaments are prohibited for three years, wars for four. Then comes the plenary indulgence, in the form already quoted above, but those who, short of paying for a substitute, contribute to the costs, receive remission "according to the quality of the subvention and their devotional disposition".[34] Here appears a scale of exact payment for an incalculable return, and such could lead to nothing but abuse. The

---

33. "Collectio de scandalis ecclesiae," ed. Autbert Stroick, *Archivum franciscanum historicum*, XXIV (1931), 40.

34. See above, note 25.

contrast between the careful provision for practical steps leading to military action, and the loose terms of the indulgence, illustrates at least the greater worldly than spiritual wisdom of the church.

C. The Full Theory of Holy War

We can best evaluate the theory by considering the case as it was argued by the distinguished Dominican scholar Humbert of Romans. He genuinely disliked war but understood the need to make a case to justify it. The case he made, while wholly circumscribed by the ordinary terms of his thinking and the contemporary commitment to the crusade, betrays from time to time an awareness of some of the real difficulties. He had the same clear picture of the unjust war that Urban stimulated in those who reported him. Instead of starting from a conception of the just war, he began by considering what makes war unjust. He said that there are three things: attacking the innocent — killing poor men and nameless farmers, ransacking hospitals and even leprosaria; fighting without reason; and fighting without authority. The war against Islam, on the contrary, was "just". The Moslems were not innocent; they were "culpable in the highest degree against the whole of Christendom"; he elaborated this no further, and to Moslem "guilt" — no nameless farmers, no hospitals — we must come back. The war was reasonable because undertaken not out of pride, avarice, or vainglory, but in defense of the faith; and defense of mere property or persons would have been justification enough. Finally, it was undertaken on the authority of the church. It was therefore *justissimum bellum,* undertaken against the most culpable of enemies, for the highest reason, and on the highest authority.

Yet Humbert knew that crusaders were by no means all penitent; there were those who carried their cross like the bad thief, as well as those who did so like the penitent thief. Moreover, Humbert was well aware that Christian practice was once very different, and that the change needed to be justified. Jesus told Peter to put up his sword, and the teaching of all the apostles and the fathers is against the use of force; he recalled the example of Maurice and his legion, who were beheaded rather than obey an unjust command, and of the innumerable martyrs. He developed a remarkable historical theory of the development of Christian practice to explain the change: "For the vine planted by the head of the household is brought to its proper growth by favor of the dew and the rains and the warmth of heaven; but it is preserved by the sword, if by chance enemies want to root it out." The powerless and the powerful, he went on, must act in different ways, the former with humility, the latter with severity; every craftsman uses the tool he has, and not that which he has not. The early Christians used miracles, the sufferings of the saints, and holy doctrine, that it might be seen that faith grew by God's agency, not man's; but when it had grown, it became necessary to defend it by the sword. The church, which lacked the early gifts of miracles and tongues and the Holy Ghost, but had power, must use it. Humbert did not deprecate this historical development. Those who object to the shedding of blood by Christians "do not themselves want to be poor, as men were in the early church, but rich; they do not want to be, as (Christians) then were, lowly, but to be held in honor; they do not want to be destitute of sustenance, as Christians then were, but to live amid pleasures." This is consciously a theory of history: "according to the series of periods and the diversity of circumstances, the church has varying situations, as the growing boy passes through varying situations before he reaches old age. Thus the church was poor, but is now rich, and many things similar; in the same way, it makes use of arms now, but did not do so then." This is an interesting, a logical, and a frank argument; does it amount to a legal theory? Almost certainly, Humbert saw this as having legal force, though we might incline rather to allot it to political theory.

Humbert in any case saw a legal defect, and cautioned that the use of the sword was confined to lay people, as the hand is the only member that can wield a sword. Using the argument of the two swords, he elsewhere stressed the necessity of rational justification of a war. Force is justified against those who rebel against the authority of the church, he wrote, because the fear of God recalls them from evil; and the infection of heretical error must be cut out like a putrid member; but the Moslems, who will not even listen to the word of the church (beheading those who tell them about their errors), are worse than rebels, who at least listen, even if they do not obey; and worse than the heretics, because they destroy body as well as soul. Jews, he added, are in a different category; their conversion is foretold by Scripture, they strengthen faith in being seen to fulfill the Scripture, when it is properly interpreted; they do not attack in arms. The Moslems' conversion no Scripture has foretold; to see them does not encourage faith, but rather gives scandal to weaker minds; more than any other unbelievers, they come strongly in arms against us. He applied the parable of the marriage feast. The Jews are those who "would not come". The idolators are those who "made light of it". The Moslems are those who treated the king's servants "shamefully and killed them". "The king was angry, and he sent his troops and destroyed those murderers and burned their city."[35] Humbert said that "from this derives the authority to advance the army against them"; this, he believed, gives his exegesis legal force.

He added that the church not only provides the justifying authority, but also grants indulgences from "all sins"; by these the crusaders would be washed as clean as martyrs are by the shedding of their blood (a large claim which, however, clearly distinguishes martyrdom from indulgence, while claiming equal effectiveness for the latter). It will be noted that there is no suggestion that the indulgence is confined to remission of pains for which penance should otherwise have been done, as Catholic apologists have maintained, even when talking about remission *a culpa et a pena*. Those who are "completely absolved", said Humbert, are "not only the dying, but the living who are good pilgrims, from all sins, great as well as small, hidden as well as open, carnal as well as spiritual, by day as well as by night, known as well as unknown." This did, of course, presuppose penitence.[36]

This is perhaps the fullest reasonable defense surviving of a canonical position which was difficult to reconcile with much Christian history and doctrine. It was a good deal closer, as we shall see in more detail, to the Moslem position. Humbert, within the limits of the method, allowed his imagination some play; he put the scholastic points for and against a proposition in a more literary form than usual, and his work gains from even this slight freedom from the classroom method. All justification of war in Christian terms is derived from the right of self-defense, and even in more sophisticated form the arguments used can still be reduced to that single issue; thus the "recovery" of the Holy Land is considered the defense of Christian land, the ill will of the enemies of God presupposes self-defense, and so on. If we come to the point of what confers the right to kill, the authority of the church, on which scholastics insist, is only part of the answer, and should rather be considered a condition. The "right" is conferred essentially by self-defense; by "reason" and by "custom" a man has the right to defend himself and his property, and still more his faith, which is his most important possession, and more important than his life on earth. Humbert often seems uneasy about these arguments, and per-

---

35. Matthew 22:1–7.

36. *De predicatione sancte crucis* (Nuremberg?, 1490), caps. 2, 8; *Opus tripartitum*, in *Appendix ad fasciculum rerum expetendarum et fugiendarum,* ed. Edward Brown (London, 1690), cap. 11.

haps stresses the wickedness of the enemy as much to evade the emotional consequences of the crusaders' cruelty and inhumanity as to establish his legal justification. In the last resort, in spite of the array of scriptural authorities, canon law was based on common sense and not on revelation, in this unlike the Moslem *jihād*. However, although the right to defend the faith by force was seen as self-evident, this argument was at least implicitly reinforced by the right of the Christian faith, as revelation, to exercise God's dominion over the world. We shall consider this "war aim" later.

Some of these arguments are found more fully, but less reasonably and certainly less attractively, expressed a few generations later, in the period of total crusading failure. When Humbert wrote there seemed to be at least some chance of saving the Latin remnant of Syria. Humbert added something to the case for killing infidels which had been put so summarily by Bernard of Clairvaux in the twelfth century and taken for granted in many bulls and canons. It was argued in still fuller detail by the English Dominican Robert Holcot, who, when he died in 1349, had lived through a period of futile attempts by the papacy to revive the crusade seriously. Though there was talk of attacking the Arab countries, there was at this date no danger of attack by any Islamic power, but the question "whether it is lawful and praiseworthy for some Christian, when in order to attack he uses force, to kill some unbeliever such as a pagan" was not altogether unreal. Alexandria was sacked after Holcot wrote.

The arguments he cites against killing unbelievers, summarized, are: God desires not the death of the sinner, but that he should be converted; the church prays for unbelievers, so they should not be killed; God is merciful and Jesus forbade Peter to use his sword; Aristotle told Alexander that he refused to shed blood because, whenever a creature kills another, the heavenly powers are moved to divine vengeance; God said, "Vengeance is mine";[37] it is forbidden to kill a bad Christian, although he is worse than a pagan who does not enjoy the restraint of Christian law; unbelief is not the unbelievers' fault, because God has not lifted the veil from their hearts; their error is invincible, because, even if they want to believe, the power of their rulers prevents them; an effect is good only if it is directed to a good end, but the

---

37. (Pseudo) Aristotle, *Secretum secretorum,* in *Opera hactenus inedita Rogeri Baconi,* fasc. V, ed. Robert Steele (Oxford, 1920), cap. 18, pp. 55–56; *The Governance of Lordschipes,* cap. 25, in *Three Prose Versions of the Secreta secretorum,* ed. Steele (EETS, ES; 1898, repr. New York, 1973), p. 61. See also *Secretum secretorum: Nine English Versions,* ed. M. A. Manzalaoui (EETS, 276; Oxford, 1977), pp. 42, 139, 324–325.

principal end is conversion, and conversion cannot be forced, because no one comes to God except by faith, but can only believe freely. The replies to these objections are: it is only the eternal death of the soul that God does not desire; the church prays for the sinner to become just, and, if he refuses, may cut him off; the sword is forbidden only without due authority, and Peter chose the wrong moment ("that was not the time"); Aristotle meant that he would not take pleasure in shedding blood, and true Christians, when they do so, take pleasure only in the end for which they do it; God's vengeance is sometimes effected through his servants; bad Christians are killed "every day"—thieves, traitors, heretics—and it is necessary only that there be just authority, rather than private decision; God will remove the veil from anyone who wants it removed; invincible error excuses only those who deserve no blame in incurring it; finally, the principal end is conversion, and extirpation only secondary. No one who believes will be killed. We can sum up all these arguments: it is a Moslem's fault that he is Moslem, and that fault is a capital offense. In that case, there would be no necessity to allow a Moslem prisoner to live if he refused to apostatize. This harsh attitude is only very slightly mitigated by the main body of the argument.

Although later Holcot distinguishes different types of *pagani,* he begins his main discussion on the assumption that he is speaking about those who rule the Holy Land—that is, the Moslems. The land was promised to Abraham and his seed, and Christians are the spiritual seed of Abraham; it is lawful to take up material arms against those who occupy our spiritual country unjustly, and thus to repel force by force. If they are killed in the course of being expelled, they are the cause of their own deaths; in the same way, a husband may kill an adulterer who does not run away from his house. Again, the outcome of what is vowed is always lawful if the thing vowed is lawful, and in this case the thing vowed is lawful according to the church militant. Again, any outcome indulgenced by the pope is lawful, and fighting against pagans is indulgenced from fault and pains (*a culpa et a pena*); and so such fighting is lawful and meritorious. A similar argument: the English church is taxed to subsidize the fighting, with the approval of the pope; therefore the end is approved by the rulers of the churches, to whom obedience is due.

The argument is prefixed by a number of definitions and distinctions. Thus, some unbelievers are subject to the church, and are associated with believers, as servants to their lords, and are ruled by them. Others are "rebels against the church, persecutors of the Christians, and insulters of Christian doctrine". This is really merely a distinction

between those under Christian and those under non-Christian governments. Then there are different ways of attacking the pagans; for example, if someone presumes to act without the authority of the church
(an allusion to Frederick II?) he cannot kill justly. Thirdly, there are
different kinds of pagans, those who have no religion "unless by chance
the law of nature"; there are also Jews, Moslems, idolators, and heretics, and these have different relations to the Christian religion. Heretics must be compelled to recant. Moslems kill anyone who preaches
against Islam, but the life of Christ cannot be taught without disprov-
ing the religion of Mohammed (a characteristic self-deception); however, those Moslems who are bound to, and tolerated by, Christians
cannot lawfully be attacked by arms, but must be granted peace according to the example set by Joshua, who enslaved the Gibeonites
as hewers of wood and drawers of water. A fortiori "pagans" may lawfully be offered protection, provided they live "sine contumelia creatoris", especially in the hope of their conversion; they cannot then lawfully be killed, though this applies only per accidens. As for those other
unbelievers, insurgents against the church and persecutors of the faith,
Christians may "attack them by force and arms, despoil them, kill them,
and devote their goods to the believers".

Jews are in a different class; Holcot does not think it lawful to kill
them, because the apostle announced their conversion at the last days,
so all, at least, may not be destroyed. The Moslems and the Jews are
not in the same case; the former persecute the Christians and turn them
out of their own towns and places, the latter are ready everywhere to
serve the Christians.[38] The war against the Moslems is just, under the
authority of the church, for many reasons: they occupy the land and
other possessions that belong to the Christians (the justification "appears proved by reason and custom"); again, it is divine law that by
right all good things of this world belong to the just (omnia bona tem-
poralia sunt justorum); again, as a corrupt member may be cut off
from the body, so may the rebels and unbelievers be cut off from the
mystical body of the redeemed human race; again, it is lawful to induce charity through terror; finally, such people—Moslems, but which?
—act worse than beasts, but beasts may be killed for the public good,
so also may evil sinners. (It is not clear whether Holcot would hold
a good act by an unbeliever to be evil.) Some of Holcot's arguments

---

38. The idea is an old one. Pope Alexander II (1061–1073), in writing about Jews who
were not to be injured, forbade a Spanish bishop to destroy a synagogue; "Dispar nimirum
est Judaeorum et Sarracenorum causa. In illos enim, qui Christianos persequuntur et ex urbi-
bus et propriis sedibus pellunt, juste pugnatur; hi vero ubique parati sunt servire" (ep. 101, in
PL, 146, col. 1387).

sound silly to us, and probably sounded severe to some of his contemporaries; he often betrays ignorance of the realities of the crusade; all that he says is nasty.[39] In an uninspired way, he elaborates Bernard of Clairvaux, but he does not innovate; he draws out what is already there. He is inferior to Humbert in intellectual power and in judgment. He takes up more thoroughly than Humbert the question of what right a Moslem has to live, and the conditions under which it is permissible to tolerate him. On these conditions there is a large canonical literature, which is the fullest expression of the legal apparatus of a "just war", and a revelation of its political purposes. Unlike many political purposes, these were in fact ultimately achieved; in the areas that the Europeans conquered permanently, Islam died out.

D. Toleration and Trade

In the Islamic law of *jihād* the end of the process, or war aim, was understood to be the death, conversion, or submission of the "infidel".[40] Crusade law to some extent resembled this, but usually, as in the scheme defended by Holcot, the submission of Moslems was barely accepted. Aquinas justified imposing force on unbelievers (where practicable) to prevent "blasphemies and evil influences", and he defined blasphemy as, in effect, any theological error publicly expressed. Toleration had no absolute status in medieval Christendom as it had (within limits strictly defined) in medieval Islam, and that is why the Moslem communities in Europe were eventually extirpated; submission was only an interim war aim. The history of James I "the Conqueror" of Aragon-Catalonia is full of Moslem surrenders to the king, representing the civil power, on his guarantee of freedom of worship.[41] This was no protection from the gradual operation of discrimination over the centuries, and canon law is our best guide to the pressures gradually exerted. The case of Moslems was generally assimilated to that of the Jews in the great collections of decretals, although a number of canons

39. *In Librum sapientie* (Basle, 1560), lectio LXV, cap. 5; Joshua 9:23; Romans 11:25. For further references see Benjamin Z. Kedar, *Crusade and Mission* (Princeton, 1984), pp. 98–99, 183–189.
40. In general see Emmanuel Sivan, *L'Islam et la croisade* (Paris, 1968).
41. Aquinas, *Summa theologiae*, 2a–2ae, qu. 10, art. 8; qu. 13, art. 1; cf. qu. 10, art. 10, and *de rationibus fidei* in *Opera omnia*, vol. 27 (Paris, 1872–1888). Cf. also *The Chronicle of James I*, tr. John Forster (London, 1883), *passim*.

specified Jews only. The main difference between the Islamic rules for Christians and Jews under Moslem rule and the Christian rules for Moslems and Jews under Christian rule lay in the original intention. The Islamic law, by introducing a special tax for *dhimmīs* and excluding them from the army, created a barrier between the majority and its dependent minorities, but the Christian rules set out deliberately to isolate "unbelieving" communities from Christian society.

Before we leave the subject of the divisions enforced between Moslems and Christians, we should consider two canons of special interest of late date. One is from the Council of Vienne (1312), incorporated into the Clementines promulgated by John XXII in 1317, which makes a number of rash incidental assertions about matters of fact; for example, that the call to prayer "invokes and extols" the Prophet's name (which might be considered accurate), and, absurdly, that Moslems "adore" Mohammed in their mosques; legal conservatism combines with propaganda to the point of self-delusion. The call to prayer is in any case understood to be "an affront to the divine name and a reproach to the Christian faith", at least when it occurs in lands subject to Christian rulers where *permixtim cum Christianis habitant Sarraceni,* glossed by the canonist John of Andrew as "said to be in Aragon and various territories in Spain". The affront lay in the Christians' hearing this fragment of Moslem worship. The decree goes on to object to the public congregation of a multitude of Moslems, which generates "scandal seriously in the hearts of the faithful"; this happens when they go to "the place where a certain Moslem was formerly buried", to "venerate and worship him". This is so vague a description of the *ḥajj* that we might think it referred to the local cult of a holy man; but John understands it as the pilgrimage to Mecca, and expresses surprise that there should be doubt as to the identity of the "certain Moslem" as Mohammed. The offense is again the appearance of the multitude of Moslem worshippers before the Christian public. John assumes that Christian rulers tolerate non-Christian religious practice "on account of their avarice, that they may take tribute". They "tolerate and suffer them (Moslems) to be and remain in their areas; sometimes the rulers suffer them to be apart, that is, separated from the Christians; sometimes they suffer and tolerate them in the same city and the same quarter." It is the latter case, of course, which gives offense, and the offense is that non-Christian worship should be seen to happen at all.[42]

---

42. *Clementis papae V constitutiones,* ii, i, in *Corpus iuris canonici,* ed. Emil L. Richter, rev. ed. by Emil A. Friedberg (Leipzig, 1879; repr. Graz, 1955), II, cols. 1180–1181.

The other decretal was issued only a few years later, by John XXII in 1317. It completes a process only half achieved by the other. It is about "the business of attacking the faithless Agarenes, by whom the kingdom of Granada is held in insult to God"; apparently God, insulted (as we have just seen) by the public profession of Islam in a mixed quarter in a Christian city, was insulted again by Moslems who worked industriously to pay tribute from a small, subordinate, but separate kingdom. The decretal begins appropriately "The Lord [is] overflowing in mercy", *copiosus in misericordia Dominus.* In response to a particular request by Peter, the infante of Castile, this decretal about the poor remnant of independent Islam in Granada has a general implication for the theology of the just war: "indeed," says Jesselin of Cassagnes in his gloss, "the defense of the church is expected to be a responsibility of the rulers of the world, and the church should be protected by their power; for it is the will of God to stimulate temporal power against heretics and other unbelievers." The "insult to God" here is defined as an injury to divine religion, a "faculty of doing harm", which God permits on account of the sins of Christians; but the "insult" and the "injury" from which the church demanded protection was just the theological "error" of those who continued to be Moslems.[43]

This offense of Granada's brings us to the last theme in the legislation for holy war, the relation of Christians to places under Moslem rule. There are two separate questions: one is the trade relationship as governed by the canonical declarations of war contraband and regulated by formal agreements between European trading powers and the Moslem states; the other is the personal situation of those Christians who lived and worked in Islamic territory, but still within reach of canon law so long as they wished to remain in the Latin church.

The prohibition of carrying arms or war materials to Islamic countries was well established, repeated in a regular formula with little variation over centuries of warfare and projected warfare; it appears first in full form in the canons of Lateran III, and was later incorporated in Gregory IX's *Decretals.* Those who carry arms, iron, or lumber for making galleys to the Moslems are as bad as the enemy or worse; so are those who serve in command of Moslem galleys and private ships. They are all excommunicated, and Christian rulers and the consuls of trading cities are warned that the goods of such people should be

43. *Extravagantes . . . Ioannis papae XXII . . .* , VIII, i, *ibid.,* cols. 1214–1215.

confiscated, and that they should themselves, if taken, be enslaved.[44] A similar but fuller canon of Lateran IV, also incorporated in the *Decretals,* added anathemas against these "false and impious" Christians who do the things forbidden by the earlier canon, and also those who give advice and help in the use of "engines", or in any other way; what this forbids is what we now call acting as foreign experts. It also required that sentences against offenders should be published in the maritime cities on Sundays and holy days; finally, the condition of pardon would be to transfer the gains made *in dispendium* to the service of the Holy Land. The *glossa ordinaria* condemns the same motivation that the original decrees attributed to such offenders; "led by blind cupidity," it says, echoing Alexander III's "harsh cupidity occupied their souls"; it argues that, because it is worse to help the enemy than to be the enemy, slavery is appropriate as punishment.[45]

Elsewhere the glossator discusses the significance of repeated excommunications. It might seem that once a man is outside the church, he is outside, and repetition adds nothing; his answer is that the effect of the first excommunication is to put the offender outside, of later excommunications to keep him there, since each sentence requires its own proper satisfaction. He draws a parallel with the penalties for usury, where the restitution must be commensurate with the offense; here more so, because the offender, guilty of "attacking" the Christian faith, sees his confiscated gain spent entirely in its defense.[46] To the modern observer, there is an implication that the merchant or "foreign expert" seeks to serve the Moslem world not only from cupidity but by preference; ordinary Mediterranean trade attacked the Christian faith in the sense that it was incompatible with the intentions of the crusade, and with the theory underlying papal policy.

Two other decretals date back to the period of the Third Crusade. The first of these deals with cases of conscience arising out of trading with the enemy: it is legitimate to go to Alexandria to redeem fellow citizens from captivity, but not to take more goods from which the Moslems could benefit than are needed for ransom. A second point is that the existence of a truce between Moslems and Christians does not justify the revival of prohibited trade with Alexandria, and merchants who swore that they would not go to Moslem countries with goods until there was peace are not excused excommunication if they

---

44. Lateran III, canon 24 (Hefele, tr. Leclercq, *Histoire des conciles,* V-2, pp. 1104–1105).

45. *Decretalium D. Gregorii papae compilatio,* V, VI, vi (in Richter and Friedberg, *op. cit.,* col. 773).

46. *Ibid.,* xvii (cols. 777–778).

do so during the truce. The gloss adds that they are not absolved from their perjury either, adding that the excommunication is *ipso iure,* and applies "in time of peace or truce". It carefully distinguishes truce from peace, the former being defined as "security of persons and property, conceded for a time". It also picks up the major ambiguity in the decretal; what if the articles to be used to ransom Christians are arms or iron? Some think that they are still exempt, but the glossator believes that this should first be referred to papal authority, not in principle, but in any particular case.[47]

The second of these decretals forbids any trade at all with the Moslems in time of war, "either in person or through agents (*per alios*), in ships or by any other means, or any material help or advice". The gloss considers that it imposes a double excommunication. The decretal concludes, and the gloss repeats, that offenders will not only be excommunicated, but also be exposed to the anger of the living God.[48] This seems to diminish a little the terrors of excommunication alone.

A later decretal of Clement V issued during the period immediately following the expulsion in 1291 of European Christians from Syria-Palestine listed more goods: "iron, horses, arms, and other forbidden goods, and also foodstuffs and wares (*mercimonia*), to Alexandria and other places of the Moslems, in the land of Egypt." It increased the abuse of both the Moslems ("dreadful and faithless nation") and the offenders ("deviating into a crooked path . . . unmindful of their own reputation and forgetful of salvation"); it piled up the list of penalties— excommunication, enslavement, perpetual infamy, testamentary incapacity, and inability to hold public office, something of a diminuendo, although the rhetoric maintains a steady frenetic level.[49] Church law naturally imputes motivation, and so tends always to read more emotionally than other kinds of law, but this law is stated emotionally by any standard. One point of making the prohibition "more absolute than absolute" was, of course, to make it inescapable to obtain a papal license to trade with Egypt, although sometimes this was withheld. We are not here concerned with the practice of the law, but the sale of expensive exemptions, amounting to a system of taxation, does affect our judgment of the theory.

In papal theory, perhaps only missionaries should have been allowed to live in Islamic territory, but some trade was allowed, even in theory,

---

47. *Ibid.,* xi (col. 775).
48. *Ibid.,* xii (col. 775); cf. *ibid.,* x (cols. 774–775).
49. *Extravagantes communes,* V, ii, i, (cols. 1289–1290).

and exemptions were given, so that it was admitted that there were and might legitimately be Christian communities living in Moslem countries, primarily for trade, not necessarily excommunicate, needing spiritual services; at certain periods, of course, there were considerable numbers of enslaved prisoners. The only profit that the popes ostensibly accepted as desirable is missionary, but trade itself has advantages both ways; the popes simply tried to insist on reserving to themselves the decision in each individual case, and gave licenses for trade limited by the number of ships and to a fixed period, for example, a year. Granted the seasonal problem of Mediterranean navigation, a year was not long in the export and import business. The sale of licenses was a taxed permission to commit an offense, which obviously reduced the whole crusading theory to absurdity.

There were, of course, many problems of conscience, for which we have some solutions by the Dominican Raymond of Peñaforte, consulted by the minister of the Friars Minor in Tunis in 1234. These are the cases. Those who claim license on the ground that their own immediate ecclesiastical superiors have not forbidden them to carry arms, iron, et cetera to the Moslems are to be excommunicated, because the decrees of the councils cover their case; the same applies to those who fight Christians. Should Spaniards who sell footwear and harness be counted as selling arms? Or those who sell rams and sheep? What about Pisans and Genoese who sell grain and legumes? These are excommunicated in times of war. Those who transport food produced by Moslems to other Moslems are excommunicated. People who bring arms for self-defense, but then sell them when they are in need, are excommunicated.

Those who sell Christians as slaves, especially if these are forced to become Moslems, are not excommunicated, but do commit mortal sin; this is also so when they steal Jews or Moslems (children presumably) and sell them as Christians. The reason why there was no excommunication for what many might think the worse offense is that this particular trade was not included specifically in the canons, and, as it was not war contraband, was not *in dispendium*. Later, in the fourteenth century, when Europeans had come to appreciate the Mamluk system, the trade in slaves came to be seen more as a kind of war contraband; the Egyptians then were said to be peaceful people, who would not carry on war if the Mamluks did not receive constant foreign recruitment. Asked about the baptism of Moslem children in the hope that they will die before they come to years of discretion, Peñaforte makes an ambiguous and unsatisfactory reply.

A more practical question was whether Christians may live with converts from Christianity, especially if they are related, some being minors, some adults, and others their own children? Happily, the reply is yes, because of either "correction", the hope of putting them right, or "necessity", presumably material necessity. Cohabitation with a heretic (Moslem?) spouse is also permitted, if there is no *contumelia creatoris;* perhaps this means here, provided the Christian spouse does not take part (or perhaps is just not seen to take part) in Moslem (or Coptic?) worship.

What about those who have been given a period of crusading for a penance, but are infirm, or poor, or afraid? Give them another penance. What of those who are held back from keeping their vow by serious business? They should not involve themselves closely with others, and, when disengaged, should fulfill the vow. Are those who steal from Moslems bound to make restitution? They are so bound. Are those who bring grain, small pieces of wood, or the like excommunicated? Only if they do so *in dispendium Terrae Sanctae,* or to attack Christians. What about clergy who give scandal by acting as merchants? They are subject to the appropriate canonical penalties. Is ignorance about what trade is forbidden an excuse? No, because the prohibitions are public, but if the offenders are ignorant, and stop when they are informed, then they are not excommunicated. If a sailor has no other means of earning his living, and takes service on a ship that is carrying contraband, is he excommunicated? Yes, but he can be absolved at discretion if he makes proper satisfaction.[50] Many of these decisions bear witness to a sensible and occasionally humane application of a harsh law which was intended to erect a powerful barrier between Moslems and Christians, and appears to a considerable extent to have succeeded.

It is beyond the scope of this chapter to examine the extent to which the canons were modified by official license, or by being ignored, but the actual correspondence of the popes fills out an otherwise incomplete picture. There is not much evidence about the life of Latin communities in North Africa, but, as we should expect, the intentions of the later canons contrast with the pre-crusading situation of the eleventh century. At the earlier date, as we saw, when an indigenous hierarchy in the Roman province of Africa just survived, Gregory VII's diplomacy shows him concerned to reach an agreement with the Ḥammādid ruler. Something of this spirit remained alive at the papal court; when, later, the local Christian church had died out, the popes, in-

---

50. "Raymundiana," in *Monumenta ordinis Fratrum Praedicatorum historica* (Rome and Stuttgart, 1898), VI, fasc. 1. doc. VIII, pp. 29 ff.

cluding those, like Gregory IX or Nicholas IV, who were most anxious for the renewal of the crusade, were concerned to ensure that the Moslem rulers at least in North Africa and the west should accept Latin clergy sent to act as chaplains to the local Christian communities. These seem to have been, from an early date, friars, especially Franciscans. Even in Egypt they served Christian prisoners, among others, but it is not clear that this service was maintained consistently.

The trading communities were relatively stable. The treaties between the commercial states and Islamic rulers, of which many, from the twelfth century onward, are extant, are strictly businesslike; they do not infringe the canons, although as Peñaforte's case-decisions illustrate, individual members of the communities must often have done so. The treaties freely use Moslem terminology, adopting the style of the country ("in the name of God the Compassionate and Merciful"); they establish a firm consular basis for trading rights, often reciprocal, and some secure the right to maintain chapels. In this situation the popes intervened amicably enough. In writing to Moslem rulers, they used phrases like "your nobility" and "your magnificence"; Gregory IX wrote to 'Abd-al-Wāḥid II, the Muwaḥḥid ruler of Morocco, "to the noble man Amiromolinus" (amīr al-mu'minīn, the commander of the faithful); we must assume that (as was often the case) this was thought to be a proper name. Several of these letters refer in more or less friendly fashion to Christians who are serving under Moslem rulers, even as soldiers.[51] It is clear that in North Africa (as distinct from Egypt) this was not always taken to be in dispendium Terrae Sanctae, and was then legal so long as it was not done to fight against Christians.

In any case, not even the shadow of toleration extended to Egypt; Egypt was an enemy country and constantly singled out as such, on strategic principles which remained dominant till the Ottoman invasion. The earlier canons that forbade trade in dispendium did not specify the Moslems against whom they were directed, but one bull of Innocent III, of the same date as Lateran IV, singled out "the lands of the Moslems who inhabit the eastern regions". A gloss of Jesselin of Cassagnes explains the phrase "the lands of Egypt" (where it occurs in the 1317 canon about Granada): "in which Christ was born, namely

51. See note 9 above; L. de Mas Latrie, Traités de paix et de commerce et documents divers (Paris, 1866-1872), II, 1-21, 367-374; Paul Riant, "Traités des Vénitiens avec l'émir d'Acre en 1304," AOL, I (1881), 406-408. Cf. Salimbene de Adam, Cronica, ed. Giuseppe Scalia (Scrittori d'Italia, 233), I (Bari, 1966), 457-458; Angelo di Spoleto, De fratribus minoribus visitantibus captivos in Babilonia (1303-4), in BOF, III, 68 ff. See also Eliyahu Ashtor, Levant Trade in the Later Middle Ages (Princeton, 1983).

in Bethlehem, brought up, in Nazareth, suffered and was buried, in Jerusalem . . . which because of the fetters of our sins is in the hands of the unbelievers."[52] What looks like a geographical error may rather be a recognition of Mamluk rule over Palestine from Cairo. Pilgrimage, because it added to the revenue of the Mamluks, was also *in dispendium,* and so required dispensation, and Egypt was a normal route to Palestine. The North African states, though the object of several startling Christian attacks, never provoked the same vituperation as Mamluk Egypt. Even though we cannot confidently assert, we can reasonably suppose, that the popes would have been ready to reach some accommodation with Islamic powers, whenever expedient, as a matter of course, were it not for the question of Palestine. This, if true, implies that the conviction that Palestine rightfully belonged to the Christians had priority in Christian theory over the argument that the Moslem religion was in itself evil. The latter originated in propaganda, although the machinery of tolerated coexistence was legal, but the former was sincerely, however perversely in a modern view, believed itself to have the force of a right at law.

E. Political Theory

These legal systems have their political implications. No imaginable papal accommodation with the Moslems of North Africa would have survived any real chance of conquering them. Just as Christians were believed to have a prescriptive right to the Holy Land, they were considered to have a lesser but still valid right to all lands that they set out to "recover". They did recover all of Spain and Sicily, and service in Spain was often (though not always) counted for purposes of penance or indulgence as equivalent to service in the east. This was law, and was simply a matter for papal decision *ad hoc.* They would have recovered any other territory of the Roman empire if they could. Behind the historical descriptions of Arab aggression in and after the seventh century lay the legal theory of "recovery"; after however long an interval, all ancient Rome was considered in some legal sense inalienably Christian. There was no territory within the reach of Christians which had not once been under Christian rule. If Iran had been

---

52. Tomassetti, *op. cit.,* Innocent III, III, 303 (no. 107, par. 14); *Extrav. Ioannis XXII,* viii, i, *s.v.* "terras Aegypti".

accessible, and conquered, what would have been the status of its Moslem inhabitants in Christian legal theory?

Beginning with Innocent IV there developed a theory of papal jurisdiction over non-Christians, and even over non-Christian states, which was soon elaborated into a theory of world monarchy by canonists busy with the task of extending papal authority. There was a steady growth in self-serving legal arguments that non-Christian states had to allow the entry of missionaries, that their Christian subjects came under direct papal authority—although it was never clear whether this was a political or only spiritual authority—and that this applied not only to those territories that had once been held by Christian rulers, but to any lands whatsoever.[53] Such discussions said nothing about subject Moslems in such states, or what might happen if such states fell into Christian hands, but there can be little doubt of the consequences. If the toleration of Moslems was only tactical, the "ultimate war aim" must inevitably have been the same as the commission to the apostles, the conversion of all unbelievers. The Jews, thanks to Romans 11:25–26, could count on being left till last, but Moslems would certainly have been reduced to submission, on the ground that non-Christians have no right to lordship and that they "persecuted" or "attacked" Christianity by existing at all (and no doubt would in any case have attacked Christendom often enough); once in submission they would have been subject to conversion, that is, compelled to listen to preaching, and to discrimination, until, as happened in Spain in the sixteenth and seventeenth centuries, and had happened in Italy in the thirteenth and fourteenth centuries, they had ceased to exist as Moslems. If we concede that "recovery" was the primary concept, then "conversion" (by war initially) was soon so firmly rooted as to become itself essential to the idea of the crusade. The political theory of the crusade was quite simply the infinite extension of Latin Christendom.

This is speculation, based on implication, but the close link between legal and political thought makes it reasonably certain. Can we speculate further? Uthred of Boldon, a monk of Durham and scholastic of the fourteenth century, was censured for discussing the possibility that Moslems, Jews, and pagans might be saved *de communi lege*; this was classed as error.[54] William Langland maintained that a "true man"

53. For further references to Innocent IV see Kedar, *op. cit.,* pp. 159–161, and on toleration generally pp. 76 ff., 146 ff., and *passim*; see also Walter Ullmann, *Medieval Papalism: the Political Theories of the Medieval Canonists* (London, 1949), pp. 114–137. For an interesting discussion of the whole concept of a "just war" see Frederick H. Russell, *The Just War in the Middle Ages* (Cambridge, Eng., and New York, 1975).

54. M.D. [i.e., David] Knowles, "The Censured Opinions of Uthred of Boldon," *Proceed-*

who follows the best law he knows, acts justly, and "lyuede as his lawe tauhte and leyueth ther be no bettere", may be saved. This specifically relates to Saracens and Jews, in spite of Langland's acceptance of traditional libels against the Prophet.[55] Aziz Atiya has drawn attention to further examples, John Gower and Honoré Bonet.[56] These opinions stand out because they were contrary to the usual opinions expressed by the lawyers. Granted the intimate connection among theology, law, and political intention, should we suppose that, if Moslems could be saved in their own "law", the compulsion to save them by conversion would disappear? Would the crusade have been confined to "recovery", perhaps only of the Holy Land? Wyclif went further, and opposed the crusade itself,[57] but he did so because the crusade, both in practice and in theory, was an instrument of papal political expansion. This idea of his was not influential, although, as Southern has shown, the originality of John Wyclif's treatment of Islam cannot be questioned.[58] Even according to the ideas aired by Uthred and Langland, however, non-believers would be protected only by their ignorance of the true religion; thus the armed crusade must still have followed the missionaries. We must conclude that "recovery" came first, both legally and politically, but that "conversion" too was an unlimited political objective that would have compelled crusaders (in law) to continue in arms to the limits of the inhabited world; and, of course, Wyclif was right; this objective for Latin Christendom was a concept inseparable from papal ambition.

The history of Frederick II, in particular, sheds light upon the theory of the papal party. Frederick preserved the Sicilian Arabs in an existence separate from the rest of his subjects for his own purposes, exploiting rather than protecting them. In Sicily itself, Innocent III had been prepared to deal with them as legitimate subjects whose loyalty, when they were loyal, should be praised; they could be dealt with through the qadis almost like a tributary people or *millet* in Islamic

---

ings of the British Academy, XXXVII (1951), 305–342, repr. in *The Historian and Character* (Cambridge, Eng., 1963), text pp. 163–165.

55. *Piers the Plowman,* ed. Walter W. Skeat (EETS; 4 vols. in 5, London, 1867–1877), B Text, Passus XII, 284–289, and XV, 389 ff., but cf. 383; C Text, XV, 209–212, and XVIII, 151 ff., 165 ff.

56. Aziz S. Atiya, *The Crusade in the Later Middle Ages* (London, 1938), pp. 187–188. Cf. Wolfram von Eschenbach, *Parzival,* ed. Albert Leitzmann in *Werke* (Tübingen, 1961–1963), VIII, 416, 25–29, and IX, 453, 11–14.

57. References in Richard W. Southern, *Western Views of Islam in the Middle Ages* (Cambridge, Mass., 1962), p. 78, and Atiya, *loc. cit.*

58. Southern, *Western Views,* pp. 79 ff.

law. Frederick, after destroying their independence, transferred them to Lucera on the mainland; he rated the life of a Moslem or a Jew at half the price of that of a Christian; he seems to have thought of them as in some sense having the same status as that of Christians in Islam, using the word *gesia* to denote a capitation tax which he imposed and which represented the *jizyah* or poll tax which Christians and Jews paid in Islam. This must have been deliberate, but Frederick did not really assimilate his Lucera Arabs to the status of *dhimmīs* in Islam, who are not required to fight; the people of Lucera, on the contrary, were required above all to provide troops who would be wholly dependent on the emperor's good will. From a Moslem or a modern point of view, pope Gregory IX was persecuting the Arabs when he insisted on their having to listen to the preaching of Dominicans, but his intention toward them was more charitable and disinterested than Frederick's; as Christians they would at least have been safer.[59]

The objections raised by the papal party to Frederick's arrangements in Palestine are also instructive. His great offenses were permitting Moslem worship in the Dome of the Rock (Qubbat aṣ-Ṣakhrah) and the Aqṣâ mosque, forbidding Christians free access to those places, and allowing the public call to prayer, as well as allowing Moslems access to Bethlehem. All these horrors were simply the admission of Moslems to the use of holy places then conceived quite wrongly to be exclusively Christian, and to public worship of their own. One other episode, out of so many told of Frederick, deserves mention here. Matthew Paris says that in Acre he had Christian girls dance before Moslems who, "it is said," had sexual relations with them; nearer the source, the Latin patriarch Gerald said that the sultan al-Kāmil, knowing that Frederick lived in Moslem style, sent him singing girls, dancing girls, and jesters, whose reputation was infamous and unmentionable among Christians, and that Frederick behaved in Arab style, in drinking (*sic*) and dressing. With Matthew Paris the (imaginary) scandal is the prostitution of Christian girls, which would indeed be contrary to the canons; with the patriarch, it was the "Arab" way of living to which he objected; he would no doubt have argued that the offense was mixed attendance at a *convivium*. All these episodes in their different ways illustrate the principles underlying the clerical concept of the crusade.[60]

59. J. L. A. Huillard-Bréholles, *Historia diplomatica Friderici secundi* (12 vols., Paris, 1852–1861), I, i, p. CCCLXXXVII; IV, i, p. 31; I, i, p. CCCLXXXVIII; V, i, p. 628; IV, i, p. 452.

60. *Ibid.,* III, 88, 101–102, 104, 109, 136, 140; V, 329, *et alibi.* Matthew Paris, *Chronica majora,* ed. Henry R. Luard (Rolls Series, 57), III, 185.

It is time to look more closely at the inevitable comparison with the law of *jihād,* itself part of the basic structure of medieval Islamic policy. In outline the two laws are closely similar. A Moslem army offers unbelievers the opportunity to accept Islam, or, failing that, to accept the status of *dhimmīs*; if they refuse both, they must fight, and, being defeated, may be enslaved or even killed. A slave who later becomes a Moslem is not necessarily freed, though it would be pious to free him. Comparing the crusade, we remember that it, too, was aimed at conversion, and that Moslems who surrendered on terms of submission were given an inferior status. Moslems captured in war (not on capitulation) would be enslaved, if not killed. The slave converted to Christianity would not automatically be freed, but it would be a pious act to free him. Obviously there is much common ground in the treatment of "infidels". So is there in the rewards of holy war. The death of the Moslem in *jihād* ensures the status of martyr (*shahīd*). The death of the crusader did not result automatically in martyrdom, because confession and absolution, absent in Islam, were necessary, but it was common to speak and think of anyone who died in the course of a crusade as a martyr. *Jihād* is more than war; it is also the struggle for one's religion. The crusade qualified as a good work, a penance, and a pilgrimage, and it was rewarded by indulgences which certainly remitted "pains and guilt". Some of them seem to imply more than later Catholic theology would allow.

The Christian or Jewish *dhimmī* was in a better situation than a conquered Moslem, in that his position was strictly regulated by a law known in advance and not dependent on the details of a capitulation; it was guaranteed by the Koran itself. It was a status of dependence, however, strictly not even second-class citizenship, but something altogether less than citizenship. The *dhimmī*'s life and property were guaranteed by the Moslem army, but he had to pay special taxes, and had to distinguish himself from Moslems by dress, and by not riding a horse or carrying weapons. As a witness he was inferior in status; his law of personal status and doctrine was determined by his bishop. The conquered Moslem had similarly to be distinguished by dress, and was inferior as a witness. Because he was unbaptized, he was not subject to canon law, and so was free to follow his own law of personal status. Some details, though similar, are not precisely the same in the two cases; Christian monarchs assumed the duty of protecting conquered Moslems on their capitulation, but these had to pay the ordinary or extraordinary taxes attached to the land they held, and those who surrendered, or negotiated a truce on terms allowing subordinate Moslem rule (of which the longest-lasting example was Granada), had to pay an exorbitant tribute. The two laws resembled each other in limiting strictly any public celebration of the religion of the other, and the erection of places of worship. On the other hand, Christians under Islamic rule were not subjected to compulsory preaching of the dominant religion, as happened in the reverse case. *Jihād* might be declared against Moslem heretics and rebels, so that if, as the popes claimed, Moslems "judaized" in declaring pork unclean, the popes themselves "islamicized" in declaring a crusade against heretics (such as the Albigensians) or against those who rebelled against their authority (the most distinguished of whom was the emperor Frederick II). Differences of detail are fewer than points of resemblance, and in any case do not obscure the close similarity of general outline.[61]

Besides the uncanny resemblances in many details, there is an overall consonance between Moslem and Christian ideas of holy war. The idea of *jihād* as spiritual struggle is much to the fore of the minds of modern Moslem theologians, and in the modern world Christians speak loosely of any good endeavor of any magnitude as a "crusade". The concept of *jihād* has not loosened quite to the same extent in Islam, but it is certainly used to define what Christians still call a "just war". It is as a theology of just war that the two ideas come closest. Even the requirement of using right means (*modus debitus*) which developed rather later in Christendom, and the idea of double effect which permits the incidental death of the innocent, are parallel to Islamic rules. We have seen that the crusade from its inception was considered the just war *par excellence,* the war which would end all other kinds of war, though in fact in time it led on to an infinite number of "just wars" and crusades for this and that alleged good end. Here we return to the starting point. Both *jihād* and crusade were designed to lead to that state of perfect peace where the world is under the rule of true religion, and the conversion of a barely tolerated remnant is imminent.

It is extremely unlikely that there was an actual Islamic influence on the Christian canons. There is no vestige or echo of specific knowledge of the Islamic law of *jihād* in any medieval writing; still less are there specific references to it, translations, questions, or discussions. In writing theology and even history there is no reticence about the use of Moslem sources, and this silence makes it certain that there was no explicit influence of Moslem jurisprudence. References do occur

61. Cf. *Encyclopedia of Islam,* vol. I (Leyden, 1908), rev. ed., vol. II (Leyden, 1965), *s.v.* "ḏjihād"; Majid Khadduri, *War and Peace in the Law of Islam* (Baltimore, 1955).

often, of course, to the "religion of violence"; generalizations are based on traditional distortions of early Islamic history, and tendentious reading of Robert of Ketton's paraphrase of the Koran, undertaken for Peter the Venerable, stressed the commands to fight unbelievers. This crude idea of *jihād* was quite unrelated to the crusade. We might say that an unacknowledged influence of Moslem jurisprudence, not even perceived by those who received it, is not impossible, but it is an unnecessarily complex assumption. The natural explanation is that those who start from the same position and go in the same direction are apt to follow much the same path. Granted the duty of converting the world, and granted that there is no objection to the use of force, at least within legally determined limits, the detailed rules seem to develop inevitably in parallel. There was of course no fundamental difference between the Christian and Moslem positions on the use of force. Christians began by not using force at all, and Humbert's theory that different stages of development require and justify different means, whether or not it is a sound theory in theology or law, is certainly good history. The real difference was that the Christian position did not require toleration, in the way that Islam is predetermined by the Koran to accept the "Peoples of the Book". Although there is something similar in the status of Jews, under Romans 11, the fact that nothing guarantees the status of Moslems — tolerated, as Holcot said, only as Gibeonite hewers of wood and drawers of water — made a political objective of total conformity possible. The proof is that Christians and Jews have survived under Islam, but not Moslems under Christian rule before the modern colonialist period; in Christendom, Jews have survived, and Moslems have not. The position of the latter was always insecure despite the reasonable terms on which so many of their cities surrendered.

In minor ways uniformity might be broken by license, by the purchase of privilege. It is ironic that in the days of effective crusading people paid the church in order not to go on "pilgrimage"; when a crusade was no longer a practical possibility, they paid for license to break the boycott, to go on pilgrimage, or to travel to Alexandria to trade. As excommunication followed excommunication and was ignored until it suited better to give way, it might seem that the weapon was cheapened beyond usefulness, but, though this may be true of the conflict between the papacy and the secular state, excommunication as the typical ecclesiastical sanction was not diminished; on the contrary, the suppression of heresy became more widespread. The fact is that excommunication was the natural mode of thought of Europeans, unquestioned till relatively late, and surviving into the seventeenth century (and vestigially much later). In the Middle Ages, those who would not keep the rules, either of recovery of the Holy Land, or of frigid relations with unbelievers, were excommunicated; above all, the unbelievers themselves began by being excommunicate. This was the justification for taking "spiritual" action against persons outside the church: to preserve Christians from contact with them. There was no secret or mystery about this. The crusade is the characteristic, even quintessential, expression of a conformist society.

The very idea of the crusade was clerical, but in that, perhaps, it differed less from *jihād,* which was the act and thought of the whole community, than might at first appear. Laymen's crusading was a series of practical wars, with little beyond a "them and us" ideology, modified by recurrent common sense, and occasionally by a little good fellowship across the barrier. The crusading ideal was quite different, a clerical intention for laymen to practise, but, though it was sometimes more, sometimes less remote from what was actually happening, laymen acquiesced, at least in the theory. Seen from the point of view of the Christian and European body politic, the crusade becomes only one aspect of the characteristic tendency of the Middle Ages, the concerted determination of the articulate classes — effectively the clerics — to establish a society so fully united as to express itself naturally in total orthodoxy. Nor is there any evidence that the bulk of the population objected to this aim; objectors seem untypical, and most of them were clerical in any case. Some degree of orthodoxy is the expression of any normal society; the peculiarity of the Middle Ages was the preponderance of clerical and theological articulate leadership.

A crusade was different from war against Moslems, as such a war was understood before Clermont, precisely in being more clerical and more theological. It was different in emphasis, and in the stronger papal initiative, expressed partly by a simple philosophy of history, but more by papal decrees elaborated in a growing collection of canons, commentaries, and theological questions. Thus the crusade must be understood as existing by virtue of its own definition; it only added a complex interpretation — at once legal and sentimental — to an already existing activity. In its turn, the papal leadership had an actual effect on events, the crusades were successfully recruited, and this recruitment, though often at a very low level, continued without break. A complex though ramshackle financial system was created.[62] Thus the existence of such a theory had helped to give a nominal body politic, "Christendom", some effective reality. The crusade was a function of

---

62. See chapter IV on finances by Fred A. Cazel, Jr., below.

"Christendom" and an important element in every approach to a papal theocracy. Strictly speaking, the crusade has no political theory of its own, but only plays an important part in the political theory of the papalists.

Moreover, the theory helped greatly to form persistent and influential European attitudes. The overall effect of the law of the crusade, including the law governing the treatment of conquered Moslems, was the political one of sealing Europe off. The relations between the Moslem world and Europe (with, in due course, America) have been uneasy up to the present day. There has been mutual respect, occasional contempt, frequent hatred, and almost constant incomprehension. We can trace this back on the European side as far as the Arab invasions of Europe through an unbroken series of misunderstandings, but, in that story, the effect of the crusading period must be considered decisive. Unmodified crusading opinions can still occasionally be heard from a few Christians, but many Moslems believe that crusade still informs the whole western attitude, and, inverted, it has certainly come to influence extremist interpretation of Islamic law.

W. M. Watt, basing his view very fairly on the evidence of contemporary Moslem historians, and especially on Ibn-Khaldūn (d. 1406), holds that the crusades were no more important to the Arabs of their time than the wars of India's Northwest Frontier to Englishmen of the imperialist age.[63] Yet, if so, the Arabs were fatally wrong; there is a clear continuous line from the crusades to the aggressive imperialism of the western European powers in the Levant and North Africa in the nineteenth century. The paternalism of the church within Europe grew into the paternalism of Europe throughout the world. Even at the height of its intolerance Europe sent experts, excommunicate but active wanderers, into the Islamic world; these are lost to history because of the effective cultural barrier which a clerical society closed behind them. The political achievement of the age was an integrated society supported by laws of exclusion; law carries no guarantee that its provisions will be put into effect, but it is likely at least over a long period to express the wishes and beliefs of a people. Crusading Europe, which retained a capacity to develop within itself, was one of the most efficiently closed societies to have flourished under civilized conditions.

63. Modern opinions: personal experience of the writer, but on extremist interpretation see also Gilles Kepel, *Le Prophète et Pharaon* (Paris, 1984), pp. 115–117, 150–158, 198–201. W. Montgomery Watt, *The Influence of Islam on Mediaeval Europe* (Edinburgh, 1970), p. 81.

II

CRUSADE PROPAGANDA

A. *The Preaching*

In 1095 Europeans were already familiar with the constituent notions of the crusade. When Urban II preached at Clermont, the Christian expansion in Spain and Sicily that had been characteristic of the third quarter of the century was well within living memory, and much of it was contemporary history even to the younger men. In spite of that, the propaganda for the eastern crusade seems to have introduced a new note of almost hysterical aggression. There had been two earlier stages. The idea of meritorious fighting against the enemies of God had been characteristic of the wars between Catholics and Arians; directed specifically against Moslems, in a somewhat imprecise form, it dated back to the ninth century, to the attacks on Rome and the settlements in southern Italy. Then European morale had only just sufficed: "lest the Arabs should behave too insolently too long, and say 'Where is their God?', God turned the hearts of the Christians, so that their desire to fight was stronger than their old desire to run away."[1]

Then with the increasing momentum of European aggression against the Arabs in the course of the eleventh century, there was a revolutionary change of tone. The companions of count Roger, like the first captors of Barbastro, were adventurers come to exploit the relative weakness of Arab Sicily and the Spain of the *taifas*; though the *Cantar del Cid* and the *Heimskringla Saga* were written later, they seem to reflect very well the spirit of the Varangian, "scourge of the Saracens", and of the Cid, who, "born in a lucky hour", made his living from the booty of the Moors.[2] These men were successful professionals who made aggression into big business. The recovery of morale was complete. It is equally and immediately obvious that they were not religious enthusiasts, and that war was in the air.

1. Liutprand of Cremona, *Antapadosis*, II, 46 (*MGH, SS,* III, 297).
2. R. Menéndez Pidal, ed., *Cantar de mio Cid* (Madrid, 1913), *passim*; Snorri Sturluson, *Heimskringla Saga,* partly translated as *King Harald's Saga* by Magnus Magnusson and Hermann Palsson (London, 1956), p. 51.

What propaganda turned such men into crusaders? The Gibbonian
— and, indeed, medieval — disillusion with the crusaders' greed for land
and booty has created a picture of them as rogues cynically exploiting
religious sentiment to their profit. For us the interesting question is
the reverse. How did the rogues come to be imbued with either the
appearance or the reality of religious motivation? This is a fruitful
perspective from which to examine again Urban's reported preaching
at Clermont. Though Gregory VII had canvassed the idea, it is evident that he did not conceive it in just the same way as did his successor. He was more concerned about papal rights in reconquered territory, more willing to envisage "coexistence" in North Africa.[3] He seems
to have thought more in terms of papal functions than of an embattled Christian commonwealth. That a reconquered area was "restored"
to Christendom was a legal concept at this stage not yet emotionally
charged. In Urban's preaching we find new notions, more especially
new sentiments, that correspond to ideas immediately and thenceforward in general use. From this point of view it matters more what Urban was understood to have said than what he actually did say. We
shall say little to distinguish the propagandist from the consumer of
propaganda, because the one is usually, and simultaneously, the other.
We are concerned only to identify the main lines of persuasion and
self-persuasion which thenceforward men of all types accepted as de-
fining their official motivation.

It is tolerably certain that Urban stressed the idea of the recovery
of Christian lands, although this has reached us in a form likely to
have appealed primarily to the more literate, and even the literary-
minded; history was a branch of literature, and the appeal to history
was strictly mythical, and myth-creating. However, it was allied with
an idea easily assimilated by the feeblest-minded and the most ignorant:
the notion of persecution, of the new wave of attacks against Christendom, comes out very strongly in the "Letter of the emperor Alexis"
faithfully reproduced in Robert of Rheims' version of Clermont;[4] and
in some form or another it is in all the accounts of the period. The
legal and liturgical notion that Christian lands, which by hypothesis
included the Holy Land, were to be "restored", and saved from a ruth-
less persecutor, acquired great new emotional force. Like all powerful

---

3. *Das Register Gregors VII.*, Erich Caspar, I, 22, 23 (*MGH, Epistolae selectae,* I, 36–39);
III, 21 (I, 287–288).

4. *Historia Hierosolimitana,* I, 1–2 (*RHC, Occ.,* III, 727–730); cf. Edmond Martène and
Ursin Durand, eds., *Thesaurus novus anecdotorum* (Paris, 1717), I, 267. For the Council of Clermont see Frederick Duncalf, "The Councils of Piacenza and Clermont," in volume I of the present work, chapter VII.

ideas, it could appeal simultaneously at all levels; on the one hand there was the reasoned catalogue of alleged history; on the other the simple image of a raping and murdering Turk.

William of Malmesbury, an admirable historian, is the first to state (ventriloquizing Urban) the historical argument fully: the enemies of God (or persecutors) inhabit one third of the world, Asia, as natives, and have come to inhabit another third, Africa; in the last third, Europe, the Christians are oppressed, and have now for three hundred years been subjugated in Spain and the Baleares. He also attributed to Urban the theory of national character determined by physique, and physique determined by climate.[5] This was supposed not only to inspire and reassure the Frenchmen of the temperate zone, but also to explain why the Turks fired their arrows from a distance, refusing to close with their enemy. It was written, of course, a generation after the event, and knowledge of Turkish tactics is clearly anticipated. Its historical perspective and historical geography probably represent long reflection upon the original propaganda, but the essence of the argument, the destiny of the Europeans to oppose the alien attack, is contained in other versions.

Guibert of Nogent's version, written like Malmesbury's after long reflection, also like Malmesbury's contains its historical disquisition, but is more scripturalized (the kings of Egypt, North Africa, and Ethiopia cut off from the Christian world); it reflects the liturgical theme of the restoration of Christian land, and even the Roman concept of an age-old struggle between east and west. Christianity was sown in the east, but the westerners, who received it last, were destined to recover Jerusalem.[6]

Robert of Rheims contrasts the French, "beloved and elect by God", phrase by phrase with the "nation of the kingdom of the Persians, a cursed nation, a foreign nation absolutely alien to God".[7] The praise of the French seems to be one of the most primitive elements in the crusading movement. Robert appeals also to the example of Charlemagne and Louis the Pious. We can class these arguments under the heading of the historical vocation of the west, which merges naturally with the theme of repelling persecution. These are two aspects of a single line of appeal, and they are reinforced by Old Testament references which tend to assimilate the crusade to biblical situations.

The religious motivation, whether to bring sin and struggle in the

---

5. *De gestis regum,* ed. William Stubbs (Rolls Series, 90), II, 393 ff.
6. *Gesta Dei per Francos,* II, 4 (*RHC, Occ.,* IV, 139).
7. *Historia Hierosolimitana,* I, 1 (*RHC, Occ.,* III, 727).

west to an end, or to achieve the pilgrimage *par excellence* in some kind of "martyrdom", constitutes the other main line of appeal. Let us again take Malmesbury's version, as representing a late stage of compilation: the "profit" of martyrdom (not necessarily death in battle) replaces the "wretched exile" of this life, and puts to practical advantage the gifts of valor which internecine war dissipates.[8] Guibert stresses this less, but retains it. The sources agree that the idea of pilgrimage as an escape from the "exile" of this life was one of Urban's themes.

It was Fulcher of Chartres who most emphasized the substitution of holy war for the petty wars and their attendant miseries in Europe, and he even saw this as Urban's principal motive. Differently expressed, this was Gibbon's explanation: the diversion of the energy of the knightly class into more profitable channels. Fulcher showed a consistent horror of war, and, as with other authors, later reflection presumably affected his memories of Clermont, an occasion which left so powerful a general impression, but so little exact recollection in its hearers.[9] The crusade was also presented as the ideal penance, and it was even seen as a chance for important men who had committed great crimes to atone without public humiliation.[10] This last point is somewhat grotesque, but in many different accounts we find the same association of ideas — unnatural internecine strife in the Christian world, the "exile" of this life, the excellence of pilgrimage, penance, and "martyrdom". Propaganda here blended with the theology of crusading which made holy war a superlatively good work. It offered, not the certainty of heaven, but at least a version of the good life attractive to the adventurous.

Does this explain the reception the preaching encountered? Urban's exact degree of emphasis, his shades of meaning, even the weight of emotional content, we cannot assess through sources which are all recollected in tranquillity and inevitably reinterpreted. Still, do the main themes justify the outburst of near-hysteria which those writers who themselves did not go on the crusade describe in such detail? One point we may take literally: when we read in Baldric of Dol that the preaching was passed down from the pope to the bishops and from them to the community, where ultimately every individual became his own preacher, we can see the process of propaganda as at once hierarchic and irre-

---

8. *De gestis regum,* II, 394–398.

9. *Fulcheri Carnotensis historia Hierosolymitana,* ed. Heinrich Hagenmeyer (Heidelberg, 1913), I, 1 (pp. 119–123). See also volume I of the present work, p. 240, and Dana C. Munro, "The Speech of Pope Urban II at Clermont, 1095," *American Historical Review,* XI (1905–1906), 231–242.

10. *Chronica Monasterii Casinensis auctore Petro (Diacono) (MGH, SS,* VII, 765).

sponsible. Self-inebriation explains the broken marriages, shattered families, and desertions from monastic vows that he and Guibert describe. The joy with which the deserted wives and parents saw their happiness broken is a gauge of hysteria; so are the mass movements — so moving to posterity — of children asking, "Is this Jerusalem?"; so are the general pictures of men of different origins and speech congregating and set in motion like a disturbed ants' nest.[11] Albert of Aachen likewise speaks of the deserted towns and castles, the empty fields and husbandless homes.

We need not ask if these accounts are exaggerated; hysterical accounts and accounts of hysteria alike need explanation. It is not clear how far the pope was responsible. Nor can we blame Peter the Hermit, whose story Albert of Aachen particularly emphasizes without explaining it, and who, as reported, seems to be a figure of myth.[12] His complex history of pilgrimages and visions, his appearance as a type of the conventional ascetic, his part in the eastward movement of rogues, fanatics, and adventurers who made up the proto-crusades — all this declines finally into his fictional appearance in the *Antioche* and *Jerusalem* poems, ribald, cunning, unscrupulously ambitious, idealistic, a sort of apotheosis of the common man. The great lords, their motives equally confused, are nevertheless more easily intelligible.[13]

The effect of propaganda which we do not know at first hand can be judged only from the recollections of those who went on the great pilgrimage. Of these the simplest and most sympathetic to the modern taste are certainly those of the author of the *Gesta Francorum*. His opening words speak of a movement of evangelical simplicity: the Lord calls on men to take up the cross — and this is conceived in terms of the gospel instruction, not of later crusading technicalities — and there is a "powerful movement" (*motio valida*) across France. The pope, the hierarchy, and priests start to preach *subtiliter* that those who want to save their souls must undertake the pilgrimage; soon the Gauls have left their homes and set off for the east.[14] This last remark was an understatement, if the other accounts which we have mentioned were

11. Guibert of Nogent, *Gesta Dei*, II, 6 (*RHC, Occ.,* IV, 142); Baldric of Dol, *Historia Jerosolimitana,* I, 6 (*RHC, Occ.,* IV, 16).

12. *Historia Hierosolymitana,* I, 2 (*RHC, Occ.,* IV, 272).

13. Richard le Pèlerin, *La Chanson d'Antioche,* ed. Paulin Paris (Paris, 1848); and ed. Suzanne Duparc-Quioc, 2 vols. (Paris, 1976, 1978); *La Conquête de Jérusalem,* ed. Célestin Hippeau (Paris, 1868); *La Chanson des chétifs* (extracts) in *La Chanson du Chevalier au Cygne,* ed. Hippeau (Paris, 1874–1877); Anouar Hatem, *Les Poèmes épiques des croisades* (Paris, 1932).

14. *Gesta Francorum,* ed. Louis Bréhier as *Histoire anonyme de la première croisade* (Paris, 1924), pp. 2–5.

at all accurate. Fulcher is clerical, stressing the council of Clermont, which the *Gesta* does not even mention, and he is courtly, impressed by the participation of the rich lords.[15]

Raymond of Aguilers, also courtly, also clerical, though ordained after he set out, totally ignores the background of the First Crusade, but explains his own story briefly. He concentrates on the events the army experienced, writing consciously to correct misrepresentations by those who did not stick it out. He clearly dissociates himself from the general state of Europe; his notorious partisanship for Peter Bartholomew, the discoverer of the "holy lance", should in no way discredit his witness to army attitudes.[16] Though the writers who themselves took part in the events they described tend to emphasize the crusade itself, rather than its inception, their reactions are entirely consistent with the alleged main lines of Urban's preaching. This is perhaps only to say that the propaganda was clear and was effective.

This is seen most clearly in their pride in being Franks and in their sense of martyrdom when facing death on pilgrimage. These points, whether they dictate or follow the official propaganda, correspond to the two key notions — the appeal to the west, and the call to a better life — reduced to their essentials. They have been modified, and almost suggest an oral tradition distinct from the writers' accounts. In the *Gesta*, martyrdom has an accidental quality which is wholly convincing. If we accept the identification of the author as a knight undistinguished in rank, he represents the presumptive target of the pope's preaching. Did it reach the target? There is a matter-of-factness in the frequent reference to the army, not only as "pilgrims" (which appears in all the accounts), but still more as "receiving martyrdom", almost a euphemism for "being killed" — "many of our men received a happy martyrdom in the course of the siege," "that day more than a thousand of our cavalry and infantry were martyred." (Conversely, Moslems are said to die "body and soul".) The poor who died of hunger were said to be dressed in heaven in martyrs' robes, although they had not died violently. In fact, when the author of the *Gesta* is reflecting, he considers every death of a "pilgrim" a kind of martyrdom, and, when he is not, he refers almost automatically to a battle casualty as a martyrdom.[17] Is this a measure of success in propaganda? The idea implied is that a crusader had put himself in danger and so, if he died as a result, died for Christ; that is, was martyred. Yet this was not ortho-

---

15. *Fulcheri Carnotensis historia Hierosolymitana,* I, 1-4, 6 (pp. 119-138, 153-163).
16. *Historia Francorum,* X (*RHC, Occ.,* III, 253-255).
17. Ed. Bréhier, pp. 10-13, 42-43, 90-91, 188-189; cf. pp. 94-95.

dox, and we must assume that the pope did not teach it; the "martyr-dom" of which the *Gesta* speaks is clearly not a theological concept. It is almost folkloric.

Practising good works as a penance was not, of course, a new idea, but as part of crusade theory it developed quickly. The indulgence was a successful experiment in the history of church discipline, and constituted a powerful inducement. In this case official theology had a widespread practical impact; we might even say that popular needs produced a radically new theology. In general, lines of argument were very persistent, but their emotional coloring fluctuated greatly. It was always obvious that the crusading movement responded to moments of crisis in Palestine. Each separate "crusade" was differentiated by its own distinct preaching. A man—or a woman—might go on the pilgrimage at any time, and it was largely the intensity of propaganda that distinguished one "crusade" from another. We think of different crusades often in terms of their leaders, who themselves merely responded, and hence contributed, to a particular movement or wave of propaganda.

It is clear that crusading and "pilgrimage" became a normal part of the political and social scene; we should not underestimate this habit of mind. Eventually it came to be taken for granted, so that there was a diminishing response to successive crises. Bruno of Asti, bishop of Segni, preached the crusade at a council in 1106, in order to revive flagging ardor. In only ten years all the excitement had faded. He was supporting Bohemond I of Antioch, whose own contribution to the propaganda is unclear, but who certainly held out worldly incentives while himself posing as an epic hero.[18] The crusade would for long have a steady appeal to merchant and soldier adventurers for sound economic and psychological reasons, as well as to religious enthusiasts. Its appeal to rulers, and perhaps to the general public, varied and ultimately waned *pari passu* with the evidence for its viability. Yet it is likely that as long as hope of crusading success lasted, it was fortified, even for the most worldly, by the conviction of God's support.

It is clear that Bernard of Clairvaux's characteristic and habitual bluff could not ensure the same enthusiasm for a war against the Arabs as it could for a project at home. His homiletic for the Second Crusade is poorly preserved, perhaps because its recruits did not succeed in the field, but we are by no means ignorant of it. It seems to have been

---

18. Suger, *Vita Ludovici grossi regis,* ed. Henri Waquet as *Vie de Louis VI le Gros* (Paris, 1964), pp. 44–45, 48–50; Orderic Vitalis, *Historia ecclesiastica,* XI, 12, ed. and tr. Marjorie Chibnall, VI (Oxford, 1978), 68–73.

dominated by a sense of outrage at physical "pollution" of the holy places and at doctrinal "persecution", as when Moslems (he supposes) say that Jesus was a deceiver because he falsely claimed to be God. This, he believes, must rouse the faithful man to fight and gain glory in victory or profit in death. There is a clear brutality in his approach. Christ is glorified in the death of the Moslem; there must be no entering into treaties with Moslems, either for money or for tribute (such as lordships?) until either their religion or their nation be destroyed. Bernard says that both swords of the faithful must be thrust into the brains of the enemies of God, and by "both swords" he means the temporal and the spiritual; in his imagery he thirsts for blood.[19]

In general the Cistercian attitude, represented also by Eugenius III himself and by Godfrey, the bishop of Langres, to whose preaching Odo of Deuil refers, seems to have leant heavily on the loss of Edessa in 1144, basically repeating Urban's "crisis of Christendom" propaganda. It seems that there was an unexpected enthusiasm when Bernard preached in the presence of the king and of some nobles to whom pope Eugenius had sent crosses. The crowds demanded so many more crosses that the preacher had to tear up his own clothes.[20] There is certainly nothing new in the substance of Bernard's propaganda, and any new development must be found in the style; there is a grim sensitivity to the danger presumed to result from a Moslem victory, and a holy pleasure in the duty to retaliate.

The persisting themes of crusade propaganda are seen clearly in a letter of archbishop Baldwin of Canterbury to his suffragans in 1185. There was again devolution of propaganda, like authority, from pope to metropolitan, and metropolitan to suffragans, and down through the hierarchy to the soldiers. Recruits were picked up as the message went down the line: Baldwin himself went to the war. The need was pressing: "Because of our sins, the enemies of the cross of Christ have become so strong that they have tried in their pride and perversion to destroy the Holy Land, the inheritance and patrimony of the Crucified, on which the Lord's feet stood, and in accordance with the complaint of the lamentation of the prophet, 'there is none to support her'." Again he puts it in a phrase: "Thus does our mother Jerusalem call to you." Nothing could better illustrate the pristine pilgrim quality, the simple piety toward the earthly scene of the life of Jesus, which still survived in the bitterness of war. In the assimilation of the church

19. *PL,* 182, cols. 651–653, 924–925.
20. Odo of Deuil, *De profectione Ludovici VII in orientem,* ed. and tr. Virginia G. Berry (*CURC,* 42; New York, 1948), pp. 8–11.

to ancient Israel we recognize another recurrent theme, specifically linking the Old Testament to the crusade, both of them seen as parts of
the long history of war between east and west. There is a sincere feeling of outrage and crisis: "The nations come to the inheritance of the
Lord and pollute his temple. . . . The tribe of them together say in
their heart: 'We will silence the name of Christ on the earth, we will
take away his place and nation; come, and in a great multitude we will
scatter the small number of Christian people'."[21] An attack so conceived would elicit an immediate will to resist; nothing could seem more
just, more simply defensive.

It can be argued that when the fruits of a successful aggression are
endangered, as when the Frankish colony in Palestine was threatened
by Saladin, it arouses more acutely bellicose reactions than the simple
instinct of self-defense in the case of an initial attack. Certainly the
west was to hold on determinedly to its acquisitions in Palestine for
many generations yet, with the ever-delusory hope of restoring a viable
state, despite the intermittent but effective pressure of the Moslems.
The Levantine colony had been a familiar political fact for a century;
it was not merely a dream of religious enthusiasts. Side by side, therefore, with the old propaganda, we note an increasing professionalism.
This was not confined to the colonists in the east, as any study of the
impact of Richard I of England upon the Palestine war must remind
us, and the preaching of Baldwin himself illustrates this point.

The *Itinerary through Wales* of Gerald of Wales is an agreeable stream
of gossip, which makes it difficult for us to remember that the party
was traveling to preach the Third Crusade in terms suited to a desperate crisis. We may attribute this contrast to the personality of Gerald,
but he was not alone, and a closer look at the preaching—such mention as this receives—shows how the new conventional appeal of the
crusade reached certain types of men in particular, among whom we
can include the archbishop, but not the writer. Gerald's brief references show the effect of propaganda on one who saw no reason to apply
it to himself. Other writers, too, even the chroniclers of the period,
reflect only an afterglow of the old inspiration. Gerald is entirely businesslike: "About three thousand men were signed with the cross" in
the course of this Welsh propaganda campaign, "well skilled in the
use of arrows and lances, and versed in military matters; impatient to
attack the enemies of the faith; profitably and happily engaged for the
service of Christ, if the expedition of the holy cross had been forwarded
with an alacrity equal to the diligence and devotion with which the

---

21. *PL,* 207, cols. 306–308 (ep. xcviii, an. 1185).

forces were collected." Gerald criticizes the authorities for failing to make good use of the recruits they were offered; all the same, he considers that a recruiting job has been well done, and he certainly describes a professional army in good morale.

It is different when he goes on to speak of Baldwin's arrival at Acre. The archbishop had been among the first to take the cross, "having heard of the insults offered to our Savior and his holy cross". As Gerald puts it, Baldwin, arrived in Palestine, found the troops attacked as well as attacking, "dispirited by the defection of the princes, and thrown into a state of desolation and despair", tormented by lack of supplies and by hunger, sick from the climate; the archbishop could only relieve them by charity, and set an example of a good death. We can deduce that by this time the familiar theme of "insults to the Savior" would appeal only to the ascetic and unworldly, such as Baldwin. Crusading should be managed like any other business operation. The attitude of the troops in the field was apathetic, and their affairs were ill-managed. There is now a cold assessment of a practical proposition, perhaps in Baldwin's mind as well as in Gerald's. The crusade, still seen as a good work, was also now a logistical job, to be done properly.[22]

We can study the professionalism of the preaching itself in a number of documents of this period and of the succeeding century. First we may take the *brevis ordinacio de predicatione sancte crucis facienda,* attributed to Philip of Oxford and dated to about 1216. What immediately strikes us is the persistence of the theme of the crusade as a way (or even the best way) of the Christian life, conceived, of course, as a pilgrimage. There is a series of short theological arguments, scholastic in method, expressly intended for amplification in the pulpit, to exemplify the need for suffering in this life.

It is only at the very end that we come to passages which take actual crusading situations into account—pieties of propaganda, but at least in a relevant setting—and at the same time suggest some emotional and rhetorical persuasion, with a reiterated *surge* and *surge ergo.* Even these passages look as if they have been chosen at random, but for that reason they are more likely to belong to the preacher's personal repertory. They still lack pithy application. Of three knights, brothers, fighting the Albigensians, two fear to die, but the third says (in the vernacular) that a day's penance (that is, death in battle) is a cheap

---

22. Giraldus Cambrensis (Gerald of Wales), *Itinerarium Kambriae,* II, 13–14, ed. James S. Dimock (Rolls Series, 21-VI), pp. 146–152.

way to God. A captured knight is suspended from the wall of a besieged place; his friends stop bombarding it for fear of hitting him;
he tells them to go on hurling stones, and the stones cut the rope that
holds him; he falls and escapes — moral, do not lack faith. A knight
wounded four times thinks of Christ's five wounds and goes again into
the battle, to die of his fifth. Another knight tells his horse, which has
often carried him into battle, that this is the first time it has carried
him into eternal life. Lastly, another knight says in French: "A horseman would sooner lose the use of his feet than his head."[23] These stories
are so unconvincing because they are meant only as bare reminders
to the preacher. This is the end of our text, and clearly is meant to
lead to the taking of the cross by the listeners around him. It is difficult to judge the quality of rhetoric that reaches us so incomplete. It
is possible to believe that what does not seem particularly apposite
or forceful to us seemed so once. It is not possible to believe that so
much theology appealed to the soldiers, and much of it must be a clerical exercise. The essential note is that the crusade was a normal component of Christian life. The way of the cross was a way of suffering;
there is no mention here, as in Bernard, of the suffering inflicted.

A much more comprehensive example of homiletic method is given
by Humbert of Romans, which combines a number of currents. Important for any study of legal theory of the crusade, his *Tractatus solemnis de predicatione*[24] is important also as propaganda. It has all
the virtues of systematic scholasticism; it is clear and inclusive, if not
exhaustive. It begins by explaining to the preacher how he will find
the matter he needs in this book, how the well-informed will be able
to complete their information, and how the emotive preacher who lacks
rational matter will find it. The preacher is advised to undertake periodic calls, "*invitationes*", to his hearers, followed by hymn-singing —
Veni Sancte Spiritus, Vexilla Regis, and such. Humbert's sermons are
direct and emotional, at once varied and repetitive, their appeal obvious. He emphasizes the "history of Islamic aggression", the story
of the rise and expansion of Islam, in much the terms that Malmesbury had attributed to Urban; other writers had used more or less the
same passage, for example, Joachim of Flora.[25] We have seen that the

23. *Quinti belli sacri scriptores minores,* ed. Reinhold Röhricht (SOL, *SH,* II-3; Geneva,
1879).

24. *Tractatus solemnis de predicatione* (Nuremberg?, 1490) (folios unnumbered), "Invitationes": cap. 1.

25. *Ibid.,* caps. 1–2 (3rd page), 4, 10, 16 ff. There are 18 pages of holy wars, 6 of Old Testament themes. Joachim, *Expositio in Apocalypsim* (Venice, 1527), fol. 163[v]. Cf. William of
Malmesbury, *De gestis regum,* II, 394.

general theme still had a very wide appeal. From this Humbert passes on to a warm condemnation of unjust war, and to a scholastic definition of the just war with an emotional content that we can only term propaganda; thus, unjust war attacks the innocent, but the crusade attacks guilty men, the Saracens; the argument continues in the same vein throughout. The stress on the "guilt" of Moslems was bound to encourage savage methods of war. The picture of Saracen aggression and Christian just resistance constitutes the *thema commune* of the whole work of preaching the crusade; it picks up from Urban not only the historical argument, but also the idea that the holy war is substituted for unholy, internecine, irresponsible war.

Humbert returns often to the history of the Moslem onslaught on the world, sometimes with a new emphasis; thus Saracens are worse than Jews, who procured the crucifixion and would not believe in the Crucified, but who did not bear arms against the worshipers of the cross; the Romans were responsible for the crucifixion, but turned to adoring the cross and did much to subjugate the world to the Crucified; but the Moslems, although they agree with the Christians in so much belief, reject the mystery of the cross, and have conquered much of the world—Asia, Africa, and even Europe as far as parts of Gaul, as we see in the history of Charles (the Great). The European aggression, which looking back from the twentieth century we see as a swing of the pendulum, is here presented as divine vindication of true religion; success vindicates and failure does not vitiate it, from Constantine, *in hoc signo,* by way of Charlemagne and Turpin to Godfrey of Bouillon and the capture of Jerusalem, and the continuing conflict thereafter. He stresses the many "martyred" Christians and the "innumerable Moslems they killed" in the glorious climax of the capture of Jerusalem in the First Crusade.

Humbert recommends to the preacher that the different kinds of crusade service should be seen in a practical, even worldly order, and should be raised before the public in that order. Service of the body—military service—comes first; next, service by property (*de propriis rebus;* the preacher is warned to take particular care over gifts); third comes verbal, or spiritual service, as by prayer. The debt that man owes of his body is explained by scholastic theological reasons, one of which is illustrated by practical terms apposite to the supposed audience: it is owed *tanquam in feudum.* We are astonished that there were not more such applications of theology to situations which the ultimate audience of these appeals might be expected to experience. Prayer for the army of the faithful is commended primarily as a useful aid toward victory. The preacher is advised to pass direct, after each aggressive passage, into an exhortation to take up the cross and follow Christ, to become a "pilgrim of the Crucified". No doubt it was well-calculated propaganda that stressed the immediate dignity of taking the cross; although this was a public penance for public sins, as Humbert says, it was also an immediate and no doubt gratifying drama with quasi-liturgical significance. It is in this connection that the preacher is recommended to bring up the theocratic idea: the church confers the cross because the church by right wields both the material and the spiritual sword. Humbert has earlier said that the evil crusader is like the bad thief whose cross does not lead to heaven. For any papalist, the example of Frederick II contrasted with that set by Louis IX. Ecclesiastical leadership was the essence of the crusading idea, and this propaganda is here for the church, narrowly conceived, rather than for Christendom in the more general sense of *populus Dei;* it was for the papacy against secular authority.

This theme is not wholly devoid of appeal to the non-churchman, or at least to the less powerful. Humbert proceeds directly to contrast the Lord who demands willing service with those lords who compel their men to follow them. Constantly Humbert reverts to the mystique of the holy war of the past, and adds to it the mystique of the Holy Land. The piety of Moslems in their own pilgrimage—the *hajj* misunderstood, supposed to be to the tomb of Mohammed the Prophet, and yet recognized as an enviable devotion—is seen as a spur to Christians whose devotion should equal and then exceed it. The major problems of theology are taken in the preacher's stride. How could God allow the rise of Mohammed? This is answered scholastically. First, it brings about a "manifestation of the faithful of Christ", as when we recognize loyal knights by their fighting strongly for the king; second, there is "good exercise": God does not want idle followers. Third, "ease of salvation": crusading gives unequaled opportunities to save one's soul.[26] All these arguments are systematized.

Humbert's *Opus tripartitum* summarized the more important points of the *De predicatione* (as he rates them): the seven motives for fighting —zeal for the divine name, zeal for the Christian religion, love for one's brethren, devotion to the Holy Land, the spiritual advantages of war, the example set by the ancients, and the graces granted by the church (indulgences and the like). The *Opus tripartitum,* Humbert's work in preparation for the Second Council of Lyons in 1274, will be considered again later. Here we should note the motives for not crusading which the *Opus* summarizes from the *De predicatione*: the seduction

26. *De predicatione,* cap. 3; *Quarta invitatio,* caps. 4, 7, 8, opening of cap. 6, caps. 9, 14, 15.

of sin, excessive fear of bodily suffering, the bad advice of men, the bad example of others, excessive love of one's own country, excessive love of one's own people, a pretended inability (on grounds of weakness, or lack of means, or unfinished business), or, finally, deficiency of faith.

A final list is of the qualities necessary for a preacher of the crusade: sanctity of life (to be worthy of his subject), the signs of penance (unfitting that he who lacks these should all day invite others to the cross and death), the assumption of the cross (to do what he recommends others to do, lest he be like the scribes and pharisees), discretion in action (the calculation of great transactions in taxation, absolutions, and dispensations requires absolute exactness), a careful solicitude (to preach effectively), a circumspect judgment (since there are so many doubtful questions involved in the business), the offerings of prayers (necessary in the least of matters, the more so in great ones), a moderate zeal (because excess of zeal has very questionable results), and, lastly, the necessary knowledge of what relates to the business[27] (this was Humbert's special contribution, the provision of homiletic material; his lack of originality did not save him from the vanity of authorship). As in all contemporary scholastic writing, more is packed into Humbert's work than we can do justice to. It is interesting for its inclusion of so much of the crusade propaganda that had preceded it, and for the scholastic bias which it gives to this familiar material. There are long lists of suitable biblical texts, many of them not immediately relevant to the theme. It is not easy to believe that the scholastic approach made effective propaganda for purposes of recruitment.

To sum up, there are certainly differences of emphasis between the propaganda associated with Urban II and that of a hundred years and more later; we must explain these changes not only in the crusading scene, but in the recruiting as well. The themes that are constant are the misery and sinfulness of this life, and the long story of holy war, from Moses and Joshua and David, through the Maccabees and, oddly, the Acts of the Apostles, to Constantine and Charlemagne, Urban and Godfrey, a sacred history perpetually renewed, for example by Louis IX. The history of Arab expansion was told in parallel, perhaps an essay in justifying the new European aggression. Urban was starting a new enterprise, and it is at least certain that his preaching was emotive. So was Bernard's. In later treatises (*De predicatione*) the periodic

---

27. *Opus tripartitum* in *Appendix ad fasciculum rerum expetendarum et fugiendarum,* ed. Edward Brown (London, 1690), II, 185 ff., and *De predicatione,* cap. 28.

hymn-singing and calls to arms provided emotional interludes in what must often have seemed dry matter. By this time a wide background of anti-Islamic polemic had created assumptions which must be understood to underlie everything that was said.

B. *The Polemic Framework*

The regular sequence of homiletic themes was supported by a set of ideas sometimes clearly stated, sometimes only hinted at. These ideas delineated the enemy as repulsive; they constituted a body of learned and popular lore which identified the Arab and Moslem world as hostile, dangerous, and harmful. Such an identification was obviously conducive to a condition of protracted warfare, and most of all if this were presented as a "just war", of which holy war is in fact the prototype.

The theme of the Arab attack upon "Asia, Africa, and parts of Europe" was supported by current accounts of the life of the Prophet Mohammed and the rise of Islam. Behind these lie accusations that violence is an essential part of the religion of Islam, which seemed no inconsistency to crusaders employed in religious violence. Also behind the propaganda for the crusade as an ascetic way of life lies a theory that Islam reverses Christian moral concepts (particularly sexual). These are the main constituents of the "Christian version" of what Islam was, and it proved so powerful a body of ideas as to survive even into our own time.[28] These ideas sealed off the mental world of Islam, really so close to the Christian, and effectively prevented contact, except in certain limited fields of immediate utility to Europe. Roughly, the development of these ideas coincides with the period of the crusades, but it is possible to write the history of either with very little reference to the other. We should not see the polemic as a crude and deliberate effort of propaganda called into being by the crusading need. Still less can we simply consider the crusades as the product of

28. Richard W. Southern, *Western Views of Islam in the Middle Ages* (Cambridge, Mass., 1962); Norman Daniel, *Islam and the West* (Edinburgh, 1966). Ugo Monneret de Villard, *Lo Studio dell' Islām in Europa nel XII e nel XIII secolo* (Vatican City, 1944), is not that brilliant scholar's best work. Correct by reference to Marie T. d'Alverny, "Deux Traductions," below (note 33), and her "Marc de Tolède, traducteur d'Ibn Tūmart," *Al-Andalus,* XVI (1951), 99–140, 259–307, and XVII (1952), 1–56, with Georges Vajda; also her *La Connaissance de l'Islam en Occident du IXe au milieu du XIIe siècle* (Spoleto, 1965); but see Ekkehart Rotter, *Abendland und Sarazenen* (Berlin and New York, 1986).

these ideas; more plausibly, we may recognize the two as jointly representative of a common impulse, but even that is an incomplete analysis. We have to see the European concept of Islam throughout the relevant period as conditioned by all the contemporary movements of thought, of which it was itself an active constituent.

The content of anti-Islamic polemic remained largely unchanged in its main lines from its first appearance in the west in the ninth century, in Spain,[29] where it derived from the resentment of Christian minorities submerged in an area of Moslem rule. The form and expression of the polemic, however, developed *pari passu* with the methods of theological, philosophical, and historical thinking of succeeding centuries. Writers struggled with absurd ingenuity to retain their inherited ideas in the face of increasing experience of Islam as it actually was.[30] This complex of notions should be seen as one compartment, a rather small and unobtrusive one, in the whole developing structure of European thought. Once that has been said, the importance of these ideas as propaganda can be seen more clearly. The Christian misconception of Islam was fitted into the main body of knowledge and opinion in which European society found expression, in such a way as to typify the enemy as the converse of the ideal Christian society—not, of course, actual Christian society. In this way propaganda sprang naturally out of the whole attitude of European society; it did not depend on any single ephemeral intellectual fashion.

This attitude to Islam was largely pseudo-historical in character; there was also a great deal of theological analysis, but it was pegged to the "history", tied directly to the sermonizing about Arab aggression, seizure of the Holy Land, and so on. It is equally true to say that the "history" was created to justify the theology. The mental process (not, of course, the ostensible argument) seems to have been this: Christianity is a religion of love, Islam is opposed to Christianity, therefore Islam is the religion of cruelty, therefore Mohammed was cruel and claimed divine justification for it, as suitable circumstances arose. A parallel process begins from the proposition that Christianity is a reli-

29. See the collection of documents dealing with the career of (St.) Eulogius, archbishop of Toledo, in *PL,* 115, cols. 703 ff., esp. *Liber apologeticus martyrum,* cols. 859–860; cf. M. C. Díaz y Díaz, "Los Textos antimahometanos mas antiguos en códices españoles," in *Archives d'histoire doctrinale et littéraire du moyen-âge,* XXXVII (1970), 149–168; Henrique Florez, *España sagrada; Theatro geográphico-histórico de la iglesia de España,* vol. XI (Madrid, 1753); *Passio S. Pelagii* in *Hrotsvithae opera,* ed. Strecher (Leipzig, 1930), pp. 54–66. See also Edward P. Colbert, *The Martyrs of Cordoba* (Washington, 1962); James Waltz, "Significance of the Voluntary Martyrs," *The Moslem World,* IX (1970), 143–159; Daniel, *Arabs and Mediaeval Europe,* 3rd ed. (London and Beirut, 1986), chap. 2.

30. Daniel, *Islam and the West,* pp. 229–270.

gion of chastity. This process is again repeated with the idea "truth" ("therefore Islam is the religion of deception"), and so on. The polemic technique, of course, is the exact converse of the mental process. It starts with the "history" of the revelation of Islam as a deception (as "unchaste", as "violent"), and works back.

Misrepresentations of the life of Mohammed and the rise of Islam fall into three classes. The first group of ideas is so fantastic that we are reduced to guessing what the sources were, and we are even uncertain that there was any source in reality at all. The early poems about Mohammed (Embrico, Walter, du Pont), and tales repeated in a large number of accounts by otherwise serious writers about the circumstances of his life and death, are both absurd and brutal, at once offensive and fantastic. The idea of a dove or bull trained to impersonate a heavenly messenger may derive respectively from Christian symbolism and Jewish superstition of the golden calf. The origin of the stories about Mohammed's death may be some dim awareness of the "apostasy of the Arabs" at the death of the Prophet; more likely, there was a deliberate effort to contrast with Jesus. Several accounts say that Mohammed foretold that he would rise on the third day; of course this is all invention. Another example of the image of Islam as a "false Christianity" is a widespread and persistent belief that the pilgrimage — the existence of which was very generally known — was to the tomb of the Prophet. There was some knowledge of the Ka'bah and of the relative importance of Mecca and Medina, but this was rare and incomplete at best. This type of attack is important only in that it occurred frequently and was an unrestrained expression of hate.[31]

The second group of misrepresentations is almost as far from reality. This revolves around a wicked Christian monk who, in a con-

31. Embrico of Mainz, *Historia de Mahumete* (*PL,* 171, cols. 1345 ff., where it is attributed to Hildebert of Le Mans), critical edition by Guy Cambier in *Embricon de Mayence, La vie de Mahomet* (Brussels, 1961); Walter of Compiègne, in du Méril, cited below, and ed. R. B. C. Huygens in *Sacris erudiri,* VIII (1956), 287–328; *Otia de Machomete,* repr. 1977 (see note 57, below); Alexandre du Pont, *Roman de Mahomet,* ed. Joseph T. Reinaud and Francisque Michel (Paris, 1831), new critical edition by Lepage (see note 57, below). Legends are recounted, for example, in Giraldus Cambrensis, *De principis instructione,* ed. George F. Warner (Rolls Series, 21–VIII), p. 69; St. Albans Chronicle, all versions; Vincent of Beauvais, *Speculum historiale,* XXIII, 39–40 (Douai, 1629); Jacobus de Varagine, *Legenda aurea,* ed. Theodor Graesse (Dresden and Leipzig, 1846), CLXXXI, *De sancto Pelagio.* Consult also Édélstand du Méril, *Poésies populaires latines du moyen-âge* (Paris, 1847); Alessandro d'Ancona, "La Leggenda di Maometto in Occidente," *Giornale storico della letteratura italiana,* XIII (1899), 199–281; Augusto Mancini, *Per lo Studio della legenda di Maometto in Occidente* (Rome, 1935); Bolesłav Ziołecki, tr. Charles Pellat, "La Légende de Mahomet au moyen-âge," *En Terre d'Islam,* III (1943). See also J. Bignami Odier and G. Levi della Vida, "Une Version latine de l'apocalypse syro-arabe de Serge-Bahira," *Mélanges d'archéologie et d'histoire,* LXII (1950), 125–148.

stantly repeated story occurring in many contexts and a number of versions, is the evil genius of a "Mohammed" conceived as rather simple. At its most absurd the Prophet himself is a rebellious cardinal of the Roman church. In every case this man contrives the content of the revelation. The source of this legend was probably the Arabic story—also legendary—of the monk Bahira, who recognized the future prophet in the young Mohammed. Christian legend distorted him into the evil genius—monk, heresiarch, cardinal—called Nicholas, or, more often, Sergius, who taught or trained a false prophet; and to the medievals the Arabic Bahira legend was a half-admission of the truth of their own absurd story; the original was not Bahira, but the bad, mad monk of their invention.[32] It is fatally easy to read any original as the perversion of its own perversion, and both versions were legendary.

Then, thirdly, we come to deal with arguments which represent the subtlest kind of deformation—unfair exaggeration and misinterpretation of admitted facts, rather than wild invention. In this category we have the more accurate accounts of the life of Mohammed, where the Arabic and Moslem sources are obvious and reasonably close. Here every divergence between Moslem and Christian sources is taken as a Moslem deviation, and so as evidence of ill intent. The guiding influence was the *Risālah* of the pseudonymous al-Kindī, a tenth-century work of oriental Christian polemic against Islam which purports simply to apply the moral criteria of Christian faith to the known facts of Mohammed's life.[33] This manages to twist a plain story into a *chronique scandaleuse,* using the technique of the gossip column and giving a free rein to malice. Nevertheless, the material it used, or abused, was authentic, and it was enormously influential, constantly recopied in summarized form in the Middle Ages; it determined the main lines of Christian attitudes almost into modern times, and has been naturally and bitterly resented by Moslems. In our own days, Christians have had to put up with similar treatment by disbelievers in Christ, and the motive of the critic in the one case, as in the other, is likely to be merely to register dissent from the religion so treated, with propagandist intent. Some of the Christian writers concerned were familiar

32. For Bahira see *Encyclopaedia of Islām*, vol. I (Leyden, 1908), *s.v.,* and rev. ed. (Leyden, 1960), *s.v.*

33. The full version of the pseudo-al-Kindī, tr. Peter of Toledo, ed. J. Muñoz y Sendino in *Miscelánea Comillas XI–XII* (1949); more accessible in MS. (best version, Paris, Arsenal, 1162; abridged version in Bibliander, *Machumetis . . . Alcoran* [Basle, 1550]). For the Cluniac corpus see James Kritzeck, *Peter the Venerable and Islam* (Princeton, 1964) and d'Alverny, "Deux traductions latines du Coran," in *Archives d'histoire doctrinale et littéraire du moyen-âge,* XVI (1947–1948), 69–131; also *Petrus Venerabilis: Schriften zur Islam,* ed., tr., and comm. Reinhold Glei (Altenberge, 1985); texts in Kritzeck, Glei, and *PL,* 189, cols. 659–720.

with irreproachably authentic Moslem sources, with a biographer like Ibn-Ishāq, and the traditionalists al-Bukhārī and Muslim.[34] It is difficult to decide whether the deformation of the truth was deliberate, but certainly it was done in order to justify the Christian inheritance of allegations about Mohammed. As more accurate information gradually became available, it tended to drive the more absurd accusations out of circulation, at any rate in learned circles, but where a fact resembled a slander it was regarded as confirming it, not as correcting it. In the case of Peter Pascual, this was a conscious argument. By setting out the two stories one after the other, he reckoned to show the priority of the "Christian" version.[35] This is the same process we have already noted, but here it is seen at its most deliberate.

Except that venom gave emotional force to hatred of Moslems, the attacks on Mohammed are really preliminary to the attacks upon the religion that he preached. We have seen that the polemic technique was to invent (or select) a story about Mohammed in order to link to it some aspect of moral teaching in which Islam and Christianity allegedly differ. The attack on Moslem teaching does not seem at any time to have been related to the perception of actual Islamic practice. We can trace written Arabic sources; we can never trace, nor would our texts by themselves allow us to suspect, that direct experience of Moslem life which we know that many Christians in fact had. This may be why the polemic was related so specifically to the original revelation and its historical circumstances; the distant past was beyond the reach of the historical techniques available. No common ground for argument was recognized, although, of course, it existed in abundance. Both Moslems and Christians accepted that everything must stand or fall by the Koran, but most Christians used only Robert of Ketton's inaccurate paraphrase, and no text or interpretation was accepted in common.

This is a situation obviously favorable to the manufacture of propa-

---

34. Particularly the *quadruplex reprobatio* (perhaps by Raymond Marti) in MS. (see Daniel, *Islam*, p. 397) and printed as *Ioannis Galensis de origine . . . Machometis* (Strassburg, 1550), but see J. Hernando Delgado, "Le 'De Seta Machometi' . . . de Richard Martin," in *Islam et chrétiens du midi* (Toulouse, 1983); and Petrus Paschasius, *Sobre el seta mahometana*, in *Obras*, ed. P. Armengol Valenzuela (Rome, 1905–1908); but see also Riccoldo of Monte Croce, a work variously known as *Disputatio, Confutatio,* or *Antialcoran,* but more properly as *Libellus contra sectam sarracenorum,* text in Jean-Marie Merigoux, "L'Ouvrage d'un frère prêcheur", in *Memorie domenicane,* n.s., XVII (Pistoia, 1986), and William of Tripoli, *De statu Saracenorum,* in Hans Prutz, *Kulturgeschichte der Kreuzzüge* (Berlin, 1883; repr. Hildesheim, 1964), appendix 1, pp. 573–598.

35. Paschasius, *Sobre . . . mahometana,* I, i, 29, and I, ii, *passim.*

ganda, and it is here that it is most clearly demonstrated that men see what they determine to see. Just as in matters of moral discipline Christians interpreted the divergences of Moslem law from Christian as license — without comparison of the actual permitted practice of the two societies — so even more unfairly they assessed the Koran in ways they would never have dared to use, or dreamed of using, to assess the Bible. For example, it was attacked as disordered, as though any prophecy could read like a scholastic treatise. Several of the Old Testament prophets read more strangely, but the point, of course, was that it was assumed that the Koran could not be the eternal word of God, and must therefore be treated as, and shown to be, an imitation. This is why Christian, and to a lesser extent Jewish, influence on Mohammed was supposed to be so important. Only in our own century have Christians begun to recognize originality in the Koran.

Most modern non-Moslem scholars have assumed, from the fact of Jewish relations with the early Moslem community, that there was a formative Jewish influence on the Koran, much more important than the more distant Christian influence. Medieval Christians took the opposite position. Whether they arrived at the theology from their historical error, or derived their history from an error in theological analysis, they conceived Islam with its positive Christology to be in the intellectual sense, if not the legal, a Christian heresy, and so they came naturally to credit the notion of there having been a Christian source of Moslem revelation. If Islam be conceived as a development from Judaism, it must, for a Christian, seem an improvement, but when it is viewed as a heresy, it must seem, not an approximation to Christianity, but a sad falling away. Even today Moslems are often hurt that Christianity does not award Islam the honorable place that Islam awards to Christianity, but in fact Islam awards Jesus honor, and Christians only toleration. This explains the vilification of Mohammed, who, for Moslems, is the bearer of the word of God, the Koran, as Mary is the bearer of the word in the Christian faith (and Mary is heartily praised in the Koran). This was precisely the trouble for western writers, who could regard praise of Jesus, expressed in terms of doctrinal deviation, only as "smearing the lip of the cup with honey, and after with deadly poison",[36] an offense against that strict orthodoxy which was a medieval preoccupation. Christians in Europe were not interested in toleration and were not grateful for the toleration of Christians in the Arab world; not to acknowledge the Christian right to rule was itself, in medieval eyes, to persecute Christianity.

36. Kritzeck, *Peter the Venerable*, p. 206.

Thus the Islamic revelation was rejected *in toto,* an ever-continuing cause of war, perpetually renewed.

The relationship between this quasi-historical, quasi-theological polemic and the state of war comes out clearly if we examine one of its most classical expressions, the summary of his own more lengthy polemic with which Riccoldo of Monte Croce ends his *Liber peregrinationis* (to Baghdad).[37] This attack immediately follows one of the most glowing testimonies to the practice of virtue by Moslems that the Middle Ages produced, and we should bear this in mind when we study Riccoldo's confused attacks on the "confusion" of Islam. In these passages he says that Islam, *lex sarracenorum* — religion was always conceived as a law, the rules for obeying God — is *larga, confusa, occulta, mendacissima, irracionabilis, et violenta.* At least three of these adjectives describe his own analysis. Thus, under *larga,* he argues that the philosophers, and above all Christ, say that the way is narrow; how then can the witness, "there is no god but God and Mohammed is his messenger", have saving power? Anyway (he goes on) such a proposition is self-evident of anything, as for example, "there is no horse . . .". Riccoldo's absurd position here is, of course, capable of being demonstrated most clearly in a language that does not lack the article: to say "there is no horse but *a* horse" or "*the* horse" immediately shows the fallacy in the argument. Under *confusa* he complains that nothing in the Koran is stated under clear headings, like scholastic categories presumably; can he have persuaded himself that it is so in the Bible, in either the New Testament or the Old? He exemplifies "confusion" from the Koran, with the complaint that in it, when God forbids something, he adds, "if you do it, God is compassionate and merciful and knows that you are weak." Does forgiveness imply inconsistency? Few today would accept this as fair criticism, and, as there is talk of confusion, we note that this point would have been appropriate, if anywhere, as laxity, under the heading *larga.*

Under *occulta* Riccoldo attacks dishonest means supposedly used by Moslems to circumvent the laws against adultery and usury; it would be easy enough to make similar criticisms of canonical evasions in the Catholic church. Under *mendacissima* he attacks chiefly passages in the Koran that are inconsistent with the text of the Bible. The first point to which Riccoldo objects as *irracionabilis* is the law of triple divorce; if an objection is to be made, it would again seem more appropriate

---

37. In *Peregrinatores medii aevi quatuor,* ed. J. C. M. Laurent (Leipzig, 1864), pp. 105 ff.: as *Itinerarius.* Based on a poor manuscript, this should be corrected by MS. Berlin Staatsbibliothek lat. 4°.446 entitled *Liber peregrinationis* and corrected by the author himself. See Emilio Panella, *Presentazione,* in *Memorie domenicane,* n.s., XVII (1986).

under the heading *larga*. He claims that learned Moslems deride the Koran in secret; it is hardly credible that this is asserted at first hand, and his sources are probably the Jacobites and Nestorians with whom he was for a time friendly. Under the same heading he goes on to explain that Islam claims to correct our biblical stories, which, if he were as logical as he claims, he would have put with his attacks on the truth of the Koran (*mendacissima*) because of its inconsistency, in detail, with the Bible. Under *violenta* he stresses that it is "most certain" that Islam will last only as long as the victory of the sword lasts. This brings him back to the life of Mohammed, and thence he wanders into subjects other than violence. Lastly, he claims that the Moslems are easily convinced and confuted in debate:[38] to this improbable claim we shall return.

Why is this attack on the unmethodical so unmethodical? It is difficult to suggest a reason, beyond the intellectual agitation induced by the subject. The fact is that Riccoldo objects to most things that he attributes to Islam, under all the epithets he lists. His perpetual inconsistencies are in fact characteristic of his approach, which can never use one single standard to judge the two religions, but which sees the same thing in Islam as a fault and in Christianity as innocent. This side of his work resembles the worst propaganda. With its considerable apparatus of learning, it pretends to show "rationally", as was said then, or "scientifically", as we should say today, that Islam is in every respect the opposite of, and so an unremitting threat to, the entire Christian structure. He typifies this polemic literature by his refusal to recognize anything good or true in the teaching of Islam (even the praise of Jesus and Mary is grudged), and in its vilification of Mohammed and his religion interchangeably. His total rejection of Moslem religion reflects in the intellectual sphere the total war that was the usual papal policy for the world. What makes this truly poignant is the contrast with Riccoldo's very honest praise of the virtues and even the religious practice of the learned Moslems he encountered. He sometimes even exaggerates these, in order to condemn Christian faults, but his account seems truthful.

Much more questionable is his unambiguous claim to have debated theology successfully with Moslems.[39] It is self-evident that Moslems could not have accepted many of his arguments as even relevant, since much that he says is a misinterpretation of an Islamic position. For

---

38. *Ibid.*, pp. 135–141; cf. also the main argument of the *Libellus contra sectam* (note 34 above).

39. Röhricht, "Lettres de Ricoldo de Monte Croce," *AOL,* II–2 (1884), 260, n. 12.

example, he makes great play with the blessing, "may God pray for Mohammed". He takes this literally and so attacks its theology. No Moslem would ever accept that the Arabic idiom here could actually bear the sense in which Riccoldo attacks it; therefore Riccoldo knew it only in written form and had never discussed it with Moslems.[40] More to the point, a public debate which involved blasphemy against the Koran (considered the uncreated word of God) and crudely sacrilegious and scurrilous attacks on Mohammed could lead only to "voluntary martyrdom" on the Cordova model, as in one case which survives in detail, of a Franciscan who mistook bad history for faith, and in a number of others known to us in more or less detail.[41] Much is pathetic in this impersonal cultural arrogance. The story of Raymond Lull, who deliberately angered Moslem mobs by attacking Mohammed, and whom the North African authorities twice saved from himself, illustrates the best that might happen in such circumstances.[42] Surviving accounts of debates between Jews and Christians show that each side dreamed its own fantasies of success.[43] An anecdote of William of Rubruck suggests the inconclusive nature of such discussions in neutral surroundings.[44] The belief that what a man himself finds so convincing must convince the world reminds us of the delusion that right must prevail in battle.

How was anti-Islamic polemic in the crusading period linked with the crusade? The polemic is not conterminous with active crusading. Naturally, it coincides with a relationship, sometimes close, sometimes distant, between Moslems and Christians, and so it coincides very generally with *jihād*. As long as the two religions existed side by side they experienced a magnetic repulsion which first took a bitter form on the Christian side, at that time materially the inferior and losing side. All the existing material—much of it, we may confidently speculate, in the form of unbroken oral tradition—was used widely and actively from the time of the First Crusade onward. Propaganda thus developed became conventional. For example, Innocent III in the course of a bull

40. *Libellus contra sectam,* cap. 9, in Merigoux, *op. cit.,* pp. 106–107, lines 209–214; and Röhricht, "Lettres," *AOL,* II-2, 288.

41. *BOF,* II, 61, 66–67, 110 ff., 143 ff.; IV, 390–394; and V, 282 ff. For Cordova see references in note 29, above.

42. Edgar A. Peers, *Ramon Lull: a Biography* (London, 1929). See the discussion of Lull in Benjamin Z. Kedar, *Crusade and Mission* (Princeton, 1984), pp. 189–199.

43. Daniel, *Islam,* p. 184, and index *s.v.* "disputation".

44. *Sinica franciscana,* vol. 1, *Itinera et relationes Fratrum Minorum saeculi XIII et XIV,* ed. Anastasius van den Wyngaert (Quaracchi, 1929), *Fr. Guilelmi de Rubruc itinerarium,* cap. XXXIII, 22 (p. 297); English translation in Christopher Dawson, *The Mongol Mission* (London and New York, 1955), p. 194.

which is simultaneously a recruiting exhortation, a legal pronounce-
ment of indulgence (as all such documents were), and a declaration
of an intention to undertake war, summarizes the usual polemic against
Mohammed in a few phrases.[45]

The crusades gave a sense of historical importance to those who
took part in them, and they aroused interest in Islam which would
otherwise have lain dormant. The most informed polemic came from
Spain, from areas where Christians had gained possession. In that sense
it is an achievement of the reconquest, and neither a cause nor a consequence of the crusades proper, but material originating in Palestine
agreed with what came from Spain, although as information it was
inferior in quality. We cannot really divide the European inheritance
in this respect. There is no doubt that this polemic served both to fill
out and to support the purely recruiting themes with which we began
this study.

C. Lay Attitudes

We can sum up all this polemic propaganda as designed to show
that the Moslems were and had always been implacable enemies, pro-
ponents of a form of religion devised to supplant and destroy Christianity. There was (in theory) no possibility of reconciliation. Moreover, every possible legal step was taken to cut Christians off from
Moslems, whether in territory under Christian rule, or in territory under Moslem rule. The authorship of most of the propaganda, and all
the intellectual propaganda, was clerical. Of course, the clergy was not
a homogeneous body; it covered a vast range of different degrees of
power, interests, skills, abilities, and cultural levels. The more intelligent propaganda (however perverse) was the work of clerics of a higher
order of ability and learning and spontaneous interest in the idea of
"Christendom". There was certainly a sense of solidarity among Christians, but this was so rarely put to the test that we cannot say how
far it existed outside the range of the theorists of Christendom. Crusading was an essential part of the papal, theological, and canonical
movement, almost as much so as the Gregorian reform which had immediately preceded it, or the investiture controversy which coincided

45. Aloysius Tomassetti, *Bullarium diplomatum et privilegiorum . . . editio* (Turin, 1857–
1872), Innocent III, III, 275 (no. 92).

with its early stages; the notion of Christendom which it both presupposed and reinforced was taken up by the scholastics. "Although the abandonment of Christendom to the Moslems must greatly touch all Christians," said Humbert, "it touches the clerical and priestly estate more, for it is they who see more clearly . . . because of their greater gift of intellect; and it concerns them more, because of the responsibility they have for Christendom."[46]

This idea of Christendom was much later than the idea of Islam. Islam was conceived as a negation set up against the church, but in one sense the opposite is true. The idea of Christendom, as at the time understood, was largely set up by the polemicists who attacked the Moslems; indeed, their "Christendom" extended in practice no further beyond the Latin west than western rule, including rule over oriental Christians considered as unreliable allies. With this theoretic picture, which is not just clerical, but papalist and scholastic, the actual interests and practice of laymen did not always coincide, and the effect of the propaganda upon them is not always discernible. The laymen, whether lords, merchants, or poor men, with the clerics dependent on them, had their own likes and dislikes, and to some extent their own propaganda.

Those who had to deal with Moslems in practice found it quite easy to treat them as human beings; this natural fact is no doubt why it seemed necessary to the canonists to set up great barriers between Moslems and Christians living beside each other in countries under Moslem or under Christian rule. Travelers, merchants, and all whose profession was not deliberately to provoke Moslems to anger, found that they got on with them well enough, and sometimes even very well, when not prevented by suspicion on both sides, arising mostly from the perpetual hostilities. The intention of the crusade propagandists was naturally to prevent this and to represent Moslems as impossible to deal with. Some of the polemic written for knightly consumption, however, even when written by clerics, at least those dependent on aristocratic patronage, was much less analytic.

We saw above that, before the crusades proper, discussion of war against Moslems lacked real hostility. The chronicles of the capture of Sicily, though committed to a church interest, show themselves more interested in personal stories (even of Arabs) and in the sequence of events, than in any attitude toward Moslems as such. In Spain, in the *Cantar del Cid,* there is absolutely no hostility to Islam at all. The Moslem gentleman (I use the word deliberately; it is his noble charac-

---

46. *Opus tripartitum,* in *Appendix . . . fugiendarum,* ed. Brown, p. 189.

ter that matters) who is manipulated by the Cid serves him loyally, admittedly much as the "lackeys of imperialism" have been said to serve their masters in our own time, but quite acceptably when judged by the standards of chivalry. The villains of the poem are Christians: it speaks for a new aristocracy against an old one, and its leading ideas are honor and booty and luck. It is far from the thought of the crusade. The Moors figure sometimes as noble enemies, but more often as the victims of the Cid's frank brigandage, and, whatever the victims felt about it, the Cid and his companions exploited them without malice.[47] At least during the period of the *taifas,* slaves and singing and dancing girls were evidently amenities of a common culture; when the other side won, the daughter of the house might become her conqueror's singing girl, if he preferred her to her ransom. Similarly, we cannot speak of crusading hatred where Arab vassals helped, as was the style of the day, to educate the sons of their Christian overlords.[48] Not indifference to religion, but a phase of confessional indifference, of often callous toleration, seems at first to have accompanied a Christian victory. Susceptibility to the clerical propaganda which exploited the more malicious Mozarab traditions (while suppressing Mozarab culture) came later, and the earlier lay attitude left no permanent mark.

Did propaganda follow, rather than precede, the crusade also in the case of the *chansons de geste,* which at first sight looks more different from that of the *Cantar del Cid* than it does on analysis? Certainly they represent something more permanent in the European imagination, an unreal but perennially popular convention that, throughout the four centuries that it survived in active form, imparted steady entertainment rather like the Wild West stories of the nineteenth century or the science fiction of the twentieth. Whether or not these poems were often based on monastic records, as Bédier has argued, most of them were meant to appeal to knightly listeners and all who admired chivalry.[49] Noble birth is important in all this literaure. When the French king buys a fine Arab slave-boy, he watches him—"Demandat mei si ere de halte gent", and when he learns that he is indeed noble, with powerful parents, treats him well. When count William is able to throw off the disguise in which he has penetrated into Arab Nîmes, and been

---

47. Menéndez Pidal, ed., *Cantar de mio Cid,* esp. cantos 126–128, 132, 25–26.

48. Reinhart P. A. Dozy, *Recherches sur l'histoire et la littérature de l'Espagne pendant le moyen-âge,* 3rd ed. (Paris and Leyden, 1881); Menéndez Pidal, *La España del Cid,* 3rd rev. ed. (Madrid, 1967), and cf. his *Poesía arabe y poesía europea* (Madrid, 1941); Reinaud, *Les Invasions des Sarrazins en France* (Paris, 1836); Daniel, *Arabs and Mediaeval Europe,* chap. 4; and see also note 62, below.

49. Joseph Bédier, *Les Légendes épiques,* 3rd ed. (4 vols., Paris, 1926–1929); cf. Jean Rychner, *La Chanson de Geste* (Geneva, 1955).

treated contemptuously as a merchant or peasant, he calls out: "Felon paien, toz vos confonde Deus! / Tant m'avez hui escharni et gabé / Et marcheant et vilain apelé; / Ge ne sui mie marcheant. . . ." Both sides understand this clearly. For an Arab knight, as for a Frank, "baseness" is as bad a fate as death: "a vostre volenté / Volentiers m'i rendrai, se jou ai seürté / Que jou n'i soie ocis et menés a vilté." The daughters (or wives) of the sultans or amirs, the ladies who change sides and marry the Christian heroes in so many of the poems, are all noble; they may change their religion, but they cannot, of course, change their class. "Birth" was necessary for any love-making: "deus puceles de molt haut parenté"; so was wealth: "Achetanz fu ses oncle, qui ot grant richeté"—four castles and as many cities. The fathers (or husbands) command large estates, even empires. An obvious example of a general trend is *Roland*'s roll-call of the enemy, king and kings' sons and dukes, besides the "amurafle" and "almaçur"; in its careful statements of properties, Climborin owns half Saragossa, Valdabron is lord of four hundred galleys.[50]

Roland, perhaps the earliest and best, certainly the best-known of the poems, is also among the most bellicose—Turpin at least seems to be an authentic crusader, though a crusading attitude is strictly confined to him; and yet in *Roland,* almost more than in any other poem, the Arab world is presented as a close analogue of European society. In most of the poems, Saracens are not only recognized as "barons", but are made out themselves to discriminate between Christians in point of birth and conduct. King Galafre in the *Couronnement de Louis* offers William of Orange fiefs and honors because of his birth—"Car tes lignages est molt de halte gent"—and of his prowess—"De tes proëces oï parler sovent". The poems assume that chess and backgammon, like love-making, are common to the two worlds; but sometimes also sup-

50. *La Chanson de Guillaume,* ed. Duncan McMillan (2 vols., Paris, 1949–1950), line 3537; Renoart's royal Saracen relatives are never forgotten, *Chanson de Guillaume,* laisse 162; *Aliscans, chanson de geste,* ed. F. Guessard and Anatole de Montaiglon (Paris, 1870), lines 4116–4117, 4386–4388; also ed. E. Wienbeck, W. Hartnacke, and P. Rasch (Halle, 1903); *La Bataille Loquifer,* ed. Monica Barnett (Oxford, 1975), lines 2947 and 3029; also ed. J. Runeberg (Helsinki, 1913); *Le Moniage Renoart,* MSS. Arsenal 6562 fol. 167 and BL MS. Royal 20.D.XI fol. 181, col. 2; cf. Runeberg, *Études sur la Geste Rainouart* (Helsinki, 1905), p. 47; *Le Charroi de Nîmes,* ed. Joseph L. Perrier (Paris, 1931; repr. 1972), lines 1360–1363; *La Chanson des quatre fils Aymon,* ed. Ferdinand Castets (Montpellier, 1909), lines 3996–3998; *Le Siège de Barbastre,* ed. Perrier (Paris, 1926), lines 5602, 5605; *La Chanson de Roland,* ed. Bédier (Paris, 1937; often reprinted), lines 1526–1528 and 1562–1564, and generally laisses 69–125; baron, vassal, etc., are used constantly in all this literature. See also *Les Textes de la Chanson de Roland,* ed. Raoul Mortier, Vol. I: *La Version d'Oxford* (Paris, 1940). On the heroines see Bédier, "La Composition de la chanson de *Fierabras,*" *Romania,* XVII (1888), pp. 48–49, and cf. Ellen Rose Woods, *Aye d'Avignon: a Study of Genre and Society* (Geneva, 1978), chaps. 2 and 3.

pose that feasting with wine is too.[51] This mistake is best considered as the product, not so much of ignorance, as of indifference to facts, combined with a set purpose to regard the Arab world as just like home. We meet more and more gallant Saracens until with the passage of time an imaginary Arab world merges with an almost equally unreal Christian one. The son of the sultan and the countess of Ponthieu, admittedly brought up as a Christian, was "preudom et boins chevaliers et hardis et cortois et larges et debounaires et ne mie orgeilleux", surely a summary of chivalric ideals. His sister remained in Egypt, "grew in very great beauty", and married a valiant Turk, and their grandson was "Salhadin, qui tant etoit courtois prince que nul plus".[52] So in the end the most chivalrous of all was a Moslem. There is plenty of generalized abuse of "pagans", but, as in the *Cantar del Cid,* the only villains were Christians — in the *chansons,* they are defectors, a Ganelon, an Ysoré, a Macaire.[53] This was not peace propaganda; it took the war for granted, and treated it like a very dangerous sport; but it was not crusade propaganda either.

The mass of the internal evidence indicates that this literature was meant simply to entertain. What we usually regard as the lowest and silliest point that propaganda reaches, the absurd theology of Mahom, Tervagan, Apollin, and the rest of the idols, can equally well be taken

51. *Chanson de Roland*: e.g., laisse 89 and lines 1604, 2686, 3172, 3637–3638; *Le Couronnement de Louis,* ed. Ernest Langlois (Paris, 1925), lines 859–860; also ed. Yvan G. Lepage, *Les Rédactions en vers du Couronnement de Louis* (Geneva, 1978). Love across cultures: *Le Siège de Barbastre,* laisse 151 ff.; *La Prise d'Orange,* ed. Claude Régnier (Paris, 1972), laisses 7, 9, 10, 13; note: "se ge nen ai la dame *et le cite*" (line 266); central episode in *Roland à Saragosse* (14th century), ed. Maria L. G. Roques (Paris, 1956); *Maugis d'Aigremont,* ed. Castets, *Revue des langues romanes,* XXXVI (1892), lines 3320–3434, where incest is averted; the queen, a captured Christian, is the hero's aunt; *La Chanson d'Aspremont,* ed. Louis Brandin (Paris, 1924; repr. 1970), lines 2635–2655, where the hero refuses more priggishly than piously; André de Mandach, *Naissance et développement de la chanson de geste en Europe,* III and IV, *Chanson d'Aspremont* (Geneva, 1975 and 1980), cross-referenced to Brandin's edition; *Aye d'Avignon,* ed. François Guessard and Paul Meyer (Paris, 1861), lines 1766–1769 and 4091–4097, Christian heroine will not, Moslem hero will, change religion. New edition, ed. S. J. Borg, *Aye d'Avignon, chanson de geste anonyme* (Geneva, 1967); cf. James R. McCormack, *Gui de Nanteuil* (Geneva and Paris, 1970). Games: in *Gaufrey, chanson de geste,* ed. F. Guessard and Polycarpe Chabaille (Paris, 1859), line 1795 and other examples; in *Gui de Warewic,* ed. Alfred Ewert (Paris, 1933), chess has a brief but essential part in the plot, lines 7969–8008, and see note 63. Wine: in *Simon de Pouille,* ed. Jeanne Baroin (Geneva, 1968), line 1480; *Gaufrey,* line 8732, etc.

52. *La Fille du Comte de Pontieu,* ed. Clovis Brunel (Paris, 1926), XXII (pp. 756–758), XXIII (pp. 780–785); *Saladin,* ed. Larry S. Crist (Textes littéraires français, 185; Geneva, 1972), I, xx, 51, cf. XXXI, 29, and *explicit*; cf. Busone da Gubbio, *L'Avventuroso Ciciliano* with *L'Ordene de Chevalerie,* ed. George F. Nott (Florence, 1832); examples of wholly fictional Arab *preux* in *Aspremont,* lines 2963, 6022, 6029, etc.

53. In *Roland;* in *Anseïs de Cartage* (*Anseïs von Karthago*), ed. Johann B. Alton (Tübingen, 1892); in *Aiol, chanson de geste,* ed. Jacques Normand and Gaston Raynaud (Paris, 1877).

as evidence of a deliberate frivolity. The number of different idols seems to increase with the passage of time, and then to tail off again, but this attitude does not correlate with any other observable change in the attitude to Islam. Sometimes the idols play more part in the story, but as far as we can tell only for the sake of the plot. Have we been guilty of anachronism and of condescension, assuming that the poets were ignorant and small-minded, when the fault lay in our own ability to interpret? The system of idols is effectively confined to this one body of literature; I do not take much account of sparse references in chronicles to idols in mosques, which may have been thoughtless reflections of the literature. It is possible for two communities to live side by side and largely in ignorance of each other, but even the most ingenious explanation of the origins of the names of the idols does not tell us why anyone wanted in the first place to invent the system of idols at all.

The poets probably thought of Islam as somehow a continuation of the religious system of ancient Rome, and of that they knew nothing save the names of some gods. The question remains, why elaborate so complex a system? If we reply, propaganda, why an attractive system of jeweled splendor? Above all, why reject the official propaganda system? The authors may have been ignorant of Moslems, but not, surely, of what other Christians knew and thought. It is not just that they ignore what the academic polemicists and theologians were saying, but, with very few exceptions in so vast a literature, they ignore the abusive folklore of Mohammed which penetrated everywhere else. To me it seems likely that they chose and knowingly adhered to a certain convention which suited the story they wanted to tell and which in fact largely determined the plot, and that they deliberately decided to take not the slightest notice of what the preachers were saying. It is possible to argue that these poems, far from being war propaganda, constitute a rejection of serious propaganda, made possible, while avoiding any suggestion of crypto-heresy, by adopting an absurd convention, but one unfavorable to Islam. In *Anseïs,* king Marsile will not desert Mohammed to save his life, out of contempt for how Christians practise their religion.[54] The poet speaks neutrally, almost ambiguously. These poems rarely come so near to satire as this, but all remain isolated from official propaganda.

Y. and C. Pellat very acutely established the absolute division among three types of polemic against Islam. One is true polemic, academic

---

54. *Anseïs,* lines 11463–11520. This episode appears in a form both more clearly satirical and more clerical in the pseudo-Turpin 13, "de ordinibus qui erant in convivio". See Hamilton M. Smyser, *The Pseudo-Turpin* (Cambridge, Mass., 1937), and C. Meredith Jones, *Historia Caroli Magni* (Paris, 1936).

"pure and applied" theology: either direct crusade propaganda, or its theoretic foundation. Another is the legendary, "folkloric" life of Mohammed. The third is the idolatry convention of the *chansons de geste* and related *romans*.[55] This division is absolute in the sense that the three categories are logically distinct. In practice they overlap, but in different ways. The legends very occasionally wander into the *chansons,* where they seem odd and out of place, but they strongly influence the academics, who were always hoping that something in the "Christian" version of events would turn out to be true, or could be made to stick. As we have seen, the legends have a distant relation to the facts as we know them from Islamic sources, sometimes so distant as to require clairvoyance to recognize, but still a relation.

We have already considered the importance of the legends in polemic, but not their character as a literary genre. One of the earliest western writers on Islam, Guibert of Nogent, calls the legends *plebeia opinio,* which we can reasonably translate as "folklore", and he tells us that he has not seen them written down. He seems not to vouch for anything that he repeats, but, after making a rather crude joke, he prescinds from it, and adds that it is not true, as some people think, that Mohammed claimed to be God. As who think? This can hardly refer to the *chansons de geste,* because a manipulated idol is not a man claiming to be God; nor is it one of the usual legends, nor does Guibert refer to it as such.[56] It may just be that a comparison with Christ is at the back of every Christian's mind, but this text does emphasize how amorphous, how protean, and sometimes untraceable this material is, penetrating sermons, chronicles, and collections, wherever the anecdotal form is appropriate. Embrico in his *Vita Mahumeti* puts it to propagandistic use maliciously and tendentiously, but Walter of Compiègne, in his *Otia de Machomete,* is more irenic, as Cambier and Lepage point out, and Alexandre du Pont's paraphrase elaborates a bosky, feudal background.[57] Legends might be used to stir up crusading sentiment, but might just as likely be repeated solely to divert.

55. Y. and C. Pellat, "L'Idée de Dieu chez les 'Sarrasins' des chansons de geste," *Studia Islamica,* XXII (1965), 5–42; cf. C. Pellat, "Mahom, Tervagan, Apollin," *Actas del primer congreso de estudios árabes* (Madrid, 1964); Henri Grégoire, "Des Dieux Cahu, Baraton, Tervagant . . . ," *Annuaire de l'Institut de philologie et d'histoire orientales et slaves,* VII (1939–1944), 451–472, and "L'Étymologie de Tervagant (Trivigant)," in *Mélanges d'histoire du théatre . . . offerts à Gustave Cohen* (Paris, 1950), 67–74; also René Basset, "Hercule et Mahomet," *Journal des savants,* n.s., I (July 1903), 391–402.

56. Guibert of Nogent, *Gesta Dei per Francos,* I, 3 (*RHC, Occ.,* IV, 127–128); see above, note 31.

57. Cambier, "Quand Gautier de Compiègne composait les *Otia de Machomete?*" *Latomus,*

The legends vary greatly, but they have in common, as I have shown, some relation to facts, however perverted, and some polemic purpose, however frivolous. Bahira-Sergius in its first form is Moslem, in its latest (cardinal) purely west European. Disgusting tales of pigs and dogs and drunkenness seem gratuitous, but probably relate to Moslem religious teaching. The magnetic tomb was picked up from Hellenistic legend, but it is a backhanded compliment to the impact of Mohammed on the European imagination that it came to be associated with him in particular.[58] Even here there is a distant authenticity in that it tended to be believed because the importance of the *hajj* was dimly apprehended. Such stories, mixed with the more authentic if equally perverted tales of the pseudo-Kindī and others, reached everywhere — except the *chansons de geste.* This can only be because the *chansons* could not repeat the legends and at the same time also maintain the system of idols which is fundamental to their only serious purpose — as we shall now see — itself interwoven with the fabric of pure entertainment.

The legends were perversions of fact, but the idols were pure fantasy, although the Arab society in which the poets imagined them was made to resemble the European even more closely than it really did. It is clear that the legends can only be propaganda, or its consequence, but the motivation of the *chansons* is less obvious. A clue is in the recurring references to Arab wealth, though they are never as frank as the *Cantar del Cid* about booty. Some of the most striking descriptions of the idols gleaming in gold and precious stones are in the *Chanson d'Antioche* ("Tous fu d'or et d'argent, moult luist et reflambie") and the *Conquête de Jérusalem,* where the royal pavilion is lighted "De l'or qui i reluist, des perres de cristal". We might blame the vulgar sensuality of the ribald Tafurs, but we first find the theme in *Roland,* and the grandest accounts come in poems of the later twelfth and the thirteenth centuries devoted to chivalry. The recurrent scene of the smashing of idols is a hardly disguised scene of loot. Wealth is emphasized in other ways. A Christian is offered great wealth to become a Moslem. The Moslem country is rich, as some contemporary travelers said,

---

XVII (1958), 531–539; cf. his "Les Sources de la *Vita Mahumeti* d'Embricon de Mayence," *Latomus,* XX (1961), 364–380, and "Embricon de Mayence (1010?–1077) est-il l'auteur de la *Vita Mahumeti?*" *Latomus,* XVI (1957), 468–479 (the Embrico of this date is questioned by Southern, *Western Views of Islam,* p. 30 note). See also Yvan G. Lepage, *Le Roman de Mahomet de Alexandre du Pont (1258) avec le texte des Otia de Machomete de Gautier de Compiègne,* établi par R. B. C. Huygens (Paris, 1977).

58. Main references at note 31 above. For the tomb see Cambier, "Les Sources," *Latomus,* XX (1961), 375–377, and Lepage, *Le Roman de Mahomet,* pp. 46–50.

and there is an idea that Moslems claim that, though God may rule in heaven, "Mahom" rules this world and makes the vegetation grow — recollections of a fertility cult?[59]

In the *chansons de geste* it is success that is important, in war especially, and is even a great moral and religious issue. Love is important, but it is interwoven with the war interest. Women, for the vulgar, are booty — "Ne doi pas estre a vos garçons livrée" — but the knight, too, who wins the sultan's daughter gains by marriage a title to his new estates that lends legality to conquest. Even Orable, surely no mere sex object, holds the hereditary title to Orange. Moslem countries were for plunder, and success was the judgment of God evinced through ordeal by battle; we must believe in the God who helps us, "En tel Dieu doit on croire, qui sa gent volt aidier."[60] In real life, Christians

59. *Chanson d'Antioche,* ed. Paris, v, 41, line 1028; ed. Duparc-Quioc, line 4878 (variant); *Conquête de Jérusalem,* ed. Hippeau, vii, 13, line 6465; *Chanson de Roland,* ed. Bédier, line 3493. Examples (by no means exhaustive) from other poems: *Les Enfances Guillaume,* ed. Patrice Henry (Paris, 1935), lines 1533–1538; *Floovant,* ed. Sven A. Andolf (Uppsala, 1941), xxv, lines 725–728; *Gaufrey,* ed. Guessard, line 8735; *Aymeri de Narbonne,* ed. Louis Demaison (Paris, 1887), lines 1224–1225; *Fierabras,* ed. Auguste Kroeber and Gustave Servois (Paris, 1860), lines 3155–3184, where the idols are brought into the narrative and destroyed in one passage; a rather fuller version in *Chanson d'Aspremont,* ed. Brandin, leads up to a distribution of broken bits among the knights, laisses 182–188, especially lines 3450–3458. Still more elaborate, in *Simon de Pouille,* ed. Baroin, the manipulator is driven out of the idols one after the other (laisses 64–67). There is a good example in the same poem of riches offered as a reward for conversion to Islam: "Trop te fera avoir et richece doner, / Trop gentil damoisselle a moiller et a per", *ibid.,* lines 1461–1462; cf. *Aye d'Avignon,* ed. Guessard, lines 1640–1642. Again, many more examples might be cited, though conversion to Christianity was also rewarded materially. Many examples also exist of Moslem wealth, idols apart, e.g., *La Chevalerie Vivien,* ed. Adolphe L. Terracher (Paris, 1923): "A Cordes tint riche cort Desrames," where are "Amoraves, riches rois coronés", lines 90, 93. Travelers: e.g., Gerard of Strassburg in Arnold of Lübeck, *Chronica Slavorum* (*MGH, SS,* XXI, 235–241); Riccoldo, *Itinerarius,* in *Peregrinatores . . . quatuor,* ed. Laurent, and Röhricht, "Lettres," *AOL,* II-2, 271–276; Simon Semeonis, in *BOF,* III; *Jacobi de Verona Liber peregrinationis,* ed. Röhricht, *ROL,* III (1895). Mahom rules: examples in *Antioche,* line 1040; *Couronnement de Louis,* line 839; *Gaufrey,* lines 8703, 8731–8732; *Chanson de Guillaume,* line 2118; *Chanson de Chevalier au Cygne,* line 4600; *Aliscans,* ed. Guessard and Montaiglon, lines 1416–1417; and *Prise d'Orange,* line 672; cf. Y. and C. Pellat, "L'Idée de Dieu".

60. Women: *Chanson d'Aspremont,* line 10906; cf. *Chanson d'Antioche,* vi, 35, line 988, "Des belles Saracines i ont fait lor delis"; Duparc-Quioc, line 6413. Aye, in the eponymous poem, is afraid of this (lines 1719–1720) but saved by Ganor (those worth ransom were no doubt safe enough), but distinguished ladies captured did marry Moslem lords in these poems, e.g., *Maugis d'Aigremont,* lines 3320–3434, and the countess of Ponthieu's daughter (*La Fille,* xi, 359–361); another version in *Le Romans de Bauduin de Sebourc,* ed. L. Napoléon Boca (Valenciennes, 1841), xiv, 657–658, "La dame de Pontieu qui Jesus renoioit / Pour l'amour d'Esmeret". God: *Conquête de Jérusalem,* vi, 16, line 5583. For the "god" who fails see the Renouart cycle, MS. Arsenal 6562 and Bibl. municipale, Boulogne-sur-Mer, 192. The association of the heiress with the estate is never more clearly put than in *Anseïs de Cartage,* lines 26–27 (the estate is all Spain). Bellisant, daughter of Charlemagne in *Otinel,* ed. F. Guessard and Henri Michelant (Paris, 1858), rewards the hero's conversion with her hand and large estates, but this way round is rare. Orable in *Prise d'Orange,* line 1400, makes her family status in Orange clear.

did not apostatize en masse at a Moslem victory; during the period of the *chansons,* only the Levant was an area of military failure, but defeat there brought a theological problem of Providence which troubled the theologians themselves. In fiction alone could Christians be sure of winning in the end, and the basis of all the plots is providential victory; the different classes of poems — the light adventure (such as *Prise d'Orange*), the serious individual adventure (*Simon de Pouille*), the fate-laden war (*Aliscans*), and the magic fantasy (*Huon de Bordeaux*) — all share this characteristic. It is here that the convention of idolatry proves its worth as literature. The thing is put to the test. The *soudan* or *amirant* or king vows offerings to the gods, but in the event they let him down. A scene in which the idols are destroyed is popular; triumph over the idols is the true climax of many poems, rather than the battle itself, which leads up to it, or the baptism of the best Saracens, which often follows. Can we call this propaganda? It is not even its effect, because the system of testing idolatry by ordeal is quite independent, in matter, of clerical argument or legendary polemic; it is unlike them because it is a reflection of actual war against Moslems, and in origin a spontaneous reaction. It extrapolates some facts of war and sets them in fantasy. If this is propaganda, it is in a very subtle sense. The poems are like *Partant pour la Syrie* or *Tipperary,* but are much more elaborate, and they never stop being entertaining as well as encouraging.[61]

There was some overlap of interests between poets and clerics, chiefly in the rewriting of history. An obscure skirmish in the Pyrenees, the Arab invasions of southern France, the sacking of the Roman suburbs, these, treated episodically or as epic, were set in a new perspective, dramatized and romanticized. The poets created an imaginary world with a complex history of its own (not unlike strange worlds in some mid-twentieth-century fictional sagas) in which not the events of history, but the impact that they made, is remembered.[62] If the history

---

61. *Prise d'Orange, Simon de Pouille,* and *Aliscans*; *Huon de Bordeaux,* ed. F. Guessard and Charles L. de Grandmaison (Paris, 1860): magic charged by Charlemagne on pp. 70–71, but the whole plot — including Oberon — is magic. Usually, the more serious the fighting (e.g., *Chanson d'Aspremont*), the more serious the religious conflict between gods, but without bitterness between knightly opponents. For other general views consult William W. Comfort, "The Literary Role of the Saracens in the French Epic," *Modern Language Association of America: Publications,* LV (1940), 628–659; Jean Frappier, *Les Chansons de geste du cycle Guillaume d'Orange* (Paris 1955 and 1965); C. Meredith Jones, "The Conventional Saracen of the Songs of Geste," *Speculum,* XVII (1942), 201–225.

62. For the invasions of southern France, especially the Guillaume cycle, but *Couronnement de Louis* joins *Fierabras* and *La Destruction de Rome,* ed. Gustave Groeber, *Romania,* II (1873), as outstanding for the Rome legend, adding Raimbert de Paris (attrib.), *La Chevalerie Ogier de Danemarche,* ed. Joseph Barrois (Paris, 1842). Attacks delivered or threatened against Paris,

in *Roland* is absurd, the Christianized Spain of the sequel, *Anseïs de Cartage,* is more so, and yet quite logical — and in its way, of course, prophetic. That fantasy of Frankish exhibitionism, the *Voyage de Charlemagne en Orient,* takes us through a nonexistent country inhabited by Turks and Persians to Byzantium; as a tourist, Charles visits Jerusalem, where there seem to be no Moslems, so he promises the patriarch to fight them in Spain. At the same time, clerics accepted the victories of poetry as fact. According to Robert of Rheims, Urban thought that Charlemagne and Louis had "destroyed the kingdom of the pagans [Turks]". Where? In the east? Or in Spain? Later, Christian Jerusalem, in *Simon de Pouille,* is embattled against Babylon (Mesopotamian, not Egyptian, Babylon), in the same general pattern, again under Charlemagne. The second crusade cycle rewrote later history as it "ought" to have been, with the conquest of Arabia, and especially Mecca, with the crossing of the Red Sea into Fairyland, now the Sudan. We do not have to suppose that anyone was deceived, or any deceit intended; these were fancies, not meant to persuade anyone to fight, though they may sometimes have had that effect; they were meant in fun.[63]

The poems encouraged people to fight in another way also inconsistent with the official propaganda. Prowess is on the whole a Pelagian virtue. Christians in the poems are defeated only because outnumbered, and are victorious only against odds, without miraculous

---

probably a confusion of Arabs with Vikings (cf. *Gormont et Isembart,* ed. Alphonse Bayot [Paris, 1921], line 472): "a Cirencestre, en voz contrees". For the false history of Spain cf. *Gui de Bourgogne,* ed. Guessard and Michelant (Paris, 1858); *Chanson de Roland,* and *Anseïs de Cartage*; and see Bédier, *Légendes,* III, *Pèlerinage,* sect. B. In general see Bédier, *ibid., passim*; Marc Bloch, *La Société féodale* (Paris, 1939–1940), part 2, chap. 6; Reinaud, *Invasions*; Gaston Paris, *Histoire poétique de Charlemagne* (Paris, 1865); Léon Gautier, *Les Épopées françaises* (Paris, 1878–1894); Paul Aebischer, *Rolandiana and Oliveriana* (Geneva, 1967); Delgado, *op. cit.;* Philippe Sénac, *Provence et piraterie sarrasine* (Paris, 1982) (with good bibliography); and the introductions to some of the critical editions of individual poems.

63. *Le Voyage de Charlemagne à Jérusalem et à Constantinople,* ed. Aebischer (Geneva, 1965); Robert of Rheims, I, 1 (*RHC, Occ.,* III, 728); *Simon de Pouille.* Second crusade cycle: *Le Bâtard de Bouillon,* ed. Robert F. Cook (Geneva, 1972), combines a number of elements that have appeared in earlier poems, but with some originality. The copulation of Baldwin and Sinamonde (it is hardly more) is closer than the usual "païenne amoureuse" story to the presumed prototype in Orderic Vitalis, *op. cit.,* X, xxi–xxiii; this union generates the Bastard, who forces his love (in marriage) on Ludie, daughter of the Amulaine and faithful lover of Corsabrin; earlier, he kills his cousin with a chessboard. The absurd "conquest of Mecca" is corrected only by the prophecy of Saladin its restorer. The magnetic tomb legend and the triumph over Mahom occur in the same episode. The strange interlude of Fairyland caps the oddities of which, however, the most interesting give a new twist to an old theme (laisses 82–89, 185, 135, 105, 101, 117–128). See also *La Fille, Chanson du Chevalier au Cygne,* and *Bauduin de Sebourc.* Consult Cook and Crist, *Le Deuxième cycle de la croisade* (Publications romaines et françaises, CXX; Geneva, 1972).

intervention. The authors seem to forget that victory is supposed to vindicate God, not their heroes' prowess, and this essential point tends to disappear from sight also in the case of the almost endless individual combats that the listeners seem to have loved. Adventure is a constant theme, perhaps increasingly important. The early-thirteenth-century romance *L'Escoufle* (by Jean Renart) is introduced by a war against the Saracens which, though only an episode, amounts to about one seventh of the whole. Two major episodes in the career of Guy of Warwick (early mid-century) are in the service of the emperor of Constantinople against the sultan of Turkey, and in the service of king Triamor of Alexandria against the giant Amorant. How could propaganda against Islam for its sexuality and violence appeal to a public that wanted to hear of violence in endless detail, varied only by episodes of love? Of course crusaders were deep in "sexuality" and "violence" from the beginning, and the secular literature suggests nothing much else. The troubadours are stylish and worldly, and when they went crusading, their motives were not more than moderately pious. A poem of Marcabru's (mid-twelfth-century) makes interesting use of the crusading theme.[64] A girl whose lover has gone to the holy war complains to Jesus that through him her sorrow grows, for the Saracen attack on him is her ruin. "The best of all the world go to serve you," she says, but the motive hardly reflects the preaching; it is not the cross, but duty—in the form of honor—and adventure that attract the men from home. We may suspect that church invective against Moslem lust was directed against the Christian laity in the first place, and that invective against Moslem violence was sometimes aimed at professionals for whom any war would do as well as a crusade.

The impact of events on professionals tends to bear this out. Most of the propaganda in the English chronicles of Richard I is directed against his European enemies; in relation to Arabs, the only obvious concern is for his reputation—the justification of his killing the prisoners, his renunciation of the pilgrimage, his personal standing with Saladin.[65] The courtly chivalry who followed him must have conceived the

64. *Poésies complètes du troubadour Marcabru,* ed. J. M. L. Dejeaune (Toulouse, 1909), pp. 108–109; Jean Renart, *L'Escoufle,* ed. Franklin P. Sweetser (Geneva, 1974), lines 1–1355 (out of 9102); *Gui de Warewic,* lines 2801 ff., 7889 ff.; *Boeve de Haumtone,* lines 1346 ff., in *Der anglonormannische Boeve de Haumtone,* ed. Albert Stimming (Halle, 1899). English versions include *The Romance of Guy of Warwick,* ed. Julius Zupitza (London, 1875–1876 and 1883–1891); *The Romance of Sir Beues of Hamtoun,* ed. Eugen Kölbing (London, 1885–1894); and the full collection of Charlemagne romances (EETS, ES, XXXIV–XLI, XLIII, XLV, L).

65. E.g., *Itinerarium . . . regis Ricardi,* ed. William Stubbs (Rolls Series, 38–I), pp. 437–438; Richard of Devizes, *Chronicon,* ed. John T. Appleby (London, 1963), pp. 74–75, and the usual sources for the Third Crusade.

heroes of the *chansons* in his image. The troubadour Gaucelm Faudit, a townsman who had gambled his fortune away, wrote, probably in sincere sorrow at the death of a patron, that "Saracens, Turks, Pagans, and Persians" feared Richard more than anyone born of a mother; it was unlikely that after his death any prince could recover the Sepulcher — "Huei mais non ai esperansa que i an / Reys ni princeps que cobrar lo saubes"; and similarly William Marshal said that the king's unexpected death prevented Richard from gaining "the lordship of Saracens and Christians and all the men of the world". In his own way as professional as Richard, Frederick II was successful in a crusade which was unacceptable to the papacy because it was not under papal leadership, nor informed by hatred of Islam. The propaganda had become integral to the crusade itself for papalists.[66]

The theme of success or failure was naturally perennial in "real life". The Second Crusade was an anticlimax. While the Latin states were still untouched, William of Tyre was oppressed by a sense of their failure. The accidental death of Frederick I at the outset of the Third Crusade seemed a wanton disaster at the hands of inscrutable Providence.[67] The Damietta crusade of 1218–1221 seemed for a brief moment to promise success. The structure of the army, directed by the legate Pelagius, as unqualified by experience as he was unsuited by temperament, parodied the structure of Christendom; and from the total failure of this crusade, after its momentary vision of an Islam destroyed, date prophecies of the end of Islam which were popular with all classes, right up to the fall of Acre, a prophetic myth that parallels the historical myth of Charlemagne. This was the self-propaganda of the whole community, giving itself to fantasy as there was less and less solid food to feed on. Yet in the recollections of Philip of Novara, who spent much of his life in the coastal remnant of the Latin states, there is no hint of danger and no whiff of crusade.[68] The threads are very tangled.

From the canons, repeated and reinforced, from instructions to confessors, from the tirades of an indignant polemicist, it is clear that neither law nor propaganda could stop Christians from mixing with

---

66. *Sur la mort de Richard* in Jean Audiau, *Nouvelle anthologie des troubadours* (Paris, 1928), p. 219, stanza vi, lines 46–47; *Histoire de Guillaume le Maréchal,* ed. Meyer (Paris, 1901), lines 11823–11828. For Frederick II see volume II of the present work, chapter XII.

67. See Humbert, below, note 78 and cf. Riccoldo, note 89; William of Tyre, *Historia rerum in partibus transmarinis gestarum,* XXI, 7, and XXIII, *praefatio* (*RHC, Occ.,* I, 1014–1017, 1032).

68. *Quinti belli sacri scriptores minores* (SOL, *SH,* II, 214–228); cf. volume II of the present work, chapter XI; Philip of Novara, *Mémoires 1218–1243,* ed. Charles Kohler (Paris, 1913; repr. 1970).

Moslems in the trading cities of the Arabs in the Mediterranean area.[69] That the evidence is negative is a success of the propaganda; we have no personal records of consuls or merchants of the period. We know more about good relations from Moslem than from Christian sources; Usāmah Ibn-Munqidh and Ibn-Jubair are obvious examples. Louis IX was the church's perfect crusader, but his devoted biographer, Joinville, is surprisingly little influenced by the official line and is a rare European witness to an attitude unsympathetic to Louis: he took the Arabs as he found them.[70]

If propaganda does indeed reflect as much as create the feelings of the society that produces it, it will be subject to different distortions in different sections of the community. Louis's failure was associated with the "crusade" of the Pastoureaux, an anticlerical insurrection which disseminated the idea that the clergy had betrayed the king and the crusade; the rich in their turn formed the idea that the revolt had itself been fomented by the Arabs. Both fantasies exemplify the natural recoil of official propaganda; the hysteria induced by a Peter the Hermit or a Fulk of Neuilly, or in the Children's Crusade, could easily degenerate into wild suspicions. Fournier's Inquisition suspected the lepers of conspiring with Arab monarchs, so that sober churchmen too were capable of paranoia under communal pressure.[71] The church wanted an official war in due feudal order, but its dogmatic and pastoral theology had no appeal for feudal leaders, except Louis. They stopped crusading except where it looked profitable. More precisely, they required feasible projects and, in terms of modern business, we can classify some fourteenth-century theories (which we shall consider shortly) as feasibility studies. The papal inflation of the crusading notion into an Albigensian Crusade or a crusade against the emperor was acceptable as relating to political reality.

If in fact the *chansons de geste* excluded the official line deliberately, that does not mean that the knightly class consciously rejected ecclesiastical teaching, but that it did not think in scholastic categories.

---

69. See chapter I, above.

70. Usāmah Ibn-Munqidh, *Memoirs of an Arab-Syrian Gentleman and Warrior in the Period of the Crusades,* tr. Philip K. Hitti (*CURC*, 10; New York, 1927), and Ibn-Jubair, *Travels,* tr. Ronald J. C. Broadhurst (London, 1952) (also *RHC, Or.,* III, 445–456, where extracts have been translated into French); John of Joinville, *Histoire de Saint Louis,* ed. Natalis de Wailly (Paris, 1868); *La Vie de St. Louis,* ed. Noel L. Corbett (Sherbrooke, Quebec, 1977); cf. Daniel, *Arabs and Medieval Europe,* pp. 183, 212–213.

71. Salimbene de Adam, *Cronica,* ed. Giuseppe Scalia (Scrittori d'Italia, 233, II [Bari, 1966], 645–646); Norman Cohn, *The Pursuit of the Millennium* (London, 1957), pp. 77, 82–87; *Le Registre d'inquisition de Jacques Fournier évêque de Pamiers (1318–1325),* ed. Jean Duvernoy II (Toulouse, 1965), pp. 135–145 (he became pope Benedict XII).

Moreover, we can overdo this; there was an overlap of attitudes, as of interests. Saladin first appears in western chronicles as the usual Arab scourge. Then two events appealed to the imagination of the west, the ransoming of poor captives at the fall of Jerusalem by Saladin and his brother al-'Ādil, and the beheading of the oath-breaking Reginald of Châtillon after Hattin; to refuse to accept him as a guest when king Guy gave him water was in accordance with the knightly code. Not only did Joinville remember this; at a moment of stress he expected Arabs to be bound by the rule of behavior he understood it to imply. In legend Saladin became a courtly hero, as we have seen, and Europe's most honored visitor, but this myth carried the clergy along with it, and clerics told satirical tales in which Saladin's disgust castigated the sins of Europe.[72] Other ideas were shared by different groups; thus the idea that Islam was a continuation of paganism is common—in very different forms admittedly—to the canonists and the *chansons de geste*.[73]

Certainly orthodox propaganda was a vehicle to express Europeans' pride in themselves and contempt for others; the church was only the chief proponent and the chief instrument of a cultural ethnocentrism in which all took part. One of the best examples of a propagandist was James of Vitry, French-born, well educated, representative of the higher clergy in the Latin state, and also of modes of thought of the early thirteenth century. He was prepared in theory, but not in practice, to attribute the loss of Jerusalem and other "Christian" lands to original sin, rather than to particular sins. His analysis of the peoples of Palestine is intelligent as well as antipathetic. It is more and more off the mark as it gets more remote from the Latins. He repeats the "orthodox" Christian attack on Mohammed and Islam, but this version of it may represent a local eastern variation of material more familiar in Spain, and occasional comments mark some fragment of actual knowledge floating in a sea of legend. Above all, he leaves us with the unmistakable impression, valid for all the crusading movement, of total Latin intolerance, an actual inability to put up with any part or parcel of alien culture, even—or especially—in the situation of a precarious colony surrounded by enemies. He speaks for a

---

72. G. Paris, "La Légende de Saladin," *Journal des Savants* (1893), pp. 284–299, 354–365, 428–438, 486–498; cf. Cook and Crist, *Le Deuxième cycle.*

73. For the canonists see above, chapter I. As far as the *chansons* are concerned, the inclusion among the supposed idols of *Apollin* (later formally assimilated as *Apollon*) and *Jupiter* confirms the delusion of continuity between antiquity and Islam; the use of the word *païen* should not be dismissed as meaningless. Cf. Roger Bacon, *Opus majus,* ed. John H. Bridges (Oxford, 1897), III, part 2, caps. ix–xiii, pp. 53–67.

whole community, but he does so in the accents of its most articulate class.[74]

There was indeed overall unity, and this articulate class controlled
the propaganda. Within the Christian community the churchmen were
always addressing their charges, never the Moslem enemy directly, nor
did they write for neutrals. The only Moslems who were converted
were those who were so unlucky as to live under Christian rule, and
the only neutrals known in the west were the Mongols, for whose conversion there was a short-lived hope, encouraged by some interesting
missions. We have already seen that the idea of a public debate was
merely another fantasy. What was the purpose of the propaganda
against the Moslem religion? W. M. Watt suggests that it represents
the "dark side" of the Christian attitude, psychologically a projection
of the sins, especially sexual sins, of the Christians upon an Islamic
scapegoat.[75] The present writer has always maintained that it both
sprang out of and served to fortify the sense of Christian European
solidarity, of which the war itself was one expression and the acceptance in theory of a severe sexual morality another.

Western Christendom wanted to establish its sense of identity. The
constant preoccupation with orthodoxy, the crusades against heretics,
and the development of the Inquisition all bear witness to the extent
to which uniformity was desired by the people who made up the society as a whole. This was not affected by division within society, or
by anticlericalism within the bounds of orthodoxy. They felt it to be
a precondition of their solidarity. To establish that a whole religion,
society, *lex,* was in every respect the reverse or denial of European society was immensely helpful in creating a mental as well as a physical
frontier. It was the best war propaganda in that it made the enemy
the proper recipients of treatment unworthy of humanity in ordinary
conditions. The evil alleged of Islam made the rules of the crusade,
of the "just war", emotionally acceptable. All war is more effective if
it is fought with hatred and if the humanity of the enemy is minimized.
In this sense the laity needed and accepted that clerical propaganda
which did not otherwise come naturally to them.

---

74. *Lettres de Jacques de Vitry,* ed. Huygens (Leyden, 1960), pp. 79–98; *Historia Hierosolymi-tana,* in Jacques Bongars, ed., *Gesta Dei per Francos* (Hanau, 1611; repr. Jerusalem, 1972), I, 1085 ff.; also Douai, 1597 (repr. Farnborough, Eng., 1971), caps. 67–83.
75. *Influence of Islam on Mediaeval Europe* (Edinburgh, 1970), p. 83.

D. *The Age of Doubt*

We come finally to the phase in which propaganda is met by counter-propaganda, arguments not only for, but also against, the crusade. These bear the marks of failure and doubt; they reveal the increasing strength of secular interests and are produced by new social developments no longer compatible with a doctrine of the crusade composed in an earlier age. The accumulation of failures affected even the theologians, and those who wanted to renew the war were faced with the classical dilemma of providential theory. In a holy war our victory is the vindication of God, but our failure must be the chastisement of our sins. Why is God now vindicated, now chastising our sins? Many agonized over this problem, to judge by the frequency with which the stock solutions are stated, up to the very end of the period of Ottoman expansion (when it became the turn of the Moslems to experience this cycle of despair).

We might date the new age of doubt from 1291 and the fall of Acre, last of the mainland territorial possessions of the Latins in Palestine. An alternative date might be 1274; the Second Council of Lyons was intended to reunite Christendom for a crusade and was a moment of useful self-questioning. Again, we might find our arbitrary date a few years earlier still, with the final failure of Louis IX at Tunis in 1270. Like the Damietta crusade of 1218, Louis's first crusade in 1249 had raised great hopes which it had quickly disappointed. The fall of Aiyūbid Cairo was no sooner rumored than Europe learned that this pious king and model crusader was a defeated prisoner.[76] Edward (I) of England, crusading at about the same time, had little thought for the kingdom of Jerusalem that was not defensive. The watershed in crusade propaganda can plausibly be said to have come when Joinville refused to join Louis's second venture, in spite of his veneration for the king and the seriousness with which he took crusading ideals. In a well-known passage he describes how Louis pressed him to take the cross again, and how he replied that the king's sergeants had oppressed and impoverished his people, and that "if I wished to do God's will, I should stay here, to help and defend my people." He considered that the king should do the same: it was a mortal sin that anyone should advise him to go, because at the time the country was at peace, both within and with its neighbors; yet, if the king went, it must deteriorate. Joinville maintained that, if the king had not gone, he might, in

---

76. Matthew Paris, *Chronica majora,* ed. Henry R. Luard (Rolls Series, 57), V, 138, and VI, 169.

spite of his weakness, have lived longer and continued his good work for the country.[77] Nothing could be more explicit than this assertion that God requires charity to begin at home; and nothing could be farther from the position of the crusade propagandists.

We may compare Humbert's preparatory work for Lyons, which was at once backward- and forward-looking; the arguments are old, his awareness of the opposition is new. He considers seven categories, first accusing objectors in general terms as "given to idleness, running away from all exertions for Christ"; there used to be an English idiomatic use of the word "slackers" which Humbert's bracing tone exactly reflects. The first particular objection that he considers is that the shedding of blood is incompatible with the Christian religion; this is based on a number of obvious New Testament texts (John 18:11, Acts 5:41, Romans 12:19, I Peter 2:23 and 3:9), but omitting the most obvious of all, Matthew 5:38 ff. He replies that the early church had no power with which to fight, but had miracles and the gifts of the Holy Ghost instead; in his own day, however, the church only had power, and must use what it had. It was obvious that Christians must resist the infidels; who would be so silly (*fatuus*) as to say otherwise? The texts cited he explained by their special circumstances; he also quoted Luke 22:36 (but not 38), adding that this is glossed to mean that Christians may sometimes use the sword, a matter not for any individual but for the church itself to decide.

The second objection is the reverse of the first: that a crusade causes the shedding of Christian blood and the death of Christians. There are innumerable casualties, "sometimes from illness, sometimes in wars, sometimes from too little or too much to eat (*ex excessu*) — and not only ordinary people, but kings and princes, and persons really useful to Christendom". He replies that people who put such arguments forward "have eyes only for what concerns their own or recent times"; they would see things very differently if they read ancient histories, about all the Arabs killed by Charles Martel or massacred in the time of Godfrey of Bouillon at the capture of Jerusalem; Charlemagne too (he thought) had killed many Arabs in the course of liberating Spain. He felt confident that a final accounting would prove that over the ages many more Moslems had been killed than Christians. He fairly pointed out that if Christians had not opposed Moslems, the Moslems who formerly inhabited Sicily, Sardinia, and Spain would have destroyed the property and lives of numberless Christians, as they did when they attacked Genoa by sea from North Africa. Anyway, Chris-

---

77. *Vie de St. Louis,* ed. Corbett, paras. 734–737.

tians are called to people heaven, not this world. Humbert does not consider the point that ancient victories were irrelevant to modern defeats, and so evades the conflict between the crudely providential view of history and the contemporary realism.

The third objection that he considers is the adverse conditions for the crusade. His choice of objections is more realistic than his replies to them. Christians in the east are few among many enemies; they are in a strange land, while their opponents are in their own (a curious admission, and seemingly inconsistent with the theory of a Christian right to the Holy Land). We are unused, he goes on, to the climate, but they are used to it; we are unused to the food, they are used to it; they know dangerous tracks and hidden routes, we do not; we are often in want, they have plenty. "As, therefore, in war, wisdom is necessary above all, it seems Christians should never attempt this kind of war." Humbert's answer is that the Moslems have the advantage in terms of worldly wisdom, but as for divine wisdom, Christians have it, and once again he brings up the numbers of Moslems successfully massacred in the past. To this third objection is connected the fourth, that, though we may well defend ourselves when the Moslems attack us, it would be better not actually to invade their lands, and even likely to prove harmful to us to do so. Humbert's answer here is that the Moslems so hate the Christians that they will let no chance to harm them pass; as they do not need to be provoked, the thing to do is to wear them out by invading their countries first. This he defends by theological argument, that it is sinful to maintain peace with the wicked. The reasons for attacking are three: to exhaust the Moslems, to introduce the worship of God into their countries, and to avoid sharing, by toleration, the guilt of their crimes. This is to give a legal answer to a pragmatic objection.

The next objection was that if Moslem nations must be extirpated, why not Jews, and also Moslems living in Christian territory, and also Tatars and barbaric nations? The conversion of the Jews, he replies, is promised (Romans 11:26) and even the Moslems under Christian rule need not be despaired of ("whether they like it or not, they can be forced to listen to preaching"); the Tatars and others do not bother us, and their conversion too is promised ("all languages should serve the Lord Jesus Christ", Daniel 7:14, adapted). Even as propaganda, Humbert's argument here is careless. Why should this last text not refer to Moslems as much as to "barbarians"? Both objection and answer here must always have seemed quibbles, and neither can be quite serious.

The sixth objection is that crusading serves no useful purpose; it only arouses the resentment of the Moslems. This cuts much closer

to the bone, but Humbert sees a triple advantage in attack: the enemies
of the Christian faith are attacked before they can themselves attack,
they are thrown into disarray, and they are frightened; these "temporal"
advantages are normal practice in war. There are also the "spiritual"
or clerical advantages; the honor of God, the salvation of Christians,
the extension of the church ("as concerns worship"), that is, the area
in which the Latin rite obtains. Moslems and Greeks under Latin rule,
he claims, live happily, cultivating their lands and paying tribute, and
can be converted gradually. His last objection resembles his second;
it is that the misfortunes of the Christians suggest that God does not
want them to go against the Moslems. There was the success of Saladin, the fortuitous death of Frederick I in a small stream, the capture
of Louis IX at Mansurah and his death at Tunis, and the dispersal by
bad weather of his fleet returning to Europe. This popular theology
is easy for the theologian to refute to his own satisfaction; such people
do not understand God's ways (the *facta divina*), it is not in this world
that God gives his rewards. A stream of biblical quotations from the
Old Testament shows how God willed the defeat of Israel.

We need not doubt that Humbert was stating actual criticisms of
the crusade that were familiar to him, and doing so quite fairly. Does
he answer them effectively? Obviously not, according to modern ideas,
and, though we must beware of anachronism, his scholastic range of
argument does not touch the more practical objections even as he himself presents them. Often, when Humbert makes an effort to meet a
practical point by appealing to ordinary knightly experience, he slides
off into theology. Wholly idealistic, Humbert is nevertheless not wholly
impractical. He wants a large permanent army to reinforce the surviving Christian centers in the east. The soldiers must be more than mercenaries, and carefully chosen, but he realizes that they will need large
stipends to maintain them at war. He proposes gracefully to leave the
laity to make their own financial offer, while he waxes at once poetical
and businesslike about the possible sources of clerical contribution.
He argues that the anti-Islamic polemic which we have discussed above
is really important; before the Second Council [of Lyons] assembles,
it will be necessary to state the facts about Islam concisely, so that
people may understand the enemy; as it is, clerics, as well as laymen,
suppose "that Moslems reckon that Mohammed is their God, which
is however false". The advice of the wise, he continues, not only the
learned but the laity, and especially the nobility, should be obtained,
and put into succinct reports; and prelates and magnates should be
sent to all countries to enlist support, especially from the other magnates. Many arguments may persuade them, says Humbert, and he takes

us back over the old familiar ground: feudal obligation to God; the examples of the Old Testament; the examples of Christian history; the need of penance; duty; nobility; shame. We must admit that in all this there has been some attempt to understand lay motivation, but there is little in the bag of tricks that was not already there.[78]

Another example from the material relating to the Second Council of Lyons is Gilbert of Tournai's *Collectio de scandalis*.[79] Its brief references to the crusade are a check on Humbert's more conventional approach. Gilbert naturally accepts in principle the necessity of destroying Moslem power, on the old theme of "restoration"—"our inheritance has been turned over to strangers" (Lamentations 5:2). In a sense his remarks are particularly traditional; he makes use of the correspondence of Peter of Blois, and also that of James of Vitry, but a radical strain is more in evidence. Of the three points to which he draws attention, one is the exploitation of the poor and of the church in order to fund the crusade; Christ, he says, cannot be liberated by the affliction of Christians. Assessors unjustly manipulate the law governing the release of various categories of crusaders from their vows; this recoils on the heads of those who preach the crusade, and who have to put up with violent criticism. Preachers who collect funds for the crusade must not be motivated by the thought of gain. It is the crusade administration, rather than the propaganda, that Gilbert criticizes; of course, he makes it clear that he supports the crusade itself, and there is no *arrière-pensée* in this. He describes the behavior of the rulers and the knightly class, of the citizens, merchants, and workers of different kinds; the ruling class fails to do justice and exploits those subject to it; merchants disregard the church and operate frauds; the rest are dishonest and do not go to church. Gilbert is like Joinville in his insistence on first putting things right at home. Neither of them really falls into any of Humbert's classes of objectors.

Of about the same date is the work of Rutebeuf, whose editor attributes the formative influence on him to Humbert. Rutebeuf's crusade polemic poetry is well within the general scope of Humbert's definitions, though sufficient variations suggest an individual assessment, and Rutebeuf cites objections to the crusade which, like Humbert's, are more convincing than their refutation. The early *Complainte d'Outremer* is the least interesting of these poems; it does seem to reflect the same tradition as Humbert's own preoccupation with the al-

---

78. *Opus tripartitum,* in *Appendix . . . fugiendarum,* ed. Brown, chaps. x–xix, xxiii, xv.
79. *Archivum franciscanum historicum,* XXIV (1931), ed. Autbert Stroick, esp. pp. 39–41.

most legendary sequence of former crusades. His *Desputizons dou Croisie et dou Descroizie* is dated in the late 1260's. The non-crusader in this debate says that the adventure is ruinous; it has reduced many to beggary; the clergy set a bad example; he would defend his country from the sultan, but will not go to hunt him out, and will do wrong to no man; and "if God is anywhere in the world, he is in France, there is no doubt". Warned to think of eternity, he is suddenly converted; this does not spring inevitably out of the sense of the poem, but seems rather a device to bring it to an end.

Rutebeuf's *Nouvele Complainte d'Outremer* is more lively than his other crusading poems, although its satirical passages contribute no surprise. The appeals to particular kings and nobles nicely combine the courtly with the pious. A long passage castigates the young squires who, instead of crusading, rob maidens of their honor; prelates on fat palfreys who preach abstinence to the poor, and clergy who live and dress well on the patrimony of the Crucified, could afford to support troops at the war. Knights at their cups threaten the sultan — "Quant la teste est bien avinee" — but next day are off hunting hares and duck; the rich townsmen buy cheap and sell dear, charge usury, and trick people, and their children spend their wealth at the brothel and the tavern while the poor starve. Rutebeuf is much taken with the theme of a golden past, and, imperceptive of the irony which no modern reader can miss, recommends to his contemporaries, as models, not only Godfrey but Bohemond and Tancred.[80] Of course, by 1270 there were no principalities for ambitious crusaders to seize, and so no Bohemond.

It is interesting to compare the contemporary view of someone actually caught up in the war; as one would expect, it is more concerned with practical problems than is anything written at the same time in Europe. Fidenzio of Padua was a Franciscan whose work was dedicated to pope Nicholas IV and, he says, explicitly commissioned by Gregory X at the Second Council of Lyons, apparently because his knowledge of the country might produce practical proposals. Probably Nicholas, if not also Gregory (who, after all, knew the situation at first hand), thought that existing proposals, originating in the west, lacked the necessary field knowledge, and Fidenzio is indeed more practical than Humbert. He lays down three basic requirements — first, forces, second, what he calls "eminence of goodness", which means, when examined in detail, sound morale, and finally, single leadership. Under the first

---

80. *Oeuvres complètes de Rutebeuf,* ed. Edmond Faral and Julia Bastin (Paris, 1959), I, 440 ff., 469 ff., 492 ff. (line 251).

heading Fidenzio often adds, after his recommendations, "and the Saracens do this also"; his military advice (and he was not a fighting priest) is largely based on his observation of Moslem success. He naturally recommends that there should be large forces, and that they should be not only well armed but professionally skilled. One aspect of morale he considers under this heading: the soldiers must be men of spirit and initiative, *fortes animo*. He considers tactics (under the heading of *sagacitas*) in the context of weaknesses he has observed. He stresses the importance of fortifications and strong points, both defensively and when in enemy territory; he rates effective intelligence next in importance, and again reminds the reader that the sultan has good spies; he demands caution, unity, and careful planning. His analysis is down to earth.

In his chapters on the need for "goodness" among Christians, commending charity, chastity, humility, mutual loyalty and compassion, unity, sobriety, legality, patience, avoidance of cupidity, and prayer, he seems to be assessing the defects he observes in terms of their opposing virtues. His "legality" is interesting; it is important especially "among those who are brought together in a single society and for the accomplishment of a single work"; it is both negative, as not injuring fellow countrymen, and positive, as serving them. Then he deals with main lines of strategy, recommending two armies, one by sea to attack Egypt, one by land (in order to split the enemy) to attack at one of a number of Syrian alternatives. He inserts a chapter on the idea of the just war, claiming the right to rule Egypt and the Holy Land "as far as the Euphrates". Much of this is new, and, insofar as it is a practical assessment of the situation, it is realistic propaganda. If it demands far more than would ever be possible, this is well devised to counteract the new opposition to crusading, the variations on the theme that it cannot be done.[81]

The period roughly from the Second Council of Lyons in 1274 to the death of Philip IV of France in 1314 was decisive in the history of crusade propaganda, because it was then that the serious intention disappeared. We are here concerned to see how the propaganda affected and was affected by the change in intention. The Genoese Galvano da Levanto serves to link the undeterred zeal of Fidenzio with the new secular approach, which he himself, however, did not share. Galvano's own attitude is unoriginal, but illustrates the practical search for leadership. Fidenzio's "mutual loyalty and compassion" is reflected in Galvano's "brotherly loyalty and compassion", and so is a sense of

---

81. *Liber recuperationis Terrae Sanctae,* in *BOF,* ser. I, II-1, 1–60.

urgency: "Lest the Christian religion succumb, it must everywhere defend itself . . . have its eye always on victory." Amid much that is old-fashioned, he looks for a leader who will give new life to the old ideal; he hopes to persuade him on grounds of principle that it is sufficiently to his advantage to do so.[82]

Most writers agreed that Acre fell because of the divided command, and that is one reason why afterward success was seen as depending on effective leadership. A distinct strand of thought stresses the sins of the people of Acre; according to Giovanni Villani, who reflects Florentine traditions, no Christian city contained "more sinners, men and women, guilty of every wickedness". John of Ypres, writing nearer the time, and himself a source of Villani's, contrasts the morals of the people with the imagined virtues of the first crusaders; he knows a good deal, though not accurate in detail, of the troubles of the succession of the Mamluk sultanate in the family of Kalavun, and so is able to point to divisions among the Moslems which were unknown to Fidenzio, in order to show that their sins, too, received punishment.[83] We shall return to the theme of Christian wickedness, which naturally is less significant for the history of events than for the history of theological propaganda.

If Fidenzio had been conscious of the need for unity of leadership, sound morale, and strategy, it was because he knew the actual situation, and the same realism occurs in other supporters of renewed fighting. Villani writes of the loss to Italian trade that resulted from the disappearance of Christian rule from the Syrian coast, but this was more a Florentine view.[84] Venice suffered less, but Venetian writers, as long as the crusade remained a serious proposition, would be keen that the armies should be carried by Venetian ships. Ptolemy of Lucca, writing retrospectively of the fall of the last coastal cities, gives two reasons in explanation, the first the "diversity of wills of the lords", who could not agree in the government or defense of Acre; the second, the stupidity of the crusaders recruited through the preaching set in train by Nicholas IV after the fall of Tripoli. They came to Acre in disorderly style, and attacked some Arab merchants, robbed them, and killed some, arousing the anger of the sultan.[85] Here are both the

---

82. *Liber sancti passagii christicolarum pro recuperatione Terrae Sanctae,* ed. Kohler, in *ROL,* VI (1898), 343–369.

83. *Cronica di Giovanni Villani a miglior lezione ridotta,* VII, 145 (Florence, 1823, II, 356). John of Ypres, *Chronicon ecclesiae Sancti Bertini,* LIII, 6, in Martène and Durand, eds., *Thesaurus novus anecdotorum,* III, 769–773.

84. *Cronica di Giovanni Villani,* pp. 355–356.

85. *Historia ecclesiastica,* in *RISS,* XI, col. 1196.

criticism of disunity and the mercantile wish that the enemy should not be provoked. Ptolemy, rather than Marino Sanudo, seems to speak for the maritime tradition.

Sanudo wrote the most monumental of all works of crusading propaganda,[86] and his enthusiasm for a point of view essentially ecclesiastical does not chime altogether harmoniously with the Venetian trading interest; his notion of a fleet-carried army to conquer Egypt would have been good business, if it had not already too often been shown to be impracticable. He is naturally well informed about Egypt's commercial needs but, like so many others, overestimates its vulnerability. After his death, the sack of Alexandria in 1365 would show that real damage could be done to Egypt, without weakening it enough to make possible a Christian conquest. For the rest, his advice is practical enough, if we grant the main strategy. Like Fidenzio, Sanudo wants to see a restoration of morale by means of a moral reformation, and he too looks to a king who should be a new Godfrey, but unite the army and people in a single rule. He offers the same advice as Fidenzio in point of tactics and effective imitation of successful Arab methods of warfare. In addition to his faith in both economic and armed war, he depends heavily on the hope of reformation, the expulsion of irreligious men and heretics, and a model state financed from the lands recaptured — once more, a repetition of the First Crusade as it was remembered by this time. His history of the crusaders is among the most thorough. He shows how Palestine has always been exposed to conquest, beginning with the Jews and running through all those who succeeded them — Greeks, Romans, Arabs, and Latins. He detours via Charlemagne, then gives the history from Godfrey to the Second Council of Lyons and the end of the kingdom of Acre. The legendary quality of these accounts is emphasized by their relative neglect of recent events. This is a good example of the revival of ancient propaganda in a new situation. Sanudo, having spent a lifetime thinking about the crusade, naturally did not ask whether it was necessary at all; when he refers to the preaching of a crusade, he thinks of the kinds of skilled men to recruit, not the arguments to persuade them. He too is both propagandist and propaganda victim. His advocacy of the strategy of invading Egypt, and of the tactics of establishing fortified places on the coast, was finally outmoded some twenty years after his death, when the

---

86. *Liber secretorum fidelium crucis,* in Bongars, *Gesta Dei per Francos,* II, 1–288. On particular points drawn from book II see part i, cap. 1 (pp. 34–35); part ii, cap. 10 (pp. 48–49); part iii, cap. 2 (p. 51); part iv, cap. 1 (pp. 53–54); part iv, cap. 19 (pp. 74–75).

papal legate, Peter Thomas, failed to persuade the army to stay in Alexandria longer than was necessary to loot and murder.

Another theme had by this time been worked into the historical legend, the story of the Mongols, seen at the time, and always afterward remembered, as a great opportunity for Christendom missed. A sentence of John Sarrasin's from Damietta in 1247 illustrates the delusion of an immediate hope: "disoient ils que Eltheltay, a tout son ost de Tartarins, seroit en l'aide au roy de France".[87] Some travelers wrote clear accounts of the Far East, the mid-century envoys John of Pian del Carpine and William of Rubruck in particular, with other clerics; there is an echo also of some of the mechanics and others who were captured by the Mongols or went to work for them and returned to Europe. John's work was reëdited by Vincent of Beauvais, and Roger Bacon gave some publicity to Rubruck's splendid book, but these authentic sources were largely ignored; Europeans exaggerated the chance that had been missed, and even continued to imagine that it still existed — this delusion survives in Sanudo.[88] At the time they underrated the lasting consequences of the Mamluk victory at 'Ain Jālūt in 1260. In the second half of the thirteenth century Mongol society was better and more accurately documented in Europe than was the Arab world with which there had been hostile contact for so long. It is difficult to define exactly the effect of the "Tartar" myth. Certainly it gave Europe an idea of a world beyond Islam, and the idea that existing conditions could be upset; it contributed to the unsettled state of mind which was increasingly dissatisfied with the traditional propaganda.

The propaganda worked itself out, exhausted by its own logic. Its greatest inherent weakness, so long as people thought in terms of holy war, was the providential problem. Riccoldo of Monte Croce arrived in Baghdad only to find evidence of the sack of Acre, where his journey had started, and of the death of his brother Dominicans, the equivalent of his family. Personal distress led him to a theological problem which he besought God — in a somewhat literary exercise — to dispel by special revelation. It was now nearly seven hundred years, he said, that Islam had flourished, and some people thought that its momentum must slow down and weaken; but, on the contrary, it was growing stronger. He demanded that God should answer him oracularly. He set the Koran on the altar before the image of Jesus and his mother,

---

87. *Lettre à Nicolas Arrode,* ed. Alfred L. Foulet (Paris, 1924), p. 2.

88. John of Pian del Carpine and William of Rubruck in *Sinica franciscana,* vol. I. Vincent of Beauvais, *Speculum historiale* (Douai, 1629, vol. V of *Biblioteca mundi,* and other editions), lib. xxxi, 3 ff.; alternates with Simon of Tournai from cap. 26. Also Sanudo, II, i, 3 (p. 36), II, iv, 28 (pp. 92–95), and cf. III, xiii, 3–9 (pp. 234–241).

and indignantly prayed, "Read, read"; "it seems to me that thou didst not want to read." In Mosul, Riccoldo bought a copy of Gregory the Great's *On the Morals of Job,* part of the loot from Acre, feeling as if he were redeeming a prisoner. He finally found his "revelation" in the work of Gregory. He read, "God speaks once"; and he realized that he must accept what he already knew as answer enough, that a Christian accepts suffering and worldly failure as normal. Here he has gone beyond the always-revived argument that worldly failure is a punishment for sin, with its delusive corollary that a revival of virtue must produce military victory. Riccoldo finally saw that success and failure have nothing to do with religion, but this made nonsense of all the most effective crusading propaganda. It is not clear that Riccoldo realized how radical he was being here. He must have realized that his praise of Moslems for practising virtues (which we considered above) was not really compatible with contemporary scholastic opinion, although he never for a moment slackened his firm hold on orthodoxy. He has learned the weakness in the historical argument of which crusade propaganda made so much. "You see that the Christians often made plans against the Moslems, and almost every design of theirs turned to their harm. For what pope, or emperor, or king made plans or arrangements over a long period against the sultan of Babylon (Cairo), against the successor of Mohammed, and was not overtaken by death or else cheated in his plan or his dispositions?"[89] This was the crux of the providential discussion.

Although the First Crusade had not been what its later admirers supposed, it had indeed offered worldly success, but this was only a memory, and Riccoldo's sense that providence was against the crusade might appeal more to the contemporaries of Philip the Fair. Although the old belief, that Christians have a right to the Holy Land, survived defiantly in Sanudo and others, the idea of not attacking the Moslems so long as they did not attack the Christians, acceptance, indeed, of a permanent cease-fire, was becoming increasingly attractive.

We may take one more example of the secular approach to the crusade in the early fourteenth century, the greatest of them, the *De recuperatione* (1306–1308) of Pierre Dubois. The first part of this work, conceived as advice to all Christendom, was dedicated to Edward I of England, because of his known concern for the Holy Land. Approaching the problem from the European end, Dubois looks at the reverse side of the theology of the crusade by discussing the unjust

89. Röhricht. "Lettres de Ricoldo de Monte Croce," *AOL,* II-2, 266–267, 269, 272, 273, 275, 277–278, 279, 281, 285, 286, 289, 293, 295.

wars of Europe which lead only to damnation. Peace and reform are the means of the crusade, or the crusade the way to peace and reform, it is not clear which. This, of course, had been Urban's own theme, but Dubois gives the papacy only a minor role. His ideas are based on the establishment of royal authority (suppression of the rebellion of great lords becomes a crusade theme in his work), and he has little sympathy with the Italian cities which acknowledge no lord. Arbitration becomes a means of promoting French authority and suzerainty. In the second part of this work, addressed to Dubois's own king, Philip IV, it becomes clearer still that the crusade, once set in train by reform, is intended to create an eastern empire for France, a project finally begun by Napoleon nearly five centuries later.

The secularity of the general scheme is shown by the reforms it proposes; only a little more than a quarter century after the orthodox Second Council of Lyons, Dubois would achieve the purposes of the crusade by very different means, including the secularization of much church property and the limitation of papal authority. Dubois would put an end to the constant flow of excommunications of recalcitrants: "It is much better to punish them in time than in eternity." Crusading is no longer an ascesis; indeed, Dubois was keen on the marriage of the clergy. He sees, of course, the need for sound financial support, and proposes to begin by using the resources of the Temple and the Hospital. His is not the old familiar concept of the crusade at all, despite the traditional language (*ardor salutis Terre Sancte*), which he uses to introduce his quite new project for colonization obliquely. Those who, instead of crusading, make war on other Catholics, and all who give them any help, will be punished; "When the war is over, the survivors, of whatever age, rank, or sex, shall be perpetually exiled from their lands and possessions, of which they shall be deprived, with whatever descendants they may have, and they shall be sent to populate the Holy Land; if they obey and freely mean to take themselves to the Holy Land, they shall be given their necessary expenses for their journey out of their confiscated property." On arrival, they were to be given lands next to the enemy. This Botany Bay concept marks the beginning of the long-cherished European intention to plant colonies in the Near East, which until recently dominated the politics of the eastern Mediterranean, and those who question any continuity between the crusading concept proper and the colonial age must at least recognize a clear link in Dubois.

His intention to populate the east with Europeans was probably stimulated by the remembered weakness of the Franks of the old Latin states, isolated amid an alien population whether Moslem or Christian Arab. Dubois thought out rough principles for apportioning land to the settlers, and rather more detailed ideas for the organization of a local militia. After a discussion of the best routes and methods for attack, he considers "those things that are required for the well-being of the colonists [*habitatores*]"; he foresees first the need for confessors speaking the language of each settler, and doctors of body as well as of soul must be ready for them before they arrive. He talks of his system of education, principally in "the languages of the Arabs and other dialects of the world", and medicine and surgery (for men and horses), to which he attaches great importance. A proper supply of interpreters must be available well in advance, and they must understand the local people—they must be, as the modern editor says, dragomans. Women were to have an important part, although considered "inferior"; girls were to obtain influence through their medical powers and knowledge, were to marry priests, who bit by bit would bring all Christians into the Roman rite, or else to marry Moslems, whom they would convert to both Christianity and monogamy. This neatly reverses an idea of Riccoldo's that captive nuns would breed enemies to Christendom. Among the advantages that would accrue would be the purchase of articles normally dear in Europe but cheap in the Levant; this ignores the economics of the Italian ports.

Dubois envisages this colonization as taking place in a world divided politically but in other ways united. "There is hardly a sane man, I think, who in these last days would credibly suppose that (as concerns temporal things) there could be one sole monarch of all the world, whom all would obey as their leader, because, if that were attempted, there would be endless wars, rebellions, and dissensions; nor would there be anyone who could settle them, because of the multitude of peoples, the remoteness and variety of places, and the natural inclination of men to disagree." He adds that those commonly called world rulers in the past had only been rulers of large areas, and then continues: "But it is likely that there could be a single prince and monarch in spiritual things, who should be spiritually effective in all directions, east, west, south, and north; which I do not see could happen unless provision be made for learning languages, in the way I have written above, or better." This spiritual power is not the pope; Dubois seems to intend a French cultural hegemony based on a colonial Latin east.[90]

90. *De recuperatione Terrae Sanctae*, ed. Angelo Diotti (Testi medievali di interesse dantesco, I; Florence, 1977), pp. 117, 119–121 (iii, 2), 121–130 (iv, 3–xi, 24), 140–144, (xxiii, 40–xxvii, 46), 150–154 (xxiv, 57–xxxviii, 61), 158–159 (xlii, 67–xliii, 69), 189–192 (lxx, 111–112), 200–201 (lxxvi, 122–lxxvii, 123), 209–211 (lxxxiii, 139–142). For all this period see Aziz S. Atiya, *The Cru-

I have dealt with Riccoldo and Dubois at some length because in their different ways they mark the end of the traditional crusade propaganda — Riccoldo its logical conclusion, Dubois the new concept that replaced it. Dubois's frank colonialism was new, but not, of course, the school of Arabic that he planned as part of it; something like it had been papal policy as early as the middle of the thirteenth century, though probably not a new project then;[91] and it was a favorite scheme of Raymond Lull's. Lull, too, was an original but, though widely read and long famed, in fact without the direct influence he longed for. His ideas of the crusade were conventional, or easily paralleled in contemporary writers. He too demanded a single war-leader, the *bellator*. His determination to preach in North Africa was finally fatal, in spite of the determination of the Moslem authorities not to martyr him. For polemic, he recommended the "al-Kindī" *Risālah*, whether in Vincent of Beauvais's shortened version, or the original in the Cluniac manuscripts, which were widely distributed; but his peculiar contribution to religious controversy, which he put into practice in North Africa, was insistently to attempt to prove the Trinity by "necessary reasons".[92] His is an interesting backwater of cultural history, though his enormous output makes him an important figure in Catalan literature.

One type of propaganda characteristic of the fourteenth century is argument supporting the papal prohibitions of trade with Mamluk Egypt and Syria. The underlying conviction that Egypt would be crucially weakened by cutting off its supplies of wood and of slaves was a miscalculation; it was a fact that Egypt needed to import these commodities, not that the supply could be effectively cut off by a simple boycott by European carriers in the Mediterranean, even if there had been no evasion of the papal prohibitions by Christian merchants, and, indeed, by papal license. So too for exports. Lull, for example, believed that a six-year boycott of the spice trade would ruin the Mamluk state. The argument was overstated, but not foolish. On paper, economic warfare looked promising, but Marino Sanudo is certainly unrepre-

---

sade in the Later Middle Ages (London, 1938), and Palmer A. Throop, *Criticism of the Crusade* (Amsterdam, 1940), for further examples and bibliography.

91. Dubois, *De recuperatione,* ed. Diotti, pp. 151–158 (xxxvi, 59–xli, 66); cf. pp. 160–169 (xlv, 71–liii, 85). Lull, *Liber de fine,* extracts in Adam Gotron, *Ramon Lulls Kreuzzügsideen* (Berlin and Leipzig, 1912), dist. 2, lib. 6. Innocent IV in Heinrich S. Denifle, *Chartularium universitatis parisiensis* (4 vols., Paris, 1889–1897), I, 212.

92. Lull, *Liber de fine,* lib. 1 and 5, in Gotron, *Ramon Lulls . . . ;* Vincent de Beauvais, *Speculum historiale,* xxiii, 40, in *Biblioteca mundi,* vol. V. For the present writer's views on Lull's "necessary reasons" see *Islam and the West,* pp. 177–180.

sentative of the great city of which he was a native in believing that
the more profitable future lay with a hypothetical crusade rather than
direct trade. Sanudo gave economic reasons, but he also emphasized
the supposed abuse of slaves, in order to arouse sexual moral repulsion. For the rest, the argument about slaves was *ad terrorem*; if the
trade succeeded, the Mamluks constituted an alarming threat; if it failed,
the peaceful Egyptians would themselves be vulnerable to threats.[93]
The vulnerability of Egypt was current if disputed doctrine in the fourteenth century (it proved true only of the landward threat from the
east), and it resulted not only in the pillage of Alexandria but in dis-
tracting attention from the early stages of the Ottoman advance. Propaganda was a conservative force.

One of the most emotive presentations of the anti-Egyptian theme
was by William Adam, a European "expert" in eastern affairs, missionary, and traveler in the east, a Dominican who was very briefly named
to the Armenian archbishopric of Sultaniyeh. He says that slaves are
needed for the army because the Egyptians themselves are given over
to carnality. The slaves supply both needs. There is a distinctly sala-
cious passage where he describes how suitable boys are prepared for
market — presumably by Christian merchants; the passage is ridiculous
and rather nasty. The propaganda here has nothing in it of observed
facts about life in Cairo; it is a propaganda picture in the worst sense,
constructed out of Christian doctrines about Moslems — propaganda,
in fact, out of propaganda. He goes on indignantly to tell the story
of a Genoese, Segurano Salvago, who used to strengthen "the persecutors of our faith" and took part in the slave trade. He was generally
"called the sultan's brother", because the sultan had addressed him in
letters as "brother and friend", a stately courtesy horrifying to the
polemicist. Segurano "was so much a Moslem that he allowed the afore-
said sin against nature to be perpetrated on his ships" and, what was
apparently more horrifying still, flew the sultan's flag "as I saw with
my own eyes". In these crimes he was aided by his relations and by
"many other Genoese".[94] This sort of propaganda is unbalanced and
without sense of proportion and it left the maritime cities unmoved.
The sultan in question is Muḥammad an-Nāṣir, whom the Franciscan
Giovanni Vitodurani praised for his severe but true justice in the protection of Latins in Cairo.[95]

The last crusading propagandists of importance were Peter Thomas,

---

93. Lull, *Liber de fine*, lib. 1, 5; Sanudo, *Liber . . . crucis*, I, *passim.*
94. *De modo Saracenos extirpandi* (*RHC, Arm.*, II, 523–525).
95. *BOF*, II, 145.

papal legate, archbishop of Cyprus, and Latin patriarch of Constantinople, and his pupil and hagiographer, Philip of Mézières, sometime chancellor of the kingdom of Cyprus. It was Peter Thomas who vainly urged the conquerors of Alexandria not to withdraw, but we do not know the details of his preaching. He proclaimed "the mystery of the cross" and "the destruction of the Saracens" in quasi-biblical rhetoric. The legendary history of St. Thomas the Apostle seems to have inspired him to dream of the conversion of the east from Islam, schism, and heresy.

Mézières planned to found a *Militia Passionis,* a special force which was in line with the ideas of Lull; it would unite the nations and estates in a good life. When the disaster of Nicopolis happened, Mézières attributed it to those familiar, but not irrelevant, excuses, disunity and sin. He was himself aware in old age that the world had lost interest in all that he had cared for most. His *Songe du vieil pèlerin* rambles, but is full of ideas; in it he concedes to the Mamluk state the virtues of peace, justice, benevolence, public order, and public charities. He advises the young Charles VI of France to send an educated squire on embassy to the sultan, in order to protect the local Christians in a peaceful way.[96] He still wished for a crusade, but had greatly mellowed; that there may be something beyond the propagandist in such a case is a lesson to remember.

In general, Europe had not ceased to wish to impose its ways on the rest of the world but was seeking new methods. There was continuing sentiment for a crusade, however, which Shakespeare reflected accurately,[97] and a purely clerical propaganda survived, and followed lines already laid down; it is interesting that Pius II, the last pope seriously to hope to see a crusade assemble, should himself have written a polemic piece against Islam in the manner of the Middle Ages. Roughly contemporary with Pius, Benedetto Aretino Accolti, a distinguished Florentine public servant and stylist, rewrote the history of the First Crusade (with an epilogue leading up to Saladin's capture of Jerusalem) in the manner of Livy.[98] The historical memory is perhaps the most persistent survival of traditional propaganda.

---

96. Philip of Mézières, *Life of St. Peter Thomas,* ed. Joseph Smet (Rome, 1954), pp. 117–141; for a modern biography see Frederick J. Boehlke, *Pierre de Thomas: Scholar, Diplomat, and Crusader* (Philadelphia, 1966). Cf. William of Machaut, *La Prise d'Alexandrie,* ed. Louis de Mas Latrie (SOL, *SH,* I), lines 3508–3529. On the *Militia* see Atiya, *Crusade in the Later Middle Ages,* pp. 140 ff.; *Le Songe du vieil pèlerin,* ed. George W. Coopland (2 vols., Cambridge, Eng., 1969), I, 230–231, and II, 210–211, 425–426. Cf. Langland, C text, XVIII, 151.

97. E.g., *Richard II,* V, vi; *I Henry IV,* I, i, cf. IV, v.

98. Pius II, *Epistola ad Morbisanum,* in Bibliander, *Machumetis . . . Alcoran* (Basle, 1550); Accolti, *De bello a Christianis gesto* (Florence, 1623).

Gradually crusading faded into pilgrimage in the older sense of the term, and, though sacrilegious attacks on Islam by Franciscan zealot missionaries continued to produce "martyrdoms",[99] for the most part a secure and inexpensive trip to Jerusalem was the height of Christian hope; resentment at delays, insults, sickness, and an inclement climate took the place of bellicosity. It is interesting that the theoretical tone of pilgrim accounts is long a continuation of crusading propaganda.

Thus crusading propaganda petered out when its main themes became irrelevant or were seen to be untrue, and new ideas replaced it. The crusade, which had begun by being the type of the Christian way of life, gave way to new forms of religion. It had never been anything but an ecclesiastical product; whatever the motives of crusaders, the official clerical line was always the only official line and the only articulate one that we know to have existed. Of course, there is plenty of evidence for its having been exploited in private interests or simply ignored. Among the most orthodox, traditional attitudes survived as long as the crusading idea survived, and the idea survived long after all practical enthusiasm for it had waned, and when it had nothing of political value to offer. If traditional historical propaganda was restated in the style of the day by Accolti, Tasso's *La Gerusalemme liberata* witnessed to the continuing appeal of the theme still later. In this way survived the expression of a papal policy long outdated. As a sentiment it would have some future value in the defense of eastern Europe and the central Mediterranean from Ottoman attack, and it would merge insensibly into the propaganda of secular colonialism; the official French line in the invasion of Algiers in 1830 still spoke of "Christendom".[100] It remains true that as long as papal leadership of western Europe in the name of "Christendom" had been a practical political project, crusading themes had been a natural expression of the unity and morale of the west. There had been an implicit "colonialism", in the modern sense, in the "cultural imperialism" of papal pronouncements even more than in the actual practice of the colonies, which were more or less well adapted to their environment.

"Cultural imperialism" played its biggest part in the European refusal to accept the basic facts about Islam, and in a total rejection of the idea of toleration. These had long-lasting effects. Conquered

---

99. *BOF,* II, 61 ff., 66–67, 110 ff., 143 ff.; IV, 390–394; and V, 282 ff. (cf. note 41 above).
100. *Papers Relative to the Occupation of Algiers by the French* (British Sessional Papers, House of Commons, 1839), L, 45–64, esp. 61, 63.

Moslems were allowed to survive, as such, only for a time, and the invidious treatment of Moslems was made possible largely by the unattractive light in which the clergy set the doctrine and the history of Islam. It is no doubt true that the laity were not much moved by theological considerations, and would have behaved as well or as badly if there had never been any propaganda at all. Yet they accepted the need for absolute orthodoxy and cultural unity in Europe, so that the part of the Mediterranean world that was Arabic in speech, and largely Moslem in religion — not, in any case, Latin, even where it was Christian — was quite unacceptable in terms of contemporary European culture. These attitudes, the product of a powerful and consistent body of propaganda, remained still powerful in the nineteenth century, when they fed the propaganda of imperialism, and they actually survive today.

Even the direct preaching cannot have been ineffective. It is not realistic to suppose that there was a total dichotomy between the official and the actual motivation. How far did the two diverge? Insofar as crusaders went to the east to forward their careers, they were doubtless mixed in motive; no one has ever found it difficult to combine the conviction of righteousness with a desire for advancement. In the Marxist sense, it is hardly possible to have feudal colonialism, and in that sense the only colonialists were the maritime cities, whose interest was purely mercantile. They needed no propaganda beyond their interests; yet, even in the periods of difficulty and failure, when their interests clashed increasingly with official doctrine, they produced literature favorable to the crusade. At all times men were willing enough to follow their interests against the church, and often, it is likely, accepted the general principles of orthodox belief without taking excommunications seriously. On the other hand, when they could combine perfect orthodoxy with a course of action that suited their interests, there was no reason why they should not draw comfort and strength from the official line. The crusade became a part of European life for those who never went crusading; the whole system of indulgences was closely involved in this. Without the crusade, kings would have lacked one acceptable means of taxing the church. To some extent, the idea became a mark of those who supported the papacy, but the monarchies also derived benefit from it. There was therefore little inclination to question the orthodox opinion. Any divergence of motive from propaganda is a tendency rather than an absolute distinction.

The Mediterranean continued divided into three main linguistic and cultural areas, and the propaganda has obscured the personal exchanges that there were among them, and particularly between Moslems and crusaders. The Greek area contracted when the Turkish culture intruded, but the propaganda barrier was maintained unbroken. In spite of it, there is enough evidence to convince us that men passed from a Latin into an Arabic culture and often passed back again, even in the Middle Ages, not only in Spain, but in the east also. From the earlier seventeenth century onward — beginning with Don Quixote — we can cull a considerable literature of people who returned from Barbary captivity; printers seem to have carried a stock of stereotype woodcuts to illustrate their stories. There is even a small literature of converts to Islam writing in Latin.[101] There is no literature of either sort from the period of the crusade. Constantine the African was, perhaps, a North African convert; in any case he antedates the crusade, and says nothing of himself. Was his successor, Afflacius, "al-Falakī"? Peter (of) Alfonso was an Arabic-speaking Jew, and he, and other Jews for that matter, converts or not, may have traveled in England.[102] Many Arabs lived in Europe, not by their own choice, and were gradually forced to become Christians. Many Latins lived on friendly terms with Arabs in Sicily and Syria; we know that best from Arabic sources. Many merchants lived and worked in Egypt, Africa, and Syria; there were also mercenary soldiers and chaplains. Only a few late accounts from travelers make up for the lack of personal accounts by European residents in the Arab world. This certainly was the Pyrrhic victory of the propaganda.

We must see crusade propaganda as essentially negative. It cut off whatever relationships might otherwise have been possible. At its worst it gave religious sanction to inhumanity which made it possible to say, for example, of Germans, "slaughter them mercilessly as if they were Saracens".[103] At best it only gave an added conviction of righteousness which boosted morale more in success than in failure. A pride in the linked achievements of various armed forces throughout history, from the ancient Jews onward, presupposed continuing success; the dangerous conviction that a holy war offered the opportunity for a whole-hearted rejection of the good things of the world often resulted in self-deception. In the last resort, all propaganda is merely the expression of hostility. The original enthusiasm which had created

101. Murad Bey, British Library, MS. Add. 19894 and Bodleian, Marsh 179; Bodin, *Colloquium Heptaplomères,* ed. Ludwig Noack (Schwerin, 1857). Cf. Fernand Braudel, *La Méditerranée et le monde à l'époque de Philippe II,* 2nd ed. (Paris, 1966).

102. Constantine legend in Peter the Deacon, *PL,* 173, col. 1034 (and his successor John Afflacius, possibly al-Falakī, but he was apparently not an astronomer); Peter (of) Alfonso, *PL,* 157, cols. 671–706.

103. Suger, *Vie de Louis VI le Gros,* pp. 222–223.

so strong a motive force and made the worst rogues in all classes call themselves an army of God was steadily eroded, but, while it lasted, it encouraged the delusion that God ensures the victory of the true believer, and from it seems to derive the tone of most modern war propaganda.

III

THE EPIC CYCLE
OF THE CRUSADES

"The Epic Cycle of the Crusades" is the name commonly given to two different cycles, composed in different centuries but related in subject matter, and both written in Old French dodecasyllabic verse. The first was apparently begun toward the end of the twelfth century by a versifier named Graindor of Douai, who rewrote and amalgamated three previously independent poems, *La Chanson d'Antioche, Les Chétifs* (the Captives), and *La Conquête de Jérusalem,* which dealt with the First Crusade. Graindor's compilation was later prefaced with an account of the fictitious youthful exploits of Godfrey of Bouillon and the story of his mythical grandfather, the swan-knight; at a later date (the middle of the thirteenth century) a sequel was added which carried the narrative from the end of the First Crusade down to the emergence of Saladin. The second cycle, composed, or at least begun, during the 1350's, comprises three separate poems, *Le Chevalier au Cygne et Godefroid de Bouillon, Baudouin de Sebourc,* and *Le Bâtard de Bouillon.*

The construction of an epic cycle over the years by different authors, usually belonging to different generations, but sometimes known to each other, conforms to a paradigm of which the best-known examples

Editions: Cycle I: *La Chanson du Chevalier au Cygne et de Godefroid de Bouillon,* ed. Célestin Hippeau (2 vols., Paris, 1874–1877); *La Chanson d'Antioche,* ed. Paulin Paris (2 vols., Paris, 1848); *La Conquête de Jérusalem,* ed. Hippeau (Paris, 1868). Cycle II: *Le Chevalier au Cygne et Godefroi de Bouillon,* ed. Frédéric de Reiffenberg and Adolphe Borgnet (4 vols., Brussels, 1844–1859); *Bauduin de Sebourc,* ed. L. Napoléon Boca (2 vols., Valenciennes, 1841); *Le Bâtard de Bouillon,* ed. Robert Cook (Geneva and Paris, 1972); *Saladin: Suite et fin du deuxième cycle de la croisade,* ed. Larry S. Crist (Geneva and Paris, 1972).

General studies: Henri Pigeonneau, *Le Cycle de la croisade et la famille de Bouillon* (Saint-Cloud, 1877); Anouar Hatem, *Les Poèmes épiques des croisades* (Paris, 1932); Suzanne Duparc-Quioc, *Le Cycle de la croisade* (Paris, 1955) (reviewed in *Le Moyen-Âge* by Claude Cahen and Robert Bossuat, LXIII, 311–328, LXIV, 139–147); Cook and Crist, *Le Deuxième cycle de la croisade: Deux études sur son développement* (Geneva, 1972).

are the cycles of Charlemagne, William of Orange, and Doon of Mayence. At the center of a soon-proliferating cycle stands a martial figure
whose prowess in many a combat has charmed a public never weary
of hearing tales about prestigious heroes who fight and slay innumerable foes. At the beginning of the fourteenth century this avid interest was crystalized in the literary and iconographic cult of the "nine
worthies" (three Jews: Joshua, David, and Judas Maccabeus; three
pagans: Hector, Alexander, and Caesar; three Christians: Arthur, Charlemagne, and Godfrey of Bouillon). The epic hero is not allowed to
remain in splendid isolation; he may be the brightest star within his
family constellation, but the deeds of his father, grandfather, brothers,
sons, nephews, and grandsons are likewise memorable and so must
be praised in epic song. Just as Charlemagne's father Pepin and his
nephew Roland are the protagonists of various *chansons de geste,* just
so Godfrey of Bouillon's ancestors, brother, cousin, and their descendants were celebrated in epics built around their persons and deeds,
real or imaginary.

Superhuman strength and supernatural happenings endow the epic
hero with a radiance that marks him as a man above other men, one
of God's elect. When his fury is aroused he can with one mighty blow
of his sword cleave an opponent and his steed in two, that is to say
into four parts, two human and two equine. Miracles accompany him
on his way, heavenly warriors battle at his side, his prayers stay the
sun in its course so that the enemy may be pursued and annihilated,
and archangels bear his soul to paradise, while devils precipitate slain
Saracens into the nethermost regions of hell. How much of all this
a medieval audience believed is somewhat beside the point. People of
those days were certainly pleased with such tales, and being entertained
were not unduly skeptical. Also, one of the fondest beliefs of the nobility was being catered to: blood will tell. Ancestors of a knight must
of necessity have been brave and strong, qualities due to be possessed
also by his relatives and descendants. Worth noticing is the explanation seemingly given in all seriousness for Eustace of Boulogne's failure to measure up to the worldly success of his brothers Godfrey and
Baldwin: when he was an infant, during his mother's absence one day
he had been suckled by a woman of low standing.

The ascription of a supernatural origin to Godfrey's family may perhaps be accounted for by many a nobleman's desire that his lineage
should not be traced back to the common people. It is worth remembering that the Lusignans, who ruled over Cyprus and Jerusalem,
claimed to be descended from the fairy Melusine. The legend of the

Trojan origin of the Franks encouraged French and English feudal families to half believe that their forefathers, in the distant past, had come from the mysterious east.[1]

When compared with William of Tyre's *Historia rerum in partibus transarinis gestarum* and its Old French sequels, the two epic cycles of the crusades have scant historical value, though they do not lack cultural significance. For three centuries, from the twelfth through the fourteenth, they fascinated the French-speaking and French-reading population of central and northern France, thus helping to nourish a lively interest in the Frankish east and in the crusades. A history of the crusades, therefore, should pay some attention to them.

To facilitate access to the first epic cycle I have deemed it advisable to give, for each of its three parts, a résumé of its contents, followed in each case by a few comments. The division into *chants* (cantos) of *Antioche* and *Jérusalem* is, of course, the invention of modern French editors, but as a means of reference it is a serviceable one.

A. *The First Cycle: Godfrey of Bouillon*

SECTION 1: THE SWAN-CHILDREN[2]

King Orient rebukes his wife for saying that the birth of twins is proof of their mother's unfaithfulness to her husband, claiming that such a belief tends to limit God's power to act as he sees fit.[3] Soon afterward queen Beatrice gives birth to septuplets: six boys and a girl, each one wearing a silver necklace. Matabrune, the queen-mother, who hates her daugher-in-law, replaces the septuplets with a litter of seven pups and has Beatrice cast into prison by the outraged king. The seven infants are abandoned on the bank of a river, where they are found by a hermit who takes care of them. Ten years later the children are discovered by one of Matabrune's servants, who steals six of the neck-

---

1. A French chronicler of the Fourth Crusade records that, when Peter of Bracieux, a Picard baron, was asked what right westerners had to eastern lands, he replied: "Don't you know that these lands belonged to our ancestors, the Trojans?" See Robert of Clari, *La Conquête de Constantinople,* ed. Philippe Lauer (Paris, 1924), cap. cvi.

2. Hippeau, vol. I, pp. 1–107.

3. Another version of the swan-children (*La Naissance du Chevalier au Cygne,* ed. Henry A. Todd [Baltimore, 1889]) calls the king Lothaire, his wife Elioxe.

laces. The children to whom they belong are transformed into swans; for several years they are fed by Elias, the seventh child, who has retained his human shape. Meanwhile Matabrune has one of the necklaces melted down by a silversmith. Young Elias succeeds in saving the life of his mother Beatrice, condemned after fifteen years' imprisonment to the stake. The swan-children, except the one whose necklace has been melted down, resume their human appearance and are christened Orient, Orion, Zacharias, John, and Rosette. Elias, whose father has abdicated in his favor, besieges Matabrune in her castle of Malbruiant. She is finally captured and burned at the stake. At the injunction of an angel Elias sets forth in a boat drawn by his brother the swan, after receiving from his mother the gift of a magic horn. On his way he slays Agolant, the dead Matabrune's brother. He enters the Rhine and reaches Nijmegen.

SECTION 2: THE SWAN-KNIGHT[4]

Duke Rainier of Saxony is laying claim before emperor Otto to the lands of the widowed duchess of Bouillon, who still lacks a champion willing to defend her rights and those of her young daughter Beatrice. The swan-knight proffers his services and succeeds in slaying Rainier, whose hostages are put to death. The Saxons seek revenge by sacking the castle of Florent, a nephew of the emperor. The swan-knight marries Beatrice, but cautions her never to ask him who he is nor whence he came, otherwise she will lose him forever. The vengeful Saxons kill Gelien, another nephew of the emperor, but the swan-knight rescues his wife from their hands. To them is born a girl, Ida, the future mother of duke Godfrey, count Eustace, and king Baldwin. The Saxons, still unappeased, besiege Bouillon but are finally routed by the emperor, whom the swan-knight has called to his aid. On the seventh anniversary of her wedding Beatrice can no longer restrain her curiosity. The swan-knight takes sorrowful leave of his wife and daughter and departs in a swan-drawn boat which has suddenly come for him. As a farewell token, he entrusts his horn to Beatrice, recommending that she take good care of it. This she fails to do. One day at the hour of noon the ducal hall bursts into flames and, amid the general confusion, a swan is seen flying away with the neglected horn. Increasing in beauty every day, Ida reaches the age of fourteen.

4. Hippeau, vol. I, pp. 107–259.

SECTION 3: GODFREY OF BOUILLON[5]

Emperor Otto holds court at Cambrai. A newcomer, young count Eustace of Boulogne, waits upon him at table with such pleasing grace that Otto grants him a boon. Eustace asks for the hand of Ida of Bouillon, whose mother Beatrice does not oppose the match and retires to a nunnery. Within two and a half years Ida gives birth to three sons, Eustace, Godfrey, and Baldwin. She insists on suckling all three, for fear that another woman's milk might prove injurious to them. One day during Ida's absence one of the babies is given the breast by a nurse. On discovering this, the frantic mother shakes the infant till he regurgitates the debasing fluid, but alas!, in later days Eustace was never to equal his two brothers. At seventeen years of age Godfrey, having received knighthood at the hands of his father, is sent to the court of emperor Otto. He champions the rights of the orphaned daughter of a castellan against her cousin, whom he slays in judicial combat. Godfrey becomes duke of Bouillon.

The scene suddenly shifts to Mecca, where a great concourse of Saracen potentates and dignitaries is assembled. The spirits of the rejoicing Moslems are dampened when Calabre, mother of Corbaran (Kerbogha), prophesies that dire things are in store for the paynim world. She names Godfrey and his brothers as the leaders of an army that will conquer Syria and Palestine. Her nephew Cornumarant, son of Corbadas and lord of Jerusalem, decides to travel to France and discover for himself whether this Godfrey is the formidable adversary his soothsaying aunt proclaims him to be. He crosses the sea disguised as a palmer, with two razor-sharp knives hidden beneath his cloak. The abbot of Saint Trond recognizes Cornumarant, whom he has seen on a pilgrimage to the Holy Land, and warns Godfrey that he is in danger of being assassinated. Godfrey sends for all his friends and retainers. Cornumarant is greatly impressed by their number. He is told that within five years Godfrey will have conquered the Holy Land. Cornumarant replies that he will ready his kingdom to meet the Christian onslaught.

Comments: It is usually assumed that the three sections of part one came into being as separate poems and were later soldered together by a *remanieur* named Renaud. The legendary tales they embody were already known to William of Tyre, since in his *Historia* (IX, 6) he refers to the swan-knight and to countess Ida's prophecy that her three

5. Hippeau, vol. II, pp. 1–189.

sons would grow up to become a duke (Godfrey), a king (Baldwin), and a count (Eustace). It should be noted here that through some curious transference the legend of the swan-knight became detached from the Godfrey epic cycle to fasten on the central figure of an entirely different cycle, that of Garin "le Lorrain", Wagner's Lohengrin (= Loherenc Garin).[6]

B. *The First Cycle: The First Crusade*

SECTION 1: THE TAKING OF ANTIOCH[7]

I: Graindor of Douai will tell how the Christian host conquered Jerusalem. The liberation of the Holy Land was prophesied by Jesus on the cross. Peter the Hermit was praying at the tomb of the Redeemer in Jerusalem when God appeared to him, commanding him to return to the lands of Christendom and announce that the time had come to free his city. Sixty thousand men assemble at Peter's behest, among them Harpin of Bourges, Richard of Caumont, John of Alis, Baldwin of Beauvais, and his brother Ernoul. Peter and his followers begin the siege of Nicaea. Soliman (Kilij-Arslan), the lord of that city, has just received reinforcements, led by Corbaran (Kerbogha), from the sultan of Persia. The Christians are defeated on the slopes of Mount Civetot, the above-named knights being taken prisoner along with Fulcher of Meulan, Richard of Pavia, the bishop of Forez, and the abbot of Fécamp. Peter, who has escaped capture, betakes himself to Rome and then to France. The pope preaches a general crusade at Clermont in Auvergne. II: Godfrey of Bouillon takes command of the Christian host. Bohemond and Tancred join up with him at Constantinople. The crusaders have difficulties with the Greek emperor, which are smoothed away by Estatin the Noseless (Taticius) and Guy the seneschal. Soliman's army is defeated and Nicaea surrenders to Estatin. III: The crusaders resume their forward march. Bohemond and his men, who had outdistanced the main army, suffer a setback. Tancred and Baldwin quarrel about the possession of Tarsus. Tancred enters Mamistra and

---

6. See Robert Jaffray, *The Two Knights of the Swan, Lohengrin and Helyas: a Study of the Legend,* with special reference to its two most important developments (New York and London, 1910).

7. *La Chanson d'Antioche,* ed. Paulin Paris.

Choros (Corycus?). Baldwin accepts an invitation from the Old Man of the Mountain to go to Rohais (Edessa) and marry his daughter. Godfrey forces his way into Artais (Artāḥ). Thanks to Enguerrand of Saint Pol, the crusaders are able to seize two towers guarding the bridge over the river Far (Orontes). Emir Garsion (Yaghī-Sīyan) prepares to defend Antioch.

IV: The crusaders encircle the city. Gontier of Aire gains possession of emir Fabur's steed. After several skirmishes, the besiegers erect a wooden tower. Dead Turks are dug up in a cemetery and decapitated, and their heads are catapulted into the city. The crusaders suffer from a shortage of food. Again the Turks attempt a sortie, again they are repulsed. At the height of the fray Godfrey cleaves one of his opponents in twain. Raimbaut Creton slaughters some two hundred Saracens who had sought refuge under the bridge over the Far. V: The Tafurs or riffraff of the army roast the bodies of the fallen Turks and eat the human flesh. When negotiations for a truce break down, the enraged Garsion orders Reginald Porquet, a recently captured Christian knight, to be hamstrung. Sansadoine (Shams-ad-Daulah), son of Garsion, is sent with a request for help to the sultan of Persia. Hardly has he arrived at the Persian court when Soliman of Nicaea shows up with a few battered stragglers. Corbaran takes command of the forces which will march to the rescue of Antioch. He is accompanied by Brohadas, one of the sultan's sons. Corbaran refuses to pay any heed to the warnings of his mother Calabre. VI: On his way to Antioch, Corbaran is unsuccessful in his attempt to storm Rohais. Meanwhile the crusaders repulse a sortie of the besieged during which the young son of emir Dacian (Fīrūz) falls into their hands. They send him back to his anxious father, who promises them his support. At this point count Stephen of Blois, having learned of Corbaran's approach, withdraws for greater security to Alexandretta. Emir Dacian informs Bohemond that he will admit the Christians into Antioch. Bohemond demands of the other leaders that they yield their share of the city to him, but Raymond of Saint Gilles refuses to forgo his rights. Dacian slays his wife, who had become suspicious of his doings, and then lowers a rope ladder fastened to a merlon. Thirty-five knights scale the walls before the ladder collapses, but they are able to open one of the gates and let the rest of the army in. Antioch, with the exception of the citadel, is taken after two days of street fighting.

VII: Corbaran and his troops arrive in view of Antioch. He writes confidently to caliph Caifas and to the sultan of Persia, but again his mother Calabre informs him that he cannot hope to prevail against the soldiers of Christ. The Franks, whose turn it is to be besieged, are tormented by the lack of food. Count Stephen of Blois advises the Greek emperor not to help the beleaguered crusaders. Peter the Provençal (Peter Bartholomew) reveals that Saint Andrew has twice appeared to him in his sleep and has designated to him the exact place where is hidden the spear with which Jesus was struck on the cross. Amid general rejoicing the Holy Lance is unearthed. A fire destroys part of Antioch. Corbaran turns down an offer to decide the issue by means of champions chosen by both sides. Emir Amidelis, who has spied on the Christians, reports back to Corbaran. VIII: The bishop of Le Puy cannot find a knight willing to carry the Holy Lance into battle: Robert of Flanders, Robert of Normandy, Godfrey of Bouillon, Tancred, Bohemond, and Hugh of Vermandois decline each in his turn an honor which would keep them from the front ranks. Raymond of Saint Gilles consents to stay inside the city to prevent Garsion from breaking out of the citadel. As the Christian leaders ride out of Antioch emir Amidelis names each one to Corbaran. The battle begins. Among the first to fall are Reginald of Tor and Odo of Beauvais. The crusaders lay about them with lance, pike, and sword. Corbaran is knocked off his horse by Robert of Normandy and Brohadas is slain by Godfrey. The poet indulges in a lengthy enumeration of Christian and Moslem warriors, adducing as his authority Richard the Pilgrim. The Red Lion (Turkish: Kîzîl Arslan), Soliman, and Sansadoine succumb under the blows of Robert of Normandy, Godfrey, and Hugh of Vermandois. Several saints are seen fighting on the Christian side. The paynims are routed, but only after Godfrey has had a narrow escape. The defenders of the citadel surrender.

SECTION 2: CORBARAN'S CAPTIVES[8]

After his defeat at Antioch Corbaran flees to Sarmasane (Kermanshah), where he returns to the bereaved sultan of Persia the body of his son Brohadas. Accused of treachery, Corbaran agrees to be put to death if any Christian chosen by him cannot defeat any two Saracens selected by the sultan, thus failing to prove his contention that the Christians are better fighters than the Moslems. On the advice of his mother Calabre he calls upon the Christian knights he has held prisoner since the battle of Civetot. Richard of Caumont consents, in exchange for his freedom and that of his companions, to do battle with Goliath of Nicaea and Sorgalé of Mecca. He slays both. Goli-

8. *Les Chétifs,* in Hippeau, vol. II, pp. 193–276.

ath's son and Sorgalé's nephew attempt with their followers to murder Corbaran and Richard of Caumont, but they are defeated by Richard and his companions. Corbaran and his newly found friends are crossing the land of king Abraham when a dragon pounces on Ernoul of Beauvais and proceeds to devour him. His brother Baldwin finally pushes his sword through the heart of the monster. Corbaran is filled with admiration and can hardly restrain himself from becoming a Christian. His nephew, son of queen Florie, is carried off by a wolf. Harpin of Bourges, another of the Christian knights once held captive by Corbaran, gives chase, only to see a huge ape wrest the child from the wolf and clamber with it into a tree. Before he at last rescues the boy, Harpin has to beat off four lions. Then he is unable to prevent five highwaymen from kidnapping the young prince, but Corbaran, who has finally arrived on the scene, manages to obtain the release of his nephew. With Corbaran's approval, the Christian knights ride toward Jerusalem. On the way they join up with the other crusaders.

SECTION 3: THE TAKING OF JERUSALEM[9]

I: Godfrey of Bouillon, several other leaders, and ten thousand knights leave the main part of the army at La Mahomerie and ride close to the holy city. While they are foraging in the valley of Jehoshaphat, they are attacked by Cornumarant and fifty thousand Saracens. At this critical juncture they are joined by Richard of Caumont, Harpin of Bourges, and the other knights formerly held captive by Corbaran. A call is sent out for help, but the Turks are driven back into Jerusalem before the arrival of the rest of the crusaders. That night Tancred and Bohemond raid Caesarea and on their way back are attacked by the emir of Ascalon. Fortunately for them several saints enter the fray on their behalf. The following day the whole army resumes its advance and reaches the top of La Montjoie, a hill from which the holy city is plainly visible. II: Godfrey and the other leaders agree on the various sectors they will occupy facing Jerusalem. King Corbadas, watching the besiegers from a high tower, is dismayed when he sees Godfrey transfix three kites with a single arrow. That night Cornumarant sallies forth with ten thousand men, but Harpin of Bourges and his companions drive them back into the city. Exhorted by the king of the Tafurs and the bishop of Marturana, the crusaders prepare a general assault.

9. *La Conquête de Jérusalem,* ed. Hippeau.

III. The king of the Tafurs is wounded, Pagan of Beauvais and Gontier of Aire are slain, and a rain of Greek fire forces the besiegers to retreat. Bohemond surprises an enemy column on its way to Acre. The Saracens send out carrier pigeons asking for assistance. These are intercepted by the Christians, who modify the terms of the messages. IV: A general assault is again attempted, but hostilities are soon suspended to allow for an exchange of prisoners. Cornumarant sets out to get help from the sultan of Persia. Baldwin of Edessa follows in hot pursuit, but is surrounded by Saracens and driven to take refuge in a marsh. His armor proves insufficient protection against the leeches, and to add to his discomfort, the Turks set fire to the dry reeds. Cornumarant receives a promise of aid from the sultan of Persia. V: The besiegers are told when and how to assault Jerusalem. They attack between the Gates of St. Stephen and David, but are unsuccessful on the first day. On the following day, a Friday, Thomas of Marle has himself hoisted up to the battlements on the spears of thirty of his men and manages to open one of the gates. The crusaders pour into the city. Corbaran surrenders the Tower of David. Godfrey is chosen as ruler of the new kingdom but refuses to wear a crown. Most of the Christian lords are about to return to their native lands when they receive news that Cornumarant is advancing on Jerusalem at the head of a huge army. VI: Corbadas and his son meet in Barbais. While foraging in the valley of Jehoshaphat, Cornumarant is taken prisoner. Raymond of Saint Gilles falls into the hands of the Turks. Corbadas tells the sultan of Persia that his son is held captive within Jerusalem. Cornumarant is exchanged for Raymond. Before he is freed he is made to witness a parade of the Christian garrison in which Godfrey has the same men file by over and over again. The sultan's army approaches Jerusalem.

VII: On the caliph's advice, the Saracens display their treasures. Eager for booty, Peter the Hermit and his followers rush forth. He is taken prisoner. Threatened with death, Peter agrees to become a Moslem. The sultan sends an envoy to Godfrey ordering him to surrender Jerusalem and abjure the Christian faith. Wishing to impress the messenger, Godfrey repeats his previous stratagem of having the same men file by several times. To cap this show of strength, he cleaves a Turk in two. After failing to take the city by storm, the paynims withdraw to Ramla. While praying in the Temple Godfrey is reassured by several signs that God's help will be forthcoming. Hugh of Vermandois and the other chieftains arrive in Jerusalem. The crusaders ride forth in the direction of Ramla. As their battalions draw near, Peter the Hermit names the leaders to the sultan: Godfrey, Robert of Normandy,

Hugh of Vermandois, Bohemond, Tancred, Rotrou of Perche, Stephen of Albermarle (Blois?), and the "king" of the Tafurs. VIII: The sultan of Persia exhorts his thirteen remaining sons to avenge the death of their brother Brohadas. The poet lists the many and sundry peoples comprising the sultan's army. The battle starts with Godfrey slaying Sinagon, the sultan's eldest son. There follows a series of jousts. Bohemond kills king Corbadas, and Lucabel, the king's brother, is slain by Tancred. Baldwin of Edessa lays low Cornumarant. Saint George and Saint Maurice are seen fighting the infidels. Peter the Hermit regains his freedom and promptly dispatches Sanguin, another of the sultan's sons. The paynims are routed. The bishop of Marturana's prayer is answered when the sun is stopped in its course and the light of day prolonged. During the pursuit, Baldwin of Edessa and Raimbaut Creton are cut off from the other knights, but are finally rescued. The sultan enters a boat at Acre and sails away to safety. Enguerrand of Saint Pol is solemnly buried. Funeral honors are also bestowed on Cornumarant, the brave enemy whose heart, when cut out from his body, fills a helmet.

Comments: Part two of Cycle I is apparently the work of a versifier named Graindor of Douai, who amalgated the compositions of three earlier poets, no one of which survives in its original form. The first of these, written by a certain Richard le Pèlerin (Richard the Pilgrim), who may have taken part in the First Crusade, told of the taking of Antioch (*La Chanson d'Antioche*); the second (*Les Chétifs*), which in its present form contains a statement that it was composed at the request of Raymond of Antioch, narrated the fictitious adventures of six followers of Peter the Hermit who through their boldness and resourcefulness supposedly won the friendship of their captor Corbaran (Kerbogha); while the third related the siege and storming of Jerusalem (*La Conquête de Jérusalem*). In laisse 1 of section 1 Graindor of Douai names himself and implies that his song has for subject the First Crusade in its entirety:

> Sirs, pray be still and end your chatter,
> If you wish to hear a noble song.
> Never has a jongleur recited a better one;
> It tells of the holy city, so worthy of reverence,
> In which God allowed his body to be wounded and harmed,
> To be struck with a lance and nailed to the cross:
> Jerusalem it is called by its right name.
> Those newly fledged jongleurs who sing this song
> Leave out its opening part,

But Graindor of Douai has no mind to do likewise,
He who has rewritten all its verses.
Now you will hear of Jerusalem
And of those who went to adore the Sepulcher,
How they assembled their armies,
In France, in Berry, in neighboring Auvergne,
Apulia, Calabria, down to Barletta on the sea,
Far-away Wales; there they gathered their forces,
And in many lands I know not by name;
Of such a pilgrimage you never heard tell.
For God they suffered many hardships;
Thirst, heat, and cold, lack of food and sleep;
Our Lord could not help but reward them
And call their souls to him on high.

The beginning of Graindor's long narrative (about twenty thousand lines), with its emphasis on the six followers of Peter the Hermit taken prisoner by Kerbogha, is evidently borrowed from *Les Chétifs*; what follows is mostly based on Richard le Pèlerin's *Chanson d'Antioche*; the lifting of the siege of Antioch brought about by the battle the crusaders won on June 28, 1098, is followed by a very lengthy segment drawn from *Les Chétifs*; when the final section, which deals with the siege of Jerusalem, is reached, there is no clear indication as to the moment Graindor ceases using the *Chétifs* and starts to paraphrase the *Conquête de Jérusalem*. Although Graindor wrote in rhymed alexandrines, it is entirely possible that one or more of his predecessors composed in a different meter and was satisfied with assonance. Any historian of the First Crusade interested in assessing the factual value of Graindor's work should always remember that his "Song of Jerusalem" represents an extensive *remaniement* of three poems which have not survived in their original form, undertaken in order to fuse their contents and thereby create the impression of a unified narrative. He should also bear in mind that Graindor's compilation has not been published as transcribed in the manuscripts, but was arbitrarily carved up in three different editions (1848, 1868, 1877) by two different editors (Paulin Paris, Célestin Hippeau).

Richard le Pèlerin must have written his *Chanson d'Antioche* not long after the First Crusade, if he is to be identified, as seems very likely, with the author of a song of Antioch who is taken to task by the chronicler Lambert of Ardres for not having included in his poem any mention of Arnold of Guines (d. 1138), presumably because that worthy had turned down the poet's request for a pair of shoes. The contents of Richard's poem can be reconstructed, at least in summary fashion, by comparing Graindor's *rifacimento* with the other accounts which derive from Richard: the Latin one by Albert of Aachen, the extant fragment from Gregory Bechada's Provençal *Canso d'Antiocha*, and the Spanish *Gran conquista de Ultramar.* Such a comparison shows that Graindor does not seem to have made any radical changes in Richard's narrative except in cantos VI and VII of his *Antioche,* for which Robert the Monk is the main source.[10]

The *Chétifs* may have been composed in Syria. According to a statement which appears in Graindor's revised version of the poem (Hippeau, II, 213), its author wrote at the request of Raymond, prince of Antioch (d. 1149), and was rewarded with a canonry at Saint Peter's in that city. Anouar Hatem claims that since the *Chétifs* manifests such intimate knowledge of Syria, its land, and its people, only a native of that country or a long-time resident could possibly be its author. Roger Goosens, though somewhat skeptical of all the local color which Hatem professes to find in the *Chétifs,* has nevertheless strengthened the case for a "Syrian" origin of the poem by pointing out that the themes, situations, and inspiration (struggles with wild animals, service of a Christian under a Saracen, desire to reconcile hostile peoples living side by side, and so forth) resemble similar material found in *Digenes Akritas* and other Byzantine epics. Urban T. Holmes and Claude Cahen, who also find themselves in general agreement with Hatem, believe that the adventures ascribed to Harpin of Bourges and his companions might well reflect the experiences of Bohemond I of Antioch and his cousin Richard of the Principate while they were prisoners of the Saracens.[11]

La Conquête de Jérusalem is the title that Hippeau chose for section 3 of Graindor of Douai's account of the First Crusade when he decided to publish it independently from the other two sections. Section 3, as is the case for the other two sections of part two, represents a revised version of older material, which at one time probably constituted an independent poem, though it may also have started as a sequel tacked on to Richard le Pèlerin's *Antioche.* The unrevised *Jérusalem,* still recognizable in the *Gran conquista de Ultramar,* was his-

---

10. See Duparc-Quioc, "La Composition de la *Chanson d'Antioche," Romania,* LXXXIII (1962), 1–29, 210–243; on p. 234 she cites Lambert's *Chronicon Ghisnense et Ardense (918–1203),* ed. Denis C. de Godefroy Ménilglaise (Paris, 1855), p. 311. She believes that the anonymous author of the *Gesta Francorum* borrowed his epic embellishments from Richard le Pèlerin. See also Lewis A. M. Sumberg, *La Chanson d'Antioche: Étude historique et littéraire* (Paris, 1968).

11. Cf. Orderic Vitalis, *Historia ecclesiastica,* X, 23 (ed. Marjorie Chibnall, V [Oxford, 1975], 350–353); Roger Goossen's review of Hatem's book in *Byzantion,* VIII (1933), 706–728; Urban T. Holmes and William M. McLeod, "Source Problems of the Chétifs," *Romanic Review,* XXVIII (1937), 99–108; and Cahen, *La Syrie du nord à l'époque des croisades et la principauté franque d'Antioche* (IFD, BO, I; Paris, 1940), pp. 568–576.

torically more accurate than its *rifacimento,* which suffers from the injection of incidents and episodes similar to those found in *Antioche* and presumably borrowed from Richard le Pèlerin (or even possibly by Graindor from his own version of *Antioche*). Anouar Hatem has attempted to prove that the older *Jérusalem* was, like the original *Chétifs,* written in the Latin Orient, but Suzanne Duparc-Quioc's counterclaim that it was composed in northern France is based on more impressive evidence.[12]

C. *The First Cycle: The Kings of Jerusalem*

Raymond of Saint Gilles, Bohemond, Tancred, Harpin of Bourges, John of Alis, the king of the Tafurs, the bishop of Forez, and the abbot of Fécamp promise Godfrey that they will stay with him in the Holy Land. Corbaran receives baptism at the hands of the bishop of Marturana, and his sister Florie (also called Matroine) becomes the wife of Godfrey. Meanwhile the siege of Acre has begun. Tancred obtains possession of Caesarea. He jousts with the emir Dodekin (Tughtigin). The resistance of Acre ends when the besiegers start catapulting beehives onto the battlements. Godfrey angers Heraclius, the patriarch of Jerusalem, by asking for relics to send his mother, countess Ida. The irate prelate does not hesitate to poison the king. Heraclius conspires with Tancred to place Bohemond on the throne, but cannot prevent Baldwin of Edessa from taking his brother's place. Heraclius dies in prison and is succeeded by Henry, archbishop of Tyre. Death also claims John of Alis and Harpin of Bourges. Baldwin is taken prisoner. In order to guarantee the payment of his ransom to the sultan of Persia, he surrenders his younger daughter Beatrice (Yvette) as a hostage. When later she returns home, she reveals that she has been ravished by Blugadas, king of Aleppo, and becomes a sister of charity at the hospital at Acre. The elder daughter, Ida, had married Amalric of Auxerre, who succeeds Baldwin on the latter's death. Amalric is king of Jerusalem for only three years. His posthumous son Baldwin inherits the crown. The widowed Ida marries Baldwin of Sebourc (Le Bourg), a cousin of Hugh of Vermandois. With his own hand Baldwin of Sebourc kills the infamous Blugadas. At this point of the narrative Saladin makes his appearance. Son of king Eufrarin of Alexandria,

12. Duparc-Quioc, *Le Cycle,* pp. 1–76, 275–390.

he becomes master of all Egypt through the assassination of his over-lord the Amulaine. At first, he makes little headway against young king Baldwin, who is ably assisted by three powerful lords, Baldwin of Falkenberg, count of Ramla, his brother Balian, count of Tripoli, and Reginald of Châtillon, castellan of Kerak. Unfortunately the young king is stricken with leprosy and cannot prevent Reginald from violating a truce both sides had promised to respect. Saladin besieges Kerak. King Baldwin manages to raise the siege and renew the truce. Soon afterward he dies without having named a successor.[13]

In the closing lines of part two of Cycle I reference is made to another poem in which the taking of Acre will be recounted, as well as the founding of the military orders. Part three does contain an account of the siege and capture of Acre, but nothing is said of the first appearance of either the Knights Templar or the Knights Hospitaller. As may be gathered from the summary given above, part three of Cycle I presents a very fanciful, yet not entirely unhistorical, recital of what took place in the Holy Land between the battle of Ascalon and the death of Baldwin IV. Godfrey of Bouillon's marriage to the fictitious Florie and the conversion of her supposed brother Corbaran are, of course, examples of unbridled fantasy. The drastic pruning down of the family tree of the kings of Jerusalem is worth noting: Godfrey's two immediate successors, his brother Baldwin I and his cousin Baldwin II, are telescoped into just one Baldwin; Baldwin II's son-in-law Fulk of Anjou and the latter's two sons, Baldwin III and Amalric, are replaced by the still more composite Amalric of Auxerre. Despite his disappearance from the roster of kings, Baldwin of Le Bourg is reborn as Baldwin of Sebourc, who will become the second husband of Ida, the supposed widow of Amalric of Auxerre. Baldwin II's eldest daughter, Melisend, and his youngest, Yvette, are now named Ida and Beatrice. Although it is historically true that Yvette was as a small child for a time a hostage in the hands of the Saracens, it is unlikely that she was sexually molested by them during her captivity, but it is indeed a fact that she later became a nun, abbess of Bethany. One may safely assume that patriarch Heraclius, who in the 1180's had for mistress the notorious Pasque de Riveti (*Madame la Patriarchesse*) and was rumored to have instigated the poisoning of William of Tyre, was the prototype of the nonhistorical patriarch Heraclius stated to have

---

13. For a detailed summary and analysis of part three of Cycle I see Émile Roy, "Les Poèmes français relatifs à la première croisade: le poème de 1356 et ses sources," *Romania,* LV (1929), 411–468.

been the contemporary and poisoner of Godfrey of Bouillon. Finally, young king Baldwin IV's leprosy and Reginald of Kerak's misdeeds correspond to the historical accounts.

D. The First Cycle: An Evaluation

Cycle I, as a whole, is difficult to assess. Quite apart from the fact that it runs to well over thirty thousand lines, it suffers from having been edited piecemeal and in incomplete form. The editor of the *Chétifs* did not attempt to give the complete text of that poem, and part three (*The Kings of Jerusalem*) lies buried in the manuscripts; it is a very late addition to Cycle I. It is different in spirit from the first two parts, which do evince a certain amount of structural unity. Whereas part three is essentially a rhymed chronicle, however distorted its chronology and presentation of facts, parts one and two are epic in character; they celebrate the heroic deeds of one man, be he the swan-knight or his grandson Godfrey of Bouillon. It should also be noted that part one leads straight into part two. The prophecies foreshadowing the exploits of Godfrey and his brothers during the First Crusade are echoed in part two by reminders of the deeds of their supposed ancestor, the swan-knight. Cornumarant, the alleged leader of the Saracens during the siege of Jerusalem by the Christians, has already appeared as Godfrey's chief antagonist in part one. In addition, there is hardly any change of ethos between the two parts, at least from a medieval point of view. In part one first the swan-knight, then his grandson Godfrey, fight to protect damsels and ladies in distress; they are the staunch champions of rightful causes, and miraculous occurrences accompany their progress through life. The same struggle in behalf of a cause which enlists divine assistance is found in part two, only here it is Christ to whom Godfrey and his companions seek to restore his inheritance. Yet it must be admitted that part two cannot compare with the *Chanson de Roland* when it comes to capturing the religious fervor and the indomitable spirit which animated the crusaders in their struggle with the Moslem world.

E. The Second Cycle

Cycle II, as already stated, belongs to the middle of the fourteenth century and comprises three different poems: *Le Chevalier au Cygne et Godefroid de Bouillon* (a title I shall shorten to *Godefroi de Bouillon*), *Baudouin de Sebourc,* and the *Bâtard de Bouillon.* As will be seen by the following comments, these three poems, without ceasing to be epics, are visibly influenced by other types of literature such as the Arthurian romance and the fabliau.

The author of *Godefroi de Bouillon* (35,180 alexandrines) has completely recast and rephrased parts one and two of Cycle I. He almost never preserves a line of one of the older epics (e.g., GB 16091 = *Jérusalem* 842, GB 16112 = 784). His account of the swan-knight and the early exploits or *enfances* of Godfrey is considerably shorter than that of his Cycle I predecessors, but, when Cornumarant appears on the scene, the *Godefroi* poet must have felt that the story as he understood it—a romance located in the Orient—had at last begun, for from then on he becomes prolix, prone to additions and embroiderings instead of his former relatively restrained self. His fancy is especially unimpeded when he describes (vv. 13832–15963) Godfrey's courting of the Saracen princess Florie, which he imagines as taking place at the very time the crusaders are advancing on Jerusalem! The climactic episode of the poem, the poisoning of Godfrey by patriarch Heraclius (vv. 27512–28537), is narrated with a certain amount of dramatic skill. Tancred is made to appear as the accomplice, however reluctant, of the murderer, and we are told that the day will come when Godfrey's mother, countess Ida of Boulogne, will exact a terrible revenge for the death of her son. On a number of occasions the *Godefroi* poet has borrowed details from William of Tyre, or more probably from the Old French translation of William's Latin text.[14]

Baudouin de Sebourc (about 23,000 alexandrines) is concerned with the *enfances* of the third ruler of the Frankish kingdom of Jerusalem, Baldwin II. The fourth son of Rose, the swan-knight's sister, Baldwin is brought up by the castellan of Sebourc in complete ignorance of his illustrious parentage. He becomes a much-traveled knight-errant, shuttling back and forth between the west and the east with surprising alacrity, the hero of many a preposterous adventure. At long last he learns that he is related to Godfrey of Bouillon and Baldwin and is in the line of succession to the throne of Jerusalem. He then settles down to what history expects of him by accepting the lordship of Edessa

14. Duparc-Quioc lists some thirty such borrowings, *Le Cycle,* pp. 110–115.

from his cousin Baldwin I. When *Baudouin de Sebourc* ends, Cycle II has not progressed chronologically beyond the point which marks the close of *Godefroi de Bouillon*: Baldwin I is still planning to attack the five Saracen rulers of Mecca, brothers who go by the names of Esclamart, Hector, Marbrun, Sardoine, and Taillefer.[15]

The *Bâtard de Bouillon* (6,546 alexandrines) opens with Baldwin I's campaign against the five kings of Mecca, his excursion to the shores of the Red Sea, and a sojourn of five years in the land of Féerie, where his hosts are king Arthur and Morgan le Fay. After Baldwin's return to Jerusalem the narrative focuses on still another Baldwin, who happens to be the illegitimate son of the king and the Saracen princess Sinamonde. The Bastard of Bouillon is the "hero" of a series of episodes which at best might be termed unfortunate. Still in his teens, he quarrels with a cousin and bashes in his skull with a chessboard; not long afterward he stabs to death his half-brother Ourry; he then proceeds to marry a Saracen girl against her wishes; when she becomes unfaithful, he allows her to be burned at the stake, and so on. The narrative shifts back to Baldwin I, only to recount his death. Tancred is dispatched to Boulogne to offer the crown to Eustace, the brother of the deceased monarch. Apprised of his arrival, countess Ida has Tancred summarily hanged. The poem closes with the ominous statement that the violent deaths of Godfrey and Tancred will so divide their respective partisans that eventually they will be unable to stem the onrushing tide of Saladin's armies. Did the Second Cycle end at this point, or did it, like the First Cycle, reach the end of the twelfth century? If we agree with those scholars who have recently given their close attention to Cycle II, we must assume that the fifteenth-century romance *Saladin* represents a prosification of a lost fourteenth-century poem which continued and completed the narrative undertaken in the *Bâtard de Bouillon*.[16]

---

15. See Edmond René Labande, *Étude sur Baudouin de Sebourc, chanson de geste: Légende poétique de Baudouin II du Bourg, roi de Jérusalem* (Paris, 1940).

16. See Cook and Crist, *Le Deuxième cycle.*

IV

FINANCING THE CRUSADES

Western Europe never wholly succumbed to those disruptive forces which threatened it with a moneyless economy. At the end of the eleventh century money was a common, but not a cheap, commodity. In the succeeding centuries the supply of money increased and money consequently cheapened; credit instruments were developed and banking practices established. During the first two crusades the scarcity of money made it rise in value as the crusaders competed with one another to obtain it by selling their goods.[1] In the thirteenth century the

The primary sources for this chapter are too scattered to permit of a comprehensive bibliography. Many chronicles of the crusades as well as a number of others have proved useful. Charters of value have been found in many cartularies and collections, both published and unpublished. Papal and royal letters and accounts have been among the most valuable sources and will be cited in the notes.

No comprehensive study of the financing of the crusades has been published, although Giles Constable has recently surveyed "The Financing of the Crusades in the Twelfth Century," in *Outremer: Studies in the History of the Crusading Kingdom of Jerusalem*, ed. Benjamin Z. Kedar *et al.* (Jerusalem, 1982), pp. 64–88. Most secondary work has been in the field of ecclesiastical support, where William E. Lunt's works are preëminent: *The Valuation of Norwich* (Oxford, 1926), *Papal Revenues in the Middle Ages* (2 vols., New York, 1934), *Financial Relations of the Papacy with England to 1327* (Cambridge, Mass., 1939), and *Financial Relations of the Papacy with England, 1327–1534* (Cambridge, Mass., 1962). His bibliographies provide the best introduction to the materials relating to the subject. Adolf Gottlob, *Die päpstlichen Kreuzzugssteuern des 13. Jahrhunderts* (Heiligenstadt, 1892), is the fullest account of papal taxes but is subject to correction. Sydney K. Mitchell, *Taxation in Medieval England* (New Haven, 1951), is also of special usefulness. On the role of the military orders the classic work is Léopold V. Delisle, *Mémoire sur les opérations financières des Templiers* (Mémoires de l'Institut national de France, Académie des inscriptions et belles-lettres, XXXIII; Paris, 1889), to which may be added Jules Piquet, *Des Banquiers au moyen âge: les Templiers* (Paris, [1939]). Robert Génestal, *Rôle des monastères comme établissements du crédit* (Paris, 1901), is still fundamental on the credit transactions of the crusaders. On the privileges of the crusaders see Émile Bridrey, *La Condition juridique des croisés et le privilège de croix* (Paris, 1900), James A. Brundage, *Medieval Canon Law and the Crusader* (Madison, Wisc., 1969), and Maureen Purcell, *Papal Crusading Policy, 1244–1291* (Leyden, 1975). It may be worthwhile to warn that L. Papa-D'Amico, *I Titoli de credito: Surrogati della moneta* (Catania, 1886), and other works based on the Collection Courtois in the Bibliothèque nationale are unreliable: cf. Alexander Cartellieri, *Philipp II. August, König von Frankreich* (4 vols., Leipzig, 1899–1922), II, 302–324.

1. August C. Krey, *The First Crusade* (Princeton, 1921), pp. 17–19. Further, the armies caused a scarcity of goods wherever they went, and the crusaders paid high prices in money which was dearly bought.

availability of more money and credit made both saving and borrowing easier. Though the situation changed thus during the crusading era, it is well to emphasize at the beginning that the crusades were always financed. When Urban II issued his call for the First Crusade, he recognized specifically that his crusaders would have to collect the money necessary for their expenses. Then and later there were some who took the vows but could not themselves find the money to pay the costs of their journey. In the financing of the crusades Innocent III saw the key to their success or failure: "If the money be not wanting, the men will not be wanting."[2]

Like the palmers who had made the pilgrimage to the Holy Land for so many centuries, the crusaders were individually responsible for carrying out their vows.[3] How could the individual crusader finance his journey? He might look first to his current income, but it will be shown later in this chapter that few crusaders had sufficient cash income both to pay their obligations at home and to support themselves decently on a crusade. If one was wealthy enough to support himself from current income, then he had to arrange to resupply himself with money as he needed it. The Holy Land lay beyond a long and dangerous passage by land or sea, and the receipt of money from home was correspondingly uncertain. On Louis IX's first crusade a shipment of money to the king was lost at sea, though at least one nobleman planned to send home to resupply himself.[4] From the middle of the twelfth century, it is true, the Templars provided facilities for the transfer of crusaders' funds, and merchants came to provide similar services by lending money in the east to be repaid in the west.

Many crusaders, however, may have hoped to support themselves with plunder. The mob led by Peter the Hermit and others like it undertook to support themselves by robbing fellow Christians in Hungary and Greece. The Jews were robbed as well as murdered by some of the crusaders. More justifiable was the booty won from the Moslems. On the First Crusade the booty of the Moslem armies defeated at Dorylaeum and at Antioch, as well as the tribute and ransom of those who had the misfortune to dwell in the path of the crusaders from Antioch to Jerusalem, all enriched the Christians. Stephen of Blois wrote home from Antioch that he had more silver and gold than when he left

2. Mansi, *Concilia,* XXII, 958.

3. On pilgrimages and pilgrims see Henry L. Savage, chapter I in volume IV of the present work. On crusaders' private financial arrangements see Constable, "The Financing of the Crusades," pp. 70–84.

4. Matthew Paris, *Chronica majora,* ed. Henry R. Luard (Rolls Series, 57), V, 239, and VI, 155–162.

France.[5] Later crusaders also benefitted by the spoils of their conquests. King Richard I of England profited enormously by his capture of Cyprus, and later in Palestine he did not scorn to capture a rich caravan. He and king Philip II Augustus of France divided the spoils of Acre, and from his share of the captives alone Philip hoped to obtain ransoms worth 100,000 bezants.[6] The capture of Damietta in 1216 and again in 1249 provided the crusading armies with quantities of precious goods, but they probably lost as much at Mansurah as they gained at Damietta.

The prudent crusader planned to finance his journey before he departed, to take great bags and chests of money with him. He could use his savings, if he had any. It has been suggested that count Robert II of Flanders may have financed his participation in the First Crusade from his treasury.[7] Stephen of Blois went on two crusades without paying any heed to his financial arrangements, and he may have had sufficient savings. Theobald III of Champagne, a century later, had saved a great treasure for the Fourth Crusade, which he bequeathed to it on his premature death.[8] And the countless legacies and gifts that were made to the crusades from the end of the twelfth century on represented increased savings. Some crusaders may have saved the whole of the cost of their journey, but two general considerations render it doubtful. First, the scarcity of money early in the crusading era militated against savings *per se*. Second, when money became more plentiful, social attitudes which had been engendered earlier continued to inhibit savings, since a chivalric society regarded money rather as a means of consumption than as a means of investment. A gentleman did not save money; he spent it. A large expenditure, such as a crusade, had to be made from his capital, whether chattels or lands. While this second consideration perhaps did not apply to the "little people", the bourgeoisie and the free peasants, one may suppose that the chevaliers, who were the crusaders *par excellence,* used what savings they might have had but that they generally found them insufficient.

5. Heinrich Hagenmeyer, ed., *Die Kreuzzugsbriefe aus den Jahren 1088–1100, mit Erläuterungen* (Innsbruck, 1901), p. 149.

6. *Itinerarium peregrinorum et gesta regis Ricardi,* ed. William Stubbs (Rolls Series, 38–1), pp. 192–204, 385–391, 232–234; Ambroise, *L'Estoire de la guerre sainte,* ed. Gaston Paris (Collection des documents inédits sur l'histoire de France; Paris, 1897), lines 4575–4586.

7. Marshall M. Knappen, "Robert II of Flanders in the First Crusade," *The Crusades and Other Historical Essays Presented to Dana C. Munro,* ed. Louis J. Paetow (New York, 1928), p. 85.

8. Geoffrey of Villehardouin, *La Conquête de Constantinople,* ed. Edmond Faral (Les Classiques de l'histoire de France au moyen-âge; 2 vols., Paris, 1938–1939), I, 36–39, 44–45; Robert of Clari, *La Conquête de Constantinople,* ed. Philippe Lauer (Les Classiques français du moyen-âge, XL; Paris, 1924), p. 4.

From the First Crusade to the last the alienation of property by crusaders reveals the failure of booty, current income, and savings to support their expeditions. A man who had a family or expected to return from the Holy Land would hesitate to dispose of the source of his and his family's livelihood, and it may be presumed that men sold their lands only as a last resort. But the examples are too numerous to name more than a few. For the First Crusade Godfrey of Bouillon sold his county of Verdun and other lands to bishop Richer, while for the Crusade of 1101 viscount Odo Arpin of Bourges sold his city and county to king Philip I of France.[9] Richard the Lionhearted sold the homage of the king of Scotland, which his father had so recently won, and swore he would sell London if he could find a buyer.[10] Fifty years later the count of Mâcon, John de Braine, sold his fief to king Louis IX.[11] Throughout the period less prominent men sold what they could of their lands, burgage tenements, and tithes.[12] As Ambroise wrote of the Third Crusade,

> And none to sell his heritage
> Delayed the holy pilgrimage.[13]

Though sales of chattels can rarely be documented from the records, the chroniclers leave no doubt that crusaders also disposed of their stock and other valuables as well. For example, Simon of Montfort sold his wood of Leicester for 1,000 pounds to finance his crusade in 1240.[14]

Crusaders preferred not to sell their property outright. Count John of Mâcon sold his fief subject to the provision of a life pension for

9. Orderic Vitalis, *Historia ecclesiastica,* ed. Auguste Le Prévost (Société de l'histoire de France; 5 vols., Paris, 1838–1855), IV, 16, 119; *Chronicon Sancti Huberti Andaginensis,* ed. Ludwig C. Bethmann and Wilhelm Wattenbach, *MGH, SS,* VIII, 615.

10. Roger of Hoveden, *Chronica,* ed. Stubbs (Rolls Series, 51), III, 13–15, 24–26; William of Newburgh, *Historia rerum Anglicarum,* ed. Richard Howlett in *Chronicles of the Reigns of Stephen, Henry II, and Richard I* (Rolls Series, 132-I), pp. 304–306.

11. *Layettes du trésor des chartes,* ed. Alexandre Teulet *et al.* (5 vols., Paris, 1863–1909), II, no. 2776.

12. E.g., *Les Registres de Grégoire IX,* ed. Lucien Auvray (Paris, 1896 ff.), II, no. 4204; Beatrice N. Siedschlag, *English Participation in the Crusades, 1150–1220* (Menasha, Wisc., 1939), appendix A, I:10, II:154, and IV:14; *Chronica monasterii de Melsa,* ed. Edward A. Bond (Rolls Series, 43), I, 220; "Document concernant les seigneurs de Ham," ed. Arthur de Marsy, *AOL,* II-2 (1884), 159–163; *Cartulaire de la léproserie du Grand-Beaulieu,* ed. René Merlet *et al.* (Chartres, 1909), no. 130; P.R.O., Great Cowcher of the Duchy of Lancaster, DL 36/1, fol. 71; P.R.O., Ancient Deeds, E 210/3197, 3282; Bibl. nat., MS. Moreau 92, fols. 34, 171–173.

13. Ambroise, *The Crusade of Richard Lion-Heart,* ed. and tr. John L. LaMonte and Merton J. Hubert (*CURC,* 34; New York, 1941), lines 67–68.

14. Matthew Paris, *Chronica majora,* IV, 7.

himself and his wife Alix. A lesser English crusader made a gift of land to a religious house in return for which the canons promised to make regular payments to his wife while he was gone on the crusade.[15] For the First Crusade duke Godfrey of Lower Lorraine sold his castle of Bouillon to bishop Otbert of Liége for 1,500 pounds with the right to redeem it if he returned, and duke Robert II of Normandy pawned his duchy to his brother king William Rufus of England for 10,000 marks which William took from the churchmen of England.[16] In 1239 Baldwin II of Courtenay, the Latin emperor of Constantinople, in his dire need, pledged his county of Namur to Louis IX for 50,000 livres of Paris; he was also to pledge to Venetian merchants his empire's holiest relic, the Crown of Thorns, and even his son and heir, Philip.[17] These are but a few famous instances of the loans by which crusaders perhaps most commonly financed their journeys. They borrowed from kings and princes, from monasteries and bishops, from lay lords and merchants, from whoever had money to lend.[18]

The terms of the loans vary. Some were interest-free, like the 70,000 livres of Tours lord Edward of England (the future king Edward I) borrowed from Louis IX in 1269.[19] A recognized form, however, gave the lender the use of the pledged land for a period of years, the income comprising his repayment. Under this *vif gage* the lender took a certain amount of risk. The more common form of loan, consequently, was the *mort gage,* which provided for the lender to have the usufruct of the land as interest, the borrower to repay the principal, usually before he got his property back.[20] From the patristic period on, the church had condemned the taking of interest on money loans as usury. The *vif gage* was not held to be usurious, since the lender was expected to regain essentially the principal of his loan. The papacy permitted clerical crusaders to pledge their benefices under these terms. Mortgages, on the other hand, fell under the condemnation of pope Eu-

15. Siedschlag, *English Participation,* appendix A, II:90.

16. On Godfrey's financial arrangements see John C. Andressohn, *The Ancestry and Life of Godfrey of Bouillon* (Bloomington, Ind., 1947), pp. 51–52; on the pawning of Normandy see Charles W. David, *Robert Curthose, Duke of Normandy* (Cambridge, Mass., 1920), pp. 91–92 and appendix D, nos. 22–24, 38, 44.

17. *Layettes du trésor des chartes,* II, no. 2744, and III, nos. 3727, 3954; Robert L. Wolff, "Mortgage and Redemption of an Emperor's Son," *Speculum,* XXIX (1954), 45–84.

18. E.g., *Cartulaire de S.-Jean-en-Vallée de Chartres,* ed. Merlet (Chartres, 1906), no. 66; *RHGF,* XII, 94–95; *Calendar of Documents Preserved in France,* ed. John H. Round (London, 1899), pp. 93, 261; Siedschlag, *English Participation,* appendix A, I:21, II:104, III:38, and IV:27; *Close Rolls, Henry III, 1234–1237* (London, 1909), pp. 385, 390, 391.

19. Jean P. Trabut-Cussac, "Le Financement de la croisade anglaise de 1270," *Bibliothèque de l'École des chartes,* CXIX (1961), pp. 113–121.

20. Génestal, *Rôle des monastères,* pp. 1–20.

genius III, and under Alexander III the papacy undertook to enforce its laws against usury. Law-abiding clergy, especially the monasteries, which had found mortgages profitable investments, gave up the business,[21] but other Christians continued to ignore or evade the prohibition of usury. The merchants of southern France and, above all, of Italy were commonly known as moneylenders. In the thirteenth century their business extended throughout Europe, and even in the Holy Land itself they made loans to needy crusaders. In addition, the Jews provided a source of money at interest, though their role in credit transactions must not be exaggerated.

The privileges of popes and princes for the crusaders reveal the great importance of credit arrangements in financing the crusades. From the First Crusade on the popes took not only the persons of the crusaders and their families but also their property under papal protection. Crusaders who found it difficult to secure the return of pledged lands were able thus to call upon the church for help. Since at the beginning of the crusades a man could not alienate his real property without the consent of his wife and heirs, nor, if it were a fief, without the consent of his lord, and since such consent was not always forthcoming for crusaders who had to borrow money for their pilgrimages, Eugenius III in 1145 conceded to crusaders the privilege of pledging lands, even fiefs, without the consent of relatives or lords, if the latter were not themselves willing to lend the money needed. At the same time Eugenius granted crusaders a moratorium on repayment of debts and sought to free them from the payment of interest on loans while they were under the cross. In 1188 Philip Augustus issued a long and detailed ordinance on crusaders' debts that gave royal authority to the "crusaders' term", as it was called, in France. Innocent III went further and ordered that crusaders should not only have a moratorium on payment of the principal of the debts but be immune from interest; creditors who took interest from crusaders should be forced to make restitution. These privileges led to the abuse of the crusade as a means of avoiding creditors, and from the middle of the thirteenth century contracts commonly included a clause renouncing the crusaders' privilege.[22] From the point of view of the crusader, whose responsibility it was to find the wherewithal for his costly expedition, respite of debts and especially prohibition of usury doubt-

---

21. *Ibid.,* pp. 78–86.
22. Bridrey, *La Condition juridique des croisés;* Edith C. Bramhall, "The Origins of the Temporal Privilege of the Crusaders," *American Journal of Theology,* V (1901), 279–292; Brundage, *Medieval Canon Law and the Crusader,* chap. VI.

less seemed only just. From the point of view of the creditors, these privileges represented a real—and usually involuntary—financial contribution to the crusades.

Finally, family and friends must often have aided the crusaders. The nature of the transactions did not require written documents to record them, and few examples can be cited. John, lord of Joinville, in describing his departure on the crusade, tells of a gift of "a great quantity of fair jewels to myself and the nine knights I had with me" made by the abbot of Saint Urbain.[23] The kings of England from Henry II to Henry III made considerable gifts to various crusaders. Henry III alone gave 500 marks to Philip d'Aubigny, one of his councillors, and more to his half-brother, Guy de Lusignan, besides a number of smaller sums to others.[24] One can have little doubt that many crusaders obtained much of their money through similar acts of generosity. Again, the social dimension of the crusades is apparent. Although the crusaders took their vows as individuals and were individually responsible for fulfilling them, the crusades were corporate, or at least collective, enterprises. As crusaders joined together to fight under the leadership of feudal lords, communal officers, national sovereigns, and the church, so they also organized their finances, thus transcending the individual.

From the beginning feudalism offered a device for the command and for the financing of crusades. The crusader who held his land of another crusader must almost automatically have followed his lord on the expedition to the Holy Land. The lord, for his part, desired to take a suitable *mesnie* with him to lend him dignity and power, and he would be willing to accept the company, not only of his vassals, but also of other men in a sort of temporary vassalage for the purposes of the crusade. In return the man might reasonably expect the lord to pay at least part of his expenses. On the First Crusade Bohemond took his followers into his service (*ad Boamundi famulatum*) and presumably paid their way.[25] At Acre both Philip Augustus and Richard took

---

23. John of Joinville, *Histoire de Saint Louis,* ed. Natalis de Wailly (Paris, 1868), p. 44.

24. *Calendar of Liberate Rolls, Henry III, 1226–1240* (London, 1917), pp. 93, 217, 471; for this Guy de Lusignan see Harold S. Snellgrove, *The Lusignans in England, 1247–1258* (Albuquerque, 1950), pp. 36–37.

25. *Gesta Francorum et aliorum Hierosolymitanorum,* ed. Rosalind Hill (London, 1962), pp. 8–9; cf. Steven Runciman, *A History of the Crusades* (3 vols., Cambridge, Eng., 1951–1954), I, 155, where Bohemond is stated to have "raised sufficient money to pay for the expenses of all that came with him", and Frederic Duncalf, "The First Crusade: Clermont to Constantinople," in volume I of the present work, p. 270, "it is not likely that he undertook to provide for any followers, except those in his personal following. . . ."

crusaders into their pay. When Philip left, he gave the command of a body of French crusaders to duke Hugh III of Burgundy along with money to pay them. Of Richard's army it has been said, "At times he was financing not only members of his own household force but mendicant pilgrims, crusaders of all social ranks whose funds had been exhausted, and apparently also knights to whom he wanted to show favors, to say nothing of the ordinary soldier of fortune whose custom it was to fight for pay."[26]

The relationship between the lord and his companions might be very loose: Geoffrey of Villehardouin condemned certain liegemen of count Baldwin of Flanders because they accepted 500 pounds from the count and then went to the Holy Land by a different way.[27] On the other hand, emperor Henry VI in 1195 published an offer to crusaders which approximated mercenary service: to 1,500 knights and the same number of sergeants he promised wages and maintenance if they would enlist in the ports of southern Italy with the masters of a fleet he was sending to the Holy Land for a year; the crusaders would have to obey the imperial commanders, to whom would also revert the *annonae* of any deceased men.[28] Henry's army, which left little mark, may have consisted both of voluntary but poor crusaders and of mercenary soldiers. On the Fifth Crusade a large part of the army at Damietta was in the pay of the papal legate Pelagius, and many were frankly mercenaries.[29] The line between the mercenary and the true crusader in the company of his lord may sometimes have been drawn fine, but it existed in the minds of the men. In 1249 Joinville was proud that he set out with a decent company of his own, but in Cyprus he was glad to accept the king's pay, and he certainly did not regard himself as a mercenary. In his household accounts king Louis distinguished between "pay of knights at wages" and "gifts and *convenances* of knights serving by the year without wages".[30]

The communal organization of the "lesser men", the middle classes, revealed itself in their crusades, which took now the character of a huge partnership, now that of a trading company, and now that of a state enterprise. Although the Italians were the most famed participants, they were not the only middle-class crusaders. From the first, expeditions of northern mariners made their way by the Strait of Gi-

---

26. Siedschlag, *English Participation,* p. 74.
27. Villehardouin, *La Conquête de Constantinople,* I, 36–37.
28. *MGH, Legum,* II (1837), 198.
29. Oliver (Scholasticus), *Die Schriften,* ed. Hermann Hoogeweg, *Bibliothek des litterarischen Vereins in Stuttgart,* CCII (Tübingen, 1894), 250–251, 260.
30. *Histoire de Saint Louis,* pp. 150–157; *RHGF,* XXI, 513–515.

braltar to the Holy Land: men of the British Isles, the Low Countries, Germany, even Scandinavia. The expedition which took Lisbon may be taken as typical of such crusades, although it was largely diverted from its original destination. The crusaders came from both sides of the North Sea and the English Channel, in large part the sailors of those seas, men neither of the chivalry nor of the peasantry. Like a commune, they elected their leaders and made policies in council and assembly. The booty won at Lisbon was shared among the members of the expedition, and presumably the other financial arrangements were similarly collective.[31]

The crusaders from the Italian cities organized their sacred expeditions like trading ventures. To participate in the First Crusade the Genoese nobles and merchants formed a *compagna* on the model of their earlier expeditions against the Moslems. The ships were provided and outfitted by subscription; each man who subscribed or went on the crusade had a certain financial interest in the profits or losses. When the expedition ended after the capture of Caesarea, the booty was divided according to the shares held by the members in the *compagna*.[32] The success of this expedition led the Genoese to finance others of a similar character over the succeeding centuries.

In Venice the state was stronger than in Genoa, as may be seen in the Venetian participation in the Fourth Crusade. Villehardouin describes the process by which the Venetians made their bargain with the French crusaders: First, the French envoys spoke to the doge and his council, who, after deliberation, made their offer to the French on the part of the Venetian state. When the envoys accepted the offer, the doge, Enrico Dandolo, had still to persuade the grand council and, finally, to sway the commons at an assembly in Saint Mark's. All Venetians shared in the costs and profits of the expedition as citizens of the state, and all were encouraged by the doge to think of themselves as sharing in the merits of the crusade.[33] The corporate principle could hardly be more completely embodied.

Unlike the centralized Venetian republic, most of the states of medieval Europe were loosely organized principalities. Medieval princes took the cross not as princes but as individuals. The crusade of Robert of Normandy, like the conquest of England by his father William I, was not that of the duchy but of the duke. Not even Louis IX of France

---

31. Osbern, *De expugnatione Lyxbonensi,* ed. and tr. C. W. David (*CURC,* 24; New York, 1936), esp. introduction, pp. 12–26.

32. Caffaro di Caschifellone, *Annali Genovesi di Caffaro e de' suoi continuatori,* ed. Luigi T. Belgrano and C. Imperiale di Sant' Angelo (5 vols., Genoa, 1890–1929), I, 5–14.

33. Villehardouin, *La Conquête de Constantinople,* I, 22–31.

could encourage or shame any very large part of his people to follow him on the crusade, much less command them. Yet by the collection of taxes to support the crusades, princes called upon their subjects as sovereigns of their states. Lords who levied the *taille,* or tallage, upon their subjects and took *aides* from their vassals could use these taxes toward financing a crusade if the occasion were accepted as lawful by their people. For his crusade in 1146 Louis VII imposed upon some of his subjects taxes which were probably *aides* and *tailles.* Count Theobald V of Blois in 1190 apparently levied a *taille* for his crusade. During the thirteenth century *aides* for going on the crusade were taken by three kings of France, counts of Champagne, counts of Nevers, a count of Poitiers, and a viscount of Limoges. The collection of the *taille* for the crusade had also become customary in France by the reign of Louis IX.[34] In England the crusade was not generally recognized as an occasion for aids and tallages, but they were sometimes asked for crusaders.[35] Outside France and England the available evidence is slight. When emperor Frederick II taxed the kingdom of Sicily in 1227-1228 and again in 1231 for his crusade, the basis of the *collecta* was the fief.[36] In 1166 the nobles of the kingdom of Jerusalem granted king Amalric an *aide* of a tenth of their movables if they did not serve in his host. In several respects, however, this levy was more like the general tax taken in France and England at the same time than the older feudal *aide.*[37]

In 1165 pope Alexander III issued a plea to the princes of western Europe for aid to the Holy Land. In response king Louis VII of France promised to give each year for five years a penny in the pound of his revenues and personal property, and the king asked his subjects lay and clerical, great and small, to contribute at the same rate (about 0.4 percent). The levy apparently did not extend to the lands of the great vassals of France unless they chose to accept it, for Henry II imposed it, with the consent of his councils, in his continental possessions as well as in England and at a somewhat higher rate (two pennies the first year and one thereafter). As provided in Henry's ordinance for his French lands, each man assessed himself under oath and deposited

34. For *aides* and *tailles* see Bridrey, *La Condition juridique,* pp. 68–70; Bibl. nat., MS. Moreau 92, f. 9. The tax of 1146 is vaguely described by the chroniclers; see the opposing interpretations of Lunt, *Valuation of Norwich,* pp. 1–2, and Mitchell, *Taxation,* p. 114. Constable, "The Financing of the Crusades," pp. 64–70, has the most recent discussion of the subject.

35. *Patent Rolls, Henry III, 1216–1225* (London, 1901), pp. 284, 318–319.

36. Richard of San Germano, *Chronica,* ed. Carlo A. Garufi (Bologna, 1936–1938), pp. 148–150, 173.

37. William of Tyre, XIX, 13 (*RHC, Occ.,* I, 903); cf. John L. LaMonte, *Feudal Monarchy in the Latin Kingdom of Jerusalem* (Cambridge, Mass., 1932), pp. 179–180.

his tax in a chest in his parish church. The parish priest and two parishioners had keys to the chest and were responsible for the delivery of the monies to the bishop. The bishops were to bring the money together as they and the king would decide. The sanctions for the collection were ecclesiastical: for fraud, excommunication; for scrupulousness, remission of one third of enjoined penance. A "first crude experiment" in compulsory almsgiving, the levy of 1166 begins the history of general taxation for financing the crusades.[38]

The peril of the Holy Land again evoked an extraordinary levy in 1183, when king Baldwin IV with the consent of a general council imposed a tax on the kingdom of Jerusalem. It was levied at the rate of one bezant on a hundred of movables and debts (and income of mercenary soldiers) and of two bezants on a hundred of the revenues of churches, monasteries, barons, and their vassals. The poor were to pay a hearth tax of one bezant or what they could; the unfree were to be taxed by their lords at the same rate. Four men were chosen in each *civitas* of the realm to assess and collect the tax, but the taxpayer might declare under oath that he was over-assessed and pay according to his own declaration.[39] Altogether the levy showed considerable development beyond that of 1166.

The kings of England and France followed the new model in levying another crusade tax on their subjects in 1185. The unit of one hundred was employed, and the annual rate was roughly the same as in Jerusalem, but the levy was taken for three years and so was the heaviest thus far collected. The sanctions remained ecclesiastical, and the tax was still administered by the clergy, though the bishops were replaced as collectors by a Templar and a Hospitaller appointed in each diocese. The exemptions of goods necessary to the taxpayer's profession presaged the Saladin Tithe.[40]

In January 1188 the two kings, Henry II and Philip Augustus, took the cross together. On the urging of the papacy, they provided for the levy of another tax upon all their subjects, clerical and lay, who did not take the cross; this was the famed Saladin Tithe.[41] The most striking feature of the tax was its rate, a tenth for one year of the value of income and movables, excluding the necessities of the taxpayer's

---

38. Lunt, *Valuation of Norwich,* pp. 2–3.

39. William of Tyre, XXII, 23 (*RHC, Occ.,* I, 1110–1112); LaMonte, *Latin Kingdom,* pp. 180–182.

40. Fred A. Cazel, Jr., "The Tax of 1185 in Aid of the Holy Land," *Speculum,* XXX (1955), 385–392.

41. See the accounts of Mitchell, *Taxation,* pp. 12–14, 64–65, 119–122, 169–171; Lunt, *Valuation of Norwich,* pp. 6–8; Cartellieri, *Philipp II. August,* II, 52–74; Bridrey, *La Condition juridique,* pp. 71–74; Round, "The Saladin Tithe," *English Historical Review,* XXXI (1916), 447–450.

profession such as the arms and horse of a knight or the books of a clerk. The novel severity of the tithe occasioned loud complaint, so much in France that Philip had to promise, for himself and his successors, never to levy such a tax again.

The administration of the tax was regulated by the two monarchs separately, and the ordinances enacted by them in their councils differ greatly. In Henry's dominions, on both sides of the Channel, the parish remained the unit of administration as theretofore, but a more elaborate machinery was established. Each taxpayer assessed himself again, but he paid his tax before committees composed of the parish priest, the rural dean, and the clerk of the baron on the local level, and of a Templar, a Hospitaller, and clerks of the bishop and king on the diocesan level. If the collectors questioned a man's payment, a sworn jury of four or six men of the parish was called to assess him. Philip's ordinance reflected the less centralized government of feudal France as compared with the governments of the Angevin dominions. Each seigneur having *haute justice* was to collect the tithes of his lay tenants. If he were a crusader, he would keep them, and a crusader who was the heir of his father or mother would have their tithes. Churchmen had to collect the tithes of their tenants and subordinates "and give them to whom they ought to give them". The sanctions of the collection were, first, a provision that crusaders might seize the tithes of those who refused to pay them, and second, that clergy and laity, including knights, should pay under oath and under threat of excommunication. But no royal enforcement like that of Henry was provided. Another much longer ordinance regulating the debts of crusaders reflects the relative importance of the two forms of finance in the minds of the French *chevalerie*.

As Philip Augustus promised, neither he nor any of his successors appear to have collected another crusade tax like the Saladin Tithe.[42] Philip and John of England, meeting in Paris in June 1201, acceded to a request of pope Innocent III to give a fortieth of their revenues for one year for the approaching Fourth Crusade, and they asked their subjects to do likewise. The method of collection in France is not known. In England the fortieth was asked as a charity, but those who refused to pay were ordered to give the king their reasons. The collection was made by counties rather than dioceses, and the sheriffs were responsible for escorting the collectors with their money and records to the

---

42. A general *collectio* was ordained by the papal legate to France during the Fifth Crusade (Bibl. nat., MS. Moreau 123, fols. 140–142), but apparently this partook more of almsgiving than tax-collecting.

New Temple at London. In this use of secular machinery, the English collection was tantamount to a tax. Both kings reserved the right to send the money to the Holy Land as they saw fit, and John ordered that it be given only to Hospitallers, Templars, and crusaders of the lands where it was collected. Philip in his ordinance specifically denied any right of distraint by the papacy, and John protested an attempt by bishop Odo of Paris to collect the fortieth in Normandy on papal authority. General taxation by the pope and the princes acting together had fallen afoul of political jealousies, which in another generation would prove fatal to this source of financial support for the crusade.[43]

In the empire hardly an echo is heard of the Saladin Tithe on the departure of Frederick Barbarossa for the Holy Land.[44] The first general tax known to have been levied in the empire was decreed by Philip of Swabia, who was king of Germany but not emperor. In a great council of the realm held in 1207, Philip ordered a general "almsgiving" for the Holy Land to be paid for five years. Freemen were asked to give as divine grace inspired them, but in the country six pence should be paid on each plow and in the towns two pence on each house. The collection may be called a tax on the non-noble lower classes but not on the freemen or nobles. The bishops were made responsible for the appointment of collectors, the nobles for enforcing the collection. The king sent messengers to collect the whole and to use it for the Holy Land.[45] Since those were troubled times in the empire and Philip was killed the next year, the universality and effectiveness of his tax are questionable.

At the Fourth Lateran Council in 1215 Innocent III called upon princes and towns to give financial aid to the Holy Land. In 1221, apparently in belated response to this request, the newly crowned emperor Frederick II levied a tax in his kingdom of Sicily for his planned crusade: from the clergy he took a twentieth of their temporal income (the pope had already collected a twentieth of ecclesiastical income) and from the laity a tenth, while the merchants also paid a twentieth of their *lucro* of the preceding year.[46] At the same time a papal legate,

43. Henri F. Delaborde, "Àpropos d'une rature dans un registre de Philippe-Auguste," *Bibliothèque de l'École des chartes,* LXIV (1903), 310; Roger of Hoveden, *Chronica,* IV, 164, 187–189; *Rotuli litterarum patentium, 1201–1216,* ed. T. Duffus Hardy (London, 1835), p. 5; cf. Mitchell, *Taxation,* pp. 131–133.

44. Cartellieri, *Philipp II. August,* II, 73–74. Gregory VIII in 1187 granted an indulgence to the citizens of Lucca, not crusaders, who gave a fortieth in aid of the Holy Land: *Regesta Honorii papae III,* ed. Pietro Pressutti (2 vols., Rome, 1888–1895), no. 900.

45. *MGH, Legum,* II, 213–214.

46. Richard of San Germano, *Chronica,* pp. 95, 97–98.

the future Gregory IX, bore the requests of the pope and the emperor for aid to the Holy Land to the cities of northern Italy. In consequence, Siena promised to collect six soldi for every hearth, while Florence promised twenty soldi for every knight's hearth, ten for every foot-soldier's hearth. Milan agreed to send twenty knights fully equipped and supplied for one year; Bologna, Brescia, Mantua, and Treviso each ten; and others fewer.[47]

In the spring of 1222 John of Brienne, regent of Jerusalem, came to England to secure aid for the Holy Land. King Henry III was a minor, but his regents called together a council of the magnates which authorized a general poll tax to be paid on November 1. The tax was levied at the rate of three marks for earls, one mark for barons, one shilling for knights, and one penny for freeholders or landless persons with chattels worth half a mark. The money was to be collected in each village by a Templar and a Hospitaller with the aid of the sheriff. Opposition to the tax appears to have necessitated another writ on November 24 which extended it to all cultivators of the land and ordered the sheriffs to distrain the taxpayers. The yield was evidently small, and arrears were ordered collected as late as January 1224.[48]

The papacy, nonetheless, favored the poll tax. Pope Honorius III in April 1223 sent an encyclical throughout western Christendom in which he asked the princes to ordain in their dominions a tax similar to those of 1207 in Germany and 1222 in England.[49] The pope asked that every household should pay one penny of Tours or its equivalent each month for three years. The collection was left up to the princes, and no ruler is known to have taken heed of the papal request. Again, in 1235 Gregory IX asked every Christian who had not taken the cross to give a penny a week to support the crusade.[50] Forty years later, Gregory X still sought to have the princes of Europe levy a universal tax for the crusade he planned.[51] He asked at least a penny a year from every person without exemption. But again the laity appear not to have consented to the levy. Such taxes as the princes of the late thirteenth century might raise, they used for purposes other than the crusades. When princes did lead crusades, they expected to have their expeditions financed largely by the clergy.

47. *Registri dei cardinali Ugolino d'Ostia e Ottaviano degli Ubaldini,* ed. Guido Levi (Rome, 1890), pp. 7, 11–12, 19–24.

48. Mitchell, *Taxation,* pp. 19–20, 35–36, 138–139.

49. *MGH, Epistolae saeculi XIII,* I, nos. 224–226.

50. *Registres de Grégoire IX,* II, no. 2664.

51. Heinrich Finke, *Konzilienstudien zur Geschichte des 13. Jahrhunderts* (Münster, 1891), p. 115.

The crusade appertained peculiarly to the church. Like the laity, individual clerics took the cross and led companies of crusaders, helped other crusaders with gifts and loans, and paid the taxes levied by their princes. But it is rather as a corporation that the church had its unique place in financing the crusades. The privileges of crusaders reveal the early concern of the church with the problem, and it evolved other, more positive methods of supporting its great enterprises.

Through the military orders of warrior-monks, the church provided directly for the defense of the Holy Land. The most important of these orders were the Knights of the Temple and the Brethren of the Hospital of St. John, although for a time the Teutonic Knights added their strength and resources to the common task. The orders formed permanent corps of crusaders stationed in the east with reserves in Europe. Each created an elaborate organization with houses of various ranks throughout Europe as well as Outremer. In the west these houses acted as recruiting stations and managed the resources of the orders locally. Early in the thirteenth century James of Vitry wrote of the orders, "They have been prodigiously increased by vast possessions both on this side of and beyond the sea, for they own villages, cities and towns. . . ."[52] The records more than bear out his statement. Each house of the orders, as James went on to say, sent "a certain sum every year for the defense of the Holy Land to their grand master", whose seat was in the east. The sum sent by preceptories of the Hospital seems normally to have been a third of their revenues, paid twice a year before the regular spring and autumn passages to the east.[53] The financial organization of the orders not only supplied their own needs, but also permitted them, especially the Templars,[54] to act as bankers for the crusades. Their part in the collection of the general taxes of 1185 and 1188 has already been noted, and they also received clerical taxes in 1201 and 1215. Their regular passages offered facilities for other crusaders to resupply themselves. Deposits with houses in the west could be withdrawn in the east, and money could also be borrowed from them in the Holy Land to be repaid in Europe. They preferred to deal in coin and apparently did not develop credit operations beyond transfers. Yet they remained the crusade bankers *par excellence,* serving the papacy and princes as well as lesser men, while their own resources gave them a prime place in the defense of the Holy Land.

52. James of Vitry, *The History of Jerusalem,* tr. Aubrey Stewart, *PPTS,* XI-2 (London, 1896), pp. 53–54.

53. Edwin J. King, *The Knights Hospitallers in the Holy Land* (London, 1931), p. 277.

54. Delisle, *Opérations financières des Templiers,* pp. 14–31, appendix xiv, xviii–xxi, xxxxviii (p. 240); cf. Piquet, *Des Banquiers.*

Around the military orders from an early date grew up confraternities, in which laymen bound themselves together to support the orders financially and otherwise. Although members of the confraternities might eventually take the vows of the orders, the corporation continued as a separate supporting body. The confraternities of the military orders perhaps provided a model for other confraternities which were actually independent crusade fraternities not associated with the older orders. The organization of a *confratria* at Châteaudun, confirmed by pope Innocent IV in 1247, may be taken as an example:[55] its members took the cross not as individuals but as a group, and they were not held to the ordinary regulations governing performance of crusade vows. They might go to the Holy Land individually, or as a group they might send money or warriors paid from the common purse. These confraternities represented an adaptation for the laity of the older military orders, unlike them in being part-time activities of the members, like them in being permanent corporations organized to support the crusade.

Ultimately the financial support of the military orders and the confraternities derived from the alms and legacies of the faithful. By his gift to one of the orders any Christian could share in the great enterprise and in the spiritual rewards promised to crusaders. As early as 1101 pope Paschal II joined with the patriarch of Jerusalem, Daimbert of Pisa, in offering an indefinite remission of penance to those who gave aid to the Hospital. Innocent II in 1131 promised remission of one seventh of enjoined penance to those who gave of their goods to the Hospital, and the same privilege was soon extended to the Temple. Confraternities also received indulgences and could pass on some of their rewards to those who supported them. Great gifts as well as innumerable small ones were made: in 1134 Alfonso I of Aragon bequeathed a third of his kingdom to the two military orders and the Holy Sepulcher; Béla of Hungary, Byzantine heir-apparent and "duke", in 1163–1169 gave 10,000 gold bezants to the Hospital; and Henry II of England sent 30,000 marks sterling to the Templars and the Hospitallers for the defense of Tyre in 1188.[56] Until the Third Crusade the Hospital and the Temple were the usual recipients of alms and legacies for the Holy Land. Later, gifts were received by the Teutonic Knights, the kings and patriarchs of Jerusalem, and others. Other crusaders

55. *Les Registres d'Innocent IV,* ed. Élie Berger (4 vols., Paris, 1884–1921), I, no. 2644.

56. *Cartulaire général de l'ordre des Hospitaliers de S. Jean de Jérusalem, 1100–1310,* ed. J. Delaville Le Roulx (4 vols., Paris 1894–1906), I, nos. 6, 91, 136, 309, 356, 360; *Cartulaire général de l'ordre du Temple, 1119?–1150,* ed. Marquis [Guigue] d'Albon (Paris, 1913), p. 381; *Itinerarium . . . regis Ricardi,* p. 26.

doubtless received alms for which the givers were granted spiritual benefits by local clergy, who certainly administered legacies for the crusade along with those for other pious purposes.

The church also developed monetary redemption of vows as a means of financing the crusades. In order that the Holy Land should suffer no loss through the inability of a crusader to fulfill his vow himself, the church early permitted him to send a substitute, both of them being entitled to the crusade indulgence. At first, redemption of vows for money, though similar to substitution in theory, was opposed by a significant body of opinion in the church. A decretal of Alexander III, incorporated in the canon law, provided for redemption by lifetime support of a pauper. On the other hand, as early as 1101 four crusaders gave lands to the Hospital in redemption of their vows. At the departure of the French army on the Second Crusade, bishops Godfrey of Langres and Arnulf of Lisieux redeemed the vows of sick and dying crusaders for money.[57] The crusaders received their full indulgence, but they were expected to give as much money as it would have cost them to make the crusade. The money was presumably used in aid of the Holy Land by the clergy who received it; much of it probably went to the military orders with the alms and legacies they received.

The loss of Jerusalem in 1187 led the church to make greater use of its penitential system for financing the crusade. Gregory VIII, followed by Clement III, offered larger indulgences to those who gave alms for the Holy Land. The pope left the execution of his mandate to the bishops, who should grant remission of sins according to the "quality of the person and the quantity of the subvention" and disburse the money to needy crusaders.[58] When archbishop Baldwin of Canterbury preached the crusade, for example, he granted an old man remission of half his enjoined penance in return for a tenth of his estate.[59] In 1198 the famous preacher Fulk of Neuilly undertook to preach the crusade in France, and he collected much money in alms. What Fulk collected he deposited in the abbey of Cîteaux, whence some of the money was sent to the Holy Land for the repair of the walls of Acre and Tyre, part was distributed to poor crusaders to de-

57. Philipp Jaffé, *Regesta pontificum Romanorum ab condita ecclesia ad annum . . . 1198,* ed. Samuel Loewenfeld *et al.* (2 vols., Leipzig, 1885–1888), II, nos. 14026, 13916; Delaville Le Roulx, *Cartulaire,* I, no. 6; John of Salisbury, *Historia pontificalis,* ed. and tr. Marjorie Chibnall (London, 1956), pp. 54–55.

58. Giraldus Cambrensis, *De principis instructione,* pp. 236–239, tr. Lunt, *Papal Revenues,* II, no. 529.

59. Giraldus Cambrensis, *Itinerarium Kambriae,* ed. James F. Dimock (Rolls Series, 21–VI), pp. 73–74.

fray the cost of equipment and transportation, and the remainder went to pay the Venetians for the fleet they prepared for the expedition.[60]

To make the collection of alms for the crusade permanent and easy, Innocent III in 1199 ordered a chest placed in every church throughout Latin Christendom, wherein the faithful might deposit their gifts to share in the remission of sins. The chests should have three locks, like those for the general taxes, the keys to be held one by the bishop, one by the priest, one by a layman. The bishops were ordered to associate with themselves a Templar and a Hospitaller as well as laymen to distribute the alms to worthy but poor crusaders who would promise to remain in the service of the cross a year or more and bring back letters attesting their stay in the Holy Land.[61] Although later popes changed these orders on disbursement of alms, the chests became fixtures in the churches of Europe.

The use of legacies and redemptions also increased during the Third and Fourth Crusades. Crusaders came to be expected to provide legacies for the fulfillment of their vows in the event of their premature death. Compacts were made, like that between Richard and Philip on the Third Crusade, that on the death of one crusader, another should receive his property and carry out the crusade for both.[62] For his crusade Richard was empowered by the pope to redeem the vows of crusaders whom he wanted to stay in England. Although Celestine III preferred substitution by men to redemption by money, Innocent III established the two systems as equal in the law of the church. The dispensation of vows was left to local prelates, but Innocent expected them to be very strict, as he was himself in the cases on which he acted. Celestine had permitted confessors to impose the vow of the cross as penance; the next step was direct absolution upon payment of money for the crusade, and this also Innocent established as a form of redemption.[63] Innocent's successors added other monies derived from the penitential system of the church: ill-gotten gains, penalties for offenses such as blasphemy, and indistinct legacies. By ill-gotten gains were meant the monies which were restored by or confiscated from usurers or thieves and which could not be restored to their victims.

---

60. Milton R. Gutsch, "A Twelfth-Century Preacher—Fulk of Neuilly," . . . *Essays Presented to Dana C. Munro,* pp. 200–205.

61. *PL,* 214, 828–832; cf. Palmer A. Throop, *Criticism of the Crusade* (Amsterdam, 1940), p. 242 and notes.

62. Matthew Paris, *Chronica majora,* II, 368–369; Roger of Hoveden, *Chronica,* III, 31, 264 (cap. XVII); cf. Lunt, *Financial Relations,* pp. 425, 433, 437, 443, 451.

63. *PL,* 206, 1135–1136; 215, 745–746, 1136–1137, 1085; 216, 493; Lunt, *Papal Revenues,* II, no. 556.

In 1237 and 1238 Louis IX of France and Theobald IV of Navarre and Champagne, with papal permission, gave to the aid of the Latin empire of Constantinople monies taken from Jewish usurers. Louis said that his predecessors had used such monies for the crusade, but thenceforth the papacy undertook to collect and control them. Indistinct legacies were those made for pious purposes not clearly specified, and these the papacy permitted to be assigned to the crusade. The income of suppressed religious orders, of some vacant benefices, and of some tithes held illegally by laymen was also ordered given for the crusade.[64]

The thirteenth-century popes concerned themselves largely with regularizing the collection and disbursement of these crusade monies. Under Gregory IX local prelates continued to collect the monies, but they were sometimes given the assistance of, sometimes frankly superseded by, papal legates. In any case, the collectors were ordered to deposit the monies with God-fearing men, report the amounts to the pope, and disburse them only by papal mandate. Thus the pope could make gifts to promising crusaders either in a specific amount or as the whole or part of the collections of an area. Crusaders exerted great pressure to obtain these monies in their own lands or neighborhoods, and the pope made numerous grants of collections in advance. To safeguard such grants, Gregory ordered the collectors to give a crusader only a third of his grant on collection, the remainder to be reserved till he had embarked or actually arrived in the east.[65] Gregory also began the diversion of these crusade monies from the Holy Land, in which he was followed by his successors. Eventually, Urban IV ordered a collector to deliver crusade monies, along with other papal revenues, to merchants for transfer to the papal camera. Boniface VIII repeated the instruction, and thenceforth papal collectors treated these funds like any others.[66]

Pope Alexander III had inspired the general levy of 1165, and from this beginning the papacy in coöperation with lay rulers had progressed in crusade taxation to the Saladin Tithe. Although the popes appealed thereafter for further general taxes upon lay and cleric alike, the results were disappointing. Taxation of the laity without the consent of

---

64. *Registres de Grégoire IX,* II, nos. 3899, 4205, 4601, 4641; Matthew Paris, *Chronica majora,* IV, 564–565; Brundage, *Medieval Canon Law,* p. 186; Purcell, *Papal Crusading Policy,* pp. 142–144.

65. *Registres de Grégoire IX, passim.* For an example of the working of the system see Sidney Painter, *The Scourge of the Clergy: Peter of Dreux, Duke of Brittany* (Baltimore, 1937), pp. 105–107.

66. Lunt, *Papal Revenues,* introduction, I, 121.

the princes was out of the question, but the clergy were rich beyond compare. From the beginning the clergy had been taxed for the crusades, and probably the largest amount of financial support had come from their treasuries and revenues. For the First Crusade William Rufus had taxed the clergy of England for the money to send Robert of Normandy to the Holy Land, and bishop Otbert of Liége had taken from his clergy the money to give Godfrey of Bouillon for his journey. In 1099 archbishop Anselm of Milan withheld a customary revenue of his clergy to support the Lombard crusade of that year. King Géza II of Hungary levied a tax upon his churchmen to bribe Conrad III to make a peaceful passage through his lands on the Second Crusade.[67] But general taxation of the Latin clergy by the popes appears only in 1188 when Clement III issued an encyclical commanding the bishops to give aid to the Holy Land and to induce or force their subordinates to contribute. In England and France this separate clerical tax was apparently merged in the general Saladin Tithe; but the letter was also sent to the clergy of Genoa, and a papal legate in Poland "imposed a tenth upon the bishops and all the clergy for the recovery of the Holy Land".[68] Thus originated papal taxation of the clergy for the crusade.

Innocent III built upon this foundation when in 1199 he levied a fortieth of the ecclesiastical income of every clerk in Latin Christendom.[69] He directed the archbishops and bishops to deal with the tax in provincial synods and then in diocesan synods to order all the clergy to assess themselves and pay the tax within three months. The bishops should collect the money in a safe place and notify the pope of the amount. The Cistercian, Premonstratensian, Grandmontine, and Car-

67. Orderic Vitalis, *Historia ecclesiastica,* IV, 16; *Chronicon S. Huberti,* in *MGH, SS,* VIII, 615; Landulfo de S. Paolo, *Historia Mediolanensis,* in *RISS,* V-3, p. 5; *The Hungarian Illuminated Chronicle,* ed. Dezsö Dercsényi (New York, 1970), facsimile 120.

68. Giraldus Cambrensis, *De principis instructione,* pp. 236–239; Mansi, *Concilia,* XXII, 581–582, 589–590; Julius von Pflugk-Harttung, ed., *Acta pontificum Romanorum inedita (97–1198)* (3 vols., Tübingen, 1881–1888), III, no. 417.

69. The fortieth is commonly considered the first papal tax for the crusades: see Edgar H. McNeal, "The Fourth Crusade," in volume II of the present work, pp. 156–157, and Joseph R. Strayer, "The Political Crusades of the Thirteenth Century," *ibid.,* II, 346. See also Gottlob, *Kreuzzugssteuern,* pp. 18–20, who did not know the letter to Genoa and dismissed the Polish evidence on *a priori* grounds. Alfonso Professione, *Contributo agli studi sulle decime ecclesiastiche e delle crociate* (Turin, 1894), p. 10, however, cited the Polish evidence as "la prima notizia di una tassa ecclesiastica per la crociata . . . ." Giuseppe Martini, "Innocenzo III ed il finanziamento delle crociate," *Archivio della R. deputazione romana di storia patria,* LXVII (1944), 314, refers to the letters to Canterbury and Genoa, but does not consider the Polish evidence; he concludes that Innocent III fully taxed the clergy but that Clement III's letters held the "premessa fondamentale". Taking all the evidence together, Clement's tax appears to be as well documented as can be expected for the period, and must take precedence over Innocent's.

thusian orders were exempted from the fortieth, but by special man-
dates the first two were commanded to pay a fiftieth of their income,
which they were to assess and collect themselves. Although Innocent
promised to treat the tax as a gift and granted an indulgence of one
fourth of enjoined penance to those who paid it faithfully, the clergy
protested vigorously, and in England much of the tax remained un-
paid six or seven years later. After the Fourth Crusade, which the fortieth was intended to support, was diverted against the papal will, the
pope seems to have sent the money to the Holy Land for use by the
military orders, the patriarch, Albert, and the king of Jerusalem, Aimery
of Lusignan. Meanwhile Innocent's own attention was diverted by the
Albigensian heresy, against which he proclaimed a crusade, and in 1209
he laid upon the clergy in southern France another tax, which his legates collected. In 1208 a similar levy had been ordered collected in Lombardy by papal "visitors". Like the fortieth, these lesser taxes were laid
by the pope on his own authority and strengthened further the system
of papal taxation of the clergy, while they also established a precedent
for diversion of clerical taxes from the Holy Land.[70]

In 1215 Innocent convened at Rome a general council of the church,
the Fourth Lateran, to provide for the succor of the Holy Land. A
long canon of the council was devoted to the organization, regulation,
and financing of the proposed expedition. While princes and towns
were asked to give aid to the Holy Land, the core of Innocent's financial program for this papal crusade was taxation of the clergy. Promising a tenth from himself and from the cardinals, the pope laid a
twentieth on the rest of the clergy for three years.[71]

When Innocent died in 1216, the execution of his plans fell to his
successor, Honorius III. In each province of Germany, Hungary, and
Spain, Honorius appointed as collectors of the tax the local masters
of the Temple and the Hospital with two dignitaries of the metropolitan chapter; they in turn were commissioned to appoint as subcollectors
in each diocese two or more clerks with a member of each military
order. Presumably like the fortieth, the monies were to be held by the
military orders until disbursed by papal mandate. Accusations of Roman misappropriation of crusade monies were rife, however; and to
avoid further scandal, Honorius determined upon a major revision of
his predecessor's plans. In February 1217 he made each bishop respon-

---

70. Martini, "Innocenzo III ed il finanziamento delle crociate"; Christopher R. Cheney,
"Master Philip the Notary and the Fortieth of 1199," *English Historical Review,* LXIII (1948),
342–350; Lunt, *Financial Relations,* pp. 240–242; Lunt, *Valuation of Norwich,* pp. 10–13; Gottlob, *Kreuzzugssteuern,* pp. 20–25, 170–177.

71. Mansi, *Concilia,* XXII, 1058–1067.

sible for the twentieth in his diocese; rendering only an account to the pope, he should send the money directly to the crusading army. The clergy exempt from episcopal authority were directed to collect the tax themselves. Decentralization, however, created other administrative problems. Toward the end of 1218, therefore, Honorius sent papal collectors directly to Spain, Germany, and Hungary, and eventually to northern Italy and to Britain; in France, where king Philip II had demanded half the collections for the Albigensian crusade, two bishops and the abbot of Cîteaux were appointed to collect and divide the tax. Although the ordinaries continued to be chiefly responsible, the papal commissioners could enforce and hasten the collection, and they had powers to deal with the exempt religious. Further, as the pope saw the need, he could direct his commissioners to give money to specified crusaders; to deposit it with the Templars, who transferred certain amounts to the east on papal order; or occasionally to send or bring it to Rome.[72]

The tax presented many other problems. The canon of the Lateran Council called for a twentieth of all "ecclesiastical revenues", a phrase which concealed grave difficulties of definition. The clergy, however, were left to assess themselves under threat of spiritual penalties, and there can be little doubt that undervaluation was common. Exemptions from the tax fill the papal registers. Besides the orders exempted from the fortieth, many other groups and individuals received exemptions for poverty, debts, or charitable function. Collections tended to be slow and uncertain. The twentieth was still being collected normally in 1221, six years after the Lateran Council. The pope had to empower many legates and prelates to absolve from papal excommunication the clergy who defaulted at the stated terms or attempted to defraud. Even of the collectors appointed directly by the pope, one proved seriously untrustworthy and others disobeyed papal orders. Disbursement was complicated because powerful crusaders received grants of the tax in their lands. Honorius complained that many magnates took the cross, took the twentieth, but neglected to go on the crusade.[73]

If the problems attendant on the administration of the twentieth were great, so were the collections. Thenceforth papal taxation became a common feature of the life of the clergy of the west, although diversion from its original purpose of supporting the crusade in the Holy Land also became common. Honorius III had diverted monies from the twentieth to the support of the Albigensian Crusade, and in 1226

---

72. Cf. Lunt, *Financial Relations,* pp. 242–247; Lunt, *Valuation of Norwich,* pp. 13–18; Gottlob, *Kreuzzugssteuern,* pp. 177–184; and the references cited therein.

73. *Regesta Honorii III, passim.*

he authorized a tenth for five years from the clergy of France for the same purpose. Gregory IX levied a tenth in 1229, not for the Holy Land, but for his war against the emperor. When he sought a thirtieth for the Holy Land in 1238, he seems to have been unsuccessful, perhaps because the next year he proclaimed a crusade against Frederick and demanded clerical taxes for it. Innocent IV convened a general council at Lyons in 1245, and the canon for the crusade, very nearly the same as that of 1215, included the levy of another twentieth for three years from all the clergy. In France and England this twentieth was superseded by a tenth which the pope granted to the kings as crusaders, and elsewhere the twentieth was directed to the "crusade" against Frederick. Although Innocent and his successors continued to tax the clergy chiefly for other purposes, Urban IV in 1262 collected for the Holy Land a hundredth for five years (the equivalent of a twentieth for one year), and Clement IV levied a tenth for three years from the French clergy when Louis IX took the cross a second time in 1267. With these taxes, the papacy improved and further centralized the administration of clerical taxation.[74]

The pontificate of Gregory X proved the climax in papal taxation of the clergy for the crusade. Although Gregory found little enthusiasm in Europe for another crusade, he nearly succeeded in organizing another great expedition before his death intervened. Like Innocent III and Innocent IV he called together another general council in 1274, and the constitutions of the council for the crusade reveal his indebtedness to his predecessors. Essentially like theirs, his financial program centered on a tenth to be collected from all the clergy for six years. Gregory's administration of the tax, most impressive in its plan and thoroughness, completed the work of his predecessors. *Declarationes dubitationum in negotio decime* were issued to define the bases of assessment. New assessments were made and in England at least proved to be much higher than earlier ones. All the lands subject to the papacy were divided into twenty-six collectorships, over each of which the pope appointed a general collector, who in turn appointed subcollectors without reference to the ordinaries. Though originally no exemptions were to be allowed, the pressure became too great, and the pope permitted the usual exemptions at the discretion of the collectors. The bitter complaints of the clergy and surviving accounts of the tax reveal the efficiency of the system and the large sums of money

74. The history of these clerical taxes of the thirteenth century is told most completely in Gottlob, *Kreuzzugssteuern*, but his research has been corrected and completed by later studies. Cf. Austin P. Evans, "The Albigensian Crusade," in volume II of the present work, p. 316; Strayer, "Political Crusades," *ibid.*, pp. 349, 352–353, 355–357, 361, 364, 371.

collected. After Gregory's death the money was largely diverted from the Holy Land. Although papal taxation of the clergy long continued, it ceased in the main to be used in support of the crusade to the Holy Land.[75]

Throughout the earlier Middle Ages devout western Christians made pilgrimages to the Holy Land. The pilgrimage unquestionably mothered the crusade: those who took the vow and wore the cross were called pilgrims, their routes to the Holy Land were the pilgrim ways, and they benefitted by the experience of the earlier pilgrims in organizing their expeditions. Yet, if the pilgrimage was mother to the crusade, the child had a lusty father in the chivalry of medieval Europe. A crusade was an armed expedition to reconquer the Holy Land for Christians, and only men with the ability and arms to fight God's battles could be effective crusaders. The simple palmer, though he accompanied the crusading armies, had not the skill or equipment of the warrior-pilgrim who may best be called a crusader. As a pilgrim, each crusader was obliged by his vow to find the means to accomplish it, and the financial basis of the crusades was the individual effort made by the crusader to finance his pilgrimage. On the other hand, the crusader's journey cost more than the palmer's: every warrior had equipment to maintain; the knight, a horse and attendants. The greater needs of crusaders gave rise to collective or corporative financing. This formed the superstructure of the vessel that carried the crusaders over the Mediterranean while individual financing made the bottom.

The First Crusade comprised several groups: the peasant mob of Peter the Hermit and others like them, the companies of knights from France and Norman Sicily, the marine expeditions from Italy and the north. Except for these last, all the evidence points to individual preparation for the crusade. At most the feudal contingents of the princes may have been feudally financed. But lesser men as well as Godfrey of Bouillon and Robert of Normandy alienated their property. The pilgrims plundered the Jews in the Rhineland and the Hungarians and Greeks on their route of march. The eastern emperor Alexius Comnenus gave them rich gifts, while booty was a prime source of con-

75. On the tenth of 1274 see Gottlob, *Kreuzzugssteuern,* pp. 94–166, 255–269; Throop, *Criticism of the Crusade,* pp. 236–286; Lunt, *Valuation of Norwich,* pp. 105–106, 551–559; Lunt, *Financial Relations,* pp. 311–346; *Rationes decimarum Italiae nei secoli XIII e XIV: Tuscia,* ed. Pietro Guidi (Vatican City, 1932); Ludovico Gatto, *Il Pontificato di Gregorio X* (Rome, 1959), chap. VI. For the history of crusade taxation after Gregory X see Ernst Hennig, *Die päpstlichen Zehnten aus Deutschland im Zeitalter des avignonesischen Papsttums und während des grossen Schismas* (Halle, 1909); Bridrey, *La Condition juridique,* p. 77; Paul Riant, *Expéditions et pèlerinages des Scandinaves en Terre Sainte au temps des croisades* (Paris, 1865), pp. 391–409.

tinuing finance. It may be supposed that crusaders received alms like the pilgrims, perhaps went as substitutes for others, but none of the later financial organization of the penitential system yet existed. Only the mariners are known to have used corporative methods of financing their expeditions. Following in the pilgrim's pattern, the crusader of 1096 generally provided for his financial support privately and individually.

During the first half of the twelfth century methods of financing crusades remained essentially the same as at the beginning. Each crusader, like the viscount of Bourges, sold his lands or saved or borrowed or plundered the money he needed to achieve his vow. However, the clergy were already being taxed to support others on the crusade. And the military orders were organized and began to accumulate the endowments which enabled them to become a standing army of crusaders in the Holy Land.

The second great expedition revealed considerable development in crusade finance, at least among the French participants. Louis VII taxed his subjects for his crusade. In his army bishops redeemed crusading vows for money, and there can be little doubt of the prevalence of substitution. The king, and very likely others, employed the financial facilities of the Templars to transport and borrow money. The wealth of both the Temple and the Hospital shows the growth of alms and legacies for the crusade. For this crusade Eugenius III issued his bull *Quantum praedecessores,* setting forth the privileges of crusaders. In all these ways social financing of the crusade had grown since the initial conquest of the land beyond the sea, yet the overwhelming impression remains that each crusader financed his own *peregrinatio* individually.

Moslem victories evoked a new response among western Christians to the problem of financing the crusades. This was universal taxation, which reached its peak with the Saladin Tithe of 1188. Presumably this tax in large part financed the Third Crusade: it was said to have yielded 70,000 pounds sterling in England alone.[76] But Henry II obtained 60,000 pounds at the same time from the Jews, and Richard I raised substantial sums in addition. The great wealth of Richard gave him a larger command than just the men of his own dominions and perhaps made possible such success as the expedition achieved. The military orders played an increasingly important role, largely supported by the papal development of the collection of alms, legacies, and redemptions of vows. Yet one cannot gainsay the primary importance of individual financing. Many crusaders pledged or sold their prop-

76. Gervase of Canterbury, *Historical Works,* ed. Stubbs (Rolls Series, 73), I, 422.

erty to pay their way. The ordinances of Philip Augustus for the crusade laid much greater emphasis on regulation of debts than on the Saladin Tithe, and Frederick Barbarossa issued an edict that no crusader should set out on the journey without complete equipment and enough money to last two years.[77]

The popes of the thirteenth century undertook to provide a more corporative financial base for the crusade. Innocent III desired a crusade not only called by the papacy, but commanded by a papal legate; in order to ensure command, the papacy had also to control the financing of the crusade. The leaders of the Fourth Crusade refused papal direction and apparently received little or none of the fortieth collected by the pope for the crusade. The legacy of the count of Champagne and the individual financial arrangements of the crusaders supported this as earlier crusades. The leaders contracted with Venice to pay 85,000 marks of Cologne to transport and feed 29,000 men and 4,500 horses for nine months. When only about half that number actually came to Venice, the leaders gave their own treasure and even borrowed what they could to pay off their debt to the Venetian state. Eventually they had to work it off by the capture of Zara, but this was hardly the kind of corporative finance envisioned by the pope.[78]

The Fifth Crusade most nearly embodied the papal plan. Going to Acre, king Andrew II of Hungary financed his expedition in the traditional way, by selling and mortgaging property, by debasing the coinage, and by taking the sacred utensils of the churches.[79] But the twentieth exacted from the clergy of all Europe provided the legate Pelagius with a sizeable command in Egypt. By July of 1220 the pope

77. *Annales Marbacenses,* in *MGH, SS,* XVII, 164; cf. *Itinerarium . . . regis Ricardi,* p. 43, which says one year.

78. The contract between Venice and the crusade leaders is printed in *Urkunden zur älteren Handels- und Staatsgeschichte der Republik Venedig mit besonderer Beziehung auf Byzanz und die Levante,* ed. Gottlieb L. F. Tafel and Georg M. Thomas (Fontes rerum austriacarum, Diplomataria et acta, XII–XIV; 3 vols., Vienna, 1856–1857; repr. Amsterdam, 1964), I, 362–373, no. 92. Villehardouin's manuscripts are curiously at variance on the total sum, though all give the fare as 4 marks per horse and 2 marks per man. Four manuscripts of the thirteenth century have a total of 85,000 marks. But two extant manuscripts of the late fourteenth century and probably two that are now lost, representing a tradition which Faral (Villehardouin, *La Conquête de Constantinople,* I, xlvi–li) believes is better than that of the earlier manuscripts and takes for the base of his text, give 94,000 marks. Faral (I, 215–217, and cf. Donald E. Queller, *The Fourth Crusade* [Philadelphia, 1977], pp. 10–11 and note 13) explains this as a first offer of the Venetians of 4 marks for each horse and knight and 2 marks for each other man, which was reduced before the contract was signed. Robert of Clari has such a story (*La Conquête de Constantinople,* pp. 7–10), but the text of Villehardouin says nothing about such bargaining and a scribal error may be all the explanation required.

79. Reinhold Röhricht, *Studien zur Geschichte des fünften Kreuzzuges* (Innsbruck, 1891), p. 24.

had sent him approximately 100,000 marks,[80] and in time his position became strong enough to enable him to lead the army to its defeat. Until that last fatal march, however, he had strong competition from other leaders whose finances were largely independent of the papacy: the king of Jerusalem, the masters of the crusading orders, and princes like the duke of Austria, Leopold VI. Oliver of Paderborn took pride in the well-supplied contingent of crusaders from his region of Cologne, and when he speaks of a "common treasury" under the legate's control, this cannot be taken to mean that the crusaders pooled all their resources. The spoils of Damietta, it is certain, were divided among the various leaders of the crusade.[81] The legate's treasury must have been filled for the most part with money from the pope, although other crusaders contributed to it.[82] Since the legate controlled no more than a fraction of the financial resources of the crusade, the ideal papal crusade failed of realization in its financing as it did in its military goal.

Later popes abandoned the principle of papal command of the crusades. They continued and extended taxation of the clergy and the collection of alms, legacies, and redemptions, but they granted the proceeds of these financial measures to lay crusaders. "Apostolic graces", as the papal grants were called, formed a prized source of support for the later thirteenth-century crusades. For his first crusade in 1248, Louis IX received all the crusade monies derived from alms, legacies, redemptions, usuries, and especially the tenth levied on the clergy of France, Lorraine, and Burgundy—all, that is, which the pope did not specifically grant to other crusaders. The king also collected *aides* from his vassals and *tailles* from his non-noble subjects. He presumably had savings to spend on the crusade plus as much of his annual revenues as he could persuade his mother, regent in his absence, to send to him.[83] The king was the greatest and the richest single crusader in the army, but his wealth, even with the backing of the church, was insufficient to finance the crusade entire. The Templars and Hospitallers provided large contingents of troops who represented another part of the corporative financial program of the church. Many crusaders other than the king received money from the church, notably his brothers Alphonse, count of Poitiers, and Robert, count of Artois; of monies

80. *MGH, Epistolae saeculi XIII,* I, no. 124.

81. *AOL,* II-2, 166. William of Chartres was master of the Temple; Garin of Montaigu, of the Hospital.

82. *MGH, Epistolae saeculi XIII,* I, no. 124; Wentworth S. Morris, "A Crusader's Testament," *Speculum,* XXVII (1952), 197: "to the treasury of the Commune of the Army one bezant."

83. Berger, *Saint Louis et Innocent IV* (Paris, 1893), pp. 185–207.

known to have been sent to Alphonse after his departure from France, roughly a fourth came from "graces". Along with the king and his brothers many crusaders probably took *aides* and *tailles*.[84] The participation of the maritime cities, mercenary though it was for the most part, was presumably financed corporatively. Yet crusaders like Joinville still alienated their property for the expedition, and not a few, among them great nobles, borrowed large sums of money from Italian merchants in Cyprus, Egypt, and Syria.[85]

Other crusades of the thirteenth century followed the same pattern of finance. For his crusade Frederick II took tax after tax from his subjects and especially from the churches of his dominions, and since he took so small an army with him when he finally went, he probably spent in the Holy Land only a fraction of what he collected. But in this as in so many things Frederick was the great exception. Papal taxation of the clergy and other papal monies provided much of the support for Richard of Cornwall in 1240 and for prince Edward of England in 1270. Edward borrowed over 100,000 livres of Tours from merchants of Cahors on the security of a clerical twentieth in England granted in 1272, and a tenth was ordered collected in 1267 to reimburse Edward and his brother Edmund for their crusade expenses. Edward also had a twentieth of movables conceded by the English barons in 1269 that yielded over 125,000 livres. He received over 10,000 li. from the Jews; the royal demesnes were tallaged; and in 1271 he was granted the revenues of all royal wardships and escheats, the regalian rights to the revenues of vacant prelacies, and the royal profits of justice. But he still had to pledge the customs of Bordeaux for four years for an unknown sum and for seven years for a loan of 70,000 li. from Louis IX.[86] Altogether, Edward may easily have spent more than half a million livres on his crusade. Louis himself raised the money for his second expedition as for the first: a tenth for three years from the French clergy and a twentieth from the French-speaking parts of Lorraine and an aid from the townsmen produced a great part of it. But he tried to recover a large loan he had made to his brother, Charles I of Anjou, and doubtless he scraped up every penny he could. Even

84. Edgard P. Boutaric, *Saint Louis et Alfonse de Poitiers* (Paris, 1870), pp. 69–77, 279–317.

85. *Layettes du trésor des chartes,* III, nos. 3769–3771, 3800, 3811, 3821, 3823, 3827, 3948, 3954, 3960.

86. Trabut-Cussac, "Le Financement de la croisade anglaise," p. 121; Mitchell, *Studies in Taxation under John and Henry III* (New Haven, 1914), 295–299; Frederick M. Powicke, *King Henry III and the Lord Edward,* 2 vols. (Oxford, 1947), II, 561–569; Simon Lloyd, "The Lord Edward's Crusade, 1270–2," in *War and Government in the Middle Ages,* ed. John Gillingham and James C. Holt (Totowa, N.J., 1984), p. 132. The money of Tours, *livres tournois,* is meant wherever li. is used.

if he did not, countless other crusaders continued to sell or pledge their lands or chattels to make the great journey.

Corporative finances remained in the thirteenth century a super-structure reared upon the solid base of individual finances. The reasons for this fact may be sought partly in the nature of the crusade, child of the individual pilgrimage and the individualistic chivalry, but partly also in the cost, which was greater not only than any individual could sustain but than any medieval state or corporation, even the church, was able or willing to afford. The evidence for the whole cost of any of the great expeditions is not forthcoming, but some idea of its magnitude can be obtained for Louis IX's first crusade. A fourteenth-century account of the French government says the crusade cost the king over 1,537,570 li.[87] It has been estimated that Louis financed between one half and three fifths of the crusaders,[88] and if this calculation is correct, the whole cost of the crusade might have been between 2,500,000 and 3,000,000 li.[89] The possibility of error in this figure is great, but it may help to put in perspective the relative value of individual and corporative sources of crusade finance. To begin with the largest corporate sums, the twentieth of their income paid by the clergy for the crusade of 1248 was probably in the neighborhood of 750,000 li. over the whole five-year period.[90] The alms, legacies, redemptions, and usuries of the church would have added somewhat more to corporative support, as did the Templars and Hospitallers. *Aides* and *tailles* added still more: his towns may have contributed as much as 274,000 li.[91] But when all allowances are made, it seems unlikely that half of the costs of the crusade came from corporative sources. The rest still had to be raised by the individual crusaders from savings, current income, or borrowings.

Something more can be said of the costs of the crusades for the various ranks of participants. For Louis's second crusade in 1270 a document has preserved the gist of the contracts made between the king and a number of crusaders he took into his pay.[92] The terms var-

87. *RHGF,* XXI, 404.

88. Strayer, "The Crusades of Louis IX," p. 494.

89. Franco Cardini, "I Costi della crociata," in *Studi in Memoria di Federigo Melis,* 5 vols. (Naples, 1978), II, 179–210, concludes that in the first quarter of the fourteenth century a modest crusade would cost more than 360,000 li., one of 40,000–50,000 combatants about 1,200,000 li. per year.

90. Gottlob, *Kreuzzugssteuern,* p. 49, gives 760,000 li.; Strayer, "The Crusades of Louis IX," p. 491, roughly 950,000 li., but I cannot replicate his calculations.

91. See William C. Jordan, *Louis IX and the Challenge of the Crusade* (Princeton, 1979), p. 98.

92. *RHGF,* XX, 305–308; but cf. *ibid.,* XXIII, 732–734.

ied greatly, an indication that many still expected to finance their journeys in part; but the king contributed from 133⅓ to 400 li. per knight for a year's service, the total being above 100,000 li. for about 500 knights. Most of these barons and knights were also promised their passage, replacement of horses, and meals in the king's palace, the cost of which can hardly have been less than a half of their stipends. The king's brother, Alphonse of Poitiers, about the same time offered to knights who would furnish their own equipment, from 160 to 180 li. a year, representing a maximum stipend of 10 sous a day, while he offered 5 sous a day to mounted bowmen.[93] All these wages were apparently supplemented by transportation and maintenance, and Alphonse specifically promised remounts to his bowmen in addition. Light cavalry thus cost half of the stipend of the chevalier and infantry a tenth or more. If Louis employed no more than 200 to 300 light cavalry and 1,600 infantry, as he did in Syria in 1250–1252, these men would have cost him well over 50,000 li. in annual stipends, plus transportation and maintenance. Transportation cost Louis over 100,000 li.,[94] and maintenance for a year would hardly have cost less. Altogether, Louis might have expected to pay 300,000 li. a year for his second expedition. On the earlier crusade, until Mansurah at least, Louis's army was larger than on the second and his campaign ran for six years. If the later account of his total costs is correct, his costs then would have averaged over 250,000 li. a year, about equal to his average annual royal revenue of 240,000 to 250,000 li. Since Louis's ordinary expenditures amounted to about half the royal revenue,[95] even with the lion's share of apostolic graces, he might have had to raise 100,000 to 125,000 li. a year from savings, current income, *aides,* and *tailles.*[96] But that was a royal expense: Henry III of England had only an average ordinary income of about 100,000 li. a year before expenditures.[97]

In the next rank among crusaders were the princes, of whom Alphonse of Poitiers may stand as an example. An extant account of his household provides exact figures from February 2 to December 10,

---

93. Boutaric, *Saint Louis et Alfonse de Poitiers,* pp. 115–116.

94. Auguste Jal, ed., *Pacta naulorum,* in *Documents historiques inédits,* ed. Jacques J. Champollion-Figeac (Collection de documents inédits; 4 vols., Paris, 1841–1848), I, 507–615. This sum is calculated on the assumption that Louis contracted with Marseilles for twenty ships, as he did in 1254, at the price offered.

95. Strayer, "The Crusades of Louis IX," p. 491 and note 6.

96. The financing of Louis IX's first crusade has been described in detail by Jordan, *Louis IX,* ch. 4.

97. James H. Ramsey, *The Dawn of the Constitution* (London, 1908), p. 297, where £30,000 is given as the ordinary revenue, but from this must be subtracted the £10,000 assigned to prince Edward from 1255.

1250, for his costs on Louis's first crusade.[98] The largest amount, 10,225 li., was spent for the hire and provisioning of ships and galleys and the wages of mariners, presumably for the journey from Damietta to Acre and thence to France. The domestic expenses of the count and countess also came to about 10,000 li. Military costs included 4,605 li. for horses, 2,529 li. for armor, and 180 li. for weapons. For the service of the barons, chevaliers, mounted bowmen, and foot-sergeants who composed his *mesnie,* Alphonse paid only about 3,000 li. The total expenditure amounted to more than 35,000 li. Since Alphonse left France seventeen months before this account began, and his expenditures before the defeat at Mansurah may have been much larger, the complete costs of his crusade must have been several times larger than those here recorded. In 1270 Alphonse raised 100,000 li. for his participation in what was generally a smaller crusade.[99] Even though Alphonse may have been extravagant, and though his expenses included his losses at Mansurah, yet his were the tastes and risks of crusader princes in the thirteenth century.

Of a baron's cost on this same crusade John of Joinville himself affords the best example. He tells of his financial preparations:

> Because I did not wish to take away with me any penny wrongfully gotten, therefore I went to Metz, in Lorraine, and placed in pawn the greater part of my land. And you must know that on the day when I left our country to go to the Holy Land, I did not hold more than one thousand livres a year in land, for my lady mother was still alive; and yet I went, taking with me nine knights and being the first of three knights-banneret. And I bring these things to your notice, so that you may understand that if God, who never yet failed me, had not come to my help, I should hardly have maintained myself for so long a space as the six years that I remained in the Holy Land.[100]

God's agent in this help was the king. When the crusaders reached Cyprus, Joinville had only 240 li. left, and the king took the proud young marshal into his pay. In July 1250 Louis again retained him for the duration of his crusade with a company composed of three knights-banneret, each with two knights as companions, making a total of ten knights. The king paid Joinville at the rate of 3,000 li. a year, of which he kept 1,200 li. for the maintenance of the whole company and paid each of the bannerets 600 li. They appear to have made their own terms with their companions, perhaps keeping something like 240 li. and giving the others 180 li. The king's officers thought Joinville asked too

98. *Layettes du trésor des chartes,* III, no. 3910.
99. Strayer, "The Crusades of Louis IX," p. 511.
100. Tr. Frank Marzials, *Memoirs of the Crusades* (London, 1908), p. 164.

much, and he agreed that his terms were high. But he reminded the king that he had lost all his possessions in Egypt including horse and armor, the implication being that he would not ask as much as he was worth if he did not have to.[101] It seems reasonable to conclude, then, that a baron could hardly take a company of ten knights on the crusade in 1250 for much less than 3,000 li. a year, and that Joinville had been very rash to attempt it if his land was worth no more than 1,000 li. a year.

For the simple knight and the lower ranks of society the stipends promised by Louis and Alphonse in 1270 afford the best measure of the costs. To knights who took their meals at his table Louis gave 160 li. a year, but to those who undertook to maintain themselves he gave wages of 10 sous a day, or 182½ li. a year. In all cases the king appears to have furnished transportation. It seems fair to say, therefore, that the simple knight in the later thirteenth century needed roughly 200 li. a year to make his pilgrimage. By the same reckoning the light cavalryman and the footsoldier needed about 100 and 20 li. respectively.

If the cost of crusades varied with the rank and wealth of the crusaders, it varied also as western Europe experienced a rise in prices and in the standard of living during the crusading era. In 1195 Henry VI offered to pay his crusaders about 90 li. a year plus their maintenance. A little earlier at Acre Philip Augustus was paying the going rate of about 72 li. a year when Richard, with his usual chivalric magnificence, offered 96 li.[102] These stipends indicate that costs increased two or three times between the Third Crusade and Louis's second expedition. So also Richard spent about 400 to 500 li. each for his ships and their sailors' wages for a year, while Louis a century later paid from 850 to 7,000 li.,[103] on the average seven to eight times as much, but the ships were probably larger. Earlier than the Third Crusade good evidence on costs fails, and the rate of increase between 1096 and 1191 cannot be stated. That costs rose, however, cannot be doubted. It is probable that the money needed by a common footsoldier with Louis IX would have sufficed a knight with Godfrey of Bouillon.

When costs of a crusade can be compared with the income of crusaders in the same period, the results are illuminating. At the time of the Third Crusade when the two kings were paying 72 and 96 li. a year to knights at Acre, it was held in England that a knight's fee should

101. Joinville, *Histoire de Saint Louis,* pp. 156–157.
102. *MGH, Legum,* II, 198; *Itinerarium . . . regis Ricardi,* pp. 213–214.
103. *Pipe Roll 2 Richard I,* ed. Doris M. Stenton (Pipe Roll Society, n.s., I; London, 1925), pp. 8–9; Jal, *Pacta naulorum,* I, 507–615.

be worth roughly 80 li. a year.[104] If a knight had only 80 li. a year income and it cost him about that to maintain himself in the Holy Land, then he had nothing with which to prepare and transport himself as well as to provide for his estate and family in his absence. In other words, current income was insufficient for the simple knight to finance a crusade. For the higher ranks of the feudality the matter is more complex: if a baron had an income of several hundred pounds, he could have gone on a crusade as a simple chevalier and paid the cost from his current income. But such a course of action would have violated the mores of the time; he was expected, in the words of Gregory IX, to take a "decent company" with him.[105] Thus Joinville set out as the leader of a company of ten knights, a number he might have supported for forty days in France, but which required him to pawn his lands and still have no more than a third enough for his crusade. Again, if 3,000 li. was the amount required for a baron to keep ten knights in the Holy Land, only a half a dozen or so of the barons of thirteenth-century England could have supported such an expedition from their current income.[106]

The crusade was the most expensive adventure of medieval chivalry, often financially ruinous to the individual crusaders. Collective and corporative methods of financing the crusades were imperative. Burghers, princes, and popes made use of such methods almost from the beginning, their individual resources being insufficient for the kind of expeditions they desired. The general taxation which reached a climax in the Saladin Tithe offered hope that a satisfactory financial structure might be created for the great enterprise. But the Saladin Tithe had no real successors. It was the model for taxation by princes for secular purposes; it was the model for taxation of the clergy by popes who found other uses for their money. The Holy Land continued to depend on armies essentially supported by private means, which were not sufficient, and the failure to develop sufficiently fast and far social methods of financing the crusades must be considered a factor in the loss of the Holy Land.

Like all wars the crusades were unproductive economically but had significant economic effects through their financing. Not only did the crusade taxes provide a model for later taxation on income and wealth, but the borrowing and lending necessary for most of the crusaders

---

104. Stubbs, *Constitutional History of England,* 6th ed. (3 vols., Oxford, 1903), I, 287–288; Round, *Feudal England* (London, 1895), p. 295: 20 pounds sterling.

105. *Registres de Grégoire IX,* I, no. 1070.

106. Painter, *Studies in the History of the English Feudal Barony* (Baltimore, 1943), pp. 170–175.

stimulated credit formation and the development of credit institutions and instruments. Indeed, the money economy as a whole must have been stimulated by these great enterprises which took so much money. The transformation of gold and silver altar ornaments into coin for crusaders may have helped to heighten the inflation that occurred during the crusades, especially in the later twelfth century. The sale of land to finance crusades most assuredly helped to make the market in real estate which was bringing about a new social order in the age of the crusades. The principal beneficiaries of all these financial transactions were the bourgeoisie, who loaned the money, bought the land, sold the provisions, furnished the transportation, and generally benefitted by the financial activity of the crusaders. The peasantry who went on the crusades may have sacrificed everything but their souls, but as a class they must have gained very materially through the greater demand for their products and the greater supply of land on the market. Those members of the lay nobility who used up their savings, or sold or pledged their lands, may sometimes have been heavy losers because of the crusades, but as a whole the nobility probably lost economic power only relatively to the gains of the burghers and peasants. It was almost certainly the clergy, and especially the monasteries, who were the chief losers, as time and again they were forced to share their wealth with the crusaders either by loans without interest or by direct taxes. In essence the crusades redistributed some of Europe's wealth out of the hands of the clergy and nobles into those of the bourgeoisie and peasantry.

V

THE INSTITUTIONS
OF THE KINGDOM
OF CYPRUS

The adoption by the kingdom of Cyprus of institutions which existed in the Latin kingdom of Jerusalem is well known to historians. Yet it is sometimes not sufficiently recognized that over a period of three centuries (1192–1489), these institutions underwent a development which profoundly modified them.

From 1192 to 1197 Cyprus formed a simple seigneury, at first in the possession of the English king; then, when Richard the Lionhearted renounced his suzerainty, and his protégé Guy of Lusignan died in 1194, Guy's brother and heir Aimery (1194–1205) was clever enough to acknowledge himself the vassal of the emperor Henry VI, who sent him a royal crown. In the same year, 1197, pope Celestine III created

There is an extensive bibliography on the history of Cyprus in earlier volumes of the present work, II, 599, and III, 340–341. The institutions of the kingdom have been briefly treated by George Hill, *A History of Cyprus,* II (Cambridge, Eng., 1948), 50–57. The high officers have been listed in the old work of Emmanuel G. Rey, *Les Familles d'outremer de Du Cange* (Paris, 1869).

Nevertheless, the sources are abundant. Besides the *Description de toute l'isle de Cypre* of Estienne de Lusignan (Paris, 1580), which, though still useful, must be used with caution, the *Livre de Philippe de Novare* and the *Livre contrefais des Assises* (published under the title *Abrégé du livre des assises de la cour des bourgeois*), have been edited in *RHC, Lois,* I, 469–571, and II, 227–352, respectively. The chronicles of Leontius Machaeras (Makhairas), *Recital concerning the Sweet Land of Cyprus, entitled "Chronicle",* ed. and tr. Richard M. Dawkins (2 vols., Oxford, 1932) (in which the translation of terms respecting institutions is not always accurate), and of Florio Bustron, *Chronique de l'île de Chypre,* ed. René de Mas Latrie, in *Collection des documents inédits sur l'histoire de France, Mélanges historiques,* V (Paris, 1886), are particularly useful. The invaluable *Histoire de l'île de Chypre sous le règne des princes de la maison de Lusignan* by Louis de Mas Latrie (3 vols., Paris, 1852–1861) should be supplemented by his "Nouvelles preuves de l'histoire de Chypre," *Bibliothèque de l'École des chartes,* XXXII (1871), 341–378; XXXIV (1873) 47–87; and XXXV (1874), 99–158; and "Documents nouveaux servants de preuves à l'histoire de l'île de Chypre," *Collection des documents inédits sur l'histoire de France, Mélanges historiques,* IV (Paris, 1882), 337–619. See also Jean Richard, *Documents chypriotes des archives du Vatican (XIVe et XVe siècles)* (Institut français d'archéa church of the Latin rite in Cyprus. Although the heirs of Isaac Comnenus (d. 1195) still laid claim to the island until 1218, the actual rise of the kingdom can be dated from 1197.[1]

Imperial suzerainty occasioned difficult years for Cyprus, when Frederick II attempted to use his rights in order to nominate regents in 1228. King Henry I (1218–1253) was released from this dependency by Innocent IV in 1247, and the kingdom was from then on fully independent; the pretender Hugh of Brienne seems to have offered to become the vassal first of Charles I of Anjou, king of Sicily, and then of James I, king of Aragon-Catalonia, in exchange for their support, but without success.[2] Some authors of crusading plans (Pierre Dubois, Manuel Piloti) proposed to transfer sovereignty to a prince who would be more useful for their plans. In 1303 there were plans for having the pope make a son of Frederick of Sicily king of Cyprus, in exchange for the

---

ologie de Beyrouth, Bibliothèque archéologique et historique, 73; Paris, 1962); "Un Évêque d'Orient latin au XIVe siècle: Guy d'Ibelin, O.P., évêque de Limassol, et l'inventaire de ses biens," *Bulletin de correspondance hellénique,* LXXIV (1950), 98–133; "Une Famille de 'vénitiens blancs' à Chypre au milieu du XVe siècle: les Audeth et la seigneurie de Marethasse," *Miscellanea in onore di Agostino Pertusi* (*Rivista internazionale di studi bizantini e slavi,* I [1981], 89–129); and *Le Livre des remembrances de la secrète du royaume de Chypre pour 1468–1469* (Nicosia, 1983). See also Francesco Balducci Pegolotti, *Pratica della mercatura,* ed. Allan Evans (Cambridge, Mass., 1936).

Among the studies of institutions, I might be permitted to cite my own articles, now reprinted in *Orient et Occident au moyen âge, contacts et relations* (London, 1976), and *Les Relations entre l'Orient et l'Occident au moyen âge* (London, 1977): "Pairie d'Orient latin: les quatre baronnies des royaumes de Jérusalem et de Chypre," *RHDFE,* ser. 4, XXVIII (1950), 67–88 (*Orient et Occident,* no. 15); "La Révolution de 1369 dans le royaume de Chypre," *Bibliothèque de l'École des chartes,* CX (1952), 108–123 (*Orient et Occident,* no. 16); "La Situation juridique de Famagouste dans le royaume des Lusignans," *Praktikon tou protou diethnous Kyprologikou Synedriou,* II (Nicosia, 1972), 221–229 (*Orient et Occident,* no. 17); "Chypre du protectorat à la domination vénitienne," *Venezia e il Levante fino al secolo XV,* ed. Agostino Pertusi, I-2 (Florence, 1972), 657–677 (*Les Relations,* no. 12); as well as books and articles cited in chapter VI of volume V of the present work, "Agricultural Conditions in the Crusader States."

On ecclesiastical institutions see below, note 57. A chapter on institutions of the Lusignan kingdom will appear in the *History of Cyprus,* to be published by Archbishop Makarios III Foundation, Nicosia.

1. On the date of Guy's death see Richard, "L'Abbaye cistercienne de Jubin et le prieuré Saint-Blaise de Nicosie," *Epeteris* of the Center of Scientific Research, Nicosia, p. 70 (repr. in Richard, *Orient et Occident,* no. 19). On the claims of Isaac's heirs see Heinrich Fichtenau, "Akkon, Zypern und das Lösegeld für Richard Löwenherz," *Archiv für österreichische Geschichte,* CXXV (1966), 11–32; Rudt de (von) Collenberg, "L'Empereur Isaac de Chypre et sa fille (1155–1207)," *Byzantion,* XXXVIII (1968), 124–177; Walther Hubatsch, "Der Deutsche Orden und die Reichslehnschaft über Cypern," *Nachrichten der Akademie der Wissenschaften in Göttingen* (Philologisch-historische Klasse, 1958), pp. 245–306.

2. *Les Registres de Grégoire X et de Jean XXI,* ed. Jean Guiraud, E. [Léon] Cadier, and Guillaume Mollat (Paris, 1892–1960), p. 343 (no. 832); Elena Lourie, "An Offer of the Suzerainty and Escheat of Cyprus to Alphonse III of Aragon," *English Historical Review,* LXXXIV (1969), 101–108.

surrender of the island of Sicily to the Angevins.[3] None of these projects amounted to anything. But after his defeat at Khirokitia in 1426, king Janus (1398–1432) had to acknowledge his dependence on the Mamluk sultan of Egypt, who, from that time on, confirmed the kings of Cyprus in their office. The republic of Venice had to obtain the consent of the sultan in 1489 in order to take possession of the island.[4]

Aimery's direct line died out in 1267. The high court recognized Hugh III (1267–1284), son of Henry of Antioch and Isabel of Lusignan, as heir to Hugh II, and thenceforth Cyprus was ruled by a branch of the princely house of Antioch. However, it took up the name and the traditions of the Lusignans: the Lusignan arms of a lion on a field of white and blue bars were quartered with the lion of Cyprus, the lion of Cilician Armenia, and the cross of Jerusalem. Further, the Lusignan colors, white and blue, were adopted for the silken cords on documents from which hung the king's seal.[5]

Rules for the succession were not firmly established. Preference was given to male heirs (in 1385 James I, a brother of Peter I, was chosen over Marietta, Peter's daughter), but Hugh III derived his rights from his mother, Isabel, and Charlotte, the daughter of John II, succeeded her father in 1458. The principle of choosing the heir closest to the last holder of the crown was retained: thus Hugh III was preferred to Hugh of Brienne, and Peter I was preferred to his nephew Hugh, the son of his older brother Guy, who had died in 1346 before their father, Hugh IV, did, although it was necessary for Hugh to have his second son, Peter, crowned in his own lifetime. Henry II (1285–1324) formally deprived the children of his brother Amalric of any claim to the throne in order to leave it to Hugh IV, the son of another brother, Guy.

In case of dispute, the high court decided. But in 1460 James (II), the illegitimate son of John II, appealed to the sultan Inal and obtained from him the investiture of the kingdom, which his half-sister Charlotte and her husband, Louis of Savoy, had been requesting. This investiture legitimized the forceful takeover which had won him the crown. Likewise the high court intervened to nominate regents. The barons were able to set aside Henry I's mother, Alice, widow of Hugh I (1205–1218), in order to commit the regency successively to Philip and to John of Ibelin. Henry II's brother Amalric, titular lord of

3. *Les Registres de Boniface VIII,* ed. Georges A. L. Digard, Maurice Faucon, André A. Thomas, and Robert Fawtier (4 vols., Paris, 1884–1939), III, 847–864 (no. 5348).

4. Richard, "Chypre du protectorat à la domination vénitienne."

5. Richard, *Documents chypriotes,* p. 133. These non-Lusignan "Lusignans", from 1267 on, are hereafter designated "de" rather than "of" Lusignan.

Tyre, obtained from the barons the government of the kingdom in place of his brother, who was declared incapable of ruling (1306).[6] It was again the liegemen who, on the death of Peter I, gave the regency to his brother John, titular prince of Antioch, whose murder queen Eleanor brought about in 1375. Was it a high court decision in 1426 to give the regency to cardinal Hugh de Lusignan when his brother Janus was captured by the Egyptians? And was there likewise such a decision in 1473 to grant Catherine Cornaro, the widow of James II, the regency in the name of her infant son James III?

Aimery of Lusignan had joined the crowns of Cyprus and Jerusalem by marrying Isabel, the widow of Henry of Champagne (1192–1197); the two crowns were separated at his death in 1205. However, when Conradin of Hohenstaufen died in 1268, Hugh III was acknowledged as his closest heir. From that time on the kings of Cyprus were simultaneously kings of Jerusalem. When the Frankish possessions in Syria were lost, Henry II had the idea of making Famagusta, which he endowed with high walls and franchises, the reflection of his lost kingdom. The cross of Jerusalem was displayed on his banners, on the seal of the bailiff of the *comerc,* and on the coins struck in the town's mint. And after he had been crowned king of Cyprus in Santa Sophia of Nicosia, each new king would go to Saint Nicholas of Famagusta to receive the crown of Jerusalem, as late as the year 1372.[7]

A third crown devolved on the king of Cyprus at the death in 1393 of Leon VI de Lusignan, king of Cilician Armenia. From then on the (de) Lusignans bore the title "king of Latin Jerusalem [with the number in order of the royal succession since Baldwin I], king of Cyprus, and king of Armenia". It is not known, however, whether the fortress of Corycus, which the kings of Cyprus held from 1360 to 1448, was regarded as forming part of the kingdom of Cilician Armenia.

The Lusignans thus considered themselves entitled to confer the offices and fiefs of each of their three kingdoms. They nominated a marshal of Armenia;[8] after they received the crown of Jerusalem, they nominated a seneschal, a constable, a marshal, a butler, and a chamberlain of Jerusalem; and after they received the crown of Cyprus,

---

6. L. de Mas Latrie, "Texte officiel de l'allocution adressée par les barons au roi Henri II pour lui notifier sa déchéance," *Revue des questions historiques,* XLIII (1888), 524–541. Cf. Charles Perrat, "Un Diplomate gascon au XIVe siècle: Raymond de Piis, nonce de Clément V en Orient," *Mélanges d'archéologie et d'histoire de l'École française de Rome,* XLIV (1927), 1–58.

7. Richard, "La Situation juridique de Famagouste."

8. John de Tabarié (Tiberias) dead in 1402; a bastard of Peter de Lusignan, the titular count of Tripoli, in 1432; see Machaeras, caps. 680–681.

they nominated titularies of these same offices, as well as an admiral, a turcopolier, a chancellor, and an auditor for the kingdom of Cyprus. In addition, after the seigneurial families of the Holy Land died out, while retaining the titles of the princes of Antioch and Galilee and the counts of Tripoli for their younger sons, Peter I and his successors accorded to their subjects the titles of counts of Edessa and of Jaffa, and lords of Sidon, of Caesarea, and of Beirut. However, these titles did not include any territorial endowment, in contrast to the first titled seigneury created in the kingdom of Cyprus, the county of Carpas (Karpassos; 1472).[9]

When Guy of Lusignan became lord of Cyprus, he concerned himself with attracting enough Franks to the island to stabilize its occupation and ensure its defense. Some came from the kingdom of Jerusalem or the other principalities of the Latin east, others came from the west, especially from Poitou. He distributed fiefs among them generously (his brother Aimery reputedly reduced the extent of these concessions). It was undoubtedly the domain of the "emperor" Isaac Comnenus, who had deprived numerous members of the Greek aristocracy of their possessions, which was thus parceled out, but many great Greek landholders, especially among the laity, and a number of Venetians were also despoiled — one tradition has it that the *archontes* had first to surrender half their possessions. In any case, it is certain that no Greek name is encountered among the vassals of the kings of Cyprus in the thirteenth century.[10]

Although generous, these feudal grants were never connected with important territories. There were no great seigneuries in Cyprus; most of them included no more than a single village (casal), or else a few scattered villages (one exception being the domain of Marethasa, belonging to the titular count of Edessa in the fifteenth century). Not all of them had even a fortified manor-house with a defense tower.

The customs of the kingdom of Jerusalem were imposed with respect to feudal law: only minor differences may be noted (as, for example, the fief being passed on only to the direct descendants of a deceased

---

9. L. de Mas Latrie, "Les Comtes de Carpas," *Bibliothèque de l'École des chartes*, XLI (1880), 375 ff., and "Documents nouveaux," pp. 421–423; Richard, "Pairie d'Orient latin."

10. The "families of archontes which, without titles or arms, comprised a Greek nobility", may have maintained "within the fold of a population hostile to the invaders their rank and their prerogatives of yester-year", to reëmerge in the 16th century: Vitalien Laurent's review of G. Hill's *History of Cyprus* in *Revue des études byzantines*, VI (1948), 269. The only Greek "noble" known up to the 16th century is Constant Synkletiko, cited in 1318 in the account book of Psimolófo, but some civil servants of the king or the churches bore names which seem to indicate a Greek aristocratic extraction.

vassal).[11] Cyprus even conserved some practices which were tending to disappear elsewhere, in particular the right of the king to compel the heiresses of a fief to remarry, by offering them a choice among three men of their rank. The manuscript of the *Assises* indicates "comme dame doit estre requise d'espouser baron".[12] This obligation was derived from that of guaranteeing the services of the fief-holder in person.

Florio Bustron has given a precise definition of the military service of the vassals. The knight had to present himself to the army with four horses, the squire with three, the man-at-arms with two, and the turcopole (who was a lightly armed horseman, originally a Syrian) with one. Where the vassal was unable to guarantee this service—as in the case of a young unmarried woman or a widow who had not remarried, although other exemptions existed—the vassal had to pay a tax called "default of service", which was assessed according to the number of fees of knights or other warriors which he or she held.[13] Under Hugh III, the vassals claimed that they were not obliged to serve the king overseas or outside the kingdom. Prince Edward of England worked out a compromise limiting the duration of such service to forty days.

In accordance with the obligation to give advice to the king, the vassals were summoned to attend his court. The high court was made up of liegemen who judged cases concerning fiefs and vassals. Its jurisdiction is specified by two custumals which particularly concern the kingdom of Cyprus: the *Livre à un sien ami* of Philip of Novara (mid-thirteenth century) and the *Livre contrefais des Assises,* or *Livre du Plédeant et du Plaidoyer,* written a century later.[14]

The high court was first of all an instrument of royal power, which elaborated the sentences promulgated by the king after the jury reported its decision to him.[15] It had charge of maintaining the rights of the king as well as judging disputes between him and his vassals. In this regard, the vassals were the guarantors of the king's acts; the *Livre*

11. *RHC, Lois,* I, 503–504; Mas Latrie, *Histoire,* I, 44–45. On the formula of homage see *RHC, Lois,* II, 385–386.

12. *RHC, Lois,* II, 389. An exemption was given to James de Fleury for his wife, allowing her to remarry anyone she chose: Richard, *Documents chypriotes,* p. 131.

13. Florio Bustron, *Chronique,* pp. 462–463; Richard, *Documents chypriotes,* p. 131; *RHC, Lois,* II, 427–434; G. Hill, *History of Cyprus,* I, 168–170. The royalty seems to have been very liberal in conceding such "defaults", which made possible concentrations of fiefs in fewer hands.

14. Maurice Grandclaude, *Étude critique sur les livres des assises de Jérusalem* (Paris, 1923), pp. 70–81, 127–135, 168–170. Philip examines only the high court; the *Livre contrefais* deals primarily with the court of the bourgeois. Other works, though probably written in Cyprus (Geoffrey le Tort, James of Ibelin), are of no special interest for the kingdom.

15. See, for example, Richard, *Documents chypriotes,* p. 155; cf. *RHC, Lois,* II, 386.

des remembrances de la secrète of 1468–1469 includes an entire chapter entitled "des chozes qui se font par la haute cour". By this time
the participation of this court was entirely formal, since it was reduced
to two or three knights who ordinarily belonged to the council of the
king. But this participation symbolized the control which the court
exercised over the development of the royal domain. In 1372 it forbade Peter II to give, sell, or exchange any elements of this domain
because he had not yet reached the age of twenty-five.[16]

The high court was also the court of first instance before which cases
concerning the monarchy itself and the royal succession were brought.
It judged the rights of claimants to the crown, proclaimed the legiti-
macy of the royal succession,[17] and nominated the regent or, as in 1432
on the death of Janus, the regency council.

It also played another role. This court, which passed sentences and
kept its own records,[18] was also the instrument by which the vassals
and rear-vassals of the king expressed themselves as a group. As in
Jerusalem, the latter formed a body which some texts, dated 1272 and
1324, called "the community of the men of Cyprus": they were the
ones to voice their claims, through James of Ibelin, about overseas
service; and it was to them that Henry II granted a "remedy", after
his restoration, "de sorte que les gens ne soient pas perdans," by drawing up two charters, "dont l'une sera au pouvoir du roi et l'autre au
pouvoir des hommes".[19]

In fact the noble class was divided. It is likely that the high court
consisted only of men of high nobility. These were the men who supported the usurpation led by Amalric of Tyre in 1306; it was the knights
of secondary rank who put Henry II back on the throne in 1310. But
it seems that the arbitrary acts of Peter I, who ignored the prerogatives of the high court and of the community of men, created unani-
mous opposition against him. He was compelled to authorize "les
hommes", among whom were his two brothers, to meet in order to
present him with a list of grievances. On the day after his assassination, this list was transformed into a "remède" adopted by the high
court, which stipulated among other things that thenceforth the *Livre
de Jean d'Ibelin* would become the law code of the realm (1369).[20] The

16. Machaeras, *Recital,* cap. 327.
17. There is a full description of the sitting of the court when Peter II was proclaimed king,
ibid., caps. 319–324.
18. *RHC, Lois,* II, 246.
19. *Ibid.,* II, 369, 419, 430.
20. I have identified this document as the outcome of the deliberation of the liegemen, in
"La Révolution de 1369". It must have been finally drawn up the day after the murder of the

juridical theory of John of Ibelin, based on the *Assise de la ligèce,* could only strengthen the control exercised by the vassals over the crown.

In reality, although there was great respect throughout this period for this *Livre* (which the Venetian administration would later have translated into Italian), the Cypriote nobility did not succeed in imposing its will on the monarchy. The vassals' rights did not prevent the regents named either by Frederick II or by John of Ibelin from exiling their adversaries and confiscating their goods, which led to the exodus of many Cypriote nobles.[21] Amalric of Tyre imprisoned and exiled his brother's followers, and Henry II cruelly revenged himself on Amalric's followers. Peter II confiscated the goods of his father's assassins, taking advantage of the fact that an attack on the island by the Genoese had defeated the party which had overthrown Peter I. John II seems to have deprived certain of his vassals of their fiefs in order to give them to others.[22] But it was the advent of James II which provoked a real revolution. The great majority of liegemen had remained loyal to Charlotte and to Louis of Savoy; James, who was besieging them in Kyrenia (1460–1464), confiscated all their fiefs and distributed them among his own supporters—Cypriote nobles, persons of lower birth, Italian or Spanish adventurers—and, when the defeated came over to his side, he gave them other fiefs, taken from the royal domain or from other vacant properties. The result of this immense upheaval was to modify profoundly the structure of the nobility, now completely shot through with new elements.[23]

Among these were the descendants of a non-Latin bourgeoisie, often of Syrian extraction, which had grown rich either in trade or in the exercise of offices in the royal administration. Already, under Peter II, Thibaut Belpharage (Abū-l-Farāj), the bailie of a casal of the royal domain, who had raised a troop of mercenaries to fight against the Genoese, was raised to the rank of knight and turcopolier of the realm, before being executed for the murder of the king's confessor, who had warned the king against giving Thibaut the castle of Corycus in fief

---

king, according to Peter W. Edbury, "The Murder of King Peter I of Cyprus (1353–1369)," *Journal of Medieval History,* VI (1980), 219–233. On the right to make common cause, claimed by the liegemen, see Machaeras, *Recital,* caps. 269–270.

21. Émile Bertaux, "Les Français d'outre-mer en Apulie et en Épire au temps des Hohenstaufen d'Italie," *Revue historique,* LXXXV (1904), 225–251.

22. At least we see the king dispose of "fiés arestés": *Documents chypriotes,* p. 146, note 2.

23. See my introduction to the *Livre des remembrances.* On the structure of the Frankish nobility before the difficulties at the end of the 14th century, cf. Rudt de (von) Collenberg, "Les Dispenses matrimoniales accordées à l'Orient latin selon les registres du Vatican d'Honorius III à Clément VII (1223–1385)," *Mélanges de l'École française de Rome: Moyen âge, Temps modernes,* LXXXIX-1 (1977), 11–93.

(1376). Thomas Parek, cited in 1382, was also "a Greek bourgeois who had become a Latin knight".[24] After James II, the Greek or Syrian families which filled the offices founded families of knights and barons who held their fiefs first from the king, then under the lordship of Venice.[25]

Unlike those of the Latin empire of Constantinople or the Norman kingdom of Sicily, the dynasty which established itself in Cyprus does not seem to have retained any of the dignities or high offices which had existed under Isaac Comnenus. The king surrounded himself with a group of high officers who bore the titles of seneschal, constable, marshal, butler, and chamberlain. The role of these officers, defined in the *Assises,* was probably not purely honorary: in 1367 the constable ordered the auction of the possessions of bishop Guy of Limassol, which was carried out by his *bannier,* and, in 1468, it was to him that a farrier engaged by the king was subject.[26] But the royal household ("nostre court") was organized into several offices which functioned apart from them. The principal office was the chamber, which was responsible both for supplies and for the upkeep of the lodgings, the clothing of the king and his servitors, and the management of the royal hunts: the huntsmen (*braconniers*) and the falconers came under the chamber. On the other hand, it was also the chamber which kept the royal treasure, and we shall find it again listed among the financial institutions. At its head was a squire, assisted by a scribe. The pantry, the butlery, and the stable constituted the three other services over which presided the *bailli de la court,* who in the fifteenth century assumed the title of *maistre de l'ostel.*

Were the constable and marshal of Cyprus in charge of the army? In 1425 the army was commanded by Henry de Lusignan, the titular prince of Galilee (although we do not know whether he was constable); the titular marshal of Jerusalem, who made decisions concerning provisioning, was Baldwin de Nores, who was above all the most trusted counselor of king Janus. The turcopoles of the royal army were theoretically subject to the turcopolier. Besides the contingents who fought

24. Machaeras, *Recital,* caps. 555–561, 564–579, 599.

25. The role of the queen, Helena Palaeologina (1442–1458), in this introduction of Greeks into the nobility has sometimes been exaggerated. It was limited to favoring certain Greeks who came with her, notably her foster-brother Thomas of the Morea, who became chamberlain of the kingdom. This is what led one titular count of Jaffa (himself married to a Cantacuzena) to complain that "the government of this kingdom has fallen entirely into the hands of Greeks and petty people." See Raffaele di Tucci, "Il Matrimonio fra Ludovico di Savoia e Carlotta di Cipro," *Bolletino storico subalpino,* XXXVII (1935), 79–83.

26. Richard, "Un Évêque d'Orient latin," pp. 131–139; *Livre des remembrances,* no. 46.

on horseback and who were equipped by the vassals of the king, the infantry comprised free men, Frankish or Greek bourgeois, Armenians, and Syrians; we know that those from Carpas were compelled to serve on horseback.[27]

From the thirteenth century on, however, the king also had to hire mercenaries. These were so numerous in the time of Peter I that the liegemen demanded in 1369 that no more than one hundred might be engaged without their consent. Beginning in 1373, however, the constable James de Lusignan had to reinforce his army with Armenian mercenaries, with Bulgarians previously in the service of Genoa, and with eight hundred men that Thibaut Belpharage hired in Venice. James II conquered his kingdom with a Moslem contingent, but he formed a permanent army by engaging some men-at-arms coming from the west with their *condottieri*: Peter of Avila commanded an *escadre* of knights, while some *condostables* had charge of the *sodées de pié*. The Venetians would later expel from the kingdom all those Franks and Sicilians whom they judged to be unreliable.

The marshal, for his part, was responsible for the material organization of the feudal army. Undoubtedly it was with regard to this that a tax called *maréchaussée* was levied on all owners of livestock: it was the marshal who had to replace horses lost by vassals in the service of the king. Moreover, his scribe (the *maréchaucier*) recorded the deeds which established fiefs in the *Livre des remembrances de la maréchaussée*: it is likely that he controlled the administration of homage.

In the thirteenth century the kings of Cyprus had no navy and had to depend on the Genoese. The fall of Acre induced Henry II to construct some warships in order to ensure the security of the coasts of Cyprus and to pursue pirates. There soon appeared an admiral of Cyprus. Hugh IV maintained six galleys in the squadron of the "Holy Union", which combatted Turkish piracy, and the arsenal of Famagusta built some warships.[28] Its activity increased under Peter I, who entrusted the office of admiral to his most faithful aide, John Monstry, whom the conspirators of 1369 pursued with hatred. Janus conducted privateering operations against the Moslems with "une galée et une galiote".[29] Finally, James II built for himself a small squadron of galleys and compelled his subjects to supply crews, and his captains

---

27. Richard, *Livre des remembrances,* Introduction. Free men also owed guard duty, especially along the coasts.

28. L. de Mas Latrie, "Nouvelles preuves," *Bibliothèque de l'École des chartes,* XXXIV, 52; Richard, *Documents chypriotes,* pp. 33–49.

29. *Emmanuel Piloti: Traité sur le passage en Terre-Sainte,* ed. Pierre H. Dopp (Louvain and Paris, 1958), p. 174.

conducted operations which the Hospitallers and the merchants complained of.

The exercise of justice belonged to the seneschal, who presided over the high court in the king's absence. Viscounts in Nicosia (and in Famagusta from the beginning of the fourteenth century) presided over the court of burgesses, which was made up of twelve jurymen drawn from the Frankish bourgeoisie. The viscount, a Frankish knight nominated by the king, had the responsibility for the administration of justice as well as the maintenance of the king's rights, according to the conditions revealed by the *Livre contrefais*; he would have the orders and the *bans* of the king published and carried out. Henry II dismissed (in 1300?) viscount Hugh Piétau and his jurymen, who had refused to have enforced an *ordenement* which was contrary to custom.[30]

An assize of 1355 reveals four bailies, those of Famagusta, Limassol, Paphos, and Cape Andreas, each of whom exercised in his "diossé" a jurisdiction analogous to that of the viscount, which extended over a vast district called the viscounty.[31] Sergeants would assist these officers; they were placed under the direction of one of them who bore the title of *mathesep* (Arabic, *maḥtasib*).

Around the time of Peter I this scheme was modified by the division of the island into twelve *contrées* at the head of which were either a viscount or a bailie, or more often a *chevetain*. A judgment rendered in 1406 by the captain and *chevetain* of Kyrenia shows that this officer was assisted by a court of four jurymen.[32]

For the non-Frankish population special courts existed. In Famagusta, whose population was predominantly Syrian, the court of the *ra'īs* seems to have ultimately supplanted the court of the viscount. But it is also known through gravestones that there were Frankish knights who bore the title of "rais des Syriens de Nicosie". For the Greeks, some documents originating in Marethasa reveal a *nomikos* and a *taboullarios,* whose titles are those of agents of the Byzantine judicial administration, some elements of which the Franks had thus conserved.[33]

---

30. *RHC, Lois,* II, 235 ff., 320–321.

31. *Ibid.,* pp. 322–324 (jurisdiction of the bailie of Famagusta); cf. Richard, "La Révolution de 1369."

32. Richard, *Livre des remembrances,* Introduction.

33. Jean Darrouzès, "Notes pour servir à l'histoire de Chypre," *Kypriakai Spoudai,* XV (1953), 88, 96–97. The first citation of a *ra'īs* by name comes in 1210: Edbury, "The 'Cartulaire de Manosque': a Grant to the Templars in Latin Syria and a Charter of King Hugh I of Cyprus," in *Bulletin of the Institute of Historical Research,* LI (1978), 175. Cf. Richard, "La Cour des syriens de Famagouste d'après un texte de 1448," *In memoriam Professeur F. Thiriet (Byzantinische Forschungen,* XII [1987], 383–398).

Each casal had its juryman, nominated by the lord from the local inhabitants, who undoubtedly assisted the seigneurial bailie in the exercise of domanial justice. It is likely that the widespread enfranchisement of the Greek bourgeoisie under Peter I resulted in the access of Greeks (and Syrians) to the functions of the jurymen of the viscount's court, initially reserved to Franks "de la loi de Rome".

With regard to the confirmation of contracts, Cyprus was still unfamiliar with notarial institutions, according to the evidence of Pegolotti around 1325, and the king recognized as valid only those enacted before the courts, such as the court of the viscount, or before other jurisdictions, such as that of the bailie of the *comerc,* which was competent in commercial matters. Beginning in 1311 at the latest, however, a new high official appeared, the auditor of Cyprus, whose role seems to have been that of authenticating the contracts which his scribe recorded in his cartulary; he also exercised the functions of the king's procurator in the high court.[34] But, in fact, it was already necessary to recognize as valid certain acts drawn up by notaries. The famous Genoese notary Lambert di Sambuceto was acting in Famagusta at the very beginning of the fourteenth century. In the fifteenth century there were numerous imperial notaries; at the very most, certain acts accepted by the latter would then receive the sanction of the viscount's court.[35]

The role of the high officers became noticeably less important in the direction of affairs. However, as early as the fourteenth century certain persons bore the title of counselor of the king. In the acts of John II and James II almost all the knights who represented the high court in the acts bore this title. And in 1452 the titular count of Jaffa, James de Fleury, was titled "chief de sonn connsel" — a title which might be compared with that of *governador del regno di Cipro,* which the admiral Muzio di Costanzo bore in 1473.[36] It seems that the king's council was a well-defined group, of which the holders of the high offices of the two realms formed a part, as also the *pourveours* and the bailie of the *secrète,* and undoubtedly other persons who were favored with dignities and pensions by the king. Without encroaching on the duties of the high court, they in effect supplanted the latter in the control of the government of the realm.[37]

34. Richard, "La Révolution de 1369," pp. 119–122.

35. According to the testament of John Audeth: cf. Richard, "Une Famille de 'vénitiens blancs'."

36. Richard, *Documents chypriotes,* p. 155; L. de Mas Latrie, "Documents nouveaux," pp. 415, 423. Florio Bustron translates the passage where George Bustron (cap. 102) calls Muzio *"vizores"* by "ch'era vice-re de Nicosia" ("Documents nouveaux," p. 602), which seems to be a misconception.

37. The sentence of 1452, cited in the preceding note, gives the composition of the high court. All its members seem to have belonged to the king's entourage.

The acts of the government were drawn up by the chancery, whose head was a chancellor, initially a notable (an ecclesiastic of high rank, later Philip of Mézières), later a simple notary, usually an Italian. It included a vice-chancellor, scribes, and a judge of the chancery, and would draw up the acts of the king according to a formulary which had evolved over the course of centuries. They were sealed with a leaden bull, which was replaced in the fourteenth century by a seal of wax on which the king was represented sitting in majesty.[38]

Although our knowledge of the administrative organization of the island is very scanty for the period of Isaac Comnenus's autonomous dominion, it may be assumed that, as in the other Byzantine provinces, the fiscal administration had been based on the division of the territory into units, the casals (*chōría*). In each casal a *katepános* levied public taxes (*dēmósion, strateia*) and there were cadastral registers (*praktika*) in which were inscribed the names of taxpayers assessed by household for the collection of the *kapnikón*. The duke had a bureau (*sékreton*) directed by a *práktōr*.

As far as can be seen, the Latins used this fiscal structure in organizing the kingdom. The division into casals provided the framework for the allocation of fiefs; and the management of the king's finances was ensured by the *secrète du roi,* or the *grande secrète* (as Philip of Novara calls it). Its head, the bailie of the *secrète,* is often called *práktoras* by Leontius Machaeras. It may be noted, moreover, that when the Mamluks took over Nicosia (1426), several officers of the *secrète* placed themselves at their disposal, and that they appointed a *práktoras.*[39]

The *secrète* formed a college. The *secrétains* assembled for deliberation; one of them had charge of the *Livre des remembrances* in which were registered the orders of the king of financial import, the leases (*apauts*) of the revenues of the royal domain, the sales or exchanges made between individuals on property held of the crown by quit-rent or otherwise, and manumissions. It was the *secrète* which authorized expenditures by issuing writs of payment (*apodixes*) on the funds of the collectors, and examined the accounts of the latter; it also put domanial revenues out to farm.

Its personnel, other than the *secrétains,* consisted of scribes, sergeants, and a judge. At its head was a bailie, who up to the time of

---

38. Richard, "La Diplomatique royale dans les royaumes d'Arménie et de Chypre," *Bibliothèque des l'École des chartes,* CXLIV (1986), 69–86.
39. For what follows, see the *Livre des remembrances,* Introduction.

James II was a Frankish knight, while the *secrétains* came from the Syrian or Greek milieu which furnished scribes for all the administrations. Finally, a treasurer of the *secrète* seems to have had charge of the money derived from the royal domain (*régale*).

Peter I had created an office of inquests, and the "master of the inquests" made decisions concerning the royal domain without asking the consent of the high court (even though the *secrète* recognized the "chozes qui se font par la haute cour"). The liegemen obtained the abolition of the office of inquests in 1369.[40] Under James II, there were two persons of the nobility who were called *pourveours dou reiaume*; one of them bore the title of the "superior of our *secrète*", and both were associated with the bailie in the commands of the king as in the deliberations of the *secrète*. These men seem to have formed a section of the royal council competent in financial matters.

The royal chamber also had its part in the management of finances: the chamberlain John de Stathia, under Peter I, and the heads of the chamber, Anthony of Bergamo and James Soulouan, under James I, had the responsibility for extraordinary taxation. From 1468 to 1472 James Zaplana was "governor of the royal chamber". A treasurer collected the sums which came from extraordinary revenues. In 1466 James II introduced a new tax, and created what was called a "new office" for the purpose.

The *régale* (the royal domain), which furnished the monarchy with its ordinary resources, included all the cities of the realm: Nicosia, Paphos, Kyrenia, Famagusta, and Limassol. Each was fortified, or at least possessed a royal castle. That of Nicosia, where the king customarily resided, was enlarged by Peter I, who added the Marguerite tower, and by Peter II, who had this tower torn down along with the "Palace of the Counts" where the royal children were lodged, in order to build the New Castle. Country residences at La Cava, Potamiou, and Akaki,[41] built in the fourteenth century, permitted the sovereign to devote himself to the hunt. The ancient fortresses of Pentadaktylos, St. Hilarion, Buffavento, and Kantara likewise belonged to the crown, as well as the Château–Franc, which James I constructed at Sígouri in order to keep an eye on the Genoese of Famagusta. Thus, with the

40. Machaeras, *Recital,* cap. 633 and note (ed. Dawkins, II, 211); Richard, "Un Évêque d'Orient latin," p. 125; "La Révolution de 1369," pp. 113–114 (where I mistakenly thought that the office of inquests might have had an essentially judicial quality).

41. Machaeras, *Recital,* caps. 87, 241, 594–597. According to George Bustron (cap. 1), after the royal palace was burned by the Mamluks (Machaeras, cap. 695), the king adopted as his residence the quarters of Richard de la Baume. Cf. Camille Enlart, *L'Art gothique et de la Renaissance en Chypre* (2 vols., Paris, 1899), II, 518–522.

exception of some towers belonging to the chief vassals and the fortified residences of the Temple and the Hospital (La Castrie and Kolossi), the king had at his disposal all the fortresses of the realm, where he placed his castellans (later captains, at least in the most important ones), and occasionally garrisons. These fortresses also served as state prisons.

In area and in revenues the royal domain was as great as or greater than those of all the vassals combined. In the diocese of Limassol the king, the vassals, and the military orders shared the territory more or less equally. The accounts of the church of Limassol for 1367 show that at this time almost all the villages of the royal domain were farmed out (in *apaut*). But in the years which followed, the king resumed their direct exploitation; royal bailies were charged with administering these villages, grouped into districts whose number, according to a list drawn up between 1510 and 1525, exceeded twenty. The *Livre des remembrances* contains acts relative to the appointment of the bailies, whose duties seem to have been essentially financial.[42]

The principal plantations of sugar cane, regarding which the king negotiated with the merchants who refined sugar, the salt beds of Larnaca, and the fisheries of the lake of Limassol belonged to the royal domain and ensured the king substantial revenues. Duties (the *gabelles*) were levied at the gates of Nicosia on the commodities taken to market; makers of fine cloth (camlet, samite) had to pay a tax when they sold their products, to which had to be affixed the bull of the royal dyeworks. Other taxes were levied on commodities put up for sale in the market. Among them figured a tax of Byzantine origin, the *comerc* (*kommérchion*), the responsibility of a particular bailie. In Famagusta, in the fourteenth century, the bailie of the *comerc* collected the dues that the merchants had to pay when landing their goods, and presided over a court which settled disputes of a commercial nature.[43]

Pegolotti, who provides evidence on these last points, also reveals how the mint of Famagusta functioned. In the thirteenth century "white bezants" were struck, after the model of the Byzantine *hyperperon*. In the fourteenth century, the bezant became a money of account, and the kings struck *deniers, gros,* and *sizains*. Financial difficulties compelled them to devalue the coinage: one devaluation undoubtedly oc-

---

42. On the dues levied by the bailies on the peasants of the villages in the royal domain, cf. volume V of the present work, chapter VI, section B. It was only in 1222 that the monarchy gave up the *chevagia et dimos* from church lands, paid up to that time by the *rustici*: L. de Mas Latrie, *Histoire,* III, 620.

43. Pegolotti, *Pratica,* ed. Evans, pp. 83–84.

curred in the first half of the fourteenth century, and another between 1440 and 1445.[44]

The initiation of extraordinary taxes probably required the consent of the liegemen and prelates, but the king tended to perpetuate their levy. Thus the *testagium,* a yearly tax of two bezants on each inhabitant of the realm (the clergy being exempt) instituted in 1292 in order to pay the soldiers and to construct boats, was not abolished until 1306 by the rebellious liegemen, after fruitless efforts by Boniface VIII.[45] Under Hugh IV the maintenance of the ships which policed the sea was financed by a levy on merchants who brought merchandise from overseas.[46] In 1369 the liegemen demanded the suppression of the taxes created by Peter I: a tax for the maintenance of soldiers, another for the arsenal of Famagusta, a levy for the fortification of Nicosia, and another for the construction of galleys.

The Genoese invasion of 1373 severely impoverished the kingdom, all the more so as it cut off its income from the revenues of Famagusta. At first it was necessary to have recourse to expedients, notably the sale of enfranchisements to some *paroikoi* (Peter I had already extensively enfranchised the *perpiriari,* the Greek burgesses of the cities).[47] Further, a tax was created of one bezant per person, the *kephalatikón;* a salt levy, which compelled each inhabitant to buy one measure of salt each year at a price fixed by the *secrète;* and finally, a "royal tithe" on fiefs and rents, which was first levied in 1388 by a mixed commission of Genoese and Cypriotes in order to pay the war indemnity exacted by Genoa.[48] The salt levy and the royal tithe continued, in spite of numerous exemptions. But it was necessary to raise new taxes after the defeat of 1426, in order to pay the tribute owed to the sultan, which aroused the opposition of subject Venetians, who attempted to evade it (1448). James II, in his turn, after having sold exemptions and enfranchisements, obtained in 1466 the right to a tax of twenty percent on wages and incomes (the *rate*) for three years.

Cyprus thus had a fiscal regime which was very similar to that of the western kingdoms. Here also the royal domain, although quite sub-

44. *Ibid.,* pp. 82–83; Richard, *Documents chypriotes,* pp. 16–17.

45. *Les Registres de Boniface VIII,* II, 143–144, 703–704 (nos. 2609, 3114, 3589); L. de Mas Latrie, "Texte officiel de l'allocution," pp. 524–541.

46. Pegolotti, *Pratica,* pp. 85–86.

47. Cf. Peter II's letter confirming the enfranchisements made by his uncles (1374): Machaeras, *Recital,* cap. 576. On the enfranchisement of the *perpiriari* dreamed up by John de Stathia see *ibid.,* cap. 157.

48. *Ibid.,* cap. 618, noting the suppression by James I, at the same time, of the office of the "taille": did this office originate with the receipt of the κεφαλατικόν?

stantial compared to the holdings of the vassals and of the church, did not suffice to permit doing without extraordinary taxation.

The presence of colonies dependent upon the merchant cities of Italy, Provence, and Catalonia did not have the same characteristics on the island as in the Frankish states of Syria. The rights which the Pisans and Venetians had acquired in the time of the Byzantines, or of Guy of Lusignan, were modest. In 1232 Genoa received the first somewhat extensive privileges, thanks to the support of John of Ibelin. But it was not until 1291, at the time of the loss of their trading establishments in Syria, that the Pisans and Catalans obtained some privileges; the Pisans established some small colonies in which a privilege of 1321 permitted them to have parish churches.[49] Venice asked for a charter of privileges in 1302, but did not acquire it until 1328. Venice aspired to its own quarters in Nicosia, Limassol, and Famagusta. In fact, it was only in Famagusta that there were communities of privileged merchants: Sicilians, Provençals, Pisans, and Barcelonans. Their main privilege was that of paying the *comerc* at a very low rate; Pegolotti recounts how he managed to obtain the same favor for the Florentines when he was the factor of the Bardi in Cyprus (1324–1326).[50] Only the Genoese and the Venetians — who enjoyed a complete franchise — had any notable establishments there: a hall where their consul presided, a church, and a street of houses.[51]

They alone also played an important role in the history of the kingdom. Venice, for example, by threatening the king with a boycott, seriously affected the operations of Peter I against the Moslems, which had compromised Venetian interests by the sack of Alexandria. The boycott would have been all the more effective since the Venetians controlled practically all the exports of two of the principal resources of the monarchy, salt and sugar.[52]

---

49. Richard, "Le Peuplement latin et syrien en Chypre au XIIIe siècle," *Byzantinische Forschungen,* VII (1979), 162–163. Aimery's diploma for the Marseillais must be dismissed as a forgery: Hans Eberhard Mayer, *Marseilles Levantehandel und ein Akkonensisches Fälscheratelier des 13. Jahrhunderts* (Tübingen, 1972). The authentic privileges given the Provençaux in 1236 (*ibid.,* pp. 193–194) make no allusion to a permanent establishment. On the Pisan churches see Richard, *Documents chypriotes,* p. 73, note 7.

50. Pegolotti, *Pratica,* pp. 70–71.

51. Venice seems to have had a consul for the Venetians in Cyprus since 1296; the title "bailie" appeared in 1306. Cf. Giovannina Majer, "Sigilli di baili veneziani in Oriente," *Archivio veneto,* 5th ser., XXIX (1941), 117–124, a list which may be completed by consulting L. de Mas Latrie, *Histoire,* III, 840. On the existence of a consul distinct from the bailie, cf. *Livre des remembrances,* no. 224, n. 1.

52. On salt cf. Jean C. Hocquet, *Voiliers et commerce du sel en Méditerranée* (Lille, 1978), pp. 227–232; on sugar see the texts in the *Livre des remembrances.* Every year, in the fall, a

These two republics had to look after not only the interests of their merchants who traded in the kingdom or who put in at its ports, but also those of a considerable number of "white Venetians" and "white Genoese". These were descendants of Syrian protégés of Venice and Genoa who had established themselves in Cyprus after fleeing the Holy Land. They claimed to enjoy the exemptions granted to the Venetians and Genoese, and that their cases should come under the jurisdiction of the consuls of Venice and Genoa. This did not prevent them from acquiring land (the *Assises* forbade the sale of land to "gens de commune") or from holding administrative offices.[53]

A quarrel between the Genoese and the Venetians, at the time of the coronation of Peter II in Famagusta, following an earlier conflict which had arisen under Peter I concerning the desertion of sailors who had claimed to be Genoese, led first to an order of the *podestà* of Genoa to his compatriots to leave the island, and then to the arrival of a Genoese fleet.[54] Peter II, captured by a ruse, had to consent to turn Famagusta over to the republic of Genoa as pledge for the payment of a heavy indemnity. This surrender was to last only twelve years, and reserved the rights of the king over the city (1374). James I had to give up Famagusta definitively on February 19, 1384. The city, with a band of territory surrounding it, was thus, in fact, independent of the kingdom until 1464. When James II repossessed it he preserved its peculiar status: the Greek bourgeoisie of the city continued to come under the jurisdiction of the court of the Syrians, and the royal writs drawn up at Famagusta were in Italian, not French.[55]

Venice, which had preserved its neutrality, maintained its privileged status in Famagusta, but its galleys put in at Larnaca when they came to pick up salt, or at Limassol to load sugar. The bailie of Venice, who represented the doge in the king's court, and who administered justice to subject Venetians, moved to Nicosia. Some Venetians began to take advantage of the difficulties of the crown, but the republic continued to be cautious in its attitude toward the Lusignans. When the Mamluks took Nicosia in 1426, the Venetian subjects gave them a warm welcome, thinking they would be treated as neutrals. But, in view of the king's

---

galea zucharorum arrived to take on sugar (Richard, "Une Famille de 'vénitiens blancs'"). Cf. Pierre Racine, "Note sur le trafic véneto-chypriote à la fin du moyen âge," *Byzantinische Forschungen,* V (1977), 307–329.

53. L. de Mas Latrie, "Nouvelles preuves," *Bibliothèque de l'École des chartes,* XXXV, 153–154; Richard, "Une Famille de 'vénitiens blancs'"; David Jacoby, "Citoyens, sujets et protégés de Venise et de Gênes en Chypre du XIIIe au XVe siècle," *Byzantinische Forschungen,* V (1977), 159–188.

54. On the first conflict see Machaeras, *Recital,* caps. 145–156.

55. Richard, "La Situation juridique de Famagouste."

need of money, the Venetian merchants and the signory itself granted some loans for which the domanial revenues constituted the security. Venetian interests were becoming increasingly tied up with the fate of the kingdom. Mark Cornaro and his brother Andrew played an important role in the service of John II; Andrew became the auditor of the kingdom under James II, who married his niece Catherine.

The bailie of Venice, who was designated every two years by the great council, and who was assisted by a vice-bailie and a council formed by visiting Venetian noblemen, was one of the important persons of the kingdom. It was his intervention which permitted Catherine to overcome the plot of November 1373. From then on, however, the republic designated two counselors to "assist" the queen permanently, while a *provveditore* commanded the Venetian troops stationed on the island. It would be sufficient, in 1489, to keep the queen at a distance and to nominate a "lieutenant of Cyprus" who, with the two counselors, formed a body of "rectors of the realm", in order to bring Cyprus effectively under the direct government of Venice.[56]

Because of the passing of the island under the domination of a Frankish dynasty, the Latin church had become the officially established church in the new kingdom of Cyprus.[57] The archbishop and the three bishops, with their chapters, seem to have received posses-

---

56. Richard, "Chypre du protectorat." The reforms introduced by Venice took careful account of the earlier constitution. With respect to the administration of justice, see L. de Mas Latrie, "Documents nouveaux," pp. 541, 554. For a layout of the administration of the island by Venice cf. G. Hill, *History of Cyprus,* III, 765-779, and L. de Mas Latrie, *Histoire,* III, *in fine.*

57. For the period of the establishment of the Latin church and its early difficulties with the Greeks, cf. volume II of the present work, pp. 623-629. In place of the short, old work of L. de Mas Latrie, "Histoire des archevêques latins de Chypre," *AOL,* II (1884), 207-328, one may substitute John Hackett, *A History of the Orthodox Church of Cyprus* (London, 1901), translated into Greek and expanded by Charilaos I. Papaïoannou (3 vols., Athens, 1923-1932), It is unfortunately marred by the assumption of a state of permanent tension between Greeks and Latins. See also G. Hill, "The Two Churches," in *History of Cyprus,* III, 1041-1104; Joseph Gill, "The Tribulations of the Greek Church in Cyprus, 1196- c. 1280," *Byzantinische Forschungen,* V (1977), 73-93. The history of the Latin church has been in part revised by the study of materials in the collection of *Instrumenta miscellanea* of the Vatican Archives, which has provided, in particular, the dossier of the succession of bishop Guy of Limassol in 1367: cf. Richard, "Un Évêque d'Orient latin," and *Documents chypriotes,* pp. 61-110. The important series of the acts of the synods of the province of Nicosia (up to 1354) has been published in Mansi, *Concilia,* XXVI, cols. 211-382. The cartulary of Santa Sophia of Nicosia, published by L. de Mas Latrie as an appendix to vol. III of his *Histoire,* was reprinted by John L. LaMonte, "A Register of the Cartulary of the Cathedral of Santa Sophia of Nicosia," *Byzantion,* V (1929-1930), 439-522. An important study of the Greek church and its relations with the Latins is Darrouzès, "Textes synodaux chypriotes," *Revue des études byzantines,* XXXVII (1979), 5-122.

sion of the cathedral churches of the four episcopal sees (Nicosia, Famagusta, Limassol, and Paphos), but without the substantial endowment which these churches had enjoyed under the Byzantine regime. Their endowment remained relatively modest; it was increased by gifts from Frankish nobles, as the cartulary of Santa Sophia of Nicosia shows. But the bulk of their revenue came from tithes which, as in the kingdom of Jerusalem, were paid by the king and by the nobles on the revenue of their domains, as well as by the holders of certain "free" lands, in accordance with the concordat of 1222. From these revenues the bishop had to ensure the maintenance of his church, the payment of the prebends of the canons and of the "assises" of the rest of the clergy, and the pay of "parochial priors" of the few parochial churches of Latin rite. However, this allowed the maintenance of only very modest cathedral chapters.[58]

As in the west, the bishops of Cyprus felt it necessary to be assisted in the exercise of their episcopal duties by auxiliary bishops. Several bishops from the Holy Land thus established themselves in Cyprus at the end of the thirteenth century and on occasion obtained the administration of episcopal sees (the see of Tortosa was even united to that of Famagusta). Later their number decreased, and it seems that only one auxiliary served as vicar *in pontificalibus* in the four dioceses: Dimanche de Deux-Lions, titular bishop of Mesembria, in 1367; Salomon Cardus and Anthony Audeth, titular bishops of Tortosa, then Nicholas de Courio, titular bishop of Hebron, who died in 1468.

The *Constitutio Cypria* of 1260 attributed to the Greek bishop the function of "vicar of the Greeks" under the Latin bishop. The Greek bishop resided in the same diocese, but in another city: Soli for the diocese of Nicosia, Lefkara for that of Limassol, Arsinoë (Polis) for that of Paphos, and Carpas for that of Famagusta. The bishop of Soli, however, enjoyed the possession of a second episcopal see, the church of St. Barnabas at Nicosia. Each of them was assisted by a chapter of Greek canons: in 1301 the deans of Soli and of St. Barnabas intrigued for the succession to the bishopric. Their endowment was likened to an episcopal *mense*. In 1321 pope John XXII increased that of the bishop of Lefkara by placing under him the monastery of the Holy Savior of Lefkara.[59] The Greek bishop had complete authority over

58. This comes from the accounts of the diocese of Limassol in 1367: Richard, *Documents chypriotes,* pp. 61 ff. The tithe levy was introduced in Cyprus by the Franks; Greek bishops were entitled, as before the conquest, to assess a hearth-tax on the followers of the Greek rite, and a *kanonikon* on the clerics.

59. Ferdinand M. Delorme and A. L. Tăutu, eds., *Acta Romanorum pontificum ab Innocentio V ad Benedictum XI (1276–1304)* (PC, Fontes, ser. 3, V-2; Vatican City, 1954), pp. 195–

the Greek priests of his diocese, and he was the judge of the Greek laity for all matters within the competence of the church's courts, which is to say for the greater part of private law. He had to swear obedience (the oath was carefully phrased, according to the compromise reached in 1260) to the Latin bishop of the diocese, but it was rare that a Latin bishop ventured to visit the person who was canonically his subordinate, as did the Dominican Bérard, bishop of Limassol in 1295, who deposed bishop Matthew of Lefkara as a "heretic".[60] It is noteworthy that some bishops, like Leo of Soli, did not hesitate to have recourse to Rome in order to strengthen their position. In the three centuries between 1260 and 1570, incidents provoked in general by excess of zeal on the part of some prelates, or of papal legates such as Peter de Pleine Chassagne in 1310 or Peter Thomas in 1360, were relatively rare; the two churches lived their parallel lives without interference. The Latin church, however, seems to have feared seeing its faithful pass to the Greek rite, and some measures were taken to prevent it. Meanwhile, the monarchy worried about limiting the access of *pariques* to the priesthood, seeing this as an indirect means of escaping their servile condition.

Among the Syrians,[61] the Melkites (*Syri*) were grouped with the Greeks and were placed under the same bishops. The Maronites, Nestorians, Jacobites, Armenians, and Copts had their own churches, notably in Famagusta and Nicosia, and their own ecclesiastical organization; they were probably not constrained to perform an act of obedience to the Latin bishop of each diocese. However, archbishop Elias summoned the heads of these communities to a provincial synod in 1340, along with the Greek bishops, in order to obtain their adherence to the canons that he promulgated; and, after the Council of Florence, representatives of the pope came to demand their adherence to the church union which had been proclaimed there.

The establishment of Latin monasticism was accomplished in stages.

198, 219–226 (nos. 119–120, 132–133); Tăutu, ed., *Acta Ioannis XXII (1317–1334)* (*ibid.*, VII-2; 1952), pp. 79–80 (no. 39).

60. Richard, *Documents chypriotes*, p. 74, notes 1, 2. Despite this deposition, Matthew seems to have remained in office until his death (archbishop John refused to carry out the sentence laid on him). He was then replaced by Olbianos, abbot of the monastery of Asomatos, who asked Bérard to confirm his election: K. Hatzipsaltis, "Ἐκ τῆς ἱστορίας τῆς ἐκκλησίας τῆς Κύπρου," *Kypriakai Spoudai,* XXII (1958), 14–15 (for the oath taken to the Latin bishop, *ibid.,* p. 18). Cf. also Darrouzès, "Textes synodaux," pp. 11–12, 20, 23. On the jurisdiction of the Greek bishop see Estienne de Lusignan, *Description,* p. 84. Greek bishoprics were reduced in number from 14 to 4, after 1220, in order to ensure exact congruence of Greek and Latin dioceses.

61. Richard, "Le Peuplement latin et syrien de Chypre."

It is not known to what extent any Latin monasteries replaced Greek monasteries; this was undoubtedly exceptional. It may perhaps have occurred in the case of the Benedictine monastery of the Cross in Cyprus (Stavrovouni), to which the monastery of St. Paul of Antioch was united after 1268, or in the case of the priory of Augustinian canons of Bellapais, which later adopted the Premonstratensian rule. But Latin monasticism was generally a matter of new foundations (the Cistercians of Beaulieu, and the Cistercian sisters of St. Theodore). The religious who were expelled by the Mamluk invasion transferred their communities to Cyprus: thus the Benedictine sisters of Our Lady of Tyre and of Our Lady of Tortosa were in Nicosia. Franciscans, Dominicans, and Carmelites then established the centers of their respective provinces of the Holy Land in Cyprus. The Temple and the Hospital, which were well endowed there, likewise established their seats in Cyprus, on a temporary basis, after the fall of Acre. The Teutonic Knights and the order of St. Thomas the Martyr (or the order of the English) also had headquarters there.[62]

The growth of Latin monasteries was paralleled by that of Greek monasteries. The concordat of 1222 had sought to limit the number of Greek monks, and it is possible that a part of their domains had been appropriated for the formation of fiefs. But the survival of large foundations which possessed some important domains, such as Kykkou, Mangana, Agros, Machaeras, and Enkleistra, and the two abbeys in Nicosia called "of the Men" (Andrio) and "of the Women" (Ienachio), is noteworthy. The Armenian prince Het̩oum, who had become a Premonstratensian, asked Clement V to unite Mangana to Bellapais. The inquiry prescribed by the pope had no effect, and Mangana kept its independence. Now and again the seigneuries subject to these monasteries may have had to pay tithes; the pope exempted them from doing so. Peter I was one of the benefactors of Kykkou, and Frankish nobles often gave evidence of their devotion to the monasteries. The Greek monasteries of Palestine, which like their Latin counterparts had lands on Cyprus, held on to them, as, for example, did that of St. Theodosius of the desert of Judaea and especially that of Sinai, which founded

---

62. Richard, *Documents chypriotes,* pp. 67–69, 111–120. The goods of the Temple, seized upon the arrest of the knights, whom Henry II punished severely for the help they had given Amalric of Tyre (Hugh III had already dealt with them heavily by taking the castle of La Castrie), were given to the Hospital, except for Psimolófo, which was given to the titular patriarch of Jerusalem, Anthony. The Hospital divided its share between the chief commandery (Kolossi) and the commanderies of Phínika and Tembros; in 1468, James II appears to have appropriated the revenues of these domains. Many knights of Rhodes entered his service.

a priory, St. Simeon of Famagusta, which pope John XXII endowed with privileges in 1334.[63]

There were also many small abbeys[64] which were incorporated into the Frankish seigneuries as they had been in the great Byzantine domains, with the Latin lord now becoming the monastery's patron, investing the abbot, and sometimes donating an icon or having a church built. In the towns, the families which occupied high administrative posts also founded monasteries or churches such as St. John of Bibi or St. Nicholas tou Soulouany. Christians of eastern rite also had their convents, such as those of the Jacobites at Omorphita (Morfittes) and of the Armenians at St. Macarius. The Ethiopian convent of Jerusalem itself had a priory at Nicosia.

The Cypriote monarchy, which had to get the Holy See to intervene on several occasions to support it in its difficulties, tried to reconcile its concern for keeping the peace between the different religious communities with its attachment to the Roman church. It does not seem to have had any serious problems with regard to the latter, with the exception of crises caused by the conflicts between the archbishops of Nicosia and the Greek episcopate before 1260. The kings of Cyprus seem to have tried to have Cypriote subjects provided with ecclesiastical benefices, though with only partial success.[65] Henry II tried in vain to have his chancellor Henry de Gibelet promoted to the archiepiscopal see. The brother of Janus, Hugh of Lusignan, was archbishop-elect of Nicosia, then became a cardinal (he played something of a role in the Council of Basel and took part in the negotiations between France, England, and Burgundy). But John II could not get the pope's agreement for the nomination to the same see of his bastard son James, who remained a postulant until he became king.

63. *Livre des remembrances,* no. 160, n. 1; Richard, "Un Monastère grec de Palestine et son domaine chypriote au début du XIIIe siècle," *Praktika* of the Second International Congress of Cypriot Studies (Nicosia, 1982). Marie of Ibelin founded the convent of Phaneromini in 1340 to house the miraculous cross of Tokhni. On the Latin foundations cf. Rudt de Collenberg, "Les Grâces papales, autres que les dispenses matrimoniales, accordées à Chypre de 1305 à 1378," *Epeteris,* VIII (1975–1977), 187–252.

64. Cf. N. Kyriazis, Τὰ μοναστήρια ἐν Κύπρῳ (Larnaca, 1970). A good example is Saint Sabas, in the diocese of Paphos, in the possession of Baldwin of Morphou in 1234. This abbey was the object of a proposed reform in 1306. It received a donation from James II in 1468 (*Livre des remembrances,* no. 117). The supposition that it belonged to the Latin rite in the 13th century is incorrect.

65. Rudt de Collenberg, "État et origine du haut clergé de Chypre avant le Grand Schisme d'après les registres des papes du XIIIe et du XIVe siècle," *Mélanges de l'École française de Rome: Moyen âge, Temps modernes,* XCI (1979), 197–332; idem, "Les Cardinaux Hugues et Lancelot de Lusignan et l'autonomie de l'église latine de Chypre, 1378–1467," *Archivum historiae pontificiae,* XX (1982), 23–128.

One remains struck by the loyalty which, on the whole, the peoples of the kingdom evinced for the Frankish dynasty. The only known popular rebellion was that of the peasants who rose up after the defeat of Khirokitia, electing several captains and even proclaiming one Alexius "king" at Lefkoniko: it was a sort of *jacquerie,* quite comparable to that which troubled the kingdom of France after Poitiers.[66] The chronicler Leontius Machaeras, in the fifteenth century, shows himself to be a devoted subject of the Lusignans.

The various communities experienced a gradual coming together. Kings and nobles made pilgrimages to Greek monasteries; the confessor of king Peter II, a Latin priest, visited his mother, a religious in the Greek convent of St. Mammas of Nicosia; the Dominican James ("Estienne") de Lusignan had a brother who was a Basilian; the Audeths, who belonged to the Jacobite rite, established religious services in the Latin and even the Greek rite, and left legacies to Coptic, Jacobite, Armenian, Maronite, Greek, and Latin churches. One of them even became a bishop in the Latin church.[67] The use of Greek was so widespread among the Franks that queen Charlotte spoke it better than French, and Hugh Boussat took his personal notes in Greek.[68] Latin priests had to take measures to prevent their flock from adopting customs appropriate to the Greek church.[69]

While the feudal institutions had been conceived for the purpose of strengthening the domination of the Frankish element, they gradually ceased to play this role. Greek and Syrian names penetrated little by little into the nobility, especially from the time of James II on. Rich burgesses had before that time acquired landed properties and become lords of fiefs. During the Venetian domination, the Synkletikos and the Sozomenos held first place among the liegemen,[70] but well before that time the royal administration had been filled with Greek and Syrian elements.

The feudal regime, though it endured until 1570, was probably no

66. Machaeras, *Recital,* caps. 636–637.

67. *Ibid.,* caps. 566–571; Richard, "Une Famille de 'vénitiens blancs'."

68. Edith Brayer, Paul Lemerle, and Vitalien Laurent, "Le Vaticanus latinus 4789," *Revue des études byzantines,* IX (1951), 47–105.

69. In a contrary sense, see the reflections of Leontius Machaeras respecting Thibaut Belpharage's conversion to the Latin rite (cap. 579). The reminder by Sixtus IV in 1472 of the rules imposed on Greek bishops by the *Constitutio* of 1260 (Mas Latrie, *Histoire,* III, 325–330) is evidence of the habitual transgression of those rules, especially with respect to episcopal jurisdiction. A 16th-century tradition has associated the name of Helena Palaeologina with a renewed audacity of the Greek clergy, but I believe that these transgressions were an older phenomenon.

70. This is not an isolated case, as can be seen by a quick look at the schedule drawn up by the Venetian administration between 1510 and 1521, which includes a list of those enfeoffed.

longer the essential characteristic of Cypriote institutions. Despite the rebellion of the liegemen against Peter I, the Lusignan monarchy maintained itself as the real master of the kingdom. Janus, John II, and James II governed without concern for the control of the high court, which was completely transformed by the very composition of the nobility. The Latin church, whose wealth remained restricted, no more represented a force of opposition than did the Greek church. The cities did not play a political role. The very crises which the kingdom experienced, with the exception of foreign interventions, were more the result of court intrigues and palace revolutions than of more profound movements. It was indeed the permanence of a well-established monarchy which guaranteed the stability of the kingdom of Cyprus, a mosaic of peoples, but of peoples among whom a true symbiosis was achieved up to 1489, and even beyond while under the domination of Venice.

VI

SOCIAL EVOLUTION
IN LATIN GREECE

Latin expansion into Byzantine territory — "Romania" — took place in several closely related fields: in addition to military and political aspects, it had also economic, demographic, and ecclesiastical repercussions. Military expansion with its political consequences is no doubt

Published sources, studies, and bibliographies bearing on Latin Greece are numerous. Therefore only publications with a direct bearing on the subject of this chapter are cited here, especially those which have been published in the last twenty years or so and present new evidence or interpretation.

Treatments of the history of Latin Greece or parts of it, accompanied by extensive bibliographies, have appeared in several recent studies. For the general background see the concise account by Kenneth M. Setton, "The Latins in Greece and the Aegean from the Fourth Crusade to the End of the Middle Ages," in *The Cambridge Medieval History*, IV-1, ed. Joan Hussey (1966), 389-420, 908-938, and the detailed treatment in the first volume of his *The Papacy and the Levant (1204-1571)* (Philadelphia, 1976). Jean Longnon has studied the Frankish states in Greece in his *L'Empire latin de Constantinople et la principauté de Morée* (Paris, 1949), and the same states to 1311 in volume II of the present work, pp. 235-274, and Peter Topping has dealt with Frankish Morea from 1311 to 1460 in volume III, pp. 104-166; see also Antoine Bon, *La Morée franque: Recherches historiques, topographiques et archéologiques sur la principauté d'Achaïe (1205-1430)* (2 vols., Paris, 1969), and the revised edition of Denis A. Zakythinos, *Le Despotat grec de Morée* (London, 1975; originally published in Paris and Athens, 1932-1953), with updated bibliographies in vol. I, pp. 359-371, and vol. II, pp. 381-403. Venetian Greece has been extensively treated by Freddy Thiriet, *La Romanie vénitienne au moyen-âge: le développement et l'exploitation du domaine colonial vénitien (XIIe-XVe siècles)*, 2nd ed. (Paris, 1975), with an updated bibliography, pp. 467-481; see also Louise Buenger Robbert, "Venice and the Crusades," in volume V of the present work, chapter IX. An extensive bibliography has been compiled by Manousos I. Manousacas, "L'Isola di Creta sotto il dominio veneziano: Problemi e ricerche," in *Venezia e il Levante fino al secolo XV*, ed. Agostino Pertusi (Atti del I Convegno internazionale di storia della civiltà veneziana; Florence, 1973), I-2, 473-514. On the history of the Catalans in Greece see Setton, in volume III of the present work, chapters VI and VII, pp. 167-277, and his *Catalan Domination of Athens, 1311-1388*, rev. ed. (London, 1975). Numerous studies published by Raymond-Joseph Loenertz, some of which have a bearing on the subject treated here, have been republished in his two volumes of *Byzantina et Franco-Graeca* (Rome, 1970-1978). The same holds true of the studies of Anthony Luttrell, republished in his *The Hospitallers in Cyprus, Rhodes, Greece and the West (1291-1440)* (London, 1978), and his *Latin Greece, the Hospitallers and the Crusades, 1291-1440* (London, 1982). Genoese Chios has not been treated here; on this subject, see the recent book by Michel Balard, *La Romanie génoise (XIIIe-début du XVe siècle)* (2 vols., Rome, 1978).

best known. It began in the early thirteenth century, during and following the Fourth Crusade, which was a turning-point in the political
history of Romania. Within a few years Frankish knights, the Venetian state, and several Italian adventurers acting on their own behalf
conquered extensive areas of the Byzantine empire, some of which re-

---

Among the sources reflecting the structure and evolution of society in the feudalized areas
of Latin Greece, the *Assizes of Romania* are the most important. This legal treatise compiled
in the Morea has been edited and translated into French by Georges Recoura, *Les Assises de
Romanie* (Paris, 1930); an English translation and a study of it have been made by Topping,
Feudal Institutions as Revealed in the Assizes of Romania, the Law Code of Frankish Greece
(Philadelphia, 1949). Corrections to the text and previous translations, as well as a thorough
study of the *Assizes,* have appeared in David Jacoby, *La Féodalité en Grèce médiévale: les 'Assises
de Romanie': Sources, application et diffusion* (Paris, 1971); see also *idem,* "Les Archontes grecs
et la féodalité en Morée franque," *Travaux et mémoires du Centre de recherche d'histoire et civilisation byzantines,* II (1967), 421–481, reprinted in his *Société et démographie à Byzance et en
Romanie latine (XIIIe–XVe siècles)* (London, 1975).

The Chronicle of the Morea presents a vivid description of feudal society in the Morea. On
the four versions of the *Chronicle,* of which the French seems definitely to be the original, see
Jacoby, "Quelques considérations sur les versions de la 'Chronique de Morée'," *Journal des Savants* (1968), pp. 133–189, reprinted in his *Société et démographie* (cited above); see also M. J.
Jeffreys, "The Chronicle of the Morea: Priority of the Greek Version," *Byzantinische Zeitschrift,*
LXVIII (1975), 304–350, whose claim it is impossible to accept on historical grounds. Although
at times faulty, the chronicle of Marino Sanudo Torsello, "Istoria del regno di Romania," in
Charles (Carl) Hopf, *Chroniques gréco-romanes inédites ou peu connues* (Berlin, 1873; repr.
1966), pp. 99–170, is an invaluable source for the Morea and especially the Aegean lordships
in the second half of the thirteenth century. The letters of Sanudo provide evidence by a contemporary till 1337, especially on Euboea: on their edition and dating see Jacoby, "Catalans,
Turcs et Vénitiens en Romanie (1305–1332): un nouveau témoignage de Marino Sanudo Torsello," *Studi medievali,* ser. 3, XV (1974), 217–223.

Documentary evidence on the Morea for the reigns of Charles I and Charles II of Anjou,
kings of Sicily, who from 1278 on interfered directly in the life of the principality, is to be found
in Riccardo Filangieri *et al.,* eds., *I Registri della cancellaria angioina,* vols. I–XXXII (Naples,
1950 ff.), which supersedes all previous publications of documents from the Angevin archives
of Naples; for the period of Charles II see also Charles Perrat and Longnon, *Actes relatifs à
la principauté de Morée, 1289–1300* (Paris, 1967). Longnon and Topping, *Documents sur le régime des terres dans la principauté de Morée au XIVe siècle* (Paris, 1969), provides invaluable
evidence on landholding, agricultural exploitation, and the status of the peasantry, which cor-
roborates the information found in the *Assizes of Romania*; see also Jacoby's review in *Byzantinische Zeitschrift,* LXIX (1976), 87–92. Ernst Gerland, *Neue Quellen zur Geschichte des lateinischen Erzbistums Patras* (Leipzig, 1903), includes documents on the Morea and Venetian
Messenia dealing with similar problems.

In view of the position of Venice in the eastern Mediterranean and particularly in Latin
Greece, it is not surprising that Venetian documents should be of utmost importance for the
whole area. They await an exhaustive examination, and most of them remain unpublished. Official documents or summaries thereof are included in the following publications (only the main
ones are mentioned here): *Urkunden zur älteren Handels- und Staatsgeschichte der Republik
Venedig mit besonderer Beziehung auf Byzanz und die Levante,* ed. Gottlieb L. F. Tafel and
Georg M. Thomas (Fontes rerum austriacarum, Diplomataria et acta, XII–XIV; 3 vols., Vienna,
1856–1857; repr. Amsterdam, 1964), and Roberto Cessi, *Deliberazioni del Maggior Consiglio
di Venezia* (3 vols., Bologna, 1931–1950), up to 1300; Giuseppe Giomo, *I 'Misti' del senato della
republica veneta, 1293–1331* (Venice, 1887). Georg M. Thomas and Riccardo Predelli, *Diploma-

mained for two centuries or more under Latin rule; such was the case with Crete, most of the Peloponnesus (Morea), Attica, Boeotia, and Euboea, as well as numerous other islands of the Aegean. This chapter deals with these areas of Greece down to about 1450.

In the political sphere, the most striking result of the Latin con-

---

tarium veneto-levantinum (2 vols., Venice, 1880-1899), and Constantin N. Sathas, *Documents inédits relatifs à l'histoire de la Grèce au moyen âge* (9 vols., Athens and Paris, 1880-1890), for the period from 1300 on. Thiriet, *Régestes des délibérations du sénat de Venise concernant la Romanie* (3 vols., Paris, 1958-1961), and *Délibérations des assemblées vénitiennes concernant la Romanie* (2 vols., Paris, 1966-1971), cover the whole period.

Venetian documents bearing exclusively on Crete have been published by Spyridon M. Theotokes, *Apophaseis Meizonos Symbolou Venetias, 1255-1689* (Athens, 1933), and *Thespismata tēs Venetikēs Gerousias, 1281-1385* (2 vols., Athens, 1936-1937), and for the last seventy of the years treated here, by Hippolyte Noiret, *Documents inédits pour servir à l'histoire de la domination vénitienne en Crète de 1380 à 1485* (Paris, 1892). Numerous files have been preserved in the Archivio del Duca di Candia, a section of the Archivio di Stato in Venice. A selection from these documents has been made by Gerland, *Das Archiv des Herzogs von Kandia* (Strassburg, 1899), and by Johannes Jegerlehner, "Beiträge zur Verwaltungsgeschichte Kandias im XIV. Jahrhundert," *Byzantinische Zeitschrift*, XIII (1904), 435-479. Systematic publication of files by the "Comitato per la pubblicazione delle fonti relative alla storia di Venezia" is slowly proceeding. P. Ratti Vidulich has edited two volumes of public documents: *Duca di Candia, Bandi (1313-1329)* (Venice, 1965), and *Duca di Candia, Quaternus Consiliorum (1340-1350)* (Venice, 1976). Freddy Thiriet has edited *Duca di Candia, Ducali e lettere ricevute (1358-1360; 1402-1405)* (Venice, 1978). Numerous unpublished documents appear in Giorgio Fedalto, *La Chiesa latina in Oriente*, vol. 3: *Documenti veneziani* (Verona, 1978).

Notarial documents reflect accurately the rhythm of daily life and provide insight into social and economic structures and institutions. Several hundred notarial registers are preserved in the Archivio del Duca di Candia; only five have been published so far, the last four in the Venetian "Fonti" series: Antonino Lombardo, ed., *Imbreviature di Pietro Scardon (1271)* (Turin, 1942); Mario Chiaudano and Lombardo, eds., *Leonardo Marcello, notaio in Candia (1278-1281)* (Venice, 1960); Raimondo Morozzo della Rocca, ed., *Benvenuto de Brixano, notaio in Candia (1301-1302)* (Venice, 1950); Lombardo, ed., *Zaccaria de Fredo, notaio in Candia (1352-1357)* (Venice, 1968); Salvatore Carbone, ed., *Pietro Pizolo, notaio in Candia (1300)* (Venice, 1978). Elisabeth Santschi has summarized several files of judicial and administrative documents, which are equally valuable, in *Régestes des arrêts civils et des mémoriaux (1363-1399) des archives du duc de Crète* (Bibliothèque de l'Institut hellénique d'études byzantines et postbyzantines de Venise, 9; Venice, 1976). Loenertz, *Les Ghisi, dynastes vénitiens dans l'Archipel, 1207-1390* (Florence, 1975), has edited and commented on an important selection of documents and other sources bearing on Crete and the Aegean islands. The same author has summarized, edited, and commented on numerous documents in several studies republished in his *Byzantina et Franco-Graeca,* especially I, 329-369, 503-536, and II, 141-393. The fifteenth-century work of Laurentius de Monachis, *Chronicon de rebus Venetis ab U.C. ad annum MCCCLIV* (Venice, 1758), is based on an intimate knowledge of documents and is most precious for Cretan history. For Catalan Greece the reader will consult the almost exhaustive collection by Antoni Rubió i Lluch, *Diplomatari de l'Orient català (1301-1409)* (Barcelona, 1947); the dating of twenty documents has been corrected by Loenertz, "Athènes et Néopatras: Régestes et notices pour servir à l'histoire des duchés catalans (1311-1394)," *AFP,* XXV (1955), 100-212, reprinted in his *Byzantina et Franco-Graeca,* II, 183-393.

Papal correspondence bearing on the Roman and Greek churches and relations between their members has appeared mainly in the calendars published by the École française de Rome; for details see Leonard E. Boyle, *A Survey of the Vatican Archives and of its Medieval Holdings*

quest was the extreme fragmentation of Romania after 1204, in marked contrast to the earlier unity of Byzantium. To a large extent, this fragmentation explains the diversity of the political and social regimes instituted by the Latins, as well as the nature and orientation of the

---

(Toronto, 1972), esp. pp. 123–127; see also the volumes edited on behalf of the PC, Fontes, ser. 3: *Vaticani* (Vatican City, 1943-1960, and Rome, 1961 ff.).

Until recently only moderate attention has been devoted to the social history of Latin Greece. This chapter aims at reconstructing the dynamics of social evolution resulting from the encounter of Latin conquerors and settlers with the indigenous population, overwhelmingly Greek; for lack of space, small minorities such as the Jews, the Slavs, the Albanians, and the Armenians have not been treated here. Besides, an attempt has been made to study feudalized and nonfeudalized areas in a comparative framework. This method has enabled us to trace Byzantine continuity in the social, legal, and institutional spheres. With the help of material relevant to Latin Greece it has thus been possible to supplement the available documentation on Byzantine Greece before 1204. This approach is illustrated in three recent studies by Jacoby, whose views differ on many points from those of previous authors: "The Encounter of Two Societies: Western Conquerors and Byzantines in the Peloponnesus after the Fourth Crusade," *American Historical Review,* LXXVIII (1973), 873–906; "Une Classe fiscale à Byzance et en Romanie latine: les inconnus du fisc, éleuthères ou étrangers," *Actes du XIVe Congrès international des études byzantines,* II (Bucharest, 1975), 139–152; and "Les États latins en Romanie: Phénomènes sociaux et économiques (1204–1350 environ)," *XVe Congrès international d'études byzantines, Rapports et co-rapports,* I: *Histoire,* sect. 3 (Athens, 1976). The present chapter relies heavily on these studies, all reprinted in Jacoby's *Recherches sur la Méditerranée orientale du XIIe au XVe siècle: Peuples, sociétés, économies* (London, 1979), as well as on the same author's other studies already cited above; see also Jacoby's "Les Gens de mer dans la marine de guerre vénitienne de la mer Egée aux XIVe et XVe siècles," in *Le Genti del mare Mediterraneo,* ed. R. Ragosta (= *XVII Colloquio internazionale di storia marittima, Napoli, 1980*) (Naples, 1981), I, 169–200. On society in Byzantine Greece shortly before the conquest and on Frankish Greece, see the studies by Jacoby just mentioned.

Recent work on the Byzantine upper class in general is by Aleksandr P. Kazhdan, *Social'nyi sostav gospodstvujushchego klassa Vizantii XI–XII vv.* (Moscow, 1974) [in Russian]; *The Byzantine Aristocracy IX to XIII Centuries,* ed. Michael Angold (BAR International Series, 221; Oxford, 1984), and especially Angold, "Archons and Dynasts: Local Aristocracies and the Cities of the Later Byzantine Empire," *ibid.,* pp. 236–253. On Byzantine Greece in particular see Judith Herrin, "Realities of Byzantine Provincial Government: Hellas and Peloponnesos, 1180-1205," *Dumbarton Oaks Papers,* XXIX (1975), 253–284. Antonio Carile, "Sulla Pronoia nel Peloponneso bizantino anteriormente alla conquista latina," *Zbornik Radova,* XVI (1975), 55–61, has contested the conclusions of Jacoby on the *pronoia.* On Frankish Greece see also Longnon, *Les Compagnons de Villehardouin: Recherches sur les croisés de la quatrième croisade* (Geneva and Paris, 1978), a mine of information on many of the Frankish conquerors and their family background; this work, however, requires additions and corrections. See also Gherardo Ortalli, *Da Canossa a Tebe: Vicende di una famiglia feudale tra XII e XIII secolo* (Padova, 1983).

On the class ethos of the Franks and the Greek feudatories in Morea see Jacoby, "La Littérature française dans les états latins de la Méditerranée orientale à l'époque des croisades: Diffusion et création," in *Essor et fortune de la chanson de geste dans l'Europe et l'Orient latin: Actes du IXe Congrès international de la Société Rencevals pour l'étude des épopées romanes (Padoue-Venise, 1982)* (Modena, 1984), pp. 617–646, and *idem,* "Knightly Values and Class Consciousness in the Crusader States of the Eastern Mediterranean," *Mediterranean Historical Review,* I (1986), 158–186. On landholders and peasants see also Angeliki E. Laiou-Thomadakis, *Peasant Society in the Late Byzantine Empire: a Social and Demographic Study* (Princeton, 1977), who refers to the pre-1204 period and Frankish Morea, yet does not always offer convincing interpretations, and Topping, "Le Régime agraire dans le Péloponnèse latin au XIVe siècle," *L'Hellén-*

economic activity and demographic currents in this area after 1204. Although the conquest resulted in a definite break in the political sphere, it did not bring about a similar phenomenon in the social or economic field. Latin Romania witnessed the encounter of various ethnic com-

---

isme contemporain, ser. 2, X (1956), 255–295, reprinted in his *Studies on Latin Greece A.D. 1205–1715* (London, 1977). Carile, *La Rendita feudale nella Morea latina del XIV secolo* (Bologna, 1974), is a partly unsuccessful attempt to deal with the society and the economy of the Morea; cf. Jacoby's review in *Byzantinische Zeitschrift,* LXXIII (1980), 356–361. See also Carile, "Rapporti fra signoria rurale e *despoteia* alla luce della formazione della rendita feudale nella Morea latina del secolo XIV," *Rivista storica italiana,* LXXXVIII (1976), 548–570.

On the Aegean see Silvano Borsari, *Studi sulle colonie veneziane in Romania nel XIII secolo* (Naples, 1966), which should be corrected and supplemented by Jacoby, *La Féodalité,* part III, and "Catalans, Turcs et Vénitiens" (both cited above). In addition to his synthesis on the Venetian empire, Thiriet has published numerous articles, several of which are now available in his *Études sur la Romanie gréco-vénitienne (Xe–XVe siècles)* (London, 1977); see especially "La Condition paysanne et les problèmes d'exploitation rurale en Romanie gréco-vénitienne," previously published in *Studi veneziani,* IX (1967), pp. 35–70, and "Villes et campagnes en Crète vénitienne aux XIVe–XVe siècles," reprinted from *Actes du IIe Congrès international des études du sud-est européen,* II (Athens, 1972), 447–459. See also Borsari, *Il Dominio veneziano a Creta nel XIII secolo* (Naples, 1963), which includes numerous excerpts of unpublished documents. Santschi has dealt in several studies with legal problems in Crete; two of them are particularly relevant: *La Notion de "feudum" en Crète vénitienne (XIIIe–XVe siècles)* (Montreux, 1976), is useful on the status of military tenures in Crete, but mistaken about "feudalism" in the island. Her study on "Quelques aspects du statut des non-libres en Crète au XIVe siècle," *Thesaurismata,* IX (1972), 104–136, is partly based on unpublished sources; it requires emendation on many points. Although dealing mainly with a later period, B. J. Slot, *Archipelagus turbatus: les Cyclades entre colonisation latine et occupation ottomane c. 1500–1718* (2 vols., Istanbul, 1982), proves useful for our purposes.

Setton has written on society in Catalan Greece in his *Catalan Domination* and in "Catalan Society in the Fourteenth Century," *Essays in Memory of Basil Laourdas* (Thessalonica, 1975), pp. 241–284. On the early years of the Catalan Company in the duchy see Jacoby, "La 'Compagnie catalane' et l'état catalan de Grèce: Quelques aspects de leur histoire," *Journal des Savants* (1966), pp. 78–103.

Slavery in the eastern Mediterranean is treated in the recent work by Charles Verlinden, *L'Esclavage dans l'Europe médiévale,* II (Ghent, 1977), which supersedes all his previous studies on the subject; see also Elizabeth A. Zachariadou, *Trade and Crusade: Venetian Crete and the Emirates of Menteshe and Aydin (1300–1415)* (Venice, 1983).

Various aspects of social, economic, and religious antagonism or accommodation between the Latins and the Greeks have been treated in numerous publications cited above and also recently in the following studies: Topping, "Viticulture in Venetian Crete (XIIIth C.)," *Fourth International Cretological Congress (1976), Acta,* II (Athens, 1981), 509–520; *idem,* "Co-existence of Greeks and Latins in Frankish Morea and Venetian Crete," republished in his *Studies on Latin Greece.* Thiriet, "La Symbiose dans les états latins formés sur les territoires de la *Romania* byzantine (1202 à 1261); phénomènes religieux," was, like the previous one, a paper for the *XVe Congrès international d'études byzantines, Rapports et co-rapports,* I, sect. 3 (Athens, 1976); see also *idem,* "Églises, fidèles et clergés en Crète vénitienne (de la conquête 1204/1211 au XVe siècle)," in *Fourth International Cretological Congress, Acta,* II, 484–500; in addition, Fedalto, *La Chiesa latina in Oriente,* I (2nd rev. ed.; Verona, 1981), and III (mentioned above); Setton, *The Papacy* (cited above). See also Laiou, "Quelques observations sur l'économie et la société de Crète vénitienne (ca. 1270–ca. 1305)," in *Bisanzio e l'Italia: Raccolta di studi in memoria di Agostino Pertusi* (Milan, 1982), pp. 177–198, and her "Observations on the Results of the Fourth Crusade: Greeks and Latins in Port and Market," *Medievalia et humanistica,* n.s., XII (1984),

munities as well as social groups and classes. The Latin conquerors
faced an indigenous population, predominantly Greek, whose social
structure, institutions, legal traditions, and mentality differed from their
own. The encounter of westerners and Byzantines resulted in continuity
in certain spheres, a break in others, and accommodation elsewhere.
An investigation of the character, stages, and limitations of this encounter requires a survey of the structure of Byzantine society before
1204, an examination of the Latin impact, and an evaluation of the
social, legal, and institutional evolution generated in both societies by
the conquest.

Recognition of the clear-cut distinction between slaves and free
men is fundamental to the understanding of Byzantine society.[1] Legally, all free men were equal; in practice, however, obvious social and
economic differences existed, yet they did not generate legal classes,
as in the west at the same period. The same holds true of imperial
privileges granted on an individual basis or collectively: the grantees
remained justiciable according to Byzantine common law. The classification of free men as "powerful" (*dynatoi*) or "weak" (*ptochoi*)
lacked precision. It is indicative of the absence of a rigid system of
social stratification and of well-defined legal classes; this was still the
case in the twelfth century. A restricted measure of social mobility
enabled men of lowly origin to gain access to the elite by displaying
efficiency in the imperial administration or the army, or by serving
powerful men. The status of the *paroikos* or dependent peasant was
somewhat exceptional in the Byzantine framework; although legally
free and answerable as such to public courts, he was subject also to
personal restrictions and was tied to his lord by links of dependence
of a legal nature.

In the western provinces, as elsewhere in the empire, land was the
major source of wealth, power, and prestige. Society was essentially
rural in character. It was dominated by an upper class lacking legal
definition, embracing great landlords, imperial officials, and imperial
dignitaries. The use of the term "archon" for all these powerful men

---

47–60. A. R. Lewis, "The Catalan Failure in Acculturation in Frankish Greece and the Islamic
World during the Fourteenth Century," *Viator*, XI (1980), 361–369, does not point to the main
reasons for this phenomenon, examined below.

This study has been prepared with the help of a grant provided by the American Philosophical
Society in 1977, and has been revised and updated since.

1. On Byzantine society and the archontes see Jacoby, "The Encounter," pp. 875–876, 879–
883, and "Les États latins," pp. 4–7, where the reader will find extensive bibliographical references. See also Kazhdan, *Social'nyi sostav*. On the Slav archontes of the Peloponnesus see below,
note 14.

clearly indicates that they were often identical. One occasionally would make a distinction between the rich landlord or *ktematikos archon* and the official in charge of civilian administration or the military officer, known respectively as *thematikos* and *tagmatikos archon,* who exercised authority from the urban center over a district which at times was limited to a city and its neighboring territory. In certain cases the emperor recognized the authority and traditional status of the chiefs of foreign populations which had settled in the empire; by conferring on them imperial titles, he strengthened their position. It is therefore not surprising that they too were considered as archontes. This was the case with the chiefs of Slav groups who preserved their tribal structure in the Peloponnesus, such as the Melings of Mount Taygetus.

The great provincial landlords were not content with the power deriving from their estates. In order to enhance their prestige and social ascendancy they strove to acquire administrative or military functions within the imperial machine of government or honorary titles in the imperial hierarchy. Imperial grants of offices and court titles ensured their coöperation. On the eve of the conquest, several great landlords of Crete and the Peloponnesus bore court titles, and some had close relations with the imperial court. A Cretan archon who was a *magistros* and "friend of the emperor" traveled to Constantinople and persuaded Isaac II Angelus (1185–1195) to grant an estate to the bishop of Calamona (Retimo) for his lifetime.[2] Leo Sgouros, an archon of Nauplia in the Peloponnesus, married the daughter of ex-emperor Alexius III Angelus (1195–1203) in 1204. The association of the archontes with the church was often quite close, since some of their relatives served as church dignitaries or officials. Besides, the patronage of ecclesiastical institutions enhanced their prestige and, occasionally, also their income, whenever they obtained the management of these institutions and their property.

Powerful archontes also developed in their own interests a network of personal bonds of dependence, yet these always retained their private nature and were never recognized by law or sanctioned by custom. They were thus basically different from western vassalage. Dependents, real or fictitious relatives, and allies occasionally constituted a large family or a real clan.[3] It is within this framework that the *archontopouloi* of Crete and the Peloponnesus were to be found. In the early thirteenth century, these were not just "sons of archontes", but a par-

2. See text in Borsari, *Il Dominio,* p. 18, note 26.
3. See an example *ibid.,* p. 60: in the late thirteenth century, four *famiglie* were supposed to include about two thousand *prole* or descendants.

ticular group situated at a lower rank than the archontes within the social elite.

Although landed property constituted the principal source of their income, many archontes resided in cities, especially in those which served as administrative, military, or ecclesiastical centers, such as Athens, Thebes, Monemvasia, Corinth, or Nauplia. Those who lived within the urban enclosure of a *kastron* or the fortified acropolis overlooking a city were sometimes called *kastrenoi* or "dwellers of a fortified city", as in Athens. Yet not all archontes lived in urban centers. The leaders of the Slav populations of the Taygetus and most of the Cretan archontes presumably resided on their rural estates, in the midst of their followers and dependents; such would also be the case after the Latin conquest. It has already been mentioned that occasionally the emperor granted privileges to individuals, to ecclesiastical institutions, or collectively to the inhabitants of a city or territory, like those of Monemvasia. These privileges, which were mostly of a fiscal nature, did not entail a definitive alienation of state prerogatives or the development of private jurisdiction.

Among the various grants awarded, the *pronoia* has drawn particular attention.[4] Literally "provision", it consisted of a concession of state revenues to an individual who collected them directly; to effect this the emperor transferred to the recipient certain peasants and the imperial land they cultivated. The *pronoia* originated in the late eleventh or early twelfth century and became more widespread under emperor Manuel I Comnenus (1143–1180). It has been claimed that the *pronoia* was the counterpart of the western fief, the basis of the imperial military system, and a major factor in the so-called "feudalization" of the empire, which allegedly led to its downfall. Furthermore, the similarity between a *pronoia* and a fief supposedly explains why the Latin conquerors found it so easy to adapt to Byzantine conditions. The foregoing examination of Byzantine society has already emphasized that it differed fundamentally from feudal society. For our purpose here it is essential to discover how widespread the *pronoia* was in the late twelfth and early thirteenth centuries in the regions of Greece conquered by the Latins.

It is rather striking that no contemporary source ever mentions the existence of *pronoiai* or *pronoia* holders. A privilege delivered in 1183 by the duke of Crete, Constantine Ducas, confirmed the property of George Skordilis and his brothers, members of an archontic family.

---

4. On the *pronoia* see Jacoby, "The Encounter," pp. 876–879, with bibliographical references to previous work on the subject.

Pronoiai are mentioned in the preamble of this document, together with patrimonial estates, in what clearly appears to be a current formula used by the imperial administration. The provisions of the privilege mention, however, only hereditary property. The preamble may therefore provide evidence as to the existence and diffusion of the *pronoia* in the empire, although not to its extent. It certainly does not prove that *pronoiai* were to be found in Crete before 1204, nor can one deduce this from a grant of Cretan imperial land made in 1170–1171.[5] The main argument in favor of a wide diffusion of the *pronoia* in the empire before 1204 rests on the Greek version of the *Chronicle of the Morea.* However, this is a late source deriving from a French original; it obviously reflects conditions existing in the second half of the fourteenth century in the principality of the Morea, an area feudalized after its conquest by the Frankish knights. The Greek *Chronicle* was presumably composed between 1341 and 1388 by a Greek archon who was firmly integrated into the class of feudatories of the principality.[6] His work is therefore not a valid source for a description of Byzantine social and institutional realities at the time of the conquest, about a century and a half earlier. In view of his social standing, it is not surprising that the author was familiar with feudal institutions. His use of *pronoia* as the equivalent of fief and of archon as the counterpart of knight may be explained by the absorption of the archontes into the feudal hierarchy of the Morea, as well as by the evolution of the Byzantine *pronoia* in the period of the Palaeologi and the knowledge thereof in the principality; indeed the *pronoia* gradually evolved into a hereditary tenure, its military nature became more pronounced, and it then resembled the western fief more than it previously had.[7]

It should also be noted that the *Assizes of Romania,* a legal treatise compiled in the Morea between 1333 and 1346, had retained various provisions of Byzantine law as they existed before the Latin conquest.[8] There is no trace, however, of the *pronoia.* Although called fiefs, the landed estates of the Greek archontes of the Morea mentioned in the Assizes were not analogous to Frankish fiefs, nor were they subject to feudal law; their transfer and succession, as well as the constitution

5. See Jacoby, "Les États latins," p. 7–8.

6. See Jacoby, "Quelques considérations," pp. 150–158 and 187 on this version; Jeffreys, "The Chronicle of the Morea," pp. 304–350, attempts to prove that the prototype was written in Greek. It is impossible, however, to deal with the subject only on a literary and philological basis. The social context has to be taken into account, and it is unlikely that Greeks should have praised the deeds of the Franks before the latter did so.

7. See especially Jacoby, "Les Archontes grecs," pp. 429–439.

8. See Jacoby, *La Féodalité,* pp. 75–82, on the dating of the *Assizes,* and pp. 32–38, on Byzantine law therein.

of a dower, reveal that they were in fact patrimonial estates governed by Byzantine law. To sum up, there is no evidence of the *pronoia* before 1204 in the territories of Greece conquered by the Latins.[9] This is rather surprising, considering the general evidence for its existence in the Byzantine empire. Specific references to Greece may be lacking because sources bearing on this region are scant, or because the diffusion of the *pronoia* in the empire may have been more limited, quantitatively and geographically, than is commonly assumed; at any rate, it is quite obvious that the *pronoia* was not the dominant form of possession of landed property at this period. The possible annexation of *pronoiai* by local archontes who assimilated them to their patrimonial estates is also to be taken into account, especially in the political context of the period immediately preceding, and contemporaneous with, the Latin conquest, with the disappearance of the curbing restraint of the imperial authority.

There can be no doubt that the weakening of the imperial government after the death of Manuel I Comnenus in 1180 enabled the expansion of the large estates, both lay and ecclesiastical, especially at the expense of the small landholders and the state. In 1198 Michael Choniates, the metropolitan of Athens, accused the *kastrenoi* inhabiting this city of using coercion to acquire land in the surrounding countryside. This evolution was accelerated at the time of the Latin conquest. Virtually independent for a few years, the great archontes were able to seize estates of the fisc and, in the Peloponnesus, also appanages of members of the imperial family, as well as property of Constantinopolitan monasteries.[10] It may be conjectured that the grant of such land to their followers enhanced their prestige and authority. The annexation of *pronoiai* at this period is not to be excluded. The Latin conquerors consulted Byzantine cadastral registers with the help of archontes, as in the Morea,[11] and gathered oral evidence, as in Crete, which enabled them to detect instances of fraud.[12] It was thus possible

9. See Jacoby, "Les Archontes," pp. 451–463; this is also the case in the areas of Coron and Modon and in the rest of the southern Peloponnesus which came under Venetian rule in 1207: *ibid.,* pp. 426–427, 438–439. Carile, "Sulla pronoia," claims that the *pronoia* existed in the Morea before 1204. However, he (on p. 58) does not take into account that the rules of succession to the "fiefs" of the archontes were entirely different from those applying to fiefs in the areas from which the knights originated.

10. On these estates in the Peloponnesus see Jacoby, "Les Archontes," pp. 423–427.

11. See the French version of the *Chronicle of the Morea, Livre de la conqueste de la princée de l'Amorée, Chronique de Morée (1204–1305),* ed. Longnon (Paris, 1911), pars. 107, 120, and the Greek Chronicle, *Chronikon tou Moreos,* ed. John Schmitt (London, 1904), verses 1649–1650, 1831–1835.

12. Texts in Borsari, *Il Dominio,* p. 17, note 26.

to discover evidence of the usurpation of land that had belonged to the imperial fisc, yet no trace of *pronoiai* was found. It may be that in the cadastral registers annexed *pronoiai* had been disguised as patrimonial estates; as they were already inscribed before 1204 under the name of their beneficiaries, such deception would have been easier than for other land. This conjecture is no doubt tempting, yet only direct evidence will enable us to ascertain the existence and diffusion of the *pronoia* in the areas of Greece conquered by the Latins. For the time being, such evidence is lacking.

The collapse of the Byzantine provincial government shortly before 1204 also had other consequences: the great archontes took over its military, fiscal, and judicial prerogatives.[13] Especially those who were invested with imperial power or bore court titles took advantage of the new situation.[14] Leo Chamaretos ruled in 1205 over Sparta and the neighboring countryside; Leo Sgouros inherited the tyrannical power of his father in Nauplia and extended his sway over Argolis and the city of Corinth, where another archon succeeded him; in the southern Peloponnesus, yet another archon from the area of Modon convinced Geoffrey of Villehardouin to conquer the peninsula together with him. In Crete the heads of great archontic families fully exercised state prerogatives in the areas which they controlled. The social standing of these archontes, the means at their disposal, their ascendancy over their clients and dependent peasants, and the support they offered to the Greek clergy facing the Latin church, all marked them as leaders of the Greek resistance to the conquerors.[15]

In the region under consideration here, it is practically impossible to get a clear view of the groups of society situated below the archontes and *archontopouloi*. Sources referring to city-dwellers other than the archontes are totally lacking. Many questions concerning the status of the peasantry remain unresolved. Peasants subject to a lord or to an ecclesiastical institution and settled on their land were known as *paroikoi*. An issue hotly debated in recent years is whether there still existed free peasants paying fiscal dues directly to the state, or whether these peasants had all been assimilated to the *demosiarioi*

---

13. On the general situation in the area see Herrin, "Realities of Byzantine Provincial Government"; the author somewhat underestimates the role of the independent archontes.

14. The leaders of Slav groups settled in the Peloponnesus had long before been granted court titles and fiscal privileges, and their traditional status and authority had thereby been strengthened: see the case of the Melings in Hélène G. Ahrweiler, "Le Sébaste, chef de groupes ethniques," *Polychronion, Festschrift Franz Dölger zum 75. Geburtstag* (Heidelberg, 1966), pp. 35–38.

15. See Jacoby, "Les États latins," p. 11.

paroikoi or dependent peasants of the state.[16] Twelfth-century evidence from Crete does not help to clarify the matter. A charter of 1197 deals with the donation of property by a Cretan to the monastery of Patmos, where the grantor became a monk. According to another charter, drafted in 1193, the vendors of a vineyard had first offered it to the holders of adjoining plots, in accordance with Byzantine law, so as to enable them to exercise their right of preëmption (*protimēsis*); thereafter, the vendors had asked two imperial officers for permission to proceed with the sale. At first glance, this would seem to indicate that they were *paroikoi* of the state, yet no such conclusion can be reached. The two Cretan charters do not inform us about the status of either the grantor or the vendors. Moreover, various sources indicate that the donation and sale of property, as well as the exercise of the right of preëmption, were not peculiar to free peasants. Finally, the transfer of immovable property was severely controlled by the state, as such property was liable to fiscal dues; this may explain why imperial officials intervened in the sale of 1193. Thus the evidence of the two Cretan charters remains inconclusive.[17] The rather meager twelfth-century sources on the Byzantine peasantry in general may be supplemented with later data from areas conquered by the Latins; this procedure is justified by the fact that various provisions of Byzantine law were preserved and applied under their rule.

There can be no doubt that even before 1204, the subjection of the *paroikos* to his lord had become very tight. The subjection of the *paroikos* may have become binding one year after he had been settled by a lord on his land. The acquisition by the lord of definitive rights to his person and that of his descendants was achieved after a period of thirty years, during which the peasant fulfilled his fiscal and manorial obligations. The exercise of a thirty-year prescription is not documented directly for the twelfth century, yet it can be inferred from later sources bearing on Latin Romania. Moreover, it is quite likely that this prescription was already applied in the eleventh century, if not earlier.

---

16. Opposing views have been expressed by George Ostrogorskij, *Quelques problèmes d'histoire de la paysannerie byzantine* (Brussels, 1956); by Johannes Karayannopulos, in his review of this study in *Byzantinische Zeitschrift*, L (1957), 167–182; and recently in *idem*, "Ein Problem der spätbyzantinischen Agrargeschichte," *Jahrbuch der österreichischen Byzantinistik*, XXX (1981), 207–237, where he also deals with the pre-1204 period; this author claims that no dependent peasantry existed in Byzantium. Laiou-Thomadakis, *Peasant Society*, pp. 142–222, 264 (especially 142–158), is of the opinion that the hereditary status of the *paroikos* was not extended to all his offspring before the fourteenth century; this would imply that the subjugation of the *paroikos* to his lord in territories held by the Latins was an innovation introduced by the conquerors. For a different interpretation, see below.

17. See Jacoby, "Les États latins," pp. 11–12.

The calculation of the thirty-year period extended not only to the subjection of the dependent person, but also to that of his descendants, at least of his male offspring. This confirms that the status of the *paroikos* was permanent during his lifetime, as well as hereditary. The *paroikos* remained legally free, in strict accordance with Byzantine law, as is clearly illustrated by the fact that he had access to, and testified in, imperial courts. Occasionally he was transferred from one lord to another, yet he could not escape his social status, while paradoxically the slave became free when emancipated by his lord. When the *paroikos* had severed the link of subjection by migrating afar and was no longer inscribed on the cadastral registers as belonging to the estate of his lord, he became "unknown to the fisc" or "free" (*eleutheros*), that is, free of any specific fiscal obligations toward the state and of dependence on a specific lord. It should be emphasized that this "freedom" was only of a fiscal nature, and was temporary; it did not extend to the social status of the *paroikos,* which remained permanent and hereditary. Indeed, the imperial administration considered the *eleutheros* as a *paroikos* of the state or *demosiarios paroikos,* and the same rule applied to persons previously not subjected to any lord, but unable to explain their fiscal status: the assimilation of the latter group to the *paroikoi* of the state implies that the Byzantine peasantry as a whole was of dependent status. The temporary nature of the "freedom" enjoyed by the *eleutheros* is illustrated by the procedure implemented by the imperial administration: once located, he was settled on imperial or state land, or else granted to an individual or an ecclesiastical institution, and became again liable to fiscal dues. He was thereby fully reintegrated into the class of the *paroikoi.*[18]

Two documents seem to contradict the assumption that the status of the *paroikos* had already become hereditary before 1204. Imperial privileges delivered respectively to the monastery of Lavra on Mount Athos in 1079 and to that of Eleousa in Macedonia in 1156 granted them the right to increase the number of *paroikoi* exempted from fiscal dues whom they held in their subjection; the additional peasants were to be selected from among their descendants.[19] The exercise of imperial rights over the descendants would seem to indicate that they did not belong to these institutions. A closer examination of these documents reveals, however, that the provisions of the grants aimed only

18. On the *eleutheros* see Jacoby, "Une Classe fiscale," pp. 139–152.

19. Texts in Paul Lemerle, André Guillou, and Nicolas G. Svoronos, *Actes de Lavra,* I [*Archives de l'Athos,* V] (Paris, 1970), pp. 215–219, no. 38, and Louis Petit, "Le Monastère de Notre Dame de Pitié en Macédoine," *Izvestija russkago arkheologicheskago instituta v Konstantinopole,* VI (1900), 28–29, 32–40; see also Ostrogorskij, *op. cit.,* pp. 28–30.

at the creation of additional exempted fiscal units. For this purpose, peasants could of course have been recruited, as in other cases, among the *paroikoi* of the state or the *eleutheroi,* who were temporarily free of tax payments and of subjection to a specific lord. The imperial government was reluctant, however, to grant manpower which it considered as belonging to the state. Instead, it was stipulated that the new fiscal units should be constituted by peasants who were already established on the monasteries' lands. The issue was thus exclusively of a fiscal nature. The status of the descendants of the exempted *paroikoi* was not at stake, and no change in their status was contemplated: they were *paroikoi* of the monasteries before the imperial grants were made, and remained so afterwards.

It is already evident by now that the subjection of the *paroikos* to his lord entailed severe restrictions on his freedom. The lord could prevent him from leaving his land. However, migration did not necessarily sever the link to the lord; subjection was maintained as long as the *paroikos* paid the customary dues incumbent upon the fiscal unit for which he was responsible. The link of the *paroikos* to his lord was thus of a personal nature; he was not tied to the soil. Some degree of mobility among the *paroikoi* is indeed attested. In certain cases, it was due to economic incentives; in others, it was prompted by the urge of the *paroikos* to find a spouse: the high excess of males in many villages, as well as ecclesiastical prohibition of marriage between relatives, inevitably led to exogamy. It is therefore not surprising that members of the same family appeared occasionally in villages of the same lord or on the estates of neighboring landlords, as well as in a nearby city.[20]

The economic and fiscal unit or *stasis* headed by the dependent peasant was liable to taxes known as *telos,* as well as to labor services or *angareia* which he owed to the state; they were occasionally transferred by the emperor to an individual or an ecclesiastical institution. As a rule, the *stasis* included land. An eleventh-century legal decision rendered by the *magistros* Cosmas specified that land held according to the *paroikikon dikaion* or "law of the *paroikos*" belonged to the lord and could not be alienated by the *paroikos.*[21] In practice, however, it was inherited, divided among heirs, or partly granted in dower. It may be assumed that in all these cases the lord did not object and possibly even agreed to the transfer of property, as long as the land was held

20. See Jacoby, "Phénomènes de démographie rurale à Byzance aux XIIIe, XIVe et XVe siècles," *Études rurales,* V-VI (1962), 177, 180–181, 184 (reprinted in Jacoby, *Société et démographie*).
21. Text in Fedor I. Uspenskij, *Actes de Vazelon* (Leningrad, 1927), pp. xxxv–xxxvi. No such problem arose when land was held under a lease, as legal conditions were then duly specified.

by people subject to him and the obligations of the fiscal unit were fulfilled. Restrictions on the rights of the *paroikos* to his lord's land did not prevent him from acquiring full ownership of land and other property by purchase or through agricultural contracts; some of these provided for the division of newly planted trees or vines between the lord on whose land they were grown and the peasant who had supplied the labor. Thus the *paroikos* could come into possession of free property even on his own lord's land. Yet if the dependent peasant died without heirs of his body, his lord succeeded to the entire immovable property situated on his domain, as well as to his chattels; this was a further mark of the *paroikos*'s subjection to his lord.[22]

The impact of the Latins on this Greek society was particularly marked in the fields of political organization and social structures closely linked to each other. The nature of the encounter of conquerors and conquered varied, however, according to the nature of the new ruling elite. Some territories were conquered by knights who imposed a feudal superstructure upon Byzantine society; other territories came almost directly under the rule of Venice or the Catalans, both with nonfeudal elites; and some territories went first through a phase of feudal rule before being occupied by Venice.

In the territories belonging to the first category, such as the Morea and the duchy of Athens, feudalism was introduced by knights who came mainly from the county of Champagne and the duchy of Burgundy;[23] in these areas of the west, feudalism was then in full bloom. In Euboea, which belonged to the third category of territories, it was introduced by knights from Lombardy and Tuscany, areas where feudalism was in regression as a result of the fierce onslaught of the communes. In many islands of the Aegean, Italian knights from these same areas, and the Venetians, imposed feudal institutions upon local society.[24]

Despite significant differences in their respective backgrounds, the French and Italian knights and the Venetian lords of the Aegean brought with them political institutions and traditions, as well as attitudes and values, common to the whole of the feudal elite in the west toward

22. See Jacoby, "Les États latins," pp. 13–14. On these agricultural contracts see Jacoby, *La Féodalité*, p. 37 and note 4; they were similar to the *complant* or *métayage* found in the west in the same period, yet in Byzantium they generated property rights.

23. See Jacoby, *La Féodalité*, pp. 29–30, 82–83, 85–86. Longnon, *Les Compagnons de Villehardouin,* shows that many crusaders were relatives or neighbors; others were vassals of the powerful feudatories.

24. See Jacoby, *La Féodalité,* pp. 185 ff., 237–239, 248–252, 271–293.

the end of the twelfth century.[25] In the areas from which they came (except for the city of Venice) society was strictly stratified, social status being virtually synonymous with legal status and transmitted by inheritance. Each class was governed by its particular legal system. Social promotion involving the crossing of class boundaries was largely restricted to the lower strata of society, when servile peasants became free. Promotion to the upper class of society was rendered most difficult by the development of class-consciousness within the ranks of the feudatories, illustrated by the ceremony of dubbing and the evolvement of the nobility into an order, with its specific rituals, morals, and obligations, as well as a particular life-style and mentality. Personal bonds of a private nature, backed within the knightly class by vassalage, provided the backbone of social and political hierarchy, while judicial and legislative authority, as well as the right of taxation, were essentially vested in private hands; the concept of a state was alien to the minds of the members of the knightly class.

All these features of political institutions and social structure were transplanted by the feudal elite to Greece. Prerogatives exercised by the Byzantine imperial government until a few years before the conquest passed into the hands of the upper echelons of the Latin knightly class. The feudal hierarchy is best known in the principality of Achaea. At most, it had only three ranks below the prince: there were his direct vassals, whether liege men or feudatories of simple homage; among the liege men the barons enjoyed a special position as his tenants-in-chief. In turn, all the liege men of this first rank could have vassals of their own, and so too could those of the second rank. Social differentiation within this Frankish elite was pronounced, and the gulf between vassals of simple homage and greater feudatories was especially marked; members of the lowest stratum, among whom sergeants were included, were not members of the knightly class. This fact goes far to explain the gradual integration of Greek archontes within their ranks and, in some cases, even within the ranks of the knightly class. Besides, Italians of non-noble descent also gained access to this class, whose nature thus evolved in the course of the thirteenth and fourteenth centuries.

A hierarchy of fiefs corresponding to that of the feudatories, knights

---

25. For what follows see Jacoby, "The Encounter," pp. 883–885, 887–888, 890, 901–902. On the integration into the feudal hierarchy of Slavs and, exceptionally in 1263, of Turkish leaders who were baptized see *ibid.,* pp. 900–901. The description of the feudal hierarchy in the present work, vol. II, p. 249, should be corrected. The social ethos of the knights was reflected in their life style, the books they read, and the literary works they composed, as well as in the wall paintings that adorned their mansions: see Jacoby, "La Littérature française" and "Knightly Values".

as well as sergeants, was also instituted. As the conquest proceeded, Latin knights assisted by Greeks consulted the Byzantine cadastral registers and divided into feudal tenements land previously held by the Byzantine fisc, the crown, and ecclesiastical institutions housed in Constantinople, land perhaps partly usurped by local archontes. The same holds true of the estates of absentee archontes or those opposing Latin rule, as well as numerous ecclesiastical properties, parts of which were secularized on various occasions. Enfeoffment of knights and mounted sergeants was restricted, however, by the prince and the barons, who were eager to preserve their political, social, and economic ascendancy. Many knights held only one fief, the standard yearly revenue of which was about 1,000 hyperpers, or part of a fief, and mounted sergeants half a fief or even less. The existence of money-fiefs and household knights further emphasizes the precarious standing of many feudatories and their dependence upon their lords.[26]

The feudal class in the Morea was more numerous than in other areas of Latin Greece and displayed strong cohesion, stability, and continuity. All these factors help to explain the important role of the Morea, especially after 1248 when its prince William II of Villehardouin received from emperor Baldwin II suzerainty over the islands of the Aegean. The main vassals of the prince, including the triarchs (*terzieri*) of Euboea, the lords of Tenos and Myconos, and the dukes of the Archipelago, participated in court gatherings convened by him and, from 1278, occasionally by his representative or bailie; they also took part in military expeditions. They were thereby closely associated with the progressive growth and diffusion in their own territories of a body of law transcribed in the *Assizes of Romania,* whose final version in French was compiled between 1333 and 1346. This private legal treatise was based partly upon custom, imported by the conquerors from their native countries as well as from the Latin empire of Constantinople and the Latin kingdoms of Jerusalem and Cyprus, where the Latins faced political and military circumstances similar to those of the Morea, and existed in a virtual state of perpetual war. In addition, the influence of royal Capetian legislation and of the Angevin kingdom of Sicily is perceptible in the *Assizes*. Byzantine private law applicable to family possessions and agricultural exploitation, as well as various rules concerning the *paroikos* or dependent persons, were also incorporated, although the conquerors severely restricted their use when it conflicted with seignorial prerogatives. Finally, the *Assizes of Romania* also embody legislation emanating from the princely court, and

---

26. See Jacoby, "The Encounter," pp. 886–887.

legal principles based on sentences pronounced by various courts of the principality. As a result of immigration after the conquest, *burgenses* or non-nobles, coming mostly from Italy, soon constituted the majority of the Latin population in the Morea. Political power remained, however, in the hands of the knightly class, and the regime instituted by the conquerors bore a decisively feudal imprint. The *Assizes of Romania* faithfully reflect the social, legal, and political realities of Frankish Morea.[27] This was not the case in all the territories of the Aegean where the *Assizes* were applied. In several of them, the process of "feudalization" was quite limited; it nevertheless had an impact on the structure of Greek society.[28]

Other territories of Romania were conquered by non-feudal elites and therefore did not witness the imposition of a feudal regime. Such was the case in areas which came under the sway of Venice; in them the commune made use of feudal institutions and terminology which it had previously applied in its territories of the Latin Orient, as in the region of Tyre. This was the case when in 1207 Venice ceded Corfu to ten members of old Venetian families, with extensive prerogatives, and in the territories around Coron and Modon, two ports in the southern Morea. Feudal terminology was also applied in Crete after 1211, the year in which Venice began the colonization of the island, which it intended to keep under its direct rule. The settlers who belonged to the old Venetian families were called in Crete *milites* or *feudati,* knights or feudatories; they were provided with military tenements called *militiae, cavalleriae,* or *feuda,* for which they owed mounted military service. The *popolani* or members of non-noble families were given smaller tenures called *serventariae* or sergeantries, liable to service on foot.

Yet the use of this terminology should not be mistaken for the introduction in Crete of a feudal regime, which was totally alien to the social and political structure of Venice and the mentality of its citizens. This is clearly illustrated by the system of government imposed upon Crete and the areas of Coron and Modon. The rule of Venice in these territories not only succeeded that of Byzantium; in many respects it also bore a striking similarity to that of the empire, and contrasted markedly with the feudal regime introduced in other Greek territories. The supreme and direct authority of the state remained unrestricted, and expressed itself in numerous spheres. Venice inherited the estates of the Byzantine fisc and its *paroikoi* or villeins (*villani*),

---

27. See Jacoby, *La Féodalité,* pp. 21–91.
28. See below, p. 200.

as well as the ownership by the state of the floating peasant population. The commune also confiscated Greek imperial monasteries and two thirds of the other Greek ecclesiastical estates, keeping one third for itself and apportioning the rest in military tenements for Latin settlers. The grant of these tenements in Crete, as well as in southern Messenia, where they seem to have been rather rare, did not restrict the authority of the state, nor did they imply any privatization of its rights and prerogatives in the judicial or fiscal spheres, as in feudalized areas. These prerogatives were exercised by means of a highly centralized administration, closely supervised by the metropolitan authorities.[29] Venetian law was enforced in all spheres and supplemented by rules adapted to the specific needs of each Venetian territory.[30]

In 1311 the duchy of Athens too was subjugated by non-feudal conquerors, members of the so-called Catalan Company, who settled exclusively in cities. The feudal regime and institutions introduced by the Frankish knights were immediately abolished, as was the use of the *Assizes of Romania*. In a way, it was as if the conquerors had succeeded directly to Byzantine rule; this was certainly the case in southern Thessaly, which was conquered by the Catalans in 1318 and 1319. At the outset, authority was vested entirely in the hands of the Catalan Company, whose institutions were supplemented by the customs of Barcelona, presumably introduced soon after the conquest; this reflects the urban character of the Catalan conquerors. No wonder, therefore, that their attitude toward the indigenous population was similar to that of the Venetians. The legal and social framework reflecting this attitude, which they created in 1311–1312, was maintained by the Catalans, in spite of their acceptance in 1312 of the kings of Sicily as supreme rulers. Sicilian rule introduced two new factors in the life of the duchy. Royal authority evidently curtailed that of the Company, which was nevertheless maintained as a corporation composed exclusively of Latin settlers and representing their predominantly urban interests. Besides, Sicilian rule introduced feudalism into the duchy. This complex regime persisted as long as the Catalan duchy existed.[31]

---

29. See Thiriet, *La Romanie,* pp. 120–133; Borsari, *Il Dominio,* pp. 27–30, 32–33, 39–40, 45–46, 109–110, 124–125; Jacoby, *La Féodalité,* pp. 225–226, 295–297, and "Une Classe fiscale," pp. 139–152; Thiriet, *La Romanie,* pp. 215–224, 251–254, deals with administration.

30. *Ibid.,* pp. 235–241. On the rules applying to military tenures in Crete see Santschi, *La Notion de "feudum",* pp. 93–167. The conditional character of these tenures and the feudal terminology applied in Crete do not warrant the conclusion of Santschi (*op. cit.,* especially pp. 185–212) that Venice introduced feudalism in the island. The basic characteristic of feudalism, the privatization of state prerogatives, is totally missing in Crete; see below.

31. See Setton, *Catalan Domination,* especially pp. 79–98, 151–165, and "Catalan Society in Greece," pp. 242–278, 283–284. On the early legislation of the Company and the continuity

The island of Euboea or Negroponte, as well as those of Tenos and Myconos, about which we are less informed, may be included in the third category of territories alluded to above. Euboea was conquered in 1205 by Boniface of Montferrat and his vassals, who prevented Venice from taking possession of the two thirds of the island it had been promised by the other leaders of the Fourth Crusade in the treaty of March 1204. During the whole of the thirteenth century, except for the years 1255–1262, the authority of Venice in Euboea was restricted to its quarter in the city of Negroponte, which was progressively extended. Although Venice actively intervened in the political and feudal affairs of the island, whose main feudal lords were its vassals from 1211 on, it wielded no direct authority over their fiefs. It is only around 1323 that Venice began its territorial expansion in the island, which culminated in 1390 with rule over the entire island.[32] At first, feudalism had coexisted in the island with Venetian rule. The imposition of the latter in areas previously governed by a feudal elite created a complex social, legal, and institutional regime, especially as Venice had to take into account existing structures. This is clearly borne out by its use of the *Assizes of Romania,* which were translated into the Venetian dialect, presumably in Euboea in the late fourteenth century. At the insistence of the feudal lords of the island, a version of the *Assizes of Romania* prepared by an official commission was sanctioned by the Venetian senate in 1452, and its dispositions acquired legal force. It soon became the only binding treatise of feudal law not only in Euboea, for which it had been prepared, but in all Venetian colonial territories, including even Corfu, which had never had any political or feudal link with the principality of Achaea. The continuity of feudal law was thereby ensured. It was applied by feudal lords as well as by Venice to feudatories, feudal tenements, and villeins. Byzantine private law regulated the civil affairs of the Greek population, restricting thereby the use of Venetian law. On the other hand, Venetian criminal and commercial law were fully enforced, as in Crete and southern Messenia.[33] A similar complex system prevailed in areas of Frankish Morea annexed by Venice, such as Nauplia and Argos in 1389, the hinterland of Coron and Modon from 1420 on, and Tenos and Myconos in 1390.[34]

The Latin population established on Byzantine soil during the pe-

---

of its institutions see Jacoby, "La 'Compagnie catalane'," pp. 87–103; on the nobility, feudalism, and the communes see Loenertz, "Athènes et Néopatras," pp. 155–212.

32. See Jacoby, *La Féodalité,* pp. 185–203, and "Catalans, Turcs et Vénitiens," pp. 217–261.
33. See Jacoby, *La Féodalité,* pp. 95–113, 201–211, 260–270, 297–299, 308.
34. *Ibid.,* pp. 213–252.

riod of the conquest was gradually reinforced in numbers by migration, and its composition became more diversified.[35] Except for the feudatories hailing from Capetian France, most new settlers, nobles as well as commoners, had lived in urban centers in the west, mainly in Italy, and were accustomed to urban life and occupations. It is therefore not surprising that they established themselves mainly in the cities of Latin Greece, especially in harbor cities, the centers of its most intense economic activity.[36] This was also the case with the settlers whom Venice sent to Crete: in addition to rural military tenements, they were provided with houses in Candia or in Canea. These settlers resided only temporarily in the villages assigned to them. In Euboea many feudatories lived in the city of Negroponte. Even knights originating from feudal areas in the west, though accustomed to a different lifestyle, favored urban settlement. True, some of them lived in isolated mountain castles or fortified rural mansions, although they resided occasionally in the houses they held in cities. Most of them, however, lived in the repaired or enlarged acropolis or *kastron* of a city or elsewhere inside the city walls, whether in the Morea or in the duchy of Athens. Significantly, after their conquest of the duchy in 1311 the Catalans acted in the same way and succeeded their Frankish predecessors in such fortified areas.

It is obvious that preference for urban settlement cannot be explained solely by economic considerations. Psychological factors of a more general nature also exerted a powerful influence in this respect: the tendency of the Latin conquerors and the western settlers who joined them to cluster behind the walls of a fortified city or acropolis arose from the urge for security of a minority group, conscious of its isolation in the midst of a numerous local Greek population. Events in Crete justified this feeling and clearly illustrate this phenomenon of aggregation: whenever a Greek rebellion threatened them, the Latins abandoned their rural holdings and took refuge in the cities.[37] It is therefore not surprising that Venetian settlement policy was aimed at increasing the numbers of Latins in urban centers. This is illustrated by the building in Crete of a new city, Canea, as well as by the grant of houses to Venetian settlers in the island in the thirteenth century, already mentioned, and even more markedly in the following century. In 1301 twenty-four Venetian families were sent from Venice to Coron

35. For what follows see Jacoby, "Les États latins," pp. 19–20.

36. Nevertheless, some Latins resided permanently in the rural area, close to Candia, where they engaged in land cultivation and the raising of animals: see Topping, "Co-existence of Greeks and Latins," p. 19.

37. An example of 1285 in Borsari, *Il Dominio,* pp. 82–83.

and Modon in order to reinforce the number of Latins residing in these cities. In 1340 Venetian citizenship restricted to Romania was granted to the Latins inhabiting the Venetian quarter of the city of Negroponte and to others who would settle there. In 1353, after the Black Death, Venice promised full and unrestricted citizenship to Latins willing to settle with their families for a period of at least ten years in the cities of Candia, Canea, Retimo, and Sitia in Crete, of Coron and Modon in the Morea, or in the Venetian quarter of Negroponte.

For lack of adequate sources, it is impossible to assess the relative numbers of the Latins and Greeks, yet the available information points to the fact that Latins remained a small minority. According to a list compiled around 1225, the principality of Achaea comprised 170 knight-fiefs and could muster some 450 mounted men. A report written in 1338 or somewhat later assessed at more than one thousand the number of knight-fiefs existing in the principality and territories subject to the suzerainty of the prince of Achaea. Even if accurate, this number is rather unimpressive, especially if the dispersion of the feudatories is taken into account. Moreover, it would be erroneous to multiply this number by a family coefficient in order to calculate the total knightly population. As all long-distance, voluntary, and individual migration is sex-selective, men accounted for an overwhelming majority among the knightly settlers; many of them arrived without a family, and subsequent immigration of relatives did not basically change the sex ratio (number of men to 100 women) within this group. The situation in this respect was worsened by the powerful class-consciousness of the feudal nobility and of the nobles hailing from Venice and other Italian cities who adopted their social ethos. Social exclusiveness, especially marked in the small group of the barons, was expressed in their matrimonial policy. Several Moreote knights married daughters of noble families in areas in the west from which they originated and later brought them over to Greece. Most of them, however, wedded Latin noblewomen from the eastern Mediterranean whose families had come from Venice, other Italian cities, France, or neighboring areas. The smallness of the knightly class and its predominantly male composition, as well as frequent marriages in its midst, gradually increased the problem of consanguinity which restricted marriage within the group, or threatened the validity of marriages already contracted. Economic considerations no doubt further limited the chances of marriage opportunities within the same group. It is significant that in 1336 pope Benedict XII justified his dispensation for a marriage in Negroponte within the forbidden degrees of consanguinity by stressing the small number of Latin nobles and his desire to prevent intermarriage with Greeks.

In Venetian Crete, the organized and imposed migration of families inaugurated in 1211, reinforced by voluntary migration, eliminated at the outset the impediment of consanguinity. Yet the groups of settlers sent from Venice to Crete were also small. In 1211 it was decided to establish 132 *militiae* and 408 sergeantries: thus the arrival of 540 families or some 2,500 persons was contemplated. However, the settlers who arrived in successive waves in 1211, 1222, 1233, and 1252 did not reach these numbers. This is confirmed by the holding of military tenements by Latins who were not Venetians, although initially only the latter were to hold them; the acquisition of several *militiae* or sergeantries by one settler also points to the same conclusion. In spite of a constant trickle of Latin settlers, the Latin population of the cities of the Venetian empire remained quite small. In 1302 Canea was almost totally empty; the year before, 24 Venetian settlers with their families, a small number indeed, departed for Coron and Modon. The population of Coron amounted in 1401 to 480 inhabitants, of whom only 80 were Latins. In the cities of the Catalan duchy of Athens, even the most populous, the Latins may not have numbered more than a few hundred.[38]

As a result of the conquest, society in Latin Romania was divided into two distinct groups: on the one hand, the Latin conquerors and the western immigrants who joined them; on the other, the indigenous Greeks and Slavs. Religious affiliation did not constitute an important factor in the relations between the members of the two communities, yet it became a basic criterion of social stratification and individual status, providing a convenient means of group identification. The Latins were those who recognized the authority of the Roman church and enjoyed the status of freemen, hence *Francus,* synonymous with *Latinus,* also meant free. The indigenous society remained faithful to the Byzantine church. It underwent a considerable change, although some thirteenth- and fourteenth-century sources seem to imply the contrary, and its internal structure was altered. In conformity with their own political and institutional traditions and concepts, the Frankish knights conceived of society as strongly stratified, each class being governed by its own set of laws. They therefore translated social realities into legal terms and ascribed to the local society a socio-legal system similar to the one proper to a feudal society. Conquerors of urban origin, such as the Venetians and the Catalans, applied a similar social stratification to the local population. On the whole, Greeks and Slavs, peas-

---

38. See Jacoby, "Les États latins," pp. 20–22.

ants and presumably city-dwellers, were relegated to the rank of villeins, regardless of their status before the conquest.

Those who escaped the process of debasement and leveling constituted numerically only a marginal element in the indigenous society: such were the archontes, the *archontopouloi,* and a few other Greek or Slav free men, as well as emancipated villeins or slaves. Thanks to their wealth, their social ascendancy, and their life-style, as well as to the fiscal exemptions they enjoyed occasionally at the time of conquest, the archontes differed considerably from the rest of the local population. They became under Latin rule a socio-legal class enjoying hereditary status and privileges. Only those who had belonged to their group, and their descendants, benefitted from this evolution; once defined, their class became practically sealed and crossing its boundaries presumably impossible. The *Assizes of Romania* forbade free Greek archontes to unfree villeins; the same holds true in Venetian Crete. The free status of archontes and *archontopouloi* is illustrated by the fact that some of them were granted military tenures. In the treaty of 1299 between Venice and Alexius Callerges, they appear alongside the Latins among those enjoying complete freedom. Moreover, the distinction between them and the villeins was recognized by Venetian courts.[39]

In spite of the cleavage existing between the conquerors and the local population, archontes and *archontopouloi* were gradually integrated, in varying degrees, into the Latin social elite. In Frankish Morea, where they were particularly numerous, this integration began at the time of the conquest, when they submitted themselves to the authority of, and performed homage and swore an oath of fealty to, the leaders of the conquerors. On a personal and legal level they were integrated among the feudatories owing simple homage, the lowest stratum in the feudal hierarchy. Yet this integration did not affect the status of their patrimonial estates, which remained hereditary and were governed as before the conquest by Byzantine law. Toward the middle of the thirteenth century the integration of several archontes proceeded beyond this first stage; they were endowed with feudal tenements, many of them quite small, which were governed by feudal law. Some archontes were even dubbed by princes or barons; as a result, they became knights and were assimilated from a legal point of view to the liege men, their new status being hereditary. In this way they achieved so-

---

39. See Jacoby, "The Encounter," pp. 889–891, and "Les États latins," pp. 23–24. Only archontes who had sufficient proof of their status were recognized as such. This was not the case with Theodore Makrembolites, who fled from Constantinople in 1204 and became a *paroikos* in Corfu: see Demetrius Chomatianus, ed. Jean B. Pitra, *Analecta sacra et classica spicilegio solesmensi parata,* VI (Rome, 1891), col. 228, no. L.

cial integration within the feudal nobility. Their holding of non-feudal land exempt from military service produced some resentment against them in the ranks of the Latin feudatories in the first half of the four-teenth century. Nevertheless, their integration continued unabated and even gained considerable impetus as time passed.

Two factors prompted the princes and barons to loosen the rigid system of social and legal stratification imposed by the Latin conquerors: the growing need for administrative personnel capable of handling the complex Byzantine fiscal system and the Greek documentation, and the lack of sufficient military forces, due especially to a decline in the number of Frankish feudatories. In the second half of the fourteenth century, the integration of some of the Greek archontes expressed it-self in their subjective identification with the values, attitudes, and class-consciousness, as well as the cause and history, of the Latin knights who had conquered the Peloponnesus and other members of their class. This is well illustrated in the Greek version of the *Chronicle of Morea,* composed between 1341 and 1388. Yet the very existence of this ver-sion, no doubt intended for Greek-speaking feudatories, emphasizes that a cultural gap persisted between Greek archontes and Frankish feudatories. Moreover, several passages in this version emphasize the distinction between Greeks and Latins, especially in the religious sphere, although the author seems to have been an Orthodox Greek who ac-cepted the supreme authority of the Roman church. Indeed, the reli-gious distinction between Latins and Greeks persisted, in spite of some manifestations of religious symbiosis which will be discussed below. Intermarriage between members of the two groups must have remained rare, certainly not common enough to obliterate Greek identity. Mixed marriages were contracted by members of the highest echelon of feu-dal society, obviously for political reasons, while others involved members of the lowest stratum of the non-noble feudatories, as im-plied by the *Assizes of Romania* (arts. 75, 125, 180). Illegitimate chil-dren born of Greek mothers who were villeins could not gain access to the feudal class, as Moreote feudal law provided that in such cases "the offspring follow the status of the mother" (art. 174).[40]

The eagerness of the archontes and other Greeks to achieve integra-tion within the Latin elite may be ascribed to economic as well as so-cial motivation. The conquerors confirmed their patrimonial estates and their hold on the peasants needed for their cultivation, which con-stituted the foundations of their power and social ascendancy, and en-dowed them with fiefs. These moves lifted the archontes to the level of

40. See Jacoby, "The Encounter," pp. 891–899, and *La Féodalité,* pp. 30–32, 108.

the Frankish feudatories and enhanced their social superiority within their own community. Administrative and military considerations already mentioned induced the princes and the barons of the Morea to encourage this process, thereby ensuring the loyalty, coöperation, and services of the Greek elite. As a result, the Greek population was deprived of an upper class willing to join the Greek church in its opposition to the Latins and to take the lead in this opposition, or to favor the Byzantine expansion in the Peloponnesus begun in 1262.[41]

A similar process of integration, although somewhat different in nature, took place in the lordships of the Aegean. The conciliatory approach of Marco I Sanudo, duke of the Archipelago (1207–1227), toward the Greeks was expressed in his religious policy and illustrated by the willingness of twenty Cretan archontes to leave their native island and join him in 1213. The smallness of the class of Latin conquerors and archontes in the duchy no doubt led, from an early stage, to the integration of Greeks of a lower rank into the class of the feudatories. The Ghisi, lords of Tenos and Myconos, awarded tenements to Greeks and Latins whom they bound to be their vassals and whom they "ennobled" in return for military service. The imposition of feudal terminology and rules constituted a legal fiction, both useful and necessary. Yet no change occurred in the economic activity of these Greek feudatories, who continued to till their land. Their particular status and social promotion produced, however, a new stratification within the indigenous society.[42]

The Venetian implantation in Crete, begun in 1211, was based on the military colonization of the island. It led to an expropriation of church land and the estates of several archontes which drove the Greeks to rise against Venice in 1212. This first rebellion ended with the departure of twenty archontes from the island, yet most of their class remained in Crete. The division within their ranks, which dated back to the period preceding the conquest, prevented them from forming a united front against Venice, thus enabling the commune to rally them progressively to its cause by granting them various concessions. The settlement reached by Venice in 1219 with two rebel leaders may be considered as the first stage in the integration of the archontes within the ranks of the Latin elite. The commune granted each of them a half *militia* in return for military service, an annual payment, and a promise of loyalty. In all respects, the two archontes were assimilated to the Latin holders of military tenements, yet at the same time they retained

---

41. See Jacoby, "The Encounter," pp. 897–903, and his "Knightly Values," pp. 163–179.
42. See Jacoby, *La Féodalité,* pp. 242–250, 284.

their patrimonial estates, as well as their social position in Greek society. The same Venetian policy was applied on several occasions after 1219. In 1224 two *militiae* were granted; in 1233, several others; and in 1252 Greeks were to be endowed with some of the fifteen available; in 1265 two *militiae* and five and a half sergeantries, each a sixth of a *militia,* were again granted. In 1299 Alexius Callerges obtained the restitution of confiscated *militiae,* and the commune granted him four more and allowed him to buy nine others, two to six of which were designated for his followers.

As in the feudal Morea, Venice integrated the archontes, yet according to its own interests, social structure, and institutions. The process of integration initiated in Crete in 1219 therefore differed markedly on many counts from that in the principality. It was neither progressive nor generalized, but took place in stages, and archontes enjoyed it only in exceptional instances, as a result of specific agreements arrived at with Venice after uprisings or as a reward for services rendered to the commune. The number of archontes benefitting from integration was therefore limited, although it steadily increased during the thirteenth century. The endowment of their followers with military tenements enhanced the social standing of the upper ranks of the archontes; so did their concern for the villeins oppressed by Latin masters, as well as for those who supported their successive rebellions and whose emancipation they managed to obtain or preserve, respectively. The concessions regarding villeins granted by Venice in 1299 to Alexius Callerges were particularly extensive. Venice even recognized the validity of the sentences pronounced by Alexius and the judges he had appointed during his long revolt, and he was allowed to receive voluntary payments and services from Greeks. All this implies considerable social ascendancy, not only over Greeks who were his followers or directly subjected to him, but also over Greeks subjected to Latin holders of military tenements or to the commune. It is therefore obvious that a network of social ties headed by the archontes existed alongside the social and legal relationship recognized by Venice.

The slow pace at which Venice succeeded in rallying the archontes to its cause explains the continuous role of the Greek church as a focus of opposition to foreign rule, both on a religious and on an ethnic level, and as a source of Greek popular resentment against the Latins. The alliance of the archontes with the Greek church, which enhanced their prestige, was also strengthened by the support lent on several occasions by the Byzantine emperors, such as John III Vatatzes and the Palaeologi, to those who rebelled. Although Venice granted military tenements to archontes in the thirteenth century, it remained suspicious of the Greeks. In principle, military tenements could be alienated only in favor of Venetians, but in practice other Latins also acquired them; alienation was strictly controlled, however, especially in order to prevent Greeks from acquiring land held by Latins or by the commune. It is thus obvious that Greeks holding military tenements could do so only with the approval of the Venetian authorities. It is significant that Venice demanded hostages to ensure the implementation of agreements, at times even from the same archontes to whom it granted *militiae*. In view of this ambivalent attitude, one of the concessions granted to Alexius Callerges in 1299 commands particular attention: the right of Alexius and those who had followed him during the rebellion to marry into Latin families. In order to evaluate properly the scope of this privilege, its context should be closely examined.[43]

There can be no doubt that Venice implemented a policy of segregation in Crete. To be sure, marriages of prominent Venetians with Greek women had already taken place earlier in the century and in some cases may have been favored by Venice. Such was certainly the case, for instance, with that of Marco Venier, holder of a *militia* in Crete, who by marrying the daughter of the Greek archon Nicholas Eudaimonoïannes acquired Cerigo in 1238 and thereby ensured Venice's control over this island.[44] George Ialina, holder of a sergeantry or sixth of a *militia* in 1271, if not earlier, married into a branch of the Venetian Gradenigo family in this period.[45] Yet when the daughters of Manuel Dragondopoulos were granted in 1272 the right to marry Latins, this was no doubt considered a major concession made by the commune.[46]

In 1293 Venice forbade all Latins holding military tenements or other land to marry into Greek families and threatened them with the loss of all their estates and with banishment from the island if they did so. Venice obviously feared that these estates might be transferred to Greeks who married Latin women. The decree stating this policy of

43. See Jacoby, "Les États latins," pp. 26–29; Borsari, *Il Dominio veneziano,* pp. 75–77, has assembled evidence about non-Venetian and Greek holders of *militiae* or *sergenteriae* in the thirteenth century.

44. See Chryssa A. Maltézou, "Le Famiglie degli Eudaimonoiannis e Venier a Cerigo dal XII al XIV secolo: Problemi di cronologia e prosopografia," *Rivista di studi bizantini e slavi,* II (1982), 208–210, 217. Cerigo was lost to emperor Michael VIII between 1261 and 1275. A member of the Venier family recovered the island between 1301 and 1309, again by marrying the daughter of a local archon: *ibid.,* pp. 212–216.

45. On the Ialinas and their economic activities in this period see Topping, "Co-existence," pp. 18–19, and Laiou, "Quelques observations," pp. 194–197. In 1301 George's son Catarinus had already attained his majority, hence the holding of the *sergenteria* by George at an earlier period.

46. Text in Cessi, *Deliberazioni del Maggior Consiglio,* II, 155, no. 72.

segregation in 1293 implied that such marriages were nevertheless taking place, although the commune was then fighting Alexius Callerges. In 1274, during the uprising of the Chortatzes clan, the commune decreed that rebellious *vasmuli* would be banished from Crete or, if found in the island, reduced forever to the status of villeins of the commune. These offspring of marriages to, and especially illegitimate unions with, Greek women, obviously were considered free, a fact confirmed by the agreement of 1299 in which they are mentioned alongside the archontes, the *archontopouloi,* and the Latins. According to Venetian practice in Crete, only the offspring, whether legitimate or not, of a Latin or a free Greek father was considered free.

Various sources seem to imply that most *vasmuli* of the upper class were the illegitimate children of Latin fathers and Greek mothers. The excess of men in the Latin population in Crete at all its social levels may well explain unions, legitimate and especially illegitimate, with Greek women. In 1319 Scopelleto Tiepolo was recognized as the illegitimate son of James Tiepolo, who had been duke of Crete in 1298, and of a Greek mother who presumably was a villein; his free status was confirmed by the authorities. In 1318 two Chortatzes attempted to prove, with the help of Greek and Latin witnesses, that they were "Latins and sons of Latins and Venetians"; they too were probably illegitimate sons of Venetian fathers. In 1302 the feudatories of Canea protested against the holding of military tenements and offices, to which they alone were entitled, by *vasmuli* and Greeks, as well as against the participation of members of these two groups in the assembly of the feudatories. Various sources seem to indicate that these *vasmuli* were favored by the Venetian officers in charge in Crete because they were the sons of Venetian noblemen, such as the Tiepolos mentioned above.

Obviously, the holding of military tenements did not ensure Greek archontes of social integration within the Latin elite. The eagerness of the Callerges and their subordinate archontes to contract mixed marriages is therefore understandable, yet the number of such marriages remained quite small, limited, it seems, to the Callerges of Milipotamo, whose members married into the noble Venetian families of Sagredo and Zeno. Other archontes remained within their own community, especially those refusing to accommodate themselves to Venetian rule; intermittent rebellions broke out in the area of Canea, and Venice remained suspicious. The acquisition by Greeks of Latin military tenures was prohibited in 1319, and in 1334 the authorities prevented Greeks from acquiring the estates of Andrew Callerges, who had died while heavily in debt. In spite of the favoritism displayed by Venetian officers toward some Greeks, few sat in the great council of Candia.[47] In the fifteenth century Venice remained as intransigent as before about segregation, and persisted in opposing the participation of Greeks in Venetian assemblies and their holding of high administrative offices. A decree to this effect was issued in Crete in 1422.[48]

It has been claimed that the agreement concluded in 1299 by Venice with Alexius Callerges opened the way to a reconciliation between Venice and the Greek community of Crete, which eventually, in the second half of the fourteenth century, generated an alliance of Venetian feudatories with the Greek archontes.[49] It is significant that members of the Gradenigo and the Venier families, who had intermarried with Greek archontic families, plotted against Venice in 1355 and were among the leaders of the Cretan rebellion in 1363. Their attitude, however, does not seem to have been shared by the majority of the Latin feudatories of the island. Nor should we be deceived by the measures they adopted in 1363. The substitution of the standard of St. Titus, patron of Crete, for that of St. Mark, patron of Venice, the license granted to Greeks to become priests if they wished, and the adoption of the Orthodox rite by Leonard Gradenigo were all measures dictated by the circumstances of the revolt and the opposition to Venice. They did not derive from a progressive rapprochement between Venetian and Greek elites (at best limited in scope), but reflected the opportunism of the Venetian leaders of the rebellion, who were fully aware of the ascendancy of the Greek archontes over their followers and dependents and of the absolute need to ensure their support.

Venice also strongly opposed the unions, whether legal or not, of Latins and Greeks within ranks of society other than the elites, yet could not entirely prevent them. Some Latin notaries and craftsmen married Greek women in the late thirteenth and early fourteenth century, learned Greek, and became hellenized, and this phenomenon no doubt increased in scope in the following period. The appearance of *vasmuli* in 1274 and 1299 as a particular group is no doubt significant, yet this is no indication as to their numerical importance. At any rate, they did not constitute a homogeneous social group; in all likelihood many, if not most, of them were illegitimate children of Latin fathers. Unlike the sons of Venetian noblemen mentioned above, the *vasmuli* whom Venice hoped to recruit for its armies in 1365, along with Turks and slaves, were no doubt the offspring of illegitimate mixed

47. See Jacoby, "Les États latins," pp. 29–31.
48. See Thiriet, *La Romanie*, p. 402.
49. *Ibid.*, pp. 135, 276–277, 301–302.

unions at the lowest ranks of society. Nevertheless Venice reacted strongly when in 1369 the authorities discovered that many Italian mercenaries recruited during the great Cretan rebellion of 1363–1366 had married Greek women of the island. The considerations which prompted Venice to oppose such unions were different from those involving members of archontic families; evidently Venice feared that women of lowly origin would escape their unfree status by marrying free men and that their marriage to the latter would undermine the mercenaries' allegiance to the state. It therefore dismissed in 1371 all mercenaries married to local Greek women, as well as all Greeks serving in the Venetian armies.[50]

This examination of the social evolution in Crete leads to the conclusion that Venice persisted in its policy of segregation there, although it could not effectively enforce its ban on intermarriage at all levels of Cretan society. The religious policy implemented by the commune in Crete also points to the continuity of its segregationist attitude. Venice considered the Latin church an instrument of government, indispensable for the strengthening of its rule over former Byzantine territories. It was to serve the interests of the state, and therefore the Venetian authorities interfered in ecclesiastical appointments and closely supervised the activity of the Latin and Greek churches. Venice was well aware of the strong opposition of the Greeks, especially the Greek clergy, to any attempt to persuade them to join the Roman church or to enforce the union of the churches proclaimed in 1369 and 1439. On the whole, therefore, it refrained from supporting any action to this effect for fear of unrest. In fact, few Greeks joined the Latin church. Venetian suspicions were aroused by Greek religious unrest, constantly stimulated by the arrival of numerous Greek priests from Byzantine territories, especially around 1450.[51] The commune's segregationist policy led to strong misgivings in Venice about the growing numbers of Latins attending services in Greek churches or having recourse to Greek priests. In 1349 the duke of Crete forcefully reiterated that such practices were prohibited, and imposed fines on all Latins and Greek priests involved in them. Significantly, this decree was to be publicly read every three months in all parts of Crete. It was promulgated anew

---

50. See Jacoby, "Les États latins," pp. 29–32; Laiou, "Quelques observations," pp. 197–198.

51. On Venetian religious policy in general see Borsari, *Il Dominio,* pp. 106–125; Fedalto, *La Chiesa,* 2nd ed., I, 377–448, and III, 9–24; Thiriet, *La Romanie,* especially pp. 283–286, 288–291, 403–406, 429–433, who has been corrected on events in the 1450's and 1460's by Manousakas, *Hē en Krētē synōmosia tou Sēphē Blastou (1453–1454) kai hē nea synōmotikē kinēsis tou 1460–1462* (Athens, 1960) [in Greek]; Thiriet, "La Symbiose," pp. 26–35, and his "Églises, fidèles et clergés," pp. 484–500.

in 1405.[52] The same problem arose again in the following years.[53] Though Venice shared the opposition of the popes to religious symbiosis, its considerations were not exclusively of a religious nature. It combatted grecization because it entailed the loss of Latin group identity and endangered the basic tenets of a rule based on segregation.

In Catalan Greece, the conquerors imposed a segregation similar to that implemented by Venice in thirteenth- and fourteenth-century Crete. In 1311 the *kastron* of Livadia was handed over to the Catalan Company by several of its inhabitants, presumably archontes. They and their descendants were rewarded with the grant of the status of Franks or Latins, thus constituting an exception to the rule. However, their full integration as freemen within the class of the conquerors was prevented, since the Company decreed in 1311–1312 that Greeks could not marry Catholic women. This ban was extended even to Greeks who had joined the Roman church. Catalan legislation was somewhat more lenient than Venetian legislation in Crete, since Latins could marry Greek women; several such marriages occurred in the upper class of Latin society.[54] The Company also prohibited, presumably in the early years of its rule, the acquisition of real estate by Greeks. The link between this provision and the interdiction of marriage of Latin women to Greeks is obvious. As in Venetian Crete, land was the source of political and military power, and its transfer to Greeks was to be prevented, or at least strictly controlled.[55] Further social integration, which was contrary to the policy of the Company, was only exceptionally granted. Such was the case in 1362, when two Greek notaries and their male offspring, though remaining Orthodox, were authorized to marry Latin women. One of them also obtained the right to acquire and alienate real estate like the Franks or Latins. In 1380 the latter privilege was also granted to the Greek mistress of the military commandant of Athens, by whom she had borne several children; she was also awarded personal freedom on the same occasion.[56] Few Greeks of the Catalan duchy of Athens seem to have joined the Roman church, and some

52. Venice, Archivio di Stato, *Duca di Candia,* busta 50, fols. 58ᵛ–59ʳ (nuova numerotazione); unsatisfactory edition by Emiliano Barbaro, *Legislazione veneta: I capitolari di Candia* (Venice, 1940), pp. 124–125.

53. Venice, Archivio di Stato, *Senato, Secreta,* reg. 7, fol. 58ʳ (unpublished), in 1418, and see below, note 91.

54. Texts in Rubió i Lluch, *Diplomatari,* pp. 352–354, nos. 268–269. On legislation in 1311–1312 see above, note 31. On Latins marrying Greek women see Setton, *Catalan Domination,* p. 252.

55. Text in Rubió i Lluch, *Diplomatari,* p. 382, no. 294; see also p. 477, no. 391.

56. See above, note 54 and last citation in note 55. He was Romeo de Bellarbre; she was Zoe of Megara.

of these were induced to do so for opportunistic reasons; their return to the Orthodox faith was punished by the confiscation of their property.[57] On the whole the Greeks remained within their community, as implied by the case of the two notaries mentioned above. The prolonged excommunication of the Latins residing in the Catalan duchy no doubt weakened the Roman church within its boundaries, but the outcry of pope Urban V in 1363 that almost all the Latins had gone over to the Orthodox rite seems to have been an overstatement.[58] As a rule, social segregation based on religious affiliation was strictly maintained in Catalan Greece.

It is significant that both in Venetian Crete and in the Catalan duchy of Athens social segregation was enforced by legislation. In spite of some variations due to different local conditions, one perceives a striking agreement between the behavior of the conquering elites of urban origin in these two areas. Everyday life and the pursuit of similar or joint economic activities brought Latins into close contact with the ruled, especially in urban centers, and hardly any factor save religion differentiated them from the Greeks, whose numbers were vastly superior. The constant threat of assimilation into the surrounding Greek society endangered their social supremacy and political prerogatives. The ruling Latin elite therefore resorted to institutionalized segregation in order to preserve the separate group identity of the Latins. The knights of the feudal Morea did not have recourse to such measures. Their class-consciousness and sense of social superiority and the strictly stratified structure of society, as well as their life-style and particular occupation, which matched their status, all created a deep gulf between them and most Greeks and ensured social segregation.

In spite of substantial differences among the various regimes established by the Latins in Romania, the evolution of the bulk of the indigenous population ran along parallel lines. Both in feudal and non-feudal areas one finds similar social institutions, rules, and phenomena, which go back in part to the Byzantine period. It would be erroneous, however, to assume that the conquest resulted solely in a change of masters for the dependent peasants. The Latins assimilated the entire subjugated indigenous population, rural as well as urban, to the *paroikoi,* or villeins (*villani*) as they were called by the Latins.[59] Only the archontes and *archontopouloi,* as well as a few free and emanci-

57. Text in Rubió i Lluch, *Diplomatari,* pp. 380–381, no. 292.
58. *Ibid.,* pp. 338–339, no. 255.
59. The equation appears in a Cretan text: see Borsari, *Il Dominio,* p. 89, note 100.

pated *paroikoi,* escaped debasement. Thus most free men sank into
a state of dependency. Moreover, in spite of continuity in the use of
the term *paroikoi,* a major change occurred in the status of these men
and women: Byzantine *paroikoi* were legally free, but under Latin rule
the villeins were considered unfree, and as such constituted a legal class
from which they could escape only by a formal act of emancipation.
The presumption of subjection was so well established that the status
of freedom became exceptional and had to be duly proven by those
who enjoyed it. In addition to its legal aspect, the subjection of the
villeins was also expressed in the attitude of the Latin lords toward
them. This attitude was similar to that of their counterparts in the west,
where the dependency of the peasantry entailed a definite note of in-
feriority and contempt. No doubt it differed from the attitude of the
Byzantine lord toward his *paroikoi*, who were legally free and had access to imperial courts. It may be assumed, however, that under the
influence of the Latins a change also occurred in the relationship of
Greek lords with their own *paroikoi.* To some extent, continuity prevailed in Venetian territories, where the commune had succeeded to
the Byzantine state: it owned villeins known as *villani comunes,* similar to the *demosiarioi paroikoi* in the empire. Moreover, the commune
assimilated to its own villeins "non-inscribed" villeins (*agrafi*) or "foreign men" (*exteri homines*), Greeks not subject to any lord; this practice was similar to that applied to the *eleutheroi* in the empire. No such
precedence in the acquisition of new manpower existed in feudalized
territories, where this former right of the state was now exercised by
all feudal lords. There were also *villani militum* included in the military tenements granted by Venice to Latins, and occasionally to Greeks.
Villeins could also be owned privately as patrimonial property if they
were *extra feudum,* not part of a military tenement. Villeins of the state
were obviously not to be found in feudalized areas, in which the prerogatives of the state had been transferred into private hands.[60]

Like the Byzantine *paroikos,* the villein inherited his status from
his father; illegitimate children born from a free father and a dependent mother were considered villeins according to feudal law, but free
under Venetian rule, in accordance with Roman law.[61] The dependence
of the villein extended to his descendants, and enforcement of the thirty-
year prescription resulted in perpetual subjection to the lord: the *Assizes*

60. See Jacoby, "Une Classe fiscale," pp. 146–151; the number of villeins heading fiscal units
in a Cretan *militia* varied from seven to twenty-five: *ibid.,* p. 149, note 54.

61. For feudal law see Jacoby, *La Féodalité,* pp. 30–31, 209, on the basis of the *Assizes of
Romania* (ed. Recoura), arts. 78, 174, 189; for Venetian rule see Santschi, "Quelques aspects
du statut," pp. 110 ff.

of Romania attest it for the Morea; it is also documented in the fifteenth century for Euboea; and in 1410 it was specified that in Crete the calculation of the period extended to the direct male ancestors of the person whose status was debated. The enforcement of the prescription in these three areas, each with a different regime, implies that it was applied continuously since the conquest, and also valid in the Byzantine period. Cases regarding the subjection of villeins were indeed decided on the basis of testimonies regarding their lineal ancestors.[62] Besides, Venetian officials in Crete were ordered to reclaim all fugitive villeins of the commune, whether heads of fiscal units or their sons inscribed on the cadastral registers within these units. The purpose of this inscription, as well as that of the eldest brother when only orphans were left, was to ensure the subjection of these villeins to their lord. It is therefore not surprising that the villein could be transferred with his wife and children, if the latter were less than sixteen years old. At this age fiscal responsibility was reached, and the son could be removed from the fiscal unit headed by his father or widowed mother, or his elder brother or sister if only orphans were registered as belonging to the fiscal unit.[63]

The subjection of the villein to his lord was extremely rigorous, regardless of whether the lord was an individual, an institution, or the state as in Venetian territory. The villein was a mere chattel who could be owned jointly by several lords, enfeoffed, held in seizin, exchanged, or sold. As his labor constituted a source of income, he might even be leased for a definite period extending from a few days, especially during the peak of the agricultural season, to several years. If he was removed by the state from a property in Venetian territory or killed by accident by a liege man in a feudal area, he was replaced by another villein. His lord was entitled to remove him from his holding and take his movable goods, provided he left him the means necessary for his sustenance and for the fulfilment of his fiscal obligations. In the case of transfer or lease for a definite period, the temporary lord exercised the prerogatives of the legitimate lord, except in the realm of criminal justice.[64]

As a rule, the lord determined where the villein should reside. In

---

62. See Jacoby, "Une Classe fiscale," pp. 143–145.

63. On this rule see texts in Borsari, *Il Dominio*, p. 91, notes 10 and 11.

64. See *Assizes of Romania* (ed. Recoura), arts. 25, 107, and also 187, 197, 211; Jacoby, "Une Classe fiscale," p. 147; Borsari, *Il Dominio*, p. 91, note 107; Thiriet, "La Condition paysanne," pp. 46–48, 56; Santschi, *La Notion de "feudum"*, p. 177, note 23; p. 178, note 28; p. 179, notes 37, 39, and 40; p. 180, note 42. On the jurisdiction exercised by the holder of a lease see Jacoby, "Les États latins," p. 37, and *La Féodalité*, p. 208.

this respect the condition of the state's villeins in Venetian Crete seems to have been somewhat better. Since the domain of the commune extended over large sections of the island, there was more room for mobility. The agreement of 1299 with Alexius Callerges specified that villeins other than those belonging to military tenements should be allowed to reside where they wished. In 1313 it was decreed that villeins of the state might dwell in Candia or in a village, at will, without fear of being regarded as villeins of feudatories; they were, however, forbidden to leave Crete or the land they held and were compelled to fulfill their obligations to the commune, such as the payment of the *villanazio,* an annual tax amounting to one hyperper imposed upon state villeins. In 1334 the Venetian authorities refused to exempt villeins inhabiting Canea from this tax, for fear that this might lead to a massive exodus of peasants from rural areas to the city. At any rate, the commune exercised strict supervision over its villeins. In 1339 those of Crete were ordered to register in the district where they had settled within fifteen days of their arrival; the following year the authorities discovered that in the area of Canea many state villeins had exhibited false privileges of enfranchisement which they had purchased, inter alia, in order to be allowed to settle wherever they wished.[65]

In spite of the restrictions imposed upon the mobility of the villeins, their migration is abundantly documented for Latin Greece. Besides economic or matrimonial considerations of an individual nature, as in the Byzantine empire, catastrophic events, as well as the general conditions prevailing in the area, explain this mobility. Frequent revolts in thirteenth-century Crete, warfare between Latins and Byzantines in the Morea, the raids of the Catalans in the peninsula and in Euboea from 1311 to 1329, the activity of Latin—and in the fourteenth and fifteenth century also of Turkish—pirates, all these increased the number of fugitive villeins. Besides, famine and recurring waves of plague after the Black Death of 1347–1348 prompted them to seek refuge elsewhere. In 1401 the Venetian authorities complained that many Greeks fearing service in the navy had fled to Anatolia. The extreme political fragmentation of Greece after 1204 no doubt provided villeins many opportunities to abandon their residence and thereby sever the link of subjection.[66]

The lord had the right to recover a villein who had abandoned his residence without permission. After locating the fugitive, he appealed

65. See Jacoby, "Les États latins," p. 38, and "Les Gens de mer," pp. 182–183.
66. See Jacoby, "Une Classe fiscale," p. 142; for the Catalans till 1329 and the Turks see also Jacoby, "Catalans, Turcs et Vénitiens," pp. 238–261. For 1401 see Noiret, *Documents inédits,* p. 116.

to a competent court in order to prove his subjection and obtain the intervention of state officials in Crete or, if in feudalized territories, that of the prince, the barons, or other feudal lords exercising high justice. In Venetian territories the state villeins were recovered by officials. Any unilateral action by the lord to reclaim his villeins was prohibited, as the Cretan feudatories were reminded in 1349. Moreover, the commune imposed heavy penalties on fugitive villeins and those who provided them with shelter, often with the intent of holding them permanently. While awaiting the verdict of the court, the fugitive was usually imprisoned at the expense of the lord who claimed him; if the lord did not provide for his sustenance, he forfeited his rights over the villein.[67]

The legal capacity of a villein was also restricted in other ways. We are particularly well informed about the Morea. He could neither contract marriage himself nor marry off his daughter, especially if the spouse was dependent upon another lord, without the permission of his own lord; the latter was compelled, however, to accept a marriage which had been contracted, even by a female villein with a free man, whereby she acquired permanent freedom. A villein was tried by his lord in civil cases, although criminal jurisdiction was the exclusive right of the prince and the barons. A villein wronged by his own lord could not lodge a complaint against him, nor appeal to a superior lord; his testimony was valid only if it concerned a portion or the boundaries of a fief, but not a liege man in a criminal case. If a villein fled, died without offspring, or willed his property without the consent of his lord, the latter inherited his goods. This rule also held in favor of a foreign lord whose land he had cultivated under a contract providing for the division of newly planted trees or vines.[68] In Venetian territories criminal justice was an exclusive prerogative of the state, and all villeins were tried in state courts, whether or not they belonged to a military tenure, an individual, or the commune. These courts also dealt with civil cases, especially those involving control over state villeins.[69] Unfortunately, there is no information about the exercise of civil justice by Latin lords or Greek archontes.

The continuity of certain aspects of the Byzantine fiscal system is well documented, yet this system underwent important changes as the

67. See Jacoby, "Une Classe fiscale," pp. 142–145; cases in Santschi, "Quelques aspects du statut," pp. 110–112, 121–122; Ratti Vidulich, *Duca di Candia, Quaternus Consiliorum,* p. 117 (February 4, 1349).

68. *Assizes of Romania* (ed. Recoura), arts. 42, 43, 125, 174–175, 184–186, 189, 198, and see above, note 67.

69. Thiriet, *La Romanie,* pp. 235–239.

Latins adapted it to their own needs and concepts. The debasement of many free men who had become villeins under Latin rule obviously entailed the imposition of heavier fiscal obligations upon them. It will be remembered that the Byzantine *paroikos* owed dues and labor services to the state. After the Latin conquest, this remained the case with Venetian state villeins only. All the other villeins, whether in Venetian or in feudal territories, were bound to provide dues and services to their lord; if the land on which they dwelt was leased to an individual or an institution, the temporary lord was entitled to collect them, as illustrated by evidence from Venetian Messenia.

The rights of the permanent or temporary lord, as well as those of the commune, also restricted the legal capacity of the villein in the economic sphere. As a rule, he could not borrow, engage in trade, or alienate movable property without the consent of his lord. The *Assizes of Romania* (art. 215) clearly distinguish between villeins who borrowed for sustenance and those who incurred commercial debts, even with the permission of their lord, which was considered more serious. A similar distinction between indebtedness and a trade operation is to be found in Venetian Crete; the villeins of the commune were allowed to borrow and to engage in trade, unless they had been explicitly forbidden to do so.

The alienation of real estate presented a particular problem, as this property was taxable and had to be registered in the cadastral registers. It was therefore necessary for villeins to obtain the agreement of their lord, or that of the commune, for villeins of the state. In 1292 a state villein living in Coron made his will after its clauses had been approved by Venetian officials. Lack of approval entailed the cancelation of sales.[70] On the other hand, the acquisition of property was not restricted, as it was indirectly of advantage to the lord. It may be assumed that in many cases, the person entering an agreement with a villein was aware of the latter's status and limitations; however, this was not always the case. In 1319 the commune ordered the official brokers operating on its behalf in Crete to disclose the status of the borrower to the other contracting party before the latter provided a loan to, or accepted surety from, a villein, to enable the lenders to protect their interests and prevent them from being defrauded by villeins. Villeins are seldom mentioned in notarial documents; either they concealed their status, or else the parties to a contract did not consider that it need be stated explicitly. In any case, it seems evident that the overwhelming majority of the Greeks involved in agricultural con-

---

70. The *stasis* could not be alienated: *Assizes of Romania* (ed. Recoura), art. 215.

tracts, loans, or the purchase of animals were villeins. It would be a mistake to consider them as free when their status is not specified;[71] cross-checking with judicial documents will no doubt confirm this assumption.

Manumission of villeins does not seem to have been practised on a large scale, except in special circumstances; such was the case in 1299 at the request of Alexius Callerges. The manumission of a villein belonging to a military tenement obviously reduced its value. It was therefore subject to approval by the prince in the Morea, presumably by the chief lord in each of the various lordships of the Aegean, or by the commune in Venetian territory. On the other hand, the Latins and the Greek archontes of Crete could free, without restriction, villeins whom they held in full ownership. In Venetian territories the commune also manumitted villeins who belonged to other lords and compensated the latter for the loss by granting them "non-inscribed" or state villeins. Manumission was granted by lords mainly as a pious act, and by the commune as a reward for services or loyalty. According to Venetian sources of the first half of the fourteenth century conditional freedom was granted in Crete to Greek sailors newly established in the island and to Greek villeins settling in Candia as long as they would serve aboard the ships of the Venetian navy.[72]

In certain cases a villein could redeem himself by paying a large sum to his lord.[73] In 1434 the Venetian senate decided that state villeins in Crete should be able to do so if they paid to the commune 50 ducats or more, which at the time amounted to some 250 hyperpers. This fiscal expedient was regarded as particularly useful because Venice was then at war in Lombardy and in urgent need of income; besides, manumission on a large scale would have reduced administrative expenses involved in the collection of the yearly *villanazio* of one hyperper. It seems unlikely, however, that many state villeins took advantage of the offer, as the sum required was huge compared with the yearly tax they paid, equivalent to the price of several oxen, even one of which peasants often found it difficult to afford.[74] Yet there can be no doubt that many

71. As assumed by Borsari, *Il Dominio,* p. 88, and by Thiriet, "La Condition," pp. 39–41.

72. See Jacoby, "Une Classe fiscale," pp. 147–148, and "Les États latins," pp. 41–42, and "Les Gens de mer," pp. 183–184.

73. A case for 60 hyperpers is mentioned in 1388: see Santschi, *La Notion de "feudum",* p. 177, note 28.

74. Text in Noiret, *Documents inédits,* pp. 363–364. For the approximate rate of exchange of the ducat around this date see Thiriet, *La Romanie,* p. 412. The price of a slave was then lower, between 27 and 40 ducats: see Verlinden, *L'Esclavage,* II, 879–881. In 1416 oxen were bought from villeins in the west and the center of Crete for 25 hyperpers, and sold in the eastern part for 60 hyperpers: see Thiriet, *La Romanie,* p. 416.

villeins aspired to freedom. In 1415 social unrest spread among the villeins of Crete, when several of them claimed that they were free men and should be treated as such.[75] No doubt the demographic contraction of the fourteenth and early fifteenth century — due to catastrophic events and the recurring plague — had increased the pressure of the lords on their villeins and, on the other hand, the awareness of the latter that the economy of the island and the prosperity of their lords depended on them. Enfranchised villeins were not always entitled to move freely. In Crete the commune occasionally imposed residence in inland cities on its former villeins. The loss of the document granting enfranchisement, disobedience, or rebellion involved a return to the unfree status.

Freedom was so exceptional that free Greeks who were not archontes or *archontopouloi* sometimes specified their status in documents, for fear of being mistakenly considered villeins. This was especially so in cases involving residence in a rural area or agricultural work. In 1301 a free Cretan Greek indebted to a Latin promised to reside for four years in a village of his and pay him dues "as do the other free inhabitants of this place"; in 1352 a plot of land was leased to four Cretan Greeks who stated explicitly that they were free. On the basis of documents bearing on the area of Patras in the northern Morea it has been claimed that communities of free peasants still existed in the fourteenth century in certain areas of Latin Greece. A closer look at these documents reveals, however, that this assumption is not warranted: a vineyard thought to be the holding of a free peasant was in fact part of a seignorial domain.[76]

Slaves frequently appear in Latin Greece.[77] The political fragmentation of the area and the frequent warfare were fully exploited by numerous pirates who raided the islands of the Aegean and the coasts of continental Greece. They were joined by Catalans from the duchy of Athens from 1311 to 1329, as well as by Turkish pirates, whose activity in the area steadily increased thereafter.[78] It is therefore surprising that Greeks constituted a majority among the slaves on the markets of Latin Greece in the first half of the fourteenth century. Gradually the proportion of Slavs from the Morea increased, and for

75. See Thiriet, *La Romanie,* p. 297.
76. See Jacoby, "Les États latins," pp. 41–42.
77. On the whole subject see Verlinden, *L'Esclavage,* II, 800–884, 974–975, Santschi, "Quelques aspects du statut," pp. 112, 114–115, 117–118, 120–122, and Zachariadou, *Trade and Crusade, passim.*
78. See above, p. 210.

a short period in the late fourteenth century Bulgarians in particular became numerous. In addition to the Black Sea the Turkish emirates of Anatolia constituted an important source of supply. The flow of slaves was considerably reduced by the Ottoman conquest in the following century.

Slaves were to be found in the Morea, in Venetian Messenia, and in the Catalan duchy of Athens, whence many of them were shipped to Crete.[79] This island was the main emporium for the slave trade to the west, although many slaves remained there. Considered mere chattels, they were owned by Latins and Greeks of all ranks of society engaged in various occupations, by members of the Catholic and Greek clergy, and even by Jews. In spite of his status, even a villein might own a slave,[80] while the reverse was of course impossible; this is a clear mark of the slave's inferior status, also implied by the *Assizes of Romania* (art. 219). Female slaves were bought for domestic purposes and served in cities as well as in rural areas; we may assume that such was also the case with most male slaves. A shortage of agricultural manpower in the second half of the fourteenth century partly explains a substantial rise in the price of male slaves; it induced the Venetian authorities to promote in 1393 and 1397 their import to Crete, in order to settle them on abandoned land held by Latin feudatories.[81] Even earlier manumitted male slaves were occasionally bound to reside in a village of their former master and to provide some amount of agricultural work for a specified number of years. All of them seem to have paid a yearly sum to their former masters.[82] In certain cases, slaves were allowed to redeem themselves, although it is not always clear how they managed to gather the means to do so.[83] In 1315 the Venetian authorities of Crete decreed that slaves who were taught by their masters the trade of a carpenter or a calker would be freed from servitude; from this text it is not clear whether the commune was opposed to any such training or approved of it. Manumission did not necessarily become effective when granted; its enforcement might be postponed for a specified period, sometimes several years. Slaves could

79. See also Setton, *Catalan Domination,* p. 87, and Santschi, "Quelques aspects du statut," p. 128, on a sale by Catalans around 1345.

80. A case in Crete (1305) in Verlinden, *L'Esclavage,* II, 825.

81. *Ibid.,* II, 877–878. Contrary to Thiriet, *La Romanie,* pp. 314–315, who relies on a shipment which arrived in Crete in August 1301, there is no reason to assume that slaves were imported then for agricultural work.

82. See Santschi, "Quelques aspects du statut," p. 122, note 50, and Verlinden, *L'Esclavage,* II, 828–830.

83. A case in 1364 for 40 hyperpers: see Santschi, *Régestes,* p. 107, no. 63.

be married. An abandoned infant slave became free if not claimed, in conformity with Roman law.[84] To sum up, although certain rules applied to slave and villein alike, the latter enjoyed a superior status.

Economic factors no doubt played an important role in shaping the pattern of daily coexistence of individuals belonging respectively to the Latin and Greek communities; these factors also generated divergent and even contrasting attitudes and feelings.

Land remained, as before the conquest, the principal source of income in Greece.[85] Whether held in full ownership or as a conditional tenement, it was mostly in the hands of the Latins, who expropriated the Greeks' land on a large scale and replaced them as landlords. In contrast to the Byzantine period, land became under Latin rule a double source of revenue for the landlords: income deriving from agricultural exploitation and income from what had been public taxes, especially in feudalized areas and, to a lesser degree, in Venetian territories, as a result of the transfer of fiscal state prerogatives into private hands. Land seems to have yielded good returns: it provided knights with means to maintain an appropriate standard of living, and its temporary or permanent acquisition was considered a good investment, as illustrated by the commercialization of military tenements in Crete.[86] On the whole, Greeks were prevented by social and legal barriers from substantially enlarging their landholding and getting their share of a prosperous agriculture increasingly geared to export. It may be assumed that this situation generated some degree of resentment within the ranks of the Greek elite, further enhanced by its exclusion from the economic benefits deriving from power positions in feudalized areas, as well as from governmental offices in Venetian territories and Catalan cities.

84. Ratti Vidulich, *Duca di Candia, Bandi,* nos. 100 and 153; Santschi, *Régestes,* p. 263, no. 1196: a case of postponement in 1388; *idem,* "Quelques aspects," p. 125, notes 60 and 61, and on the status of offspring in cases of mixed parentage, *ibid.,* pp. 114–115, 117–120.

85. On the economy of Latin Greece see Jacoby, "Les États latins," pp. 42–48. On the Morea in particular see numerous documents in Filangieri, *I Registri,* and Longnon and Topping, *Documents*; also Bon, *La Morée franque,* pp. 320–325; Carile, *La Rendita feudale,* pp. 80–183, and "Rapporti fra signoria rurale e *despoteia*," pp. 548–570, as well as the reviews by Jacoby of Longnon and Topping, *Documents,* and of Carile's book (see bibliography above). On Venetian territories see Borsari, *Il Dominio,* pp. 67–103, and his *Studi,* pp. 107–132; Laiou, "Quelques observations," pp. 177–198, and her "Observations on the Results of the Fourth Crusade," pp. 47–54, 57; Zachariadou, *Trade and Crusade*; Thiriet, *La Romanie,* pp. 309–349, 410–428. Notarial documents and Venetian complaints about piracy provide evidence of the extensive reliance of Greek traders who were Venetian or foreign subjects on ships belonging to Venetians. On piracy see especially Gareth Morgan, "The Venetian Claims Commission of 1278," *Byzantinische Zeitschrift,* LXIX (1976), 411–438.

86. Presumably because of the rise in grain prices; some prices paid in the thirteenth century for military tenures are recorded by Borsari, *Il Dominio,* opposite p. 84.

In the Morea the archontes benefitted from grants of land, generally on a moderate scale, and some of them served in the princely and seignorial administration; these two economic facets of integration into the ruling elite provided them with partial compensation for the loss of their social standing.

The holding of large estates by the Latins influenced not only the attitude of the Greek elite toward them, but also that of the peasants. The constant presence of Latin lords on these lands or in their vicinity, or, in the case of Italian landholders in the Morea, of their agents engaged in improving agricultural exploitation, their endeavor to ensure growing profits in a true commercial spirit, and a manpower shortage due to demographic contraction all brought heavy pressure to bear on the dependent peasantry, especially in Crete. The ethnic cleavage in the island was exacerbated by economic factors; it is therefore not surprising that Cretan peasants were often willing to join the archontes and the Greek clergy in opposing Venetian rule.

On the other hand, the expanding demand in Venice for agricultural products from Greece, grain and wine in particular, as well as raisins, cheese, wool, and hides, encouraged the cultivation of numerous plots of land and the raising of animals by landowners, lessees, and sharecroppers belonging to almost all ranks of society. It also afforded seasonal work for hired laborers. Latins and Greeks appear side by side, at times as partners, in numerous business contracts involving investments, loans, and labor in agriculture and the raising of animals.[87] The same holds true with the manufacturing of goods and the supply of services, as well as local and regional commerce on land and at sea. Greeks, however, suffered from various restrictions in maritime trade. Villeins were not allowed to leave the territory in which they lived. Thus, for instance, those of Crete were barred from traveling outside the island. In addition, Venetians and especially Venetian citizens seem to have acquired since the 1270's at the latest a dominant position in regional maritime transportation. This activity was partly integrated into the pattern of long-distance commerce and transportation dominated by itinerant traders and ships operating from Venice, and enjoying a favored status and the commune's protection. Some members of prominent Venetian families such as the Corners, Ghisi, Morosini, and Sanudos, who had settled in Crete, also participated in regional

87. See above, note 36. The production and trade of Cretan grain was stimulated in 1281 and the following decades by massive purchases made by the commune at guaranteed prices higher than those on the free market.

trade and shipping. In fourteenth-century Morea Florentine and south Italian traders largely monopolized the export of agricultural produce and its transportation to the Angevin kingdom of Sicily.

Activity related to manufacturing, trade, and shipping was mainly concentrated in urban centers. By crossing class and community boundaries, similar or joint economic activity led to social intercourse, tempered ethnic tensions somewhat, and opened the way to accommodation on a daily level between Greek and Latin city-dwellers. It is precisely this phenomenon that so worried the ruling elites in non-feudal territories and prompted them to enforce institutionalized ethnic segregation, as illustrated in Venetian Crete from the thirteenth century on and in the Catalan duchy of Athens in the fourteenth century.

This rapprochement occasionally extended to another sphere of daily life. Within a few years after the conquest, the Greek clergy was deprived of its higher ranks and of educated priests, who fled Latin rule,[88] yet it displayed a considerable vitality. Two factors explain its influence on the Greek community, especially in rural areas. Greek monks and Greek priests were to be found in cities and villages alike; besides, the latter lived among the laymen and shared their fate, as most priests were villeins.[89] This situation contrasted sharply with that of the Latin clergy. Catholic priests were not numerous enough to attend to the religious needs of the Latin population, which was scattered all over Latin Greece, often in very small groups: in 1210 Othon de la Roche, the "great lord" of Athens, asked pope Innocent III to provide priests for all castles and villages in which twelve Catholics were settled.[90] Besides, Latin priests were seldom present in rural areas or inland cities; most of them resided in coastal cities, where the major part of the Latin population dwelt. Finally, members of the higher Latin clergy were often absent from their sees and offices.[91] It is therefore not surprising that growing numbers of Latins turned to Greek priests and attended their religious services. It may safely be assumed, however, that this religious symbiosis was not generalized and occurred only in places where Latins were few. In 1322 pope John XXII com-

88. For continental Greece see Herrin, "Realities of Byzantine Provincial Government," p. 263, and Thiriet, "La Symbiose," pp. 21, 29, 33; for Crete, see Borsari, *Il Dominio,* pp. 105–108.

89. See above, note 51; Thiriet, "La Symbiose," pp. 21–26, and his "Églises, fidèles et clergés," pp. 489–499, as well as Santschi, "Quelques aspects du statut," pp. 121–122 for Crete, and numerous cases in Longnon and Topping, *Documents.*

90. As mentioned in a letter of Innocent III, an. XIII, ep. 16, in *PL,* 216, col. 216.

91. Sathas, *Documents inédits,* II, 236–237, 245; Noiret, *Documents inédits,* pp. 191–192, 267, 305–306; Fedalto, *La Chiesa,* III, nos. 450–451, 512, 558–560, 582, 595, 668; Thiriet, *La Romanie,* pp. 405–406; and his "Églises, fidèles et clergés," pp. 491–493.

plained bitterly that in the Morea Latins mingled with Greeks at religious services.[92] The same phenomenon is attested in Crete by numerous sources, yet it is significant that a decree issued in 1349 specifically prohibited minor Venetian officials in the inland areas from having recourse to Greek priests.[93] It remains to be seen what impact this process had on the relations between the Latins and the Greek population.

The social, legal, and institutional framework established by the Latins in their respective territories shortly after the conquest no doubt conditioned to a large extent the attitudes and behavior of the Latin rulers and settlers toward the indigenous population, and vice versa. In spite of the diversity of regimes, certain basic features were common to all areas of Latin Greece: such were legal and social stratification and, broadly speaking, the deterioration in the status and condition of the Greeks. Daily coexistence affected, however, the pattern of relations between the two communities and their respective members, yet not to the same degree or in the same manner everywhere. In feudalized areas coexistence produced legal and social, but not religious or cultural, integration of the Greek elite into the Latin upper class. In non-feudal areas, even this limited integration remained exceptional. Institutionalized segregation was steadily enforced by Venice in Crete, yet proved effective at the level of the elites only. It seems to have been more successful in the Catalan duchy of Athens. Whatever the case, in the period under consideration here intermarriage seems to have remained a marginal phenomenon in Latin Greece, and coexistence never developed into an assimilation of the Latins to the Greek population.

In the fourteenth century the crossing of religious boundaries occurred in both directions, yet was apparently limited in scope.[94] More important in this respect was the religious symbiosis spreading in inland areas, which, however, was restricted to common religious practice. It derived no doubt from the practical needs of Latins and did not necessarily imply a change in religious affiliation, nor was it tanta-

---

92. Letter in Caesar Baronius, *Annales ecclesiastici,* XXIV (Bar-le-Duc, 1872), cols. 187–188.

93. See above, note 52. Common religious services in cities were quite exceptional: see Thiriet, "Le Zèle unioniste d'un franciscain crétois et la riposte de Venise (1414)," *Polychronion* (above, note 14), pp. 496–504.

94. See above, notes 51 and 57; also especially Thiriet, "Églises, fidèles et clergés," pp. 493–495, and Laiou, "Quelques observations," pp. 197–198, who refers to mixed marriages which no doubt promoted the Latins' acculturation.

mount to conversion to Orthodoxy. Furthermore, it did not generate mutual accommodation between the Greek and Latin communities at large, nor did the spreading knowledge of the Greek language among Latins or social and economic intercourse between them and the Greeks, attested from the thirteenth century on, achieve this result. About 1220 Greek priests of Latin Morea coöperated with their fellow Greeks of Epirus,[95] and in 1244 Greek monks living in the duchy of Athens collaborated with those of Epirus or Nicaea.[96] About 1330, more than a century after the imposition of Latin rule, Marino Sanudo, an acute observer of Latin Greece, described the situation in Cyprus, Crete, Euboea, Rhodes, and other islands, as well as in the Morea, as follows: "Although these places are subjected to the rule of the Franks and obedient to the Roman church, almost all the population is Greek and is inclined toward this sect [the Greek Orthodox church], and their hearts are turned toward Greek matters, and when they can show this freely, they do so."[97] Venice was perfectly aware of this crucial fact, which explains its segregationist policy and its reluctance to enlist Greeks in the armed forces and navy, unless absolutely necessary, on a temporary basis, and on a limited scale.[98]

It has been claimed that Venice's attitude toward its Greek subjects became more lenient from the late fourteenth century on, against the background of the Ottoman advance in the Balkans.[99] This statement requires some qualifications. It is true that the commune became somewhat more attentive to the wishes of the Greek population in its territories and adopted a more flexible attitude on practical matters, such as the training of Greek archers in order to ensure the coastal defense of Crete.[100] With that it is significant, as noted above, that it basically maintained its stance on mixed marriages, the participation of Greeks and *vasmuli* in political assemblies, and their holding of high state offices, as well as on religious symbiosis. The anti-Venetian unrest stimulated in Crete and Corfu from the mid-fifteenth century on by the arrival of Greek priests from Byzantine and Turkish territories leads to the conclusion that Sanudo's statement about the Greek attitude towards the Latins remained largely valid in this period. He had rightly

95. See Demetrius Chomatianus, ed. Pitra, VII, cols. 87–98, no. 22.

96. *Les Registres d'Innocent IV,* ed. Élie Berger, I (Paris, 1884), pp. 112–113, no. 657 (April 29, 1244).

97. "Istoria del Regno di Romania," ed. Hopf, *Chroniques gréco-romanes,* p. 143.

98. On its vacillating policy on this last matter see Jacoby, "Les États latins," p. 29, and "Les Gens de mer," pp. 181–185, 191; also Thiriet, *La Romanie,* pp. 402–403.

99. Thiriet, *La Romanie,* pp. 301–302, 395 ff.

100. See Jacoby, "Les Gens de mer," p. 185.

perceived that Greek religious affiliation was the source of Greek ethnic awareness.[101] It is only later, in the sixteenth century, that Latin
acculturation proceeded further, and accommodation between Latins
and Greeks emerged in the territories remaining under Venetian rule.

101. For this reason Greek priests may have pretended to know no language other than their
own, as suggested by a trial held in Candia in 1410: see Thiriet, "Églises, fidèles et clergés," pp.
495–496.

VII

THE OTTOMAN TURKS AND THE CRUSADES, 1329–1451

A. *Turkish Settlement and Christian Reaction, 1329–1361*

The fall of Acre in 1291 did not end the crusader peril for the Moslem world. Western Christendom was still unchallenged at sea in the eastern Mediterranean, and its forces had the advantage of being able to land at any time anywhere on the coasts, which therefore remained

General works on Ottoman history include Joseph von Hammer-Purgstall, *Geschichte des osmanischen Reiches* (10 vols., Pest, 1827–1835; repr. Graz, 1963), largely superseded; Johann W. Zinkeisen, *Geschichte des osmanischen Reiches in Europa* (7 vols., Hamburg, 1840–1863; repr. Darmstadt, 1963), still important for Ottoman relations with Europe; Nicola Jorga (Nicolae Iorga), *Geschichte des osmanischen Reiches nach den Quellen dargestellt* (5 vols., Gotha, 1908–1913; repr. 1963), based on contemporary sources and archives, still essential; and İsmail H. Uzunçarşili, *Osmanli tarihi* (4 vols., Ankara, 1947–1959).

General histories relevant to the Ottomans are Wilhelm Heyd, *Histoire du commerce du Levant au moyen-âge,* tr. Furcy Reynaud (2 vols., Leipzig, 1885–1886; repr. Leipzig, 1936, Amsterdam, 1967); Ludwig Pastor, *The History of the Popes from the Close of the Middle Ages,* tr. Frederick I. Antrobus; vols. I–VI (London, 1891 ff.); and Aziz S. Atiya, *The Crusade in the Later Middle Ages* (London, 1938).

Other histories relevant to our subject include Frederick W. Hasluck, *Christianity and Islam under the Sultans* (2 vols., Oxford, 1929); *Mélanges offerts à M. Nicolae Iorga par ses amis de France* . . . (Paris, 1933); Dorothy M. Vaughan, *Europe and the Turk: a Pattern of Alliances, 1350–1700* (Liverpool, 1954); and Franz Babinger, *Aufsätze und Abhandlungen zur Geschichte Südosteuropas und der Levante,* I, Südosteuropa (Schriften der Südosteuropa-Gesellschaft, no. 3; Munich, 1962).

A long list of Ottoman documents published in various countries is contained in the introduction to Jan Reychman and Ananiasz Zajaczkowski, *Handbook of Ottoman-Turkish Diplomatics,* tr. Andrew S. Ehrenkreutz, ed. Tibor Halasi-Kun (The Hague and Paris, 1968). Journals frequently publishing Ottoman documents include *Târîkh-i Osmânî encümeni mecmuasî* (Istanbul, 1908–1931), *Belleten* (Turkish Historical Society, Ankara; since 1937), *Tarih vesikalari* (Ankara, 1941–1961), *Tarih dergisi* (Faculty of Letters, University of Istanbul; since 1950), *Prilozi, za orijentalnu filologiju* (Orientalni Institut u Sarajevo; annually since 1950), *Monumenta turcica historiam Slavorum meridionalium illustrantia* (*idem;* since 1957), *Fontes historiae Bulgariae,* ser.

the boundaries between Islam and Christendom. The Christian's pre-dominance on the sea was acknowledged by the Mamluks.[1] In fact, in the period after 1291 a blockade—ordered by pope Nicholas IV (1288-1292)—of Egypt, Syria, and Turkey seriously threatened to cut the supply lines of commodities vital to the Mamluks—arms, timber,

---

XV–XVI: *Fontes turcici* . . . (Sofia, since 1964), and *Belgeler* (Turkish Historical Society, Ankara; since 1964). See also *Arşiv Kîlavuzu* (2 vols., Istanbul, 1938–1940), incomplete guide to the collections of documents in the Topkapî Sarayî archives (TKS); M. Tayyib Gökbilgin, *XV-XVI. asìrlarda Edirne ve Paşa Livâsi* (Istanbul, 1952), a collection of archival documents important for pious foundations in Rumelia, Ottoman biography, and finances; *Sûret-i defter-i sancak-i Arvanid,* ed. Halil Inalcik (Turkish Historical Society; Ankara, 1954), Ottoman survey book of Albania, dated 1432; and Ahmed Ferîdûn (Beg), ed., *Münşe'ât es-selâṭîn* (2 vols., Istanbul, 1858), critically analyzed by Irène Beldiceanu-Steinherr, *Recherches sur les actes des règnes des sultans Osman, Orkhan et Murad I* (Munich, 1967).

Western collections of documents are Ernest Charrière, ed., *Négociations de la France dans le Levant* (4 vols., Paris, 1848); Georg E. Müller, ed., *Documenti sulle relazioni delle città toscane coll' Oriente cristiano e coi turchi fino all' anno MDXXXI* (Documenti degli archivi toscani, no. 3; Florence, 1879); Vladimir Lamansky, ed., *Secrets d'état de Venise* (St. Petersburg, 1884; repr. New York, 1968); Iorga, *Notes et extraits pour servir à l' histoire des croisades au XVe siècle* (6 vols., Paris and Bucharest, 1899–1916); and Freddy Thiriet, ed., *Régestes des délibérations du sénat de Venise concernant la Romanie* (3 vols., Paris and The Hague, 1958–1961).

Western memoirs of interest include G. Georgiades Arnakis, "Gregory Palamas among the Turks and Documents of his Captivity as Historical Sources," *Speculum,* XXXVI (1951), 104–118; *Reisen des Johannes Schiltberger* . . . , ed. Karl F. Neumann (Munich, 1859), tr. J. Buchan Telfer as *The Bondage and Travels of Johannes Schiltberger . . . in Europe, Asia, and Africa, 1396–1427,* with notes by Philipp Bruun (Hakluyt Series; London, 1879): he was captured in 1396 and served the sultan for six years; Bertrandon de la Brocquière, *Voyage d'Outremer,* ed. Charles Schefer (Paris, 1892); and "Donado da Lezze" (Giovanni-Maria Angiolello), *Historia turchesca (1300–1514),* ed. Ion Ursu (Bucharest, 1910).

For Ottoman chroniclers see Babinger, *Die Geschichtsschreiber der Osmanen und ihre Werke* (Leipzig, 1927). The earliest surviving account of Ottoman history in Turkish is in Ahmedî's dedication of the *Iskendernâme* to the contender Suleiman (1402–1411); the text was last published by Nihal Atsìz in *Osmanlì tarihleri* (Istanbul, 1949), pp. 1–35 (rhymed summary, with historical data too brief and too vague). Early Ottoman traditions, apparently composed in chronicle form under Orkhan (1326–1362), are lost, but their contents are partially known from compilations made under Bayazid II (1481–1512). 'Âshìk Pasha-zâde summarized them in faithful detail in his *Tevârîkh-i Âl-i 'Othmân,* ed. Atsìz as *'Âşìkpaşazâde tarihi* (Istanbul, 1949), pp. 79–318; tr. Richard F. Kreutel, *Vom Hirtenzelt zur hohen Pforte* (Vienna and Cologne, 1959); legendary folk tales are mixed in with genuine historical accounts, necessitating critical use of this important source.

The second and third compilations—Rûhî (or Pseudo-Rûhî) and the anonymous chronicler—used some of the same sources as the first. For discussion see Inalcik, "The Rise of Ottoman Historiography," in *Historians of the Middle East,* ed. Bernard Lewis and Peter M. Holt (London, 1962), pp. 152–167; Victor L. Ménage, "The Beginnings of Ottoman Historiography," *ibid.,* pp. 168–179; and *idem, Neshrî's History of the Ottomans: the Sources and Development of the*

---

1. David Ayalon, "Baḥriyya," *Encyclopaedia of Islâm,* 2nd ed., I (Leyden, 1960), 945–946; *idem,* "The Wâfidiya in the Mamluk Kingdom," *Islamic Culture,* XXX (1951), 89–104; Inalcik, "The Rise of the Turcoman Maritime Principalities in Anatolia, Byzantium, and Crusades," *Byzantinische Forschungen,* IX (1985), 179–217.

iron, and most important of all, slaves. Since these materials and slaves were imported from Turkey or through the Aegean Sea from the Black Sea, the islands of the eastern Mediterranean acquired major importance in western strategy. As a result of this new situation, the *uj* (frontier) Turcomans in Anatolia, dependent on the export to Egypt of

---

Text (London, 1964). The section on Ottoman history added by Enverî to *Le Destân d'Umur Pacha* (see below) is an original compilation of the earlier chronicles which sheds new light on various controversial points.

On the Turkish principalities in Anatolia see Uzunçarşili, *Anadolu beylikleri,* 2nd ed. (Ankara, 1969), a general survey; Paul Wittek, *Das Fürstentum Mentesche: Studien zur Geschichte Westkleinasiens im XIII.–XV. Jahrhundert* (Istanbul, 1934); Barbara Flemming, *Landschaftsgeschichte von Pamphylien, Pisidien und Lykien im Spätmittelalter* (Wiesbaden, 1964); Mustafa C. Varlik, *Germiyan-oğullari tarihi, 1300–1429* (Ankara, 1974); Tuncer Baykara, *Denizli tarihi* (Istanbul, 1969); Himmet Akin, *Aydin-oğullari tarihi hakkinda bir araştirma* (Istanbul, 1946); Claude Cahen, "Pour l' Histoire des turcomanes d'Asie mineure au XIIIe siècle," *Journal asiatique,* CCXXXIX (1951), 325–354; Adnan S. Erzi, "Akkoyunlu ve Karakoyunlu tarihi hakkinda araştirmalar," *Belleten,* XVIII (1954), 179–221; John Woods, *The Aqquyunlu: Clan, Confederation, Empire* (Minneapolis and Chicago, 1976); Faruk Sümer, *Kara Koyunlular,* I (Ankara, 1967); Şehabeddin Tekindağ, "Son Osmanli-Karaman münasebetleri hakkinda araştirmalar," *Tarih dergisi* (1963), 43–76; and M. Yaşar Yücel, *Kadi Burhâneddin Ahmed ve devleti, 1344–1398* (Ankara, 1970).

For a comprehensive analysis of conditions in Selchükid Anatolia and the frontier areas see the pioneering works of Mehmed Fuad Köprülü, "Bemerkungen zur Religionsgeschichte Kleinasiens," *Mitteilungen zur osmanischen Geschichte,* I (1921–1922), 203–222; "Köprülüzâde Mehmed Fuad's Werk über die ersten Mystiker in der türkischen Literatur," *Körösi Csoma Archiv,* II (1927–1932), 281–310, 406–422; *Les Origines de l'empire ottoman* (Paris, 1935); and "Osmanli imperatorluğunun etnik menşei meselesi," *Belleten,* VII (1943), 219–303. Köprülü's work has been expanded by Friedrich Giese, "Das Problem der Enstehung des osmanischen Reiches," *Zeitschrift für Semitistik und verwandte Gebiete,* II (1924), 246–271; by Franz G. Taeschner, "Beiträge zur Geschichte der Achis in Anatolien," *Islamica,* IV (1929), 1–47, and *idem,* "Aḫī," in *Encyclopaedia of Islām,* rev. ed., I (Leyden, 1960; repr. 1967), 321–323; and by Wittek, "Deux chapîtres de l'histoire des Turcs de Roum," *Byzantion,* XI (1936), 285–319, and *idem, The Rise of the Ottoman Empire* (London, 1958). See also Ernst Werner, *Die Geburt einer Grossmacht: die Osmanen (1300–1481), ein Beitrag zur Genesis des türkischen Feudalismus* (Berlin, 1966).

On the struggle for the Aegean see Max Silberschmidt, *Das orientalische Problem zur Zeit der Entstehung des türkischen Reiches nach venezianischen Quellen, 1381–1400* (Leipzig and Berlin, 1923); Irène Mélikoff-Sayar, tr., *Le Destân d'Umur Pacha: Düstûrnâme-i Enverî* (Bibliothèque byzantine, Documents, no. 2; Paris, 1954); Paul Lemerle, *L'Émirat d'Aydin, Byzance et l'Occident: Recherches sur "La geste d'Umur Pacha"* (Bibliothèque byzantine, Études, no. 2; Paris, 1957), basic for 1330–1348; and Angeliki E. Laiou, "Marino Sanudo Torsello, Byzantium and the Turks," *Speculum,* XLV (1970), 374–392.

On Timur, the Ottomans, and the west see M. Halil Yinanç, "Bayazid I," *İslâm Ansiklopedisi,* II (Istanbul, 1943), 369–371; Marie M. Alexandrescu-Dersca, *La Campagne de Timur en Anatolie (1402)* (Bucharest, 1942), reviewed by Inalcik in *Belleten,* XI (1947), 341–345; Zeki V. Togan, "Timurs Osteuropapolitik," *ZDMG,* CVIII-2 (1958), 279–298; Tekindağ, *Berkuk devrinde Memlûk sultanligi* (Istanbul, 1961); Yücel, "Timur tehlikesi," *Belleten,* XXXVII (1973), 159–190; and Anatoly P. Novosel'tsev, "On the Historical Evolution of Timur," *Voprosy isotorii,* II (1973), 100–115.

No systematic and objective history of Ottoman-Byzantine relations exists. For partial treatments see Oskar Halecki, *Un Empereur de Byzance à Rome: Vingt ans de travail pour l'union des églises et pour la défense de l'empire d'Orient, 1355–1375* (Warsaw, 1930; repr. London, 1972); Peter Charanis, "Internal Strife at Byzantium during the XIVth Century," *Byzantion,* XV

their timber and slaves, were brought into a closer relationship with the Mamluks.

One crucial development in the ensuing period of struggle between Islam and Christendom was the rise in the first half of the fourteenth century of Turkish navies manned by sea ghazis,[2] who were later to

---

(1940), 208-230; *idem,* "The Strife among the Palaeologi and the Ottoman Turks, 1370-1402," *Byzantion,* XVI (1942-1943), 286-314; George Ostrogorsky, *History of the Byzantine State,* tr. Joan M. Hussey (London, 1956); John W. Barker, *Manuel II Palaeologus, 1391-1425: a Study in Late Byzantine Statesmanship* (New Brunswick, N.J., 1969); Apostolos E. Bakalopoulos, *Origins of the Greek Nation, 1204-1461,* tr. Ian Motes, vol. I (New Brunswick, 1970); and Laiou, *Constantinople and the Latins: the Foreign Policy of Andronicus II, 1282-1328* (Cambridge, Mass., 1972).

Byzantine chroniclers are indispensable for Ottoman history before 1451; John Cantacuzenus's memoirs, *Historiarum libri IV,* ed. Ludwig Schopen (*CSHB,* 3 vols., Bonn, 1828-1832; also in *PG,* vol. CLIII), are analyzed by Valentin Parisot, *Cantacuzène, homme d'état et historien* (Paris, 1845), and by Lemerle, *L'Émirat,* in the light of Nicephorus Gregoras (1290-1360) and other contemporary sources. For the period 1360-1400 no Byzantine chronicle comparable to these two exists. For 1400-1462 the most important source is Ducas (Doukas), *Historia byzantina,* ed. Immanuel Bekker (*CSHB,* Bonn, 1834; also in *PG,* vol. CLVII), tr. Harry J. Magoulias as *Decline and Fall of Byzantium to the Ottoman Turks (Historia turco-byzantina, 1341-1462)* (Detroit, 1975). Ducas should be supplemented by George Sphrantzes, *Chronicon minus,* ed. Bekker (*CSHB,* Bonn, 1838; also in *PG,* vol. CLVI), tr. Marios Philippides as *The Fall of the Byzantine Empire* (Amherst, 1980). For 1420-1463 see also Laonicus Chalcocondylas, *Historiarum demonstrationes,* ed. Eugen Darkó (2 vols. in 3, Budapest, 1922-1927; cf. Akdes Nimet (Kurat), *Die türkische Prosopographie bei Laonikos Chalkokondyles* (Hamburg, 1933). Charles (Karl) Hopf, *Chroniques gréco-romanes inédites ou peu connues* (Berlin, 1873; repr. 1966), is still useful.

For the Ottomans and the Balkans a systematic bibliography is the *Bibliographie d'études balkaniques* (Sofia, since 1966). Each Balkan country publishes a journal devoted to Balkan studies: *Balkan Studies* (Salonika, since 1960), *Revue des études sud-est européennes* (Bucharest, since 1962), *Studia albanica* (Tirana, since 1963), *Études balkaniques* (Sofia, since 1964), *Balcanica* (Belgrade, since 1969), and *Güney-Doğu Avrupa araştirmalari* (Istanbul, since 1972). See also Constantin Jireček, *Geschichte der Bulgaren* (Prague, 1876); Stanoje Stanojević, "Die Biographie Stefan Lazarevićs von Konstantin dem Philosophen als Geschichtsquelle," *Archiv für slavische Philologie,* XVIII (1896), 409-472, source tr. Matthias Braun as *Lebensbeschreibung des Despoten Stefan Lazarević . . .* (Göttingen, 1956); Stojan Novaković, *Die Serben und Türken,* tr. K. Kezdimirović (Semlin, 1897); Ferdinand Šišić, "Die Schlacht bei Nikopolis (25 September 1396)." *Wissenschaftliche Mittheilungen aus Bosnien und der Hercegovina,* VI (1898), 291-327; Jireček, *Geschichte der Serben* (2 vols., Gotha, 1911-1918; repr. Amsterdam, 1967); Constantin Marinescu (Marinesco), "Alphonse V, roi d'Aragon et de Naples, et l'Albanie de Scanderbeg," *Mélanges de l'École roumaine en France,* I (Paris, 1923), 7-135; Ilie Minea, "Vlad Dracul şi vremea sa," *Cercetari istorce,* II (1923), 1-135; Atiya, *The Crusade of Nicopolis* (London, 1934); Francisc Pall, "Marino Barlezio: uno storico humanista," *Mélanges d'histoire générale,* II (Cluj, 1938), 135-318; Braun, "Türkenherrschaft und Türkenkampf bei den Balkanslaven," *Welt als Geschichte,* III-IV (1940), 124-139; Georg Städtmüller, *Geschichte Südosteuropas* (Munich, 1950); Ivan Dujčev, "La Conquête turque et la prise de Constantinople dans la littérature slave contemporaine," *Byzantinoslavica,* XIV (1953), 14-54; XVI (1955), 318-329; and XVII (1956), 276-340; Branislav Djurdjev, "Bosna," in *Encyclopaedia of Islām,* rev. ed., I, 1261-1275; Inalcik, "Arnavutluk," *ibid.,* I, 650-658; *idem,* "Iskender Beg," *ibid.,* IV-1 (1973-1975), 138-140; Bariša Krekić, *Dubrovnik (Raguse) et le Levant au moyen âge* (Paris and The Hague, 1961); Giuseppe Valentini, ed., *Acta albanica veneta, saeculorum XIV et XV* (20 vols., Munich, 1967-1974); and Inalcik,

2. Al-'Umarī, *Masālik al-abṣar fī mamālik al-amṣar,* ed. Taeschner (Leipzig, 1929), pp. 43-52.

form the nucleus of Ottoman sea power. The emergence of these sea ghazis can be seen as a continuation of the Turkish expansion movement toward the west. Turkish azebs (from Arabic *'azab,* bachelor, youth), the fighting men on these flotillas, were identical in origin, motivation, and organization to the frontier ghazis. One of the first results of this new set of circumstances was a northward shift of the main field of action, eventually leaving Egypt and Syria out of the actual struggle.

The Turkish conquest of western Anatolia from the Byzantines in

"L'Empire ottoman," (*Actes du premier Congrès international des études balkaniques et sud-est européennes . . . [Sofia, 1966],* Éditions de l'Académie bulgare des sciences, 1967-1971, III (*Histoire,* 1969).

On Hungary, Austria, and the Ottomans see Josef von Aschbach, *Geschichte Kaiser Sigmunds* (4 vols., Hamburg, 1838); Alfons Huber, "Ludwig I. von Ungarn und die ungarischen Vassallenländer," *Archiv für österreichische Geschichte,* LXVI (1884), 1-44, printed separately (Vienna, 1885); Leopold Kupelwieser, *Die Kämpfe Ungarns mit der Osmanen bis zur Schlacht bei Mohács, 1526,* 2nd ed. (Vienna, 1899); Gustav Beckmann, *Der Kampf Kaiser Sigmunds gegen die werdende Weltmacht der Osmanen, 1392-1437* (Gotha, 1902); Iorga, "Du Nouveau sur la campagne turque de Jean Hunyadi en 1448," *Revue historique du sud-est européen,* III (1926), 13-27; and Lajos Elekes, *Hunyadi* (in Hungarian; Budapest, 1952).

On the papacy, Italy, and the Ottomans the basic reference is now Kenneth M. Setton, *The Papacy and the Levant, 1204-1571* (4 vols., Philadelphia, 1976-1985). Older works still useful include Lodovico Sauli, *Storia della colonia dei genovesi in Galata* (2 vols., Turin, 1831); Samuele Romanin, *Storia documentata di Venezia* (10 vols., Venice 1853-1861; repr. 1925); Iorga, *Philippe de Mézières, 1327-1405* (Paris, 1896); Camillo Manfroni, *La Battaglia di Gallipoli e la politica veneta-turca* (Venice, 1902); *idem, Storia della marina italiana dal trattato di Ninfeo alla caduta di Costantinopoli* (3 vols., Leghorn, 1902-1903); Francesco Cerone, "La Politica orientale di Alfonso di Aragona," *Archivio storico per le provincie napoletane,* XXVII (1902), 3-93, 380-456, 555-634, 774-852, and XXVIII (1903), 154-212; and William Miller, *The Latins in the Levant: a History of Frankish Greece (1204-1566)* (London, 1908; repr. 1964).

More recent works include Pall, "Ciriaco d'Ancona e la crociata contro i Turchi," AR, *BSH,* XX (1938), 9-60; Babinger, "Le Vicende veneziane nella lotta contro i Turchi durante il secolo XV," *Civiltà veneziana del quattrocento* (Florence, 1957), pp. 51-73; Anthony Luttrell, "The Crusade in the Fourteenth Century," *Europe in the Late Middle Ages,* ed. John R. Hale, John R. L. Highfield, and Beryl Smalley (London, 1965), pp. 122-154; Eugene L. Cox, *The Green Count of Savoy* (Princeton, 1967); Paolo Preto, *Venezia e i Turchi* (Florence, 1975); Michel Balard, *La Romanie génoise (XIIe-début du XVe siècle)* (2 vols., Rome and Genoa, 1978); and "Le Relazioni tra l'Italia e la Turchia", special issue of *Il Veltro,* XXIII/2-4 (1979).

On the crusade of Varna see the anonymous chronicle, *Gazavât-i Sultân Murâd b. Mehemmed Han,* ed. Inalcik and M. Oğuz (Ankara, 1978); Lajos Fekete, "Das Fethnâme über die Schlacht bei Varna," *Byzantinoslavica,* XIV (1953), 258-270; O. Székely, "Hunyadi János elsö török hadjáratai (1441-1444)," *Hadtörténelmi Közlemények,* XX-XXII (1919-1921), 1-64; Pall, "Autour de la Croisade de Varna: la question de la paix de Szeged et de sa rupture (1444)," AR, *BSH,* XXII (1941), 144-158; Halecki, *The Crusade of Varna: Discussion of Controversial Problems* (New York, 1943); and Jan Dąbrowski, "L'Année 1444," *Bulletin international de l'Académie polonaise des sciences et des lettres: Classe d'histoire et de philosophie,* supp. no. 6 (Cracow, 1951).

For the Ottoman adoption of Hussite *wagenburg* tactics see M. Wulf, *Die hussitische Wagenburg* (Berlin, 1889); Jan Durdík, *Hussitisches Heerwesen* (Berlin, 1961); and *Gazavât-i Sultân Murâd,* ed. Inalcik and Oğuz.

the second half of the thirteenth century had not caused serious alarm in the west, since western Christendom was then primarily concerned with the fate of the last remnants of the crusader states on the Syrian coast and with the restoration of the Latin empire in Constantinople. The Turkish warrior-nomads had been active on the Selchükid-Byzantine frontiers for a long period of time without making a determined attempt at invasion, and, in any case, their repulsion was thought not to be a difficult task for the Byzantine state. In the crusade projects drawn up around 1300 the Turkish invasion of western Anatolia was regarded as a minor question to be dealt with by the crusader army on its way to Palestine.

Today most historians try to explain the collapse of Byzantine rule in western Anatolia by focusing on certain "unwise" policies of the Byzantine government. But it seems clear that the fundamental reason for the collapse is the mass migration of the Turcomans (Türkmen) westward in the last decades of the thirteenth century, an event reminiscent of the first Turkish invasion of Anatolia after the battle of Manzikert (1071). Christian Europe became aware of the significance of the Turkish advance only in the early fourteenth century, when Latin possessions and commercial traffic came increasingly under attack by the Turcoman ghazis, fighters for Islamic holy war (*jihād*) operating on the Aegean Sea. Thus, with Islam issuing a direct challenge to Europe on the sea, an entirely new situation arose in the long struggle between Islam and Christendom.

The gravity of the threat on the Aegean was clearly seen by Marino Sanudo "Torsello" (1270–1337). A tireless propagandist for a general crusade against Egypt since 1306, Sanudo had by 1320 developed the view that the first objective of a crusade should be the expulsion of the Turks from the Aegean.[3] Indeed, coupled with an effective military organization and with the revival of the holy war, the mass movement of the Turks toward the west assumed, after the first successes, such a magnitude that there was soon talk of a Turkish peril for all Europe.

When a new Turkey with great demographic potential and a heightened holy war ideology emerged in the old Selchükid (Seljuk) frontier zone, east of a line from the mouth of the Dalaman (Indos) river to that of the Sakarya (Sangarius), a thrust by this explosive frontier society against the neighboring Byzantine territory in western Anatolia was almost inevitable.

---

3. Laiou, "Marino Sanudo Torsello," p. 380. Cf. Atiya, "The Crusade in the Fourteenth Century," in volume III of the present work, p. 10.

This westward expansion had been accomplished in four stages: the seasonal transhumance movements of Turcoman nomadic groups into the Byzantine coastal plains; the organization of small raiding groups under ghazi leaders, mostly of tribal origin, for booty raids or for employment as mercenaries; the emergence of successful leaders capable of bringing local chiefs together as their clients, for conquest and for the establishment of *beyliks* (principalities) in the conquered lands, on the model of the principalities founded in the old Selchükid frontier zone; and finally, the involvement of these ghazi beyliks, with definite political and economic goals, in the regional struggle for supremacy in the Aegean and in the Balkans.

In the 1320's and 1330's, Turkish groups acting as ghazi raiding parties or mercenary companies joined together under the command of powerful leaders such as Umur Pasha (1334–1348) of the Aydin dynasty or Orkhan (1326–1362) and his eldest son, Suleiman Pasha, of the Ottoman house; only through them could the Byzantines hope to acquire sizable mercenary aid from Anatolia. Through alliance with the Byzantines the Turcoman begs in turn could provide employment and booty for the ever-growing number of ghazis gathering under their banners for raids on an increasingly larger scale in the Balkans. At this stage neither Umur nor Orkhan was interested in conquest or settlement of overseas lands.

Between 1329 and 1337, while Umur was launching his spectacular sea expeditions from Smyrna, the Ottomans, fighting against the Byzantines in northwestern Anatolia, were also making important conquests, including Nicaea on March 2, 1330, and Nicomedia in 1337. Their first significant advances came during the period 1329–1334, when Umur too was engaged in hostilities with the Byzantines. Though our sources give no hint of an alliance or actual coöperation between Umur and Orkhan, circumstances made them natural allies in this period, and again from 1342 to 1346, when Umur was giving strong support to John VI Cantacuzenus against his rivals in Constantinople.[4] The efforts of the latter to secure military aid from Orkhan failed; instead, with the assistance of Ottoman troops, Cantacuzenus was able to seize all the Black Sea ports except Sozopolis from the hands of his enemies. The marriage of his daughter Theodora to Orkhan in June 1346 cemented Cantacuzenus's alliance with the Ottoman principality, by

4. For this period see Lemerle, *L'Émirat d'Aydin*, pp. 145–174, 204–217. Lemerle relies on the translation into French by Mélikoff-Sayar, *Le Destân d'Umur Pacha*. Cf. Luttrell, "The Hospitallers at Rhodes, 1306–1421," in volume III of the present work, pp. 293–295; Inalcik, *op. cit.* (in note 1, above).

then the strongest of the Turcoman states. Once in full power in Constantinople (February 3, 1347), however, Cantacuzenus appeared to turn to a policy of coöperation with the Latins against the Turks, offering in 1348 to continue the Byzantine alliance with pope Clement VI (1342-1352) and Humbert II of Viennois (d. 1355).[5] This policy, however, was intended primarily to thwart the plans of Stephen IV Dushan, the Serbian king (1331-1355), who in 1345 had proclaimed himself "emperor of the Serbs and Greeks".

By 1347 Dushan's advances had become a major threat to the existence of the empire, as he was seeking Venetian assistance in the conquest of Constantinople.[6] Under the circumstances Cantacuzenus had to maintain close relations with the Ottomans, the only source from which he could expect substantial military aid; it was this situation that led to the Turkish settlement in Europe.

While the Turks of Aydin were effectively neutralized by the capture of the castle at Smyrna (Izmir), which the pope had decided to keep as a check upon them, the Ottoman Turks were becoming more and more involved in Balkan affairs, especially after they had firmly established themselves in Karasi, facing Thrace.[7] Umur's death in the spring of 1348 led to Aydin's decline as a threat to the Latins, but it also served to strengthen the position of the Ottomans, bringing under their banner an increasing number of *ghazis*. The leaders of the *ghazā* in Karasi appear to have collaborated with the Ottomans to bring about the union of the two states, and the Ottoman conquests in Thrace in the next decade were to be basically the work of ghazis from Karasi.

Immediately after the first conquests in Karasi, the area was made into an Ottoman *uj* (frontier) sanjak with Biga (Pegae) as its center, under the leadership of Suleiman Pasha, an ardent advocate of frontier warfare (*ghazā*), who was to become responsible for the shaping of Ottoman western policy. The new frontier sanjak had important sea bases at Lampsacus (Lapseki), Aydinjik (near Cyzicus), and Kemer (Keramides?), which from Byzantine times had sheltered corsairs who preyed on the merchant ships traveling between the Dardanelles and the Bosporus. In 1352 the principal Ottoman army was to embark from Kemer for their conquest of the isthmus of the Gallipoli peninsula.

---

5. See Raymond J. Loenertz, "Ambassades grecs auprès du Pape Clément VI (1348)," in *Orientalia Christiana periodica*, XIX (1953), 178-196; Lemerle, *L'Émirat*, pp. 224-226; Setton, *The Papacy and the Levant*, I, 212-215. Cf. Deno Geanakoplos, "Byzantium and the Crusades, 1261-1354," in volume III of the present work, pp. 63-65.

6. Jireček, *Geschichte der Serben*, I, 386-387, 396; Thiriet, *Régestes*, I, no. 189.

7. Lemerle, *L'Émirat*, pp. 219-222. The area around Pergamum (Bergama) and Troy facing the Dardanelles appears to have been organized as a frontier sanjak under a branch of the Karasi dynasty, first under Yakhshi Beg and then under Suleiman Beg.

We cannot tell with certainty which of the Turkish groups active in Thrace in this period came from the Ottoman dominions. On two occasions Byzantine historians speak specifically of Ottoman armies sent over to Thrace: the first came shortly after the meeting of Orkhan with Cantacuzenus at Scutari (Üsküdar) in 1346, when Suleiman Pasha, at the head of an army of ten thousand, was sent to Thrace against the Serbs. Evidently the Ottoman soldiery engaged rather in the usual booty raids, and soon returned home to Anatolia. In 1350, when Stephen Dushan threatened Thessalonica, a second large Ottoman army, reportedly twenty thousand in number, again under Suleiman Pasha, proceeded along the Aegean coast of Thrace together with the Byzantine forces under Matthew Cantacuzenus, son of John VI, while John VI Cantacuzenus and co-emperor John V Palaeologus sailed by sea to Thessalonica. Before the armies reached their objective, however, Orkhan stated that he was threatened by Turkish emirs, his neighbors in Anatolia, and called Suleiman back; after a raid into Bulgaria, the latter returned.

A crisis parallel to that of Byzantium also helped to make possible the Ottoman passage into Europe: the conflict between Genoa and Venice over the Byzantine heritage in the eastern Aegean. The Venetian-Genoese war (1350–1355), which caused the dissolution of the anti-Turkish coalition in the Aegean, gave rise to a new power alignment in the area. While the Venetians moved closer to Cantacuzenus and king Peter IV of Aragon-Catalonia (1336–1387) and his Catalans in the Levant, the Genoese allied themselves with the leading Turkish emirs, Khiḍr (Hizir) Beg of Aydîn and the Ottoman Orkhan. During the war the Turkish emirs provided the Genoese not only with badly needed provisions but also with military aid. Cantacuzenus, always hoping that Byzantine sovereignty might be reëstablished in Chios and the two Phocaeas, then in Genoese hands, actually concluded a treaty of alliance with Venice in May 1351. Venice promised to mediate between the emperor and Stephen Dushan.

Both the Venetians and the Genoese sought the alliance of the Ottomans in this all-out war for the control of the waterways to the Black Sea. The Ottomans controlled the Asiatic side of the Bosporus, and their aid to Pera was of crucial importance. Despite the solicitations of the Venetians and Cantacuzenus, the Ottomans chose to support the Genoese, a logical policy for them to follow since the Venetians were known to be the principal contender against Turkish westward expansion in this period, while the Genoese showed themselves to be generally coöperative. Apparently the Genoese-Ottoman treaty was the first treaty concluded between the Ottomans and a western nation.

(The document itself is not extant, and its exact date is not known.) During the war the Ottomans supplied the Genoese with one thousand archers, who were stationed at Pera and on the Genoese ships.[8]

The Ottomans apparently took part in the defense of Pera in the summer of 1351, when, following a surprise attack by the Venetians, the city was besieged by joint Venetian-Byzantine forces. Orkhan himself, at the head of his army, arranged an interview with the Genoese admiral Paganino Doria at Chalcedon to the south of the Bosporus.[9] The major clash between the two parties took place on the Bosporus on February 15, 1352. Judging from a Genoese document of a later date, praising the role Orkhan played on the occasion,[10] he must have taken an active part in this crucial battle between the Genoese armada under Doria and the allied fleets of Venice and Aragon. Abandoned by his allies and surrounded in Constantinople by victorious Ottoman and Genoese forces, Cantacuzenus had to accept a treaty of peace with Doria, signed May 6, 1352, which forbade the use of Greek territories or seamen by the Venetians against the Genoese, and recognized the Genoese possession of Pera within its new limits.[11]

Thanks to Genoese assistance, the Ottomans were provided with a safe means of crossing the Straits whenever they wished, aboard Genoese ships, while the Genoese in turn secured Ottoman protection for Pera and commercial privileges within Ottoman dominions. A first example of this coöperation occurred in 1352 when the Ottoman forces under Suleiman and his brother Khalil were ferried across the Bosporus on Genoese ships for raids into Greek territories in Thrace.[12] Commercial ties between Pera and Bursa (Brusa) would be of considerable benefit to the development of both cities. Bursa was soon to become a terminus for caravans bringing silk from Iran, and the silk trade was one of the sources of Pera's renewed prosperity. Pera, in turn, was to be the Ottomans' market for obtaining western commodities, principally the fine woolens much in demand in the Near East.

In 1352 the Ottomans were still at war with Byzantium. Their collaboration with the Genoese in the siege of Constantinople, coupled with the invasion of Thrace by an Ottoman army under Suleiman, must

---

8. Camillo Manfroni, "Le Relazioni fra Genova, l'impero bizantino e i Turchi," *Atti della Società ligure di storia patria,* XXVIII (ser. 3, I; 1896), 710–713, cited by Iorga, *Geschichte,* I, 192; Heyd, tr. Raynaud, I, 506.

9. Iorga, "Latins et Grecs d'Orient et l'établissement des Turcs en Europe," *Byzantinische Zeitschrift,* XV (1906), 211.

10. Luigi T. Belgrano, "Prima serie di documenti reguardanti le colonie di Pera," *Atti della Società ligure,* XIII (1877–1884), 127, 129, cited by Heyd, tr. Raynaud, I, 507.

11. Documents published by Sauli, *Della Colonia dei genovesi in Galata,* II, 216.

12. Iorga, *Geschichte,* I, 192.

have been decisive in inducing Cantacuzenus to abandon his western allies. He hastened to make peace with the Ottomans, still with the idea that he could use them as he had Umur's ghazis, to further his own interests in protecting the empire against Stephen Dushan and in replacing the Palaeologi on the Byzantine throne. Dushan, in turn, chose to protect John V Palaeologus (1341/1391) in the civil war which broke out again in Thrace in the summer of 1352 and lasted through the summer of 1356. Allied to the Venetians in return for a promise to relinquish the island of Tenedos, John V mobilized a Serbian-Bulgarian army in Demotica to set out against Matthew Cantacuzenus in Adrianople. Suddenly an Ottoman army of ten thousand men under Suleiman arrived to oppose the allied army, and inflicted a crushing defeat on it at Pythion in October 1352.[13] This was the first Ottoman victory over the Serbs, who were to be until 1389 the major contenders against Ottoman expansion into the Balkans.

John V Palaeologus fled, and took shelter at Tenedos under Venetian protection, finally leaving Cantacuzenus free to claim the throne. Suleiman then entered Adrianople as an ally of Cantacuzenus, which the Ottoman epic fancies as the first "conquest" of the city by the Ottomans. Suleiman returned home after this meeting, but he left behind a small Turkish force that took up winter quarters in a site reportedly assigned by Cantacuzenus, at Tzympe (Jinbi), a small fortress on the coast north of Gallipoli. As a bridgehead on the western shores of the Marmara sea, the occupation of Tzympe was important as a harbinger of the Turkish settlement in Europe to come.

The historian Nicephorus Gregoras asserted that Cantacuzenus himself gave the Turks the fortress, and that they lived in Tzympe with their families under a qadi with their own mosque, forming a military colony in the pay of Cantacuzenus.[14] The latter, in reply, tried to absolve himself of responsibility for the incident by saying that the fortress was taken by the Ottoman Turks during the events of 1351–1352.[15] In Ottoman tradition Tzympe was captured by surprise by a small group (seventy men) with the aid of a native Greek.[16] However that may be,

---

13. Jireček, *loc. cit.* The Ottoman tradition on Suleiman's victory over the Serbs is to be found in Pseudo-Rûhî (Oxford, Bodleian Library, MS. Marsh 313), fols. 21–22; on this source see Inalcik, "The Rise of Ottoman Historiography," pp. 152–167.

14. Iorga, *Geschichte,* I, p. 194.

15. Iorga, "Latins," p. 213. The Venetian accusation that the Genoese with two small ships took the Turks across the Straits, and thus were responsible for their settlement in Europe (Heyd, *op. cit.,* II, 44–45) must have some truth in it. We know that Suleiman's forces were transported to Thrace by the Genoese in 1351.

16. *Düstûrnâme-i Enverî,* ed. Yînanç (Istanbul, 1928), p. 82.

once settled in Tzympe[17] Eje Beg, accompanied by Melik Beg, the converted son of Asen, Greek lord of Gallipoli, ferried fresh forces amounting in a few days to two thousand men from the Anatolian to the European coast on Greek ships found in the port of Tzympe. Asen, failing to overcome them, shut himself in his castle. In Biga Suleiman Pasha put the new frontier thus established around Tzympe under the command of Eje Beg, who, it seems, had formulated the original plan to organize the ghazis under the protection of the Ottoman state into a permanent settlement on the European side of the Dardanelles.[18]

A new and decisive development in the settlement of Turks in Thrace was, according to the Ottoman sources, the transfer under Suleiman Pasha himself of a regular army, three thousand in number, by ship from Kemer to Kozlu-Dere, a valley near Tzympe that led up to the Hexamilion on the heights dominating the isthmus of the Gallipoli peninsula. Suleiman set up headquarters at Bolayîr on the heights of the isthmus and organized his ghazis into two fronts, one against Gallipoli under Eje Beg and Ghāzī Fāḍil, the other against Thrace under Hajji Ilbegi and Evrenos (Evrenuz), all from Karasi. Gallipoli was put under constant pressure by the ghazis, who also tried to cut off its sea communications.[19] In the north Suleiman Pasha succeeded by 1354 in subduing the area between Saros bay and Megali-Agora (Migal-Kara), thus penetrating deep into Thrace.

Determined to maintain themselves in Thrace, the Ottomans pursued their traditional policy of *istimālet,* whereby they tried to win over the native population through friendly and conciliatory treatment, while deporting to Anatolia any Greek military elements capable of organizing resistance.

The Turkish settlement in Thrace caused consternation in Byzantium, but the situation was militarily hopeless. The number of Byzan-

---

17. According to Enverî, *Düstûrnâme,* p. 83, the first fortress conquered by the Ottomans in Thrace was not Tzympe but Akcha-Burgos. A village by the name of Akcha-Burgoz in the Kozlu-Dere area near Gallipoli is mentioned in the Ottoman survey book of Gallipoli dated 1476 (Istanbul, Belediye Library, Cevdet no. O-79). In the 'Âshîk Pasha-zâde account (*op. cit.,* p. 124) Akcha-Limon or Akcha-Burgoz became the target of Ottoman attacks, but only after the conquest of Jinbi (Tzympe). The Ottomans, he says, after settling at Jinbi, burned the ships lying at Akcha-Limon.

18. The Ottoman tradition ascribes the original idea to the Ottoman leaders, Suleiman or (more likely) Orkhan. Allegedly Eje Beg met Suleiman in Biga, or Suleiman met his father, Orkhan, at Bursa, and got the idea for a permanent conquest of Thrace. These stories were evidently later additions intended to ascribe the original idea to the Ottoman house.

19. They let no ships arrive or disembark at Gallipoli ('Âshîk Pasha-zàde, *op. cit.,* p. 124).

tine and Catalan soldiers employed by the empire had greatly diminished, as Cantacuzenus himself admitted, as a result of the recent civil
war, so the emperor had for some time been dependent on the Turkish
troops sent by his son-in-law Orkhan. The only means left to him to
exert pressure on Suleiman were diplomatic, through Orkhan. It appears that Orkhan and the emperor finally signed a treaty providing
for the evacuation of the area occupied in Thrace in return for the
payment to Suleiman of ten thousand gold pieces.[20]

The earthquake of March 2, 1354, which demolished the walls of
Gallipoli and other fortifications in the area, completely altered the
situation. Exposed to the raids of the surrounding Turks, most of the
towns' population either took shelter in the few fortified places still
left standing or fled to Constantinople by sea. The ghazis immediately took possession of Gallipoli and other abandoned sites. The Ottoman tradition says that on this occasion "since there were innumerable
'Frenks' (Catalan mercenaries?) in Gallipoli, it was impossible to capture it. There was nothing more for the ghazis to do but pray for its
fall. And then, early one morning the walls suddenly collapsed. Its
commander left in a ship."

Suleiman was in his capital, Biga, in Anatolia, when the earthquake
occurred. He hurried quickly to Gallipoli and took steps to secure the
Turkish presence in the newly occupied places, repairing fortifications
and bringing more ghazis and whole colonies of settlers from Anatolia to settle in and reinforce the defenses of the abandoned towns.[21]
While he was there, he led his ghazis on a raid for booty into Bulgaria,
though sparing Byzantine lands out of respect, apparently, for the recent peace treaty with the emperor.

In the face of Cantacuzenus's protest to Orkhan that Suleiman's
occupation of Byzantine cities was against the terms of their peace
treaty, Suleiman replied that he had not taken them by force but had
simply occupied some abandoned towns. It appears that there was quite
a lengthy exchange of views before Orkhan, in exchange for forty thousand gold pieces, agreed to try to persuade his son to heed the emper-
or's demands. For Cantacuzenus this was a critical issue, upon which
his very survival on the Byzantine throne depended, as he was accused
by his opponents of "delivering the empire and the Christians into the
hands of the Turks".[22] The people of Constantinople were in a state

---

20. Cantacuzenus, *op cit.*, III, 163, refers repeatedly to such a treaty.
21. On this point 'Âshik Pasha-zâde, *loc. cit.*, and Cantacuzenus, *loc. cit.*, concur; see in
particular the important document in Beldiceanu-Steinherr, *Recherches*, pp. 135–148.
22. Nicephorus Gregoras, *Byzantina historia*, II, ed. Schopen (*CSHB*, Bonn, 1830), 3rd rev.
ed., by Immanuel Bekker (Bonn, 1855), p. 224.

of great agitation, anticipating that the Turks might even attack the city, when on November 22, 1354, John V Palaeologus suddenly appeared from his exile on Tenedos. In the face of the threatening mobs of the city, Cantacuzenus had no recourse but to resign.

With the fall of Cantacuzenus, Byzantine politics took on a more belligerent orientation, the first stage of which, it was believed, ought to be the resumption of negotiations with pope Innocent VI (1352–1362) for a crusade against the Turks, in exchange for the union of the churches. As early as December 20, 1355, John V Palaeologus, formally promising the union of the churches, always a precondition for papal coöperation, asked for immediate military aid (five galleys and fifteen transport ships with five hundred horse and a thousand footmen within six months), and the preparation of a large-scale crusade against the Turks.[23] That the emperor was in a desperate position was further shown by his promise to send his son Manuel as a hostage to the pope's court at Avignon. At this point, however, it was difficult for the pope even to secure money to maintain the defenses of Smyrna, always his primary concern.

In the summer of 1356, letters sent by the pope to Venice, Genoa, Cyprus, and the Hospitallers asking them to give military aid to the emperor were left unanswered. Even Venice, which was expected to be the most concerned about the Ottoman menace to Byzantium, remained passive. The Ottoman occupation of Gallipoli coincided first with Venice's war against Genoa, and then—despite the efforts of Peter Thomas, the papal nuncio, to bring about peace, while in Buda on his way to Constantinople in 1356—with resumption of the war between Venice and Hungary in April 1357. It is true that the Venetian bailie in Constantinople warned his government in time about the imminent danger created by the Ottoman settlement in Thrace. As early as 1354, during the panic caused by the news that Gallipoli had fallen, the bailie had written that the Greeks of Constantinople thought they had best put themselves under the protection of a strong Christian government such as Venice, Hungary, or Serbia.[24] The short-sighted and avaricious senate, however, was interested not in considering any steps to be taken against the Ottomans, but rather in forcing the emperor to pay heavy interest on its loans and to strengthen the existing ruinous trade privileges.

---

23. Halecki, *Un Empereur de Byzance à Rome*, pp. 29–38; see also Setton, *The Papacy*, I, 225–226.

24. Iorga, "Latins," pp. 217–218; letter published by Jireček, *Geschichte der Bulgaren*, p. 309. The bailie was Matthew Venier.

Although Peter Thomas's mission to Constantinople as the pope's nuncio, which lasted from the end of May to November 1357, did not produce the results hoped for by both sides, it is significant nevertheless as the first sign of papal awareness of the immediacy of the Ottoman threat to Byzantium. Following Peter Thomas's mission the pope began to mention Romania and Constantinople side by side with Smyrna as areas that had to be defended against the Turks. It is safe to say that it was at this time that western Europe began to see the Ottomans as the principal enemies of Christendom, and to make Gallipoli one of the principal targets of crusading activities.

When Peter Thomas arrived in Constantinople in the spring of 1357, he found that the emperor was away on campaign against the Ottomans, who had advanced rapidly through Thrace since the fall of Gallipoli in March 1354. As both Byzantine and Ottoman sources recount, immediately following the earthquake and subsequent capture of Gallipoli Suleiman busied himself in creating a strong Turkish bridgehead there. One of the earliest Ottoman traditions says: "[after the capture of Gallipoli] Suleiman sent word to his father: 'Now a great number of people of the Islamic faith are needed here so that the conquered fortresses can be settled and the country around them be made to flourish. We need also many *ghāzī yoldash* (ghazi companions) to garrison and reinforce the conquered fortresses.' Orkhan agreed with the proposal. First they deported over to Rumelia the Arab nomads who had arrived in Karasi. These remained for some time in the area around Gallipoli . . . [while Suleiman made further conquests in Thrace]. Every day new immigrants came over from Karasi. Settling down, these commenced ghazi activities. Briefly speaking, Islam was so strengthened that whenever they attacked, the infidels were unable to resist them."[25]

The capture by Phocaean corsairs of prince Khalil, the eleven-year-old son of Orkhan, in the early summer of 1357,[26] and the sudden death of Suleiman soon afterward, put Orkhan in a difficult position, compelling him to come to an agreement with John V, as it was only through him that Orkhan could hope to secure the release of his son from captivity. From Gregoras's detailed account of the event it becomes clear that the agreement involved Orkhan's promise to cease all aggression against Byzantine territory, to stop any aid to Matthew Cantacuzenus in Thrace, to reimburse all expenses incurred in the outfitting of ships to be sent against the Phocaeans, and to cancel the

25. 'Âshik Pasha-zâde, *op. cit.,* p. 124; Inalcik, "*Arab* Camel Drivers in Western Anatolia in the Fifteenth Century," *Revue d'histoire maghrebine,* X (1983), 256–270.

26. Between early June and July; see John's letter in Setton, *The Papacy,* I, 228.

outstanding debts of the emperor.[27] It appears that John V even hoped to recover the territory occupied by the Ottomans in Thrace, since the aggressive Suleiman was now dead. Thus in his answer to the pope's letter dated July 21, 1357, the emperor was able to communicate to Innocent VI some signs of success over his enemies and high hopes for the future.[28] For the ghazis the agreement, signed under duress, was a great sacrifice. It meant the cessation of warfare and the abandonment of the Turks who had recently settled in Thrace.

After his rescue of Khalil from the corsairs in the early summer of 1358,[29] John V conceived a plan that would maintain peace with the Ottomans. Following the example of Cantacuzenus, he secured Orkhan's agreement to the engagement of his daughter Irene, then almost ten years old, to the Ottoman prince in Constantinople. He then returned Khalil to his father at Nicomedia. Furthermore, he had the promise of the old Orkhan that Khalil was to succeed him on the throne at his death. After Suleiman's death prince Murad, with his tutor Lala Shahin, took his place in Gallipoli as frontier lord. Khalil, in his appanage in Nicaea, died soon afterward, in 1359.

The Ottoman tradition[30] is important for the historian of the crusades since it seems to corroborate a disputed account given by Philip of Mézières, the biographer of Peter Thomas, on the crusaders' campaign against the Ottomans in 1359. Back in Constantinople in the autumn of 1359 as the pope's apostolic legate in the east, Peter Thomas had brought with him a small crusading force composed of Hospitallers, Venetians, Genoese, and English soldiers on Venetian galleys. He found John V engaged in hostilities with the Ottomans, Khalil having by that time returned home, and perhaps died. According to Philip the crusaders, joined by Greek forces, captured and burned Lampsacus, an Ottoman transit port on the Asiatic side of the Dardanelles. During their return to their ships they were attacked by Turks waiting in ambush. Fleeing in disorder with the legate at their head, the Christians barely escaped a massacre.

Turkish tradition mentions an engagement on the plain adjoining

---

27. Ostrogorsky, "Byzance, état tributaire de l'empire turc," *Zbornik radova Vizantoloskog Instituta,* V (1958), 49–58.

28. Setton, *The Papacy,* I, 228.

29. See Parisot, *Cantacuzène,* pp. 298–309; Iorga, "Latins," p. 219, but the date given there, 1356, is erroneous.

30. Anonymous, *Tevārīkh-i Āl-i 'Othmān,* ed. Giese as *Die altosmanischen anonymen Chroniken . . . ,* I (Breslau, 1922), 18; a ghazi tradition in Oruj, *Tevārīkh-i Āl-i 'Othmān,* ed. Franz Babinger (Hanover, 1925), p. 19, makes Umur Pasha encourage Suleiman not to abandon his conquests in Europe.

Saros bay on the Aegean, and gives the impression that it occurred shortly after the death of Suleiman in 1357. At that time the Byzantines might have made a show of force there just to intimidate the ghazis into evacuating. But it is also plausible that in 1359 the crusaders made an attack at Saros bay as well as at Lampsacus. At any rate, this was the first Ottoman engagement with a crusading force, and seems to show that Philip's account is in general reliable.

A vigorous Ottoman onslaught started in Thrace under the leadership of prince Murad and his tutor Lala Shahin in 1359. Matthew Villani reports[31] that in 1359 Turks appeared before the walls of Constantinople, the first Ottoman threat against the imperial capital. He may have been referring to an event that is described in *The Anonymous Ottoman Chronicles*[32] as Murad's surrounding a fortress "near Istanbul" in A.H. 761 (October 23, 1359–October 13, 1360).[33] The following year the Ottoman army systematically occupied the fortresses on the two main roads between Constantinople and Adrianople, isolating the latter city and finally forcing it to surrender in the early spring of 1361.[34] To facilitate their rapid occupation of Thrace and its capital Adrianople, the Ottomans appear to have shrewdly made Matthew Cantacuzenus's cause their own, claiming that they were acting to protect the rights of the house of Cantacuzenus in the district of Adrianople, from which he had been driven out. The Ottoman ruler seems to have been exploiting his traditional role as a "supporter" of the rights of Cantacuzenus, his brother-in-law, and it would seem that there were still partisans of the Cantacuzeni in the region.

In connection with the Ottoman offensive between 1359 and 1361, the report of a conspiracy between Lala Shahin and the partisans of Cantacuzenus against John V's life should be mentioned. Rumors of the conspiracy reached Italy at the beginning of 1360, with emphasis on the role played by the Ottomans, who were suspected of desiring through it to lay hands on the imperial city.[35] Orkhan died in 1362, and was succeeded by his son Murad I (1362–1389).

31. Matthew Villani, "Istoria," *RISS,* XIV (Milan, 1729), 549–550; he also tells us that in 1358 the Hospitallers of Rhodes destroyed a Turkish fleet of 29 vessels returning from a raid on the Thracian coast.

32. See note 30.

33. See Inalcik, "The Conquest of Edirne," in *The Ottoman Empire: Conquest, Organization and Economy* (London, 1978), no. III, p. 195.

34. *Ibid.,* pp. 195–199; Beldiceanu-Steinherr, "La Conquête d'Andrinople par les Turcs," *Travaux et mémoires,* I (Paris, 1965), 431–461, assumes that Hajji Ilbegi and other frontier begs in Thrace acted independently of the Ottomans and conquered Adrianople about 1369.

35. See Parisot, *Cantacuzène,* pp. 306–308; Iorga, "Latins," pp. 220–221.

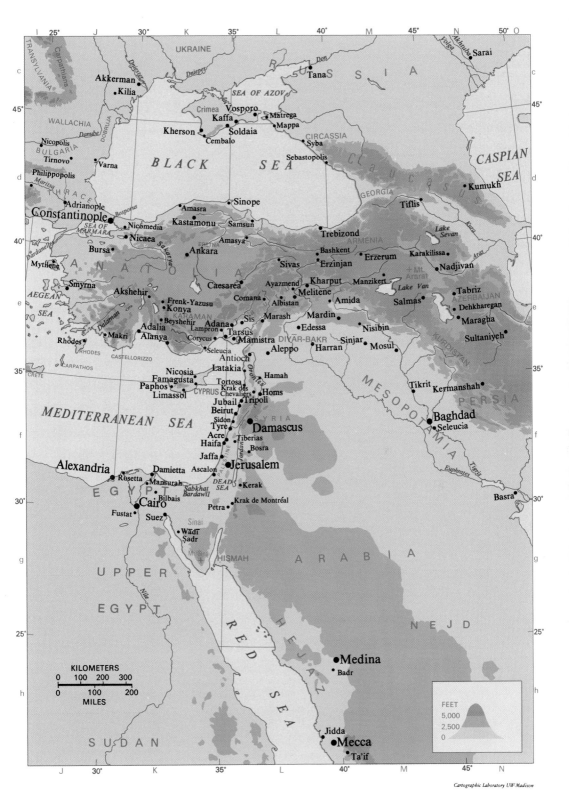

1. The Near East

2. Western Europe

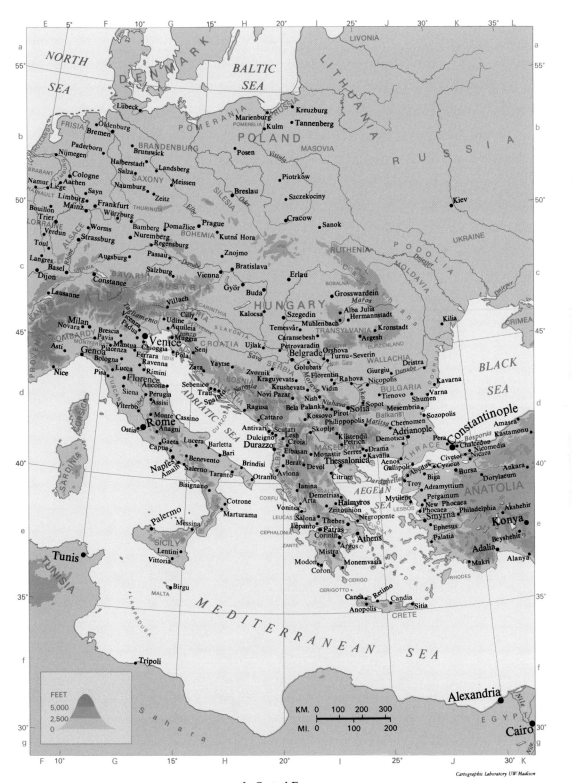

3. Central Europe

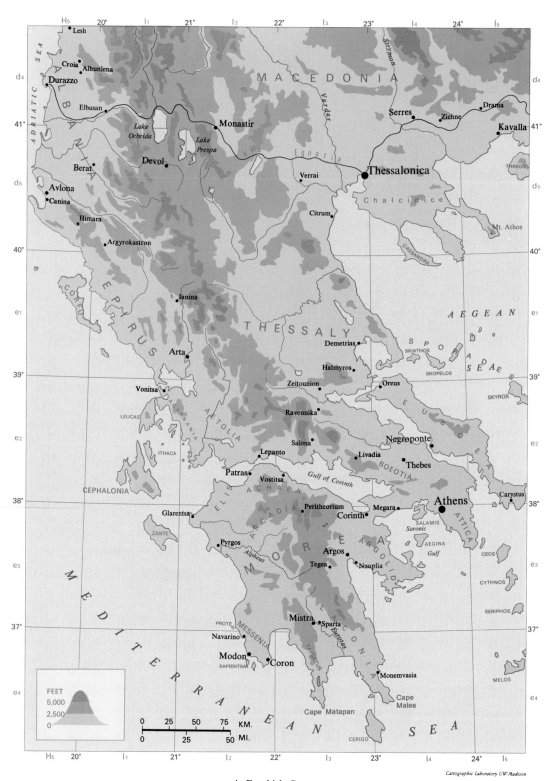

4. Frankish Greece

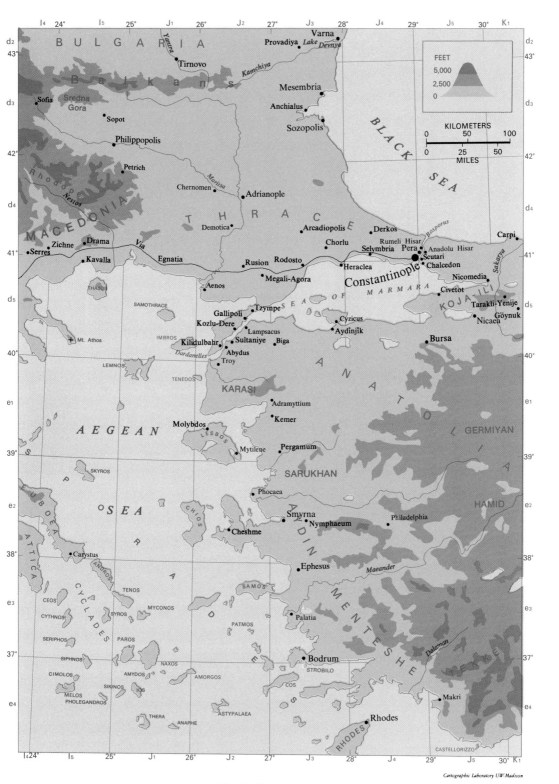

5. The Straits and the Aegean

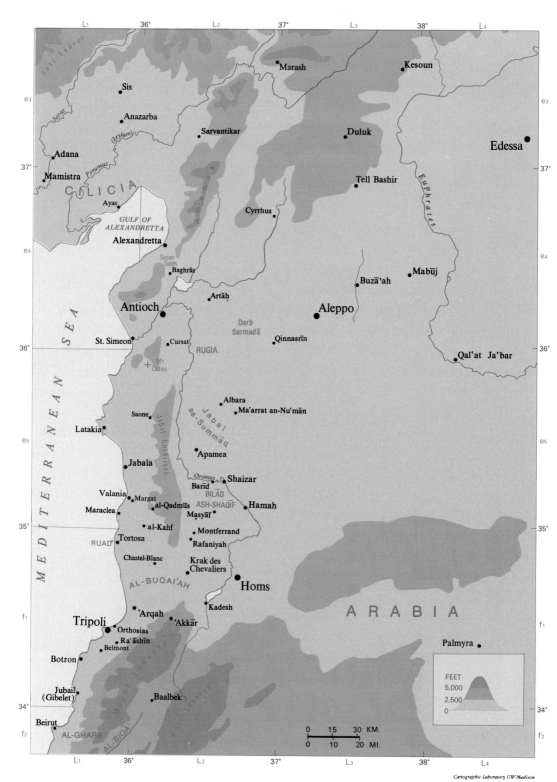

6. Northern Syria

L₁   36°   L₂   37°   L₃   38°   L₄

Anti-Taurus

Marash   Kesoun

Sis

e₃   e₃

Anazarba

Sarus

Sarvantikar   Duluk

Ceyhan

Adana   Edessa

37°   Mamistra   Tell Bashir   37°

Pyramus

CILICIA

Ayas   Cyrrhus   Euphrates

GULF OF ALEXANDRETTA

e₄   Buzāʿah   Mabūj   e₄

Alexandretta

Syrian Gates

Baghrās

Artāh

Antioch   Aleppo

SEA

Darb Sarmadā

St. Simeon   Cursat   Qinnasrīn

36°   RUGIA   Qalʿat Jaʿbar   36°

Mt. Casius

MEDITERRANEAN

Albara

Ma'arrat an-Nuʿmān

Saone   Jabal as-Summāq

e₅   Latakia   e₅

Apamea

Jabala

Orontes   Shaizar

Barīd

Valania   BILĀD

Margat   ASH-SHAQĪF   Hamah

Maraclea   al-Qadmūs

al-Kahf   Masyāf

35°   Montferrand   35°

RUAD   Tortosa   Rafaniyah

Chastel-Blanc   Krak des Chevaliers

AL-BUQAIʿAH

Homs   A R A B I A

f₁   ʿArqah   Kadesh   f₁

Tripoli   ʿAkkār

Orthosias   Palmyra

Raʾāshīn

Belmont

Botron

Jubail (Gibelet)

Baalbek

34°   FEET   34°

Beirut   5,000

f₂   AL-GHARB   AL-BIQĀ   2,500   f₂

0

0   15   30 KM.

0   10   20 MI.

L₁   36°   L₂   37°   L₃   38°   L₄

Cartographic Laboratory UW-Madison

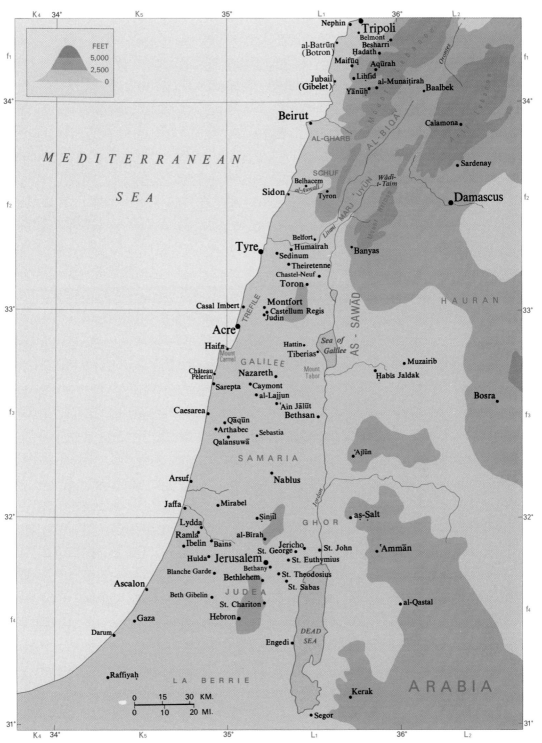

FEET
5,000
2,500
0

f₁

34°

Nephin
Tripoli
al-Batrūn
(Botron)
Belmont
Besharri
Ḥadath
Maifūq
Aqūrah
Jubail
(Gibelet)
Lihfid
al-Munaiṭirah
Yānūḥ
Baalbek

Beirut

Calamona

AL-GHARB

MEDITERRANEAN

SCHUF

Sardenay

SEA

Belhacem
al-Anwali
Sidon
Tyron

Wādi-
l-Taim

Damascus

f₂

Belfort
Humairah
Tyre
Sedinum
Theiretenne
Chastel-Neuf
Toron

Banyas

33°

Montfort
Casal Imbert
Castellum Regis
Judin

AS - SAWĀD

HAURAN

Acre
Haifa

Hattin
Tiberias

Sea of
Galilee

Muzairib

GALILEE

Mount
Carmel

Château
Pèlerin
Nazareth
Sarepta
Caymont
al-Lajjun
'Ain Jālūt
Bethsan

Mount
Tabor

Ḥabis Jaldak

Bosra

Caesarea
Qāqūn
Arthabec
Qalansuwā
Sebastia

'Ajlūn

SAMARIA

Arsuf
Nablus

Jaffa
Mirabel

as-Ṣalt

Sinjil

GHOR

32°

Lydda
Ramla
Ibelin
Bains
al-Bīrah
Jericho
St. George
St. John
'Ammān

Hulda
Jerusalem
Blanche Garde
Bethany
Bethlehem
St. Euthymius
St. Theodosius

St. Sabas

al-Qastal

Ascalon
Beth Gibelin
JUDEA
St. Chariton

f₄

Gaza
Hebron

Darum
DEAD
SEA
Engedi

Raffiyaḥ
LA BERRIE
Kerak
ARABIA

0   15   30 KM.
0   10   20 MI.

Segor

31°

Cartographic Laboratory U.W. Madison

7. Palestine

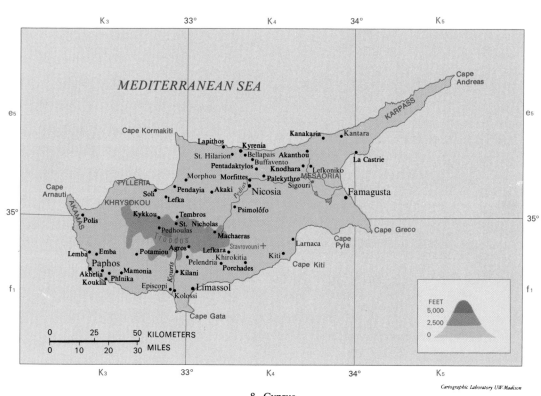

MEDITERRANEAN SEA

e₅

Cape
Andreas

KARPASS

Cape Kormakiti

Lapithos   Kyrenia   Kanakaria   Kantara

St. Hilarion   Bellapais   Akanthou   La Castrie

Pentadaktylos   Buffavento
Knodhara   Lefkoniko

Cape
Arnauti   PYLLERIA   Morphou   Morfittes   Palekythro   MESAORIA

KHRYSOKOU   Soli   Pendayia   Akaki   Pedieos   Nicosia   Sigouri   Famagusta

AKAMAS   Lefka

35°   Polis   Kykkou   Tembros   Psimolófo   35°

    St. Nicholas

Pedhoulas   Cape Greco

Troodos   Machaeras

Lemba   Emba   Potamiou   Agros   Lefkara   Stavrovouni   Larnaca   Cape
Pyla

Paphos   Khirokitia   Kiti

Akhelia   Mamonia   Pelendria   Porchades   Cape Kiti

Koukliá   Phlnika   Kilani

    Episcopi   Limassol

f₁   Kolossi   f₁

Cape Gata

| 0 | 25 | 50 | KILOMETERS |
| 0 | 10 | 20 | 30 | MILES |

FEET
5,000
2,500
0

Cartographic Laboratory UW/Madison

8. Cyprus

9. Venice and the Levant in 1300

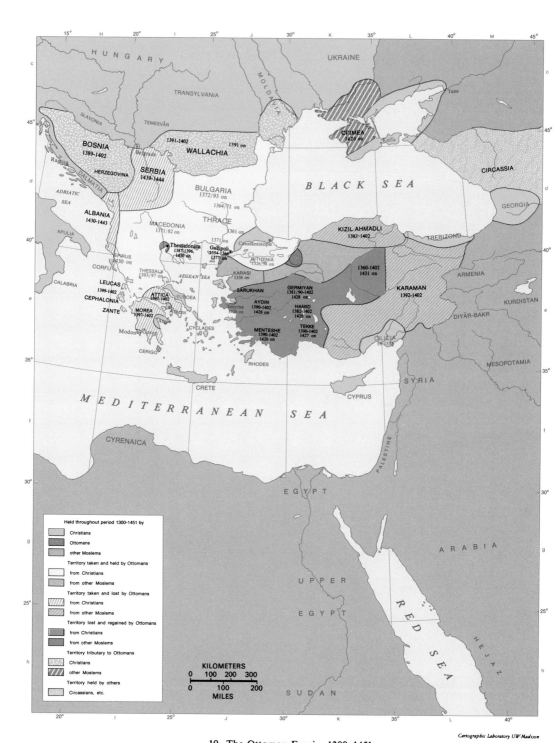

15°   20°   25°   30°   35°   40°   45°

c

HUNGARY

UKRAINE

TRANSYLVANIA

MOLDAVIA

Tana

SLAVONIA

TEMESVÅR

CRIMEA
1420 on

Kaffa

BOSNIA
1389-1402

Belgrade

1391-1402

1391 on

CIRCASSIA

Ragusa

DALMATIA

HERZEGOVINA

SERBIA
1439-1444

WALLACHIA

BLACK SEA

d

ADRIATIC
SEA

BULGARIA
1372/93 on

GEORGIA

1364/72 on

ALBANIA
1430-1443

MACEDONIA
1371/82 on

THRACE

KIZIL AHMADLI
1393-1402

TREBIZOND

APULIA

1371 on

1361 on

Constantinople

ARMENIA

EPIRUS
1430 on

Thessalonica
1387-1396,
1430 on

Gallipoli
1354-1366
1377 on

BITHYNIA
1326/38 on

1360-1402
1431 on

KARAMAN
1392-1402

CORFU

THESSALY
1393/97 on

AEGEAN SEA

KARASI
1336 on

KURDISTAN

CALABRIA

LEUCAS
1399-1402

SARUKHAN

GERMIYAN
1381/90-1402
1428 on

DIYÂR-BAKR

CEPHALONIA

ATTICA
1397-1402

EUBOEA

AYDIN
1390-1402
1426 on

HAMID
1382-1402
1426 on

ZANTE

MOREA
1397-1402

Athens

Smyrna
1426 on

MENTESHE
1390-1402
1426 on

TEKKE
1390-1402
1427 on

CILICIA
1375 on

Modon Coron

CYCLADES

MESOPOTAMIA

CERIGO

RHODES

SYRIA

CRETE

CYPRUS

MEDITERRANEAN SEA

PALESTINE

CYRENAICA

EGYPT

ARABIA

UPPER

EGYPT

RED SEA

SUDAN

HEJAZ

Held throughout period 1300-1451 by

Christians

Ottomans

other Moslems

Territory taken and held by Ottomans

from Christians

from other Moslems

Territory taken and lost by Ottomans

from Christians

from other Moslems

Territory lost and regained by Ottomans

from Christians

from other Moslems

Territory tributary to Ottomans

Christians

other Moslems

Territory held by others

Circassians, etc.

KILOMETERS
0   100   200   300

0   100   200
MILES

Cartographic Laboratory U.W. Madison

10. The Ottoman Empire 1300–1451

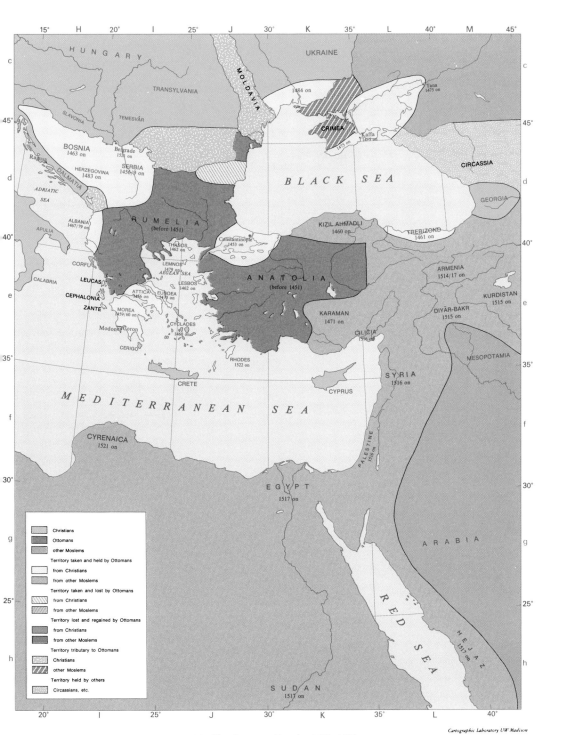

11. The Ottoman Empire 1451–1522

Legend:

- Christians
- Ottomans
- other Moslems

Territory taken and held by Ottomans
- from Christians
- from other Moslems

Territory taken and lost by Ottomans
- from Christians
- from other Moslems

Territory lost and regained by Ottomans
- from Christians
- from other Moslems

Territory tributary to Ottomans
- Christians
- other Moslems

Territory held by others
- Circassians, etc.

Map labels:

HUNGARY
TRANSYLVANIA
MOLDAVIA
UKRAINE
Tana 1475 on
SLAVONIA
TEMESVÁR
CRIMEA
Kaffa 1475 on
BOSNIA 1463 on
Belgrade 1521 on
SERBIA 1456/9 on
CIRCASSIA
Ragusa
DALMATIA
HERZEGOVINA 1483 on
BLACK SEA
ADRIATIC SEA
GEORGIA
ALBANIA 1467/79 on
RUMELIA (before 1451)
KIZIL AHMADLI 1460 on
TREBIZOND 1461 on
APULIA
CORFU
THASOS 1462 on
Constantinople 1453 on
ARMENIA 1514/17 on
CALABRIA
LEMNOS 1479-80 on
AEGEAN SEA
LESBOS 1462 on
ANATOLIA (before 1451)
KURDISTAN 1515 on
LEUCAS
ATTICA 1456 on
EUBOEA 1470 on
CEPHALONIA
ZANTE
MOREA 1459/60 on
KARAMAN 1471 on
DIYĀR-BAKR 1515 on
Modon Coron
CYCLADES 1460 on
CILICIA 1516 on
MESOPOTAMIA
CERIGO
RHODES 1522 on
SYRIA 1516 on
CRETE
CYPRUS
MEDITERRANEAN SEA
PALESTINE 1516 on
CYRENAICA 1521 on
EGYPT 1517 on
ARABIA
RED SEA
SUDAN 1517 on
HEJAZ 1517 on

Cartographic Laboratory UW Madison

12. Mongols and Missions in the Thirteenth Century

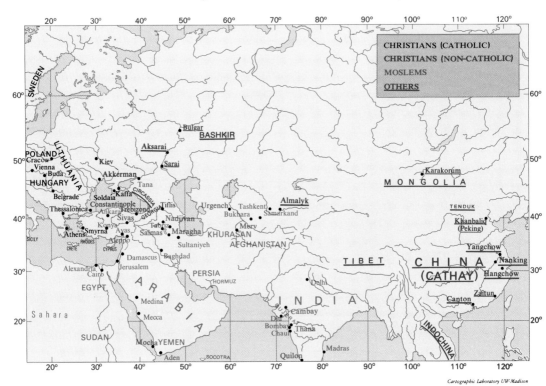

13. Missions and Mongols in the Fourteenth Century

B. Ottoman Conquests and the Crusade, 1361–1421

In the papal declarations of the second half of the fourteenth century propaganda for the crusade began to be formulated as a defensive struggle to save Europe from the Turks. But actually this meant, at this period, to protect the Latin possessions and interests in Greece and the Aegean Sea against the growing Turkish threat. Also it meant to save Byzantium and eastern Christendom, since the aid was expected to entail the submission of the Greek church to Rome, with resulting advantages for the papacy's position in the west. Throughout the period 1300–1453, however, the campaigns against the Turks turned into full-fledged crusades only when they coincided with the interests of the Venetian colonial empire in the Levant or those of Hungary for its sphere of influence in the Balkans. For Venice it was vital to keep its control over the coasts and islands strategically important for its sea communications with the Levant: Dalmatia, Albania, the Ionian islands, the Morea, and the Aegean, while Hungary under the Angevin king Louis I "the Great" (1342–1382) embarked upon building an empire from the Adriatic to the Black Sea with complete control of the Danubian countries: Dalmatia, Serbia, Bosnia, Wallachia, and Moldavia.

It is therefore important for the historian of the crusades to find out at what particular times these two great powers found the Ottomans a major threat to their interests, and, in the face of this challenge, how they intensified their activities to establish their own control in the threatened areas and consequently tried to mobilize the forces of Christian Europe in "crusades". In the following pages we shall focus our attention on these points.

During the Ottoman expansion in the Balkans the Serbs, Venetians, and Hungarians had to deal first with the frontier begs, and when these Christian states made a major attempt at driving them away they were faced with the Ottoman army under the sultan, the ghazi of the ghazis. The Ottoman military frontier zones in the Balkans moved forward in successive waves: first, from 1354 to 1361, as far as the Maritsa river; second, from 1361 to 1383, up to the Balkan mountain range, to Sredna Gora in the north and to the Strymon (Struma) river in the south; third, from 1383 to 1393, in the Dobruja, along the Danube, and in the Skoplje-Kossovo area; and fourth, from 1393 to 1454, in Albania, Thessaly, upper Serbia, and Vidin. At each shift of the military frontier the hinterland came under the direct rule of the Ottoman central government. It was only under Mehmed II (1451–1481) that the Morea, Serbia, and Bosnia would be annexed to the Ottoman empire, making the Balkans south of the Danube a compact Ottoman territory with the exception of some ports or strongholds still under Venetian or Hungarian control. However, it was only with the conquests of Bayazid I "the Thunderbolt" (1389–1402), who extended the Ottoman boundaries to the Danube in the north, Skoplje and southern Albania in the west, and Thessaly in the south, that Hungary and Venice felt, for the first time, the Ottoman threat to their zones of interest as an imminent danger.

In the case of Venice it should be pointed out that as a result of Bayazid's annexation of the maritime beyliks of western Anatolia in 1389–1390 the Ottomans had become a threatening sea power in the Aegean, and Bayazid challenged the Venetians on the sea and the Straits by converting Gallipoli into a fortified arsenal and naval base on the Dardanelles and by building a castle, Anadolu-Hisar, on the Bosporus. It was these developments that finally led to the crusade of Nicopolis in 1396.

Hungarian designs on the Balkans go back to the Angevin king Louis I "the Great" (1342–1382), who benefitted in the period 1362–1364 from the Ottoman advance into Bulgaria by extending his sway over the lands south to the Danube. The Byzantine emperor John V Palaeologus saw Hungary as a powerful ally in his plans to recapture Anchialus (Pomorie) and Mesembria (Nesebur) on the Black Sea from the Bulgarians and to drive the Turks out of Europe. In 1365 Hungarian and Byzantine envoys were at the papal court in Avignon to promote a crusade against the Ottomans, and, in his bull of January 22, 1366, pope Urban V (1362–1370) declared a crusade the avowed purpose of which was the expulsion of the Turks from Europe. In the winter of 1365–1366 the emperor himself made a surprise visit to Buda, the Hungarian capital, to induce Louis to move.[36]

In the face of the Hungarian-Byzantine threat, Bulgaria saw no alternative but to make peace and an alliance with the Ottomans. The latter supplied tsar John Alexander (1331–1371) with forces or let him use Turkish mercenaries on the Danube against the Hungarians, and on the Black Sea coasts against the Byzantines in the period 1365–1367.

---

36. Ostrogorsky, tr. Hussey, pp. 478–480; see the important study by Petăr Nikov, "The Turkish Conquest . . . " (in Bulgarian), *Izvestija na Istoričeckoto Družestvo,* VII–VIII (1928), 41–112; Setton, *The Papacy,* I, 286–291.

In response to the pope's call to a crusade the count of Savoy, Amadeo VI, a cousin of the Byzantine emperor, arrived with a crusading fleet of twenty galleys (stronger than previously thought by historians)[37] at the Dardanelles. He captured Gallipoli from the Ottomans late in August 1366; then, passing to the Black Sea, he took Anchialus and Mesembria from the Bulgarians for the Byzantines in October, and finally laid siege to Varna, though still awaiting the promised crusader army of the Hungarian king. The crusading plan to go to the aid of the Byzantines was eventually postponed, and in 1367 Ottoman forces appeared before Sozopolis, which had been conquered by Amadeo VI in the previous year. In 1367 the Bulgarians, with the support of Ottoman forces, also threatened the Hungarians in Vidin, and the Hungarian king had to ask the coöperation of the Wallachian voivode Vlad I (ca. 1360–1372) against them.[38] By then the Byzantines had become more apprehensive of Louis's crusading plans than of the Turks. The Angevin king's plans included the conversion to Catholicism of the Orthodox peoples of the Balkans and the capture of Constantinople. The first move by Louis was the subjection of the Bulgarians to his sovereignty, and the establishment of his control in the Vidin area. In 1366 he had created the banat of "Bulgaria", which included Vidin, Orshova, Mühlenbach (Sebesh), and Temesvár.[39] In April 1367 the Byzantine emperor hastily made peace with the Bulgarian tsar John Alexander, which displeased Louis. Hungarian possession of Vidin did not last long, and Louis's crusade project remained only a dream.

It is not correct that after the conquest of Adrianople (Edirne) in 1361 Murad, then still only a prince, had made it the capital city of the Ottoman state. Upon the death of his father Orkhan in March 1362 Murad I had hurriedly come to Bursa (the capital until 1402), and had then moved to defend the Ankara area against the Anatolian emirs of Eretna and Karaman. Lala Shahin, commander-in-chief of the Ottoman forces in Rumelia, in coöperation with the frontier begs Evrenos and Hajji-Ilbegi, was responsible for the Ottoman activities in Europe into the 1370's. Because of the fall of Gallipoli in 1366 and the constant threat from the Byzantine stronghold of Pegae (Kara-Biga) on the southern Marmara coast, Murad found it risky to cross over to Europe before 1373. Thus, despite initial advances in the Maritsa valley and toward the Serbian principality of Serres in the south, the

---

37. Setton, *The Papacy,* I, 294.

38. Iorga, *Geschichte,* I, 230–231; for the oft-repeated legend of Louis I's crusade against the Ottomans see Gheorghe I. Bratianu, "L'Expédition de Louis I de Hongrie contre le prince de Valachie Radu I Basarab," *Revue historique du sud-est européen,* II (1925), 4–6.

39. Huber, "Ludwig I. von Ungarn," p. 30.

Ottoman begs remained in general on the defensive. This situation also explains why they chose coöperation with the Bulgarian tsar and why the Byzantines embarked upon feverish efforts to drive the Turks out of Thrace in the period 1366–1371. These Byzantine activities had been preceded by contact through the patriarch Callistus with the despot John Ugljesha, prince of Serres, in 1363–1364, and by intense Byzantine diplomatic activity in the courts of the pope and the Hungarian king to promote a crusade in 1365–1366; they were highlighted by John V Palaeologus's visit to Italy and conversion to Latin Catholicism in Rome in 1369.

A Serbian army under Ugljesha and his brother Vukashin attempted to take Adrianople in 1371. The Ottoman frontier forces inflicted a crushing defeat on the Serbs by a surprise night attack at Chernomen on September 26, killing both brothers. "With the defeat of Maritsa (Chernomen) began the Turkish domination over the southern Slavs."[40] Turkish raiders overran Macedonia and invaded as far as Thessaly and Albania.[41] An interesting document[42] granting protection and exemption from taxes to the monks of the monastery of Saint John Prodrome near Serres attests to the Ottoman influence in Macedonia in 1372/ 1373. According to the early Ottoman traditions Murad I, on his way to the Dardanelles to support the ghazis who had informed him of the Serbian attack on Adrianople, had first to stop and reduce Pegae, which threatened his retreat.[43] Thus it can be said that in 1371 the Byzantine-Serbian alliance was a fact, and while the frontier begs of Rumelia had to meet the Serbian army, Murad had to fight the Byzantines at Pegae.

The Ottoman victory at Chernomen seems to have caused alarm at the threat of an Ottoman invasion of Italy. Exaggerated rumors spread about Ottoman plans for conquering Albania and the ports on the Adriatic.[44] The pope invited France, England, and Flanders to unite for a crusade, and wanted the Christian rulers in the Levant, including the Byzantine emperor, to send delegates to a meeting at Thebes to discuss joint action against the Ottomans, but no such meeting took place.

King Louis of Hungary, however, showed his concern by taking an

40. Jireček, *Geschichte der Serben*, II, 438; Halecki, *Empereur*, pp. 188–212.

41. Dujčev, "La Conquête turque," *Byzantinoslavica, loc. cit.*

42. Elizabeth A. Zachariadou, "Early Ottoman Documents of the Prodromos Monastery (Serres)," *Südost-Forschungen*, XXVIII (1969), 1–12.

43. A close critical examination of the early Ottoman traditions has not yet been done; see Inalcik in *Historians of the Middle East*, pp. 152–167.

44. Setton, *The Papacy*, I, 328–329.

oath to go on a crusade the following year, and asked the Venetians and Ragusans to build galleys for him. But his intentions were of another nature. The Ottoman victory at Chernomen and ensuing raids served Louis's old plans to strengthen Hungarian control over the Danubian lands. Louis's "crusade" was actually one against Orthodox "schismatic" peoples of Serbia, Bosnia, and Bulgaria. By May of 1356, following the dismemberment of Stephen Dushan's empire, Louis had already declared a crusade against "schismatics".[45] Under the king's protection the Franciscans were zealously pursuing their conversion efforts in the Balkans. This policy totally alienated the Orthodox population and princes in the Balkans from Hungary, and prepared the way for the Ottomans, who often appeared with their policy of *istimālet* or "reconciliation" as protectors of the Orthodox church and local princes. Actually the Hungarians and Turks, pressing the Slavic nations from north and south, were helping each other's advance until the day they faced each other. However, in 1373 Murad at the request of the Venetian senate sent a force of 5,000 mercenaries against the Hungarians in Dalmatia.[46]

After Chernomen the Serbian princes in Macedonia—Mark Kraljevich, the despot Dragash Dejanovich, and his brother Constantine—agreed to pay tribute and to serve in the Ottoman army. Serres came back under Greek rule under Manuel Palaeologus, the future emperor, but the frontier beg Evrenos established a march there under Delü Balaban, who carried on ghazi warfare against Manuel. Not only the Serbian princes of Macedonia and the new Bulgarian tsar Shishman, but also emperor John V after his return from Italy (October 28, 1371), had to recognize Murad's suzerainty after Chernomen.[47] The emperor's visit to Italy and his conversion to Catholicism had failed to bring about a naval crusade, or secure the coöperation of Hungary, which was considered the only land power capable of driving the Turks back to Anatolia. By the time of John V's visit to Europe the Ottomans seem to have supported an anti-western faction in Byzantium, with Andronicus IV, the ambitious son of the emperor, at its head. From then on the Ottoman ruler, as suzerain of the Byzantine emperor, shrewdly manipulated and profited from disputes for power in the Palaeologian family, which erupted as civil wars in 1373, 1376–1379, and 1390.

45. Huber, "Ludwig I. von Ungarn," p. 27.
46. *RISS,* XVII (1760), col. 176, cited by Herbert A. Gibbons, *The Foundation of the Ottoman Empire: a History of the Osmanlis . . . (1300–1403)* (Oxford, 1916), p. 149; for early relations between Murad I and Venice see Thiriet, *Régestes,* I, no. 423 (1365).
47. Charanis, "The Strife among the Palaeologi and the Ottoman Turks," p. 292.

Murad also exploited the fierce rivalry between the Venetians and the Genoese for possession of Tenedos in the war of Chioggia, 1378–1381. In October 1376, when Andronicus promised Tenedos, key to the Dardanelles, to the Genoese, Venice occupied the island. Andronicus captured Constantinople and the Byzantine throne with Ottoman and Genoese support. At the beginning of 1377 he delivered Gallipoli to the Ottomans after ten years of Byzantine possession. Those Byzantines favoring the western alliance and a crusade were against the surrender of Gallipoli, but the populace and senate approved Andronicus's decision. As a vassal of Murad, the emperor was not actually in a position to block the passage of the Turks anyhow. In the face of the coöperation among Murad, Andronicus, and the Genoese, Venice took John V's side. But the latter could recover his throne (July 1, 1379) only after promising more favorable tributes of vassaldom to Murad—a military contingent for his campaigns, a yearly payment higher than before, and the surrender of Philadelphia, Byzantium's last important possession in inland Anatolia.[48]

The rapid Ottoman expansion was considerably assisted by the defeatism and hopelessness among the Greeks and other Balkan nations. In his criticisms, the pro-western Demetrius Cydones reflects this psychology by attacking those coöperating with the Turks among the high-placed while, he says, the populace, especially city dwellers in the grip of poverty and shortages, also favored Ottoman rule. The church was openly discussing whether the Turks were preferable to the pope or not. On various occasions the Greek church was unwilling to give up its income from land rents to finance military preparations against the Ottomans. Turkish sovereignty was often presented as an inevitable consequence of divine judgment for the sins of the Christians.[49] The Ottomans steadily promoted the same idea, and in their *istimālet* propaganda they promised a peaceful and prosperous existence under their rule; in general, they delivered what they had promised.

From 1373 on, assured of Byzantine coöperation, the sultan could cross with his army over to Europe without fear of being cut off from Anatolia. The Ottomans were encouraged by international developments in this period. Following the death in September 1382 of Louis

48. *Ibid.,* p. 299; Peter Schreiner, "Zur Geschichte Philadelphias im 14. Jahrhundert (1293–1390)," *Orientalia Christiana periodica,* XXXV (1969), 404–405.

49. Dujčev, "La Conquête turque," pp. 486–489; Speros Vryonis, *The Decline of Medieval Hellenism in Asia Minor and the Process of Islamization from the Eleventh through the Fifteenth Century* (Berkeley, Los Angeles, London, 1971), pp. 408–421; Ihor Ševčenko, *La Vie intellectuelle et politique à Byzance sous les premiers Paléologues* (Brussels, 1962).

I of Hungary, who had styled himself "king of Serbia, Dalmatia, and Bulgaria", Hungary was in the grip of an internal struggle for succession. Even the Serbian knez Lazar I (1371–1389) in the Morava valley and Bosnia, who supported the Angevins for the Hungarian throne, was involved in the struggle against Louis's successor Sigismund (1385–1437).[50] At the same time, the rivalry between Venice and Hungary for Dalmatia prevented these two powers from acting jointly against the Ottomans for the whole period until 1394. Also the Genoese-Venetian rivalry over Tenedos and the waterways to the Black Sea, which caused a destructive war between the two republics, neutralized these maritime powers in respect to the Ottomans, who had been allied to the Genoese since 1352. The diplomatic revolution leading to the Hungarian-Venetian alliance would come only after the Ottoman occupation of Bulgaria in 1393.[51]

By the treaty of June 8, 1387, with Genoa, Murad I renewed commercial privileges granted previously by Orkhan.[52] Genoese documents of the period show that the Ottomans maintained close commercial relations with the Genoese and were visiting Pera. It also appears that the Ottoman Porte did not openly challenge Venice during Murad's reign (1362–1389). The republic continued to purchase wheat from the Ottoman territories (Thrace?) and even hoped to be allowed by Murad to establish a colony at Scutari, just across from the rival Genoese colony at Pera, making diplomatic attempts in 1365, 1368, and 1384.[53] In brief, the Ottomans succeeded in maintaining the neutrality of the Italian maritime powers which were in control of the Straits during the period when Murad embarked upon his extensive conquests in the Balkans.

In 1383 Murad, crossing the Straits, established his headquarters in Adrianople and sent an army under the grand vizir Khayreddin Pasha and Evrenos to conquer the rich coastal plains and cities of western Thrace between the lower Nestos (Mesta) and the Strymon (Struma). The Ottomans employed their navy under Azeb Beg to cut off aid from the sea. Kavalla (Christopolis), Drama, Zichne, and Serres in this region, which had been under blockade for many years, surrendered on terms.[54] The raiders extended their activities as far as Albania and the

50. Jireček, *Geschichte der Serben*, II, 117.
51. The best analysis of Venetian diplomacy of this period is still Silberschmidt, *Das orientalische Problem 1381–1400*.
52. Heyd, tr. Raynaud, II, 259–260.
53. *Ibid.*
54. The city of Serres was taken only in 1383 but the countryside had already come under the control of the Ottoman frontier forces under Delü Balaban in 1372. The Ottoman chronicles

Morea, and Thessalonica and other cities were attacked. After the campaign of 1383, however, the center of the new Ottoman march under Evrenos was Serres, and the Strymon river became the new border.

In 1385 a larger campaign in the Balkans was organized under the sultan. The operations were conducted in two directions. An army under the beglerbeg of Rumelia and Evrenos invaded Macedonia and took the plain of Thessalonica; though without success against the city itself, it captured Verrai (Fere or Kara-Ferye in Turkish sources). Monastir surrendered and raiders forayed as far as Charles I Tocco's territory in Epirus.[55]

While the army under the beglerbeg was advancing on the ancient Via Egnatia, the main army under Murad himself followed the famous military route in the Maritsa valley toward Danubian Serbia. He was able to cross the historic pass of the Nishava river and in the autumn of 1385 he captured Nish,[56] only fifty miles from knez Lazar's capital, Krushevats. The Serbian ruler saw no alternative to accepting the Ottoman overlordship under the heavy conditions of dispatching a contingent of one thousand men to Murad's campaigns and paying fifty okka[57] (about 140 pounds) of silver annually as tribute. At this time Hungary was too involved in its internal struggle over the succession to intervene.

The course of events leading to the historic battle of Kossovo-Polje is described thus in the earliest Ottoman tradition.[58] In 1385 the Karamanids, taking advantage of the absence of Murad and the Anatolian forces, had invaded the disputed area in Hamid which had been conquered by the Ottomans in 1381. In the summer of 1386 Murad's Ottomans defeated the Karamanid Alāeddin Ali in a pitched battle

---

make this distinction; see particularly the conquest of "Siroz" (Serres) in the anonymous *Tevârîkh-i Âl-i 'Othmân* (Paris, Bibl. nat., MS. suppl. turc 1047), fol. 19^v; I cannot agree with the interpretation of Beldiceanu-Steinherr, "La Prise de Serrès," *Acta historica, Societas academica Dacoromana,* IV (1965), 15-24. The date of the final conquest is established by Ostrogorsky, "La Prise de Serrès par les Turcs," *Byzantion,* XXXV (1965), 302-319; and *idem, Serska Oblast* (Belgrade, 1965), pp. 126-160.

55. Ottoman compilations of the late fifteenth century by Idrīs and Neshrī confuse the chronology and order of events. 'Āshìk Pasha-zâde and the anonymous chronicles are more faithful to their original sources. My chronology is based on a critical study of these sources. The date of the conquest of Verrai (787/1385) is confirmed in Christian sources; see Jireček, *Geschichte der Serben,* II, 107, and Silberschmidt, *op. cit.,* pp. 95-96.

56. Serbian annals (see Jireček, *Geschichte der Serben,* II, 118) give the date as 1386.

57. 50,000 okka in Neshrī, *Ğihānnümā: Die altosmanische Chronik des Mevlānā Mehemmed Neschri,* ed. Theodor Menzel and Taeschner, I (Leipzig, 1951), 58, but only 50 *okka* in Idrīs.

58. Neshrī, *op. cit.,* p. 71; and Enverî, *Düstûrnâme,* pp. 85-87; for Serbian annals on Kossovo see Gavro A. Skrivanić, *Kosovska Vitka* (Četinje, 1956); *Lebensbeschreibung des Despoten Stefan Lazarević von Konstantin dem Philosophen,* tr. Braun.

at Frenk-Yazusu, where the Serbian contingent fought on the left wing.[59] Upon the return home of the Serbian contingent, which complained of harsh treatment in the Ottoman army, Lazar renounced his allegiance to Murad and tried to bring about a coalition of the subjected Balkan states against the Ottomans. The defeat at Plochnik on August 27, 1388, of an Ottoman frontier force under Kavala Shahin,[60] who had invaded Bosnia in collaboration with Balsha, lord of Scutari, encouraged tsar Shishman and despot Dobrotich, the Bulgarian rulers, and Tvrtko I, ruler of Bosnia (1353-1391), to form a coalition with Lazar. This was followed by an agreement between Sigismund, king of Hungary, and Lazar, who accepted the obligations of vassalage as under Louis I.[61]

In order to secure his rear in his campaign against Serbia, Murad sent Ali Pasha Chandarlī, the new grand vizir, against Shishman and Dobrotich in the autumn of 1388. Ali, at the head of the forces of Rumelia, made a swift raid into Bulgaria, and in the spring of 1389, when Murad crossed the Dardanelles, Ali continued operations in Danubian Bulgaria, where tsar Shishman had taken refuge in Nicopolis. Tirnovo, the capital of Shishman, surrendered (but was not occupied) and the tsar finally submitted in Nicopolis. Then Ali Pasha joined the sultan's army near Philippopolis (Plovdiv; Filibe) and the whole army marched in the direction of Kossovo-Polje. The Christian lords of Küstendil (Konstantin) and Timok (Saraj) joined Murad's army. The Anatolian emirates, including Karaman, had responded to his call and sent contingents for this crucial confrontation between the forces of Islam and Christendom.

The Serbian army included contingents from Bosnia under Vlatko Vukovich and from Croatia under ban John Horvath, as well as mercenaries or volunteers comprising "Franks, Vlachs, Albanians, Hungarians, Czechs, and Bulgarians". In the western Balkans (Ragusa, Albania, and Bosnia) cannon was known by 1380, and reliable Ottoman and Serbian sources attest to its use at the battle of Kossovo in the summer of 1389.[62] The Ottoman victory at Kossovo marks the estab-

59. A contemporary Ottoman source in Neshrī, *op. cit.,* p. 59, dates it as the spring of 788/ 1386. Another contemporary source, 'Azīz Astarābādī, *Bazm u Razm,* ed. Köprülü (Istanbul, 1928), p. 313, is not clear here in its chronology; it contains complementary details on Murad's conquests in Tekke.

60. Kavala Shahin is often confused with Lala Shahin, beglerbeg of Rumelia under Murad I.

61. Huber, "Die Gefangennehmung der Königinnen Elisabeth und Maria von Ungarn und die Kämpfe König Sigismunds gegen die Neapolitanische Partei und die übrigen Reichsfeinde in den Jahren 1386-1395," *Archiv für österreichische Geschichte,* LXVI (1885), 523; Jireček, *Geschichte der Serben,* II, 119.

62. See D. Petrovič, "Fire-arms in the Balkans," in *War, Technology and Society in the Middle East,* ed. Vernon J. Parry and Malcolm E. Yapp (London, 1975), pp. 164-172.

lishment of Ottoman overlordship in Serbia and the beginning of the Ottoman-Hungarian rivalry over this key area between the Balkans and Central Europe. On the battlefield Murad I was assassinated, and Lazar was captured and executed.

Stephen, the new knez (1389–1427), and his mother Militsa under the threat of Hungarian invasion readily accepted the protection of and vassalage to Bayazid I, the new sultan, and her daughter despina (lady) Olivera was given in marriage to Bayazid. Ottoman garrisons were stationed in the important fortresses on the Danube, including Golubats. In the autumn of 1389 Sigismund invaded Serbia and took Borach (Bor) and Chestin in upper Serbia. The following summer Ottoman-Serbian forces fought together against the Hungarian bans.[63]

Bayazid had to return to Anatolia in haste since the Anatolian vassal emirs, in alliance with Alāeddin Ali of Karaman and Burhāneddin of Sivas (Sebastia), upon learning of the death of Murad I at Kossovo had initiated an uprising.[64] Bayazid was occupied in Anatolia warring against the emirs from 1389 to 1392. During this period he annexed the maritime emirates of Sarukhan, Aydin, and Menteshe in western Anatolia and the old Selchükid emirates of Germiyan, Hamid, and Kastamonu, and extended his control to the Amasya region, where he was challenged by the powerful sultan of Sivas. By his conquests in Anatolia Bayazid established his authority and greatly increased his power, and in 1393 he returned to the Balkans to assert his sovereignty over the Christian vassal states, which had, during his absence, slackened their ties to the Ottoman state and come into the orbit of Hungary and Venice.

The urgent problem for the Ottomans was to reassert control over Danubian Bulgaria. In 1391 with Sigismund's support Mircea cel Bătrân ("the Old"), voivode of Wallachia (1386–1418), had invaded northern Bulgaria as far as Karnobad, while Bayazid was occupied in Anatolia. In late 1392 Bayazid exchanged embassies with Ladislas, king of Naples (1386–1414), a rival of Sigismund for the Hungarian throne.[65] The following summer Bayazid invaded Bulgaria, taking Tirnovo on July 17, 1393, and placed tsar Shishman in Nicopolis as an Ottoman vassal to guard against Hungarian-Wallachian encroachments. Prior to his campaigns into Greece, Hungary, and Wallachia, Bayazid called all the Ottoman vassal princes to a meeting in the winter of 1393–1394

---

63. Jireček, *Geschichte der Serben,* II, 124.
64. The main source is Astarābādī, *Bazm u Razm,* pp. 383, 387–388.
65. Silberschmidt, *op. cit.,* pp. 47–48.

to make sure of their loyalty and coöperation;[66] the meeting place was Verrai, not "Serrai" (Serres) as reported in some Byzantine sources.[67] As the new Byzantine emperor, Manuel II (1391–1425), himself confirms, the appearance of the vassal princes before the sultan was a custom and condition of Ottoman suzerainty.

Bayazid's next moves were an invasion of Thessaly and the county of Salona on February 20, 1394, and the occupation of Thessalonica on April 21. Bayazid's insistence on direct control of the strategic cities and areas in the Balkans frightened his vassals.

Though authoritarian in his dealings with his vassals, Bayazid had shown a conciliatory attitude toward Venice after the annexation of the emirates of western Anatolia in the winter of 1389–1390. In May 1390 he reconfirmed the capitulations made under the Aydin dynasty, in response to the mission of Francis Querini. Venice would not have opposed the Ottomans if its commercial privileges and maritime security had been guaranteed. But in 1391 the corsairs of western Anatolia, now under Ottoman control, had begun their attacks against Venetian possessions in the Aegean and the Morea, forcing the senate to take new defense measures and send protests to the sultan. Construction of galleys in Constantinople, Thessalonica, and other ports for the Ottoman navy in the spring of 1392 caused great concern in Venice. Manuel II was then acting as a loyal vassal of the sultan and appeared to be using Ottoman power to block Venetian dominance in the Aegean and the Straits.

As under Umur Pasha half a century earlier, the Turkish navy had once again become an aggressive and threatening power. In the spring of 1392 the Venetian senate gave orders to their "captain of the Gulf" to proceed to the Aegean and attack Ottoman warships on the open sea. The reappearance of the threat of Turkish sea power under Bayazid led Venice to consider reviving the Latin League in the Aegean, with the participation of Lesbos, Chios, Rhodes, and Cyprus.

In the summer of 1392 the Ottoman navy sailed to the Black Sea to coöperate with Bayazid's army against Suleiman, emir of Kastamonu, so Venetian apprehension of an immediate Ottoman attack faded. In 1394 after the Verrai meeting Venice welcomed Manuel's request for aid against the sultan, who wanted to establish full control of Constantinople.

---

66. See Barker, *Manuel II,* pp. 112–122.

67. The fact that the meeting-place was Verrai, not Serrai (Serres), was first indicated by Karl Hopf, and after him by Silberschmidt, *op. cit.,* p. 95. In the Ottoman sources the date is given (mistakenly) as after 798/1395.

The despot Theodore Palaeologus (1382–1407) had become an Ottoman vassal in 1388, in order to gain Ottoman support for his struggle against the Latin barons, and especially for his fight against Venice for Argos. According to the famous inscription of Parori, he said he was ruling in the Morea in the name of the sultan.[68] But when, after the meeting of Verrai, Bayazid required the surrender of Argos and other strategic places in the Morea, Theodore managed to flee to the Morea, where he made an alliance with Venice against the Ottomans by the agreement of Modon on May 2, 1394. He surrendered Argos to the Venetians and then with their assistance captured Monemvasia from the Ottoman garrison.[69]

But the major event leading to the crusade was Bayazid's invasion of Hungary in 1394. We learn from a later Ottoman document[70] that in that year the Ottoman army under the sultan himself entered Hungary near Belgrade,[71] attacked Slankamen, Titel, Becskerek, Temesvár, Carashova, Caransebesh, and Mehadia deep in Transylvania, and then turned south into Wallachia in the direction of Nicopolis. There Mircea barred the way to the Ottoman army at the mountain pass of Rovine near Argesh, his capital. On October 10, 1394, Bayazid's army escaped disaster only after a fierce battle at Argesh in which the vassal Serbian princes Mark Kraljevich and Constantine Dejanovich and several Ottoman begs fell.[72] The sultan crossed the Danube at Nicopolis on ships supplied by tsar Shishman, who was placed there by Bayazid in 1393 when Tirnovo, his capital, was occupied by the Ottomans. Suspicious of Shishman's secret relations with Mircea and Sigismund,[73]

68. Loenertz, "Pour l'histoire du Péloponnèse au XIVe siècle (1382–1404)," *Études byzantines,* I (1943), 169–171; Turks from western Anatolia had appeared in the Morea as mercenaries or allies since the time of Michael IX Palaeologus (1294–1320). According to Loenertz, Ottoman Turks interfered in Moreote affairs following their conquest of Thessalonica in 1387. Theodore went to Murad's court to offer his allegiance in 1388.

69. *Ibid.,* 183–184.

70. See *Actes du Xe Congrès international d'études byzantines* (Istanbul, 1956), p. 220; the original is in the Topkapİ Sarayİ archives, no. 6374. Apparently it was a report prepared for Mehmed II for a campaign in Hungary or Wallachia.

71. The Topkapİ document says that there was no fortress at Belgrade at that time whereas the Paris anonymous (Bibl. nat., MS. suppl. turc 1047) speaks of the siege of Belgrade for a month.

72. On the basis of a document dated October 1395 concerning a donation made by Helen for the soul of her father, Constantine Dejanovich, G. S. Radojčić, "La Chronologie de la bataille de Rovine," *Revue historique du sud-est européen,* V (1928), 136–139, puts the date of the battle as May 17, 1395, the date of Constantine's death as found in Serbian annals. But now the Topkapİ document provides new details supporting October 1394. On the battle itself Enverî, *Düstûrnâme,* p. 88, gives interesting details.

73. According to von Aschbach, *Geschichte Kaiser Sigmunds,* I, 99, tsar Shishman had shifted to the Hungarian side.

Bayazid, once across the river, seized and executed Shishman on June 3, 1395,[74] and appointed Vlad voivode of Wallachia. Mircea took refuge in Transylvania in March 1396 and joined Sigismund in Kronstadt (Brashov). Together they descended on the Danube and in May recaptured Little Nicopolis on the north bank, opposite Nicopolis, and installed a Hungarian garrison. The Hungarian army was, however, harassed by Vlad on his way back home.[75]

Thus in 1393-1395 the whole of Bulgaria was annexed to the Ottoman empire, and Wallachia came under an Ottoman vassal prince.[76] On the Danube front Dristra (Silistra) and the Dobruja, long disputed between Bulgarian and Wallachian princes, became the seat of an Ottoman frontier lord. Nicopolis, which was in Ottoman hands, became the key fortress for control of Bulgaria and Wallachia. Farther to the west at Vidin, the Bulgarian tsar Sracimir (Sratsimir) was a loyal vassal of the sultan, and an Ottoman garrison was stationed there. To restore Hungarian influence and control in the area, Sigismund saw that he needed the support of the whole of Christian Europe, and especially of Venice. Just at this juncture Venice, as we have seen, abandoned its neutral attitude and decided to enter the struggle and to support any joint undertaking against the Ottomans.

The Ottoman invasion of Hungary in 1394 aroused genuine concern in pope Boniface IX (1389-1404) in Rome.[77] In October the pope issued, upon Sigismund's appeal, a bull for a crusade against the Ottomans.[78] On December 23 a Byzantine envoy arrived in Venice requesting aid and urging war against Bayazid. In early 1395 Venice became the center of the negotiations for a crusade. Reversing its cautious policy vis-à-vis the Ottomans, the senate decided to try full coöperation with Hungary. Venice also promised to send a fleet to the Dardanelles to cut off Ottoman communication between Anatolia and Rumelia. Sigismund secured a Burgundian-French contingent for the crusade, but there were rumors in France that John Galeazzo Visconti of Milan, threatened by the French, had exchanged embassies of friendship with the Ottoman sultan.[79] Ladislas of Naples, the rival of Sigismund, was another Italian ruler in contact with "the enemy of Christendom". A

74. The Topkapi document, no. 6374.
75. Von Aschbach, *op. cit.,* p. 92.
76. The Topkapi document claims that Mircea was a tributary of the sultan prior to the campaign of 1394.
77. Setton, *The Papacy,* I, 342-343.
78. Sigismund's letter to the pope in October 1394, mentioning Bayazid's invasion of Hungary, must have been written before the battle of Argesh on October 10.
79. See Setton, *The Papacy,* I, 347 and note 94.

Byzantine-Hungarian alliance was signed in Buda in February 1396 and Venice was informed about it in March.

Without this Balkan background the crusade of Nicopolis cannot be adequately explained. Western participation in the crusade appears to be grossly exaggerated in western accounts. The crusaders from western Europe, "une multitude de chevaliers sans experience, sans ordre,"[80] was apparently quite a small contingent, and yet they intended "to conquer the whole of Turkey and march into the empire of Persia, . . . the kingdom of Syria, and the Holy Land of Jerusalem".

Vlad of Wallachia, an Ottoman vassal, was attacked from the north by Stephen Lackovich, the voivode of Transylvania, but the Serbs under Stephen Lazarevich joined Bayazid's army. The Ottoman strategy was to delay the advance of the crusaders by resisting them in the fortified cities, in order to give the sultan, who was at the head of his army besieging Constantinople, time to gather his forces. The crusaders met resistance at Vidin and Rahova in late August and were held up by a stiff defense at the stronghold of Nicopolis (September 8-10). Bayazid surprised the crusaders at Nicopolis, and the ensuing pitched battle ended in a complete victory for the sultan (September 25, 1396),[81] who won fame throughout Islam as a ghazi.

Sigismund, Philibert of Naillac (soon to be grand master of the Hospitallers), and a few other leaders escaped down the Danube in a small boat, and John of Nevers and several other captive nobles were held for ransom, but most of the crusaders who survived the battle were enslaved or slaughtered by the infuriated sultan. The shocked reaction of western Europe to this disaster led to disillusion with the crusade idea and refusal to participate in similar expeditions for nearly half a century.

Venice took part in the crusade, but the small Venetian fleet of four galleys under Thomas Mocenigo, captain of the Gulf, was instructed not to engage in military operations beyond the northern Aegean and to stay with the members of the Aegean league—Rhodes, Chios, and Lemnos. By his naval preparations at Gallipoli and strict ban on wheat export to Venice, Bayazid had taken measures against the republic.[82]

80. Iorga, *Histoire des roumaines,* III (Bucharest, 1937), 362.

81. See the discussion of the size of the crusader army in Setton, *The Papacy,* I, 351–353. Delbrück's estimate of ten thousand for the Ottoman army is confirmed by the Ottoman anonymous (Paris 1047), fols. 22^r-22^v: "upon the news of the invasion Bayazid hurried to Nicopolis taking with him an army of ten thousand select troops." Each man had a pair of horses to go at maximum speed. At Tirnovo Rumelian forces joined the sultan. For details of the battle see Setton, *The Papacy,* I, 353–355.

82. Silberschmidt, *op. cit.,* pp. 158–160.

After Nicopolis Venice had to take more serious steps to protect Constantinople and Euboea.

After his victory Bayazid turned against Byzantium, which he held responsible for the crusade; now its conquest appeared easier than ever. The sultan's pressure on Constantinople in October 1396 is confirmed by Venetian and Genoese documents, as well as by the Ottoman chronicles.[83] Venice feared that the fall of Constantinople was quite imminent, and hastily sent instructions dated October 29, 1396, to Mocenigo to take appropriate measures.[84] Ottoman tradition makes it clear that immediately after the battle of Nicopolis Bayazid turned his army against Constantinople and demanded the surrender of the city. Negotiations were concluded by the emperor's pledging allegiance, with the payment of a yearly tribute of ten thousand gold ducats and the establishment of a Turkish quarter in Constantinople with a qadi and a mosque. (Our source adds that the Moslems from Göynük and Tarakli-Yenije who were settled in the quarter were driven out of the city after Bayazid's defeat at Ankara by Timur [Tamerlane] in 1402.) Apparently the sultan never gave up his intention of taking the city, but temporarily acquiesced to the peace offer of the emperor[85] at a time when pressing problems in Anatolia confronted him.

While Bayazid was occupied in Anatolia, first in conquering Karaman territory and then in fighting against sultan Burhāneddin of Sivas in the Amasya area in 1397, and the following year in capturing several cities in the Euphrates valley from the Mamluks, Manuel II was busy sending diplomatic missions to try to persuade the courts of France, Rome, and Venice to send a crusade to deliver Constantinople from its fate.[86] In 1397 Venice was seriously concerned about the alleged plans of the ex-emperor John VII to surrender the city, and took naval measures to prevent it.[87] Marshal John Boucicault's fruitless expedition (1399) and Manuel II's visit to European capitals in quest of aid (1400-1403) did not bring about any change in the situation.[88]

83. *Ibid.*; Thiriet, *Régestes,* I, no. 914.

84. *Ibid.,* nos. 917, 918; but Silberschmidt, *op. cit.,* p. 165, thinks that references in the documents belong to the period before the battle of Nicopolis; cf. Setton, *The Papacy,* I, 358. The letter of the vicarius of Pera thanking the Venetians is dated October 28, 1396; for the sultan's siege of Constantinople after Nicopolis see 'Āshĭk Pasha-zâde, *op. cit.,* 67–68; Neshrī, *op. cit.,* p. 90.

85. In his letter dated July 1, 1397 (see Barker, *Manuel II,* pp. 154–155), Manuel II speaks of three years of hard times in the war against Bayazid I.

86. *Ibid.,* pp. 149–160.

87. *Ibid.,* pp. 138–146.

88. Setton, *The Papacy,* I, 370–385; Barker, *Manuel II,* pp. 154–199.

Manuel's departure for Europe made the sultan furious,[89] and he forthwith demanded that John VII surrender the city.[90] A naval league against the Ottomans comprising the Hospitallers, the Genoese of Chios, and James Crispo, the duke of the Archipelago (1397–1418), was then considered by the Venetian senate.[91] Byzantium's salvation, however, would come from the east. In 1400 Timur captured Sivas, an Ottoman city since 1398, and on July 28, 1402, he defeated Bayazid at the battle of Ankara and made him a prisoner;[92] he died in captivity a few months later, probably by suicide.

Between 1402 and 1413 Bayazid's sons Suleiman (in Adrianople), Mehmed (at Amasya), and 'Isa (at Bursa) fought for the succession. Their civil wars kept them too weak and divided to threaten Constantinople, Venice, or Hungary, which enjoyed the respite without making any serious effort to strengthen their defenses against the inevitable resurgence of Ottoman power. The eventual winner, Mehmed I, ruled for eight more years, but deliberately made no military or diplomatic moves to destroy the unwonted calm.

C. *The Struggle for the Balkans, 1421–1451*

During the civil war, however, Byzantium had learned the most efficient way to check Ottoman aggressiveness and obtain concessions. At the accession on June 25, 1421, of Mehmed I's son Murad II, who was declared sultan in Bursa at the age of seventeen,[93] Manuel II set Mustafa, Murad's uncle, free in the Balkans, where he was joined by many leaders of the Ottoman forces, including powerful frontier begs.

Mustafa had agreed to return to the emperor Gallipoli, the rich coastal plains of Thrace, Thessaly, and the Black Sea coasts, thus restoring the Byzantine empire to its boundaries prior to Bayazid I's conquests. The Turkish dynasties in Anatolia, which Timur had restored to their principalities, also rebelled against Murad II. The young sultan had to recognize the occupation of Hamid-ili by the Karamanids. Juneyd,

89. See patriarch Matthias's letter, end of 1399, *ibid.,* pp. 203–205.

90. Thiriet, *Régestes,* II, no. 981.

91. See Iorga, *Notes et extraits,* I, 105–106, 115.

92. On Timur's campaign see Alexandrescu-Dersca, *La Campagne de Timur en Anatolie (1402).*

93. For Murad II see Inalcik, "Murād II," *Islâm Ansiklopedisi,* VIII (Istanbul, 1960), 598–615.

a pretender to the principality of Smyrna, had joined Mustafa in Rumelia. The Ottoman state was again in danger of dissolution.

Under the circumstances, Murad's government at Bursa followed the same conciliatory policy with the Christian states as his father's had in 1413. It was ready to accept all the Byzantine demands, except the surrender to the emperor of Gallipoli and of Mehmed's two infant sons as hostages. Murad made agreements with Serbia and Hungary through his ambassadors as his father Mehmed I had done against Musa, his rival in Rumelia in 1413. Venice approached both sides to make the most of the situation. It wanted Venetian merchants to receive the same treatment that they enjoyed in Constantinople and an export permit for 10,000 *modii* (about 20,000 tons) of wheat annually from the Ottoman possessions.[94]

In the final encounter near Bursa (end of January or early February 1422), Mustafa lost the day as a result of the defection of the frontier begs and of Juneyd, whom Murad recognized as sovereign in Smyrna. With the Genoese ships brought by John Adorno, podestà of New Phocaea, Murad was able to cross the Dardanelles and capture and execute his uncle in Adrianople.[95]

In the spring the victorious sultan came to lay siege to Constantinople. Supported by guns and a navy, this siege, from June 20 to September 6, 1422, was the most serious theretofore made against the Byzantine capital. Venice was alarmed, and took measures to protect its merchant ships trading with the Black Sea ports from Ottoman naval forces. However, the proposal of a naval demonstration against the sultan before Constantinople was rejected by the senate. At this point the cautious doge Thomas Mocenigo (1414–1423) tried to avoid a war against the Ottomans. His bailie in Constantinople, Benedict Emo, was instructed to offer mediation for peace negotiations between the sultan and the emperor.[96] At any rate, military aid to Byzantium under siege could not be sent before the following spring. But help came to Byzantium from Anatolia. The Germiyanids, Karamanids, and Jandarids responded favorably to a Byzantine diplomatic move for an attack on the Ottoman territories in Anatolia. These Anatolian emirs convinced Ilyas, the tutor of Murad II's brother Mustafa, who was then only thirteen years old and living in Germiyan, to rebel and sent forces to support him.[97] Upon hearing the news, following an unsuc-

94. Thiriet, *Régestes,* II, no. 1825, instructions to Benedict Emo dated October 10, 1421.
95. Inalcik, "Murād II," p. 60.
96. Thiriet, *Régestes,* II, nos. 1854, 1855, dated August 26, 1422.
97. A newly discovered Ottoman source, Osman Turan, *Tarihî Takvîmler* (Ankara, 1954), pp. 20, 60, is particularly important for the younger Mustafa's activities; cf. Ducas, tr. Magoulias,

cessful final assault on August 26, the sultan lifted the siege of Constantinople.

The Ottoman threat had led Manuel II to seek closer relations with the west, and in particular with pope Martin V (1417–1431). In response the pope sent messages to various western rulers requesting aid to Byzantium, and his legate, the Franciscan Anthony of Massa, arrived in Constantinople on September 10, 1422, to negotiate church union, but these negotiations were not fruitful. More practical results were expected from diplomatic contacts with Venice and Hungary.

Since 1411 Sigismund, "emperor of the Romans and king of Hungary", had championed the deliverance of Balkan Christians and Byzantium,[98] and since 1416 Manuel II had been trying to reconcile Hungary and Venice for the purpose of starting a crusade against the Ottomans. In this effort, Manuel was joined by king Vladislav II Jagiello of Poland (1386–1434), who had received the Byzantine ambassador Philanthropenos in August 1420.[99]

Actually, Venice shrewdly made the most of the crisis of 1421–1423. In the wake of the Ottoman siege of Constantinople, the senate agreed to strengthen the Byzantine fleet by ten galleys (October 1422). In the Morea, Venetians sought to take over the remnants of the Frankish principalities[100] and threatened to join the Greeks in order to hold the Ottoman forces at the newly constructed Hexamilion wall on the isthmus.[101] In the spring of 1423 Murad was still threatening the Byzantine empire. Now free of challenges from his rivals in Anatolia and his brother Mustafa (late January 1423) Murad sent Turakhan, the powerful frontier beg in Thessaly, to invade the Morea on May 22, 1423, and destroy the Hexamilion fortifications.[102] Turakhan's cam-

---

p. 164; Iorga, *Notes et extraits,* I, 324; *idem,* "Sur les deux Prétendants Mustafa," *Revue historique du sud-est européen,* X (1933), 12–13.

98. Barker, *Manuel II,* pp. 327–329, 369.

99. *Ibid.,* pp. 336–339.

100. Setton, *The Papacy,* II (Philadelphia, 1978), 12–14.

101. Barker, *Manuel II,* pp. 310–314.

102. *Ibid.,* p. 369, note 121; see especially *"Tarihî Takvîmler."* Defeated by the forces sent by Murad II under Mihal-oghlu, Murad's brother Mustafa took refuge in Constantinople (September 30, 1422). With the emperor's support he went to Selymbria (Silivri), apparently hoping for coöperation from dissidents in Rumelia. But under the attack of the Rumelian forces, he retreated to Koja-ili (the Nicomedia area) where he was recognized as sultan. Nicaea (Iznik) opened its gates to him. Mustafa threatened Bursa, and seems to have established his control over the greater part of Ottoman Anatolia. On the advice of his tutor Yörgüj Pasha, Murad II set out from Adrianople and attacked Mustafa in Nicaea in winter. Taken by surprise and betrayed by his tutor Ilyas, Mustafa was captured and executed (February 20, 1423). Murad's forces had to fight against the Jandarid and Karamanid forces during his action against Mustafa.

paign was apparently a move to discourage an attack on the rear of the Ottomans, who were now concentrating their forces on Thessalonica, which had been under blockade since the spring of 1422. But, to the disappointment of the Ottomans, Thessalonica, the second city of the Byzantine empire, passed by agreement under Venetian sovereignty on September 14, 1423. Since the city had been under Ottoman rule from 1387 to 1402, and paid a tribute of 100,000 *akcha* to the sultans while under the Byzantine rule thereafter, the Ottomans considered the Venetian occupation a hostile act. The Venetian ambassador, Nicholas Giorgio, sent to make an agreement, was arrested in the winter of 1424, and the Venetian offer to pay a tribute of 1,500–2,000 ducats for the city was rejected. An Ottoman army estimated to consist of five thousand men was holding the city under siege.

The Venetian-Ottoman war for Thessalonica lasted seven years, with dangerous implications for the Ottomans. While on the one hand the republic made several diplomatic attempts to have the sultan recognize the Venetian occupation of Thessalonica in return for some concessions and payment of tribute,[103] on the other hand it tried to instigate a crusade or form a regional coalition against the Ottomans. A Venetian fleet under Peter Loredan was at Gallipoli in June 1424, blocking the Straits to all Ottoman ships.

To divert Ottoman forces, Venice then encouraged Juneyd in the Smyrna area to rise against Murad. The Ottoman sultan had difficult times in his war against this energetic fighter, who attempted to raise the Karamanids and other emirs in Anatolia against the Ottomans. Given this dangerous situation, Murad had to sign a peace treaty with Byzantium (February 22, 1424) which accepted payment of a yearly tribute of 300,000 *akcha* (about 10,000 gold ducats) and the return of lands occupied since 1402 on the coasts of the Marmara, Aegean, and Black Seas except the castles of Mesembria, Derkos, and Zeitounion (Lamia).

In collaboration with Venice, Juneyd planned to send Ismail, an Ottoman pretender, to Rumelia, but Murad again secured Genoese coöperation to blockade Juneyd from the sea. Juneyd's elimination in 1425 deprived Venice of an efficient ally. In the spring of 1425 the Ottoman-Venetian war flared up on the Thessalonica front. The Venetians occupied Cassandra and Kavalla and at the same time attempted to use a "false" Mustafa as a pretender to the throne. In 1426 the Ot-

---

For Turakhan's raid into the Morea see Iorga, *Notes et extraits,* I, 497, and Peter Topping's account in volume III of the present work, p. 164; cf. Setton, *ibid.,* III, 269.

103. See Setton, *The Papacy,* II, 22–26.

toman corsairs from Palatia (Balat) and Ephesus (Ayasoluk) struck Euboea, Modon, and Coron while war spread in Albania with the Ottoman siege of Durazzo.

During the crisis of 1421–1424, the Ottoman frontier lords on the Danube and in Macedonia, southern Bosnia, and Albania had been able to protect Ottoman interests in the buffer zones against Hungary and Venice. During this period, while the buffer states—the Serbian despotate, the kingdom of Bosnia, and the voivodate of Wallachia—were forced to accept suzerainty or give up strategic points to Hungary and Venice, the Ottoman frontier lords had supported rival parties or pretenders in these buffer states and intensified their raids into these countries.

Coupled with the energetic stand of the Ottoman frontier lords, the war between Hungary and Venice for Dalmatia relieved the Ottomans of the danger of a "crusade" in the Balkans during this period.

Venice, however, became the principal beneficiary of the changing conditions in the Balkans. In addition to having seized the Dalmatian ports of Zara, Spalato (Split), Sebenico (Shibenik), and Traù (Trogir) from Hungary between 1412 and 1420, the republic had extended its sway in northern Albania and Montenegro following the death of Balsha in 1421. This policy had led Venice into war against Stephen Lazarevich, the Serbian despot, in the years 1421–1423.[104] In this fight Stephen found Ottoman frontier forces an efficient ally, and from then on he recognized Murad as his suzerain. By the peace treaty signed on August 12, 1423, however, the despot had to recognize Venetian occupation of Scutari, Alessio (Lesh), and Dulcigno. Later, in 1426, the Ottoman frontier lord Ilyas Beg was included in the treaty as a witness or guarantor.[105] This expansion of Venetian control can be considered as a counter to the Ottoman expansion in Albania—the occupation of Croia (Akchahisar) in 1415, and that of Avlona, Berat, and Pyrgos in 1420.

Hungary also exploited the situation by reinforcing its position in Serbia, Bosnia, and Wallachia in the period 1419–1429. During this period Sigismund was particularly active in extending Hungarian control in the northern Balkans and lower Danubian basin, even claiming sway over northern Bulgaria by supporting a Bulgarian prince's claim to the throne.

---

104. Iorga, *Geschichte*, I, 394; Stanojević, "Die Biographie Stefan Lazarevićs," pp. 459–470.
105. Ilyas Beg may be Ilyas, *subashi* of Chartalos near Berat; see *Sûret-i defter-i sancak-i Arvanid*, ed. Inalcik, timar no. 261.

Mircea had died in 1418 and his sons Michael and then Dan II recognized Hungarian suzerainty in Wallachia. The situation apparently caused great concern in Murad's court, and the sultan ordered frontier forces to support Radu II ("the Simple", or "the Bald"), another son of Mircea, against his brother, culminating in the invasion of Wallachia in 1423.[106] Hungarians and Ottomans fought on the Danube as supporters of their respective candidates for the Wallachian throne. Following his attempt at an agreement in 1424, the sultan, now freed of his Anatolian enemies, organized a large-scale campaign against Wallachia and Hungary under the beglerbeg of Rumelia with the participation of all the frontier lords. At the head of his army, Sigismund himself encountered the Ottoman army at Golubats and Orshova, and blocked their way.[107] The Venetians in Thessalonica received with joy the news of the Ottoman failure on the Danube.[108]

Upon the termination of the truce in 1426, the Ottoman-Hungarian rivalry over Wallachia and Serbia escalated. First the Ottomans drove Dan away from Wallachia early in 1427, and Sigismund had to come to reinstate him on the Wallachian throne in the spring. His forces then retook Giurgiu and crossed the Danube. There Sigismund built the fortress Szentgyörgy, and settled German forces as a barrier against the Ottomans. At this point, the death of the Serbian despot Stephen Lazarevich on July 19, 1427, and the dispute over his heritage brought the rivalry of the two powers on the Danube to a point of crisis. Stephen had arranged his succession in favor of George Brankovich, lord of upper Serbia, under Hungarian protection; Brankovich would be a vassal of the Hungarian king, by an agreement signed in May 1426.[109] According to the agreement upon the death of Stephen, Hungary would inherit Belgrade, Golubats, and the banat of Machva on the west side of the Danube. Even before the death of Stephen in 1427, the Ottomans had reacted against this arrangement and, by invading George's lands, had forced him to recognize Ottoman suzerainty, to cede the area between Krushevats and Kossovo, to wed his daughter Mara to

---

106. Anonymous, *Tevârîkh-i Āl-i 'Othmân* (Paris, Bibl. nat., MS. suppl. turc, 1047), p. 38, tells us that following the execution of his brother Mustafa (early 1423) Murad II ordered a massive attack against Wallachia, and that he then made peace with "Drakula" on condition of the payment of a tribute; according to Iorga, *Geschichte*, I, 390, Ottoman forces advanced as far as Kronstadt (Brashov).

107. Sigismund was at Orshova on August 16, 1425; Iorga, *Geschichte*, I, 391. The anonymous *Tevârîkh* claims an Ottoman surprise attack and victory at Golubats against the king's forces in 828/1425.

108. Iorga, *Geschichte*, I, 391.

109. Jireček, *Geschichte der Serben*, II, 159; Ignaz A. Fessler, *Geschichte von Ungarn*, ed. Ernst Klein, II (Leipzig, 1869), 372-373.

the sultan, and to guarantee coöperation against the Hungarians.[110] The Ottomans, in return, had promised George military aid against his rival, king Tvrtko II of Bosnia, who had laid siege to Srebrenitsa.

In the summer of 1427, frontier forces under Ishak Beg of Skoplje staged a raid into Bosnia, and went as far as Croatia. Under the pressure of the Ottoman frontier forces Tvrtko II had accepted Hungarian protection since 1422,[111] and now demanded aid. After the death of Stephen in July, the Ottomans and Hungarians moved to invade Serbia to prevent each other from taking over the land. While Sigismund occupied Belgrade in the autumn of 1427, the Ottoman forces invaded upper Serbia, capturing Krushevats and Golubats, as well as the island of "Jan-adasï" (identified as New Orshova) in the Danube. As noted above, Murad had already forced Brankovich, the new Serbian despot (1427–1456), to recognize Ottoman suzerainty, and to pay tribute. But now the despot chose as his heir Frederick of Cilly, Sigismund's son-in-law.[112]

When military action around Thessalonica was intensified, the Venetian senate had accepted the necessity of an alliance with Hungary (October 1425). Now not only Byzantium but also Florence[113] and Savoy, as well as Poland, urged Hungary to reach an agreement with Venice.

Sigismund organized his conquests into two *banats* (military frontier provinces), Machva and Belgrade, against the Ottomans. Opposite Golubats (Galambócz), now in Ottoman hands, he built the fortress Lászlóvár.[114] Thus a strong defense line was created against the Ottomans from Giurgiu on the lower Danube to Severin, while Wallachian, Serbian, and Bosnian princes recognized the protection and suzerainty of the Hungarian king. Sigismund once again emerged as the champion of a crusade against the Ottomans. Planning his crowning as emperor in Rome, he declared his determination to reach a full agreement with the pope to achieve peace and unity in Italy so that he could eradicate the Hussite heresy, and, as an ultimate goal, could fight against the Ottomans and deliver the Holy Land.[115]

110. The main source is Neshrī, *op. cit.,* pp. 161–162.
111. In 1410 Sigismund entered Bosnia and was crowned "king of Bosnia and Serbia"; see Jireček, *Geschichte der Serben,* II, 147.
112. Fessler, *op. cit.,* II, 374. Frederick succeeded his father Hermann II in 1435 and died in 1454.
113. Beckmann, *Der Kampf,* pp. 92–93; see Iorga, *Notes et extraits,* I, 351–357, 409–410; Setton, *The Papacy,* II, 25; Barker, *Manuel II,* pp. 375–379.
114. Fessler, *op. cit.,* II, 374.
115. For his words to the Florentine embassy in September 1427, see Beckmann, *Der Kampf,* p. 92.

In April 1428 a strong army of twenty-five to thirty thousand Hungarians and six thousand Wallachians under voivode Dan II, as well as Lithuanian contingents, arrived before Golubats. The Turkish fleet on the Danube was eliminated. Murad rushed with fresh forces to the aid of the hard-pressed Golubats, and Sigismund decided not to risk a pitched battle as he had done at Nicopolis in 1396.

A cease-fire for the retreat of the Hungarian army to the west side of the Danube was agreed upon early in June 1428. Continued negotiations eventually resulted in a three-year truce between the two powers. While Sigismund took pains to explain to Venice and pope Martin V his reasons for making peace with Murad, the Ottoman sultan in his turn tried to prove to sultan Barsbay of Egypt (1422-1438) that the peace was necessary and that Serbia and Bosnia were once again forced to recognize Islamic overlordship.[116]

The Ottomans now controlled Serbia through their strongholds of Golubats and Krushevats, as well as Ishak Beg's forces in Skoplje. Brankovich built for himself a new capital at Smederevo (Semendria) between Golubats and Belgrade,[117] and accepted full vassalage to the sultan—payment of a yearly tribute of 50,000 gold ducats and provision of an auxiliary force of two thousand for the sultan's expeditions.

Sigismund, taking advantage of the Ottoman crisis and the intensification of the Ottoman pressure on the buffer states, resumed in the period 1421-1428 efforts to realize the plan of a Danubian empire originated by Louis the Great. The struggle resulted in a compromise, or rather a postponement of the question, because of the powerful Ottoman reaction. The Ottomans, when they found themselves in a better position, would resume their aggressive policy in the region against Hungary, and this would give rise to a series of crusading activities in the west, on Hungarian initiative.

Disappointed by the armistice between the Hungarians and the Turks, Venice's hopes revived when new developments threatened the Ottomans on their eastern borders. During the Ottoman siege of Golubats the Karamanids, apparently in collaboration with Hungary,[118] had moved against the Ottomans, forcing Murad to surrender the much-disputed Hamid area. Through the mediation of the king of Cyprus, Janus (1398-1432), Venice entered into negotiations for an alliance

---

116. The sultan's letter is in Ferîdûn, *op. cit.,* I, 303-305.

117. The anonymous *Tevârîkh* gives the date as 831 (October 22, 1427-November 11, 1428).

118. István Katona, *Historia critica . . . regum Hungariae: Stirpis mixtae* (12 vols., Pest *et alibi,* 1778-1810), V, 505, cited by Iorga, *Notes et extraits,* I, 505.

with the Karamanids.[119] But the most disturbing news for the Ottomans was the campaign of Shāhrukh, son of Timur, in Anatolia,
which gave rise to great expectations throughout Christian Europe.
Since 1416 Shāhrukh (1405–1447) had showed his determination to sustain the status quo established by Timur in Anatolia and not let the
Ottomans press and annex the Anatolian emirates, those of the Karamanids and Jandarids in particular. The contemporary sources attribute to him a grandiose plan to invade the Ottoman dominions in Anatolia and Rumelia and return to Azerbaijan via Moldavia and Kaffa.[120]
But in 1429, when he invaded eastern Anatolia, his immediate concern
was to crush the rising power of the Turcoman Karakoyunlu there,
which threatened Timurid rule in Azerbaijan.

The common danger brought the Ottomans and Mamluks much
closer to each other. Apart from the Timurid threat, the project of
a Karamanid-Cypriote-Venetian alliance was against the interests of
the Mamluks, who had invaded Cyprus in 1426 and made king Janus
a vassal, while the Karamanids were considered to be under Mamluk
protection. At any rate, this Mamluk-Ottoman rapprochement would
continue in the future, and turn against western Christendom, Rhodes
in particular, in the coming decades.

On March 29, 1429, Venice finally declared war against the Ottomans,
whose growing naval power and continual attacks on Euboea and other
Venetian possessions in the Aegean had become distressing. By early
March a Turkish fleet had appeared before Thessalonica.[121] The senate believed that the Ottomans had decided to finish this dispute once
and for all.

During the long struggle for Thessalonica, the Ottoman tactics consisted of naval attacks on the Venetian possessions and merchant marine in the Aegean,[122] while sustaining a long blockade which aimed
to force the city to surrender by ruining its trade and starving its inhabitants, a tactic successfully used by the Ottomans against other cities
with strong fortifications and large populations since the fall of Bursa

119. Iorga, *Geschichte,* I, 406; *idem, Notes et extraits,* I, 502; the senate's decision is dated
August 30, 1424.

120. Ferîdûn, *op. cit.,* I, 152.

121. Iorga, *Notes et extraits,* I, 486–488; the Ottomans succeeded in capturing two Venetian
ships; the report is dated March 29, 1429. Venice, at this time, attempted to use the false "Mustafa", pretender to the Ottoman throne, in Thessalonica to cause defections in Murad's army;
see *ibid.,* I, 489–490, dated May 10, 1429.

122. The Ottoman attack on Euboea, Modon, and Coron in the spring of 1428 was particularly destructive, reminiscent of the raids of Umur Pasha in the previous century; see Setton,
The Papacy, II, 37.

in 1326. As vividly reflected in Venetian correspondence, Venice had to feed the city by sea, mainly from Crete, and eventually the starving populace turned against their new masters. The Ottomans had sympathizers and supporters among the Greeks, especially the Greek clergy.

Venetian tactics were to cut off the Ottomans' passage between Anatolia and Rumelia at the Dardanelles, to support the Karamanids, and to chase the Ottoman fleet away from Thessalonica.[123] In June 1429 the senate offered Sigismund a new project of alliance with emphasis on the occupation of the Dardanelles and Gallipoli.[124] During the summer and autumn Murad had to watch with anxiety Shāhrukh's movements on his borders in Anatolia, and be content with the raids of his frontier forces in the Morea and Albania, while the Venetian fleet under Andrew Mocenigo threatened Gallipoli.

Shāhrukh's victory against the Karakoyunlu in the battle of Salmas on September 17-18, 1429, emboldened the Venetians, who reminded Murad of the danger from the east.[125] Shāhrukh returned to Azerbaijan for the winter, and Murad called the Anatolian forces under the able general Hamza, conqueror of Smyrna, to Europe in February 1430. Thessalonica was taken on March 29, 1430. In his letter to his friend the Mamluk sultan Barsbay, Murad II presented it as a victory for Islam, and considered it as the elimination of a great danger to the Ottoman state.[126]

The fall of Thessalonica came as a surprise to the Venetians; Silvestro Morosini was then cruising off the coast of Epirus. In the summer of 1430, while Shāhrukh was still in Azerbaijan, the Venetian fleet attacked Gallipoli and cut off all communications on the Straits. Acting on behalf of the sultan, Hamza signed a peace treaty in July 1430 (ratification September 4, 1430). Venice recognized the Ottoman possession of Thessalonica, and guaranteed security for Ottoman communications on the Straits. By agreeing to pay a yearly tribute of 236 ducats Venice also recognized Ottoman overlordship at Patras, where Latin rule was challenged by the Greeks and Turks. For his part, the sultan recognized Venetian sovereignty over its Albanian possessions — Durazzo, Scutari, and Antivari (Bar). Seven years of occupation of Thessalonica and the resulting Ottoman war had cost the republic over 700,000 ducats.

---

123. Iorga, *Notes et extraits,* I, 490, instructions to the captain-general Andrew Mocenigo, dated May 15, 1429; for the Karamanids see *ibid.,* I, 503.

124. *Ibid.,* I, 494.

125. *Ibid.,* I, 505, note 5.

126. Ferîdûn, *op. cit.,* I, 198.

The capture of Thessalonica marked the resumption of an aggressive Ottoman policy in the Balkans, the first goal being the strengthening of their rule in Albania and Epirus. The despotate of Ianina (Yanya) was occupied, and Charles II Tocco accepted Ottoman suzerainty over Arta in 1430, while Venice took the Ionian islands of Leucas (Santa Maura), Zante, and Cephalonia under its protection.

In the following year Turakhan made his power over the Morea felt by demolishing the Hexamilion fortifications once again. But Albania would be the main arena of the Ottoman-Venetian rivalry in the ensuing half century. So close to Italy and so vitally important for Venetian communication with the world outside the Adriatic Sea, Albania received sustained attention and support from Venice, Naples, and the papacy against the establishment of Ottoman rule, and this support — in addition to the particular characteristics of the land and people — was responsible for the long and stiff resistance the Ottomans encountered.

Albania was considered by the Ottomans as a base to invade Italy and by the Italian states as their first defense line and as a bridgehead for a crusade against the Ottomans. During the fifteenth century the papacy's growing concern and zeal to organize crusades against the Ottomans was more related to the direct Ottoman threat to the papal states than to the deliverance of the Holy Land. The Aragonese kings of Naples fought in Albania against the Ottomans for their own security from the 1430's on,[127] and an Ottoman invasion of the Ancona area was felt to be an imminent danger throughout the second half of the fifteenth century. It was, however, the Venetians' naval superiority, as well as their building of strong defense lines on the islands in the Adriatic and Ionian seas and along the Albanian coasts, that really deterred the Ottomans from an invasion and gave a sense of security to the Italians. The Ottomans almost never planned or attempted an invasion of Italy without first eliminating the Venetian factor either by an agreement or by direct occupation of the Venetian bases in the area. Interestingly enough, throughout this period from 1430 on Ottoman diplomacy tried to further its Albanian policy by taking advantage of dissensions among the Italian states, between Venice and Milan or between the papacy and Venice or Naples. In any event, the period from 1430 to 1479 witnessed a crucial struggle between Venice and the Ottomans for the control of the Albanian coasts, the first defense line of Venice and Italy.

Thanks to an unusual wealth of documentation on Albania from

127. See Cerone, "La Politica orientale di Alfonso di Aragona," *loc. cit.;* Marinescu, "Alphonse V," pp. 7–135.

the Italian archives for this period,[128] and to the recently discovered Ottoman surveys of the country,[129] we are now able to evaluate the Italian involvement as well as internal conditions of the Albanian insurrections from 1432 on. Following their conquest of Thessalonica and Ianina the Ottomans made a survey of Albania in 1431-1432. The Ottoman survey book of 1432, which includes additional entries down to the mid-fifteenth century, shows that several Albanian seigneurial families were deprived of part of their lands, which were given to the Ottoman timar-holders, and Albanian clans in general resented being subjected to Ottoman taxation and the control of a centralist administration. Since the Ottomans could not establish complete control of the seacoast, and since Venetians gave refuge and aid to the rebels, rebellion became endemic in Albania in this period. But the actual situation was much more complex because Albanian lords shifted their loyalty between Venice and the Ottomans according to circumstances. Moreover, as was the case in the Morea, Serbia, and Bosnia, the Ottoman frontier begs in Albania acted as local lords, and achieved a kind of political equilibrium in the region.

During the Thessalonica war the northern Albanian lord John Castriota, father of Scanderbeg, had accepted Venetian protection, but after the fall of Thessalonica the Ottomans forced him to recognize the sultan's overlordship. The rebellion in southern Albania, apparently a direct outcome of the Ottoman survey of 1432, proved to be much more serious.[130] Under the leadership of local lords Thopia Zenevisi and George Araniti, whose lands had been given to Ottoman soldiers, a series of insurrections broke out in the coastal and mountainous areas, and Ottoman timar-holding sipahis were massacred. Despite several repressions at the hands of the Ottoman frontier begs, Albanian rebellion simmered until 1443, when Scanderbeg turned against the Ottomans and took on the leadership of the Albanian resistance.[131]

Emerging at a time when Christian Europe was ardently preparing for a crusade to drive out the Ottomans from the Balkans, Scanderbeg was destined to become the symbol of the crusade (once a Moslem, he had returned to Christianity), and later, after his successful guerrilla warfare against the Ottomans, and defeating four armies under the sultans in 1448, 1450, 1466, and 1467, he would be acclaimed

128. See Valentini, *Acta albanica veneta*, vols. XV-XX.

129. The Ottoman survey of Albania dated 1432 is printed in *Sûret-i defter-i sancak-i Arvanid*, ed. Inalcik.

130. See Inalcik, "Arnavutluk'ta Osmanlî Hakimiyetinin yerleşmesi ve Iskender Bey Isyanînin Menşei," *Fâtih ve Istanbul*, I-2 (1953), 152-175.

131. For Scanderbeg see Inalcik, "Iskender Beg," pp. 138-140.

throughout Italy as the defender of the faith and of Europe. In 1450 pope Nicholas V (1447–1455) called on all the Christian powers to assist him. Scanderbeg finally had to acknowledge the suzerainty of king Alfonso I of Naples (March 26, 1451) and agree to hand Croia over to the king's forces. In 1457 pope Calixtus III appointed Scanderbeg "captain-general of the Holy See". But historical reality was far from the Christian or humanistic Europe's image of him. Most of the time he acted as a mercenary or clan chief subsidized by Venice, the king of Naples, or the pope. Also, far from achieving national unity, he restricted his sphere of activity to northern Albania. Once, in 1438, an Ottoman *subashi* of Croia himself, he had rebelled against the sultan in 1443 to recover his father's domains, when the Ottoman sovereignty in the Balkans was on the verge of collapse. Scanderbeg's ambition was often challenged by other Albanian clan chiefs, resulting in local feuds.

While the Ottomans and the Italian powers, including the papacy, confronted each other in the sensitive area of Albania, the real front of the struggle between Christian Europe and the Ottoman empire was the middle Danube, though these two fronts were often connected, as when in 1434 Sigismund made contact with the defeated Albanian lords. Later, in 1448, John Hunyadi would try to combine his operations in the Balkans with Scanderbeg's. After the capture of Thessalonica, the Ottoman pressure had increased to strengthen Turkish control of the buffer states of Wallachia, Serbia, and Bosnia. Through his embassy in 1431, Sigismund had in his turn asked the sultan to recognize his overlordship of these countries.

In 1434 the Hungarian king got the upper hand in the struggle for supremacy by receiving in his court the allegiance of the rulers of Serbia and Bosnia, and the king's protégé, Vlad II "the Devil" (or "the Dragon", Dracul), replaced the Ottoman favorite, his brother Aldea, in Wallachia. The following year Shāhrukh's renewed campaign against the Karakoyunlu in eastern Anatolia and the Karamanid attack against the Ottomans were most encouraging news for the king.[132] Shāhrukh invited all the Anatolian emirs, including Murad II, to recognize his overlordship in July 1435. To punish the Karamanids, Murad waited for the return of Shāhrukh with his powerful army to Central Asia.

Sigismund died January 9, 1437, and Hungary plunged into an internal crisis over the succession. A terrible peasant insurrection against excessive exploitation by feudal lords broke out in Transylvania in the

132. Iorga, *Geschichte,* I, 417.

spring of 1437, culminating in the battle of Bobalna. Ottoman pressure was one of the excuses to increase the tax burden on the peasantry. The Ottomans thought it was time to attack and restore their power in the middle Danube against Hungary. In 1438 the sultan himself at the head of his army invaded Hungary. According to an Ottoman document[133] Murad crossed the Danube at the Kamen, near Vidin, bombarded Severin, attacked Mehadia and Mühlenbach, and after following the river Maros (Muresh) laid siege to Hermannstadt (Szeben), the center of Transylvania, while his raiders forayed all over the land. He returned through Wallachia and crossed the Danube at Giurgiu. In this campaign the Serbian and Wallachian princes, as loyal vassals, led the Ottoman army. The Transylvanian peasantry profited from the Ottoman invasion to take up arms against their rulers again in 1438.[134]

Believing that Hungarian resistance had collapsed, the Ottomans occupied the Serbian despotate; Smederevo fell August 27, 1439, and the frontier beg Isa of Skoplje laid siege to Yaytse (Jajce), capital city of Bosnia, and forced king Tvrtko II to pay a yearly tribute of 2,500 ducats. The Serbian silver mines at Novo Brdo, vitally important for supplying silver to Italy via Ragusa, were captured by the Ottomans, and in 1439 the export of silver to the west was prohibited.[135] In 1440 Murad II, in order to crown his successes, attempted to capture Belgrade, the gate to central Europe, which had been occupied and fortified by the Hungarians since 1427. His defeat at Belgrade and the emergence of John Hunyadi swung the pendulum in the reverse direction. Hunyadi reorganized the Hungarian frontier forces, and, perhaps more important, took into his service Hussite mercenary troops who with their *wagenburg* tactics were to revolutionize warfare in the Balkans. Ottoman raiders, invading Transylvania under the frontier lord Mezid, were crushed in 1441, and the reinforced Ottoman army of Rumelia under the beglerbeg Shehābeddin, which was sent to make up for the defeat in the following year, failed miserably. Hunyadi's victories set off vibrations throughout Christian Europe and heightened the crusading spirit in the west.[136]

133. Inalcik, "Byzantium and the Origins of the Crisis of 1444 under the Light of Turkish Sources," *Actes du XIIe Congrès international des études byzantines,* II (Belgrade, 1964), 159-163.

134. Stefan Pasco, *La Révolte populaire de Transylvanie des années 1437-1438* (Bucharest, 1964), pp. 34-107.

135. The Ottoman conquest of Novo Brdo, a center of silver production, took place on June 27, 1441; see Jireček, *Geschichte der Serben,* II, 178.

136. Pope Eugenius IV (1431-1447) celebrated the victories entailing "a vast slaughter of the infidels" as signs of God's clemency for Christians; see Setton, *The Papacy,* II, 68.

The negotiations for the union of the Greek church with Rome and for a crusade were taken up in Rome more zealously than ever when, in the wake of the fall of Thessalonica, the Byzantines had serious fears of the Ottoman capture of Constantinople. The Golden Horn was then closed off by the chain at its entrance. Emperor John VIII Palaeologus (1425–1448) himself left for Italy on November 24, 1437, to attend the council in Ferrara (and then, from February 1439 on, in Florence) and finally to conclude the union of the Latin Catholic and Greek Orthodox churches. This time high dignitaries of the Greek church, including the patriarch Joseph II, accompanied the emperor. The union of the churches was declared in Florence on July 6, 1439. For the crusade, the real objective of the Greeks, a plan was offered to the council by John Torcello (or Torzello), the emperor's "chambellan".[137] In their efforts to persuade the west to launch a crusade, the Greeks claimed that to defeat the Ottomans it was sufficient to invade the Balkans with a crusading army of 80,000. In the Balkans, he added, not only would the regular forces of the Serbian despotate, the Greeks of the Morea, and the Albanians join the crusaders, but also Christian soldiers in the service of the sultan, 50,000 in number, would desert to the side of the west. According to Torcello, the bulk of the Ottoman soldiery were not as well armed as the westerners. To sell the project the Greeks further asserted that the recovery of the Holy Land would be an easy task for the westerners after the Ottomans' defeat.[138]

The union was the decision of the ruling elite, who saw the sole hope for the salvation of Byzantium in full coöperation with the west. It was, however, a decisive step which opened a critical period ending with the fall of Byzantium.[139] Thus far the emperors, anticipating the protests of the conservative Orthodox masses and a strong reaction on the part of the Ottomans, had acted with caution on this matter. As soon as John VIII was back in Constantinople, the sultan sent an envoy to inquire about what had occurred in Florence. The emperor tried to conceal the real political objective of the union,[140] but as is clear from the contemporary Ottoman sources[141] the Ottomans were fully aware of the negotiations for preparation of a crusade against

137. On Torcello see *ibid.,* II, 68, note 103.
138. Torcello's report is in Bertrandon of La Brocquière, ed. Schefer, and see La Brocquière's criticisms, pp. 263–274; cf. Setton, *The Papacy,* II, 69, note 107.
139. Sphrantzes, ed. Bekker, p. 173; ed. Vasile Grecu (Bucharest, 1966), p. 178.
140. Ducas, *op. cit.,* tr. Magoulias, p. 181.
141. *Ghazavât-i Sultân Murâd,* pp. 2–4; see also Ferîdûn, *op. cit.,* I, 613–614, and Paris, Bibl. nat., MS. arabe no. 4434, fols. 133^v–138^v.

themselves, and from this time on a strong party, mostly from among the military leaders, claimed that unless Byzantium were eliminated there would be no security and no future for the Ottoman state. In *Ghazavāt-i Sultan Murād,* a recently discovered, well-informed account of the events between 1439 and 1444, the crusades of 1443 and 1444, as well as the Karamanid attacks in Anatolia, are all attributed originally to the activities of Byzantine diplomacy. Though basically reflecting the view of the anti-Byzantine party, the claim is largely confirmed by our western sources, which tell us about activities of Byzantine diplomats in Rome, Venice, and Buda in those years.[142]

Hungary, exposed directly to Ottoman attacks after the Ottoman occupation of Serbia, was prepared, under the leadership of the regent John Hunyadi, to launch a decisive war against the Ottomans. In their efforts toward this end, the Hungarian aristocracy agreed in 1440 to have Ladislas (Vladislav III), king of Poland, as their king (László IV), provided that he vigorously pursue the struggle against the Ottomans. Hungary found that Byzantium was equally interested in the launching of a general crusade. As early as February 1442 the Byzantine envoy, John Torzello, was in Venice with the mission of visiting Buda, Rome, and other European capitals for the realization of such a crusade.[143] Once the union was realized pope Eugenius IV (1431-1447) showed great enthusiasm for the crusade. In February 1442 he appointed cardinal Julian Cesarini as papal legate to Hungary; on January 1, 1443, he invited the Christian rulers to a general crusade against the Ottomans, and in May 1443 he named his nephew Francis Condulmer commander of the fleet to coöperate with the crusader army from Hungary.[144] Although Venice was typically cautious enough not to engage in a direct conflict with the Ottomans, it was supporting the preparations, and agreed to build a crusading fleet of ten galleys when funds were made available.[145]

Encouraged by the Ottoman reverses in the Balkans and by the Byzantine emperor,[146] the Karamanid Ibrahim Beg had made raids into the disputed territory of Akshehir (Philomelium) and Beyshehir in late 1442, and again in the spring of 1443. Murad II forced him to sign

142. See Iorga, *Notes et extraits,* II (Paris, 1899), index, p. 580, *s.v.* Jean VIII Paléologue; Halecki, *The Crusade of Varna,* pp. 32-82. Halecki tries to prove that there was no confirmation by king Ladislas of Hungary at Szegedin of the treaty of Adrianople of June 12, 1444. Dąbrowski, "L'Année 1444," was critical of Halecki's thesis, and *Ghazavât-i Sultân Murâd* now supplies Ottoman evidence that Halecki is incorrect; see below, note 149.

143. Iorga, *Notes et extraits,* II, 83; Thiriet, *Régestes,* III, no. 2568.

144. Setton, *The Papacy,* II, 68-69.

145. Thiriet, *Régestes,* III, nos. 2608, 2628; Setton, *The Papacy,* II, 75, note 131.

146. *Ghazavât,* p. 4.

a peace agreement after a swift and particularly brutal raid into Karaman in the summer of 1443, and then returned to Rumelia in the autumn. The crusaders' army under Ladislas, the Hungarian king, John
Hunyadi, voivode of Transylvania, and George Brankovich, despot of
Serbia, crossed the Danube at Belgrade early in October, when the Ottoman provincial cavalry had been scattered and returned home. The
crusading enthusiasm inspired by Hunyadi led a great number of volunteers to join the regular forces of the Hungarian magnates. The
whole army, estimated to consist of 25,000 men, included an important mercenary force hired with funds given by the Serbian despot,
and, in addition, a contingent of 8,000 Serbian and 5,000 Polish soldiers. As in 1396, the bulk of the army consisted of Hungarians,
which demonstrates the fact that the "crusade" was basically a Hungarian undertaking.

The Ottoman chronicle, *Ghazavāt,*[147] clarifies many important points
concerning "the long campaign". In explaining the successes of the
Christian army, the Ottoman sources in general emphasize the disagree-
ment and lack of coöperation between the Ottoman frontier forces
under Turakhan and the sipahi army under Kasim, beglerbeg of Rumelia. These sources are silent, however, on the most important battle
of the whole campaign, which took place at Bolvani in the plain of
Nish on November 3, 1443. Here the Ottoman forces mustered under
Turakhan and Kasim were defeated in their attempt to halt the advance
of the crusaders. Pirot and Sofia soon fell and, according to *Ghazavāt,*
Bulgarians welcoming and helping the invading army elected a "vla-
dika" as their head in Sofia. The sultan, who had been in Sofia, had
burned down the city before his retreat. In a letter to the Venetian senate from Sofia dated December 4, 1443, cardinal Cesarini proclaimed
the "flight of the sultan".

To protect the Maritsa valley leading to his capital, Adrianople, the
sultan fortified all the passes through the Balkan range, and met the
crusader army at Zlatitsa pass. Exhausted by cold and hunger, the Christian army was beaten at the battle of Zlatitsa and forced to retreat on
December 12, 1443.

In pursuit of the enemy, the sultan fell upon the Christian army at
Melshticha near Sofia on December 24.[148] His attack failed mainly because the crusaders sheltered themselves in their camp, surrounded by
war-wagons reinforced by guns. It was this tactic which made possible

---

147. For a comparison of the information supplied by *Ghazavât* with western sources, see
my notes in the edition of the work (Ankara, 1978), pp. 94–110.

148. *Ghazavât,* 23–25, states that sultan Murad was present at the battle.

the long retreat under constant attack by the harassing Ottoman forces. On January 2, 1444, at the mountain pass at Kunovitsa, between Pirot and Nish, Hunyadi inflicted a defeat on the pursuing Ottoman army; among the captives was Mahmud, husband of the sultan's sister. The retreating crusader army reached Belgrade on January 25. When he reached Buda safely the king dismounted and went barefoot to the church in gratitude to God. The pope sent a consecrated cap and sword to the king, and throughout Europe the victory was celebrated with great joy and religious fervor. Never before had a Christian army advanced so deep into Ottoman territory. Following the crusade, the Ottoman military structure throughout the Balkans seemed to dissolve as local lords in Ottoman service tried to gain their independence, among them Scanderbeg in Albania and despot Constantine Palaeologus in the Morea. Vlad II Dracul turned against the Ottomans and recognized Hungarian suzerainty, thus impairing the Ottoman position in Bulgaria.

During the summer of 1444 there was panic among the Turks in Rumelia and, as *Ghazavāt* put it, the well-to-do were leaving Rumelia for Anatolia. There, however, the Karamanid Ibrahim Beg had renewed his attack and occupied the territory in dispute in the spring of 1444. The sultan had made contact with the king of Hungary as early as January 1444, promising to revive the Serbian despotate as a buffer between the two countries.[149] The sultan's wife Mara, George Brankovich's daughter, played an important role in the opening of negotiations in March and April of 1444. Hoping to recover his despotate, Brankovich did everything possible to realize this peace. He attempted to persuade Hunyadi to work for peace by giving up to him his own small domain in Hungary (Vilagos and 120 villages). Actually, Hunyadi agreed to this to gain time to prepare the crusade. "The long campaign" was to be completed in 1444, and the Ottomans driven out of the Balkans. Later, Hunyadi was to be promised the kingdom of Bulgaria. It is obvious that for him "peace" was a war trick.

The Hungarian-Serbian embassy to the sultan concluded a peace treaty in Adrianople on June 12, 1444. The sultan had to agree to the revival of the Serbian despotate, which had been annexed to the Ottoman empire in 1439. The Ottomans even had to surrender Golubats, the principal Ottoman fortress on the Danube since 1427. In return, the king recognized Ottoman rule over Bulgaria. The Hungarians and

---

149. For the treaty of Adrianople (or Szegedin) and the period between 1443 and 1451 in general, see Inalcik, *Fâtih devri üzerinde tetkikler ve vesikalar* (Ankara, 1954).

the Ottomans both promised not to cross the Danube to attack. The Serbian despot was to remain under the sultan's suzerainty as a tributary prince. Vlad Dracul was included in the peace treaty as an Ottoman tributary prince but under Hungarian protection. The sultan solemnly ratified the treaty by oath in the presence of the ambassadors. In order to take the oaths from the king, the despot, and Hunyadi and to implement the surrender of the fortresses in Serbia to the despot, the sultan sent Balta-oghlu Suleiman[150] to Hungary. By the peace treaty Hungary had attained the objectives it had pursued for decades. Beyond this, any continuation of war would have to be a real crusade to eliminate Ottoman rule in the Balkans and rescue Constantinople.

Already, however, on April 15, 1444, the king had given his oath in the presence of cardinal-legate Cesarini to continue the crusade that summer.[151] But there was strong opposition in Hungary to the continuation of the war. In April the Hungarian diet did not approve the preparations for war. Those in favor of peace gave priority to improvement of internal conditions in Hungary and Poland, while the war party believed in the potential success of a crusade and its advantages for the king's position in Hungary. The pope's legate Cesarini and John de' Reguardati, the Venetian envoy in Buda, vigorously supported the partisans of war. Already, in the winter, the Venetian senate had formally notified the king of its resolution to join the crusade and send a fleet to the Straits to cut off Ottoman communications between Asia and Europe; this fleet left Venice on June 15, 1444. At this point Venice expected the imminent collapse of the Ottoman empire, and planned to occupy Gallipoli, Thessalonica, Albania, and even some ports on the Black Sea. The news of the departure of the fleet reached Hungary in July and definitely had a strong influence on the decision to go to war. In his letter dated July 30, 1444, John VIII Palaeologus told the king that it was the most opportune moment to destroy the Ottomans, since Murad II had crossed over to Anatolia, and that the peace treaty had thus served its real purpose.

Despot Constantine in the Morea promised his military coöperation with the crusaders, and had already taken the offensive. Byzantine diplomacy also appears to have been responsible for the coöperation of the Karamanids with the despot and Hungary.[152] Within the Balkans Scanderbeg and Ghin Zenevisi in Albania, as well as the Albanians and Vlachs in Thessaly, were in rebellion, and king Tvrtko II

150. Later, in 1453, the Ottoman admiral at the siege of Constantinople.
151. See above, note 142.
152. Inalcik, *Fâtih devri,* p. 33.

of Bosnia had recovered Srebrenitsa. All these developments during the summer made the Hungarian court believe that the chances for success of a crusade could not be better at any other time.

Murad II had crossed over to Anatolia against the Karamanids on July 12, 1444, but instead of fighting he signed a peace treaty with them in early August at Yenishehir, giving up the long-disputed area to them. Then, believing he had guaranteed peace in the east and west by eliminating the main issues of conflict with the Hungarians and the Karamanids, he abdicated in favor of his son Mehmed II, then only twelve years old, thus leaving all power in the hands of the grand vizir Chandarlï Khalil. A fierce rivalry soon broke out between Khalil and the tutors of the young sultan for power in Adrianople. The Byzantine emperor then released the Ottoman pretender Orkhan, who went to the Dobruja to win over the frontier raiders to his cause. An uprising of the Hurūfī dervishes in Adrianople occurred at the same time, in the summer of 1444. This chaotic state of affairs in the Ottoman empire was used as a further argument by those in the Hungarian capital advocating a crusade.

On August 15, 1444, at Szegedin, by taking the oath in the presence of Balta-oghlu Suleiman, the sultan's ambassador, king Ladislas completed the formal ratification of the treaty concluded in Adrianople on June 12.[153] The king did so upon the insistence of the despot, since otherwise Balta-oghlu would not evacuate and surrender the fortresses in Serbia. On August 4, 1444, while negotiations continued at Szegedin on this key point, the king proclaimed under oath a manifesto to the Christian world about his firm decision to continue war against the Ottomans. The Venetian senate, however, thought this was not a sufficient guarantee, and decided to act cautiously in its relations with the sultan. It can be concluded that Ladislas, and Hunyadi in particular, were determined to continue the war against the Ottomans in 1444, but did not want to jeopardize their diplomatic success of the recovery of the Serbian despotate for the sake of a "formality". Besides, cardinal Cesarini assured the king that an oath sworn to an "infidel" without the pope's approval was not canonically binding, and reminded him of the possibility of excommunication if he violated his solemn promises for the crusade.[154]

The crusaders' army, 16,000 men under Ladislas and Hunyadi, crossed the Danube near Belgrade on September 18-22, 1444. The Serbian

153. *Ibid.,* pp. 1-53; Pall, "Ciriaco d'Ancona," pp. 42-43; *idem,* "Autour de la croisade de Varna," p. 152.

154. Zinkeisen, *Geschichte,* I, 672-674.

despot George Brankovich remained neutral. According to *Ghazavāt* the native Bulgarian peasants again coöperated with the invading army. The Wallachian army, 4,000 to 7,000 strong, under Vlad Dracul, joined the crusaders near Nicopolis. The Christian high command decided to capture Adrianople, the Ottoman capital, without wasting time on the way at the fortresses of Vidin, Nicopolis, Tirnovo, and Provadiya (Pravidi), which put up stiff resistance, while Shumen and Petrich were taken by storm. On November 9 the Christian army besieged and took Varna on the Black Sea, where it was to establish contact with the crusading fleet, which included eight papal, six or eight Venetian, four Burgundian, and two Ragusan galleys.[155] The fleet was not successful in blocking the passage of the Anatolian army under Murad, who was hastily called from Bursa to assume the high command on October 20, 1444.

The Ottoman army forced the crusaders to a pitched battle before Varna on November 10. All passages for possible retreat of the Christian army were intercepted. At the battle, both wings of the Ottoman army were routed, and then Ladislas with his heavy cavalry charged straight on Murad's camp, where the decisive battle took place. The scattered Ottoman cavalry gathered around the sultan's flag and fought back. "When the king," *Ghazavāt* says, "saw that the Christian troops began to scatter in defeat around him, he was panicked and did not know what to do. Although he tried to rearrange his troops he failed. While he was running to and fro alone one of the Ottoman soldiers struck him a strong blow with a mace, which threw him off his horse. The janissaries and azebs crowded around him and struck him with their axes." Ladislas's death was followed by a general debacle of the crusader army. Hunyadi, however, was able to retreat safely, thanks to his *wagenburg* tactics.

There is a consensus that Varna was a turning point in eastern European history. In Poland, those opposing the idea of a crusade against the Ottomans got the upper hand,[156] and Hungary entered another crisis of succession. Now Ottoman control in the Balkans was reëstablished more firmly than ever. Murad II resumed the Ottoman throne in 1446 as a result of grand vizir Khalil's maneuvers against his rivals, Zaganuz and Shehābeddin, tutors of the young sultan Mehmed II. In order to reassert Ottoman sovereignty, Murad embarked upon a series of campaigns against despot Constantine in the Morea (autumn 1446) and Scanderbeg in Albania (1448 and 1450). Hunyadi did not give up

---

155. Setton, *The Papacy,* II, 85–86. On the crusade of Varna see below, chapter VIII.
156. Halecki, *From Florence to Brest* (Rome, 1958), pp. 75–76.

his struggle against the Ottomans after Varna. In 1445, while a Venetian fleet under Alvise Loredan came to watch the Ottomans on the Dardanelles, the Wallachian voivode Vlad Dracul, with the support of Hunyadi, reconquered Giurgiu from the Ottomans, and the following year Vlad defeated an invading army under the frontier beg Davud (spring 1446).

In 1448, when Murad attacked Scanderbeg in Albania, Hunyadi invaded Serbia as far as Kossovo, where a fierce three-day battle ended with Ottoman victory (October 17–20, 1448). In this connection, two points should be made: first, by now the Ottomans had learned *wagenburg* (in Turkish *tabur-jengi*) tactics and increased their firepower. Second, since the 1444 agreement of Yenishehir the Karamanids had coöperated with the Ottomans; a Karamanid contingent fought against the Hungarians at Kossovo in 1448. Also, in this period, a sense of solidarity and friendship ruled the relations between the Ottomans and the Mamluks, who were both threatened by the Timurid Shāhrukh and by the crusaders. The Mamluks, suzerains of the kings of Cyprus since 1426, tried unsuccessfully to subjugate the Hospitallers of Rhodes by sending a fleet against the island in the summer of 1444.

Perhaps most important of all, the defeat at Varna sealed the fate of Byzantium. The union of the churches and the idea of the crusade suffered a deep setback in all the Graeco-Slavic world. The Greeks and other Balkan peoples accommodated themselves to the idea of living under an Islamic state rather than under the Catholic Venetians and Hungarians. It should be added that by this time the Ottoman state was fully transformed into a classic Islamic sultanate with all its underpinnings, and that an actual social revolution was introduced into the Balkans by a state policy efficiently protecting the peasantry against local exploitation and the dominance of feudal lords and extending an agrarian system based on state ownership of land and its utilization in small farms in the possession of peasant households. As early as 1432, Bertrandon of La Brocquière, a Burgundian spy, had observed that Murad II had immense resources in his hands with which to conquer Europe if he wished to do so.[157]

---

157. *Le Voyage d'Outremer* (Belgrade, 1950), p. 110: "s'il vouloit exquiter la puissance qu'il a et sa grant revenue, veu la petite résistence qu'il treuve en la crestienté, ce seroit à luy légiere chose à en conquester une grant partie."

VIII

THE CRUSADE OF VARNA

The defeat of the crusaders under king Sigismund at Nicopolis on September 25, 1396, ended, for almost half a century, any concerted military opposition to Ottoman expansion in the Balkans. The European provinces that had been overrun by the Turks remained tributary

The letters of Aeneas Sylvius Piccolomini, a secretary to Frederick III in Vienna, were edited by Rudolf Wolkan, *Der Briefwechsel des Eneas Silvius Piccolomini* (Fontes rerum austriacarum, Abteilung II, vols. LXI, LXII, LXVII, and LXVIII; Vienna, 1909-1918). His writings, *Opera quae extant omnia,* were published in Basel, 1551 (repr. Frankfurt am Main, 1967). The *Commentaries* were translated into English by Florence A. Gragg and Leona C. Gabel (Smith College Studies in History, vols. XXII, XXV, XXX, XXXV, XLIII; Northampton, Mass., 1937-1957). The Latin text of the *Commentarii de gestis Concilii Basiliensis* was published with English translation by Denys Hay and Wilfrid K. Smith (Oxford, 1967).

Some of the sources for the crusades in the fifteenth century have been treated by Nicolae Iorga, *Notes et extraits pour servir à l'histoire des croisades au XVe siècle* (6 vols., Paris, 1899-1916). The deliberations of the Venetian senate have been abstracted by Freddy Thiriet, *Régestes des délibérations du sénat de Venise concernant la Romanie* (3 vols., Paris and The Hague, 1958-1961).

The principal Greek sources for the events are Laonicus Chalcocondylas, *De Origine ac rebus Turcorum* (ed. Immanuel Bekker, *CSHB,* Bonn, 1843, and ed. Eugen [Jeno] Darkó, *Historiarum demonstrationes,* 2 vols. in 3, Budapest, 1922-1927), George Sphrantzes, *Chronicon minus* (*PG,* 156, and ed. Vasile Grecu, Bucharest, 1966), and Ducas, *Historia byzantina* (ed. Bekker, *CSHB,* Bonn, 1834, and ed. Grecu, *Istorija turco-bizantină 1341-1462,* Bucharest, 1958).

The naval campaign is narrated by John (Jehan) of Wavrin, uncle of the Burgundian admiral Waleran of Wavrin, as *Recueil des croniques et anchiennes istories de la Grant Bretaigne, a present nomme Engleterre,* ed. William Hardy and Edward L. C. P. Hardy (Rolls Series, 39; 5 vols., 1864-1891; repr. Nendeln, Liechtenstein, 1965-1972). The records of expenditures for the Burgundian fleet are in the Archives du Nord, Lille, and have been partially abstracted by Henri and Bernard Prost, *Inventaires mobilières et extraits des comptes des ducs de Bourgogne de la maison Valois, 1363-1477* (2 vols., Paris, 1902-1913). An examination of the archives was published by Léon E. S. J. de Laborde, *Les Ducs de Bourgogne: Études sur les lettres, les arts et l'industrie pendant le XVe siècle* . . . (part 2, 3 vols., Paris, 1849-1852).

The deliberations of the Reichstag for Albert II were edited by Gustav Beckmann, *Deutsche Reichstagsakten* (vol. XIII, Stuttgart, 1925), and by Helmut Weigel (*ibid.,* vol. XIV, Stuttgart, 1935; both vols. repr. Göttingen, 1957); those for Frederick III by Hermann Herre, Ludwig Quidde, and Walter Kämmerer (vols. XV–XVII, Stuttgart, 1963), containing valuable reports on the progress of Turkish arms. The acts of Frederick III in the Haus-, Hof-, und Staatsarchiv, Vienna, Joseph Chmel, ed., *Regesta chronologico-diplomatica Friderici IV. Romanorum regis (imperatoris III.)* (Vienna, 1838; repr. Hildesheim, 1962), and supplemented by Adolph Bachmann, ed., *Urkunden und Aktenstücke zur österreichischen Geschichte im Zeitalter Kaiser Friedrichs III. und König Georgs von Böhmen, 1440-1471* (Fontes rerum austriacarum: Diplomataria et acta, XLII, part 2; Vienna, 1879). See Heinrich Koller, *Das Reichsregister König Albrechts II.* (Vi-

vassal states, while sultan Bayazid I concentrated on consolidating his control over Anatolia, in which the Ottoman state had emerged as the most powerful among the many Turkish principalities.[1] Consolidation meant conquest of the Selchükid and Turcoman emirates that had

enna, 1955), and Johannes Janssen, ed., *Frankfurts Reichscorrespondenz, 1376-1519* (Freiburg, 1864-1872), for reports of Albert's campaigns.

Documentary material relating to Poland has been edited by Augustin Theiner in three important series: *Vetera monumenta historica Hungariam sacram illustrantia* (2 vols., Rome, 1859-1860), *Vetera monumenta Poloniae et Lithuaniae* (4 vols., Rome, 1860-1864), and *Vetera monumenta Slavorum meridionalium historiam illustrantia* (2 vols., Rome, 1863-1875). August Sokołowski and Joseph Szujski, eds., *Monumenta medii aevi historica res gestas Poloniae illustrantia* (19 vols., Cracow, 1874-1927; repr. New York and London, 1965) contain II-1, 2 (1876), XII (1891), XIV (1894), *Codex epistolaris saeculi decimi quinti,* vol. I-1: ann. 1384-1444, ed. Sokołowski; vol. I-2: ann. 1444-1492, ed. Szujski; vol. 2: ann. 1385-1445, ed. Anatoli Lewicki; vol. 3: ann. 1392-1501, ed. Lewicki. See also August Cieszkowski, ed., *Fontes rerum polonicarum e tabulario reipublicae venetae,* series I, fasc. 2, *Acta Vladislao Jagiellonicae regnante* (Posen, 1890).

The most important narrative source for the history of Poland in this period is Jan Długosz, *Historia polonica* (2 vols., Leipzig, 1711-1712). Długosz (1415-1480) was secretary to bishop Zbigniew Oleśnicki, a conciliarist opposed to Eugenius's policies, a view that is reflected in Długosz's work, written at the bishop's request. Another historian of Poland, Martin Kromer, wrote a history of Poland inspired by Długosz, *De Origine et rebus gestis Polonorum* (Basel, 1559). Kromer was secretary to bishop Peter Gamrat of Cracow (1538-1545) and then to prince Sigismund Augustus, and in a position to use archival material.

Filippo Buonaccorsi of San Gimignano (1437-1496), called Callimachus, was educated in Rome and fled to Poland when implicated in a plot against pope Paul II. He lived in the house of Gregory of Sanok, became Latin tutor to the princes of Poland, and wrote a life of Oleśnicki and a history of the reign of Vladislav III, *Philippi Callimachi experientis historia rerum gestarum in Hungaria et contra Turcos per Vladislaum Poloniae et Hungariae regem,* ed. Saturnin Kwiatkowski (Monumenta Poloniae historica, VI; Cracow, 1893), 19-162, and Irmina Lichońska, ed., *Historia de rege Vladislao* (Zaklad Nau o Kulturze Antycsnej PAN. Bibliotheca latina medii et recentioris aevi, III, Warsaw, 1959).

Of the Hungarian sources János Thurocz (Johannes de Thwrocz), a prothonotary at the court of Matthias Corvinus, wrote a history of Hungary, *Chronica Hungarorum* (Vienna, 1711, in *Scriptores rerum Hungaricarum,* I, and a Hungarian edition, ed. László Geréb, in *Monumenta Hungarica,* Budapest, 1957); although it was based on contemporary sources, it is not always reliable. A more accurate source is Antonio Bonfini, *Historia Pannonica: sive Hungaricarum rerum decades IV et dimidia* (Cologne, 1690), a history of Hungary to 1496, the first thirty chapters of which survive.

A fascinating memoir of the civil war in Hungary by Elizabeth's lady-in-waiting is *Aus den Denkwürdigkeiten der Helene Kottannerin, 1439-1440,* ed. Stephan F. L. Endlicher (Leipzig, 1846). Some interesting reactions to the Turkish incursions in Transylvania are in Franz Zimmerman and Carl Werner, eds., *Urkundenbuch zur Geschichte der Deutschen in Siebenbürgen* (4 vols., Hermannstadt, 1892-1937). For Ragusan-Hungarian relations see József Gelcich and Lajos Thallóczy, eds., *Diplomatarium relationum reipublicae ragusanae cum regno Hungariae* (Budapest, 1887).

The Ottoman sources for this period are sparse, and those which speak of Varna add relatively little; see chapter VII, above, for their evidence. Idrīs wrote a history in Persian from 1310 to his own time in 1502 entitled *Eight Paradises (Hasht Bihisht)* at the request of sultan Selim I. Neshrī wrote a history, *Ǧihānnümā: die altosmanische Chronik des Mevlānā Meḥemmed Neschri,* ed. Theodor Menzel and Franz G. Taeschner (2 vols., Leipzig, 1951-1955), which

1. See Halil Inalcik, chapter VII, above.

evolved during four centuries of Turkish invasions. Bayazid conquered and annexed the two largest of these states, Karaman (1397) and Sivas (1398), thereby extending an empire that stretched from the Euphrates to the Danube.

---

provides a fairly reliable chronology of events. Sadeddin (1536-1599) wrote a universal history entitled *Crown of History,* relying heavily on Neshrī and valuable for the policies of Murad II; part of his history was translated into French by Antoine Galland in the 18th century as *Annales ottomanes,* and exists in manuscript in the Bibliothèque nationale, Salle des manuscrits, Fonds français 6074 and 6075.

For the struggle with the Turks in Hungary before Varna see Beckmann, *Der Kampf Kaiser Sigmunds gegen die werdende Weltmacht der Osmanen, 1392-1437* (Gotha, 1902), and Wilhelm Wostry, *König Albrecht II., 1437-1439* (2 vols. in Prager Studien aus dem Gebiete der Geschichts-wissenschaft, XII and XIII; Prague, 1906-1907). In addition to the older multivolume works on Ottoman history by Iorga and Joseph von Hammer-Purgstall, valuable recent studies are Halil Inalcik, *The Ottoman Empire: the Classical Age, 1300-1600,* tr. Norman Itzkowitz and Colin Imber (New York, 1973), and Ernst Werner, *Die Geburt einer Grossmacht: die Osmanen* (Berlin, 1966). Three articles give insight into the methods and objectives of Turkish conquest: David Angelov, "Certains Aspects de la conquête des peuples balkaniques par les Turcs," *Byzantinoslavica,* XVII (1956), 220-275; Ömer Lütfi Barkan, "Les Déportations comme méthode de peuplement et de colonisation dans l'empire ottoman," *Revue de la Faculté des sciences économiques de l'Université d'Istanbul,* XI (1949-1950), 67-131; and Inalcik, "Ottoman Methods of Conquest," *Studia Islamica,* II (1954), 103-129.

For Cesarini's life see Paul Becker, *Giuliano Cesarini* (Kallmünz, 1935); Heinrich Fechner, *Giuliano Cesarini, 1398-1444: bis zur seiner Ankunft in Basel am 9. September 1431* (Marburg, 1907); Ernest F. Jacob, "Giuliano Cesarini," *Bulletin of the John Rylands Library,* LI (1968), 104-121; Roger Mols, "Julien Cesarini," *Dictionnaire d'histoire et de géographie ecclésiastiques,* XII (1953), cols. 220-249; the funeral oration of Poggio Bracciolini in Angelo Mai, ed., *Spicilegium romanum,* X (1844), 374-385; and Vespasiano da Bisticci, *The Vespasiano Memoirs: Lives of Illustrious Men of the Fifteenth Century,* tr. William George and Emily Waters (London, 1926).

A careful study of Polish objectives in 1440 is Vincenz Zarkzewski, *Wladislaw III. Königs von Polen Erhebung auf den ungarischen Thron* (Leipzig, 1867). For the diplomatic negotiations see David Angyal, "Die diplomatische Vorbereitung der Schlacht von Varna (1444)," *Ungarische Rundschau für historische und soziale Wissenschaften,* II (1913), 518-524. See Franz Babinger, "Von Amurath zu Amurath: Vor- und Nachspiel der Schlacht bei Varna, 1444," *Oriens,* III (1950), 229-265 (repr. in his *Aufsätze und Abhandlungen zur Geschichte Südosteuropas . . . ,* I, Munich, 1962), for the abdication of Murad II. For the battles and expeditions see Alfons Huber, "Die Kriege zwischen Ungarn und den Türken, 1440-1443," *Archiv für österreichische Geschichte,* LXVIII (1886), 159-207, and Leopold Kupelwieser, *Die Kämpfe Ungarns mit den Osmanen bis zur Schlacht bei Mohács (1526),* 2nd ed. (Vienna, 1899).

For discussions of the alleged peace of Szegedin see Angyal, "Le Traité de paix de Szeged avec les Turcs (1444)," *Revue de Hongrie,* VII (1911), 255-268; Jan Dąbrowski, "L'Année 1444," *Bulletin international de l'Académie polonaise des sciences et des lettres: Classe d'histoire et de philosophie,* supp. no. 6 (Cracow, 1951); Francisc Pall, "Autour de la croisade de Varna: la question de la paix de Szeged et de sa rupture (1444)," AR, *BSH,* XXII (1941), 144-158; and Oskar Halecki, *The Crusade of Varna: a Discussion of Controversial Problems* (New York, 1943). For the letters and reports of Ciriaco see Pall, "Ciriaco d'Ancona e la crociata contro i Turchi," AR, *BSH,* XX (1938), 57-68. For the politics of Alfonso V of Aragon see Francesco Cerone, "La Politica orientale di Alfonso di Aragona," *Archivio storico per le provincie napoletane,* XXVII (1902), 3-93, 380-456, 555-634, 774-852, and XXVIII (1903), 154-212; Constantin Marinescu, "Alphonse V, roi d'Aragon et de Naples, et l'Albanie de Scanderbeg," *Mélanges de l'École roumaine en France,* I (Paris, 1923), 7-135; and three articles by Pall: "Les Relations entre la Hon-

The Islamic world now had two major powers, each claiming hegemony. Timur the Lame (1369-1405) had established his empire in Central Asia and on the Iranian plateau, and as heir of the Īl-khānid power claimed sovereignty over Anatolia. The dispossessed Anatolian emirs fled to Timur's court, appealing for the restoration of their territories and charging Bayazid with violating the faith of Islam by attacking fellow Moslems engaged in the holy war. In 1402 Timur moved his army into Anatolia, and Bayazid wheeled to meet him on the Anatolian plateau. At Ankara on July 28 the Ottomans were decisively defeated and Bayazid was taken prisoner, remaining a captive until his death in 1403.

The political situation was suddenly altered radically: the emirates were restored and the remaining Ottoman territory was divided by Timur among Bayazid's sons Suleiman, Musa, and 'Isa. The impetus toward further Ottoman conquest was removed for a generation as internecine strife occupied the Turkish princes. Musa eliminated 'Isa and, in 1411, Suleiman, only to be defeated and killed in 1413 by his younger brother Mehmed I. After the latter's death in 1421 two claimants surfaced; his son Murad II besieged Constantinople in 1422, but lifted the siege to fight and defeat his "uncle" Mustafa (called "the Impostor") in 1423, thereby emerging as sultan (1421-1451) of a unified empire.[2]

After the defeat at Nicopolis king Sigismund pursued a defensive policy in the Balkans until his death in 1437. One notable exception to this policy occurred in 1428 when he began fortifying Golubats, intending to make it a Hungarian stronghold and establish control over northern Serbia, nominally a vassal of Hungary, while a civil war raged between rival claimants to the Serbian throne. The Ottomans had re-

---

grie et Scanderbeg," *Revue historique du sud-est européen,* X (1933), 111–141, "Le Condizioni e gli echi internazionali della lotta antiottomana del 1442–1443, condotta da Giovanni di Hunedoara," *Revue des études sud-est européennes,* III (1965), 432–463, for the wars of 1442–1443, and "Skanderbeg et Ianco de Hunedoara," *ibid.,* VI (1968), 5–21. There is a detailed account of the crusade of Varna in Kenneth M. Setton, *The Papacy and the Levant (1204–1571),* II, *The Fifteenth Century* (Philadelphia, 1978), chap. 3, with extensive archival material.

For the Burgundian naval campaign see Marinescu, "Philippe le Bon, duc de Bourgogne, et la croisade," *Actes du VIe Congrès international d'études byzantines,* I (1950), 147–168; *idem,* "Du Nouveau sur 'Tirant lo Blach'," *Estudis Románics,* IV (1953–1954), 137–205; Johanna D. Hintzen, *De Kruistochtplannen van Philips den Goede* (Rotterdam, 1918); Roger Degryse, "De Bourgondische expedities naar Rhodos, Constantinopel en Ceuta, 1441–1465," *Académie de marine de Belgique: Communications (Mededelingen der Akademie van marine van België),* XVII (1965), 227–265; L. Nicolau d'Olwer, "Un Témoignage catalan du siège de Rhodes en 1444," *Estudis universitaris catalans,* XII (1927), 376–387, for the Burgundian participation in the defense of Rhodes; and Iorga, "Les Aventures 'sarrazines' des français de Bourgogne au XVe siècle" (Cluj, 1926; repr. in *Mélanges d'histoire générale,* I [1927], 9–56).

2. Max Silberschmidt, *Das orientalische Problem zur Zeit der Entstehung des türkischen Reiches nach venezianischen Quellen, 1381-1400* (Leipzig and Berlin, 1923).

garded Serbia as a tributary state since 1389, when Murad I defeated
the Serbs at Kossovo Polje. Thus challenged, Murad II led an army
against Golubats, which he captured, almost taking Sigismund prisoner
in the process. A peace was made which recognized George Brankovich as the despot (1427–1456) of a Serbian kingdom that served as
a buffer between the two powers. Sigismund now established Belgrade
as the bulwark of Hungarian defense against the Turks; Murad fortified Golubats, while Brankovich established himself at Smederevo,
at the confluence of the Danube and Morava rivers. Sigismund concentrated his efforts on fighting the Hussites, who at Domažlice on
August 14, 1431, decisively defeated a crusading army led by the papal
legate, cardinal Julian Cesarini.

When the peace between Hungary and Serbia expired in 1431 Sigismund claimed territory in Serbia, Bosnia, and Bulgaria. These small
principalities found themselves caught in a conflict between two empires with little chance of continued independent existence. By 1434
Murad had decided on a more aggressive policy in the Balkans. His
objective was to expand the Ottoman territory and transform tributary vassal states into provinces of the Ottoman empire, a pattern followed in subsequent expansion.[3] The more immediate objectives of
the new aggressiveness were to halt Venetian advances in the Morea
(Peloponnesus), occupy the strategic Serbian fortresses as a prelude
to an attack on Transylvania, and strengthen Ottoman control over
Wallachia. Byzantium still attempted to play the role of a great empire, although the territory of the "empire" amounted to little more
than the capital and the Morea. The Ottomans repeatedly besieged
Constantinople, but their sieges were doomed to failure since the city
could be supplied by sea and the Ottomans had not yet developed a
significant naval force.[4]

The Byzantines sought aid from Catholic Europe; however, they
realized that little was to be expected from the west until the schism
that had since 1054 separated the Latin and Orthodox churches was
healed. Moreover, the disunity of western Europe, competing nation-
alisms, and the desolation caused by the Hundred Years War had con-

3. Josef von Aschbach, *Geschichte Kaiser Sigmunds,* IV (Hamburg, 1845), 269 ff.; Paul Wittek, "De la Défaite d'Ankara à la prise de Constantinople," *Revue des études islamiques,* XII
(1938), 1–34; Constantin Jireček, *Geschichte der Serben,* II (Gotha, 1918; repr. Amsterdam, 1967),
125, 164. On Sigismund's crusades against the Hussites see Frederick G. Heymann in volume
III of the present work, chapter XVII.
4. Inalcik, *The Ottoman Empire,* pp. 17 ff., and Werner, *Die Geburt einer Grossmacht,*
pp. 219 ff.

vinced the Byzantines that any significant military aid was highly un-likely.[5] The only source from which Byzantium could expect concerted military action was the papacy, so Manuel II Palaeologus had con-tinued negotiations concerning union, sending emissaries to the Coun-cil of Constance.[6] With the removal of the Ottoman threat after An-kara, all initiative for union had vanished, and negotiations were postponed. Manuel made few effective diplomatic overtures to the west between 1402 and 1417, though he did send representatives to the Council of Constance, but not to the Council of Pisa. He concentrated his efforts in the east, recovering Thessalonica, rebuilding the Hexa-milion wall, and consolidating Byzantine power in the Morea.

The Byzantines could not, however, reasonably expect aid to be sent until union was achieved, an objective that Manuel nevertheless at-tempted to postpone and otherwise prevent from reaching fruition. He realized that for the Byzantine populace and clergy this was an unacceptable price to pay for military aid, and he warned his son and heir that it was an unattainable objective.[7]

The accession of Murad II meant for Byzantium a period of renewed warfare. Almost immediately Constantinople was besieged, from June 10 to September 6, 1422, but the city could not be taken as long as the Turks could not maintain a naval blockade. In the following year the Turks destroyed the Hexamilion, overran the Morea, and attacked Thessalonica. In a desperate effort to save the city, the despot Androni-cus Palaeologus gave it to the Venetians, from whom Murad II, never-theless, captured it in 1430. And yet the conciliatory gestures of pope Martin V (1417–1431), including the suggestion of convening an ecu-menical council that would have met the requirements of the Greeks and defraying the cost of the Byzantine delegates, met with evasive-ness in Constantinople. On July 1, 1425, Manuel died and John VIII became sole emperor (d. 1448), and negotiations continued. When Mar-

5. John W. Barker, *Manuel II Palaeologus (1391–1425): a Study in Late Byzantine States-manship* (New Brunswick, N.J., 1969), pp. 290 ff.

6. Raymond J. Loenertz, "Les Dominicains byzantins Théodore et André Chrysobergès et les négociations pour l'union des églises grecque et latine de 1415 à 1430," *AFP,* IX (1939), 5–61. In early 1416 Manuel sent a delegation led by Nicholas Eudaimonoïoannes, his son Androni-cus, and John Bladynteros.

7. On June 15, 1422, Martin V appointed Anthony of Massa as apostolic nuncio to Con-stantinople. Although he had an audience with Manuel on September 16, by November 14, with Manuel recovering from a stroke, John VIII and the patriarch replied that only an ecumenical council could settle the differences between the churches. On November 8, 1423, these discus-sions were reported to the fathers at Pisa, and further discussions were postponed. Cf. Gill, *op. cit.,* pp. 327–330.

tin V died on February 20, 1431, a Greek embassy was en route to Rome to discuss a union council. It turned back at Gallipoli when news of the pope's death reached the emissaries.

Eugenius IV (1431–1447) continued Martin's policies, and fully accepted the concept of convening an ecumenical council to end the schism and reunite the Latin Catholic and Greek Orthodox churches. In competition with the conciliarist prelates of the Council of Basel, who "deposed" him on January 24, 1438, he conducted lengthy and intricate negotiations with John VIII, resulting in the emperor's arrival at Ferrara in March 1438, accompanied by the patriarch Joseph II and other Greek prelates. On April 9 the council, considered by the papacy but not by the conciliarists a continuation of the Council of Basel, was formally opened. Early in 1439 fear of the plague led it to move to Florence, where intensive discussion culminated in a decree of union, signed on July 5 by Latin and Greek participants, including the emperor.

This act of union represented an agreement based on political necessity, which was accepted by the higher Greek clergy. It did not take into account the hatred of the Latins by the Byzantine population and the regular clergy, who would unite successfully to prevent its implementation. Nevertheless, Eugenius could point to a very solid achievement, one which tipped the scales decisively in his favor in his struggle with the conciliarists. Thereafter Eugenius steadily reëstablished papal authority. He could claim the overwhelming acceptance of union by the Byzantine hierarchy, supported by the patriarchs of Alexandria, Antioch, and Jerusalem, as well as envoys of Alexius IV Comnenus, the emperor of Trebizond, the Georgians, Ruthenians, and Wallachians. John left Florence on August 26 and sailed from Venice on October 19, arriving home on February 1, 1440, only to learn of his wife's death and to face strong opposition to union.

In January 1439, well before the formal consummation of union, John VIII had had Isidore of Kiev open negotiations for aid from the papacy and the western rulers. Eugenius had responded with a delegation of three cardinals, who promised that the pope would provide the Greeks with transport and with three hundred soldiers and two ships as a permanent garrison for Constantinople. If the city were attacked, Eugenius would send ten ships for a year or twenty for six months, and if an army were needed the pope would attempt to have the European rulers send contingents to form a united army. John agreed to these proposals and requested that this agreement be placed in writing and sealed, and that arrangements be made with banks in Venice,

Genoa, and Florence for its fulfillment.[8] All parties to these negotiations realized that if Constantinople were to be adequately defended, both a land army and a naval squadron acting in unison would be needed.

Any land offensive against the Ottomans would have to cross the Balkans, presumably starting from a base in Hungary, which was part of emperor Sigismund's domains. Sigismund of Luxemburg had acquired a claim to the Hungarian crown in 1385 by his marriage to Maria, daughter of king Louis the Great of Poland and Hungary, and in 1387 had been recognized as king by the Hungarian estates. He had added the title "king of the Romans" in 1410 and that of Bohemia in 1419, though the latter was not accepted by the Czechs until 1436, after a series of unsuccessful crusades against the Hussites. He was finally crowned emperor in 1433. After Maria's death he had married Barbara of Cilly, who in 1410 bore him a daughter, Elizabeth, the heiress to his kingdoms. In 1411 he obtained from the Hungarian estates the promise that they would recognize the right of Elizabeth to the throne and elect a man to rule with her, a stipulation that was to be important during the events of 1439–1440. Elizabeth married Albert V of Hapsburg, duke of Austria, in 1422, and in 1434 the estates agreed to Sigismund's proposal that Albert should succeed him, though insisting on a formal election at the time of his accession.[9]

By late autumn 1437 Sigismund was in Prague, sick, and realized he was dying. He sent a message to Elizabeth and Albert to meet him at Znojmo in Bohemia, where he planned to hold a meeting of the Bohemian magnates and elicit from them recognition of the couple's rights to the throne. He reached the city on November 21, gravely ill, and obtained the promises he sought, although a formal election would still be necessary. He died on December 9 and was buried in Grosswardein (Nagyvárad) in Hungary. At his death the imperial throne and

8. Georg Hofmann, ed., *Epistolae pontificiae ad Concilium Florentinum spectantes,* 3 parts (Rome, 1940–1946), II, 67, in *Concilium Florentinum, Documenta et scriptores.* On June 5 Eugenius indicated to John that loans of 10,000 florins had been negotiated from Florence and Venice. On September 23 Eugenius wrote to John VIII mentioning the promises that had been made; cf. *ibid.,* II, 113–115 and 117–120, where the pope wrote to the Council of Basel, on October 7, outlining his plans for a crusading army supported by a fleet.

9. The original agreements are lost, and we are dependent for our information on a letter written by Elizabeth during the civil war to Frederick III, published in Adam F. Kollarius (Kollár), ed., *Analecta monumentorum omnis aevi Vindobonensia,* I (Vienna, 1761), 915 ff. The 1434 agreement is also mentioned in a letter from Gaspar Schlick to Frederick III, in *Deutsche Reichstagsakten,* IX, 421. For the arrangements at Sigismund's death see W. Ebstein, "Die letzte Krankheit des Kaisers Sigismunds," *Mitteilungen der Instituts für österreichische Geschichtsforschung,* XX (1906), 678–682.

those of Hungary and Bohemia fell vacant. The papacy now sought to encourage and support the claims of Albert to Sigismund's possessions in the hope that Hungary, Bohemia, Germany, and Austria would be united, and thereby more effectively oppose Ottoman expansion.

After the burial Albert and Elizabeth went from Grosswardein to Bratislava to meet with the Hungarian estates, which made Albert promise to devote his energy to Hungary and not to accept the German crown without their express permission. He was to reside in Hungary and to keep the border between Austria and Hungary unchanged, lest Hungary become absorbed into the empire. In mid-December 1437 Albert and Elizabeth accepted these conditions and were elected king and queen of Hungary; they were crowned on January 1, 1438. On March 18 Albert was unanimously elected "king of the Romans", and with Hungarian approval he accepted the German throne on April 29. As for Bohemia, the estates were divided between adherents of Albert and of Casimir, the thirteen-year-old brother of king Vladislav III (Władysław) of Poland. Albert was elected king by a majority of the diet on December 27, 1437, but the Utraquists—the radical Hussites led by archbishop John Rokycana—held a rump election in March 1438 and elected Casimir king.

Albert accepted this throne in Vienna on April 16; then on April 20 the Polish estates accepted the throne for Casimir and opened hostilities by sending two armies into Bohemia in support of his claims. At this time the most powerful person at the Polish court was the bishop of Cracow, Zbigniev Oleśnicki, a devoted conciliarist who worked to have the abuses of the church corrected by the council. He sought the union of Poland and Hungary, under Polish hegemony, but opposed Casimir's acceptance of the Bohemian throne from the Hussite "heretics". Albert was crowned in Prague on June 29, and on August 12 defeated the Polish invaders at Kutná Hora. A Polish army of possibly twelve thousand men under Vladislav then invaded Silesia, but was thrown back by the Hungarians under Stephen Rozgonyi, who in October stopped another Polish army which had advanced to within one mile of Breslau. Although the Polish estates led by Oleśnicki urged Vladislav to make peace, his Polish army again invaded Silesia in the early summer of 1439 while the Ottomans were attacking Transylvania and Serbia, convincing Albert and the Germans that the Poles and Turks had formed an unholy alliance. Finally a truce was arranged under papal auspices, since the Ottoman threat had now assumed serious proportions.[10]

10. See Janssen, *Frankfurts Reichscorrespondenz*, I, 465, for Vladislav's appeal for recog-

In the summer of 1438, as the Council of Florence debated theology and Albert was occupied in Bohemia, Murad II crossed into Europe with a large army, intent on subjugating Transylvania. He compelled Vlad II Dracul, the voivode of Wallachia (d. 1446) and a vassal of Hungary, to accompany him with his army. Although unsuccessful in attempts to take Hermannstadt (Sibiu) and Kronstadt (Brashov), the Turks burned and pillaged for over six weeks, and captured, by unreliable contemporary estimates, between seventy and eighty thousand prisoners.[11] Fearing that the sultan planned to attack Serbia and Hungary, Albert invested John Hunyadi with the banat of Szöreny and the responsibility for defending the border.

Murad then demanded that George Brankovich, despot of Serbia, surrender to him the city of Smederevo, on the Danube east of Belgrade. Brankovich fortified the city but then, realizing that it could not withstand a siege, fled to Ragusa and on to Hungary, leaving his son Gregory to defend the city. At the end of May 1439 Murad invaded Serbia, besieged Smederevo, and sent raiding parties to devastate the territory between the Danube and Temesvár. Albert summoned the royal army and the Hungarian nobles to join him at Szegedin, which he reached on July 29, finding there only twenty-five thousand men. Defections and dysentery reduced their number to six thousand, too few to relieve Smederevo, which Gregory surrendered to Murad on August 29.[12] The sultan decided on a permanent extension of the empire, establishing Bosnia and Albania as Ottoman provinces under a governor at Skoplje.

Albert withdrew to Buda and traveled toward Vienna, fatally ill with

nition of Casimir's rights to the throne. On April 20, 1438, Eugenius appointed John Zengg and John Berardi, archbishop of Taranto, as his legates to the peace negotiations: *Deutsche Reichstagsakten,* XIV, 246–247. Oleśnicki led the Polish delegation and Gaspar Schlick represented Albert; cf. Otto Hufnagel, "Caspar Schlick als Kanzler Friedrichs III.," *Mitteilungen des Instituts für österreichische Geschichtsforschung,* VIII, Ergänzungsband (1911), 253–261. A second truce was arranged on May 24 to last until September 25; see György Fejér, ed., *Codex diplomaticus Hungariae ecclesiasticus ac civilis,* XI (Budapest, 1844), 234 and 240, for a letter of Vladislav and Casimir dated June 4 from Cracow, to the papal legates promising to observe the truce.

11. *Deutsche Reichstagsakten,* XIII-2, 524–525, which also contains reports of the Turkish destruction. Vlad Dracul had been created voivode by 1436, and Albert continued to address him as a vassal; see Iorga, *Histoire des roumains et de la romanité orientale,* IV (Paris, 1937), 45–72, and Gustav Gündisch, "Die Türkeneinfälle in Siebenbürgen bis zur Mitte des 15. Jahrhunderts," *Jahrbücher für Geschichte Osteuropas,* II (1937), 393–412. Albert had been warned by the Ragusans on March 8 that the Turks were preparing an expedition across the Danube; see Gelcich and Thallóczy, *Diplomatarium,* pp. 422–423. Albert, however, continued to divert large numbers of troops to the northern border, fearing a Polish attack; cf. Imre Navy, ed., *Codex diplomaticus patrius,* II (Prague, 1865), 287–288.

12. Iorga, *Geschichte des osmanischen Reiches,* I (Gotha, 1908), p. 423.

dysentery. After writing a will to safeguard the heritage of the child Elizabeth was expecting, he died at Neszméty on October 27, 1439, at the age of forty-two. His preoccupation with securing the crowns of three kingdoms had permitted the Turks to expand their Balkan conquests at the expense of Hungary, and had thwarted Eugenius's hopes for a crusade. The struggles over the succession to the Hungarian throne were to delay the crusade for another five years, and diverted the energies of the papacy to involvement in Hungarian and Polish affairs.

Elizabeth sought to have herself proclaimed regent in Austria and Hungary, but she realized that Bohemia would not accept her nor her future child. On February 22, 1440, she gave birth at Bratislava to a son, Ladislas (V) "Posthumus". After Albert's death the Hungarians had invoked the agreement of 1411 and opened negotiations in Cracow for Elizabeth's marriage to the sixteen-year-old Vladislav III of Poland, which remained stalled during her pregnancy. Then, on March 8, these negotiations culminated in a treaty recognizing Vladislav as king Ladislas (László) IV of Hungary, but the thirty-six-year-old Elizabeth refused to accept him as husband or king, and appealed for recognition of her son Ladislas, whom she placed under the guardianship of duke Frederick III of Hapsburg, Albert's successor as king of the Romans (1440–1452, emperor 1452–1493). Both Ladislas and Vladislav were crowned by the rival Hungarian factions, which were respectively supported by the Austrian and Polish armies.[13] As Elizabeth and Vladislav opened hostilities, Murad II besieged Belgrade, the key fortress protecting Hungary. Under the command of János Thallóczy the garrison defended the fortress for six months, during which the Turks reportedly lost thirty thousand men.[14]

For two years the civil war continued indecisively, with actual warfare limited to occasional skirmishing as each army devastated the lands of its adversaries. Elizabeth steadily lost ground, as her support in Hungary was eroded by the open illegality of her actions and the destructiveness of her German troops and Bohemian mercenaries, while Vladislav and Oleśnicki won her adherents over with acts of leniency and grants of clemency.[15] In the spring of 1441 Eugenius attempted

13. Elizabeth was supported by the voivode Desiderius Losonczy and by the Székler counts Michael Kusoli, Francis Csáky, and Stephen Rozgonyi; cf. István Katona, *Historia critica . . . regum Hungariae: Stirpis mixtae,* XII (Pest, 1791), 924.

14. Długosz, *Historia polonica,* XII, col. 748, describes Belgrade, ". . . quod est quidam portus, et primus in Ungariam introitus, obsidione vallaverat, . . .", and cf. Thurocz, *Chronica Hungarorum,* I, cap. 35.

15. Katona, *op. cit.,* XIII, 150, and Długosz, *Historia polonica,* XII, col. 759. Elizabeth sold

unsuccessfully to negotiate a truce; on February 12, 1442, with the civil war at its height, he appointed cardinal Julian Cesarini legate to Hungary with a twofold commission: to establish peace and to organize the crusade against the Turks, under the leadership of Vladislav.[16]

After an effort to enlist Venetian support for the planned crusade, and an unsuccessful attempt to meet Frederick III in Vienna, Cesarini joined Vladislav at Buda on May 27, and with Oleśnicki away at Cracow soon became the principal adviser of the young and highly impressionable king.[17] By August he had arranged a ten-month truce and a meeting between the two monarchs to enter into a permanent peace. On November 24 Vladislav and Elizabeth met at Györ, where they negotiated for three weeks under Cesarini's auspices; on December 16 they signed a treaty of peace. Suddenly, on December 24, 1442, Elizabeth died; her supporters claimed she had been poisoned on Vladislav's orders.[18] Cesarini sought to have the treaty accepted by Frederick, who was carrying on the war in the name of Ladislas, but not until May 1444 did Frederick confirm it, under pressure from Eugenius. Only then was Vladislav free to turn his full attention to the Ottoman threat.

Following his unsuccessful attempt on Belgrade in 1440, Murad had taken Novo Brdo with its valuable silver mines in 1441, while Turkish raiding parties plundered as far as Belgrade before being defeated by Hunyadi, who pursued them to Smederevo.[19] In 1442 Murad sent Mezid Beg into Transylvania with a large army, which plundered and burned as far as Hermannstadt (Sibiu) and then moved northwestward. On March 18 they defeated Hunyadi near Alba Julia (Weissenburg), killing its bishop George Lepès, but a week later Hunyadi and Nicholas of Ujlak (called Ujláki) decisively defeated them at Szent Imre, killing

---

the royal jewels to pay her mercenaries, who plundered everywhere. Kollár, *Analecta,* II, 832, indicates that on August 3 she pawned the "house crown" for 2,500 florins. By December she had borrowed 2,000 gulders against her Austrian estates, and by 1442 she had sold Oldenburg to Frederick for 8,000 florins; cf. József Teleki, *Hunyadiak kora magyarországon* (12 vols., Pest, 1852–1894), X, 112–113, and Ignaz A. Fessler, *Geschichte von Ungarn,* ed. Ernst Klein (Leipzig, 1869), 463 ff.

16. Hofmann, *Epistolae,* III, 92–93.

17. See Mols, "Julien Cesarini," *loc. cit.,* and the funeral oration of Poggio, which is factual but undistinguished, in Mai, *loc. cit.* See Cieszkowski, *op. cit.,* pp. 61–62, for the response of the Venetian senate to Cesarini. For the truce see Elizabeth's letter of August 14 to Nicholas Ban and Stephen Báthori from Bratislava (Pressburg).

18. Cf. Jacob Caro, *Geschichte Polens,* IV (Gotha, 1875), p. 331, in *Geschichte der europäischen Staaten,* and Ladislaus von Szalay, *Geschichte Ungarns,* III (Budapest, 1875), 51, for a discussion of the allegations.

19. Werner, *op. cit.,* p. 227, and Inalcik, *The Ottoman Empire,* p. 20. See Wilhelm Schmidt, *Die Stammburg der Hunyade in Siebenbürgen* . . . (Hermannstadt, 1865). At Vladislav's accession Hunyadi was count of Temesvár; he was named voivode of Transylvania by Vladislav (1440–1456).

Mezid Beg.[20] Later in 1442 Hunyadi defeated two other Ottoman armies which had been devastating Wallachia.[21] On January 8, 1443, Cesarini wrote to Venice announcing the treaty signed by Vladislav and Elizabeth, the latter's death, and Hunyadi's third victory on December 7.[22]

The legate and the Venetians had been planning, throughout the fall of 1442, a crusade consisting of a land army setting out from Hungary supported by a fleet stationed in the Dardanelles.[23] The fleet's objectives were to cut communications between Anatolia and Europe, protect Constantinople, and join with the crusaders to capture the Turkish fortresses on the Danube while the main Ottoman forces were kept in Anatolia. In the reign of Murad II his European fortresses and cities were normally garrisoned sufficiently to defend the area; however, the sultan's army was kept in Anatolia during the winter months, coming to Europe only for a specific campaign. Thus a crusading army stood a good chance of overwhelming the Turkish garrisons if a naval blockade was established in the Dardanelles, since the Ottomans did not possess a navy to oppose a fleet. Constantinople could always be supplied by sea during a siege and communications with the west kept open. On September 15 the Ragusans offered, in a letter to Cesarini, to arm one galley to join a fleet in support of a land army for the duration of the campaign; they estimated that a fleet of twenty-eight ships would be required to blockade the Dardanelles effectively.[24]

On January 1, 1443, with the civil war ended, Eugenius issued a bull levying a tenth on the entire church in order to raise funds for arming a fleet.[25] On January 2 the Venetian senate wrote to duke Philip III of Burgundy (1419–1467) requesting aid for the crusade, and on Janu-

20. Thurocz, *op. cit.,* ch. 37, and Chalcocondylas, ed. Bekker, p. 253. Katona, *op. cit.,* XIII, 216, gives the inscription from the tomb of the bishop in Alba Julia from which we know the date of the battle, "die bis nono Martii anno domini millesimo CCCCXL secundo"; and cf. Kupelwieser, *Die Kämpfe,* pp. 62 ff.

21. *Monumenta Hungariae historica,* series I, XXIII, 141. For a description of the battle see Iorga, *Geschichte des osmanischen Reiches,* I, 425 ff., and Köhler, *Die Schlachten,* p. 39.

22. Iorga, *Notes et extraits,* III, 100–101; the senate responded to Cesarini, and pointed out that the tithe was yielding insufficient funds for the fleet. The vice-chancellor, Francis Condulmer, had come to Venice on August 2 without funds, and thus little could be done. The Venetians stated that the delays were detrimental to the Christian cause.

23. Cesarini was in Venice in late March, and explained his objectives to doge Francis Foscari (1423–1457); cf. Domenico Caccamo, "Eugenio IV e la crociata di Varna," *Archivio della Società romana di storia patria,* LXXIX (3rd series, X; Rome, 1956), 45–46.

24. Iorga, *Notes et extraits,* II, 390.

25. Hofmann, *Epistolae,* III, 68–75. The bull mentions the glorious victories in Hungary and the necessity of having a land army and a fleet to fight the Turks. The cardinals have agreed to give a tenth of the income from their benefices and Eugenius has given one fifth of his income from annates and "servitia communia".

ary 9 Eugenius requested ten galleys from Venice, to be armed at papal expense and sent to the Dardanelles. On April 3 the senate wrote Eugenius, confirming their offer to provide the ten galleys if the pope would pay to have them armed.[26] On May 8 Eugenius appointed his nephew, cardinal Francis Condulmer, legate and captain-general of the papal fleet.[27] On June 14 Eugenius and Alfonso of Aragon and Naples concluded peace and an agreement whereby Alfonso was to send six galleys to the Dardanelles for six months; they were, however, never sent. By July both the pope and the senate realized that preparations for a crusade could not be completed in 1443, and on December 17 Eugenius wrote to Ragusa that he hoped to have a fleet in the Dardanelles by the following summer.[28]

In addition to the pope and Venice duke Philip of Burgundy supported the crusade. Since the crusade of Nicopolis in 1396, when Philip's father John the Fearless was taken prisoner, the idea of a military expedition against the Turks had been a recurrent theme of Burgundian eastern policy. In 1421 Philip and the duke of Bedford, John of Lancaster, had sent Gilbert of Lannoy to the east, and in 1432 Philip had dispatched Bertrandon of La Broquière to Palestine, Syria, and Anatolia to report on the military situation.[29] In 1439 John VIII sent his chamberlain John Torcello to the duke with a plan for a war against Murad and the deliverance of the Holy Land.

Philip was also supporting the Knights Hospitaller in defense of Rhodes against the Mamluks of Egypt. In 1440 Murad signed a treaty with the Mamluks aimed at Rhodes. The lack of a navy had prevented the Ottomans from attacking the knights, who could not be placed on the defensive by Egyptian warships. Early that year sultan Jakmak aẓ-Ẓāhir (1438–1453) sent a fleet of nineteen galleys against Castellorizzo, an island belonging to the Hospitallers off the coast of southwestern Anatolia. The knights dispatched eight galleys and four smaller ships, and forced the Mamluks to retire. On September 25, 1440, an Egyptian fleet appeared off Rhodes, but soon retired to Cyprus, and

26. Iorga, *Notes et extraits*, III, 121–122. Leonard Venier was the Venetian ambassador at the papal court. The previous October 30 the senate had learned of Hunyadi's victories from Vladislav; see *ibid.*, III, 105–106. News of the last victory was circulated throughout western Europe: Huber, "Die Kriege," pp. 159–207.

27. Hofmann, *Epistolae*, III, 78–80.

28. Iorga, *Notes et extraits*, III, 128–129. On May 20, 1443, the Venetians wrote to Condulmer stressing the importance of having a fleet in the Dardanelles to support the crusading army; see *ibid.*, III, 126–127, and III, 134, for Leonard Venier's letter of July 6 concerning sending a fleet the following year.

29. Deno Geanakoplos, "Byzantium and the Crusades, 1354–1453," in volume III of the present work, p. 98.

then to Egypt. The knights prepared to repel a second expected attack and appealed to the duke of Burgundy, who sent three ships under Geoffrey of Thoisy.[30] This squadron sailed from Sluis to Bruges, then to Lisbon, where Geoffrey inspected some ships the duke was having built there, then into the Mediterranean and the Black Sea. Little fighting occurred, and the squadron returned to Villefranche in mid-1442, Geoffrey having gained some knowledge of the eastern Mediterranean.[31]

Meanwhile, the Byzantine envoy Theodore Caristinus again visited the duke at Chalon-sur-Saône early in 1443 and appealed to him to send warships in support of the planned crusade. Philip responded by sending an emissary to Venice to request four galleys, which he would pay to have armed. He informed Caristinus of this decision and offered to send in addition the three galleys and one galiot that were being built at Villefranche and two of the ships that had been sent to Rhodes, making a total of ten ships to form the Burgundian squadron. Thus by the spring of 1443 diplomatic efforts had resulted in commitments for a fleet of twenty-one ships, including one from the Ragusans, seven less than the Ragusan government deemed necessary to establish an effective blockade of the Dardanelles.[32]

As preparations for the fleet progressed, Cesarini sought to have the army mobilized. In early January 1443 and again on April 9 he addressed the estates in Buda, urging them to undertake an expedition against the Turks, who had been defeated by Hunyadi in 1442, and informing them of the tithe levied by the pope to support a fleet. At first the estates declined to take action, postponing a decision until their next meeting in June. During that meeting letters arrived from Ragusa and from Hunyadi in Belgrade, informing the Hungarians that sultan Murad II had crossed to Anatolia, handed over the government to his young son Mehmed (II), and retired to Bursa. Hunyadi advised them that the Rumelian fortresses were lightly garrisoned and that an

---

30. Ettore Rossi, *Storia della marina dell' ordine di San Giovanni di Gerusalemme, di Rodi e di Malta* (Rome, 1926), p. 19. Thoisy, whose appointment is dated March 25, 1441, had accompanied Lannoy to the Levant; he was a Knight Hospitaller and governor of the ducal galleys.

31. Marinescu, "Philippe le Bon," p. 154, and "L'Île de Rhodes au XVe siècle et l'ordre de Saint-Jean de Jérusalem d'après des documents inédits," *Miscellanea Giovanni Mercati,* V (Studi e testi, 125; Vatican City, 1945), 382–401.

32. This number is based on the estimate made by the Ragusans in a letter to Eugenius dated February 10, 1444, found in Bariša Krekić, *Dubrovnik (Ragusa) et le Levant au moyen âge* (Paris and The Hague, 1961), p. 336, and Gelcich and Thallóczy, pp. 451–454. The diplomatic efforts of that spring were intense indeed. Theodore Caristinus had visited the duke of Burgundy, while Eugenius had effectively put together an alliance of Venice, the papacy, Burgundy, and Ragusa. Even Alfonso of Aragon had joined. See Marinescu, "Notes sur quelques ambassadeurs byzantins," *Annuaire de l'Institut de philologie et d'histoire orientales et slaves,* X (1950), 421.

army of thirty thousand could drive the Turks out of Europe.[33] These reports led the estates to vote a subsidy and support for a crusade.

The sources for the first "long expedition" are sparse. We have a letter from Hunyadi to Ujláki, Vladislav's report to the doge of Venice, a poem by Michael Beheim, and the chronicles of Callimachus, Długosz, and Chalcocondylas.

Vladislav issued a royal summons to his vassals, and Cesarini and Brankovich left Buda with the royal army on July 22, 1443. Długosz reports that the king spent the rest of the summer arming his men, obtaining horses, and awaiting the contingents he had summoned from Poland and Wallachia.[34] Estimates of the size of the army range from Beheim's of fourteen thousand to Długosz's of twenty-five thousand (which is too large), with about six hundred supply wagons. The army moved southeast, probably passing through Szegedin, crossing the Danube at Petrovaradin (Peterwardein), and sometime in October arriving at Belgrade, where they joined forces with Hunyadi, designated by Vladislav as "capitaneus exercitus generalis". From Belgrade the army proceeded southeast to the Turkish stronghold of Kraguyevats, which they captured and burned. Thence the army continued southeast along the Morava river to Aleksinats, where news reached them of the approach of a Turkish force. Vladislav and Cesarini decided to encamp while the two voivodes, John Hunyadi and Ujláki, reconnoitered with a force of twelve thousand men.

The voivodes reached Nish, which was held by a small Turkish garrison, and took the city, which they plundered and burned. They learned that three Turkish armies were converging on Nish to meet and march against the crusaders, but succeeded in defeating all three before they could link up. On November 3 word was brought that yet another Turkish force, combined with the remnants of the defeated armies, was advancing past Hunyadi's left flank toward the royal camp. Hunyadi returned to Nish, where he defeated this fourth attack,[35] capturing Murad's chancellor and many Ottoman officers. Hunyadi, it is

---

33. Chmel, *Materialien zur österreichischen Geschichte aus Archiven und Bibliotheken* (Vienna, 1837), I-2, 114 ff.

34. Długosz, *Historia polonica*, XII, col. 755, ". . . plures gentes ex regno Poloniae et terris Wallachiae." See the poem of Michael Beheim in Thomas von Karajan, ed., *Quellen und Forschungen zur vaterländischen Geschichte, Literatur und Kunst* (Vienna, 1849), pp. 35–36, and Ducas, ed. Bekker, p. 217, for estimates on the number of troops.

35. Kupelwieser, *Die Kämpfe*, pp. 69 ff. Hunyadi wrote of his exploits to Ujláki on November 8 when he had returned to the royal camp; see Katona, *op. cit.*, XIII, 251–254. He states that he had twelve thousand men, had captured Nish, and had defeated the force under Isa Beg,

said, took four thousand prisoners and brought the king nine Ottoman banners as trophies. Vladislav wrote to Venice of victories over
Ottoman armies numbering thirty thousand men. We are not sure of
the precise dates, but Aeneas Sylvius states that these battles all took
place by November 3, 1443.[36]

Hunyadi returned to camp sometime before November 9, when he
wrote to Ujláki. The army now marched southeast from Nish past Bela
Palanka and Pirot to Sofia, which they reached in late November or
early December. They stormed the city, which they sacked, plundering
and burning everything.[37]

Then the crusaders advanced toward the Maritsa river, through the
pass of Trajan's Door, planning to attack Philippopolis (Plovdiv) and
then march down river to the Turkish administrative headquarters in
Rumelia at Adrianople (Edirne). Murad, who had resumed the throne
and crossed the Straits with a large army, had his troops block the key
pass, through which the old Roman road ran to Adrianople. The Hungarians swung east toward the Zlatitsa pass into the Topolnitsa valley,
but this pass was blocked by trees and ice and defended by an army
under Murad's son-in-law Khalil Pasha, beglerbeg of Anatolia.[38] The
Hungarians attempted unsuccessfully to force the pass, and were halted
for three days at the castle of Sladagora. The sources agree that the
main battle took place on December 24, 1443, lasting all day and into
the night. The crusaders used artillery in an attempt to dislodge the
Turks, who threw trees, boulders, and ice into the pass and showered
arrows down on them. From subsequent negotiations we know that
the sultan's son-in-law was taken prisoner.[39] Unable to advance farther in winter, short of food and supplies, the crusaders decided to
return to Hungary and attempt another expedition in the spring.

As the crusaders returned to Hungary the sultan sent Kasim Pasha
at the head of Rumelian cavalry and Anatolian troops to attack the

---

a second pasha, and Turakhan Beg. He had captured many Turkish prisoners and released Christian
prisoners, among whom were many nobles.

36. Information on these battles is given by Aeneas Sylvius in a letter dated January 15,
1444 (in Wolkan, *Der Briefwechsel*, LXI-2, p. 281). In a letter to bishop Leonard Laiming of
Passau, dated October 28, 1445, *ibid.*, pp. 562–579, he states that thirty thousand Turks were
killed.

37. Thurocz, *op. cit.*, chap. 40.

38. Ducas, ed. Bekker, p. 218. The Turkish historian Sadeddin describes the route taken;
see the French translation, *Annales ottomanes*, p. 85.

39. Długosz, *Historia polonica*, XII, cols. 776 ff., gives an account of this battle. Aeneas
Sylvius describes the battle in his letter of October 28, 1445, saying that Hunyadi and his men
tried to force the pass. Chalcocondylas, ed. Bekker, p. 413, states that the Hungarians could
not get through the pass and were forced to turn back because of a lack of supplies; cf. Ducas,
ed. Bekker, p. 219.

crusader army, which they followed over the Iskar and the Nishava, joining battle at the Kunovitsa pass. Brankovich was guarding the rear, which the Turks attacked. Hunyadi and Vladislav, who were already through the pass, left the wagons guarded by infantry and joined the battle near the river on the eastern side of the pass. The engagement ended in a complete victory for the crusaders. The battle, the last of the "long expedition", took place on January 5, 1444, under a full moon.[40] Short of supplies and horses, the crusaders burned much of their baggage and wagons before returning to Belgrade, where Hunyadi and his men remained for the winter. He refused Brankovich's request to winter in Serbia and help him reconquer it. Vladislav and Cesarini returned to Buda, where they arrived in February and were greeted as conquering heroes. A service of thanksgiving was held in the cathedral, where a "Te Deum" was sung and the captured Turkish weapons were displayed. The victories were announced to the European princes, long accustomed to hearing only of Christian defeats at the hands of the Turks.

One result of the victorious campaign of 1443 was the successful revolt of the Albanians under George Castriota, known as Scanderbeg (d. 1468). Castriota had been sent from Albania as a hostage to the sultan's court and trained at the military academy of Enderum in Adrianople, where his accomplishments earned him the title of beg (tacked onto his Turkish name of Iskander as Scanderbeg). He was co-commander of one of the armies defeated by Hunyadi near Nish. After the battle he fled to Albania, where he gathered forces and captured Croia from the Turks. By the summer of 1444 he was leading a revolt against the Turks with the aid of the Venetians and Alfonso V of Aragon, king of Naples. Some historians have claimed that Scanderbeg formed an alliance with Vladislav, but this has been proved false through letters included by Aeneas Sylvius in his work describing the events of Kossovo in 1448 (which Marinus Barletius, who first printed them, confused with Varna in 1444).[41] Scanderbeg was in no position at the time of the second campaign to create any sort of diversion in support of the crusade.

Letters of congratulation and embassies arrived in Buda during the next few months praising the victories and urging the king to undertake another expedition in the spring.[42] The victories had demonstrated

40. Kupelwieser, *op. cit.*, pp. 75–77.

41. Pall, "Les Relations entre la Hongrie et Scanderbeg," pp. 111–141, and "Skanderbeg et Ianco de Hunedoara," pp. 5–21.

42. Cesarini wrote to the Venetians about the victories, and on January 15, 1444, the senate decided to send a secretary to Buda to offer the republic's congratulations; see Iorga, *Notes et*

that Turkish arms were not invincible. The sultan had, however, been able to halt the crusaders by crossing into Rumelia with his army. It was now clear that any future success against the Turks would depend on preventing the Ottoman forces from crossing the Dardanelles, which could be accomplished only by a naval blockade. Without a navy the Ottomans were powerless to challenge such a blockade.

Now work on the galleys was accelerated, with the objective of having a fleet in Levantine waters for the 1444 campaigning season.[43] The victories of the so-called "long expedition" of 1443 resulted in an upsurge of diplomatic efforts to gain military support. On February 8 Ragusa offered to arm two galleys to join the combined fleet, and on the tenth in a letter to Eugenius urged the pope to hasten the arming of his galleys so that they would be stationed in the Dardanelles by summer, when the crusaders were in the field, since this was the only way to halt the transfer of Turkish reinforcements from Anatolia. They also advised Eugenius to urge Vladislav to have his army in the field by the time the fleet would be ready.[44]

On March 3 the Venetian senate learned that Cesarini and Vladislav had returned to Buda. They appointed John de' Reguardati emissary on March 6, instructing him to proceed there with all possible speed; even his route was specified. He was to assure Cesarini that the senate had done all in its power to have the papal galleys armed, and had already prepared the hulls and levied the tithe in its territories. He was to encourage the Hungarians to undertake a second expedition; he was to keep Venice's allies informed of progress on the galleys and to report back to Venice on preparations undertaken in Hungary; and he was to negotiate for the territories requested by Venice when victory was attained.[45]

On March 13 the senate decided to have ten galleys chosen in the

---

extraits, III, 145–147. On March 25, 1444, Alfonso of Naples sent a letter of congratulations based on information he had received from Ragusa; see Gelcich and Thallóczy, Diplomatarium, pp. 363–364.

43. Iorga, Notes et extraits, III, 156–157. On January 15, 1444, the senate sent an emissary to Buda and voted to permit the collection of the tithe in Venetian territory. On February 2 they urged Condulmer to arm those galleys for which he had funds; see ibid., III, 149–150. Meanwhile the Ragusans wrote to Eugenius on February 18, offering to arm two galleys which would join the allied fleet, and urging the pope to complete the arming of his galleys.

44. Krekić, Dubrovnik, p. 336; Gelcich and Thallóczy, Diplomatarium, 451–454. The Ragusans acknowledged the pope's letters of November 9, December 13 and 17, in which he solicited support and named Christopher Garatoni as legate.

45. Sime Ljubić, ed., Listine o odnošajïh izmedju južnoga slavenstva i mletačke republike, III, in Monumenta spectantia historiam slavorum meridionalium, IX (Zagreb, 1878), 183–186, for the appointment of John de' Reguardati. On March 26 Reguardati was further empowered to present his credentials to Brankovich: ibid., 186–187.

arsenal, armed, and dispatched as quickly as possible, even though funds from the pope had not arrived; Condulmer was authorized to select the commanders for these papal galleys, subject to the senate's approval. On March 21 the Venetians voted to permit Condulmer to spend the twelve hundred ducats collected in Venice on arming the papal galleys.[46] The senate had also ordered the preparation of four galleys for the duke of Burgundy, informing him on March 21 that his envoys had found them ready, and that the ten unarmed galleys were ready for the pope. The senate and the duke were concerned about Eugenius's preparations, and they responded to his inquiries of February 10. With Condulmer in Venice, the senate expressed the hope that their arming would soon begin. The senate knew nothing certain about efforts by any other Italian cities, but claimed that these fourteen galleys would suffice to guard the Dardanelles. Venice would not promise to send Venetian ships for a predetermined time, although the republic was prepared to offer some of the galleys at sea near Gallipoli.[47] On April 20 duke Philip appointed Waleran of Wavrin captain-general of the "auxiliary army" (i.e., the Burgundian squadron) being sent to Constantinople, and instructed him to go to Venice to oversee the work on the galleys requested by him. Sometime after April 20 he left Bruges with thirty-one Burgundian emissaries with money for sixty days for the trip from Bruges to Venice.[48]

On May 12 the senate wrote to Reguardati in Buda that the papal galleys would sail from Venice in a few days, to be joined in the Levant by Venetian ships. They reported that the Burgundian envoy, Wavrin, had arrived in Venice to oversee the arming of the four ducal galleys and had informed the senate that Philip the Good was having an additional three galleys and one galiot refurbished at Nice (more accurately, at Villefranche), to be joined by another warship. The senate instructed Reguardati to urge Vladislav to start the expedition soon, since the time was favorable and the galleys were being completed; however, they could accomplish nothing without the land army that they were meant to support. On the same day the Venetians responded to Cesarini's letters of April 25 and 28 informing them of Vladislav's firm intention to undertake a second expedition in the summer. The senate reported to Cesarini on the imminent departure of the papal, Venetian, and Burgundian galleys.[49]

46. Iorga, *Notes et extraits,* III, 162–163, and Thiriet, *Régestes,* III, 110. Cf. Cieszkowski, *op. cit.,* 1–3, 85–89, and Ljubić, *Listine,* XXI, 187.

47. Cieszkowski, *op. cit.,* I-3, 85–89.

48. Archives du Nord, Lille, reg. B1983, fol. 90[v].

49. Iorga, *Notes et extraits,* III, 167–168, and Thiriet, *Régestes,* III, 111–112.

Thus, throughout the spring of 1444 the Venetians were encouraging the Hungarians to begin a second offensive, pressing the arming of the papal galleys, and overseeing the departure of their own ships. After the encouraging news from Hungary the Venetians decided to commit their own galleys, thus engaging the sultan in a full-scale war. They realized that any delay in the departure of the fleet would be disastrous, and so ordered the galleys to sail no later than May 21 under penalty of heavy fine to the patrons, while protesting vigorously to Condulmer the lack of payment for the arming of the papal galleys.[50]

On June 4 and 5 the legate informed the senate that the papal galleys were armed, and that some had sailed and others were ready to sail, while two galleys were still awaiting the remainder of their rigging. On June 17 the doge wrote to the duke of Crete, Thomas Duodo, instructing him to use the tenth collected there to purchase biscuit and bread for the fleet.[51] By June 17 the Venetian galleys were prepared to sail, and the senate instructed their captain, Alvise Loredan, that both he and Wavrin, as commander of the Venetian and Burgundian galleys, would be under Condulmer's command. The republic, however, wanted to avoid war with the Mamluks, which would endanger their Levantine possessions, so Loredan was not to attack Mamluk ships at sea; the fleet had been armed for war only against the Turks. Loredan was not to allow the galleys to touch at Rhodes although Condulmer would probably request them to do so. The galleys were not to attack Mamluk ships encountered in the Dardanelles supporting the Ottomans, nor were the Burgundian galleys to be allowed to go to Rhodes, as had been agreed to by duke Philip.[52]

We know from a letter of the senate to Cesarini dated July 4 that Condulmer sailed from Venice on June 22 with seven papal galleys and eight Venetian galleys; the Burgundian galleys were to leave in two or three days. The senate agreed to Cesarini's request to send eight or more galleys from those that were to be stationed in the Dardanelles up the Danube to Nicopolis to support the crossing of the crusaders.[53] The

---

50. Iorga, *Notes et extraits,* III, 169–170. On May 25 the senate accused the pope of delaying work on the galleys. The Venetians reminded Condulmer of their efforts, and remarked that the galleys should fly the banner of St. Mark since they were armed with Venetian money.

51. Iorga, *Notes et extraits,* III, 172–173, and Thiriet, *Régestes,* III, 112. The fleet was expected in Ragusa by early July, and preparations were under way there for its reception; see Krekić, *Dubrovnik,* p. 339.

52. Iorga, *Notes et extraits,* III, 173–174, and Thiriet, *Régestes,* III, 114. The senate threatened the patrons with death if they disobeyed these orders.

53. Iorga, *Notes et extraits,* III, 175–176. This plan was discussed in Venice before the fleet sailed and had there received Wavrin's support. This letter was addressed to Condulmer, who was at Pola.

Venetians again wrote to Reguardati instructing him how to proceed in the negotiations concerning those territories requested by Venice, which included Gallipoli and Thessalonica. The Byzantine envoy, who had denigrated Venice's contributions, was to be reminded that the republic had spent thirty thousand ducats for the papal fleet in addition to six to eight galleys sent under the banner of St. Mark.[54]

By July 5 the two Ragusan galleys had been outfitted and were ordered to sail the next day. The great council gave instructions that the funds collected from the clergy of Ragusa were to be given to Condulmer to be used for provisioning the galleys en route. With victory in the air the Ragusans now put in their bid for territories they wanted.[55]

Wavrin left Venice on July 6 with one galley; on July 7 the senate ordered two other Burgundian galleys to sail during the night, while the last was to leave at noon on the eighth.[56] The Burgundians had promised the Byzantine ambassador to send four additional ships, and early in 1443 the duke had appointed Geoffrey of Thoisy and Regnault de Confide, a Knight Hospitaller, captains of the three galleys and one galiot that were at Villefranche. They were to oversee the arming and repair of these ships and sail to the Adriatic to join Wavrin, under whose command they were to proceed to the Dardanelles.[57] At the same time the duke chose Alfonso de Oliveria, a gentleman of the household of the Portuguese-born duchess Isabella, to oversee the arming of the two additional ships at Villefranche.

In the summer of 1444 rumors were in the air of a planned Mamluk attack on Rhodes. The grand master, John of Lastic, appealed to Eugenius, who had the cardinal "of Thérouanne", Jean le Jeune (Johannes Juvenis), write to Wavrin at Venice requesting him to go to Rhodes to aid the knights and then to proceed to the Dardanelles. This the Venetians forbade, instructing Loredan not to touch at Rhodes. Wavrin communicated this to the cardinal of Thérouanne, who wrote to Geoffrey and Regnault directing them to sail directly to Rhodes. They left

54. *Ibid.,* III, 177–178.

55. *Ibid.,* III, 175, and Thiriet, *Régestes,* III, 114; Krekić, *Dubrovnik,* pp. 339–340. The Ragusans wanted Avlona and Canina and the surrounding areas. On June 8, 1444, the great council wrote to Vladislav and Cesarini about territory.

56. Iorga, *Notes et extraits,* III, 179. John of Wavrin, ed. Hardy, V, 39–41, is confused in his chronology; he states that Loredan and Condulmer sailed on July 22, instead of a month earlier. He has Waleran of Wavrin leaving Venice on July 25. For Wavrin's departure date see also his letter in the Archives du Nord, Lille, reg. B1984, 1444, and Hintzen, *De kruistochtplannen,* pp. 38–41.

57. Archives du Nord, Lille, reg. 1986, no. 59.240; the appointment was made at Bruges. For a full discussion see Degryse, "De Bourgondische expedities . . . ," pp. 227–265.

Villefranche in July and sailed along the coast of North Africa to Lampedusa, where news reached them that a Mamluk fleet had attacked Rhodes. The Burgundians sailed to the island, where they engaged the Egyptian fleet and then joined the knights in a successful defense of the city, after which they sailed on September 28 to join Wavrin at Constantinople.[58]

By July 17 the two Ragusan galleys had joined the papal-Venetian galleys at Modon in the southern Morea, and on August 19 the Ragusan government instructed its captain to remain with the fleet for six months.[59] By late August the fleet had reached the Dardanelles, as the Ragusans reported to their ambassador at the Bosnian court on August 20, informing him that the galleys would be at Gallipoli by the end of the month. From the information reaching them the Ragusans thought that more than twenty-five galleys would be in the Dardanelles by early September, and this was an accurate estimate: ten papal galleys, eight Venetian, two Ragusan, four Burgundian under Wavrin, four Burgundian ships under Geoffrey of Thoisy, and another two under Oliveria made a total of thirty ships.[60] It was a fleet sufficiently large to blockade the Dardanelles effectively and prevent an Ottoman army from crossing.

In the spring and summer of 1444 peace negotiations were begun between Murad II on the one hand and Vladislav, Hunyadi, and Brankovich on the other. These negotiations caused apprehension among Hungary's allies, and have remained a subject of contention not only among contemporary writers but among historians ever since.[61]

Although the "long expedition" did not achieve a lasting success, it had reversed the almost uninterrupted series of Ottoman victories.

58. For an account of Geoffrey of Thoisy's activities see Marinescu, "Du Nouveau sur 'Tirant lo Blanch'," pp. 137–205; Iorga, "Les Aventures 'sarrazines'," pp. 9–56. The Mamluks attacked the city of Rhodes on August 10, 1444, and besieged it for forty days. After a decisive battle on September 10 the Mamluks withdrew on September 14. The news of the unsuccessful siege reached Venice on October 14. Jean le Jeune, bishop of Thérouanne (1436–1451), was created a cardinal in 1439 but kept his bishopric.

59. Krekić, *Dubrovnik,* p. 341. On July 14 the Venetian senate permitted the government of Corfu to open negotiations with the Turks and the inhabitants of Avlona (Valona) and Argyrokastron in order to obtain these places and to offer the Turks pensions if they had already left their castles. The approach of the fleet had caused panic among the Turkish garrisons: Iorga, *Notes et extraits,* III, 179–180.

60. Krekić, *Dubrovnik,* p. 341.

61. The significant modern literature on the negotiations at Szegedin includes Halecki, *The Crusade of Varna;* Dąbrowski, *L'Année 1444;* Pall, "Ciriaco d'Ancona e la crociata contro i Turchi"; Angyal, "Le Traité de paix de Szeged," pp. 374–392; and particularly Pall, "Autour de la croisade de Varna," pp. 144–158, where he convincingly disproves the thesis of Halecki.

In the spring of 1444 Murad was thus under attack from the Hungarians, in Albania, in the Morea, and from Ibrahim Beg in Karaman. While Vladislav and Cesarini were en route back to Buda in January 1444, a Turkish emissary arrived in camp and requested the king to set a date for the reception of an embassy from the sultan. Again in March a Greek monk arrived from Brankovich's daughter Mara, one of Murad's wives, repeating the sultan's offer to restore her father as despot, and to return his sons Gregory and Stephen, who had been blinded.[62] He found these proposals acceptable, since he urged the Hungarian diet to accept peace when it met in Buda in mid-April. Vladislav and Cesarini did not want peace and, on April 25 and 28, the legate wrote to Venice that the king and the barons had sworn to him that they would lead another expedition against the Turks in the summer.[63] The senate accepted this assurance and continued with the preparations for the fleet. Nevertheless, sometime in May and June emissaries did arrive in Adrianople from Vladislav, Brankovich, and Hunyadi, even though the latter was voivode and a vassal of the king. Our sources for these negotiations are the reports of Ciriaco de' Pizzicolli (1391–1452) of Ancona, an Italian humanist who was present in Adrianople at the sultan's court in May and June, and who sent reports to his friend Andreolo Giustiniani-Banca of Chios, enclosing copies of important official documents.

Around June 12 Ciriaco wrote to his friend that Vladislav's Serbian emissary Stojka Gisdanich arrived in Adrianople with Vitislao, representing John Hunyadi; Athanasius Frashak, metropolitan of Semendria (Smederevo), and another unnamed emissary; and Bogdan, Brankovich's chancellor, escorted by sixty horsemen. Gisdanich's credentials were dated April 24 — nine days after Vladislav had sworn to lead an expedition — and empowered him to conclude a treaty, which was to be sworn to by Murad in the royal emissary's presence.[64] In his report on these negotiations the papal collector Andreas de Palatio wrote that Hunyadi and Brankovich were carrying on these negotiations without consulting the king.[65] However, the letters of credence prove other-

---

62. Krekić, *Dubrovnik,* p. 337. On March 5, 1444, the government of Ragusa placed a boat at the disposal of a monk who is described as a messenger from Mara. He was to be taken to Spalato (Split) and from there to the despot George; the grand council confirmed this decision on March 6.

63. Venice, Sen. Secreto, Reg. 16, fol. 91; see Giuseppe Valentini, *Acta Albaniae veneta saeculorum XIV et XV,* XVIII (Munich, 1974), no. 4962, p. 174, for the senate's reply to Cesarini dated May 12, 1444.

64. Reprinted in Halecki, *The Crusade of Varna,* p. 85.

65. Lewicki, *Codex epistolaris,* II, 460, and Długosz, *Historia polonica,* XII, col. 701, who repeats the statement ". . . tractatum pacis . . . habuerunt inconsulto rege."

wise. It is probable that Vladislav regarded the embassy as unimportant, as merely a tactic to induce the sultan to leave Rumelia.

Brankovich requested the release of his sons, the return to him of the conquered towns and fortresses, particularly Golubats on the Danube, and the granting of favorable terms to Vlad Dracul, voivode of Wallachia. Brankovich and Vlad were, however, to remain Turkish vassals. Negotiations stalled on the surrender of Golubats, which with Belgrade guarded the routes that armies invading Hungary would take. On June 12 Murad agreed to all the requests and swore to a ten-year truce, appointing Suleiman Beg and Varnas, a Greek, his emissaries to Vladislav to obtain his oath. On that day Murad wrote to Vladislav informing him of his emissaries' appointment and looking forward to a ten-year peace.[66] Murad wanted peace with the Hungarians so that he could move his army to Anatolia, without concern about an attack on his European provinces. By granting generous terms to Brankovich he deprived the allies of the Serbian army, and ruptured the alliance erected by Cesarini.

Ciriaco wrote to the Hungarians of the threat to Murad in Anatolia, and reported the events to John VIII Palaeologus. The Byzantines had planned to create a diversion by attacking the Turks from the Morea, the attack to be led by the two despots, the emperor's brothers Theodore (now lord of Selymbria) and Constantine Dragases, who was the more powerful in the Morea.

In February 1444 Constantine successfully established his power north of the isthmus of Corinth, crossed the Hexamilion, and reduced Boeotia and Thebes.[67] The Byzantines had been encouraged by the victories of 1443, and were alarmed at the news of a peace treaty, but not seriously enough to halt their attack. Only the Ragusans instructed their ambassador in Buda to secure the city's interests in any peace that was concluded.[68]

The treaty that had been negotiated in Adrianople on June 12 was concluded in the hope of inducing the sultan to cross to Anatolia, thereby assuring the forthcoming crusade a greater chance of success. This was recognized by Ciriaco, who wrote a letter to John Hunyadi that same day from Adrianople, informing him of what had occurred and wishing him success on the forthcoming expedition.[69] Ciriaco had

66. See Halecki, *The Crusade of Varna,* pp. 88–90, for the sultan's letter of June 12, 1444, to Vladislav. The Turks agreed also to return prisoners.

67. Dionysios A. Zakythinos, *Le Despotat grec de Morée,* I (Paris, 1932; repr. London, 1975), 230 ff.

68. Iorga, *Notes et extraits,* II (Paris, 1899), 403.

69. Halecki, *The Crusade of Varna,* pp. 86–87, and Johann A. Fabricius, *Bibliotheca latina mediae et infimae aetatis,* ed. Giovanni A. Mansi, VI (Padua, 1754), addenda, p. 13.

met the Christian envoys, and still looked forward to a crusade. He did not expect the peace to be kept by the allies, and when he reached Constantinople on June 24 he wrote again to Hunyadi more openly than he had been able to from Adrianople. In this letter he spoke of the peace which Murad had had to accept in order to protect Rumelia from attack while he was fighting Ibrahim Beg. Ciriaco reported that the sultan did not believe the peace would last long. Indeed Adrianople's defenses were being strengthened. As soon as Karaman had been subdued Murad would invade Hungary, and take revenge for the crusaders' victories. This peace was simply a means by which the sultan could buy time. Again Ciriaco urged the voivode to attack the Turks that year.[70]

The treaty had meant as little to Vladislav, who, throughout June and July, continued to prepare for the crusade. He wrote to the Florentines and the king of Bosnia, Stephen VI Thomas, reassuring them of his preparations for a second expedition.[71] Vladislav had been informed by letters and by the return of his envoy of the agreement concluded at Adrianople, by which he was bound by the letters he had given Gisdanich. He was invited to come to Szegedin on August 1, where he would meet the Turkish envoys and swear to the treaty. Vladislav arrived there sometime in late July, and what occurred there is best described in the most reliable contemporary accounts: the report of the Venetian ambassador Reguardati and Cesarini's report to the senate, which was summarized in the instructions it sent to Alvise Loredan on September 9. Reguardati's report to the senate confirms Cesarini's, thereby establishing its accuracy, and both were used by the senate as the basis of the instructions issued to the captain of their fleet. The senate was concerned about the negotiations; Loredan was, nevertheless, instructed to support the crusaders if they should set out. Whatever had occurred the Venetians continued to plan for hostilities against the Turks.[72]

There has been controversy among modern historians about whether or not Vladislav ratified the treaty of June 12 in Szegedin in late July. Some Polish historians have attempted to prove that he did not ratify it and, therefore, did not perjure himself in the manifesto he issued on August 4. Nevertheless, it has been convincingly demonstrated that Vladislav did just that. He ratified the treaty around July 26, then swore

---

70. Halecki, *The Crusade of Varna*, pp. 90–91, and Pall, "Ciriaco d'Ancona," p. 645.

71. Iorga, II, 404–405, for Vladislav's letter to Florence on July 2, 1444, and Iorga, II, 407, for the letter of July 24 to the king of Bosnia, in which Vladislav again confirmed his intention to lead the crusade.

72. Iorga, *Notes et extraits*, III, 187. The text is in Ljubić, XXI, 871–873.

a few days later to lead a crusade.[73] Even if Vladislav had not ratified the treaty, this would have broken the promise given in the letter to his emissary Gisdanich of April 24, and thus, one way or another, this emotional young king had perjured himself. Other contemporary sources charged that the king had indeed perjured himself, and these sources had unusually good access to persons close to the events.[74]

On August 4 Vladislav issued a manifesto in which he renewed his oath to lead a crusade, naming September 1 as the date on which this crusade would start out. It mentions the closed and sworn treaty and the arrival of the Turkish emissaries who sought his oath. Throughout the events of the spring and summer the king had behaved in a confusing and often contradictory manner. On April 15 he promised the diet to lead a crusade, yet on the 24th he issued letters to Gisdanich giving promises to the sultan. By July he assured the Florentines of his intentions to fight, and on the 25th left for Szegedin to receive Turkish emissaries who would obtain his oath to confirm the treaty. Then on August 4 he again swore to lead a crusade.

Hunyadi had used the negotiations as a tactic to induce Murad to go to Anatolia at the head of his army. It also provided him the time to make sure the allied fleet would be in the Straits by the time the land army took the offensive. Eugenius had put together a powerful naval alliance that could effectively mount a blockade, although it was not always certain he was one of its most consistent supporters.

News of the peace caused doubts among the allies. Wavrin learned of it from some Turks at Gallipoli. Cesarini put these doubts to rest by writing to Condulmer, to whom he stated that peace had not been concluded. On September 5 he wrote to John VIII Palaeologus, who was further reassured by letters from Vladislav and Hunyadi. Ciriaco of Ancona wrote to king Alfonso at Naples, and wrote to Cesarini on September 19 informing him of the victory of the Knights Hospitaller over the Mamluk fleet, in which the Burgundians had played a prominent part.[75]

What is certain is that George Brankovich had achieved his own objective through the peace negotiations. He ratified the treaty on August 15, after Vladislav had decided to proceed with the crusade. Murad

73. See Pall, "Ciriaco d'Ancona," pp. 62–63, for the convincing arguments advanced to support the ratification of the treaty by Vladislav.

74. Aeneas Sylvius Piccolomini wrote of the king's perjury; see Wolkan, *Der Briefwechsel,* epistolae 170, 172–174, 186–189. For Wavrin's testimony see Hardy, ed., *Croniques,* V (1864), 41–43.

75. From a copy of Ciriaco's *Commentarii odeporici* in the Bibl. Apost. Vaticana, Cod. lat. 5250, fols. 11^r–11^v, cited by Setton, *Papacy and the Levant (1204–1571),* II, 87, note 22.

had also bought time and had succeeded in splitting the alliance. Brankovich's defection resulted in the loss to the Hungarian army of 8,000 men, almost a third of the entire force of the "long expedition". This loss was to prove a fatal one to the crusaders. He entered Smederevo on August 22, and soon thereafter his sons were restored to him.[76] In addition to depriving the crusaders of important forces, the remaining Turkish garrisons were strengthened by the soldiers freed from defending the Serbian fortresses. Some places along the crusaders' route would now be able to withstand their attack.

The neutrality of Serbia also meant that the crusaders, rather than cross the mountains to Adrianople, would have to take the route down the Danube across Bulgaria to the Black Sea, and from there to Constantinople to join the fleet. This route was protected by well-garrisoned castles and cities, necessitating long sieges and the resulting delays. Once the land forces had joined the fleet then, in conjunction, they would attempt to conquer the Ottoman strongholds.

Throughout the spring of 1444 Vladislav prepared for war and assured his allies of his intentions, in spite of the negotiations. The Hungarian nobles, as we have seen, were summoned to a diet in Buda on April 15 to discuss support for a crusade, for which it voted approval and levied a special tax. Some of the most powerful ecclesiastical and lay magnates agreed to accompany the king. Venice was informed of these events by Reguardati by early May.[77] However, the negotiations at Adrianople in June and the meeting in Szegedin in late July delayed the expedition beyond the normal campaigning season, and thereby seriously impaired its chances for success. The sultan crossed to Anatolia on July 12, and thus the delay in the commencement of the expedition had achieved the important objective of removing Murad across the Straits. It had, however, also given him the time he needed to attack Karaman and end the danger there by concluding a peace treaty. The two months of June and July were to prove a serious loss to the crusaders; however, the fleet was in position in the Straits by late July.

Our main source for the route of the crusaders and the climactic battle is Andreas de Palatio, the papal collector of the tithe, who accompanied Vladislav and was an eyewitness to the battle. His letter from Posen dated May 16, 1445, describes these events in detail.[78]

Vladislav was still in Buda on July 24 when he wrote to the king of

76. Halecki, *The Crusade of Varna,* p. 55.
77. Iorga, *Notes et extraits,* III, 167–168.
78. Printed by Lewicki, *Codex epistolaris,* II, no. 308.

Bosnia.[79] In early July he had planned to have his troops assembled at Grosswardein by the 15th. At Szegedin on August 4 he issued a manifesto designating September 1 for the start of the expedition. His Polish subjects, however, opposed his undertaking another expedition against the Turks. When the Polish diet met at Piotrków on August 26, Oleśnicki led the campaign to have the magnates request the return of the king to Poland. Cesarini's influence over the king meant that a successful crusade would strengthen the pope's position, a result completely at odds with Oleśnicki's support of the conciliarists. Moreover, there were serious problems in Poland—a dispute with Lithuania over Podolian territory that he asserted required the return of the king. Vladislav had written to the diet reporting the peace terms offered at Adrianople, and on August 26 the diet sent a message urging him to accept the terms and return to Poland.[80] This the king refused to do, replying to the diet on September 22 en route to Varna. The king was, however, supported by Polish nobles who had accompanied him: Jan Koniecpolski, the chancellor, and Peter of Szczekociny, the vice-chancellor, who together directed the foreign policy of Poland. The decision of the diet did deprive Vladislav of some Polish reinforcements, which were not significant even in 1443.

The commencement of the crusade caused panic in Adrianople. Orkhan, a grandson of Bayazid who had taken refuge with the Byzantines, was freed and went to the Dobruja, where he attempted to raise a revolt against Murad. In Adrianople the sultan's twelve-year-old son was not able to control events when a power struggle broke out between the grand vizir Chandarlï Khalil and his rivals Zaganuz and the beglerbeg of Rumelia. Then a fire in Adrianople, caused by rioting of the janissaries, destroyed a considerable part of the city.[81]

From Szegedin the crusaders proceeded to Temesvár and headed southeast, crossing the Danube at Orshova on September 20 with sixteen thousand knights and two thousand wagons.[82] The army had much the same contingents as the previous year, although depleted by the defection of the eight thousand Serbs.

On September 24 they crossed the Timok river, which formed the frontier with the Ottoman vassal state of Bulgaria, and reached Florentin, then marched to Vidin on the Danube by September 26. It was

79. See Iorga, *Notes et extraits,* II, 407, for the report of the Ragusan ambassadors at the Bosnian court to their government.

80. Lewicki, *Codex epistolaris,* I, 141–142. The estates reminded Vladislav that they had agreed to his acceptance of the Hungarian throne because of the Turkish threat.

81. Inalcik, *The Ottoman Empire,* pp. 20–21.

82. Długosz, *Historia polonica,* XII, col. 800; Iorga, *Notes et extraits,* III, 188–189.

decided that, because of the time of year and the necessity of joining the fleet, they would not attempt to take the city. The route led east to Nicopolis; to turn south there across the Balkan mountains would have been the quickest; however, the two thousand wagons prevented them from taking this route.

On October 16 the army reached Nicopolis. Since Vladislav did not have sufficiently powerful artillery to attack the strong walls, he contented himself with burning the suburbs. Vlad Dracul, the voivode of Wallachia, had met the king near Nicopolis with four thousand mounted soldiers who were to accompany the crusaders under the command of Vlad's two sons. He was apparently shocked to realize the smallness of the crusading forces, and Długosz reports that Vlad attempted to persuade Vladislav to turn back by remarking that Murad was able to bring more men on a hunting party than Vladislav had brought for a crusade.[83] Vlad, who had offered no support the previous year, was probably supporting Vladislav as a result of Hunyadi's efforts at Adrianople to have Wallachia included in the agreements and accorded favorable terms.

The crusaders remained at Nicopolis for two or three days, then followed a Roman road to the coast. It it possible that the army marched along the Danube, crossing the Yantra river, turning southeast to Shumen (Szumla) and thence east to Novi Pazar. Callimachus has Hunyadi leading the army with three thousand Hungarians and the Wallachians, followed by the wagons with the king leading the remainder of the troops.[84] The crusaders plundered and burned all along their route, not even sparing the Orthodox churches. On October 24, according to Długosz, Vladislav addressed an offer to the Turkish strongholds of Shumen, Mahoracz, Provadiya, Varna, Kavarna, and Galata offering the defenders safe conduct to Adrianople if they surrendered these places without a struggle; he used Turkish prisoners to deliver his messages,[85] which were spurned.

Around October 25, according to Michael Beheim, the crusaders were at Shumen, where they assaulted the city for two days, capturing it the third day. A tower with fifty Turkish soldiers was bitterly defended until the crusaders set it on fire, thereby killing the defenders. Here Vladislav encamped for seven days. He sent a detachment of five hundred men to attack Tirnovo, but three hundred of them were lost in the unsuccessful attack on the town.

83. Długosz, *Historia polonica,* XII, col. 800; Palatio, in Lewicki, *Codex epistolaris,* II, 24.
84. Callimachus, ed. Kwiatowski, pp. 146–147.
85. Michael Beheim in von Karajan, ed., *Quellen,* p. 133.

On November 4 the crusaders again started out, crossing an arid plateau and reaching a castle (possibly near Kaspichan) which was taken by storm. The army remained here for two days besieging and then plundering the castle. On November 7 the army arrived at the city and castle of Provadiya, which was located atop a high mountain.[86] The crusaders opened a breach in the wall through which they gained entrance, capturing the castle and — according to Palatio's report — killing five thousand Turks. There Cesarini received a letter from Francis Condulmer reporting that the sultan had made peace with the emir of Karaman and on October 16 had crossed the Bosporus with his army, consisting of thirty thousand to forty thousand men.[87]

En route to the Dardanelles Wavrin's galleys had stopped at Tenedos (Bozja–ada) to search for the site of ancient Troy,[88] arriving at the entrance to the Dardanelles two days later. There Gauvin Quiéret, carrying the duke's pennant, landed and successfully engaged the Turks. Then the Burgundians sailed to Gallipoli, where they joined with the papal fleet and where they found cardinal Condulmer suffering from fever. Condulmer and Wavrin, each with two galleys, sailed to Constantinople to meet with John VIII. Wavrin left the Burgundian galleys under the command of Gauvin Quiéret and Peter Vas, who together with the papal galleys maintained the blockade at Gallipoli. Here in late September they were joined by the galleys from Rhodes under Geoffrey of Thoisy.[89] By September 19 the victory at Rhodes was known to Ciriaco at Constantinople. On September 27 he visited the Christian fleet at Gallipoli.

At Constantinople, according to John (Jehan) of Wavrin's chronicle, the plan of the blockade was decided upon. The papal galleys, those of Venice, and two Burgundian galleys were to patrol between Gallipoli and Lampsacus, in the Dardanelles. Some of the galleys, possibly the Ragusan, were stationed in the Bosporus. Early in October news reached the fleet that the sultan was marching toward the Dardanelles with the intention of forcing a crossing there. Wavrin left the galleys under Vas and returned to Constantinople with Quiéret to confer with the galley captains stationed there.[90] Wavrin and the others realized that the gal-

---

86. Callimachus, ed. Kwiatowski, p. 148. Długosz, *Historia polonica,* XII, col. 802, and Leunclavius, *Historiae musulmanae Turcorum* (Frankfurt, 1591), p. 513, confirm that the city was taken by storm.

87. Estimate of the number of men in the sultan's army taken from the funeral oration delivered by Poggio Bracciolini, in Mai, *Spicilegium,* X, 374–384.

88. Wavrin, ed. Hardy, V, 38.

89. Degryse, "De Bourgondische expedities," p. 236.

90. Wavrin, ed. Hardy, V, 44–45, and Adrien Huguet, "Un Chevalier picard à la croisade de Constantinople, 1444–1445: Gauvin Quiéret, Seigneur de Dreuil," *Bulletin trimestriel de la*

leys stationed in the Bosporus were in serious danger of being sunk by cannon which the sultan had had mounted on the Asiatic shore. The strait was narrow enough to enable the Turks thereby to prevent the ships from remaining on patrol there. During Wavrin's inspection the Turks demonstrated the effectiveness of this tactic by firing on them from the Anatolian fortress of Anadolu Hisar.[91] Quiéret and Jean Bayart, another Burgundian, returned to John VIII to persuade him of the necessity of having Byzantine troops secure the European shore of the Bosporus: "Il est impossible que galees se puissent tenir au destroit tant que les deux rivages seront occupez par les Turcqz." So pitiful was the state of the emperor's resources that all he could promise was two Byzantine galleys; he had no other support to give.

Unable to cross at the Dardanelles, the sultan and his army marched to the Bosporus. On October 15 Khalil Pasha with seven or eight thousand Turkish soldiers, with cannon and artillery, were taken across by the Genoese of Pera in their boats[92] and occupied the European shore of the Bosporus.

On October 16 the sultan arrived at the Anatolian shore with what Wavrin estimates at three or four thousand soldiers and five to six hundred camels. During the night the Turks had moved cannon into place on the European shore, and on the morning of the sixteenth they began bombarding the galleys. The fleet attempted to advance but, being bombarded from both shores, was forced to retire. Moreover, it was hampered by adverse winds and the unwillingness of the Venetians to risk their ships' being sunk by cannon. Thus, the fleet made no serious attempt to prevent Murad's forces from crossing. The sultan with his troops then crossed under the walls of Anadolu Hisar, the narrowest point of the strait, where Europe and Asia almost touch. On the evening of the sixteenth a storm arose which forced the Christian galleys into port, thereby enabling the hardier Turks to cross over unopposed. The Byzantine galleys, which had attempted to come close to shore, were badly damaged by the cannon. The fleet had waited in vain for two or three months for the arrival of the crusaders. Had Vladislav not delayed crossing the Danube until the third week in September,

---

Société des antiquaires de Picardie, XXXVIII (1939), 42 ff. "Peter Vas" was a Castilian named Pedro Vasquez de Saovecha.

91. Wavrin, ed. Hardy, V, 47, ". . . la mer y estoit si estroite que une cullevrine porroit tyrer dun bort à l'autre, cest a scavoir de la Turquye en Grece, et de Grece en Turquye, et que journelement les Turcqz du neuf chastel tyroient canons quy passoient par dessus les galees." See *ibid.,* pp. 47–51, for the crossing by the Turks.

92. The Genoese participation is documented in Wavrin, ed. Hardy, V, 49; Eugenius wrote in 1444, "Genuenses Amuratem in Europam trajicere partiuntur," in Raynaldus, *Annales ecclesiastici,* ad. ann. 1444, ed. Theiner, vol. XXVIII (Paris, 1887), 293.

but crossed on September 1, the crusading army could have been at Constantinople by October 16 and effectively prevented the Ottoman crossing.

Murad joined his son Mehmed and Khalil Pasha, who had gathered all the available troops in Rumelia, numbering seven to eight thousand additional men. Loredan dispatched a letter to Cesarini, but by the time it reached him Murad was already close to Varna.

Meanwhile, on November 8 the crusaders stormed the castle of Michelich, perhaps located on the upper Devnya lake about four miles from the sea.[93] Palatio reports that a detachment of crusaders found and burned on the Kamchiya river a Turkish flotilla of twenty-eight ships, which were apparently to be used on the Danube. On November 9 the king arrived at Varna, where the city and Galata, Marcropolis, and Kavarna surrendered to him, the Turkish garrisons having fled. Vladislav and the crusaders encamped in front of the city. On the evening of November 9 the crusaders saw the campfires of the Turks about half a mile away. Vladislav ordered the outposts of the camp to be strengthened, all soldiers to remain armed, and a council of war to be called for the early morning of November 10.

Murad had arrived in Adrianople in late October and from there marched to Nicopolis, whence he followed the crusaders; on November 5 he was at Shumen.[94] On the night of November 9 he encamped in the position from which he intended to attack, controlling the heights above Varna with the crusading army between him and the sea. The only line of retreat, to the north, was a wasteland.

The crusaders decided to take the offensive, and formed their line in a crescent stretching from the lake in front of the walls of the city back toward the Black Sea. On the far left was Hunyadi, with five banners of his soldiers and the Hungarian barons. In the middle was Vladislav with his Hungarian and Polish troops.[95] Here where the king's banner flew, together with the banner of St. George carried by Stephen Báthori of Transylvania, some two thousand troops were stationed. The right wing was composed of Hungarian troops under five banners, including Cesarini's. Between the king and Cesarini were stationed the banners of the bishop of Bosnia, Rafael Herczeg; Simon Rozgonyi, bishop of Erlau; and Francis Thallóczy, ban of Croatia. At the far right were John Dominis, bishop of Grosswardein, and some Polish

---

93. Michael Beheim in Karajan, ed., *Quellen,* p. 135.
94. Długosz, *Historia polonica,* XII, col. 803.
95. Palatio, in Lewicki, *Codex epistolaris,* II, 29.

troops. Hunyadi kept a reserve force of Wallachians behind the center of the line. The entire line stretched for about five thousand feet and thus was inadequately defended by twenty-five thousand men. The army had only light artillery, which consisted of small-caliber cannon and catapults and which do not seem to have been used in the battle.

Opposite the left wing of the crusaders the sultan stationed the European mounted cavalry under Davud Pasha, to the left of which were the Anatolian mounted troops under Karaja Beg. Facing the right of the crusader line were the *akinjis,* irregular mounted troops who served for plunder and fought in a freewheeling manner, outside the discipline of the regular Turkish soldiers, and the azebs, Turkish footsoldiers from the provinces. In the center behind the mounted Anatolian and European cavalry stood the sultan, surrounded by the janissaries. The cavalry were arranged in rectangles, each divided into squadrons.[96] The Ottoman army may have numbered sixty thousand, although it is uncertain how many men the sultan actually had under his command.

For three hours after stationing themselves the crusaders awaited the Turkish attack. The battle began with an attack by the *akinjis* and azebs on the crusaders' right wing, which was thrown back by Rozgonyi and Thallóczy. Reportedly at one point Murad contemplated flight from the battlefield, and was constrained by his janissaries. When the *akinjis* attacked, the Anatolian sipahis moved forward; after the first assault failed the *akinjis* again attacked, engaging the forces under Thallóczy and Simon Rozgonyi. Then Cesarini and Thallóczy were attacked from the left by the sipahis; their lines broke and they sought the refuge of the wagon barricade. The bishops of Grosswardein and Erlau could not maneuver quickly enough and were caught between the city and the lake. Both attempted to make it across the swampy terrain to Galata and failed; apparently they were killed.[97] The Turks reached the seacoast and the barricade of 2,000 wagons, defended by only two hundred men.

Meanwhile Hunyadi and Vladislav attacked the Anatolian sipahis, driving them back some four thousand feet, killing Karaja Beg, and effectively driving the Anatolians from the field. The camels of the sultan's army apparently frightened the horses of the crusaders, preventing the king and Hunyadi from moving forward. Hunyadi placed Vladislav in his former position, requesting him not to move without his instructions. The left wing of the crusader army was engaged in battle with the Rumelian sipahis. Hunyadi charged to the attack there,

96. Kupelwieser, *Die Kämpfe,* pp. 96–97.
97. Długosz, *Historia Polonica,* XII, cols. 804–805.

leaving the king with his household troops as a reserve force. This attack resulted in a forward movement of the Hungarian force, driving the entire right wing of the Ottoman cavalry from the field and leaving only the janissaries with Murad in the center.

Chalcocondylas relates Vladislav's Polish troops urged him to attack the janissaries and not to allow Hunyadi all the glory of victory.[98] Vladislav charged into the janissaries, who unhorsed him and beheaded him, placing his head on a lance held above the army. Hunyadi was unable to come to Vladislav's aid quickly enough, and when the news of the king's death spread the army panicked and fled the field. The wagon barricade may not have been taken until the next day, when Stephen Báthori was killed. The Turks did not follow the retreating crusaders; Murad remained for three days on the battlefield and then returned to Adrianople. Sometime during the battle or soon thereafter Cesarini was killed. Various reports of his death circulated; the only certain fact is that he did not leave the area alive.[99] Hunyadi fled and reached the Danube, where he was taken prisoner by Vlad Dracul, who released him after some time.

Incredibly, the crusading army had nearly carried the day. Had Brankovich and his 8,000 Serbs been at Varna with Vladislav, it is possible that the victory might have been a Christian one. The Turks had suffered heavy losses, and had turned possible defeat into victory through the reckless act of the king. Even then the triumph was not immediately evident when, at the day's end, both armies withdrew to their camps. Indeed it was reported that Murad was not sure that he was the victor for three days. But if the Turks had suffered heavily, the crusaders had been crippled. They could not have withstood another battle. At Varna the Turks had employed muskets for the first time.[100]

The failure of the crusade sealed the fate of Byzantium nine years later. Varna brought the Turks to the walls of Belgrade in 1448 and to the walls of Vienna in a generation.

98. Chalcocondylas, ed. Bekker, p. 337.

99. Callimachus, ed. Kwiatkowski, p. 159, states that Cesarini was killed while fleeing the battlefield. Wavrin, ed. Hardy, V, 57, says that Cesarini made it to the Danube where he was drowned by the Wallachians; Thurocz, *op. cit.,* p. 257, says merely that he was killed. On June 1, 1445, Aeneas Sylvius wrote to Guiniforta Barziza in Milan that Cesarini was killed by the Hungarians (in Wolkan, *Der Briefwechsel,* LXI-2, 506); Długosz, *Historia polonica,* XII, col. 810, says that he was killed by the Wallachians. By November 13, 1444, news of the battle had reached Vienna, since on that date Aeneas Sylvius wrote to the duke of Milan reporting that the fleet was being accused of treachery. They were, however, not able to keep guard because of a lack of provisions, and Murad was able to cross into Europe with forty thousand men. He reported that there was no certain news about Vladislav and that Cesarini had been killed (in Wolkan, *Der Briefwechsel,* LXI-2, pp. 487–490).

100. Inalcik, *The Ottoman Empire,* p. 21.

IX

THE OTTOMAN TURKS
AND THE CRUSADES,
1451–1522

A. *Mehmed the Conqueror's Empire,*
1451–1481

At the accession of Mehmed II to the throne in 1451 all the enemies of the Ottomans were confident, remembering the desperate condition of the Turkish state during his first sultanate (1444–1446).[1] Ottoman client states in the Balkans and Anatolia, as well as Byzantium,

Besides the works cited in the bibliographical note to chapter VII, above, the following are useful for the period 1451–1522: Robert Schwoebel, *The Shadow of the Crescent: the Renaissance Image of the Turk (1453–1517)* (New York, 1967); Alessio Bombaci, "Nuovi firmani greci di Maometto II," *Byzantinische Zeitschrift,* XLVII (1954), 298–319; Konstantin Mihailović, *Memoirs of a Janissary,* tr. Benjamin Stolz and Svat Soucek (Ann Arbor, Mich., 1975) — he was captured in 1455 and returned to Christendom in 1463; T. Spandouyn Cantacasin, *Petit traicte de l'origine des Turcqz,* ed. Charles Schefer (Paris, 1896), important for the organization of the Ottoman state under Bayazid II; Carl Göllner, *Turcica: die europäischen Türkendrucke des XVI. Jahrhundert,* vol. I, 1501–1550 (Bucharest and Berlin, 1961); Michael Critobulus (Kritovoulos), *History of Mehmed the Conqueror,* tr. Charles T. Riggs (Princeton, 1954); Johannes Hofer, *Johannes von Capestrano: ein Leben im Kampf die Reform der Kirche* (Innsbruck *et alibi,* 1936); Georg Voigt, "Johannes von Capistrano, ein Heiliger des fünfzehnten Jahrhundert," *Historische Zeitschrift,* X (1863), 19–96; Franz Babinger, *Der Quellenwert der Berichte über den Entsatz von Belgrad, am 21/22 Juli 1456* (Munich, 1957); Wilhelm Franknoi, *Mathias Corvinus, König von Ungarn, 1458–1490* (Freiburg im Breisgau, 1891); Heinrich Ulmann, *Kaiser Maximilian I.,* vol. I (Stuttgart, 1884); Babinger, "Kaiser Maximilians I. 'geheime Praktiken' mit den Osmanen (1510/11)," *Südost-Forschungen,* XV (1956), 202–236; Constantin Marinescu, "Le Pape Calixtus III (1455–1458), Alfonse d'Aragon roi de Naples, et l'offensive contre les Turcs," *Bulletin historique de l'Académie roumaine,* XIX (1935), 77–97; and Göllner, "Zur Problematik der Kreuzzüge und der Türkenkriege im 16. Jahrhundert," *Revue des études sud-est européennes,* XIII (1975), 97–115.

On Mehmed the Conqueror see Critobulus and Bombaci (above), and Tursun Beg (a high official, close to the sultan), *The History of Mehmed the Conqueror,* publ. with tr. by Halil Inalcik and Rhoads Murphey (Minneapolis and Chicago, 1978), the most detailed and authoritative

1. For the first sultanate of Mehmed II, 1444–1446, and for the period 1451–1453 see Inalcik, *Fâtih devri,* pp. 55–136.

311

issued threats and even launched attacks against the Ottomans. In Anatolia Ibrahim Beg of Karaman not only seized control of several fortresses in the Hamid area, but also encouraged pretenders to intensify their activities in the provinces of Germiyan, Aydîn, and Menteshe. Under these threatening circumstances Mehmed II moved to confirm the treaties made during his father's reign with the Serbs and the Byzantines. He agreed to cede Alaja-Hisar (Krushevats) and some other frontier fortresses to the Serbian despot George Brankovich (1427–1456). As for the Byzantine emperor Constantine XI (1448–1453), not only did he take control of areas extending as far as Chorlu, but he also demanded that a yearly payment of 300,000 *akcha* should be paid to meet the expenses of the pretender Orkhan Chelebi, who was sequestered in Constantinople.

Mehmed sent Karaja Pasha to Sofia to counter a possible attack by the Hungarians, while he himself set out with the army in May to deal with the situation in Anatolia. As Mehmed marched eastward the Byzantine envoys made new demands on him, threatening to release the pretender Orkhan Chelebi. By ceding the port and fortress of Alanya, Mehmed sought to make a peaceful settlement with the Karamanid Ibrahim Beg, and he made preparations for a prompt return to Adrianople (Edirne). When the janissaries demanded increased wages, he reorganized the corps, giving decisive evidence of his resoluteness and power. But as a ghazi leader he needed prompt military

book in Turkish on Mehmed; Ibn-Kemāl, *Tevârikh-i Âl-i Osman, Defter VII,* ed. Şerafeddin Turan (Ankara, 1954), the most important compilation by an Ottoman historian; Inalcik, *Fâtih devri üzerinde tetkikler ve vesikalar,* I (Ankara, 1954), emphasizing Christian timar-holders in Mehmed II's early years; Babinger, *Mehmed the Conqueror and his Time,* tr. Ralph Manheim, ed. William C. Hickman (Princeton, 1978), with added footnotes on works published after the original 1953 German edition; reviewed by Inalcik in *Speculum,* XXXV (1960), 408–427; and Inalcik, "Mehmed II," in *İslâm Ansiklopedisi,* VII (1955), 506–535.

On Jem see Louis Thuasne, *Djem-Sultan* (Paris, 1892), still the basic work, well documented; Hans Pfefferman, *Die Zusammenarbeit der Renaissancepäpste mit den Türken* (Winterthur, 1946); İsmail H. Ertaylan, *Sultan Cem* (Istanbul, 1951); Babinger, *Spätmittelalterliche frankische Briefschaften aus dem grossherrlichen Seraj zu Stanbul* (Munich, 1963); Inalcik, "A Case Study in Renaissance Diplomacy: the Agreement between Innocent VIII and Bayezid II on Djem Sultan," *Journal of Turkish Studies,* III (1979), 209–230; and J. Lefort, *Documents grecs dans les archives de Topkapi Sarayi, contribution à l'histoire de Cem Sultan* (Ankara, 1981).

For military technology see David Ayalon, *Gunpowder and Firearms in the Mamluk Kingdom: a Challenge to a Medieval Society* (London, 1956), reviewed by Inalcik in *Belleten,* XXI (1957), 501–512; Dj. Petrović, "Firearms in the Balkans," in *War, Technology, and Society in the Middle East,* ed. Vernon J. Parry and Malcolm E. Yapp (London, 1975), pp. 164–194; Inalcik, "The Socio-political Effects of the Diffusion of Firearms in the Middle East," *ibid.,* pp. 195–217; and the old but still useful article by John H. Lefroy, "The Great Cannon of Muhammad II. (A.D. 1464), Recently Presented to the British Government by the Sultan . . . ," *The Archaeological Journal,* XXV (1868), 261–280.

victories as proof of his ability and his commitment to restoring Islamic superiority in the Balkans.

In order to establish his authority Mehmed and his former tutor Zaganuz resolved to take the offensive. On returning from the Karaman campaign he gave orders to Chandarli Khalil Pasha in August 1452 for the construction of a fortress, Rumeli-Hisar, on the European shore of the Bosporus opposite Anadolu-Hisar, as a first step toward a siege of Constantinople. Thus the city was completely cut off from the sources of its food supply in the Black Sea, and reinforcements to the Ottoman army could pass unhindered from Anatolia.

Chandarli Khalil Pasha, a capable diplomat, had already taken steps to ensure Venice's neutrality by renewing the terms of the Venetian-Ottoman agreement on September 10, 1451, and had accommodated Venetian demands with regard to the question of wheat export, a sensitive issue for Venice. Similarly, a three-year armistice with Hungary had been signed on November 20, 1451, again granting concessions. In the fall of 1452 the Ottoman frontier lords in the Morea took the offensive, but although the Byzantine emperor had sent an envoy to Venice in the winter of 1451–1452 he had been unsuccessful in stirring the west into military action. There was a general belief in Christian Europe at this time that the Ottomans would not immediately undertake the siege of Constantinople.

Actually Mehmed II thought that the grand vizir, Chandarli Khalil, presented the greatest obstacle to his plan for the conquest of Constantinople. Chandarli feared that in the event of a successful conquest he would lose all his influence, whereas a major military setback would place the Ottoman state in a dangerous position. The young sultan believed that Chandarli might not fully coöperate with him in his attack. In a war council before the siege, the sultan's warlike policy was received with enthusiasm by those such as Zaganuz who expected their own power to benefit from the changes which victory would bring. The more cautious party, represented by Chandarli Khalil, laid stress on the impregnability of the walls, as well as on the dangers from the west, but the war party, with the sultan at its head, was in the majority and Chandarli had to acquiesce.

During the actual siege, which lasted for fifty-four days (April 6–May 29), these opposing viewpoints would again come to the fore at two critical junctures. The outcome of the siege depended largely on the time factor. Both the Byzantines and the Ottomans were influenced throughout the course of the siege by rumors of the approach of land or sea forces in aid of the city. In the final week of May word that

John Hunyadi had crossed the Danube and that a crusader fleet had set out for the Bosporus was spread among the Ottoman army. These rumors and the sultan's attempts to secure the surrender of the city through peace offers engendered concern and unrest among the Ottoman troops, who criticized the young Mehmed for "exposing his people and the state to utter destruction by entering into an undertaking whose accomplishment was impossible". In the war council which was then convened Chandarlī again drew attention to the dangers involved in provoking the western world, and emphasized the necessity of ending this dangerous war by reaching some sort of understanding with the Byzantines. Chandarli's arguments were countered by Zaganuz, who stated his conviction that the Christian rulers would, as in the past, fail to unite for common action, and that even if they were able somehow to field an army the superior Ottoman forces were equal to the challenge. Thereupon, the decision was taken to make a general assault on May 29, and it was left to Zaganuz to organize the attack. The sultan proclaimed it in these terms: "the stones [buildings] and the land of the city and the city's appurtenances belong to me; all other goods and property, prisoners and foodstuffs are booty for the troops." Three days of sack were granted.[2]

The western and the Turkish sources agree that the eventual success of the Ottomans came chiefly as the result of two events: the breaching of the walls by the Ottoman artillery bombardment, and the disputes which arose between the Byzantines and the Latins defending the city. After the wounding and withdrawal from the fight of the Genoese supreme commander John Giustiniani-Longo the whole defense collapsed. The Ottoman army entered the city through a large breach made by bombardment in the wall. Emperor Constantine was killed in hand-to-hand combat. The Ottoman and Byzantine sources also agree in reporting that Mehmed the Conqueror (Fātih) felt sadness as he toured the looted city, his future capital. The inhabitants were enslaved and taken away, either into the tents of the army outside the city or onto ships. After he visited Hagia Sofia he proclaimed "to his vizirs and

2. For Christian sources on the conquest see Edwin A. Pears, *The Destruction of the Greek Empire and the Story of the Capture of Constantinople by the Turks* (London, 1903); Steven Runciman, *The Fall of Constantinople* (London, 1965); Babinger, *Mehmed the Conqueror and his Time,* tr. Manheim, pp. 82–103; Agostino Pertusi, *La Caduta di Costantinopoli: le testimonianze dei contemporanei* (Verona, 1976); J. R. Melville, *The Siege of Constantinople by the Turks: Seven Contemporary Accounts* (Amsterdam, 1977); and the bibliography in *Byzantinische Zeitschrift,* XLVI–XLIX (1953–1956). For eastern sources see Inalcik, "Mehmed II," *İslâm Ansiklopedisi,* VII, 510–511; the most important Ottoman source for the conquest is Tursun Beg, ed. Inalcik and Murphey. See also Giovanni B. Picotti, "Sulle Navi papali in Oriente al tempo della caduta di Costantinopoli," *Nuovo archivio veneto,* XI (1911), 413–437.

his commanders and his officers that henceforth his capital was to be Istanbul".

The conquest of Constantinople opened a new chapter in the history of crusading activities in Europe. Until the death of Mehmed II in 1481 the popes did their utmost to convince the western nations that organization of a crusade under papal leadership was the most immediate and pressing task facing Europe. In this new phase of crusading activities the keynote was that now western Christendom itself was in direct danger from an aggressive Islam and that a crusade, if launched, would defend Europe and its Christian civilization. The immediate goal of a crusade was no longer the deliverance of the holy places but of Constantinople, and the expulsion of the Turks from Europe. In his vow for a crusade Calixtus III (1455–1458) would seek forgiveness for postponing for a time the sacred goal of recapturing the holy places.

The Ottoman success radically altered the strategic situation at the expense of Christian Europe. For western Christendom, perhaps the most important consequence of the Ottoman conquest was the loss of European control of the Straits, which deprived the west of an important strategic advantage, the ability to cut communications between the European and Asiatic territories of the Ottoman empire. Though this strategy had never proved as effective as crusading plans had called for it to be, largely because of Genoese intransigence, nevertheless it had had a restraining effect on the Ottomans. Even more important than its effect on military strategy, Ottoman control of the Straits isolated the Italian colonies on the shores of the Black Sea and left them at the mercy of the Ottomans.

In his plans to build a "universal" empire, Mehmed fully appreciated the strategic significance of the Straits as a check on Venetian seapower. During his thirty-year reign he created a series of defense lines from Tenedos to the Black Sea to make Istanbul invulnerable from the sea. With bases at Gallipoli, İzmit (Nicomedia), and Istanbul, and protected by these strong defenses, his strengthened navy became a real challenge to Venetian seapower and an effective instrument in his empire-building. In 1454 Mehmed sent his navy, fifty vessels in all, to the Black Sea to compel the submission of the states and colonies there. The navy first attacked Akkerman, forcing the submission on October 5, 1455, of Peter III Aron, voivode of Moldavia, to the sultan with a yearly tribute of 2,000 gold ducats.

As a result of his capture of the seat of the Caesars, Mehmed considered himself their successor, and laid claim to all the territories which the Byzantine emperors had formerly ruled. The inspiration for his expanded empire may be linked to several sources, including the Turco-Mongol concept of empire and the Islamic caliphate, but we know for certain that the possession of the Byzantine throne carried a great personal significance for Mehmed. In directing his conquests against the Christian world of the west, Mehmed was now able to justify his claim to be the successor to the Roman empire. The idea of founding a "universal" empire always lay behind Mehmed's plans in his efforts to pursue his conquests and military campaigns and to raise the ruined city of Istanbul to the status of a great and wealthy capital city, sometimes at the expense of the other cities of his realm.

As successor to the Byzantine emperor, Mehmed concentrated his immediate efforts on eliminating, one by one, all the dynasts who were in a position to lay claim to the throne of Byzantium. First he disposed of David Comnenus, the last emperor of Trebizond (1458–1461, d. 1463), next the two despots in the Morea, and then the Gattilusi family in Lesbos and Aenos, whose sons had married into the Palaeologian house.

In the concept and methods of Mehmed II's conquests the outstanding feature is his abandonment of the beylik system of semiautonomous rule by local magnates and princes in Rumelia and Anatolia in favor of outright annexation, by which he attempted to accelerate the process of establishing a centralized empire. By so doing Mehmed revived the aggressive policy of Bayazid I (1389–1402), which had been abandoned in favor of a policy of compromise during the civil war of 1402–1413 and the sultanates of Mehmed I (1413–1421) and Murad II (1421–1451). The capture of Constantinople had signified the final victory of the group of military men who pursued a policy of war and annexation over the group favoring caution and compromise. It was not until somewhat later in his reign that Mehmed was able to realize his centralizing ambitions in Anatolia, but he proceeded without delay in the Balkans.

Following the old Ottoman policy Mehmed incorporated into the imperial war machine the pre-Ottoman military groups.[3] Both among the timariot cavalry forces and as separate and intact groups, Christian soldiers played an important role in his army. The proportion of Christian timar-holders in the Balkan provinces as recorded in the survey registers of Mehmed II's time ranged from three percent to over thirty percent. The *voyniks,* who had constituted a group of lesser importance as peasant-soldiers, were present in large numbers in Bulgaria,

---

3. See Inalcik, *Fâtih devri,* pp. 137–184; *idem,* "Ottoman Methods of Conquest," in *The Ottoman Empire: Conquest, Organization and Economy* (London, 1979), art. I, pp. 122–127.

Macedonia, Albania, and Serbia. The registers also show that the system of rewarding certain groups with tax exemption in return for service to the state was to a large extent preserved under the Ottoman regime. Mehmed's reason for leaving the local institutions and groups intact in certain areas such as Serbia and Bosnia was his concern to preserve these areas as secure and loyal frontier zones along the borders with Hungary.

During Mehmed II's reign more than at any other time the Ottoman state took on the role of champion in the holy war against the Christian world. He was aware that in the west the idea of European unity and of combining forces in a crusade was embodied by the pope, whom the Ottomans considered their arch-enemy. The cornerstone of Mehmed's strategy was to avoid a crusade from the west, and in particular to escape the necessity of battling simultaneously on two fronts, in Rumelia and in Anatolia.

The fall of Constantinople was looked upon as a major disaster in the west, and stirred up a strong reaction throughout Europe. Pope Nicholas V (1447–1455) was successful in establishing peace and a league among the Italian states in 1454, and invited all the governments in Europe to the preparation of a crusade. There is no doubt that the Ottoman court was well informed about these initiatives. Mehmed quickly moved to sign a treaty with Venice on April 18, 1454, in order to neutralize the republic and ensure that it would not provide the naval support on which success of the crusader plans so heavily depended. Venice for its part benefitted from the treaty, which recognized its trade privileges within the Ottoman empire, with only a minimal customs fee of two percent for goods entering and leaving the empire. The republic also retained the right to maintain a bailie in Istanbul as a permanent representative at the Porte to look after Venetian interests. By agreeing to pay tribute for their colonies in the Black Sea and in the Aegean, the Genoese also reached an understanding with the sultan. However, the Knights Hospitaller of Rhodes, on the direct orders of the pope, announced that they would never pay a yearly tribute. An Ottoman naval campaign of 1454 into the Aegean under the command of Hamza Beg accomplished little.

It appears that in January 1455, when Mahmud Pasha was appointed grand vizir, a more decisive policy toward the Aegean islands, aimed at direct Ottoman control, was adopted.[4] Mehmed had already declared war against Rhodes and Chios, and now, accusing Domenico Gattilusio,

---

4. Enverî, *Düstûrnâme,* ed. M. Halil Yinanç (Istanbul, 1928), p. 103.

the lord of Lesbos, of siding with the Chians, he also threatened him with invasion. Lesbos managed to secure a reprieve by agreeing to raise its tribute to ten thousand ducats.[5] Still pursuing the new more aggressive policy, however, the Ottomans occupied Old Phocaea in December 1455 and Aenos toward the end of January or February 1456, in addition to the islands of Imbros and Samothrace, which belonged to a branch of the Gattilusi family. The Ottoman initiative seems to have been prompted by both a dynastic rivalry over the possession of these islands and Ottoman concern over an attack by the crusader fleet which was being readied by the pope.[6] Under the eunuch Ismail the Ottoman fleet also occupied Lemnos upon the invitation of the Greek islanders, who rose up against Nicholas Gattilusio in May 1456. The unsuccessful intervention against the islanders by Nicholas's brother Domenico, prince of Lesbos, enraged the sultan.

The fate of the northern Aegean islands had become a major concern in the papal court too. After the fall of Imbros and Samothrace the island of Lesbos itself was in imminent danger. Domenico sent urgent appeals for aid to Genoa and the pope.[7] Genoa sent a warship with reinforcements, and Calixtus III gave priority to this issue, giving orders to accelerate the pace of preparations of the papal fleet. Alarmed by the implications of the Ottoman advance for the security of Euboea, Venice considered for a moment the occupation of Lemnos and Imbros for itself.[8] The sultan's new policy of direct control was obviously motivated by his concern to safeguard his western flank and Istanbul before setting out against Belgrade, as planned for the following spring. Control of these islands was to be one of the principal issues between the Ottomans and Christian Europe for the next two centuries. Actually preparations for such a naval attack had been on the drawing board ever since the fall of Constantinople in 1453.

Despite the peace achieved in Italy by the treaty of Lodi on April 9, 1454, and conclusion of a defensive and aggressive alliance against the Ottomans for a period of twenty-five years among the Italian powers on February 25, 1455,[9] realistic statesmen such as Francis Sforza, duke of Milan (1450–1466), Cosimo de' Medici in Florence (1434–1464), and

5. Ducas, *Decline and Fall of Byzantium to the Ottoman Turks . . . 1341–1462,* tr. Harry J. Magoulias (Detroit, 1975), p. 254.

6. Critobulus, tr. Riggs, pp. 105–106.

7. William Miller, "The Gattilusi of Lesbos (1355–1462)," *Byzantinische Zeitschrift,* XXII (1913), 433.

8. *Ibid.*

9. Ludwig Pastor, *The History of the Popes from the Close of the Middle Ages,* tr. Frederick I. Antrobus, II (London, 1894), 273–276.

Alfonso I of Naples (1442-1458) were not convinced by the exaggerated reports of an imminent Ottoman invasion. Outside Italy in Christian Europe we find the same indifference to the pope's call for the crusade. While Venice and the papacy were interested in heightening crusading zeal for their own purposes, these potentates coolly considered the Ottoman threat as a check against the ambitions of their powerful rivals in Italy. Their indifference has puzzled modern historians, but in actuality an Ottoman invasion of Italy in 1453 was only a remote possibility, in view of the fact that the Christian powers, principally Venice and Aragon, had a clear naval superiority in the Mediterranean. In addition, Christian outposts in Albania, the Morea, and the Aegean posed a serious obstacle in the way of any Ottoman advance. Also Hungary, which was threatening the Ottomans in Serbia, had become Mehmed's main concern at this time.

The preparation of the papal fleet, for which the date of departure had been fixed as March 1, 1456, was as usual delayed by various mishaps. The fleet, consisting of sixteen galleys with 5,000 soldiers and 300 cannon,[10] was finally able to put out to sea only in mid-June 1456. One goal of the expedition was to divert some of the Ottoman forces from the Hungarian front, and another was to release Chios and Lesbos from their submission to the sultan, and secure their coöperation in recapturing the northern Aegean islands occupied by the Ottomans. In this way the revival of the Christian League against the Turks in the Aegean would be realized.

Chios, however, would not agree to repudiate its allegiance to the sultan and join the papal forces. It had already agreed to pay Mehmed 30,000 ducats in indemnity and to raise its yearly tribute to 10,000 ducats.[11] The Chians were anxious not to jeopardize their trade with the sultan's dominions, which was vital to their existence.

The papal fleet occupied Lemnos and Imbros by agreement and Thasos by force, and left garrisons for their defense. The Turkish navy was absent during all these operations, obviously because it was engaged on the Black Sea during the Belgrade campaign in the summer and because of the mariners' annual abandonment of their ships in the autumn. Despite a tendency among western historians to minimize the importance of this papal intervention in the Aegean, the sources indicate that it created a grave situation for the Ottomans, especially in view of developments in Lesbos. Upon the arrival of the crusaders'

---

10. Nicolae Iorga, *Geschichte des osmanischen Reiches nach den Quellen . . .* , I (Gotha, 1908), 85; Pastor, *op. cit.,* II, 256; Ducas, tr. Magoulias, p. 256.

11. Ducas, tr. Magoulias, pp. 254-255.

navy at Mytilene, Domenico and Nicholas Gattilusio, as Critobulus
informs us, declared their repudiation of the sultan's authority.[12] Nicholas, who had been expelled from Lemnos by Mehmed, advocated a
policy of resistance to the Ottomans. Twelve triremes of the papal fleet
stayed on at Mytilene.[13]

Mehmed sent a powerful fleet under Ismail, governor of Gallipoli
and admiral of the fleet, against the Gattilusi in the spring of 1457.[14]
Judging from the great preparations for the Ottoman fleet, it can be
said that the sultan had in mind annexing Lesbos as he had the other
northern Aegean islands. The papal squadron retreated to Chios. The
Ottoman admiral laid siege to the fortress of Molybdos without result
and subsequently left the island, returning to Gallipoli on August 9.
Domenico, declaring that the papal navy was incapable of protecting
him, turned to the sultan and offered his submission by sending a tribute; in 1458 Nicholas accused him of aiding Mehmed, and had him
executed. During the course of 1457 both the Chians and William II
Crispo, the duke of the Archipelago, had followed in Lesbos's footsteps and agreed to submit to the Ottomans.[15]

Lemnos and Thasos, still in Christian hands, were put by the pope
under the protection of the grand master of the Hospitallers after the
return of the papal fleet to Italy in 1458. The Venetians and the Catalans each wanted these strategic islands for themselves, but Calixtus
III refused their request. After Calixtus died, the new pope, Pius II
(1458–1464), planned to put them under the Genoese.[16] At any rate,
in 1457–1459 the Latins were trying to create on these islands bases
for defense and for attack against the Ottomans, but in 1459–1460
Mehmed occupied them, ending the squabbles. A compromise with
the Greek population, who resented the Latin occupation, enabled the
sultan to take over these islands easily: he agreed that the despot Demetrius Palaeologus, an Ottoman protégé in the Morea, would take
possession of the islands in return for recognition of Ottoman suzerainty, with the payment of a yearly tribute of three thousand ducats.
Upon the conclusion of the agreement Zaganuz Pasha, the new Otto-

12. See Critobulus, tr. Riggs, pp. 138–139. Miller, *op. cit.*, pp. 435–436, thinks that the Gattilusi continued paying their tribute to the sultan, but the tribute was taken to the sultan in August 1456 (Ducas, p. 256) before the papal fleet arrived at Mytilene in the autumn.

13. Ducas, tr. Magoulias, p. 256; Miller, *op. cit.*, p. 434, thinks that the fleet departed in
August.

14. The fleet comprised 156 sail and carried cannon and siege engines.

15. For the dates see Miller, *op. cit.*, p. 435; Critobulus, tr. Riggs, p. 139, puts it after the
campaign against the Morea in 1458.

16. Miller, *op. cit.*, p. 434.

man admiral, came with the fleet and without difficulty occupied Thasos and Samothrace with the coöperation of the local Greek notables. In 1460, when the sultan conquered the Morea, the four islands and Aenos were granted as an appanage to Demetrius.[17]

Despite paying tribute to the sultan to prevent an attack, Nicholas Gattilusio, the new master of Lesbos, took every measure to put the island in readiness while he urgently requested aid from Genoa. The sultan, accusing Nicholas of making secret agreements with the Italians and letting the Catalan corsairs use the island as a base,[18] made a decisive attack on Lesbos in 1462. While the grand vizir Mahmud arrived with a powerful fleet[19] and began the siege of the fortified city of Mytilene, the sultan himself came by land with the main part of the army and made camp on the mainland at Ayazmend in August. The walls were not able to withstand Mehmed's powerful artillery, and once the lower fortress Melanoudion had succumbed, Nicholas surrendered.[20] The whole island was immediately put under direct Ottoman rule.[21] Although a Venetian fleet was closely following the Otto-

17. The main source for all this is Critobulus, tr. Riggs, pp. 143-145, 149, 159-160, who was personally involved in the negotiations. Emphasis should be put on the agreement with the Greeks; the point is missed in Miller, Babinger, and Kenneth M. Setton, *The Papacy and the Levant (1204-1571)*, II (Philadelphia, 1978), 223-224, 238.

18. Critobulus, tr. Riggs, p. 180.

19. According to Ducas, tr. Magoulias, p. 261, the Ottoman fleet then consisted of 7 warships and 60 triremes. According to an Ottoman survey of Gallipoli dated 1479 (Istanbul, Belediye Library, Cevdet K. no. 079), the Ottoman fleet based there was composed of four types of ships: *kadirga* (galley), *galyata* (galliot), *kayik* (fusta), and *at-gemisi* (cargo ship). Captains of *kadirgas* numbered 32, of *galyatas* 5, of *kayiks* 11, and of *at-gemisis* 59. Transports were also called *palandarie* or *parandarie*. The *bölük,* crew, of the admiral's flagship included 20 *azebs* or marines, 7 *mehters* or the military band, and 5 *kumis* (for *comte* see Auguste Jal, *Archéologie navale* [Paris, 1840], p. 474); each *kadirga* included an average of 196 *kürekjis* (oarsmen) and 100 *jenkjis* (fighters). For the naval terms mentioned above see Henry R. Kahane and Andreas Tietze, *The Lingua Franca in the Levant: Turkish Nautical Terms of Italian and Greek Origin* (Urbana, 1958); and Hans A. von Burski, *Kemāl Re'īs: ein Beitrag zur Geschichte der türkischen Flotte* (diss., Bonn, 1928), pp. 34-36.

In 1453 at the siege of Constantinople Mehmed II's navy was composed of 12 galleys, 20 galliots, 70 fuste, and 20-25 *palandarie*. According to Critobulus, *op. cit.,* p. 96, in 1454, in the expedition against Rhodes, the fleet under Hamza numbered "eighty warships besides quite a few cargo ships and other ships carrying cannon". In 1480 the fleet under Gedik Ahmed heading for Otranto included 28 *galee* and 104 *fuste et palandarie* with 4,000 cavalry; see "Donado da Lezze" (Giovanni-Maria Angiolello), *Historia turchesca,* ed. Ion Ursu (Bucharest, 1910), p. 110.

20. Critobulus, tr. Riggs, p. 183.

21. For the *reaya*'s status and taxation under Ottoman rule see the regulation of Midilli (Mytilene) published by Ömer Lütfi Barkan, *XV. ve XVI. inci asirlarda osmanli imparatorluğunda ziraî ekonominin hukukî ve malî esaslari,* I, *Kanunlar* (Istanbul, 1943), 332-338; cf. the regulation of Lemnos published by Heath W. Lowry, "A Corpus of Extant Kanunnames for the Island of Limnos . . . ," *Journal of Ottoman Studies,* I (1980), 41-60.

man military operations, it was under orders to avoid direct confrontation with the Ottoman forces.[22]

Pius II showed himself just as enthusiastic and determined as Calixtus III for a general crusade of all Christian nations "to free Europe from the disgrace of Turkish domination". According to Ferdinand Gregorovius, "the deliverance of Constantinople was the ideal of his pontificate."[23] The congress summoned by the pope for this purpose convened at the time when the Ottomans were in the process of evicting the papal forces from the northern Aegean islands.[24]

The news of the fall of the Serbian despotate in June 1459 and the arrival in Mantua of the envoys from the directly threatened kingdoms of Hungary and Bosnia galvanized a short-lived Christian European alliance. To muster the forces needed to overcome the now powerful army of the Ottomans was considered impossible, yet, prompted by cardinal Bessarion, a Greek refugee in Rome, the decision was taken to declare a general crusade of European nations for three years starting in 1460. However, before setting out on his campaign against Trebizond, Mehmed was able to sign an armistice with the Knights Hospitaller of Rhodes.

Meanwhile in Albania the struggle against the Ottomans continued. Up until 1463, when Venice openly took the Albanian rebels under its own protection, both the king of Naples and the pope were actively involved on that front. They provided the rebel leader Scanderbeg with money and supplies and even sent troops. Before setting out on the Trebizond campaign, however, Mehmed also negotiated an armistice agreement with Scanderbeg.

The pope had convinced Hungary, the Ottomans' major rival in Europe, that it should participate fully in the planned crusade. Conflict between the Ottomans and Hungary was inevitable because of the rivalry over Serbia. In 1451 when Mehmed II came to the throne the Serbian despot George Brankovich had seized the fortress of Alaja-Hisar (Krushevats) and its environs, but on learning of the Ottoman capture of Constantinople he offered to return it. The sultan responded by sending an ultimatum in which he laid hereditary claim to all knez Lazar's former territories in the Morava river valley including Smederevo and Golubats, but promised to give up to Brankovich the Vuchitrn-Lab region (Vilk-ili), which had belonged to the despot's father, Vuk.

---

22. Miller, *op. cit.,* p. 439; Ottoman eyewitness accounts are given by Enverî in *Düstûrnâme,* pp. 100–101, and Tursun Beg, *op. cit.,* pp. 101a–103a.

23. Pastor, *op. cit.,* III, 19, 78.

24. *Ibid.,* III, 85–96.

During Mehmed's campaign into the Morava river valley in 1454, the fortresses of Omol (Omolridon) and Sifrije-Hisar (Ostrovitsa) were captured by the Ottomans, and the despot took refuge in Hungary. When the Ottoman army withdrew, John Hunyadi from Belgrade and the Serbs in the Kossovo area turned to the offensive in the fall of 1454. Hunyadi devastated the Vidin-Nish area, but the Serbs were beaten in the south.

In Mehmed's second Serbian campaign in 1455 he concentrated his forces against southern Serbia and Vilk-ili. He took possession of a number of silver-producing towns, Trepcha, Novo Brdo (June 1, 1455), and the Lab valley. The despot's desperate appeal for a crusade did not yield any result and he had to give up all hope of recovering the silver mines of Novo Brdo, the source of his wealth and power. By limiting his demands to the return of Vilk-ili to the Ottomans, Mehmed managed to reach a unilateral peace agreement with Brankovich to the exclusion of the Hungarians. The despot also agreed to pay a very large yearly tribute and to provide troops.

Once the Serbian despotate was neutralized, Mehmed II prepared a major campaign to oust the Hungarians from Belgrade and invaded Hungary in 1456. Twenty-one cannons, as well as a fleet of two hundred vessels, sixty-four of them galleys, were to be used in the campaign. Although internal dissension and hostility with the emperor Frederick III (1452–1493) weakened Hungary's defense, it received strong support from the papacy with the declaration of a crusade against the Ottomans and the sending of a papal fleet to the Aegean. The fiery preachings of the Franciscan friar John of Capistrano and the arrival of crusaders whom he had recruited from among the populace of Hungary and Germany gave the movement much the appearance of the earliest crusades. Mehmed's huge army caused panic in Italy, where many thought that Hungary could not resist the sultan's attack and that he intended to move his army into Italy after conquering Hungary.[25]

Although Mehmed's guns demolished Belgrade's defenses and a group of janissaries actually entered the city, Hunyadi was able to bring in reinforcements by breaking the blockade on the Danube (July 14). Thus the general assault was repulsed (July 21) and the sultan was forced to retreat (July 23).[26]

25. Setton, *The Papacy,* II, 178.

26. While Catholic sources (see Babinger, *Der Quellenwert,* and Setton, *The Papacy,* II, 179–182) give credit for the victory to John of Capistrano and his "crusaders", the Ottoman chronicles (especially Tursun, Ibn-Kemāl, and Idrīs) confirm the Venetian and Hungarian sources by relating Hunyadi's key role. The Ottoman sources stress that Hunyadi first upset the sultan's

This major victory sent powerful vibrations throughout Christian Europe. Pope Calixtus III wrote that now he looked forward "not only to the recovery of Constantinople but also to the liberation of Europe, Asia, and the Holy Land."[27] The activity of the pope's fleet in the Aegean in 1457 was thought to be a preliminary to the deliverance of Constantinople. Pope Pius II made contact with Uzun Hasan, ruler of the Akkoyunlu Turcomans (1466–1478), and the Georgians in an attempt to encircle the Ottomans from the east.[28]

In 1456 George Brankovich died and a dispute over the Serbian succession brought on a new crisis, with Mehmed supporting George's son Gregory against his brother Lazar II (1456–1458). About this time another dispute which had arisen between the two Greek despots in the Morea, Demetrius and Thomas Palaeologus, had confused the situation in the south, so Venice intervened and claimed the Morea as part of its own sphere of influence. In Albania too the situation had deteriorated for the Ottomans in 1457, when Scanderbeg defeated the Ottoman forces in Albunlena. In response to these threats the sultan in the spring of 1458 sent Isa Beg with reinforcements against Scanderbeg, while he himself set out for the Morea with an army, and he dispatched the pretender Gregory to Serbia with an army under Mahmud Pasha. In response to a number of concessions on the part of Mahmud Pasha the Serbs surrendered a few fortresses in various parts of the country, including Golubats. However, an army under the personal command of the Hungarian king Matthias Corvinus (Hunyadi, 1458–1490) in nearby Smederevo continued to pose a threat, and Mahmud withdrew his forces to the area around Nish.

At this juncture the sultan, having conquered those areas in the Morea formerly subject to emperor Constantine XI, arrived with his forces in Skoplje (Üsküb) and met with Mahmud Pasha. Matthias, following his father's example, waited to act until the onset of autumn and the expected annual disbanding of the Ottoman army. Mehmed II,

---

plan by his victory over the Ottoman fleet on the Danube; he was able to bring his army to the fortress by ship. After a week of intensive cannon fire, the sultan gave the order for a general assault. The janissaries who entered the city were isolated and eliminated by Hunyadi; the assault ended in complete failure. Now the Ottoman tactic was to lure Hunyadi with his small army out of Belgrade by a feigned retreat. Hunyadi was not, however, deceived, as the Ottoman eyewitness historian Tursun makes clear. As Christian sources tell us, those attacking the Ottomans in their trenches were John of Capistrano's "crusaders". According to the Ottoman sources these first succeeded, and advanced as far as the sultan's camp, but then were repulsed and massacred.

27. Setton, *The Papacy,* II, 183, note 89: the pope's letter to archbishop Antonio Forcilioni of Florence written in August 1456.

28. Anthony Bryer, "Ludovico da Bologna and the Georgian and Anatolian Embassy of 1460–1461," *Bedi Kartlisa (Revue de Kartvelogie),* XIX–XX (1965), 179–198; John Woods, *The Aqquyunlu . . .* (Minneapolis and Chicago, 1976), p. 101.

however, responded with exceptional measures, and remained in Skoplje until at least November 1458. The king, who crossed the Danube and attacked Tahtalu, was forced by the Ottomans to retreat. In the spring of the following year the sultan himself led an army into the field against Smederevo. The Serbs came to Sofia in June 1459 to surrender the keys to the fortress; the Serbian despotate was once again annexed to the Ottoman empire. Next Mehmed crossed to Anatolia and took Amasra (Amastris) on the Black Sea from the Genoese without a battle.

Pope Pius II received the news of the surrender of Smederevo as an unmitigated disaster for the west, and consequently during the deliberations at the Congress of Mantua in 1459 the launching of a crusade was officially announced. As a result of the establishment of despot Thomas's control over the Morea with western support, Pius regarded the Morea as an excellent base for operations against the Ottomans. The sultan, however, invaded the Morea in 1460 and annexed the entire region, with the exception of a few fortresses on the coasts which belonged to Venice. The capture of Argos by the Ottomans finally convinced the Venetians of the necessity of declaring war (July 28, 1463).

Meanwhile, new developments in Wallachia and Bosnia had made inevitable the outbreak of an open conflict between the Hungarians and the Ottomans. In 1461 Mehmed had sought to regain the allegiance of the voivode of Wallachia, but Vlad III Tepesh ("the Impaler") had responded by allying himself with the king of Hungary instead, and even went so far as to take advantage of the sultan's absence during the Trebizond campaign to attack Ottoman outposts across the Danube. Consequently, in the summer of 1462 Mehmed invaded Wallachia, and appointed in Vlad's place his brother Radu III ("the Handsome"), who was living in the Ottoman palace. The king of Bosnia, Stephen Tomashevich (1461–1463), who espoused the western Catholic cause against the Ottomans, did not hesitate to hand some fortresses over to the Hungarians (1462). But because of the internal religious division his situation was hopeless, and Bosnia too was conquered by the sultan in 1463.

By 1463 this uninterrupted series of invasions convinced the Ottomans' two great rivals, Hungary and Venice, that the time had come for decisive action on their part. At long last the pope's efforts bore fruit, and Venice and Hungary signed a mutual offensive and defensive pact. The pope now believed that the crusade would become a reality. Signing an agreement with Venice and Burgundy, he set May

1464 as the date for the departure of a crusade. A plan was even prepared for dividing the lands of the Ottoman empire among the Christian states in case of victory. It provided that Venice would take the
Morea, Boeotia, Attica, and the coastal part of Epirus; Scanderbeg
would take Macedonia; the remaining parts of the former lands of the
Byzantine empire (mainly Thrace and Thessaly) would be divided between the Greek dynasts; and Hungary would take all of Serbia, Bosnia, Bulgaria, and Wallachia.

The western powers, promising Scanderbeg financial support, persuaded him to go on the offensive, thereby disregarding the terms of
his agreement with the sultan. The major rival to Ottoman power in
eastern Anatolia, Uzun Hasan, ruler of the Akkoyunlu Turcomans,
entered into negotiations with Venice for a pact against the sultan. As
early as the autumn of 1463 the allies began their offensive. Venice retook Argos in September and the walls of the Hexamilion were quickly
reinforced. A number of towns and cities in the Morea rose up in revolt and sided with the Venetians, and the Moslems remaining in the
peninsula had to take refuge in a few fortresses over which they maintained control. On December 16 the king of Hungary attacked and
captured the Bosnian capital Yaytse (Jajce). The Venetian fleet patrolled
the waters outside the Dardanelles, threatening to strike at any moment.

Mehmed, faced with these threats on all sides, took drastic steps.
Despite the fact that winter was already near, he immediately sent Mahmud Pasha with a strong army to the Morea. In order to strengthen the
empire's naval forces he established a new shipyard at Kadîrga-limanî
in Istanbul, and in order to assure the safety of Istanbul he ordered
that matching fortresses be built on either side of the Dardanelles at
Kilidulbahr and Sultaniye (Chanakkale). The Venetians were defeated
in the Morea, and were once again forced to give up the peninsula to
the Ottomans. While the sultan himself was on the way to the Morea
to reinforce Mahmud Pasha, on reaching Zeitounion he learned of the
successful conclusion of the campaign and changed the direction of
his march toward Bosnia. In the summer of 1464 he besieged Yaytse
in an attempt to expel the Hungarians but was unsuccessful. On his
return to Sofia in September he learned of the Hungarian king's entry
into Bosnia and sent a force under the command of Mahmud Pasha,
who forced Matthias to withdraw. Thus Mehmed had achieved success in meeting the allied threats on every front. Pope Pius II, who
had hoped to lead the crusader army in person, died at Ancona August 15, 1464, and the crusade collapsed.

During 1465 Mehmed opened peace negotiations with Venice and
Hungary because of the need to deal with the confused situation in

Karaman, but no agreement could be reached. In the spring of 1466 he set out against Albania to punish Scanderbeg. After conducting operations against the Albanians in the highlands, he constructed a strong fortress, Elbasan, in the low country in central Albania, as a base against those Albanians who were continuing resistance from their strongholds in the mountains. After the sultan's departure Scanderbeg, with support troops sent by Venice, defeated Balaban Beg, who was pressing the fortress of Croia, and besieged the newly constructed fortress of Elbasan. Outraged by Scanderbeg's actions, the sultan himself set out on his second Albanian campaign in 1467. In order to intimidate his enemies, he attacked the Albanians mercilessly and sent raiding parties against the Venetian ports, including Scutari and Durazzo. Thus Albania became one of the principal arenas of the Venetian-Ottoman war. Venice achieved little military benefit from the alliance with king Matthias, but as a result of the agreements reached with Uzun Hasan and Pir Ahmed, the emir of Karaman, it was now possible to mobilize a large land force in Asia against the sultan.

Before Uzun Hasan emerged as an ally, Venice had taken advantage of the sultan's Karaman campaign of 1468. In 1469 Venice had sent out its fleet from Euboea and struck repeated blows against the Rumelian coastline. The islands of Lemnos and Imbros were occupied, and the important commercial centers of Aenos and New Phocaea were sacked and burned. Then the Venetian fleet moved on to the Morea and, after capturing the fortress of Vostitsa, reinforced it as a base for future actions. At this time the Ottoman fleet had been occupied in operations in the Black Sea against the Genoese.

This daring attack led Mehmed to a decision to retaliate with a major blow against the enemy, and he chose Negroponte on Euboea as the target of his attack. During this campaign the Ottomans achieved tactical superiority, and while his fleet monitored the movements of the Venetian fleet, a land force under the personal command of the sultan built a bridge linking the island with the mainland; thus he was able to bring over his army, which succeeded in subduing the fortress on July 11, 1470. The loss of Negroponte aroused great concern not only among the Venetians but throughout the west, and there was general fear that the Ottomans had now established complete control of the Aegean. On Christmas day 1471 pope Sixtus IV (1471-1484) assigned six cardinals to the task of stimulating interest in Europe for the launching of a crusade against the Turks. A pact was signed between Venice and Naples for the formation of a crusader fleet, but the rest of Europe remained aloof.

Aware of the dangerous situation during his campaigns in the east, the sultan tried to neutralize his western rivals by peace offensives. In July 1471 he sent an envoy to Venice to offer peace. Since he insisted on complete control of the Aegean islands, the Morea, and Albania, and in particular on the payment of a yearly tribute, the negotiations broke down in March 1472.

Uzun Hasan, engaged in a life-and-death struggle with the Ottomans, the outcome of which would determine the future of eastern Anatolia, readied himself for battle with every military and diplomatic weapon at his disposal.[29] In the winter of 1470–1471 an Akkoyunlu embassy visited Venice, Rome, and Naples seeking an agreement against the Ottomans. Under the impact of the fall of Negroponte, and despite the sultan's peace offensive in 1471 and 1472, Venice reached an agreement with Uzun Hasan which included the following cardinal points. To aid Uzun Hasan with firearms Venetian ships would bring arms and a small landing party to the coast of Karaman, to be met there by forces sent by Uzun Hasan. After his expected victory Uzun Hasan was to become master of most of Anatolia and make the Ottoman sultan promise to refrain from building fortresses on the coasts and to allow free access for Venetian shipping into the Black Sea. In addition to this, he was to secure the return to Venice of the Morea and Euboea as well as Lesbos. The Venetians assured Uzun Hasan that they were capable of entering the Straits and capturing Istanbul. In the summer of 1472 an Akkoyunlu-Karamanid army invaded Ottoman territory as far as Akshehir in central Anatolia, but on August 14 the invading army was routed by the Ottomans.

The large crusader fleet, composed of about 87 galleys from Venice, Naples, Rhodes, the papacy, and Cyprus, had been wreaking havoc along the Mediterranean shores of the Ottoman territories all summer. Adalia (Antalya) was sacked and burned in August and Smyrna (İzmir) on September 13. In the spring of 1473 the fleet, in coöperation with the forces of the Karamanid Kasim Beg, took the fortresses of Corycus, Sïgïn, and Seleucia (Silifke). The sultan took all possible measures to counter the Akkoyunlu-Christian attack. In the winter he had hastily sent a force of raiders (akïnjïs) from Rumelia to the area around Sivas, and in the spring he arrived in person with his large army and advanced in the direction of Erzinjan against Uzun Hasan. The Akkoyunlu were cut off from communication with the Christian force which landed at Corycus, near Tarsus on the Mediterranean coast.

---

29. For Uzun Hasan and his struggle against Mehmed II see Woods, *The Aqqunyunlu,* pp. 87–137.

At the decisive battle of Bashkent on August 11, 1473, Mehmed emerged triumphant and imposed harsh terms on Uzun Hasan. The latter was to cede the fortress of Kara-Hisar and to promise never again to violate Ottoman territory.

Mehmed took a defensive stance vis-à-vis Hungary in the period 1471–1473. Despite Matthias's attempts at intervention, the sultan managed to build a strongly fortified castle on the Danube at Shabats (Bögürdelen) to ensure the security of Bosnia. In the years after 1471 he sent his raiding forces not against Hungary but against the Austrian lands of Matthias's rival emperor Frederick III, and even sent an envoy to Matthias proposing peace. In 1473 a Hungarian envoy was sent in return but he was kept waiting until the completion of the Uzun Hasan affair, and was not granted an audience with the sultan.

After his victory against Uzun Hasan Mehmed listened to the envoy's demands, which included the abandonment or demolition of the two fortresses on the Danube, the Avala (Havāle) ramparts opposite Belgrade and the fortress of Golubats (Gügerjinlik). Not only were these demands rejected by the sultan, but he countered with a demand of his own for the ceding of the fortress of Yaytse in Bosnia, and ordered a raid against Hungarian territory. In this raid (winter 1474) Mihaloghlu Ali advanced as far as Varád. Because of his ongoing war with Poland, Matthias was unable to capitalize on the opportunity in 1473, and had to leave the raid of 1474 unanswered. It was not until 1475 that the king was free to launch his counterattack. He captured the fortress of Shabats on February 15, 1476.

Meanwhile the sultan, who was busily making preparations for a campaign against Moldavia, made an offer of peace. Disregarding the offer, the Hungarian king proceeded to build three wooden forts on the Danube for the purpose of gaining control of the Smederevo region. The sultan, upon his return from the Moldavian campaign, immediately set out for Smederevo, disregarding the exhaustion of his troops, and demolished the three forts. Thereafter Hungary was neutralized by Matthias's war against the Hapsburgs. Not only did Matthias withhold his support from the Venetians, but he let his father-in-law, the king of Naples, make an agreement with the sultan. But after formalizing the peace with Venice in 1479 the Ottoman raids against Hungary were resumed. While the frontier begs attacked Transylvania the new governor of Bosnia, Davud Pasha, accompanied by a large *akĭnjĭ* force, crossed the Sava river and carried out extensive raids in Hungary.

From 1474 on the sultan intensified the war against Venice. In 1477

Suleiman Pasha was sent against the Venetian possession Lepanto, but as a result of the timely arrival of naval assistance it was able to resist capture. Evrenuz-oghlu Ahmed blockaded the Venetian fortress of Croia in Albania, and managed to repel naval reinforcements as they attempted to land on the shore. In the autumn of 1477 Iskender Pasha, the governor of Bosnia, led an army against Venetian territory in northern Italy and advanced over the Isonzo and Tagliamento rivers, wreaking havoc on the plain opposite the city of Venice itself. In the following year a similar raid was carried out against Friuli.

Finally in April 1478 the sultan himself set out on campaign against the Venetians in Albania. Proceeding directly to Scutari he immediately besieged the fortress, which resisted all the assaults. After cutting off access to it from the sea by a blockade Mehmed returned with the main part of the army. Helpless to save Scutari and fearful because of the recent raids for Venice itself, the republic resumed peace negotiations in December 1478. On January 15, 1479, a peace treaty was signed, bringing an end to this long war; its principal provisions were that Venice agreed to evacuate Scutari and hand it over to the Ottomans, gave up claims to Croia and the islands of Lemnos and Euboea, and agreed to pay a yearly tribute of 10,000 gold ducats, in return for which it was to enjoy freedom to engage in commerce.

Since the sultan had by this peace treaty effectively neutralized the major enemy sea power, he was now able to turn his attacks against Rhodes, Italy, and the papacy without worry. The rivalries existing among Naples, Venice, and Milan, as well as their general opposition to the policies of the papacy, played into Mehmed's hands, and Venice encouraged him to take immediate action against the kingdom of Naples.

In the spring of 1480 he sent Mesih Pasha with a fleet against Rhodes while simultaneously launching Gedik Ahmed Pasha with another fleet against southern Italy, thus opening a new phase in his conquests. After a fierce ninety-day siege starting on May 23, 1480, the Ottomans were forced to retreat from Rhodes with severe losses.

Gedik Ahmed, the conqueror of Karaman and the Crimea, managed to capture the islands of Leucas (Santa Maura), Cephalonia, and Zante belonging to the Tocco dynasty, and also found an opportunity to meddle in the internal politics of the kingdom of Naples in 1479. In the summer of 1480 he set out from Avlona with a fleet of 132 ships carrying 18,000 men and on August 11 captured Otranto. After reinforcing the fortress and transforming it into a base for operations, he began carrying out raids. The capture of Otranto was regarded as the first step toward the capture of Rome, and the pope fell into a panic, even thinking of fleeing to safety outside Italy. Gedik Ahmed returned to Rumelia in order to collect fresh troops for renewed attacks, but in the spring of 1481, as he was preparing to cross the Adriatic with reinforcements, the news of Mehmed's death was sent by his son, the new sultan Bayazid II (1481-1512), along with an urgent request for his return to the capital to meet the threat posed by Bayazid's brother Jem Sultan.[30] Otranto was quickly retaken by the Neapolitans, and Italy was spared further Ottoman invasions.

B. The Ottomans, the Crusade, and Renaissance Diplomacy, 1481–1522

The death of Mehmed the Conqueror on May 3, 1481, gave rise to an internecine struggle for the throne between his sons Bayazid and Jem. Bayazid II, supported by Ishak Pasha, Gedik Ahmed, and the janissaries, who had rebelled at the death of Mehmed, succeeded in taking control of the capital. Jem's attempts to challenge his brother's control in the years 1481 and 1482 met with defeat at the hands of Bayazid, who had collected the main forces of the empire under his banner. The state of civil war in the Ottoman empire gave rise to great expectations in the Christian world. The papacy was hopeful that the civil war would lead to a territorial division of the empire,[31] and it was believed that this was the most opportune time to strike a decisive blow against the Ottomans. After his final defeat at Ankara in June 1482, Jem took refuge in Rhodes, relying on the promise of the Hospitallers that he would be transferred to Rumelia to continue the fight.

Actually the Hospitaller grand master, Peter of Aubusson, kept him as a prisoner because Bayazid made generous offers to the knights in exchange for their promise to keep him guarded.[32] Up until the time of his agreement with the knights of Rhodes (December 14, 1482), fol-

---

30. This analysis of Mehmed II's relations with Christian Europe is based in general on Inalcik, "Mehmed II," in İslâm Ansiklopedisi, VII, 506–535; also on Babinger, Mehmed the Conqueror, and Setton, The Papacy, II, 108–363; see my review of Babinger's book in Speculum, XXXV (1960), 408–427.

31. Johann W. Zinkeisen, Geschichte des osmanischen Reiches in Europa, II (Gotha, 1854; repr. Darmstadt, 1963), 498; for the civil war see the contemporary eyewitness Angiolello in "Donado da Lezze," ed. Ursu, pp. 164–183.

32. Thuasne, Djem-Sultan, pp. 80–95; obviously Jem was deceived by the knights. See his biography, Vāḳi'āt, ed. Mehmed Arif (Istanbul, 1914), pp. 7–8.

lowing the execution of the overbold Gedik Ahmed Pasha (November 18), sultan Bayazid's position both internally and internationally was weak, as the janissaries, the 'ulema, and other factions reacted against any continuation of Mehmed II's centralizing policy. The knights of Rhodes immediately began negotiations with the other leaders of the Christian world for the undertaking of a crusade against the Ottomans. There were two courses open to the western powers: they could either follow a war policy and send a crusader army against the Ottomans with Jem as a figurehead, or else simply use the threat of sending Jem to check the sultan, forcing him to seek peaceful relations with the west. In effect, the sum of 45,000 gold pieces sent annually by the Ottoman sultan, ostensibly for the maintenance expenses of prince Jem, acted as a kind of tribute which softened the stance of the western powers and led them to choose the second alternative.[33] Nevertheless, the position of Jem as a hostage in the hands of European states gave rise to new developments in relations between western governments and the Ottomans.

The Ottoman diplomatic efforts were on the whole successful in realizing their primary aims, which were to prevent a crusade and to keep Jem from joining forces with either the Mamluk sultan of Egypt or the king of Hungary, the two principal rivals of the Ottomans, who were both in a position to use Jem in a most effective way against Bayazid. To achieve this goal, the Ottomans made use of diplomatic means as well as military threats, seeking to exploit for their own benefit the rivalries existing among the Christian powers in Europe. During this period the Ottomans did everything in their power to deepen the divisions between the Italian states, encouraging and giving their support to the weaker states in their struggle against the dominant powers in the Italian scene. These weaker states constantly used the threat of Ottoman intervention on their behalf as a check against the incursions of their enemies.

Bayazid confirmed the peace treaty with Venice on January 16, 1482. Several new concessions not present in the 1479 agreement were added at this time, a sign that Bayazid indeed felt the need for continuation of peaceful relations with this maritime power.[34] The advantageous terms granted to the Venetians achieved the effective neutralization of

---

33. Pfefferman, *Die Zusammenarbeit,* pp. 84–90.

34. Bayazid agreed to forego the 10,000-gold-piece tribute paid by the Venetians to Mehmed II and lowered the customs duties for Venetians from five percent to four; see Bombaci, "Nuovi firmani greci di Maometto II," pp. 298–319.

the republic, which was perennially the Ottomans' principal rival on the sea, as the Hungarians were on the land.

Since both the Ottomans and the Venetians were at war with the king of Naples, the agreement took the form of an alliance. From the Ottoman documentation[35] it appears that Bayazid would even have been content to have Jem in the custody of Venice. The Venetian authorities kept the sultan informed of Jem's movements in Italy and France, and of the progress of the major powers' intentions and plans, but naturally all this was done in such a way as to influence Bayazid's policy in favor of Venetian interests. Taking care to preserve their friendly relations with the Ottomans, the Venetians, as a rule, would not participate in the councils being convened to make plans for a crusade. But they too appreciated the value of the custody of Jem in western hands as a check on Ottoman actions, especially on the sea.

Under the circumstances, the peace agreement concluded in 1484 between Bayazid and Ferdinand (Ferrante) I, the king of Naples (1458-1494), can be considered a further Ottoman diplomatic success. The invasion of Otranto by the Ottomans in 1481 had caused panic in Italy. The news of Mehmed II's death had reached the pope on June 2, 1481. Sixtus IV did not, however, relax his efforts to organize a general crusade against the Ottomans. This crusade was to be joined by all Italy, and, if possible, by the entire Christian world. After recapturing Otranto from the Ottomans on September 21, 1481, king Ferdinand, following the traditional policy of the Aragonese dynasty, set about stirring up a rebellion in Albania. Accordingly, Klada set out from Naples, captured the Albanian coastal fortresses of Himara and Sopot, and established contact with Albanian leaders in 1481. Despite the pope's wish that the crusader naval force which set sail to subdue the Turkish garrison at Otranto be sent on against Avlona,[36] the Ottoman naval base in Albania, his desires were not heeded. By this time the papacy had already made plans to arrange with Venice for the removal of Ferdinand from the throne of Naples.[37] Because of the ensuing war of Ferrara in Italy, enthusiastic invitations for a crusade following the capture of Jem by the Hospitallers produced no result.

Hüseyn Beg, Bayazid's ambassador to European governments in con-

35. Letter in Ertaylan, *Sultan Cem,* from Topkapi Sarayi archives (cited hereafter as TKS), no. 5457: "why do the Venetians not capture Jem while there is a chance for it? It is time for them to show their friendship"; cf. Vladimir Lamansky, *Secrets d'état de Venise* (St. Petersburg, 1884; repr. New York, 1968), p. 202; Thuasne, *Djem,* p. 106.

36. Pastor, *The History of the Popes,* tr. Antrobus, IV (London, 1894), 342.

37. *Ibid.,* IV, 374. It is noteworthy that the 500 Ottoman soldiers who joined Naples' forces as mercenaries played a significant role in the battle of Campomorto (1482).

nection with Jem's affairs, reported that the king of Naples was very anxious to make peace with the sultan.[38] Ferdinand enthusiastically acknowledged the receipt of the peace and friendship offers of Bayazid and stressed "the friendship and brotherhood which exists between the two of us".[39] He also added useful information about Jem which he had collected through his spies.

The Ottomans, however, in the winter of 1484, probably as a result of Venetian encouragement, prepared a large fleet, and it gave rise to the fear of an imminent Ottoman invasion in Italy. Thereupon the pope informed Ferdinand about his move to prepare a crusader fleet and invited the Italian states, excluding Venice, to contribute to the expenses, estimated at 200,000 ducats.[40] Actually, this was a plan to organize an Italian coalition under the pope's leadership, against Venice as well as the Ottomans. Ottoman diplomacy, in its turn, skillfully made use of the fear aroused by the naval preparations to guarantee Jem's firm detention. In the following years the Hospitallers and Venice were able to keep the Ottoman fleet from entering the Aegean by use of the threat of sending a crusader army with Jem. It appears that in these years, Bayazid's great fear was that Mamluk sultan Ka'itbay of Egypt (1468–1496) might gain control of Jem. Bayazid, therefore, made attempts to have his brother assassinated. The grand master Peter of Aubusson, judging from his correspondence with Bayazid,[41] purported to coöperate with this plan in order to obtain extra money from the sultan.

All during this period Bayazid sought particularly active diplomatic relations with all Christian governments involved with Jem and the proposed crusade. He created a spy network to keep himself informed of political developments in various countries of the west.[42] Since the sultan personally conducted all these activities, the seraglio replaced the *divan* (imperial council) in foreign affairs.

In order to assure himself of Jem's confinement, Bayazid addressed a letter to the French king in which he said: "It has been agreed between us and the grand master that a specified amount of money shall

38. TKS, no. 5457, reproduced by Ertaylan, *op. cit.,* p. 189. It can be dated May 1484; cf. Thuasne, *Djem,* pp. 104, 110.

39. TKS, no. 5680, reproduced by Ertaylan, *op. cit.,* p. 203.

40. Thuasne, *Djem,* pp. 125–126.

41. *Ibid.,* pp. 126, 129.

42. The point is clarified by the reports in the Topkapí Saraýi archives, partially published by Ertaylan; Selâhettin Tansel, *Sultan II Bayezid'in Siyasi Hayati* (Istanbul, 1966); Turan, "Barak Reis'in şehzade Cem meselesile ilgili olarak Savoie'ya gönderilmesi," *Belleten,* XXVI (1962), 539–555; and Victor L. Ménage, "The Mission of an Ottoman Secret Agent in France in 1486," *Journal of the Royal Asiatic Society* (1965), pp. 112–132; Lefort, *Documents grecs . . . Cem Sultan.*

be regularly sent to him for the livelihood of my brother on condition that he be kept guarded in a safe place within your domains and never let leave for another country. . . . Our hope is that friendship between the two of us be established."[43] However, Hüseyn Beg, Bayazid's envoy in the west, was not able to see the ailing king Louis XI, who died on August 30, 1483, after which events took a new turn.

At the time of Bayazid's accession to the throne in May 1481, the Ottoman state was at war not only with the king of Naples and the knights of Rhodes, but also with Hungary. Bayazid's first move was to announce a campaign against Hungary and to order his troops to assemble at Sofia under the command of the beglerbeg of Rumelia.[44] Actually these activities might be considered as a strategy to combine under his command the military forces of the empire for the impending struggle for the throne. Taking advantage of the situation Stephen "the Great", the voivode of Moldavia (1457–1504), entered Wallachia in the summer of 1481 and marched as far as Turnu on the Danube, raiding the Ottoman territory to the south of the river. In the autumn king Matthias Corvinus of Hungary too gathered a large force along his southern borders (according to his letter, 32,000 men), entered Serbia, and advanced as far as Krushevats.[45] This raid greatly worried the Ottoman government, and the grand vizir Davud Pasha hurriedly returned to Sofia from the battle against Jem.[46] Frontier warfare continued in 1482 and 1483.[47] The king of Hungary controlled all northern Bosnia, including Yaytse, and further planned to occupy Herzegovina and establish it as an independent kingdom for his bastard son.[48] In the meantime he was awaiting aid from Italy and Germany to complete the large-scale preparations for war against the Ottomans.

Despite Matthias's moves to take Jem into his custody, Jem was transferred to France, whence he later made fruitless attempts to es-

43. TKS, no. 6071, in Ertaylan, *op. cit.,* p. 186; it must have been written in early 1484. Hüseyn was in France in the summer of 1483, and returned to Rhodes on January 28, 1484; see Thuasne, *Djem,* pp. 110–115.

44. *Rüstem Pasha tarihi,* MS. in Istanbul, University Library, 45a.

45. Constantin Jireček, *Geschichte der Serben,* II (Gotha, 1918; repr. Amsterdam, 1967), 251.

46. Ibn-Kemāl, vol. VIII, MS. 12b; Iorga, *Geschichte,* II (Gotha, 1909), 261.

47. During the period 1481–1483 Turkish raiders in the Austrian districts of Carinthia and Styria were particularly active; see Leopold Kupelwieser, *Die Kämpfe Ungarns mit den Osmanen bis zur Schlacht bei Mohács, 1526,* 2nd ed. (Vienna, 1899); Franz Ilwolf, "Die Einfälle der Osmanen in die Steiermark," *Mittheilungen des historischen Vereines für Steiermark,* IX (1859), 179–205; Wilhelm Neuman, "Die Türkeneinfälle nach Kärnten," *Südost-Forschungen,* XIV (1955), 84–109.

48. Zinkeisen, *op. cit.,* II, 499–500; Kupelwieser, *loc. cit.*

cape to Hungary and to enter Rumelia.[49] On their part, the knights of Rhodes took great precautions to assure that Jem would not escape or be kidnapped.[50] The danger of Jem's entering the Balkans through Hungary was ever-present. Bayazid was well aware of the plan through the reports of his spies.[51] With this in mind, he sent a sizeable force with orders to build two fortresses on the banks of the Morava river, located on the main route of advance of Hungarian armies through Serbia into the heart of the Balkans. The sultan himself waited in readiness in Sofia until the completion of the two fortresses in the spring of 1483.[52] Finally, in the autumn of 1483, Matthias signed a five-year armistice with the sultan and turned all his military might against the German emperor, whom he accused of attempting to instigate the Ottomans to attack him. After a series of victorious battles he entered Vienna in June 1485. It is noteworthy that during this period the Ottoman frontier warfare against Hungary stopped. It was agreed that raids involving less than four hundred men should not be considered a cause of war.

In fact, Bayazid did not want to be involved in a dangerous war against Hungary, the mainstay of the crusading armies. In order to strengthen his own control over the Ottoman throne, however, he was obliged to initiate a holy war against Christians; the janissaries were exerting pressure on him to declare such a war. He chose to attack the weakest Christian enemy, and made his war objective the principality of Moldavia. In his effort to establish control of Wallachia, Stephen, though an Ottoman vassal, had rebelled and launched an attack against the Ottomans in 1481. But before initiating the campaign, the sultan had to be certain of the Hungarians' neutrality, and therefore made the offer to Matthias of a five-year armistice, no mention being made of Moldavia. Bayazid conducted a successful campaign in Moldavia, and annexed Kilia and Akkerman to his empire (1484).

Matthias, who was fully involved in the west with the war against the emperor, was obliged to renew his armistice with the sultan and to recognize the de facto situation and be content with the sultan's promises that Stephen would be "treated well".[53] The Moldavian voi-

---

49. *Vāḳi'āt*, pp. 8, 23; see Inalcik, "A Case Study," and document TKS 6071, in Ertaylan, *op. cit.*, p. 195. Jem sent his agents to Hungary in early 1483 (Thuasne, *Djem*, p. 108).

50. *Ibid.*, pp. 106–112.

51. Document TKS 607, in Ertaylan, *op. cit.*, p. 173; Thuasne, *Djem*, p. 108.

52. These two fortresses were called Ibn-Kemāl Koblos and Hiram (today Rama) cf. Iorga, *Geschichte*, II, 261.

53. Matthias threw the blame for the Moldavian defeat on his chancellor, Peter Váradi, the archbishop of Kalocsa, whom he accused of neglecting the terms of the peace agreements made with the sultan of 1483. It is difficult to ascertain whether the Ottomans undertook the Mol-

vode was left no alternative but to turn to Poland for assistance in his struggle against the Ottomans.

In May 1485 Jem had been moved to the Hospitaller castle of Bois-lamy, but early in 1486 the grand master and Innocent VIII (1484–1492) agreed in theory that he should be brought to Italy. In 1487 the pope began serious efforts to bring Jem to Rome as a solution to his domestic problems. The war with Ferdinand had again taken a serious turn, posing a severe problem for the papacy. Ferdinand then tried to present himself as Bayazid II's ally in Italy, giving the sultan his full coöperation in the matter of Jem.[54] From then on, the king steadily informed the Ottoman court on the project of the pope for a crusade with Jem. By pursuing this policy of friendship with the sultan, he protected his lands from the danger of Ottoman raids, thus being able to concentrate his forces against the pope. The plans for coöperation with the Ottomans envisaged by the condottiere Boccolino Guzzoni, who had captured Osimo in the papal territory, caused great concern in Rome. Guzzoni first approached the Ottoman governors in Albania, and finally established relations with the sultan in 1487. Word spread that Guzzoni was prepared to seize the March of Ancona in the papal territory, Jem's planned place of residence.[55] It seems that Guzzoni's offers were not taken seriously in Istanbul.[56] All the same, the pope tried to take advantage of the alarm aroused in Italy by the incident, and to get Venice to move into action against Ferdinand of Naples. The papacy's best chance was to bring Jem to Rome and take command of a crusade participated in by the Christian states of Europe. While the pope, Matthias, and the Egyptian sultan were each striving to get hold of Jem and to use him for their respective political objectives, Bayazid now saw that it was best to keep Jem in France.[57]

davian campaign with the advance knowledge of Matthias. For Matthias's policy of appeasement toward Bayazid in his later years see György Hazai, "Urkunde des Friedensvertrages zwischen König Matthias Corvinus und dem türkischen Sultan, 1488," *Beiträge zur Sprachwissenschaft, Volkskunde und Literatur (Steinitz Festschrift)* (Deutsche Akademie der Wissenschaften, Berlin, no. 5; 1965), pp. 141–145.

54. The pope claimed that members of the Neapolitan aristocracy, tired of Ferdinand's oppression, thought of calling the Ottomans to their aid, and that the pope dissuaded them (Pastor, *op. cit.,* IV, 260).

55. Thuasne, *Djem,* pp. 138–141.

56. *Ibid.,* pp. 150–157.

57. Bayazid II promised to send the French king some sacred relics from Istanbul, which became an object of diplomacy during this period; see Babinger, "Reliquienschacher am Osmanenhof im XV Jahrhundert," *Bayerische Akademie der Wissenschaften, Philosophisch-historische Klasse: Sitzungsberichte, Jahrgang 1956,* II (Munich, 1956); *idem,* "Sultan Mehmed II. und ein Heiliger Rock," *ZDMG,* CVIII (1958), 266–278.

In his attempts to obtain Jem, the Mamluk sultan chose as his go-between Lorenzo de' Medici (1469–1492), apparently because of Lorenzo's influence in the courts of France and the papacy, as well as his extensive banking operations. In the spring of 1488 Lorenzo Spinelli, one of Lorenzo de' Medici's agents in France, offered the French king one hundred thousand gold ducats in the name of Ka'itbay for the delivery of Jem.[58] Since papal nuncios had already been granted permission to take Jem to Rome by the French government, which believed that this was in the best interest of Christendom, the Egyptian and Hungarian requests were declined. In order to foil his enemies' plans, Bayazid had instructed his envoy, Anthony Ciritho, to say that he was ready to sign a peace agreement with king Charles VIII of France (1483–1498) and to make peace with the entire Christian world, as well as to pay a considerable sum of money.[59] Moreover, Bayazid offered a military alliance, promising the king aid against his enemies. Even more surprising was the Ottoman sultan's promise to deliver the city of Jerusalem to the French, after its capture from the Mamluks. All of this would be in exchange for the king's promise to keep Jem guarded in France.[60] The sultan's offers impressed the king's council, and orders were sent out to stop Jem on his way to Rome. But in the end the nuncios succeeded in putting Jem aboard a boat belonging to the knights of Rhodes, bound for the papal state. The Ottoman prince entered Rome on March 13, 1489.

Jem's transfer from French territory to Rome to be put directly under the pope's custody was considered in Istanbul as the beginning of a crusade, and caused alarm. Bayazid II, sending an envoy to Rhodes, declared the transfer of Jem to Rome a breach of the pact between the Porte and the order, and took a threatening attitude toward the Hospitallers. On the other hand, the negotiations of the Mamluk ambassador in France and later in Rome to obtain Jem to use against the Ottomans were followed with anxiety that this was a greater and more immediate danger.

The Mamluks of Egypt were involved from the beginning in the intense international struggle to obtain Jem to use him in their fight against the Ottomans. Especially after war broke out between the Ottomans and the Mamluks in 1485, Ka'itbay, sultan of Egypt (1468–

---

58. Thuasne, *Djem,* p. 193; Babinger, "Lorenzo de Medici e la corte ottomana," *Archivio storico italiano,* CXXI (1963), 353–354; *idem, Spätmittelalterliche Briefschaften,* p. 68.

59. Ernest Charrière, *Négociations de la France dans le Levant,* I (Paris, 1848), cxxiv; Babinger, "Reliquienschacher," pp. 17–18.

60. Thuasne, *Djem,* pp. 217–218.

1496), did his utmost to bring Jem to Egypt.[61] After Jem's transfer to Rome in 1489, he seemed to prefer to join Ka'itbay, a Moslem ruler, rather than Matthias, for his fight against Bayazid. Even if Ka'itbay could not use Jem directly in the Egyptian campaign against the Ottomans, Jem's participation in a crusade from the west would divert Ottoman forces from the Egyptian front. This coöperation between Christian Europe and the Islamic state of Egypt, once the sole protagonist of Moslem holy war against Christendom, indicates that during the fifteenth century, in the east as well as in the west, political expediency superseded strict religious idealism.

Now that Jem was in Rome, the power and influence of the pope were greatly enhanced, and papal diplomacy became increasingly complex. While Matthias was pressing the pope to deliver Jem to him as the only power capable of fighting against the Ottomans, the pope declared his decision to convene a congress to be attended by the delegates of all the Christian states in Europe to prepare a crusade.[62] At the same time, the Egyptian ambassador in Rome proclaimed Ka'itbay's willingness to join an anti-Ottoman league, should Jem be delivered to him, and promised to return all the Christian territories conquered by the Ottomans.

The *Türkenkongress,* which opened in Rome on March 25, 1490, was the logical outcome of the papal diplomacy of bringing Jem to Rome. The pope declared that this was the most favorable moment to take action against the Ottomans. It was believed that Jem was prepared, in the event that he obtained the Ottoman throne through Christian help, to withdraw from the Balkans, even to give up Istanbul.[63] Sultan Ka'itbay of Egypt would be invited to participate in the war against the Ottomans. But with the unexpected death of Matthias Corvinus on April 6, 1490, all the plans for the crusade fell through. In addition, the struggle between Charles VIII and the emperor Maximilian (1493-1519), as well as that between Ferdinand of Naples and Innocent VIII, started up once again.

While the Ottoman war against the Mamluks in Cilicia continued, a crusader attack from the west would have created a most dangerous situation for the Ottoman empire. Ottoman tactics all during the Jem

---

61. Jem's mother Chichek Khatun, a refugee in Egypt, was urging the sultan through his wife to free her son and bring him to Egypt; see an intelligence from Egypt to Bayazid II: TKS no. 6008/3, signed by Ya'kub; for Chichek Khatun in Egypt see Ibn-Iyās, *Badā'i az-zuhūr fī wakāi' ad-duhūr,* ed. Mohamed Mostafa, III (Cairo, 1963), 390.

62. Pastor, *Geschichte der Päpste,* III (Freiburg, 1899), 218-224.

63. Francesco Cognasso, "Il Sultano Djem alla corte di Alessandro VI," *Popoli,* II (1942), 96-103.

crisis were to neutralize the west by aggressive diplomacy, sending envoys with lavish promises, presents, money, and relics on the one hand, and to discourage Christian attack by showing strength by building up a strong navy ready to strike and launching large-scale raids on the Danube and Bosnian frontier on the other hand. Friendly relations were sustained with Venice, whose seapower was thought to be of crucial importance for a crusade against the Ottoman empire.

In the face of the dangerous situation following Jem's transfer to Rome in 1489, Bayazid used the same tactics and found Innocent VIII quite amenable to negotiation. The grand master of Rhodes, Peter of Aubusson, who was the central figure in east-west relations during the Jem crisis, now offered his mediation in drafting an agreement between the sultan and the pope. Bayazid promptly sent his envoy to Rhodes.[64] The prime concern of the grand master and the pope at that time apparently was to neutralize an Ottoman offensive against Rhodes and Italy. Moreover the pope, always short of money, wanted to receive a regular and substantial income for acting as custodian of Jem Sultan.[65] The earliest document attesting to Innocent VIII's interest in establishing relations with the sultan is dated December 21, 1489.

To negotiate with Bayazid, the pope employed Giovanni Battista Gentile, a Genoese merchant in Istanbul.[66] In a letter dated May 17, 1490,[67] the sultan wrote to Innocent VIII that through the grand master he had learned with great satisfaction of the transfer of Jem to Rome, and that he was hoping that an agreement about his custody would soon be reached with the pope. Later a Genoese Dominican, Leonard of Chiavari, who apparently lived in Pera, was employed as an envoy in the pope's relations with the sultan.[68] In the late spring or summer of 1490, Leonard came to Rome in the company of an Ottoman envoy to negotiate the terms of Jem's custody.

Upon the transfer of Jem into the custody of the pope in Rome, the Porte had lost the guarantee under the pact with the grand master of Rhodes that Jem would not be delivered to the enemies of Bayazid II. Innocent, in his turn, needed an agreement with the sultan to receive the yearly payment of forty thousand gold ducats which he was entitled

---

64. Thuasne, *Djem,* p. 264.

65. For the pope's financial difficulties see Pastor, *op. cit.,* III, 270–272, 281–285; Thuasne, *Djem,* p. 189; Pfefferman, *op. cit.,* p. 89.

66. Babinger, *Spätmittelalterliche Briefschaften,* pp. 64–75.

67. *Ibid.,* pp. 68–69.

68. *Ibid.,* pp. 69–71.

to receive in accordance with the concord signed with the French king.[69]

Bayazid had chosen for this crucial mission an important man of his court, the *kapiji-bashi* Mustafa Beg, and was ready to send him to the pope via Rhodes in March. But because of Innocent's crusade maneuver, the Ottoman embassy was delayed four months, until the *Türkenkongress* ended its sessions in Rome on July 30, 1490.

Mustafa's visit to Rome made it possible for Bayazid to establish direct contact with the pope and to disclose the secret practices and pretensions of the grand master. Mustafa's disclosures proved that Peter of Aubusson was concealing his special agreements with the sultan, which were all secret and verbal, and that he had received much more money than was stipulated in the written agreement. Also, in another meeting between Mustafa and Innocent, in the presence of the cardinals, Mustafa's clarifications demonstrated that the grand master's claim that Bayazid II wanted only the Hospitallers to be the guardians of Jem was not true. It became evident that in all his dealings Peter had regarded Jem as his own personal prisoner rather than the prisoner of the order or of any other authority.

In his letter to the pope,[70] Bayazid II said that he was pleased to learn that Jem had been conveyed to Rome, and hoped that Jem was being maintained at the Vatican on the same terms as the grand master had undertaken his custody some years before. The sultan's ambassador declared that if the conditions were accepted, which meant the relinquishment of the idea of using Jem in a crusade against the Ottoman empire, the sultan would keep peace with Christendom. Mustafa himself, in the information he gave to the historian Idrīs,[71] claimed to have made an agreement with the pope, sworn to by an oath as is required in the Christian religion, to the effect that Innocent would keep Jem in custody and not let him attack Bayazid's lands, and that in return the sultan would not harm the pope's country.[72]

In the secret instructions given by the pope to his envoy,[73] his nephew

69. Setton, *The Papacy,* II, 406.

70. The letter was written in Greek; for a Latin version of it see Setton, *The Papacy,* II, 418, note 7.

71. *Hasht Bihisht,* TKS, MS. Hazine 1655.

72. For many years the Ancona area within the papal state was a target of Ottoman raids; see Iorga, *Notes et extraits pour servir à l'histoire des croisades au XVe siècle, 1470-1500,* V (Bucharest, 1915), 157-159, 163-164; Jean Delumeau, "Un Ponte fra Oriente e Occidente: Ancona nel Cinquecento," *Quaderni storici,* XIII (Ancona, 1970), 26-48; Setton, *The Papacy,* II, 397.

73. See the text of this important document in Setton, *The Papacy,* II, 419, note 10, and 421, note 13.

Giorgio Bocciardi, Innocent gave details of how the "pension" or "tribute" should be paid—in Venetian gold ducats every year on December 1. The pope's dispatch of a nuncio to collect Jem's pension can be considered as a positive indication that an agreement, verbal and secret, was reached between the pope and Mustafa.[74]

As a result of the agreement made by Mustafa in Rome in January 1491, the Ottoman Porte believed that a crusade was not likely in the near future, and this belief must have encouraged the Turks to resume their aggressive policy against Hungary. The internal conflicts and Maximilian's invasion of Hungary following Matthias Corvinus's death in 1490 had created extremely favorable conditions for the Ottomans to consolidate their position on the Danube. Inactive for a long time, the frontier forces were impatient to resume their raids into Hungary, which they believed was now incapable of putting up serious resistance. The Hungarian ambassador to the sultan, Emerich Czobor, was unsuccessful in his attempt to renew the truce ending in 1491.[75]

In the same year Bayazid II concluded a peace agreement with Egypt and made large-scale preparations for a campaign on land and sea for 1492. The secret preparations, construction of a large fleet—"eighty sails including thirty galleys"[76]—in particular, gave rise to speculations in Italy about the real target of the Ottomans. Venice and Naples took defensive measures, and both demanded that, for their common safety, the pope use the instrument in his hands, Jem Sultan.[77] By June the Venetians were reassured about the sultan's plans.[78]

Suleiman Pasha, the Ottoman frontier lord at Smederevo, had invited the Hungarian ban of Machva, Nicholas of Ujlak, an opponent of king Ladislas VI (1490–1516), to recognize Ottoman suzerainty, and surrender Belgrade, promising to add to his possessions the Ottoman fortresses of Alaja-Hisar (Krushevats) and Zvornik. Bayazid, who himself did not give much credit to the reportedly favorable disposition of the ban, suggested that, in case the ban changed his mind about surrendering Belgrade, the army should change its destination toward the Adriatic Sea to crush Albanian rebels and subjugate Montenegro. When in Sofia at the head of his army, he received the news that the Hungarian ban had indeed changed his mind, and that the Hungarians were united to resist the sultan, so he set out with the bulk of his

74. See Inalcik, "A Case Study in Renaissance Diplomacy," pp. 209-230.
75. See Ignaz A. Fessler, *Geschichte von Ungarn*, ed. Ernst Klein, III (Leipzig, 1874), 249.
76. According to a Venetian intelligence report of May 7, 1492; see Setton, *The Papacy*, II, 425. In Idrīs: 20 coques, 5 barcas, 80 galleys, and about 200 smaller ships or transports.
77. See Setton, *The Papacy*, II, 425-426.
78. *Ibid.*, II, 426, note 26.

army to invade northern Albania. On the Hungarian front, raids under the frontier begs Mihal-oghlu Ali and Suleiman Pasha, as well as the blockade of Belgrade, were foiled by stiff Hungarian resistance.

Before he left Istanbul for this campaign on April 6, 1492, Bayazid had shown his intention to keep peace with the pope by sending an envoy to Innocent VIII with 40,000 gold ducats along with valuable relics, including the alleged iron head of the lance which pierced Jesus's side at the crucifixion, which Innocent had specifically requested through his ambassador Bocciardi. The delivery of the 40,000 ducats and the generous gifts was indeed a positive indication of Bayazid's appeasement policy toward the pope and of the existence of an agreement between the two parties about the custody of Jem and keeping peace.

Venice, the only maritime power able to curb the Ottomans, chose to avoid conflict, and continued to honor the 1479 agreement. It was undoubtedly Venice among all the western powers which best exploited the Jem situation vis-à-vis the Ottomans. While functioning as an indispensable source of information for the sultan concerning Jem's position in Europe, Venice used the conflict between the Ottomans and Mamluks, nominal suzerains of Cyprus, and in 1489 managed to bring the island under its direct rule.[79] Neither the Mamluks nor the Ottomans, who were at war with each other, were in a position to challenge the Venetian takeover of Cyprus. While the pope was encouraged by the republic to enter into negotiations with the Mamluk sultan for the delivery of Jem, a Venetian ambassador, Peter Diedo, was hurriedly sent to Cairo to explain to the Mamluk sultan Ka'itbay that the Venetian claim of sovereignty over Cyprus was a move taken only to prevent the island's falling into the hands of the Ottomans. Further, Diedo claimed that since the Mamluks lacked a fleet to protect Cyprus, Venetian possession of the island would be beneficial to both parties. Venice agreed to all the conditions which had been imposed by the Mamluks on the Lusignan dynasty of Cyprus, including the payment of a yearly tribute of 8,000 gold ducats.

The loss of Cyprus to Venice was, until 1571, an irreparable setback to the Ottomans in the eastern Mediterranean. Furthermore, Venice strengthened its position on the vital waterway between Avlona and Italy by forcing the Porte to recognize Venetian sovereignty over the island of Zante by an agreement reached on April 22, 1494. It also strengthened the fortifications of Corfu, key point of the Venetian mari-

---

79. See George F. Hill, *A History of Cyprus,* III (Cambridge, Eng., 1948), 735–747. The Ottomans made their first raids on the island after the Venetian takeover.

time empire. Thus a naval operation against Venetian possessions in the Morea and the Adriatic Sea, as well as an Ottoman attack on Italy, was made strategically impractical, and the threat from Avlona, the only important Ottoman base outside the Dardanelles, was greatly reduced.

From 1491 on, however, Venetian-Ottoman relations had become increasingly strained. The rivalry for control of the Albanian and Montenegrin coast, as well as the uneasy situation in the Morea, where Venice controlled the most important ports and naval bases, including Navarino, Modon, Coron, Monemvasia, and Nauplia, were among the factors which created an explosive atmosphere. The arrival of the Ottoman fleet on the Albanian coast and the unexpected invasion of Albania by an army under the command of the sultan himself posed a direct threat to Italy and the Venetian possessions in the Adriatic Sea. A Venetian fleet was sent to Corfu, and the fortifications on the island were substantially strengthened. The landing of an Ottoman frontier force at Gasha, only fifteen miles from Senj itself, caused alarm in Venice, and the republic requested that the pope demand, using the threat of Jem, that the sultan evacuate the fortress.[80] By 1493 the fear of an Ottoman invasion of Italy brought Venice, Milan, and the papacy closer together, and a league was formed on April 25. Venice now actively supported the pope in his crusade effort, and assured him of its full participation. It even requested that the pope mention in the agreement that Jem would be handed over to Venice. The republic promised to open hostilities as soon as Maximilian declared war against the Ottomans, for according to Venetian strategy, Austria had replaced Hungary as the strongest land power in such a crusade.

The resumption of *ghazā* activities by the Ottomans had annoyed not only Venice but also Maximilian, who after the death of Matthias Corvinus in 1490 had emerged as the protector of the Christian lands in Central Europe. Maximilian, as a result of the large-scale attacks of the Ottoman frontier forces against neighboring lands on the Danube, became an ardent advocate of a crusade against the Ottomans.[81] On the eve of the French invasion of Italy, he even favored the idea of Jem's delivery to the Mamluk sultan in exchange for promises to join the Christian league.[82]

---

80. Thuasne, *Djem,* pp. 321–322.

81. Joseph Plösch, "Der St. Georgsritterorden und Maximilians I. Türkenpläne," in *Festschrift Professor Karl Eder zum 70. Geburtstag,* ed. Helmut J. Mezler-Andelberg (Innsbruck, 1959), pp. 33–55.

82. For Maximilian's instructions to his ambassador to Rome, Marquard Breisacher, see Thuasne, *Djem,* pp. 441–446.

Ottoman aggressiveness after 1492 can be explained by several factors. The Ottomans had concluded peace with Egypt in 1491, at the urgent request of the Ḥafṣid ruler Zakarīyā' II of Tunisia, alarmed by the Spanish *reconquista*. The fall of Granada on January 31, 1492, celebrated as a Christian retaliation for the conquest of Constantinople, gave rise to intensification of the *ghazā* spirit in the Islamic world in general. Moreover, following the death of Matthias Corvinus and the ensuing internal confusions in Hungary, the Ottomans hoped to capture Belgrade, thus increasing pressure through the frontier forces' operations against the Austrian and Hungarian dominions.

In 1492, during a large-scale raid in Croatia, heavy Ottoman casualties, reportedly ten thousand men, were suffered when the army fell into a trap near Villach. But the successful raid in 1493 under the able general Ya'kub Pasha, governor of Bosnia, into Slovenia, Croatia, and lower Styria was crowned with his victory at Corbova (Krbava) on September 9.[83] In the following year the large-scale raids continued in Croatia and Transylvania, and Paul Kinizsi, Hungarian frontier commander, made retaliatory raids into Ottoman Serbia. Thus a serious situation had arisen in Central Europe too, about which pope Alexander VI (1492–1503) expressed great concern during his negotiations with the Porte. A truce between Hungary and the Ottomans was concluded only at the beginning of 1495, when Charles VIII's invasion of Italy caused a general reaction against France in Europe. The Ottomans then concentrated their forces against Poland.

In 1494 the pope and the king of Naples had united against the French in an attempt to stop Charles VIII in his invasion of Italy, and had used the threat of Ottoman intervention. Now Alexander's Italian policy was in open conflict with the crusade plan. In response, the pope's adversaries, Charles VIII and the pro-French cardinals, denounced the pope for betraying the interest of Christendom by establishing secret ties with the Ottoman sultan. Indeed, the papal policy of attempting to use Ottoman power against its immediate enemies, while at the same time continuing its crusade plans, is a spectacular example of Renaissance Italy's pragmatic balance-of-power diplomacy.

Threatened by a French invasion, the new king of Naples, Alfonso II (1494–1495), now backed by the pope,[84] hurried his agent Camillo Pandone to Istanbul to request military aid, a contingent of six thou-

---

83. Milan Japunčić, *Kratka povijest Like e Krbave* (Gospic, 1936); Johann C. von Engel, *Staatskunde und Geschichte von Dalmatien, Croatien und Slawonien* (Halle, 1798), pp. 564–567; details in Ottoman sources—Idrīs, Ibn-Kemāl, and the anonymous chroniclers.

84. The pope for his part wrote to Bayazid II that Alfonso's territories should be spared;

sand Ottoman soldiers. He said he was ready to pay them, that is, to employ them as mercenaries, a practice employed for centuries by other Christian governments in Byzantium and the Balkans.

Alexander's envoy, the Genoese Giorgio Bocciardi, was already in Istanbul.[85] Using the excuse that he needed money immediately in order to prepare the resistance against the French invasion of Italy, the pope requested that the year's allowance for Jem be sent in advance. The pope's envoy told Bayazid that the French king planned to capture Jem, take the kingdom of Naples, and from there attack the Ottoman empire.[86] Alexander also called on Bayazid as a true friend to put pressure on Venice to abandon its neutrality and join the resistance against the French.[87] Bayazid reacted promptly and sent three ambassadors to Italy to encourage the papacy, Naples, and Venice to resist Charles VIII. The ambassadors arrived in Italy in November 1494, at the time when Charles entered Florence (November 17). In Venice, on November 21, the Ottoman envoy, who was anxiously watched by the French ambassador Philip of Commines, criticized the republic for its neutrality and threatened to launch an Ottoman attack on Italy should Venice refuse to join the resistance.

On November 20 Kasim Chawush, who had been sent with the money requested for Jem (40,000 gold ducats), accompanied by Bocciardi, was attacked by French partisans near Ancona. All the money and the sultan's letters to the pope were captured.[88] The next day in Florence, the French king, attempting to rival Maximilian, made a declaration before his march to Rome that his purpose in this campaign was to fight the Turk and deliver the holy places, and that his expedition to Naples was only a necessary first step.[89] In order to humiliate Alexander, the seized letters, five in number, together with Bocciardi's testimony about the fulfillment of his embassy, were immediately published in Florence. The document most incriminating for the head of the church was the sultan's letter proposing that the pope assassinate

---

see Thuasne, *Djem,* p. 326. On Ottoman-papal relations in the period 1489–1495 in general, now see Setton, *The Papacy,* II, 381–482.

85. He left Rome in June and stayed in Istanbul till the end of September 1494; see Thuasne, *Djem,* p. 320.

86. In September Charles VIII invited Peter of Aubusson to come to Rouen from Rhodes to give him his expert opinion on the king's plan for a crusade against the Ottomans; see Thuasne, *Djem,* p. 328.

87. *Ibid.,* pp. 325–327; Pastor, *op. cit.,* V, 427.

88. Pietro Ferrato, *Il Marchesato di Mantova e l'imperio ottomano alla fine del secolo XV* (Mantua, 1876); Hans J. Kissling, *Sultan Bajezid's II. Beziehungen zu Markgraf Francesco II. von Gonzaga* (Munich, 1965), p. 40.

89. Paul Durrieu, "La Délivrance de la Grèce projetée en France à la fin du quinzième siècle," *Revue d'histoire diplomatique,* XXVI (1912), 333–351.

Jem and offering 300,000 ducats for the delivery of the corpse to the sultan's men at one of the Ottoman ports.[90] Bayazid also promised that no Christian state would be the subject of attack, and in order to show his good faith, the sultan had even taken an oath on the Koran in the presence of Bocciardi. While there is no doubt about the authenticity of the other letters, written in Greek with the sultan's monogram, this particular one, in Latin, is believed by some scholars to be a forgery.

Deserted by the Christian powers, the pope finally had to agree, on January 15, 1495, to all the points insisted upon by the French king, as preliminary to his plan for the crusade against the Ottomans—the delivery of Jem and free passage through the papal territory for the occupation of the kingdom of Naples. Charles VIII entered Naples in triumph on February 22. Three days later Jem suddenly died, evoking the usual accusations of murder; the basis for the containment of Bayazid died with him. Charles abandoned plans for a crusade against the Turks, and turned his attention to his European enemies, but not until 1499 was Jem's body returned to Bayazid by Frederick, king of Naples (1497–1501).

The anti-French coalition of March 31, 1495, linking pope Alexander VI, emperor Maximilian, Venice, Milan, and Ferdinand and Isabella of Spain in a so-called Holy League against Islam, was followed by the outbreak of the Italian wars, involving western Christendom in a long internal struggle from which sultan Suleiman I, "the Magnificent" (1520–1566), would benefit by expanding his empire into Central Europe. The new pattern of diplomacy in the west, introduced in Renaissance Italy during the fifteenth century, would in the sixteenth bring the Ottoman empire into the European state system in an alliance with France against the Hapsburgs.

After Jem's death the Ottomans continued to be one of the important elements in the balance of power in Italy.[91] They followed with great concern the progress of the negotiations for an alliance between Venice and Louis XII against Milan, for an alliance between the great naval power, Venice, and France might indeed lead to the realization of a crusade. Bayazid took a supportive attitude toward the anti-Venetian dispositions of Naples, Mantua, and Florence, rivals of the republic. In return for Ottoman military assistance—that is, the

90. Thuasne, *Djem,* p. 339, says, "son authenticité ne saurait être en doute"; for a discussion of the problem see Pastor, *op. cit.,* V, 427–428; Kissling, *op. cit.,* p. 42; Setton, *The Papacy,* II, 457.
91. See Setton, *The Papacy,* II, 508–542.

supplying of mercenary forces — these states offered to pay annually 50,000 gold ducats.

The Ottoman government strictly enforced its prohibition of grain export to Venice, which was of vital importance to the republic. Anxious to avoid the outbreak of a war with the Ottoman empire, Venice brought forth several proposals for conciliation. In 1497–1498 the Venetian ambassador Andrew Zanchani offered a yearly tribute of 3,000 gold ducats for the peaceful possession of Cephalonia and Cattaro (Kotor), while agreeing to give up its claims on the territory of Montenegro. However, in confirmation of its sovereignty over the coastal areas in Montenegro, Venice sent out a fleet to the bay of Cattaro in June 1497.[92]

The Ottomans realized throughout the period of the Jem affair that without a strong navy they could not feel secure in their position in the Balkans and exert an effective influence on the course of events in Italy. After 1489 the Ottomans feverishly pursued their efforts to strengthen their fleet. In 1497 they started the construction at the Istanbul shipyards of two huge köke (coques or naves) of 1800 tons, considered to be the largest warships of the time.[93] On June 16, 1499, the Ottoman fleet finally set out from the Dardanelles toward Tenedos (Bozja-ada), causing alarm to spread from Rhodes to Egypt and Venice. After the arrest of all the Venetian subjects in the Ottoman dominions, which meant a declaration of war against Venice, it was learned that the real objective of the expedition was the Morea. While a sizeable force was sent as a distraction against the Venetian possessions in Dalmatia and Albania under Iskender Pasha, the frontier commander in Bosnia, another army under the command of the beglerbeg of Rumelia, Mustafa, was simultaneously directed toward Lepanto.

The success of the military operations depended on the ability of the Ottoman navy to repulse the Venetian sea forces and to complete the encirclement of Lepanto from the sea. The sultan himself, on the summer pastures of Greece, impatiently awaited news of the arrival

92. On the Venetian-Ottoman war of 1499–1503 our main source, Marino Sanudo, *I Diarii,* I–III, ed. Guglielmo Berchet (Venice, 1879), has been exploited by historians since Joseph von Hammer-Purgstall and Zinkeisen, and more recently by Sydney N. Fisher, *The Foreign Relations of Turkey, 1481–1512* (Urbana, 1948), pp. 51–89, and Setton, *The Papacy,* II, 511–514. As for the main contemporary Ottoman sources, Idrīs, Ibn-Kemāl, and the anonymous Tevārīh have been used most recently by Tansel, *op. cit.,* pp. 176–226. Ottoman *ghazānāmes* dealing with each individual campaign are listed by Agâh S. Levend, *Gazavâtnâmeler* (Ankara, 1956), 19–22. A critical use of these sources is still needed.

93. On the sultan's fleet and the two coques, the Ottoman and Venetian sources give details; in particular see von Burski, *op. cit.,* pp. 33–40. The Ottoman fleet, 260 or 300 vessels, was larger than the Venetians' fleet, but the latter had a greater number of warships.

of the fleet. As the Ottomans had no base in the Morea, the fleet experienced great difficulty and delays in getting supplies and reinforcements along the way to Lepanto. At the sea battle, which took place near the island of Prote (Prodano or Barak-ada) on August 12, 1499, the Venetians were not successful in intercepting the Ottoman fleet, and suffered losses. On three separate occasions the Venetian fleet, reinforced by the French and Rhodian squadrons, attempted to block the progress of the Ottoman navy toward the Gulf of Corinth. From each of these skirmishes the Ottomans emerged successful. On August 25, after thirty-three days of constant pursuit by the allied fleet, the Ottoman sea forces eventually reached Lepanto, and the Venetian fleet withdrew to its base at Corfu. On seeing the arrival of the Turkish navy and the withdrawal of the Venetian fleet, the commander of the place surrendered on August 28, 1499. The victory was particularly significant since it was the first time that the Ottoman navy had been able to challenge the Venetians successfully on the open sea.

The fall of Lepanto caused deep concern about the Ottoman danger in Europe. In the autumn of 1499 pope Alexander VI appealed to the European states to unite for a crusade and in May 1500 ordered the collection of a crusading tithe. In his crusading bull of June 1, 1500, he put stress on the danger of the invasion of Italy by the Ottomans, since he said that the Ottomans now had a stronger navy and had started to seize all the strategic ports on the coasts.[94] The Venetians, for their part, were doing their utmost to convince Ladislas, the Hungarian king, to join the crusade and fully to involve the French king Louis XII, their ally (1494–1500), in the Venetian war against the sultan; a French squadron had already coöperated with Venice against the Ottomans in 1499. Venetian diplomats were also trying to induce John Albert, king of Poland (1492–1501), to join the crusade, since as a result of the king's ambitions in Moldavia, Poland had twice been invaded by large armies under the frontier beg Bali Beg in 1498. Bayazid thought he could foil the crusading plans by diplomacy, sending one envoy to pressure the Hungarian king to sign a peace treaty and another one to Rome in February 1500 to try to see the pope.[95]

In the following year, when the Venetians and French made proposals of peace, the Ottomans responded haughtily, demanding the payment of an annual tribute as well as the surrender of Coron, Modon, and Nauplia in the Morea. In the face of these excessive demands, Venice sought to convert its war against the Ottomans into a

---

94. Setton, *The Papacy,* II, 526–527.
95. *Ibid.,* II, 524.

full-scale European crusade. Now the pope undertook serious steps for its preparation among the Christian nations, including Wallachia, Moldavia, and even Russia. On his part, Bayazid encouraged Venice's rivals in Italy and permitted the establishment of a Florentine consul in Istanbul, besides promising a large amount of military aid to Naples—but insisting in return that they surrender Otranto. Thus, after having eliminated the Jem question, the Ottomans unhesitatingly returned once more to the expansionist policy of the time of Mehmed the Conqueror.

In the following campaign season the Ottoman goal was the capture of the fortresses of Modon and Coron in the Morea. As a result of the delays in the arrival of the heavy artillery transported by the ships, the siege of Modon, heavily fortified by the Venetians, was drawn out. Although the siege had begun in March, the fleet did not arrive until July 17; only after its arrival was the fortress surrounded by both land and sea. Despite the intervention of the Venetian fleet Modon fell after a final assault on August 10, 1500. Following the Ottoman capture of Modon, Coron surrendered without resistance a week later.

Upon the arrival of the news of the fall of Modon and Coron, the pope dispatched three legates to European governments to urge them to join the crusade and coöperate in collecting crusading tithes. Alexander was particularly eager to join the French in Naples against king Frederick (1497–1501) for the partition of the kingdom of Naples, so he joined the French-Spanish League on June 29, 1501. The allies declared that the partition was a necessary step to secure peace and unity against the Ottomans, while Frederick put his hopes in the sultan's intervention and aid. Lodovico, duke of Milan, who was also known as the sultan's protégé, tried to break the Venetian-French alliance by promising Venice his good offices for a peace with the Porte.

A crusader fleet composed of French, Venetian, papal, and Spanish ships set out in the fall and easily seized the island of Cephalonia and the fortress of Navarino (on December 3, 1500), which had been in Ottoman hands since August. The Ottomans were on the alert, however, and had assigned Khadim Ali to guard the Morea while Iskender Pasha attacked the Venetian possessions in Dalmatia.

In 1501 Christian fleets individually undertook raids, causing the Ottomans difficulties. The Venetian forces, attempting to land at Avlona, were destroyed on August 15, 1501, by the Ottomans, who then conquered Durazzo. An allied squadron of eighty ships, including forty galleys, landed forces on Lesbos and began the siege of Mytilene, its capital. This move threatened Istanbul itself. The French ships, twenty-six in number, set sail for the Dardanelles to block the arrival of the

Turkish navy, according to an Ottoman report.[96] The Ottomans experienced great difficulties in bringing reinforcements to the besieged from Anatolia. Besides, since it was outside the regular campaign season, it was hard for the Ottomans to mobilize the navy. Eventually, when a land army under Hersek-zade and the beglerbeg of Anatolia reached the shores opposite the island, they found that the enemy had already raised the siege and left the island with their fleet. Meanwhile on May 28 an Ottoman fleet, under the command of the famous seaman Kemāl Re'īs, captured Navarino in coöperation with the land forces. In this battle three galleys and one galleon were captured from the Christians. The Spanish fleet under the command of Gonsalvo Fernando, raiding the Anatolian coasts, inflicted great damage by burning and plundering. Ottoman sources report that in July 1501 the Christian fleet landed at Cheshme near Smyrna and slaughtered the population.[97]

It is noteworthy that in these years the Christian nations attacking the Ottoman homeland and the Dardanelles demonstrated, on the whole, their naval superiority and control of the seas. In 1502 this became even more pronounced. While a Venetian fleet was making a surprise attack against Thessalonica and Makri (on the Thracian coast), the main allied fleet — Rhodes, France, the pope, and Venice — made a landing at the island of Leucas (Santa Maura) and seized the fortress. Under these circumstances the Ottomans were well disposed toward Venetian peace offers. In 1502, while Bayazid threatened Venice with the preparation of a huge armada of five hundred ships, his vizirs mentioned to Valerio Marzello, the Venetian bailie, now released from prison, the advantages of peace. At the same time, the Hungarian ambassador in Istanbul was exerting pressure on the sultan for peace, and a treaty was concluded at Istanbul on August 10, 1503.

An agreement with Venice was drawn up in September 1502 and signed December 14, but due to the Ottoman insistence on the return of Leucas and on payment of a war indemnity, the final ratification act was delayed until August 10, 1503. In the end Venice agreed to return Leucas and, as in the 1479 treaty, to pay an annual sum of 10,000 gold ducats to the Ottomans. In return, the Ottomans agreed to permit the residence of a permanent bailie in the Ottoman capital and to return the goods confiscated during the war, as well as to give up the island of Cephalonia to the Venetians. The Ottomans, however, retained their conquests in the Morea — Lepanto, Modon, and Coron — and Durazzo in Albania.

96. Tansel, *op. cit.*, p. 220 (TKS, no. 5027, facsimile copy, no. 23).
97. Tansel, *op. cit.*, p. 217.

The conclusion of the peace agreement between the Ottomans and the Venetians met with the disapproval of the pope and the rest of the Christian world. Without Venice the crusade could not be continued. Despite the efforts of pope Julius II (1503–1513) Venice remained faithful to the peace with the sultan. At the same time, following in the footsteps of Timur and Uzun Hasan, Shāh Ismāʻīl (1501–1524), the founder of the Ṣafavid dynasty in Persia and a formidable rival of the Ottomans in the east, approached Venice for a joint attack against the Ottoman empire. In 1508 the shah's ambassador to Venice was well received by the doge, Leonard Loredan (1501–1521). While expressing interest in future coöperation with Persia, the doge explained that it was not the time for Venice to break off the peace agreement with the Ottomans.

The next few years were marked by intense diplomatic activity but no major hostilities. The League of Cambrai against Venice (1508) tried to enlist both Hungarian and Ottoman support. The emperor Maximilian I promised Dalmatia to Hungary, but it chose neutrality in Europe and a peace treaty with the Turks, for one year in 1510 and then for five years in 1512. Maximilian declared himself, at the diet of Augsburg in the spring of 1510, the leader of still another crusade against the Turks, but secretly attempted to secure joint action with the Ottomans against Venice, which in turn requested Turkish frontier forces for use as mercenary troops.[98] Neither side achieved its objective.

Paralyzed by a struggle for the succession among the Ottoman princes, and by a terrible insurrection in 1511 of the Turcoman Kîzîlbash heretics in Anatolia, the sixty-four-year-old sultan Bayazid II had to pursue a peace policy in Europe, making sure that none of the rival powers emerged strong enough to launch a crusade. Shāh Ismāʻīl of Persia threatened his eastern borders, and, as spiritual leader of a powerful ṣūfī order, helped incite the Turcoman revolt. Bayazid was thus fully occupied in defending the empire and developing its commercial and economic strength. Having established Ottoman naval power in the Aegean and eastern Mediterranean, he supported the "Moriscos" of Spain and the Moslems of North Africa against Spanish attacks, sending sea-ghazis who eventually became the Barbary corsairs.[99]

In the Indian Ocean the Portuguese not only terrorized Moslem merchants and pilgrims, but entered the Red Sea and threatened Mecca and Medina. A Mamluk fleet was destroyed by the Portuguese in 1509

---

98. Babinger, "Kaiser Maximilian," pp. 206, 221, 223–233.

99. See Andrew Hess, "The Moriscos: an Ottoman Fifth Column in Sixteenth-Century Spain," *American Historical Review,* LXXIV (1968), 1–25; *idem, The Forgotten Frontier: a History of the Sixteenth-Century Ibero-African Frontier* (Chicago and London, 1978); and James T. Monroe, "A Curious Morisco Appeal to the Ottoman Empire," *Al-Andalus,* XXXI (1966), 281–303.

at Diu, off the Gujerat coast, and the Egyptian sultan Kansuh al-Ghūrī had to accept aid and experts from his Ottoman foes to build a new fleet at Suez to drive the Portuguese out of the Red Sea.[100]

Bayazid's orderly administration, resembling that of his grandfather, Murad II, rather than that of his father, Mehmed II, earned him the sobriquet 'Adlī, "the Law-Abiding", in contrast to his father's "the Conqueror". His son Selim I "the Grim" (Yavuz), despising Bayazid's pacific policies, won the janissaries' support and deposed his father in April 1512. By massive military campaigns he defeated the Ṣafavids of Persia in 1514 and destroyed the Mamluk state in 1516-1517,[101] doubling the territory and financial resources of the empire by annexing eastern Anatolia, Syria, Egypt, and the Hejaz. He thus won the distinction of being the protector of the holy cities of Mecca and Medina, and assigned his admiral Selman in 1517 to defend Jidda against a Portuguese fleet. Selim completed the transformation from a frontier state to a powerful empire, easily a match for the Holy Roman empire of Maximilian I (1493-1519) and Charles V (1519-1556). During his brief reign he paid little attention to Europe, however, and thus does not figure importantly in crusades history.

At his premature death in 1520 he was succeeded by his son Suleiman I "the Magnificent" (or "the Law-Giver", Kanuni; d. 1566), who in true ghazi fashion inaugurated his reign with the conquests of Belgrade (August 30, 1521) and Rhodes[102] (December 20, 1522). He was to challenge Charles V successfully both in central Europe and on the Mediterranean, and to consolidate the Ottoman position in the European state system as a secret ally of Francis I of France against the Hapsburgs. Charles would attempt to revive the crusade against both Suleiman and Francis, but this had become a different world, in which the crusading idea was anachronistic and irrelevant, long before its final failure in 1556. The capture of Belgrade and Rhodes may be considered either as the final victories of the Islamic counter-crusade or as the start of a new phase of the continuing struggle between the Ottoman empire and western Christendom.

100. See Inalcik's review of Ayalon, *Gunpowder and Firearms in the Mamluk Kingdom,* in *Belleten,* XVII (1956), 501-505.

101. See Mustafa M. Ziada, "The Mamluk Sultans, 1291-1517," in volume III of the present work, chapter XIV; Inalcik, "The Rise of the Ottoman Empire," in *The Cambridge History of Islam,* vol. I, *The Central Islamic Lands,* ed. Peter M. Holt, Ann K. S. Lambton, and Bernard Lewis (Cambridge, Eng., 1970), pp. 314-319.

102. See Ettore Rossi, "The Hospitallers at Rhodes, 1421-1523," in volume III of the present work, pp. 332-339; Inalcik, "The Heyday and Decline of the Ottoman Empire," in *The Cambridge History of Islam,* I, 324; and Setton, *The Papacy and the Levant,* vol. III (Philadelphia, 1984).

X

CRUSADER COINAGE
WITH GREEK OR LATIN
INSCRIPTIONS

Throughout the crusades the great eastward movement of armies and pilgrims was accompanied by a heavy and persistent flow of money. This we can judge from the ill-recorded evidence of hoards deposited in the area of the crusading states, and, more generally, from the profound economic and monetary changes in both western Europe and the Levant, of which the crusades were the apparent cause. Each of the crusader states in Syria and Palestine issued in due course its own currency—three of the four on a substantial scale—and other minor and more ephemeral currencies were issued by Frankish authorities in the area from time to time. The direct monetary consequences of the crusades, therefore, were not negligible.

On the other hand, the princes who led the First Crusade came from lands in which money did not yet play a major economic role, a fact reflected in contemporary assessments of the importance of things. Financial matters do not therefore figure largely in the accounts of the

---

The principal work on the coinage of the crusades is Gustave Schlumberger, *Numismatique de l'Orient latin* (Paris, 1878–1882; repr. Graz, 1954). This was founded upon and superseded the pioneering work of F. de Saulcy, *Numismatique des croisades* (Paris, 1847). Schlumberger's work is one of the great classics of nineteenth-century numismatic scholarship, and it is still the indispensable handbook for the study of the coins of the crusades, but two factors have made it out of date. The progress of research in Byzantine and related numismatics, particularly in the later period, has resulted in the removal to the Byzantine sphere of several coins which Schlumberger attributed to the Franks; and the discovery in recent years of much new material (the result of growing world-wide interest and trade in coins) has made coins abundant which Schlumberger thought rare and has produced some altogether new ones.

Schlumberger's book covered the whole of the Latin east. If this chapter were to cover the monetary background of every Christian state to which attention has been given in the volumes of *A History of the Crusades,* it would have had to go even further to treat the coinages, for example, of the emerging Spanish kingdoms or of the Teutonic Knights in the Baltic. Even to have covered the coins of the Latin east in the generally accepted sense, including Lusignan Cyprus, the knights of the Hospital at Rhodes, the Genoese in Chios and Lesbos (Mytilene),

chroniclers. Since, moreover, no mint records of the crusader states are extant, we are largely dependent upon the numismatic evidence, on the surviving coins and the circumstances of their survival, for our knowledge of the circulating medium among the crusaders, and how it changed in the two centuries from the Council of Clermont to the fall of Acre.

There were, as far as we know, no coins struck by the crusaders while they were actually on their way to Jerusalem. Armies have a constant need for money, but they rarely mint it for themselves, and never do so when they are on the move. The money that the crusaders had, therefore, they either took with them, often exchanging it on the way, or received by way of subsidy from the Byzantine emperor, or looted, or acquired in the form of ransom payments.

A. *The Money They Took with Them*

Before they started on the expedition, the princes made estimates of the traveling money which they would need.[1] Peter the Hermit col-

---

and the Franks in Greece and the Latin empire of Constantinople, would have involved a complete revision of Schlumberger and the writing of a work on a scale comparable to that of the original.

It has been thought best therefore to limit the scope of this chapter to the money and coinage of the crusaders in the strictest sense, namely to the Latin states in Syria and Palestine from the First Crusade until 1291. This leaves scope for a brief but reasonably complete and illustrated catalogue of the coins known to have been minted by the Franks in those states.

For information outside the scope of this chapter, but relating to the monetary background of areas treated in volumes II and III of *A History of the Crusades,* the reader is referred to Jacques Yvon's contributions on the Latin Orient, published in the second volumes of the International Numismatic Commission's *Survey of Numismatic Research 1960–65* (Copenhagen, 1967) and *1966–71* (New York, 1973).

Important public collections of coins of the crusaders are to be found in the Cabinet des Médailles of the Bibliothèque nationale, Paris, in the Department of Coins and Medals of the British Museum, London, in the American Numismatic Society, New York, and in the Israel Museum, Jerusalem.

The author is grateful to those curators of public collections and private owners who have allowed him access to their cabinets. He particularly wishes to thank Mr. John J. Slocum, who has given him not only that privilege, but generous advice and hospitality as well. However, it must also be recorded that there is important material which is so far unpublished and which the author has not seen. In the present state of crusader numismatics many of the attributions in the catalogue may have to be revised in the light of fuller knowledge. For information on some sizeable financial transactions during the Third Crusade the reader is referred to the "Acre Archive" in Sotheby's Sale Catalogue of Western Manuscripts, London, 23rd June 1987, pp. 28–35, which was published too late to be incorporated in this chapter.

1. William of Tyre, *Historia rerum in partibus transmarinis gestarum,* I, xvii (*RHC, Occ.,*

lected gifts from the devout princes of Christendom to minister to the necessities of the poor and needy during their pilgrimage. The wagon containing this entire treasure was carried off by Bulgarian raiders as the pilgrims were on their way to Constantinople.[2]

Raymond of Aguilers gives a list of the coins that the crusaders principally used among themselves: "Pictavini, Cartenses, Mansei, Lucenses, Valentinenses, Mergoresi et duo Pogesi pro uno istorum"[3] — the billon deniers of Poitou, of Chartres, of Le Mans, of Lucca, of Valence, of Melgueil, and of Le Puy, these last being worth one half the value of the others.

It is instructive to compare this list, which accords, so far as it goes, with the western coins of the late eleventh and early twelfth centuries which turn up in stray finds in Syria and Palestine, with the roll of the leaders of the crusade and the coins which they and their followers used in their homelands. Although there were no kings among them, most of the leaders from France exercised the *jus monetae*. Within the empire this right was not so widely distributed at that time, but the leaders from Germany and Italy also were closely connected with those who did exercise rights of coinage.

These then are the coinages which the leaders issued or with which they were associated at home:

Godfrey of Bouillon and Baldwin of Boulogne: The dukes of Lower Lorraine as such did not issue coins, nor did Godfrey strike any for his territory of Bouillon. In France, however, their father Eustace II struck a scanty coinage as count of Boulogne, and possibly their brother Eustace III did also.[4]

Bohemond, Tancred, and Richard of the Principate: None of these princes issued coins in southern Italy. However, Robert Guiscard, father of Bohemond and grandfather of Tancred, and Roger Borsa, Bohemond's half-brother, issued extensive coinages in copper and some gold coins also. Their uncle, Roger, struck a similar coinage as count of Sicily.[5]

I, 47). William's statement may amount to no more than an intelligent man's belief that no one would go on a crusade without a little forethought about the probable cost. Doubtless most crusaders' forward financial planning consisted in laying hands on whatever cash they could get.

2. *Ibid.,* I, xxi (*RHC, Occ.,* I, 55).

3. Raymond of Aguilers, *Historia Francorum qui ceperunt Iherusalem,* xxvi (*RHC, Occ.,* III, 278). Another MS reads: ". . . Manses, Luccenses, Valanzani, Melgorienses, . . .".

4. Faustin Poey d'Avant, *Les Monnaies féodales de France* (Paris, 1858–1862), III, 372.

5. Giulio Sambon, *Repertorio generale delle monete coniate in Italia . . .* (Paris, 1912), IV, II, III.

Raymond of Toulouse: Raymond passed as the richest of the crusading leaders. The actual coinage of Toulouse in the name of Raymond himself was not very extensive, but his overlordship included many other mints. The most important of these was undoubtedly that where he exercised the right of coinage as count of Melgueil.[6] Two who took service with Raymond were also possessors of mints of their own. Gaston of Béarn inherited from his father Centulle the mint of Morlaas, which struck (always in the name of Centulle) the most prolific currency in Gascony.[7] Gerard of Roussillon was the heir to a somewhat sparser coinage. He succeeded to the county of Roussillon in 1102, and deniers are extant bearing his name; these are mentioned by the name of *rosellos* in a charter of 1112.[8]

Robert of Flanders: The coinage of the counts of Flanders dates from the end of the tenth century, but it was not yet of great extent or importance by 1100. The various coins of Robert himself, and those struck by his countess Clementia of Burgundy as regent during his absence on the crusade, are known in only a few examples.[9]

Robert of Normandy: The coinage of Normandy had much degenerated by 1100. The light and much-debased Norman denier was of only local importance by that time, and was supplemented even in Normandy by the heavier and more highly valued deniers of neighboring Maine and Anjou.[10]

Adhémar of Monteil, Bishop of Le Puy: The anonymous coinage of Le Puy was extensively used in Auvergne. These coins, which were of low intrinsic value, passed at one half the value of the denier of Melgueil. The vernacular expression *pougeoise* came in due course to signify a fractional coin, both among the Franks in the east and in the kingdom of France.[11]

---

6. *Ibid.,* II, 286. The coinage of Melgueil remained in the hands of the counts of Toulouse until 1215, when as a consequence of the Albigensian Crusade it was granted by Innocent III to the bishop of Maguelonne.

7. *Ibid.,* II, 160.

8. A. Engel and Raymond Serrure, *Traité de numismatique du moyen âge* (Paris, 1894), II, 447.

9. Serrure, "Une Page de l'histoire monétaire de la Flandre (1070–1100)," *Revue belge de numismatique* (1880), p. 188; W. Engels, "Der Fund von Liesborn i. Westf.," *Zeitschrift für Numismatik,* XXV (1906), 227–244; Claude Richebé, *Les Monnaies féodales d'Artois du Xe au début du XIVe siècle* (Paris, 1963), pp. 42–45, 169–170.

10. Poey d'Avant, *op. cit.,* I, 26–32. For the coins of Anjou and Maine see *ibid.,* I, 199–216.

11. *Ibid.,* I, 337–342.

Hugh of Vermandois: The single specimen of a denier in the name of Hugh is of doubtful authenticity. There is, however, a series of anonymous deniers of Saint Quentin, the principal city of the county of Vermandois, some of which date from this period;[12] this was a coinage of moderate importance. Hugh's brother, Philip I, issued a fairly extensive coinage as king of France.[13]

Stephen of Blois: The coins of Stephen's county of Chartres and the related issue of his county of Blois formed one of the most important currencies in France at the end of the eleventh century.[14]

Baldwin of Hainault: No coins are known for Baldwin as count of Hainault, but he struck a few pieces at Saint Omer, as claimant to the county of Flanders. They are as rare as the coins of Robert.

The coins therefore which Raymond of Aguilers mentions correlate tolerably well with the coinage traditions of the leaders of the crusade. The coins in his list which remain to be accounted for are the coins of Poitou, of Lucca, and of Valence.

The deniers of Poitou were one of the most plentiful coinages of France; the Poitevin mint of Melle was supplied from Carolingian times by the silver mine there.[15] The Poitevin connection with the crusade was always strong, and of course the count of Poitou, William of Aquitaine, was a leader of the abortive crusade of 1101.

The deniers of Valence were, with those of Vienne (also frequently found in Syria and Palestine), one of the principal currencies of the Rhône valley.[16] Valence lay on the main route which would be followed

---

12. *Ibid.,* III, 383–384.

13. Jean Lafaurie, *Les Monnaies des rois de France* (Paris, 1951), pp. 6–11.

14. Poey d'Avant, *op. cit.,* I, 229–241.

15. *Ibid.,* II, 1–30.

16. *Ibid.,* III, 7. For the coins of Vienne see *ibid.,* III, 36. The association of deniers of Valence with the Latin east is discussed in D. M. Metcalf, "Coins of Lucca, Valence, and Antioch," *Hamburger Beiträge zur Numismatik* (1968–1969; published 1972), pp. 433–470. Deniers of Valence were also present in the Barbarossa hoard recently discovered in Cilicia; see Wolfgang Hess in *Münchner Jahrbuch der bildenden Kunst,* 3rd ser., XXXV (1984), 252–254. Information on this hoard, which was probably deposited by German crusaders accompanying the emperor Frederick Barbarossa on the Third Crusade, has become available too late for inclusion in the text of this chapter. It will be published in detail by Dr. Ulrich Klein of the Württembergisches Landesmuseum, Stuttgart.

The biggest single element in the hoard, which is entirely of silver, is made up of pfennigs of Philip of Heinsberg, archbishop of Cologne, and coins of similar standard struck by Frederick himself at his mint at Aachen. A significant portion consists of episcopal issues from Strassburg and the Lotharingian bishoprics of Metz and Toul, and pfennigs struck at the archbishop of Salzburg's mint at Friesach in the eastern Alps. There is a useful contribution from the Swaby any pilgrim of northern or central France making the pilgrimage by way of Provence or Italy. It will be recalled also that the cleric Bernard of Valence became the first Latin patriarch of Antioch.

The mint of Lucca was one of the four imperial mints of Italy, and the only one situated in Tuscany. Its significance for the crusades is that it supplied the coinage for Pisa, which under the direction of its archbishop Daimbert was the first of the Italian maritime communes to give naval and economic support to the movement.

Briefly therefore it can be stated that of the coins mentioned by Raymond of Aguilers, the *pictavini* were contributed originally by the Poitevins, the *cartenses* by the followers of Stephen, the *mansei* by Robert's Normans, the *lucenses* came with the fleet, the *valentinenses* and *pogesi* with the Provençals and those who traveled down the Rhône valley, and the *mergoresi* were originally brought by the followers of Raymond of Saint Gilles. All are found in Palestine and Syria.[17]

There is nothing in the chronicler's list to represent the home coinage of the Lorrainers and the Flemings on the one hand or of Bohemond's Normans on the other. To some extent this may reflect the fact that Raymond of Aguilers was with the Provençal army, but the surviving coins confirm his account. It must be assumed that these others brought less of their own money with them, which would have made them more heavily dependent upon subsidies. In Bohemond's case we may note that his kinsfolk's coinage in southern Italy was mostly copper, which does not usually travel, being reckoned rather worthless far from home.

What the Normans did bring with them, however, was a generation's experience of Byzantine money and minting practice in the outer marches of the empire. Moving in effect from one Byzantine frontier area to another, at Antioch and Edessa (where they were an important element in count Baldwin's following) they were quick to resume the striking of coins on their own. Their coins, though of the local pattern, were yet not so different from those to which they were accustomed in Italy.

---

bian abbeys and bishoprics, and from Würzburg, as well as English sterlings and coins from France, Italy, Cilician Armenia, and Antioch.

17. Dorothy H. Cox, *The Tripolis Hoard of French Seignorial and Crusaders' Coins* (ANS, NNM, no. 59; New York, 1933), pp. 34–48; Metcalf, "Some Hoards and Stray Finds from the Latin East," ANS, *Museum Notes,* XX (1975), 141–152.

B. *The Money They Encountered en Route*

The specie which the crusaders first met in quantity was Byzantine coin acquired in the form of subsidies. William of Tyre records[18] how at Constantinople duke Godfrey, one of the leaders less well provided with funds from his own land, received from the emperor Alexius as much gold coin as two men could carry on their shoulders and ten measures "de aereis denariis". Fulcher of Chartres, in what may be another account of the same episode, tells us that after the capture of Nicaea "jussit imperator de auro suo et argento atque palliis proceribus nostris dari, peditibus quoque distribui fecit de nummis suis aeneis, quos vocant tartarones."[19] These coins were the copper *tetartera,* which were placed at the lowest point in the scale of Alexius's newly reformed coinage.

The monetary reforms of Alexius have only recently been elucidated.[20] His coinage embodied a far more sophisticated monetary system than any which the Franks, except probably Bohemond's Normans, had experienced before. It was based upon the gold hyperpyron, 20½ carats fine. The fractional pieces were an electrum coin, valued at one third of the gold, and a billon piece, the *aspron trachy* or *staminon,* valued at one forty-eighth. The copper *tetartera* were in the system below these three, but their precise value in relation to them has not been established. In the frontier areas, some of the pre-reform coinage of earlier emperors, which included gold coins substantially less pure than the hyperpyron, was still in circulation along with the reformed coinage.

In describing the cost of living during the siege of Antioch in the winter of 1097–1098, the anonymous historian of the First Crusade mentions that the price of a donkey was eight *purpurati* (hyperpyra) "qui appreciabantur cxx solidis denariorum".[21] This quotation of an exchange rate which is equivalent to 180 deniers for one hyperpyron, or to 3¾ deniers for one billon *aspron trachy,* implies that an exchange market was already well established. However, the first actual record of an exchange transaction between crusaders and Byzantines dates not from the First Crusade but from the Second. Odo of Deuil records[22]

---

18. William of Tyre, II, xii (*RHC, Occ.,* I, 89).

19. Fulcher of Chartres, *Historia Hierosolymitana,* I, x (ed. Heinrich Hagenmeyer, Heidelberg, 1913; *RHC, Occ.,* III, 333–334).

20. Michael F. Hendy, *Coinage and Money in the Byzantine Empire 1081–1261* (Dumbarton Oaks, 1969).

21. *Gesta Francorum et aliorum Hierosolimitanorum,* ed. Louis Bréhier (Paris, 1924), p. 76.

22. Odo of Deuil, *De profectione Ludovici VII in Orientem,* III, IV, ed. and tr. Virginia G. Berry (*CURC,* 42; New York, 1948), pp. 40, 66.

the bewilderment of his economically untutored countrymen when they were first confronted by the intricacies of the Byzantine coinage. He also suggests that they were given a very bad rate of exchange against their own money. Indeed it would not be surprising if the Franks were cheated from time to time by the Byzantine money-changers. However, when in 1147, under the walls of Constantinople, the pilgrims received one copper *staminon* (by which name Odo must intend the billon *aspron trachy* of the reformed coinage) for two of their deniers, instead of having to give five deniers as they had done at the imperial frontier and as they were to do again as they crossed Anatolia, it appears that they were treated by the emperor Manuel to an especially favorable rate. In any case they got a better bargain than their grandfathers had at Antioch fifty years earlier.

Underlying Odo's complaint, which is couched in rather obscure language as if the chronicler himself did not really grasp what the issue was, there appears to have been a complete misapprehension on the part of the Franks as to the nature of Byzantine subsidiary coinage. Their own deniers were worth their intrinsic value and no more. The Byzantine billon on the other hand was worth one forty-eighth of a hyperpyron not intrinsically but because a powerful government was to maintain that as its value, which was a much more advanced monetary concept.

At least no misunderstanding arose in the valuation of gold, to the use of which the crusaders took readily, although gold coin was not generally available in their homelands. As they moved east they encountered Byzantine gold of both the reformed and the pre-reform coinage. In William of Tyre's story of count Baldwin II of Edessa, who pledged his beard and tricked his Armenian father-in-law, Toros, into redeeming it for him, the ransom price is stated in gold *michaelitae,* the debased gold *nomismata* struck by Michael VII.[23] Later, when Baldwin as king of Jerusalem was ransomed for a sum of one hundred thousand of these coins, William described them as the principal currency of those regions.[24] It was only much later, when Baldwin III was married to Theodora, niece of the emperor Manuel, in 1158, that William mentioned the hyperpyron as making up part of the bride's dowry.[25]

The coinage of the Saracens when the Franks first encountered it was in as much disarray as their political system. Like the coinage of the Byzantine empire it was based upon gold, the silver having been drawn away, presumably by the high value given to it in Latin Christen-

23. William of Tyre, XI, xi (*RHC, Occ.,* I, 471).

24. *Ibid.,* XIII, xv (*RHC, Occ.,* I, 576); Cécile Morrisson, "Le Michaèlaton et les monnaies à la fin de XIe siècle," *Travaux et mémoires,* III (1968), 369–374.

25. William of Tyre, XVIII, xxii (*RHC, Occ.,* I, 857).

dom, as much as a century before the First Crusade.[26] The most plentiful Islamic gold coinage in the area consisted of dinars struck by the eleventh-century Fāṭimid caliphs at mints in Egypt and Syria.[27] The Franks became accustomed to give and to receive these coins, to which they gave the name *besanti sarracenati,* in ransom payments and tribute. In due course they themselves came to strike imitations of them.

The only coins struck by the emirs and atabegs with whom the crusaders first came into immediate contact were copper pieces for local circulation.[28] There is no evidence that the Franks used these in their own transactions, but it is to be noted that the very first coins that the Frankish leaders struck in their own names were likewise copper coins of low value for local use.

C. The Coins Minted by the Crusaders

The actual minting of coins by the crusaders themselves was instituted shortly after their settlement in the east and continued, with some intermission, until their expulsion nearly two centuries later. Their minting operations may be divided broadly into three phases. The first phase, a period of crude quasi-Byzantine copper coinage in the northern states of Edessa and Antioch, began a year or two after the First Crusade and ended soon after the eclipse of the Normans at the "field of blood" in 1119. The second phase, a period of typically Frankish denier coinage at Antioch, Jerusalem, and Tripoli, ran from about 1140 until after Hattin. The last phase, characterized by new monetary experiments and some proliferation of minting authorities, lasted from the Frankish revival until the extinction of the Latin settlements in 1291.

THE FIRST PHASE

The coinage of the first phase is limited to Edessa and Antioch. All the coins are made of copper and are struck on thick flans. They run

26. Andrew M. Watson, "Back to Gold—and Silver," *Economic History Review,* 2nd ser., XX (1967), 1 ff.

27. See George C. Miles, *Fatimid coins in the Collection of the University Museum, Philadelphia, and the American Numismatic Society* (ANS, NNM, no. 121; New York, 1951).

28. Stanley Lane-Poole, *Coins of the Urtuki Turkumans* (International Numismata Orientalia; London, 1875); Paul Casanova, "Numismatique des Danichmendites," *Rev. numis.,* 3rd ser., XII (1894), 307–321, 433–460; XIII (1895), 389–402; and XIV (1896), 210–230, 306–315.

in series, starting with clean blanks, but thereafter overstruck one on the other. The inscriptions are in Greek at Edessa, in Greek or Latin at Antioch. It appears that the weight of the coins was not particularly important, since the weight range within each issue is very large.

We cannot tell which were the very first coins minted in the name of the leaders of the crusade. There are coins of both Edessa and Antioch which, on numismatic evidence, must date from before 1104. From their general aspect it seems clear that they were struck more for the use of the native population than for the Franks.

Edessa, of course, was not conquered from the Turks, but was taken over from its Armenian ruler by Baldwin of Boulogne's coup d'état. Its inhabitants, according to William of Tyre, were native "Chaldaeans" and peaceful Armenians ignorant of the use of arms and familiar only with the business of trading.[29] The Armenian rulers of the city had not, however, struck coins.

We cannot tell whether the decision to issue coins there was taken by Baldwin I or Baldwin II. Documentary evidence is lacking. The numismatic evidence, so far as it goes, would tend to put the initial date after rather than before 1100, the year when Baldwin I departed to become king of Jerusalem. Yet the decision to institute a coinage accords rather well with what we know of Baldwin I — his thirst for sovereignty and his single-minded intention to acquire and efficiently to administer a state in the Levant. Since Edessa, of all the crusading states, was the least dislocated by the shocks of the crusade, it is not impossible to envisage the issue of coins there before 1100.

There is nothing very Frankish about the first Edessene coins.[30] By numismatic convention they are called *folles,* by analogy with the Byzantine copper coins of the period immediately before Alexius's reform, which they much resemble. In weight, in general aspect, and presumably in purpose, though not in type, they also resemble copper coins issued at this time by Turkish atabegs and emirs ruling neighboring districts of northern Syria. They weigh mostly 6½ to 8½ grams, and they proceed in a succession of issues, each overstruck on a previous one.

This practice of overstriking was normal in the Byzantine empire at this epoch, and is also found in the copper coinage struck by Bohemond's kin in southern Italy.[31] We do not know the reason for it.

---

29. William of Tyre, XVI, iv (*RHC, Occ.,* I, 708).

30. John Porteous, "The Early Coinage of the Counts of Edessa," *Numis. Chr.,* 7th ser., XV (1975), 169–182.

31. Philip Grierson, "The Salernitan Coinage of Gisulf II (1052–1077) and Robert Guiscard (1077–1085)," *Papers of the British School at Rome,* XXIV (new ser., XI; 1956).

It cannot be because there were no facilities for making fresh blanks, since in the case of Edessa, at least, the first coins of each series are struck on fresh blanks. Presumably it was an economy measure, since the value of the coins was not high and the issues were frequently changed. From our point of view, the advantage of the practice is that it enables us to set out the issues in the correct order and to date them approximately, but the coins are hard to decipher, and the overstrikes make the later issues quite hideous.

There were at least seven issues (nos. 1–7) and probably more in the early years, though some of these are represented now by only a handful of surviving specimens. The first (pl. I, no. 1) was struck on clean blanks and in a wholly Byzantine style. It is identified as a coin of Baldwin by the reverse inscription — BΛΔN in the angles of a jeweled cross.

There follow one more issue in Baldwin's name (pl. I, no. 2) and three (pl. I, nos. 3–5) in the name of Richard of the Principate, Bohemond's cousin, who was regent of Edessa from 1104 to 1108 when Baldwin II was a prisoner of the Turks. The inscriptions are in Greek. Baldwin's coin reads XBBK in the angles of a cross, initials which may be taken to signify Χρίστε βοήθει Βαλδουίνῳ κώμη. Richard's legends are all variations on the theme Κύριε βοήθει Ρικάρδῳ, Lord save Richard. A touch of Frankishness begins to creep in with the design of Richard's third (pl. I, no. 5): the circular inscription around the cross is common on western deniers of this period but unknown on the Byzantine coinage.

The next issue (pl. II, no. 6) is anonymous. It could be Richard's or Baldwin II's. The type, however, is interesting: it is the first appearance on the crusader coinage of an armed knight. The only precedent for this figure, so characteristic in our eyes of these military states, and destined to become, in one aspect or another, one of the classic types of the Latin coinage in Syria, is a coin of count Roger of Sicily[32] which dates from about twenty years before. Richard's followers in Edessa would have been familiar with the Sicilian coin, and the adoption of this type at Edessa may be ascribed to Italo-Norman influence.

Incidentally, what little we know of Richard (his rapacity toward his Edessene subjects is almost all that is recorded of him)[33] gives us a possible clue as to the purpose of these frequent type changes, three at least in three years. It seems likely that they were some kind of reve-

---

32. Sambon, *op. cit.,* no. 876.
33. Matthew of Edessa, *Chronicle* (*RHC, Arm.,* I, 80–81).

nue device: we may suppose that coin was called in at intervals and a fee charged for its reissue in a new form.

About the year 1110 the last of the large Edessene coins was struck, a piece (pl. II, no. 7) reverting to a more Byzantine style with a jeweled cross on the obverse and count Baldwin's name and title in Greek written across the field on the reverse. There was then a change. The weight of the Edessene coinage was reduced to an average 4½ grams and a new series was begun on clean blanks. All these issues (pl. II, nos. 8–11) bear the name Baldwin and the image of the count in armor. The first and most sophisticated shows the count holding a cross in his hand and the inscription ΒΑΛΔΟΥΙΝΟC ΔΟΥΛΟ CTAΫ, Baldwin servant of the Cross. The later issues, all overstruck, are somewhat cruder. On none of them does Baldwin have a territorial title, but they must come from Edessa, since their source is always northern Syrian. The weight reduction may reflect the ruler's desire to bring his coinage into line with that of Antioch.

There are no coins which can be ascribed with any certainty to the counts Joscelin. The last coins of Edessa, as our knowledge stands at present, belong to a curious issue (pl. II, no. 12) nearly all the surviving specimens of which appear to come from a single hoard, as yet unpublished. They are of copper, but may be alloyed with a little silver. They apparently come in two distinct weights, though the standard of each is so erratic as to admit the possibility that all are of one denomination. The inscription is in Greek: CTAYPOC NIKA, the Cross conquers, and ΒΑΛΔΟΥΙΝ XOMI, count Baldwin. They are struck with neat dies, but on blanks which are often rough and some of which may bear traces of a Kufic inscription.

In most aspects, especially in their Greek inscription, their absence of territorial title, and their erratic weight standard, these still belong to the first phase of crusading coinage. In other respects, however — in the thin fabric of the lighter ones, the circular inscription around the cross, and the possible presence of silver in the alloy — they look forward to coins of the second phase. With one possible exception, they are the only Edessene coins to point to this transition.

The exception, a doubtful one, is represented by a single unprovenanced and broken coin (pl. II, no. 13). This, although not certainly part of the Edessene series, is probably best considered here, since it appears to link the last coinage of count Baldwin with the period after he became king of Jerusalem. It is a billon coin and it has a Greek inscription on either side: + ΒΑΛΔΟΥΙΝΟC ΔΕCΠΟΤΗC in five lines and $\overline{IX}$ $\overline{XC}$ NIKA disposed in the angles of a cross. The title clearly points to a date after Baldwin's becoming king of Jerusalem, but the fabric and the language of the inscription suggest that it should be ascribed to one of the northern Frankish states. Metcalf and Willis[34] classify the piece without comment as a coin of Antioch struck by Baldwin during his years of regency in the principality (1119–1126). However, the coin may equally well belong to Edessa, to the eighteen-month interval between Baldwin's consecration as king at Easter 1118 and his investiture of Joscelin with that county in the late summer of 1119. That the coin was struck in the kingdom of Jerusalem is possible but unlikely.[35]

In considering the coinage of Antioch we must recall that the city on the Orontes, unlike Edessa, was once an imperial mint. However, as there is no evidence that the mint was reopened when the city was recovered by Byzantine arms in 969, the issue of coinage there by the crusaders is probably independent of that earlier tradition and should be interpreted as an assertion of sovereignty on their part. The Antioch mint seems never to have been a bone of contention between the prince and the emperor in the long dispute about the prince's status and Byzantine overlordship. It was not, however, until well into the reign of Roger of Salerno that the coins gave the ruler any title; before that their only territorial reference was the image of St. Peter, first patriarch and patron saint of Antioch, which appeared on five of the first eleven issues.

All the early copper coins of Antioch are of the light but erratic weight standard of the later armed-man coins of Edessa. There are some rare issues among them, but as a rule they are more plentiful than those of Edessa. The order of the principal issues is reasonably clear and is established by the pattern of overstrikes. Four issues of Tancred (nos. 16–19) as regent for Bohemond I are followed by three of Roger (nos. 20–22) and maybe two of Bohemond II (nos. 15?, 23).

The first of Tancred's coins (pl. III, no. 16) shows a bust of St. Peter, neatly engraved, and a reverse inscription in Greek, Lord save thy servant Tancred. Such use of the local patron saint is found in the provincial coinage of the Byzantine empire; St. Theodore appears on the

---

34. Metcalf and P. J. Willis, "Crusader Coins in the Museum of the Order of St. John, at Clerkenwell," *Numis. Chr.,* 7th ser., XIX (1979), 136.

35. The inscription allows the hypothesis that this is a coin of Baldwin I, the first Latin emperor of Constantinople, whose seal, with the same legend, is engraved on the title page of Rénier Chalon, *Recherches sur les monnaies des comtes de Hainaut* (Brussels, 1848). However, the fabric of the coin is quite unlike that of Byzantine coins at the time of the Latin conquest.

coinage of Trebizond at just this time.[36] The parallel is strikingly reinforced by the similarity in appearance of Theodore on the Trebizond coins to the bust of Tancred himself as he appears on his second issue (pl. III, no. 17) at Antioch. This portrait has sometimes been said to show Tancred wearing a turban, and therefore to demonstrate how quickly the crusading princes adopted oriental manners.[37] The prototype of the Greek soldier-saint is a more convincing explanation of Tancred's bizarre appearance.

Tancred's third issue (pl. III, no. 18) has the reverse inscription ÐSFŦ for Domine Salvum Fac Tancredum, the Latin transcription of the invocation κύριε βοήθει which is found on coins of both Antioch and Edessa. On account of its Latin legend this coin was once ascribed to the principality of Galilee, which Tancred held as a fief of Godfrey of Bouillon before 1100. That ascription is still sometimes made, but it cannot be correct since the coins have been found with others at Antioch[38] and take their due place in the succession of overstrikes, forming the undertype of coins of Roger and of Tancred's last issue (pl. III, no. 19), a coin of conventional Byzantine aspect with a bust of Christ on the obverse and Tancred's name in Greek on the reverse.

Roger made three successive issues of copper coins, the first two (pl. III, nos. 20, 21) with Greek inscriptions, the third (pl. III, no. 22) with a Latin one. All share the essentially Byzantine iconography of the early crusader coins, but the first two bear images not used by Roger's predecessors, the Virgin orans and St. George slaying the dragon. The St. George coin is chiefly remarkable for its reverse legend, which sets out Roger's title as prince of Antioch. It is the only coin of the first phase to state a territorial title, and it may possibly be interpreted as an example of the assertiveness characteristic of usurpers.

The problems of the early coinage of Antioch center upon the attribution of coins in the name of Bohemond. One of these indeed (pl. III, no. 23), a coin with the reverse inscription BAIMYNΔOC set in the angles of a cross, is not difficult, since it occurs overstruck on coins of Roger. This must therefore be ascribed to Bohemond II and, since it follows hard on Roger's coins, to the early part of his reign before his arrival in the east in 1126 to take up his inheritance. This close se-

36. Simon Bendall, "The Mint of Trebizond under Alexius I and the Gabrades," *Numis. Chr.,* 7th ser., XVII (1977), 132.

37. For a rehearsal of the role of this coin as evidence for the rapid orientalization of the crusaders see Raymond C. Smail, *Crusading Warfare 1097–1193* (Cambridge, Eng., 1978), p. 41, note 1.

38. Dorothy B. Waage, *Antioch-on-the-Orontes,* IV, part 2 (Princeton, 1952), 69.

quence is an incidental but not weighty argument against the attribution of the BAΛΔOYINOC ΔЄCΠOTHC coin (pl. II, no. 13) to this
period at Antioch.

Two other coins bearing the name Bohemond or an abbreviation
of it are more difficult to place. One of these (pl. III, no. 14) shows
a bust of St. Peter on the obverse and the letters BHMT in the angles
of a floriate cross on the reverse. Schlumberger ascribed it to Bohemond I.[39] The main arguments for giving so early a date to this rather
scarce coin are its primitive style and the arrangement of the brief inscription about the cross, like that on Baldwin's first coin of Edessa
(pl. I, no. 1). There is also the negative argument that this coin is not
found overstruck on Tancred's coins. However, it would be reassuring
if a specimen could be found overstruck by one of Tancred's issues.

For the other coin in Bohemond's name (pl. III, no. 15) there is even
less on which to build a hypothesis. It exists in a single specimen, unpublished until now. On the obverse we find St. Peter again, but neatly
engraved in the style rather of Tancred's first issue (pl. III, no. 16) than
of the coin (no. 14) just considered. The reverse inscription is in Latin:
BO[AMV]NDVS SERVVS XP̄I. The coin is overstruck, but the undertype is not identifiable.

This may be the immediate predecessor of Tancred's first issue, or
it may come just after that issue, in which case Tancred's first St. Peter
coins must be put back to before Bohemond's release from his Danishmendid prison in 1102. That, however, would suppose that there
was a plentiful issue (no. 16) by Tancred during his first regency, an
interlude of two years from which this coin (no. 15) is the sole sur-
vivor, and then a resumption of prolific coinage (nos. 17–19) by Tancred with his second regency in 1104. It makes more sense to suppose
that all Tancred's issues followed hard upon each other.

It is tempting, in the absence of further evidence, to relate the new
coin to Tancred's first St. Peter coin, which it so much resembles in
iconography, in style, and in the meaning, if not the language, of the
inscription. However, even if new evidence is discovered which makes
it necessary to ascribe it after all to Bohemond II after 1119, still this
piece, the most uncompromisingly Latin of all the coins of the first
phase, interestingly reinforces the two points which must strike anyone who examines the early coinage of the crusaders. One is the close
parallel with the coinage of the Normans in southern Italy, which is
also an overstruck coinage in copper given to insouciant alternation
between Greek and Latin. The second point is the genuine religious

39. Schlumberger, *Numismatique*, p. 43.

fervor which these coins transmit, counterbalancing to some extent the evidence of the crusaders' boundless rapacity which emerges from some accounts of the crusade: Lord save thy servant Tancred; Baldwin the servant of the Cross; Bohemond the servant of Christ. We are accustomed to the appearance of the saints in the iconography of later medieval coinage, and the Κύριε βοήθει invocation is found on the coins of the Byzantine emperor and on the seals, though not the coins, of the Normans in Italy. But even if their inscriptions do contain an element of ostentatious humility which may have had a political purpose, these coins, with their absence of territorial title, are still impressive. There is something in them of that spirit which allegedly prompted Godfrey of Bouillon to refuse a crown in the city where his God had worn a crown of thorns.

THE SECOND PHASE

During the twelfth century the coinage of western Christendom consisted almost entirely of silver or billon deniers (*denari,* pence, or *pfennige*) issued at various weights and fineness by different feudal authorities. One of its characteristics was a tendency to crystalize into what are known to numismatists as "immobilized types" — forms and designs remaining essentially unchanged for decades on end. The principal coinages of France and those of the imperial mints of Italy were prime examples of this.

Coinage in western Christendom[40] was the king's monopoly if he could enforce it, but if not, not. In France the *jus monetae* was still widely distributed, a legacy of the breakdown of political cohesion in late Carolingian times. A number of coinages, notably those of the counts of Anjou and Champagne in the north and those of the counts of Toulouse and dukes of Aquitaine in the south, were more important than the king's own, but royal authority was gradually strengthened, and by the end of the century royal coinage was predominating. In Germany, on the other hand, the imperial prerogative was weakened and dispersed, so that by 1200 the imperial mints were at best competing as equals with those of the great feudatories, notably the ecclesiastical servants of the empire and the secular lords of the march. In northern Italy coinage, to begin with, was largely restricted to the

---

40. For a general discussion of twelfth-century coinage in western Christendom see Grierson, *Monnaies du moyen âge* (Fribourg, 1976), pp. 111–151, and Porteous, *Coins in History* (London and New York, 1969), pp. 53–80.

imperial mints—Pavia, Milan, Verona, and Lucca—but increasingly the communes either asserted or were granted their own minting privileges. Only in England, in southern Italy, and in the Spanish kingdoms was the right of coinage more or less exclusively held in royal hands.

Among the crusaders coinage was not exclusively royal insofar as the *jus monetae* was vested in all four rulers of the Latin states. They, however, kept it to themselves, permitting even less encroachment by their barons during the twelfth century than did the king of England. Nor did the privileges and immunities granted to the Italian communes within certain cities extend to the operation of a mint. Yet otherwise, in monetary as in political affairs, the principal outside influences in the Latin states came from France and the maritime communes of Italy.

It is not in itself surprising that twelfth-century Frankish princes should have issued silver and billon coinage. That rulers in Syria and Palestine should do so, however, implied an important reversal of the economic and monetary trends of nearly two centuries. Such coins were quite exceptional in that part of the world, and their appearance there was a sign that in the wake of the crusaders' conquest silver, the valued currency of the west, was drawn eastward. This was either because the west was sending heavy subsidies for their support, or because the Latins established in their new lands economies which, in monetary terms, were an eastward extension of the system already operating in the west. Probably both causes were at work, but they worked slowly; if the crusading princes did not start to issue silver coinage on a regular basis before about 1140, this was because until then there was little silver about. Even when regular silver coinage was established, it was accompanied by far more subsidiary issues of copper coinage than was ever normal in the west.

It may be that some of the earliest silver coins struck by the crusaders were in fact imitations of western coins. It has been argued that some of the cruder and later varieties of the *denaro* of Lucca, the *lucensis* of Raymond of Aguilers' catalogue, were actually struck by the Pisans, and that some may even have been minted in the Holy Land, where various hoards of them have been found.[41] The existence of a denier of Chartres from an eastern source and with a retrograde inscription possibly adds a little more weight to this theory that the first silver minted by the crusaders consisted of copies of the coins which they had brought with them.[42] It raises, however, the important juridical

41. Metcalf, *loc. cit.*
42. This coin, which is unpublished, is in the author's collection.

question whether they were issued by the Latin princes or minted *sub rosa* by the Italian communities.

The first deniers of Frankish type and bearing the name of a crusading prince are apparently coins of Bertrand (Bertram) of Tripoli (pl. VIII, no. 65). A very rare anonymous coin of the same type and with the same reverse legend (pl. VIII, no. 66) is also ascribed to Bertrand. Since Bertrand died in 1112, the coins ascribed to him are outliers, struck quite early during what we have called the first phase of crusading coinage and antedating all other Frankish deniers by at least twenty-five years. They cannot therefore be fitted into any neat pattern of monetary development in the Latin states, and they are the more extraordinary in that Pons, Bertrand's more active and longer-lived successor, apparently struck no coins in twenty-four years. Bertrand's coins, which are closely related in type to those which he struck as count of Toulouse before he left for Tripoli in 1109, are represented by only a handful of surviving specimens.

Regular coinage of silver deniers seems to have begun more or less contemporaneously in Antioch and Jerusalem about 1140. The new phenomenon appears to reflect two facts: a steady enough inflow of silver to sustain coinage of this kind and the presence of a Frankish population big enough to demand it.

At Antioch the denier coinage was instituted by Raymond of Poitiers some time after his marriage in 1136 to Constance, the successor of Bohemond II. His issue came after a period of some fifteen years in which there was either no coinage at all, or at most some irregular issues of anonymous copper coinage of thin fabric but otherwise of primitive aspect (pl. IV, nos. 24–26), which may be ascribed to these years on the somewhat inadequate ground that they fit in badly almost anywhere else.

Raymond's new coins (pl. IV, no. 27) have on the obverse a neat profile bust and the circular inscription RAMVNDVS; the reverse simply gives the name of the city ANTIOCHIЄ around a short cross. A profile portrait was quite exceptional in French coinage at that date, but normal in England, whence Raymond was summoned to Antioch in 1136, and also in Navarre and Aragon, kingdoms bordering on his native Aquitaine.[43]

Several varieties of Raymond's denier have been noted.[44] It was evi-

43. Another possible prototype for the profile portrait is the head of St. Maurice as it appeared on the deniers of Vienne.

44. Metcalf, "Billon Coinage of the Crusading Principality of Antioch," *Numis. Chr.,* 7th ser., IX (1969), 255.

dently struck over quite a long period, and maybe at varying fineness. A copper coin (pl. IV, no. 28) is also ascribed to Raymond.

Raymond was succeeded in 1149 by his son Bohemond III. To him are ascribed a series of deniers (pl. IV, no. 30) bearing the name BOAMVNDVS with a profile portrait similar to that on Raymond's coins in the last phase of their evolution. Their reverse inscription reads ANTIOCHIA, a change in spelling which may be helpful for the classification of the anonymous copper coinage (pl. IV, no. 29; pl. V, nos. 35–36). The bare-head deniers of Bohemond continued in issue for some fourteen years, during which there was a gradual deterioration in their execution.[45]

About 1163 the bare-head coins were replaced by a new issue whose principal feature was a profile bust wearing chain-mail and a helmet marked with a cross. The form of this helmet, with its prominent nasal, is very similar to that shown in two well-known illustrations of crusaders in action dating from about 1170, the mural in the Templar church at Cressac (Charente) and the miniature plan of Jerusalem in a manuscript in the Royal Library, The Hague.[46] As a coin type, however, this armed bust is unprecedented.

The helmet deniers (pl. IV, no. 31; pl. V, nos. 33, 38, 39) remained in issue as an immobilized type until the 1220's. At least eight distinct issues have been noted and their relative chronology established, although their precise order is not beyond dispute.[47]

Both the bare-head and the helmet deniers were accompanied by sporadic issues of minor coinage in copper or very debased billon of varying types (pl. IV, nos. 29, 32; pl. V, nos. 34–37, 40). By a misleading convention these have also been labeled deniers. It is much more likely that they were fractional pieces, *mailles* or *pougeoises,* forming part of a comprehensive monetary system.

King Fulk struck a plentiful coinage in his home county of Anjou.[48] His followers from France no doubt carried large numbers of *deniers angevins* to Palestine, where they figure prominently among the finds of Frankish coins.[49] Fulk, however, struck no coins of his own as king

---

45. *Ibid.,* p. 248; Metcalf, "Coins of Lucca . . . ," p. 455.

46. Both illustrated in Thomas S. R. Boase, *Kingdoms and Strongholds of the Crusaders* (London, 1971), pp. 62, 85.

47. Derek F. Allen, "Coins of Antioch &c. from Al Mina," *Numis Chr.,* 5th ser., XVII (1937), 200–210; Metcalf, "The Mağarik Hoard of 'Helmet' Coins of Bohemund III of Antioch," ANS, *Museum Notes,* XVI (1970), 95–109, and "Billon Coinage of Antioch," *ibid.,* XVI, 256; Roberto Pesant, "The ANS Hoard of Antioch Deniers," *ibid.,* XVIII (1972), 73.

48. Poey d'Avant, *op. cit.,* I, 204.

49. Metcalf, "Some Hoards and Stray Finds . . . ," p. 145. See also the story quoted in vol-

of Jerusalem, and quite possibly struck no coins in Jerusalem at all.

If he did, there are two issues of coins which could be ascribed to him, though both are anonymous. One of these (pl. VII, no. 58) features a church steeple symbolically towering over two flanking minarets; on the other (pl. VII, no. 60) a patriarchal cross is set between two palm branches and stars. Both are scarce, but the recent discovery of a fractional *maille* or *obole* for each (nos. 59, 61) suggests that they were normal and regular issues and not just temporary or emergency strikings. Their weight of about one gram for the deniers and some of their stylistic features suggest a fairly early date, and their provenance, where this is known, suggests that they circulated in the Latin kingdom. However, their rarity and the near-indecipherability of their inscriptions are more suggestive of the tail-end of a coinage than the beginning of one. Their placing here in the coinage of the crusades is very tentative.[50]

More characteristic of the confident beginning of a new coinage by a vigorous political power are deniers and *oboles* with the obverse inscription RЄX BALDVINVS and the Tower of David on the reverse (nos. 41–44). These are among the most plentiful of all crusader coins, and it says much for the intractability of crusading numismatics, without documents or satisfactory hoard evidence, that it is not even certain whether they were introduced by Baldwin II or Baldwin III. The more generally held opinion is that the initiative was Baldwin III's, but it may be that they were started by Baldwin II and continued as an immobilized type through the reigns of Fulk and Baldwin III. If this second alternative proved to be the case, the anonymous coins (nos. 58–61) described in the last paragraph would probably have to be pushed further back in time, making them almost contemporary with the rare deniers of Bertrand of Tripoli (pl. VIII, no. 65).

The Baldwin coins are divided into two classes, one of coarser style (pl. VI, nos. 41, 42) and another of neater workmanship (pl. VI, nos. 43, 44) whose letter-forms incorporate many annulets and curlicues. The very earliest deniers, of coarse workmanship, read DЄ hIЄRVSALЄM instead of DЄ IЄRVSALЄM on the reverse.[51]

---

ume IV of the present work, p. 9. Of course *deniers angevins* were also struck by king Richard and carried out with the Third Crusade; see Cox, *op. cit.,* pp. 5–7.

50. Arnold Spaer, "Two Rare Crusader Coins of the Latin Kingdom of Jerusalem," *Numis. Chr.,* 7th ser., XVII (1977), 184. For the *oboles* see *idem,* "Two Crusader Oboles," *ibid.,* CXLII (1982), 160.

51. The fullest treatment of the Baldwin deniers is in Metcalf, "Coinage of the Latin Kingdom of Jerusalem in the Name of Baudouin," *Numis. Chr.,* 7th ser., XVIII (1978), 71. They are also discussed in Yvon, "Monnaies et sceaux de l'Orient latin," *Rev. numis.,* 6th ser., VIII (1966), 89.

Amalric continued the issue of deniers and *oboles,* and some of his coins also have the same curious letter-forms as we find on some of the Baldwin pieces. Amalric's coins (pl. VI, nos. 45, 46) read AMAL-RICVS REX; on the reverse the Tower of David is replaced by a schematic representation of the church of the Holy Sepulcher. They continued as an immobilized type probably until well after Saladin's conquest of Jerusalem in 1187. It would be surprising in the light of normal medieval practice if Baldwin IV had reverted to the Tower of David type of his namesake and uncle. The hoard evidence, such as it is, contradicts this idea.

The last coins of the Latin kingdom before Hattin are copper coins in the name of Guy (pl. VI, no. 49). The type is interesting: a crowned facing bust of the king on the obverse and a domed building on the reverse. Schlumberger identified this building as the Templum Domini (the Dome of the Rock), since its form is quite distinct from the church of the Holy Sepulcher as shown on the Amalricus deniers, while it approximates closely to the Dome of the Rock as it appears today and as it is represented alongside the Holy Sepulcher and the Tower of David on the reverse of the royal seals of the kings of Jerusalem.[52] However, the building on Guy's coin has an opening in the roof, which was a feature of the Holy Sepulcher but not of the Dome of the Rock. Representations of all these buildings are conventional rather than realistic, and the Holy Sepulcher in particular is shown in a wide variety of forms in documents of the period. The assumption must be that the building more sacred to the crusaders was intended in this instance.[53]

It has usually been assumed that the mint for the coinage of the kingdom was at Jerusalem itself. Yet the existence of two quite distinct styles for the Baldwin deniers points to the possibility of two mints.[54] Acre and Tyre have been proposed in place of the capital, but the question is still quite open. More recently Beirut has also been suggested as the possible mint of an enigmatic late-twelfth-century issue of anonymous copper coins which bear the inscription TVRRIS DAVIT and were once attributed to the siege of Jerusalem in 1187 (pl. VI, no. 48);[55] these coins, which have the Tower of David on the obverse and an eight-

---

52. Schlumberger, Ferdinand Chalandon, and Adrien Blanchet, *Sigillographie de l'Orient latin* (Paris, 1943), p. 2.

53. I am indebted to the Rev. John Wilkinson for this observation.

54. This question is discussed in Metcalf, "Coinage of the Latin Kingdom," *loc. cit.*

55. Christopher Sabine, "The *Turris Davit* Coinage and the Regency of Raymond III of Tripoli (1184–6)," *Numis. Chr.,* 7th ser., XVIII (1978), 85.

pointed star on the reverse, show characteristics of both Tripoli and the Latin kingdom.

The most extraordinary of all the coins of Jerusalem (if coins they be) are gold pieces struck in the names of Baldwin and Amalric,[56] and possibly even Fulk. They do not fit into the neat pattern of typically Frankish coinage of the second phase. Indeed they fit into no normal numismatic pattern whatsoever, since they survive only in fragmentary form.

A reconstruction of the fragments, some of which are segmental while others are irregularly shaped bits, points to coins of about the size of a dinar. One side has a hexagram and the legend CIVITATIS : HIERVSALEM; another side has a star device and the legend +SIGNVM BALDVINI REGIS. There are variant inscriptions, one of which seems to include the name AMALRICVS, while another suggests FVLCONIS. This is the only gold which bears the name of a crusading ruler or principality. The practice of cutting up coins in order to make fractional values was not abnormal elsewhere in the twelfth century, but this is the only instance in which the complete pieces do not survive. We may speculate whether they were struck specifically in order to be cut up, and if so, why. As the fragments have almost always been found in groups, it is unlikely that they were intended for scattering as alms.

The twelfth-century coinage of Tripoli was less prolific and less rich than that of Antioch or Jerusalem. It was, as we have seen, exceptional in its early beginnings with the scanty coinage of count Bertrand. Thereafter there was no identifiable coinage for thirty years. Even then, when Jerusalem and Antioch began their heavy coinages of silver, Raymond of Tripoli (we cannot even be sure whether it was Raymond II or Raymond III) made only sporadic issues of small copper and very debased billon coins (nos. 67–69). Only one issue of reasonably fine deniers (no. 70) appears to have been made before 1187, and that was by no means plentiful.

The principal characteristics of the Tripolitan coinage are the large number of anonymous issues and the heavy Provençal influence in the choice of designs. What appears to be the earliest coin of Raymond of Tripoli, a copper *pougeoise* (perhaps) of very erratic weight (pl. VIII,

---

56. J. D. Brady, "A Firm Attribution of Latin Gold Coinage to Twelfth-Century Jerusalem," ANS, *Museum Notes,* XXIII (1978), 133. This covers only some of the fragments, of which more have since become available. A good selection is in the collection of the American Numismatic Society, New York.

no. 67), has a short cross pattée with an annulet at each end of the cross; a cross resembling this was adopted for the arms of the count of Toulouse. Another early piece (pl. VIII, no. 68), of very debased billon or copper, has on it a paschal lamb with a processional cross. This type was first used by Alfonso Jordan on coins which he struck as count of St. Gilles (1112–1148);[57] a similar coin of Alfonso Jordan's successor Raymond V (1148–1194) has been found near Tripoli.[58] Finally, the type of the crescent moon and star (no. 69; pl. VIII, no. 70), which was to become the Tripolitan type par excellence and was used for the only good deniers of Raymond III, was closely related to deniers struck by Raymond V of Toulouse and St. Gilles for his marquisate of Provence.[59] The confusing duplication of names as of coin-types is itself a measure of the continuing relationship between Tripoli and the Midi.

One more design commonly found on the coins of Tripoli is the city gate or castle. This, which is not unlike the Tower of David but has a door in it, was presumably derived from the count's seal, which in common with the seals of many other barons had a representation of a tower on the reverse.[60]

The castle coins (pl. IX, nos. 73, 75) are all anonymous, as also are some of the crescent and star coins (pl. VIII, no. 72). It has been assumed that these must have been struck during one of the periods when the count was in captivity, and Raymond III's long imprisonment from 1164 to 1171 is especially cited as their probable date of issue. Probably those years, when there were heavy issues at Jerusalem and Antioch, were also a period of minting activity at Tripoli, but there is no reason especially to associate the anonymous issues with Raymond's absence. Anonymous coinage was commonplace in the Levant as in the west in the twelfth century, and in an age of immobilized types, when even the death of a ruler did not necessitate the removal of his name from the coinage, still less need his name be removed because he was confined in a Saracen prison.

In the years before Saladin's conquest only one baron of the Latin kingdom, the lord of Sidon, appears to have struck a coinage of his own. There are some rare deniers rather doubtfully attributed to Gerard (fl. 1153–1164) (pl. XI, no. 94). More certainly attributable are almost equally scarce deniers of his son Reginald (pl. XI, no. 93), which

57. Poey d'Avant, op. cit., II, 253.
58. The coin (ibid., no. 3718) is in Mr. Slocum's collection.
59. Ibid., II, 255.
60. Schlumberger et al., Sigillographie, p. 59.

bear his name RENALDVS and a castle on one side, an arrow on the other. The castle doubtless derived from Reginald's seal;[61] the arrow was a canting symbol devised for Sidon (Saiète — *sagitta*). These coins probably date from before Hattin, since Reginald lost his barony in the same campaign as Guy of Lusignan lost his kingdom. However, he was subsequently regranted part of his fief by Saladin, and his coins therefore may possibly date from the obscure period which elapsed between this recovery and his death about 1204. Whichever date is correct, and whether he usurped or was granted the right of coinage, his action shows how the barons were encroaching upon the royal power in those years; yet the fact that his was the only baronial mint to be established so early shows in a sense how respected the regalian right still was, in spite of the incapable hands in which it rested for much of the time.

A list of baronies allegedly enjoying minting rights was compiled by Schlumberger.[62] This was based upon a misreading of the *Assises*, which were in any case too late to be a reliable authority. The right of *coin* referred to in that document was the right to the use of a lead seal, not the right to a mint.

THE THIRD PHASE

Saladin's conquest of Jerusalem, by taking away so much of the territory of the Latin states, profoundly altered their economy. Thereafter they appear as precarious but wealthy maritime communities, necessarily concentrating on commerce but engaged also in some industry and specialized agriculture. They enjoyed a final hectic prosperity during the years of political détente with Saladin's successors, until the approach of the Mongols ruined the commerce of the hinterland on which they depended economically, and the rising power of the Mamluks extinguished them altogether.

Their prosperity was an extension of the increasing economic activity of the whole of Latin Christendom. In this expansion the lead was taken by Italy, and in no field so obviously as that of monetary change and development.[63] The old quasi-imperial coinages of north-

---

61. *Ibid.*, p. 57.
62. Schlumberger, *Numismatique*, p. 108. The argument that Schlumberger was mistaken in this was first advanced by Raoul Chandon de Briailles, "Le Droit de *coins* dans le royaume de Jérusalem," *Syria*, XXIII (1942–1943), 244–257.
63. For thirteenth-century coinage in Europe see Grierson, *Monnaies du moyen âge*, pp. 155–204, and Porteous, *Coins in History*, pp. 83–101.

ern Italy declined in importance as minting rights were granted to the communes, among them Genoa in 1139 and Pisa in the reign of Frederick Barbarossa. The coinage of Venice in particular grew in scope and importance, and in 1201 Enrico Dandolo introduced the silver *grosso* of 24 *denari* in order to facilitate the heavy payments for material and wages which the republic was making in the course of fitting out the Fourth Crusade.[64] A monetary development which was crucial to the advance of the commercial revolution in Europe was thus directly linked to the history of the crusades.

Within a few years many other Italian communes, Genoa, Pisa, and Ancona among them, followed Venice's lead in the issue of larger-multiple coins. Finally in 1252 Genoa and Florence began to mint gold,[65] a sign that the eastward flow of silver which had marked the earlier phase of the crusades was now matched by a counterflow of gold.

The principal characteristic of French coinage during the same period was the increasing extension of the royal money at the expense of the feudal, a change which was largely brought about by the policy of Philip Augustus; it was in Philip's royal currency, the *livre tournois,* that major financial business was transacted during the Third Crusade. Not all the feudal coinages were eclipsed, however, and those which survived were, if anything, more plentiful and more vigorous than before. Among them were those of some notable crusaders: the Poitevin and Aquitanian deniers of king Richard I,[66] the deniers of Provins and Troyes struck by count Henry of Champagne and his successors,[67] the coins of Hugh IV, duke of Burgundy,[68] and those of Hervey of Donzi, count of Nevers.[69] The coins of Provins and Troyes, which were the currency in which the business of the Champagne fairs was transacted, would have enjoyed a wide circulation in any case, but the abundance of the others may well be connected with the financing of crusading expeditions.

---

64. N. Papadopoli, *Le Monete di Venezia* (Venice, 1893), I, 81; see also Donald E. Queller, "A Note on the Re-organization of the Venetian Coinage by Doge Enrico Dandolo," *Rivista italiana numismatica,* LXXVII (1975), 167–172.

65. Roberto S. Lopez, *Settecento anni fa: il ritorno all' oro nel occidente duecentesco* (Naples, 1955), and "Back to Gold, 1252," *Economic History Review,* 2nd ser., IX (1956–1957), 227–228.

66. L. M. Hewlett, *Anglo-Gallic Coins* (London, 1920), p. 9.

67. Poey d'Avant, *op. cit.,* III, 242–252.

68. *Ibid.,* III, 196.

69. *Ibid.,* I, 314. The correlation between those who struck feudal coins in France and those who went on the Third and Fifth Crusades is treated in Cox, *op. cit.* For the German coins that were taken on the Third Crusade see note 16. Two notable German crusaders whose coins are present in the Barbarossa hoard are the emperor Frederick himself and bishop Godfrey of Würzburg.

The introduction of heavy silver and gold coinage in France was the work of Louis IX, who in 1266 instituted the silver *gros tournois* and the gold *écu*.[70] Louis's monetary reform illustrates the curious interaction of the Latin states with France in monetary matters, since about the same time Bohemond VI of Tripoli and Antioch introduced a silver *gros* of the same weight and fineness as the *gros tournois.* The appearance of the *gros tournois,* with its concentric circles of inscription, also seems to derive from that of coins circulating in the east with which Louis and his crusading companions would have been familiar.

The counterpart of these important monetary changes in the west was the reappearance of silver coinage and the relative decline of gold in the east.[71] This was heralded by Saladin's resumption of silver coinage at Damascus in 1174–1175.[72] The Selchükids (Seljukids) of Rūm took it up in 1185–1186,[73] and the Christian kings of Cilician Armenia some fifteen years later.[74] The Nicaean coinage of Theodore Lascaris (1202–1222) was predominantly silver,[75] while that of Trebizond was exclusively so from the reign of Manuel I (1238–1263).[76] Only in Egypt did the older pattern persist, with a plentiful coinage of gold dinars and little else until the end of the Aiyūbid dynasty in 1252.[77]

Quite apart therefore from the political upheaval caused by Saladin's conquest, important changes were to be expected in the currency of the Latin states. Nevertheless, for a few years the coinages of Antioch and Tripoli at least continued with little alteration. Both principalities persisted with their "immobilized" coinages, Antioch with the helmet deniers and Tripoli with the star deniers. On the latter the barely perceptible substitution of BAMVNDVS (pl. IX, no. 74) for RAMVNDVS (pl. VIII, no. 71) marked Bohemond of Antioch's assumption of power soon after the death of Raymond III in 1187. De-

70. Blanchet and A. Dieudonné, *Manuel de numismatique française* (Paris, 1916), II (by Dieudonné), 115, 147, 225.

71. Watson, *op. cit.,* pp. 5–6.

72. Paul Balog, *The Coinage of the Ayyubids* (London, 1980), p. 36.

73. Stanley Lane-Poole, *Catalogue of Oriental Coins in the British Museum* (London, 1877), III, no. 92.

74. Paul Z. Bedoukian, *Coinage of Cilician Armenia* (ANS, NNM, no. 147; New York, 1962), pp. 10, 50.

75. Hendy, *op. cit.,* p. 228.

76. Otto Retowski, *Die Münzen der Komnenen von Trapezunt* (republished with an introduction by W. Hahn, Brunswick, 1974).

77. Andrew S. Ehrenkreutz, "The Standard of Fineness of Gold Coins Circulating in Egypt at the Time of the Crusades," *Journal of the American Oriental Society,* LXXIV (1954), 162–166.

niers of Bohemond, as later abbreviated to BAMVND' (pl. IX, no. 76), are the most abundant of all Tripolitan issues. As some of the later helmet deniers of Antioch are also among the commoner varieties of that common type, it seems that both coinages were issued with renewed vigor after 1200. At Antioch an issue of helmet deniers in the name of Raymond Roupen (pl. V, no. 38) signals the years of his control there from 1216 to 1219.

In the kingdom of Jerusalem, Saladin's conquest and the removal of king Guy temporarily destroyed the juridical basis on which the coinage had been produced until then. Gradually, however, the kingdom was reconstituted; the extent to which the royal coinage too was reconstituted depends upon the interpretation which is put upon the Holy Sepulcher deniers in the name of Amalricus (pl. VII, no. 52). We have seen that these coins probably continued in issue as an immobilized type through the reigns of Baldwin IV and Baldwin V. It is reasonable to suppose that, like the helmet deniers of Antioch, they continued still longer, possibly until the 1220's. The best argument for this is that hoards deposited in the 1220's contain large numbers of them.[78] The theory is also supported by the fact that certain coins of John of Brienne (pl. VII, no. 55) are of the same type.

Apart from the Holy Sepulcher deniers, the coins of the Latin kingdom struck after 1187 are rather scanty. Some are anonymous. At one time it was argued that the TVRRIS DAVIT coppers (pl. VI, no. 48) were siege pieces struck at Jerusalem after Hattin but before Saladin took the city, but it has been pointed out that they were struck over a longer period than that theory would allow.[79] They do appear, however, to have been struck somewhere in the Latin kingdom in the closing years of the twelfth century, as does an anonymous billon denier (pl. VI, no. 47) with a patriarchal cross on the obverse which reads MONETA REGIS and REX IERL'M. The ascription of this one, however, to the crusaders' encampment before Acre, when the kingdom was in dispute between Guy of Lusignan and Conrad of Montferrat, is possibly too fanciful.[80] Anonymous coinage at this period is not so exceptional that we must necessarily ascribe it to a time of political vacuum. It is probably safer to assume that, when political conditions were critically uncertain, no coins were issued at all.[81]

---

78. H. Longuet, "La Trouvaille de Kessab en Orient latin," *Rev. numis.,* 4th ser., XXXVIII (1935), 163–181. See also the table in Yvon, "Monnaies et sceaux," p. 96.

79. Sabine, "The *Turris Davit* Coinage," p. 90.

80. Schlumberger, *Numismatique,* p. 91.

81. For the siege of Jerusalem it must be allowed that the account of Ernoul (*RHC, Occ.,*

The first coins which can be given a definite place in the renascent kingdom are copper *pougeoises* in the name of Henry of Champagne (pl. VI, nos. 50, 51). These show his modest feudal title, COMES HENRICVS, and, exceptionally for Frankish coins,[82] the denomination and the mint: PVGES D'ACCON. Two issues are extant, a fairly plentiful one with fleur de lis reverse (pl. VI, no. 50) and a rare one, represented now by a single specimen, with a hexagram in place of the fleur (pl. VI, no. 51). Both of these motifs are found on the French feudal coinage, but neither, curiously enough, in Henry's own county of Champagne.[83]

There are three issues of coins in the name of John of Brienne (nos. 53–55), the last coins struck for the Latin kingdom in the king's name. All are exceptional in one way or another. Two of John's issues are datable. These are billon deniers with a crowned facing bust and the prominent mint name of Damietta (pl. VII, nos. 53, 54). John occupied Damietta in 1219. He was at pains to assert his regalian rights there against the papal legate, Pelagius, and his authorization of these coins probably had as much to do with that struggle as with economic requirements. Nevertheless, the coins would have been useful for paying an army which had been campaigning in the Nile delta for eighteen months, and the bullion for them presumably came from the captured city.

The other coin of John (pl. VII, no. 55) has no mint-name, and the type is the conventional Holy Sepulcher of the Amalricus deniers. The importance of this piece lies in its weight, which at 2.70 grams is about three times that of the average denier. Fortunately another and even rarer coin (pl. VII, no. 56) of the same type and weight (but without John's name) gives us the denomination. This coin was a *dragma* or *dirhem*, in one sense a forerunner of the dirhems that were to be struck at Acre with Arabic inscriptions, but in another sense the first silver

---

II, 70) is both specific and circumstantial: Balian of Ibelin and the patriarch, acting in concert, ordered that the Holy Sepulcher be stripped of its silver covering and that this silver be coined for payment to the knights and sergeants defending the city. Sabine, "Numismatic Iconography of the Tower of David and the Holy Sepulchre," *Numis. Chr.,* 7th ser., XIX (1979), 129, marshals the arguments for ascribing an identifiable and separate issue of coins to this event, but his article, although informative on the iconography of the coins in question (no. 62), falls short of proving the case. There is no reason to suppose that special coins were struck. Indeed, the authorities might be thought to have had other preoccupations than the designing of a new coinage, and it is more likely that the mint went ahead with coins that it was already equipped to make, namely *Amalricus* deniers. However, either way, it is curious to reflect that some of these coins may be made of silver taken from the very monument that figures on the reverse.

82. But not at all exceptional for Arabic coins.

83. The hexagram (star of David) coin is published by Spaer, "Two Rare Crusader Coins," p. 185, who also discusses the origin of the motifs of both issues.

grosso of the Latin Orient. It was struck only some ten or fifteen years after Enrico Dandolo's Venetian *grosso,* and antedated almost every other such coin in Italy.

A curious parallel to John's *dirhem,* unpublished until now, is found in the coinage of Tripoli. This is a coin of the BAMVND' star type (pl. IX, no. 77), of fine silver and probably weighing, when struck,[84] something over two grams, or about the same as a Venetian *grosso.* This coin cannot be dated surely within twenty years, but a date before rather than after 1240 seems likely. Wherever it is finally put, it confirms the view that the late "economic" phase of the Latin states was a time for monetary experiment.

It has sometimes been maintained that in the years after 1187 the regalian rights of the kings of Jerusalem were much weakened and that the "Livre au Roi",[85] which appeared to reassert those rights, was in fact expressing a nostalgic yearning for conditions which were gone for good.[86] One reason given for this is the proliferation of baronial coinage in these years. The evidence does not support this argument. There was no wholesale usurpation of the royal monopoly of minting. A strict examination of the baronial coins reduces the number of issuing baronies to three — Beirut, Tyre, and Sidon.

The coinage of Beirut (nos. 84–88) consists of deniers in the name of John of Ibelin and anonymous copper pieces which, to judge from their appearance, are probably contemporary.[87] The obverse type of all of them is a castle or city gate, doubtless taken, like the similar type for Reginald of Sidon and the counts of Tripoli, from the lord's seal.[88] John's coinage was no brief emergency issue: there are two distinct deniers with minor varieties of each, and they are at least as well minted as any other coins of the Latin kingdom. It is an attractive theory to associate this coinage with John's dispute with the emperor Frederick, but deniers of both types are found in the Kessab and Tripolis hoards, both of which are associated with the Fifth Crusade, and

---

84. The only known surviving coin, which is in the author's collection, is badly chipped. It weighs 1.90 grams, but an original weight of 2.00–2.20 grams is a fair estimate.

85. *Livre au Roi,* xvi (*RHC, Lois,* I, 617). The passage reads: "nul hom ne deit aver port, euvreneour ne monee labourant, fors li rois, par dreit ne par l'assize." The minting of coins was a crime punishable by loss of fief.

86. For a statement of this point of view see Jonathan Riley-Smith, *The Feudal Nobility and the Kingdom of Jerusalem 1174–1277* (London, 1973), p. 147.

87. But this was not Schlumberger's judgment; see *Numismatique,* p. 118. Nos. 84, 85, and 88 are shown on pl. X.

88. Schlumberger *et al., Sigillographie,* p. 40.

are thought to have been deposited about 1221.[89] Surprisingly, therefore, since John of Brienne was a strong king who knew his rights and his relations with John of Ibelin were not bad, this coinage seems to have begun and maybe ended some years before the lord of Beirut became heavily engaged in constitutional disputes with his suzerain. Whatever the cause of its issue, the Beirut coinage was not continued by John's successors.

The coinage of Tyre is all very late. Philip of Montfort was granted the lordship in 1246 by Henry I of Cyprus acting as regent of the kingdom; Philip was succeeded by his son John in 1270. By the time Philip was invested with Tyre, the lordship accounted for half the total area of the Latin kingdom, and the king's regalian rights were indeed of less account than they once were.

Two issues of coins are known for Philip (pl. X, nos. 89, 90) and two for John (pl. X, nos. 91, 92), all rare and rather ill-struck in copper.[90] Three of them feature a portico with columns. At first sight this appears to be a throwback to an early Frankish coinage type, the so-called temple type of Charlemagne.[91] In practice it is more likely that the building shown is the edicule of the Holy Sepulcher as restored in 1048.[92]

The most extensive, and also the most puzzling, of the baronial coinages is that of Sidon (pl. XI, nos. 93–99). It is not plentiful, but it comprises several different types, most of which are difficult to date. As we have seen, Sidon's coinage started early, but after Saladin's conquest Reginald's coinage probably ceased, and the city was not recovered by the Franks until 1227. Reginald's heir, Balian, was closely associated with the royal government; he was appointed one of Frederick's lieutenants in 1229, and held that position either alone or jointly until his death ten years later. At first he occupied a central position politically, mediating between Frederick and John of Ibe-

89. See Longuet, *op. cit.,* p. 175, and Cox, *op. cit.,* p. 55. There exist so few coins certainly struck in the Latin states in the years 1220–1230 that it would be possible to give a post-1225 date to both hoards, if that were necessary. However, the presence of seven coins of Henry I of Cyprus (1218–1253) in Kessab, and their absence from Tripolis, argues against the later date for Tripolis. It should be accepted therefore that the Ibelin coinage dates from the reign of John of Brienne.

90. The coins of Tyre are reclassified by A. John Seltman, "Some Crusader Coins," *Spink's Numismatic Circular,* LXXIV (1966), 61.

91. For a discussion of this type see Grierson, "Money and Coinage under Charlemagne," in *Karl der Grosse,* I, *Persönlichkeit und Geschichte* (ed. W. Braunfels *et al.,* Düsseldorf, 1965), p. 519.

92. J. Wilkinson, "The Tomb of Christ: an Outline of its Structural History," *Levant,* IV (1972), 83–97.

lin's baronial party, but after 1235 he threw in his lot with his peers.

For some years after Balian's death his widow Margaret seems to have exercised authority at Sidon. In the only contemporary account of the coinage of Sidon, Joinville[93] refers to it as the lady Margaret's currency. Her son Julian is credited with little political ambition. After he assumed control he found that the lordship's revenues were not enough to support its feudal obligations, and he turned Sidon over to the Templars in 1260.

It is probably safe to assume that the currency to which Joinville referred, in which Louis made his offering at the tomb of Walter of Brienne in Sidon in 1252, was the coinage of anonymous deniers of reasonably good billon which read D · E · N · I · E · R · D · E · S · E · E · T · E · and show an unidentified domed building on the reverse (pl. XI, no. 99). These are the only coins of Sidon plentiful enough to warrant Joinville's description of them as a proper currency, the only ones also which are fit for a king's offering.

From this it may be deduced that all the other coins (nos. 93–98) of Sidon are of poor quality. They survive for the most part in such bad condition, and their legends are so garbled, that we can identify them as from Sidon only by the arrow, which first figured on the coins of Reginald. The persistence of this device owes less to continuity than to the aptness of the pun on the city's name.

All conclusions about the coinage of Sidon must be tentative. It is unlikely that Balian would have resumed coinage in defiance of Frederick's regalian rights as long as he was actually a royal official giving even half-hearted support to Frederick's policies. It is unlikely therefore that any of these later Sidon coins were struck before about 1235. The appearance of the good billon deniers, which in fabric are rather like coins struck by Frederick himself in Sicily, is consistent with their having been minted some time during the two decades 1235–1255. The poor-quality arrow coins and the related issues may be subsidiary pieces dating from the same time, but they are more likely later, the monetary expression of Julian's financial difficulties.

The modest coinages of Beirut, Tyre, and Sidon comprise the whole story of baronial minting in the Latin kingdom. The attribution of coins to Toron stems from a misreading of certain Montfort coins of Tyre.[94] A coin is published (pl. VII, no. 63) for the mint of Jaffa,[95] but since it is anonymous and Jaffa was intermittently in the hands

---

93. John of Joinville, *Mémoires,* ed. Francisque Michel (Paris, 1858), p. 140.
94. Seltman, *op. cit.,* p. 61.
95. Schlumberger, *Numismatique,* p. 110.

of the crown, this must be assumed to be a royal issue until proved otherwise. The myth of a more substantial baronial coinage originated partly from these misattributions, but chiefly from Schlumberger's misinterpretation of the *Assises of Jerusalem* and the long list of potential baronial mints which consequently appeared in his standard work on the subject.

Nevertheless, if the baronial coinages of the Latin kingdom in the thirteenth century seem scanty, they should be seen against a background of royal and princely coinage that is far from plentiful. There are no coins of the Latin kingdom in the name of Frederick or of his son Conrad, though Sicilian coins of both of them are common, many bearing the title of king of Jerusalem;[96] and these, to judge from thirteenth-century finds, began to play a significant part in the monetary circulation of the Latin states at this epoch.[97] The most important coinages minted at this time in Palestine were the coins with Arabic inscriptions struck at Acre. There are no coins of Antioch which can be said with certainty to come after the last of the helmet deniers, which date from not much after 1230.

At this late stage most of the circulating medium in what remained of the Latin states was provided from abroad. The increasing importance of Sicilian coinage in the area has already been mentioned. Among Italian coinages, those of Genoa and Venice were also much in evidence. The crusades of the brother and son successively of Henry III of England were the probable cause of the transfer of Henry's fine silver pence to the area in fair numbers. Even the new coinage of Portugal, which was a port of call for crusaders coming by sea from northern Europe, found its way into the local circulation. Less surprisingly, the coins of Cyprus were introduced in increasing quantity. Almost no country of western Christendom goes quite unrepresented in the stray finds of coins of this period in the Latin east, but still France predominates, as it did from the time of the First Crusade.[98]

Yet the mints of the Latin states could still display surprising originality. One example of this is an anonymous gold dinar (pl. VII, no. 57) showing the Agnus Dei and an appropriate Latin inscription. Since the coin is not only anonymous, but also carries no indication of where it was minted, it is only because of the oriental provenance of the few surviving specimens that it can be attributed to the Latin states at all.[99]

96. Sambon, *op. cit.,* V, IIB, IIC.
97. Metcalf, "Some Hoards and Stray Finds," p. 148.
98. *Ibid.,* pp. 142–148.
99. This coin was published by Grierson, "A Rare Crusader Besant with the Christus Vincit

It was probably struck during the reaction against Arabic inscriptions and Islamic professions of faith on the coinage which took place after the visitation of Odo of Châteauroux and the ensuing strictures of Innocent IV.[100]

The most vigorous revival of minting activity in these latter days of the crusading states occurred at Tripoli. After the plentiful issues of BAMVNDVS deniers (pl. IX, nos. 74, 76) and the solitary *dirhem/gros* (pl. IX, no. 77) mentioned above, almost nothing was minted at Tripoli except possibly some anonymous pieces with garbled legends (no. 64) and some rare and debased deniers (no. 78; pl. IX, no. 79) whose late date is indicated by their French inscriptions. Then one of the last two counts, probably Bohemond VI, introduced a substantial *gros* of fine silver weighing 4.20 grams (pl. IX, no. 80). The first issue of these coins was of entirely traditional Tripolitan type, with an eight-pointed star as the main feature of the reverse. On a second issue (pl. IX, no. 82), by Bohemond VII certainly (the regnal number is stated, for once), the star was replaced by a handsome castle.

The significance of these coins is that the *gros* was of exactly the same weight as the French *gros tournois*. The normal presumption would be that the greater prince influenced the lesser in a matter such as this, and that the Tripolitan coin was first issued some time after Louis's reform of 1266. This is still probable. However, the Tripolitan money differed from the French in that each issue was accompanied by an identical coin of half its weight (2.10 grams) (pl. IX, nos. 81, 83). We have seen that a coin of this weight, equal to that of a Venetian *grosso,* was struck at Tripoli some years earlier (pl. IX, no. 77). Some of the initiative therefore certainly lay with the counts of Tripoli, and, once that point is granted, the possibility has to be taken seriously that the larger Tripolitan *gros* was the prototype for the *gros tournois* and not vice versa. This would involve counting the smaller coin as the *gros* and valuing the larger one as a double *gros,* a reversal of the conventional position.[101]

So far as coinage is concerned, Tripoli is the only one of the Latin

---

Legend," ANS, *Museum Notes,* VI (1954), 169–178, and it was reconsidered by Yvon, "Monnaies et sceaux," pp. 89–91.

100. See chapter XI, below.

101. It is a modern idea to conceive of these denominations as "double" or "half". Medieval practice was to refer to a certain value in money of account, such as *gros* of 6 deniers or *gros* of 12 deniers. Even so, the medieval mind might work by progression, either from the larger coin to the smaller or from the smaller to the larger. The history of the Tripolitan coinage suggests that this began with the smaller *gros* and proceeded to the larger. The French on the other hand started with the *gros tournois* and did not produce a smaller *gros* until some twenty years later.

states which went down with its colors flying. The Aleppo hoard, which is thought to consist largely of booty carried off from the sack of Acre, was made up entirely of gold coins from western Christendom. Monetarily speaking, Acre at the close was a Frankish outpost and nothing more. But the castle coins of Bohemond VII, whose design, the castle and the cross, is so traditional to crusader coinage and so symbolic of crusading life, are among the finest of all the coins ever struck by the Franks in Syria and Palestine. They are also the last. Part of their beauty today lies in the fact that they mostly survive in fine condition. They were not in circulation for long before Tripoli surrendered to the onslaught of the Mamluks.

CORPUS OF COINS

County of Edessa

BALDWIN I (1098–1100) or BALDWIN II (1100–1104)

1. Æ (Pl. I)
   Obv. Bust of Christ facing, between $\overline{\text{IC}}$ $\overline{\text{XC}}$.
   Rev. Jeweled cross on two steps; B Λ Δ N in angles.
   6.5–8.7 g.
   Numis. Chr., 7-XV (1975), 177; Schlumberger 20 (pl. I, 5).

BALDWIN II (1100–1104)

2. Æ (Pl. I)
   Obv. Bust of Christ facing.
   Rev. Long cross on two steps, the arms flanked by two pellets;
   X B B K in angles.
   7.2 g.
   Numis. Chr., 7-XV (1975), 178.

RICHARD OF THE PRINCIPATE, regent (1104–1108)

3. Æ (Pl. I)
   Obv. Bust of Christ facing, between $\overline{\text{IC}}$ $\overline{\text{XC}}$, within beaded outer
   circle.
   Rev. KE | BOHΘ | PIKAP | ΔW in four lines across the field, within
   beaded outer circle.
   4.5–8.3 g.
   Numis. Chr., 7-XV (1975), 178; Schlumberger (pl. II, 2).

4. Æ (Pl. I)
   Obv. Broad jeweled cross potent, within beaded outer circle. No
   inscription.
   Rev. KE | BOHΘ | PIKAP | ΔW in four lines across the field, with-
   in beaded outer circle.
   4.6–7.6 g.
   Numis. Chr., 7-XV (1975), 178; Schlumberger (pl. II, 1).

5. Æ (Pl. I)

   Obv. Bust of Christ facing, between I̅C̅ X̅C̅, within outer circle.

   Rev. Short cross within inner circle; **KЄBPHKAPΔ** in outer circle.

   5.0–7.0 g.

   Numis. Chr., 7-XV (1975), 179.

RICHARD OF THE PRINCIPATE, regent, or BALDWIN II (*ca.* 1108)

6. Æ (Pl. II)

   Obv. Armed man standing to left, holding a drawn sword before his face and a long shield behind him, all within outer circle. No inscription.

   Rev. Patriarchal cross within outer circle; large pellets in the middle angles of the cross; two arcs ending in trefoils springing from the outer circle and ending in the lower angles. No inscription.

   6.3–10.2 g.

   Numis. Chr., 7-XV (1975), 179; Schlumberger 18 (pl. I, 1 & 2).

BALDWIN II, restored (1108–1118)

7. Æ (Pl. II)

   Obv. Broad jeweled cross potent, within outer circle. No inscription.

   Rev. **BAΛΔ | OVINO | KOMH** (or variant) in lines across the field, within outer circle.

   4.6–9.3 g.

   Numis. Chr., 7-XV (1975), 180; Schlumberger 19 (pl. I, 3 & 4).

8. Æ (Pl. II)

   Obv. Armed man walking to left, holding up a small cross in his right hand and with his left hand on the hilt of his sword; **BAΓΔOVINOCΔO ⱂΛOC⳦V⁻**, all within outer circle.

   Rev. Long cross fleury standing on floriate base; pellet in each angle of the cross; all within outer circle. No inscription.

   3.2–4.2 g.

   Schlumberger 21 (pl. I, 7).

9. Æ (Pl. II)

   Obv. Armed man walking to left, as no. 8. Inscription placed irregularly in the field reading downward: **BAΓ** before the figure, **ΔOIN** behind it.

   Rev. Cross fleury standing on floriate base; usually a pellet in each angle of the cross and a pellet at each end. No inscription.

   2.4–4.6 g.

   Schlumberger 21 (pl. I, 8 & 9).

10. Æ (Pl. II)

Obv. Armed man standing facing, holding a long cross in his right hand and resting his left on a patterned shield. Inscription reading downward: **ΒΑΓΔ** to left of the figure, **Ν** to right.

Rev. Short cross, **Β Η Δ Ν**, each letter placed at one end of the cross.

2.2–4.9 g.

Schlumberger 21 (pl. I, 10 & 11).

11. Æ (Pl. II)

Obv. Armed man standing facing, with a drawn sword in his right hand and a long cross in his left. Inscription about the figure in the field **Β Λ**, all within outer circle.
Δ Ν

Rev. Bust of Christ facing, between I$\overline{\text{C}}$ X$\overline{\text{C}}$.

2.4–3.8 g.

Schlumberger 22 (pl. I, 12).

12. Billon (Pl. II)

Obv. Short cross pattée with forked left arm and a pellet at each of the other ends, all within inner circle. + **ϹΤΑVΡΟϹΝΙΚΑ** within outer circle.

Rev. + **ΒΑ** | **ΓΔΟV** | **ΙΝΧΟ** | **ΜΙ** (or variant) in four lines across the field, within outer circle.

0.9–5.4 g. This exceptional weight range may comprise two distinct denominations, one in the range 1.0–2.0 g. and the other in the range 3.5–5.5 g.

Rev. numis., 3-XV (1897), 533.

Edessa or Antioch

BALDWIN II, king of Jerusalem (1118–1131)

13. Billon (Pl. II)

Obv. + | **ΒΑΛΔ** | **ΟVΙΝΟϹ** | **ΔΕϹΠΟ** | **ΤΗϹ**.

Rev. Long cross I$\overline{\text{X}}$ X$\overline{\text{C}}$ ΝΙ ΚΑ in angles.

2.38 g. (broken).

Numis. Chr., 7-XIX (1979), 136.

Principality of Antioch

BOHEMOND I (1098–1100, 1102–1104)

14. Æ (Pl. III)

Obv. Nimbate bust of St. Peter facing, holding a long cross over his left shoulder. Vertical inscription in field: P to left of bust, $\overset{T}{\underset{E}{\Pi}}\overset{O}{}$ to right; all within beaded outer circle.

Rev. Long cross fleury standing on floriate base; B H M T in angles; all within beaded outer circle.

3.3–5.4 g.

Schlumberger 43 (pl. II, 4).

BOHEMOND I (1098–1100, 1102–1104) or BOHEMOND II (1119–1130)

15. Æ (Pl. III)

Obv. Nimbate bust of St. Peter facing, holding long cross, jeweled at the ends, over his right shoulder; ☉ to left; all within beaded outer circle.

Rev. BO⋀ | NDVS | SERVVS | XPI in four lines across the field, in beaded outer circle.

3.78 g.

One specimen in private collection.

TANCRED, regent (1100–1102, 1104–1112)

16. Æ (Pl. III)

Obv. Nimbate bust of St. Peter facing, holding long cross over his left shoulder. Inscription in field: $\overset{O}{\Pi E}$ to left, $\overset{P}{\overset{O}{C}}$ to right of bust; all within beaded outer circle.

Rev. + | KEBOI | ΘHTOΔV | ⋀OCOVT | ANKPI | + in six lines across the field, within beaded outer circle.

1.9–6.5 g. A piece weighing 2.55 g. is struck on a scyphate flan.

Schlumberger 44 (pl. II, 6).

17. Æ (Pl. III)

Obv. Facing bust of Tancred, bearded, wearing a bonnet tipped with a jeweled cross and holding a drawn sword over his right shoulder. KEBOIΘI TANKPIT. (or KE BOHΘI TOC ΔOV⋀ON TAN, or variant), all within beaded outer circle.

Rev. Long cross pommée standing on floriate base. IC XC NI KA in angles, all within one or two beaded outer circles.

1.8–9.2 g.

Schlumberger 45 (pl. II, 7).

18. Æ (Pl. III)

    Obv. St. Peter nimbate, standing, his right hand in benediction, his left holding a processional cross. Vertical inscription: SPE to left of figure, ꞆPV to right; all within beaded outer circle.

    Rev. Long cross, ᗺSFꞆ in angles; all within beaded outer circle.
2.6–4.3 g.
Schlumberger (pl. V, 1).

19. Æ (Pl. III)

    Obv. Bust of Christ facing, between I͞C X͞C within outer circle.

    Rev. Long cross pommée on floriate base, TA NK P H in angles; all within outer circle.
1.9–5.7 g.
Schlumberger 45–46 (pl. II, 8).

ROGER OF SALERNO (1112–1119)

20. Æ (Pl. III)

    Obv. The Virgin Mary orans, wearing a jeweled mantle; M͞H Θ͞Y by her head.

    Rev. + | ΚΕΒΟΗΘ | ΕΙΤωϹω | ΔΟΥΛωΡ | ΟΤΓΕΡΙω | + (or variant) in four or five lines across the field, within outer circle.
2.4–7.0 g.
Schlumberger 48 (pl. II, 11).

21. Æ (Pl. III)

    Obv. St. George nimbate, mounted on a horse galloping to right, and spearing a dragon. Inscription in field: ⊘ to left, ΓΕωΡΓΙΟϹ to right; all within beaded outer circle.

    Rev. + | ΡΟΤ3ΕΡ | ΠΡΙΓΚΠ | ΟϹΑΝΤΙ | ΟΧΙ (or variant) in four or five lines across the field; within beaded outer circle.
2.6–5.7 g.
Schlumberger 48 (pl. II, 12).

A specimen in the Bibliothèque nationale weighing 5.05 g. is overstruck on a follis of emperor Leo VI (Schlumberger, pl. II, 13).

22. Æ (Pl. III)

    Obv. Christ standing, blessing; I͞C X͞C by his head; all within outer circle.

    Rev. Long cross with a pellet at each end; D͞N͞E SA͞L F͞T R͞O in angles; within beaded outer circle.
2.3–5.0 g.
Schlumberger 47 (pl. II, 10).

BOHEMOND II (1119–1130)

23. Æ (Pl. III)

> *Obv.* Bust of St. Peter, nimbate, facing, with long cross over his left shoulder. Vertical inscription in field: $\frac{\Theta}{\Pi}$ to left, ЄT to right of bust.
>
> *Rev.* Long cross springing from floriate base with pellet at each of the other three ends; BA IM YN ΔOC in angles; all within beaded outer circle.
>
> 2.6–4.9 g.
>
> Schlumberger 49 (pl. II, 14).

ANONYMOUS (period *ca.* 1120–1150)

24. Æ (Pl. IV)

> *Obv.* Bust of St. Peter, nimbate, facing, holding a long cross over his right shoulder. Inscription on either side of bust; ⊘ ΠЄ; all within outer circle.
>
> *Rev.* Cross moline with fleurs or trefoils facing inward in the angles, within beaded outer circle. No inscription.
>
> 0.9–1.4 g.
>
> Schlumberger 493 (pl. XIX, 1 shows variant with the cross on the apostle's left shoulder).

25. Æ (Pl. IV)

> *Obv.* Armed man holding banner, on horse galloping to left. No inscription.
>
> *Rev.* Long cross pattée; A N T O in angles.
>
> 0.8–1.0 g.
>
> Schlumberger 56 (pl. III, 11). This type is probably derived from that of the seal of the princes of Antioch, the earliest recorded example of which is of Raymond of Poitiers (Schlumberger *et al.*, *Sigillographie,* 33).

26. Æ (Pl. IV)

> *Obv.* As no. 25, but mounted figure to right.
>
> *Rev.* As no. 25.
>
> 0.8 g.
>
> Unpublished.

RAYMOND OF POITIERS (1136–1149)

27. Æ or billon denier (Pl. IV)

Obv. Bare head to right, within beaded inner circle, the neck breaking through the circle; + RAITVNDVS.

Rev. Short cross pattée in beaded inner circle; + ANTIOCHIE.

0.7–0.9 g.

Numis. Chr., 7-IX (1969), 255, which postulates five varieties distinguished by their lettering and the extent to which the neck breaks
through the inner circle.

28. Æ (Pl. IV)

Obv. Three bars disposed in Y shape; curiously formed RAⳡ in
angles.

Rev. AN | TIOC | HIE in three lines across the field.

1.0–1.3 g.

Schlumberger 51 (pl. II, 19).

ANONYMOUS (period *ca.* 1140–1180)

29. Æ (Pl. IV)

Obv. Cross with pellet in each angle, within beaded inner circle; +
PRINCEPꙄ.

Rev. Abstract ornamental design incorporating small cross, bar,
and loop, all within beaded inner circle. + ANTIOCHIE,
sometimes retrograde.

0.8–1.0 g.

Schlumberger 58 (pl. III, 15). The spelling ANTIOCHIE suggests
an early date, but the epigraphy and fabric suggest a date nearer to
1180.

BOHEMOND III (1149–1201)

30. Billon denier (Pl. IV)

Obv. Bare head to right, within beaded inner circle;
+ BOAMVNDVS.

Rev. Cross (sometimes with pellet in first angle) within beaded
inner circle; + ANTIOCHIA.

0.6–1.0 g.

Numis. Chr., 7-IX (1969), 248 ff., which postulates three consecutive
issues distinguished by the modeling of the head and the epigraphy,
and dates them to the years 1149–1163.

31. Billon denier (Pl. IV)

    Obv. Helmeted bust to right, with cross on helmet and chain-mail on neck; crescent to left and five-pointed star to right of head; all within beaded inner circle. + BOΛMVNDVS.

    Rev. Cross with crescent in second angle, within beaded inner circle. + ΛNTIOCHIΛ.

    0.8–1.1 g.

    Numis. Chr., 5-XV (1935), 200–210; *ibid.,* 7-IX (1969), 261. This appears to be the earliest of the helmet deniers and dates from *ca.* 1163.

ANONYMOUS (period *ca.* 1163–1180)

32. Æ (Pl. IV)

    Obv. Helmeted bust to right, with cross on helmet and chain-mail on neck; branches on either side. No inscription.

    Rev. Grid of four lines crossing at right angles with a pellet or annulet in each compartment; all within a tressure of eight arches. No inscription.

    0.3–0.6 g.

    Schlumberger 59 (pl. III, 17).

BOHEMOND III (1149–1201) or BOHEMOND IV (1201–1232)

33. Billon denier (Pl. V)

    Obv. Helmeted bust to left, with cross on helmet and chain-mail on neck; crescent to left and five-pointed star to right of head; all within beaded inner circle. + BOΛMVNDVS.

    Rev. Cross with crescent in second angle, within beaded inner circle. + ΛNTIÓCHIΛ   (or ΛMTIOCHIΛ).

    0.8–1.1 g.

    Numis. Chr., 5-XVII (1937), 200–210; *ibid.,* 7-IX (1969), 257–267; ANS, *Museum Notes,* XVI (1970), 95–109. Eight varieties of this immobilized type, dating from *ca.* 1163 to *ca.* 1220, have been classified, distinguished by the style of portrait, punctuation, and epigraphy.

34. Æ (Pl. V)

    Obv. Fleur de lis between pellets, within inner circle;

    + BOΛMVNDVS.

    Rev. Cross with pellet or star in each angle; +ΛNTIOCHIΛ.

    0.6–0.9 g.

    Schlumberger 52 (pl. III, 1). This appears to have been the principal fractional accompaniment to the helmet deniers. The several unclassified varieties were perhaps changed pari passu with the helmet issues.

ANONYMOUS (period *ca.* 1200)

35. Æ (Pl. V)

Obv. Three-towered castle with double-doored gate; three small bushes in the foreground. No inscription.

Rev. ΛN │ TIOC │ HIΛ in three lines across the field, the inscription divided by thin lines.

0.6–0.8 g.

Schlumberger 57 (pl. III, 12).

36. Æ (Pl. V)

Obv. Ƨ and four pellets in beaded inner circle; + PRINCEPS, sometimes retrograde.

Rev. Cross with crescent in one angle and pellets in the others; within beaded inner circle. +ΛNTIO·hIΛ (or variant).

0.6–1.0 g.

Schlumberger 58 (pl. III, 16).

BOHEMOND IV (1201–1232)

37. Billon or Æ (Pl. V)

Obv. Cross pattée with annulet at each end and pellet in each angle, within beaded inner circle; + BOΛMVNDVS.

Rev. Crescent and six-pointed star, within beaded inner circle; + ΛNTIOCHIΛ or variant.

1.0 g.

Schlumberger 53 (pl. III, 3).

RAYMOND ROUPEN (1216–1219)

38. Billon denier (Pl. V)

Obv. As no. 33; + R V : P : INVƧ :

Rev. As no. 33.

0.6–1.1 g.

Numis. Chr., 7-IX (1969), 265.

BOHEMOND IV (1201–1232) or BOHEMOND V (1232–1251)

39. Billon denier (Pl. V)

Obv. As no. 33.

Rev. As no. 33.

0.6–0.9 g.

Numis. Chr., 5-XVII (1937), 200–210; *ibid.,* 7-IX (1969), 257–267. This last (post *ca.* 1220) issue of the helmet denier is distinguished from earlier varieties by its cruder style and lighter weight. It is unlikely to have been struck much after 1232.

40. Æ (Pl. V)

Obv. B in sometimes beaded inner circle; + BOΛMVNDV or
IOΛMVNDV (one variety reads + ΛIITIOCHEI).

Rev. Cross in inner circle; + ΛNTIOCHIΛ (or blundered version;
e.g., one variety reads NDOIT).

0.7–0.8 g.

Schlumberger 37 (pl. III, 13 & 14).

Kingdom of Jerusalem

BALDWIN III (1143–1162)

41. Billon denier (Pl. VI)

Obv. Cross in beaded inner circle; ⦂ (or +) REX BΛLDVINVS.

Rev. Tower in beaded inner circle; ⦂ (or +) DE IERVSΛLEM (variants read ⦂DE hIERVSΛLEM and DE bIERVSΛLEM).

0.95 g. (average).

Numis. Chr., 7-XVIII (1978), 71; *Rev. numis.,* 6-VIII (1966), 92. The
two variants seem likely to be the earliest issues.

42. Billon maille or obole (Pl. VI)

Obv. As no. 41; ⦂   REX BΛLDVINVS.

Rev. As no. 41; ⦂   (or +) DE IERVSΛLEM.

0.45 g. (average).

Numis. Chr., 7-XVIII (1978), 75; *Rev. numis.,* 6-VIII (1966), 92.

43. Billon denier (Pl. VI)

Obv. As no. 41; REX BΛLDVINVS, neat lettering; X and Λ decorated
with annulets.

Rev. As no. 41; + DE IERVSΛLEM, neat lettering; Λ decorated with
annulets.

0.97 g. (average).

Numis. Chr., 7-XVIII (1978), 78; *Rev. numis.,* 6-VIII (1966), 92.

44. Billon maille or obole (Pl. VI)

Obv. As no. 43.

Rev. As no. 43.

0.48 g. (average).

Numis. Chr., 7-XVIII (1978), 79; *Rev. numis.,* 6-VIII (1966), 92.

AMALRIC (1162–1175) and his successors (to *ca.* 1200)

45. Billon denier (Pl. VI)
Obv. Cross with pellets or annulets in second and third angles, all within beaded inner circle; ◦ AMALRICVS REX.
Rev. Holy Sepulcher in beaded inner circle; + DE IERVSALEM.
0.9 g. (average).
Schlumberger 85.

46. Billon maille or obole (Pl. VI)
Obv. As no. 45.
Rev. As no. 45.
0.4 g. (average).
Schlumberger 85.

ANONYMOUS (period *ca.* 1190)

47. Billon denier (Pl. VI)
Obv. Patriarchal cross between A and ⍵, within beaded inner circle; MONETA REGIS.
Rev. Cross in beaded inner circle; + REX IERL'M (or IERNM).
0.6–0.8 g.
Schlumberger 91 (pl. III, 27); *Rev. numis.,* 2-X (1865), 297.

48. Æ (Pl. VI)
Obv. Tower of David, sometimes between two annulets or pellets, within beaded inner circle; T·V·R·R·I·S· with annulets or pellets between letters.
Rev. Eight-pointed star within beaded inner circle; + ·D·A·V·I·T· with annulets or pellets between letters.
0.6–0.9 g.
Numis. Chr., 7-XVIII (1978), 85–92.

GUY OF LUSIGNAN (1186–1192)

49. Æ (Pl. VI)
Obv. Facing head, crowned and bearded, within beaded inner circle; + REXGVIDOD.
Rev. Domed building within beaded inner circle; EIERVSALEGN.
0.9–1.4 g.
Schlumberger 88 (pl. III, 25). Schlumberger identified the building on the reverse as the Dome of the Rock as shown on seals of the kingdom, but the indication of a hole in the dome suggests that the Holy Sepulcher is represented.

HENRY OF CHAMPAGNE (1192–1197)

50. Æ pougeoise, Acre (Pl. VI)

    Obv. Cross pattée with annulet in each angle, within beaded inner circle; + COGⴄЄS HENRICVS.

    Rev. Fleur de lis within beaded inner circle; + PVGЄS ÐⴀCCON.

    0.7–1.5 g. A piedfort in the Bibliothèque nationale weighs 9.6 g.

    Schlumberger 92 (pl. III, 28).

51. Æ pougeoise, Acre (Pl. VI)

    Obv. As no. 50.

    Rev. Hexagram with a circle at its center and annulets in the angles, within beaded inner circle; + PVGЄS DⴀCCON.

    0.8 g.

    Numis. Chr., 7-XVII (1977), 185.

AIMERY OF LUSIGNAN (1197–1205) and his successors (to *ca.* 1220)

52. Billon denier (Pl. VII)

    Obv. Cross with annulets in first and fourth angles, within inner circle; ⴀMⴀLRICVS RЄX.

    Rev. Holy Sepulcher, in inner circle; + DЄ IЄRVSⴀLЄM.

    0.6 g. (average).

    Cox (ANS, NNM, no. 59; 1933), p. 50; *Rev. numis.,* 4-XXXVIII (1935), 167.

JOHN OF BRIENNE (1210–1225)

53. Billon denier, Damietta (Pl. VII)

    Obv. Head facing, wearing triangular crown with pendants, in inner circle; + IOHⴀNNЄS RЄX.

    Rev. Cross with annulets in second and third quarters, in inner circle; + DⴀMIЄTⴀ.

    0.6–0.8 g.

    Rev. numis., 4-XXXVI (1933), 173; Schlumberger (Supplement) 6 (pl. XX, 4). This coin and the next must date from the Franks' occupation of Damietta in 1219.

54. Billon denier, Damietta (Pl. VII)

    Obv. Crowned head facing, in inner circle; + DⴀMIⴀTⴀ (or variant punctuation).

    Rev. Cross with pellets or annulets in second and third quarters, within inner circle; + IOhЄS ፧ RЄX.

    0.6–0.9 g.

    Rev. numis., 4-XXXVI (1933), 173; Schlumberger 93 (pl. III, 31).

55. Æ dragma or dirhem (Pl. VII)

    Obv. Cross with pellets or annulets in second and third quarters, within inner circle; + IOHANNES REX.

    Rev. Holy Sepulcher, within inner circle; + DEIERVSALEM.

    2.2–2.8 g. There is a pierced specimen (2.6 g.) struck on a scyphate flan.

    Schlumberger 92 (pl. III, 30). In view of the mint signature on the next coin it seems reasonable to ascribe this one also to Acre.

ANONYMOUS (period *ca.* 1220–1240)

56. Æ dragma or dirhem, Acre (Pl. VII)

    Obv. Cross pattée, sometimes with pellet or annulet in second quarter, within inner circle; DRAGMA·ACCONSIS (ACCONEN or ACCONENS).

    Rev. Holy Sepulcher, within inner circle; + SEPVLCHRI ɤ DOMINI (various punctuation).

    2.1–2.5 g.

    Schlumberger (Supplement) 4 (pl. XX, 3).

Kingdom of Jerusalem (?)

The coins in this section are certainly coins of the Latin states in Syria and Palestine, but the evidence on which they are attributed specifically to the kings of Jerusalem is by no means conclusive.

57. A′ dinar (Pl. VII)

    Obv. Paschal Lamb nimbate to left, holding standard, within inner circle. Inscription in two circles: + AGNVS : DEI : QVI : LLIT ; (inside) + PECCATA : ๛VnDI.

    Rev. Cross with pellet in first angle within inner circle. Inscription in two circles: + XPISTVS : VINCIT : XPISTVS REG ; (inside) + XPISTVS I๛PERAT.

    3.3–3.6 g.

    Rev. numis., 6-VIII (1966), 89.

58. Billon denier (Pl. VII)

    Obv. Cross pattée within inner circle; + SΛИΛCƆOΛ (?).

    Rev. Church towering over two flanking minarets. No inscription.

    0.8–1.0 g.

    Numis. Chr., 7-XVIII (1977), 184.

59. Billon obole.
    Obv. Cross pattée within beaded inner circle. ∾. N ∧.
    Rev. Church towering over two flanking minarets. No inscription.
    0.41 g.
    Numis. Chr., 8-II (1982), 160.

60. Billon denier (Pl. VII)
    Obv. Patriarchal cross on block between two branches and stars.
        No inscription.
    Rev. Cross pattée, in beaded inner circle; +⁚ CRV⁚ CIS⁚ (or +
        V⁚CRVCIS, retrograde).
    0.7–1.1 g.
    Schlumberger 493 (pl. XIX, 3); *Numismatic Circular* (Feb. 1966), p.
    32.

61. Billon obole.
    Obv. Patriarchal cross on block between two branches and stars.
        No inscription.
    Rev. Cross pattée in beaded inner circle. + CRVS.∾CIV retrograde.
    0.35 g.
    Numis. Chr., 8-II (1982), 160.

62. Billon denier.
    Obv. Tower of David with four flags, two protruding from each
        side, within inner circle. + TVRRIS DA̅VIT (?), retrograde.
    Rev. Holy Sepulcher, showing rock tomb and edicule, within inner
        circle; + [SEPVLCHRVM] DOMINI (?).
    1.0–1.2 g.
    Numis. Chr., 7-XIX (1979), 122.

63. Billon denier, Jaffa (Pl. VII)
    Obv. Cross pattée in inner circle; +∘DENA̅RIVS∘.
    Rev. Building with high central tower and lower flanking towers, in
        inner circle; +∘ IOPPENSIS.
    0.7 g.
    Schlumberger 110 (pl. IV, 29). The question whether this coin was
    struck by royal authority or that of a count of Jaffa still remains
    open.

64. Billon denier.
    Obv. Two vertical bars with a small cross above and an annulet
        below, all within inner circle. + IIOIIOII or variant.
    Rev. Cross pattée with pellet in each angle, within inner circle. Sim-
        ilar inscription.
    0.4–0.5 g.
    Numis. Chr., 7-XX (1980), 100. Schlumberger ascribed this coin to
    Tripoli, and others have followed him, but the evidence for any
    attribution is slight. It is probably to be dated after 1230.

County of Tripoli

BERTRAND (1109–1112)

65. Æ or billon denier (Pl. VIII)
Obv. Cross pattée within beaded inner circle; + B·TRⱯⱮDVS CO.
Rev. TⱯS and four pellets within inner circle; + TRIPOLISCIVI.
0.8 g.
Schlumberger 100 (pl. IV, 1).

ANONYMOUS (period *ca.* 1112)

66. Æ denier (Pl. VIII)
Obv. Cross within beaded inner circle; + TRI∴PO∴LIS.
Rev. TⱯS and two pellets within inner circle; + TRIPOVISCIVI.
0.8 g.
Schlumberger 101 (pl. IV, 2).

RAYMOND II (1136–1152) or RAYMOND III (1152–1187)

67. Æ (Pl. VIII)
Obv. Cross with single pellets or annulets in the upper angles and three in the lower angles, within beaded inner circle; MONETⱯ TRIPOLIS.
Rev. Short cross pattée with annulet at each end; ꞦAIMVNDI COMITIS (or COMITI').
0.8–1.2 g. (but there exists an exceptional piece of 2.3 g.).
Schlumberger 101 (pl. IV, 3). The author is not inclined to accept the theory that these coins were struck by Raymond of St. Gilles.

68. Æ (Pl. VIII)
Obv. Cross with pellet in each angle, within beaded inner circle; + RⱯIMVNDVS COMⒺS.
Rev. Lamb (or horse?) to left with processional cross behind, within beaded inner circle; + CIVITⱯS TRIPOLIS or + TRIPO-LIS CIVITⱯS.
0.9–1.1 g.
Schlumberger 103 (pl. IV, 8); see also Poey d'Avant, II, 253 for the related coins of the county of Saint Gilles.

69. Æ
Obv. Crescent and star of eight rays with pellets between the rays, within inner circle; + RⱯMVNDVS.
Rev. Cross with three pellets at each end and scepters in each angle. No inscription.
1.2 g.
Schlumberger 102 (pl. IV, 5).

RAYMOND III (1152–1187)

70. Billon denier (Pl. VIII)

    Obv. Cross with pellets in first and second angles, within beaded
    inner circle; + RΛMVNDVS COMS. Initial cross and letters
    ΛMNDS and C decorated with pellets and/or double bars.

    Rev. Crescent and star of eight rays with pellets between the rays;
    CIVITΛS TRIPOLIS. Letters CS and PO decorated as on obv.

    0.9–1.0 g.

    Schlumberger 102 (pl. IV, 4).

RAYMOND III and his successors (to *ca.* 1200)

71. Billon denier (Pl. VIII)

    Obv. Cross pattée within beaded inner circle; ⊞ RΛMVNDVS
    COMS.

    Rev. Star of eight rays with annulets in angles, in beaded inner
    circle; ⊞ CIVITΛS TRIPOLIS.

    0.6–0.9 g.

    Cox (ANS, NNM, no. 59; 1933), p. 55.

ANONYMOUS (period *ca.* 1180–1200)

72. Æ (Pl. VIII)

    Obv. Crescent and star of eight rays with pellets between the rays,
    within beaded inner circle; CIVITΛS TRIPOLIS (or variant).

    Rev. Long cross, the ends branching into fleurons of three pellets;
    in the angles scepters with pellets at the tip. No inscription.

    0.9–1.3 g.

    Schlumberger 103 (pl. IV, 6).

73. Æ (Pl. IX)

    Obv. Crenelated gate or castle with double doorway, within beaded
    inner circle; + CIVITΛS (or variant).

    Rev. Cross with circle at the center, globules at the ends, and cres-
    cents in the angles, set either straight or saltire-wise in beaded
    inner circle; + TRIPOLIS.

    0.6–0.9 g.

    Schlumberger 103 (pl. IV, 9, 10, 11).

BOHEMOND (IV of ANTIOCH) (*ca.* 1187–1232)

74. Billon denier (Pl. IX)

    Obv. As no. 71; + (or ⊞) BΛMVNDVS COMS.

    Rev. As no. 71.

    0.81 g. (average).

    Rev. numis., 4-XXXVIII (1935), 175.

ANONYMOUS (period *ca.* 1200–1230)

75. Æ (Pl. IX)
    Obv. Cross with circle at center, globules at the ends, and pellets in each angle, within beaded inner circle; + CIVITΛS.
    Rev. Crenelated tower, in beaded inner circle; + TRIPOLIS.
    0.6–1.1 g.
    Schlumberger 103 (pl. IV, 12, 13, 14). This type comprises several varieties, distinguished principally by the conformation of the tower on the reverse.

BOHEMOND (IV of ANTIOCH) (*ca.* 1187–1232)
BOHEMOND (V of ANTIOCH) (1232–1251)
BOHEMOND (VI of ANTIOCH) (1251–1274)

76. Billon denier (Pl. IX)
    Obv. Cross pattée within inner circle; + or · BΛMVND'COMS.
    Rev. Star of six (or sometimes eight) rays with annulets or pellets between the rays, within inner circle; + or : CIVITΛS TRIPOL'.
    0.4 g. (average).
    Schlumberger 104 (pl. IV, 18). Some varieties have a pellet in the first angle of the cross.

77. Æ gros (Pl. IX)
    Obv. Cross in beaded inner circle; + BΛMVND'COMS.
    Rev. Eight-pointed star with annulets in angles, within beaded inner circle; + CIVITΛS TRIPOL'.
    1.9 g. (broken).
    Unpublished.

78. Billon denier.
    Obv. Cross pattée, in beaded inner circle; + BΛMVND' COMS.
    Rev. Star of six rays, annulets between the rays, in inner circle; + CITE TRIPOL.
    0.4 g.
    Unpublished (Bibliothèque nationale, no. 4154).

79. Billon denier (Pl. IX)
    Obv. Cross pattée, in inner circle; + B-O·COMS:
    Rev. As no. 78.
    0.3–0.4 g.
    Schlumberger 105 (pl. IV, 25).

BOHEMOND (VI of ANTIOCH) (1251–1274)

80. Æ gros (of tournois weight) (Pl. IX)

   Obv. Cross pattée in frame of four arches and four angles with drops in the spandrels; all within beaded inner circle; + ˙BOEMVNDVS **:** COMES.

   Rev. Star of eight rays with pellets between set in tressure of eight arches with drops in the spandrels; all within beaded inner circle; + CIVITⱭS **:** TRIPOL·I·

   4.2 g.

   Schlumberger 105 (pl. IV, 19).

81. Æ gros (of Venetian or half-tournois weight) (Pl. IX)

   Obv. As no. 80.

   Rev. As no. 80.

   2.1 g.

   Schlumberger 105 (pl. IV, 20).

BOHEMOND (VII OF ANTIOCH) (1274–1287)

82. Æ gros (of tournois weight) (Pl. IX)

   Obv. Cross pattée in tressure of twelve arches, all within beaded inner circle; + SEPTIMUS·BOEMVNDVS·COMES.

   Rev. Three-towered castle in tressure of twelve arches, all within beaded inner circle; + CIVITⱭS **:** TRIPOLIS **:** SYRIE.

   4.3 g.

   Schlumberger 106 (pl. IV, 21).

83. Æ gros (of Venetian or half-tournois weight) (Pl. IX)

   Obv. As no. 82.

   Rev. As no. 82.

   2.1 g.

   Schlumberger 105 (pl. IV, 22).

Lordship of Beirut

JOHN OF IBELIN (1198–1236)

84. Billon denier (Pl. X)

    Obv. Cross with crescents in first and fourth angles and annulets in second and third, all within beaded inner circle; + IOﬁS DE IBELIﬄO (or BELIﬄO).

    Rev. Twin-towered gate within beaded inner circle; + CIVITᴧS BERITI.

    0.8–1.0 g.

    Rev. numis., 4-XXXVIII (1935), 175; 6-VIII (1966), 97; Cox (ANS, NNM, no. 59; 1933), p. 53.

85. Billon denier (Pl. X)

    Obv. Cross, sometimes with crescent in second and third angles, within inner circle; + IOhᴧﬄNES.

    Rev. City gate, in inner circle; + DE BERITI.

    0.6–0.7 g.

    Schlumberger 118 (pl. V, 10).

86. Billon denier.

    Obv. Cross pattée with annulets in first and fourth angles, within beaded inner circle; + IOhS DYBELIﬄO.

    Rev. Crenelated tower, annulet below, within beaded inner circle; + DﬄS BERITEﬄS.

    0.9 g.

    Rev. numis., 6-VIII (1966), 97.

ANONYMOUS (period *ca.* 1200–1250)

87. Æ

    Obv. Towered city gateway, in inner circle; + DE BᴧRVTh.

    Rev. Interlace pattern interspersed with pellets. No inscription.

    0.6–1.4 g.

    Schlumberger 111 (pl. V, 27).

88. Æ (Pl. X)

    Obv. Towered city gateway, within inner circle; + DE BERITEHSIE (or + DE BEROTOLE).

    Rev. Interlace pattern interspersed with annulets. No inscription.

    0.6–1.25 g.

    Schlumberger 111 (pls. V, 12, & XX, 11).

Lordship of Tyre

PHILIP OF MONTFORT (1246–1270)

89. Æ (Pl. X)

> *Obv.* Cross with pellet or annulet in each angle, within beaded inner circle; + PhЄLIPЄ.
>
> *Rev.* Building with tall steeple between two pellets or annulets, all within beaded inner circle; SIRЄ·D·SVR.
>
> 0.7–1.3 g.
>
> *Numismatic Circular* (March 1966), p. 61.

90. Æ (Pl. X)

> *Obv.* Cross within beaded inner circle; : +:PhЄLIPЄ.
>
> *Rev.* Portico of four columns, within beaded inner circle; + DЄ SVR.
>
> 1.1–1.5 g.
>
> Schlumberger 28 (pl. V, 14).

JOHN OF MONTFORT (1270–1283)

91. Æ (Pl. X)

> *Obv.* Cross within beaded inner circle; + IOh SIRЄ.
>
> *Rev.* Portico of four columns, within beaded inner circle; + DЄ SVR.
>
> 1.1–1.4 g.
>
> *Numismatic Circular* (March 1966), p. 62.

92. Æ (Pl. X)

> *Obv.* Cross within beaded inner circle; + IOh SIRЄ.
>
> *Rev.* Portico of two columns with arched doorway between, within beaded inner circle; + DЄ ᴧVR.
>
> 1.2–1.3 g.
>
> *Numismatic Circular* (March 1966), p. 62.

Lordship of Sidon

REGINALD GRENIER (d. *ca.* 1204)

93. Billon denier (Pl. XI)
    Obv. Tower within inner circle; + RENⱭLDVS.
    Rev. Arrow pointing left, within inner circle; + SYDONIⱭ.
    0.8–1.3 g.
    Schlumberger 114 (pl. V, 3). This coin is probably to be ascribed to
    the period before Saladin's capture of Sidon in 1187, but Reginald
    survived until about 1204 and by then the Franks had recaptured
    part of the lordship and maybe controlled the city. A date after
    1187, though unlikely, cannot be ruled out for these coins.

ANONYMOUS (date uncertain)

94. Æ (Pl. XI)
    Obv. Arrow between groups of three pellets, within inner circle; +
        S Ʀ A D.
    Rev. Six-pointed star-like figure with globules at the ends, within
        inner circle; + ·S·I·D·O·N·
    0.9 g.
    Bibliothèque nationale (no. 4177); cf. Schlumberger (Supplement) 7
    (pl. XX, 6). Schlumberger ascribes the coin engraved in this plate,
    which shows the reverse inscription retrograde, to Gerard, father of
    Reginald and lord of Sidon in the mid-twelfth century. The inscrip-
    tion on the obv. of the BN coin is by no means so convincing.
    Compared with the neat reverse legend it appears to be deliberately
    obscure, and the case for the reading GIRARDVS is by no means
    conclusive. Were it not for the ambiguity of the obverse inscription
    there would be no difficulty in classifying this with the other coins of
    Sidon with blundered legends, for which the mid-thirteenth century
    seems the likely date.

ANONYMOUS (after 1220?)

95. Æ (Pl. XI) ·
    Obv. Arrow between groups of three pellets, within inner circle;
        ///SYD//N.
    Rev. Holy Sepulcher, within inner circle; inscription illegible ///Ɐ///.
    0.7–1.0 g.
    Schlumberger 114 (pl. V, 7).

96. Æ (Pl. XI)

    Obv. Formless building (presumably Holy Sepulcher) surmounted by a cross, within inner circle. Garbled inscription.

    Rev. Arrow between two pellets within inner circle. Garbled inscription //// V੧O ////.

    0.7–1.0 g.

    Schlumberger 115 (pl. V, 6).

97. Æ (Pl. XI)

    Obv. Arrow between groups of three pellets, within inner circle. Inscription illegible.

    Rev. Six-pointed star-like figure with globules at the ends, within inner circle. Inscription illegible.

    0.5–1.0 g.

    Schlumberger 114 (pl. V, 4 & 5).

98. Æ (Pl. XI)

    Obv. Arrow pointing downward between two crosslets and four annulets, within outer circle. No inscription.

    Rev. Six-pointed star-like figure with globules at the ends, within outer circle. No inscription.

    0.6–1.2 g.

    Numismatic Circular (March 1966), p. 62.

99. Billon denier (Pl. XI)

    Obv. Cross pattée in inner circle; + ·D·Є·N·I·Є·R·

    Rev. Holy Sepulcher, in inner circle; + ·D·Є·S·Є·Є·T·Є·

    0.4–0.8 g.

    Schlumberger 115 (pl. V, 8).

I. Coinage of the county of Edessa

410

6   7

8   9

10   11

12   13

II. Coinage of the county of Edessa

411

14 15

16 17

18 19

20 21

22 23

III. Coinage of the principality of Antioch

412

24

25   26

27

28   29

30   31   32

IV. Coinage of the principality of Antioch

413

33

34

35

36

37

38

39

40

V. Coinage of the principality of Antioch

414

41

42

43

44

45

46

47

48

49

50

51

VI. Coinage of the kingdom of Jerusalem

415

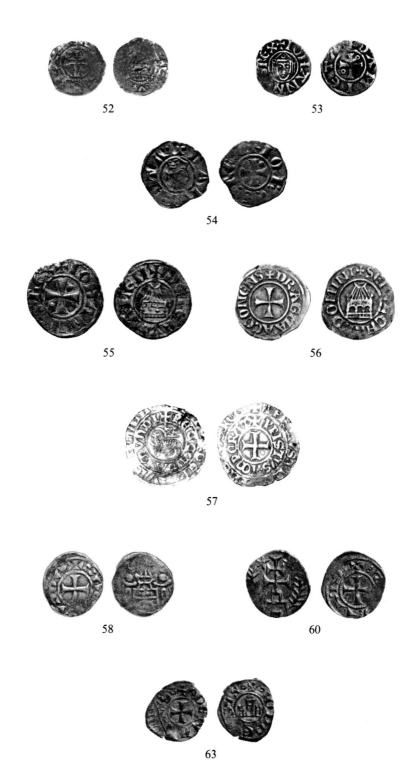

52

53

54

55

56

57

58

60

63

VII. Coinage of the kingdom of Jerusalem

416

65

66

67

68

70

71

72

VIII. Coinage of the county of Tripoli

417

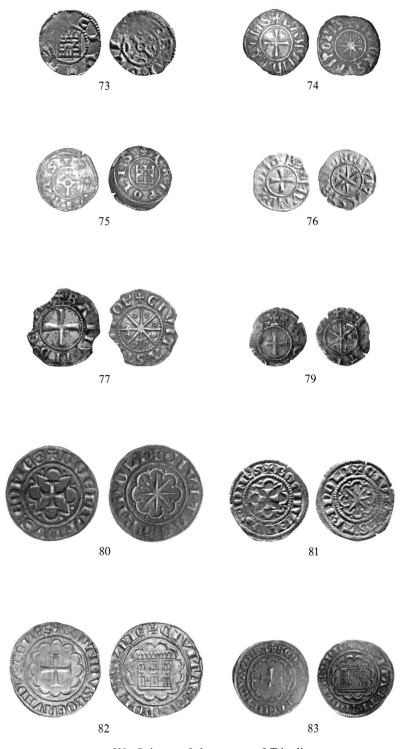

73 74 75 76 77 79 80 81 82 83

IX. Coinage of the county of Tripoli

Beirut

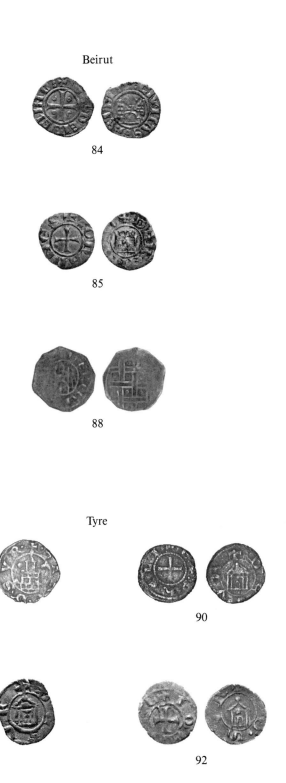

84

85

88

Tyre

89

90

91

92

X. Coinage of the lordships of Beirut and Tyre

93   94

95   96

97   98

99

XI. Coinage of the lordship of Sidon

420

XI

CRUSADER COINAGE
WITH ARABIC INSCRIPTIONS

A. *The Islamic Context*[1]

CURRENCY IN THE MOSLEM WORLD

In the Islamic lands, the crusaders encountered monetary systems quite different from the one they knew in Latin Europe, where the only coins until the thirteenth century were small, often debased, silver deniers (pennies). The Moslems, in contrast, used gold dinars, silver dirhams, and copper *fulūs* (*fals* in the singular). Not every part of the Islamic world had coins in all three metals at the same time. Systems varied from place to place, even within the realms of dynasties such as the Fāṭimids, Aiyūbids, and Mamluks, and evolved during the two centuries the crusaders were in Syria.

Some features, nevertheless, were general among the Moslems whom the crusaders met. In the Moslem lands, as elsewhere in pre-modern

For the coinage of the major Islamic dynasties in contact with the crusaders, see, for the Fāṭimids, George C. Miles, *Fatimid Coins in the Collections of the University Museum, Philadelphia, and the American Numismatic Society* (ANS, Numismatic Notes and Monographs, no. 121; New York, 1951), a catalogue of one major collection only but with references to all previous work; for the Aiyūbids, Paul Balog, *The Coinage of the Ayyubids* (Royal Numismatic Society Special Publication, no. 12; London, 1980); for the Mamluks, *idem, The Coinage of the Mamluk Sultans of Egypt and Syria* (ANS, Numismatic Studies, no. 12 [New York, 1964]). Both these latter are corpuses, including all coins known at the time of publication. The standard reference for all the Arabic coins of the crusaders is Paul Balog and Jacques Yvon, "Monnaies à légendes arabes de l'Orient latin," *Rev. numis.,* 6th ser., I (1958), 133–168; the abbreviation BY used frequently below indicates the variety numbers established by them. The most recent general classification of the crusader gold varieties is Adon A. Gordus and D. M. Metcalf, "Neutron Activation Analysis of the Gold Coinages of the Crusader States" (similarly, GM), in *Metallurgy in Numismatics,* ed. Metcalf and W. A. Oddy, I (London, 1980), 119–150, summarized with some additional refinements by Metcalf, *Coinage of the Crusades and the Latin East in the Ashmolean Museum, Oxford* (London, 1983), pp. 9–14, 42–44. For the crusader Arabic dirhams, the standard survey is Michael L. Bates, "Thirteenth Century Crusader Imitations of Ayyubid Silver Coinage: a Preliminary Survey," in *Near Eastern Numismatics, Iconography, Epigraphy and History: Studies in Honor of George C. Miles,* ed. Dickran K. Kouymjian (Beirut, 1974), pp. 393–409.

1. This section is by Bates.

economies, precious metal coins were struck from bullion or non-current coins that were brought to the mint by the government or by private persons. Charges for materials and labor were levied proportionately on the coins struck from the material brought in by the customer. Private persons had to pay a government seigneurage (mint tax) in addition. As a result, the amount of bullion in the coins received by the customer was less than the amount of bullion brought in. In other words, coins were a manufactured product with a value (buying power) greater than an equivalent amount of the raw material from which they were made. The difference in value between coins and the bullion in them was fundamentally a result of the mint charges, but was also affected by such factors as inconvenience of minting, transport charges to the mint, reluctance of individuals to reveal holdings of precious metals, and many other intangible factors which can be summed up as the result of supply and demand in a given place at a given time. As legal tender, only current coins could be used for payments to the government and in most transactions between private parties, and this legal constraint was sufficient to keep their money value above their intrinsic (metal) value. If a coin issue was demonetized (abolished as legal tender), its value would drop to the value of the bullion in each coin, causing a loss to the possessors at the time of demonetization.

In a minting regime such as that described, coins can be exchanged by count only if the proportional variation in weight of individual coins is less than the difference between the value of the raw metal in them and their value as coins. If coins circulate by count, and some coins vary from the normal weight by more than total mint costs, it may become profitable to withdraw these heavier coins from circulation to melt and return to the mint, obtaining more coins with a higher money value from the same amount of bullion. There may be a tendency to set aside heavier coins, with a higher intrinsic value, for savings, while returning lighter coins to circulation, and it may become profitable to clip the edges of coins, retaining the same money value while profiting from the bullion value of the clippings. These practices, if they become common, will result in a general lowering of the average weight of the issue in circulation and thereby force weighing of payments in self-defense.

For a government to force its coins to circulate by count, it must either set minting charges high, creating a large difference between their bullion value and their money value, or control the weight of its coins very precisely.[2] Some Moslem coinages are known to have circulated

2. For a fuller discussion of monetary theory relating to pre-modern mints see Gilles P.

by count, suggesting that one of the two latter conditions obtained, but in the crusader period most precious metal issues were weighed out in transactions. A payment of 100 dinars, for example, took the form of an amount of coins equal in weight to 100 times the current standard weight of the dinar, an amount which might be more or less than 100 individual coins. The process of weighing was recognized as an inconvenience, but was considered normal. Almost every transaction required a balance, with standard weights supplied or regulated by the government.[3] To alleviate the inconvenience somewhat, coins were often sealed in purses, with a label indicating the content by weight; these purses, if sealed by government agencies or reputable money-changers, could be passed from hand to hand like large-denomination notes today. A form of check, *ruq'ah,* also was used in payments.[4] It is important to realize, therefore, that while the words "dinar" and "dirham" meant respectively "a gold coin" or "a silver coin", a payment of a certain number of dinars or dirhams meant transferral of that many weight units of the coinage in question—the number of coins was immaterial.

Because the intrinsic value of precious metal coins was close—even though not equal—to their monetary value, it would have been impossible for any government to guarantee effectively the relationship of denominations in two different metals. To do so would have meant to back up the relationship by standing ready to exchange either for the other at a set rate, but this was impossible in practice because of fluctuations in the prices of the metals. (It is impossible even in the twentieth century, as shown by the abandonment by all governments of precious metal coins with a defined legal tender value. The fixed relationships of modern coins and notes are possible only because their intrinsic worth is far less than their nominal value.)

Hennequin, "Problèmes théoriques et pratiques de la monnaie antique et médiévale," *Annales islamologiques,* X (1972), 1–51.

3. The major exception in the crusader era was the new dirham coinage introduced by Saladin in Syria and Egypt in the late twelfth century, which circulated by count at least some of the time. Other exceptions would include most copper coins, which were probably sold by the mint against payment in silver or gold coins at a price far above the value of the copper in them, many small transactions (a Syrian market manual of Saladin's time refers to a rule that transactions of less than four coins could be by count), and informal payments—no one weighed a coin before tossing it to a beggar. On the other hand, no eastern Mediterranean Islamic gold coinage of the period 1092–*ca.* 1420 could have circulated by count, although the western Mediterranean dinars of the type introduced by the Muwaḥḥids probably did.

4. Solomon D. F. Goitein, *A Mediterranean Society,* 3 vols. (Berkeley, 1967–1978), I, 229–266, discusses means of payment in 10th–13th-century Egypt and Syria in detail. For the evidence for weighing see also Bates, "The Function of Fāṭimid and Ayyūbid Glass Weights," *Journal of the Economic and Social History of the Orient,* XXIV (1981), 70–81.

In the Moslem world and almost all pre-modern economies, current gold and silver coins were related in value only by the marketplace, like different national currencies today. Governments could fix values only in certain transactions (for example, in denominating salaries in one currency while paying them in another) and sometimes might attempt to decree relationships in private transactions, but such decrees were widely evaded and impossible to enforce. In normal times values were fairly stable, so that people could have a notional rate for the relationship of the dinar and the dirham, but in any substantial transactions involving both coins the exchange rate had to be set by negotiation. The value of foreign coins in local currency was also determined by supply and demand, not by precious metal content; moreover, if payments were made by weight, local weights would have been used to measure foreign coins, so that varying coin weight standards would have no effect on value. To be sure, metal content set a floor value for any coin, but its actual equivalency in local currency was set in the marketplace.

ISLAMIC GOLD COINAGE

The major Moslem mints for gold coinage in the vicinity of the crusaders were Cairo and Alexandria in Egypt, and Mosul and Baghdad (named Madīnat as-Salām on coins) in Mesopotamia. A few other mints in the region issued gold occasionally. For gold coinage, the Euphrates was a clear dividing line between two different systems. The dinars of Mosul (pl. XII, no. 1) and Baghdad (pl. XII, no. 2) did not circulate in Syria and did not influence the coinage of the crusaders. The issues of both these mints continued the Selchükid Iranian tradition. For the eleventh and first half of the twelfth centuries, their coins are rather scarce, but after about 1160 the representation of both becomes more continuous, while for the thirteenth century (until the Mongol conquest) the coins of these mints are common, large, well engraved, and quite pure, although completely irregular in weight,[5] a general characteristic of gold coins east of the Euphrates from the tenth to the fourteenth centuries.

Egypt first minted gold coins under Islam in 786 and immediately became one of the principal centers of gold coinage in the Moslem world, issuing dinars continuously and abundantly throughout the 'Ab-

---

5. Arlette Nègre, "Le Monnayage d'or des sept derniers califes abbasides," *Studia islamica,* XLVII (1978), 165–175.

bāsid, Ṭūlūnid, and Ikhshīdid periods.[6] In northwestern Africa and Sicily the Fāṭimid monetary system included dinars, quarter dinars, and small silver dirhams. These coins were distinguished from those of the Sunnī ʿAbbāsid realms by the presence of certain Shīʿī inscriptions, by different weight standards, and especially by a design so obviously different that even illiterates in Arabic could distinguish the two coinages.

The conquest of Egypt by the Fāṭimids resulted in the introduction of their monetary system there, replacing the previous ʿAbbāsid-style coinage. Under al-Muʿizz (in Egypt, 969–975) and al-ʿAzīz (975–996), the Fāṭimid dinar was closely controlled in weight, and is said by a contemporary to have circulated by count,[7] but under al-Ḥākim (996–1021) a series of changes began. In A. H. 400 (1009/10), and then again in 404, the design of the dinar was substantially altered. The coinage of his successor, aẓ-Ẓāhir (1021–1036), was at first much like the last issues of al-Ḥākim, but new major changes were made in 420 (1029/30) and 424 or 425. Again, the earliest coinage of al-Mustanṣir (1036–1094) is like the third type of aẓ-Ẓāhir, but changes in arrangement and content of inscriptions were made in 430 (1038/9), 435 (pl. XII, no. 3), and 439, while in 440 (1048/9; pl. XII, no. 4) and 474 (1081/2; pl. XII, no. 5) radically different designs were introduced. Under al-Mustaʿlī (1094–1101) in Muḥarram 490 (1096/7),[8] another substantive change was made in the design of the gold coinage (pl. XII, no. 6). Thereafter Fāṭimid gold coinage was unchanged in appearance until the end of the dynasty (pl. XII, no. 7), except for the issues of aẓ-Ẓāfir (1149–1154).

The purpose of these new issues is not clear in every instance, and there is no need to discuss them in detail here, but it can be said in general that such obvious changes in the appearance of the coinage were not merely cosmetic, but marked changes in the monetary function of the coins. Contemporaries, it is clear, regarded the different issues as different monies, related to each other by fluctuating exchange rates;[9] put another way, each new issue became the standard current legal tender, while the previous issue was usable only to pay off debts

6. Egypt may have minted dinars before 786, but they cannot as yet be identified. Dinars of the late Ikhshīdid period are scarce today, perhaps as a result of the recoinage of gold forced after the Fāṭimid conquest, which would have brought most of the previously circulating dinars to the melting pot (Ibn-Muyassar, *Akhbār Miṣr,* ed. Ayman Fuʾad Sayyid, II [Cairo, 1981], 164).

7. Al-Maqdisī (al-Muqaddasī), *Aḥsān at-taqāsīm fī maʿrifat al-aqālīm,* ed. Martin J. de Goeje (Bibliotheca geographorum arabicorum, III; Leyden, 1906), p. 240.

8. Ibn-Muyassar, *op. cit.,* II, 65.

9. For example, Goitein, *op. cit.,* I, 239, citing a Geniza document of about 1060 which distinguishes between "lined" dinars (the issue or issues of 425–440) and "concentric" dinars (the

denominated in it, or for export, or as bullion. The kinds of monetary change that the new types marked might have included changes in the weight standard or metal alloy of the dinars or of the silver dirhams (which were changed in parallel with the dinars), changes in the way standards of alloy or weight were enforced, changes in the terms on which coins were issued from the mint, or changes in the weight standards used to measure out payments. The determination of which of these factors was behind any particular change rests upon a more careful study of Fāṭimid coinage than has yet been made, as well as a reëxamination of the written sources.

Al-Mustanṣir's coinage was the prototype for one group of crusader imitations, although most of the imitations do not precisely reproduce any of his coins. Balog and Yvon cite an issue struck from 1043 to 1047 (pl. XII, no. 3) as prototype for their crusader varieties 3–16,[10] but there does not seem to be any good reason for this short-lived issue to have been selected in particular. BY 3–16 have only four horizontal lines of inscription on the obverse, unlike any of al-Mustanṣir's issues. It is more realistic to say that these imitations merely reproduce, after a fashion, a coin type introduced first in 1043 or 1044 but retained with variations until 1048 or 1049, then reintroduced in 1081 or 1082 and retained until al-Mustanṣir's death in 1094. All the dinars of these years have the words "'Alī" and "Ma'add" at the top of the obverse and reverse field inscriptions, as do the imitations, but none of the originals have only three lines of inscription below these words as do the imitations. Probably the crusader die cutters attempted to reproduce only the general appearance of the prototype, condensing four or five lines into three. Most of these imitations are extremely barbarous, and their makers could have had no idea of the meaning of the inscriptions they attempted to copy. Very likely the coin they had before them was an example of al-Mustanṣir's last issue, which was struck in Egypt and Syria for about twelve years and ended only some three years before the First Crusade (the type was retained for a few years after al-Mustanṣir's death, but no longer with his name or the words "'Alī" and "Ma'add").

The concentric inscription type that interrupted the "'Alī-Ma'add" type may also have been imitated, but very sparingly if at all. Balog and Yvon list only one such coin in their corpus.[11] There may, how-

issue of 440–474), as well as between Damascus and Egyptian dinars of the same kind. These latter seem to the modern observer to be externally identical except for the mint names.

10. Balog and Yvon, *op. cit.,* pp. 145–146.

11. BY 1, a coin in the American Numismatic Society (0000.999.14974); its attribution is problematic (pl. XVI, no. 45); see below, p. 455.

ever, be others still attributed to the Fāṭimids in various collections. One example might be a dinar of Miṣr, 443, in the British Museum with a gold fineness of only 89.1 percent according to Oddy's measurement.[12] All the crusader imitations of al-Mustanṣir's issues are attributed in the next section to the county of Tripoli.

The last Fāṭimid type, beginning in 490 (1096/7), bears the words ʿāl ghāyah, "high standard (of fineness)" (pl. XII, no. 6),[13] and this issue, like its predecessor, was initially higher in fineness, probably as close to pure gold as technology permitted at the time, although this standard was not always maintained during the issue's century of life. On the other hand, the ʿāl ghāyah coins do not seem to have been struck to any weight standard. This mattered little, since dinars were usually weighed in payment.

It was this type that was most extensively imitated by the crusaders, specifically the issues of the caliph al-Āmir (1101–1130), whose dinars would have been the most common in circulation in the earliest years of the crusading principalities. According to Metcalf's chronology (below, pp. 441–448), these imitations would have begun at a date around the middle of the twelfth century and continued until the third quarter of the thirteenth; they are attributed to the kingdom of Jerusalem.

Egypt's rulers took pride in the high quality of their gold coinage, and the mint discriminated against foreign gold coins, even those of nearly the same level of purity. Generally speaking, this high quality was maintained: with few exceptions, Fāṭimid gold coins are better than 90 percent pure, and most are as pure as contemporary technique permitted.[14] Nevertheless, it would be gathered from what has been said that the picture of the Fāṭimid dinar as the "dollar of the Middle Ages", absolutely standard in weight and purity from the beginning to the end of the dynasty, is seriously misleading. Both the weight standard (or the standard of the weights used to measure transactions) and the purity of the Fāṭimid dinar were changed from time to time; contemporaries were well aware of these variations, but to reconstruct the exact sequence of changes will require a more minute study of the coinage than has yet been made.[15]

Egyptian dinars issued under the Aiyūbid sultan Saladin do not seem

12. Oddy, "The Gold Contents of Fāṭimid Coins Reconsidered," *Metallurgy in Numismatics,* I (London, 1980), 116, no. 811, plate 9.

13. For *ghāyah* as a synonym for "fineness", or more precisely "intended fineness", see Ibn-Khaldūn, *Al-muqaddimah,* I, ed. Étienne M. Quatremère, *Notices et extraits des manuscrits de la Bibliothèque nationale,* XVI (Paris, 1858), 407; Fr. trans. William MacGuckin de Slane, *ibid.,* XIX (1862), 460; Eng. trans. Franz Rosenthal (Bollingen Series, no. 43, New York, 1958), I, 464.

14. Oddy, *op. cit.,* pp. 99–118.

15. For a fuller discussion of these problems see Bates, "The Function," pp. 86–91.

to be materially different from those of the last Fāṭimids. The change in government and religion led to some modifications in the inscriptions and small changes in the arrangement, but the basic coin design, with brief central horizontal inscriptions surrounded by prominent circular legends, is much the same (pl. XII, no. 8). It has been asserted that Saladin abandoned standard weight for his gold coinage, but this in fact had happened long before, in 490 (1096/7); if the range of variation of Saladin's dinars is larger than that of al-'Āḍid's, this is probably a result of the larger number of coins available for study. It has also been asserted that Saladin debased his dinars significantly, but some of the low-fineness coins assigned to him may be crusader imitations. The alleged debasement of the dinar in his reign cannot be confirmed until careful numismatic study has separated his genuine coins from their crusader imitations.[16]

It was not until the reign of al-'Ādil Abū-Bakr I (1200–1218) that any substantive change in the appearance of the Aiyūbid dinar is seen (pl. XII, no. 9). In the first year of his reign a new dinar type with long horizontal inscriptions and a single marginal legend was introduced, or rather revived from the eleventh century. The mint alternated between the old and new designs during al-'Ādil's reign, but by the time of al-Kāmil (1218–1238) the new type was definitively adopted and maintained until after 713 (1313/4). Major variations on this type include the introduction of Naskhī script instead of Kufic after 622 (1225/6), and aẓ-Ẓāhir Baybars' use of a lion or leopard on dinars as his personal symbol (pl. XIII, no. 10), an innovation not maintained by his successors. There is no evidence to suggest that any of the changes after Saladin's time reflected a change in the weight standard, fineness, or other monetary functions of the Egyptian dinar, but the Aiyūbid and Mamluk gold coinage has yet to be examined rigorously on these points.

Miṣr, the official name of Fusṭāṭ, the commercial center of the Cairo metropolis, is the usual mint name on Fāṭimid Egyptian dinars. In 516 (1122/3), however, unspecified problems at the Fusṭāṭ mint led to the opening of an additional mint in the administrative center al-Qāhirah, that is, in Cairo properly speaking.[17] After 525 (1130/1) this mint ceased

---

16. Cf. Andrew S. Ehrenkreutz, "The Standard of Fineness of Gold Coins Circulating in Egypt at the Time of the Crusades," *Journal of the American Oriental Society*, LXXIV (1954), 162–166, a work published before the existence of crusader imitations of Aiyūbid gold was suspected.

17. Al-Maqrīzī, *Kitāb al-mawā'iẓ wa-l-i'tibar fī dhikhr al-khiṭaṭ wa-l-āthār* (Cairo, 1270/ 1853), I, 445. An issue of al-Ḥākim dated 394 (1003/4) is also known from a mint in Cairo, but this mint apparently operated only in this year for some special purpose.

operation, but in the troubled times of al-'Āḍid (1160–1171) a mint was again opened in Cairo and produced the bulk of his issues. This was apparently the only mint in the city under the Aiyūbids and Mamluks. A second regular mint was established in Egypt at Alexandria in 465 (1072/3)[18] and operated regularly into the fifteenth century. A mint also operated in Qūṣ in Upper Egypt from 517 (1123/4) to 519.

In eleventh-century Syria a number of towns had mints for the Fāṭimids: Aleppo, Damascus, Tiberias, Ramla (which used the name *Filasṭīn*, Palestine, on coins), Tyre, Tripoli, Acre, and Ascalon.[19] Of these, only Tyre may have minted continuously throughout the Fāṭimid period, but even there the record has gaps. The first four mints mentioned, all located inland, apparently ceased to operate in the 1060's, probably as a result of the Selchükid conquests in Syria. Production of Fāṭimid dinars was left to the port cities Tyre, Tripoli, and Acre—the latter issued dinars for the first time just as the inland mints were closing down, perhaps not coincidentally. The last recorded date for Acre and Tripoli is 495 (1101/2) while production at Ascalon began in 503 (1109/10), at the time of Tripoli's capture by the crusaders, and continued until 510 (1116/7). The last date recorded for Tyre is 517 (1123/4) (pl. XIII, no. 11),[20] just before it was taken by the crusaders (1124). According to a much later Arab writer, the crusaders kept the mint of Tyre open for three years after its conquest, striking coins in the name of al-Āmir.[21] *Dīnār Ṣūrī*, "Tyre dinar", was the generic Arabic term for the crusader Arabic gold coins, but only a small proportion of these imitations actually bear the mint-name Ṣūr.[22] These last three major Fāṭi-

18. The various references in the literature to issues of Alexandria before 465 are all to be dismissed; those that have been carefully examined have turned out to be misattributions. For example, the coin of the University Museum, Philadelphia, ascribed by Miles to the year 435 (Miles, *Fatimid Coins*, no. 259, pl. III; the coin is on loan to the American Numismatic Society, 1002.1.1083; pl. XVI, no. 46) is an imitation or counterfeit; its date is indistinct, but its type was not introduced until 474 (1081/2). It may well be a crusader imitation, as its gold fineness is approximately 78.5 percent by specific gravity measurement, the same as that of many crusader bezants.

19. The table in Miles, *op. cit.*, pp. 50–51, is still valid for the termination dates of Fāṭimid Syrian issues, except for Ṣūr (Tyre).

20. The unique dinar of that date is unpublished, in the collection of the American Numismatic Society (1955.131.1).

21. Ibn-Khallikān, *Kitāb wafāyat al-a'yan*, ed. Iḥsān 'Abbās (Beirut, n.d.), V, 301; Fr. trans. MacGuckin de Slane (Paris, 1843–1845), III, 456; see below, p. 441.

22. It seems odd that only a few crusader bezants can be assigned to Tyre, as will be seen below. Robert Irwin, "The Supply of Money and the Direction of Trade in Thirteenth-Century Syria," in *Coinage in the Latin East: the Fourth Oxford Symposium on Coinage and Monetary History*, ed. Peter W. Edbury and Metcalf (BAR International Series, no. 77; Oxford, 1980), p. 91, has explained this anomaly with the suggestion that from the late twelfth century, if not earlier, the word Ṣūrī was a calque on the French term "de Syrie".

mid Syrian mints for gold – Tyre, Tripoli, and Acre – are also the most likely locations for the mints that issued the crusader gold imitations.

After the Fāṭimid dinar mints closed, Moslem Syria had little gold coinage of its own. The mint of Damascus began issuing dinars in 530 (1135/6) and continued for about ten years, striking coins of Fāṭimid style with the names of the 'Abbāsid caliphs and the Selchükid sultans of the east, but these coins are quite scarce today, suggesting a small issue (pl. XIII, no. 12).[23] In 583 (1187/8) dinars were struck for Saladin in Damascus, perhaps to process the booty from Jerusalem and his other conquests in that year, but no other Moslem Syrian gold coins are known until the reign of Baybars (1260–1277).[24] For the most part, Syrians used imported Egyptian or crusader (Ṣūrī) dinars in the twelfth and thirteenth centuries.[25]

In addition to the mints listed in Syria, Egypt, and Mesopotamia, there are also a very few Rūm Selchükid issues in gold, from Konya beginning as early as 573 (1177/8), and from Sivas.[26]

23. Ibn-al-Qalānisī, *Dhail ta'rikh Dimashq,* ed. Henry F. Amedroz (Leyden, 1908), p. 257; trans. Roger Le Tourneau, *Damas de 1075 à 1145* (Damascus, 1952), p. 236 (where the text's description of the metal content of the coins is misconstrued as a list of denominations). Published examples of this series are few; one is in Stanley Lane-Poole, *Catalogue of Oriental Coins in the British Museum* (London, 1887–1890), III, 45, no. 88.

24. For the Damascus dinar issue of Saladin see Balog, *Ayyubids,* p. 77, no. 79. The first Damascus dinar of Baybars, with an illegible date, has recently been discovered in the collection of the Kuwait National Museum. Otherwise, Mamluk gold coinage in Damascus is known only from the reign of Kalavun (1279–1290) onward (*idem, Mamluk Sultans,* p. 120). The dinar attributed to Filasṭīn, 592, by Balog, *Ayyubids,* p. 108, no. 201 (now in the collection of the Kuwait National Museum, where it was reëxamined by one of the present authors), is surely misread. The mint name is somewhat unclear but is probably al-Iskandarīyah (Alexandria). It is, incidentally, not impossible that the reintroduction of gold minting at Damascus was a response to the cessation of crusader gold minting in or shortly after 1258.

25. Eliyahu Ashtor, *Histoire des prix et des salaires dans l'Orient médiéval* (Paris, 1969), pp. 239–240, and Irwin, *op. cit.,* pp. 91–93, provide many citations for the use of *Miṣrī* and *Ṣūrī* dinars. For example, the waqfs founded by Nūr-ad-Dīn (d. 1174) yielded in the year 608 (1211/2) 9,000 Ṣūrī dinars per month (Abū-Shāmah, *Kitāb ar-raudatain fī akhbār ad-daulatain,* ed. Muḥammad Ḥilmī Muḥammad Aḥmad [Cairo, 1956], I, 23). A waqf, of course, is a Moslem pious endowment for some worthy cause, so this is surely an example of the use of Ṣūrī dinars among Moslems, which Irwin denies. Another example cited by Irwin himself is a statement of the price of grain in Damascus in 1178/9 in Ṣūrī dinars. The debate over the use of crusader coins by Moslems has perhaps been overdrawn. Since Syria had no mint for gold during most of the 12th and 13th centuries, and since it is known that crusader bezants came into the Moslem territories as tribute, indemnities, and perhaps even trade payments, it can only be assumed that these bezants were used by Moslems in further transactions among themselves. The only alternatives would have been reserving such coins for return transactions with the crusaders or sending them to the Moslem mints in Egypt and Mesopotamia for recoinage. It does not necessarily follow that crusader coins predominated in the gold money in circulation, and only a tiny minority of transactions were large enough to make gold coins appropriate.

26. İbrahim and Cevriye Artuk, *İstanbul arkeoloji muzeleri teşhirdeki islâmî sikkeler kataloğu* (Istanbul, 1970), no. 1060 (Konya, 573), and *passim.*

ISLAMIC SILVER COINAGE

The eleventh and most of the twelfth centuries have been regarded as an era of "silver famine" for the Moslem Near East, with little or no silver coinage, but this is a misconception, as shown not only by the frequent references in Arabic written sources to transactions in dirhams, but also by the increasing repertoire of silver coins of Egypt and Syria found by numismatists once they began looking for them.[27] It is nevertheless true that the full-weight good silver dirham of the eighth to tenth centuries vanishes from the central Islamic lands in the eleventh and twelfth centuries, and it seems that many areas, especially east of the Euphrates, almost totally ceased coinage in silver for some time. The silver coinage of Egypt and Syria that survives from this period is difficult to study for a variety of reasons,[28] and the present state of numismatic knowledge is fragmentary indeed. Only a few generalizations can be made at this time. The region east of the Euphrates can be dealt with summarily: dirhams disappear completely, as far as is now known, in the early eleventh century (except in the farthest east) and do not reappear until the thirteenth century.

The type of small dirham characteristic of Egypt and Syria in the Fāṭimid era first appeared in Sicily or North Africa under the Aghlabids in the ninth century. This coinage was continued by the Fāṭimids and introduced by them to Egypt and Syria when they conquered these lands in 969. It is difficult to say if Egypt had any substantial dirham coinage before that date, for only a handful of Egyptian Ikhshīdid dirhams are known. As with the absence of late Ikhshīdid dinars, the paucity of Ikhshīdid dirhams may be a result of the recoinage forced at the beginning of the Fāṭimid period. On the other hand, Egypt had no Islamic silver coinage at all before 787, and Egyptian dirhams are rare throughout the 'Abbāsid and Ṭūlūnid eras.

---

27. Claude Cahen, "Monetary Circulation in Egypt at the Time of the Crusades and the Reform of Al-Kāmil," in *The Islamic Middle East (700–1900)*, ed. Avram L. Udovitch (Princeton, 1981), pp. 315–334; Balog, "History of the Dirhem in Egypt from the Fatimid Conquest until the Collapse of the Mamluk Empire, 358–922 H./968–1517 A.D.," *Rev. numis.*, 6th ser., III (1961), 109–146.

28. The silver coins of the period are small and much alloyed with copper, making them especially liable to corrosion, which usually renders the inscriptions partially illegible. Judging by those that survive, they were not particularly well struck to begin with; the dies are larger than the coin blank, so that only a part of the inscription appears on the coin. Sometimes most of the coin surface is blank, with only one or two letters to be seen. As a result, only a small proportion of the coins can be attributed with certainty to a specific date and place. These small dark-colored bits have often been overlooked or ignored in scientific archeological excavations, and they are of no interest at all to the illicit diggers who, for better or worse, are the main source for numismatic finds from the Near East.

In the reign of al-Ḥākim difficulties which are not yet clearly understood occurred, ending up in the recoinage of A.H. 400 (1009/10), when, for the first time, the gold coinage was changed in appearance during a caliph's reign.[29] It is possible, in fact, that this and the subsequent changes in the design of the gold coinage mentioned above are related much more to changes in the silver coinage than in the dinar. At any rate, the evolution of Fāṭimid silver coinage in the eleventh century will not be understood until the metrology and silver content of each of the successive types is studied separately. The general picture, however, is one of decline in the fineness of the silver, accompanied naturally by lower exchange rates against the dinar, which remained relatively constant in fineness.[30] At the end of the century, references to dirhams in Egypt are seldom encountered in the written sources, while surviving examples of such dirhams from the late years of al-Mustanṣir and the reign of al-Mustaʿlī are few.

The new dinar type introduced in 490 (1096/7) was accompanied by a new dirham.[31] The designs of the two denominations are similar, but there was also a change in the fabrication of dirhams. Previously they were thin and circular, probably cut or punched out of silver sheets before striking, but after 490, and until the beginning of the thirteenth century, dirhams were struck on squarish chunks of silver cut by a chisel from a long ribbon-shaped ingot. Usually two opposite edges of the coins can be seen to be cut, but sometimes "tongue-shaped" dirhams are found with three rounded edges and one cut, evidently the end of an ingot.[32] This dirham type endured into the Aiyūbid era with only the necessary changes in inscription (pl. XIII, no. 16).

Several contemporary descriptions of the Aiyūbid Egyptian mint specify that these dirhams were to be 30 percent silver and 70 percent

29. Al-Maqrīzī, *Ighāthat al-ummah bi-kashf al-ghummah,* ed. Muḥammad Muṣṭafâ Ziyādah and Muḥammad ash-Shaiyāl (Cairo, 1940), pp. 15–16, 64–65. The problems arose in 397, according to the first passage, or 399, according to the second, but al-Maqrīzī does not say that the change in the coinage occurred in the same year, only that the situation continued until the reform. The change in the appearance of the coinage does not come until 400.

30. Balog, "History," p. 122; Goitein, *op. cit.,* I, 368–392.

31. Both old- and new-type dirhams are known from the reign of al-Mustaʿlī (a new-type black dirham is published by Balog, "Études numismatiques de l'Égypte musulmane: Périodes fatimite et ayoubite, nouvelles observations sur la technique du monnayage," *Bulletin de l'Institut d'Égypte,* XXXIII (1951), 7–8; the ANS has another (1953.48.3; pl. XIII, no. 14), as well as a dirham of the older type (1971.132.15; unpublished, pl. XIII, no. 13). Ibn-Muyassar, *op. cit.,* II, 65, mentions a reform of the dinar in 490, and it seems reasonable to suppose that the new dirhams were introduced at the same time. The change is, probably wrongly, attributed to al-Āmir's reign by as-Suyūṭī, *Ḥusn al-muḥāḍarah,* II, 156 (ed. 1299, II, 205).

32. Balog, "Études numismatiques de l'Égypte musulmane, III: Fatimes, Ayoubites, premiers Mamelouks, leurs techniques monétaires," *Bulletin de l'Institut d'Égypte,* XXXV (1953), 401–429.

copper, a statement largely confirmed by a small number of modern analyses.[33] It seems likely that this was the intended fineness from the beginning. The weights of these little coins are quite irregular, ranging from less than half a gram up to more than two grams; for payments, they were weighed against a standard of about 2.95 grams per monetary dirham. The exchange rate during the twelfth and early thirteenth centuries was between 35 and 40 monetary dirhams per dinar.[34] In the Aiyūbid period, when these dirhams had to be distinguished from other silver coins, they are often identified specifically as "black" dirhams, but this term is seldom used earlier — they are simply called dirhams. A small number of larger round-flan dirhams of twelfth-century Fāṭimid Egypt survive; these have the same design and inscriptions as the square coins, vary widely in weight (from 2.25 to 3.60 grams), and judging by appearance (which can be misleading) have the same silver purity as the square coins (pl. XIII, no. 15).[35] Probably these should be regarded only as an alternate physical form of the standard dirham with the same monetary value (weight for weight). These Fāṭimid large black dirhams are not to be confused with the new dirhams introduced by Saladin, discussed below. The latter were a currency separate from the black dirham and intended to replace it. Aiyūbid large black dirhams have not been found.

In 622 (1225/6), under the Aiyūbid sultan al-Kāmil, a change was made in the small dirhams because of certain difficulties with the existing silver issues, but as contemporary sources make clear, the change was only in the method of manufacture.[36] The new "round" or

33. Ibn-Mammātī, *Qawāwīn ad-dawāwīn*, ed. 'Azīz Suryāl 'Atīyah (Cairo, 1943), pp. 331–333; al-Makhzūmī, *Minhāj*, trans. Cahen, "La Frappe des monnaies en Égypte au VIe/XIIe siècle d'après le *Minhaj* d'al-Makhzumi," in *Near Eastern Numismatics, Iconography, Epigraphy and History: Studies in Honor of George C. Miles*, ed. Dickran K. Kouymjian (Beirut, 1974), p. 338; Ibn-Ba'rah, *Kashf al-asrār al-'ilmīyah bi-dār aḍ-ḍarb al-miṣrīyah*, ed. 'Abd-ar-Raḥmān Fahmī (Cairo, 1966), pp. 83–84, 87, trans. Ehrenkreutz, "Extracts from the Technical Manual on the Ayyubid Mint in Cairo," *Bulletin of the School of Oriental and African Studies*, XV (1953), 440–442. For modern analyses see Balog, "History," pp. 122, 128.

34. Goitein, *op. cit.*, I, 379–383. It is often asserted that the rate 40 : 1 corresponds to a rate for pure silver (*nuqrah*) dirhams of 13⅓ : 1, but this is mathematically incorrect; 40 : 1 for 30 percent fineness is equal to 12 : 1 for pure silver. An exchange rate of 13⅓ : 1 is attested only for the second half of the 13th century (*ibid.*, I, 386–387, 390); on the other hand, 12 : 1 is attested by one document of the twelfth century (*ibid.*, I, 387, no. 90).

35. Balog, "Notes on Some Fatimid Round-Flan Dirhams," *Numis. Chr.*, 7th ser., I (1961), 175–179.

36. Described by Ibn-Ba'rah, *op. cit.*, pp. 83–84, who states that they are to be 30 percent silver. The change may have been a restoration of the black dirham standard, for al-Kāmil's early dirhams are different in fabric and design from previous black dirhams and may have been less fine or otherwise unsatisfactory. Al-Kāmil has been unfairly accused of a "colossal fraud" because al-Maqrīzī, two centuries later, erroneously states that his new dirhams were two-thirds

"globular" black dirhams were made by striking blanks produced by pouring molten alloy over a cone so that the drops fell into water; their fineness, however, was unchanged. These continued to be struck in Egypt until the reign of Baybars. In his reign or later, the older cut-ribbon technique was reintroduced. The last known are from the reign of aṣ-Ṣāliḥ Ismā'īl (1342-1345).[37] Although the fabric of Mamluk black dirhams is similar to earlier ones, it is not known if their fineness was the same.

In the eleventh century Fāṭimid dirhams were also issued at Syrian mints, apparently according to the same system that obtained in Egypt. Silver minting did not, however, cease in Syria at the time of the closure of the Fāṭimid gold mints mentioned above, although it seems to have diminished considerably. Debased silver coins are known bearing the names of Tughtigin of Damascus (497-522: 1104-1128), Alp Arslan (507-508: 1113-1115) of Aleppo (but probably struck in Damascus) (pl. XIII, no. 17),[38] and the Börid Ismā'īl of Damascus (526-529: 1132-1135), as well as dirhams corresponding to the brief gold series from Börid Damascus, 530-540 (1135-1146). Generally the designs of these coins are inspired by contemporary or past Fāṭimid issues, but the names on them are those of Selchükids, the 'Abbāsid caliphs, and local Turkish Syrian rulers. Their debasement is such that it is difficult to be certain in some instances whether they are intended to be dirhams or copper *fulūs,* but at least some are surely billon (heavily alloyed silver.)[39] One billon issue of Aleppo, probably of 479-487 (1086-1095), is also known.[40] More of these coins will probably be found as numismatists become aware of their existence, but nevertheless they seem to be excessively scarce and probably were not issued in large quantities. None are known after 541 (1146/7). Neither these nor the preceding Fāṭimid silver issues were imitated by the crusaders, probably because the Franks' own small debased pennies fulfilled the same monetary function.

---

silver while they are in fact less than one-third, but there is no evidence that al-Kāmil himself made such an absurd claim, which would have fooled no one.

37. Balog, *Mamluk Sultans,* p. 172, no. 284.

38. Kamāl-ad-Dīn, *Kitāb zubdat al-ḥalab fī ta'rīkh Ḥalab,* in *RHC, Or.,* III, 604, mentions that Alp Arslan's name was put on the coinage of Damascus after his conquest of the city in 508 (1115); the ANS coin of Alp Arslan is probably this issue.

39. Only a few examples of these series have been published: Lane-Poole, *Catalogue,* IX, 296, no. 3051 (a billon dirham of Tughtigin); Coskun Alptekin, "Selçuklu paralari," *Selçuklu Arastirmalari Dergisi,* III (1971), 551, no. 209A (a billon dirham of Damascus, ca. 530-540). Others exist in public and private collections.

40. Lutz Ilisch, "Unedierte Silbermünzen der Salğūqen und ihren Nachfolger aus Nordsyrien," *Münstersche Numismatische Zeitung,* XII, no. 1 (March 1982), 10, no. 1.

Saladin's conquests in Syria began a new era in the history of the Islamic dirham. He introduced for the first time in two centuries the minting of full-weight good silver dirhams at Damascus, where the earliest recorded date on his new dirhams is 571 (1175/6), the year after his occupation of the city (pl. XIII, no. 18).[41] By the following year, 572 (1176/7), silver dirhams were being struck in Aleppo with the name of the Zengid atabeg, Ismāʿīl ibn-Maḥmūd (pl. XIV, no. 20).[42]

Saladin's new dirhams departed from previous Islamic practice in having the main inscriptions on both sides enclosed in a square, which was in turn enclosed in a circle with subsidiary inscriptions in the sectors between the square and the circle.[43] When Saladin took Aleppo in 1183, he introduced full dirhams there as well, but with the central inscriptions enclosed in a hexagram, or "seal of Solomon", like pl. XIV, no. 21, a coin of his son aẓ-Ẓāhir.[44] Dirhams with one or the other of these designs were struck at several Aiyūbid mints in Syria (including, at one time or another, Gaza, Hamah, and Homs) as well as in towns in upper Mesopotamia and beyond, including Akhlat, Harran, Ḥiṣn Kaifā, Manbij, Mardin, Maiyafariqin, Nisibin, and Edessa (ar-Ruhāʾ). They were issued by the Artukids as well as by Aiyūbid princes, and also by the crusaders, as will be seen (pl. XIII, no. 19, a coin of Damascus, 1242/3, is one of the prototypes for the crusader dirhams). Both the square-type and hexagram-type dirhams were accompanied by analogous half dirhams, which probably circulated at par with the full dirhams (on a weight-for-weight basis) and are not to be confused with the black dirhams of Egypt, a separate currency.

In Shauwāl 583 (1187), Saladin ordered the introduction of these dirhams in Egypt to replace the Egyptian black dirhams, intending to relieve the populace of the necessity of weighing dirhams in transactions. The innovation did not succeed, however, possibly because the fineness of the new dirhams (in Egypt) was not consistent: some were pure silver and others only half silver.[45] At either fineness, the

---

41. Ignatz Pietraszewski, *Numi Mohammedani,* I (Berlin, 1843), 111, no. 406.

42. Unpublished, in the ANS collection (1951.108.4). A published example, of 574, is in Lane-Poole, *op. cit.,* III, 213, no. 603.

43. The design was new for dirhams, but was adapted from the prestigious Muwaḥḥid gold dinar of the western Mediterranean.

44. This design was quite new, and was noted by the historian Ibn-abī-Ṭaiy (quoted by Abū-Shāmah, *op. cit.* [Cairo, 1288/1871], II, 47).

45. The variation in fineness probably explains the conflicting reports by al-Maqrīzī: in the *Shudhūr al-ʿuqūd fī dhikr an-nuqūd,* ed. and trans. Daniel Eustache, "Études de numismatique et de métrologie musulmanes," *Hespéris Tamuda,* X (1969), 128–129, he states that the new dirhams were half silver and half copper, but in the *Kitāb as-sulūk li-maʿrifat duwal al-mulūk,* ed. Ziyādah (Cairo, 1956) I, 99, the new dirhams are said to be of pure silver. These coins are very

new dirhams with their stable weight might have been acceptable and
have replaced the irregular black dirhams as intended, but the populace apparently considered unreliability in alloy a greater disadvantage
than the inconvenience of weighing out the black dirhams with their
stable 30 percent silver content. The black dirham continued to be issued in Egypt throughout the Aiyūbid period and into the Mamluk
era, but full dirhams, of Damascus type, were also struck in Egypt
under al-'Ādil I and from the 1240's until 1260; their fineness is unknown.

In the latter year Baybars introduced a new dirham, analogous in
appearance to his gold coinage and with 70 percent silver. This was
the standard silver issue of the rest of the thirteenth and first half of
the fourteenth century in both Egypt and Syria (pl. XIV, no. 23).[46]

Following Saladin's initiative, silver coinage spread to Anatolia, Mesopotamia, and Iran in the thirteenth century. The Selchükids of Rūm
produced massive issues of dirhams from Anatolian mints, with a design quite different from Saladin's; Cilician Armenia issued quantities
of silver trams; and the 'Abbāsid caliphs began minting dirhams in the
1230's. Under the Mongols, silver coinage became the standard currency of Iran by the end of the thirteenth century, in complete contrast
to the situation only a century before. None of these coinages, however, is relevant to that of the crusaders.

ISLAMIC COPPER COINAGE

In general, copper coinage disappeared in the Moslem world in the
ninth century, not to reappear until the twelfth or later. Egypt, for example, had no copper coinage after 872. In areas without copper currency, everyday transactions were probably carried out with cut-up dirhams, with standard commodities, or by accumulating transactions at
neighborhood merchants until the total bill was large enough to pay
with a dirham. In Fāṭimid and Aiyūbid Egypt, the small somewhat debased dirhams had a value low enough for everyday minor purchases.

There are, however, exceptions to this general situation. One area

---

scarce today. The two in the ANS were analyzed by Professor Adon A. Gordus of the University
of Michigan Department of Chemistry. One (1972.250.14), dated 585, contained 52 percent silver, while a second (1917.215.1328; pl. XIV, no. 22), of 586, was 97.7 percent fine. Note that the
later coin is the purer, but it would be hazardous to draw conclusions as to the temporal sequence of the two fineness levels from only two examples.

46. Balog, *Mamluk Sultans;* Bates, "The Coinage of the Mamlūk Sulṭān Baybars I: Additions and Corrections," ANS, *Museum Notes,* XXII (1977), 161–181.

where copper persisted longer than elsewhere, and returned sooner, was northern Syria. The earliest datable issue in the crusader period bears the name of Rîdvan, ruler of Aleppo (1095–1113; pl. XIV, no. 24), but there are many anonymous coins of fabric and style similar to this issue, some of which may be earlier than his reign (pl. XIV, no. 25).[47] These coins are irregular in shape, but most often polygonal, with straight edges; the blanks appear to have been cut from thin sheets of copper with shears. They bear images of various kinds—a lion, elephant, or bird—or complicated geometrical figures. Their inscriptions are sparse and often cryptic. On the basis of provenance and a general similarity of style, they have generally been attributed to the Selchükids of Syria, and perhaps because of Rîdvan's name, Aleppo is regarded as their center of manufacture, but until they have been carefully studied, these identifications should be accepted only tentatively. These coins are probably the original *qirṭās,* a term that is known first in an account of the death of Rîdvan, who left behind dinars of gold, black dirhams, silver coins, and *qirṭās.*[48] This notice and others throughout the twelfth and into the thirteenth century suggest that *qirṭās,* which means literally "papyrus" or by extension any rough brown paper, came to designate copper coinage in general in twelfth-century Syria. Looking at the coppers of the Selchükids of Syria, one can see how the appellation may have arisen, because either the thin sheets of copper or the thin, often rectangular, coins themselves may have brought to mind sheets of brown paper.

It is not known how long these coins were struck. They were probably replaced by a copper issue of the Zengid Nūr-ad-Dīn (1146–1174) struck on normal round flans with images borrowed from Byzantine coppers, but with his name and title in Arabic (pl. XIV, no. 26). These are generally attributed to Aleppo. Nūr-ad-Dīn also initiated copper coinage in Damascus, with a purely inscriptional issue bearing his name and the caliph's in bold tall script (pl. XIV, no. 27). The mint and date of issue are inscribed in the margin of these coins, but the dates most often are illegible; the earliest so far recorded is 558 (1162/3).[49] This particular Damascus issue was also called *qirṭās* and was continued by Saladin and his successors until 611 (1214/5), when it was abolished,[50]

---

47. Miles, "Islamic Coins," in *Antioch-on-the-Orontes,* IV, 1, *Ceramics and Islamic Coins,* ed. Frederick O. Waage (Princeton, 1948), pp. 119–121.

48. Ibn-abī-Ṭaiy, quoted in Ibn-al-Furāt, *Ta'rīkh ad-duwal wa-l-mulūk,* ms. Vienna I, 75 *verso* (this reference was provided by Professor Claude Cahen).

49. Nikita Elisséeff, *Nur ad-Din: un grand prince musulman de Syrie au temps des croisades (511–569 H./1118–1174)* (Damascus, 1967), III, 821, noting a coin in the Damascus Museum.

50. Al-Maqrīzī, *Sulūk,* I, 180.

but small copper coinage continued to be called *qirṭās* in Damascus until at least as late as 720 (1320/1).[51]

Since the crusader states of northern Syria also issued copper coins beginning in the early twelfth century, and Latin Europe had no indigenous copper coinage, the possibility exists of some influence between the crusader coppers and the early polygonal *qirṭās*. The two series, however, are, with rare exceptions, not very similar in appearance. The crusader coppers are adaptations of Byzantine types, while the images on the Moslem coins are neither Byzantine nor Frankish but rather traditional Near Eastern. The crusader coins are also dissimilar in fabric, being struck on round, probably cast, flans, although a few thin polygonal crusader coppers are known, perhaps overstruck on Moslem *qirṭās*.[52] It is not even clear which series antedates the other, since Miles's tentative attribution of a Moslem issue to the time of the Selchükid Malik-Shāh (d. 485/1092) is unconfirmed. At most, it may be that the crusaders conquered a population using copper coins and issued their own coppers to meet an existing economic need. A single reference indicates that the Moslems referred to the crusader coppers also as *qirṭās*.[53]

There are two other important Moslem copper coinages of the crusader era. One, the large image-bearing coppers of eastern Anatolia and northern Mesopotamia, evidently began as a Moslem adaptation of the heavy anonymous coppers of Byzantium, because the earliest issues, under the Dānishmendids Amīr Ghāzī (1104–1134) and Muḥammad (1134–1140; pl. XIV, no. 28), bear only Byzantine inscriptions and images.[54] Later issues have Arabic inscriptions combined with a wide range of different images, including Byzantine images from coins or wall paintings, types copied from pre-Islamic coins (Greek [pl. XIV, no. 29], Roman, Parthian, and Sāsānid), personifications of planets and other astronomical phenomena, and traditional Near Eastern royal images. Such coppers were struck by Dānishmendids, Artukids, Zengids, Aiyūbids, Rūm Selchükids, and several minor Moslem dynasties. It has often been suggested that the use of images on this coinage evinces crusader influence, or issuance for trade with the crusaders, but in fact

---

51. *Ibid.*, II, 205, where the coins are described as "*fulūs* which are called *qirṭās*"; see Ashtor, *op. cit.*, pp. 242, 247, 260, and 263 for other references to *qirṭās* in the 13th century.

52. Gustave Schlumberger, *Numismatique de l'Orient latin* (Paris, 1878), plate II, nos. 4–5; Metcalf, *Coinage of the Crusades,* plate 3, no. 40.

53. Ash-Shaizarī, *Nihāyat ar-rutbah fī ṭalab al-ḥisbah,* ed. al-Bāz al-ʿArīnī (Cairo, 1946), p. 75.

54. Estelle J. Whelan, "A Contribution to Danishmendid History: the Figured Copper Coins," ANS, *Museum Notes,* XXV (1980), 133–166.

there are no images derived from Latin Europe, or any other evidence linking these coins with the crusaders. Rather, the large coppers are generally found only in the regions where they were struck, and must have had an important place in the local monetary systems, judging by the abundance of surviving specimens. The large coppers gradually disappear during the thirteenth century, subsequent to (perhaps because of) the introduction of dirhams in their region.[55]

Copper coinage was reintroduced to Egypt in 622 (1225) by the Aiyūbid sultan al-Kāmil. Initial difficulties resulted in several withdrawals of the new currency under the Aiyūbids, but by the time of the Mamluks copper *fulūs* were an accepted part of Egypt's currency. These Egyptian coppers, however, do not seem to have circulated outside Egypt and have little relevance to the crusaders.[56]

B. *Crusader Arabic Gold Issues*[57]

The kings of Jerusalem and the counts of Tripoli struck, in addition to billon deniers of western pattern, gold coinages for their domains. These coins, called *bizantii saraceni* or *bizantii saracenati* in the Latin sources, were issued in considerable quantities. From sometime before the reign of Baldwin III (1143–1163) until 1251 these bezants imitated more or less faithfully Moslem dinars, especially those of the Fāṭimid caliphs al-Mustanṣir and al-Āmir. The issues of these long-reigning caliphs can be presumed, although there is no useful archaeological evidence, to have been the normal currency in Syria in the first decades after the establishment of the Latin kingdom. After 1251 the inscriptions on the coins were Christian, but still in Arabic. The imitations of al-Mustanṣir's coinage (prototype, pl. XII, nos. 3, 5) are probably to be attributed to the northern principalities, while the coinage of the kingdom of Jerusalem was exclusively of the type of al-Āmir (prototype, pl. XII, no. 6). The best of the imitations are

55. The best general catalogue and discussion of this series in its historical context is *idem, The Public Figure: Political Iconography in Medieval Mesopotamia,* Ph.D. dissertation, New York University, 1979.

56. Hassanein Rabie, *The Financial System of Egypt, A.H. 564–741/A.D. 1169–1341* (London, 1972), pp. 182–184, 188–189, 195–197; Jere L. Bacharach, "Circassian Monetary Policy: Copper," *Journal of the Economic and Social History of the Orient,* XIX (1976), 32–47; Balog, *Ayyubids,* pp. 156–160. The argument put forward by Balog and others that glass jetons were used as small change in Egypt is contested by Bates, "The Function," *passim.*

57. This section was written by Metcalf, with additions and modifications by Bates.

elegant and legible, but the inscriptions and dates they bear are those of the prototype and irrelevant to their historical interpretation. Other specimens are blundered and meaningless to varying degrees. The evidence for their geographical and chronological attribution is therefore from finds of these coins in association in hoards; from analyses of their metal fineness, the relative proportions of trace elements in their alloys, and their weight standards; and from contemporary literary texts, Latin and Arabic.[58]

The official status of these coins (which have long been recognized as belonging in some sense to the crusader principalities)[59] is proved by documentary sources, in which they are sometimes referred to explicitly as, for example, *bisancii auri saracenati de moneta regis Hierusalem* (gold saracenate bezants of the coinage of the king of Jerusalem). They were intended to circulate within the Latin states, and there is little if any evidence to suggest that they enjoyed an international role, except that they are sometimes found in Cilician Armenia, and finds and literary references show that they were used in the Moslem hinterland of the crusader states, for Moslem Syria had little gold coinage of its own in the twelfth and thirteenth centuries. The idea that they were widely current in the Mediterranean world, however, is a *canard*. They were, rather, one element (the other being billon) in a national coinage under tight control.

Although the bezants were imitations, they were not intended to deceive.[60] Their weight standards were less than the nominal Islamic dinar of 4.25 grams, and although Moslem gold coins of the twelfth and thirteenth centuries fluctuate in weight, few drop below 4.0 grams, while the bezants virtually never exceed that weight. Those who were wealthy enough to use gold coins would have had no trouble in distinguishing the two currencies, which in any case did not normally mingle in circulation. Moreover, the alloy of the bezant was quite different from that of the dinar. Fāṭimid dinars of the crusader period, including the prototypes of the crusader imitations, were usually as pure as the workmen's skill could make them, while nearly all of the imitations have finenesses of 80 percent or less. The debased alloys of the bezants were in no way either fraudulent or incompetent: they reflected decisions to give the coins a certain intrinsic value.

---

58. For a more detailed discussion of the evidence for the attributions to be proposed here see Gordus and Metcalf, *op. cit.,* and Metcalf, *Coinage of the Crusades,* pp. 9–14, 42–44.

59. The first to identify them was Henri Lavoix, in 1865; see Balog and Yvon, *op. cit.,* p. 133.

60. Cf. Ehrenkreutz, "Arabic Dinars Struck by the Crusaders, a Case of Ignorance or of Economic Subversion," *Journal of the Economic and Social History of the Orient,* VII (1964), 165–182.

For the most part, the alloy variations were parallel in the northern and southern crusader states. From about the middle of the twelfth century the alloy was, by medieval standards, controlled within a perfectly acceptable variation of 1–2 percent, and the bezant deserved its high reputation. It was a far more valuable coin than the silver or billon deniers that were universal in western Christendom, and it answered the needs, no doubt, of a merchant class that would otherwise have found it convenient to use Byzantine or Arabic gold pieces. To the economic historian, the significant aspect of the evidence of the bezants is that gold should have flowed into the mints of the Latin east in quantities sufficient to strike so many coins.

THE GOLD COINAGE OF THE KINGDOM OF JERUSALEM

The most important evidence for the relative chronology of the gold coinage of the kingdom of Jerusalem is furnished by analysis of the gold content of the bezants. Nearly all the bezants imitating the coinage of al-Āmir can be divided into two groups, one of close to 80 percent fineness and another of about 68 percent. Hoard evidence, as well as the fact that the dated Christian Arabic coinage of 1251 and after is also of about 68 percent fineness, indicate that the latter coins are the later in time. The small remaining body of coins with fineness above 80 percent can reasonably be placed at the beginning of the sequence. Establishing an absolute chronology for these series is more problematic.

The date of the beginning of gold coinage in the kingdom is difficult to estimate. Ibn-Khallikān, a century and a half later (but presumably using an earlier source), records that when the city of Tyre eventually fell to the Franks in 1124 the crusaders continued for three years to strike coins in the name of al-Āmir, at the end of which time they ceased to do so.[61] Since no coins of Tyre have survived bearing the year 518, the Moslem date of the capture of the city, and only one is known of the previous year, it is difficult to assume that the crusaders simply continued to strike the Moslem issue current at the time of the conquest, for at least one or two might be expected to have survived. In any case Acre, which seems to have been a more important mint for the crusaders than Tyre, was conquered in 1104, and had had a Moslem mint at least until 1101. It is theoretically possible that the minting of gold by the crusaders might have begun at Acre even before the conquest of Tyre. The earliest evidence from the Latin side

---

61. Ibn-Khallikān, *Wafāyat, loc. cit.* (n. 21).

is a *colleganza* of July 1142, which makes it certain that crusader bez-ants were already being struck in the kingdom of Jerusalem before the accession of Baldwin III: it refers to a debt to be paid at Acre in *bizancios saracenatos bonos auri de rege illius terrae de pesa secun-dum consuetudinem illius terrae*[62] (saracenate bezants of good gold of the king of that country and of a weight according to the custom of that country).

If, then, the crusaders began issuing gold coins sometime between 1104 and 1142, what were these coins? Among issues identified so far as crusader imitations, there is only one variety which, by reason of its high gold content, is a likely candidate for an issue of the kingdom of Jerusalem in the period before the introduction of coins of 80 per-cent fineness about the middle of the twelfth century. This is BY 26, a relatively rare group, which amalgamates two very different styles of coinage, one small and compact (pl. XV, no. 30), the other on larger flans, with stiff, thin lettering and a wide empty border between the two circles of the legend (pl. XV, no. 31). Four specimens of the large-flan variety range from 91 to 97.4 percent in fineness, while three small-flan coins are lower, from 82.5 to 88.1 percent.[63] Both styles imitate the coinage of al-Āmir, but they are rather different from one another in appearance. The tall, elegant script and wide border of the large-flan coins is unlike any other crusader imitations, and indeed rather unlike the Fāṭimid prototype; the very earliest issues of al-Āmir, just after 1101, have a wider space between inner and outer inscriptions than his later dinars, but their script is nothing like the large-flan BY 26. The small-flan coins included in BY 26 are, on the contrary, much like the later crusader issues and resemble also their Fāṭimid proto-types. Probably the two varieties should be reclassified separately, with the small-flan coins seen as precursors of the Acre coinage of the king-dom of Jerusalem, and the large-flan coins reserved for further con-sideration. This small handful of known specimens seems insufficient to fill the entire span of years during which they may have been issued. It may be, however, that there were originally many more, and that the adoption of the 80 percent standard was accompanied by a recoin-age that called in most of the existing bezants to the melting pot.

The date of the introduction of the 80 percent standard is quite un-certain. The aftermath of the Second Crusade, 1148, seems to be the earliest possible occasion. A later date, up to just before 1165, would

---

62. Raimondo Morozzo della Rocca and Antonino Lombardo, eds., *Documenti del com-mercio veneziano nei secoli XI—XIII* (Regesta chartarum Italiae, XXVIII [1940]), no. 81.
63. More fully discussed in Gordus and Metcalf, *op. cit.,* pp. 139–140.

fit the numismatic evidence as well, and perhaps accord with the references to *bisancios . . . de moneta regis Hierusalem* which begin in 1161.[64] The date 1165 as *ante quem* is suggested by a document of that year which speaks of *bisancios . . . novos* and *veteres;* the *novi* are perhaps the 80 percent coins, while *veteres* are those of higher fineness. It must be admitted, however, that *novi* is a term used over a wide range of dates, and its interpretation is not without difficulties. Still, it seems safe at least to say that the bezants of 80 percent fineness were introduced probably in the reign of Baldwin III, or under Amalric (1163–1174) at the latest.

The date of the reduction in fineness from 80 to 68 percent can almost certainly be put in the second half of the twelfth century, and one historical occasion immediately presents itself as probable: the time of Saladin's conquests, or about 1186–1188. The events of 1187 and 1188 shattered the Latin kingdom; Guy (1186–1192) evidently found it impossible to issue proper silver coinage, and the financial crisis may have necessitated a change in the gold currency as well. The date is supported by further references in documents of 1190, 1192, and 1194 to "new bezants". Further possible support is provided by a hoard said to be from Latakia, if this provenance is reliable, for that city fell to Saladin in July 1188 and the hoard contained two coins of the reduced standard along with thirty-nine of the 80 percent standard. It seems likely, therefore, to have been concealed just at the time of danger from Saladin, placing the beginning of the new coinage at least some months earlier.[65]

The coins to be attributed to this phase are BY 25 (pl. XV, no. 32), BY 27a–d (pl. XV, no. 33), BY 27f, BY 20–21 (pl. XV, no. 34), and BY 22–24 (pl. XV, no. 35). All of these are imitations of the coinage of al-Āmir, although the type was standard in Egypt throughout most of the twelfth century. They can be divided, largely on the basis of differences in the ratio of silver to copper as minor constituents of the alloy, into three groups which probably correspond to different mints: Acre and Tyre no doubt account for most of the production, but there are problems in deciding which group belongs to which mint. Perhaps BY 25 and 27 belong to Acre, BY 20–21 possibly to Tyre, while BY 22–24 remain uncertain and may be the product either of the same mint as BY 20–21 or of a third mint.[66] BY 25 is listed by Balog and

---

64. Yvon, "Besants sarracénats du roi de Jérusalem," *Bulletin de la Société française de numismatique* (1961), pp. 81–82; Gordus and Metcalf, *op. cit.,* p. 138.

65. Gordus and Metcalf, *op. cit.,* pp. 130–131.

66. The rather complicated arguments for mint attribution are set out in detail by Gordus and Metcalf, *op. cit.,* pp. 132–136.

Yvon among the "legible" imitations, while BY 27 begins the listing of "imitations grossières", completely illegible, but there is little obvious difference among the many bezants assigned to these two classes. Nor for that matter is there any great visual distinction between the groups assigned to Acre, Tyre, and a possible uncertain mint. They are tentatively assigned on the basis of consistent differences in the ratio of silver to copper as alloying elements, and, in the case of BY 20–21, on the fact that a large proportion of these coins were in a hoard said to have been found near Tyre.[67] The existence of a mint at Tyre at least until 1190–1192 is shown by a Venetian document of a later date referring to its closure or relocation in this period.[68] Probably a definitive classification of these coins can be made only on the basis of a complete die study in conjunction with the results of metal analysis. It seems likely that the bezants of the second phase initially were intended to be of 20 Byzantine carats weight, about 3.74 grams, and to contain 16 carats of gold, 3½ carats of silver, and ½ carat of copper, with some falling away from these standards as time went on.[69]

The bezants of the third phase of the coinage of the kingdom of Jerusalem have the same prototype as those of the second phase and are superficially similar, but in this instance it is easy to distinguish the two phases visually: the coins of phase 3 (BY 27e–f and 28–32; pl. XV, no. 36) are markedly more barbarous in execution, with much thicker letters, executed as it were with a blunt instrument. Many of them have little symbols added in the central field of the obverse or reverse, such as a point, a pair of points, or a small crescent. They are also distinguished by their lower fineness, ranging mostly from 67 to 70 percent gold, with a few specimens as low as 64 percent, and by generally lower weights, ranging mostly from 3.25 to 3.5 grams. It seems possible that the mint intended to produce a coin of 18 carats weight, with 12 carats of gold, 4 carats of silver, and 2 of copper, resulting in a fineness of two-thirds gold, although the coins in general contain slightly more gold and less copper than this prescription would yield. The discrepancy may be explained by error in the analytical technique, by irregularities at the mint, or by use of a different alloy formula.[70] Another indication of the assumed fineness of these coins is provided by the Moslem writer an-Nābulusī, who in his discussion of problems in the Egyptian mint written about 1242 men-

67. Balog and Yvon, "Deux trésors de monnaies d'or des croisés," ANS, *Museum Notes,* XI (1964), 301–302. See above, note 22.
    68. Metcalf, *Coinage of the Crusades,* p. 12.
    69. Gordus and Metcalf, *op. cit.,* p. 143.
    70. See *ibid.,* pp. 141–142, for full discussion.

tions that Ṣūrī dinars were accepted by the mint at a rate of 60 Egyptian mithqals per 100 Ṣūrī mithqals;[71] that is, a given weight of Ṣūrī dinars was valued at 60 percent of the value of an equal weight of Egyptian dinars (which were assumed by the mint to be pure gold). If we assume that this figure was the final result to the customer, taking into account the 5 percent minting charge which was standard a few years earlier (according to Ibn-Baʿrah[72]), it appears that the Ṣūrī dinar was rated as if 65 percent gold. This is well within the actual fineness range of phase 3 dinars, and if one assumes also that the Egyptian mint slightly underestimated the fineness of foreign dinars, as appears from Ibn-Baʿrah's tabulation, the figure is not inconsistent with an estimated intended fineness of two-thirds gold.

Probably nearly all these are products of the Acre mint, an assumption based on their similarity in weight, fineness, and silver/copper ratio

71. An-Nābulusī, *Lumaʿ al-qawāwīn al-mudīyah,* ed. Cahen, *Bulletin des études orientales,* XVI (1958–1960), 53.

72. Ibn-Baʿrah, *op. cit.,* pp. 58–61; Ehrenkreutz, "Standard," p. 163. Ehrenkreutz's proposal that Ibn-Baʿrah also refers to the Ṣūrī dinar is in error. The very obscure word that Ehrenkreutz read "Ṣūrī" has been read "Yaʿqūbī" by two subsequent editors of the text (Fahmī, editor of the complete manuscript, and Ḥusayn Muʾnis, who edited this passage in his edition of ʿAlī ibn-Yūsuf al-Ḥākim, *Ad-dauḥah al-mustabakah fī dawābiṭ dār as-sikkah* [Madrid, 1960], p. 58, no. 2); that is, the term "Yaʿqūbī" is used twice in the text, and the two first lines of the tabulation by Ehrenkreutz both refer to the same issue, which is to be identified as North African, not crusader. On the other hand, another entry in Ibn-Baʿrah's list of the values of various gold issues set by the Egyptian mint may conceal, within some apparent corruption of the text, a reference to the Ṣūrī dinar. This is the next to last coin, named in the manuscript "tūrī" or "thūrī" dinar, neither term having any evident meaning. Fahmī and Muʾnis, the editors of the text, both suggest emending this term to "Nūrī", meaning dinars struck by a ruler named Nūr-ad-Dīn; the issues of the Zengid atabegs of Mosul might be meant, but these seem to be mentioned already under the term "atabākī". Ehrenkreutz suggested a similarity of "tūrī" with the word he read "ṭūrī" in an-Nābulusī's text, which is in fact Ṣūrī (it is the reference under discussion above). It is barely possible that Ṣūrī could somehow be transformed by a copyist into "tūrī"; the letters ṣ and t are not similar in Arabic, but the rest of the word is the same.

A peculiarity of this passage is that, in this one instance, the various figures given by Ibn-Baʿrah do not jibe. He says that this coin lost 10 percent in refining which, after deduction of the standard 5 percent mint charges, left 85 mithqals per hundred to the customer. This figure is anomalous because Ibn-Baʿrah's listing is in order of fineness; 85 percent should come near the top of the list, not at the bottom. Moreover, Ibn-Baʿrah gives the dirham value of each of the coins he lists, based on a standard of 40 dirhams per Egyptian mithqal; the "tūrī" dinar is said to be worth 24 dirhams, but this figure is quite wrong if the coin is valued at 85 percent of the Egyptian mithqal. Ehrenkreutz resolved these contradictions by emending the loss in minting from 10 to 35, but this is opposed by the text's statement that 85 mithqals were left to the customer. We would propose another solution, based on the fact that the 24-dirham ratio given by the text corresponds exactly to a value of 60 mithqals per hundred, the same as the figure found in an-Nābulusī for the Ṣūrī dinar. It may be that the original text of Ibn-Baʿrah had entries for both a Nūrī and a Ṣūrī dinar. The mithqal values given in the present manuscript are not unreasonable for the dinars of Mosul (if that is the correct identification of the tūrī/thūrī/nūrī dinar) while the dirham value given could have pertained originally to the Ṣūrī dinar. The similarity of the two words may well have led some copyist to conflate the two entries.

to the bezants with Christian Arabic inscriptions, which bear the authentic mint name Acre. One analyzed example of the class BY 20–21 has only a 58 percent fineness, and may represent the phase 3 coinage of the Tyre mint. As suggested, this series comes after the imitations with 80 percent and begins probably shortly before the concealment of the Latakia hoard (1188?). The date may also have been not long before the closure of the Tyre mint (1190–1192), but the new bezants need not have been introduced immediately after the termination of the old, especially considering the sharp break in style between the two. There may have been a period of months or years between the end of one and the beginning of the next, while the crusaders reorganized after the defeats of 1187. As for the termination of phase 3, it is reasonable to believe that it continued until the visit of the papal legate Odo in 1250, because the introduction of Christian Arabic crusader gold immediately afterward makes no sense otherwise.

In the spring of 1250 Odo, bishop of Châteauroux, arrived in Syria in the entourage of Louis IX and reported to pope Innocent IV on the monetary practices of the Franks in Syria. His report has not survived, but the response of Innocent IV is still extant.[73] In it the pope takes notice of the striking of bezants and drachms (silver coins) by the Christians of Acre and Tripoli with the name of Mohammed and the date of the era of his birth (*sic*). The practice was forbidden, under pain of excommunication.

Even before Innocent's letter arrived, Odo, probably with Louis's support, put a stop to the purely imitative coinage. In response, the mint of Acre began the production of a new type of bezant, much like the old in its general appearance,[74] weight standard, and fineness, but bearing inscriptions in legible Arabic proclaiming Christian instead of Moslem doctrines (pl. XV, no. 37). On one side, the outer margin states the place and date of issue: "struck in Acre in the year one thousand two hundred, one and fifty, of the Incarnation of our Lord the Messiah." The inner circular inscription proclaims "Father, Son, and Holy Ghost" and the central inscription continues, in two lines, "one

---

73. It is quoted by Lavoix, *Monnaies à légendes arabes frappées en Syrie par les croisés* (Paris, 1877), pp. 52–53.

74. Balog and Yvon, "Monnaies," p. 158, take issue with Lavoix's statement that the prototype for these coins is the same dinar of al-Āmir that served as prototype for the imitations. They assert rather that the prototype is the "contemporary" Aiyūbid gold coinage. This is nonsense; the coins are nothing like contemporary Aiyūbid coins except in their cursive Arabic script, but this latter feature is only a result of the fact that the inscriptions for the first time are original, not copied from an old prototype, and therefore naturally in contemporary script. Otherwise the design, with a small central field surrounded by two circular inscriptions, is identical to that of the imitations that preceded them.

godhead".[75] On the other side, the outer and inner circular inscriptions read: "We are glorified by the Cross of our Lord Jesus the Messiah, in whom is our salvation and our life and our resurrection, and in whom is our deliverance and pardon."[76] On this same side, the central inscription of the imitations is replaced by a cross, and smaller crosses mark the beginnings of all circular inscriptions on both sides of the coin. The year 1251 is the earliest known for this series; none are yet known with the date 1252, but the years 1253–1258 are all represented.[77] If these dates are authentic, it would appear that the devastation of Acre by the war of Saint Sabas brought the minting of gold to an end.

The fineness of these coins seems to be the same as the preceding series, ranging from 62.4 to 68.7 percent. An Italian list of Mediterranean gold coins and their finenesses[78] gives for the *bisanti d'Acri colla croce* a fineness of 16⅓ carats, or in some manuscripts 15⅔ (also 16 *meno* ⅓). The former figure, in the earliest manuscript, is equivalent to 68 percent, which seems rather high in comparison to the coins' average fineness of 65.85 percent. The lower figure, in the next three manuscripts in chronological order, corresponds better at 65.28 percent. Possibly the copyist of the earliest of the extant manuscripts mistakenly substituted *et* for *meno*.

The only crusader gold issue which might be attributable to the years after 1258 is the very rare Agnus Dei coinage (pl. XV, no. 38), which is neither an imitation nor inspired by a Moslem issue, but which has the same fineness and silver/copper ratio as the Christian Arabic issues of Acre. It has been attributed by Grierson[79] to Antioch, and to the period of Louis's stay in Syria, 1250–1254. It seems unlikely, however,

75. The latter phrase has been gratuitously corrected by earlier catalogers, who assumed that the Arabic word *ilāh,* "god, divinity, godhead", was an error for *Allāh,* "God". Considering that the remainder of the inscriptions on the coins are perfectly literate, there is no reason to think that the spelling was accidental in this one instance.

76. The word *takhalluṣ,* "deliverance", is misspelled *taḥalluṣ* in the Arabic version of the inscriptions by both Lavoix, *op. cit.,* p. 54, and Balog and Yvon, "Monnaies," p. 158. Presumably the latter merely copied a typographical error in the earlier work. The difference is only a single dot.

77. In comparison, the corresponding silver coins, discussed below, are known only for the year 1251.

78. Found in six manuscripts ranging in date from *ca.* 1350 to *ca.* 1480, edited by the late Allan Evans in an unpublished typescript deposited after his death in the American Numismatic Society. The earliest of these manuscripts is Riccardiano 2236, fol. 43ʳ, giving 16⅓ carats as the fineness of the coin; those with variant forms of the fineness are Datini 1174, fol. 24ᵛ (dated *ca.* 1380, with 15⅔ carats) and Conventi G, VII, 1137, fol. 249ʳ (dated 1418, with 16 less ⅓ carats). The authors are grateful to Dr. Alan Stahl for bringing this material to their attention.

79. Philip Grierson, "A Rare Crusader Bezant with the *Christus vincit* Legend," ANS, *Museum Notes,* VI (1954), 169–178.

that Antioch, which so far as we can judge had never minted gold bezants, would have initiated such a major departure from the traditional bezant at so early a date. Rather than a precedent for the design of the gros tournois and the French *écu d'or,* might the Agnus Dei issue not have been rather an echo of the latter coin, introduced perhaps at Acre in 1266 or more probably at Tripoli after 1268? There seems no compelling reason against a date after 1266, and the Agnus Dei issue might well be a parallel to the silver gros of Tripoli of that era.[80]

There are numerous references in the documents and histories to saracenate bezants and Ṣūrī dinars after 1258 up into the 1280's, with the latest in 1302–1303.[81] It seems possible that the crusader bezants, in the absence of any abundant competitor, continued to circulate for some time after their minting ceased. Damascus began to mint gold coins in the reign of Baybars, after 1260, but Mamluk Syrian dinars seem to have been produced only irregularly and in small quantities.

THE GOLD COINAGE
OF THE NORTHERN CRUSADER STATES

The coins discussed so far are all imitations or adaptations of a single prototype, the dinars of the Fāṭimid caliph al-Āmir. All these have been attributed to the kingdom of Jerusalem. There is another group of bezants, copied from the coinage of the eleventh-century caliph al-Mustanṣir, which seem to represent a regular and substantive series, struck over a long period of time in large quantities, although they are not so abundant as the al-Āmir imitations. These are evidently the official gold coinage of another of the crusader principalities, and the only question is whether they were minted at Antioch or Tripoli, or both. Thirteenth-century documents mention both *bisantii tripolitani* and *bisantii antiocheni,* but it is not quite certain—since the territories were under united rule—whether these imply a mint in each place or are merely legal phrases. The analytical evidence makes the hypothesis of two mints unlikely, although it does not rule it out. Stylistically, the al-Mustanṣir imitations all seem to belong to a single series; numismatists would be at a loss to know how they could be attributed to two mints. Most decisive, at least for the mid-thirteenth century, is the papal letter responding to the complaints of Odo of Châteauroux, for while it forbids the manufacture of imitations in all the cru-

---

80. Gordus and Metcalf, *op. cit.,* p. 133.
81. Irwin, *op. cit.,* p. 92.

sader territories — Jerusalem, Tripoli, and Antioch — it mentions only Acre and Tripoli as the cities where they were being made. The actual coins used in Antioch, described for legal purposes as bezants of Antioch, were most likely issues of the prince of that principality (who also was count of Tripoli), struck at Tripoli.[82]

Similarly the *bissancii sarracinati d'Armenie* that are frequently referred to in notarial acts from the port of Ayas in Cilician Armenia[83] are, we may be sure, the expression of a legal standard of quality rather than coins minted in Cilicia. Later in the thirteenth century they may even have become merely "ghost monies", an accounting device for recording sums that were paid in silver currencies.

The prototype for the imitations of al-Mustanṣir's dinars, as discussed in the previous section, is not precisely identifiable. They resemble any of several of his dinar varieties with broad central fields containing several horizontal inscriptions.[84] All the imitations have a semblance, at least, of the words "Ma'add" and "'Alī" at the top of the field; these are usually the only words that can be read except by direct comparison to one of the originals. All have an empty band surrounding the field and an outer marginal inscription which is also nearly illegible. They can be divided into several groups on the basis of their gold content, and this classification, as well as increasing barbarity of style, suggests a chronological arrangement from highest to lowest gold fineness, like the bezants of Jerusalem. The hoard evidence, slender as it is, supports this hypothesis, suggesting also that the sequence of reductions was at least roughly parallel.[85]

The earliest gold coinage of Tripoli is probably BY 2, characterized by high fineness and relatively careful workmanship. Unlike the remainder of the al-Mustanṣir imitations, BY 2 has five horizontal lines of inscription on each side, and stylistically it also stands out. It can be divided into two subvarieties which are similar in their rendering of the letter shapes but with subtle differentiation in style, best seen on the illustration. Among those analyzed by Gordus, the two ANS specimens represent one subvariety, with finenesses of 97.9 (pl. XVI, no. 39) and 86.6 percent, while the Paris specimen, representing the other subvariety (the one illustrated by Balog and Yvon), falls between them

---

82. Gordus and Metcalf, *op. cit.*, pp. 132–133.

83. Paul Z. Bedoukian, *The Coinage of Cilician Armenia* (ANS, Numismatic Notes and Monographs, no. 147; New York, 1962), p. 45. On "ghost monies" see Carlo M. Cipolla, *Money, Prices, and Civilization in the Mediterranean World* (Princeton, 1956), pp. 38–51.

84. A single coin imitates al-Mustanṣir's concentric legend issue; it is doubtful whether it belongs with the other imitations of his dinars. See below, p. 455.

85. Gordus and Metcalf, *op. cit.*, pp. 128–131.

with a fineness of 92.5 percent (another example of this subvariety, not the one analyzed, pl. XVI, no. 40). It differs markedly from the other two in its ratio of silver to copper. The coins of this group, however, are definitively linked as the products of a single mint not only by certain idiosyncrasies of letter form but also by the presence of three oblique strokes crossing the empty band between field and margin on both sides of the coin. These strokes link this group, in turn, to the remainder of the issues attributed to Tripoli, many of which also have markings in this area (although not oblique strokes).[86]

The remaining bezants of Tripoli form a fairly homogeneous series. All have only four lines of inscription on obverse and reverse, and many, though not all, have marks of some kind — small circles or dots — in the empty band around the field. Neither the presence or absence of markings nor their arrangement when present seems to have any relationship to differences that can be established on other grounds, but the marks nevertheless may have had some secret significance for mint personnel and others. Although the field inscriptions, except for the words "'Alī" and "Ma'add", are complete gibberish, they are nonetheless regular from one coin to the next. For example, the last line of the reverse (arbitrarily defined as the side with "Ma'add") always has a distinctive pattern which can best be described as two vertical wedge-shaped lines, a circle with a tail, a circle, and two more wedge shapes (reading Arabic-fashion from right to left). This simplified rendering of the Arabic becomes more condensed on the latest issues, but its gradual evolution can be easily traced when a number of specimens are examined. From their style one may judge that this is a continuous series of coins from a single mint.

It can be subdivided into four groups. The first (BY 3 and BY 4?) is of relatively finer workmanship. Only two of these were analyzed by Gordus and Metcalf; both were examples of BY 3 with 89.7 and 82.9 percent gold. This level of gold fineness overlaps with the fineness of BY 2 and suggests that BY 3 followed it very closely. Both BY 2 and BY 3 can be seen as analogues of the phase 1 coinage of the kingdom of Jerusalem, and probably can be assigned to the first half, or at least to the first two-thirds, of the twelfth century. BY 4 is associated with BY 3 on the basis of style.

The next group, BY 5-6, resembles BY 3-4 greatly, but there is a distinct decline from one to the next in workmanship. BY 5-6 are classified by Balog and Yvon as the first in the series "monnaies d'imita-

---

86. *Ibid.,* p. 140. BY 1 is there included with BY 2 as a possible early production of the Tripoli mint, but it cannot be that early, as it has Saladin's name on it. See below, p. 455.

tion grossière". One example of each of BY 5 and 6 was analyzed, with 71.3 and 73.6 percent gold, respectively. The number of coins so far analyzed is small, making definitive conclusions hazardous, but if, as seems almost certain from comparison of the engraving of the two groups, BY 3–4 was followed chronologically by BY 5–6, then there was, as in the kingdom of Jerusalem, a change from a higher but irregular standard of alloy to one that was lower but more tightly controlled. It appears probable that BY 5–6 are analogous to the phase 2 bezants of Jerusalem. The change in gold standard may have taken place at about the same time.

The last two groups have in common a much cruder style than the previous issues (Balog and Yvon introduce them as "plus grossière encore") and a considerable reduction in gold content, ranging for the two groups together from 57 to 67 percent, with the first group concentrated around 62 percent and the second about 60.6 percent. On both the letters are much thicker and more abbreviated than before — like the phase 3 coins of the kingdom, they seem to have been engraved with a blunt instrument. The first of these two groups (BY 7–12; pl. XVI, no. 41) can be easily distinguished from the second (BY 13–16; pl. XVI, no. 42) by the presence on the latter of the letters B and T on obverse and reverse in the same position as the words "Ma'add" and "'Alī" on earlier issues. Some of the B-T bezants also have a small cross on one side or the other, worked inconspicuously into the pseudo-Arabic inscription.[87] These two groups can plausibly be assigned to the era of Jerusalem's phase 3, that is, to the period between Saladin's conquests and the edict of Innocent IV forbidding imitations of Moslem coins.

These Tripoli bezants, although lower in fineness than those of Acre, are heavier on the average; it seems possible at least that they were also intended to contain 12 carats of gold, but to weigh 19 instead of 18 carats (with 4½ carats of silver and 2½ of copper).[88] These are quite possibly the same *bisante saracinato* mentioned in the Italian merchants' list previously cited[89] with a fineness of 15 carats (62.5 percent) and a value of 12 per ounce (of Florentine florins). This latter relation-

87. There is no significant distinction to be drawn between the B-T bezants with and without the cross; both dies of at least one specimen without cross were used separately in combination with other dies containing the cross (Balog and Yvon, "Monnaies," pp. 142–143).

88. Gordus and Metcalf, *op. cit.,* pp. 132, 142.

89. Above, note 78. *Bisanti saracinati d'oro* of the same fineness are also in another merchants' list edited by Evans from several manuscripts, of which the earliest is Archivio di Stato di Firenze, Manoscritti 75, fol. 288[r], assigned by him to 1320; another is that of Pegolotti's *La Pratica della mercatura* of 1320–1340 (ed. Evans, Cambridge, Mass., 1936, p. 288). This latter tradition does not give the relationship to the florin.

ship, according to Evans's calculations, indicates a weight standard of 3.78 grams, since the florin, 24 carats fine, weighed one-eighth of an ounce of 28.33 grams.

The letters B and T have been much discussed, without any definitive conclusion. Most previous proposals are eliminated by the analysis data, which put these coins clearly in the thirteenth century, probably at the very end of the series of imitations. The coins with B and T may, indeed, be contemporary with the Christian Arabic bezants of Acre, issued 1251–1258.[90] This attribution makes it reasonable to conjecture that B and T stand for *Boemundus* and *Tripolis* (as found in the obverse and reverse of the Latin silver coins). They are still essentially imitations, it is true, but their inscriptions are so completely barbarous that no real trace of their original Islamic import remains, so they may have been considered permissible within the terms of the papal edict. If they do in fact come from the period after the edict, there is no reason to assume that they ended in precisely the same year as the gold coinage of Acre; Tripoli did not fall to the Mamluks until 1289.

OTHER GOLD ISSUES OF THE CRUSADERS

The arrangement proposed above accounts for the great majority of the surviving bezants: roughly 160 out of about 200 published specimens. There remain a number of coins that seem certainly to be attributable to the crusaders, but cannot be fitted into the two major minting sequences. One such group are the coins in the Latakia hoard which seem to be dinars of ʿAlī ibn-Muḥammad (an eleventh-century ruler of Yemen) bearing the mint name Zabīd and the date 451 (1059/ 60; pl. XVI, no. 43). Although Balog and Yvon considered these authentic, Miles already in 1967 labeled them imitations which he suspected would eventually be classed as crusader coins.[91] Their presence in a hoard of the late twelfth century, as well as their gold content of 77.2 to 81.1 percent, is sufficient evidence for their identification as crusader issues. The gold content is the same as the issues of the kingdom of Jerusalem in the second half of the twelfth century, but it seems very unlikely that any of the royal mints would have struck a quite different type of bezant. Tentatively, one might suggest that the

90. The two series are found together in at least one hoard, described by Grierson, "Rare Crusader Bezant," p. 174.
91. Balog and Yvon, "Deux trésors," p. 299; Miles, "Some Hoards," p. 190.

Yemeni imitations were issued by Reginald of Châtillon from a mint at his fortress Kerak. Reginald's strategic ambitions in the Red Sea might accord with the choice of a Yemeni issue as prototype, and his independent character would make him an appropriate candidate to flout the royal minting rights of the young leper king Baldwin IV (1174–1185).[92] Possibly other dinars currently attributed to Yemen in the eleventh and twelfth centuries will prove on reëxamination to be crusader imitations also.

Another mysterious group of objects are the cut gold fragments that have been found in several hoards, often in association with full-size bezants. These include both imitations of Fāṭimid dinars and pieces with Latin inscriptions and geometric designs. These latter are known only as fragments, never as full coins. They have been interpreted as coins of the Latin kingdom from the time of Baldwin III and Amalric,[93] but this identification remains problematic.

It is extremely unlikely that these curious pieces were an official coinage. Although many have a wedge shape with one circular edge, suggesting a fragment cut from a circular disc like a coin, the majority are four-sided or irregular as if cut from strips or plates. They seem to come from a period (contemporary with the second phase of the bezants) when there was a regular and plentiful gold coinage. The alloy of the cut pieces that have been analyzed is from 50.4 to 62.1 percent,[94] lower than in any of the full-size bezants, and their weight is quite irregular, from 0.34 to 1.08 grams. The style and quality of the engraving of the Latin pieces, however, are typical of the royal mints. Several letters can be closely matched on deniers of Baldwin III, pointing to a date before 1167 for these objects. None of the Arabic fragments has been die-linked or matched with any specific variety of the full-size bezants, but the relatively fine style of the small fragments of inscription that can be seen is typical of the bezants of the twelfth

---

92. Gordus and Metcalf, *op. cit.,* p. 136.

93. Jeremiah D. Brady, "A Firm Attribution of Latin Gold Coinage to Twelfth-Century Jerusalem," ANS, *Museum Notes,* XXIII (1978), 133–147; *idem,* "A Hoard of Latin Gold Fragments of Baldwin of Jerusalem," in *Actes du 9ème Congrès International de Numismatique (Berne, Septembre 1979,* II: *Numismatique du Moyen Âge et des Temps Modernes,* ed. Tony Hackens and Raymond Weiller (Louvain-la-Neuve and Luxembourg, 1982), pp. 829–840; *idem,* "A Statistical Analysis of the Gold Fineness of a New Hoard of Crusader Latin Coinage of the Twelfth Century," *PACT: Revue du groupe européen d'études pour les techniques physiques, chimiques, et mathématiques appliquées à l'archéologie,* V (1981): *Statistics and Numismatics: Table ronde . . . ,* ed. Charlotte Carcassonne and Tony Hackens, pp. 391–398. Despite the fact that some of these pieces have the royal titulature *de Iervsalem,* it does not follow that they were struck in that city.

94. Gordus and Metcalf, *op. cit.,* p. 150. Another group, analyzed by Brady, "Hoard," p. 832, and "Analysis," *passim,* had a fineness range of 55.6 to 70.3 percent, leading him to suggest that these are earlier in date than the cut pieces from the Marash hoard.

century (some of the fragments may be pieces of genuine Moslem coins, although none has yet been so identified). There are several examples of fragments with Arabic on one side and Latin on the other, of which one in the ANS is the largest.[95] The latter is apparently of the type with several horizontal lines of inscription characteristic of Tripoli bezants, but other fragments are clearly of the small-central-field type of the kingdom of Jerusalem.

Even though these may be a product of one or more official mints, it does not follow that they were intended as coins. It has been suggested that they were made to be used in making payments by weight, to make up small deficiencies, or that they were used for payments of a fraction of a bezant, but this hardly can account for the creation of a large variety of Latin designs which were never struck as full-size coins. Another suggestion, which perhaps makes more sense, is that they were made for sale to pilgrims who wanted to offer gold at a shrine without a substantial expenditure.[96] At the same time, finds of these pieces with bezants in hoards suggest that the fragments had some monetary value. They may be related to the *pezzetti di bisanti,* "little pieces of bezants", with a fineness of 11¾ carats (48.96 percent) mentioned in the series of merchants' lists of 1350–1480.[97] The twelfth-century fragments are unlikely to be the same pieces mentioned in the fourteenth-century texts (in any case their fineness is slightly higher than any stated by the lists), but might be their monetary ancestors.

Only the Latin fragments have been studied in detail. The central designs on the majority are a "matrix" or "grid" on the obverse and a "star" on the reverse. These rather complicated interlaced figures have been drawn in full only by Miles.[98] The inscriptions include, on the obverse, BALDVINVS or AMALRICVS (REX), or SIGNUM AMALRICI or BALDVINI REGIS. The most common reverse inscription is IERVSALEM or HIERVSALEM CIVITAS, with variants. A number of fragments have letter combinations which cannot be fitted into

95. ANS 1981.36.1 (pl. XVI, no. 44; *Annual Report of the American Numismatic Society,* 1981, p. 19, no. 32), part of a group (from a hoard?) of 19 fragments. Others are in Metcalf, *Coinage of the Crusades,* plates 8–9, nos. 141, 225.

96. First suggested by Arthur J. Seltman, "Coins of the Crusades," *Spink's Numismatic Circular,* LXXIV (1966), 32–33; see Metcalf, *Coinage of the Crusades,* p. 31.

97. Edited by Evans, as cited above, note 78. *Pezzi di bisanti,* with a fineness of 12 carats, are also mentioned by the other manuscript tradition, including Pegolotti, *loc. cit.,* along with *pezzi di Tripoli* of 11 carats (45.83 percent). Another money in the former list is the *roelle sanza crocie . . . cioe bisanti* with a fineness of 11⅝ carats (48.25 percent), which are listed in only one of the six manuscripts, Datini 1174, the same one that describes the bezants with cross as *bisanti roelle* and gives the fineness of the latter as 15⅔ carats.

98. "Some Hoards," p. 195; these are only examples, as the designs on the fragments studied later often differ in detail.

the commonly found inscriptions; these may be parts of additional titulature, or of other names, possibly COMES HENRICVS or COMES RAIMVNDVS (Raymond III of Tripoli as regent of the kingdom, 1184–1186?).[99]

As for the Arabic fragments, the prevailing type is an imitation of the coinage of al-Āmir, like the full-size bezants of the Latin kingdom, and the fine style is like the bezants of the twelfth century. The Arabic fragments are like the Latin ones, however, in that no fragment has yet been observed to correspond precisely to any known full-size bezant—that is, it looks as if special dies were engraved to strike the Arabic fragments just as for the Latin ones (but a rigorous study has yet to be made). The Arabic side of the ANS bilingual piece (pl. XVI, no. 44) appears most similar to BY 2, identified as an early issue of Tripoli, but in truth the two widely separated pointillate circles surrounding the central area are paralleled on no other bezant, prototypical dinar, or fragment, and the same feature on the Latin side of the piece is also found on no other fragment. Obviously a great deal of study and much new material will be needed before it will be possible to speak with confidence of the full range of designs and inscriptions of these mysterious little bits.

The remaining imitations not yet attributed are all isolated small groups or unique coins with no obvious connection to any other issues. These include:

1. BY 1, a coin in the American Numismatic Society (0000.999.14974; pl. XVI, no. 45), which is unique among all the known imitations in copying the design of al-Mustanṣir's issue of 1048–1082, with three concentric circular inscriptions and no central field inscriptions. The inscriptions (which Balog and Yvon ignored as having "aucune signification, l'artisan franc n'ayant pas connu l'arabe") are legible, copied from the dinars of Saladin during the caliphate of the 'Abbāsid al-Mustaḍī (1174–1180). The visual difference between this latter coinage and the concentric type of al-Mustanṣir is that Saladin's coinage has two short lines of inscription in the center, which the imitation omits. BY 1 also has less silver than copper as alloying element, quite different from any crusader imitation analyzed, and finally its epigraphical style is unlike that of the other imitations. Since it is clearly not a genuine Moslem coin, it seems reasonable to attribute it to the Franks, but it may well be an issue of a very short-lived mint, perhaps private, from a place and time unguessable. Its fineness, 94.3 percent, suggests an early date, but it cannot be earlier than the accession of Saladin (1174).

99. Metcalf, *Coinage of the Crusades*, p. 32.

2. A bezant imitating with some fidelity the Egyptian dinars of Saladin with the name of the caliph an-Nāṣir, struck from 1180 to 1193. The imitation is described but not assigned a number by Balog and Yvon.[100] The alloy of the piece is not known. Its weight is 3.31 grams, within the range of the phase 3 bezants attributed above to the late twelfth and thirteenth centuries. This is the only imitation of an Aiyūbid dinar identified so far. Its existence raises the possibility that other dinars now attributed to Saladin, less crude in execution, might upon reëxamination turn out to be crusader imitations, which in turn may explain in part the debasement and irregular, often low, weight of the Egyptian dinar in Saladin's reign noted by Ehrenkreutz.[101]

3. A number of coins, mostly found in hoards along with bezants, as for example the five "authentic Fāṭimid" dinars of the Latakia hoard, which can now be confidently attributed as bezants on the basis of the results of neutron activation analysis and a reëxamination of the pieces.[102] These bezants are rather diverse, with mint names including Miṣr, al-Iskandarīyah (Alexandria), and al-Muʿizzīyah al-Qāhirah (Cairo), and dates including 508, 510, 514, 515, 516, and 518 (1114–1125; all within the reign of al-Āmir). Their weights and fineness are typical of bezants of the second phase at Acre. The engraving of their dies is, obviously, sufficiently skillful to fool experienced numismatists, but armed with the knowledge of their deficient weight and alloy, one can see that they do not have the finished appearance of similar dinars of full weight and alloy.

These good-quality imitations seem likely to be attributable to a subsidiary mint of the Latin kingdom, perhaps Tyre, but there is no certainty that all should be assigned to the same mint or era. Once again, further study is needed. These are surely not the only crusader imitations to be found among Fāṭimid dinars hitherto considered authentic. Oddy's tables show a number of debased issues, many of which were catalogued as Fāṭimid by Lane-Poole.[103] It seems likely that most of these are crusader bezants. Of special interest are the low-alloy dinars

---

100. "Monnaies," pp. 152–153, fig. 52.

101. Ehrenkreutz, "The Crisis of Dinar in the Egypt of Saladin," *Journal of the American Oriental Society,* LXXVI (1956), 178–184.

102. Balog and Yvon, "Deux trésors," p. 299; Gordus and Metcalf, *op. cit.,* pp. 129–130. Miles, in 1970, accepted the reattribution of four of these five coins, but considered one of them, no. 5 of the hoard, "unmistakably a genuine dinar". Despite his authoritative opinion, a careful comparison of this coin with other dinars of the same mint and period has convinced Bates that this dinar is indeed an imitation. The other analyzed bezants of the same category are Gordus and Metcalf, nos. 80–90.

103. Oddy, *op. cit.,* tables 3, 4, and 5; Oddy (pp. 107, 109) raises the possibility of a crusader attribution of these coins.

of Tripoli with dates around 460 (1067/8); if these can be proven to be imitations, they would represent a new major variety in the bezant series.

In summary, then, the combined evidence of metal analysis, metrology, hoards, visual examination of the coins, Latin documents, and Arabic texts indicates the general organization and evolution of the crusader imitation bezants. Two major series, from the kingdom of Jerusalem and the county of Tripoli, can be identified and put into a reasonably well-defined chronological sequence from the mid-twelfth century until after the middle of the thirteenth. At the same time this new understanding of the history of the crusader bezant raises further questions and problems for numismatic research.

C. Crusader Arabic Silver Issues[104]

Within a generation or two after the arrival of the first crusaders in Syria, they had begun to issue gold coins imitating those of the Moslems and copper coins analogous to those of Byzantium and northern Syria (although with Latin inscriptions), but there were no crusader imitation silver coins in the twelfth century. This is not surprising, for two simple reasons. First, the silver coinage of the Moslem world at the time of the first crusades, especially in Syria, was evidently scanty, consisted of small coins considerably alloyed and low in value, and was unlikely to make any impression on newcomers. Second, and probably more important, the crusaders already had their own silver coinage in western Europe, the penny, also a small and often debased coin. The gold and copper coins of Syria were new to the crusaders, but the little debased dirhams filled no role that could not be played by pennies imported from Europe or struck by the crusaders themselves.

The situation changed radically after Saladin's invasion of Syria in 1174. One of his earliest innovations was the initiation of minting of full-weight good silver dirhams at Damascus, Homs, Hamah, and Aleppo. Judging by the quantity of surviving examples, Saladin's new dirham coinage was not issued in large amounts at first, but increased in volume during his reign and under his immediate successors. From the turn of the thirteenth century, Aiyūbid Syrian dirhams become quite common. Minting of full dirhams also spread to other Moslem

104. This section was written by Bates.

lands: Egypt, Anatolia, and Mesopotamia. One possible interpretation of the process is that the new dirhams in the late twelfth century took some time to become established as an important part of the monetary system, but as they did so, they created a demand for silver coinage which had the effect of drawing silver to the mints from bullion stocks in Syria itself and from outside. This hypothesis has its importance for the understanding of the crusader Arabic silver coinage, as will be seen.

The Frankish states on the Syrian littoral must inevitably have been drawn into the process of expansion of the use of full dirhams in Syria. It seems reasonable to assume that Aiyūbid dirhams would have come to the Franks in transactions with the Moslems, and that these coins would come to be used not only for return transactions but also in exchanges among Franks—not, to be sure, for the transactions of daily life in the marketplace, but in large commercial dealings. At any rate, it is certain that the minting of dirhams spread not only to Aiyūbid Syria's Moslem neighbors but also to the crusaders, beginning in 1216. It is also certain that these crusader dirhams were issued in large quantity and had an important economic role.

Who precisely issued these coins, and what exactly their economic role was, are questions the answers to which are less clear. Three major series of crusader dirhams exist, two that imitate Aiyūbid dirhams and one of Aiyūbid type but with Christian inscriptions.[105] The dates on these coins are not those of the prototypes, but follow a regular sequence and seem to be authentic in most cases. The three series follow in chronological sequence without overlapping. Until about 1245, the crusader dirhams are homogeneous at any given time, without subvarieties, indicating production from a single mint. It seems plausible, therefore, that the dirhams were produced either by an official mint or with official authorization. Since the third series (that with Christian inscriptions) bears the mint-name 'Akkā (Acre), it seems plausible that this was the mint for all the crusader dirhams. In sum, the dirhams, like the crusader gold bezants, seem to have been an officially sanctioned coinage of the kingdom of Jerusalem.

The economic role of the dirhams, however, was different from that of the bezants. The bezant, as argued previously, was intended as a

---

105. Metcalf, *Coinage of the Crusades,* p. 29, lists two additional series as possible crusader dirhams, possibly at the suggestion of Mr. Stephen Album. It should be made clear that series B and D on that page were not identified as such by Bates, "Thirteenth Century Crusader Imitations," although Metcalf's note 8 on page 28 might seem to imply otherwise. No evidence has been presented for the attribution of these two series to the crusaders, or even for the existence of Metcalf's series D.

separate currency from the Fāṭimid dinars it imitated. The crusader dirhams, in contrast, were clearly intended to circulate along with Aiyūbid dirhams. The imitations, until about 1245, are visually indistinguishable from their prototypes except by their anomalous dates, which in any case are often not visible because of irregularities of striking. When the date is illegible, it is impossible today to identify any single dirham by itself as an imitation or a prototype; it must have been impossible for contemporaries as well. Unlike the bezants, these dirhams are found in hoards mixed with authentic Moslem issues.[106]

There is nothing deceptive or fraudulent in this close similarity. Aiyūbid dirhams from different mints, with different designs and inscriptions, circulated indiscriminately together, if hoard evidence is to be believed, and mixed with these are found also dirhams of another dynasty, the Artukids, with designs like those of the Aiyūbids but with clear inscriptional indication of their origin. Since any dirham with one of the few Aiyūbid designs seems to have been accepted at parity, it was rational for the crusaders also to issue their version of this standard coinage. By doing so they could convert silver into coinage without the disadvantage of having to transport it to a Moslem mint and pay mint charges to Moslems. Although the system by which the crusaders regulated the weight of their dirhams was different from the Moslem system, and their average weight was slightly lower, the silver content of a typical crusader dirham was roughly the same as that of the Moslem issues. The only element of deception was the use of Moslem designs and inscriptions to ensure acceptance of the coins. Had the crusaders used distinctive designs, or even the same design with overtly Christian inscriptions, the coins would probably have been treated as a separate currency by Moslems and not accepted at parity. This consideration perhaps explains why the last crusader dirham series, issued with crosses and Christian inscriptions in conformity with the letter of pope Innocent, was short-lived and soon replaced by a revival of the imitative coinage, slightly modified to comply with the papal injunction while passing unrecognized by the Moslems.

The first series of crusader dirhams, so far as is now known, were imitations of the coinage of aẓ-Ẓāhir Ghāzī, son of Saladin and ruler of Aleppo from 1186 until his death in 1216. The specific prototype was struck from 598 to 613 (1201–1216; pl. XIV, no. 21). It has the hexagram or "seal of Solomon" design which was standard at Aleppo,

---

106. Balog, "La Trouvaille du Fayoum," *Bulletin de l'Institut d'Égypte* XXXIV (1951–1952), 17–55; Bates, "Crusader Imitations," p. 395; Enrico Leuthold, Jr., "Monete con leggende in arabo — islamiche e de' Crociati — in un ripostiglio del XIII secolo," *Rivista italiana di numismatica,* 5th ser., XIX (1971), 175–184.

with the main inscriptions framed in a six-pointed star enclosed in a circle. Az̧-Z̧āhir's name and titles are in the star on one side of the coin, and those of his overlords, the Aiyūbid sultan al-'Ādil and the 'Abbāsid caliph an-Nāṣir, are on the other. The mint name and date are on the side with az̧-Z̧āhir's name in the six small triangular segments between the points of the star and the circle, and the Moslem declaration of faith is on the other side in the same location.[107] The coinage included smaller half dirhams as well. These include half dirhams with the same hexagram design but with abbreviated versions of the titles of az̧-Z̧āhir and an-Nāṣir on the two sides, without al-'Ādil's name, and also halves struck with full-dirham dies.

Crusader imitations of both dirhams and half dirhams are known, differing from the prototype only in bearing dates after 613 (1216; pl. XVI, nos. 47–48). Every year from 614 to 630 (1217–1233) is represented, and also the year 638 (1240/1).[108] These coins have the mint name "Ḥalab" (Aleppo) and the names of az̧-Z̧āhir, who died in 1216, al-'Ādil, who died in 1218, and the caliph an-Nāṣir, who died in 1225. Meanwhile, Aleppo itself produced normal dirhams covering the same span of years bearing the names of az̧-Z̧āhir's successors al-'Azīz (1216–1236) and an-Nāṣir (1236–1260), along with the appropriate names of their overlords and the caliphs.[109] It is impossible, therefore, that the dirhams with az̧-Z̧āhir's name and dates after 613 could have been issues of the Aleppo mint, or official issues of any Moslem mint.

Their anachronistic dates are the principal basis for the attribution of the posthumous Aleppo dirhams to the crusaders, by analogy with the subsequent crusader issue imitating Damascus dirhams, which also has impossible dates along with, on some examples, small crosses as definitive proof of Christian origin; but the dates are not the only evidence. Further support is provided by statistical study of their metrology and metal content. The data on which this study was based are as yet unpublished, but can be summarized here. Numismatists determine the weight standard of a coinage issue by the frequency-distribution method, which consists essentially of dividing the weight range of known examples into equal intervals (usually 0.05 gram) and counting the number of coins in each interval. The resulting series can be set out in tabular form or graphed. This technique indicates the mode, that is, the interval including most coins, which is the safest indicator of the mint's intended weight standard. The distribution of weights also

---

107. Balog, *Coinage of the Ayyubids,* nos. 599, 601–628.
108. *Ibid.,* nos. 629–654, lists representative specimens of each date.
109. *Ibid.,* nos. 686–706, 724–757.

provides evidence as to the means by which the weights of individual coins were controlled by the mint. The result of such studies on genuine Aiyūbid dirhams is always the same if the number of specimens is sufficient: the number of coins in each interval increases gradually as the weight increases, up to the modal weight range, and then drops off sharply. In other words, there are many coins with less than the modal weight, the presumed weight standard of the mint, and few coins with more. This distribution, which produces an asymmetrical ("skewed") graph, is an indication that the weight of coins was controlled individually by the mint, or else that people culled the coins that they found in circulation. Overweight coins were trimmed down to standard, or remelted and restruck, while underweight coins were allowed to be issued.

Similar studies of the crusader dirhams that imitate Aiyūbid issues of Damascus, the attribution of which is certain, produce a different distribution: the graph, depending on the number of specimens in the sample, approaches the shape of the classical bell-shaped curve, with nearly equal numbers of coins above and below the modal interval. This curve is characteristic of mint regulation of weight in mass, with a certain number of coins per weight unit (pound or mark of silver) regardless of the weight of individual specimens. The contrast between the Aiyūbid and the crusader dirhams, given that they often circulated together, allows us to deduce that the heavy coins were removed by the mint before entering circulation. In the specific instance at hand, the weight distribution of the dirhams of az̧-Z̧āhir's lifetime and those of his son al-'Azīz both conform to the highly skewed curve of other Aiyūbid dirhams, while the distribution of the weights of the posthumously dated dirhams is quite symmetrical, as on the other dirham issues of the crusaders. The quantitative results of the two studies show that the standard in az̧-Z̧āhir's lifetime was 2.95–3.00 grams, while the imitations (considering only those up to 630) were issued at an average weight of about 2.83 grams.

As to fineness,[110] analyses of eighteen dirhams of az̧-Z̧āhir Ghāzī and seven of his son al-'Azīz Muḥammad show that, between the Moslem years A.H. 600 and 625, the standard of fineness at the Aleppo mint was maintained at a very high level, with none of the coins below 97.2 percent silver; sixteen of the twenty-five imitations analyzed were below this figure, ranging in all from 98.6 down to 94.2 percent until

---

110. The analyses discussed here and throughout this section were made by Professor Adon A. Gordus of the University of Michigan Department of Chemistry, by neutron activation analysis of streaks. Professor Gordus is not responsible for any of the present interpretations of his data.

626, and between 90.5 and 95.5 percent from 628 to 638. This difference does not prove, in itself, that the imitations were produced by the crusaders, but it makes it unlikely that they were issues of the Aleppo mint. Moreover, this difference in fineness is the clue to the precise beginning of the imitations. One might expect at first that the imitations began during aẓ-Ẓāhir's lifetime, but judging by the consistent and tightly controlled fineness of the dirhams issued in his lifetime, compared to the lower fineness of the posthumous dirhams, this is not the case—except for the year of his death, 613. Five dirhams of that year were analyzed, of which four were struck with the same dies (proof of origin from the same mint); their fineness range, from 93.6 to 97.4 percent silver, is decidedly lower than that of the preceding dirhams of aẓ-Ẓāhir and the subsequent dirhams of al-'Azīz, while at the same time congruent with the range of the posthumous dirhams. It would seem, therefore, that all five coins are imitations; these represent the entire holdings of the ANS for the year 613.

One may conclude that the imitation dirhams began to be struck in precisely the year that aẓ-Ẓāhir died, 613 (1216).[111] In this date lies the clue to the possible reason for the beginning of the imitative coinage. In the early years of the thirteenth century aẓ-Ẓāhir was in alliance with the crusaders, specifically with the counts of Tripoli, Bohemond III and IV. Among his various agreements was a treaty with Venice in 604 (1207/8) which provided that Venetian merchants could have access to the mint at Aleppo to have coins struck from any silver bullion they might bring to the city.[112] This was probably the most convenient and cheapest access to a dirham mint available to the Franks at the time. Indeed, the existence of this clause in the treaty implies that without treaty rights, the Franks had no direct access to Moslem

111. It is not impossible that authentic dirhams of aẓ-Ẓāhir of 613 will be found (he died nearly at the middle of that year), but they will be identifiable only by their higher silver fineness, and then only tentatively because the range of fineness of the two coinages overlaps somewhat.

112. Wilhelm Heyd, "Ueber die angeblichen Münzprägungen der Venetianer in Accon, Tyrus, and Tripolis," *Numismatische Zeitschrift*, XI (1979), 239, is the best discussion of this clause of the treaty; see also Irwin, "Supply," p. 88. Heyd, whose article in a somewhat obscure publication has been widely ignored, demolishes the assumption that this treaty and others like it gave the Franks the right to operate mints. From this treaty, and another with the king of Cilician Armenia that gives the Venetians the right to strike coins on the same terms as they did in Acre, Schlumberger (*Numismatique de l'Orient latin,* pp. 137–138) argued that the Venetians not only operated mints in various Moslem and Armenian cities, but operated the mint in Acre that struck the imitative coinages, both gold and silver. Heyd demonstrates that these treaties gave the Venetians only the valuable right to take gold or silver to the local mint to be struck into local coinage on regulated terms; otherwise, their bullion would have had to be sold to middlemen. The treaty with aẓ-Ẓāhir, for example, specifies a charge of 5 percent.

mints,[113] leaving them with the alternative of selling bullion for what it would bring in dirhams in the marketplace.

Relations between az̲-Z̲āhir and the crusaders began to cool in his later years, and the alliance with Tripoli was definitely ended at his death in 1216.[114] Probably the arrangement with the Venetians also terminated at this time. It seems entirely possible that the Venetians, or other crusaders, had become familiar with the dirhams they had been obtaining from the Aleppo mint and decided to begin making their own. It was proposed above, because of the continuity of this series of imitations with the later ones culminating in an issue with the mint-name Acre, that all these imitations should be regarded as issues of the mint there of the kingdom of Jerusalem. If so, it would seem that the Venetian privileges at the mint of Aleppo from 1207 to 1216 had a wide monetary impact for all the crusader states, sufficient to induce the royal mint to take up production of these coins after the termination of the agreement, or that the Venetians depended on these coins to the extent that they insisted on their minting in Acre. Alternatively, however, it must be admitted that the possibility of a north Syrian mint such as Tripoli for the Aleppo imitations is attractive. It cannot be excluded that these dirhams may not be directly connected with the imitations of Damascus coinage that followed them so closely in time.

The first period of issue of Aleppo imitations extended, then, from 613 to 630 (1216–1233). Toward the end of this span of years, in 628 and 629, the fineness of these dirhams had begun to decline, judging by one specimen from each of those years with 90.6 and 93.0 percent silver respectively. The last year of minting in 630 is also the beginning of a general dearth of Moslem dirhams until 637, suggesting that silver had become scarce in those years throughout Syria. In 638 (1240/1), however, imitations of Aleppo dirhams appear again, still with the same design and inscriptions (pl. XVI, no. 49). The occasion for this reappearance is suggested by a comparison of the metal content of these imitations with that of the coinage of Damascus in the same year. A feature of silver coins in the pre-modern era is the presence of small amounts of gold, ranging sometimes to more than 1 percent. This occurs because gold is a normal trace element in silver ore, but usually in amounts not detectable by medieval technology. Because it is chemically similar to silver, it is not removed by the refining process. As a

113. Such clauses were frequent in treaties between Franks and Moslems; see Irwin, *loc. cit.*, and Heyd, *passim.*

114. Mary Nickerson Hardwicke, "The Crusader States, 1192–1243," in volume II of the present work, pp. 526–540.

result, coins that come from a single source of silver will have a small but consistent amount of gold as an impurity. This may indicate that the coins in question were all made from ore from a single mine or ore vein, but it is of course also true that coins from the same batch of melted silver will have approximately the same level of gold content, even if that silver came from disparate sources. Four Aleppo imitations and nine dirhams of Damascus have been analyzed, and all fell into the same narrow range of gold impurity level, from 0.29 to 0.36 percent for the imitations and 0.26 to 0.36 for the Damascene coins. In no other instance was there such a close correspondence between crusader and Moslem coins. In fact, the range of gold impurity for Syrian dirhams in the Aiyūbid era is normally quite wide, ranging from 0.30 to 1.20 percent, with issues of every mint spread throughout this range. This diversity is not surprising, as Syria has no native source of silver and must have imported its bullion from a variety of sources. In this context, the similarity of the imitations and the coinage of Damascus in 638 is remarkable.

There is an obvious historical explanation for this phenomenon: in early 638 (July–August 1240) aṣ-Ṣāliḥ Ismāʿīl, the Aiyūbid ruler of Damascus, entered into an alliance with the crusaders, which continued in force for a few months only. Under the terms of the treaty, the crusaders were permitted to come to Damascus to buy arms and supplies.[115] It seems likely that it was specifically to provide funds for this "shopping expedition" that the minting of Aleppo imitations was revived, and it would seem furthermore that the bulk of the silver brought to the mint at Damascus in this year was made up of these crusader dirhams. The fineness of the imitations, ranging from 90.5 to 95.5 percent silver, is no worse than that of the coinage of Damascus itself in the same year, from 89.5 to 96.5 percent, but one can imagine that the imitation dirhams, by this time obsolete in type by a quarter-century, were discriminated against by the Damascenes, who converted them as rapidly as possible into current coin (possibly the crusaders themselves were allowed to bring silver to the Damascus mint, although this is not explicitly stated).

The second series of crusader Arabic dirhams imitates the Damascus issue begun by aṣ-Ṣāliḥ Ismāʿīl in the year of his first alliance with

---

115. R. Stephen Humphreys, *From Saladin to the Mongols: the Ayyūbids of Damascus, 1193-1260* (Albany, N.Y., 1977), pp. 265–269; cf. Sidney Painter, "The Crusade of Theobald of Champagne and Richard of Cornwall, 1239-1241," in volume II of the present work, p. 479, and Hamilton A.R. Gibb, "The Aiyubids," *ibid.,* p. 707. Humphreys' dating is used here, because the alliance was formed after the accession of aṣ-Ṣāliḥ Aiyūb as sultan in the last month of 637 (July 1240).

the crusaders (pl. XIII, no. 19). Both prototype and imitation have the main inscriptions in a square enclosed in a circle at the rim of the coin. One side has the name and titles of aṣ-Ṣāliḥ in the square, with the mint city and the date in the four segments between the square and outer circle. The other side has the name and titles of the caliph al-Mustanṣir in the square and the Moslem profession of faith in the segments. This issue was struck from 638 (1240/1) until 640 (1242), when al-Mustanṣir died. As normal in Syria, the issue was accompanied by half dirhams of the same pattern, struck with special half-dirham dies with abbreviated inscriptions or with full-dirham dies.[116]

The crusader imitations of this issue closely reproduce the central inscriptions of the prototype, but vary in one way or another in their marginal inscriptions. On the basis of these variations the imitations can be classified into six types, which should be regarded as separate issues and will be discussed individually. Since the distinguishing inscriptions are small and at the edge of the coins, they are easily effaced by carelessness in striking, which was usual at both the crusader and the Moslem mints, and when this happens it is impossible to distinguish visually an imitation from the prototype. Even when visible, the distinguishing characteristics of the imitations are inconspicuous, and were probably not noticed by the people who used these coins. The modern numismatist who knows what to look for can sort out a few imitations and a few authentic prototypes from any large groups of coins of this type, but the rest can be identified as crusader or Moslem only by close comparison of unidentified with identified coins to establish die identities. The majority of known specimens of the cru-

116. All these are listed in Balog, *Ayyubids*, nos. 801–807, along with dirhams of 635 and 637, but it is doubtful that these earlier dates really exist, because of the intrusion of crusader imitations into the corpus of dirhams attributed to aṣ-Ṣāliḥ (see the listing in Bates, "Crusader Imitations," p. 403; at least two of the imitations in that list are cataloged by Balog as genuine), and because of the similarity of the numerals "seven" and "nine" as written on these coins. Although aṣ-Ṣāliḥ was ruler of Damascus for some months in 635, it is probable that he, like his brother al-Ashraf Mūsâ before him, acknowledged al-Kāmil as overlord on coins, even though al-Kāmil did not recognize his accession, besieged the city, and took it from him. No Arabic source mentions that aṣ-Ṣāliḥ issued coins in his own name, and had he done so, thereby openly rebelling against al-Kāmil, it is unlikely that the two would have come to terms as they did (Humphreys, *op. cit.*, pp. 232–237). When aṣ-Ṣāliḥ came to power in Damascus again in 637, he acknowledged al-ʿĀdil II of Egypt as overlord and is specifically said to have kept his name on the coins (Humphreys, *op. cit.*, pp. 257–258). It is unlikely that aṣ-Ṣāliḥ began issuing coins with his own name until after the overthrow of al-ʿĀdil II and the accession of his enemy aṣ-Ṣāliḥ Aiyūb on the eighth day of the last month of 637 (Humphreys, *op. cit.*, p. 264). Allowing some time for the news to reach Damascus and for aṣ-Ṣāliḥ Ismāʿīl to decide on a policy, it becomes unlikely that coins in his name began before 638. At least one of Balog's entries for 635, the British Museum specimen, is a crusader imitation and the readings of the other two have yet to be confirmed. The coins Balog assigned to 637 could just as well be 639.

sader imitations have been identified and classified through die identities with fully legible examples.

Type I (pl. XVII, no. 50): this is by far the largest issue among the Damascus imitations, comprising about 65 percent of all identified specimens.[117] Dirhams of this type are identical in every respect to the prototype, including the mint identification *Dimashq,* "Damascus", but they have the dates 641, 644, and perhaps 647,[118] which are all after the death of the caliph al-Mustanṣir named on them; at the same time the Damascus mint produced dirhams with the name of his successor. This anachronism is odd, but does not in itself prove a crusader origin for these coins. There are numerous instances of such anachronisms resulting at Moslem mints from the accidental combination of old and new dies ("muling"), although these are mostly isolated single coins. In the case of the aṣ-Ṣāliḥ imitations of Type I, however, there are hundreds of examples. The attribution to the crusaders is further supported by analogy with other types that have clear indication of Christian origin, by a high incidence of barbarity or illiteracy in the marginal inscriptions, and by metrological and metallurgical differences from the prototype. There are also analogous half dirhams, like the prototype half dirhams.

The various dates of Type I are closely linked by shared dies for the undated side of the coin, suggesting that minting was more or less continuous throughout the years 641 to 644 or 647 (1243–1247 or 1243–1250).[119] The dates then might sometimes be fictitious, but it seems obvious that 641 (1243/4) would not be the earliest year found on the imitations if it was not in fact the first year of issue. The reasonable supposition that imitations might have begun while the prototype was still being issued, and thus be indistinguishable by date from the prototypes, is simply not supported by the die evidence, for nearly all the

117. Judging by the number of specimens recorded by Bates, "Crusader Imitations," p. 404. The number of surviving specimens today is largely a result of hoard finds; a single find of a large hoard including a particular issue can change the proportions overnight. Nevertheless, the number of dies reported for the different types of the Damascus imitations is proportional in most cases to the number of existing specimens, suggesting that the number of surviving coins is roughly proportional to the original size of the issues. The exception is Type V, with a much higher proportion of dies to number of specimens than the others, indicating that this issue may have been larger than its representation in 1974 would indicate.

118. Leuthold, *op. cit.,* p. 183, read the dates 642, 643, 645, and 648 as well, but these readings are rejected by Bates, *op. cit.,* pp. 406–407, where the questions involved are discussed in full. The dates 641 and 644 are clear and generally accepted by all scholars. The cursive script makes the reading 647 speculative.

119. This conclusion lends support to the dates suggested by Leuthold, but unfortunately all the coins on which he reads these dates have more clearly legible die duplicates that disprove his readings.

coins of this type with dates of 640 and before are interlinked by the use of a small number of obverse and reverse dies, and none of them as yet can be linked to any of the coins with posthumous dates. Moreover, there are metallurgical differences between the coins dated 640 and earlier, as a group, and those dated 641 and after. It would seem, therefore, that as in the case of the Aleppo imitations, the issuers of the Damascus imitations deliberately selected an obsolete prototype. It is not obvious why this particular prototype was chosen, but there may be some connection with the renewed alliance between aṣ-Ṣāliḥ and the Franks of Acre in spring 1244 (late 641).[120]

The date 647, if it is rightly read, has support from historical circumstances as the terminal date for Type I (and for the first phase of issue of all the Damascus imitations), because it was in late 647 (spring 1250) that bishop Odo of Châteauroux arrived in Syria to find the Franks striking coins bearing the names of Moslem rulers and Moslem religious inscriptions. There are no crusader coins with Moslem dates after 647, or any with the Christian year 1250, suggesting that Odo's intervention put a stop to all minting for a time.

Types II, III, and IV: all three of these types are known only in small quantities (6, 8, and 2 respectively were known in 1974[121]). Their economic importance is therefore slight, but they are of interest because their marked divergences from the common Type I issue and the absence of any die links between any of these types raise the possibility that they were issued at different mints (which might mean only different workshops in the same city). Type II (pl. XVII, no. 51), which seems to be dated 643 (1245/6, a very problematic reading), differs from Type I only in having differently arranged and very barbarous marginal inscriptions.

Type III (pl. XVII, no. 52) is more interesting: the date 643 on it is almost certain, and the dirhams of this type are characterized by the presence of inconspicuous crosses in the margins. All known die varieties have a cross in the topmost segment of the side with the date, between the two Arabic words for "in the name of" and "God" that precede the statement of place and date of minting. On the other side, all have also an interesting modification of the name of the Moslem prophet in the marginal inscription "Mohammed is the messenger of God." As modified, the only possible reading of the name is *Mikhā'īl*, the Arabic equivalent of the name Michael. Did the die cutters, or

120. Humphreys, *op. cit.,* p. 274; Steven Runciman, "The Crusader States, 1243–1291," in volume II of the present work, p. 561; Gibb, *op. cit.,* p. 709.
121. Bates, "Crusader Imitations," p. 404.

their superintendents, really intend to say that "Michael is the messenger of God"? Could this refer to the archangel Michael? Since on some of these coins the name *Mikhā'īl* (which is written in two separate letter groups in Arabic) is divided by a small cross, it would seem likely that the engravers knew what they were doing. Even before Odo, it seems, some Christians were uncomfortable with a coinage that completely aped Moslem practice, or perhaps the date is fictitious and the type to be assigned to the period after the papal interdiction of Moslem inscriptions. This series also was accompanied by an analogous half-dirham issue (pl. XVII, no. 53).

Type IV (pl. XVII, no. 54) is quite anomalous, as the only imitation with modified central inscriptions, shortening one of aṣ-Ṣāliḥ's titles from *'Imād-ad-Dunyā wa-d-Dīn* (pillar of society and religion) to *'Imād-ad-Dīn,* a common and perfectly legitimate elision among Moslems. The date is apparently to be read 644 (1246/7). Given that only two examples are known, it is only analogy that supports the attribution of this issue to the crusaders, but unless the date is fictitious, it suggests the existence of a third mint in addition to the main Type I mint.

Types V and VI come after an intervening issue with Christian inscriptions, making it appropriate to postpone their discussion.

Bishop Odo's intervention led to the introduction of a third crusader dirham series with overtly Christian inscriptions and with crosses, corresponding to the similar issue in gold of 1251–1258 described in the previous section of this chapter. The silver coinage had a much shorter life span, limited to 1251 only.[122] The relative success of the new bezants as compared to the dirhams may be explained by the different monetary roles of the two currencies. The bezants, which imitated obsolete Fāṭimid coins, were unlike any contemporary issue and were well known to Moslems as Frankish in origin. The new bezants, therefore, may well have been equally acceptable despite their overtly Christian symbols. The imitative crusader dirhams, however, closely resembled current Moslem coins and were evidently meant to circulate indiscriminately with them (as they successfully did, if hoard evidence is to be believed). The new crusader dirhams with Christian inscriptions and crosses could not pass as ordinary Moslem coins, resulting in their rejection by Moslems, or at best in their being discounted against current Moslem dirhams.

Balog and Yvon list thirteen varieties of Christian dirhams and four

122. A dirham of 1252 and another of 1253 have been mentioned in print, but these readings cannot be accepted (*ibid.,* p. 408). The marginal inscriptions of these coins are cursively engraved and often poorly impressed, making it easy to be misled in reading them.

varieties of the accompanying half dirhams, [123] but the principal division is into three groups: those with a central cross on one side surrounded by a circle, those with a central cross but no circle, and those without a cross (pl. XVII, nos. 55–58). All these have the same Arabic inscriptions, which are mostly different from those on the bezants. The design is the same as that of the second series of Damascus imitations, with central inscriptions in a square surrounded by a circle and subsidiary inscriptions in the spaces between the square and the circle, a very common type for thirteenth-century Syrian dirhams. On the side designated by Balog and Yvon as the obverse, the inscription in the margin states the place and date of issue: "struck in Acre in the year one thousand two hundred, one and fifty, of the Incarnation (of the Messiah)" (some varieties omit the words in parentheses). The central inscription on this side is not found on the bezants: "one God, one faith, one baptism." On the other side, the central inscription proclaims "Father, Son, and Holy Ghost: one godhead", [124] and the marginal inscription states "His is the glory forever and ever, amen amen." [125] The half dirhams omit the obverse central inscription as well as the mint date formula; instead the reverse central inscription is divided between the two sides and the reverse marginal inscription is repeated on both margins (pl. XVII, no. 58). In addition to these inscriptions and the crosses, these coins are extensively ornamented with a variety of fleurs-de-lys, small crescents, arabesques, and diacritical marks drawn from the repertoires of both Moslem and Christian craftsmen.

Presumably because these dirhams were not readily accepted by Moslems, the crusader mint revived the issue of imitations of aṣ-Ṣāliḥ Ismāʿīl's coinage of Damascus, but with some modifications. It is probably no coincidence that one type of these renewed imitations bears the date 1253, when Innocent's letter arrived in Syria; taken literally, it forbade only the emission of coins with the name of Mohammed and his "birth date" (the Moslem year), and thereby opened the way to revival of imitative coins without the objectionable features. These are classified as Types V and VI of the second series. Both replace the Moslem profession of faith in the margin with the simple statement "in the name of God the merciful, the compassionate", a very common Moslem formula but one to which no monotheist could object. Type V (pl. XVII, no. 59) has the Christian date "one thousand and

123. Balog and Yvon, "Monnaies," pp. 161–167, nos. 42–48.

124. As with the corresponding gold issue, the Arabic word *ilāh*, "godhead", has been falsely corrected by previous catalogers to *Allāh;* see note 75 above.

125. This inscription also has previously been misread: the first word is not *Allāh*, which would result in the meaning "God is the glory", but simply *lahu*, "To Him is the glory."

two hundred and three and fifty", but with the fictitious mint name
Damascus, while Type VI (pl. XVII, no. 60) reverts to the original Moslem year of the Damascus imitations, 641. Despite this latter date, Type
VI clearly belongs to the same period as Type V, not only because of
the shared religious formula but also because of similarities of style
in the engraving of the marginal inscriptions on both sides of the coins.
Possibly the date 641 was acceptable because it was fictitious, or possibly no one cared enough to enforce the papal injunction on this point.
Because there are no die links between the two types, the possibility
of two separate mints or workshops is raised again, but the similarity
of the types indicates that there was no great distance between their
places of manufacture. One would even say that the same die engravers were at work. It is also possible that the dirhams dated 641 came
after those dated 1253, and continued to be struck for a while, perhaps until the end of the Christian bezants in 1258, or even later.

In weight standard and fineness, the Damascus-type crusader dirhams were lower than their prototype, the coins of Damascus 1239–
1242, but about equal to contemporary issues of Damascus and Aleppo
after 1243. The general pattern for all three of these mints (Damascus,
Aleppo, and the crusader mint) is similar: weight and fineness decline
in the 640's (1242–1252) and decline further after 650 (1252/3). For
Damascus, 637–640, the weight standard indicated by the mode is
about 2.90–2.95 grams, while for the first large crusader issue, Type
I, it is about 2.80–2.85, but the two coinages are closer in average weight,
at 2.87 and 2.83 grams respectively. Moreover, the modal weight of
the issues of Damascus, 641–647, the same Moslem years as Type I,
is 2.85–2.90, much nearer to the crusader standard. In fineness, the
crusader Type I coins range from 79.6 to 94.2 percent silver, while the
prototypes range from 84.9 to 96.5 and the coinage of Damascus in
the same years as the crusader issue ranges from 78.6 to 96.7 percent.
The crusader dirhams with Christian inscriptions are higher in fineness than the close imitations, ranging from 85.8 to 96.9 percent, but
the subsequent imitations, Types V and VI, return to the range of Type
I, from 70.5 to 91.9 percent, with only one coin out of twenty above
90 percent. Similarly at Damascus, the four analyzed dirhams after
650 (1252/3) range only from 73.1 to 80.2 percent, while at Aleppo
in the same era the range is from 74.4 to 83.2.

Several features of these data are remarkable: the wide range in
fineness among all these dirhams, the apparent general decline, and
the close correspondence of issues at the three major Syrian mints.
Since all these coins are found mixed together in hoards, contemporaries must have ignored the differences between individual coins, but

it would seem likely that the value of all these dirhams was discounted to compensate for the unreliability of weight and fineness. By 1260 the monetary situation had reached a crisis. According to Abū-Shāmah, Damascus was flooded with Frankish dirhams reported to contain only 15 percent silver, and the danger that these dirhams would be suppressed caused everyone to spend them as quickly as possible, which made prices rise to extraordinary levels. At the end of the year these dirhams were prohibited and exchanged for current Damascus coin, but at a considerable discount.[126] According to the manuscripts of Abū-Shāmah's history, these dirhams were known as *bāqīyah* or *bāfīyah,* a word which is not understood but which must be a name denoting the origin of the coins, either by place or by issuing authority. It has been emended more than once to *yāfīyah,* "Jaffan", but it hardly seems likely that a place as small as Jaffa, and so far away, could have emitted enough dirhams to flood the market in Damascus.

The only Frankish silver coins of the time were the Arabic imitations and the Frankish pennies, which might have been called dirhams by the Moslems. It seems improbable that the pennies would have circulated to any extent among Moslems, but as far as is now known, the imitations never dropped so low as 15 percent silver. On the other hand, no crusader imitations of about 1260 have been analyzed, or even identified as such. Type VI, which was attributed above to about the same period as Type V, dated 1253, might still have been issued as late as 1260. The lowest fineness of the eight Type VI dirhams analyzed was 75.6 percent, but all these specimens came from a hoard datable to about 1255, before the time of which Abū-Shāmah writes. At present, the identity of the *bāqīyah* dirhams remains a mystery.[127]

At the least, Abū-Shāmah's passage is evidence that crusader dirhams were still being issued as late as 1260, that by that time they had an important role in the monetary economy of Damascus (if not all of Moslem Syria), and that the Moslems were aware that these coins came from the Franks but used them anyway. The importance of the crusader dirhams is not surprising. A preliminary die study of the crusader issues has counted so far 94 obverse and 110 reverse dies for the imitations of Aleppo dirhams, and 142 obverse and 142 reverse dies for the Damascus imitations. The current consensus among numisma-

---

126. Abū-Shāmah, *Tarājim rijāl al-qarnain (as-sādis wa-s-sābi')* (also known as *Dhail 'alâ ar-raudatain*), ed. Muḥammad Zahīd ibn-al-Ḥasan al-Kautharī (Cairo, 1947), p. 211; *RHC, Or.,* V, 203.

127. The passage and its analogues in other Arab writers are discussed in more detail by Irwin, *op. cit.,* pp. 94–95. Also a mystery are the Beirut dirhams of 1261 mentioned by a historian cited by Irwin.

tists estimates a possible production for a single die of ten to twenty thousand coins, suggesting at least one to two million Aleppo imitations and about 1,400,000 to 2,800,000 Damascus-type dirhams. These are conservative estimates, because it is likely that many dies remain to be discovered, and the number of dies does not include those for the half dirhams of each series. Also, the dies of the dirhams with Christian inscriptions have not been studied and counted. Assuming an average weight of about 2.8 grams, and an average fineness of 95 percent for the Aleppo coins, the silver content of the Aleppo imitations would amount to about 2.5 to 5 metric tons, while for the Damascus coins, with the same average weight but an average fineness of only 85 percent, the total issue would be about 3.4 to 6.8 metric tons of silver.

These figures should not be taken with great seriousness, considering the many assumptions that went into their calculation, but it seems safe to say that at least five to ten metric tons of silver went into the making of the crusader Arabic dirhams. This silver did not come from Syria, which has no mines. Some of it might have come from Anatolia, imported by the crusaders through Cilician Armenia, and some might also have come from Byzantine territory, but it seems reasonable to deduce that the bulk of this silver came from western Europe. There is direct evidence for movement of silver from Europe to Syria in the form of coins found in the latter region, and indirect evidence in the existence of special taxes collected in many European countries for the support of the crusaders and in documents referring to the export of silver.[128] It does not necessarily follow that all the silver that supplied the thirteenth-century Islamic revival of silver coinage came from Europe, but it does seem clear that the crusader imitations of Aiyūbid silver coinage must have contributed substantially to the stock of silver in Moslem Syria.

There are in addition a few other crusader Arabic coins that can only be mentioned here. These exist in only one or two specimens, and have not been studied beyond their first publication by Balog and Yvon.[129] Two examples are known of an issue of billon, BY 49, which has on one side an equal-armed barred cross with small wedge-shaped figures, described as crosses, in the four quadrants, and on the other side an Arabic inscription that has been read *duriba bi-Quds,* "struck in Jerusalem". The reading is not entirely certain, but the language of the inscription together with the cross is perhaps sufficient evidence

128. Much of this evidence is collected by Andrew M. Watson, "Back to Gold — and Silver," *Economic History Review,* 2nd ser., XX (1967), 7–21.

129. Balog and Yvon, "Monnaies," pp. 167–168.

for the attribution of these two little coins to the crusaders; they might have been tokens of some sort rather than true coins. Somewhat similar is a unique copper coin, BY 50, with an equal-armed cross, the branches ending in fleurs-de-lys, and on the other side an Arabic inscription read as "struck in Acre". Again, the reading is not completely satisfactory. One further copper, BY 51, has been struck with dinar dies; it is probably a counterfeit.

LIST OF COINS
ILLUSTRATED

All coins are in the cabinet of the American Numismatic Society, and are its property except as noted: UM = University Museum, Philadelphia; HSA = Hispanic Society of America, New York City.

THE ISLAMIC CONTEXT

1. al-Mauṣil (Mosul), 567 (1171/2), dinar. 1972.288.115.
2. Madīnat as-Salām (Baghdad), 613 (1216/7), dinar. 1002.1.455(UM).
3. Miṣr (al-Fusṭāṭ), 438 (1046/7), dinar. 1002.1.925(UM).
4. Miṣr, 442 (1050/1), dinar. 1974.26.207.
5. Miṣr, 482 (1089/90), dinar. 1002.1.961(UM).
6. Miṣr, 506 (1112/3), dinar. 1917.215.32.
7. al-Muʿizzīyah al-Qāhirah (Cairo), 565 (1169/70), dinar. 1002.1.1024(UM).
8. al-Qāhirah (Cairo), 571 (1175/6), dinar. 1002.1.1028(UM).
9. al-Iskandarīyah (Alexandria), 608 (1211/2), dinar. 1962.126.21.
10. al-Iskandarīyah, 661 (1262/3), dinar. 1002.1.1(UM).
11. Ṣūr (Tyre), 517 (1123/4), dinar. 1955.131.1.
12. Dimashq (Damascus), 531 (1136/7), dinar. 1969.98.1.
13. (Egypt, 1094–1097), dirham. 1971.132.15.
14. (Egypt, 1097–1101), dirham. 1953.48.3.
15. Miṣr, 556 (1160/1), dirham. 1965.9.1.
16. (Egypt, 1180–1193), dirham. 1917.215.1329.
17. (Damascus, 1113–1115), dirham. 1936.72.1.
18. Dimashq, 573 (1177/8), dirham. 1936.105.1.
19. Dimashq, [640] (1242/3), dirham. 1917.215.1357.
20. Ḥalab (Aleppo), 572 (1176/7), dirham. 1951.108.4.
21. Ḥalab, 602 (1205/6), dirham. 1937.1.6.
22. al-Qāhirah, 586 (1190/1), dirham. 1917.215.1328.
23. Dimashq, Ṣafar 667 (Oct./Nov. 1268), dirham. 1002.1.1977(UM).
24. (Syria [Aleppo?], 1095–1113), fals. 1967.249.3.

25. (Syria [Aleppo?], 1078–1117?), fals. 1973.102.1.
26. (Aleppo, 1146–1174), fals. 1954.112.1.
27. (Damascus, 1146–1174), fals. 1971.89.41.
28. (Sivas, 1134–1142), fals. 1002.1.411(UM).
29. al-Jazīrah (Mosul?), 575 (1179/80), fals. 1002.1.663(UM).

CRUSADER ARABIC GOLD

30. BY 26, small flan; GM 7. 1969.78.1.
31. BY 26, large flan; GM 1. 1933.45.3.
32. BY 25; GM 17. 1969.78.2.
33. BY 27d; GM 65. 1957.114.19.
34. BY 21; GM 83. 1924.69.16.
35. BY 23–24; GM 94. 1969.78.4.
36. BY 27e; GM 111. 1950.70.2.
37. BY 40; GM 153. 1917.215.627.
38. Agnus Dei; GM 183. 1952.115.4.
39. BY 2, variant; GM 9. 1965.87.4.
40. BY 2. 1962.125.6.
41. BY 12. 1978.64.644.
42. BY 15; GM 170. 1001.57.4533(HSA).
43. Yemeni type, GM 105. 1957.114.2.
44. bilingual fragment. 1981.36.1.
45. BY 1; GM 8. 0000.999.14974.
46. Miles, *Fatimid Coins,* 259 ("al-Iskandarīyah, 435").
    1002.1.1083(UM).

CRUSADER ARABIC SILVER

47. "Ḥalab", 619 (1222), dirham. 1972.75.16.
48. "Ḥalab", 618 (1221/2), half dirham. 1971.76.622.
49. "Ḥalab", 638 (1240/1), dirham. 1971.76.584.
50. "Dimashq", 641 (1243/4), dirham. Bates Type I.C. 1917.215.1379.
51. "Dimashq", 643? (1245/6?), dirham. Bates Type II.B. 1917.215.1389.
52. "Dimashq", 643 (1245/6), dirham. Bates Type III.A. 1971.76.198.
53. "Dimashq", [643 (1245/6)], half dirham. Bates half dirham Type
    II. 1971.76.334.
54. "Dimashq", 644 (1246/7), dirham. Bates Type IV. 1971.76.201.
55. ʿAkkā, 1251, dirham. BY 42. 1925.163.2.
56. ʿAkkā, 1251, dirham. BY 45. 1954.121.1.

57. 'Akkā, 1251, dirham. BY 47b. 1917.215.2549.
58. 'Akkā, 1251, half dirham. BY 44a. 1942.23.1152.
59. "Dimashq", 1253. Bates Type V. 1971.76.248.
60. "Dimashq", "641". Bates Type VI. 1949.163.262.

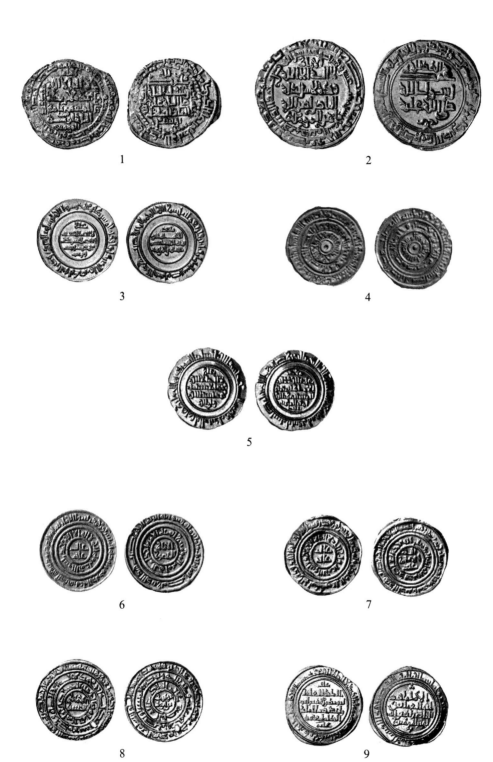

XII. Islamic gold coinage

10

11

12

13

14

15

16

17

18

19

XIII. Islamic gold and silver coinage

478

20

21

22

23

24

25

26

27

28

29

XIV. Islamic silver and copper coinage

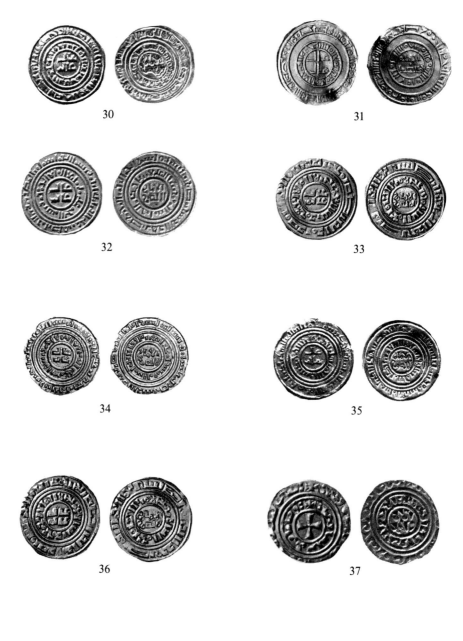

30

31

32

33

34

35

36

37

38

XV. Crusader gold coinage: Jerusalem

480

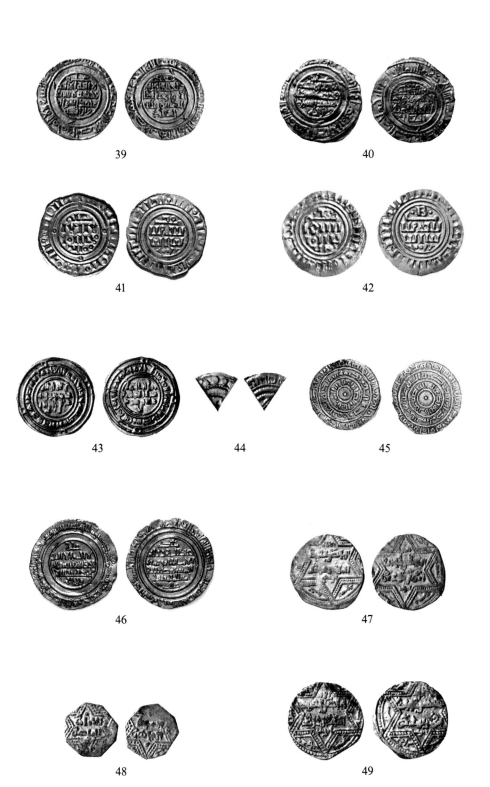

39   40

41   42

43   44   45

46   47

48   49

XVI. Crusader gold and silver coinage

50

51

52

53

54

55

56

57

58

59

60

XVII. Crusader silver coinage

GAZETTEER
AND NOTE ON MAPS

This gazetteer has been prepared to fill a variety of functions. Every relevant place-name found in the text or on the maps is here alphabetized and identified, variant spellings and equivalent names in other languages are supplied, and the map location is indicated. Thus it not only serves as an index to the maps and a supplement to them, but is itself a source for reference on matters of historical geography and changing nomenclature.

In the gazetteer, alphabetization is by the first capital letter of the form used in maps and text, disregarding such lower-case prefixes as al- and such geographical words as Cape, Gulf, Lake, Mount, and the like. The designation "classical" may mean Greek, Latin, biblical, or other ancient usage, and the designation "medieval" generally means that the name in question was in common use among speakers of various languages during the crusades, or appears in contemporary sources.

On the maps may be found nearly every place name occurring in the text of this volume or of volume V, since the same maps appear in both volumes. Exceptions include a few places whose exact locations are unknown, a few outside the regions mapped, several in areas overcrowded with names, and some of minimal importance or common knowledge.

All maps for this volume have been designed and prepared in the University of Wisconsin Cartographic Laboratory under the direction of Onno Brouwer, assisted by David DiBiase. Base information was compiled from U.S.A.F. Jet Navigation Charts at a scale of 1:2,000,000. Historical data have been supplied by Dr. Harry W. Hazard (who also compiled the gazetteer) from such standard works as Sprüner-Menke, Stieler, Andree, and Baedeker for Europe, Lévi-Provençal for Moslem Spain, Rubió i Lluch and Bon for Frankish Greece, and Honigmann, Dussaud, Deschamps, Cahen, and LeStrange for the Near East. Additional information was found in *The Encyclopaedia of Islām* (old and new editions) and *İslâm Ansiklopedisi,* in Yāqūt and other Arabic sources, in The Columbia Lippincott Gazetteer of the World, on Michelin and Hallweg road maps, and of course in the text of this volume.

Aachen (German), Aix-la-Chapelle (French): city—F2b5: 2, 3.

Abyssinia: region—see Ethiopia.

Achaea (Latin), Achaïa (classical Greek), Akhaïa (modern Greek): district of northern Morea—I2e2: 4.

Acre; Ptolemaïs (classical), Saint Jean d'Acre (medieval), 'Akkā (Arabic), 'Akko (Israeli): city, port—L1f3: 1, 7.

Adalia or Satalia (medieval), Attalia (classical), Antalya (Turkish): port—K1e4: 1, 3.

Adana (classical, Armenian, Turkish): city—L1e3: 1, 6.

Aden; 'Adan (Arabic): port—N1j3: 12, 13.

Adrianople; Hadrianopolis (classical), Edirne (Turkish): city—J2d4: 1, 3, 5.

Adriatic Sea; Hadria or Mare Hadriaticum (Latin)—GHd: 2, 3, 4.

Aegean Sea; Aigaion Pelagos (Greek), Mare Aegaeum (Latin), Ege Denizi (Turkish)—IJe: 1, 3, 4, 5.

Aegium: town—see Vostitsa.

Aenos or Aenus (classical), Enos or Menas (medieval), Enez (Turkish): town—J2d5: 3, 5.

Aetolia (Latin), Aitōlia (classical Greek), Aitolía (modern Greek): district of central Greece—I2e2: 4.

Afghanistan: region, now a nation, east of northern Persia—QRSef: 12, 13.

Agros (Greek): Greek Orthodox monastery—K4f1: 8.

Aguilers (medieval), Aighuile or Aiguilhe (French): village just north of Le Puy (E4c5: 2).

Aigaion Pelagos—see Aegean Sea.

'Ain Jālūt (Arabic: well of Goliath), Geluth or Well of Harod (medieval), 'En Harod (Israeli): village—L1f3: 7.

Aire-sur-l'Adour (French): town—D5d2: 2.

Aix-la-Chapelle: city—see Aachen.

Akaki (Greek): village—K4e5: 8.

Akcha-Burgos; Akça-Burgos or -Burgoz (Turkish): village near Kozlu-Dere (J2d5: 5).

Akcha-Limon; Akça-Limon (Turkish): port north of Gallipoli (J2d5: 5).

Akhlat or Ahlat (Turkish), Akhlāṭ or Khilāṭ (Arabic), Khlat (Armenian): town—M3e2: 1.

'Akkā, 'Akko: city, port—see Acre.

Akkerman (medieval), Belgorod Dnestrovski (Russian): port—K1c4: 1.

Aksarai or Sarai-Berke (Tatar): town, now unimportant—N2c2: 13.

Akshehir; Akşehir (Turkish: white city), Philomelium (Latin), Philomēlion (medieval Greek): town—K2e2: 1, 3.

Alamut; Alamūt (Persian, Arabic): fortress—O1e4: 12.

Alanya (Turkish), Scandelore or Candeloro (medieval), 'Ala'īyah or 'Alāyā (Arabic): port—K2e4: 1, 3.

Alaşehir: town—see Philadelphia.

Alba Julia (Latin), Weissenburg (German), Gyulafehérvár (Hungarian), Alba Iulia (Rumanian): town—I4c4: 3.

Albania (medieval), Shqipni or Shqipri (Albanian): region NW of Epirus, now a nation—Hd: 3, 4.

Albano Laziale (Italian): town 14 miles SE of Rome (G3d4: 2, 3).

Albermarle (French): town, probably fictitious (or error for Blois).

Albunlena (medieval): battlefield—H5d4: 4.

Aleksinats; Aleksinac (Serbian): town 17 miles NNW of Nish (I2d2: 3).

Aleppo (Italian), Beroea or Chalybon (classical), Halab (Arabic), Haleb (Turkish): city—L3e4: 1, 6.

Alessio: town—see Lesh.

Alexandretta (medieval), İskenderun (Turkish): port—L2e4: 6.

Alexandretta, Gulf of; Sinus Issicus (classical), İskenderun Körfezi (Turkish)—L1e4: 6.

Alexandria (classical), al-Iskandarīyah (Arabic): city, port — J5f4: 1, 3.

Algiers; al-Jazā'ir (Arabic): city — E4d4: 2.

Alis (medieval): possibly Alès (formerly Alais), 25 miles NW of Nîmes (E5d2: 2).

Alpheus (Latin), Alpheios (classical Greek), Charbon (medieval), Alfíos (modern Greek): river — I2e3: 4.

Alps: mountain range — FGc: 2, 3.

Alsace (French), Alsatia (Latin), Elsass (German): region west of the upper Rhine — Fc: 2, 3.

Altoluogo: town — see Ephesus.

Amalfi (Italian): port — G5d5: 3.

Amanus (Latin), Gavur, Alma, or Elma Daği (Turkish): mountain range — L2e4: 6.

Amasra (Turkish), Amastris (classical): port — K3d4: 1, 3.

Amasya (Turkish), Amasia (classical): town — L1d5: 1.

Amida (classical), Āmid or Diyār-Bakr (Arabic), Diyarbekir or Diyarbakir (Turkish): town — M1e3: 1.

Amiens (French): city — E3c1: 2.

Anadolu-Hisar (Turkish: castle of Anatolia): fortress — J5d4: 5.

Anaphe; Anaphē (classical Greek), Namfio (medieval Italian), Anáfi (modern Greek): island — J1e4: 5.

Anatolia; Asia Minor (Latin), Romania or Rūm (medieval), Anadolu (Turkish): region south of the Black Sea — JKLde: 1, 3, 5.

Anchialus (Latin), Axillo (medieval), Akhyoli (Turkish), Pomoriye (Bulgarian): port — J3d3: 5.

Ancona (Italian): port — G4d2: 2, 3.

Andalusia; al-Andalus (Arabic), Andalucia (Spanish): region of southern Spain — CDe: 2.

Andreas, Cape, or Cape Saint Andrew; Le Chief (medieval): NE tip of Cyprus — K5e5: 8.

Andros (classical), Andro (medieval Italian), Andria (Turkish), Ándros (modern Greek): island — I5e3: 5.

Angoulême (French): town — E1c5: 2.

Anjou (French): region of NW France — D5c3: 2.

Ankara (Turkish), Ancyra (classical), Angora (medieval): town, now city — K3e1: 1, 3.

Antalya: port — see Adalia.

Antioch; Antiochia (classical), Anṭākiyah (Arabic), Antakya (Turkish): city — L2e4: 1, 6.

Antivari (Italian), Antebarium (Latin), Bar (Serbian): port — H5d3: 3.

Apulia (classical), Puglia or Puglie (Italian): region of SE Italy — Hd: 3.

Aquitaine (French), Aquitania (classical): region of western France — Dcd: 2.

Arabia (classical), Jazīrat al-'Arab (Arabic): peninsular region east of the Red Sea — LMNgh: 1, 6, 7.

Aragon; Aragón (Spanish), Araghūn (Arabic): region of NE Spain — DEd: 2.

Aral Sea; Aral'skoye More (Russian) — PQcd: 12, 13.

Arcadia (classical), Mesaréa (medieval), Arkadhía (modern Greek): district of northern Morea — I2e3: 4.

Archipelago (from Greek Aigaion Pelagos): islands of the Aegean Sea (IJde: 5).

Ardeal: region — see Transylvania.

Ardres (French): town 18 miles NE of Boulogne (E2b5: 2).

Argesh; Curtea de Argeş (Rumanian): town — I5c5: 3.

Argolid or Argolis (classical), Argolís (modern Greek): district of eastern Morea — I3e3: 4.

Argos (classical), Árgos (modern Greek): town — I3e3: 3, 4.

Argyrokastron (Greek), Gjirokastër (Albanian): town — I1d5: 4.

Arles (French), Arelas (classical): city — E5d2: 2.

Armenia (classical), Hayastan (Armenian), Ermenistan (Turkish): region north of Lake Van—Md: 1.

Armenia, Cilician: kingdom—KLe: 9.

Arnauti, Cape: western tip of Cyprus—K3e5: 8.

Arsinoë: town—see Polis.

Arsuf; Apollonia-Sozusa (classical), Arsur (medieval), Arsūf (Arabic), Tel Arshaf (Israeli): town, now abandoned for Herzliyya—K5f3: 7.

Arta (medieval), Ambracia (classical), Árta (modern Greek), Narda (Turkish): town—I1e1: 3, 4.

'Artāḥ (Arabic), Artesia (classical), Artais (medieval): town, now unimportant—L2e4: 6.

Artois (French): district of northern France—E3b5: 2.

Ascalon; Ashkelon (biblical), 'Asqalān (Arabic), Tel Ashqelon (Israeli): port, now abandoned for modern Ashqelon—K5f4: 1, 7.

Asia Minor (classical): region equivalent to western Anatolia.

Asti (Italian), Hasta (classical): town—F4d1: 2, 3.

Athens; Athēnai (classical Greek), Cetines or Satines (medieval), Athínai (modern Greek): city—I4e3: 3, 4.

Athens: duchy—Ie: 9.

Athlith, 'Atlīt: castle—see Château Pèlerin.

Athos, Mount; Áyion Óros (modern Greek): Greek Orthodox monastery—I5d5: 4, 5.

Atlantic Ocean—BCc: 2.

Atlas, High; Aṭlas (Arabic): mountain range—Cf: 2.

Attica (Latin), Attikē (classical Greek), Attikí (modern Greek): district of eastern Greece—I4e3: 4, 5.

Aubusson (French): town 44 miles NNE of Limoges (E2c5: 2).

Augsburg (German): city—G1c2: 2, 3.

Austria; Ostmark (German): region east of Bavaria, smaller than modern nation—GHc: 2, 3.

Auvergne (French): region of southern France—Ecd: 2.

Auxerre (French): town—E4c3: 2.

Avala or Havale (Serbian): mountain 9 miles south of Belgrade (I1d1: 3).

Avignon (French), Avenio (classical): city—E5d2: 2.

Avila; Avela (classical), Ávila de los Caballeros (Spanish): town—D1d5: 2.

Avlona (medieval), Aulon (classical), Valona (Italian), Vlonë or Vlorë (Albanian): port—H5d5: 3, 4.

Axillo: port—see Anchialus.

Ayas (medieval), Lajazzo (Italian), Yumurtalik (Turkish): port—L1e4: 6.

Ayasoluk: town—see Ephesus.

Ayazmend (Turkish): port—L4e2: 1.

Aydin (Turkish): district of western Anatolia, equivalent to classical Lydia—Je: 5.

Aydinjik (Turkish): port—J3d5: 5.

Azerbaijan; Ādharbādhagān or Āzerbaijān (Persian): region of NW Persia and SE Transcaucasia—Ne: 1.

Azov: port—see Tana.

Azov, Sea of; Azovskoye More (Russian)—Lc: 1.

Baalbek; Heliopolis (classical), Ba'labakk (Arabic): town—L2f1: 6, 7.

Babylon: town—see Fustat.

Baffa: castle—see Sígouri.

Baghdad; Baghdād (Arabic): city—M5f2: 1.

Baisān: town—see Bethsan.

Baleares (Spanish): island group—Ede: 2.

Balkan Mountains—Id: 3, 5.

Balkans: peninsular region east of the Adriatic Sea.

Balkhash, Lake—STc: 12, 13.

Baltic Sea—HIab: 2, 3.

Bar: port—see Antivari.

Barbais (French): unidentified town, probably fictitious.

Barbary: the coast of North Africa.

Barbastro (Spanish), Barbashtrū (Arabic): town—E1d3: 2.

Barcelona (Spanish), Barcino (classical), Barshilūnah (Arabic): city, port—E3d4: 2.

Bari (Italian), Barium (classical): port—H2d4: 3.

Barletta (Italian): port—H2d4: 3.

Baruth: port—see Beirut.

Basel (German), Basle or Bâle (French): city—F3c3: 2, 3.

Bashkent or Kara Hisar (Turkish): battlefield—L5e1: 1.

al-Batrūn: town—see Botron.

Bavaria; Bayern (German): region of southern Germany—Gc: 2, 3.

Béarn (French): district of sw France—Dd: 2.

Beaufort: crusader castle—see Belfort.

Beaulieu-sur-Dordogne (French): town and monastery 41 miles NNE of Cahors (E2d1: 2).

Beauvais (French): town—E3c1: 2.

Becskerek (Hungarian): town 54 miles SSE of Szegedin (I1c4: 3).

Bedford: town—D5b3: 2.

Beirut; Berytus (classical), Bairūt (Arabic), Baruth (medieval): port—L1f2: 1, 6, 7.

Bela Palanka (Serbian): town—I3d2: 3.

Belfort or Beaufort (medieval), Shaqīf Arnūn or Qal'at ash-Shaqīf (Arabic: fort of the rock): crusader castle—L1f2: 7.

Belgorod Dnestrovski: port—see Akkerman.

Belgrade; Beograd (Serbian: white town): city—I1d1: 3.

Bellapais or Bella Paise (medieval): monastery—K4e5: 8.

Benevento (Italian), Beneventum (Latin): town—G5d4: 3.

Berat (Albanian), Pulcheriopolis (classical), Bellagrada (medieval): town—H5d5: 3, 4.

Bergamo (Italian): town 28 miles NE of Milan (F5c5: 3).

Berry (French): district of central France—Ec: 2.

Bethany; al-'Āzarīyah (Arabic), 'Eizariya (Israeli): abbey and fort—L1f4: 7.

Bethlehem (biblical), Ephrata (classical), Bait Laḥm (Arabic: house of flesh): town—L1f4: 7.

Bethsan or Bessan (medieval), Scythopolis or Bethshan (classical), Baisān (Arabic), Bet She'an (Israeli): town—L1f3: 7.

Beyoğlu: port—see Pera.

Beyshehir; Beyşehir (Turkish): town—K2e3: 1, 3.

Biga or Biğa (Turkish), Pegae (Latin), Pēgai (medieval Greek): town—J3d5: 3, 5.

al-Biqā' (Arabic: the hollow), Coele-Syria (classical), Bekaa (modern): district of central Lebanon—L1f2: 6, 7.

Bithynia (classical): district of NW Anatolia—Jde: 10.

Bitolj: town—see Monastir.

Black Sea; Mare Euxinus (Latin), Kara Deniz (Turkish), Chernoye More (Russian)—JKLd: 1, 3, 5.

Blois (French): town—E2c3: 2.

Bobalna: district north of Grosswardein—Ic: 3.

Bodrum or Budrum (Turkish), Halicarnassus (classical), Petroúnion (modern Greek): town—J3e3: 5.

Boeotia (Latin), Boiōtia (classical Greek), Voiotía (modern Greek): district of eastern Greece—I4e2: 4.

Bohemia; Čechy (Czech): region north of Austria—GHc: 2, 3.

Boislamy (French): castle near Aubusson.

Bokhārā: city—see Bukhara.
Bolayîr (Turkish): village 8 miles NE of Gallipoli (J2d5: 5).
Boldon: town 13 miles NNE of Durham (D4b1: 2).
Bolgar: town—see Bulgar.
Bologna (Italian): city—G2d1: 2, 3.
Bolvani (medieval): castle near Nish (I2d2: 3).
Bombay: city and port—S3i2: 12, 13.
Borach; Boraç (Turkish), Bor (Serbian): town 38 miles WNW of Vidin (I3d2: 3).
Bordeaux (French), Burdigala (classical): city, port—D5d1: 2.
Bosnia; Bosna (Serbian, Turkish): region west of Serbia—Hd: 3.
Bosporus (classical), Karadeniz Boğazî (Turkish: Black Sea strait)—J5d4: 1, 3, 5.
Botron (medieval), Botrys (classical), al-Batrūn (Arabic): town—L1f1: 6, 7.
Bouillon (French): town—F1c1: 2, 3.
Boulogne-sur-Mer (French): port—E2b5: 2.
Bourcq: castle—see Le Bourg.
Bourges (French): town—E3c3: 2.
Bourgogne: region—see Burgundy.
Bozja-ada: island—see Tenedos.
Brabant (French, Flemish): district east of Flanders—EFb: 2, 3.
Bracieux (French): village 10 miles ESE of Blois (E2c3: 2).
Brandenburg (German): district of northern Germany—Gb: 2, 3.
Bratislava (Slovakian), Pressburg (German), Pozsony (Hungarian): city—H3c2: 3.
Braunschweig: city—see Brunswick.
Bremen (German): city, port—F4b2: 2, 3.
Brescia (Italian): city—G1c5: 3.
Breslau (German), Wrocław (Polish): city—H3b4: 3.
Brienne-la-Vieille (French): village 20 miles ENE of Troyes (E5c2: 2).
Brindisi (Italian), Brundisium (Latin): port—H3d5: 3.
British Isles: England, Wales, Scotland, Ireland and smaller islands.
Brittany; Bretagne (French), Breiz (Breton): region of NW France—Dc: 2.
Bruges (French), Brugge (Flemish): port, now city—E4b4: 2.
Brunswick; Braunschweig (German): city—G1b3: 2, 3.
Brusa: city—see Bursa.
Buda (Hungarian), Ofen (German): city, now part of Budapest—H5c3: 3.
Buffavento (medieval): castle—K4e5: 8.
Bugia; Saldae (classical), al-Bijāyah (Arabic), Bougie (French): port—F1e4: 2.
Bukhara; Bokhārā (Persian), Bukhārā (Arabic): city—Q5el: 12, 13.
Bulgar or Bolgar; Bolgary (Russian, formerly Uspenskoye): town, now village—N5b3: 12.
Bulgaria; Moesia (classical), Blgariya (Bulgarian): region south of the lower Danube, larger than modern nation—IJd: 1, 3, 5.
Burgundy; Bourgogne (French): region of eastern France, extending farther south than now—EFc: 2.
Burhaniye: port—see Kemer.
Bursa (Turkish), Prusa (classical), Brusa (medieval): city—J5d5: 1, 3, 5.
Byblos: town—see Jubail.
Byzantium: city—see Constantinople.

Caen (French): city—D5c1: 2.
Caesarea ad Argaeum or Mazaca (classical), Kayseri (Turkish): city—L1e2: 1.
Caesarea Maritima or Palaestinae (classical), Cesaire (medieval), Qaisārīyah (Arabic), Qesari (Israeli). port, now abandoned for Sedot Yam—K5f3: 7.
Caffa: port—see Kaffa.
Cahors (French): town—E2d1: 2.

Cairo: al-Qāhirah (Arabic: the victorious): city—K2f5: 1, 3.

Calabria (Italian): region of sw Italy—He: 3.

Calamona: town—see Retimo.

Cambrai (French): town—E4b5: 2.

Campomorto (Italian): battlefield sse of Rome (G3d4: 3).

Çanakkale: town—see Sultaniye.

Candeloro: port—see Alanya.

Candia: island—see Crete.

Candia (medieval), Heracleum (Latin), Iráklion (modern Greek): port—J1e5: 3.

Canea (classical), Khanía (modern Greek): port—I5e5: 3.

Canina (medieval), Bullis or Byllis (classical), Kanine (Albanian): town, now unimportant—H5d5: 4.

Canterbury: city—E2b4: 2.

Canton; Kwangchow or Kuang-chou (Chinese): city, port—AA4g2: 13.

Capistrano or Capestrano (Italian): village 75 miles ene of Rome (G3d4: 3).

Capua (Italian): town—G5d4: 3.

Caransebesh; Caransebeş (Rumanian): town—I3c5: 3.

Carashova; Caraşova (Rumanian): town 23 miles sw of Caransebesh (I3c5: 3).

Caria: region—see Menteshe.

Carinthia; Kärnten (German): region south of medieval Austria—Gc: 2, 3.

Carpas: district—see Karpass.

Carpathians; Carpates (classical), Karpaty (Czech, Polish), Carpatii (Rumanian): mountain range—IJc: 1, 3.

Caspian Sea—NOde: 1.

Cassagnes (French): village near Sarlat, 32 miles nnw of Cahors (E2d1: 2).

Cassandra; Pallene (classical), Kassándra (modern Greek): peninsula—I4e1: 4.

Castellorizzo; Megisto (classical), Meis (Turkish), Castelrosso (Italian), Kastellórizo
(modern Greek): island—J5e4: 1, 5.

Castile; Castilla (Spanish), Qashtālah (Arabic): region of north central Spain—Dde: 2.

Catalonia; Cataluña (Spanish), Catalunya (Catalan): region of ne Spain—Ed: 2.

Cathay: region—see China.

Cattaro (Italian), Kotor (Serbian): port—H4d3: 3.

Caucasus; Kavkaz (Russian): mountain range—MNd: 1.

Caumont-sur-Durance (French): village 8 miles ese of Avignon (E5d2: 2).

Celje: town—see Cilly.

Central Asia: region extending from the Aral Sea to Mongolia.

Ceos; Keōs (classical Greek), Tzía (medieval), Zea (Italian), Morted (Turkish), Kéa
(modern Greek): island—I5e3: 4, 5.

Cephalonia (Latin), Kephallēnia (classical Greek), Kephallōnia (medieval Greek), Ke-
fallinía (modern Greek): island—I1e2: 3, 4.

Cerigo (Italian), Cythera (Latin), Kythēra (classical Greek), Kíthira (modern Greek):
island—I3e4: 3, 4.

Cerines: town—see Kyrenia.

Cesaire: port—see Caesarea.

Cetines: city—see Athens.

Ceuta (Spanish), Septa (classical), Sabtah (Arabic): port—C5e5: 2.

Chalcedon (Latin), Kalkhēdōn (classical Greek), Khalkēdōn (medieval Greek), Kadiköy
(Turkish): town—J5d5: 3, 5.

Chalcis: port—see Negroponte.

Chalon-sur-Saône (French): town—E5c4: 2.

Champagne (French): region of ne France—EFc: 2.

Charbon: river—see Alpheus.

Chartalos (medieval): town near Berat (H5d5: 4).

Chartres (French): city—E2c2: 2.

Château Pèlerin (French), Athlith (medieval), 'Atlīt (Arabic), 'Aṭlit (Israeli): crusader castle—K5f3: 7.

Châteaudun (French): town 27 miles ssw of Chartres (E2c2: 2).

Châteauroux (French): town—E2c4: 2.

Châtillon-sur-Loing (French): town, now part of Châtillon-Coligny, 32 miles west of Auxerre (E̦4c3: 2).

Chernomen; Črnomen (Bulgarian), Çirman, Çermen, or Sîrf Sindigi (Turkish: destruction of the Serbs), Orménion (modern Greek): battlefield—J2d4: 3, 5.

Cherson: port—see Kherson.

Cheshme; Çeşme (Turkish): town—J2e2: 5.

Chestin; Çestin (Serbian): town 10 miles sw of Kraguyevats (I1d1: 3).

Chiavari (Italian): town 16 miles ESE of Genoa (F4d1: 3).

China; Cathay (medieval): region of eastern Asia—W/CCe/h: 12, 13.

Chios (classical), Scio (Italian), Sakiz (Turkish), Khíos (modern Greek): island—J1e2: 5.

Chorlu; Çorlu (Turkish), Tzurulum (Latin): town—J3d4: 5.

Choros (medieval): unidentified port in Cilicia, possibly Corycus (K5e4: 1).

Christopolis: port—see Kavalla.

Cilicia (classical): region of southern Anatolia—KLe: 6.

Cilly; Celje (Slovene): town—H1c4: 3.

Circassia: region north of western Caucasus—LMd: 1.

Cirencester: town 27 miles NE of Bath (D3b4: 2).

Cîteaux (French): abbey—F1c3: 2.

Citó: town—see Zeitounion.

Civetot (medieval), Cibotus (classical): port, now abandoned—J5d5: 3, 5.

Clairvaux (French): abbey—E5c2: 2.

Clarence: town—see Glarentsa.

Clari (medieval), Cléry-sur-Somme (French): town 27 miles east of Amiens (E3c1: 2).

Clermont (French): town, now part of Clermont-Ferrand—E4c5: 2.

Cluny (French): abbey—E5c4: 2.

Cologne (French), Colonia Agrippinensis (Latin), Köln (German): city—F2b5: 2, 3.

Commines or Comines (French), Kamen (Flemish): town 10 miles NNW of Lille (E4b5: 2).

Compiègne (French): town 33 miles east of Beauvais (E3c1: 2).

Compostela or Santiago de Compostela (Spanish), Campus Stellae (Latin), Shant Ya'qūb (Arabic): town and shrine—C2d3: 2.

Constance (French), Konstanz (German): town—F5c3: 2, 3.

Constantinople; Byzantium or Constantinopolis (classical), İstanbul (Turkish): city—J4d4: 1, 3, 5.

Corbova (medieval), Krbava (Serbian): region of western Croatia.

Cordova; Córdoba (Spanish), Qurṭubah (Arabic): city—D1e3: 2.

Corfu; Corcyra (Latin), Kerkyra (classical Greek), Corfù (Italian), Kérkira (modern Greek): island—H5e1: 3, 4.

Corinth; Korinthos (classical Greek; now Palaiá Kórinthos: Old Corinth): city—I3e3: 3, 4.

Corinth, Gulf of; Korinthiakós Kólpos (modern Greek)—I3e2: 4.

Cornwall: region of sw England—CDb: 2.

Coron (medieval), Korōnē (medieval Greek), Koróni (modern Greek): port—I2e4: 3, 4.

Corsica; Cyrnus (classical), Corse (French): island—Fd: 2, 3.

Corycus (classical), Goṛigos (Armenian), Le Courc (medieval), Korgos (Turkish): port—K5e4: 1.

Cos; Lango or Stanchio (medieval Italian), Stankoi (Turkish), Kós (modern Greek): island—J3e4: 5.

Courtenay (French): village 32 miles WNW of Auxerre (E4c3: 2).

Cracow; Cracovia (Latin), Kraków (Polish): city—H5b5: 3.

Cremona (Italian): town—G1c5: 2.

Cressac (French): village near Blanzac, 13 miles ssw of Angoulême (E1c5: 2).

Crete; Candia (medieval), Krētē (medieval Greek), Kandia (Turkish), Kríti (modern Greek): island—IJef: 1, 3.

Crimea; Gazaria (medieval), Krym (Russian): peninsula—K4c5: 1, 3.

Croatia; Meran (medieval), Hrvatska (Croatian): region north of Dalmatia—Hc: 3.

Croia (Italian), Kroja (Serbian), Akça-Hisar (Turkish), Krujë (Albanian): town—H5d4: 3, 4.

Cyclades (classical), Kikládhes (modern Greek): island group—IJe: 3, 5.

Cyprus (Latin), Kypros (medieval Greek), Kîbrîs (Turkish), Kípros (modern Greek): island—Kef: 1, 8.

Cyrenaica (classical), Barqah (Arabic): region west of Egypt—If: 10, 11.

Cyzicus (classical), Kapîdağ (Turkish): town, now abandoned—J3d5: 3, 5.

Dalaman: river—J5e3: 1, 5.

Dalmatia (medieval), Dalmacija (Croatian): region east of the Adriatic Sea, equivalent to classical Illyria—Hd: 3.

Damascus (classical), Dimashq or ash-Sha'm (Arabic: the left): city—L2f2: 1, 7.

Damietta; Dimyāṭ (Arabic): port—K2f4: 1.

Danube; Donau (German), Duna (Hungarian), Dunav (Serbian, Bulgarian), Dunărea (Rumanian): river—G5c2, J3d1: 1, 2, 3.

Dardanelles; Hellespontus (classical), Çanakkale Boğazî (Turkish): strait—J2d5: 1, 3, 5.

Deabolis: town—see Devol.

Dead Sea; Baḥr Lūṭ (Arabic: sea of Lot), Yam Hamelah (Israeli)—L1f4: 1, 7.

Delhi; Dillī (Hindi), Dihlī or Dehlī (Persian): city—T3g2: 12, 13.

Demotica; Didymoteichon (classical), Dēmotika (medieval Greek), Dhidhimótikhon (modern Greek): town—J2d4: 3, 5.

Denmark; Danmark (Danish): region of Scandinavia, then including southern part of modern Sweden—FGab: 2, 3.

Derkos (medieval): fortress—J4d4: 5.

Deuil (French): town 8 miles north of Paris (E3c2: 2).

Devizes: town 18 miles east of Bath (D3b4: 2).

Devnya, Lake—J3d2: 5.

Devol; Deabolis or Diabolis (medieval): town, now abandoned—I1d5: 3, 4.

Didymoteichon: town—see Demotica.

Dieudamour: castle—see Saint Hilarion.

Dijon (French): city—F1c3: 2, 3.

Dilmān: town—see Salmas.

Dimashq: city—see Damascus.

Diu: port—S1h5: 13.

Diyār-Bakr (Arabic): region of the upper Tigris—Le: 1.

Diyār-Bakr, Diyarbekir: town—see Amida.

Dnieper; Borysthenes (classical), Dnepr (Russian): river—K3c4: 1.

Dniester; Tyras (classical), Dnestr (Russian), Nistru (Rumanian): river—J5c4: 1.

Dobruja: region east of lower Danube—Jd: 1, 3.

Domažlice (Czech), Taus (German): town—G3c1: 3.

Don; Tanaïs (classical): river—L5c3: 1.

Donzi or Donzy-le-Pré (French): town—E4c3: 2.

Dorylaeum (classical): town, now abandoned in favor of Eskishehir—K1e1: 3.

Douai (French): town 12 miles south of Lille (E4b5: 2).

Douro (Portuguese), Duero (Spanish), Duwīruh (Arabic): river—C3d4: 2.

Drama: town—I5d4: 3, 4, 5.
Dreux (French): town 21 miles NNW of Chartres (E2c2: 2).
Dristra (medieval), Durostorum (classical), Silistre (Turkish), Silistra (Rumanian), Silistria (Bulgarian): town—J3d1: 3.
Dubrovnik: port—see Ragusa.
Dulcigno (Italian), Ulcinj (Serbian): port—H5d4: 3.
Durazzo (Italian), Epidamnus or Dyrrachium (classical), Draj (Turkish), Dürres (Albanian): port—H5d4: 3, 4.
Durham: city—D4b1: 2.

Ebro (Spanish), Ibruh (Arabic): river—D4d3: 2.
Edessa; Rohais or Rochais (medieval), ar-Ruhā' (Arabic), Urfa (Turkish): city—L4e3: 1, 6.
Edirne: city—see Adrianople.
Eger: city—see Erlau.
Egypt; Miṣr (Arabic): region of NE Africa—JKf: 1, 3.
Elbasan (medieval, Albanian): town—I1d4: 3, 4.
Elbe (German), Labe (Czech): river—G2b2: 2.
Elis; Êlis or Ēleia (classical Greek), Ilía (modern Greek): district of NW Morea—I2e3: 4.
Emel: river—see Imil.
England; Britannia (Latin): region—Db: 2.
English Channel; La Manche (French)—CDbc: 2.
Enkleistra (Greek): Greek Orthodox monastery in Cyprus, location uncertain.
Enos or Enez: town—see Aenos.
Ephesus (classical), Altoluogo (medieval), Ayasoluk (Turkish): city, now unimportant—J3e3: 3, 5.
Epirus (Latin), Ēpeiros (classical Greek), Ípiros (modern Greek): region west of Thessaly—Ie: 3, 4.
Eretna (Turkish): district east of Ankara—Ke: 1.
Erlau (German), Eger (Hungarian): city—I1c3: 3.
Erzerum; Theodosiopolis (classical), Garin (Armenian), Erzurum (Turkish): city—M2e1: 1.
Erzinjan (Turkish), Arsinga (classical), Arzenga (medieval): town—L5e1: 1.
Estanor: port—see Pera.
Estives: city—see Thebes.
Ethiopia or Abyssinia; Ityopya (Amharic): region of east central Africa—not in region mapped.
Euboea (classical), Evripos (medieval Greek), Negroponte (Italian), Egripos (Turkish), Évvoia (modern Greek): island—I4e2: 3, 4, 5.
Euphrates (classical), al-Furāt (Arabic), Fîrat Nehri (Turkish): river—N1f4: 1; L4e4: 6.

Falkenberg; Fauquembergues (French): village 24 miles ESE of Boulogne (E2b5: 2).
Famagusta; Ammōkhostos (classical Greek), Famagosta (medieval Italian): port—K4e5: 1, 8.
Fécamp (French): abbey, now town, 38 miles NW of Rouen (E2c1: 2).
Ferrara (Italian): city—G2d1: 2, 3.
Fethiye: port—see Makri.
Fez; Fās (Arabic): city—D1f1: 2.
Filistīn: region—see Palestine.
Flanders; Vlaanderen (Flemish): region of northern France and Belgium—EFb: 2.
Flora or Floris (medieval), Fiore (Italian): abbey near Cosenza, 47 miles WNW of Cotrone (H3e1: 3).
Florence; Firenze (Italian): city—G2d2: 2, 3.
Florentin (Bulgarian): town—I3d1: 3.

Foglia, Foça: port—see Phocaea.
Forez (French): district east of Clermont (E4c5: 2).
France: region, smaller than modern nation.
Frankfurt am Main (German): city—F4b5: 2, 3.
Frenk-Yazusu (Turkish): battlefield—K3e3: 1.
Friesach (German): town 65 miles NW of Cilly (H1c4: 3).
Frisia; Friesland (Dutch, German): region of northern Netherlands and NW Germany—
    Fb: 2, 3.
Friuli (Italian): district of NE Italy—Gc: 2, 3.
Fustat; al-Fusṭāṭ (Arabic), Babylon (medieval): town—K2f5: 1.

Gadres: town—see Gaza.
Galata (Bulgarian): suburb SE of Varna (J3d2: 5).
Galilee; Hagalil (Israeli): region of northern Palestine—L1f3: 7.
Galilee, Sea of, or Lake Tiberias; Buḥairat Ṭabarīyah (Arabic), Yam Kinneret (Israeli)—
    L1f3: 7.
Gallipoli (medieval), Callipolis (classical), Gelibolu (Turkish): town—J2d5: 3, 5.
Gascony; Gascogne (French): region of SW France—Dde: 2.
Gasha (medieval): unidentified port 15 miles from Senj (G5d1: 3).
Gastría: castle—see La Castrie.
Gata, Cape: southern tip of Cyprus—K4f1: 8.
Gaza (classical), Gadres (medieval), Ghazzah (Arabic): town—K5f4: 7.
Gazaria: peninsula—see Crimea.
Geluth: village—see ʿAin Jālūt.
Genoa; Genua (Latin), Genova (Italian): city, port—F4d1: 2, 3.
Georgia or Grusia (medieval), Sakartvelo (Georgian): region east of the Black Sea
    and south of the Caucasus—MNd: 1.
Germany; Alamannia or Allemania (medieval), Deutschland (German): region of north
    central Europe—FGbc: 9.
Germiyan (Turkish): district of west central Anatolia—JKe: 5.
Gibelet: town—see Jubail.
Gibraltar, Strait of; az-Zuqāq (Arabic)—C5e5: 2.
Giurgiu (Rumanian), San Giorgio (Italian), Szentgyörgy (Hungarian): town—J1d2: 3.
Glarentsa; Chiarenza or Clarence (medieval), Cyllene (Latin), Kyllēnē (classical Greek),
    Killíni (modern Greek): town—I2e3: 4.
Golden Horn; Chrysoceras (classical), Haliç (Turkish): bay between Constantinople
    and Pera (J4d4: 5).
Golubats; Golubac (Serbian): town—I2d1: 3.
Göynük (Turkish): town—K1d5: 5.
Granada (Spanish), Ighranāṭah or Gharnāṭah (Arabic): city—D2e3: 2.
Greco, Cape—K5f1: 8.
Greece; Hellas (Greek), Graecia (Latin): region west of the Aegean Sea, smaller than
    modern nation.
Grosswardein (German), Nagyvárad (Hungarian), Oradea (Rumanian): city—I2c3: 3.
Guadalquivir (Spanish), al-Wādī al-Kabīr (Arabic: the great river): river—C5e3: 2.
Guadiana (Spanish, Portuguese), Wādī Ānah (Arabic): river—C4e2: 2.
Guines or Guînes (French): town 16 miles NE of Boulogne (E2b5: 2).
Gujerat or Gujarat: district of western India—Sh: 13.
Gurganj: city—see Urgench.
Gurghiu: town—see Szent Imre Görgény.
Györ (Hungarian), Raab (German): town—H3c3: 3.

Habsburg: castle—see Hapsburg.
Haifa; Cayphas or Caiffa (medieval), Ḥaifā (Arabic), Ḥaifa (Israeli): port—L1f3: 1, 7.

Hainault; Hainaut (French), Henegouwen (Flemish): district east of Artois — EFb: 2, 3.
Ḥalab, Haleb: city — see Aleppo.
Halicarnassus: town — see Bodrum.
Hamah; Epiphania or Hamath (classical), Ḥamāh (Arabic): city — L2e5: 1, 6.
Hamid (Turkish): district of west central Anatolia — Ke: 5.
Hangchow or Hang-chou (Chinese), Quinsai (medieval): city, port — CClf5: 13.
Hapsburg; Habsburg (German): castle sw of Brugg, 29 miles east of Basel (F3c3: 3).
Harod, Well of — see 'Ain Jālūt.
Harran or Haran (Turkish), Carrhae (classical), Ḥarrān (Arabic): town — L5e4: 1.
Hattin, Horns of; Madon (classical), Ḥaṭṭīn or Ḥiṭṭīn (Arabic): battlefield, hill — L1f3: 7.
Hauran; Ḥaurān (Arabic): district of SE Syria — L2f2: 7.
Hauteville (French): village 55 miles wsw of Caen (D5c1: 2).
Hebron (classical, Israeli), Ḥabrūn or Khalīl (Arabic), Saint Abraham (medieval): town — L1f4: 7.
Heinsberg (German): town 21 miles north of Aachen (F2b5: 2).
Hejaz; al-Ḥijāz (Arabic): region of western Arabia — Lgh: 1.
Hellespont(us): strait — see Dardanelles.
Heracleum: port — see Candia.
Hermannstadt (German), Szeben or Nagyszeben (Hungarian), Sibiu (Rumanian): town — I5c5: 3.
Hermon, Mount; al-Jabal ash-Shaikh or Jabal ath-Thalj (Arabic: the hoary, or snow-covered, mountain) — L1f2: 7.
Herzegovina; Hercegovina (Serbian), Hersek (Turkish): district NW of Montenegro — Hd: 3.
al-Ḥijāz: region — see Hejaz.
Himara or Himarë (Albanian), Chimaera (classical), Chimara (Italian): town — H5d5: 4.
Hiram or Rama (medieval): fort on Morava near Danube.
Ḥiṣn al-Akrad: fortress — see Krak des Chevaliers.
Ḥiṣn Kaifā (Arabic), Castrum Cepha (classical), Hasankeyf (Turkish): town — M2e3: 1.
Hohenstaufen (German): castle, now destroyed, 75 miles south of Würzburg (F5c1: 3).
Holland (Dutch): region north of Brabant — Eb: 2, 3.
Holy Land — see Palestine.
Homs; Emesa (classical), Ḥimṣ (Arabic): city — L2f1: 1, 6.
Hoveden (medieval) or Howden: town 80 miles north of Leicester (D4b3: 2).
Hungary; Magyarország (Hungarian): region of central Europe — HIc: 3.

Ianina or Janina (medieval), Yanya (Turkish), Ioánnina (modern Greek): town — I1e1: 3, 4.
Ibelin (medieval), Jabneel or Jamnia (classical), Yabnâ (Arabic), Yavne (Israeli): village — K5f4: 7.
Iconium: city — see Konya.
Imbros; Lembro (medieval Italian), İmroz (Turkish): island — J1d5: 5.
Imil, Emel, or Yemel (Russian): river — Uc: 12, 13.
India: region of southern Asia — R/Vf/j: 12, 13.
Indian Ocean: M/Xhij: 12, 13.
Indo-China: peninsular region of SE Asia — YZlm: 12, 13.
Ionian Sea — HIe: 3.
Iran; Īrān (Persian): modern nation comprising most of medieval Persia.
Ireland; Hibernia (Latin), Eire (Gaelic): island — Cb: 2.
Iskar or Iskŭr (Bulgarian): river flowing past Sofia to the Danube — I5d2: 3.
Iskenderun: port — see Alexandretta.
Isonzo (Italian), Soča (Croatian): river east of Aquileia — G5c5: 3.
İstanbul: city — see Constantinople.

Istria (classical), Istra (Croatian, Slovene): peninsula—Gc: 3.
Italy; Italia (Latin, Italian): peninsular region, now a nation.
Ithaca (Latin), Ithakē (classical Greek), Itháki (modern Greek): island—I1e2: 4.
İzmir: city, port—see Smyrna.
İzmit: town—see Nicomedia.
İznik: town—see Nicaea.

Jaffa or Joppa; Yāfā (Arabic), Yafo (Israeli): port, now joined to Tel Aviv—K5f3: 1, 7.
Jajce: town—see Yaytse.
Jan-adasĭ (Turkish), New Orshova: island in the Danube sw of Orshova (I3d1: 3).
Janina: town—see Ianina.
Jehoshaphat or Josaphat; valley, possibly Kidron, but probably north of Jerusalem (L1f4: 7).
Jericho; Arīḥā or ar-Rīḥā (Arabic): town—L1f4: 7.
Jerusalem; Hierosolyma (classical), al-Quds ash-Sharīf (Arabic), Yerushalayim (Israeli): city—L1f4: 1, 7.
Jidda; Jiddah (Arabic): port—L5h4: 1.
Joinville (French): town 37 miles wsw of Toul (F1c2: 2).
Joppa: port—see Jaffa.
Jordan; al-Urdunn (Arabic): river—L1f3: 1, 7.
Josaphat: valley—see Jehoshaphat.
Jubail (Arabic: small mountain), Byblos (classical), Gibelet (medieval): town—L1f1: 1, 6, 7.
Judea: region of central Palestine—L1f4: 7.

Kadĭköy: town—see Chalcedon.
Kaffa or Caffa (medieval), Theodosia (classical), Feodosiya (Russian): port—L1c5: 1.
Kalocsa (Hungarian): town—H4c4: 3.
Kamchiya (Bulgarian): river—J2d3: 5.
Kamen (Bulgarian): river flowing into Danube NW of Vidin (I3d2: 3).
Kangurlan: town—see Sultaniyeh.
Kantara; al-Qanṭarah (Arabic: the bridge), Kantára (modern Greek): town—K4e5: 8.
Kara Hisar: battlefield—see Bashkent.
al-Karak: fortress—see Kerak.
Karakorum (Tatar), Holin (Chinese): city, now abandoned—Y3c3: 12, 13.
Karaman (Turkish): region of south central Anatolia—Ke: 1.
Karasi; Karasĭ or Karesi (Turkish): district of NW Anatolia—Je: 5.
Karnobad or Karnobat (Bulgarian): town 32 miles west of Anchialus (J3d3: 5).
Kärnten: region—see Carinthia.
Karpass or Karpassos (Greek), Carpas (medieval): peninsular district—K5e5: 8.
Kaspichan (Bulgarian): village 12 miles east of Shuman (J2d2: 3).
Kastamonu (Turkish), Castra Comnenon or Kastamuni (medieval): town—K4d4: 1, 3.
Kavalla; Neapolis Datenon (classical), Christopolis (medieval), Kaválla (modern Greek): port—I5d5: 3, 4, 5.
Kavarna (Bulgarian): resort town—J4d2: 3.
Kayseri: city—see Caesarea.
Kemer or Keramides (medieval), Burhaniye (Turkish): port—J2e1: 5.
Kerak; Kir-hareseth (classical), Krak des Moabites or Krak of Moab (medieval), al-Karak (Arabic): fortress, now town—L1f4: 1, 7.
Kerch: port—see Vosporo.
Kermanshah; Kermānshāh (Persian), Sarmasane (medieval): city—N2f1: 1.
Kesoun; Ḳesoun (Armenian), Cesson (medieval), Kaisūn (Arabic), Keysun (Turkish): fortress, now town—L3e3: 6.
Ketton: town 25 miles east of Leicester (D4b3: 2).

Khanbaliq (Mongolian), Chi, Yenking, or Chungtu (classical Chinese), Cambaluc (medieval), Peking, Pei-ching, Beijing, or Peiping (modern Chinese): city—BB1e1: 12, 13.

Kharput or Harput (Turkish), Kharpert (Armenian), Ḥiṣn Ziyād or Zaid (Arabic): fortress, now town—L5e2: 1.

Kherson or Cherson (medieval Russian), Chersonesus Heracleotica (classical), Korsun (Slavic): port, now ruined (not modern Kherson on the Dnieper)—K4d1: 1.

Khirokitia; Khirokitía or Khoirokitía (modern Greek): battlefield—K4f1: 8.

Khurasan; Khorāsān (Persian): region of NE Persia—PQe: 12, 13.

Kiev (Russian): city—K1b5: 3.

Kilia (medieval), Kiliya (Russian): town—J5c5: 1, 3.

Kilidulbahr (Turkish): fort—J2d5: 5.

Kîzîl Ahmadlî (Turkish): tribal region in northern Anatolia—Kd: 10, 11.

Koblos or Palanka (medieval): fort on Morava opposite Hiram.

Koja-ili (Turkish): district around Nicomedia—Jd: 5.

Köln: city—see Cologne.

Kolossi (medieval), Kolóssi (modern Greek): fortress—K3f1: 8.

Konya (Turkish), Iconium (classical, medieval): city—K3e3: 1, 3.

Kossovo; Kosovo (Serbian): town—I2d3: 3.

Kossovo-Polje; Kosovo Polje (Serbian: field of blackbirds): battlefield near Kossovo (I2d3: 3).

Kotor: port—see Cattaro.

Kozlu-Dere (Turkish): port—J2d5: 5.

Kraguyevats; Kragujevac (Serbian): town—I1d1: 3.

Krak de Montréal (medieval), ash-Shaubak (Arabic): fortress, now village—L1f5: 1.

Krak des Chevaliers (medieval), Ḥiṣn al-Akrād (Arabic: stronghold of the Kurds): fortress—L2f1: 1, 6.

Krak of Moab, or des Moabites: fortress—see Kerak.

Kraków: city—see Cracow.

Kroja: town—see Croia.

Kronstadt (German), Braşov (Rumanian): town (recently called Stalin)—J1c5: 3.

Krushevats; Kruševac (Serbian), Alaja-Hisar (Turkish): town—I2d2: 3.

Kunovitsa; Kunovica (Serbian): town and mountain near Nish (I2d2: 3).

Kurdistan; Kurdistān (Persian, Arabic): region between Armenia and Persia—MNe: 1.

Küstendil; Konstantin-ili (Turkish), Kyustendil (Bulgarian): town—I3d3: 3.

Kutná Hora (Czech), Kuttenberg (German): town—H1c1: 3.

Kykkou (Greek): Greek Orthodox monastery—K3e5: 8.

Kyrenia; Cerines (medieval), Kerýnia, (modern Greek): town—K4e5: 8.

La Broquière or La Bro(c)quière (French): village 65 miles SW of Toulouse (E2d2: 2).

La Castrie (medieval), Gastría (modern Greek): castle—K4e5: 8.

La Cava (Italian): castle SE of Nicosia (K4e5: 8).

La Montjoie (French): hill overlooking Jerusalem (L1f4: 7).

La Sola: town—see Salona.

Lab (Serbian): river flowing SE of Vuchitrn.

Laconia (Latin), Lakōnia or Lakōnikē (medieval Greek), Lakonía (modern Greek): district of SE Morea—I3e4: 4.

Lajazzo: port—see Ayas.

Lampedusa (Italian): island—G3e5: 3.

Lampron (Armenian), Namrun (Turkish): fortress—K5e3: 1.

Lampsacus (classical), Lapseki (Turkish): village—J2d5: 5.

Lancaster: city—D3b1: 2.

Lango: island—see Cos.

Langres (French): town—F1c3: 2, 3.

Languedoc (French): region of southern France—Ecd: 2.

Lannoy (French): town 9 miles NW of Tournai (E4b5: 2).

Laodicea: port—see Latakia.

Laon (French): town—E4c1: 2.

Larnaca; Lárnaka (modern Greek): town—K4f1: 8.

Lastic (French): village near Saint Flour, 39 miles west of Le Puy (E4c5: 2).

Lászlóvár (Hungarian): fortress opposite Golubats (I2d1: 3).

Latakia; Laodicea ad Mare (classical), al-Lādhiqīyah (Arabic): port—L1e5: 1, 6.

Lausanne (French): town—F2c4: 2, 3.

Le Bourg or Bourcq (French): castle in Vouziers canton, Ardennes, near Rethel, NE of Rheims (E5c1: 2).

Le Chief: see Cape Andreas.

Le Courc: port—see Corycus.

Le Mans (French): city—E1c3: 2.

Le Puy-en-Velay (French), Podio (medieval Latin): town—E4c5: 2.

Lebanon, Mount; Jabal Lubnān (Arabic)—L2f1: 6, 7.

Lefkara (medieval Greek): town—K4f1: 8.

Lefkoniko; Lefkonikó (modern Greek): town—K4e5: 8.

Leicester: town—D4b3: 2.

Lembro: island—see Imbros.

Lemnos; Lēmnos (medieval Greek), Stalimene (medieval), Límnos (modern Greek): island—J1e1: 5.

Leon; León (Spanish): region of northern Spain—CDd: 2.

Leontes: river—see Litani.

Lepanto (Italian), Naupactus (classical), Epaktos (medieval Greek), Návpaktos (modern Greek): port—I2e2: 3, 4.

Lesbos (classical), Mytilēnē (medieval Greek), Metelino (medieval Italian), Midülü (Turkish), Lésvos (modern Greek): island—J2e1: 5.

Lesh; Lezhe (Albanian), Lissus (classical), Alessio (Italian): town—H5d4: 3, 4.

Leucas or Leukas (classical), Leucadia or Santa Maura (medieval), Levkás (modern Greek): island—I1e2: 3, 4.

Liége or (recently) Liège (French), Luik (Flemish): city—F1b5: 2, 3.

Lille (French), Ryssel (Flemish): city—E4b5: 2.

Limassol; Nemesos (medieval Greek), Lemesós (modern Greek): port—K4f1: 1, 8.

Limoges (French): city—E2c5: 2.

Lisbon; Lisboa (Portuguese), Ushbūnah (Arabic): city, port—C1e2: 2.

Lisieux (French): town 45 miles WSW of Rouen (E2c1: 2).

Litani; Leontes (classical), al-Lītānī (Arabic): river—L1f2: 7.

Lithuania; Lietuva (Lithuanian): region east of Poland, larger than modern state—IJab: 3.

Livadia; Lebadea or Levadeia (classical), Levádhia (modern Greek): town—I3e2: 5.

Livonia; Livland (German): district NE of Riga—IJa: 3.

Lodi (Italian): town 18 miles SE of Milan (F5c5: 3).

Loire (French): river—E3c3: 2.

Lombardy; Lombardia (Italian): region of NW Italy—Fcd: 2, 3.

London: city, port—D5b4: 2.

Lorraine (French), Lothringen (German): region of eastern France—EFc: 2, 3.

Lorraine, Lower: district of southern Belgium (EFbc).

Low Countries: Netherlands and part of Belgium.

Lübeck (German): city, port—G1b2: 2, 3.

Lucca (Italian): town—G1d2: 2, 3.

Lucera (Italian): town—H1d4: 3.

Lusignan (French): town—E1c4: 2.

Luxemburg or Letzeburg; Luxembourg (French): region, now independent, south of Belgium.

Lydda (classical), Saint George (medieval), al-Ludd (Arabic), Lod (Israeli): town — K5f4: 7.

Lydia: district — see Aydin.

Lyons; Lyon (French): city — E5c5: 2.

Mabûj: town — see Manbij.

Macedonia (classical), Makedhonía (modern Greek), Makedonija (Serbian): region west of Thrace — Id: 3, 4, 5.

Machaeras or Makhairas (Greek): Greek Orthodox monastery — K4f1: 8.

Machaut or Machault (French): village 22 miles ENE of Rheims (E5c1: 2).

Machva; Mačva (Serbian), Macsó (Hungarian): district south of Sava river (H4d1: 3).

Mâcon (French): town — E5c4: 2.

Madras: city, port — U1m2: 12, 13.

Maeander (classical), Büyük Menderes (Turkish): river — J4e3: 5.

al-Maghrib: region — see North Africa.

Maguelonne (French): port, now unimportant — E4d2: 2.

Mahoracz (Bulgarian): fortress between Provadiya and Shumen.

Maine (French): region of NW France — Dc: 2.

Mainz (German), Mayence (French): city — F4b5: 2, 3.

Maiyafariqin; Martyropolis (classical), Maiyāfāraqīn (Arabic), Miyafarkin or Silvan (Turkish): town — M2e2: 1.

Majorca; Mallorca (Spanish), Mayūrqah (Arabic): island — Ee: 2.

Makri (medieval), Fethiye (Turkish): port — J5e4: 1, 3, 5.

Malatia, Malatya: city — see Melitene.

Malmesbury: town 90 miles west of London (D5b4: 2).

Malmsey, Malvasia: fortress — see Monemvasia.

Malta; Melita (classical), Mālitah (Arabic): island — G5e5: 3.

Mamistra (medieval), Mopsuestia (classical), Msis (Armenian), Misis (Turkish): town — L1e4: 1, 6.

Manbij or Mabūj (Arabic), Hierapolis (classical), Membij (Turkish): town — L3e4: 6.

Mangana: Greek Orthodox monastery in outskirts of Nicosia (K4e5: 8).

Mansurah; al-Manṣūrah (Arabic): town — K2f4: 1.

Mantua; Mantova (Italian): city — G1c5: 3.

Manzikert; Mandzgerd (West) or Mantskert (East Armenian), Malazgirt (Turkish): town — M3d1: 1.

Maragha; Marāgheh (Persian): town — N2e3: 1.

Marash (Armenian, Turkish), Germanicia (classical), Mar'ash (Arabic): town — L2e3: 1, 6.

Marcropolis (Bulgarian): town near Varna (J3d2: 5).

Mardin (Turkish), Māridīn (Arabic): town — M1e3: 1.

Marethasa: valley east of Tylleria (K3e5: 8).

Margat (medieval), al-Marqab (Arabic: the watch-tower): fortress — L1e5: 6.

Marienburg (German), Malbork (Polish): fortress, now town — H5b1: 3.

Maritsa; Hebrus (classical), Evros (medieval Greek), Meriç (Turkish): river — J2d5: 1, 3, 5.

Marle (French): village 14 miles NNE of Laon (E4c1: 2).

Marmara, Sea of; Propontis (classical), Marmara Denizi (Turkish) — J4d5: 5.

Maros (Hungarian), Marisus (classical), Mureş (Rumanian): river flowing by Alba Julia — IJc: 3.

al-Marqab: fortress — see Margat.

Marrakesh; Marrākush (Arabic): city — C2f4: 2.

Marseilles; Massalia (classical Greek), Massilia (Latin), Marseille (French): city, port — F1d2: 2.

Marturana (medieval), Martirano (Italian): town — H2e2: 3.

Marv: city — see Merv.

Massa (Italian): town 28 miles NW of Pisa (G1d2: 3).

Maṣyāf or Maṣyāth or Maṣyād or Miṣyāf (Arabic): fortress — L2e5: 6.

Matapan, Cape; Taenarum (Latin), Metōpon (medieval Greek), Ákra Taínaron (modern Greek) — I3e4: 4.

Mayence: city — see Mainz.

Mecca; Makkah (Arabic): city — L5h4: 1.

Medina; al-Madīnah (Arabic: the city): city — L5h1: 1.

Mediterranean Sea — D/Ldef: 1, 2, 3, 4, 6, 7, 8.

Megali-Agora (medieval), Malkara or Migal-Kara (Turkish): town — J2d5: 5.

Megara; Mégara (modern Greek): town — I4e3: 4.

Mehadia (Rumanian): village 12 miles north of Orshova (I3d1: 3).

Meissen (German): town — G4b4: 2, 3.

Melgueil (French): medieval county around Mauguio, 7 miles east of Montpellier (E4d2: 2).

Melitene (classical), Melden (Armenian), Malatia (medieval), Malatya (Turkish): city — L4e2: 1.

Melle (French), Metallum (classical): town — E1c4: 2.

Melshticha (Bulgarian): battleground about 12 miles west of Sofia (I4d3: 3).

Menas: town — see Aenos.

Menteshe (medieval), Muğla (modern Turkish): region of western Anatolia equivalent to classical Caria — Je: 5.

Meran: region — see Croatia.

Merv or Marv (Persian), Margiana (classical): city — Q2e3: 12, 13.

Mesaréa: district — see Arcadia.

Mesembria (medieval), Misivri (Turkish), Nesebar (Bulgarian): town — J3d3: 3, 5.

Mesopotamia (classical), al-‘Iraq (Arabic): region between the Tigris and the Euphrates — LMNef: 1.

Messenia; Messēnē (medieval Greek), Messíni (modern Greek): district of sw Morea — I2e4: 4.

Messina (Italian): port — H1e2: 3.

Metelino: island — see Lesbos.

Metz (French): city — F2c1: 2.

Meulan (French): town 23 miles WNW of Paris (E3c2: 2).

Mézières (French): town, now attached to Charleville, 50 miles NE of Rheims (E5c1: 2).

Michelich (Bulgarian): castle west of Varna (J3d2: 5).

Micone: island — see Myconos.

Midi (French): southern France (DEd: 2).

Milan; Milano (Italian): city — F5c5: 2, 3.

Milipotamo (Greek): unidentified locality in Crete.

Misis: town — see Mamistra.

Miṣr: region — see Egypt.

Mistra (medieval), Myzithra (medieval Greek), Mistrás (modern Greek): town — I3e3: 4.

Mocha; Mukhā (Arabic): port — M4j2: 13.

Modon (medieval), Methōnē (medieval Greek), Methóni (modern Greek): port — I2e4: 3, 4.

Moldavia; Boghdan (Rumanian): region east of the Carpathians — Jc: 3.

Molybdos (classical), Mólivdhos (modern Greek): port — J2e1: 5.

Monastir; Bitolj (Serbian): town — I2d4: 3, 4.

Monemvasia; Minōa (classical Greek), Malvasia or Malmsey (medieval), Monemvasía (modern Greek): fortress, now town — I4e4: 3, 4.

Monferrato: district — see Montferrat.

Mongolia; Meng-ku (Chinese): region north of China — V/BBbcd: 12, 13.

Montaigu-sur-Champeix or Montaigut-le-Blanc (French): castle 10 miles SSE of Clermont (E4c5: 2).

Monte Cassino (Italian): abbey—G4d4: 3.

Monte (di) Croce (Italian): village near Florence (G2d2: 3).

Monteil (French): village, now Monteil-au-Vicomte, 30 miles NW of Nice (F3d2: 2).

Montenegro (Italian: black mountain), Crna Gora (Serbian): district north of Albania—HId: 3.

Montferrat (French), Monferrato (Italian): district of NW Italy—F4c5: 2, 3.

Montfort (French), Starkenberg (German), Qal'at al-Qurain (Arabic): castle—L1f2: 7.

Montfort-l'Amaury (French): town 25 miles WSW of Paris (E3c2: 2).

Montpellier (French): town—E4d2: 2.

Montréal (French): fief around Krak de Montréal (L1f5: 1).

Morava (Serbian): river—I2d2: 3.

Moravia; Morava (Czech): region SE of Bohemia—Hc: 9.

Morea (medieval), Peloponnesus (Latin), Peloponnēsos or Moreas (medieval Greek), Pelopónnisos (modern Greek): peninsular region of southern Greece—I3: 3, 4.

Morfittes (medieval), Omorphita (Greek), Küçük Kaimakli (Turkish): village—K4e5: 8.

Morlaàs (French): town 18 miles south of Aire (D5d2: 2).

Morocco; al-Maghrib al-Aqsâ (Arabic: the farthest west): region of NW Africa—CDf: 2.

Morphou; Mórphou (modern Greek): town—K3e5: 8.

Mosul; al-Mauṣil (Arabic), Musul (Turkish): city—M4e4: 1.

Mühlenbach or Mühlbach (German), Sebeş (Rumanian), Szászsebes (Hungarian): town—I4c5: 3.

Myconos (classical), Micone (medieval Italian), Mokene (Turkish), Míkonos (modern Greek): island—J1e3: 5.

Mytilene: island—see Lesbos.

Mytilene; Mytilēnē (classical Greek), Mitylēnē (medieval Greek), Mitilíni (modern Greek): town—J2e1: 1, 3, 5.

Nablus; Shechem or Neapolis (classical), Nābulus (Arabic): town—L1f3: 7.

Nagyvárad: city—see Grosswardein.

Naillac (French): chateau at Le Blanc, 35 miles east of Poitiers (E1c4: 2).

Namfio: island—see Anaphe.

Namur (French): town—E5b5: 2, 3.

Nanking or Nan-ching (Chinese): city—BB4f3: 13.

Naples; Napoli (Italian): city, port—G5d5: 3.

Naples: kingdom—Hd: 9.

Narbonne (French): town—E4d2: 2.

Naupactus: port—see Lepanto.

Nauplia (classical), Návplion (modern Greek): port—I3e3: 4.

Navarino (Italian), Pylos (classical Greek), Zonklon (medieval): port, now superseded by New Navarino—I2e4: 4.

Navarre (French), Navarra (Spanish): region of northern Spain—Dd: 2.

Naxos; Nicosia (medieval Italian), Naksa (Turkish), Náxos (modern Greek): island—J1e4: 5.

Nazareth; an-Nāṣirah (Arabic): town—L1f3: 7.

Near East: region from Egypt to Persia and Turkey to Aden.

Negroponte: island—see Euboea.

Negroponte (medieval Italian: black bridge), Chalcis (classical), Khalkís (modern Greek): port—I4e2: 3, 4.

Nejd; Najd (Arabic): region of central Arabia—MNg: 1.

Neopatras: duchy—Ie: 9.

Nestos (Greek), Nestus (Latin), Kara Su (Turkish), Mesta (Bulgarian): river flowing into the Aegean opposite Thasos—I5d4: 5.

Neszméty (Hungarian): town 37 miles NW of Buda (H5c3: 3).

Neuilly-sur-Marne (French): town 10 miles east of Paris (E3c2: 2).

Nevers (French): town—E4c4: 2.

Newburgh: town—D2a4: 2.

Nicaea (classical), İznik (Turkish): town—J5d5: 1, 3, 5.

Nice (French), Nizza (Italian): port—F3d2: 2.

Nicomedia (classical), İzmit (Turkish): town—J5d5: 1, 3, 5.

Nicopolis (medieval), Nikeboli (Turkish), Nikopol (Bulgarian): town—I5d2: 1, 3.

Nicosia; Levkōsia (medieval Greek), Nicosía (modern Greek): city—K4e5: 1, 8.

Nijmegen (Dutch): town—F1b4: 3.

Nile; Baḥr an-Nīl (Arabic): river—K3g4: 1; K1f4: 3.

Nîmes (French): city—E5d2: 2.

Nish; Niš (Serbian), Niş (Turkish), Naissus or Nissa (classical): town—I2d2: 3.

Nishava; Nisava (Serbian): river flowing past Pirot into the Morava—I3d2: 3.

Nisibin or Nusaybin (Turkish), Nisibis (classical), Naṣībīn or Nuṣaibīn (Arabic): town—M2e3: 1.

Nogent-sur-Marne (French): town 7 miles east of Paris (E3c2: 2).

Normandy; Normandie (French): region of northern France—DEc: 2.

North Africa; al-Maghrib (Arabic: the west): region from Morocco to Cyrenaica, north of the Sahara.

North Sea—DEFab: 2, 3.

Novara (Italian): town—F4c5: 3.

Novgorod (Russian: new city): city—K2a2: 12.

Novi Pazar or Raška (Serbian), Rascia (Latin): town—I1d2: 3.

Novo Brdo (Serbian): mine 20 miles east of Kossovo (I2d3: 3).

Noyon (French): town 29 miles west of Laon (E4c1: 2).

Nuremberg; Nürnberg (German): city—G2c1: 2, 3.

Ochrida, Lake; Lychnitus Lacus (classical), Ohridske Jezero (Serbian)—I1d4: 4.

Oder (German), Odra (Czech, Polish): river—H1b3: 2.

Oldenburg (German): city—F4b2: 2, 3.

Omol (medieval): fortress in the Morava valley (Id: 3).

Omorphita: village—see Morfittes.

Oradea: city—see Grosswardein.

Orange (French): town 13 miles north of Avignon (E5d2: 2).

Oreus (Latin), Ōreos (medieval Greek), Oreoí (modern Greek): town—I4e2: 4.

Orléans (French): town—E2c3: 2.

Orontes (classical), al-ʿĀṣī (Arabic: the rebellious), Far (medieval): river—L2e5: 1, 6, 7.

Orshova; Orşova (Rumanian): town—I3d1: 3.

Osimo (Italian), Auximum (classical): town 9 miles south of Ancona (G4d2: 3).

Ostia (Italian): port, now village—G3d4: 2, 3.

Ostrovitsa; Ostrovica (Serbian), Sifrije-Hisar (Turkish): fortress 30 miles north of Zara (H1d1: 3).

Otranto (Italian): town—H4d5: 3.

Outremer (French: overseas), Ultramare (Latin): the Latin states in Syria and Palestine.

Oxford: town—D4b4: 2.

Paderborn (German): town—F4b4: 2, 3.

Padua; Padova (Italian): city—G2c5: 2, 3.

Palatia (medieval), Miletus (classical), Balat (Turkish): port, now abandoned—J3e3: 3, 5.

Palermo (Italian), Balarm (Arabic): city, port—G4e2: 3.

Palestine; Palaestina (classical), Filistīn (Arabic): region west of the Dead Sea and the Jordan—KLf: 1.

Palestrina (Italian): town—G3d4: 3.

Palmyra or Tadmor (classical), Tadmur, now Tudmur (Arabic): caravan town—L4f1: 6.

Papal States—Gd: 9.

Paphos (medieval), Páphos (modern Greek): town—K3f1: 1, 8.

Paris (French): city—E3c2: 2.

Parori; Paróri (modern Greek): village 1 mile east of Mistra (I3e3: 4).

Passau (German): town—G4c2: 2, 3.

Patmos; Patmo (Italian), Batnos (Turkish), Pátmos (modern Greek): island—J2e3: 5.

Patras (medieval), Pátrai (modern Greek): port—I2e2: 3, 4.

Pavia (Italian): town—F5c5: 2, 3.

Pedhoulas; Pedhoulás or Pedoulás (modern Greek): town—K3f1: 8.

Pegae: town—see Biga.

Peking: city—see Khanbaliq.

Peloponnesus: peninsular region—see Morea.

Peñaforte (Spanish): castle near Villafranca del Panadés, 25 miles west of Barcelona (E3d4: 2).

Pentedaktylos (Greek): monastery—K4e5: 8.

Pera or Estanor (medieval), Beyoğlu (Turkish): port—J4d4: 3, 5.

Perche (French): district west of Chartres—E1c2: 2.

Pergamum (classical), Bergamo (Turkish): town—J3e1: 3, 5.

Persia (classical), Īrān (Persian): region of sw Asia—NOef: 1.

Persian Gulf; Khalīj-i-Fars (Persian), Khalīj al-'Ajam (Arabic)—NOg: 12, 13.

Perugia (Italian): town—G3d2: 3.

Petra Deserti (classical): ancient city—L1f5: 1.

Petrich (Bulgarian), Petritzos (medieval Greek): castle—I5d4: 3, 5.

Petrovaradin (Serbian), Peterwardein (German): town—H5c5: 3.

Philadelphia (classical), Alaşehir (Turkish): town—J4e2: 3, 5.

Philippopolis (classical), Plovdiv (Bulgarian), Filibe (Turkish): town—I5d3: 1, 3, 5.

Philomelium: town—see Akshehir.

Phínika (modern Greek): village—K3f1: 8.

Phocaea (classical), Foglia (Italian), Foça (Turkish): port, now abandoned for New Phocaea—J2e2: 3, 5.

Phocaea, New; Yenifoça (Turkish): port—J2e2: 3, 5.

Piacenza (Italian): town—F5c5: 2.

Pian del Carpine or Piano della Magione (Italian), Plano de Carpini (Latin), Plano-carpino (medieval): village 9 miles wNw of Perugia (G3d2: 3).

Picardy: Picardie (French): region of northern France—Eb: 2.

Piis (French): village about 40 miles se of Bordeaux (D5d1: 2).

Piotrków (Polish): town—H5b4: 3.

Pirot (Bulgarian): town—I3d2: 3.

Pisa (Italian): port, now city—G1d2: 2, 3.

Planocarpino: village—see Pian del Carpine.

Plochnik; Pločnik (Serbian): battlefield 15 miles wsw of Nish (I2d2: 3).

Plovdiv: town—see Philippopolis.

Podio: town—see Le Puy.

Podolia: region north of Moldavia—Jc: 3.

Poitiers (French): town—E1c4: 2.

Poitou (French): region of western France—DEc: 2.

Poland; Polska (Polish): region east of Germany—HIb: 3.

Polanka: fort—see Koblos.

Polis (medieval), Arsinoë (classical): town—K3e5: 8.

Pomerania; Pommern (German): region of ne Germany—GHb: 2, 3.

Pomoriye: port—see Anchialus.
Ponthieu (French): district of western Picardy (Eb: 2).
Porto (Italian): village 13 miles sw of Rome (G3d4: 3).
Portugal; Lusitania (classical): region west of southern and central Spain, now a
    nation—Cde: 2.
Posen (German), Poznán (Polish): city—H2b3: 3.
Potamiou; Potamioú (modern Greek): village—K3f1: 8.
Prague; Praha (Czech): city—G5b5: 2, 3.
Prespa, Lake; Brygius Lacus (classical), Brygēis Limnē (medieval Greek), Prespansko
    Jezero (Serbian)—I1d5: 4.
Pressburg: city—see Bratislava.
Prote (Serbian), Prodano (Italian), Barakada (Turkish): island—I2e3: 4.
Provadiya (Bulgarian), Probaton (medieval), Provadi (Turkish): town—J3d2: 5.
Provence (French): region of SE France—EFd: 2, 3.
Provins (French): town 40 miles WNW of Troyes (E5c2: 2).
Prussia; Preussen (German), Prusy (Polish): region of NE Germany—HIb: 3.
Psimolófo (medieval Greek), Psomolóphou (modern Greek): village—K4e5: 8.
Pskov (Russian), Pleskau (German): city—J4a3: 12.
Puglia or Puglie: region—see Apulia.
Pylos: port—see Navarino.
Pyramus (classical), Chahan (Armenian), Jeyhan (Turkish): river—L1e4: 6.
Pyrenees; Pyrénées (French), Pirineos (Spanish): mountain range—DEd: 2.
Pyrgos (Greek): town—I2e3: 4.
Python or Pithion (Greek), Egri-Kuleli-Burgaz (Turkish): town 20 miles south of
    Adrianople (J2d4: 5).

Qal'at ash-Shaqīf: crusader castle—see Belfort.
Qūṣ (Arabic), Apollonopolis Parva (classical): town—K3g5: 1.

Raab: town—see Györ.
Ragusa (medieval), Dubrovnik (Serbian): port—H4d3: 3.
Rahova or Rakhova (medieval), Oryakhovo (Rumanian): town—I4d2: 3.
Ramla; Rama or Rames (medieval), ar-Ramlah (Arabic: the sandy): town—K5f4: 7.
Rascia, Raska: town—see Novi Pazar.
Ravenna (Italian): town—G3d1: 2, 3.
Red Sea; al-Baḥr al-Aḥmar (Arabic)—Lgh: 1.
Regensburg (German), Ratisbon (medieval): town—G3c1: 2, 3.
Retimo (medieval), Calamona or Rethymnon (classical), Réthimnon (modern Greek):
    town—I5e5: 3.
Rheims; Reims (French): city—E5c1: 2.
Rhine; Rijn (Dutch), Rhein (German), Rhin (French): river—F3b5: 2; F3c2: 3.
Rhineland: region of the middle Rhine.
Rhodes; Rhodos (classical Greek), Rhodus (Latin), Ródhos (modern Greek): city,
    port—J4e4: 1, 5.
Rhodes; Rhodos (classical Greek), Rhodus (Latin), Rodos (Turkish), Rodi (Italian),
    Ródhos (modern Greek): island—Je: 1, 3, 5.
Rhodope; Rhodopē (classical Greek), Rodhópi (modern Greek), Rodopi (Bulgarian):
    mountain range—I5d4: 5.
Rhone; Rhône (French): river—E5c5: 2.
Riga; Rīga (Lettish): city—I5a4: 12.
Rodez (French): town—E3d1: 2.
Rohais or Rochas: city—see Edessa.
Romania: region—see Anatolia.
Romans-sur-Isère (French): town 11 miles north of Valence (E5d1: 2).

Rome; Roma (Italian): city—G3d4: 2, 3.
Rosetta; Rashīd (Arabic): port—K1f4: 1.
Rouen (French): city—E2c1: 2.
Roussillon (French): district north of the eastern Pyrenees—E3d3: 2.
Rovine (Rumanian): village 28 miles north of Temesvár (I2c5: 3).
Rubruck (Flemish): village 33 miles WNW of Lille (E4b5: 2).
Rūm: region: see Anatolia.
Rumeli-Hisar (Turkish: castle of Rumelia): fortress—J5d4: 5.
Rumelia; Rumeli (Turkish): Ottoman territory in Europe—IJde: 11.
Russia; Rus (medieval), Russiya (Russian): region of eastern Europe—JKLMbc: 1, 3.
Ruthenia (medieval): region of eastern Europe, not equivalent to modern (till 1945) Czechoslovakian province—IJc: 3.

Sabina (Italian): district 35 miles north of Rome (G3d4: 3).
Sachsen: region—see Saxony.
Sagitta: port—see Sidon.
Sahara; aṣ-Ṣaḥrā' (Arabic): desert—DEFGfg: 2, 3.
Saint Abraham: town—see Hebron.
Saint Albans; Verulamium (Latin): town 20 miles NNW of London (D5b4: 2).
Saint Andrew, Cape: see Cape Andreas.
Saint Bertin (French): abbey 17 miles east of Boulogne (E2b5: 2).
Saint George: town—see Lydda.
Saint Gilles-du-Gard (French): village 10 miles west of Arles (E5d2: 2).
Saint Hilarion or Dieudamour (French), Áyios Ilárion (modern Greek): castle—K4e5: 8.
Saint Jean d'Acre: city, port—see Acre.
Saint Nicholas (tou Soulouaiy); Áyios Nikólaos (modern Greek): village—K3f1: 8.
Saint Omer (French): town—E3b5: 2.
Saint Pol-sur-Ternoise (French): town 34 miles north of Amiens (E3c1: 2).
Saint Quentin (French): town 26 miles NW of Laon (E4c1: 2).
Saint Simeon (medieval), as-Suwaidīyah (Arabic), Süveydiye (Turkish): port—L1e4: 6.
Saint Theodosius; Dair Ibn-'Ubaid (Arabic): Greek Orthodox monastery—L1f4: 7.
Saint Trond (French): town—F1b5: 2.
Saint Urbain (French): abbey near Vassy, 42 miles WSW of Toul (F1c2: 2).
Sakarya (Turkish), Sangarius (classical): river—K2e1: 1; K1d5: 5.
Salamanca (Spanish), Salmantiqah (Arabic): city—C5d5: 2.
Salerno (Italian): port—G5d5: 3.
Salisbury: city—D4b4: 2.
Salmas, Selmas, or Salamastrum (medieval), Salmās, Dilmān, or Shāhpūr (Persian): town—M5e2: 1.
Salona or La Sala (medieval), Amphissa (classical), Amfíssa (modern Greek): town—I3e2: 3, 4.
Salonika or Saloníki: city—see Thessalonica.
as-Salṭ (Arabic): town—L1f3: 7.
Salzburg (German): city—G4c3: 2, 3.
Samaria (classical): district of northern Palestine—L1f3: 7.
Samarkand; Samarqand (Persian, Arabic): city—R2e1: 12, 13.
Samothrace; Samothrakē (classical Greek), Samothráki (modern Greek): island—J1d5: 5.
Sangarius: river—see Sakarya.
San Germano Vercellese (Italian): village 22 miles NW of Montferrat (F4c5: 3).
San Gimignano (Italian): town 18 miles SW of Siena (G2d2: 3).
Sanok (Polish): town—I3c1: 3.
Santa Maura: island—see Leucas.

Santiago de Compostela: shrine — see Compostela.

Saone (medieval), Ṣahyūn or Ṣihyaun (Arabic): crusader castle — L2e5: 6.

Saragossa; Caesaraugusta (classical), Zaragoza (Spanish), Saraqusṭah (Arabic): city — D5d4: 2.

Sarai or Sarai-Batu (Tatar), Sarāi (Persian: palace): town, now abandoned — N3c3: 1.

Sarai-Berke: town — see Aksarai.

Sardinia; Sardegna (Italian): island — Fde: 2, 3.

Sarmasane: city — see Kermanshah.

Saronic Gulf; Saronikós Kólpos (modern Greek) — I4e3: 4.

Saros Bay; Saros Körfezi (Turkish): bay north of Gallipoli peninsula (J2d5: 5).

Sarukhan (Turkish): district of western Anatolia — Je: 5.

Sarus (classical), Sahan (Armenian), Seyhan (Turkish): river — L1e3: 6.

Satalia: port — see Adalia.

Satines: city — see Athens.

Sava or Save (Croatian), Sau (German), Száva (Hungarian): river — H4d1: 3.

Savoy; Savoie (French): region of SE France — Fc: 2, 3.

Saxony; Sachsen (German): region of northern Germany — Gb: 2, 3.

Scandelore: port — see Alanya.

Scandinavia: region comprising Denmark, Sweden, and Norway.

Schwaben: region — see Swabia.

Scio: island — see Chios.

Scotland; Scotia (Latin): region north of England — CDa: 2.

Scribention: town — see Sopot.

Scutari (Italian), Chrysopolis (classical), Üsküdar (Turkish): port — J5d4: 5.

Scutari (Italian), Scodra (classical), Shkodër (Albanian): port — H5d3: 3.

Sebastia: city — see Sivas.

Sebenico (Italian), Šibenik (Serbian): port — H1d2: 3.

Sebeş: town — see Mühlenbach.

Segna: port — see Senj.

Segni (Italian): town 30 miles ESE of Rome (G3d4: 3).

Seine (French): river — E5c2: 2.

Seleucia Trachea (classical), Selevgia (Armenian), Silifke (Turkish): port, now town — K4e4: 1.

Selmas: town — see Salmas.

Selymbria (medieval), Silivri (Turkish): port — J4d4: 5.

Semendria: town — see Smederevo.

Senj (Serbian), Segna (Italian), Zengg (German): port — G5d1: 3.

Serbia; Srbija (Serbian): region east of Dalmatia — HId: 3.

Serres (medieval), Sérrai (modern Greek): town — I4d4: 3, 4, 5.

Sevan, Lake (Russian), Gökçe Gölü (Turkish) — N1d5: 1.

Severin (Rumanian): district north of Orshova — Icd: 3.

Seville; Hispalis (classical), Sevilla (Spanish), Ishbīliyah (Arabic): city — C5e3: 2.

Shabats; Šabac (Serbian), Bögürdelen (Turkish): town 40 miles west of Belgrade (I1d1: 3).

Shaizar (medieval Arabic), Larissa (classical), Saijar (modern Arabic): fortress, now town — L2e5: 6.

Shaqīf Arnūn: castle — see Belfort.

ash-Shaubak: fortress — see Krak de Montréal.

Shumen; Šumen (Bulgarian), Sumni (Turkish): town, now Kolarovgrad — J2d2: 3.

Šibenik: port — see Sebenico.

Sibiu: town — see Hermannstadt.

Sicily; Sicilia (Italian), Ṣiqillīyah (Arabic), Trinacria (medieval): island — Ge: 2, 3.

Sidon; Sagitta (medieval), Ṣaidā' (Arabic): port — L1f2: 1, 7.

Siebenbürgen: region — see Transylvania.

Siena (Italian): town—G2d2: 2, 3.
Siğin (Turkish): fortress on the coast of Cilicia (Ie: 6).
Sígouri or Sívouri (modern Greek), Baffa (medieval): castle—K4e5: 8.
Silesia; Schlesien (German), Śląsk (Polish), Slezsko (Czech): region north of Moravia—
     Hb: 3.
Silifke: port—see Seleucia.
Silistria or Silistra: town—see Dristra.
Silivri: port—see Selymbria.
Silvan: town—see Maiyafariqin.
Silves (Portuguese), Shilb (Arabic): town—C2e3: 2.
Sinai; Sīnā' (Arabic): peninsula—Kfg: 1.
Sinai, Mount, or Mount Horeb; Jabal Mūsâ (Arabic: mountain of Moses)—K4g2: 1.
Sinope; Sinōpē (medieval Greek), Sinop (Turkish): port—L1d3: 1.
Sis (Armenian, medieval), Kezan (Turkish): town—L1e3: 1.
Sitia or Seteia (Greek): town—J2e5: 3.
Sivas; Sebastia (classical), Sîvas (Turkish): city—L3e1: 1.
Skoplje; Üsküb (Turkish), Skopje (Serbian): town—I2d4: 3.
Sladagora (Bulgarian): castle near Zlatitsa.
Slankamen (Serbian): village 18 miles NNW of Belgrade (I1d1: 3).
Slavonia: district east of Croatia—Hc: 3.
Slovenia: region NW of Croatia—GHc: 3.
Sluis (Flemish, Dutch), L'Écluse (French): port, now town, 10 miles NE of Bruges
     (E4b4: 2).
Smederevo (Serbian), Semendria (German): town 24 miles ESE of Belgrade (I1d1: 3).
Smyrna (classical), İzmir (Turkish): city, port—J3e2: 1, 3, 5.
Socotra; Suqūṭrâ (Arabic): island—Q4/5j3: 13.
Sofia; Sardica (classical), Triaditia (medieval Greek), Sredec (Serbian), Sofiya
     (Bulgarian): city—I4d3: 3, 5.
Soli (Greek): town, now abandoned—K3e5: 8.
Sopot (Bulgarian), Scribention (medieval): town—I5d3: 3, 5.
Sozopolis (medieval), Apollonia (classical), Sözeboli or Uluborlu (Turkish), Sozopol
     (Bulgarian): town—J3d3: 3, 5.
Spain; Hispania (classical), España (Spanish): region south of the Pyrenees.
Spalato (medieval), Split (Serbian): port—H2d2: 3.
Sparta or Lacedaemon (Latin), Spartē or Lakedaimōn (classical Greek), Spárti (mod-
     ern Greek): town—I3e3: 4.
Sporades; Sporádhes (modern Greek): island group—IJe: 3, 4, 5.
Srebrenitsa; Srebrenica (Serbian): town 75 miles SW of Belgrade (I1d1: 3).
Sredna Gora (Bulgarian): mountain range—Id: 5.
Stalimene: island—see Lemnos.
Stanchio or Stankoi, island—see Cos.
Starkenberg: castle—see Montfort.
Stavrovouni; Stavrovoúni (modern Greek): mountain—K4f1: 8.
Strassburg (German), Strasbourg (French): city—F3c2: 2, 3.
Strymon; Strymōn (classical Greek), Strimón (modern Greek), Struma (Bulgarian):
     river—I4d4: 4.
Styria; Steiermark (German): region of southern Austria—GHc: 3.
Sudan; as-Sūdān (Arabic: the Negro lands): region south of Egypt—JKh: 1.
Suez; as-Suwais (Arabic): port—K3g1: 1.
Sultaniye (medieval Turkish), Çanakkale (modern Turkish): port—J2d5: 5.
Sultaniyeh; Sulṭānīyeh (Persian), Kangurlan (Mongol): town—N4e4: 1.
Ṣūr: port—see Tyre.
Suzdal (Russian): city—M1a4: 12.
Swabia; Schwaben (German): region of SW Germany—Fc: 2, 3.

Sweden; Sverige (Swedish): region of Scandinavia, smaller than modern nation — GHa: 12, 13.

Syria (classical), ash-Sha'm or Sūriyah (Arabic): region east of the Mediterranean — Lf: 1.

Szczekociny (Polish): town — H5b5: 3.

Szegedin (Hungarian): city, now Szeged — I1c4: 3.

Szent Imre Görgény (Hungarian), Gheorgheni or Gurghiu (Rumanian): town 100 miles NE of Hermannstadt (I5c5: 3).

Szentgyörgy: town — see Giurgiu.

Szöreny (Hungarian): district roughly equivalent to Severin (Icd: 3).

Tabriz; Tabrīz (Persian): city — N2e2: 1.

Tagliamento (Italian): river flowing into the Adriatic 12 miles east of Caorle — G3c4: 3.

Tagus (classical), Tajo (Spanish), Tejo (Portuguese), Tājuh (Arabic): river — C3e1: 2.

Tana (medieval), Tanaïs (classical), Azov (Russian): port — L5c3: 1.

Tannenberg (German), Stębark (Polish): village — I1b2: 3.

Taraklï-Yenije (Turkish): village — K1d5: 5.

Taranto (Italian): port — H3d5: 3.

Tarsus (classical, Turkish), Darsous (Armenian): city — K5e4: 1.

Tashkent; Binkāth or Tāshkand (Arabic): city — R5d4: 12, 13.

Taurus (classical), Toros Dağlarï (Turkish): mountain range — Le: 1.

Taus: town — see Domažlice.

Taygetus (classical), Pentedaktylon (medieval Greek), Taïyetos (modern Greek): mountain range — I3e3: 4.

Tbilisi; city — see Tiflis.

Tekke (Turkish): region of SW Anatolia, equivalent to classical Pamphylia — Je: 5.

Tell Bashir; Tall Bāshir (Arabic), Turbessel (medieval), Tilbeshar (Turkish): fortress — L3e4: 6.

Tembros or Tembria (Greek): village — K3e5: 8.

Temesvár (Hungarian): district of western Rumania — Ic: 10, 11.

Temesvár (Hungarian), Timişoara (Rumanian): town — I2c5: 3.

Tenduk (medieval), Tozan (Mongol): district of Mongolia — AAd: 13.

Tenedos; Tenedo (medieval Italian), Bozja-ada (Turkish): island — J1e1: 5.

Tenos; Tēnos (classical Greek), Tine (medieval Italian), İstendil (Turkish), Tínos (modern Greek): island — J1e3: 5.

Thabaria: town — see Tiberias.

Thasos; Thásos (modern Greek): island — I5d5: 3, 5.

Thebes; Thēbai (classical Greek), Estives (medieval), Thívai (modern Greek): city — I4e2: 3, 4.

Thérouanne (French): village 29 miles east of Boulogne (E2b5: 2).

Thessalonica (medieval), Therma (classical), Solun (Macedonian), Salonika (Italian), Thessaloníki or Saloníki (modern Greek): city, port — I3d5: 3, 4.

Thessaly; Thessalia (classical), Vlachia (medieval), Thessalía (modern Greek): region of northern Greece — Ie: 3, 4.

Thoisy-la-Berchère (French): village 30 miles WSW of Dijon (F1c3: 2).

Thrace; Thracia (Latin), Thrakē (classical Greek), Trakya (Turkish), Thráki (modern Greek): region south of Bulgaria — Jd: 1, 3, 5.

Thuringia; Thüringen (German): region of central Germany — Gb: 2, 3.

Tiberias (classical), Thabaria (medieval), Ṭabarīyah (Arabic), Tevarya (Israeli): town — L1f3: 1, 7.

Tiberias, Lake — see Galilee, Sea of.

Tibet: region north of India — UVWfg: 12, 13.

Tiflis; Tiflīs (Persian), Tbilisi (Georgian): city — M5d4: 1.

Tigris (classical), Dijlah (Arabic), Dijle (Turkish): river — N2f4: 1.

Timişoara: town—see Temesvár.

Timok (medieval), Saraj (Turkish), Zaječar (Serbian): town 30 miles wsw of Vidin (I3d2: 3).

Tine or Tínos: island—see Tenos.

Tirnovo; Ternovum (Latin), Tirnova (Turkish), Trnovo (Bulgarian): town—J1d2: 1, 3, 5.

Titel (Serbian): village 29 miles NNW of Belgrade (I1d1: 3).

Toledo (Spanish), Toletum (classical), Ṭulaiṭulah (Arabic): city—D1e1: 2.

Topolnitsa (Bulgarian): river flowing past Philippopolis (I5d3: 5) to Maritsa.

Tor (French): town, probably fictitious.

Toroge (medieval), Tour Rouge (French): unidentified place, probably in Spain.

Toron (medieval): fortress—L1f2: 7.

Tortosa; Antaradus (classical), Anṭarṭūs or Ṭarṭūs (Arabic): port—L1f1: 1, 6.

Tortosa (Spanish), Dertosa (classical), Ṭurṭūshah (Arabic): town—E1d5: 2.

Toul (French): town—F1c2: 2, 3.

Toulouse (French): city—E2d2: 2.

Tournai (French), Doornijk (Flemish): town—E4b5: 2.

Tours (French): town—E1c3: 2.

Trajan's Door; Kopula Derbend (Bulgarian): pass 40 miles SE of Sofia (I4d3: 3).

Transylvania; Siebenbürgen (German), Erdély (Hungarian), Ardeal (Rumanian): region SE of medieval Hungary—IJc: 1, 3.

Traù (medieval), Trogir (Serbian): port—G2d2: 3.

Trebizond; Trapezus (classical), Trapezunt (medieval), Trabzon (Turkish): city, port—L5d5: 1.

Trebizond: empire—Ld: 9.

Trepcha; Trepča (Serbian): mine 24 miles NNW of Kossovo (I2d3: 3).

Treviso (Italian): town 16 miles NNW of Venice (G3c5: 3).

Trier (German), Trèves (French): city—F2c1: 2, 3.

Trinacria: island—see Sicily.

Tripoli; Oea (classical), Ṭarābulus al-Gharb (Arabic): port—G4f3: 3.

Tripoli; Tripolis (classical), Ṭarābuluṣ (Arabic): city, port—L1f1: 1, 6, 7.

Trnovo: town—see Tirnovo.

Trogir: port—see Traù.

Troy; Ilium, Ilion, or Troia (classical): site of ancient city, at village of Hisarlik—J2e1: 3, 5.

Troyes (French): town—E5c2: 2.

Tunis; Tūnis (Arabic): city—G1e4: 2, 3.

Tunisia; Ifrīqiyah (Arabic): region of North Africa—FGef: 2, 3.

Turkey; Türkiye (Turkish): modern nation, comprising Anatolia and parts of Thrace, Armenia, and Kurdistan.

Turnu (Rumanian), Drubeta (classical): town, now Turnu-Severin—I3d1: 3.

Tuscany; Toscana (Italian): region of central Italy—Gd: 2, 3.

Tusculum (Latin): town, now abandoned, 12 miles SE of Rome (G3d4: 3).

Tyre; Tyrus (classical), Ṣūr (Arabic), Tyr (Israeli): port—L1f2: 1, 7.

Tzía: island—see Ceos.

Tzurulum: town—see Chorlu.

Tzympe (classical), Jinbi or Çimenlik (Turkish): port north of Gallipoli (J2d5: 5).

Ujlak (Croatian), Ilok (Turkish): village—H5c5: 3.

Ukraine; Ukraina (Russian): region of sw Russia—Kc: 1, 3.

Ulcinj: port—see Dulcigno.

Upper Egypt: region along the Nile south of Cairo—JKg: 1.

Urfa: city—see Edessa.

Urgench (Russian), Urgenç (Turkish), Gurganj (Persian), al-Jurgānīyah (Arabic), now Kunya Urgench: city, now abandoned for Novo Urgench—Q1d4: 13.

Üsküdar: port—see Scutari.

Valence (French): town — E5d1: 2.
Valencia (Spanish), Balansiyah (Arabic): city, port — D5e1: 2.
Valona: port — see Avlona.
Van, Lake; Van Gölü (Turkish) — M3e2: 1.
Varád; probably Varasd (Hungarian), Varaždin (Croatian), Warasdin (German): town 50 miles east of Cilly (H1c4: 3).
Vardar (medieval), Axius (classical): river — I3d4: 4.
Varna (medieval, Bulgarian): port, recently called Stalin — J3d2: 1, 3, 5.
Venice; Venezia (Italian): city, port — G3c5: 2, 3.
Verdun (French): town — F1c1: 2, 3.
Vermandois (French): district of eastern Picardy (Eb: 2).
Verona (Italian): city — G2c5: 2.
Verrai (medieval), Véroia (modern Greek), Fere or Kara-Ferye (Turkish): town — I3d5: 4.
Via Egnatia (medieval): road across Balkans from Durazzo to Constantinople — HIJd: 4, 5.
Vidin (Bulgarian): town — I3d2: 3.
Vienna; Wien (German): city — H2c2: 3.
Vienne (French): town — E5c5: 2.
Viennois (French): district of sw France, now called Dauphiné — Fc: 2.
Vilagos; Világos (Hungarian), Șiria (Rumanian): village 40 miles NNE of Temesvár (I2c5: 3).
Vilk (Serbian): district around the Lab valley.
Villach (German): town — G4c4: 2, 3.
Villefranche-sur-Mer (French), Villafranca (Italian): port — F3d2: 2.
Villehardouin (French): castle near Troyes (E5c2: 2).
Vistula; Wisƚa (Polish), Weichsel (German): river — H5b3: 3.
Viterbo (Italian): city — G3d3: 2, 3.
Vitry-en-Artois (French): village 25 miles south of Lille (E4b5: 2).
Vivar or Bivar or Viver (Spanish): town — D5e1: 2.
Vlachia: region — see Thessaly and Wallachia.
Volga (Russian), Itil (Tatar): river — N3c4: 1.
Vonitsa (medieval Greek), Bonditza (medieval), Vónitsa (modern Greek): town — I1e2: 3, 4.
Vosporo (medieval), Kerch (Russian): port — L2c5: 1.
Vostitsa (medieval), Aegium (Latin), Aíyion (modern Greek): town — I3e2: 4.
Vuchitrn; Vučitrn (Serbian): town 15 miles NNW of Kossovo (I2d3: 3).

Wales; Cambria (Latin), Cymru (Welsh): region west of England — Db: 2.
Wallachia; Vlachia (medieval), Valachia (Rumanian), Eflak (Turkish): region north of Bulgaria — IJd: 1, 3.
Warwick: town — D4b3: 2.
Wavrin (French): town 18 miles west of Tournai (E4b5: 2).
Weissenburg: town — see Alba Julia.
Wessex: region of southern England.
Wien: city — see Vienna.
Winchester: city — D4b4: 2.
Worms (German): town — F4c1: 2, 3.
Wrocƚaw: city — see Breslau.
Würzburg (German): city — F5c1: 2, 3.

Yangchow or Yang-chou (Chinese): city, port — BB5f3: 13.
Yantra (Bulgarian): river — J1d2: 5.
Yaytse; Jajce (Serbian): town — H3d1: 3.
Yemen; al-Yaman (Arabic: the right-hand): region of sw Arabia — MNi: 12, 13.

Yenishehir; Yenişehir (Turkish): town, now Çankaya, 1 mile south of Ankara (K3e1: 3).
Ypres (French), Ieper (Flemish): town 17 miles NNW of Lille (E4b5: 2).

Zabīd (Arabic): town—M4j1: 12.
Zaitun (medieval), Tsinkiang or Chin-chiang (Chinese): port—BB4h1: 12, 13.
Zaječar: town—see Timok.
Zante (Italian), Zacynthus (Latin), Zákinthos (modern Greek): island—I1e3: 3, 4.
Zara (Italian), Jadera (classical), Zadar (Croatian): port—H1d1: 3.
Zaragoza: city—see Saragossa.
Zea: island—see Ceos.
Zeitounion; Lamia (classical), Gitonis or Citó (medieval), Zitouni (medieval Greek),
    Lamía (modern Greek): town—I3e2: 3, 4.
Zichne (Greek): town—I4d4: 4, 5.
Zlatitsa (Bulgarian): pass 3 miles north of Zlatitsa.
Zlatitsa (Bulgarian): town 42 miles east of Sofia (I4d3: 3).
Znojmo (Czech), Znaim (German): town—H2c2: 3.
Zonklon: port—see Navarino.
Zvornik (Serbian): town—H5d1: 3.

SELECT BIBLIOGRAPHY
OF THE CRUSADES

compiled by Hans Eberhard Mayer
and Joyce McLellan
edited by Harry W. Hazard

Contents

Introductory Note

A bibliographer is a prisoner of circumstances. This applies to many aspects of his activities and starts with completeness. I did not try to achieve it in this bibliography because it would have meant to duplicate, and more than duplicate, my 1960 *Bibliographie zur Geschichte der Kreuzzüge,* which would not have served any practical purpose, even if space limitations had permitted. On the other hand, while reference must be made to my earlier volume, this bibliography had to be somewhat more comprehensive in scope because the chapters of the six volumes give much more consideration to North Africa, Spain, Prussia, and Bohemia than I did there. Apart from including sections on the wars in these countries, I have attempted to make the bibliography more comprehensive for the more modern publications. In other words, from the older literature on the subject I have selected only those books and studies which seem to me to be either standard works in the field or, at least, of considerable importance to it. Another criterion for inclusion has been that works should be included which would lead the researcher easily to much of the previous literature concerning this or that special subject within the general topic. Thus, a book such as Gustave Schlumberger et al., *Sigillographie de l'Orient latin* (1943), made it possible to exclude almost everything written on the seals of the Latin east before that year. I know, however, that my criteria for the inclusion of less recent works of research are to some extent arbitrary; I must again plead as an excuse the restrictions imposed by considerations of space, which no editor can allow without limits, as well as the fact that this general bibliography had to reflect to some extent what individual authors had cited as source material and scholarly literature in their chapters. If they felt that such titles merited citation, I was to a certain extent bound, not that I would have disagreed with them very often, but this meant that I had to make sacrifices in other places where I was completely on my own.

I have made two previous bibliographical efforts in the field of the crusades, and, for literature up to about the year of publication of each, I should like to refer the reader to them for more detailed information: (1) Hans E. Mayer, *Bibliographie zur Geschichte der Kreuzzüge* (Hanover, 1960), containing publications approximately up to 1958, and continued, as a *bibliographie raisonnée,* by (2) Hans E. Mayer, "Literaturbericht über die Geschichte der Kreuzzüge: Veröffentlichungen 1958–1967," *Historische Zeitschrift:* Sonderheft 3 (1969), pp. 641–731. I had intended to provide the next installment after another ten years had elapsed. Before they had done so I was asked by the general editor, Dr. Kenneth M. Setton, to join in this international venture, and I gladly agreed to his request. This bibliography, then, also constitutes the second continuation of my *Bibliographie* of 1960, although the new is mixed with a generous selection of the old. With regard to significant new publications since 1967, I have attempted to list them through 1982 with sundry (but not systematically collected) additions of more recent publications. I hope that the bibliographical material put together here will be of value to students of the field.

There are a number of other and more specific dilemmas of a bibliographer with which everyone who has done this kind of work is familiar, and I shall not try to give an exhaustive list. While middle names of authors are normally given only as initials, every effort has been made to extend the first given names of authors who use only their initials. It is English scholars in particular who seem to be elusive on this point, presenting me with a number of "unbreakable codes"; I apologize for this slight inconsistency and inconvenience. Another problem was that of reprints and translations: I have listed them where they came to my knowledge, but no systematic effort has been made to be comprehensive in this respect because both reprints and translations are very hard for the bibliographer to trace, as they are not reported broadly enough in the review sections of scholarly journals or in periodic bibliographies.

A special case is that of the Collected Studies series of Variorum Reprints in London. Thanks to the firm's catalogues, issued twice a year, they are quite easy to track down, and a good number of them are pertinent to this bibliography. They gave me an unexpected opportunity to alleviate the space problem. Generally speaking, in the cases either of such individual collected studies, be they published by Variorum or another publishing house, or of collective volumes of papers, I have included only the volume as a whole, not the individual papers. But no rule should be followed without exceptions, so I have dispensed with this principle in the cases of some authors whose work is particularly important to the subject of the crusades. The most notable exceptions are Claude Cahen, Joshua Prawer, Jean Richard, and Kenneth M. Setton. If in their cases only the volumes of collected studies had been listed, the bibliography would not have shown the extent of their outstanding contributions to the field.

I shall only mention but not discuss the problem of transliteration from oriental languages (and also from Slavonic ones with a Cyrillic alphabet or from Greek). Every bibliographer knows that there is simply no solution to this problem which would yield consistency. The *History of the Crusades* does have a standard transliteration system for Arabic, etc., but this was useless for me if I was dealing with a book where Arabic words had already been transliterated on the title page according to the French or German or another fashion. I could no longer change this, but I trust that orientalists will understand this predicament. This leads me to another problem which is not oriental in character at all, but somewhat irritating. Some names of authors appear in their publications in various forms, which is not surprising where transliteration enters the picture once more. I enter them under a standardized form, with specific variants in parentheses, as "Ostrogorski (here, Ostrogorsky)" or "Hopf, Carl (here, Charles)".

The titles of sources and of certain specialized categories are arranged according to subject matter. This is not always easy because some titles could as easily be classified in one section as in another. But I had to make a choice, as I could not list any titles twice. I have put such titles into those sections to which they seemed to be most pertinent. The system of arrangement by subject matter is maintained from the big sections to the small subsections and the development of the system can easily be followed in the headings of sections and subsections. The latter are sufficiently small to abandon, within each subsection, the arrangement by subject matter in favor of an alphabetical arrangement which will impose no hardships on the reader. However, it seemed to be more appropriate to list the papal documents by successive pontificates rather than alphabetically by the names either of editors or of popes.

Titles of secondary works are listed alphabetically by author (or by editor if there is no author listed), and chronologically for each author; all are cross-indexed by primary subject matter. Titles without author or editor named are listed at the end, followed by selective cross-indexes of subjects and of co-authors, editors, and translators. A list of abbreviations for periodicals or series occurring frequently in this bibliography will be found appended to this introductory note. Dr. McLellan and I supplied almost all the bibliographical materials and we are responsible for any errors contained therein. Dr. Hazard is responsible for the way these materials are here arranged for presentation as well as for several additional entries (as is Dr. Norman Zacour) and for the indexes. He is also responsible for the editorial decision, based on the *Chicago Manual of Style* and followed throughout all six volumes of this work, to capitalize in French, Italian, and Spanish titles the second word of a title, if the first word is a definite or an indefinite article.

It would have been impossible for me to compile this bibliography if I had not had the help of Dr. Joyce McLellan. She checked and rechecked the titles to be included within the larger framework of preparing my old *Bibliographie* for a possible new edition. Her accuracy was as much to be admired as her persistence. She justly appears as co-author of this bibliography, and my sincerest thanks must be extended to her here, all the more so since I have completely lost track of her whereabouts. My thanks are also due to the Fritz Thyssen Stiftung for having provided the funds for Dr. McLellan to work with me. Our joint thanks are due to the staff of the Bayerische Staatsbibliothek in Munich, which never failed to respond to our frequent requests, many of which were not easy to accommodate.

Hans E. Mayer

Abbreviations Used in Bibliography

Abh. Gött.	Abhandlungen der philologisch-historischen Klasse der Akademie (earlier, Gesellschaft) der Wissenschaften zu Göttingen
ABS Athens	*Annual of the British School at Athens*
AF Praed.	*Archivum Fratrum Praedicatorum*
Amer. HR	*American Historical Review*
AO Latin	*Archives de l'Orient latin*
AOSMM	*Annales de l'ordre souverain militaire de Malte*
Arch. Ven.	*Archivio veneto*
BC Hell.	*Bulletin de correspondance hellénique*
BÉ Char.	*Bibliothèque de l'École des chartes*
B Éc. HÉ	Bibliothèque de l'École des hautes-études
BÉFAR	Bibliotheque des Écoles françaises d'Athènes et de Rome
Bibl. AH	Bibliothèque archéologique et historique
BTSOF	Biblioteca bio-bibliografica della Terra Santa e dell' Oriente francescano
Byz. F	*Byzantinische Forschungen*
Byz. Z	*Byzantinische Zeitschrift*
Cah. Civ. Méd.	*Cahiers de civilisation médiévale*
Cath. HR	*Catholic Historical Review*
CD inédits	Collection des documents inédits sur l'histoire de la France
Col. URC	Columbia University Records of Civilization: Sources and Studies
CRAIBL	*Comptes-rendus des séances de l'Académie des inscriptions et belles-lettres*
CSH Byz.	Corpus scriptorum historiae Byzantinae
D Oaks P	*Dumbarton Oaks Papers*
DRH Cr.	Documents relatifs à l'histoire des croisades
Eng. HR	*English Historical Review*
Fonti SI	Fonti per la storia d'Italia
Fonti SV	Fonti per la storia di Venezia
Forsch. DG	*Forschungen zur deutschen Geschichte*
Gött. Nach.	*Nachrichten der Akademie (earlier, Gesellschaft) der Wissenschaften zu Göttingen; I, Philologisch-historische Klasse*
Hist. Stud., ed. Ebering	Historische Studien, ed. Emil Ebering
Hist. Z	*Historische Zeitschrift*
HJ Görres.	*Historisches Jahrbuch der Görresgesellschaft*
H of C	*A History of the Crusades* (the present work; see Setton 1955)
Isr. Expl. J	*Israel Exploration Journal*
JA	*Journal asiatique*
JESHO	*Journal of the Economic and Social History of the Orient*
J Med. H	*Journal of Medieval History*
MAIBL	*Mémoires de l'Institut (national) de France, Académie des inscriptions et belles-lettres*
Med. AA	Medieval (earlier, Mediaeval) Academy of America
MÉF Rome	*Mélanges d'archéologie et d'histoire de l'École française de Rome*

MGH	Monumenta Germaniae historica
SS.	Scriptores
SS. rer. Germ.	Scriptores rerum Germanicarum
Migne, *PG*	Migne, Jacques P., ed., *Patrologiae cursus completus: Series Graeco-Latina*
Migne, *PL*	Migne, Jacques P., ed., *Patrologiae cursus completus: Series Latina*
MIÖG	*Mitteilungen des Instituts für österreichische Geschichtsforschung*
MS Antiq. F	*Mémoires de la Société nationale des antiquaires de France*
O Chr. P	*Orientalia christiana periodica*
Outremer	(see Kedar 1982-2)
Pal. DVHL	Palästinahefte des deutschen Vereins vom Heiligen Lande
PC, Fontes	Fontes pontificiae commissionis ad redigendum Codicem iuris canonici orientalis
PPTS	Palestine Pilgrims' Text Society
QDA Pal.	*Quarterly of the Department of Antiquities in Palestine*
QFIAB	*Quellen und Forschungen aus italienischen Archiven und Bibliotheken*
RÉ Byz.	*Revue des études byzantines*
Rev. hist.	*Revue historique*
Rev. QH	*Revue des questions historiques*
RHC,	*Recueil des historiens des croisades:*
Arm.	*Historiens arméniens*
Lois	*Lois*
Occ.	*Historiens occidentaux*
Or.	*Historiens orientaux*
RH Droit FÉ	*Revue historique de droit français et étranger*
RHL Lang.	*Revue historique et littéraire de Languedoc*
RHSEE	*Revue historique de sud-est européen*
R Ital. SS.	Rerum Italicarum scriptores
RO Chr.	*Revue de l'Orient chrétien*
RO Latin	*Revue de l'Orient latin*
Rolls Series	Rerum Britannicarum medii aevi scriptores: The Chronicles and Memorials of Great Britain and Ireland during the Middle Ages
SB Wien	*Sitzungsberichte der philosophisch-historischen Klasse der Österreichischen* (earlier, *Kaiserlichen*) *Akademie der Wissenschaften*
SOL, *SG*	Société de l'Orient latin: *Série géographique*
SOL, *SH*	Société de l'Orient latin: *Série historique*
Studium BF	Pubblicazioni dello Studium Biblicum Franciscanum
Varior. Repr., CS	Variorum Reprints: Collected Studies
VSWG	*Vierteljahrschrift für Sozial- und Wirtschaftsgeschichte*
ZDPV	*Zeitschrift des deutschen Palästinavereins*
Z Kirch.	*Zeitschrift für Kirchengeschichte*

Bibliography – General Works

BIBLIOGRAPHIES

A1. Argenti, Philip P., *Bibliography of Chios from Classical Times to 1936* (Oxford, 1940).

A2. Atiya, Aziz S., *The Crusade: Historiography and Bibliography* (Bloomington, Ind., 1962).

A3. Bautier, Robert H., "Sources pour l'histoire du commerce maritime en Méditerranée du XIIe au XVe siècle," in *Les Sources de l'histoire maritime en Europe, du moyen âge au XVIIIe siècle: Actes du Quatrième colloque international d'histoire maritime, tenu à Paris du 20 au 23 mai 1959,* ed. Michel Mollat et al. (Bibliothèque générale de l'École pratique des hautes-études, VIe section; Paris, 1962), pp. 137-179.

A4. Beatty, Alfred C., *The A. Chester Beatty Library: a Catalogue of the Armenian Manuscripts, with an introduction by Sirarpie Der Nersessian* (2 vols., Dublin, 1959).

A5. Cobham, Claude D., *An Attempt at a Bibliography of Cyprus,* new ed. by George E. Jeffery (Nicosia, 1929).

A6. Croussouloudis, Nicolas, "Bibliographie de l'église latine de Chio," Βαλκανικὴ Βιβλιογραφία, V (Salonica, 1976, published 1979), 1-196.

A7. Dessubré, M., *Bibliographie de l'ordre des Templiers (imprimés et manuscrits)* (Bibliothèque des initiations modernes; Nieuwkoop, 1966).

A8. Fumagalli, Giuseppe, *Bibliografia Rodia* (Biblioteca di bibliografia italiana, 14; Florence, 1937).

A9. Haaf, Rudolf ten, *Kurze Bibliographie zur Geschichte des Deutschen Ordens 1198-1561* (Göttingen, 1949).

A10. Hellwald, Ferdinand de, *Bibliographie méthodique de l'ordre souverain de St.-Jean de Jérusalem* (Rome, 1885).

A11. Jouhate, J., "La Croisade contre les Albigeois: étude bibliographique," *Revue historique, scientifique et littéraire de Département du Tarn,* 2-XXIII (1906), 101-121.

A12. Lampe, Karl H., *Bibliographie des Deutschen Ordens bis 1959* (Quellen und Studien zur Geschichte des Deutschen Ordens, 3; Bonn and Godesberg, 1975).

A13. Mayer, Hans E., *Bibliographie zur Geschichte der Kreuzzüge* (2nd unrevised ed., Hanover, 1965).

A14. Mayer, Hans E., "Literaturbericht über die Geschichte der Kreuzzüge: Veröffentlichungen 1958-1967," *Hist. Z,* Sonderheft 3 (Munich, 1969), pp. 641-731.

A15. Mizzi, Giuseppe (here, Joseph), "A Bibliography of the Order of St. John of Jerusalem (1925-1969)," *The Order of St. John in Malta: XIII Council of Europe Exhibition* (Malta, 1970), pp. 108-204.

A16. Neu, Heinrich, *Bibliographie des Templer-Ordens, 1927-1965, mit Ergänzungen zur Bibliographie von M. Dessubré* (Bonn, 1965).

A17. Pearson, James D., *Index Islamicus 1906-1955* (Cambridge, Eng., 1958); five supplements (Cambridge, Eng., and London, 1962-1983).

A18. Pillet, Alfred, *Bibliographie der Troubadours,* supplemented, continued, and ed. by Henry Carstens (Schriften der Königsberger Gelehrten Gesellschaft, Sonderreihe 3; Halle, 1933).

A19. Röhricht, Reinhold, *Bibliotheca geographica Palaestinae: Chronologisches Ver-zeichnis der von 333 bis 1878 verfassten Literatur über das Heilige Land mit dem Versuch einer Kartographie* (Berlin, 1890), repr. with supplements by David H.K. Amiran (Jerusalem, 1963).

A20. Rossi, Ettore, *Aggiunta alla Bibliographie méthodique de l'ordre souverain de St.-Jean de Jérusalem di Ferdinand de Hellwald* (Rome, 1924).

A21. Seibt, Ferdinand, *Bohemica: Probleme und Literatur seit 1945* (*Hist. Z,* Bib-liographisches Sonderheft 4; Munich, 1970).

A22. Thomsen, Peter, *Die Palästina-Literatur: eine internationale Bibliographie in systematischer Ordnung:* vol. 1, *Systematische Bibliographie der Palästina-Literatur* (7 vols., for 1895–1945, and vol. A, for 1878–1894; Leipzig and Berlin, 1908–1972).

A23. — *Harvard University, Library. Crusades: Classification Schedule, Classified Listing by Call Numbers, Alphabetical Listing by Author or Title, Chrono-logical Listing* (Widener Library shelflist, vol. 1; Cambridge, Mass., 1965).

RESEARCH AIDS

B1. Amiran, David H.K., et al., eds., *Atlas of Israel: Cartography, Physical Geo-graphy, Human and Economic Geography, History* (Jerusalem and Amster-dam, 1970).

B2. Baudrillart, Alfred, et al., eds., *Dictionnaire d'histoire et de géographie ecclési-astiques* (Paris, 1912–).

B3. Brice, William C., ed., *An Historical Atlas of Islam* (Leyden, 1981).

B4. Buchberger, Michael, *Lexikon für Theologie und Kirche,* rev. ed. by Josef Hofer and Karl Rahner (10 vols. and *Register,* Freiburg im Breisgau, 1957–1967).

B5. Dulaurier, Édouard F., *Recherches sur la chronologie arménienne technique et historique:* vol. 1, *Chronologie technique* (Bibliothèque historique armé-nienne, 1; Paris, 1859).

B6. Edler, Florence, *Glossary of Mediaeval Terms of Business, Italian Series, 1200–1600* (Cambridge, Mass., 1934).

B7. Eubel, Conrad, *Hierarchia catholica medii aevi, sive Summorum pontificum, S.R.E. cardinalium, ecclesiarum antistitum series, ab anno 1198 usque ad annum 1431 perducta e documentis tabularii praesertim Vaticani collecta, digesta, edita* (2nd ed., vols. 1, 2, Münster, 1913–1914).

B8. Fliche, Augustin, et al., eds., *Histoire de l'église depuis les origines jusqu'à nos jours* (Paris, 1934–).

B9. Freeman-Grenville, Greville S. P., *The Muslim and Christian Calendars, being Tables for the Conversion of Muslim and Christian Dates from the Hijra to the Year A.D. 2000* (London and New York, 1963).

B10. Gams, Pius B., *Series episcoporum ecclesiae catholicae* (2 vols., Regensburg, 1873–1886).

B11. Hazard, Harry W., *Atlas of Islamic History,* 3rd rev. ed. with maps executed by Hereward Lester Cooke jr. and J. M. Smiley (Princeton Oriental Studies, 12; Princeton, 1954).

B12. Johns, Cedric N., *Palestine of the Crusades: a Map of the Country . . . with Historical Introduction and Gazetteer* (Survey of Palestine, 3rd ed., Jaffa, 1946).

B13. Le Quien, Michel, *Oriens christianus, in quatuor patriarchatus digestus; quo exhibentur ecclesiae, patriarchae, caeterique praesules totius Orientis* (3 vols., Paris, 1740).

B14. Naz, Raoul, et al., eds., *Dictionnaire de droit canonique, avec un sommaire de l'histoire et des institutions et de l'état actuel de la discipline* (7 vols., Paris 1935–1965).

B15. Prawer, Joshua, and Meron Benvenisti, "Palestine under the Crusaders" (map with commentary and bibliography), in *Atlas of Israel* (Jerusalem and Amsterdam, 1970), section IX, "History", ed. Michael Avi-Yonah, no. 10; larger version published separately by the Survey of Israel as *The Crusader Kingdom of Jerusalem* (1972).

B16. Wüstenfeld, Heinrich F., and Eduard Mahler, *Vergleichungs-Tabellen zur muslimischen und iranischen Zeitrechnung mit Tafeln zur Umrechnung orient-christlicher Ären;* 3rd rev. ed. of *Vergleichungs-Tabellen der mohammedanischen und christlichen Zeitrechnung* unter Mitarbeit von Joachim Mayr, newly ed. by Bertold Spuler (Mainz and Wiesbaden, 1961).

B17. Zambaur, Eduard von (here, de), *Manuel de généalogie et de chronologie pour l'histoire de l'Islam* (Hanover, 1927).

B18. — *The Encyclopaedia of Islam,* new ed., prepared by a number of leading Orientalists (Leyden, 1960–   ); supp., fasc. 1 ff. (Leyden, 1980–   ); index to vols. 1–3 (Leyden, 1979).

HISTORIOGRAPHY

C1. Beddie, James S., "Some Notices of Books in the East during the Crusades," *Speculum,* VIII (1933), 240–242.

C2. Brincken, Anna D. von den, *Die "Nationes Christianorum orientalium" im Verständnis der lateinischen Historiographie von der Mitte des 12. bis in die zweite Hälfte des 14. Jahrhunderts* (Kölner historische Abhandlungen, 22; Cologne and Vienna, 1973).

C3. Brundage, James A., "Recent Crusade Historiography: Some Observations and Suggestions," *Cath. HR,* XLIX (1964), 493–507.

C4. Dölger, Franz, and Alfons M. Schneider, *Byzanz* (Wissenschaftliche Forschungsberichte, Geisteswissenschaftliche Reihe 5; Berne, 1952).

C5. Gabrieli, Francesco, *Arab Historians of the Crusades,* tr. E. J. Costello (London, 1984).

C6. Krey, August C., "A Neglected Passage in the Gesta and its Bearing on the Literature of the First Crusade," in *The Crusades and Other Historical Essays Presented to Dana C. Munro,* ed. Louis J. Paetow (New York, 1928), pp. 57–78.

C7. LaMonte, John L., "Some Problems in Crusading Historiography," *Speculum,* XV (1940), 57–75.

C8. Lewis, Bernard, "The Sources for the History of the Syrian Assassins," *Speculum,* XXVII (1952), 475–489.

C9. Lewis, Bernard, and Peter M. Holt, eds., *Historians of the Middle East* (London and New York, 1962).

C10. Luttrell, Anthony, "Greek Histories Translated and Compiled for Juan Fernández de Heredia, Master of Rhodes, 1377–1396," *Speculum,* XXXV (1960), 401–407.

C11. Luttrell, Anthony, "The Hospitallers' Historical Activities," *AOSMM*, XXIV (1966), 126–129; XXV (1967), 6 unnumbered pages; XXVI (1968), 13 unnumbered pages.

C12. Mayer, Hans E., "America and the Crusades," *Proceedings of the American Philosophical Society*, CXXV (1981), 38–45.

C13. Moresco, Mattia, and Gian Piero Bognetti, *Per l'edizione dei notai liguri del secolo XII* (Genoa, 1938).

C14. Morgan, David O., ed., *Medieval Historical Writing in the Christian and Islamic Worlds* (London, 1982).

C15. Salibi, Kamal S., *Maronite Historians of Mediaeval Lebanon* (American University of Beirut: Publications of the Faculty of Arts and Sciences, Oriental Series, 34; Beirut, 1959).

C16. Sauvaget, Jean, *Introduction à l'histoire de l'Orient musulman; éléments de bibliographie,* reëd. by Claude Cahen (Initiation à l'Islam, 1; Paris, 1961).

C17. Waeger, Gerhart, *Gottfried von Bouillon in der Historiographie* (Geist und Werk der Zeiten, 18; Zurich, 1969).

HISTORIOGRAPHY — INDIVIDUAL AUTHORS

C18. Andrea, Alfred J., "Walter, Archdeacon of London, and the *Historia occidentalis* of Jacques de Vitry," *Church History,* L (1981), 141–151.

C19. Bromiley, Geoffrey W., "Philip of Novara's Account of the War between Frederick II of Hohenstaufen and the Ibelins," *J Med. H,* III (1977), 325–337.

C20. Brunel, Clovis, "David d'Ashby, auteur méconnu des 'Faits des Tartares'," *Romania,* LXXIX (1958), 39–46.

C21. Buckler, Georgina, *Anna Comnena* (Oxford, 1929).

C22. Buridant, Claude, ed., *La Traduction de l'"Histoire orientalis" de Jacques de Vitry* (Bibliotheque française et romane, sér. B: Éditions critiques de textes, 19; Paris, 1986).

C23. Cannuyer, C., "La Date de rédaction de l'Historia orientalis de Jacques de Vitry (1160/70–1240), évêque d'Acre," *Revue d'histoire ecclésiastique,* LXXVIII (1983), 65–72.

C24. Dondaine, Antoine, "Ricoldiana: notes sur les oeuvres de Ricoldo da Montecroce," *AF Praed.,* XXXVII (1967), 119–179.

C25. Faral, Edmond, "Geoffroy de Villehardouin: la question de sa sincérité," *Rev. hist.,* CLXXVII (1936), 530–582.

C26. Friedman, Lionel J., *Text and Iconography for Joinville's Credo* (Med. AA, Publ. 68; Cambridge, Mass., 1958).

C27. Funk, Philipp, *Jakob von Vitry: Leben und Werke* (Beiträge zur Kulturgeschichte des Mittelalters und der Renaissance, 3; Leipzig and Berlin, 1909).

C28. Giese, Wolfgang, "Asienkunde für den kreuzfahrenden Westen: die 'Flos historiarum terre Orientis' des Hayto von Gorhigos (O. Praem.) aus dem Jahre 1307," in *Secundum regulam vivere: Festschrift für P. Norbert Backmund,* ed. Gert Melville (Windberg, 1978), pp. 245–264.

C29. Guzman, Gregory G., "Simon of St.-Quentin and the Dominican Mission of the Mongol Baiju: a Reappraisal," *Speculum,* XLVI (1971), 232–249.

C30. Guzman, Gregory G., "Simon of Saint-Quentin as Historian of the Mongols and Seljuk Turks," *Mediaevalia et humanistica,* n.s., III (1972), 155–178.

C31. Guzman, Gregory G., "The Encyclopedist Vincent of Beauvais and his Mongol Extracts from John of Plano Carpini and Simon of St.-Quentin," *Speculum,* XLIX (1974), 287–307.

C32. Kedar, Benjamin Z., "Gerard of Nazareth, a Neglected Twelfth Century Writer in the Latin East: a Contribution to the Intellectual and Monastic History of the Crusader States," *D Oaks P,* XXXVII (1983), 55–77.

C33. Knoch, Peter, *Studien zu Albert von Aachen: der erste Kreuzzug in der deutschen Chronistik* (Stuttgarter Beiträge zur Geschichte und Politik, 1; Stuttgart, 1966).

C34. Kugler, Bernhard, *Albert von Aachen* (Stuttgart, 1885).

C35. Laiou, Angeliki E., "Marino Sanudo Torsello, Byzantium and the Turks," *Speculum,* XLV (1970), 374–392.

C36. Morgan, Margaret R., *The Chronicle of Ernoul and the Continuations of William of Tyre* (Oxford Historical Monographs; London, 1973).

C37. Morgan, Margaret R., *La Continuation de Guillaume de Tyr (1184–1197)* (DRH Cr., 14; Paris, 1982).

C38. Morgan, Margaret R., "The Rothelin Continuation of William of Tyre," in *Outremer* (1982), pp. 244–257.

C39. Morris, Colin, "Geoffroy de Villehardouin and the Conquest of Constantinople," *History,* LIII (1968), 24–34.

C40. Oehler, Hans, "Studien zu den Gesta Francorum," *Mittellateinisches Jahrbuch,* VI (1970), 58–97.

C41. Rousset, Paul, "Rutebeuf poète de la croisade," *Revue d'histoire ecclésiastique suisse,* LX (1960), 103–111.

C42. Swietek, Francis R., "Gunther of Pairis and the Historia Constantinopolitana," *Speculum,* LIII (1978), 49–79.

HISTORIOGRAPHY – WILLIAM OF TYRE

C43. Crawford, Robert W., "William of Tyre and the Maronites," *Speculum,* XXX (1955), 222–228.

C44. Davis, Ralph H.C., "William of Tyre," in *Relations between East and West in the Middle Ages,* ed. Derek Baker (Edinburgh, 1973), pp. 64–75.

C45. Desobry, [l'abbé], "L'Histoire des croisades de Guillaume de Tyr et ses continuateurs: Manuscrit 843 de la Bibliothèque municipale d'Amiens," *Bulletin trimestriel de la Société des antiquaires de Picardie,* LIII (1969/1970), 220–235.

C46. Edbury, Peter W., and John G. Rowe, "William of Tyre and the Patriarchal Election of 1180," *Eng. HR,* XCIII (1978), 1–25.

C47. Edbury, Peter W., and John G. Rowe, *William of Tyre, Historian of the Latin East* (Cambridge Studies in Medieval Life and Thought, 4th ser., no. 8; Cambridge, Eng., 1988).

C48. Folda, Jaroslav, "Manuscripts of the History of Outremer by William of Tyre: a Handlist," *Scriptorium,* XXVII (1973), 90–95.

C49. Hiestand, Rudolf, "Zum Leben und zur Laufbahn Wilhelms von Tyrus," *Deutsches Archiv,* XXXIV (1978), 345–380.

C50. Huygens, Robert B.C., "Guillaume de Tyr étudiant: un chapître (XIX, 12) de son 'Histoire' retrouvé," *Latomus,* XXI (1962), 811–829.

C51. Huygens, Robert B.C., "La Tradition manuscrite de Guillaume de Tyr," *Studi medievali,* 3-V (1964), 281–373.

C52. Huygens, Robert B.C., "Pontigny et l'Histoire de Guillaume de Tyr," *Latomus,* XXV (1966), 139–142.

C53. Huygens, Robert B.C., "Editing William of Tyre," *Sacris erudiri,* XXVII (1984), 461–473.

C54. Krey, August C., "William of Tyre, the Making of an Historian in the Middle Ages," *Speculum,* XVI (1941), 149–166.

C55. Lacroix, Benoît, "Guillaume de Tyr: unité et diversité dans la tradition latine," *Études d'histoire littéraire et doctrinale,* 4-XIX (1968), 201–215.

C56. Mayer, Hans E., "Zum Tode Wilhelms von Tyrus," *Archiv für Diplomatik,* V–VI (1959–1960), 182–201.

C57. Schwinges, Rainer C., *Kreuzzugsideologie und Toleranz: Studien zu Wilhelm von Tyrus* (Monographien zur Geschichte des Mittelalters, 15; Stuttgart, 1977).

C58. Vessey, David W.T.C., "William of Tyre and the Art of Historiography," *Mediaeval Studies,* XXXV (1973), 433–455.

C59. Vessey, David W.T.C., "William of Tyre: Apology and Apocalypse," *Hommages à André Boutémy,* ed. Guy Cambier (Collection Latomus, 145; Brussels, 1976), pp. 390–403.

HISTORICAL GEOGRAPHY AND TOPOGRAPHY

D1. Abel, Félix M., "Naplouse, essai de topographie," *Revue biblique,* XXXII (1923), 120–132.

D2. Abel, Félix M., *Géographie de la Palestine* (Études bibliques; 2 vols., Paris, 1933, 1938).

D3. Alishan, Leound (here, Léonce) M., *Sissouan, ou l'Arméno-Cilicie: description géographique et historique . . .* (Venice, 1899).

D4. Baedeker, Karl, *Grèce: manuel du voyageur* (Leipzig, 1910).

D5. Baedeker, Karl, *Palestine et Syrie: manuel du voyageur,* 4th ed. (Leipzig, 1912).

D6. Baldi, Donato, ed., *Enchiridion locorum sanctorum,* 2nd ed. (Jerusalem, 1955).

D7. Berchem, Max van, and Edmond Fatio, *Voyage en Syrie* (Mémoires publiés par les membres de l'Institut français d'archéologie du Caire, vols. 37–38; 2 vols., text and plates, Cairo, 1914–1915).

D8. Beyer, Gustav, "Das Gebiet der Kreuzfahrerherrschaft Caesarea in Palästina siedlungs- und territorialgeschichtlich untersucht," *ZDPV,* LIX (1936), 1–91.

D9. Beyer, Gustav, "Neapolis (nāblus) und sein Gebiet in der Kreuzfahrerzeit: eine topographische und historisch-geographische Studie," *ZDPV,* LXIII (1940), 155–209.

D10. Beyer, Gustav, "Die Kreuzfahrergebiete von Jerusalem und S. Abraham (Hebron)," *ZDPV,* LXV (1942), 165–211.

D11. Beyer, Gustav, "Die Kreuzfahrergebiete Akko und Galilaea," *ZDPV,* LXVII (1944–1945), 183–260.

D12. Beyer, Gustav, "Die Kreuzfahrergebiete Südwestpalästinas," *Beiträge zur biblischen Landes- und Altertumskunde (hervorgegangen aus der ZDPV),* LXVII (1946–1951), 148–192, 249–281.

D13. Beyer, Gustav, "Civitas Ficuum," *ZDPV,* LXIX (1953), 75–85, with an addition by Albrecht Alt, *ibid.,* 85–87.

D14. Combe, Étienne, *Alexandrie musulmane: notes de topographie et d'histoire* (Cairo, 1933).

D15. Conder, Claude R., and Horatio H. Kitchener, eds., *Map of Western Palestine* (Palestine Exploration Fund, Survey of Western Palestine, 26 sheets; London, 1880); accompanying volumes: 1. Claude R. Conder and Horatio H. Kitchener, *The Survey of Western Palestine: Memoirs of the Topography, Orography, Hydrography and Archaeology,* ed. with additions by E. H. Palmer (3 vols., London, 1881–1883); 2. Charles Warren and Claude R. Conder, *The Survey of Western Palestine: Jerusalem* (London, 1884); 3. Edward H. Palmer, *The Survey of Western Palestine: Arabic and English Name Lists* (London, 1881); 4. Trelawney Saunders, *An Introduction to the Survey of Western Palestine: its Waterways, Plains and Highlands* (London, 1881); 5. Edward Hull, *The Survey of Western Palestine: Memoir on the Geology and Geography of Arabia Petraea, Palestine and Adjoining Districts* (London, 1886); 6. Henry B. Tristram, *The Survey of Western Palestine: the Fauna and Flora of Palestine* (London, 1884); 7. Claude R. Conder, *Mediaeval Topography of Palestine: the Survey of Western Palestine; Special Papers on Topography, Archaeology, Manners and Customs,* ed. Charles Wilson (London, 1881); 8. Henry C. Stewardson, *The Survey of Western Palestine: a General Index* (London, 1888).

D16. Conder, Claude R., *The Survey of Eastern Palestine: Memoirs of the Topography, Orography, Hydrography, Archaeology etc.:* I, *The 'Adwân Country* (London, 1889).

D17. Dussaud, René, *Topographie historique de la Syrie antique et médiévale* (Bibl. AH, 4; Paris, 1927).

D18. Dussaud, René, Paul Deschamps, and Henri Seyrig, *La Syrie antique et médiévale illustrée* (Bibl. AH, 17; Paris, 1931).

D19. Favreau, Marie L., "Die Kreuzfahrerherrschaft 'Scandalion' (Iskanderûne)," *ZDPV,* XCIII (1977), 12–29.

D20. Favreau-Lilie, Marie L., "Landesausbau und Burg während der Kreuzfahrerzeit: Safad in Obergalilaea," *ZDPV,* XCVI (1980), 67–87.

D21. Finbert, Elian J., *Les Guides bleus: Israel* (Paris, 1961).

D22. Fischer, Hans, "Geschichte der Kartographie von Palästina," *ZDPV,* LXII (1939), 169–189; LXIII (1940), 1–111.

D23. Fischer, Wolfdietrich, and Jürgen Schneider, eds., *Das Heilige Land im Mittelalter: Begegnungsraum zwischen Orient und Okzident* (Schriftenreihe des Zentralinstituts für fränkische Landeskunde und allgemeine Regionalforschung an der Universität Erlangen-Nürnberg, 22; Neustadt an der Aisch, 1982).

D24. Gaudefroy-Demombynes, Maurice, *La Syrie à l'époque des Mamelouks d'après les auteurs arabes: description géographique, économique et administrative* (Bibl. AH, 3; Paris, 1923).

D25. Giese, Wolfgang, "Stadt- und Herrscherbeschreibungen bei Wilhelm von Tyrus," *Deutsches Archiv,* XXXIV (1978), 381–409.

D26. Goodwin, Jack C., *An Historical Toponymy of Cyprus,* 3rd ed. (Nicosia, 1978).

D27. Guérin, Victor, *Description géographique, historique et archéologique de la Palestine, accompagnée de cartes détaillées:* I, *Judée* (3 vols., Paris, 1868); II, *Samarie* (2 vols., 1874); III, *Galilée* (2 vols., 1880).

D28. Hartmann, Richard, "Die Herrschaft von al-Karak: ein Beitrag zur historischen Geographie des Ostjordanlandes," *Der Islam,* II (1911), 129–142.

D29. Hennig, Richard, *Terrae incognitae: eine Zusammenstellung und kritische Bewertung der wichtigsten vorkolumbischen Entdeckungsreisen an Hand der darüber vorliegenden Originalberichte,* 2nd ed. (4 vols., Leyden, 1944–1956).

D30. Herde, Peter, "Die Schlacht bei Tagliacozzo: eine historisch-topographische Studie," *Zeitschrift für bayerische Landesgeschichte,* XXV (1962), 679–744.

D31. Heydenreich, Ludwig H., "Ein Jerusalem-Plan aus der Zeit der Kreuzfahrer," in *Miscellanea pro arte: Hermann Schnitzler zur Vollendung des 60. Lebensjahres am 13. Januar 1965,* ed. Peter Block and Joseph Hoster (Schriften des Pro Arte Medii Aevi, Freunde des Schnütgen-Museums E.V.; Düsseldorf, 1965), pp. 83–90.

D32. Jacoby, David, "Crusader Acre in the Thirteenth Century: Urban Layout and Topography," *Studi medievali,* 3-XX (1979), 1–45.

D33. Jacoby, David, *Recherches sur la Méditerranée orientale du XIIe au XVe siècle: Peuples, sociétés, économies* (Varior. Repr., CS, 105; London, 1979).

D34. Jacoby, David, "Montmusard, Suburb of Crusader Acre: the First Stage of its Development," in *Outremer* (1982), pp. 205–217.

D35. Kimble, George H.T., *Geography in the Middle Ages* (London, 1938).

D36. Kob, Konrad, "Zur Lage von Hormoz: ein territorialgeschichtliches Problem der Kreuzfahrerzeit, *ZDPV,* LXXXIII (1967), 136–164.

D37. Koder, Johannes, *Negroponte: Untersuchungen zur Topographie und Siedlungsgeschichte der Insel Euboia während der Zeit der Venezianerherrschaft* (Denkschriften der Österreichischen Akademie der Wissenschaften, 112 = Veröffentlichungen der Kommission für die Tabula imperii Byzantini, 1; Vienna, 1973).

D38. Kopp, Clemens, "Beiträge zur Geschichte Nazareths," *Journal of the Palestine Oriental Society,* XIX (1939–1940), 82–119.

D39. Kretschmer, Konrad, *Die italienischen Portolane des Mittelalters: ein Beitrag zur Geschichte der Kartographie und Nautik* (Veröffentlichungen des Instituts für Meereskunde und des geographischen Instituts an der Universität Berlin, 13; Berlin, 1909).

D40. Le Strange, Guy, *Palestine under the Moslems: a Description of Syria and the Holy Land from A.D. 650 to 1500, Translated from the Works of the Mediaeval Arab Geographers* (London, Boston, and New York, 1890); new ed. with introduction by Walid Khalidy (Beirut, 1965; repr. New York, 1975).

D41. Makhouly, Maim, and Cedric N. Johns, *Guide to Acre* (Government of Palestine, Department of Antiquities; 2nd rev. ed., Jerusalem, 1946).

D42. Mas Latrie, Louis de, "Notice sur la construction d'une carte de l'île de Chypre," *BÉ Char.,* XXIV (1863), 1–50.

D43. Mayer, Hans E., "Die Kreuzfahrerherrschaft 'Arrābe," *ZDPV,* XCIII (1977), 198–212.

D44. [Meistermann, Barnabé], *Le Mont Thabor: notices historiques et descriptives, par le P. Barnabé, d'Alsace* (Paris, 1900).

D45. Meistermann, Barnabé, *Guide du Nil au Jourdain par le Sinaï et Petra sur les traces d'Israël* (Paris, 1909).

D46. Meistermann, Barnabé, *Guide de Terre Sainte* (3rd ed., Paris, 1935); 1st ed. tr. as *New Guide to the Holy Land* (London, 1907).

D47. Meyer, Justus, "Es-Samariya, ein Kreuzfahrersitz in Westgaliläa," *Jahrbuch des römisch-germanischen Zentralmuseums Mainz,* XI (1964), 198–202.

D48. Mittmann, Siegfried, *Beiträge zur Siedlungs- und Territorialgeschichte des nördlichen Ostjordanlandes* (Abhandlungen des Deutschen Palästinavereins; Wiesbaden, 1970).

D49. Philippson, Alfred, *Das byzantinische Reich als geographische Erscheinung* (Leyden, 1939).

D50. Philippson, Alfred, Herbert Lehmann, and Ernst Kirsten, *Die griechischen Landschaften: eine Landeskunde* (4 vols. in 8 parts, Frankfurt, 1950–1959).

D51. Pitcher, Donald E., *An Historical Geography of the Ottoman Empire from Earliest Times to the End of the Sixteenth Century* (Leyden, 1972).

D52. Prawer, Joshua, "Mappōth historiōth shel 'Akō" [Historical Maps of Acre], *Eretz Israel,* II (1953), 175–184, plates XX–XXIII.

D53. Prawer, Joshua, "The Jerusalem the Crusaders Captured: a Contribution to the Medieval Topography of the City," in *Crusade and Settlement,* ed. Peter W. Edbury (Cardiff, 1985), pp. 1–16.

D54. Probst, Hermann, *Die geographischen Verhältnisse Syriens und Palästinas nach Wilhelm von Tyrus, Geschichte der Kreuzzüge* (Das Land der Bibel: Gemeinverständliche Hefte zur Palästinakunde, 4, Hefte 5–6, and 5, Heft 1; Leipzig, 1927).

D55. Ramsay, William M., *The Historical Geography of Asia Minor* (Royal Geographical Society: Supplementary Papers, 4; London, 1890).

D56. Rey, Emmanuel G., "Étude sur la topographie de la ville d'Acre au XIIIe siècle," *MS Antiq. F,* XXXIX (= 4-IX; 1878), 115–145; "Supplément à l'étude sur la topographie de la ville d'Acre au XIIIe siècle," *MS Antiq. F,* XLIX (= 5-IX; 1888), 1–18.

D57. Rey, Emmanuel G., "Note sur les territoires possédés par les Francs à l'est du lac de Tibériade, de la Mer Morte et du Jourdain," *MS Antiq. F,* 5-I (1880), 86–94.

D58. Richard, Jean, "Questions de topographie tripolitaine," *JA,* CCXXXVI (1948), 53–59.

D59. Röhricht, Reinhold, "Studien zur mittelalterlichen Geographie und Topographie Syriens," *ZDPV,* X (1887), 195–345; Nachträge XI (1888), 139–142; XII (1889), 33–35; XVIII (1895), 82–87; XIX (1896), 61–62.

D60. Röhricht, Reinhold, "Karten und Pläne zur Palästinakunde aus dem 7. bis 16. Jahrhundert," *ZDPV,* XIV (1891), 8–11, 87–92, 137–141; XV (1892), 34–39, 185–188; XVIII (1895), 173–182.

D61. Sauvaget, Jean, *Alep* (Paris, 1941).

D62. Sauvaget, Jean, "Le Plan antique de Damas," *Syria,* XXVI (1949), 314–358.

D63. Savignac, Raphael, "Ou'airah," *Revue biblique internationale,* XII (1903), 114–120.

D64. Schmidt, Otto H., "Ortsnamen Palästinas in der Kreuzfahrerzeit: Ortsnamenregister zu den Aufsätzen von Prutz, Beyer und Kob in der ZDPV 4–83," *ZDPV,* LXXXVI (1970), 117–164.

D65. Schur, Nathan, *Jerusalem in Pilgrims' and Travellers' Accounts* (Jerusalem, 1980).

D66. Spuler, Bertold, and Ludwig Forrer, *Der Vordere Orient in islamischer Zeit* (Wissenschaftliche Forschungsberichte: Geisteswissenschaftliche Reihe, 21; Berne, 1954).

D67. Tomaschek, Wilhelm, "Zur historischen Topographie Kleinasiens im Mittelalter," *SB Wien,* CXXIV-8 (1891), 1–106.

D68. Van Millingen, Alexander, *Byzantine Constantinople, the Walls of the City and Adjoining Historical Sites* (London, 1899).

D69. Vincent, Louis H., and Félix M. Abel, *Jérusalem: recherches de topographie, d'archéologie et d'histoire* (2 vols. in 4, Paris 1912-1926).

D70. Wright, John K., *The Geographical Lore of the Time of the Crusades: a Study in the History of Medieval Science and Tradition in Western Europe* (American Geographical Society, Research Series Publications, 15; New York, 1925).

D71. Yule, Henry, *Cathay and the Way Thither; being a Collection of Medieval Notices of China* (Works issued by the Hakluyt Society, 2nd ser., 38, 33, 37, 41; new ed., 4 vols., London, 1913-1916; rev. ed. by Henri Cordier, 4 vols., London, 1925-1930).

D72. — *Les Guides bleus: Égypte: le Nil égyptien et soudanais du Delta à Khartoum* (Paris, 1956).

D73. — *Les Guides bleus: Moyen Orient: Liban, Syrie, Jordanie, Iraq, Iran* (Paris, 1965).

D74. — [State of Israel,] Prime Minister's Office, Department for Landscaping and the Preservation of Historic Sites, *Acre: the Old City: Survey and Planning* (Kesten Report, Jerusalem, 1962).

NUMISMATICS AND SIGILLOGRAPHY

E1. Allen, Derek, "Coins of Antioch, etc., from al-Mina," *Numismatic Chronicle,* 5-XVII (1937), 200-210.

E2. Balog, Paul, and Jacques Yvon, "Monnaies à légendes arabes de l'Orient latin," *Revue numismatique,* 6-I (1958), 133-168.

E3. Balog, Paul, "History of the Dirhem in Egypt from the Fāṭimid Conquest until the Collapse of the Mamlūk Empire, 358-922 H./968-1517 A.D.," *Revue numismatique,* 6-III (1961), 109-146.

E4. Bates, Michael L., and David M. Metcalf, "Crusader Coinage with Arabic Inscriptions," *H of C,* VI (1989), 421-482.

E5. Bedoukian, Paul Z., *Coinage of Cilician Armenia* (Numismatic Notes and Monographs, 147; New York, 1962).

E6. Bedoukian, Paul Z., "Coins of the Baronial Period of Cilician Armenia (1080-1198)," *American Numismatic Society Museum Notes,* XII (1966), 139-145.

E7. Bellinger, Alfred R., and Philip Grierson, eds., *Catalogue of the Byzantine Coins in the Dumbarton Oaks Collection and in the Whittmore Collection* (Dumbarton Oaks Catalogues; 3 vols. in 5, Washington, 1966-1973).

E8. Brady, J. D., "A Firm Attribution of Latin Gold Coinage to Twelfth Century Jerusalem," *American Numismatic Society Museum Notes,* XXIII (1978), 133-147.

E9. Casanova, Paul, "Numismatique des Danichmendites," *Revue numismatique,* 3-XII (1894), 307-321, 433-460; 3-XIII (1895), 389-402; 3-XIV (1896), 210-230, 306-315.

E10. Chandon de Briailles, Raoul, "Le Droit de 'coins' dans le royaume de Jérusalem," *Syria,* XXIII (1942-1943), 244-257.

E11. Cox, Dorothy H., *The Tripolis Hoard of French Seignorial and Crusaders' Coins* (New York, 1933).

E12. Duplessy, J., and David M. Metcalf, "Le Trésor de Samos et la circulation monétaire en l'Orient latin aux XIIe et XIIIe siècles," *Revue belge de numismatique,* CVIII (1962), 173–207.

E13. Edbury, Peter W., and David M. Metcalf, eds., *Coinage in the Latin East: the Fourth Oxford Symposium on Coinage and Monetary History* (British Archaeological Reports, International Series, 77; Oxford, 1980).

E14. Ehrenkreutz, Andrew S., "The Standard of Fineness of Gold Coins Circulating in Egypt at the Time of the Crusades," *Journal of the American Oriental Society,* LXXIV (1954), 162–166.

E15. Goodacre, Hugh G., *A Handbook of the Coinage of the Byzantine Empire* (3 vols., London, 1928–1933).

E16. Grierson, Philip, "A German Crusader's Hoard of 1147 from Side (Turkey)," in *Lagom: Festschrift für Peter Berghaus zum 60. Geburtstag* (Münster, 1981), pp. 195–203.

E17. Hazard, Harry W., *The Numismatic History of Late Medieval North Africa* (Numismatic Studies, 8; New York, 1952).

E18. Hazard, Harry W., "Late Medieval North Africa: Additions and Supplementary Notes," *American Numismatic Society Museum Notes,* XII (1966), 195–221.

E19. Jacoby, David, "Some Unpublished Seals from the Latin East," *Israel Numismatic Journal,* V (1981), 83–88.

E20. Karst, Josef (here, Joseph), *Précis de numismatique géorgienne* (Publications de la Faculté des lettres de l'Université de Strasbourg, 81; Paris, 1938).

E21. Lilburn, Alistair, "A Parcel Apparently from an Early Hoard of 'Helmet' Deniers of Bohemund III of Antioch," *Numismatic Chronicle,* CXLI (1981), 163–166.

E22. Mas Latrie, Louis de, "Notice sur les monnaies des rois de Chypre de la maison de Lusignan," *BÉ Char.,* V (1843–1844), 118–142, 413–437.

E23. Mayer, Hans E., *Das Siegelwesen in den Kreuzfahrerstaaten* (Bayerische Akademie der Wissenschaften, Philosophisch-historische Klasse: Abhandlungen, n.s., 83; Munich, 1978).

E24. Metcalf, David M., "The Currency of *Deniers Tournois* in Frankish Greece," *ABS Athens,* LV (1960), 38–59.

E25. Metcalf, David M., "Coins of Lucca, Valence and Antioch: Some New Stray Finds from the Time of the Crusades," *Hamburger Beiträge zur Numismatik,* XXII–XXIII (1968–1969), 443–470.

E26. Metcalf, David M., "Billon Coinage of the Crusading Principality of Antioch," *Numismatic Chronicle,* 7-IX (1969), 247–267.

E27. Metcalf, David M., "The Magaracik Hoard of 'Helmet' Coins of Bohémond III of Antioch," *American Numismatic Society Museum Notes,* XVI (1970), 95–109.

E28. Metcalf, David M., "Some Hoards and Stray Finds from the Latin East," *American Numismatic Society Museum Notes,* XX (1975), 139–152.

E29. Metcalf, David M., "Coinage of the Latin Kingdom of Jerusalem in the Name of Baudouin," *Numismatic Chronicle,* CXXXVIII (1978), 71–84.

E30. Metcalf, David M., "Crusader Coinage Associated with the Latin Patriarchates of Jerusalem and Antioch," *Numismatic Circular,* LXXXVII (1979), 445–446.

E31. Metcalf, David M., "The Gros grand and the Gros petit of Henry II of Cyprus," *Numismatic Chronicle,* CXLII (1982), 83–100.

E32. Metcalf, David M., *Coinage of the Crusades and the Latin East in the Ash-molean Museum, Oxford* (Oxford, 1983).

E33. Morgan, Jacques de, *Manuel de numismatique orientale de l'antiquité et du moyen âge,* ed. Karapet J. Basmadjian, vol. 1 (Paris, 1923-1936).

E34. Pesant, Roberto, "The A.N.S. Hoard of Antioch Deniers," *American Numis-matic Society Museum Notes,* XVIII (1972), 73-85.

E35. Porteous, John, "Crusader Coinage with Greek and Latin Inscriptions," *H of C,* VI (1989), 354-420.

E36. Retowski, Otto F., *Die Münzen der Komnenen von Trapezunt* (Moscow, 1910; republ. Brunswick, 1974, with introduction by W. Hahn).

E37. Sabine, C. J., "The *Turris Davit* Coinage and the Regency of Raymond III of Tripoli (1184-6)," *Numismatic Chronicle,* CXXXVIII (1978), 85-92; CXLI (1981), 156-158.

E38. Sabine, C. J., "The Billon and Copper Coinage of the Crusader County of Tripoli, *c.* 1102-1268," *Numismatic Chronicle,* CXL (1980), 71-112.

E39. Sabine, C. J., "The Sequence of the 'Bare Head' Type of Bohemund III of An-tioch," *Numismatic Chronicle,* CXLI (1981), 158-163.

E40. Schlumberger, Gustave, *Numismatique de l'Orient latin* (Paris, 1878; repr. Graz, 1954); *Supplément* (Paris, 1882).

E41. Schlumberger, Gustave, *Sigillographie de l'empire byzantin* (Paris, 1884).

E42. Schlumberger, Gustave, Ferdinand Chalandon, and Adrien Blanchet, *Sigillogra-phie de l'Orient latin* (Bibl. AH, 37; Paris, 1943).

E43. Spaer, Arnold, "Archbishop Baldwin II of Caesarea," *Numismatic Chronicle,* CXL (1980), 193-194.

E44. Yvon, Jacques, "Monnaies et sceaux de l'Orient latin," *Revue numismatique,* 6-VIII (1966), 89-107.

EPIGRAPHY

F1. Berchem, Max van, "Épigraphie des Assassins de Syrie," *JA,* 9-IX (1897), 453-501.

F2. Chamberlayne, Tankerville J., *Lacrimae nicossienses: Recueil d'inscriptions fu-néraires, la plupart françaises, existant encore dans l'île de Chypre, suivi d'un armorial chypriote et d'une description topographique et archéologique de la ville de Nicosie,* vol. I (Paris, 1894).

F3. Clermont-Ganneau, Charles, "La Pierre de Bethphage: fresques et inscriptions des croisés recemment découvertes auprès de Jérusalem (d'après une com-munication du frère Liérin de Hamme et du capitaine G. Guillemot)," *Revue archéologique,* n.s., XXXIV (1877), 366-388.

F4. Colin, Gabriel, *Corpus des inscriptions arabes et turques de l'Algérie: 1. Dé-partement d'Alger* (Bibliothèque d'archéologie africaine, 4; Paris, 1901).

F5. Combe, Étienne, Jean Sauvaget, and Gaston Wiet, *Répertoire chronologique d'épigraphie arabe* (Publications de l'Institut français d'archéologie orien-tale du Caire; 16 vols. and index, Cairo, 1931-1975).

F6. Hamilton, Robert W., "Note on a Mosaic Inscription in the Church of the Na-tivity," *QDA Pal.,* VI (1936-1937), 210-211.

F7. Houdas, Octave V., and René Basset, "Épigraphie tunisienne," *Bulletin de cor-respondance africaine (École supérieure des lettres d'Alger),* I (1882-1883), 161-200.

F8. Jalabert, Louis, René Mouterde, Claude Mondésert, and Jean Paul Rey-Coquais, *Inscriptions grecques et latines de la Syrie* (Bibl. AH, 12, 32, 46, 52, 61, 66, 78, 89; 8 vols., Paris, 1929–1970).

F9. Mercier, Gustave, *Corpus des inscriptions arabes et turques de l'Algérie: 2.* Département de Constantine (Bibliothèque d'archéologie africaine, 5; Paris, 1902).

F10. Sandoli, Sabino de, *Corpus inscriptionum crucesignatorum Terrae Sanctae (1099–1291)* (Studium BF, 21; Jerusalem, 1974).

F11. Thomsen, Peter, "Die lateinischen und griechischen Inschriften der Stadt Jerusalem und ihrer nächsten Umgebung," *ZDPV,* XLIII (1920), 138–158; XLIV (1921), 1–61; supplement, LXIV (1941), 203–256.

F12. Waddington, William, *Inscriptions grecques et latines de la Syrie* (Paris, 1870).

Bibliography — Sources

COLLECTIONS (OF SOURCES)

G1. Amari, Michele, ed., *Biblioteca arabo-sicula: Ossia raccolta di testi arabici che toccano la geografia, la storia, le biografie e la bibliografia della Sicilia* (Leipzig, 1857); *Appendice* (Leipzig, 1875).

G2. Bartholomaeis, Vincenzo de, ed., *Poesie provenzali storiche relative all' Italia* (Fonti SI, 71, 72; 2 vols., Rome, 1931).

G3. Bongars, Jacques, ed., *Gesta Dei per Francos, siue orientalium expeditionum, et regni Francorum Hierosolimitani historia a variis, sed illius aevi scriptoribus, litteris commendata* (2 parts in 1 vol., Hanau, 1611).

G4. Bouquet, Martin, et al., eds., *Recueil des historiens des Gaules et de la France* (24 vols., Paris, 1738–1904).

G5. Boutaric, Edgard, ed., "Notices et extraits des documents inédits relatifs à l'histoire de France sous Philippe le Bel," *Notices et extraits des manuscrits de la Bibliothèque nationale*, XX-2 (1862), 83–237.

G6. Chabot, Jean B., et al., eds., *Corpus scriptorum Christianorum Orientalium* (Paris, Leipzig, Rome, Louvain, and Beirut, 1903–).

G7. Chroust, Anton, ed., *Historia de expeditione Friderici imperatoris et quidam alii rerum gestarum fontes eiusdem expeditionis: Quellen zur Geschichte des Kreuzzuges Kaiser Friedrichs I.* (MGH, SS. rer. Germ., n.s., 5; Berlin, 1928).

G8. Cobham, Claude D., ed. and tr., *Excerpta Cypria: Materials for a History of Cyprus*, 2nd ed. (Cambridge, Eng., 1908).

G9. Dulaurier, Édouard F., ed., *Bibliothèque historique arménienne: choix des principaux historiens arméniens* (3 vols., Paris, 1858–1859).

G10. Eidelberg, Schlomo, tr., *The Jews and the Crusaders: the Hebrew Chronicles of the First and Second Crusades* (Madison, 1977).

G11. Gildemeister, Johannes, ed., "Beiträge zur Palästinakunde aus arabischen Quellen," *ZDPV*, IV (1881), 85–92; VI (1883), 1–12; VII (1884), 143–172, 215–230; VIII (1885), 117–145; cf. also his "Des 'Abd al-ghânî al-nâbulusî Reise von Damascus nach Jerusalem," *Zeitschrift der deutschen morgenländischen Gesellschaft*, XXXVI (1882), 385–400.

G12. Golubovich, Girolamo, ed., *Biblioteca bio-bibliografica della Terra Santa e dell' Oriente francescano* (5 vols., Quaracchi, near Florence, 1906–1926); *Nuova serie,* ed. Golubovich (14 vols., Quaracchi, 1921–1939); *Serie 3,* ed. Golubovich and Giulio Zanello (2 vols., Quaracchi, 1928–1948); *Serie 4,* ed. Martiniano Roncaglia (2 vols., Cairo, 1954).

G13. Halphen, Louis, and René Poupardin, eds., *Chroniques des comtes d'Anjou* (Collection de textes pour servir à l'étude et à l'enseignement d'histoire, 48; Paris, 1913).

G14. Heisenberg, August, ed., *Neue Quellen zur Geschichte des lateinischen Kaisertums und der Kirchenunion* (Sitzungsberichte der Bayerischen Akademie der Wissenschaften, Philosophisch-philologische und historische Klasse, Jahrgang 1922, 5. Abhandlung; Jahrgang 1923, 2. und 3. Abhandlung; Munich, 1923; incomplete, but published together as one volume).

G15. Hofmann, Georg, Joseph Gill, et al., eds., *Concilium Florentinum: Documenta et scriptores* (10 vols., Rome, 1940–1971).

G16. Hopf, Carl (here, Charles), ed., *Chroniques gréco-romanes inédites ou peu connues* (Berlin, 1873; repr. 1966).

G17. Houtsma, Martijn T., ed., *Recueil de textes relatifs à l'histoire des Seldjoucides* (4 vols., Leyden, 1886-1902).

G18. Huici Miranda, Ambrósio, ed., *Las Crónicas latinas de la Reconquista* (2 vols., Valencia, 1913).

G19. Huici Miranda, Ambrósio, ed. and tr., *Colección de crónicas árabes de la reconquista* (Instituto General Franco de estudios e investigación hispano-árabes; 4 vols., Tetuan, 1951-1955).

G20. Kaňák, Miloslav, and František Šimek, eds., *Křižovnický rukopis: Staré letopisy české z rukopisu Křižovnickeho* (Živá díla minulosti, sv. 24; Prague, 1959).

G21. Khitrowo, [Sofia] de, ed. and tr., *Itinéraires russes en Orient* (SOL, *SG,* 5; Geneva, 1889).

G22. Komroff, Manuel, ed., *Contemporaries of Marco Polo* (New York, 1928).

G23. Kötzschke, Rudolf, ed., *Quellen zur Geschichte der ostdeutschen Kolonisation im 12. bis 14. Jahrhundert* (2nd ed., Leipzig, 1931).

G24. Langlois, Victor, ed., *Collection des historiens anciens et modernes de l'Arménie* (2 vols., Paris, 1868-1869).

G25. Laurent, Johann (here, Johannes) C.M., ed., *Peregrinatores medii aevi quatuor: Burchardus de Monte Sion, Ricoldus de Monte Crucis, Odoricus de Foro Julii, Wilbrandus de Oldenborg . . .* (2nd ed., Leipzig, 1873), with appendix, *Mag. Thietmari peregrinatio.*

G26. Mansi, Giovanni D., ed., *Sacrorum Conciliorum nova et amplissima collectio* (31 vols., Florence and Venice, 1759-1798); rev. ed. by Jean P. Martin and Louis Petit (53 vols., Paris, Arnheim, and Leipzig, 1901-1927; repr. Paris, 1960-1962).

G27. Melville, J. R., *The Siege of Constantinople by the Turks: Seven Contemporary Accounts* (Amsterdam, 1977).

G28. Michelant, Henry V., and Gaston Raynaud, eds., *Itinéraires à Jérusalem et descriptions de la Terre Sainte rédigés en français aux XIe, XIIe et XIIIe siècles* (SOL, *SG,* 3; Geneva, 1882).

G29. Migne, Jacques P., ed., *Patrologiae cursus completus: Series latina* (221 vols. and 4 vols. of registers, Paris, 1841-1864); *Series graeco-latina* (167 vols., Paris, 1857-1876).

G30. Molinier, Auguste, and Titus Tobler, eds., *Itinera Hierosolymitana et descriptiones Terrae Sanctae bellis sacris anteriora et latina lingua exarata* (SOL, *SG,* 1-2; Geneva, 1879).

G31. Müller, Ulrich, ed., *Kreuzzugsdichtung* (Deutsche Texte, 9; Tübingen, 1969).

G32. Muratori, Lodovico A., ed., *Rerum Italicarum scriptores* (25 vols., Milan, 1723-1738); new ed. by Giosuè Carducci et al. (Città di Castello and Bologna, 1900-   ).

G33. Neubauer, Adolf, and Moritz Stern, eds., *Hebräische Berichte über die Judenverfolgungen während der Kreuzzüge,* tr. Seckel Baer (Quellen zur Geschichte der Juden in Deutschland, 2; Berlin, 1892).

G34. Niebuhr, Barthold G., Immanuel Bekker, et al., eds., *Corpus scriptorum historiae Byzantinae* (50 vols., Bonn, 1828-1897).

G35. Papadopulos-Kerameus, Athanasius, ed., *Fontes historiae imperii Trapezuntini* (vol. 1 [all published], St. Petersburg, 1897).

G36. Pertz, Georg H., et al., *Monumenta Germaniae historica inde ab anno Christi quingentesimo usque ad annum millesimum et quingentesimum auspiciis societatis aperiendis fontibus rerum Germanicarum medii aevi* (Hanover, Weimar, Stuttgart, Cologne, Berlin, Zurich, and Dublin, 1826-   ).

G37. Peters, Edward, ed., *Christian Society and the Crusades, 1198-1229: Sources in Translation* . . . (Philadelphia, n.d.).

G38. Pimenta, Alfredo, ed., *Fontes medievais da história de Portugal:* vol. 1. *Anais e crónicas* (Lisbon, 1948).

G39. Riant, Paul E.D., ed., *Exuviae sacrae Constantinopolitanae: Fasciculus documentorum minorum ad Byzantina lipsana in Occidentem saeculo XIIIo translata spectantium et historiam quarti belli sacri imperiique gallo-graeci illustrantium* (2 vols., Geneva, 1877-1878); supplement: *La Croix des premiers croisés, la sainte lance et la sainte couronne,* ed. Fernand de Mély (Paris, 1904).

G40. Röhricht, Reinhold, ed., *Quinti belli sacri scriptores minores* (SOL, *SH,* II-3; Geneva, 1879).

G41. Röhricht, Reinhold, ed., *Testimonia minora de quinto bello sacro* (SOL, *SH,* 3; Geneva, 1882).

G42. Sandoli, Sabino de, ed., *Itinera Hierosolymitana crucesignatorum (saec. XII-XIII)* (Studium BF, Collectio maior, 24; 4 vols., Jerusalem, 1978-1984).

G43. Silva Tarouca, Carlos de, ed., *Crónicas dos sete primeiros reis de Portugal* (Fontes narativas da historia portuguesa, 1; Lisbon, 1952).

G44. Theiner, Augustin, ed., *Vetera monumenta historica Hungariam sacram illustrantia* (2 vols., Rome, 1859-1860).

G45. Theiner, Augustin, ed., *Vetera monumenta Slavorum meridionalium historiam illustrantia* (2 vols., Rome and Zagreb, 1863-1875).

G46. Tobler, Titus, ed., *Descriptiones Terrae Sanctae ex saeculo VIII., IX., XII., et XV.* (Leipzig, 1874).

G47. Töppen, Max, ed., *Scriptores rerum prussicarum: die Geschichtsquellen der preussischen Vorzeit bis zum Untergange der Ordensherrschaft* (5 vols., Leipzig, 1861-1874).

G48. Wilkinson, John, ed., *Jerusalem Pilgrims before the Crusades* (Warminster, 1978).

G49. Wyngaert, Anastaas (here, Anastasius) van den, ed., *Sinica franciscana:* vol. 1. *Itinera et relationes Fratrum Minorum saeculi XIII et XIV* (Quaracchi, 1929).

G50. — *Acta sanctorum quotquot toto urbe coluntur,* by the Société des Bollandistes (70 vols., Antwerp and Brussels, 1643-1940).

G51. — *Archives de l'Orient latin* (Société de l'Orient latin; 2 vols., Paris, 1881-1884; repr. New York, 1978).

G52. — *Documents relatifs à l'histoire des croisades,* ed. by the Académie des inscriptions et belles-lettres (15 vols., Paris, 1946-1984).

G53. — *Fonti per la storia d'Italia,* ed. by the Istituto storico italiano (from 1934 on with the addition: per il medio evo), (101 vols., Rome, 1887-1972).

G54. — *Palestine Pilgrims' Text Society* (13 vols. and index, London, 1896-1907; repr. New York, 1971).

G55. — *Portugaliae monumenta historica: Scriptores* (vol. 1 [all published], Lisbon, 1856-1861).

G56. — *Recueil des historiens des croisades,* ed. by the Académie des inscriptions et belles-lettres: *Historiens occidentaux* (5 vols., Paris, 1844-1895); *Histo-*

riens orientaux (5 vols., Paris, 1872–1906); *Historiens grecs* (2 vols., Paris, 1875–1881); *Documents arméniens* (2 vols., Paris, 1869–1906); *Lois: Les Assises de Jérusalem* (2 vols., Paris, 1841–1843).

G57. — *Rolls Series: Rerum britannicarum medii aevi scriptores, or Chronicles and Memorials of Great Britain and Ireland during the Middle Ages,* published under the direction of the Master of the Rolls (251 vols., London, 1858–1896).

NARRATIVE SOURCES — WESTERN LANGUAGES

H1. Achard d'Arrouaise, "Poème sur le temple de Salomon: fragment inédit," ed. Albert C. Clark, *RO Latin,* XII (1909–1911), 263–274.

H2. Adam, William (falsely "Brocardus"), "Directorium ad passagium faciendum," *RHC, Arm.,* II (Paris, 1906), 365–517.

H3. Albert of Aachen, "Historia Hierosolymitana," *RHC, Occ.,* IV (Paris, 1879), 265–713. See also C33, C34.

H4. Alfonso VII, king of Castile and Leon, "Continuación de los documentos generales de la história de España: Chrónica latina del Emperador Don Alfonso VII," ed. Henrique Florez, *España sagrada: Theatro geográfico-histórico de la iglesia de España,* vol. XXI (Madrid, 1766), pp. 307–409.

H5. Alfonso X, king of Castile and Leon, *Primera crónica general estoria de España que mandó componer Alfonso el Sabio y se continuaba bajo Sancho IV en 1289,* ed. Ramón Menéndez Pidal, with Antonio G. Solalinde, Manuel Muñoz Cortés, and José Gómez Pérez (2 vols., Madrid, 1955).

H6. Alfonso de Palencia, *Crónica de Enrique IV escrita en latín,* tr. Antonio Paz y Melia (Collección de escritores castellanos, 126, 127, 130, 134; 4 vols., Madrid, 1904–1909).

H7. Amadi, Francesco, and Diomedes Strambaldi, *Chroniques d'Amadi et de Strambaldi,* ed. René de Mas Latrie (CD inédits, 1st ser., Histoire politique; 2 vols., Paris, 1891–1893).

H8. Ambroise, *L'Estoire de la guerre sainte: Histoire en vers de la troisième croisade, 1190–1192,* ed. Gaston Paris (CD inédits; Paris, 1897); tr. Edward N. Stone as "History of the Holy War," in *Three Old French Chronicles of the Crusades* (University of Washington Publications in the Social Sciences, 10; Seattle, 1939); tr. Merton J. Hubert as *The Crusade of Richard Lion-Heart by Ambroise,* with notes and documentation by John L. LaMonte (Col. URC, 34; New York, 1941).

H9. Angiolello, Giovanni M. ("Donado da Lezze"), *Historia turchesca (1300–1514),* ed. Ion Ursu (Bucharest, 1910).

H10. Arnold of Lübeck, *Chronica Slavorum a. 1172–1209,* ed. Johann M. Lappenberg (MGH, SS. rer. Germ., 14; Hanover, 1868).

H11. Aubrey of Trois Fontaines, *Chronica,* ed. Paul Scheffer-Boichorst (MGH, SS., 23; Hanover, 1874; repr. Stuttgart, New York, 1963), pp. 631–950.

H12. Aymar ("Haymarus Monachus"), patriarch of Jerusalem, *De expugnata Accone liber tetrastichus,* ed. Paul E.D. Riant (Lyons, 1866).

H13. Baldric of Bourgueil, bishop of Dol, "Historia Jerosolimitana," *RHC, Occ.,* IV (Paris, 1879), 1–111.

H14. Bartolf of Nangis, "Gesta Francorum Iherusalem expugnantium," *RHC, Occ.,* III (Paris, 1866), 487–543.

H15. Bartoš, Písař ("Bartossek of Drahonicz"), *Chronicon: Kronika Bartoška z Dra-honic,* ed. Jaroslav Goll (Fontes rerum bohemicarum, 5; Prague, 1907), pp. 589–624.

H16. Benjamin of Tudela, *The Itinerary,* ed. and tr. Marcus N. Adler (2 vols., London, 1907).

H17. Bernáldez, Andrés, *Memorias del reinado de los Reyes Católicos que escribía el bachiller Andrés Bernáldez,* ed. Manuel Gómez-Moreno and Juan de Mata Carriazo (Biblioteca Reyes Católicos: Crónicas; Madrid, 1962).

H18. Bernard, abbot of Clairvaux, "Opera omnia," ed. Jacques P. Migne, *PL,* vols. 182–185 (Paris, 1854–1855). New ed.: *Opera,* ed. Jean Leclercq, Charles H. Talbot, and Henricus M. Rochais; 8 vols. so far, but including the particularly important letters (Rome, 1957–1975).

Bernard le Trésorier, *see* Ernoul.

H19. Bertrandon de la Broquière, *Voyage d'Outremer,* ed. Charles Schefer (Paris, 1892).

H20. Bouhours, Dominique, *Histoire de Pierre d'Aubusson, grand-maistre de Rhodes* (Paris, 1676; 4th ed. with additions by M. de Billy, Paris, 1806); tr. as *The Life of the Renowned Peter of Aubusson, Grand Master of Rhodes, Containing Those Two Remarkable Sieges of Rhodes by Mohamet the Great, and Solyman the Magnificent* (London, 1679).

H21. Burchard of Mount Sion, "Descriptio Terrae Sanctae," ed. Johann C.M. Laurent, in *Peregrinatores medii aevi quatuor* (2nd ed., Leipzig, 1873), pp. 1–100; tr. Aubrey Stewart as *A Description of the Holy Land [A.D. 1280]* (PPTS, XII-1; London, 1896; repr. New York, 1971).

H22. Bustron, Florio, *Chronique de l'île de Chypre,* ed. René de Mas Latrie (CD inédits, Mélanges historiques, 5; Paris, 1886).

H23. Caffaro di Caschifellone, *Annali genovesi di Caffaro e de' suoi continuatori, dal MXCIX al MCCXCIII,* ed. Luigi T. Belgrano and Cesare Imperiale di Sant' Angelo (Fonti SI, 11–14b; 5 vols., Genoa, 1890–1929).

H24. Caffaro di Caschifellone, *Brevis regni Ierosolymitani historia,* ed. Georg H. Pertz (MGH, SS., 18; Hanover, 1863; repr. Stuttgart, New York, 1963), pp. 49–56.

H25. Cosmas of Prague, *Chronica Boemorum: die Chronik der Böhmen des Cosmas von Prag,* ed. Bertold Bretholz (MGH, SS. rer. Germ., n.s., 2; 2nd [unchanged] ed., Berlin, 1955).

H26. Dandolo, Andrea, *Chronica per extensum descripta aa. 46-1280 d.C.,* ed. Ester Pastorello (R Ital. SS., n.s., 12, part 1; Bologna, 1938).

H27. Daniel, *Putešestviya . . . ,* tr. [Sofia] de Khitrowo as "Vie et pèlerinage de Daniel, hégoumène russe, 1106–1107," in *Itinéraires russes en Orient* (SOL, SG, 5; Geneva, 1889); tr. Charles W. Wilson as *The Pilgrimage of the Russian Abbot Daniel in the Holy Land, circa 1106–1107 A.D.* (PPTS, IV-3; London, 1895; repr. New York, 1971).

H28. Desclot, Bernardo, *Crònica,* ed. M. Coll i Alentorn (Els nostres clâssica col-lecció, 62–64, 66, 69–70; 5 vols., Barcelona, 1949–1951); tr. Frank L. Crich-low as *Chronicle of the Reign of King Pedro III of Aragon . . . by Bernat Desclot* (2 vols., Princeton, 1928–1934).

H29. Dubois, Pierre, *De recuperatione Terre Sancte: traité de politique générale,* ed. Charles V. Langlois (Collection de textes pour servir à l'étude et à l'enseigne-ment de l'histoire, 9; Paris, 1891); also ed. Angelo Diotti (Testi medievali di interesse dantesco, 1; Florence, 1977).

H30. Durant, Guillaume (here, Guilelmus Durantis), "Bib. nat. ms. lat. 7470: Informacio brevis super hiis que viderentur ex nunc fore providenda quantum ad passagium divina favente gracia faciendum," ed. Paul Viollet, in *Histoire littéraire de la France,* XXXV (Paris, 1921), pp. 129–134.

H31. Ekkehard of Aura, "Hierosolymita," *RHC, Occ.,* V (Paris, 1895), 1–40; also ed. Heinrich Hagenmeyer (Tübingen, 1877).

H32. Ephraim bar Jacob, "Bericht des Ephraim bar Jacob," in *Hebräische Berichte über die Judenverfolgungen während der Kreuzzüge,* ed. Adolf Neubauer and Moritz Stern (Quellen zur Geschichte der Juden in Deutschland, 2; Berlin, 1892).

H33. Ernoul, *Chronique d'Ernoul et de Bernard le Trésorier,* ed. Louis de Mas Latrie (Société de l'histoire de France; Paris, 1871; repr. Brussels, 1974). See also C36.

H34. Falcandus, Hugo, *La Historia; o, Liber de regno Sicilie e la epistola ad Petrum Panormitane ecclesie thesaurarium di Ugo Falcando,* ed. Giovanni B. Siragusa (Fonti SI, 22; Rome, 1879).

H35. Fidenzio of Padua, "Liber recuperationis Terrae Sanctae," *BTSOF,* 1-II, part 1 (Fonti generali per la storia de' secoli XIII e XIV; Quaracchi, 1913), pp. 1–60.

H36. Fretellus, Rorgo, *Rorgo Fretellus de Nazareth et sa description de la Terre Sainte,* ed. Petrus C. Boeren (Koninklijke Nederlandse Akademie van Wetenschapen, Afdeling Letterkunde, Verhandelingen, n.s., 105; Amsterdam, 1980); tr. James R. MacPherson as *"Fetellus" (circa 1130 A.D.)* (PPTS, V-1; London, 1896; repr. New York, 1971).

H37. Fulcher of Chartres, *Historia Hierosolymitana (1095-1127),* ed. Heinrich Hagenmeyer (Heidelberg, 1913); tr. Frances R. Ryan, ed. Harold S. Fink as *A History of the Expedition to Jerusalem 1095-1127* (Knoxville, 1969).

H38. Geoffrey of Villehardouin, *La Conquête de Constantinople,* ed. and tr. Edmond Faral, 2nd ed. (Les classiques de l'histoire de France au moyen-âge, 18, 19; 2 vols., Paris, 1961). See also C25, C39.

H39. Gerhoh (here, Gerhohus) of Reichersberg, *Gerhohi Reichersbergensis praepositi Opera hactenus inedita,* ed. Friedrich Scheibelberger (Linz, 1875); ed. Ernst Sackur as *Gerhohi praepositi Reichersbergensis: De investigatione Antichristi* (MGH, Libelli de Lite imperatorum et pontificum saeculis XI et XII conscripti, 3; Hanover, 1897), pp. 304–395.

H40. Gervase, abbot, "Gervasii, Praemonstratensis Abbatis, ad Innocentium (III) Epistolae," in *Recueil des historiens des Gaules et de la France,* XIX (Paris, 1880), pp. 604–605, 618–620.

H41. Guibert of Nogent, "Historia quae dicitur Gesta Dei per Francos," *RHC, Occ.,* IV (Paris, 1879), 113–263.

H42. Gunther of Pairis, *De expugnatione Constantinopolitana,* ed. Paul E.D. Riant (Geneva, 1875). See also C42.

H43. Henry of Livonia, *Heinrici Chronicon Lyvoniae, 1186-1227,* ed. Wilhelm Arndt (MGH, SS., 23; Hanover, 1874; repr. Stuttgart and New York, 1963), pp. 231–332; tr. James A. Brundage as *The Chronicle of Henry of Livonia* (Madison, 1961).

H44. Henry of Valenciennes, *Histoire de l'empereur Henri de Constantinople,* ed. Jean Longnon (DRH Cr., 2; Paris, 1948).

H45. Hernando del Pulgar, *Crónica de los reyes católicos, por su secretario Fernando* (sic) *del Pulgar,* ed. Juan de Mata Carriazo (Collección de crónicas españolas, 5–6; 2 vols., Madrid, 1943).

H46. Humbert of Romans, *Opus tripartitum,* in *Appendix ad fasciculum rerum expetendarum et fugiendarum; prout ab O.G. editus est Coloniae, A.D. 1535 . . . ab innumeris mendis repurgatus . . . una cum appendice . . . scriptorum veterum (quorum pars magna nunc primum e MSS. codicibus in lucem prodit), qui Ecclesiae Romanae errores et abusus detegunt et damnant, necessitatemque Reformationis urgent: Opera et studio Edwardi Brown* (2 vols., London, 1690).

H47. James I, king of Aragon, *Chronica o comentaris del rey en Jacme primer rey Darago,* ed. Mariano Aguiló y Fuster (Biblioteca Catalana; Barcelona, 1878); tr. John Forster as *The Chronicles of James I, King of Aragon, Surnamed the Conqueror (Written by Himself),* introd., annotated, etc. by Pascual de Gayangos (2 vols., London, 1883).

H48. James of Vitry, "Historia Hierosolimitana (Historia orientalis, liber tertius)," ed. Jacques Bongars in *Gesta Dei per Francos* (2 vols. in 1, Hanau, 1611), I, 1047–1145; excerpts tr. Aubrey Stewart as *The History of Jerusalem, A.D. 1180* [error for *ca.* 1220] (PPTS, XI-2; London, 1896; repr. New York, 1971). See also C18, C27.

H49. James of Vitry, *Lettres de Jacques de Vitry (1160/1170–1240), évêque de Saint-Jean-d'Acre,* ed. Robert B.C. Huygens (Leyden, 1960).

H50. John of (here, Jean de) Joinville, *Histoire de Saint Louis,* ed. and tr. into modern French by Natalis de Wailly (Société de l'Histoire de France, Publications; Paris, 1868; repr. New York and London, 1965); ed. Noel L. Corbett as *La Vie de Saint Louis* (Sherbrooke, Quebec, 1977); tr. Joan Evans (London, 1938). See also C26.

H51. John of Pian del Carpine (here, Johannes de Plano Carpini), *Historia Mongolorum: Viaggio ai Tartari nel 1245–47,* ed. Giorgio Pullè (Milan, 1929); tr. Jean Becquet and Louis Hambis as *Histoire des Mongols* (Paris, 1965). See also C31.

H52. John of Salisbury, *Historiae pontificalis quae supersunt,* ed. Reginald Lane Poole (Oxford, 1927); ed. and tr. Marjorie Chibnall (London, 1956).

H53. John of (here, Johann von) Würzburg, "Descriptio Terrae Sanctae," ed. Titus Tobler, *Descriptiones Terrae Sanctae ex saeculo VIII, IX, XII, et XV* (Leipzig, 1874), pp. 108–192; tr. Aubrey Stewart as *Description of the Holy Land (A.D. 1160–1170)* (PPTS, V-2; London, 1896; repr. New York, 1971).

H54. John "the Deacon", *Chronicon Venetum et Gradense usque ad a. 1008,* ed. Georg H. Pertz (MGH, SS., 7; Hanover, 1846; repr. Stuttgart, New York, 1963), pp. 1–47.

H55. Laurence of Březová, *Laurentii de Brzezonia Historia Hussitica: Vavřince z Březove Kronika Husitská,* ed. Jaroslav Goll (Fontes rerum bohemicarum, 5; Prague, 1893), pp. 327–534.

H56. Louis IX, king of France, "Epistola Sancti Ludovici regis de captione et liberatione sua," ed. François Duchesne, in *Historiae Francorum scriptores a Philippo Augusto rege usque ad regis Philippi dicti pulchri tempora,* vol. V (Paris, 1649), pp. 428–432.

H57. Lucas of Tuy, "Chronica mundi ab origine mundi usque ad eram MCCLXXIV," ed. Andreas Schott, in *Hispaniae illustratae, seu rerum urbiumque Hispaniae, Lusitaniae, Aethiopiae et Indiae scriptores varii,* vol. IV (Frankfurt, 1608), pp. 1–116.

H58. Ludolf of Suchem (here, von Sudheim), *De itinere Terrae Sanctae liber . . . ,* ed. Ferdinand Deycks (Bibliothek des litterarischen Vereins in Stuttgart, 25;

Stuttgart, 1851), pp. 1–104; tr. Aubrey Stewart as *Description of the Holy Land . . . A.D. 1350* (PPTS, XII-3; London, 1895; repr. New York, 1971).

H59. Lull, Raymond, *Opera omnia,* ed. Ivo Salzinger (8 vols., Mainz, 1721–1742).

H60. Malaterra, Gaufredus, *De rebus gestis Rogerii Calabriae et Siciliae comitis et Roberti Guiscardi ducis fratris eius auctore Gaufredo Malaterra monacho Benedictino,* ed. Ernesto Pontieri (R Ital. SS., n.s., 5, part 1; Bologna, 1928).

H61. Martin da Canal, *Les Estoires de Venise: Cronaca veneziana in lingua francese dalle origini al 1275,* ed. and tr. Alberto Limentani (Civiltà veneziana, Fonti e testi, 12 [= 3rd ser., 3]; Florence, 1972).

H62. Muntaner, Raymond, *The Chronicle of Muntaner,* tr. Anna Goodenough (Works issued by the Hakluyt Society, Series 2, 47, 50; 2 vols., London, 1920–1921).

H63. Nicholas of Calvi, "Niccolò da Calvi e la sua Vita d'Innocenzo IV con una breve introduzione sulla istoriografia pontificia nei secoli XIII e XIV," ed. Francesco Pagnotti, *Archivio della R. Società romana di storia patria,* XXI (1898), 7–120.

H64. Niger, Radulfus, *De re militari et triplici via peregrinationis Ierosolimitane (1187/1188),* ed. Ludwig Schmugge (Beiträge zur Geschichte und Quellenkunde des Mittelalters, 6; Berlin, 1977).

H65. Odo of Deuil, *De profectione Ludovici VII in orientem,* ed. and tr. Virginia G. Berry (Col. URC, 42; New York, 1948); also ed. Henri Waquet as Eudes de Deuil, *La Croisade de Louis VII roi de France* (DRH Cr., 3; Paris, 1949).

H66. Odoric of Pordenone, "Liber de Terra Sancta," ed. Johann C.M. Laurent, in *Peregrinatores medii aevi quatuor* (2nd ed., Leipzig, 1873), pp. 143–158.

H67. Oliver, *Historia Damiatina,* ed. Hermann Hoogeweg as *Die Schriften des Kölner Domscholasters, späteren Bischofs von Paderborn und Kardinal-Bischofs von S. Sabina, Oliverus* (Bibliothek des litterarischen Vereins in Stuttgart, 202; Tübingen, 1894), pp. 159–282; tr. John J. Gavigan, *The Capture of Damietta by Oliver of Paderborn* (Philadelphia, 1948; repr. New York, 1980).

H68. Orderic Vitalis, *Historiae ecclesiasticae libri tredecim,* ed. Auguste Le Prevost and Léopold Delisle (Société de l'histoire de France; 5 vols., Paris, 1838–1855); new ed. and tr. Marjorie Chibnall, 6 vols. (Oxford, 1969–1980).

H69. Osbern, "De expugnatione Lyxbonensi," ed. William Stubbs, *Chronicles and Memorials of the Reign of Richard I,* vol. I (Rolls Series, 38-1; London, 1864), pp. cxlii–clxxxii; ed. and tr. Charles W. David (Col. URC, 24; New York, 1936).

H70. Otto of Freising, *Chronica; sive, Historia de duabus civitatibus,* ed. Adolf Hofmeister (MGH, SS. rer. Germ., 45; 2nd ed., Hanover and Leipzig, 1912).

H71. Otto of Freising, *Gesta Friderici imperatoris,* ed. Georg Waitz and Bernhard von Simson (MGH, SS. rer. Germ., 46; 3rd ed., Hanover and Leipzig, 1912).

H72. Paris, Matthew, *Chronica maiora,* ed. Henry R. Luard (Rolls Series, 57; 7 vols., London, 1872–1883); tr. John A. Giles as *Matthew Paris's English History from the Year 1235 to 1273* (Bohn's Antiquarian Library; 3 vols., London, 1852–1854; repr. New York, 1968).

H73. Pegolotti, Francesco Balducci, *La Pratica della mercatura,* ed. Allan Evans (Med. AA, Publ., 24; Cambridge, Mass., 1936).

H74. Peter of Dusburg, *Chronik des Preussenlandes,* ed. and tr. Klaus Scholz and Dieter Wojtecki (Ausgewählte Quellen zur deutschen Geschichte des Mittelalters, 25; Darmstadt, 1984).

H75. Peter of Les Vaux-de-Cernay, *Hystoria Albigensis,* ed. Pascal Guébin and Ernest Lyon (3 vols., Paris, 1926–1939).

H76. Petrus Ansolinus de Ebulo, *De rebus Siculis carmen,* ed. Ettore Rota (R Ital. SS., n.s., 31, part 1; Città di Castello, 1904–1910).

H77. Philip of Mézières, "Epistre lamentable et consolatoire sur le fait de la desconfiture lacrimable du noble et vaillant roy de Honguerie par les Turcs devant la ville de Nicopoli en l'empire de Boulguerie," in *Chroniques de France, d'Angleterre, d'Espaigne, de Bretaigne, de Gascogne, de Flandres et lieux circonvoisins* by Jean Froissart, *Oeuvres,* ed. Joseph M.B.C. Kervyn de Lettenhove, vol. XVI (Brussels, 1872), pp. 444–523.

H78. Philip of Mézières, *Le Songe du vieil pèlerin,* ed. George W. Coopland (2 vols., Cambridge, Eng., 1969).

H79. Philip of Mézières, "Neuf chapîtres du 'Songe du vieil pèlerin' de Philippe de Mézières relatifs à l'Orient," ed. Edgar Blochet, *RO Chr.,* IV (1899), 364–379, 605–614; V (1900), 144–154.

H80. Philip of Mézières, *The Life of St. Peter Thomas,* ed. Joseph Smet (Textus et studia historica Carmelitana, 2; Rome, 1954).

H81. Philip of Novara, *Mémoires,* in *Les Gestes des Chiprois,* ed. Gaston Raynaud (SOL, *SH,* 5; Geneva, 1887), pp. 25–138; also in *RHC, Arm.,* II (Paris, 1906), 651–872; portion ed. Charles Kohler (Les Classiques français du moyen-âge, 10; Paris, 1913; repr. 1970); tr. John L. LaMonte and Merton J. Hubert as *The Wars of Frederick II against the Ibelins in Syria and Cyprus* (Col. URC, 25; New York, 1936). See also C18.

H82. Ralph of Caen, "Gesta Tancredi in expeditione Hierosolymitana," *RHC, Occ.,* III (Paris, 1866), 587–716.

H83. Ralph of Diceto, *Opera historica: the Historical Works of Master Ralph de Diceto,* ed. William Stubbs (Rolls Series, 68; 2 vols., London, 1876).

H84. Raymond of Aguilers, *Historia Francorum qui ceperunt Iherusalem,* tr. and ed. John H. Hill and Laurita L. Hill (Memoirs of the American Philosophical Society, 71; Philadelphia, 1968).

H85. Riccoldo of Monte Croce, *Il Libro della peregrinazione nelle parti d'Oriente di frate Ricoldo da Montecroce,* ed. Ugo Monneret de Villard (Institutum historicum Fratrum Praedicatorum, Dissertationes historicae, 13; Rome, 1949). See also C24.

H86. Riccoldo of Monte Croce, "Lettres sur la prise d'Acre, 1291," ed. Reinhold Röhricht, *AO Latin,* II-2 (1884), 258–296.

H87. Richard of Holy Trinity, *Itinerarium peregrinorum et gesta regis Ricardi auctore, ut videtur, Ricardo canonico Sanctae Trinitatis Londoniensis,* ed. William Stubbs in *Chronicles and Memorials of the Reign of Richard I,* vol. I (Rolls Series, 38-1; London, 1864).

H88. Richard of San Germano, *Chronica a. 1189–1243,* ed. Georg H. Pertz (MGH, SS., 19; Hanover, 1866; repr. Stuttgart, New York, 1963), pp. 321–384; also ed. Carlo A. Garufi (Bologna, 1936–1938).

H89. Robert of Clari, *La Conquête de Constantinople,* ed. Philippe Lauer (Les classiques de l'histoire de France au moyen-âge; Paris, 1924); Italian translation by Anna Maria Nada Patrone as *La Conquista di Costantinopoli (1198–1216)* (Collana storica di fonti e studi, 13; Genoa, 1972).

H90. Robert of Rheims, "Historia Hierosolimitana," *RHC, Occ.,* III (Paris, 1866), 721–882.

H91. Rodrigo of Toledo, "Rerum in Hispania gestarum libri IX," ed. Andreas Schott, *Hispaniae illustratae seu rerum urbiumque Hispaniae, Lusitaniae, Aethiopiae et Indiae scriptores varii,* vol. II (Frankfurt, 1603), pp. 25–195.

H92. Roger of Hoveden, *Chronica,* ed. William Stubbs (Rolls Series, 51; 4 vols., London, 1868–1871).

H93. Roger of Wendover, *Flores historiarum,* ed. Henry G. Hewlett (Rolls Series, 84; 3 vols., London, 1886–1889); tr. John A. Giles as *Flowers of History: the History of England from the Descent of the Saxons to A.D. 1235* (Bohn's Antiquarian Library; 2 vols., London, 1849; repr. New York, 1968).

H94. Romuald II, archbishop of Salerno, *Annales* (MGH, SS., 19; Hanover, 1866; repr. Stuttgart, New York, 1963), pp. 387–461.

H95. Rutebeuf, *Oeuvres complètes de Rutebeuf, trouvère du XIIIe siècle,* ed. Achille Jubinal (new ed., 3 vols., Paris, 1874–1875); also ed. Edmond Faral and Julia Bastin (2 vols., Paris, 1959). See also C41.

H96. Saewulf, in *Relations des voyages de Guillaume de Rubruk, Jean du Plan Carpin, Bernard le Sage, Saewulf, . . . ,* ed. Francisque Michel and Thomas Wright (Publications de la Société de géographie [= Extrait du 4e vol. des Mémoires de la Société de géographie]; Paris, 1839), pp. 237–274; Latin ed. and English tr. (without title) by [William R.B. Brownlow], bishop of Clifton (PPTS, IV-2; London, 1896; repr. New York, 1971).

H97. Salimbene de Adam, *Cronica,* ed. Oswald Holder-Egger (MGH, SS., 32; Hanover, 1905–1913, repr. 1963), pp. 1–652; also ed. Giuseppe Scalia (Scrittori di Italia, 233; 2 vols., Bari, 1966); tr. Joseph L. Baird et al. as *The Chronicle . . .* (Medieval and Renaissance Texts and Studies, 40; Binghamton, N.Y., 1986).

H98. Sánchez Candeira, Alfonso, ed. and tr. "Las Cruzadas en la historiografía española de la época: Traducción castellana de una redacción desconocida de los 'Anales de Tierra Santa'," *Hispania,* XX (1960), 325–367.

H99. Sanudo, Marino (Torsello, or the Elder), "Istoria del regno di Romania sive regno di Morea," ed. Carl (here, Charles) Hopf, *Chroniques gréco-romanes inédites ou peu connues* (Berlin, 1873), pp. 99–170. See also C35.

H100. Sanudo, Marino (Torsello, or the Elder), "Liber secretorum fidelium crucis super Terrae Sanctae recuperatione et conservatione," ed. Jacques Bongars, *Gesta Dei per Francos* (2 vols. in 1, Hanau, 1611), II, 1–288; separate reprint ed. Joshua Prawer (Jerusalem, 1972); portion tr. Aubrey Stewart as *Secrets for True Crusaders to Help Them to Recover the Holy Land* (PPTS, XII-2; London, 1896; repr. New York, 1971).

H101. Sanudo (or Sanuto), Marino (the Younger), *I Diarii di Marino Sanuto (MCCCCXCVI-MDXXXIII) dall' autografo Marciano ital. cl. VII cod. CDXIX-CDLXXVII,* ed. Guglielmo Berchet, Federico Stefani, Nicolò Barozzi, Rinaldo Fulin, and Marco Allegri (58 vols., Venice, 1879–1903).

H102. Sanudo (or Sanuto), Marino (the Younger), *Le Vite dei Dogi di Marin Sanudo,* ed. Giovanni Monticolo (R Ital. SS., n.s., 22, part 4; Città di Castello, 1900).

H103. Simon of Saint-Quentin, *Histoire des Tartares,* ed. Jean Richard (DRH Cr., 8; Paris, 1965). See also C29–31.

Strambaldi, Diomedes, *see* Amadi, Francesco.

H104. Suger, abbot of St. Denis, *Oeuvres complètes,* ed. Albert Lecoy de La Marche (Société de l'histoire de France; Paris, 1867).

H105. Suger, abbot of St. Denis, *Vie de Louis VI le Gros par Suger, suivie de l'histoire du roi Louis VII*, ed. Auguste Molinier (Collection de textes pour servir à l'étude et à l'enseignement de l'histoire, 4; Paris, 1887); also ed. Henri Waquet (Paris, 1964).

H106. Thaddeus of Naples, *Hystoria de desolacione et conculcacione civitatis Acconensis et tocius Terre Sancte in A.D. MCCXCI*, ed. Paul E.D. Riant (Geneva, 1873).

H107. Theoderic (here, Theodoricus), *Libellus de locis sanctis*, ed. Marie L. and Walther Bulst (Editiones Heidelbergenses, 18; Heidelberg, 1976); tr. Aubrey Stewart as *Theoderich's Description of the Holy Places (circa 1172 A.D.)* (PPTS, V-4; London, 1896; repr. New York, 1971).

H108. Tudebode, Peter (Petrus Tudebodus), *Historia de Hierosolymitano itinere*, ed. John H. Hill and Laurita L. Hill, revised by Jean Richard (DRH Cr., 12; Paris, 1977); tr. Hill and Hill (Memoirs of the American Philosophical Society, 101; Philadelphia, 1974); also in *RHC, Occ.*, III (Paris, 1866), 1-117.

H109. Vincent of Beauvais, *Speculum quadruplex, naturale, doctrinale, morale et historiale* (4 vols., Douai, 1624). See also C31.

H110. Walter the Chancellor, *Bella Antiochena*, ed. Heinrich Hagenmeyer (Innsbruck, 1896).

H111. William of Machaut, *La Prise d'Alexandrie, ou Chronique du roi Pierre Ier de Lusignan*, ed. Louis de Mas Latrie (SOL *SH*, 1; Geneva, 1877; repr. Brussels, 1974).

H112. William of Malmesbury, *De gestis regum Anglorum*, ed. William Stubbs (Rolls Series, 90; 2 vols., London, 1887-1889).

H113. William of Puylaurens, "Guillaume de Puylaurens et sa chronique," ed. J. Beyssier, in *Troisièmes mélanges d'histoire du moyen âge publiés sous la direction de M. le Professeur Luchaire* (Université de Paris, Bibliothèque de la Faculté de Lettres, 18; Paris, 1904), pp. 85-175.

H114. William of Rubruck, in *Relations des voyages de Guillaume de Rubruk, Jean du Plan Carpin, Bernard le Sage, Saewulf, . . .*, ed. Francisque Michel and Thomas Wright (Publications de la Société de géographie [= Extrait du 4e vol. des Mémoires de la Société de géographie]; Paris, 1839), pp. 9-200.

H115. William of Tudela, *La Chanson de la croisade contre les Albigeois*, ed. Paul Meyer (2 vols., Paris, 1875-1879).

H116. William of Tyre, *Historia rerum in partibus transmarinis gestarum edita a venerabili Willermo Tyrensi archiepiscopo*, in *RHC, Occ.*, I-1, 2 (Paris, 1844); tr. and annotated by Emily A. Babcock and August C. Krey as *A History of Deeds Done Beyond the Sea* (Col. URC, 35; 2 vols., New York, 1943; repr. New York, 1976); new ed. (as *Guillaume de Tyr*) by Robert B.C. Huygens with source identification and determination of dates by Hans E. Mayer and Gerhard Rösch (Corpus Christianorum, Continuatio mediaevalis, 63, 63A; 2 vols., Turnhout, 1986). See also C43-C59.

H117. — "An Account of the Battle of Hattin, Referring to the Frankish Mercenaries in the Oriental Moslem States," ed. Jean Richard, *Speculum*, XXVII (1952), 168-177.

H118. — *Annales Barenses*, ed. Georg H. Pertz (MGH, SS., 5; Hanover, 1844; repr. Stuttgart, New York, 1963), pp. 51-56.

H119. — *Annales Beneventani*, ed. Georg H. Pertz (MGH, SS., 3; Hanover, 1839; repr. Stuttgart, New York, 1963), pp. 173-185.

H120. — *Annales Casinenses,* ed. Georg H. Pertz (MGH, SS., 19; Hanover, 1866; repr. Stuttgart, New York, 1963), pp. 303–320.

H121. — *Annales Cavenses,* ed. Georg H. Pertz (MGH, SS., 3; Hanover, 1839; repr. Stuttgart, New York, 1963), pp. 185–197.

H122. — "Annales de Terre Sainte," ed. Reinhold Röhricht and Gaston Raynaud, *AO Latin,* II-2 (1884), 427–461.

H123. — *Annales Herpibolenses,* ed. Georg H. Pertz (MGH, SS., 16; Hanover, 1859; repr. Stuttgart, New York, 1963), pp. 1–12.

H124. — *Annales Palidenses,* ed. Georg H. Pertz (MGH, SS., 16; Hanover, 1859; repr. Stuttgart, New York, 1963), pp. 48–98.

H125. — "Anonymi Chronicon Terrae Sanctae s. Libellus de expugnatione," ed. Hans Prutz, in *Quellenbeiträge zur Geschichte der Kreuzzüge* (Danzig, 1876), pp. 57–103.

H126. — *Anonymous Pilgrim V. 2,* tr. Aubrey Stewart (PPTS, VI-1; London, 1894; repr. New York, 1971), pp. 27–36.

H127. — "Chronicon Maurinacense," in *Recueil des historiens des Gaules et de la France,* vol. XII (Paris, 1877), pp. 68–88.

H128. — *Chronicon Venetum quod vulgo dicunt Altinate,* ed. Heinrich Simonsfeld (MGH, SS., 14; Hanover, 1883; repr. Stuttgart, New York, 1963), pp. 1–97.

H129. — *Continuatio Guilelmi Tyrii,* ed. Marianne Salloch as *Die lateinische Fortsetzung des Wilhelm von Tyrus* (Diss., Berlin; Greifswald, 1934).

H130. — *Das Itinerarium peregrinorum: eine zeitgenössische englische Chronik zum dritten Kreuzzug in ursprünglicher Gestalt,* ed. Hans E. Mayer (MGH, Schriften, 18; Stuttgart, 1962); *cf.* the review by Marie L. Bulst, *Hist. Z,* CXCVIII (1964), 380–387; also Mayer, "Zum Itinerarium peregrinorum," *Deutsches Archiv,* XX (1964), 210–221; Bulst, "Noch einmal das Itinerarium peregrinorum," *Deutsches Archiv,* XXI (1965), 593–606; and Mayer, "Zur Verfasserfrage des Itinerarium peregrinorum," *Classica et Mediaevalia,* XXVI (1965), 279–292.

H131. — *De constructione castri Saphet: Constructions et fonctions d'un château fort franc en Terre Sainte,* ed. Robert B.C. Huygens (Koninklijke Nederlandse Akademie van Wetenschapen, Afdeling Letterkunde, Verhandelingen, n.s., 111; Amsterdam, 1981); *cf.* "Un Nouveau texte du traité 'De constructione castri Saphet'," ed. Robert B.C. Huygens, *Studi medievali,* 3-VI, fasc. 1 (1965), 355–387.

H132. — "De excidio urbis Acconis lib. II.," in *Veterum scriptorum et monumentorum historicorum, dogmaticorum, moralium amplissima collectio,* ed. Edmond Martène and Ursin Durand, vol. V (Paris, 1724), cols. 757–784.

H133. — *De expugnatione Terrae Sanctae libellus,* ed. Joseph Stevenson as appendix to Ralph of Coggeshall, *Chronicon Anglicanum* (Rolls Series, 66; London, 1875), pp. 209–262.

H134. — "Ein Bericht über die Eroberung von Byzanz im Jahre 1204," ed. Heinrich Simonsfeld, *Abhandlungen aus dem Gebiet der klassischen Altertumswissenschaft: Wilhelm von Christ zum sechzigsten Geburtstag, dargebracht von seinen Schülern* (Munich, 1891), pp. 63–74.

H135. — "Ein Tractat über das heilige Land und den dritten Kreuzzug," ed. Georg M. Thomas, *Sitzungsberichte der Königlich Bayerischen Akademie der Wissenschaften,* II (1865), 141–171.

H136. — "Ein zeitgenössisches Gedicht auf die Belagerung Accons," ed. Hans Prutz, *Forsch. DG,* XXI (1881), 449–494.

H137. — "Epistola de morte Friderici imperatoris," ed. Anton Chroust, in *Quellen zur Geschichte des Kreuzzuges Kaiser Friedrichs I.* (MGH, SS. rer. Germ., n.s., 5; Berlin, 1928), pp. 173-178.

H138. — *Gesta Francorum et aliorum Hierosolimitanorum,* ed. and tr. Louis Bréhier as *Histoire anonyme de la première croisade* (Les classiques de l'histoire de France au moyen-âge, 4; Paris, 1924); ed. and tr. Rosalind M.T. Hill as *The Deeds of the Franks and the Other Pilgrims to Jerusalem* (Medieval Texts; London and New York, 1962). See also C6, C40.

H139. — "Gesta Innocentii [III]," ed. Jacques P. Migne, *PL,* vol. 214, cols. 18-227.

H140. — *Gesta obsidionis Damiate,* ed. Oswald Holder-Egger (MGH, SS., 31; Hanover, 1903), pp. 463-503.

H141. — "Historia de expeditione Friderici imperatoris (Der sogenannte Ansbert)," ed. Anton Chroust, *Quellen zur Geschichte des Kreuzzuges Kaiser Friedrichs I.* (MGH, SS. rer. Germ., n.s., 5; Berlin, 1928), pp. 1-115.

H142. — "Historia de profectione Danorum in Hierosolymam," ed. Martin C. Gertz, *Scriptores minores historiae Danicae medii aevi,* vol. II (Copenhagen, 1918-1920), pp. 443-492.

H143. — "Historia peregrinorum," ed. Anton Chroust, *Quellen zur Geschichte des Kreuzzuges Kaiser Friedrichs I.* (MGH, SS. rer. Germ., n.s., 5; Berlin, 1928), pp. 116-172.

H144. — *Illustrazioni della spedizione in Oriente di Amedeo VI (il Conte Verde),* ed. Federigo E. Bollati di Saint-Pierre (Biblioteca storica italiana, 5 [i.e., 6]; Turin, 1900).

H145. — "L'Estoire d'Eracles empereur et la conqueste de la terre d'Outremer," *RHC, Occ.,* II, 1-481; continued as "Continuation de Guillaume de Tyr de 1229 à 1261, dite du manuscrit de Rothelin," *RHC, Occ.,* II, 483-639. New edition, mainly from Ms. D, for the years 1184-1197 as: *La Continuation de Guillaume de Tyr (1184-1197),* ed. Margaret R. Morgan (DRH Cr., 14; Paris, 1982). See also C37, C38.

H146. — *La Chanson d'Antioche composée au commencement du XIIe siècle par le pèlerin Richard, renouvelée sous le règne de Philippe Auguste par Graindor de Douai,* ed. Paulin Paris (2 vols., Paris, 1848); ed. Suzanne Duparc-Quioc as *La Chanson d'Antioche: 1. édition du texte d'après la version ancienne* (Paris, 1977); *2. Étude critique* (DRH Cr., 11; 2 vols., Paris, 1978).

H147. — *La Chanson du Chevalier au Cygne et de Godefroid de Bouillon,* ed. Célestin Hippeau (2 vols., Paris, 1874-1877).

H148. — *La Conquête de Jerusalem,* ed. Célestin Hippeau (Paris, 1868).

H149. — *Le Romans de Bauduin de Sebourc,* ed. L. Napoléon Boca (2 vols., Valenciennes, 1841).

H150. — "Les Chroniques vénitiennes de la Marcianne," ed. Freddy Thiriet, *MÉF Rome,* LXXIV (1954), 241-292.

H151. — *Les Gestes des Chiprois (1095-1209),* ed. Gaston Raynaud (SOL, SH, 5; Geneva, 1887).

H152. — *Libro de los fechos et conquistas del principado de la Morea compilado por comandamiento de Don Johan Ferrandez de Heredia,* ed. Alfred Morel-Fatio (SOL, SH, 4; Geneva, 1885).

H153. — *Livre de la conqueste de la princée de l'Amorée: Chronique de Morée (1204-1305),* ed. Jean Longnon (Paris, 1911).

H154. — "Memoria Terre Sancte," ed. Charles Kohler, *Mélanges pour servir à l'histoire de l'Orient latin et des croisades* (Paris, 1906), pp. 516-567.

H155. — "Narratio de itinere navali peregrinorum Hierosolymam tendentium et Silviam capientium," ed. Charles W. David, *Proceedings of the American Philosophical Society,* LXXXI (1939), 591–676.

H156. — "The Chronicle of Reims," tr. Edward N. Stone, in *Three Old French Chronicles of the Crusades* (University of Washington Publications in the Social Sciences, 10; Seattle, 1939).

H157. — "Une Lettre apocryphe sur la bataille de Smyrne (1346)," ed. Nicolae Iorga, *RO Latin,* III (1895), 27–31.

H158. — "Versione italiana inedita de la Cronaca di Morea," ed. Carl (here, Charles) Hopf, *Chroniques gréco-romanes inédites ou peu connues* (Berlin, 1873), pp. 414–468.

NARRATIVE SOURCES – GREEK

I1. Acropolites, George, *Opera,* ed. August Heisenberg (2 vols., Leipzig, 1903).

I2. Alexius I Comnenus, emperor, *Alexii I Comneni Romanorum imperatoris ad Robertum I Flandriae comitem epistola spuria,* ed. Paul E.D. Riant (Geneva, 1879).

I3. Attaliates, Michael, *Historia,* ed. Immanuel Bekker (CSH Byz.; Bonn, 1853).

I4. Bryennius, Nicephorus, *Commentarii,* ed. Augustus Meinecke (CSH Byz.; Bonn, 1836).

I5. Chalcocondyles, Laonicus, *Historiarum demonstrationes,* ed. Eugen Darkó (2 vols. in 3, Budapest, 1922–1927).

I6. Choniates, Michael, archbishop of Athens, *Τὰ σωζόμενα τὰ πλεῖστα ἐκδιδόμενα νῦν τὸ πρῶτον κατὰ τοὺς ἐν Φλωρεντία, Ὀξωνίῳ, Παρισίς καὶ Βιέννῃ κώδικας,* ed. Spiridon P. Lampros (2 vols., Athens, 1879–1880; repr. Groningen, 1968).

I7. Choniates, Nicetas, *Historia,* ed. Ioannes A. (= Jan L.) Van Dieten (Corpus fontium historiae Byzantinae, 11, Series Berolinensis; 2 vols., Berlin and New York, 1975).

I8. Cinnamus, John (here, Ioannes Kinnamos), *Epitome rerum ab Ioanne et Alexio* [sic] *Comnenis gestarum,* ed. Augustus Meinecke (CSH Byz.; Bonn, 1836); tr. Charles M. Brand as *Deeds of John and Manuel Comnenus by John Kinnamos* (Col. URC, 95; New York, 1976).

I9. Comnena, Anna, *Alexiade: Règne de l'empereur Alexis I Comnène (1081–1118),* ed. Bernard Leib (Collection byzantine publ. sous le patronage de l'Association Guillaume Budé; 3 vols., Paris, 1937–1945); Vol. 4: *Index,* by Paul Gautier (Paris, 1976); tr. Elizabeth A.S. Dawes, *The Alexiad . . .* (London, 1928; repr. New York, 1978). See also C21.

I10. Ducas, *Istoria turco-bizantina (1341–1462),* ed. with Rumanian transl. by Vasile Grecu (Scriptores byzantini, 1; Bucharest, 1958); tr. Harry J. Magoulias as *Decline and Fall of Byzantium to the Ottoman Turks . . . 1341–1462* (Detroit, 1975).

I11. Eustathius, archbishop of Thessalonica, *La Espugnazione di Tessalonica,* ed. Stilpon Kyriakidis with Italian transl. by Vincenzo Rotolo (Istituto siciliano di studi bizantini e neoellenici, Testi, 5; Palermo, 1961).

I12. Gregoras, Nicephorus, *Byzantina historia,* ed. Ludwig Schopen and Immanuel Bekker (CSH Byz.; 3 vols., Bonn, 1829–1855).

I13. John (here, Joannes) VI Cantacuzenus, emperor, *Historiarum libri IV,* ed. Ludwig Schopen (CSH Byz.; 3 vols., Bonn, 1828–1832).

I14. Machaeras, Leontius, *Recital concerning the Sweet Land of Cyprus, Entitled 'Chronicle',* ed. and tr. Richard M. Dawkins (2 vols., Oxford, 1932; repr. New York, 1980).

I15. Pachymeres, George, *De Michaele et Andronico Palaeologis libri XIII,* ed. Immanuel Bekker (CSH Byz.; 2 vols., Bonn, 1835).

I16. Phocas, John, *Ekphrasis . . . ,* tr. Aubrey Stewart as *The Pilgrimage of Joannes Phocas in the Holy Land (in the Year 1185 A.D.)* (PPTS, V-3; London, 1896; repr. New York, 1971).

I17. Prodromos, Theodore, "Scripta miscellanea," in Migne, *PG,* 133, cols. 1221–1424.

I18. Psellus, Michael, *Chronographie ou histoire d'un siècle de Byzance (976–1077),* ed. and tr. Émile Renauld (2 vols., Paris, 1926–1928).

I19. Psellus, Michael, "Epistulae," in *Michaeli Pselli scripta minora,* ed. Eduard Kurtz and Franz Drexl, vol. II (Orbis Romanus, 13; Milan, 1941).

I20. Psellus, Michael, "Un Discours inédit de Psellos: Accusation du Patriarche Michel Cérulaire devant le synod (1059)," ed. Louis Bréhier, *Revue des études grecques,* XVI (1903), 375–416; XVII (1904), 35–76.

I21. Sphrantzes, George, *Chronicon minus,* ed. Immanuel Bekker (CSH Byz.; Bonn, 1838); ed. Vasile Grecu (Bucharest, 1966); tr. Marios Philippides as *The Fall of the Byzantine Empire* (Amherst, 1980).

I22. Theophylactus, archbishop of Bulgaria, "Epistolae," in Migne, *PG,* 126, cols. 307–558.

I23. Zonaras, John, *Annales,* ed. Moritz Pinder (CSH Byz.; 2 vols.), and vol. 3, ed. Theodor Büttner-Wobst as *Epitome historiarum* (Bonn, 1841–1897).

I24. — *Cecaumeni strategicon et incerti scriptoris de officiis regiis libellus,* ed. Vasily G. Vasil'evsky (Zapiski istoriko-philologieskago phakultete imperatorskago S.-Peterburgskago Universiteta, 38, 1896).

I25. — *To Chronikon tou Moreos: the Chronicle of the Morea,* ed. John Schmitt (Byzantine Texts, ed. John B. Bury, 5; London, 1904; repr. New York, 1979; new ed. by Petros P. Kalonaros as *Τὸ Χρονικὸν τοῦ Μορέως: Τὸ ἑλληνικὸν κείμενον* (Athens, 1941; repr. Athens, 1966).

NARRATIVE SOURCES – ARABIC

J1. 'Abd-al-Wāḥid al-Marrākushī, *The History of the Almohades, Preceded by a Sketch of the History of Spain from the Times of the Conquest till the Reign of Yusef ibn-Téshufin, and of the History of the Almoravides,* ed. Reinhart P. Dozy (2nd ed., Leyden, 1881).

J2. Abū-l-Fidā', *Annales muslemici arabice et latine,* ed. Johann J. Reiske and Jacob G.C. Adler (5 vols., Copenhagen, 1789–1794).

J3. Abū-l-Ḥasan 'Alī ibn-Abī-Bakr al-Harawī, *Guide des lieux de pèlerinage,* tr. Janine Sourdel-Thomine (Institut français de Damas; Damascus, 1957).

J4. Abū-Shāmah, Shihāb-ad-Dīn, *Kitāb ar-rauḍatain fī akhbār ad-daulatain,* ed. Abū-s-Su'ūd 'Abd-Allāh (2 vols. in 1, Cairo, 1871–1875); extracts tr. A. C. Barbier de Meynard as "Le Livre des deux jardins," *RHC, Or.,* IV–V (Paris, 1848, 1906).

J5. Badr-ad-Dīn al-Ainī, "Extraits du livre intitulé le Collier de perles," *RHC, Or.,* II-1 (Paris, 1887), 181–250.

J6. Bahā'-ad-Dīn Ibn-Shaddād, *Kitāb an-nawādir as-sulṭānīyah* . . . , ed. with Latin transl. by Albert Schultens as *Vita et res gestae sultani Alamalichi Alnasiri Saladini* (Leyden, 1732); ed. and tr. as "Anecdotes et beaux traits de la vie du Sultan Youssof (Salâh ed-Dîn)" in *RHC, Or.,* III (Paris, 1884), pp. 1–370; tr. Charles W. Wilson and Claude R. Conder as *"Saladin"; or, What Befell Sultan Yusuf* . . . (PPTS, XIII; London, 1897; repr. New York, 1971).

J7. Ibn-'Abd-aẓ-Ẓāhir, Muḥī-ad-Dīn, *Ar-rauḍ aẓ-ẓāhir fī sīrat al-Malik aẓ-Ẓāhir,* ed. and tr. Syedah F. Sadeque as *Baybars I of Egypt* (Dacca, 1956; repr. New York, 1980).

J8. Ibn-abī-Dīnār, Muḥammad ibn-abī-l-Qāsim, *Al-mu'nis fī akhbār Ifrīqiyah wa-Tūnis,* tr. Edmond Pellissier and Gaston Rémusat as *Histoire de l'Afrique* (Exploration scientifique de l'Algérie pendant les années 1840, 1841, 1842, no. 7; Paris, 1845).

J9. Ibn-abī-Zar' al-Fāsī, 'Alī ibn-'Abd-Allāh, *Annales regum Mauritaniae, a condito Idrisidarum imperio ad annum fugae 726, ab Abu-l Hasan Ali ben Abd Allah ibn Abi Zer' Fesano vel ut alii malunt, Abu Muhammed Salih ibn Abd el Halim Granatensi conscriptos ad librorum manuscriptorum fidem,* ed. Carl J. Tornberg (2 vols. in 1, Uppsala, 1843–1846); tr. Auguste Beaumier as *Roudh el-Kartas: Histoire des souverains du Maghreb (Espagne et Maroc) et annales de la ville de Fès* (Paris, 1860).

J10. Ibn-al-Aḥmar, Ismā'īl ibn-Yūsuf, *Histoire des Benî Merîn, rois de Fâs, intitulée Rawḍat en-nisrîn (Le jardin des églantines) par Ibn el-Aḥmar,* ed. and tr. Ghaousti Bouali and Georges Marçais (Publications de la Faculté des lettres d'Alger, Bulletin de correspondance africaine, 1st ser., 55; Paris, 1917).

J11. Ibn-al-Athīr, abū-l-Ḥasan 'Alī ibn-Muḥammad, "Histoire des Atabecs de Mosul," *RHC, Or.,* II-2 (Paris, 1876), 1–375.

J12. Ibn-al-Athīr, abū-l-Ḥasan 'Alī ibn-Muḥammad, *Kitāb al-kāmil fī-t-ta'rīkh: Ibn el-Athiri chronicon, quod perfectissimum inscribitur,* ed. Carl J. Tornberg (14 vols., Uppsala, 1851–1853, and Leyden, 1862–1876; repr. Beirut, 1965–   ).

J13. Ibn-al-Furāt, Nāṣir-ad-Dīn Muḥammad ibn-'Abd-ar-Raḥīm, *Ayyubids, Mamlukes and Crusaders: Selections from the Tārīkh al-duwal wa'l-mulūk,* text and tr. by Ursula and Malcolm C. Lyons; historical introd. and notes by Jonathan S.C. Riley-Smith (2 vols., Cambridge, Eng., 1971).

J14. Ibn-al-Jauzī, Abū-l-Farāj, *Al-muntaẓam fī ta'rīkh al-mulūk,* vol. X (Hyderabad, 1939/1940).

J15. Ibn-al-Khatīb, Lisān-ad-Dīn abū-'Abd-Allāh Muḥammad ibn-'Abd-Allāh, *Correspondencia diplomática entre Granada y Fez (siglo XIV): Extractos de la "Raihana alcuttab" (mss. de la Biblioteca del Escorial),* ed. and tr. Mariano Gaspar y Remiro (Granada, 1916).

J16. Ibn-al-Khatīb, Lisān-ad-Dīn abū-'Abd-Allāh Muḥammad ibn-'Abd-Allāh, *Ta'rīkh al-Maghrib al-'arabī fī-l-'asr al-wasīf* (Casablanca, 1964).

J17. Ibn-al-Qalānisī, *Dhail ta'rīkh Dimashq,* ed. Henry F. Amedroz (Beirut, 1908); portion ed. and tr. Roger Le Tourneau as *Damas de 1075 à 1145: traduction d'un fragment de l'Histoire de Damas d'Ibn al-Qalānisī* (Institut français de Damas; Damascus, 1952); portion tr. Hamilton A.R. Gibb as *The Damascus Chronicle of the Crusades* (London, 1932; repr. London, 1967; repr. New York, 1980).

J18. Ibn-as-Sāʿī, ʿAlī ibn-Anjab, *Al-Djamiʿ al-Mukhtasar (Annales et biographies) d'Ibn as-Sâʿi al-Khâzin,* ed. Anastās Mari, al-Kirmilī (Baghdad, 1934).

J19. Ibn-Bībī, Yaḥyâ ibn-Muḥammad, *Histoire des Seldjoucides d'Asie Mineure d'après l'abrégé du Seldjouk-nāmeh d'Ibn Bibi,* ed. Martijn T. Houtsma (Recueil de textes relatifs à l'histoire des Seldjoukides, 3 [Texte turque]; 4 [Texte persan]; Leyden, 1902).

J20. Ibn-ʿIdhārī al-Marrākushī, *Histoire de l'Afrique et de l'Espagne, intitulée Al-buyano 'l-Mogrib, par Ibn-Adhárí (de Maroc), et fragments de la Chronique d'aríb (de Cordoue),* ed. Reinhart P. Dozy (Ouvrages arabes, publiés par R.P.A. Dozy; 2 vols., Leyden, 1848–1851).

J21. Ibn-Iyās, Muḥammad ibn-Aḥmad, *An Account of the Ottoman Conquest of Egypt in the Year A.H. 922 (A.D. 1516) Translated from the Third Volume of the Arabic Chronicle of Muhammed ibn Ahmed ibn Iyās, an Eye-Witness of the Scenes he Describes,* tr. William H. Salmon (Oriental Translation Fund, n.s., 25; London, 1921).

J22. Ibn-Jubair, Muḥammad, *Rihlah,* ed. William Wright (E.J.W. Gibb Memorial Series, 5; London, 1852); revised by Martin J. de Goeje (Leyden, 1907); tr. Maurice Gaudefroy-Demombynes as *Voyages* (DRH Cr., 4–7; 4 vols. in 2, Paris, 1949–1965); tr. Ronald J.C. Broadhurst as *The Travels of Ibn Jubayr* (London, 1952).

J23. Ibn-Khaldūn, abū-Zaid ʿAbd-ar-Raḥmān ibn-Muḥammad, *Kitāb al-ʿibar wa-dīwān al-mubtada' wa-l-khabar fī aiyām al-ʿArab* . . . (Cairo, 1867–1878; repr. in 7 vols., Beirut, 1958–1966); tr. William MacGuckin de Slane as *Histoire des Berbères et des dynasties musulmanes de l'Afrique septentrionale par Abou-Zeid Abd-er-Rahman ibn-Mohammed ibn Khaldun,* new ed. by Paul Casanova (4 vols., Paris, 1925–1956).

J24. Ibn-Shaddād, ʿIzz-ad-Dīn, *Al-aʿlāq al-khaṭīrah fī dhikr umarā' ash-Shaʿm wa-l-Jazīrah,* tr. Anne-Marie Eddé-Terrasse as *Description de la Syrie du Nord* (Institut français de Damas; Damascus, 1984).

J25. Ibn-Taghrībirdī (or Ibn-Taghribardī), abū-l-Maḥāsin Yūsuf, *Abû l'Maḥâsin ibn Taghrî Birdî's Annals Entitled an-Nujûm az-zahirâ fī mulûk Miṣr wal-Kâhirâ,* vol. I, parts 1 and 2, and vol. II, parts 1 and 2, ed. Theodoor W.J. Juynboll and Benjamin F. Matthes (Leyden, 1852–1861); vol. II, part 2, nos. 1–3; vol. III, part 1, no. 1; vol. V, nos. 1–4; vol. VI, part 1, nos. 1–3, and part 2, nos. 1–2; vol. VII, nos. 1–3, and indices and glossary ed. William Popper (University of California Publications in Semitic Philology, 2, 3, no. 1, 5–7; Berkeley, 1909–1929); tr. William Popper as *History of Egypt 1382–1469 A.D.* (University of California Publications in Semitic Philology, 13, 14, 17–19, 22–24; 8 vols., Berkeley, 1954–1963; repr. New York, 1976).

J26. Ibn-Wāṣil, Jamāl-ad-Dīn abū-ʿAbd-Allāh Muḥammad, *Mufarrij al-kurūb fī akhbār Banī Aiyūb,* ed. Jamāl-ad-Dīn ash-Shaiyal (here, Ǧamal ad-Dīn aš-Šayyal; 3 vols., Cairo, 1953/1954–1960/1961).

J27. Al-Idrīsī, abū-ʿAbd-Allāh Muḥammad ibn-Muḥammad, *Géographie d'Edrisi,* tr. Pierre A. Jaubert (2 vols., Paris, 1836–1840); partial transl. by Johannes Gildemeister as "Beiträge zur Palästinakunde aus arabischen Quellen: 5. Idrīsī," *ZDPV,* VIII (1885), 117–145, with 25 pp. of Arabic text; partial transl. by Reinhart P. Dozy and Martin J. de Goeje as *Description de l'Afrique et de l'Espagne* (Leyden, 1866).

J28. ʿImād-ad-Dīn al-Iṣfahānī, *Conquête de la Syrie et de la Palestine par Saladin*

(Al-fatḥ al-qussī fī-l-fatḥ al-qudsī), ed. Carlo de Landberg (vol. I, Leyden, 1888), tr. Henri Massé (DRH Cr., 10; Paris, 1972).

J29. al-Jazarī, Shams-ad-Dīn, abū-ʿAbd-Allāh Muḥammad ibn-Ibrāhīm, *Taʾrīkh al-Jazarī,* tr. Jean Sauvaget as *La Chronique de Damas, années 689–698 H.* (B Éc. HÉ, 294; Paris, 1949).

J30. Kamāl-ad-Dīn ibn-al-ʿAdīm, "Kamāl al-Dīn's Biography of Rāšid al-Dīn Sinān," ed. and tr. Bernard Lewis, *Arabica,* XIII (1966), 225–267.

J31. Kamāl-ad-Dīn ibn-al-ʿAdīm, *Zubdat al-ḥalab fī taʾrīkh Ḥalab,* ed. Sami ad-Dahhān (2 vols., Damascus, 1951–1968).

J32. al-Maqdisī (here, al-Muqaddasī), Shams-ad-Dīn Muḥammad ibn-Aḥmad, *Aḥsan at-taqāsīm fī maʿrifat al-aqālīm (La meilleure répartition pour la connaissance des provinces),* ed. Martin J. de Goeje (Bibliotheca geographorum arabicorum, III: Leyden, 1906); tr. André Miquel (Institut français de Damas; Damascus, 1963); portion tr. Guy Le Strange as *Description of Syria . . .* (PPTS, III-3; London, 1896; repr. New York, 1971).

J33. al-Maqqarī, Aḥmad ibn-Muḥammad, *The History of the Mohammedan Dynasties in Spain, Extracted from the Nafhu-t-tíb min ghosni-l-Andalusi-r-rattíb wa táríkh Lisánu-d-Dín Ibni-l-Khattíb, by Ahmed ibn Mohammad al-Makkarí, a Native of Telemsán,* tr. and ed. Pascual de Gayangos y Arce (2 vols., London, 1840–1843).

J34. al-Maqrīzī, Taqī-ad-Dīn abū-l-ʿAbbās Aḥmad ibn-ʿAlī, *Chronicle of Aḥmad ibn ʿAli al-Maḳrīzī Entitled Kitāb al-sulūk li-maʿrifat duwal al-mulūk,* ed. Muḥammad M. Ziyādah (10 vols., Cairo, 1934–1973; incomplete).

J35. al-Maqrīzī, Aḥmad ibn-ʿAlī, "Histoire d'Égypte," tr. Edgar Blochet, *RO Latin,* VI (1898), 435–489; VIII (1900–1901), 165–212, 501–553; IX (1902), 6–163, 466–530; X (1903–1904), 248–371; XI (1905–1908), 192–239; publ. separately (Paris, 1908).

J36. al-Maqrīzī, Aḥmad ibn-ʿAlī, *Histoire des sultans mamlouks de l'Égypte écrite en arabe par Taki-eddin Ahmed-Makrizi,* tr. Étienne M. Quatremère (2 vols. in 4 parts, Paris, 1837–1845).

J37. al-Maqrīzī, Aḥmad ibn-ʿAlī, *History of the Ayyūbid Sultans of Egypt,* tr. Ronald J.C. Broadhurst (Boston, 1980).

J38. al-Maqrīzī, Aḥmad ibn-ʿAlī, *Kitāb al-mawāʿiz wa-l-iʿtibār bi-dhikr al-khiṭaṭ wa-l-āthār,* ed. Muḥammad Riyādah (2 vols., Cairo, 1853/1854).

J39. al-Murtaḍâ, Muwaḥḥid ruler, "Une Lettre de l'Almohade Murtaḍâ au Pape Innocent IV," ed. Eugène Tisserant and Gaston Wiet, *Hespéris,* VI (1926), 27–53.

J40. an-Nasawī, Muḥammad ibn-Aḥmad, *Histoire du sultan Djelal ed-Din Mankobirti, prince du Kharezm,* ed. Octave V. Houdas (2 vols., Paris, 1891–1895).

J41. an-Nuwairī, Muḥammad ibn-Qāsim, *Kitāb al-ilmām bi-l-iʿlām,* ed. Aziz S. Atiya (Osmania Oriental Publications Bureau, al-Silsilah al-jadīdah min al-maṭbūʿāt, 9-14; 6 vols., Hyderabad, 1968–1973).

J42. Shihāb-ad-Dīn ibn-Faḍl-Allāh al-ʿUmarī, "Quelques passages du ʿMasalik el absar' relatifs au Maroc," ed. Maurice Gaudefroy-Demombynes, in *Mémorial Henri Basset: Nouvelles études nord-africaines et orientales, publiées par l'Institut des hautes-études marocaines,* I (Publication de l'Institut des hautes études marocaines, 17; Paris, 1928), pp. 269–280.

J43. Sibṭ Ibn-al-Jauzī, *Mirʾāt az-zamān (A.H. 495–654) by Šams ad-Dīn Abū ʾl-Muẓaffar Yūsuf ben Qizughlū ben ʿAbdallāh, Commonly Known by the Surname of Sibṭ Ibn al-Jauzī: a Facsimile Reproduction of Manuscript No. 136 of the Landberg Collection of Arabic Manuscripts Belonging to Yale University,* ed. James R. Jewett (Chicago, 1907).

J44. Usāmah Ibn-Munqidh, *Kitāb al-'itibar,* ed. Hartwig Dérenbourg as *Un Émir syrien au moyen âge;* vol. 2, *Autobiographie d'Ousâma* (Publications de l'École des langues orientales vivantes, 2nd ser., 13; Paris, 1886); ed. Philip K. Hitti (Princeton Oriental Texts, 1; Princeton, 1930); tr. Hitti as *An Arab-Syrian Gentleman and Warrior in the Period of the Crusades . . .* (Col. URC, 10; New York, 1929; repr. Beirut, 1964); tr. into German by Gernot Ritter as *Usāma ibn Munqidh, ein Leben im Kampf gegen Kreuzritterheere* (Tübingen and Basel, 1978).

J45. Yaḥyâ Ibn-Khaldūn, *Histoire des Beni 'Abd el-Wâd, rois de Tlemcen jusqu'au règne d'Abou H'ammou Moûsa II, par Abou Zakarya Yah'îa Ibn Khaldoun,* ed. Alfred Bel (2 vols., Algiers, 1904–1911).

J46. az-Zarkashī, Muḥammad ibn-Ibrāhīm, *Chronique des Almohades et des Hafçides, attribuée à Zerkechi,* tr. Edmond Fagnan (Constantine, 1895).

J47. — "Une Chronique chiite au temps des croisades," ed. Claude Cahen, *CRAIBL* (1935), pp. 258–269.

J48. — "Une Chronique syrienne du VIe–XIIe siècle: le Bustān al-Jami," ed. Claude Cahen, *Bulletin d'études orientales de l'Institut français de Damas,* VII–VIII (1937–1938), 113–158.

NARRATIVE SOURCES – ARMENIAN

K1. Grigor of Akanc', *History of the Nation of the Archers (the Mongols),* ed. and tr. Robert P. Blake and Richard N. Frye; with Francis W. Cleaves, *The Mongolian Names and Terms in the History of the Nation of the Archers* (Cambridge, Mass., 1954).

K2. Heṭoum ("Hayton"), lord of Goṙigos (Corycus), "La Flor des Estoires de la terre d'Orient, ou Flos historiarum terre Orientis," *RHC, Arm.,* II (Paris, 1906), 111–363. See also C28.

K3. Matthew of Edessa, *Chronique de Matthieu d'Édesse (962–1136) avec la continuation de Grégoire le Prêtre, jusqu'en 1162,* ed. and tr. Édouard Dulaurier (Bibliothèque historique arménienne, 2; Paris, 1858).

K4. Sempad, constable, *Smpada Sbarabedi Darekirk'* (The Chronicle of the Constable Sempad), ed. Seropé Akelian (Venice–San Lazzaro, 1956); tr. Sirarpie Der Nersessian as "The Armenian Chronicle of the Constable Smpad or of the 'Royal Historian'," *D Oaks P,* XIII (1959), 141–168; tr. Gérard Dédéyan as *La Chronique attribuée au connétable Smbat* (DRH Cr., 13; Paris, 1980).

NARRATIVE SOURCES – SYRIAC

K5. Bar Hebraeus, *Chronicon ecclesiasticum,* ed. and tr. (into Latin) Jean B. Abbeloos and Thomas J. Lamy (3 vols., Paris and Louvain, 1872–1877); also ed. and tr. Ernest A.W. Budge as *The Chronography of Gregory Abû'l Faraj, the Son of Aaron, the Hebrew Physician Commonly Known as Bar He-*

braeus, Being the First Part of his Political History of the World (2 vols., London, 1932; repr. Amsterdam, 1976).

K6. Michael the Syrian, *Chronique de Michel le Syrien, patriarche jacobite d'Antioche (1166–1199),* ed. and tr. Jean B. Chabot (4 vols., Paris, 1899–1924).

K7. — *Chronicon ad annum Christi 1234 pertinens,* ed. Jean B. Chabot (Corpus scriptorum Christianorum orientalium, Scriptores Syri, 36–37; Paris, 1916–1920).

K8. — "The First and Second Crusade from an Anonymous Syriac Chronicle," tr. Arthur S. Tritton and Hamilton A.R. Gibb, *Journal of the Royal Asiatic Society* (1933), pp. 69–101, 273–305.

K9. — *The Monks of Kûblâi Khân, Emperor of China: or, the History of the Life and Travels of Rabban Ṣâwmâ, and Markos, who as Mar Yahbh-Allâhâ III became Patriarch of the Nestorian Church in Asia,* ed. and tr. Ernest A.W. Budge (London, 1928); also ed. and tr. Jean B. Chabot as "Histoire du patriarche Mar Jabalaha III et du moine Rabban Çauma," *RO Latin,* I (1893), 567–610; II (1894), 73–142, 235–304, 630–638, 641–643 (publ. separately, Paris, 1895).

NARRATIVE SOURCES — PERSIAN

K10. Juvainī, 'Alā'-ad-Dīn 'Aṭā Malik, *The History of the World-Conqueror, by 'Ala' ad-Din, 'Aṭa-Malik Juvaini, Translated from the Text of Mirza Muhammad Qazvini,* ed. John A. Boyle (UNESCO collection of representative works: Persian series; 2 vols., Manchester, 1958).

K11. Nāṣir-i-Khusrau, *Sefer nameh,* ed. and tr. Charles Schefer as *Relation du voyage de Nassiri Khosrau en Syrie, en Palestine, en Égypte, en Arabie et en Perse pendant les années de l'hégire 437–444 (1035–1042)* [error for 1047–1054] (Publications de l'École des langues orientales vivantes, 2nd ser., I; Paris, 1881); portion also tr. Guy Le Strange as *Diary of a Journey through Syria and Palestine* (PPTS, IV-1; London, 1893; repr. New York, 1971).

K12. Rashīd-ad-Dīn Faḍl-Allāh, *Geschichte Ġāzān-Hān's aus dem Ta'rīḫ-i mubārak-i Gazānī des Rašid al-Dīn Faḍlallāh b. 'Imad ad-Daula Abūl-Ḫair,* ed. Karl Jahn (E.J.W. Gibb Memorial Series, n.s., 14; London, 1940); ed. Karl Jahn as *Geschichte der Ilhāne Abāgā bis Gaihatū (1265–1295)* (Abhandlungen der deutschen Gesellschaft der Wissenschaften und Künste in Prag: Philosophisch-historische Abteilung, 11; Prague, 1941).

K13. Rashīd-ad-Dīn Faḍl-Allāh (here, Rašīd al-Dīn Faẓl Allāh), *Die Frankengeschichte,* tr. Karl Jahn (Denkschriften der philosophisch-historischen Klasse der Österreichischen Akademie der Wissenschaften, 129 [= Veröffentlichungen der Iranischen Kommission, 4]; Vienna, 1977).

K14. ash-Shamī, Niẓām-ad-Dīn, *Histoire des conquêtes de Tamerlan intitulée Zafarnāme,* ed. Felix Tauer (Monografie archivu orientálního, 5, parts 1, 2; 2 vols., Prague, 1937–1956).

NARRATIVE SOURCES — TURKISH

K15. Enveri, *Le Destân d'Umur Pacha: Dusturname-i Enveri,* ed. Irène Mélikoff-Sayar (Bibliothèque byzantine: Documents, 2; Paris, 1954).

K16. Neshrī, Muḥammad, *Jihânnümâ,* ed. Theodor Menzel and Franz G. Taeschner as *Ğihānnümā: Die altosmanische Chronik des Mevlānā Meḥemmed Neschri* (2 vols., Leipzig, 1951–1955).

K17. Tursun Beg, ed. and tr. Halil Inalcik and Rhoads Murphey as *The History of Mehmed the Conqueror* (Minneapolis and Chicago, 1978).

K18. — *Gazavât-i Sultân Murad b. Mehemmed Han,* ed. Halil Inalcik and M. Ogüz (Ankara, 1978).

NARRATIVE SOURCES – MONGOLIAN

K19. — *Die geheime Geschichte der Mongolen aus einer mongolischen Niederschrift des Jahres 1241 von der Insel Kode'e im Keluren-Fluss,* tr. Erich Haenisch (2nd rev. ed., Leipzig, 1948).

K20. — *Yüan-ch'ao pi-shih: Histoire secrète des Mongols,* ed. and tr. Paul Pelliot (Paris, 1949).

DOCUMENTS – POPES

L1. Jaffé, Philipp, ed., *Regesta pontificum romanorum ab condita ecclesia ad annum p. Chr. natum 1198,* 2nd ed., ed. Wilhelm Wattenbach, Samuel Löwenfeld, et al. (2 vols., Leipzig, 1885–1888).

L2. Potthast, August, ed., *Regesta pontificum romanorum inde ab anno p. Chr. n. 1198 ad annum 1304* (2 vols., Berlin, 1873–1875).

L3. Delorme, Ferdinand M., and Aloysius L. Tăutu, ed., *Acta romanorum pontificum ab Innocentio V ad Benedictum XI (1276–1304)* (PC, Fontes, 3rd ser., V-2; Vatican City, 1954).

L4. Tomassetti, Aloysius, ed., *Bullarium diplomatum et privilegiorum sanctorum romanorum pontificum Taurinensis editio locupletior facta* (25 vols., Turin, 1857–1872).

L5. Pertz, Georg H., and Carl Rodenberg, eds., *Monumenta Germaniae historica . . . : Epistolae saeculi XIII e regestis pontificum romanorum* (3 vols., Berlin, 1883–1894).

L6. Brackmann, Albert, et al., ed., *Regesta pontificum romanorum: Germania pontificia sive repertorium privilegiorum et litterarum a Romanis pontificibus ante annum MCLXXXXVIII Germaniae ecclesiis, monasteriis, civitatibus singulisque personis concessorum* (7 vols. in 8, Berlin, 1911–1935 and Göttingen, 1978–1987).

L7. Kehr, Paul, ed., *Regesta pontificum romanorum: Italia pontificia sive repertorium privilegiorum et litterarum a Romanis pontificibus ante annum MCLXXXXVIII Italiae ecclesiis, monasteriis, civitatibus singulisque personis concessorum* (10 vols.; vol. 9 ed. Walther Holtzmann, vol. 10 ed. Dieter Girgensohn; Berlin, 1906–1962, and Zurich, 1975).

L8. Brackmann, Albert, "Papsturkunden in Deutschland," *Gött. Nach.* (1902), pp. 193–223; (1904), pp. 94–138.

L9. Erdmann, Carl, *Papsturkunden in Portugal* (Abh. Gött., n.s., XX, 3; Berlin, 1927).

L10. Holtzmann, Walther, *Papsturkunden in England* (Abh. Gött., n.s., 25; 3rd ser., 14, 33; 3 vols., Berlin, 1930–1935, and Göttingen, 1952).

L11. Kehr, Paul, "Papsturkunden in Italien," *Gött. Nach.* (1896), pp. 277–308, 357;

(1897), pp. 175-216, 223-233, 349-389; (1898), pp. 6-44, 45-97, 237-334, 349-396; (1899), pp. 197-249, 251-282, 283-337; (1900), pp. 1-75, 111-197, 198-269, 286-344, 360-436; (1901), pp. 57-115, 117-170, 196-228, 239-271; (1902), pp. 67-129, 130-167, 169-192, 393-558; (1903), pp. 1-49, 50-115, 116-161, 505-591, 592-641; (1904), pp. 139-203; (1905), pp. 321-380; (1908), pp. 223-304; (1909), pp. 435-517; (1910), pp. 229-288; (1911), pp. 267-335; (1912), pp. 321-383, 414-480; (1924), pp. 156-193.

L12. Kehr, Paul, *Papsturkunden in Spanien: Vorarbeiten zur Hispania pontificia:* I. *Katalanien* (Abh. Gött., n.s., 18-2; Berlin, 1926); II. *Navarra und Aragon* (*ibid.,* 22-1; Berlin, 1928).

L13. Ramackers, Johannes, *Papsturkunden in den Niederlanden* (Abh. Gött., 3rd ser., 8-9; 2 vols., Berlin, 1933-1934).

L14. Wiederhold, Wilhelm, *Papsturkunden in Frankreich,* parts 1-7 (*Gött. Nach.,* Beihefte; Berlin, 1906, 1907, 1910, 1913); cont. in Hermann Meinert, Johannes Ramackers, and Dietrich Lohrmann, *Papsturkunden in Frankreich, Neue Folge* (Abh. Gött., n.s., 3; 3rd ser., 21, 23, 27, 35, 41, 95; 7 vols., Berlin and Göttingen, 1937-1976).

L15. Rodenberg, Carl, ed., *Epistolae saeculi XIII e regestis pontificum romanorum selectae* (MGH, Epistolae; 3 vols., Berlin, 1883-1894).

L16. Lupprian, Karl E., *Die Beziehungen der Päpste zu islamischen und mongolischen Herrschern im 13. Jahrhundert anhand ihres Briefwechsels* (Studi e testi, 291; Vatican City, 1981).

L17. Röhricht, Reinhold, "Zur Correspondenz der Päpste mit den Sultanen und Mongolenchanen des Morgenlandes im Zeitalter der Kreuzzüge," *Theologische Studien und Kritiken,* LXIX (1891), 357-369.

L18. — "Documents relatifs à Guillaume Adam, archevêque de Sultanieh, puis d'Antivari, et son entourage, 1318-46," *RO Latin,* X (1903-1904), 38-48.

L19. — *Vatikanische Quellen zur Geschichte der päpstlichen Hof- und Finanzverwaltung 1316-1378,* ed. by the Görres-Gesellschaft (8 vols., Paderborn, 1910-1972).

DOCUMENTS — INDIVIDUAL POPES (Chronological)

L20. Caspar, Erich, ed., "Die Kreuzzugsbullen Eugens III. [1145-1153] (mit Anhang: Der Text der Kreuzzugsbulle Eugens III. vom 1. März 1146, Trastevere [J-L. 8796] hergestellt von P. Rassow)," *Neues Archiv der Gesellschaft für ältere deutsche Geschichtskunde,* XLV (1924), 285-305.

L21. Hageneder, Othmar, and Anton Haidacher, eds., *Die Register Innocenz' III.* [1198-1216], with a separate index by Alfred A. Strnad (Publikationen der Abteilung für historische Studien des Österreichischen Kulturinstituts in Rom, sect. II, part I; 2 vols., Graz and Cologne, 1964, and Graz, Vienna, and Cologne, 1968).

L22. Haluščynskyj, Theodosyj T., ed., *Acta Innocentii III (1198-1216) e registris Vaticanis aliisque fontibus . . .* (PC, Fontes, 3rd. ser., II; Vatican City, 1944).

L23. Pressutti, Pietro, ed., *Regesta Honorii papae III* [1216-1227] (2 vols., Rome, 1888-1895).

L24. Tǎutu, Aloysius L., ed., *Acta Honorii III (1216-1227) et Gregorii IX (1227-1241) e registris Vaticanis aliisque fontibus* (PC, Fontes, 3rd. ser., III; Vatican City, 1950).

L25. Auvray, Lucien, ed., *Les Registres de Grégoire IX [1227–1241]: Recueil des bulles de ce pape* (BÉFAR, 2nd ser.; 3 vols. and tables, Paris, 1896–1955).

L26. Matanić, Athanasius, "Bulla missionaria 'Cum hora jam undecima' eiusque juridicum 'Directorium apparatus'," *Archivum Franciscanum historicum,* L (1957), 364–378.

L27. Berger, Élie, ed., *Les Registres d'Innocent IV* [1243–1254] (BÉFAR, 2nd ser.; 4 vols., Paris, 1884–1921).

L28. Haluščynskyj, Theodosyj T., and Meletius M. Wojnar, eds., *Acta Innocentii IV (1243–1254) e registris Vaticanis aliisque fontibus . . .* (PC, Fontes, 3rd ser., IV-1; Rome, 1962).

L29. Bourel de la Roncière, Charles, Joseph de Loye, Auguste Coulon, and Pierre de Cenival, eds., *Les Registres d'Alexandre IV [1254–1261]: Recueil des bulles de ce pape* (BÉFAR, 2nd ser.; 3 vols., Paris, 1895–1959).

L30. Guiraud, Jean, ed., *Les Registres d'Urbain IV (1261–1264): Recueil des bulles de ce pape* (BÉFAR, 2nd ser.; 4 vols. and tables, Paris, 1901–1958).

L31. Jordan, Édouard, ed., *Les Registres de Clément IV (1265–1268): Recueil des bulles de ce pape* (BÉFAR, 2nd ser.; 1 vol. and tables, Paris, 1893–1945).

L32. Guiraud, Jean, and Léon Cadier, eds., *Les Registres de Grégoire X (1271–1276) et de Jean XXI (1276–1277): Recueil des bulles de ces papes* (BÉFAR, 2nd ser.; 1 vol. and tables, Paris, 1892–1960).

L33. Gay, Jules, and Suzanne Vitte, eds., *Les Registres de Nicolaus III (1277–1280): Recueil des bulles de ce pape* (BÉFAR, 2nd ser.; Paris, 1898–1938).

L34. *Les Registres de Martin IV (1281–1285): Recueil des bulles de ce pape,* ed. by Membres de l'École française de Rome (BÉFAR, 2nd ser.; Paris, 1901–1935).

L35. Prou, Maurice, ed., *Les Registres d'Honorius IV [1285–1287]: Recueil des bulles de ce pape* (BÉFAR, 2nd ser.; Paris, 1888).

L36. Langlois, Ernest, ed., *Les Registres de Nicolas IV [1288–1292]: Recueil des bulles de ce pape* (BÉFAR, 2nd ser.; 2 vols., Paris, 1886–1905).

L37. Digard, Georges, Maurice Faucon, Antoine Thomas, and Robert Fawtier, eds., *Les Registres de Boniface VIII [1294–1303]: Recueil des bulles de ce pape* (BÉFAR, 2nd ser.; 4 vols., Paris, 1907–1939).

L38. Grandjean, Charles, ed., *Le Registre de Benoît XI: Recueil des bulles de ce pape* [1303–1304] (BÉFAR, 2nd ser.; Paris, 1905).

L39. *Regestum Clementis papae V* [1305–1314], ed. by Monks of the Order of St. Benedict (9 vols. and appendix, Rome, 1885–1892); Yvonne Lanhers and Cyrille Vogel, *Tables des Registres de Clément V publiés par les Bénédictins* (BÉFAR, 3rd ser.; Paris, 1957).

L40. Mollat, Guillaume, and G. de Lesquen, eds., *Jean XXII (1316–1334): Lettres communes . . .* (BÉFAR, 3rd ser.; 16 vols., Paris, 1904–1947).

L41. Coulon, Auguste, and Suzanne Clemencet, eds., *Jean XXII (1316–1334): Lettres secrètes et curiales relatives à la France* (BÉFAR, 3rd ser.; 3 vols., Paris, 1901–1972).

L42. Vidal, Jean M., ed., *Benoît XII (1334–1342): Lettres communes et curiales analysées d'après les registres dits d'Avignon et du Vatican* (BÉFAR, 3rd ser.; 3 vols., Paris, 1903–1911).

L43. Daumet, Georges, ed., *Benoît XII (1334–1342): Lettres closes, patentes et curiales se rapportant à la France* (BÉFAR, 3rd. ser.; Paris, 1920).

L44. Vidal, Jean M., and Guillaume Mollat, eds., *Benoît XII (1334–1342): Lettres closes et patentes intéressant les pays autres que la France* (BÉFAR, 3rd ser.; 2 vols., Paris, 1899–1950).

L45. Déprez, Eugène, ed., *Clément VI (1342–1352): Lettres closes, patentes et curiales se rapportant à la France* (BÉFAR, 3rd ser.; 2 vols., Paris, 1901–1961).

L46. Déprez, Eugène, ed., *Innocent VI (1352–1362): Lettres patentes, closes et curiales se rapportant à la France* (BÉFAR, 3rd ser.; Paris, 1909).

L47. Gasnault, Pierre, Marie H. Laurent, and Nicole Gotteri, eds., *Innocent VI (1352–1362): Lettres secrètes et curiales* (BÉFAR, 3rd ser.; 4 vols., Paris, 1959–1976) (incomplete).

L48. *Urbain V (1362–1370): Lettres communes*, ed. by Membres de l'École française de Rome, M. H. Laurent, M. Hayez, A. M. Hayez, et al. (BÉFAR, 3rd ser.; 10 vols., Paris, 1954–1985).

L49. Lecacheux, Paul C., and Guillaume Mollat, eds., *Urbain V (1362–1370): Lettres secrètes et curiales se rapportant à la France* (BÉFAR, 3rd ser.; Paris, 1902–1955).

L50. Mirot, Léon, and Henri Jassemin, eds., *Grégoire XI (1370–1378): Lettres secrètes et curiales relatives à la France* (BÉFAR, 3rd ser.; Paris, 1935); tables by Guillaume Mollat and Edmond R. Labande (Paris, 1957).

L51. Mollat, Guillaume, ed., *Grégoire XI (1370–1378): Lettres secrètes et curiales intéressant les pays autres que la France* (BÉFAR, 3rd ser.; 3 fascicles, Paris, 1962–1965).

DOCUMENTS — CRUSADES AND THE HOLY LAND

M1. Barag, Dan, "A New Source Concerning the Ultimate Borders of the Latin Kingdom of Jerusalem," *Isr. Expl. J*, XXIX (1979), 197–217.

M2. Bautier, Robert H., "La Collection de chartes de croisade dite 'Collection Courtois'," *CRAIBL* (1956), pp. 382–386.

M3. Belgrano, Luigi T., ed., *Documenti inediti riguardanti le due crociate di San Ludovico IX* (Geneva, 1859).

M4. Cahen, Claude, "Une Lettre d'un prisonnier musulman des Francs de Syrie," in *Études de civilisation médiévale: Mélanges offerts à Edmond R. Labande* (Poitiers, 1974), pp. 83–87.

M5. Constable, Giles, "Medieval Charters as a Source for the History of the Crusades," in *Crusade and Settlement*, ed. Peter W. Edbury (Cardiff, 1985), pp. 73–89.

M6. Delaville Le Roulx, Joseph, "Chartes de la Terre Sainte," *RO Latin*, XI (1905–1908), 181–191.

M7. Deschamps, Paul, "Études sur un texte latin énumérant les possessions musulmanes dans le royaume de Jérusalem vers l'année 1239," *Syria*, XXIII (1942–1943), 86–104.

M8. Goitein, Solomon D.F., "Contemporary Letters on the Capture of Jerusalem by the Crusaders," *Journal of Jewish Studies*, III (1952), 162–177.

M9. Hagenmeyer, Heinrich, ed., *Epistulae et chartae ad historiam primi belli sacri spectantes quae supersunt aevo aequales ac genuinae: Die Kreuzzugsbriefe aus den Jahren 1088–1100* (Innsbruck, 1901).

M10. Hiestand, Rudolf, "Zwei unbekannte Diplome der lateinischen Könige von Jerusalem aus Lucca," *QFIAB*, L (1971), 1–57.

M11. Holt, Peter M., "The Treaties of the Early Mamluk Sultans with the Frankish States," *Bulletin of the School of Oriental and African Studies*, XLIII (1980), 67–76.

M12. Kedar, Benjamin Z., "The Passenger List of a Crusader Ship, 1250: Towards the History of the Popular Element on the Seventh Crusade," *Studi medievali*, 3-XIII (1972), 267–279.

M13. Rey, Emmanuel G., *Recherches géographiques et historiques sur la domination des Latins en Orient* (Paris, 1877).

M14. Riant, Paul E.D., "Inventaire critique des lettres historiques de croisades," *AO Latin*, I (1881), 1–224.

M15. Riant, Paul E.D., "Les Archives des établissements latins d'Orient," *AO Latin*, I (1881), 705–710.

M16. Richard, Jean, "Un Recueil de lettres sur la huitième croisade," *Bulletin de la Société nationale des antiquaires de France* (1960), pp. 182–187.

M17. Richard, Jean, "Le Comté de Tripoli dans les chartes du fonds des Porcellet," *BÉ Char.*, CXXX (1972), 339–382.

M18. Röhricht, Reinhold, ed., *Regesta regni Hierosolymitani, 1097–1291* (Innsbruck, 1893); *Additamentum* (Innsbruck, 1904; both repr. New York, 1960).

DOCUMENTS – CRUSADES AND HOLY LAND ECCLESIASTICAL INSTITUTIONS

M19. Bresc-Bautier, Geneviève, ed., *Le Cartulaire du chapître du Saint-Sépulcre de Jérusalem* (DRH Cr., 15; Paris, 1984).

M20. Bruel, Alexandre, "Chartes d'Adam, abbé de Notre-Dame du Mont-Sion, concernant Gérard, évêque de Valanea, et le prieuré de Saint-Samson d'Orléans (1289)," *RO Latin*, X (1903-1904), 1–15.

M21. Cahen, Claude, "Un Document concernant les Melkites et les Latins d'Antioche au temps des croisades," *RÉ Byz.*, XXIX (1971), 285–292.

M22. Chalandon, Ferdinand, "Un Diplôme inédit d'Amaury I, roi de Jérusalem, en faveur de l'abbaye du Temple-Notre-Seigneur (1166)," *RO Latin*, VIII (1900-1901), 311–317.

M23. Delaborde, Henri F., ed., *Chartes de Terre Sainte provenant de l'abbaye de Notre Dame de Josaphat* (BÉFAR, 19; Paris, 1880).

M24. Delaville Le Roulx, Joseph, "Tîtres de l'hôpital des Bretons d'Acre," *AO Latin*, I (1881), 423–433.

M25. Hiestand, Rudolf, *Vorarbeiten zum Oriens pontificius III: Papsturkunden für Kirchen im Heiligen Lande* (Abh. Gött., ser. 3, no. 136; Göttingen, 1985).

M26. Kohler, Charles, "Chartes de l'abbaye de Notre-Dame de la vallée de Josaphat en Terre-Sainte (1108–1291)," *RO Latin*, VII (1899), 108–222.

M27. Marsy, Arthur de, "Fragment d'un cartulaire de l'ordre de Saint-Lazare, en Terre Sainte," *AO Latin*, II-2 (1884), 121–157.

M28. Mayer, Hans E., "Sankt Samuel auf dem Freudenberge und sein Besitz nach einem unbekannten Diplom König Balduins V.," *QFIAB*, XLIV (1964), 35–71.

M29. Mayer, Hans E., "Die Stiftung Herzog Heinrichs des Löwen für das Hl. Grab," in *Heinrich der Löwe,* ed. Wolf D. Mohrmann (Veröffentlichungen der Niedersächsischen Archivverwaltung, 39; Göttingen, 1980), pp. 307–330.

M30. Petit, Ernest, "Chartes de l'abbaye cistercienne de Saint-Serge de Giblet en Syrie," *MS Antiq. F,* 5-VIII (1887), 20–30.

M31. Rey, Emmanuel G., "Chartes de l'abbaye du Mont Sion," *MS Antiq. F,* 5-VIII (1887), 31–56.

M32. Richard, Jean, "Le Chartrier de Sainte-Marie-Latine et l'établissement de Raymond de Saint-Gilles à Mont-Pèlerin," in *Mélanges d'histoire du moyen âge (dédiés à la mémoire de) Louis Halphen* (Paris, 1951), pp. 605–612.

M33. Richard, Jean, "La Fondation d'une église latine en Orient par Saint Louis: Damiette," *BÉ Char.,* CXX (1962), 39–54.

M34. Rozière, Eugène de, ed., *Cartulaire de l'église du Saint-Sépulcre de Jérusalem* (Paris, 1849; repr. in Migne, *PL,* 155 [Paris, 1880], cols. 1105–1262).

DOCUMENTS – KNIGHTS HOSPITALLER

N1. Delaville Le Roulx, Joseph, *Les Archives, la bibliothèque et le trésor de l'ordre de Saint-Jean de Jérusalem à Malte* (BÉFAR, 32; Paris, 1883).

N2. Delaville Le Roulx, Joseph, ed., *Cartulaire général de l'ordre des Hospitaliers de S. Jean de Jérusalem (1100–1310)* (4 vols., Paris, 1894–1906).

N3. Delaville Le Roulx, Joseph, "Inventaire des pièces de Terre Sainte de l'ordre de l'Hôpital," *RO Latin,* III (1895), 36–106.

N4. Gabaretta, Anthony Z., and Giuseppe (here, Joseph) Mizzi, compilers, *Catalogue of the Records of the Order of St. John in the Royal Malta Library* (13 vols., Malta, 1964–1976).

N5. Hiestand, Rudolf, *Vorarbeiten zum Oriens pontificius: I. Papsturkunden für Templer und Johanniter: Archivberichte und Texte* (Abh. Gött., 3rd ser., 77; Göttingen, 1972).

N6. Hiestand, Rudolf, *Vorarbeiten zum Oriens pontificius: II. Papsturkunden für Templer und Johanniter: Neue Folge* (Abh. Gött., 3rd ser., 135; Göttingen, 1984).

N7. Mizzi, Giuseppe, "Di Alcune bolle papali sconosciute riguardanti l'ordine Gerosolimitano," *AOSMM,* XXIV (1966), 37–43.

N8. [Pauli, Sebastiano, ed.,] *Codice diplomatico del sacro militare ordine Gerosolimitano oggi di Malta* (2 vols., Lucca, 1733–1737).

N9. Prutz, Hans, *Malteser Urkunden und Regesten zur Geschichte der Tempelherren und der Johanniter* (Munich, 1883).

DOCUMENTS – KNIGHTS TEMPLAR

N10. Albon, Guigue A.M.J.A. (marquis) d', ed., *Cartulaire général de l'ordre du Temple 1119?–1150: recueil des chartes et des bulles relatives à l'ordre du Temple,* vol. I (Paris, 1913); *Fascicule complémentaire* (Paris, 1922).

N11. Delaville Le Roulx, Joseph, *Documents concernant les Templiers extraits des archives de Malte* (Paris, 1882).

N12. Delaville Le Roulx, Joseph, "Bulles pour l'ordre du Temple tirées des archives de S. Gervasio de Cassolas," *RO Latin,* XI (1905–1908), 405–439.

N13. Edbury, Peter W., "The Cartulaire de Manosque: a Grant to the Templars in Latin Syria and a Charter of King Hugh I of Cyprus," *Bulletin of the Institute of Historical Research,* LI (1978), 174–181.

N14. Léonard, Émile G., *Introduction au cartulaire manuscrit du Temple (1150–1317), constitué par le marquis d'Albon et conservé à la Bibliothèque nationale, suivie d'un tableau des maisons françaises du Temple et de leurs précepteurs* (Paris, 1930).

N15. Lizerand, Georges, *Le Dossier de l'affaire des Templiers* (Les classiques de l'histoire de France au moyen âge; Paris, 1923).

N16. Michelet, Jules, ed., *Le Procès des Templiers* (CD inédits; 2 vols., Paris, 1841–1851).

N17. Riley-Smith, Jonathan S.C., "The Templars and the Castle of Tortosa in Syria: an Unknown Document concerning the Acquisition of the Fortress," *Eng. HR*, LXXXIV (1969), 278–288.

See also N5, N6, N9.

DOCUMENTS – TEUTONIC KNIGHTS

N18. Joachim, Erich, *Regesta historico-diplomatica ordinis S. Mariae Theutonicorum, 1198-1525,* ed. Walther Hubatsch (2 parts and index in 5 vols., Göttingen, 1948–1965).

N19. Predelli, Riccardo, "Le Reliquie dell' archivio dell' ordine teutonico in Venezia," *Atti del Reale istituto veneto di scienze, lettere ed arti,* LXIV (1904–1905), 1379–1463.

N20. Prutz, Hans, "Eilf Deutschordens-Urkunden aus Venedig und Malta," *Altpreussische Monatsschrift,* XX (1883), 385–400.

N21. Strehlke, Ernst, ed., *Tabulae ordinis Theutonici ex tabularii regii Berolinensis codice potissimum* (Berlin, 1869); 2nd ed. with preface and discussion of manuscript by Hans E. Mayer (Toronto, 1975).

DOCUMENTS – CILICIAN ARMENIA

O1. Langlois, Victor, ed., *Le Trésor des chartes d'Arménie, ou cartulaire de la chancellerie royale des Roupéniens, comprenant tous les documents relatifs aux établissements fondés en Cilicie par les ordres de chevalerie institués pendant les croisades et par les républiques marchandes d'Italie* (Venice, 1863).

O2. Maleczek, Werner, "Ein unbekannter Brief König Leos II. von Armenien an Papst Innocenz III.," *Römische historische Mitteilungen,* XIII (1971), 13–25.

DOCUMENTS – BYZANTINE EMPIRE

P1. Dölger, Franz, and Peter Wirth, eds., *Regesten der Kaiserurkunden des oströmischen Reiches von 565-1453* (Corpus der griechischen Urkunden des Mittelalters und der neueren Zeit, ser. A, part 1; 5 vols., Munich and Berlin, 1924–1965); part 3, *Regesten von 1204 bis 1282,* 2nd rev. ed. by Peter Wirth (Munich, 1977).

P2. Dölger, Franz, ed., *Aus den Schatzkammern des heiligen Berges: 150 Urkunden und 50 Urkundensiegel aus zehn Jahrhunderten* (Munich, 1948).

P3. Florinskiĭ, Timofeĭ D., ed., *Afonskie Akty* (St. Petersburg, 1880).

P4. Grumel, Venance, and Vitalien Laurent, eds., *Les Actes des patriarches* (Le patriarcat byzantin: recherches de diplomatique, d'histoire et de géographie ecclésiastiques: 1st ser., Les régestes des actes du patriarcat de Constantinople, vol. 1; 4 fascicules, Bucharest and Paris, 1932–1971).

P5. Laurent, Vitalien, and Jean Darrouzès, eds., *Dossier grec de l'union de Lyon (1273-1277)* (Archives de l'Orient chrétien, 16; Paris, 1976).

P6. Miklosich, Franz von, and Joseph Müller, eds., *Acta et diplomata Graeca medii aevi sacra et profana* (6 vols., Vienna, 1862-1890).

P7. Petit, Louis, ed., *Actes de l'Athos* (St. Petersburg, 1903; repr. Amsterdam, 1964).

P8. Rouillard, Germaine, and Paul Collomp, eds., *Actes de Lavra: édition diplomatique et critique d'après les descriptions, photographies et copies de Gabriel Millet et Spiridon de Lavra* (Archives de l'Athos, publiées sous la direction de Gabriel Millet; Paris, 1937).

P9. Sathas, Constantin (here, Konstantinos) N., ed., *Μνήμεια Ἑλληνικῆς ἱστορίας: Documents inédits relatifs à l'histoire de la Grèce au moyen-âge* (9 vols., Athens and Paris, 1880-1890).

P10. Theiner, Augustin, and Franz von Miklosich, eds., *Monumenta spectantia ad unionem ecclesiarum Graecae et Romanae* (Vienna, 1872).

P11. Waha, M. de, "La Lettre d'Alexis Comnène à Robert Ier le Frison: une revision," *Byzantion,* XLVII (1977), 113-125.

P12. Will, Cornelius, ed., *Acta et scripta quae de controversiis ecclesiae Graecae et Latinae saeculi XI composita exstant* (Leipzig, 1861).

DOCUMENTS—FRANKISH GREECE

Q1. Chabot, Eugène M., "Un Document relatif à l'expédition de la compagnie catalane en Orient (1304)," *Le Moyen-âge,* XXIII (= 3-XIV; 1910), 198-203.

Q2. Dennis, George T., "Three Reports from Crete on the Situation in Romania, 1401-1402," *Studi veneziani,* XII (1970), 243-265.

Q3. Gerland, Ernst, *Neue Quellen zur Geschichte des lateinischen Erzbistums Patras* (Bibliotheca scriptorum graecorum et romanorum Teubneriana: Scriptores sacri et profani, 5; Leipzig, 1903).

Q4. Loenertz, Raymond J., "Athènes et Néopatras: régestes et notices pour servir à l'histoire des duchés catalans, 1311-1394," *AF Praed.,* XXV (1955), 100-212, 428-431.

Q5. Loenertz, Raymond J., "Hospitaliers et Navarrais en Grèce (1376-1383): régestes et documents," *O Chr. P,* XXII (1956), 319-360.

Q6. Loenertz, Raymond J., "Athènes et Néopatras: régestes et documents pour servir à l'histoire ecclésiastique des duchés catalans (1311-1395)," *AF Praed.,* XXVIII (1958), 5-91.

Q7. Longnon, Jean, and Peter W. Topping, eds., *Documents sur le régime des terres dans la principauté de Morée au XIVe siècle* (École pratique des hautes-études: Documents et recherches sur l'économie des pays byzantins, islamiques et slaves et leurs relations commerciales au moyen âge, 9; Paris and The Hague, 1969).

Q8. Perrat, Charles, and Jean Longnon, eds., *Actes relatifs à la principauté de Morée, 1289-1300* (CD inédits, Octavo series, 6; Paris, 1967).

Q9. Pokorny, Rudolf, "Zwei unedierte Briefe aus der Frühzeit des lateinischen Kaiserreichs von Konstantinopel," *Byzantion,* LV (1985), 180-209.

Q10. Rubió y Lluch, Antoni, *Diplomatari de l'Orient català, 1301-1409: collecció de documents per la història de l'expedició catalana a Orient i dels ducats d'Atenes i Neopàtria* (Barcelona, 1947).

DOCUMENTS — CYPRUS

R1. LaMonte, John L., "A Register of the Cartulary of the Cathedral of Santa Sophia of Nicosia," *Byzantion,* V (1929-1930), 439-522.

R2. Mas Latrie, Louis de, "Nouvelles preuves de l'histoire de Chypre sous le règne des princes de la maison de Lusignan," *BÉ Char.,* XXXII (1871), 341-378; XXXIV (1873), 47-87; XXXV (1874), 99-158.

R3. Mas Latrie, Louis de, *Documents nouveaux servant de preuves à l'histoire de l'île de Chypre sous le règne des princes de la maison de Lusignan* (CD inédits, Mélanges historiques, 4; Paris, 1882), 337-619.

R4. Poncelet, Édouard, "Compte du domaine de Gautier de Brienne au royaume de Chypre," *Bulletin de la Commission royale d'histoire,* XCVIII (1934), 1-28.

R5. Richard, Jean, *Chypre sous les Lusignans: documents chypriotes des archives du Vatican (XIVe et XVe siècles)* (Bibl. AH, 73; Paris, 1962).

R6. Richard, Jean, ed., *Le Livre des remembrances de la secrète du royaume de Chypre (1468-1469),* with Theodore Papadopoullos (Centre de recherches scientifiques: Sources et études de l'histoire de Chypre, 10; Nicosia, 1983).

DOCUMENTS — VENICE

S1. *Benvenuto de Brixano, notaio in Candia (1301-1302),* ed. Raimondo Morozzo della Rocca (Fonti SV, Sezione 3: Archivi notarili; Venice, 1950).

S2. *Domenico, prete di S. Maurizio, notaio in Venezia (1309-1316),* ed. Maria Francesca Tiepolo (Fonti SV, Sezione 3: Archivi notarili; Venice, 1970).

S3. *Felice de Merlis, prete e notaio in Venezia ed Ayas (1315-1348),* vol. I, ed. Andreina Bondi Sebellico (Fonti SV, Sezione 3: Archivi notarili; Venice, 1973).

S4. *Leonardo Marcello, notaio in Candia (1278-1281),* ed. Mario Chiaudano and Antonino Lombardo (Fonti SV, Sezione 3: Archivi notarili; Venice, 1960).

S5. *Moretto Bon, notaio in Trebisonda, Venezia (1403-1408),* ed. Sandro de' Colli (Fonti SV, Sezione 3: Archivi notarili; Venice, 1963).

S6. *Nicola de Boateriis, notaio in Famagosta e Venezia (1355-1365),* ed. Antonino Lombardo (Fonti SV, Sezione 3: Archivi notarili; Venice, 1973).

S7. *Pietro Pizolo, notaio in Candia (1300),* ed. Salvatore Carmone (Fonti SV, Sezione 3: Archivi notarili; Venice, 1978).

S8. *Zaccaria de Fredo, notaio in Candia (1352-1357),* ed. Antonino Lombardo (Fonti SV, Sezione 3: Archivi notarili; Venice, 1968).

S9. Badoer, James (Giacomo), *Il Libro dei conti (Costantinopoli 1436-1440) di Giacomo Badoer,* ed. Tommaso Bertelè and Umberto Dorini (Il Nuovo Ramusio; raccolta di viaggi; testi e documenti relativi ai rapporti fra l'Europa e l'Oriente, 3; Rome, 1956).

S10. Baracchi, Antonio, and Rinaldo Fulin, "Le Carte del mille e del millecento che si conservano nel R. archivio notarile di Venezia," *Arch. Ven.,* VI (1873), 293-307; VII (1874), 80-98, 352-369; VIII (1874), 134-153; IX (1875), 99-115; X (1875), 332-351; XX (1880), 51-80, 314-330; XXI (1881), 106-120; XXII (1881), 313-332.

S11. Cessi, Roberto, ed., *Deliberazioni del Maggior Consiglio di Venezia* (Atti delle assemblee costituzionali italiane dal medio evo al 1831; 3rd ser., Parlamenti

e consigli maggiori dei comuni italiani, Sezione 1; 3 vols., Bologna, 1931–
1950).

S12. Krekić, Bariša, *Dubrovnik (Raguse) et le Levant au moyen âge* (École pratique
des hautes études, VI section: Documents et recherches sur l'économie des
pays byzantins, islamiques et slaves et leurs relations commerciales au moyen
âge, 5; Paris, 1961).

S13. Martin, M. E., "The Venetian-Seljuk Treaty of 1220," *Eng. HR,* XCV (1980),
321–330.

S14. Mas Latrie, Louis de, *Traités de paix et de commerce et documents divers concernant les relations des Chrétiens avec les Arabes de l'Afrique septentrionale
au moyen âge* (Paris, 1866); *Supplément* (Paris, 1872).

S15. Mas Latrie, Louis de, *Commerce et expéditions militaires de la France et de
Venise au moyen âge* (CD inédits, Mélanges historiques, 3; Paris, 1880).

S16. Morozzo della Rocca, Raimondo, and Antonino Lombardo, eds., *Documenti
del commercio veneziano nei secoli XI–XIII* (Regesta chartarum Italiae, 28–
29 [= Documenti e studi per la storia del commercio e del diritto commerciale italiano, 19-20]; 2 vols., Rome and Turin, 1940).

S17. Morozzo della Rocca, Raimondo, and Antonino Lombardo, eds., *Nuovi documenti del commercio veneto dei secoli XI–XIII* (Deputazione di storia patria
per le Venezie: Monumenti storici, n.s., 7; Venice, 1953).

S18. Noiret, Hippolyte, ed., *Documents inédits pour servir à l'histoire de la domination vénitienne en Crète de 1380 à 1485* (BÉFAR, 61; Paris, 1892).

S19. Predelli, Riccardo, and Pietro Bosmin, eds., *I Libri commemoriali della repubblica di Venezia; Regesti (1293-1787)* (Reale deputazione veneta di storia
patria: Monumenti storici, Ser. 1, Documenti 1, 3, 7–8, 10-11, 13, 17; 8 vols.,
Venice, 1876-1914).

S20. Tafel, Gottlieb L.F., and Georg M. Thomas, eds., *Urkunden zur älteren Handels-
und Staatsgeschichte der Republik Venedig mit besonderer Beziehung auf
Byzanz und die Levante* (Fontes rerum Austriacarum, Sectio II, 12-14; 3 vols.,
Vienna, 1856-1857).

S21. Thiriet, Freddy, ed., *Régestes des délibérations du sénat de Venise concernant
la Romanie* (École pratique des hautes études: Documents et recherches sur
l'économie des pays byzantins, islamiques et slaves et leurs relations commerciales au moyen âge, 1, 2, and 4; 3 vols., Paris and The Hague, 1958–
1961).

S22. Thiriet, Freddy, ed., *Délibérations des assemblées vénitiennes concernant la
Romanie* (École pratique des hautes études: Documents et recherches sur
l'économie des pays byzantins, islamiques et slaves et leurs relations commerciales au moyen âge, 8, 11; 2 vols., Paris and The Hague, 1966-1971).

S23. Thomas, Georg M., and Riccardo Predelli, eds., *Diplomatarium veneto-levantinum sive acta et diplomata res Venetas Graecas atque Levantinas illustrantia,
1300-1451* (Reale Deputazione veneta di storia patria: Monumenti storici,
Ser. 1, Documenti 5, 9; 2 vols., Venice, 1880-1899).

DOCUMENTS – GENOA

S24. *Bonvillano (1198),* ed. J. E. Eierman, Hilmar C. Krueger, and Robert L. Reynolds (R. Deputazione di storia patria per la Liguria, Notai liguri del secolo
XII, 3; Genoa, 1939).

S25. *Giovanni di Guiberto (1200–1211),* ed. Margaret W. Hall-Cole, Hilmar C. Krueger, R. G. Reinert, and Robert L. Reynolds (R. Deputazione di storia patria per la Liguria, Notai liguri del secolo XII, 5; 2 parts, Genoa, 1940).

S26. *Guglielmo Cassinese (1190–1192),* ed. Margaret W. Hall, Hilmar C. Krueger, and Robert L. Reynolds (R. Deputazione di storia patria per la Liguria, Notai liguri del secolo XII, 2; 2 parts, Genoa, 1938).

S27. *Lanfranco (1202–1226),* ed. Hilmar C. Krueger and Robert L. Reynolds (Società ligure di storia patria, Notai liguri del secolo XII e del secolo XIII, 6; 3 parts, Genoa, 1951–1953).

S28. *Oberto Scriba de Mercato (1186),* ed. Mario Chiaudano (R. Deputazione di storia patria per la Liguria, Notai liguri del secolo XII, 4; Genoa, 1939).

S29. *Oberto Scriba de Mercato (1190),* ed. Mario Chiaudano and Raimondo Morozzo della Rocca (R. Deputazione di storia patria per la Liguria, Notai liguri del secolo XII, 1; Genoa, 1938).

S30. Balard, Michel, *Gênes et l'Outremer:* 1. *Les actes de Caffa du notaire Lamberto di Sambuceto 1289–1290;* 2. *Actes de Kilia du notaire Antonio di Ponzo 1360* (École pratique des hautes études [vol. 2, École des hautes études en sciences sociales]: Documents et recherches sur l'économie des pays byzantins, islamiques et slaves et leurs relations commerciales au moyen âge, 12, 13; 2 vols., Paris, The Hague, and New York, 1973–1980).

S31. Barker, John W., "Miscellaneous Genoese Documents on the Levantine World of the Late Fourteenth and Early Fifteenth Centuries," *Byzantine Studies,* VI (1979), 49–82.

S32. Bigoni, Guido, "Quattro documenti genovesi sulle contese d'Oltremare nel secolo XIII," *Archivio storico italiano,* 5-XXIV (1899), 52–65.

S33. Brătianu, Gheorghe I., *Actes des notaires génois de Péra et de Caffa de la fin du treizième siècle (1281–1290)* (Académie roumaine, Études et recherches, 2; Bucharest, 1927).

S34. Chiaudano, Mario, and Mattia Moresco, eds., *Il Cartolare di Giovanni Scriba* (Documenti e studi per la storia del commercio e del diritto commerciale italiano, 1–2; 2 vols., Turin, 1935; repr. Turin, 1970).

S35. Desimoni, Cornelio, "Actes passés en 1271, 1274 et 1279 à l'Aias (Petite Arménie) et à Beyrouth par devant des notaires génois," *AO Latin,* I (1881), 434–534.

S36. Desimoni, Cornelio, "Actes passés à Famagouste de 1299 à 1301 par devant le notaire génois Lamberto di Sambuceto," *AO Latin,* II-2 (1884), 3–120; cf. *RO Latin,* I (1893), 58–139, 275–312, 321–353.

S37. Desimoni, Cornelio, "Quatre titres des propriétés des Génois à Acre et à Tyr," *AO Latin,* II-2 (1884), 213–230.

S38. Holt, Peter M., "Qalāwūn's Treaty with Genoa in 1290," *Der Islam,* LVII (1980), 101–108.

S39. Imperiale di Sant' Angelo, Cesare, ed., *Codice diplomatico della repubblica di Genova* (Fonti SI, 77, 79, 89; 3 vols., Rome, 1936–1942).

DOCUMENTS—PISA

S40. Froux Otten, Catherine, "Les Pisans en Égypte et à Acre dans la seconde moitié du XIIIe siècle: documents nouveaux," *Bollettino storico pisano,* LII (1983), 163–190.

S41. Müller, Joseph (here, Giuseppe), ed., *Documenti sulle relazioni della città toscane coll' Oriente cristiano e coi Turchi fino all' anno 1531* (Documenti degli archivi toscani, 3; Florence, 1879; repr. Rome, 1966).

DOCUMENTS — NAPLES AND SICILY

S42. Capasso, Bartolomeo, *Inventario cronologico-sistematico dei registri angioini conservati nell' archivio di stato in Napoli* (Naples, 1894).

S43. Carini, Isidoro, and Raffaele Starrabba, *Gli Archivi e le biblioteche di Spagna in rapporto alla storia d'Italia in generale e di Sicilia in particolare* (2 vols., Palermo, 1884–1897).

S44. Cosentino, Giuseppe, ed., *Codice diplomatico di Federico III di Aragona, re di Sicilia 1355–1377*: vol. I. *1355–1360* (Documenti per servire alla storia di Sicilia, 1st ser., Diplomatica, 9; Palermo, 1885; all published).

S45. Durrieu, Paul, *Les Archives angevines de Naples: étude sur les registres du roi Charles I (1265–1285)* (BÉFAR, 46, 51; 2 vols., Paris, 1886–1887).

S46. Giudice, Giuseppe del, ed., *Codice diplomatico del regno di Carlo I et II d'Angio dal 1265 al 1303* (3 vols., Naples, 1863–1902).

S47. Jamison, Evelyn M., "Documents from the Angevin Registers of Naples: Charles I," *Papers of the British School at Rome,* XVII (1949), 87–180.

S48. Lefèvre, R., *La Crociata di Tunisi del 1270 nei documenti del distrutto archivio angioino di Napoli* (Istituto italo-africano, Quaderni della rivista "Africa", 5; Rome, 1977).

S49. Travali, Giuseppe, *I Diplomi angioini dell' archivio di stato di Palermo* (Documenti per servire alla storia di Sicilia, 1st ser., Diplomatica, 7; Palermo, 1886).

S50. — *Codice diplomatico dei re aragonesi di Sicilia Pietro I, Giacomo, Federico II, Pietro II e Ludovico dalla rivoluzione siciliana del 1282 sino al 1355*, vol. I ed. Giuseppe La Mantia; vol. II ed. Antonino di Stefano and Francesco Giunta (Documenti per servire alla storia di Sicilia, 23, 24; Palermo, 1918–1954).

S51. — *I Registri della cancellaria angioina ricostruiti da Riccardo Filangieri con la collaborazione degli archivisti napoletani* (Accademia Pontaniana, Naples, Testi e documenti di storia napoletana, 1–30; 30 vols., Naples, 1950–1971).

DOCUMENTS — AMALFI

S52. Camera, Matteo, *Memorie storico-diplomatiche dell' antica città e ducato di Amalfi* (2 vols., Naples, 1876–1881; repr. Salerno, 1972).

DOCUMENTS — MARSEILLES

T1. Blancard, Louis, ed., *Documents inédits sur le commerce de Marseille au moyen-âge* (2 vols., Marseilles, 1884–1885).

T2. Mayer, Hans E., *Marseilles Levantehandel und ein akkonensisches Fälscheratelier des 13. Jahrhunderts* (Bibliothek des Deutschen historischen Instituts in Rom, 38; Tübingen, 1972).

DOCUMENTS – SPAIN

U1. Bofarull y Mascaro, Prospéro, et al., eds., *Collección de documentos inéditos del Archivo general de la corona de Aragon* (41 vols., Barcelona, 1847–1910).

U2. Finke, Heinrich, ed., *Acta Aragonensia, Quellen zur deutschen, italienischen, französischen, spanischen, zur Kirchen- und Kulturgeschichte: aus der diplomatischen Korrespondenz Jaymes II. (1291–1327)* (3 vols., Berlin, 1908–1922); "Nachträge und Ergänzungen zu den Acta Aragonensia I–III," *Gesammelte Aufsätze zur Kulturgeschichte Spaniens,* VII (Spanische Forschungen der Görresgesellschaft, ser. I, 7; Münster, 1938), pp. 326–346.

U3. González, Julio, ed., *Regesta de Fernando II* (Consejo superior de investigaciones cientificas, Instituto Jerónimo Zurita; Madrid, 1943).

U4. Huici Miranda, Ambrósio, ed., *Colección diplomática de Jaime I el Conquistador* (3 vols., Valencia, 1916–1922).

DOCUMENTS – GERMAN EMPIRE

V1. Aronius, Julius, ed., *Regesten zur Geschichte der Juden im fränkischen und deutschen Reiche bis zum Jahre 1273* (Quellen zur Geschichte der Juden in Deutschland, 3–4; 2 vols., Berlin, 1887–1902).

V2. Böhmer, Johann F., *Regesta imperii: IV. Ältere Staufer: Abt. 3. Die Regesten des Kaiserreichs unter Heinrich VI. 1165 (1190)–1197,* compiled by Gerhard Baaken (Graz and Cologne, 1972).

V3. Böhmer, Johann F., *Regesta imperii: V. Die Regesten des Kaiserreichs unter Philipp, Otto IV., Friedrich II., Heinrich (VII.), Conrad IV., Heinrich Raspe, Wilhelm und Richard: 1198–1272,* ed. Julius Ficker and Eduard Winkelmann (3 vols. in 5, Innsbruck, 1881–1901).

V4. Hampe, Karl, ed., *Acta pacis ad S. Germanum anno MCCXXX initae: die Aktenstücke zum Frieden von S. Germano, 1230* (MGH, Epistolae selectae, 4; Berlin, 1926).

V5. Holtzmann, Walther, "Papst-, Kaiser- und Normannenurkunden aus Unteritalien," *QFIAB,* XXXV (1955), 46–85.

V6. Huillard-Bréholles, Jean L.A., *Historia diplomatica Friderici secundi* (6 parts in 12 vols., Paris, 1852–1861).

V7. Zinsmaier, Paul, "Nachträge zu den Kaiser- und Königsurkunden der Regesta imperii 1198–1272," *Zeitschrift für die Geschichte des Oberrheins,* CII (= n.s., LXIII: 1954), 188–273.

DOCUMENTS – HUNGARY

W1. Gelcich, József, and Lajos Thallóczy, eds., *Diplomatarium relationum reipublicae ragusanae cum regno Hungariae* (Budapest, 1887).

DOCUMENTS – BALKANS

X1. Iorga, Nicolae, *Notes et extraits pour servir à l'histoire des croisades au XVe siècle* (6 vols., Paris and Bucharest, 1899–1916).

LEGAL SOURCES

Y1. *Armenisches Rechtsbuch,* ed. Josef Karst (2 vols., Strassburg, 1905).

Y2. *Assises d'Antioche, reproduites en françois,* ed. Leound (here, Léonce) M. Alishan (Gheuant Alishanian) (Venice, 1876).

Y3. *Constitutiones et acta publica imperatorum et regum,* vols. 1–3, ed. Ludwig Weiland and Jakob Schwalm (MGH, Legum, sectio 4; Hanover and Leipzig, 1893–1906).

Y4. *Deutsche Reichstagsakten unter Kaiser Sigmund* (Deutsche Reichstagsakten, 7–10; 4 vols., Munich and Gotha, 1878–1906).

Y5. *Die Statuten des Deutschen Ordens,* ed. Max Perlbach (Halle, 1890); tr. Indrikis Sterns as *The Statutes of the Teutonic Knights: a Study of Religious Chivalry* (diss., University of Pennsylvania; Philadelphia, 1969).

Y6. *Die ursprüngliche Templerregel,* ed. Gustav Schnürer (Studien und Darstellungen aus dem Gebiet der Geschichte, III-1; Freiburg im Breisgau, 1903).

Y7. *Gli Statuti marittimi veneziani fino al 1255,* ed. Riccardo Predelli and Adolfo Sacerdoti (Venice, 1903, separate edition; originally printed in *Nuovo archivio veneto,* n.s., IV [1902], 113–161, 267–291; V [1903], 161–251, 314–356).

Y8. *Gli Statuti veneziani di Jacopo Tiepolo del 1242 e le loro glosse,* ed. Roberto Cessi (Memorie del R. Istituto di scienze, lettere ed arti, XXX-2; Venice, 1938).

Y9. *Ius Graeco-Romanum,* ed. Karl E. Zachariae von Lingenthal (7 vols., Leipzig, 1856–1884).

Y10. *La Règle du Temple,* ed. Henri de Curzon (Société de l'histoire de France; Paris, 1886).

Y11. "Les Assises de Jérusalem ou recueil des ouvrages de jurisprudence composés pendant le XIIIe siècle dans les royaumes de Jérusalem et de Chypre," ed. [Auguste] Beugnot, *RHC, Lois,* I (Paris, 1841), 22–644; II (Paris, 1849), 19–537.

Y12. *Les Assises de Romanie,* ed. Georges Recoura (B Éc. HÉ, 258; Paris, 1930).

Y13. *Les Livres des Assises et des usages dou reaume de Jérusalem; sive, Leges et instituta regni Hierosolymitani,* vol. I, ed. Eduard H. von Kausler (Stuttgart, 1839).

Y14. *Liber consuetudinum imperii Romaniae: Feudal Institutions as Revealed in the Assizes of Romania, the Law Code of Frankish Greece,* tr. and ed. Peter W. Topping (Philadelphia, 1949; repr. New York, 1980).

Y15. *Liber iurium reipublicae Genuensis,* ed. Ercole Ricotti (Historiae patriae monumenta, 7, 9; 2 vols., Turin, 1854–1857).

Y16. Sempad, constable (Smbat Sparapet), *Sudebnik* (Middle Armenian Lawbook), ed. A. G. Galstian (Erivan, 1958).

Y17. "Statuti della colonia genovese di Pera," ed. Vincenzo Promis, *Miscellanea di storia italiana,* XI (1870), 513–780.

Y18. "Statuti e ordinamenti sul governo del Banco di San Giorgio a Famagosta," ed. Vito Vitale, *Atti della Società ligure di storia patria,* LXIV (1935), 390–454.

Y19. *Statuti inediti della città di Pisa dal XII al XIV secolo,* ed. Francesco Bonaini (3 vols., Florence, 1854–1870).

Y20. *The Councils of Urban II: 1. Decreta Claromontensia,* ed. Robert Somerville (Annuarium historiae conciliorum, Supplementum 1; Amsterdam, 1972).

Secondary Works

'Abd-ar-Rāziq, 'Alī, *Islam and the Fundamentals of Authority: a Study of the Caliphate and Government in Islam,* tr. Charles C. Adams (Chicago, 1928).

Abel, Félix M., "Le Couvent des Frères Prêcheurs à St.-Jean d'Acre," *Revue biblique,* XLIII (1934), 265-284.

Abel-Rémusat, Jean Pierre, "Mémoires sur les relations politiques des princes chrétiens et particulièrement des rois de France avec les empereurs mongols," *MAIBL,* VI (1822), 396-469; VII (1824), 335-438.

Abulafia, David, "Henry Count of Malta and his Mediterranean Activities, 1202-1230," in *Medieval Malta: Studies on Malta before the Knights,* ed. Anthony L. Luttrell (London, 1975), pp. 104-125.

Abulafia, David, "Crocuses and Crusaders: San Gimignano, Pisa and the Kingdom of Jerusalem," in *Outremer* (1982), pp. 227-243.

Abulafia, David, "Invented Italians in the Courtois Charters," in *Crusade and Settlement,* ed. Peter W. Edbury (Cardiff, 1985), pp. 135-143.

Aguado Bleye, Pedro, *Manual de historia de España,* rev. ed. by Cayetano Alcázar Molina (Grandes biografías; 3 vols., Madrid, 1969-1971).

Ahrweiler, Hélène, *Byzance et la mer: la marine de guerre, la politique et les institutions maritimes de Byzance aux VIIe-XVe siècles* (Bibliothèque byzantine, Études, 5; Paris, 1966).

Airaldi, Gabriella, and Benjamin Z. Kedar, *I Comuni italiani nel regno crociato di Gerusalemme: Atti del colloquio "The Italian Communes in the Crusading Kingdom of Jerusalem"* (Jerusalem, May 24-May 28, 1984) (Collana storica di fonte e studi, 48; Genoa, 1986).

Alishan, Leound M. (here, Léonce), *Léon le Magnifique, premier roi de Sissouan ou de l'Arméno-Cilicie,* tr. Georges Bayan (Venice, 1888).

Alishan, Leound M. (here, Léonce), *L'Armeno Veneto: Compendio storico e documenti delle relazioni degli Armeni coi Veneziani: 1. Primo periodo, secoli XIII-XIV: Compendio storico; 2. Primo periodo, secoli XIII-XIV: Documenti* (2 vols., Venice, 1893).

Allen, William E.D., *A History of the Georgian People from the Beginning down to the Russian Conquest in the Nineteenth Century* (London, 1932).

Allmendinger, Karl-Heinz, *Die Beziehungen zwischen der Kommune Pisa und Ägypten im hohen Mittelalter* (VSWG, 54, Beiheft; Wiesbaden, 1967).

Almagià, Roberto, et al., *Nel VII Centenario della nascità di Marco Polo* (Istituto veneto di scienze, lettere, ed arti; Venice, 1955).

Almeida, Fortunato de, *História de Portugal* (6 vols., Coimbra, 1922-1929).

Alphandéry, Paul, and Alphonse Dupront, *La Chrétienté et l'idée de croisade: 1. Les premières croisades; 2. Recommencements nécessaires (XIIe et XIIIe siècles)* (Bibliothèque de synthèse historique: L'évolution de l'humanité, 38, 38bis; 2 vols., Paris, 1954, 1959).

Altaner, Berthold, *Die Dominikanermissionen des 13. Jahrhunderts: Forschungen zur Geschichte der kirchlichen Unionen und der Mohammedaner- und Heidenmissionen des Mittelalters* (Breslauer Studien zur historischen Theologie, 3; Habelschwerdt, 1924).

Altaner, Berthold, "Sprachkenntnisse und Dolmetscherwesen im missionarischen und diplomatischen Verkehr zwischen Abendland (päpstliche Kurie) und Orient im 13. und 14. Jahrhundert," *Z Kirch.,* LV (1936), 83-126.

Altaner, Berthold, "Zur Kenntnis des Arabischen im 13. und 14. Jahrhundert," *O Chr. P,* II (1937), 427-452.

Alverny, Marie T. d', "La Connaissance de l'Islam en Occident du IXe au milieu du XIIe siècle," in *L'Occidente e l'Islam nell' alto medioevo,* II (Spoleto, 1965), pp. 577-602, 791-803.

Alverny, Marie T.d', "Alain de Lille et l'Islam: le Contra Paganos," in *Islam et Chrétiens du Midi (xiie—xive s.)* (Cahiers de Fanjeaux, 18; Toulouse, 1983), pp. 301-350.

Amari, Michele, *Storia dei musulmani di Sicilia,* 2nd ed. by Carlo A. Nallino (Biblioteca siciliana di storia, letteratura ed arte; 3 vols., Catania, 1933-1939).

Ambraziejuté, Maria, *Studien über die Johanniterregel* (Freiburg [in Switzerland], 1929).

Andrea, Alfred J., "Conrad of Krosigk, Bishop of Halberstadt, Crusader and Monk of Sittichenbach: his Ecclesiastical Career, 1184-1225," *Analecta Cisterciensia,* XLIII (1984), 11-91.

Andrea, Alfred J., "Cistercian Accounts of the Fourth Crusade: Were They Anti-Venetian?," *Analecta Cisterciensia,* XLIV (1985), 3-41.

Andressohn, John C., *The Ancestry and Life of Godfrey of Bouillon* (Indiana University Publications, Social Science Series, 5; Bloomington, 1947; repr. Freeport, N.Y., 1972).

Andrews, Kevin, *Castles of the Morea* (Gennadeion Monographs, 4; Princeton, 1953; repr. Amsterdam, 1978).

Angelov, David, "Certains aspects de la conquête des peuples balkaniques par les Turcs," *Byzantinoslavica,* XVII (1956), 220-275.

Angold, Michael, *A Byzantine Government in Exile: Government and Society under the Laskarids of Nicaea (1204-1261)* (London, 1975).

Angyal, David, "Le Traité de paix de Szeged avec les Turcs (1444)," *Revue de Hongrie,* IV-7 (1911), 255-268, 374-392.

Antoniadis-Bibicou, Hélène, *Recherches sur les douanes à Byzance; l'"octava", le "kommerkion" et les commerciaires* (Cahiers des Annales, 20; Paris, 1963).

Antuña, Melchor M., "Campañas de los Almohades en España," *Religión y cultura,* XXIX (1935), 347-373.

Archer, Thomas A., "On the Accession Dates of the Early Kings of Jerusalem," *Eng. HR,* IV (1889), 89-105.

Argenti, Philip P., *The Occupation of Chios by the Genoese and their Administration of the Island, 1346-1566* (3 vols., Cambridge, Eng., 1958).

Argenti, Philip P., "The Mahona of the Giustiniani: Genoese Colonialism and the Genoese Relationship with Chios," *Byz. F,* VI (1979), 1-35.

Arkel de Leeuw van Weenen, Andrea van, and Krijne Ciggaar, "St. Thorlac's in Constantinople, Built by a Frankish Emperor," *Byzantion,* XLIX (1979), 428-446.

Armingaud, Jean J.M., "Venise et le Bas-Empire," *Archives des missions scientifiques et littéraires,* 2-IV (1867), 299-443.

Arnold, Thomas W., and Alfred Guillaume, eds., *The Legacy of Islam* (Oxford, 1931).

Arnold, Udo, "Jerusalem und Akkon: zur Frage von Kontinuität oder Neugründung des Deutschen Ordens 1190," *MIÖG,* LXXXVI (1978), 416-432.

Arnold, Udo, "Entstehung und Frühzeit des Deutschen Ordens: zu Gründung und innerer Struktur des Deutschen Hospitals von Akkon und des Ritterordens in der ersten Hälfte des 13. Jahrhunderts," in *Die geistlichen Ritterorden Europas,* ed. Josef Fleckenstein and Manfred Hellmann (Vorträge und Forschungen, 26; Sigmaringen, 1980), pp. 81-107.

Aschoff, Volker, *Über den byzantinischen Feuertelegraphen und Leon den Mathematiker* (Deutsches Museum, Abhandlungen und Berichte, 48; Munich, 1980).

Ashtor, Eliyahu, "Républiques urbaines dans le Proche-Orient à l'époque des croisades?," *Cah. Civ. Méd.,* XVIII (1975), 117-131.

Ashtor, Eliyahu, and Benjamin Z. Kedar, "Una Guerra fra Genova e i Mamlucchi negli anni 1380," *Archivio storico italiano,* CXXXIII (1975), 3-44.

Ashtor, Eliyahu, *A Social and Economic History of the Near East in the Middle Ages* (London, 1976).

Ashtor, Eliyahu, "Il Commercio levantino di Ancona nel basso medioevo," *Rivista storica italiana,* LXXXVIII (1976), 213-253.

Ashtor, Eliyahu, "Observations on Venetian Trade in the Levant in the XIVth Century," *Journal of European Economic History,* V (1976), 533-586.

Ashtor, Eliyahu, "The Venetian Cotton Trade in Syria in the Later Middle Ages," *Studi medievali,* 3-XVII (1976), 675-715.

Ashtor, Eliyahu, "Levantine Sugar Industry in the Later Middle Ages — an Example of Technological Decline," *Israel Oriental Studies,* VII (1977), 226-276.

Ashtor, Eliyahu, "L'Exportation de textiles occidentaux dans le Proche Orient musulman au bas moyen âge (1370-1517)," in *Studi in memoria di Federigo Melis,* ed. L. de Rosa (Naples, 1978), II, 303-377.

Ashtor, Eliyahu, *Studies on the Levantine Trade in the Middle Ages* (Varior. Repr., CS, 74; London, 1978).

Ashtor, Eliyahu, "Europäischer Handel im spätmittelalterlichen Palästina," in *Das Heilige Land im Mittelalter,* ed. Wolfdietrich Fischer and Jürgen Schneider (Neustadt an der Aisch, 1982), pp. 107-126.

Asmar, Camille, "L'Abbaye de Belmont dite Deir el Balamand," *Bulletin du Musée de Beyrouth,* XXV (1972, publ. 1975), 1-69.

Astuti, Guido, "L'Organizzazione giuridica del sistema coloniale e della navigazione mercantile delle città italiane nel medio evo," in *Mediterraneo e Oceano Indiano: Atti del VI colloquio di storia marittima* (Civiltà veneziana, Studi, 23; Florence, 1970), pp. 57-90.

Atiya, Aziz S., *The Crusade of Nicopolis* (London, 1934; repr. New York, 1978).

Atiya, Aziz S., *The Crusade in the Later Middle Ages* (London, 1938).

Atiya, Aziz S., *A History of Eastern Christianity* (London and Notre Dame, 1968).

Atiya, Aziz S., "The Crusade in the Fourteenth Century," *H of C,* III (1975), 3-26, and "The Aftermath of the Crusades," *ibid.,* 647-666.

Ayalon, David, *Studies on the Mamlūks of Egypt (1250-1517)* (Varior. Repr., CS, 62; London, 1977).

Babinger, Franz, "Von Amurath zu Amurath: Vor- und Nachspiel der Schlacht bei Varna," *Oriens,* III (1950), 229-265.

Babinger, Franz, *Mehmed der Eroberer und seine Zeit: Weltenstürmer einer Zeitenwende,* 2nd ed. (Munich, 1959); tr. Ralph Manheim, ed. William C. Hickman, as *Mehmed the Conqueror and his Time* (Bollingen Series, 96; Princeton, 1978).

Bach, Erik, *La Cité de Gênes au XIIe siècle* (Classica et mediaevalia dissertationes, 5; Copenhagen, 1955).

Baethgen, Friedrich, *Die Regentschaft Papst Innozenz III. im Königreich Sicilien* (Heidelberger Abhandlungen zur mittleren und neueren Geschichte, 44; Heidelberg, 1914).

Bagatti, Bellarmino, *I Monumenti di Emmaus (el-Qubeibeh) e dei dintorni: risultato degli scavi e sopralluoghi negli anni 1873, 1887-90, 1900-02, 1940-44* (Studium BF, 4; Jerusalem, 1947).

Bagatti, Bellarmino, "Le Pitture medievali della pietra di Betfage," *Studii biblici fran-ciscani Liber annuus,* I (1950–1951), 228–246.

Bagatti, Bellarmino, *Gli Antichi edifici sacri di Betlemme, in seguito agli scavi e re-stauri praticati dalla Custodia di Terra Santa (1948–1951)* (Studium BF, 9; Jerusa-lem, 1952).

Bagatti, Bellarmino, and Emmanuele Festa, *Il Golgata e la croce: ricerche storico-archeologiche* (Studium BF, Collectio minor, 21; Jerusalem, 1978).

Baker, Derek, ed., *Relations between East and West in the Middle Ages* (Edinburgh, 1973); includes Gill, Riley-Smith.

Baker, John N.L., *Medieval Trade Routes* (London, 1938).

Balard, Michel, "Les Génois en Asie centrale et en Extrême-Orient au XIVe siècle: un cas exceptionnel," in *Économies et sociétés au moyen âge: Mélanges offerts à Édouard Perroy* (Paris, 1973), pp. 681–689.

Balard, Michel, *La Romanie génoise (XIIe–début du XVe siècle)* (BÉFAR, 235 [= Atti della Società ligure di storia patria, n.s., 18], 2 vols., Rome and Genoa, 1978).

Balbis, Giannino, "Il Medioevo genovese tra Mediterraneo e Mar Nero," *Nuova ri-vista storica,* LXI (1977), 182–193.

Balducci, Hermes, *La Chiesa di S. Maria del Borgo in Rodi, fondata dal gran maestro Hèlion de Villeneuve; La cattedrale di Rodi; La chiesa di Santa Caterina della Lin-gua d'Italia* (Pavia, 1933).

Baldwin, Marshall W., "Ecclesiastical Developments in the Twelfth Century Crusad-ers' State of Tripolis," *Cath. HR,* XXII (1936), 149–171.

Baldwin, Marshall W., *Raymond III of Tripolis and the Fall of Jerusalem (1140–1187)* (Princeton, 1936; repr. New York, 1978).

Baldwin, Marshall W., "The Latin States under Baldwin III and Amalric, 1143–1174," *H of C,* I (1955, 2nd ed. 1969), 528–561, and "The Decline and Fall of Jerusalem," *ibid.,* 590–621.

Baldwin, Marshall W., "Missions to the East in the Thirteenth and Fourteenth Cen-turies," *H of C,* V (1985), 452–518.

Ballesteros, Manuel, "La Conquista de Jaén por Fernando III el Santo," *Cuadernos de historia de España,* XX (1953), 63–138.

Ballesteros y Beretta, Antonio, *Historia de España y su influencia en la historia uni-versal,* 2nd ed. (10 vols., Barcelona, 1922–1944).

Ballesteros y Beretta, Antonio, "La Reconquista de Murcia, 1243–1493," *Boletín de la Real Academia de la historia,* CXI (1942), 133–150.

Baltrušaitis, Jurgis, *Études sur l'art médiéval en Géorgie et en Arménie* (Paris, 1929).

Baltrušaitis, Jurgis, *Le Problème de l'ogive et l'Arménie* (Paris, 1936).

Banescu, Nicolae, *Le Déclin de Famagouste: fin du royaume de Chypre: notes et docu-ments* (Institut roumain d'études byzantines, n.s., 4; Bucharest, 1946).

Banús y Comas, Carlos, *Expedición de Catalanes y Aragoneses a Oriente a principios del siglo XIV* (Madrid, 1929).

Barasch, Moshe, *Crusader Figural Sculpture in the Holy Land: Twelfth Century Ex-amples from Acre, Nazareth and Belvoir Castle* (Ramat Gan and New Brunswick, 1971).

Barasch, Moshe, "An Unknown Work of Medieval Sculpture in Acre," *Scripta Hiero-solymitana,* XXIV (1972), 72–105.

Barber, Malcolm C., "James of Molay, the Last Grand Master of the Order of the Temple," *Studia monastica,* XIV (1972), 91–124.

Barber, Malcolm C., *The Trial of the Templars* (Cambridge, Eng., 1978).

Barber, Malcolm, "The Pastoureaux of 1320," *Journal of Ecclesiastical History,* XXXII (1981), 143–166.

Barkan, Ömer Lütfi, "Les Déportations comme méthode de peuplement et de colonisation dans l'empire ottoman," *Revue de la Faculté des sciences économiques de l'Université d'Istanbul,* XI (1949–1950), 67–131.

Barker, John W., *Manuel II Palaeologus (1391–1425): a Study in Late Byzantine Statesmanship* (Rutgers Byzantine series; New Brunswick, 1969).

Bartol'd, Vasiliĭ V., *Turkestan down to the Mongol Invasion,* tr. Bartol'd and Hamilton A.R. Gibb, 2nd ed. (E.J.W. Gibb Memorial Series, 2, 5; London, 1928).

Bartol'd, Vasiliĭ V. (here, Wilhelm), *Zwölf Vorlesungen über die Geschichte der Türken Mittelasiens,* tr. Theodor Menzel (Die Welt des Islams, 14–17; 4 vols., Berlin, 1932–1935).

Bartoš, František M., *Husitská revoluce* (České dějiny, díl 2, č. 7-8; 2 vols., Prague, 1965–1966); ed. and tr. John Klassen as *The Hussite Revolution, 1424–1437* (East European Monographs, 203; Boulder, Colo., 1986).

Basmadjian, Karapet J., "Les Lusignans de Poitou au trône de la Petite Arménie," *JA,* 10-VII (1906), 520–524.

Baynes, Norman H., and Henry St. L.B. Moss, eds., *Byzantium: an Introduction to East Roman Civilisation* (Oxford, 1948).

Beaumont, André A., "Albert of Aachen and the County of Edessa," in *The Crusades and Other Historical Essays Presented to Dana C. Munro,* ed. Louis J. Paetow (New York, 1928), pp. 101–138.

Beck, Hans G., *Die byzantinische Kirche im Zeitalter der Kreuzzüge (Handbuch der Kirchengeschichte,* ed. Hubert Jedin, vol. V-2; Freiburg, 1968).

Beck, Marcel, "Alexios Komnenos zwischen Türken und Normannen," in *Legende, Mythos, Geschichte: die Schweiz und das europäische Mittelalter* (Frauenfeld, 1978), pp. 74–84.

Beck, Marcel, "Kreuzzug und Imperium zur Zeit der Staufer," in *Legende, Mythos, Geschichte: die Schweiz und das europäische Mittelalter* (Frauenfeld, 1978), pp. 85–117.

Beck, Marcel, "Die geschichtliche Bedeutung der Kreuzzüge," in *Legende, Mythos, Geschichte: die Schweiz und das europäische Mittelalter* (Frauenfeld, 1978), pp. 118–139.

Becker, Carl H., "The Expansion of the Saracens," *Cambridge Mediaeval History,* vol. II (Cambridge, Eng., 1913; repr. 1926, 1964), pp. 329–390.

Bédier, Charles M.J. (here, Joseph), and Pierre Aubrey, eds., *Les Chansons de croisade* (Paris, 1909).

Bédier, Charles M.J. (here, Joseph), *Les Légendes épiques: recherches sur la formation des chansons de geste,* 3rd ed. (4 vols., Paris, 1926–1929).

Beebe, Bruce, "The English Baronage and the Crusade of 1270," *Bulletin of the Institute of Historical Research,* XLVIII (1975), 127–149.

Beldiceanu-Steinherr, Irène, "La Conquête d'Andrinople par les Turcs," *Travaux et mémoires,* I (Paris, 1965), 431–461.

Belperron, Pierre, *La Croisade contre les Albigeois et l'union du Languedoc à la France (1209–1249)* (Paris, 1942).

Benvenisti, Meron, *The Crusaders in the Holy Land* (Jerusalem, 1970; New York, 1972).

Benvenisti, Meron, "Bovaria — Bariyya: a Frankish Residue on the Map of Palestine," in *Outremer* (1982), pp. 130–152.

Béraud-Villars, Jean M.E., *Les Normands en Méditerranée* (Paris, 1951).

Berchem, Max van, "Notes sur les croisades: 1. Le royaume de Jérusalem et le livre de M. Röhricht," *JA,* 9-XIX (1902), 385-456.

Berlière, Ursmer, "Die alten Benedictinerklöster im Heiligen Lande," *Studien und Mitteilungen aus dem Benediktiner- und Cistercienserorden,* IX (1888), 113-130, 260-272, 473-492.

Bernhard, Ludger, "Die Legitimität des Lateinischen Kaiserreiches von Konstantinopel in jakobitischer Sicht," *Jahrbuch der Österreichischen byzantinischen Gesellschaft,* XVI (1967), 133-138.

Bernhardi, Wilhelm von, *Konrad III.* (Jahrbücher der deutschen Geschichte; Leipzig, 1883).

Berry, Virginia G., "The Second Crusade," *H of C,* I (1955, 2nd ed. 1969), 463-512.

Bertram, Martin, "Johannes von Ancona: ein Jurist des 13. Jahrhunderts in den Kreuzfahrerstaaten," *Bulletin of Medieval Canon Law,* n.s., VII (1977), 49-64.

Bertrand, Paul, *Histoire des chevaliers-hospitaliers de Saint-Lazare* (Paris, 1932).

Besta, Enrico, "La Cattura dei Veneziani in Oriente per ordine dell' imperatore Emmanuele Comneno e le sue conseguenze nella politica interna ed esterna del comune di Venezia," *Antologia veneta,* I (1900), 35-46, 111-123.

Bettin, Hans, *Heinrich II. von Champagne: seine Kreuzfahrt und Wirksamkeit im Heiligen Lande (1190-1197)* (Hist. Stud., ed. Ebering, 85; Berlin, 1910).

Beumann, Helmut, *Heidenmission und Kreuzzugsgedanke in der deutschen Ostpolitik des Mittelalters* (Wege der Forschung, 6; Darmstadt, 1963).

Bezold, Friedrich von, *König Sigmund und die Reichskriege gegen die Husiten bis zum Ausgang des dritten Kreuzzugs* (3 vols. in 1, Munich, 1872-1877).

Bezold, Friedrich von, *Zur Geschichte des Husitentums: Culturhistorische Studien* (Munich, 1874).

Bezzola, Gian A., *Die Mongolen in abendländischer Sicht (1120-1270): ein Beitrag zur Frage der Völkerbegegnungen* (Berne, 1974).

Bikai, Patricia M., "A New Crusader Church in Tyre," *Bulletin du Musée de Beyrouth,* XXIV (1971), 83-90.

Billioud, Joseph, "De la Date de la perte de Chypre par la branche légitime des Lusignans, 1464," *Le Moyen-âge,* XXXIV (= 2-XXV; 1923), 66-71.

Bishko, Charles Julian, "The Spanish and Portuguese Reconquest, 1095-1492," *H of C,* III (1975), 396-456.

Bishko, Charles J., *Studies in Medieval Spanish Frontier History* (Varior. Repr., CS, 124; London, 1980).

Blake, E. O., "The Formation of the 'Crusade Idea'," *Journal of Ecclesiastical History,* XXI (1970), 11-31.

Blochet, Edgard, "Les Relations diplomatiques des Hohenstaufen avec les sultans d'Égypte," *Rev. hist.,* LXXX (1902), 51-64.

Boase, Thomas S.R., *Castles and Churches of the Crusading Kingdom* (London and New York, 1967).

Boase, Thomas S.R., *Kingdoms and Strongholds of the Crusaders* (London, 1971).

Boase, Thomas S.R., "Ecclesiastical Art in the Crusader States in Palestine and Syria: A. Architecture and Sculpture; B. Mosaic, Painting, and Minor Arts," *H of C,* IV (1977), 69-139, and "Military Architecture in the Crusader States . . . ," *ibid.,* 140-164.

Boase, Thomas S.R., "The Arts in Cyprus: A. Ecclesiastical Art," *H of C,* IV (1977), 165-195, and "The Arts in Frankish Greece and Rhodes: A. Frankish Greece," with David J. Wallace; "B. Rhodes," *ibid.,* 208-250.

Boase, Thomas S.R., ed., *The Cilician Kingdom of Armenia* (Edinburgh and London, 1978).

Boehlke, Frederick J., *Pierre de Thomas: Scholar, Diplomat, and Crusader* (Philadelphia, 1966).

Boehm, Laetitia, "De Karlingis imperator Karolus, princeps totius Europae: zur Orientpolitik Karls I. von Anjou," *Historisches Jahrbuch,* LXXXVIII (1968), 1–35.

Böhm, Ludwig, *Johann von Brienne, König von Jerusalem, Kaiser von Konstantinopel* (Diss., Heidelberg, 1938).

Bolton, Brenda M., "A Mission to the Orthodox? the Cistercians in Romania," in *The Orthodox Churches and the West* (Oxford, 1976), pp. 169–181.

Bon, Antoine, "Forteresses médiévales de la Grèce centrale," *BC Hell.,* LXI (1937), 136–208.

Bon, Antoine, "Note additionelle sur les forteresses médiévales de la Grèce centrale," *BC Hell.,* LXII (1938), 441–442.

Bon, Antoine, "La Prise de Kalamata par les Francs en 1205," *Revue archéologique,* 6-XXIX–XXX (= Mélanges d'archéologie et d'histoire offerts à Charles Picard . . . , I; 1949), 98–104.

Bon, Antoine, *Le Péloponnèse byzantin jusqu'en 1204* (Bibliothèque byzantine, Études, 1; Paris, 1951).

Bon, Antoine, "Recherches sur la principauté d'Achaïe (1205–1430)," in *Études médiévales offerts à M. le doyen Augustin Fliche . . .* (Publications de la Faculté des lettres de l'Université de Montpellier, 4; Vendôme, 1953), pp. 7–21.

Bon, Antoine, *La Morée franque: recherches historiques, topographiques et archéologiques sur la principauté d'Achaïe (1205–1430)* (BÉFAR, 213; 2 vols., Paris, 1969).

Boockmann, Hartmut, *Der Deutsche Orden: Zwölf Kapitel aus seiner Geschichte* (Munich, 1981).

Borg, Alan, "Observations on the Historiated Lintel of the Holy Sepulchre, Jerusalem," *Journal of the Warburg and Courtauld Institutes,* XXXII (1969), 25–40.

Borg, Alan, "The Holy Sepulchre Lintel," *Journal of the Warburg and Courtauld Institutes,* XXXV (1972), 389–390.

Borg, Alan, "The Lost Apse Mosaic of the Holy Sepulchre," in *The Vanishing Past: Studies of Medieval Art, Liturgy and Metrology Presented to Christopher Hohler,* ed. Alan Borg and Andrew Martindale (British Archaeological Reports, International Series, 111; Oxford, 1981), pp. 7–12.

Borsari, Silvano, "Federico II e l'Oriente bizantino," *Rivista storica italiana,* LXIII (1951), 279–291.

Borsari, Silvano, *Il Dominio veneziano a Creta nel XIII secolo* (Naples, 1963).

Borsari, Silvano, "Il Commercio veneziano nell' impero bizantino nel XII secolo," *Rivista storica italiana,* LXXVI (1964), 982–1011.

Borsari, Silvano, *Studi sulle colonie veneziane in Romania nel XIII secolo* (Naples, 1966).

Borsari, Silvano, "Per la Storia del commercio veneziano col mondo bizantino nel XII secolo," *Rivista storica italiana,* LXXXVII (1976), 104–126.

Borst, Arno, *Die Katharer* (MGH, Schriften, 12; Stuttgart, 1953).

Bosch, Ursula V., *Kaiser Andronikos III. Palaiologos: Versuch einer Darstellung der byzantinischen Geschichte in den Jahren 1321–1341* (Amsterdam, 1965).

Bosio, Giacomo, *Dell' Istoria della sacra religione ed ill[ustrissi]ma militia di S. Giovanni Gierosolimitano,* 2nd ed. (3 vols., Rome and Naples, 1621–1684).

Bourrilly, V. L., "Essai sur l'histoire politique de la commune de Marseille des origines à la victoire de Charles d'Anjou (1264)," *Annales de la Faculté des lettres d'Aix,* XII (1919-1920), 1-240; XIII (1921-1922), 23-308.

Boutaric, Edgard, *La France sous Philippe le Bel: étude sur les institutions politiques et administratives de moyen âge* (Paris, 1861).

Boutaric, Edgard, "La Guerre des Albigeois et Alphonse de Poitiers," *Rev. QH,* II (1867), 155-180.

Boutaric, Edgard, *Clément V, Philippe le Bel et les Templiers* (Paris, 1872).

Boyle, John A., "The Il-Khans of Persia and the Princes of Europe," *Central Asiatic Journal,* XX (1976), 25-40.

Brader, David, *Bonifaz von Montferrat bis zum Antritt der Kreuzfahrt (1202)* (Hist. Stud., ed. Ebering, 55; Berlin, 1907).

Branca, Vittore, ed., *Storia della civiltà veneziana: 1. Dalle origini al secolo di Marco Polo* (Florence, 1979).

Brand, Charles M., "The Byzantines and Saladin, 1185-1192, Opponents of the Third Crusade," *Speculum,* XXXVII (1962), 167-181.

Brand, Charles M., "A Byzantine Plan for the Fourth Crusade," *Speculum,* XLIII (1968), 462-475.

Brand, Charles M., *Byzantium Confronts the West, 1180-1204* (Cambridge, Mass., 1968).

Brandenburg, Erich, *König Sigmund und Kurfürst Friedrich I. von Brandenburg* (Berlin, 1891).

Brătianu, Gheorghe I., *Recherches sur le commerce génois dans la Mer Noire au XIIIe siècle* (Paris, 1929).

Brătianu, Gheorghe I., *Études byzantines d'histoire économique et sociale* (Universitatea Mihaileană din Iaşi, Studii de istorie generală, 4; Paris, 1938).

Brătianu, Gheorghe I., *Les Vénetiens dans la Mer Noire au XIVe siècle: la politique du Sénat en 1332-33 et la notion de latinité* (Academia romana, Bucharest, Études et recherches, 11; Bucharest, 1939).

Braune, Michael, "Die mittelalterlichen Befestigungen der Stadt Tortosa/Ṭarṭūs: Vorbericht der Untersuchungen 1981-1982," *Damaszener Mitteilungen,* II (1985), 45-54.

Bray, Jennifer R., "The Medieval Military Order of St. Katherine," *Bulletin of the Institute of Historical Research,* LVI (1983), 1-6.

Bredero, Adriaan H., "Studien zu den Kreuzzugsbriefen Bernhards von Clairvaux und zu seiner Reise nach Deutschland im Jahre 1146," *MIÖG,* LXVI (1958), 331-343.

Bredero, Adriaan H., "Jérusalem dans l'Occident médiéval," in *Mélanges offerts à René Crozet à l'occasion de son soixante-dixième anniversaire,* ed. Pierre Gallais and Yves Jean Riou, vol. I (Poitiers, 1966), pp. 259-271.

Bréhier, Louis, *L'Église et l'Orient au moyen-âge: les croisades* (Bibliothèque de l'enseignement d'histoire ecclésiastique; 6th ed., Paris, 1928).

Bréhier, Louis, *Le Monde byzantin* (Bibliothèque de synthèse historique: L'évolution de l'humanité, 32-32ter; 3 vols., Paris, 1947-1950).

Bresc-Bautier, Geneviève, "Les Imitations du Saint-Sépulcre de Jérusalem (IXe-XVe s.): archéologie d'une dévotion," *Revue d'histoire de la spiritualité,* L (1974), 319-324.

Breton, René, "Monographie du château de Markab, en Syrie," *Mélanges de l'Université Saint-Joseph,* XLVII (1972), 251-274.

Bridge, Antony, *The Crusades* (London, 1980).

Bridrey, Émile, *La Condition juridique des croisés et le privilège de croix* (Paris, 1900).

Briggs, Martin S., *Muhammadan Architecture in Egypt and Palestine* (Oxford, 1924).

Brockelmann, Carl, *Geschichte der islamischen Völker und Staaten* (2nd ed., Munich and Berlin, 1943); tr. Joel Carmichael and Moshe Perlmann as *History of the Islamic Peoples* (New York, 1947).

Brockman, Eric, *The Two Sieges of Rhodes, 1480-1522* (London, 1969).

Brooks, Neill C., *The Sepulchre of Christ in Art and Liturgy, with Special Reference to the Liturgic Drama* (University of Illinois Studies in Language and Literature, VII, no. 2; Urbana, 1921).

Brown, Elizabeth A.R., "The Cistercians in the Latin Empire of Constantinople and Greece, 1204-1276," *Traditio,* XIV (1958), 63-120.

Brown, Horatio F., "The Venetians and the Venetian Quarter in Constantinople to the Close of the Twelfth Century," *Journal of Hellenic Studies,* XL (1920), 68-88.

Brundage, James A., "Adhemar of Puy: the Bishop and his Critics," *Speculum,* XXXIV (1959), 201-212.

Brundage, James A., "An Errant Crusader: Stephen of Blois," *Traditio,* XVI (1960), 380-395.

Brundage, James A., "The Crusade of Richard I: Two Canonical 'Quaestiones'," *Speculum,* XXXVIII (1963), 443-452.

Brundage, James A., "A Note on the Attestation of Crusaders' Vows," *Cath. HR,* LII (1966), 234-239.

Brundage, James A., "'Cruce Signari': the Rite for Taking the Cross in England," *Traditio,* XXII (1966), 289-310.

Brundage, James A., "The Crusader's Wife: a Canonistic Quandary," *Studia Gratiana,* XII (= Collectanea Stephan Kuttner, 2; 1967), 425-441.

Brundage, James A., "The Crusader's Wife Revisited," *Studia Gratiana,* XIV (= Collectanea Stephan Kuttner, 4; 1967), 241-251.

Brundage, James A., "The Votive Obligations of Crusaders: the Development of a Canonistic Doctrine," *Traditio,* XXIV (1968), 77-118.

Brundage, James A., *Medieval Canon Law and the Crusader* (Madison, 1969).

Brundage, James A., "The Army of the First Crusade and the Crusade Vow: Some Reflections on a Recent Book," *Mediaeval Studies,* XXXIII (1971), 334-343.

Brundage, James A., "Marriage Law in the Latin Kingdom of Jerusalem," in *Outremer* (1982), pp. 258-271.

Brundage, James A., "St. Anselm, Ivo of Chartres, and the Ideology of the First Crusade," in *Les Mutations socio-culturelles au tournant des XIe–XIIe siècles: Études Anselmiennes (IVe session)* (Paris, 1984), pp. 175-187.

Brunschvig, Robert, *La Berbérie orientale sous les Ḥafṣides des origines à la fin du XV siècle* (Publications de l'Institut d'études orientales d'Alger, 8, 11; 2 vols., Paris, 1940-1947).

Bryer, Anthony A.M., "The Fate of George Komnenos, Ruler of Trebizond (1266-1280)," *Byz. Z,* LXVI (1973), 332-350.

Bryer, Anthony A.M., "Greeks and Türkmens: the Pontic Exception," *D Oaks P,* XXIX (1975), 113-148.

Bryer, Anthony A.M., *The Latins in the Euxine* (XVe Congrès international d'études byzantines: Rapports et co-rapports: 1. Histoire: pt. 3. La symbiose dans les états latins formés sur les territoires byzantins: phénomènes sociaux, économiques, religieux et culturels; Athens, 1976).

Buchon, Jean A., *Recherches et matériaux pour servir à une histoire de la domination française aux 13e, 14e et 15e siècles dans les provinces demembrées de l'empire grec à la suite de la 4e croisade* (2 vols., Paris, 1840).

Buchon, Jean A., *La Grèce continentale et la Morée: voyage, séjour et études historiques en 1840 et 1841* (Paris, 1843).

Buchon, Jean A., *Nouvelles recherches historiques sur la principauté française de Morée et ses hautes baronnies à la suite de la 4e croisade* (2 vols. and atlas, Paris, 1843).

Buchon, Jean A., *Recherches historiques sur la principauté francaise de Morée et ses hautes baronnies* (2 vols., Paris, 1845).

Buchthal, Hugo, "The Painting of Syrian Jacobites in its Relation to Byzantine and Islamic Art," *Syria,* XX (1939), 136–150.

Buchthal, Hugo, *Miniature Painting in the Latin Kingdom of Jerusalem, with Liturgical and Palaeographical Chapters* by Francis Wormald (Oxford, 1957).

Buckley, James M., "The Problematical Octogenarianism of John of Brienne," *Speculum,* XXXII (1957), 315–322.

Buisson, Ludwig, *Erobererrecht, Vasallität und byzantinisches Staatsrecht auf dem ersten Kreuzzug* (Berichte aus den Sitzungen der Joachim-Jungius-Gesellschaft der Wissenschaften, 2, no. 7; Hamburg, 1985).

Bulst-Thiele, Marie L., "Templer in königlichen und päpstlichen Diensten," in *Festschrift Percy Ernst Schramm zu seinem siebzigsten Geburtstag . . .,* ed. Peter Classen and Peter Scheibert, vol. I (Wiesbaden, 1964), pp. 289–308.

Bulst-Thiele, Marie L., "Zur Geschichte der Ritterorden und des Königreichs Jerusalem im 13. Jahrhundert bis zur Schlacht bei La Forbie am 17. Oktober 1244," *Deutsches Archiv,* XXII (1966), 197–226.

Bulst-Thiele, Marie L., *Sacrae domus militiae Templi Hierosolymitani magistri: Untersuchungen zur Geschichte des Templerordens 1118/19–1314* (Abh. Gött., 3rd ser., 86; Göttingen, 1974).

Bulst-Thiele, Marie L., "Die Mosaiken der Auferstehungskirche in Jerusalem und die Bauten der Franken im 12. Jahrhundert," *Frühmittelalterliche Studien,* XIII (1979), 442–471.

Burns, Robert I., "The Catalan Company and the European Powers, 1305–1311," *Speculum,* XXIX (1954), 751–771.

Burns, Robert I., *The Crusader Kingdom of Valencia: Reconstruction on a Thirteenth Century Frontier* (2 vols., Cambridge, Mass., 1967).

Burns, Robert I., *Islam under the Crusaders: Colonial Survival in the 13th Century Kingdom of Valencia* (Princeton, 1973).

Burns, Robert I., *Medieval Colonialism: Postcrusade Exploitation of Islamic Valencia* (Princeton, 1975).

Burns, Robert I., *Moors and Crusaders in Mediterranean Spain* (Varior. Repr., CS, 73; London, 1978).

Burns, Robert I., *El Reino de Valencia en el siglo XIII (iglesia y sociedad)* (2 vols., Valencia, 1982; revision of *The Crusader Kingdom of Valencia).*

Burns, Robert I., *Muslims, Christians and Jews in the Crusader Kingdom of Valencia* (Cambridge, Mass., 1983).

Bury, John B., "The Lombards and Venetians in Euboia (1205–1303)," *Journal of Hellenic Studies,* VII (1886), 309–352; VIII (1887), 194–213; IX (1888), 91–117.

Bury, John B., "Roman Emperors from Basil II to Isaac Komnenos," in *Selected Essays of J. B. Bury,* ed. Harold Temperley (Cambridge, Eng., 1930), pp. 126–214.

Buschhausen, Helmut, *Die süditalienische Bauplastik im Königreich Jerusalem von König Wilhelm II. bis Kaiser Friedrich II.* (Österreichische Akademie der Wissenschaften, phil.-hist. Klasse, Denkschriften, 108; Vienna, 1978).

Busse, Heribert, "Vom Felsendom zum Templum Domini," in *Das Heilige Land im Mittelalter*, ed. Wolfdietrich Fischer and Jürgen Schneider (Neustadt an der Aisch, 1982), pp. 19–32.

Byrne, Eugene H., "Genoese Trade with Syria in the 12th Century," *Amer. HR*, XXV (1919–1920), 191–219.

Byrne, Eugene H., "The Genoese Colonies in Syria," in *The Crusades and Other Historical Essays Presented to Dana C. Munro*, ed. Louis J. Paetow (New York, 1928), pp. 139–182.

Byrne, Eugene H., *Genoese Shipping in the Twelfth and Thirteenth Centuries* (Med. AA, Monographs, 1; Cambridge, Mass., 1930).

Caddeo, Rinaldo, et al., eds., *Storia marittima dell' Italia, dall' evo antico ai nostri giorni*, vol. I (Milan, 1942).

Caggese, Romolo, *Roberto d'Angiò e i suoi tempi* (2 vols., Florence, 1922–1930).

Cagigas, Isidro de las, *Minorías étnico-religiosas de la edad media española* (4 vols., Madrid, 1947–1949).

Cahen, Claude, "La Campagne de Mantzikert d'après les sources musulmanes," *Byzantion*, IX (1934), 613–642.

Cahen, Claude, "Le Diyâr Bakr au temps des premiers Urtukides," *JA*, CCXXVII (1935), 219–276.

Cahen, Claude, *La Syrie du Nord à l'époque des croisades et la principauté franque d'Antioche* (Institut français de Damas, Bibliothèque orientale, 1; Paris, 1940).

Cahen, Claude, "La Première pénétration turque en Asie Mineure (seconde moitié du XIe s.)," *Byzantion*, XVIII (1948), 5–67.

Cahen, Claude, "Notes sur l'histoire des croisades et de l'Orient latin: 1. En quoi la conquête turque appelait-elle la croisade?," *Bulletin de la Faculté des lettres de l'Université de Strasbourg*, XXIX (1950–1951), 118–125.

Cahen, Claude, "Notes sur l'histoire des croisades et de l'Orient latin: 2. Le régime rural syrien au temps de la domination franque," *Bulletin de la Faculté des lettres de l'Université de Strasbourg*, XXIX (1950–1951), 286–310.

Cahen, Claude, "Notes sur l'histoire des croisades et de l'Orient latin: 3. Orient latin et commerce du Levant," *Bulletin de la Faculté des lettres de l'Université de Strasbourg*, XXIX (1950–1951), 328–346.

Cahen, Claude, "Le Commerce anatolien au début du XIIIe siècle," in *Mélanges d'histoire du moyen âge (dédiés à la mémoire de) Louis Halphen*, ed. Charles E. Perrin (Paris, 1951), pp. 91–101.

Cahen, Claude, "Pour l'Histoire des Turcomanes d'Asie mineure au XIIIe siècle," *JA*, CCXXXIX (1951), 325–354.

Cahen, Claude, "L'Évolution de l'iqṭāʿ du IXe au XIIIe siècle: contribution à une histoire comparée des sociétés médiévales," *Annales: Économies, sociétés, civilisations*, VIII-1 (1953), 25–52.

Cahen, Claude, "Notes sur les débuts de la futuwwa d'an-Nasir," *Oriens*, VI (1953), 18–22.

Cahen, Claude, "An Introduction to the First Crusade," *Past and Present* (1954), no. 6, pp. 6–29.

Cahen, Claude, "L'Islam et la croisade," *Relazioni del X Congresso internazionale di scienze storiche, Roma 1955: 3. Storia del medio evo* (Florence, 1955), pp. 625–635.

Cahen, Claude, "The Turkish Invasion: the Selchükids," *H of C*, I (1955, 2nd ed. 1969), 135–176.

Cahen, Claude, "La Féodalité et les institutions politiques de l'Orient latin," in *Oriente ed Occidente nel medio evo: Convegno di scienze morali, storiche e filologiche 27 maggio−1° giugno 1956* (Accademia nazionale dei Lincei, Fondazione Alessandro Volta, Atti dei convegni, 12; Rome, 1957), pp. 167-191.

Cahen, Claude, "Le Premier cycle de la croisade (Antioche, Jérusalem, Chétifs)," *Le Moyen-âge,* LVII (1957), 312-328.

Cahen, Claude, "Mouvements populaires et autonomisme urbain dans l'Asie musulmane du moyen âge," *Arabica,* V (1958), 225-250; VI (1959), 25-56, 233-265.

Cahen, Claude, "Zur Geschichte der städtischen Gesellschaft im islamischen Orient des Mittelalters," *Saeculum,* IX (1958), 59-76.

Cahen, Claude, "Selğukides, Turcomans et Allemands au temps de la troisième croisade," *Wiener Zeitschrift für die Kunde des Morgenlandes,* LVI (1960), 21-31.

Cahen, Claude, "The Turks in Iran and Anatolia before the Mongol Invasions," *H of C,* II (1962, 2nd ed. 1969), 661-692, and "The Mongols and the Near East," *ibid.,* 715-732.

Cahen, Claude, "À Propos des coutumes du marché d'Acre," *RH Droit FÉ,* 4-XLI (1963), 287-290.

Cahen, Claude, "L'Alun avant Phocée: un chapître d'histoire économique islamo-chrétienne au temps des croisades," *Revue d'histoire économique et sociale,* XLI (1963), 433-447.

Cahen, Claude, "Douanes et commerces dans les ports méditerranéens de l'Égypte médiévale d'après le Minhādj d'al-Makhzūmī," *JESHO,* VII (1964), 217-314.

Cahen, Claude, *Pre-Ottoman Turkey: a General Survey of the Material and Spiritual Culture c. 1071-1330,* tr. J. Jones-Williams (New York, 1968).

Cahen, Claude, "Saint-Louis et l'Islam," *JA,* CCLVIII (1970), 3-12.

Cahen, Claude, "La Politique orientale des comtes de Flandre et la lettre d'Alexis Comnène," *Mélanges d'Islamologie: Volume dédié à la mémoire de Armand Abel,* ed. Pierre Salmon (Leyden, 1974), pp. 84-90.

Cahen, Claude, *Turcobyzantina et Oriens christianus* (Varior. Repr., CS, 34; London, 1974).

Cahen, Claude, "Amalfi en Orient à la veille, au moment et au lendemain de la première croisade," in *Amalfi nel medioevo* (Salerno, 1977), pp. 271-283.

Cahen, Claude, "Le Commerce d'Amalfi dans le Proche-Orient musulman avant et après la croisade," *CRAIBL* (1977), pp. 291-300.

Cahen, Claude, *Les Peuples musulmans dans l'histoire médiévale* (Damascus, 1977).

Cahen, Claude, *Orient et Occident au temps des croisades* (Paris, 1983).

Camera, Matteo, *Istoria della città e costiera di Amalfi* (Naples, 1836).

Campbell, George A., *The Knights Templars: their Rise and Fall* (London, 1937; repr. New York, 1980).

Canale, Michele G., *Della spedizione in Oriente di Amedeo VI di Savoia, detto il conte verde* (Genoa, 1887).

Canard, Marius, "L'Impérialisme des Fatimides et leur propagande," *Annales de l'Institut d'études orientales d'Alger,* VI (1942-1947), 156-193.

Cantarino, Vicente, "The Spanish Reconquest: a Cluniac Holy War Against Islam?," in *Islam and the Medieval West: Aspects of Intercultural Relations,* ed. Khalil S. Semaan (Albany, N.Y., 1980), pp. 82-109.

Capmany y de Montpalau, Antonio de, *Memorias históricas sobre la marina, comercio y artes de la antigua ciudad de Barcelona* (4 vols., Madrid, 1779-1792).

Cardini, Franco, "La Crociata nel duecento: l'Avatāra' di un ideale," *Archivio storico italiano,* CXXXV (1977), 101-139.

Cardini, Franco, "La Repubblica di Firenze e la crociata di Pio II," *Rivista di storia della chiesa in Italia,* XXXIII (1979), 455–482.

Cardini, Franco, "Pelegrinaggi medievali in Terra Santa," *Rivista storica italiana,* XCIII (1981), 5–10.

Cardini, Franco, "La Société italienne et les croisades," *Cah. Civ. Méd.,* XXVIII (1985), 19–33.

Carile, Antonio, "Partitio terrarum imperii Romanie," *Studi veneziani,* VII (1965), 125–305.

Carile, Antonio, *La Rendita feudale nella Morea latina del XIV secolo* (Bologna, 1974).

Carile, Antonio, "La Cancellaria sovrana dell' impero latino di Costantinopoli (1204–1261)," *Studi veneziani,* n.s., II (1978), 37–73.

Carile, Antonio, *Per una Storia dell' impero latino di Costantinopoli (1204–1261)* (Il mondo medievale: Sezione di storia bizantina e slava, 2; 2nd ed., Bologna, 1978).

Carile, Antonio, "Movimenti di popolazione e colonizzazione occidentale in Romania nel XIII secolo alla luce della composizione dell' esercito crociato nel 1204," *Byz. F,* VII (1979), 5–22.

Carile, Antonio, "Signoria rurale e feudalesimo nell' impero latino di Costantinopoli (1204–1261)," in *Structures féodales et féodalisme dans l'Occident méditerranéen (Xe–XIIIe siècles: Bilan et perspectives de recherches)* (Collection de l'École française de Rome, 44; Rome, 1980), pp. 667–678.

Caro, Georg, *Genua und die Mächte am Mittelmeer 1257–1311: ein Beitrag zur Geschichte des 13. Jahrhunderts* (2 vols., Halle, 1895–1897); Italian tr. as *Genova e la supremazia sul Mediterraneo (1257–1311)* (Atti della Società ligure di storia patria, n. s., 14–15; 2 vols., Genoa, 1974–1975).

Carra de Vaux, Bernard, *Les Penseurs de l'Islam* (5 vols., Paris 1921–1926).

Cartellieri, Alexander, "L'Ordonnance de Philippe-Auguste sur la dîme de la croisade de 1184," *Rev. hist.,* LXXIII (1900), 61–63; *cf. ibid.,* LXXVI (1901), 329–330.

Cartellieri, Alexander, *Philipp II. August, König von Frankreich: 2. Der Kreuzzug (1187–1191)* (Leipzig and Paris, 1906).

Cartellieri, Otto, *Abt Suger von Saint-Denis (1081–1151)* (Hist. Stud., ed. Ebering, 11; Berlin, 1898).

Caspar, Erich, *Roger II. (1101–1154) und die Gründung der normannisch-sicilischen Monarchie* (Innsbruck, 1904).

Caspar, Erich, *Hermann von Salza und die Gründung des Deutschordensstaats in Preussen* (Tübingen, 1924).

Cate, James Lea, "A Gay Crusader," *Byzantion,* XVI (1942–1943), 503–526.

Cate, James Lea, "The Crusade of 1101," *H of C,* I (1955, 2nd ed. 1969), 343–367.

Cauwenbergh, Étienne van, *Les Pèlerinages expiatoires et judiciaires dans le droit communal de la Belgique au moyen âge* (Université de Louvain, Recueil de travaux publiés par les membres des conférences d'histoire et de philologie, 48; Louvain, 1922).

Cazel, Fred A., "The Tax of 1185 in Aid of the Holy Land," *Speculum,* XXX (1955), 385–392.

Cazel, Fred A., "Financing the Crusades," *H of C,* VI (1989), 116–149.

Cerone, Francesco, "La Politica orientale di Alfonso di Aragona," *Archivio storico per le provincie napoletane,* XXVII (1902), 3–93, 380–456, 555–634, 774–852; XXVIII (1903), 154–212.

Cerone, Francesco, *L'Opera politica e militare di Ruggiero II in Africa ed in Oriente* (Catania, 1913).

Cerone, Francesco, "La Sovranità napoletana sulla Morea e sulle isole vicine," *Archivio storico per le province napoletane,* XLI (1916), 5–64, 193–266; XLII (1917), 5–67.

Cerulli, Enrico, *Etiopi in Palestina: Storia della comunità etiopica di Gerusalemme* (Collezione scientifica e documentaria a cura del Ministero dell' Africa italiana, 12, 14; 2 vols., Rome, 1943–1947).

Cervellini, Giovanni B., "Come i Veneziani aquistarono Creta," *Nuovo archivio veneto,* n.s., XVI (1908), 262–278.

Cessi, Roberto, "Venezia e l'acquisto di Nauplia ed Argo," *Nuovo archivio veneto,* XXX (1915), 147–173.

Cessi, Roberto, *Venezia ducale: 1. Duca e popolo* (Venice, 1940).

Cessi, Roberto, *Le Colonie medioevali italiane in Oriente: I. La conquista* (Bologna, 1942).

Cessi, Roberto, "Venezia e la quarta crociata," *Arch. Ven.,* 5-XLVIII–XLIX (1951), 1–52.

Cessi, Roberto, *Politica ed economia di Venezia nel Trecento* (Storia e letteratura, 40; Rome, 1952).

Cessi, Roberto, "L'Eredità di Enrico Dandolo," *Arch. Ven.,* XCI (1960), 1–25.

Cessi, Roberto, *Storia della repubblica di Venezia* (Biblioteca storica principato, 23, 26; new ed., 2 vols., Milan and Messina, 1968).

Chabot, Jean B., "Notes sur les relations du roi Argoun avec l'Occident," *RO Latin,* II (1894), 566–638.

Chalandon, Ferdinand, *Les Comnène: étude sur l'empire byzantin au XIe au XIIe siècles* (Mémoires et documents publiés par la Société de l'École des chartes, 4; 2 vols., Paris, 1900–1912; repr. New York, 1960).

Chalandon, Ferdinand, *Histoire de la domination normande en Italie et en Sicile* (2 vols., Paris, 1907).

Chalandon, Ferdinand, *Histoire de la première croisade jusqu'à l'élection de Godefroi de Bouillon* (Paris, 1925).

Chandon de Briailles, Raoul, "Lignages d'Outre-Mer: les seigneurs de Margat," *Syria,* XXV (1946–1948), 231–258.

Chapman, Conrad, *Michel Paléologue, restaurateur de l'empire byzantin (1261-1282)* (Paris, 1926).

Charanis, Peter, "Byzantium, the West and the Origin of the First Crusade," *Byzantion,* XIX (1949), 17–36.

Charanis, Peter, "On the Social Structure and Economic Organization of the Byzantine Empire in the 13th Century and Later," *Byzantinoslavica,* XII (1951), 94–153.

Charanis, Peter, "Aims of the Medieval Crusades and How they Were Viewed by Byzantium," *Church History,* XXI (1952), 123–134.

Charanis, Peter, "Economic Factors in the Decline of the Byzantine Empire," *Journal of Economic History,* XIII (1953), 412–424.

Charanis, Peter, "The Byzantine Empire in the Eleventh Century," *H of C,* I (1955, 2nd ed. 1969), 177–219.

Charanis, Peter, *The Armenians in the Byzantine Empire* (Lisbon, 1963).

Charon, J., "L'Église grecque melchite catholique," *Échos d'Orient,* IV (1900–1901), 268–275, 325–333; V (1901–1902), 18–25, 82–89, 141–147, 203–206, 264–270, 332–343; VI (1903), 16–24, 113–118, 198–207, 298–307, 379–386; VII (1904), 21–26.

Chasin, Martin, "The Crusade of Varna," *H of C,* VI (1989), 276–310.

Chazan, Robert, "Emperor Frederick I, the Third Crusade and the Jews," *Viator,* VIII (1977), 83–93.

Chazan, Robert, *European Jewry and the First Crusade* (Berkeley, 1987).

Cheetham, Nicolas, *Medieval Greece* (New Haven and London, 1981).

Chéhab, Maurice H., *Tyr à l'époque des croisades:* 1. *Histoire militaire et diplomatique* (forming, in two parts, vols. XXVII and XXVIII of the *Bulletin du Musée de Beyrouth;* Paris, 1975); 2. *Histoire sociale, économique et religieuse* (forming, in two parts, vols. XXXI and XXXII of the *Bulletin du Musée de Beyrouth;* Paris, 1979).

Chevalier, Ulysse, *La Croisade du dauphin Humbert II 1345–1347: discours prononcé à la fête du cinquantenaire de la Société d'archéologie de la Drôme, 10 février 1920* (Paris, 1920).

Christiansen, Eric, *The Northern Crusades: the Baltic and the Catholic Frontier, 1100–1525* (Minneapolis, London, and Basingstoke, 1980).

Christin, Pierre, *Étude des classes inférieures d'après les Assises de Jérusalem* (Poitiers, 1912).

Chrysostomides, Julian, "Venetian Commercial Privileges under the Palaeologi," *Studi veneziani,* XII (1970), 267–356.

Citarella, Armand O., "The Relations of Amalfi with the Arab World before the Crusades," *Speculum,* XLII (1967), 299–312.

Citarella, Armand O., "Patterns in Medieval Trade: the Commerce of Amalfi before the Crusades," *Journal of Economic History,* XXVIII (1968), 531–555.

Clapham, Alfred W., "The Latin Monastic Buildings of the Church of the Holy Sepulchre, Jerusalem," *Antiquaries Journal,* I (1921), 3–18.

Clément, Olivier, "Byzance et le concile de Lyon," Κληρονομία, VII (1975), 254–272.

Clermont-Ganneau, Charles, *Études d'archéologie orientale* (B Éc. HÉ, 44, 113; 2 vols. in 4 parts, Paris, 1880–1897).

Clermont-Ganneau, Charles, *Recueil d'archéologie orientale* (8 vols., Paris, 1888–1924).

Clermont-Ganneau, Charles, *Archaeological Researches in Palestine during the Years 1873–1874,* tr. Aubrey Stewart and John Macfarlane (2 vols., London, 1896–1899).

Cocheril, Maur, "Essai sur l'origine des ordres militaires dans la péninsule ibérique," *Collectanea ordinis Cisterciensium reformatorum,* XX (1958), 346–461; XXI (1959), 228–250, 302–329.

Cognasso, Francesco, "Un Imperatore bizantino della decadenza: Isaaco II Angelo," *Bessarione,* Anno 19, fasc. 31 (1915), 29–60.

Cohn, Willy, *Die Geschichte der normannisch-sizilischen Flotte unter der Regierung Rogers I. und Rogers II. (1060–1154)* (Historische Untersuchungen, 1; Breslau, 1910; repr., together with two other relevant studies by Cohn, in his *Die Geschichte der sizilischen Flotte 1060–1266* (Aalen, 1978).

Cohn, Willy, *Hermann von Salza* (Abhandlungen der Schlesischen Gesellschaft für vaterländische Cultur, 4; Breslau, 1930).

Combe, Étienne, *Alexandrie au moyen âge* (Alexandria, 1928).

Conant, Kenneth J., "The Original Buildings at the Holy Sepulchre in Jerusalem," *Speculum,* XXXI (1956), 1–48.

Conder, Claude R., *The Latin Kingdom of Jerusalem 1099 to 1291 A.D.* (London, 1897; repr. New York, 1973).

Congar, Yves M.C., "Henri de Marcy, abbé de Clairvaux, cardinal-évêque d'Albano et légat pontifical," *Studia Anselmiana,* XLIII (= Analecta monastica: Textes et études sur la vie des moines au moyen âge; 5th ser., Rome, 1958), pp. 1–90.

Coniglio, Giuseppe, "Amalfi e il commercio amalfitano nel medio evo," *Nuova rivista storica,* XXVIII–XXIX (1944–1945), 100–114.

Conrad, Hermann, "Gottesfrieden und Heeresverfassung in der Zeit der Kreuzzüge:

ein Beitrag zur Geschichte des Heeresstrafrechts im Mittelalter," *Zeitschrift der Savigny-Stiftung für Rechtsgeschichte, Germanistische Abt.,* LXI (1941), 71–126.

Constable, Giles, "A Note on the Route of the Anglo-Flemish Crusaders of 1147," *Speculum,* XXVIII (1953), 525–526.

Constable, Giles, "The Second Crusade as Seen by Contemporaries," *Traditio,* IX (1953), 213–279.

Constable, Giles, "The Financing of the Crusades," in *Outremer* (1982), pp. 64–88.

Constable, Giles, "Opposition to Pilgrimage in the Middle Ages," *Studia Gratiana,* XIX (1976; Mélanges G. Fransen, I), 123–146.

Cook, Robert F., and Larry S. Crist, *Le Deuxième cycle de la croisade: deux études sur son développement: Les textes en vers; Saladin* (Publications romanes et françaises, 120; Geneva, 1972).

Cook, Robert F., *"Chanson d'Antioche": chanson de geste: le cycle de la croisade est-il épique?* (Purdue University Monographs in Romance Languages, 2; Amsterdam, 1980).

Cosack, Harald, "Konrads III. Entschluss zum Kreuzzug," *MIÖG,* XXXV (1914), 278–296.

Cosack, Ulrich, *Die Eroberung von Lissabon im Jahre 1147: eine Episode aus der Geschichte des zweiten Kreuzzuges* (Diss., Halle, 1875).

Coüasnon, Charles, *The Church of the Holy Sepulchre in Jerusalem* (Schweich Lectures of the British Academy, 1972; tr. J. P. and Claude Ross, London, 1974).

Coulton, George G., *Crusades, Commerce and Adventure* (London, Edinburgh, and New York, 1930).

Cowdrey, Herbert E.J., "Pope Urban II's Preaching of the First Crusade," *History,* LV (1970), 177–188.

Cowdrey, Herbert E.J., "Cluny and the First Crusade," *Revue bénédictine,* LXXXIII (1973), 285–311.

Cowdrey, Herbert E.J., "The Mahdia Campaign of 1087," *Eng. HR,* XCII (1977), 1–29.

Cowdrey, Herbert E.J., "Pope Gregory VII's 'Crusading' Plans of 1074," in *Outremer* (1982), pp. 27–40.

Cowdrey, Herbert E.J., *Popes, Monks and Crusaders* (London, 1984).

Cowdrey, Herbert E.J., "Martyrdom and the First Crusade," in *Crusade and Settlement,* ed. Peter W. Edbury (Cardiff, 1985), pp. 46–56.

Cox, Eugene L., *The Green Count of Savoy* (Princeton, 1967).

Cramer, Valmar, "Kreuzpredigt und Kreuzzugsgedanke von Bernhard von Clairvaux bis Humbert von Romans," *Das Heilige Land in Vergangenheit und Gegenwart,* I (1939; = Pal. DVHL, 17–20), 43–204.

Cramer, Valmar, *Der Ritterorden vom Hl. Grabe von den Kreuzzügen bis zur Gegenwart* (Pal. DVHL, 46–48; Cologne, 1952).

Crescini, Vincenzo, *Rambaut de Vaqueiras et le marquis Boniface de Montferrat* (Toulouse, 1901).

Creswell, Keppel A.C., *The Works of Sultan Baibars al-Bunduqdârî in Egypt* (Cairo, 1926).

Creswell, Keppel A.C., *Early Muslim Architecture: Umayyads, Early 'Abbāsids and Tūlūnids* (2 vols., Oxford, 1932–1940).

Creswell, Keppel A.C., "Fortification in Islam before A.D. 1250," *Proceedings of the British Academy* (1952), pp. 89–125.

Creswell, Keppel A.C., *The Muslim Architecture of Egypt:* 1. *Ikhshīds and Fātimids, A.D. 939–1171;* 2. *Ayyūbids and Early Bahrite Mamluks, A.D. 1171–1326* (2 vols., Oxford, 1952–1959).

Croussouloudis, Nicolas, "Les Origines de l'église de Chio et les différentes listes de ses évêques," *Κληρονομία,* IX (1977), 338-369.

Crozet, René, "Le Voyage d'Urbain II et ses négociations avec le clergé de France (1095-1096)," *Rev. hist.,* CLXXIX (1937), 271-310.

Curtis, Edmund, *Roger of Sicily and the Normans in Lower Italy, 1016–1154* (Heroes of the Nations; London and New York, 1912; repr. New York, 1973).

Cutler, Alan, "The First Crusade and the Idea of Conversion," *Muslim World,* LVIII (1968), 155-164.

Dąbrowski, Jan, *Władysław I Jagiellończyk na Węgrzech, 1440-1444* (Rozprawy historyczne Towarzystwa Naukowego Warszawskiego, 2, zesz 1; Warsaw, 1922).

Dąbrowski, Jan, "L'Année 1444," *Bulletin international de l'Académie polonaise . . . ; Classe d'histoire et de philosophie,* supp. 6 (Cracow, 1951).

Dade, Erwin, *Versuche zur Wiedererrichtung der lateinischen Herrschaft in Konstantinopel im Rahmen der abendländischen Politik (1261 bis etwa 1310)* (Diss., Jena; Würzburg and Jena, 1938).

Dagron, Gilbert, "Minorités ethniques et religieuses dans l'Orient byzantin à la fin du Xe et au XIe siècle: l'immigration syrienne," *Travaux et mémoires du Centre de recherche d'histoire et civilisation de Byzance,* VI (1976), 177-216.

Dalleggio d'Alessio, Eugenio (here, Eugène), "Les Sanctuaires urbains et suburbains de Byzance sous la domination latine, 1204-1261," *RÉ Byz.,* XI (1953), 50-61.

Dalleggio d'Alessio, Eugenio, "Listes des podestats de la colonie génoise de Péra (Galata) des prieurs et sous-prieurs de la Magnifica Communità," *RÉ Byz.,* XXVII (1969), 151-157.

Dalman, Gustaf, *Arbeit und Sitte in Palästina* (Schriften des Deutschen Palästina-Instituts, 3, 5, 6, 8-10; Zugleich Beiträge zur Förderung christlicher Theologie, 2nd ser., 14, 15, 27, 29, 33, 36, 41, 48; 7 parts in 8 vols., Gütersloh, 1928-1942).

Daly, William M., "Christian Fraternity, the Crusaders, and the Security of Constantinople, 1097-1204: the Precarious Survival of an Ideal," *Mediaeval Studies,* XXII (1960), 43-91.

Daniel, Norman, *Islam and the West: the Making of an Image* (Edinburgh, 1960).

Daniel, Norman, "The Legal and Political Theory of the Crusade," *H of C,* VI (1989), 3-38, and "Crusade Propaganda," *ibid.,* 39-97.

Danstrup, John, "The State and Landed Property in Byzantium to ca. 1250," *Classica et Mediaevalia,* VIII (1946), 222-262.

Datta, Pietro L., *Spedizione in Oriente di Amedeo VI, conte di Savoia* (Turin, 1826).

Dauvillier, Jean, "L'Expansion de l'église syrienne en Asie centrale et en Extrême-Orient," *L'Orient syrien,* I (1956), 76-87.

Dauvillier, Jean, "Guillaume de Rubrouck et les communautés chaldéennes d'Asie centrale," *Annuaire de l'École des législations religieuses* (1951-1952), II, 36-42; revised version in *L'Orient syrien,* II (1957), 223-242.

Dauvillier, Jean, "La Papauté, l'union des églises et les missions en Orient durant le moyen âge: à propos d'un ouvrage récent," *Revue d'histoire ecclésiastique,* LXXIV (1979), 640-651.

David, Charles W., *Robert Curthose, Duke of Normandy* (Harvard Historical Studies, 25; Cambridge, Mass., 1920; repr. New York, 1982).

Dawson, Christopher H., ed., *The Mongol Mission: Narratives and Letters of the Franciscan Missionaries in Mongolia and China in the Thirteenth and Fourteenth Centuries,* tr. by a Nun of Stanbrook Abbey (The Makers of Christendom; London and New York, 1955; repr. New York, 1980).

Day, Gerald W., "Manuel and the Genoese: a Reappraisal of Byzantine Commercial

Policy in the Late XIIth Century," *Journal of Economic History,* XXXVII (1977), 289–301.

Day, Gerald W., "Byzantine-Genoese Diplomacy and the Collapse of Emperor Manuel's Western Policy 1168–1171," *Byzantion,* XLVIII (1978), 393–405.

Day, John, *Les Douanes de Gênes, 1376–1377* (2 vols., Paris, 1963).

Dean, Bashford, "A Crusaders' Fortress in Palestine: a Report of Explorations Made by the Museum 1926," *Bulletin of the Metropolitan Museum of Art,* XXII-2 (1927).

Defrémery, Charles F., "Nouvelles recherches sur les Ismaéliens ou Bathiniens de Syrie, plus connus sous le nom d'Assassins, et principalement sur leurs rapports avec les états chrétiens d'Orient," *JA,* 5-III (1854), 373–421; 5-V (1855), 5–76.

Delaruelle, Étienne, "Essai sur la formation de l'idée de croisade," *Bulletin de la littérature ecclésiastique publié par l'Institut catholique de Toulouse,* XLII (1941), 24–45, 86–103; XLV (1944), 13–46, 73–90; LIV (1953), 226–239; LV (1954), 50–63.

Delaruelle, Étienne, "L'Idée de croisade chez Saint Louis," *Bulletin de littérature ecclésiastique publié par l'Institut catholique de Toulouse,* LXI (1960), 241–257.

Delaruelle, Étienne, "L'Idée de croisade dans la littérature clunisienne du XIe siècle et l'abbaye de Moissac," *Annales du Midi,* LXXV (1963), 419–439.

Delaruelle, Étienne, *L'Idée de croisade au moyen âge* (Turin, 1980).

Delaville Le Roulx, Joseph, *La France en Orient au XIVe siècle: expéditions du maréchal Boucicaut* (BÉFAR, 44, 45; 2 vols., Paris, 1886).

Delaville Le Roulx, Joseph, "L'Ordre de Montjoye," *RO Latin,* I (1893), 42–57.

Delaville Le Roulx, Joseph, *Les Hospitaliers en Terre Sainte et à Chypre (1100–1310)* (Paris, 1904).

Delaville Le Roulx, Joseph, *Les Hospitaliers à Rhodes jusqu'à la mort de Philibert de Naillac (1310–1421)* (Paris, 1913).

Delbrück, Hans, *Geschichte der Kriegskunst im Rahmen der politischen Geschichte: 3. Das Mittelalter,* 2nd ed. (Berlin, 1923).

Delehaye, Hippolyte, *Les Origines du culte des martyrs,* 2nd ed. (Subsidia hagiographica, 20; Brussels, 1933).

Delisle, Léopold, *Mémoire sur les opérations financières des Templiers* (*MAIBL,* XXXIII-2; Paris, 1889).

Demirkent, Isin, *Urfa haçli kontluğu tarihi (1098–1118)* (Istanbul Universitesi edebiyat fakültesi yayînlarî, no. 1896; Istanbul, 1974).

Dennett, Daniel C., "Pirenne and Muhammad," *Speculum,* XXIII (1948), 165–190.

Dennett, Daniel C., *Conversion and Poll Tax in Early Islam* (Cambridge, Mass., 1950).

Dennis, George T., *The Reign of Manuel II Palaeologus in Thessalonica, 1382–1387* (Orientalia christiana analecta, 159; Rome, 1960).

Dennis, George T., "The Correspondence of Rodolfo de Sanctis, Canon of Patras, 1386," *Traditio,* XVII (1961), 285–321.

Dennis, George T., *Byzantium and the Franks, 1350–1420* (Varior. Repr., CS, 150; London, 1982).

Der Nersessian, Sirarpie, *Manuscrits arméniens illustrés des XIIe, XIIIe et XIVe siècles de la Bibliothèque des Pères Mekhitharistes de Venise* (2 vols., Paris, 1936–1937).

Der Nersessian, Sirarpie, *Armenia and the Byzantine Empire: a Brief Study of Armenian Art and Civilisation* (Cambridge, Mass., 1945).

Der Nersessian, Sirarpie, "The Kingdom of Cilician Armenia," *H of C,* II (1962, 2nd ed. 1969), 630–659.

Der Nersessian, Sirarpie, *Études byzantines et arméniennes: Byzantine and Armenian Studies* (Fundaçâo Calouste Gulbenkian, Bibliothèque arménienne de la Fondation Calouste Gulbenkian; 2 vols., Louvain, 1973).

Deschamps, Paul, "Au Temps des croisades: le château de Saone dans la principauté d'Antioche," *Gazette des beaux-arts,* 6-IV (1930), 329-364.

Deschamps, Paul, "La Sculpture française en Palestine et en Syrie à l'époque des croisades," *Mémoires et monuments de la fondation Piot,* XXXI (1930), 91-118.

Deschamps, Paul, "Un Chapiteau roman du Berry, imité à Nazareth au XIIe siècle," *Mémoires et monuments de la fondation Piot,* XXXII (1932), 119-126, and pl. XI.

Deschamps, Paul, *Les Châteaux des croisés en Terre Sainte:* 1. *Le Crac des Chevaliers;* 2. *La défense du royaume de Jérusalem;* 3. *La défense du comté de Tripoli et de la principauté d'Antioche* (Bibl. AH, 19, 34, 90; 3 vols. and 3 albums of plates, Paris, 1934-"1973" – vol. 3 actually published in 1977).

Deschamps, Paul, "Le Château de Servantikar en Cilicie, le défilé de Marris et la frontière du comté d'Édesse," *Syria,* XVIII (1937), 379-388.

Dib, Pierre, *Histoire de l'église maronite* (Mélanges et documents, I; 2 vols., Beirut, 1962).

Dichter, B., *The Orders and Churches of Crusader Acre* (Acre, 1979).

Dickerhof, Harald, "Über die Staatsgründungen des ersten Kreuzzuges," *Historisches Jahrbuch,* C (1980), 95-130.

Diehl, Charles, "Les Fresques de l'église d'Abou-Gosch," *CRAIBL* (1924), pp. 89-96.

Diehl, Charles, *La Société byzantine à l'époque des Comnènes: Conférences faites à Bucarest (avril 1929)* (Paris, 1929).

Diehl, Charles, ed., *Histoire de l'art byzantin:* 1. Charles Diehl, *La Peinture byzantine* (Paris, 1933); 2. Jean Ebersolt, *Monuments d'architecture byzantine* (Paris, 1934); 3. Louis Bréhier, *La Sculpture et les arts mineurs byzantins* (Paris, 1936).

Digard, Georges A.L., *Philippe le Bel et le Saint-Siège de 1285 à 1304* (2 vols., Paris, 1936).

Dirimtekin, Feridun, *İstanbul'un fethi* (T. C. İstanbul Belediyesi İstanbul fethinin 500 üneil yil dön ümünü kutlulama yayîn larîndar, sayi 6; Istanbul, 1949).

Dodu, Gaston J., *Histoire des institutions monarchiques dans le royaume latin de Jérusalem, 1099-1291* (Paris, 1894; repr. New York, 1978).

Dölger, Franz, "Das Fortbestehen der 'ἐπιβολή in mittel- und spätbyzantinischer Zeit," in *Studi in memoria di Aldo Albertoni,* II (Padua, 1934), pp. 3-11.

Dölger, Franz, *Beiträge zur Geschichte der byzantinischen Finanzverwaltung, besonders des 10. und 11. Jahrhunderts* (Byzantinisches Archiv, 9; 2nd ed., Hildesheim, 1960).

Donaver, Federico, *La Storia della repubblica di Genova* (3 vols., Genoa, 1913-1914).

Donovan, Joseph P., *Pelagius and the Fifth Crusade* (Philadelphia, 1950; repr. New York, 1976).

Dossat, Yves, "Le Comté de Toulouse et la féodalité languedocienne à la veille de la croisade albigeoise," *Revue du Tarn,* IX (1943), 75-90.

Dossat, Yves, "La Société méridionale à la veille de la croisade albigeoise," *RHL Lang.,* I (1944), 66-87.

Dossat, Yves, "Le Clergé méridional à la veille de la croisade albigeoise," *RHL Lang.,* I (1944), 263-278.

Dossat, Yves, "Cathares et Vaudois à la veille de la croisade albigeoise," *RHL Lang.,* II (1945), 390-397; III (1946), 70-83.

Dossat, Yves, "Alfons de Poitiers et la préparation financière de la croisade de Tunis: les ventes de forêts (1268-1270)," in *Septième centenaire de la mort de Saint-Louis: Actes des colloques de Royaumont et de Paris* (Paris, 1976), pp. 121-232.

Dournovo, Lidiia A., *Armenian Miniatures,* with preface by Sirarpie Der Nersessian, tr. Irene J. Underwood (London, 1961).

Dräseke, Johannes, "Der Kircheneinigungsversuch des Kaisers Michael VIII. Paläo-logos," *Zeitschrift für wissenschaftliche Theologie,* XXXIV (1891), 325–355.

Dräseke, Johannes, "Zum Kircheneinigungsversuch des Jahres 1439," *Byz. Z,* V (1896), 572–586.

Dräseke, Johannes, "Bischof Anselm von Havelberg," *Z Kirch.,* XXI (1900), 160–185.

Dräseke, Johannes, "Der Übergang der Osmanen nach Europa im XIV. Jahrhundert," *Neue Jahrbücher für das klassische Altertum,* XXXI (1913), 476–504.

Dressaire, Léopold, "Les Peintures executées au XIIe siècle sur les colonnes de la ba-silique de Bethléem," *Jérusalem,* XXVII (1932), 365–369.

Du Cange, Charles Du Fresne, *Les Familles d'Outremer,* ed. Emmanuel G. Rey (CD inédits, 18; Paris, 1869).

Du Mesnil du Buisson, Robert, "Les Anciennes défenses de Beyrouth," *Syria,* II (1921), 235–257, 317–327.

Ducellier, Alain, *La Façade maritime de l'Albanie au moyen âge: Durazzo et Valona du XIe au XVe siècle* (Documents et recherches sur l'économie des pays byzantins, islamiques et slaves et leurs relations commerciales au moyen âge, 13; Thessalonica, 1981).

Dufourcq, Charles E., *L'Espagne catalane et le Maghrib au XIIIe et XIVe siècles de la bataille de Las Navas de Tolosa (1212) à l'avènement du sultan mérinide Abou-l-Hassan (1331)* (Bibliothèque de l'École des hautes études hispaniques, 37; Paris, 1966).

Dujčev, Ivan, "La Conquête turque et la prise de Constantinople dans la littérature slave contemporaine," *Byzantinoslavica,* XIV (1953), 14–54; XV (1955), 318–329; XVI (1956), 276–340.

Dujčev, Ivan, "La Spedizione catalana in Oriente all' inizio del secolo XIV ed i Bul-gari," *Annuario de estudios medievales,* IX (1974–1979), 425–437.

Dujčev, Ivan, "Car Kalojan, bitkata pri Odrin prez april 1205 g. i nejnite setnini [Tsar Kaloyan, the Battle of Odrin in April 1205, and its Consequences]," *Voenno-istoričeski Sbornik,* XLVIII (1979), 107–123.

Dulaurier, Édouard F., "Étude sur l'organisation politique, religieuse et administra-tive du royaume de la Petite-Arménie," *JA,* 5-XVII (1861), 377–437; 5-XVIII (1861), 289–357.

Dunbar, J. G., and W.W.M. Boal, "The Castle of Vahga," *Anatolian Studies,* XIV (1964), 175–184.

Duncalf, Frederic, "The Peasants' Crusade," *Amer. HR,* XXVI (1920–1921), 440–453.

Duncalf, Frederic, "The Pope's Plan for the First Crusade," in *The Crusades and Other Historical Essays Presented to Dana C. Munro,* ed. Louis J. Paetow (New York, 1928), pp. 44–56.

Duncalf, Frederic, "The Councils of Piacenza and Clermont," *H of C,* I (1955, 2nd ed. 1969), 220–252, and "The First Crusade: Clermont to Constantinople," *ibid.,* 253–279.

Duparc-Quioc, Suzanne, *Le Cycle de la croisade* (Paris, 1955).

Ebersolt, Jean, *Orient et Occident: recherches sur les influences byzantines et orien-tales en France avant et pendant les croisades,* 2nd ed. (Paris, 1954).

Edbury, Peter W., "The Ibelin Counts of Jaffa: a Previously Unknown Passage from the 'Lignages d'Outremer'," *Eng. HR,* LXXXIX (1974), 604–610.

Edbury, Peter W., "Feudal Obligations in the Latin East," *Byzantion,* XLVII (1977), 328–356.

Edbury, Peter W., "The Crusading Policy of King Peter I of Cyprus, 1359-1369," in

The Eastern Mediterranean Lands in the Period of the Crusades, ed. Peter M. Holt (Warminster, 1977), pp. 90–105.

Edbury, Peter W., "The Disputed Regency of the Kingdom of Jerusalem 1264/6 and 1268," *Camden Miscellany,* XXVII (= Camden, 4th series, 22; 1979), 1–47 (with partial new edition of the *Documents relatifs à la successibilité au trône et à la régence*).

Edbury, Peter W., "The Murder of King Peter I of Cyprus (1359–1369)," *J Med. H,* VI (1980), 219–233.

Edbury, Peter W., "John of Ibelin's Title to the County of Jaffa and Ascalon," *Eng. HR,* XCVIII (1983), 115–133.

Edbury, Peter W., ed., *Crusade and Settlement: Papers Read at the First Conference of the Society for the Study of the Crusades and the Latin East and Presented to R. C. Smail* (Cardiff, 1985); includes Abulafia, Cowdrey, Grabois, B. Hamilton, Housley, Kedar, Loud, Mayer, Pringle, Richard, Riley-Smith, Schein, Tyerman, D53.

Egami, Namio, "Olon-Sume et la découverte de l'église catholique romaine de Jean de Montecorvino," *JA,* CCXL (1952), 155–167.

Egidi, Pietro, "I Capitelli romanici di Nazaret," *Dedalo,* I-3 (1920–1921), 761–776.

Ehrenkreutz, Andrew S., "The Crisis of the Dīnār in the Egypt of Saladin," *Journal of the American Oriental Society,* LXXVI (1956), 178–184.

Ehrenkreutz, Andrew S., "Arabic Dinars Struck by the Crusaders: a Case of Ignorance or of Economic Subversion?," *JESHO,* VII (1964), 167–182.

Ehrenkreutz, Andrew S., *Saladin* (Albany, N.Y., 1972).

Ehrhard, Albert, "Das griechische Kloster Mar-Saba in Palästina: seine Geschichte und seine litterarischen Denkmäler," *Römische Quartalschrift für christliche Altertumskunde und Kirchengeschichte,* VII (1893), 32–79.

Eickhoff, Ekkehard, *Friedrich Barbarossa im Orient: Kreuzzug und Tod Friedrichs I.* (Deutsches archäologisches Institut, Abt. Istanbul; Istanbuler Mitteilungen, Beiheft 17; Tübingen, 1977).

Elisséeff, Nikita, *Nūr ad-Dīn: un grand prince musulman de Syrie au temps des croisades (511–569 H./1118–1174)* (Institut français de Damas; 3 vols., Damascus, 1967).

Elisséeff, Nikita, *L'Orient musulman au moyen âge, 622–1260* (Paris, 1977).

Elm, Kaspar, "Fratres et sorores Sanctissimi Sepulchri: Beiträge zu fraternitas, familia und weiblichem Religiosentum im Umkreis des Kapitels vom Hlg. Grab," *Frühmittelalterliche Studien,* IX (1975), 287–333.

Elm, Kaspar, "Kanoniker und Ritter vom Heiligen Grab: ein Beitrag zur Entstehung und Frühgeschichte der palästinensischen Ritterorden," in *Die geistlichen Ritterorden Europas,* ed. Josef Fleckenstein and Manfred Hellmann (Vorträge und Forschungen, 26; Sigmaringen, 1980), pp. 141–169.

Enlart, Camille, "Quelques monuments d'architecture gothique en Grèce," *Revue de l'art chrétien,* 4-VIII (1897), 309–314.

Enlart, Camille, "Les Monuments et souvenirs nationaux à l'étranger: expansion de l'art français: Abbaye de Lapais (Chypre) (District de Cérines)," *L'Ami des monuments et des arts,* XII (1898), no. 68, pp. 222–233.

Enlart, Camille, "Expansion de l'art français à travers le monde: les monuments français de l'île de Chypre: Église métropolitaine de Sainte-Sophie à Nicosie," *L'Ami des monuments et des arts,* XII (1898), nos. 69–70, pp. 259–277.

Enlart, Camille, *L'Art gothique et de la Renaissance en Chypre* (2 vols., Paris, 1899).

Enlart, Camille, "L'Abbaye cistercienne de Belmont en Syrie," *Syria,* IV (1923), 1–22.

Enlart, Camille, *Les Monuments des croisés dans le royaume de Jérusalem: Architecture religieuse et civile* (Bibl. AH, 7–8; 2 vols. and 2 albums of plates, Paris, 1925–1928).

Ephtimiou, M. B., "Greeks and Latins of Thirteenth Century Cyprus," *Greek Orthodox Theological Review,* XX (1975), 35–52.

Erbstösser, Martin, *Die Kreuzzüge: eine Kulturgeschichte,* 2nd ed. (Leipzig, 1980).

Erdmann, Carl, "Der Kreuzzugsgedanke in Portugal," *Hist. Z,* CXLI (1930), 23–53.

Erdmann, Carl, *Die Entstehung des Kreuzzugsgedankens* (Forschungen zur Kirchen- und Geistesgeschichte, 6; Stuttgart, 1935); tr. Marshall W. Baldwin and Walter Goffart as *The Origin of the Idea of Crusade* (Princeton, 1977).

Errera, Carlo, "I Crociati veneziani in Terra Santa dal concilio di Clermont alla morte di Ordelafo Falier," *Arch. Ven.,* XXXVIII (1889), 237–277.

Eszer, Ambrosius K., *Das abenteuerliche Leben des Johannes Laskaris Kalopheros: Forschungen zur Geschichte der ost-westlichen Beziehungen im 14. Jahrhundert* (Schriften zur Geistesgeschichte des östlichen Europa, 3; Wiesbaden, 1969).

Evans, Austin P., "The Albigensian Crusade," *H of C,* II (1962, 2nd ed. 1969), 277–324.

Evert-Kappesowa, Halina, "La Société byzantine et l'union de Lyon," *Byzantinoslavica,* X (1949), 28–41.

Evert-Kappesowa, Halina, "Une Page de l'histoire des relations byzantino-latines: le clergé byzantin et l'union de Lyon (1274–1282)," *Byzantinoslavica,* XIII (1952–1953), 68–92.

Evert-Kappesowa, Halina, "Une Page de l'histoire des relations byzantino-latines: 1. Byzance et le St. Siège à l'époque de l'union de Lyon; 2. La fin de l'union de Lyon," *Byzantinoslavica,* XVI (1955), 297–317; XVII (1956), 1–18.

Every, George, *The Byzantine Patriarchate, 451–1204,* 2nd rev. ed. (London, 1962); repr. New York, 1980).

Fabre, Abel, "La Sculpture provençale en Palestine au XIIe siècle," *Échos d'Orient,* XXI (1922), 45–51.

Fallmerayer, Jacob P., *Geschichte des Kaiserthums von Trapezunt* (Munich, 1827).

Faris, Nabih A., ed., *The Arab Heritage* (Princeton, 1946).

Faris, Nabih A., "Arab Culture in the Twelfth Century," *H of C,* V (1985), 3–32.

Fasoli, Gina, "Problemi di storia medievale siciliana," *Siculorum Gymnasium,* n.s., IV (1951), 1–20.

Fasolo, Furio, "La Chiesa di S. Maria del Castello di Rodi," *Atti del XV Congresso di storia dell' architettura: Malta, 11–16 settembre 1967: L'architettura a Malta dalla preistoria all' ottocento* (Rome, 1970), pp. 275–300.

Faure, Claude, "Le Dauphin Humbert II à Venise et en Orient (1345–1347)," *MÉF Rome,* XXVII (1907), 509–562.

Favreau, Marie L., *Studien zur Frühgeschichte des Deutschen Ordens* (Kieler historische Studien, 21; Stuttgart, 1974).

Favreau, Marie L., "Zur Pilgerfahrt des Grafen Rudolf von Pfullendorf: ein unbeachteter Originalbrief aus dem Jahre 1180," *Zeitschrift für die Geschichte des Oberrheins,* CXXIII (= n.s., LXXXIV: 1975), 31–45.

Favreau, Marie L., "Die italienische Levante-Piraterie und die Sicherheit der Seewege nach Syrien im 12. and 13. Jahrhundert," *VSWG,* LXV (1978), 461–510.

Favreau, Marie L., "Graf Heinrich von Champagne und die Pisaner im Königreich Jerusalem," *Bullettino storico pisano,* XLVII (1978), 97–120.

Favreau, Marie L., "Graf Heinrich von Malta, Genua und Boemund IV. von Antiochia: eine urkundenkritische Studie," *QFIAB,* LVIII (1978), 181–215.

Favreau-Lilie, Marie L., "The Teutonic Knights after the Fall of Montfort (1271): Some Reflections," in *Outremer* (1982), pp. 272–284.

Favreau-Lilie, Marie L., "La Cacciata dei Pisani dal regno di Gerusalemme sotto la reggenza di Enrico conte di Champagne e un diploma di Boemondo IV conte di Tripoli per il comune di Pisa," *Bollettino storico pisano,* LIV (1985), 107–115.

Fedalto, Giorgio, *Simone Atumano, monaco di studio, arcivescovo latino di Tebe (secolo XIV)* (Storia del Cristianesimo, 2; Brescia, 1968).

Fedalto, Giorgio, *La Chiesa latina in Oriente* (Studi religiosi, 3; 3 vols., Verona, 1973–1978; rev. ed., vol. 1, Verona, 1981).

Fedalto, Giorgio, "La Chiesa latina nel regno di Tessalonica: 1204–1224, 1423–1430," Ἐπετηρὶς Ἑταιρείας Βυζαντινῶν Σπουδῶν, XLI (1974), 88–102.

Fedalto, Giorgio, *Perchè le crociate: saggio interpretativo* (Il mondo medievale: Sezione di storia bizantina e slava, 3; Bologna, 1980).

Fedden, Robin, and John Thomson, *Crusader Castles* (London, 1957).

Ferrard, Christopher G., "The Amount of Constantinopolitan Booty in 1204," *Studi veneziani,* XIII (1971), 95–104.

Fichtenau, Heinrich, "Akkon, Zypern und das Lösegeld für Richard Löwenherz," *Archiv für österreichische Geschichte* (= Bausteine zur Geschichte Österreichs), CXXV (1966), 11–32.

Fiey, Jean M., "Le Pèlerinage des Nestoriens et des Jacobites à Jérusalem," *Cah. Civ. Méd.,* XII (1969), 113–126.

Fiey, Jean M., *Chrétiens syriaques entre croisés et Mongols* (Orientalia christiana analecta, 97; Rome, 1974), pp. 327–341.

Fiey, Jean M., *Chrétiens syriaques sous les Mongols (Il-Khanat de Perse, XIIIe–XIVe siècles)* (Corpus scriptorum christianorum orientalium, 362 [= Subsidia, 44]; Louvain, 1975).

Fink, Harold S., "The Role of Damascus in the History of the Crusades," *Muslim World,* XLIX (1959), 41–53.

Fink, Harold S., "The Foundation of the Latin States, 1099–1118," *H of C,* I (1955, 2nd ed. 1969), 368–409.

Finke, Heinrich, *Papsttum und Untergang des Templerordens* (Vorreformationsgeschichtliche Forschungen, 4–5; 2 vols. in 1, Münster, 1907).

Fischel, Walter J., "The Spice Trade in Mamluk Egypt: a Contribution to the Economic History of Medieval Islam," *JESHO,* I (1958), 157–174.

Flahiff, George B., "Deus non vult: a Critic of the Third Crusade," *Mediaeval Studies,* IX (1947), 162–188.

Fleckenstein, Josef, and Manfred Hellmann, eds., *Die geistlichen Ritterorden Europas* (Konstanzer Arbeitskreis für mittelalterliche Geschichte, Vorträge und Forschungen, 26; Sigmaringen, 1980); includes U. Arnold, Elm, Hiestand, Luttrell, Mayer, Melville, Prawer.

Fleckenstein, Josef, "Die Rechtfertigung der geistlichen Ritterorden nach der Schrift 'De laude novae militiae' Bernhards von Clairvaux," in *Die geistlichen Ritterorden Europas,* ed. Fleckenstein and Manfred Hellmann (Vorträge und Forschungen, 26; Sigmaringen, 1980), pp. 9–22.

Fliche, Augustin, "Les Origines de l'action de la papauté en vue de la croisade," *Revue d'histoire ecclésiastique,* XXXIV (1938), 765–775.

Folda, Jaroslav, "The Fourth Crusade, 1201–1203 (Some Reconsiderations)," *Byzantinoslavica,* XXVI (1965), 277–290.

Folda, Jaroslav, "A Crusader Manuscript from Antioch," *Rendiconti della Pontificia accademia romana di archeologia,* 3-XLII (1969–1970), 283–298.

Folda, Jaroslav, *Crusader Manuscript Illumination at Saint Jean d'Acre, 1275-1291* (Princeton, 1976).

Folda, Jaroslav, "Painting and Sculpture in the Latin Kingdom of Jerusalem, 1099-1291," *H of C,* IV (1977), 251-280, and "Crusader Art and Architecture: a Photographic Survey," *ibid.,* 281-354.

Folda, Jaroslav, "Three Crusader Capitals in Jerusalem," *Levant,* X (1978), 139-155.

Folda, Jaroslav, ed., *Crusader Art in the Twelfth Century* (British Archaeological Reports, International Series, 152; Oxford, 1982).

Folda, Jaroslav, with Pamela French and Pierre Coupel, "The Crusader Frescoes at Crac des Chevaliers and Marqab Castle," *D Oaks P,* XXXVI (1982), 177-210.

Folda, Jaroslav, *The Nazareth Capitals and the Crusader Shrine of the Annunciation* (Monographs on the Fine Arts, 42; University Park, Pa., and London, 1986).

Forbes-Boyd, Eric, *In Crusader Greece: a Tour of the Castles of the Morea* (New York, 1964).

Forey, Alan J., "The Order of Mountjoy," *Speculum,* XLVI (1971), 250-266.

Forey, Alan J., *The Templars in the Corona de Aragón* (University of Durham Publications; London, 1973).

Forey, Alan J., "The Military Order of St. Thomas of Acre," *Eng. HR,* XCII (1977), 481-503.

Forey, Alan J., "The Military Orders in the Crusading Proposals of the Late-Thirteenth and Early-Fourteenth Centuries," *Traditio,* XXXVI (1980), 317-345.

Forey, Alan J., "The Failure of the Siege of Damascus in 1148," *J Med. H,* X (1984), 13-23.

Forey, Alan J., "The Military Orders and the Spanish Reconquest in the Twelfth and Thirteenth Centuries," *Traditio,* XL (1984), 197-234.

Formentini, Ubaldo, *Genova nel basso impero e nell' alto medioevo* (Storia di Genova dalle origini al tempo nostro, 2; Milan, 1941).

Forstreuter, Kurt, *Der Deutsche Orden am Mittelmeer* (Quellen und Studien zur Geschichte des Deutschen Ordens, 21; Bonn, 1967).

Forsyth, George H., and Kurt Weitzmann, *The Monastery of Saint Catherine at Mount Sinai: the Church and Fortress of Justinian* (Ann Arbor, 1973).

Fotheringham, John K., "Genoa and the Fourth Crusade," *Eng. HR,* XXV (1910), 26-57.

Fotheringham, John K., *Marco Sanudo, Conqueror of the Archipelago* (Oxford, 1915).

Foulet, Alfred, "The Epic Cycle of the Crusades," *H of C,* VI (1989), 98-115.

France, John, "The Crisis of the First Crusade from the Defeat of Kerbogha to the Departure from Arqa," *Byzantion,* XL (1970), 276-308.

France, John, "An Unknown Account of the Capture of Jerusalem," *Eng. HR,* LXXXVII (1972), 771-783.

Frances, E., "Alexis Comnène et les privilèges octroyés à Venise," *Byzantinoslavica,* XXIX (1968), 17-23.

Frankenberger, Otakar, *Naše velká armáda* (3 vols. in 1, Prague, 1921).

Frazee, Charles A., "The Catholic Church in Constantinople, 1204-1453," *Balkan Studies,* XIX (1978), 33-49.

Friedman, Elias, *The Latin Hermits of Mount Carmel: a Study in Carmelite Origins* (Institutum Historicum Teresianum, Studia, 1; Rome, 1979).

Friendley, Alfred, *The Dreadful Day: the Battle of Mantzikert, 1071* (London, 1981).

Frolow, Anatole, "La Déviation de la quatrième croisade vers Constantinople," *Revue de l'histoire des religions,* CXLV (1954), 168-187; CXLVI (1954), 67-89; CXLVII (1955), 50-61.

Frolow, Anatole, *La Relique de la Vraie Croix: recherches sur le développement d'un culte* (Archives de l'Orient chrétien, 7; Paris, 1961).

Frolow, Anatole, *Les Reliquaires de la Vraie Croix* (Archives de l'Orient chrétien, 8; Paris, 1965).

Fulin, Rinaldo, "Venezia e la quarta crociata, dissertazione del dottore Lodovico Streit," *Arch. Ven.,* XVI (1878), 46-49, 239-271.

Furber, Elizabeth Chapin, "The Kingdom of Cyprus, 1191-1291," *H of C,* II (1962, 2nd ed. 1969), 599-629.

Gäbler, Ulrich, "Der Kinderkreuzzug vom Jahre 1212," *Schweizerische Zeitschrift für Geschichte,* XXVIII (1978), 1-14.

Gabriel, Albert, *La Cité de Rhodes MCCCX-MDXXII* (2 vols., Paris, 1921-1923).

Gabriel, Albert, *Monuments turcs d'Anatolie* (2 vols., Paris, 1931-1934).

Gabrieli, Francesco, "Arabi di Sicilia e Arabi di Spagna," *al-Andalus,* XV (1950), 27-45.

Gabrieli, Francesco, "Le Crociate viste dall' Islàm," in *Concetto, storia, miti e immagini del medio evo,* ed. Vittore Branca (Civiltà veneziana: Aspetti e problemi, 7; Florence, 1973), pp. 183-198.

Gadolin, A. R., "Alexis I Comnenus and the Venetian Trade Privileges: a New Interpretation," *Byzantion,* L (1980), 439-446.

Galey, John, *Sinai und Katarinenkloster* (Stuttgart, 1979); tr. as *Sinai and the Monastery of St. Catherine* (London, 1980).

Ganshof, François L., "Recherches sur le lien juridique qui unissait les chefs de la première croisade à l'empereur byzantin," in *Mélanges offerts à M. Paul E. Martin* . . . (Geneva, 1961), pp. 49-63.

García de Valdeavellano y Armicis, Luis, *Curso de historia de las instituciones españolas: de los orígenes al final de la edad media* (Madrid, 1968).

García-Larragueta, Santos A., *El Gran priorado de Navarra de la orden de San Juan de Jerusalén, siglos XII-XIII* (2 vols., Pamplona, 1957).

Gardner, Alice, *The Lascarids of Nicaea: the Story of an Empire in Exile* (London, 1912).

Gariador, Benoît, *Les Anciens monastères bénédictins en Orient* (Lille and Paris, 1912).

Garufi, Carlo A., "Ruggiero II e la fondazione della monarchia in Sicilia," *Archivio storico siciliano,* n.s., LII (1932), 1-33.

Gatto, Ludovico, *Il Pontificato di Gregorio X, 1271-1276* (Istituto storico italiano per il medio evo, Studi storici, fasc. 28-30; Rome, 1959).

Gaudefroy-Demombynes, Maurice, *Les Institutions musulmanes,* 3rd ed. (Bibliothèque de philosophie scientifique; Paris, 1946).

Gay, Jules M.M., *L'Italie méridionale et l'empire byzantin depuis l'avènement de Basile Ier jusqu'à la prise de Bari par les Normands (867-1071)* (BÉFAR, 90; Paris, 1904).

Gay, Jules M.M., *Le Pape Clément VI et les affaires d'Orient (1342-1352)* (Paris, 1904).

Geanakoplos, Deno J., "The Council of Florence (1438-1439) and the Problem of Union between the Greek and Latin Churches," *Church History,* XXIV (1955), 324-346.

Geanakoplos, Deno J., *Emperor Michael Palaeologus and the West, 1258-1282: a Study in Byzantine-Latin Relations* (Cambridge, Mass., 1959).

Geanakoplos, Deno J., *Byzantine East and Latin West: Two Worlds of Christendom in Middle Ages and Renaissance; Studies in Ecclesiastical and Cultural History* (New York and Oxford, 1966).

Geanakoplos, Deno J., "Byzantium and the Crusades, 1261-1354," *H of C*, III (1975), 27-68, and "Byzantium and the Crusades, 1354-1453," *ibid.*, 69-103.

Geanakoplos, Deno J., *Medieval Western Civilization and the Byzantine and Islamic Worlds: Interaction of Three Cultures* (Lexington, Mass., and Toronto, 1979).

Génestal, Robert, *Rôle des monastères comme établissements du crédit* (Paris, 1901).

Gerland, Ernst, "Kreta als venetianische Kolonie (1204-1669)," *HJ Görres.*, XX (1899), 1-24.

Gerland, Ernst, "Histoire de la noblesse crétoise au moyen âge," *RO Latin*, X (1903-1904), 172-247; XI (1905-1908), 7-144; published separately (Paris, 1907).

Gerland, Ernst, "Der vierte Kreuzzug und seine Probleme," *Neue Jahrbücher für das klassische Altertum*, XIII (1904), 505-514.

Gerland, Ernst, *Geschichte des lateinischen Kaiserreiches von Konstantinopel: 1. Geschichte der Kaiser Balduin I. und Heinrich (1204-1216)* (Geschichte der Frankenherrschaft in Griechenland, 2 [all published]; Homburg vor der Höhe, 1905).

Germain, Alexandre C., *Histoire de la commune de Montpellier depuis ses origines jusqu'à son incorporation à la monarchie française* (3 vols., Montpellier, 1851).

Germain, Alexandre C., *Histoire du commerce de Montpellier antérieurement à l'ouverture du port du Cette* (2 vols., Montpellier, 1861).

Germer-Durand, J., "La Sculpture franque en Palestine," *Conférences de Saint-Étienne 1910-1911* (École pratique d'études bibliques: Études palestiniennes et orientales, 5; Paris, 1911), pp. 233-257.

Gero, Stephen, "The Byzantine Church and the West: a Survey of Recent Research," *Greek Orthodox Theological Review*, XXIII (1978), 69-82.

Gerola, Giuseppe, *Monumenti veneti nell' isola di Creta: ricerche e descrizione* (4 vols., Venice, 1906-1932).

Gerola, Giuseppe, "I Monumenti medioevali delle tredici Sporadi," *Annuario della Reale scuola archeologica di Atene e delle missioni italiane in Oriente*, I (1914), 169-356; II (1916), 1-101.

Gerola, Giuseppe, "Il Restauro dello spedale dei cavalieri a Rodi," *L'Arte*, XVII (1914), 333-360.

Gerola, Giuseppe, "Il Contributo dell' Italia alle opere d'arte militari rodiesi," *Atti del Reale istituto veneto di scienze, lettere ed arti*, LXXXIX (1929/1930), 1015-1027.

Gerola, Giuseppe, "I Francescani di Creta al tempo del dominio veneziano," *Collectanea franciscana*, II (1932), 301-361.

Gervaso, Roberto, ed., *La Storia delle crociate* (3 vols., Milan, 1978).

Gibb, Hamilton A.R., "The Achievement of Saladin," *Bulletin of the John Rylands Library*, XXXV (1952-1953), 44-60.

Gibb, Hamilton A.R., "The Caliphate and the Arab States," *H of C*, I (1955, 2nd ed. 1969), 81-98.

Gibb, Hamilton A.R., "Zengi and the Fall of Edessa," *H of C*, I (1955, 2nd ed. 1969), 449-462, and "The Career of Nūr-ad-Dīn," *ibid.*, 513-527, and "The Rise of Saladin, 1169-1189," *ibid.*, 563-589.

Gibb, Hamilton A.R., "The Aiyūbids," *H of C*, II (1962, 2nd ed. 1969), 693-714.

Giesebrecht, Wilhelm von, *Geschichte der deutschen Kaiserzeit* (6 vols., Brunswick and Leipzig; vols. 1-3, 5th ed., 1881-1890; vol. 4, 4th ed., 1877; vols. 5-6, 1st ed., 1880-1895).

Gieysztor, Alexander, "The Genesis of the Crusades: the Encyclical of Sergius IV," *Mediaevalia et humanistica*, V (1948), 3-23; VI (1950), 3-34.

Gill, Joseph, "Greeks and Latins in a Common Council: the Council of Florence (1438-1439)," *O Chr. P,* XXV (1959), 265-287.

Gill, Joseph, *The Council of Florence* (Cambridge, Eng., 1959; repr. New York, 1982).

Gill, Joseph, *Eugenius IV, Pope of Christian Union* (London, 1961).

Gill, Joseph, "Franks, Venetians and Pope Innocent III 1201-1203," *Studi veneziani,* XII (1970), 85-106.

Gill, Joseph, "Innocent III and the Greeks: Aggressor or Apostle?," in *Relations between East and West in the Middle Ages,* ed. Derek Baker (Edinburgh, 1973), pp. 95-108.

Gill, Joseph, "The Tribulations of the Greek Church in Cyprus 1196-c. 1280," *Byz. F,* V (1977), 73-93.

Gill, Joseph, *Byzantium and the Papacy, 1198-1400* (New Brunswick, N.J., 1979).

Gill, Joseph, *Church Union: Rome and Byzantium (1204-1453)* (London, 1979).

Gilles, Henri, "Législation et doctrine canoniques sur les Sarrasins," in *Islam et Chrétiens du Midi (xiie-xive s.)* (Cahiers de Fanjeaux, 18; Toulouse, 1983), pp. 195-213.

Gillingham, John, *Richard the Lionheart* (London, 1978); tr. Rudi Heeger as *Richard Löwenherz* (Düsseldorf, 1981).

Gillingham, John, "Richard I and the Science of War in the Middle Ages," *War and Government in the Middle Ages: Essays in Honour of J. O. Prestwich,* ed. John Gillingham and J. C. Holt (Woodbridge, 1984), pp. 78-91.

Gindler, Paul, *Graf Balduin I. von Edessa* (Halle, 1901).

Giunta, Francesco, *Aragonesi e Catalani nel Mediterraneo* (2 vols., Palermo, 1953-1959).

Giurescu, Constantin C., "The Genoese and the Lower Danube in the XIIIth Century," *Journal of European Economic History,* V (1976), 587-600.

Gjuzelev, V., "Bŭlgarskata dŭržava i Nikeja v borbas sreštu latinskata carigradska imperija (1204-1261 g.) [The Bulgarian Kingdom and Nicaea in the Fight against the Latin Empire of Constantinople]," *Izvestija na Nacionalnija Istoričeski Musej,* II (1978), 7-37.

Gleber, Helmut, *Papst Eugen III. (1145-1153) unter besonderer Berücksichtigung seiner politischen Tätigkeit* (Beiträge zur mittelalterlichen und neueren Geschichte, 6; Jena, 1936).

Godfrey, John, *1204: the Unholy Crusade* (Oxford, 1980).

Goitein, Solomon D.F., "New Light on the Beginnings of the Kārim Merchants," *JESHO,* I (1958), 175-184.

Goitein, Solomon D.F., *A Mediterranean Society: the Jewish Communities of the Arab World as Portrayed in the Documents of the Cairo Geniza* (3 vols., Berkeley, Los Angeles, and London, 1967-1978).

Goldmann, Zeev, "The Hospice of the Knights of St. John in Akko," *Archaeology,* XIX (1966), 182-189.

Goldziher, Ignaz, *Vorlesungen über den Islam,* 2nd rev. ed., ed. Franz Babinger (Heidelberg, 1925).

Golubovich, Girolamo, "San Francesco e i Francescani in Damiata (5 Nov. 1219-2 Febb. 1220)," *Studi francescani,* XXIII (n.s., XII; 1926), 307-330.

Goñi Gaztambide, José, *Historia de la bula de la cruzada en España* (Victoriensia, 4; Vitoria, 1958).

Gonzaga de Azevedo, Luiz, *História de Portugal* (6 vols., Lisbon, 1935-1940).

González, Julio, *Alfonso IX* (2 vols., Madrid, 1944).

González, Julio, "Las Conquistas de Fernando III en Andalucia," *Hispania,* VI (1946), 515-631.

González, Julio, *El Reino de Castilla en la época de Alfonso VIII* (Consejo superior de investigaciones científicas, Escuela de estudios medievales: Textos, 25-27; 3 vols., Madrid, 1960).

Goss, Vladimir P., and Christine V. Bornstein, eds., *The Meeting of Two Worlds: Cultural Exchange between East and West during the Period of the Crusades* (Studies in Medieval Culture, 21; Kalamazoo, 1986).

Gotron, Adam, *Ramon Lulls Kreuzzugsideen* (Abhandlungen zur mittleren und neueren Geschichte, 39; Berlin and Leipzig, 1912).

Gottlob, Adolf, *Die päpstlichen Kreuzzugssteuern des 13. Jahrhunderts: ihre rechtliche Grundlage, politische Geschichte und technische Verwaltung* (Heiligenstadt, 1892).

Gottlob, Adolf, "Hat Papst Innocenz III. sich das Recht zuerkannt, auch die Laien zu Kreuzzugszwecken zu besteuern?," *HJ Görres.,* XVI (1895), 312-319.

Gottlob, Adolf, *Kreuzablass und Almosenablass: eine Studie über die Frühzeit des Ablasswesens* (Kirchenrechtliche Abhandlungen, ed. Ulrich Stutz, 30-31; Stuttgart, 1906).

Gottschalk, Hans L., *Al-Malik al-Kāmil von Egypten und seine Zeit: eine Studie zur Geschichte Vorderasiens und Egyptens in der ersten Hälfte des 7./13. Jahrhunderts* (Wiesbaden, 1958).

Gottschalk, Hans L., "Die ägyptische Sultanin Šağarrat ad-Durr in Geschichte und Dichtung," *Wiener Zeitschrift für die Kunde des Morgenlandes,* LXI (1967), 41-61.

Gottwald, J., "Die Kirche und das Schloss Paperon in Kilikisch-Armenien," *Byz. Z,* XXXVI (1936), 86-100.

Gottwald, J., "Die Burg Til im südöstlichen Kilikien," *Byz. Z,* XL (1940), 89-104.

Gottwald, J., "Burgen und Kirchen im mittleren Kilikien," *Byz. Z,* XLI (1941), 82-103.

Gough, Michael, "Anazarbus," *Anatolian Studies,* II (1952), 85-150.

Graboïs, Aryeh (here, Ariyeh), "Le Privilège de croisade et la régence de Suger," *RH Droit FÉ,* 4-XLII (1964), 458-465.

Graboïs, Aryeh, "La Cité de Baniyas et le château de Subeibeh pendant les croisades," *Cah. Civ. Méd.* XIII (1970), 43-62.

Graboïs, Aryeh, (here, Ariyeh), "Les Pèlerins occidentaux en Terre Sainte et Acre: d'Accon des croisés à Saint-Jean d'Acre," *Studi medievali,* 3-XXIV (1983), 247-264.

Graboïs, Aryeh, "The Crusade of King Louis VII: a Reconsideration," in *Crusade and Settlement,* ed. Peter W. Edbury (Cardiff, 1985), pp. 94-104.

Graetz, Heinrich, *Geschichte der Juden von den ältesten Zeiten bis auf die Gegenwart* (11 vols., Leipzig and Vienna, 1923).

Grandclaude, Maurice, *Étude critique sur les livres des assises de Jérusalem* (Paris, 1923).

Gray, George Z., *The Children's Crusade: an Episode of the 13th Century* (New York, 1870; London, 1871).

Grégoire, Henri, "L'Opinion byzantine et la bataille de Kossovo," *Byzantion,* VI (1931; offert à Sir William Mitchell Ramsay), 247-251.

Grégoire, Henri, "The Question of the Diversion of the Fourth Crusade, or an Old Controversy Solved by a Latin Adverb," *Byzantion,* XV (1940/41), 158-166.

Gregorovius, Ferdinand, *Geschichte der Stadt Athen im Mittelalter von der Zeit Justinians bis zur türkischen Eroberung* (2 vols., Stuttgart, 1889); tr. into Greek by Spyridon P. Lampros as Ἱστορία τῆς πόλεως Ἀθηνῶν κατὰ τοὺς μέσους αἰῶνας ἀπὸ τοῦ Ἰουστινιανοῦ μέχρι τῆς ὑπὸ τῶν Τούρκων καταστήσεως (3 vols., Athens, 1904-1906).

Greilsammer, Myriam, "Structure and Aims of the Livre au Roi," in *Outremer* (1982), pp. 218–226.

Grierson, Philip, "The Debasement of the Bezant in the Eleventh Century," *Byz. Z,* XLVII (1954), 379–394.

Groh, Friedrich, *Der Zusammenbruch des Reiches Jerusalem 1187–1189* (Jena, 1909).

Grousset, René, *Histoire des croisades et du royaume franc de Jérusalem* (3 vols., Paris, 1934–1936).

Grousset, René, *Histoire de l'Arménie, des origines à 1071* (Bibliothèque historique; Paris, 1947).

Grumel, Venance, "La Chronologie des patriarches grecs de Jérusalem au XIIIe siècle," *RÉ Byz.,* XX (1962), 197–201.

Grunebaum, Gustav E. von, *Medieval Islam: a Study in Cultural Orientation,* 2nd ed. (Chicago, 1953).

Grunzweig, Armand, "Philippe le Bon et Constantinople," *Byzantion,* XXIV (1954), 47–61.

Gual Camarena, Miguel, "Precedentes de la reconquista valenciana," *Consejo superior de investigaciones científicas, Escuela de estudios medievales, Sección de Valencia: Estudios medievales,* 1, fasc. 5 (Valencia, 1952), pp. 163–246.

Guardione, Francesco, *Sul Dominio dei ducati di Atene e Neopatria dei re di Sicilia* (Palermo, 1895).

Guilland, Rodolphe, "Les Appels de Constantin XI Paléologue à Rome et à Venise pour sauver Constantinople (1452–1453)," *Byzantinoslavica,* XIV (1953), 226–244.

Guilland, Rodolphe: Widely scattered writings on the administrative history of the Byzantine empire, of which unfortunately no collected reprint is available. These articles are too numerous to be listed here. The reader is referred to the bibliography of Guilland's writing 1938–1957 in *Byzantion,* XXV–XXVII (1955–1957), 695–696.

Gutsch, Milton R., "A Twelfth Century Preacher — Fulk of Neuilly," in *The Crusades and Other Historical Essays Presented to Dana C. Munro,* ed. Louis J. Paetow (New York, 1928), pp. 183–206.

Guyard, Stanislas, "Un Grand maître des Assassins au temps de Saladin," *JA,* 7-IX (1877), 324–489.

Hackett, John, *A History of the Orthodox Church of Cyprus from the Coming of the Apostles Paul and Barnabas to the Commencement of the British Occupation, A.D. 45–A.D. 1878* (London, 1901); tr. into Greek and expanded by Charilaos I. Papaioannou (3 vols., Athens, 1923–1932).

Hagenmeyer, Heinrich, *Peter der Eremite: ein kritischer Beitrag zur Geschichte des ersten Kreuzzuges* (Leipzig, 1879).

Hagenmeyer, Heinrich, "Chronologie de la première croisade 1094–1100," *RO Latin,* VI (1898), 214–293, 490–549; VII (1899), 275–339, 430–503; VIII (1900–1901), 318–382. Continued as "Chronologie de l'histoire du royaume de Jérusalem," *RO Latin,* IX (1902), 318–365; X (1903–1904), 372–405; XI (1905–1908), 145–180, 453–485; XII (1909–1911), 68–103, 283–326.

Hagspiel, Gereon H., *Die Führerpersönlichkeit im Kreuzzug* (Geist und Werk der Zeiten, 10; Zurich, 1963).

Halecki, Oscar, *Un Empereur de Byzance à Rome: Vingt ans de travails pour l'union des églises et pour la défense de l'empire d'Orient, 1355–1375* (Towarzystwo naukowe Warszawskie Rozprawy, 8; Warsaw, 1930; repr. London, 1972).

Halecki, Oscar, *The Crusade of Varna: a Discussion of Controversial Problems* (Polish Institute Series, 3; New York, 1943).

Haller, Johannes, "Kaiser Heinrich VI.," *Hist. Z,* CXIII (3-XVII; 1914), 473-504.

Haller, Johannes, *Das Papsttum: Idee und Wirklichkeit,* rev. ed. (5 vols., Urach and Stuttgart, 1950-1953).

Hamilton, Bernard, "Rebuilding Zion: the Holy Places of Jerusalem in the Twelfth Century," *Studies in Church History,* XIV (1977), 105-116.

Hamilton, Bernard, "The Armenian Church and the Papacy at the Time of the Crusades," *Eastern Churches Review,* X (1978), 61-87.

Hamilton, Bernard, "Women in the Crusader States: the Queens of Jerusalem (1100-1190)," in *Medieval Women: Dedicated and Presented to Rosalind M.T. Hill on the Occasion of her Seventieth Birthday,* ed. Derek Baker (Studies in Church History, Subsidia, 1; Oxford, 1978), pp. 143-174.

Hamilton, Bernard, "A Medieval Urban Church: the Case of the Crusader States," in *The Church in Town and Countryside,* ed. Derek Baker (Studies in Church History, 16; Oxford, 1979), pp. 157-170.

Hamilton, Bernard, *Monastic Reform, Catharism and the Crusades (900-1300)* (Varior. Repr., CS, 97; London, 1979).

Hamilton, Bernard, *The Latin Church in the Crusader States: the Secular Church* (London, 1980).

Hamilton, Bernard, "Ralph of Domfront, Patriarch of Antioch (1135-40)," *Nottingham Medieval Studies,* XXVIII (1984), 1-21.

Hamilton, Bernard, "The Titular Nobility of the Latin East: the Case of Agnes of Courtenay," in *Crusade and Settlement,* ed. Peter W. Edbury (Cardiff, 1985), pp. 197-203.

Hamilton, Robert W., *The Church of the Nativity, Bethlehem: a Guide,* 2nd rev. ed. (Jerusalem, 1947; repr. 1968).

Hamilton, Robert W., *The Structural History of the Aqsa Mosque: a Record of Architectural Gleanings from the Repairs of 1938-1942* (London and Jerusalem, 1949).

Hammer-Purgstall, Josef von, *Die Geschichte der Assassinen aus morgenländischen Quellen* (Stuttgart and Tübingen, 1818).

Hampe, Karl, *Urban IV. und Manfred (1261-1264)* (Heidelberger Abhandlungen zur mittleren und neueren Geschichte, 11; Heidelberg, 1905).

Hampe, Karl, *Geschichte Konradins von Hohenstaufen* (Historische und bibliographische Nachträge . . . unter Berücksichtigung der Forschungsergebnisse seit 1894 von Hellmut Kämpf; 2nd ed., repr. Leipzig, 1942).

Hampe, Karl, *Deutsche Kaisergeschichte in der Zeit der Salier und Staufer,* 10th ed., ed. Friedrich Baethgen (Heidelberg, 1949).

Hampel, Emil, *Untersuchungen über das lateinische Patriarchat von Jerusalem von Eroberung der heiligen Stadt bis zum Tode des Patriarchen Arnulf (1099-1118)* (Diss., Erlangen; Breslau, 1899).

Hanotaux, Gabriel, "Les Vénitiens ont-ils trahi la chrétienté en 1202?," *Rev. hist.,* IV (1877), 74-102.

Hanotaux, Gabriel, ed., *Histoire de la nation égyptienne* (7 vols., Paris, 1931-1940).

Hansbery, Joseph E., "The Children's Crusade," *Cath. HR,* XXIV (1938), 30-38.

Hansen, Joseph, *Das Problem eines Kirchenstaates in Jerusalem* (Diss., Freiburg, Switzerland; Luxemburg, 1928).

Hardwicke, Mary Nickerson, "The Crusader States, 1192-1243," *H of C,* II (1962, 2nd ed. 1969), 522-554. See also Nickerson.

Hartmann, Angelika, *An-Nāṣir li-Dīn Allāh (1180-1225): Politik, Religion, Kultur in der späten 'Abbasidenzeit* (Studien zur Sprache, Geschichte und Kultur des islamischen Orients, n.s., 8; Berlin and New York, 1975).

Hartmann, Johannes, *Die Persönlichkeit des Sultans Saladin im Urteil der abendländischen Quellen* (Hist. Stud., ed. Ebering, 239; Berlin, 1939).

Hartmann, Richard, *Der Felsendom in Jerusalem und seine Geschichte* (Zur Kunstgeschichte des Auslands, 69; Strassburg, 1909).

Harvey, William, *The Church of the Holy Sepulchre: Structural Survey, Final Report* (London, 1935).

Hasluck, Frederick W., "Monuments of the Gattelusi," *ABS Athens,* XV (1908-1909), 248-269.

Hasluck, Frederick W., "Frankish Remains at Adalia," *ABS Athens,* XV (1908-1909), 270-273.

Hasluck, Frederick W., "The Latin Monuments of Chios," *ABS Athens,* XVI (1909-1910), 137-184.

Hasluck, Frederick W., "Datcha-Stadia-Halikarnassos," *ABS Athens,* XVIII (1911-1912), 211-216.

Hatem, Anouar, *Les Poèmes épiques des croisades: genèse, historicité, localisation: essai sur l'activité littéraire dans les colonies franques de Syrie au moyen âge* (Paris, 1932).

Hauck, Albert, *Kirchengeschichte Deutschlands,* 8th (unchanged) ed. (5 vols., Berlin, 1954).

Haussig, Hans W., "Die Mittelmeerpolitik Kaiser Michael VIII.," *Actes du XIVe Congrès international des études byzantines,* II (Bucharest, 1975), pp. 109-111.

Hauziński, Jerzy, "Fryderyk II Hohenstauf i asasyni: mało znany epizod w relacji Muhammada al-Hamawi [Frederick II of Hohenstaufen and the Assassins: a Little-Known Episode in the Report of Muḥammad al-Hamawī]," *Ars Historica: Prace z dziejów powszechnych i Polski* (Universytet im.Adama Mickiewicza w Poznaniu, Seria historia, 71; Poznań, 1976), pp. 229-239.

Hauziński, Jerzy, *Muzułmańska sekta asasynów w europejskim piśmiennictwie wieków średnich* [The Islamic Sect of the Assassins in European Medieval Literature] (Universytet im.Adama Mickiewicza w Poznaniu, Seria historia, 74; Poznán, 1978).

Hauziński, Jerzy, *Polityka orientalna Fryderyka II Hohenstaufa* [The Eastern Politics of Frederick II of Hohenstaufen] (Universytet im.Adama Mickiewicza w Poznaniu, Seria historia, 79; Poznań, 1978).

Hayek, Dimitri, *Le Droit franc en Syrie pendant les croisades: Institutions judiciaires* (Paris, 1925).

Hazard, Harry W., "Caesarea and the Crusades," in *The Joint Expedition to Caesarea Maritima:* vol. I. *Studies in the History of Caesarea Maritima,* ed. Charles T. Fritsch (Bulletin of the American Schools of Oriental Research, Supplemental Studies, 10; Missoula, Montana, 1975), pp. 79-114.

Hazard, Harry W., "Moslem North Africa, 1049-1394," *H of C,* III (1975), 457-485.

Hecht, Winfried, *Die byzantinische Aussenpolitik zur Zeit der letzten Komnenenkaiser (1180-1185)* (Neustadt an der Aisch, 1967).

Heers, Jacques, "Il Commercio nel Mediterraneo alla fine del secolo XIV e nei primi anni del secolo XV," *Archivio storico italiano,* CXIII (1955), 157-209.

Hefele, Karl J. von, *Conciliengeschichte,* tr. Henri M. Leclercq as *Histoire des conciles* (12 vols., Paris, 1907-1952).

Hehl, Ernst D., *Kirche und Krieg im 12. Jahrhundert: Studien zu kanonischem Recht und politischer Wirklichkeit* (Monographien zur Geschichte des Mittelalters, 19; Stuttgart, 1980).

Heisenberg, August, *Nikolaos Mesarites: die Palastrevolution des Johannes Komnenos* (Programm des K. Alten Gymnasiums zu Würzburg für das Studienjahr 1906–7; Würzburg, 1907).

Helbig, Adolph H., *Al-Qāḍī al-Fāḍil, der Wezir Saladins: eine Biographie* (Berlin, 1909).

Hellenkemper, Hansgerd, *Burgen der Kreuzritterzeit in der Grafschaft Edessa und im Königreich Kleinarmenien* (Geographica historica, 1; Bonn, 1976).

Hendrickx, Benjamin, "Les Chartes de Baudouin de Flandre comme source pour l'histoire de Byzance," *Byzantina,* I (1969), 59–80.

Hendrickx, Benjamin, "Recherches sur les documents diplomatiques non conservés concernant la quatrième croisade et l'empire latin de Constantinople pendant les premières années de son existence (1200–1206)," *Byzantina,* II (1970), 107–184.

Hendrickx, Benjamin, "À Propos du nombre des troupes de la quatrième croisade et de l'empereur Baudouin I," *Byzantina,* III (1971), 29–40.

Hendrickx, Benjamin, "Baudouin IX de Flandre et les empereurs byzantins Isaak II l'Ange et Alexis IV," *Revue belge de philologie et d'histoire,* XLIX (1971), 482–489.

Hendrickx, Benjamin, "Les Institutions de l'empire latin de Constantinople (1204–1261): la chancellerie," *Acta Classica: Proceedings of the Classical Association of South Africa,* XIX (1976), 123–131.

Hendrickx, Benjamin, "Les Institutions de l'empire latin de Constantinople (1204–1261): la cour et les dignitaires," *Byzantina,* IX (1977), 187–217.

Hendrickx, Benjamin, and C. Matzukis, "Alexios V Doukas Mourtzouphlos: his Life, Reign and Death (?–1204)," *Ἑλληνικά,* XXXI (1979), 108–132.

Hendy, Michael F., "Byzantium, 1081–1204: an Economic Reappraisal," *Transactions of the Royal Historical Society,* 5-XX (1970), 31–52.

Henschel-Simon, E., "Note on a Romanesque Relief from Jerusalem," *QDA Pal.,* XII (1945–1946), 75–76, and pl. XXIV.

Herculano de Carvalho e Araujo, Alexandre, *História de Portugal desde o começo da monarchia até o fim do reinado de Affonso III,* 7th ed., ed. David Lopes (Lisbon, 1914–1916).

Herde, Peter, "Die Kämpfe bei den Hörnern von Hittīn und der Untergang des Kreuzritterheeres (3. und 4. Juli 1187)," *Römische Quartalschrift für christliche Altertumskunde und Kirchengeschichte,* LXI (1966), 1–50.

Herde, Peter, "Christians and Saracens at the Time of the Crusades: Some Comments of Contemporary Medieval Canonists," *Studia Gratiana,* XII (Collectanea Stephan Kuttner, 2; 1967), 359–376.

Herde, Peter, *Karl I. von Anjou* (Urban Taschenbücher, 305; Stuttgart, 1979).

Herde, Peter, "Taktiken muslimischer Heere vom ersten Kreuzzug bis 'Ain Djalut (1260) und ihre Einwirkung auf die Schlacht bei Tagliacozzo (1268)," in *Das Heilige Land im Mittelalter,* ed. Wolfdietrich Fischer and Jürgen Schneider (Neustadt an der Aisch, 1982), pp. 83–94.

Herquet, Karl, *Juan Ferrandez [sic] de Heredia, Grossmeister des Johanniterordens, 1377–1396* (Mühlhausen, 1878).

Herquet, Karl, "Chronologie der Grossmeister des Hospital-Ordens," *Wochenblatt der Johanniter Ordens-Balley Brandenburg,* XXI (1880), 63–65; "Nachträge . . . ," pp. 201–204.

Herquet, Karl, *Chronologie der Grossmeister des Hospitalordens während der Kreuzzüge* (Berlin, 1880).

Herzfeld, Ernst E., and Samuel Guyer, *Monumenta Asiae Minoris antiqua:* vol. II. *Meriamlik und Korykos: Zwei christliche Ruinenstätten des rauhen Kilikiens* (Manchester, 1930).

Herzog, Anni, *Die Frau auf den Fürstenthronen der Kreuzfahrerstaaten* (Berlin, 1919).

Herzsohn, I.J.P., *Der Überfall Alexandriens durch Peter I., König von Jerusalem und Cypern* (Diss., Bonn, 1886).

Heyd, Wilhelm, *Geschichte des Levantehandels im Mittelalter* (2 vols., Stuttgart, 1879); tr. Furcy Raynaud as *Histoire du commerce du Levant au moyen-âge* (2 vols., Leipzig, 1885–1886; repr. Leipzig, 1936, and Amsterdam, 1967).

Heymann, Frederick G., *John Žižka and the Hussite Revolution* (Princeton, 1955).

Heymann, Frederick G., "The Crusades against the Hussites," *H of C,* III (1975), 586–646.

Heynen, Reinhard, *Zur Entstehung des Kapitalismus in Venedig* (Münchener volkswirtschaftliche Studien, 71; Stuttgart and Berlin, 1905; repr. New York, 1971).

Heywood, William, *A History of Pisa* (Cambridge, Eng., 1921).

Hiestand, Rudolf, "Chronologisches zur Geschichte des Königreichs Jerusalem um 1130," *Deutsches Archiv,* XXVI (1970), 220–229.

Hiestand, Rudolf, "Legat, Kaiser und Basileus: Bischof Kuno von Praeneste und die Krise des Papsttums von 1111/1112," in *Aus Reichsgeschichte und Nordischer Geschichte,* ed. Horst Fuhrmann, Hans E. Mayer, and Klaus Wriedt (Kieler historische Studien, 16; Stuttgart, 1972), pp. 141–152.

Hiestand, Rudolf, and Hans E. Mayer, "Die Nachfolge des Patriarchen Monachus von Jerusalem," *Basler Zeitschrift für Geschichte und Altertumskunde,* LXXIV (1974), 109–130.

Hiestand, Rudolf, "Kaiser Konrad III., der zweite Kreuzzug und ein verlorenes Diplom für den Berg Thabor," *Deutsches Archiv,* XXXV (1979), 82–126.

Hiestand, Rudolf, "Chronologisches zur Geschichte des Königreichs Jerusalem im 12. Jahrhundert," *Deutsches Archiv,* XXXV (1979), 542–555.

Hiestand, Rudolf, "Die Anfänge der Johanniter," in *Die geistlichen Ritterorden Europas,* ed. Josef Fleckenstein and Manfred Hellmann (Vorträge und Forschungen, 26; Sigmaringen, 1980), pp. 31–80.

Hiestand, Rudolf, "Reconquista, Kreuzzug und heiliges Grab: die Eroberung von Tortosa 1148 im Lichte eines neuen Zeugnisses," *Gesammelte Aufsätze zur Kulturgeschichte Spaniens,* XXXI (1984), 136–157.

Hiestand, Rudolf, "Saint-Ruf d'Avignon, Raymond de Saint-Gilles et l'église latine du comté de Tripoli," *Annales du Midi,* IIC (1986), 327–336.

Hill, George, *A History of Cyprus* (4 vols., Cambridge, Eng., 1940–1952).

Hill, John H. and Laurita L., "Contemporary Accounts and the Later Reputation of Adhémar, Bishop of Puy," *Mediaevalia et humanistica,* IX (1955), 30–38.

Hill, John H. and Laurita L., *Raymond IV de Saint-Gilles, comte de Toulouse* (Toulouse, 1959), tr. as *Raymond IV, Count of Toulouse* (Syracuse, N.Y., 1962).

Hillgarth, Jocelyn N.A., *The Problem of a Catalan Mediterranean Empire 1229–1327* (Eng. HR, supplement 8; London, 1975).

Hillgarth, Jocelyn N.A., *The Spanish Kingdoms 1250–1516* (2 vols., Oxford, 1978).

Hilsch, Peter, "Der Deutsche Ritterorden im südlichen Libanon: zur Topographie der Kreuzfahrerherrschaften Sidon und Beirut," *ZDPV,* XCVI (1980), 174–189.

Hindley, Geoffrey, *Saladin* (New York, 1976); German tr. by Miriam Magal as *Saladin: Ritter des Islam* (Wiesbaden, 1978).

Hintlian, K., *History of the Armenians in the Holy Land* (Jerusalem, 1976).

Hirsch, Richard, *Studien zur Geschichte König Ludwigs VII. von Frankreich (1119–1160)* (Leipzig, 1892).

Hitti, Philip K., *History of Syria, including Lebanon and Palestine,* 2nd ed. (London and New York, 1957).

Hitti, Philip K., *Lebanon in History,* 2nd ed. (New York and London, 1962).

Hitti, Philip K., *History of the Arabs from the Earliest Times to the Present,* 10th ed. (New York and London, 1970).

Hitti, Philip K., "The Impact of the Crusades on Eastern Christianity," in *Medieval and Near Eastern Studies in Honor of Aziz Suryal Atiya,* ed. Sami A. Hanna (Leyden, 1972), pp. 211–217.

Hitti, Philip K., "The Impact of the Crusades on Moslem Lands," *H of C,* V (1985), 33–58.

Hodgson, Marshall G.S., *The Order of the Assassins: the Struggle of the Early Nizârî Ismâ'îlîs against the Islamic World* (The Hague, 1955; repr. New York, 1980).

Hofmann, Georg, "Die Konzilsarbeit in Ferrara," *O Chr. P,* III (1937), 110–140, 403–455.

Hofmann, Georg, "Die Konzilsarbeit in Florenz," *O Chr. P,* IV (1938), 157–188.

Hohlweg, Armin, "Der Kreuzzug des Jahres 1444: Versuch einer christlichen Allianz zur Vertreibung der Türken aus Europa," in *Die Türken in Europa* (Göttingen, 1979), pp. 20–37.

Hohlweg, Armin, "Kaiser Johannes VIII. Palaiologos und der Kreuzzug des Jahres 1444," *Byz. Z,* LXXIII (1980), 14–24.

Holmes, Urban T., and William M. McLeod, "Source Problems of the *Chétifs,* a Crusade *Chanson de geste,*" *Romanic Review,* XXVIII (1937), 99–108.

Holmes, Urban T., *Daily Living in the Twelfth Century* (Madison, 1952).

Holmes, Urban T., "Life among the Europeans in Palestine and Syria in the Twelfth and Thirteenth Centuries," *H of C,* IV (1977), 3–35.

Holt, Peter M., Ann K.S. Lambton, and Bernard Lewis, eds., *The Cambridge History of Islam:* vol. I. *The Central Islamic Lands* (Cambridge, Eng., 1970).

Holt, Peter M., "Qalāwūn's Treaty with Acre in 1283," *Eng. HR,* XCI (1976), 802–812.

Holt, Peter M., ed., *The Eastern Mediterranean Lands in the Period of the Crusades* (Warminster, 1977); includes Edbury, Irwin, Riley-Smith, Smail.

Holt, Peter M., "Saladin and his Admirers: a Biographical Assessment," *Bulletin of the School of Oriental and African Studies,* XLVI (1983), 235–239.

Holtzmann, Walther, "Studien zur Orientpolitik des Reformpapsttums und zur Entstehung des ersten Kreuzzuges," *Historische Vierteljahrschrift,* XXII (1924–1925), 167–199.

Holtzmann, Walther, "Die Unionsverhandlungen zwischen Kaiser Alexios I. und Papst Urban II. im Jahre 1089," *Byz. Z,* XXVIII (1928), 38–67.

Holtzmann, Walther, "Quellen und Forschungen zur Geschichte Friedrich Barbarossas: 3. Zu den Anfängen des dritten Kreuzzuges," *Neues Archiv der Gesellschaft für ältere deutsche Geschichtskunde,* XLVIII (1930), 384–413.

Hölzle, Peter, *Die Kreuzzüge in der occitanischen und deutschen Lyrik des 12. Jahrhunderts* (Göppinger Arbeiten zur Germanistik, 278; 2 vols., Göppingen, 1980).

Honig, Rodolfo, *Rapporti tra Federico II e Gregorio IX rispetto alla spedizione in Palestina* (Bologna, 1896).

Honigmann, Ernst, *Die Ostgrenze des byzantinischen Reiches von 363–1071 nach griechischen, syrischen und armenischen Quellen* (Corpus Bruxellense historiae Byzantinae, 3; Brussels, 1935).

Hoogeweg, Hermann, "Der Kreuzzug von Damiette 1218–1221," *MIÖG,* VIII (1887), 188–218; IX (1888), 249–288.

Hopf, Carl, "Geschichtlicher Überblick über die Schicksale von Karystos auf Euboea in dem Zeitraume von 1205–1470," *SB Wien,* XI (1853), 555–606.

Hopf, Carl, "Geschichte der Insel Andros und ihrer Beherrscher in dem Zeitraume von 1205–1566," *SB Wien,* XVI (1855), 23–131.

Hopf, Carl, "Urkunden und Zusätze zur Geschichte der Insel Andros und ihrer Beherrscher in dem Zeitraume von 1207–1566," *SB Wien,* XXI (1856), 221–262.

Hopf, Carl, "Veneto-byzantinische Analekten," *SB Wien,* XXXII-3 (1859), 363–528.

Hopf, Carl, "Griechenland im Mittelalter und in der Neuzeit: Geschichte Griechenlands vom Beginn des Mittelalters bis auf unsere Zeit," in *Allgemeine Encyklopädie der Wissenschaften und Künste,* ed. Johann S. Ersch and Johann G. Gruber, Section I, vol. LXXXV (1867), pp. 67–465; LXXXVI (1868), pp. 1–190.

Hopf, Carl, *Les Giustiniani, dynastes de Chios,* tr. Étienne A. Vlasto (Paris, 1888).

Horn, Elzear, *Ichnographiae locorum et monumentorum veterum Terrae Sanctae (1724–1744),* 2nd ed. of the Latin text with English translation by Eugene Hoade and preface and notes by Bellarmino Bagatti (Studium BF, 15; Jerusalem, 1962).

Horst, Heribert, *Die Staatsverwaltung der Grossselǧūqen und Ḫōrazmšāhs* (Wiesbaden, 1964).

Hotzelt, Wilhelm, *Kirchengeschichte Palästinas im Zeitalter der Kreuzzüge 1099–1291* (Pal. DVHL, 29–32; Cologne, 1940).

Hotzelt, Wilhelm, "Gregor X., der letzte Kreuzzugspapst (1271–1276)," *Das Heilige Land in Vergangenheit und Gegenwart,* III (Pal. DVHL, 33–36; 1941), 92–110.

Housley, Norman J., "The Franco-Papal Crusade Negotiations of 1322–3," *Papers of the British School at Rome,* XLVIII (1980), 166–185.

Housley, Norman J., "Angevin Naples and the Defense of the Latin East: Robert the Wise and the Naval League of 1334," *Byzantion,* LI (1981), 548–556.

Housley, Norman J., "Politics and Heresy in Italy: Anti-Heretical Crusades, Orders and Confraternities, 1200–1500," *Journal of Ecclesiastical History,* XXXIII (1982), 193–208.

Housley, Norman J., *The Italian Crusades: the Papal-Angevin Alliance and the Crusades against Christian Lay Powers, 1254–1343* (Oxford and New York, 1982).

Housley, Norman J., "Charles II of Naples and the Kingdom of Jerusalem," *Byzantion,* LIV (1984), 527–535.

Housley, Norman J., "Crusades against Christians: their Origins and Early Development, c. 1000–1216," in *Crusade and Settlement,* ed. Peter W. Edbury (Cardiff, 1985), pp. 17–36.

Housley, Norman, *The Avignon Papacy and the Crusades, 1305–1378* (Oxford, 1986).

Howorth, Henry H., *History of the Mongols from the Ninth to the Nineteenth Century* (5 vols., London, 1876–1888, 1927).

Hubatsch, Walther, "Der Deutsche Orden und die Reichslehnschaft über Cypern," *Gött. Nach.* (1955), pp. 245–306.

Hubatsch, Walther, "Montfort und die Bildung des Deutschordensstaates im Heiligen Lande," *Gött. Nach.* (1966), pp. 161–199.

Hüffer, Georg, "Die Anfänge des zweiten Kreuzzuges," *HJ Görres.,* VIII (1887), 391–429.

Huici Miranda, Ambrósio, "Los Almohades en Portugal (Conferência feita em assembleia geral ordinária de 29 de Abril de 1953)," *Anais,* 2-V (1954), 9-51.

Huici Miranda, Ambrósio, "Las Campañas de Ya'qūb al-Mansūr en 1190 y 1191 (Conferência feita em assembleia geral ordinaria de 1 de Maio de 1953)," *Anais,* 2-V (1954), 53-74.

Huici Miranda, Ambrósio, *Historia política del imperio Almohade* (Instituto General Franco de estudios e investigación hispano-árabe; 2 vols., Tetuan, 1956-1957).

Huici Miranda, Ambrósio, *Las Grandes batallas de la reconquista durante las invasiones africanas (Almoravides, Almohades y Benimerines)* (Madrid, 1956).

Humphreys, R. Stephen, *From Saladin to the Mongols: the Ayyubids of Damascus, 1193-1260* (Albany, N.Y., 1977).

Hussey, Joan M., *Church and Learning in the Byzantine Empire, 867-1185* (London, 1937).

Hussey, Joan M., "The Byzantine Empire in the Eleventh Century: Some Different Interpretations," *Transactions of the Royal Historical Society,* 4-XXXII (1950), 71-85.

Hussey, Joan M., "Byzantium and the Crusades, 1081-1204," *H of C,* II (1962, 2nd ed. 1969), 123-151.

Hussey, Joan M., Donald M. Nicol, and G. Cowan, eds., *The Byzantine Empire: 1. Byzantium and its Neighbours; 2. Government, Church and Civilisation* (Cambridge Medieval History, IV; 2 vols., Cambridge, Eng., 1966-1967).

Huygens, Robert B.C., *Latijn in "Outremer": een blik op de Latijnse letterkunde der Kruisvaarderstaten in het Nabije Oosten* (Leyden, 1964).

Huygens, Robert B.C., "Monuments de l'époque des croisades: Réflections à propos de quelques livres récentes," *Bibliotheca orientalis,* XXV (Leyden, 1968), 9-14.

Huygens, Robert B.C., "La Campagne de Saladin en Syrie du Nord (1188)," in *Colloque d'Apamée de Syrie: bilan de recherches archéologiques* (Brussels, 1974), pp. 273-283.

Ilgen, Theodor, *Markgraf Conrad von Montferrat* (Marburg, 1880).

Inalcik, Halil, "Ottoman Methods of Conquest," *Studia Islamica,* II (1954), 103-129.

Inalcik, Halil, *The Ottoman Empire: the Classical Age, 1300-1600,* tr. Norman Itzkowitz and Colin Imber (New York, 1973).

Inalcik, Halil, "The Ottoman Turks and the Crusades, 1329-1451," *H of C,* VI (1989), 222-275, and ". . . 1451-1522," *ibid.,* 311-353.

Iorga, Nicolae, *Philippe de Mézières, 1327-1405, et la croisade au XIVe siècle* (B Éc. HÉ, 110; Paris, 1896; repr. London, 1973).

Iorga, Nicolae, "Latins et Grecs d'Orient et l'établissement des Turcs en Europe (1342-1362)," *Byz. Z,* XV (1906), 179-222.

Iorga, Nicolae, *Brève histoire de la Petite Arménie: l'Arménie cilicienne: Conférences et récit historique* (Paris, 1930).

Iorga, Nicolae, *France de Chypre* (Collection de l'Institut néo-hellénique de l'Université de Paris, 10; Paris, 1931).

Iorga, Nicolae, *Histoire des Roumains et de la romanité orientale,* vol. IV (Bucharest, 1937).

Irmscher, Johannes, "Les Francs — représentants de la littérature en grec vulgaire," *Byz. F,* VII (1977), 57-66.

Irwin, Robert, "Iqṭā' and the End of the Crusader States," in *The Eastern Mediterranean Lands in the Period of the Crusades,* ed. Peter M. Holt (Warminster, 1977), pp. 62-77.

Ivanov, Wladimir, *A Brief Survey of the Evolution of Ismailism* (Leyden, 1952).

Jackson, Peter, "The Crisis in the Holy Land in 1260," *Eng. HR,* XCV (1980), 481-513.

Jackson, Peter, "The End of Hohenstaufen Rule in Syria," *Bulletin of the Institute of Historical Research,* LIX (1986), 20-36.

Jackson, Peter, "The Crusades of 1239-41 and their Aftermath," *Bulletin of the School of Oriental and African Studies,* L (1987), 32-60.

Jacob, E. F., "The Bohemians at the Council of Basel, 1433," in *Prague Essays, Presented by a Group of British Historians to the Caroline University of Prague on the Occasion of its Six-Hundredth Anniversary,* ed. R. W. Seton-Watson (Oxford, 1949), pp. 81-123.

Jacobs, Wilhelm, *Patriarch Gerold von Jerusalem: ein Beitrag zur Kreuzzugsgeschichte Friedrichs II.* (Diss., Bonn; Aachen, 1905).

Jacoby, David, "Un Régime de coseigneurie gréco-franque en Morée: les 'Casaux de parçon'," *MÉF Rome,* LXXV (1963), 111-125.

Jacoby, David, "La 'Compagnie catalane' et l'état catalan de Grèce: quelques aspects de leur histoire," *Journal des Savants* (1966), pp. 78-103.

Jacoby, David, "Les Archontes grecs et la féodalité en Morée franque," *Centre de recherche d'histoire et civilisation byzantines: Travaux et mémoires,* II (1967), 421-481.

Jacoby, David, "Les Quartiers juifs de Constantinople à l'époque byzantin," *Byzantion,* XXXVII (1967), 167-227.

Jacoby, David, *La Féodalité en Grèce médiévale: les "Assises de Romanie": sources, application et diffusion* (École pratique des hautes études: Documents et recherches sur l'économie des pays byzantins, islamiques et slaves et leurs relations commerciales au moyen âge, 10; Paris and The Hague, 1971).

Jacoby, David, "Les Juifs vénitiens de Constantinople et leur communauté du XIIIe au milieu du XVe siècle," *Revue des études juives,* CXXXI (1972), 397-410.

Jacoby, David, "The Encounter of Two Societies: Western Conquerors and Byzantines in the Peloponnesus after the Fourth Crusade," *Amer. HR,* LXXVIII (1973), 873-906.

Jacoby, David, "Catalans, Turcs et Vénitiens en Romanie (1305-1332): un nouveau témoignage de Marino Sanuto Torsello," *Studi medievali,* 3-XV (1974), 217-261.

Jacoby, David, *Société et démographie à Byzance et en Romanie latine (XIIIe-XVe siècles)* (Varior. Repr., CS, 35; London, 1975).

Jacoby, David, "Une Classe fiscale à Byzance et en Romanie latine: les inconnus du fisc, éleuthères ou étrangers," in *Actes du XIVe Congrès international des études byzantines, Bucarest, 6-12 septembre 1971,* II (Bucharest, 1975), pp. 139-152.

Jacoby, David, *Les États latins en Romanie: phénomènes sociaux et économiques (1204-1350 environ)* (XVe Congrès international d'études byzantines: rapports et co-rapports: 1. Histoire: part 3. La symbiose dans les états latins formés sur les territoires byzantins: phénomènes sociaux, économiques, religieux et culturels; Athens, 1976).

Jacoby, David, "Citoyens et protégés de Venise et de Gènes en Chypre du XIIIe au XVe siècle," *Byz. F,* V (1977), 159-188.

Jacoby, David, "L'Expansion occidentale dans le Levant: les Vénitiens à Acre dans la seconde moitié du treizième siècle," *J Med. H,* III (1977), 225-264.

Jacoby, David, *Recherches sur la Méditerranée orientale du XIIe au XVe siècle: Peuples, sociétés, économies* (Varior. Repr., CS, 105; London, 1979).

Jacoby, David, "Les Vénitiens naturalisés dans l'empire byzantin: un aspect de l'expansion de Venise en Romanie du XIIIe au milieu du XVe siècle," *Travaux et mémoires du Centre de recherche d'histoire et de civilisation de Byzance,* VIII (1981), 219–235.

Jacoby, David, "Les Gens de mer dans la marine de guerre vénitienne de la mer Egée aux XIVe et XVe siècles," in *Le Genti del Mare Mediterraneo,* ed. R. Ragosta (= *XVII Colloquio internazionale di storia marittima, Napoli, 1980;* Naples, 1981), I, 169–200.

Jacoby, David, "Venetian Anchors for Crusader Acre," *The Mariner's Mirror,* LXXI (1985), 5–12.

Jacoby, David, "The Kingdom of Jerusalem and the Collapse of Hohenstaufen Power in the Levant," *D Oaks P,* XL (1986), 83–101.

Jacoby, David, "Social Evolution in Frankish Greece," *H of C,* VI (1989), 175–221.

Jacoby, Zehava, "The Tomb of Baldwin V, King of Jerusalem (1185–1186), and the Workshop of the Temple Area," *Gesta,* XVIII-2 (1979), 3–14.

Jacoby, Zehava, "A Newly Discovered Crusader Fragment in Jerusalem," *Isr. Expl. J,* XXX (1980), 202–204.

Jacoby, Zehava, "Le Portail de l'église de l'Annonciation de Nazareth au XIIe siècle," *Monuments et mémoires de la Fondation Eugène Piot,* LXIV (1981), 141–194.

Jacoby, Zehava, "The Workshop of the Temple Area in Jerusalem in the Twelfth Century: its Origins, Evolution and Impact," *Zeitschrift für Kunstgeschichte,* XLV (1982), 325–394.

Jacopozzi, Nazzareno, "Dove sia avvenuta la visita di San Francesco d'Assisi al Sultano el-Kamel," *Congrès international de géographie, Le Caire—Avril 1925,* V (1926), 141–156.

Jahn, Hans, *Die Heereszahlen in den Kreuzzügen* (Diss., Berlin, 1907).

Janin, Raymond, *Les Églises separées d'Orient* (Bibliothèque catholique des sciences religieuses; Paris, 1929).

Janin, Raymond, "Au Lendemain de la conquête de Constantinople: les tentatives d'union des églises, 1204–1214," *Échos d'Orient,* XXXII (1933), 5–21, 195–202.

Janin, Raymond, "Les Sanctuaires de Byzance sous la domination latine (1204–1261)," *Études byzantines,* II (1944), 134–184.

Janin, Raymond, "Les Sanctuaires des colonies latines à Constantinople," *RÉ Byz.,* IV (1946), 163–177.

Janin, Raymond, "L'Église latine à Thessalonique de 1204 à la conquête turque," *RÉ Byz.,* XVI (= Mélanges Sévérien Salaville; 1958), 206–216.

Janin, Raymond, *Le Siège de Constantinople et le patriarcat oecuménique: les églises et les monastères,* 2nd ed. (La géographie ecclésiastique de l'empire byzantin; Paris, 1969).

Janin, Raymond, *Les Églises et les monastères des grands centres byzantins (Bithynie, Hellespont, Latros, Galèsios, Trébizonde, Athènes, Thessalonique)* (La géographie ecclésiastique de l'empire byzantin; Paris, 1975).

Jansen, Reinhard, "Die historischen Grundlagen zu 'Os Lusiadas' VIII, 18," *Aufsätze zur portugiesischen Kulturgeschichte,* V (Portugiesische Forschungen der Görresgesellschaft, ser. 1; 1965), 228–247.

Jansen, Reinhard, "Heinrich von Bonn: die Erinnerung an die Kreuzfahrer aus dem römischen Reich in der portugiesischen Legendentradition," *Rheinische Vierteljahresblätter,* XXX (1965), 23–29.

Janssens, Émile, *Trébizonde en Colchide* (Brussels, 1969).

Jeanroy, Alfred, *La Poésie lyrique des troubadours (Histoire externe et interne)* (2 vols., Toulouse and Paris, 1934).

Jeffery, George E., *A Description of the Historic Monuments of Cyprus: Studies in the Archaeology and Architecture of the Island* (Nicosia, 1918).

Jegerlehner, Johannes, "Der Aufstand der kandiotischen Ritterschaft gegen das Mutterland Venedig 1363-1365," *Byz. Z*, XII (1903), 78-125.

Jegerlehner, Johannes, "Beiträge zur Verwaltungsgeschichte Kandias im XIV. Jahrhundert," *Byz. Z*, XIII (1904), 435-479.

Jireček, Constantin, *Geschichte der Serben* (2 vols., Gotha, 1911-1918; repr. Amsterdam, 1967).

John, Eric, "A Note on the Preliminaries of the Fourth Crusade," *Byzantion*, XXVIII (1958), 95-105.

Johnen, Joseph, "Philipp von Elsass, Graf von Flandern, 1157 (1163)-1191," *Bulletin de la Commission royale d'histoire de Belgique*, LXXIX (1910), 341-467.

Johns, Cedric N., "Excavations at Pilgrims' Castle ('Atlīt)," *QDA Pal.*, I (1931-1932), 111-129; II (1932-1933), 41-104; III (1933-1934), 145-164; IV (1934-1935), 122-137; V (1935-1936), 31-60; VI (1936-1938), 121-152.

Johns, Cedric N., "The Attempt to Colonize Palestine and Syria in the Twelfth and Thirteenth Centuries," *Journal of the Royal Central Asian Society*, XXI (1934), 288-300.

Johns, Cedric N., "The Abbey of St. Mary in the Valley of Jehoshaphat, Jerusalem," *QDA Pal.*, VIII (1939), 117-136.

Johns, Cedric N., *A Guide to the Citadel of Jerusalem* (Jerusalem, 1944).

Johns, Cedric N., *A Guide to 'Atlit* (Jerusalem, 1947).

Johnson, Edgar N., "The Crusades of Frederick Barbarossa and Henry VI," *H of C*, II (1962, 2nd ed. 1969), 87-122.

Johnson, Edgar N., "The German Crusade on the Baltic," *H of C*, III (1975), 545-585.

Joranson, Einar, "The Great German Pilgrimage of 1064-1065," in *The Crusades and Other Historical Essays Presented to Dana C. Munro*, ed. Louis J. Paetow (New York, 1928), pp. 3-43.

Jordan, Édouard, *Les Origines de la domination angevine en Italie* (Paris, 1909).

Jordan, Édouard, *L'Allemagne et l'Italie aux XIIe et XIIIe siècles* (Histoire générale: Histoire du moyen âge, IV-1; Paris, 1939).

Jordan, William C., "Supplying Aigues-Mortes for the Crusade of 1248: the Problem of Restructuring Trade," in *Order and Innovation in the Middle Ages: Essays in Honor of Joseph R. Strayer*, ed. William C. Jordan, Bruce McNab, and Teofilo R. Ruiz (Princeton, 1976), pp. 165-172.

Jordan, William C., *Louis IX and the Challenge of the Crusade: a Study in Rulership* (Princeton, 1979).

Jugie, Martin, "Le Voyage de l'empereur Manuel Paléologue en Occident (1399-1403)," *Échos d'Orient*, XV (1912), 322-332.

Jugie, Martin, *Le Schisme byzantin: aperçu historique et doctrinal* (Paris, 1941).

Julien, Charles A., *Histoire de l'Afrique du Nord: Tunisie, Algérie, Maroc*, reédited by Christian Courtois and Roger Le Tourneau (Bibliothèque historique; 2 vols., Paris, 1951-1952).

Jurewicz, Oktawiusz, *Andronikos I. Komnenos* (Amsterdam, 1970).

Kafesoğlu, Ibrahim, *Sultan Melikşah devrinde büyük Selçuklu imperatorluğu* (İstanbul Universitesi edebiyat fakültesi yayînlarî, no. 569; Istanbul, 1953).

Kahl, Hans D., "Heidnisches Wendentum und christliche Stammesfürsten: ein Blick in die Auseinandersetzung zwischen Gentil- und Universalreligion im abendländischen Hochmittelalter," *Archiv für Kulturgeschichte*, XLIV (1962), 72-119.

Kahl, Hans D., *Slawen und Deutsche in der brandenburgischen Geschichte des zwölften Jahrhunderts* (Mitteldeutsche Forschungen, 30; 1 vol. in 2, Cologne and Graz, 1964).

Kairophylas, Kostas (here, Costas Kerofilas), *Amedeo VI di Savoia nell' impero bizantino* (Rome, 1926).

Kairophylas, Kostas, Ἱστορία τῶν Ἀθηνῶν ὑπὸ τοὺς Βυζαντινοὺς καὶ Φράγκους *(330–1456)* (Athens, 1933).

Kaminsky, Howard, *A History of the Hussite Revolution* (Berkeley, 1967).

Kantorowicz, Ernst, *Kaiser Friedrich II.* (2 vols., Berlin, 1927–1931).

Kap-Herr, Hans von, *Die abendländische Politik Kaiser Manuels mit besonderer Rücksicht auf Deutschland* (Strassburg, 1881).

Karalevskij, Cyril P., "Antioche," in *Dictionnaire d'histoire et de géographie ecclésiastiques,* III (1924), cols. 563–703.

Karayannopulos, Johannes, "Die kollektive Steuerverantwortung in der frühbyzantinischen Zeit," *VSWG,* XLIII (1956), 289–322.

Karayannopulos, Johannes, *Das Finanzwesen der frühbyzantinischen Zeit* (Südosteuropäische Arbeiten, 52; Munich, 1958).

Karpozilos, Apostolos D., *The Ecclesiastical Controversy between the Kingdom of Nicaea and the Principality of Epiros (1217–1233)* (Salonica, 1973).

Kawerau, Peter, *Die jakobitische Kirche im Zeitalter der syrischen Renaissance: Idee und Wirklichkeit,* 2nd ed. (Deutsche Akademie der Wissenschaften zu Berlin, Institut für griechisch-römische Altertumskunde: Berliner byzantinische Arbeiten, 3; Berlin, 1960).

Kawerau, Peter, *Ostkirchengeschichte:* III. *Das Christentum in Europa und Asien im Zeitalter der Kreuzzüge* (Corpus scriptorum Christianorum orientalium, 442: Subsidia, 65; Louvain, 1982).

Kedar, Benjamin Z., "The General Tax of 1183 in the Crusading Kingdom of Jerusalem: Innovation or Adaptation?," *Eng. HR,* LXXXIX (1974), 339–345.

Kedar, Benjamin Z., and Aharon Kaufman, "Radiocarbon Measurements of Medieval Mortars: a Preliminary Report," *Isr. Expl. J,* XXV (1975), 36–38.

Kedar, Benjamin Z., *Merchants in Crisis: Genoese and Venetian Men of Affairs and the Fourteenth Century Depression* (New Haven and London, 1976).

Kedar, Benjamin Z., and Chr. Westergard-Nielsen, "Icelanders in the Crusader Kingdom of Jerusalem: a Twelfth Century Account," *Mediaeval Scandinavia,* XI (1978–1979, appeared 1983), 193–211.

Kedar, Benjamin Z., and W. G. Mook, "Radiocarbon Dating of Mortar from the City Wall of Ascalon," *Isr. Expl. J,* XXVIII (1978), 173–176.

Kedar, Benjamin Z., and Sylvia Schein, "Un Projet de passage particulier proposé par l'ordre de l'Hôpital 1306–1307," *BÉ Char.,* CXXXVII (1979), 211–226.

Kedar, Benjamin Z., "Ein Hilferuf aus Jerusalem vom September 1187," *Deutsches Archiv,* XXXVIII (1982), 112–122.

Kedar, Benjamin Z., Hans E. Mayer, and Raymond C. Smail, eds., *Outremer—Studies in the History of the Crusading Kingdom of Jerusalem Presented to Joshua Prawer* (Jerusalem, 1982); includes Abulafia, Benvenisti, Brundage, Constable, Cowdrey, Favreau-Lilie, Greilsammer, Mayer, Richard, Riley-Smith, Runciman, Schein, Smail, C36, D34.

Kedar, Benjamin Z., "The Patriarch Eraclius," in *Outremer* (1982), pp. 177–204.

Kedar, Benjamin Z., "Mercanti genovesi in Alessandria d'Egitto negli anni sessanta del secolo XI," *Miscellanea di studi storici,* II (Collana storica di fonti e studi, 38; Genoa, 1983), 21–30.

Kedar, Benjamin Z., "Palmarée, abbaye clunisienne du XIIe siècle en Galilée," *Revue bénédictine,* XCIII (1983), 260–269.

Kedar, Benjamin Z., *Crusade and Mission: European Approaches toward the Muslims* (Princeton, 1984).

Kedar, Benjamin Z., "Ecclesiastical Legislation in the Kingdom of Jerusalem: the Statutes of Jaffa (1253) and Acre (1254)," in *Crusade and Settlement,* ed. Peter W. Edbury (Cardiff, 1985), pp. 225–230.

Kedar, Benjamin Z., and [R.] Denys Pringle, "La Fève: a Crusader Castle in the Jezreel Valley," *Isr. Expl. J,* XXXV (1985), 164–179.

Kenaan, Nurith, "Local Christian Art in Twelfth Century Jerusalem," *Isr. Expl. J,* XXIII (1973), 167–175, 221–229.

Kennan, Elizabeth, "Innocent III and the First Political Crusade," *Traditio,* XXVII (1971), 231–251.

Kestner, E., *Der Kreuzzug Friedrichs II.* (Diss., Göttingen, 1873).

Khatchatrian, A., "L'Architecture arménienne – essai analytique," *Vostan: Cahiers d'histoire et de civilisation arménienne,* I (1948-1949), 57–144.

Khowaiter, Abdul A., *Baibars the First: his Endeavours and Achievements* (London, 1978).

Kindlimann, Sibyl, *Die Eroberung von Konstantinopel als politische Forderung des Westens im Hochmittelalter* (Geist und Werk der Zeiten, 20; Zurich, 1969).

King, David J.C., "The Taking of Le Krak des Chevaliers in 1271," *Antiquity,* XXIII (1949), 83–92.

King, David J.C., "The Defences of the Citadel of Damascus: a Great Mohammedan Fortress of the Time of the Crusades," *Archaeologica,* XCIV (1951), 57–96.

Kisch, Guido, *The Jews in Medieval Germany: a Study of their Legal and Social Status* (Chicago, 1949).

Kittel, E. E., "Was Thibaut of Champagne the Leader of the Fourth Crusade?," *Byzantion,* LI (1981), 557–565.

Kleemann, Gustav, *Papst Gregor VIII. (1187)* (Jenaer historische Arbeiten, 4; Bonn, 1912).

Kling, Gustav, *Die Schlacht bei Nikopolis im Jahre 1396* (Diss., Berlin, 1906).

Knappen, Marshall M., "Robert II of Flanders in the First Crusade," in *The Crusades and Other Historical Essays Presented to Dana C. Munro,* ed. Louis J. Paetow (New York, 1928), pp. 79–100.

Knebel, Wilhelm, *Kaiser Friedrich II. und Papst Honorius III. in ihren gegenseitigen Beziehungen von der Kaiserkrönung Friedrichs bis zum Tode des Papstes (1220-1227)* (Münster, 1905).

Knoch, Peter, "Kreuzzug und Siedlung: Studien zum Aufruf der Magdeburger Kirche von 1108," *Jahrbuch für die Geschichte Mittel- und Ostdeutschlands,* XXIII (1974), 1–33.

Koch, Adolf, *Hermann von Salza, Meister des Deutschen Ordens* (Leipzig, 1885).

Kohler, Charles, "Rerum et personarum quae in Actis Sanctorum Bollandistis et Analectis Bollandianis obviae ad Orientem Latinum spectant index analyticus," *RO Latin,* V (1897), 460–561.

Kohler, Charles, *Mélanges pour servir à l'histoire de l'Orient latin et des croisades* (2 vols., Paris, 1900-1906).

Köprülü, Mehmet F., "Bizans müesseselerinin Osmanlī müesseselerine te'siri hakkinda bâzi mülâhazalar (Remarques sur l'influence des institutions byzantines sur les institutions ottomanes)," *Türk hukuk ve iktisat tarihi mecmuasi,* I (1931), 165–298.

Köprülü, Mehmet F., *Les Origines de l'empire ottoman* (Paris, 1935).

Kötting, Bernhard, *Peregrinatio religiosa: die Wallfahrten in der Antike und das Pil-gerwesen in der alten Kirche* (Forschungen zur Volkskunde, 33–35; Münster, 1950).

Krekić, Bariša, *Dubrovnik, Italy, and the Balkans in the Late Middle Ages* (Varior. Repr., CS, 125; London, 1980).

Kremer, Alfred von, *Culturgeschichte des Orients unter den Chalifen* (2 vols., Vienna, 1875–1877).

Kretschmayr, Heinrich, *Geschichte von Venedig* (in *Allgemeine Staatsgeschichte*, ed. Karl G. Lamprecht et al.; Sect. 1, Geschichte der europäischen Staaten, XXXV, 1–3; 3 vols., Gotha, 1905–1934; repr. Stuttgart, 1964).

Kritzeck, James, *Peter the Venerable and Islam* (Princeton Oriental Studies, 23; Princeton, 1964).

Krueger, Hilmar C., "The Italian Cities and the Arabs before 1095," *H of C*, I (1955, 2nd ed. 1969), 40–53.

Kugler, Bernhard, *Boemund und Tankred, Fürsten von Antiochien: ein Beitrag zur Geschichte der Normannen in Syrien* (Tübingen, 1862).

Kugler, Bernhard, *Studien zur Geschichte des zweiten Kreuzzuges* (Stuttgart, 1866).

Kugler, Bernhard, *Analecten zur Geschichte des zweiten Kreuzzuges,* in *Tübinger Uni-versitätsschriften aus dem Jahre 1876–1877* (Tübingen, 1878).

Kugler, Bernhard, *Neue Analekten zur Geschichte des zweiten Kreuzzuges,* in *Tübinger Universitätsschriften aus dem Jahre 1882–1883* (Tübingen, 1883).

Kugler, Bernhard, *Geschichte der Kreuzzüge,* 2nd ed. (Allgemeine Geschichte in Ein-zeldarstellungen, sect. 2, part 5; Berlin, 1891).

Kühn, Fritz, *Geschichte der ersten lateinischen Patriarchen von Jerusalem* (Leipzig, 1886).

Kühnel, Bianca, "Steinmetzen aus Fontevrault in Jerusalem: eine Bauplastikwerkstatt der Kreuzfahrerzeit," *Wiener Jahrbuch für Kunstgeschichte,* XXXIII (1980), 83–97.

Labande, Edmond R., *Étude sur Baudouin de Sebourc, chanson de geste: légende poétique de Baudouin II du Bourg, roi de Jérusalem* (Paris, 1940).

Labande, Edmond R., "Recherches sur les pèlerins dans l'Europe des XIe et XIIe siècles," *Cah. Civ. Méd.,* I (1958), 159–169, 339–347.

Labib, Subhi Y., "Geld und Kredit: Studien zur Wirtschaftsgeschichte Aegyptens im Mittelalter," *JESHO,* II (1959), 225–246.

Labib, Subhi Y., "Handelsgeschichte Ägyptens im Mittelalter," *Saeculum,* XIII (1962), 166–178.

Labib, Subhi Y., *Handelsgeschichte Ägyptens im Spätmittelalter, 1171–1517* (*VSWG,* Beihefte, 46; Wiesbaden, 1965).

Lacroix, Benoît, "Deus le volt!: la théologie d'un cri," in *Études de civilisation médié-vale: Mélanges offerts à Edmond R. Labande* (Poitiers, 1974), pp. 461–470.

Ladero Quesada, Miguel A., *Milicia y economía en la guerra de Granada: el cerca de Baza* (Universidad de Valladolid, Falcultad de filosofía y letras: Estudios y docu-mentos: Cuadernos de historia medieval, 22; Valladolid, 1964).

Ladero Quesada, Miguel A., *Castilla y la conquista del reino de Granada* (Universi-dad de Valladolid, Secretariado de Publicación (Thesis, Valladolid, 1967).

Lafond, Jean, "Découverte de vitraux historiés du moyen âge à Constantinople," *Ca-hiers archéologiques,* XVIII (1968), 231–238.

Laiou, Angeliki E., *Constantinople and the Latins: the Foreign Policy of Andronicus II, 1282–1328* (Harvard Historical Studies, 88; Cambridge, Mass., 1972).

Laiou-Thomadakis, Angeliki E., *Peasant Society in the Late Byzantine Empire: a So-cial and Demographic Study* (Princeton, 1977).

Lambton, Ann K.S., *Contributions to the Study of Seljuq Institutions* (London, 1939).

Lamma, Paolo, *Comneni e Staufer: ricerche sui rapporti fra Bisanzio e l'Occidente nel secolo 12* (Studi storici, 14-18, 22-25; Rome, 1955-1957).

Lammens, Henri, "Les Nosairis dans le Liban," *RO Chr.,* VII (1902), 452-477.

Lammens, Henri, *La Syrie: précis historique* (2 vols., Beirut, 1921).

LaMonte, John L., "The Communal Movement in Syria in the Thirteenth Century," in *Anniversary Essays in Mediaeval History by Students of Charles Homer Haskins,* ed. Charles H. Taylor (Boston and New York, 1929), pp. 117-131.

LaMonte, John L., *Feudal Monarchy in the Latin Kingdom of Jerusalem, 1100 to 1291* (Med. AA, Monographs, 4; Cambridge, Mass., 1932).

LaMonte, John L., "To What Extent Was the Byzantine Empire the Suzerain of the Latin Crusading States?," *Byzantion,* VII (1932), 253-264.

LaMonte, John L., "John d'Ibelin, the Old Lord of Beirut, 1177-1236," *Byzantion,* XII (1937), 417-448.

LaMonte, John L., "The Rise and Decline of a Frankish Seigneury in the Time of the Crusades," *RHSEE,* XV (1938), 301-322.

LaMonte, John L., "The Viscounts of Naplouse in the Twelfth Century," *Syria,* XIX (1938), 272-278.

LaMonte, John L., "The Lords of Le Puiset on the Crusades," *Speculum,* XVII (1942), 100-118.

LaMonte, John L., "The Lords of Sidon in the Twelfth and Thirteenth Centuries," *Byzantion,* XVII (1944-1945), 183-211.

LaMonte, John L., "The Lords of Caesarea in the Period of the Crusades," *Speculum,* XXII (1947), 145-161.

LaMonte, John L., and Norton Downs, "The Lords of Bethsan in the Kingdoms of Jerusalem and Cyprus," *Mediaevalia et humanistica,* VI (1950), 57-75.

Lampros, Spyridon P., *Παλαιολόγεια καὶ Πελοποννησιακά,* ed. I. K. Bogiatzides (4 vols. in 2, Athens, 1912-1930).

Landon, Lionel, *The Itinerary of King Richard I, with Studies on Certain Matters of Interest Connected with his Reign* (Publications of the Pipe Roll Society, 51 [= n.s., 13]; London, 1935).

Lane Poole, Austin, *From Domesday Book to Magna Carta, 1087-1216* (Oxford History of England, 3; Oxford, 1951).

Lane Poole, Stanley, *A History of Egypt in the Middle Ages,* 4th ed. (London, 1925).

Lane Poole, Stanley, *Saladin and the Fall of the Kingdom of Jerusalem* (Heroes of the Nations, 24; new ed., New York and London, 1926; repr. New York, 1978).

Langè, S., *Architettura delle crociate in Palestina* (Como, 1956).

Langendorf, Jean-Jacques, and Gérard Zimmermann, "Trois monuments inconnus des croisés: I. La chapelle du Château de Montréal (Jordanie); II. L'octogone du Château de Tripoli (Liban); III. La forteresse de Séléfké (Turquie)," *Genava,* n.s., XII (1964), 123-165.

Langlois, Charles V., *Le Règne de Philippe III, le Hardi* (Paris, 1887).

Langlois, Victor, *Essai historique et critique sur la constitution sociale et politique de l'Arménie sous les rois de la dynastie roupénienne* (Mémoires de l'Académie impériale des sciences de St.-Pétersbourg, 6-III, 3; St. Petersburg, 1860).

Laurent, Joseph, *Byzance et les Turcs seldjoucides dans l'Asie occidentale jusqu'en 1081* (Annales de l'est, 28, pt. 2; Nancy, Paris, and Strassburg, 1913).

Laurent, Joseph, "Arméniens de Cilicie: Aspiétès, Oschin, Ursinus," in *Mélanges offerts à M. Gustave Schlumberger* (Paris, 1924), pp. 159-168.

Laurent, Joseph, "Des Grecs aux croisés: étude sur l'histoire d'Édesse entre 1071 et 1098," *Byzantion,* I (1924), 367–449.

Laurent, Marie H., "Grégoire X et Marco Polo (1267–1271)," *MÉF Rome,* LVIII (1941–1946), 132–144.

Laurent, Vitalien, "La Croisade et la question d'Orient sous le pontificat de Grégoire X (1272–1276)," *RHSEE,* XXII (1945), 105–137.

Laurent, Vitalien, "L'Idée de la guerre sainte et la tradition byzantine," *RHSEE,* XXIII (1946), 71–98.

Lavisse, Ernest, ed., *Histoire de France depuis les origines jusqu'à la Révolution* (9 vols. in 18 parts, repr. Paris, 1901–1911; repr. New York, 1967).

Lavocat, Louis L.L., *Procès des frères et de l'ordre du Temple d'après les pièces inédites publiées par M. Michelet et des documents imprimés anciens et nouveaux* (Paris, 1888).

Lawrence, Thomas E., *Crusader Castles* (2 vols., London, 1936).

Le Viere Leiser, G., "The Crusader Raids in the Red Sea in 578/1182–83," *Journal of the American Research Center in Egypt,* XIV (1977), 87–100.

Leclercq, Jean, "Gratien, Pierre de Troyes et la seconde croisade," *Studia Gratiana,* II (1954), 583–593.

Leclercq, Jean, *Recueil d'études sur Saint Bernard et ses écrits* (Storia e letteratura, 92, 104, 114; 3 vols., Rome, 1962–1969).

Leclercq, Jean, "L'Encyclique de St.-Bernard en faveur de la croisade," *Revue bénédictine,* LXXXI (1971), 282–308; "Addition," *ibid.,* LXXXII (1972), 312.

Leclercq, Jean, "Pour l'histoire de l'encyclique de Saint Bernard sur la croisade," in *Études de civilisation médiévale: Mélanges offerts à Edmond R. Labande* (Poitiers, 1974), pp. 479–490.

Lehmann, Johannes, *I Crociati,* tr. Colombo Pilone (Milan, 1978).

Leib, Bernard, *Rome, Kiev et Byzance à la fin du XIe siècle: rapports religieux des Latins et des Gréco-Russes sous le pontificat d'Urbain II (1088–1099)* (Paris, 1924).

Leib, Bernard, "Les Patriarches de Byzance et la politique religieuse d'Alexis Ier Comnène (1081–1118)," *Recherches de science religieuse,* XL (1952; Mélanges Jules Lebreton, II), 201–221.

Lemerle, Paul, "La Domination vénitienne à Thessalonique," *Fontes Ambrosiani,* XXVII (= Miscellanea Giovanni Galbiati, 3; Milan, 1951), pp. 219–225.

Lemerle, Paul, "Byzance et la croisade," *Relazioni del X Congresso internazionale di scienze storiche, Roma 1955:* vol. 3. *Storia del medioevo* (Florence, 1955), pp. 595–620.

Lemerle, Paul, *L'Émirat d'Aydin, Byzance et l'Occident: recherches sur "La geste d'Umur Pacha"* (Bibliothèque byzantine, Études, 2; Paris, 1957).

Lemerle, Paul, "Recherches sur le régime agraire à Byzance: la terre militaire à l'époque des Comnènes," *Cah. Civ. Méd.,* II (1959), 265–281.

Lemmens, Leonhard, *Die Franziskaner im Heiligen Lande:* 1. *Die Franziskaner auf dem Sion (1336–1551),* 2nd ed. (Franziskanische Studien, Beiheft 4; Münster, 1925).

Lemmens, Leonhard, "De Sancto Francisco Christum praedicante coram sultano Aegypti," *Archivum Franciscanum historicum,* XIX (1926), 559–578.

Lemmens, Leonhard, *Geschichte der Franziskanermissionen* (Missionswissenschaftliche Abhandlungen und Texte, 12; Münster, 1929).

Lenel, Walter, *Die Entstehung der Vorherrschaft Venedigs an der Adria mit Beiträgen zur Verfassungsgeschichte* (Strassburg, 1897).

Lenel, Walter, "Zur älteren Geschichte Venedigs," *Hist. Z,* XCIX (1907), 473–514.

Lenel, Walter, *Venetianisch-istrische Studien* (Strassburg, 1911).

Léonard, Émile G., *Histoire de Jeanne Ire, reine de Naples, comtesse de Provence (1343-1382): la jeunesse de la reine Jeanne* (Mémoires et documents historiques publiés par ordre de . . . prince Louis II de Monaco; 2 vols., Monaco, 1932).

Léonard, Émile G., *Les Angevins de Naples* (Paris, 1954).

Leonhardt, Wilhelm, *Der Kreuzzugsplan Kaiser Heinrichs VI.* (Diss., Giessen; Leipzig, 1913).

Lévi-Provençal, Évariste, *Histoire de l'Espagne musulmane,* 2nd ed. (3 vols., Paris and Leyden, 1950-1953).

Lewis, Archibald R., *Naval Power and Trade in the Mediterranean, A.D. 500-1100* (Princeton Studies in History, 5; Princeton, 1951).

Lewis, Archibald R., "The Catalan Failure in Acculturation in Frankish Greece and the Islamic World during the Fourteenth Century," *Viator,* XI (1980), 361-369.

Lewis, Bernard, "Saladin and the Assassins," *Bulletin of the School of Oriental and African Studies,* XV (1953), 239-245.

Lewis, Bernard, "The Ismā'īlites and the Assassins," *H of C,* I (1955, 2nd ed. 1969), 99-132.

Lewis, Bernard, *The Arabs in History,* new ed. (London, 1958).

Lewis, Bernard, *The Assassins: a Radical Sect in Islam* (New York, 1968).

Lewis, Bernard, "The Mongols, the Turks and the Muslim Polity," *Transactions of the Royal Historical Society,* 5-XVIII (1968), 49-68.

Lewis, Bernard, "Palestine: on the History and Geography of a Name," *International History Review,* II (1980), 128-130.

Lilie, Ralph-Johannes, "Die Schlacht bei Myriokephalon (1176): Auswirkungen auf das byzantinische Reich im ausgehenden 12. Jahrhundert," *RÉ Byz.,* XXXV (1977), 257-275.

Lilie, Ralph-Johannes, *Byzanz und die Kreuzfahrerstaaten: Studien zur Politik des byzantinischen Reiches gegenüber den Staaten der Kreuzfahrer in Syrien und Palästina bis zum Vierten Kreuzzug (1096-1204)* (Poikila byzantina, 1; Munich, 1981).

Lilie, Ralph-Johannes, "Der erste Kreuzzug in der Darstellung Anna Komnenes," *Varia II* (Poikila byzantina, 6; Bonn, 1987), pp. 49-148.

Limentani, Alberto, "Reliquie antico-francesi nella Biblioteca Antoniana," *Memorie dell' Accademia Patavina, Classe di scienze morali, letteratura ed arti,* LXXIX (1961/1962), 3-28.

Lindner, Rudi P., *Nomads and Ottomans in Medieval Anatolia* (Indiana University Ural and Altaic Series, 144; Bloomington, 1983).

Lloyd, Simon, "The Lord Edward's Crusade, 1270-2: its Setting and Significance," *War and Government in the Middle Ages: Essays in Honour of J. O. Prestwich,* ed. John Gillingham and J. C. Holt (Woodbridge, 1984), pp. 120-133.

Loenertz, Raymond J., "Les Missions dominicaines en Orient au XIVe siècle et la Société des Frères Pérégrinants pour le Christ," *AF Praed.,* II (1932), 1-83; III (1933), 1-55; IV (1934), 1-47.

Loenertz, Raymond J., "Pour l'histoire du Péloponnèse au XIVe siècle (1382-1404)," *Études byzantines,* I (1943), 152-196.

Loenertz, Raymond J., "Généalogie des Ghisi, dynastes vénitiens dans l'Archipel (1207-1390)," *O Chr. P.* XXVIII (1962), 121-172, 322-335.

Loenertz, Raymond J., "Les Seigneurs terciers de Négropont de 1205 à 1280," *Byzantion,* XXXV (1965), 235-276.

Loenertz, Raymond J., *Byzantina et Franco-Graeca: articles parus de 1935 à 1966,* reëd. with the collaboration of Peter Schreiner (Storia e letteratura, 118, 145; 2 vols., Rome, 1970-1978).

Loenertz, Raymond J., "Aux Origines du despotat d'Épire et de la principaute d'Achaïe," *Byzantion,* XLIII (1973), 360-394.

Loenertz, Raymond J., *La Société des Frères Pérégrinants: étude sur l'Orient domini-cain* (Institutum historicum Fratrum Praedicatorum: Dissertationes historicae, 7; Rome, 1937); continued as "La Société des Frères Pérégrinants de 1374 à 1475: étude sur l'Orient dominicain, II," *AF Praed.,* XLV (1975), 107-145.

Loenertz, Raymond J., *Les Ghisi: dynastes vénitiens dans l'Archipel 1207-1390,* ed. with Peter Schreiner (Civiltà veneziana, Studi, 26; Florence, 1975).

Loerke, William C., "The Monumental Miniature," *The Place of Book Illumination in Byzantine Art* (Princeton, 1975), pp. 61-97.

Lojacono, Pietro, "La Chiesa conventuale di S. Giovanni dei Cavalieri in Rodi: studio storico-architettonico," *Clara Rhodos,* VIII (1936), 245-288.

Lojacono, Pietro, "Il Palazzo del gran maestro in Rodi: studio storico-architettonico," *Clara Rhodos,* VIII (1936), 289-365.

Løkkegaard, Frede, *Islamic Taxation in the Classic Period with Special Reference to Circumstances in Iraq* (Copenhagen, 1950).

Lomax, Derek W., "Las Milicias cistercienses en el reino de Léon," *Hispania,* XXIII (1963), 29-42.

Lomax, Derek W., *La Orden de Santiago, 1170-1273* (Madrid, 1965).

Lomax, Derek W., *The Reconquest of Spain* (London, 1978).

Longnon, Jean, *Les Français d'Outre-mer au moyen-âge: essai sur l'expansion fran-çaise dans le bassin de Méditerrannée,* 2nd ed. (Paris, 1929).

Longnon, Jean, "Le Rattachement de la principauté de Morée au royaume de Sicile en 1267," *Journal des Savants* (1942), pp. 134-143.

Longnon, Jean, "Problèmes de l'histoire de la principauté de Morée," *Journal des Savants* (1946), pp. 77-93, 147-161.

Longnon, Jean, "L'Organisation de l'église d'Athènes par Innocent III," *Archives de l'Orient chrétien,* I (Mémorial Louis Petit; 1948), 336-346.

Longnon, Jean, *L'Empire latin de Constantinople et la principauté de Morée* (Biblio-thèque historique; Paris, 1949).

Longnon, Jean, "La Reprise de Salonique par les Grecs en 1224," *Actes du VIe Con-grès international des études byzantines (Paris 1948),* I (1950), pp. 141-146.

Longnon, Jean, "The Frankish States in Greece, 1204-1311," *H of C,* II (1962, 2nd ed. 1969), 235-274.

Longnon, Jean, "La Vie rurale dans la Grèce franque," *Journal des Savants* (1965), pp. 343-357.

Longnon, Jean, "Les Vues de Charles d'Anjou pour la deuxième croisade de Saint-Louis: Tunis ou Constantinople?," in *Septième centenaire de la mort de Saint-Louis: Actes des colloques de Royaumont et de Paris* (Paris, 1976), pp. 183-195.

Longnon, Jean, "Sur les Croisés de la quatrième croisade," *Journal des Savants* (1977), pp. 119-127.

Longnon, Jean, *Les Compagnons de Villehardouin: recherches sur les croisés de la quatrième croisade* (Centre de recherches historiques et de philologie de la IVe section de l'École pratique des hautes études, sect. 5, vol. 30; Geneva and Paris, 1978).

Lopez, Roberto S., *Genova marinara nel Duecento: Benedetto Zaccaria, ammiraglio e mercante* (Biblioteca storia principato, 17; Messina and Milan, 1933).

Lopez, Roberto S., *Storia delle colonie genovesi nel Mediterraneo* (Istituto nazionale fascista di cultura: Studi giuridici e storici; Bologna, 1938).

Lopez, Roberto S., "Mohammed and Charlemagne: a Revision," *Speculum,* XVIII (1943), 14–38.

Lopez, Roberto S., "Silk Industry in the Byzantine Empire," *Speculum,* XX (1945), 1–42.

Lopez, Roberto (here, Robert) S., "The Trade of Medieval Europe: the South," in *The Cambridge Economic History of Europe,* ed. Moisi M. Postan and Edwin E. Rich, vol. II (Cambridge, Eng., 1952), pp. 257–354.

Lopez, Roberto (here, Robert) S., "The Norman Conquest of Sicily," *H of C,* I (1955, 2nd ed. 1969), 54–67.

Lopez, Roberto S., *Byzantium and the World around it: Economic and Institutional Relations* (Varior. Repr., CS, 85; London, 1978).

Lot, Ferdinand, *L'Art militaire et les armées au moyen âge en Europe et dans le Proche-Orient* (2 vols., Paris, 1946).

Lotter, Friedrich, *Die Konzeption des Wendenkreuzzuges: ideengeschichtliche, kirchen-rechtliche und historisch-politische Voraussetzungen der Missionierung von Elb- und Ostseeslawen um die Mitte des 12. Jahrhunderts* (Vorträge und Forschungen, special vol. 23; Sigmaringen, 1977).

Loud, G. A., "The *Assise sur la Ligece* and Ralph of Tiberias," in *Crusade and Settlement,* ed. Peter W. Edbury (Cardiff, 1985), pp. 204–212.

Lounghis, T. C., "The Failure of the German-Byzantine Alliance on the Eve of the First Crusade," *Δίπτυχα,* I (1979), 158–167.

Luchaire, Achille, "L'Ordonnance de Philippe-Auguste sur la dîme de la croisade de 1185," *Rev. hist.,* LXXII (1900), 334–338.

Luchaire, Achille, *Innocent III: la croisade des Albigeois* (Paris, 1905).

Luchaire, Achille, *Innocent III: la question d'Orient,* 2nd ed. (Paris, 1911).

Luke, Harry, "The Kingdom of Cyprus, 1291–1369," *H of C,* III (1975), 340–360, and ". . . 1369–1489," *ibid.,* 361–395.

Lunt, William E., *Financial Relations of the Papacy with England* (Med. AA, Publication nos. 33, 74: Studies in Anglo-Papal Relations during the Middle Ages, 1–2; 2 vols., Cambridge, Mass., 1939–1962).

Luttrell, Anthony, "The Knights Hospitallers of Rhodes and their Achievements in the Fourteenth Century," *Revue de l'ordre souverain militaire de Malte,* XVI (1958), 136–142.

Luttrell, Anthony, "Venice and the Knights Hospitallers of Rhodes in the Fourteenth Century," *Papers of the British School at Rome,* XXVI (= n.s., XIII; 1958), 195–212.

Luttrell, Anthony, "Actividades económicas de los Hospitalarios de Rodas en el Mediterráneo occidental durante el siglo XIV," *VI Congreso de historia de la Corona de Aragón* (Madrid, 1959), pp. 175–183.

Luttrell, Anthony, "Interessi fiorentini nell' economia e nella politica dei Cavalieri Ospedalieri di Rodi nel trecento," *Annali della Scuola normale superiore di Pisa,* 2nd ser.: *Lettere, storia e filosofia,* XXVIII (1959), 317–326.

Luttrell, Anthony, "The Aragonese Crown and the Knights Hospitallers of Rhodes, 1291–1350," *Eng. HR,* LXXVI (1961), 1–11.

Luttrell, Anthony, "Emmanuele Piloti and Criticism of the Knights Hospitallers of Rhodes, 1306–1444," *AOSMM,* XX (1962), 11–17.

Luttrell, Anthony, "Fourteenth-Century Hospitaller Lawyers," *Traditio,* XXI (1965), 449–456.

Luttrell, Anthony, "The Crusade in the Fourteenth Century," in *Europe in the Late Middle Ages,* ed. John R. Hale, John R.L. Highfield, and Beryl Smalley (London, 1965), pp. 122–154.

Luttrell, Anthony, "Intrigue, Schism and Violence among the Hospitallers of Rhodes, 1377–1384," *Speculum,* XLI (1966), 30–48.

Luttrell, Anthony, "The Latins of Argos and Nauplia, 1311–1394," *Papers of the British School at Rome,* XXXIV (= n.s., XXI: 1966), 34–55.

Luttrell, Anthony, "Feudal Tenure and Latin Colonization at Rhodes, 1306–1415," *Eng. HR,* LXXXV (1970), 755–775.

Luttrell, Anthony, "Notes on the Chancery of the Hospitallers of Rhodes, 1314–1332," *Byzantion,* XL (= Hommage au R.P.R.J. Loenertz; 1970), 408–420.

Luttrell, Anthony, "The Hospitallers in Cyprus after 1291," Πρακτικὰ τοῦ πρώτου διεθνοῦς Κυπρολογικοῦ συνεδρίου, II (Nicosia, 1972), pp. 161–171.

Luttrell, Anthony, ed., *Medieval Malta: Studies on Malta before the Knights* (London, 1975).

Luttrell, Anthony, "The Hospitallers of Rhodes, 1306–1421," *H of C,* III (1975), 278–313.

Luttrell, Anthony, "The Servitudo Marina at Rhodes 1306–1462," in *Serta Neograeca: Amsterdamer Beiträge zur neugriechischen Literatur, Geschichte und Kunst,* ed. K. Th. Dimaras and Peter Wirth (Amsterdam, 1975), pp. 50–65.

Luttrell, Anthony, "Slavery at Rhodes: 1306–1440," *Bulletin de l'Institut historique belge de Rome,* XLVI–XLVII (1976–1977), 81–100. ˙

Luttrell, Anthony, *The Hospitallers in Cyprus, Rhodes, Greece and the West (1291–1440)* (Varior. Repr., CS, 77; London, 1978).

Luttrell, Anthony, "Gregory XI and the Turks 1370–1378," *O Chr. P,* XLVI (1980), 394–417.

Luttrell, Anthony, "The Hospitallers of Rhodes: Prospectives, Problems, Possibilities," in *Die geistlichen Ritterorden Europas,* ed. Josef Fleckenstein and Manfred Hellmann (Vorträge und Forschungen, 26; Sigmaringen, 1980), pp. 243–266.

Luttrell, Anthony, *Latin Greece, the Hospitallers and the Crusades, 1291–1440* (Varior. Repr., CS, 158; London, 1982).

Luttrell, Anthony, "The Benedictines and Malta: 1363–1371," *Papers of the British School at Rome,* L (1982), 146–165.

Luzzatto, Gino, *Storia economica d'Italia: 1. L'antichità e il medioevo* (Biblioteca storica, 20; Rome, 1949).

Luzzatto, Gino, *Studi di storia economica veneziana* (Padua, 1954).

Luzzatto, Gino, *Storia economica di Venezia dall' XI al XVI secolo* (Venice, 1961).

Lyons, Malcolm C., and David E.P. Jackson, *Saladin: the Politics of the Holy War* (University of Cambridge Oriental Publications, 30; Cambridge, Eng., 1982).

Macek, Josef, *Prokop Veliký* (Živá díla minulosti, sv. 22; Prague, 1953).

Macek, Josef, *Tábor v husitském revolučnim hnutí* (Práce Československé akademie věd. Sekce filosofie a historie, 1–2; 2 vols.; vol. I, 2nd ed., vol. II, 1st ed., Prague, 1955–1956).

Macek, Josef, *The Hussite Movement in Bohemia,* tr. Vilém Fried and Ian Milner (2nd enlarged ed., Prague, 1958; repr. New York, 1980).

Macquarrie, Alan, *Scotland and the Crusades 1095–1560* (Edinburgh, 1985).

Maggiorotti, Leone A., *Architetti e architettura militari,* vol. I (L'Opera del genio italiano all' estero; [4th ser.] Gli architetti militari; Rome, 1933).

Magnocavallo, Arturo, *Marin Sanudo il Vecchio e il suo progetto di crociata* (Bergamo, 1901).

Magoulias, Harry J., "A Study in Roman Catholic and Greek Orthodox Church Relations on the Island of Cyprus between the Years A.D. 1196 and 1360," *Greek Orthodox Theological Review*, X (1964), 75–106.

Mähl, Sibylle, "Jerusalem in mittelalterlicher Sicht," *Die Welt als Geschichte*, XXII (1962), 11–26.

Maiuri, Amedeo, "Il Castello di S. Pietro nel Golfo d'Alicarnasso," *Rassegna d'arte antica e moderna*, n.s., VIII (= XXI; 1921), 85–92.

Maiuri, Amedeo, "L'Ospedale dei cavalieri di Rodi," *Bollettino d'arte del Ministero della pubblica istruzione*, n.s., I (= XV; 1921), 211–226.

Maiuri, Amedeo, *Rodi: Guida dei monumenti e del Museo archeologico . . .*, (2nd ed., Milan, 1921).

Maiuri, Amedeo, "I Castelli dei cavalieri di Rodi a Cos e a Budrúm (Alicarnasso)," *Annuario della Reale scuola archeologica di Atene e delle missioni italiane in Oriente*, IV–V (1921–1922 [pub. 1924]), 275–343.

Maiuri, Amedeo, and G. Jocapich, "Monumenti di arte cavalleresca," *Clara Rhodos*, I (1928), 127–181.

Maltézou, Chryssa A., "Il Quartiere veneziano di Costantinopoli (scali marittimi)," *Θησαυρίσματα*, XV (1978), 30–61.

Manfroni, Camillo, *Storia della marina italiana dalle invasioni barbariche al trattato di Ninfeo* (Leghorn, 1899).

Manfroni, Camillo, *Storia della marina italiana dal trattato di Ninfeo alla caduta di Costantinopoli (1261–1453)* (3 vols., Leghorn, 1902–1903).

Manfroni, Camillo, *I Colonizzatori italiani durante il medio evo e il rinascimento:* vol. I. *Dal seccolo XI al XIII* (Rome, 1933).

Mann, Jacob, *The Jews in Egypt and in Palestine under the Fāṭimid Caliphs: a Contribution to their Political and Communal History Based Chiefly on Genizah Material Hitherto Unpublished* (2 vols., London, 1920–1922; repr. New York, 1970).

Mansilla, Demetrio, "El Cardenal hispano Pelayo Gaitán (1206–1230)," *Anthologica Annua*, I (1953), 11–66.

Manvelichvili, Alexandre, *Histoire de Géorgie* (Paris, 1951).

Marçais, Georges, *La Berbérie musulmane et l'Orient au moyen âge* (Les grandes crises de l'histoire; Paris, 1946).

Marinescu, Constantin, "Philippe le Bon, duc de Bourgogne, et la croisade 1453–1467," *Bulletin des études portugaises et de l'Institut français au Portugal*, n.s., XIII (1949), 3–28.

Marinescu, Constantin, "Philippe le Bon, duc de Bourgogne, et la croisade (1419–1453)," *Actes du VIe Congrès international d'études byzantines (Paris 1948)*, I (Paris, 1950), pp. 147–168.

Markowski, Michael, "Crucesignatus: its Origins and Early Usage," *J Med. H*, X (1984), 157–165.

Martin, Jean P., "Les Premiers princes croisés et les Syriens jacobites de Jérusalem," *JA*, XII (1888), 471–490; XIII (1889), 33–80.

Martin, José-Luis, "Orígenes de la orden militar de Santiago (1170–1195)," *Anuario de estudios medievales*, IV (1967), 571–590.

Martini, Giuseppe, "Innocenzo III ed il finanziamento delle crociate," *Archivio della R. deputazione romana di storia patria*, LXVII (1944), 309–335; repr. in *Nuova rivista storica*, LXV (1981), 191–208.

Mas Latrie, Louis de, "Des Relations politiques et commerciales de l'Asie Mineure avec l'île de Chypre sous le règne des princes de la maison de Lusignan," *BÉ Char.*, VI (1844), 301–330, 485–521; VII (1845–1846), 121–142.

Mas Latrie, Louis de, *Histoire de l'île de Chypre sous le règne des princes de la maison de Lusignan* (3 vols., Paris, 1852–1861; repr., 4 vols., Famagusta, 1970).

Mas Latrie, Louis de, "La Terre au delà du Jourdain et ses premiers seigneurs," *BÉ Char.*, XXXIX (1878), 416–420, and "Errata" on p. 588.

Mas Latrie, Louis de, *L'Île de Chypre: sa situation présente, ses souvenirs du moyen-âge* (Paris, 1879).

Mas Latrie, Louis de, "Les Comtes de Jaffa et d'Ascalon du XIIe au XIXe siècle," *Rev. QH*, XXVI (1879), 181–200.

Mas Latrie, Louis de, "Le Fief de la chamberlaine et les chambellans de Jérusalem," *BÉ Char.*, XLIII (1882), 647–652.

Mas Latrie, Louis de, "Les Seigneurs du Crac de Montréal appelés d'abord seigneurs de la terre au delà du Jourdain," *Arch. Ven.*, XXV (= n.s., XIII; 1883), 475–494.

Mas Latrie, Louis de, "Histoire des archevêques latins de l'île de Chypre," *AO Latin*, II-1 (1884), 207–328.

Mas Latrie, Louis de, "Les Patriarches latins d'Antioche," *RO Latin*, II (1894), 192–205.

Mas Latrie, Louis de, "Les Seigneurs d'Arsur en Terre Sainte," *Rev. QH*, n.s., XI (= LV; 1894), 585–597.

Massignon, Louis, "La 'Futuwwa' ou 'pacte d'honneur artisanal' entre les travailleurs musulmans au moyen âge," *La Nouvelle Clio*, IV (1952), 171–198.

Mata Carriazo, Juan de, *Historia de la guerra de Granada*, in *Historia de España*, ed. Ramón Menéndez Pidal: vol. 17. *La España de los reyes católicos (1474–1516)*, vol. 1, by Luis Suárez Fernándes and Juan de Mata Carriazo, part 3 (Madrid, 1969), pp. 385–914.

Matton, Raymond, *Rhodes* (Collection de l'Institut français d'Athènes, 62: Villes et paysages de Grèce, vol. 1; Athens, 1949).

Mayer, Hans E., "Zur Beurteilung Adhémars von Le Puy," *Deutsches Archiv*, XVI (1960), 547–552.

Mayer, Hans E., "Das Pontifikale von Tyrus und die Krönung der lateinischen Könige von Jerusalem: zugleich ein Beitrag zur Forschung über Herrschaftszeichen und Staatssymbolik," *D Oaks P*, XXI (1967), 141–232.

Mayer, Hans E., "On the Beginnings of the Communal Movement in the Holy Land: the Commune of Tyre," *Traditio*, XXIV (1968), 443–457.

Mayer, Hans E., "Zwei Kommunen in Akkon?," *Deutsches Archiv*, XXVI (1970), 434–453.

Mayer, Hans E., "Kaiserrecht und Heiliges Land," in *Aus Reichsgeschichte und Nordischer Geschichte*, ed. Horst Fuhrmann, Hans E. Mayer, and Klaus Wriedt (Kieler historische Studien, 16; Stuttgart, 1972), pp. 193–208.

Mayer, Hans E., "Studies in the History of Queen Melisende of Jerusalem," *D Oaks P*, XXVI (1972), 93–182.

Mayer, Hans E., and Marie L. Favreau, "Das Diplom Balduins I. für Genua und Genuas goldene Inschrift in der Grabeskirche," *QFIAB*, LV/LVI (1976), 22–95.

Mayer, Hans E., *Bistümer, Klöster und Stifte im Königreich Jerusalem* (MGH, Schriften, 26; Stuttgart, 1977).

Mayer, Hans E., "Die Kanzlei Richards I. von England auf dem dritten Kreuzzug," *MIÖG*, LXXXV (1977), 22–35.

Mayer, Hans E., "Ibelin versus Ibelin: the Struggle for the Regency of Jerusalem 1253–1258," *Proceedings of the American Philosophical Society*, CXXII (1978), 25–57.

Mayer, Hans E., "Latins, Muslims and Greeks in the Latin Kingdom of Jerusalem," *History*, LXIII (1978), 175–192.

Mayer, Hans E., "Die Seigneurie de Joscelin und der Deutsche Orden," in *Die geist-lichen Ritterorden Europas,* ed. Josef Fleckenstein and Manfred Hellmann (Vor-träge und Forschungen, 26; Sigmaringen, 1980), pp. 171–216.

Mayer, Hans E., "Ein Deperditum König Balduins III. von Jerusalem als Zeugnis seiner Pläne zur Eroberung Ägyptens," *Deutsches Archiv,* XXXVI (1980), 549–566.

Mayer, Hans E., "Jérusalem et Antioche au temps de Baudouin II," *CRAIBL* (1980), pp. 717–734.

Mayer, Hans E., "Carving up Crusaders: the Early Ibelins and Ramlas," in *Outremer* (1982), pp. 101–118.

Mayer, Hans E., "Henry II of England and the Holy Land," *Eng. HR,* XCVII (1982), 721–739.

Mayer, Hans E., "The Concordat of Nablus," *Journal of Ecclesiastical History,* XXXIII (1982), 531–543.

Mayer, Hans E., *Kreuzzüge und lateinischer Osten* (Varior. Repr., CS, 171; London, 1983).

Mayer, Hans E., *Probleme des lateinischen Königreichs Jerusalem* (Varior. Repr., CS, 178; London, 1983).

Mayer, Hans E., "John of Jaffa, his Opponents and his Fiefs," *Proceedings of the American Philosophical Society,* CXXVIII (1984), 134–163.

Mayer, Hans E., *Mélanges sur l'histoire du royaume latin de Jérusalem* (Mémoires de l'Académie des inscriptions et belles-lettres, n.s., 5; Paris, 1984).

Mayer, Hans E., *Geschichte der Kreuzzüge* (Urban-Bücher, 86; 6th ed., Stuttgart, 1985); rev. tr. by John Gillingham as *The Crusades* (Oxford, 1972; 2nd ed., 1988).

Mayer, Hans E., "Die Herrschaftsbildung in Hebron," *ZDPV,* CI (1985), 64–81.

Mayer, Hans E., "The Double County of Jaffa and Ascalon: One Fief or Two?," in *Crusade and Settlement,* ed. Peter W. Edbury (Cardiff, 1985), pp. 181–190.

Mayer, Hans E., "The Origins of the County of Jaffa," *Isr. Expl. J,* XXXV (1985), 35–45.

Mayer, Hans E., "The Origins of the Lordships of Ramla and Lydda in the Kingdom of Jerusalem," *Speculum,* LX (1985), 537–552.

Mayer, Hans E., "The Succession to Baldwin II of Jerusalem: English Impact on the East," *D Oaks P,* XXXIX (1985), 139–147.

Mayer, Hans E., "Guillaume de Tyr à l'école," *Mémoires de l'Académie des sciences, arts et belles-lettres de Dijon,* CXXVII (1985–1986, published 1988), 257–265.

Mayer, Hans E., "Die Legitimät Balduins IV. von Jerusalem und das Testament der Agnes von Courtenay," *HJ Görres.,* CVIII (1988), 63–89.

McGinn, Bernard, "Iter sancti sepulchri: the Piety of the First Crusaders," in *Essays in Medieval Civilization,* ed. Bede K. Lackner and Kenneth R. Philip (The Walter Prescott Webb Memorial Lectures, 12; Austin and London, 1978), pp. 33–72.

McLeod, William, "Castles of the Morea in 1467," *Byz. Z,* LXV (1972), 353–363.

McNeal, Edgar H., and Robert L. Wolff, "The Fourth Crusade," *H of C,* II (1962, 2nd ed. 1969), 153–185.

Megaw, A.H.S., "The Arts in Cyprus: B. Military Architecture," *H of C,* IV (1977), 196–207.

Meinardus, Otto F., *The Copts in Jerusalem* (Cairo, 1960).

Melinkian-Chirvani, Assadullah S., "Venise entre l'Orient et l'Occident," *Bulletin d'études orientales,* XXVII (1974), 109–126.

Melville, Marion, *La Vie des Templiers,* 2nd ed. (Paris, 1974).

Melville, Marion, "Les Débuts de l'ordre du Temple," in *Die geistlichen Ritterorden Europas,* ed. Josef Fleckenstein and Manfred Hellmann (Vorträge und Forschungen, 26; Sigmaringen, 1980), pp. 23–30.

Menager, Léon R., *Amiratus—ἀμηρᾶς: l'émirat et les origines de l'amirauté (XIe-XIIIe siècles)* (École pratique des hautes études, Paris: Bibliothèque générale, Sect. 6; Paris, 1960).

Menéndez Pidal, Ramón, *La España del Cid,* 3rd rev. ed. (Madrid, 1967).

Mercier, Ernest, *Histoire de l'Afrique septentrionale (Berbérie) depuis les temps les plus reculés jusqu'à la conquête française (1830)* (3 vols., Paris, 1888-1891).

Mercier, Maurice, *Le Feu grégeois, les feux de guerre depuis l'antiquité, la poudre à canon* (Paris and Avignon, 1952).

Mertens, Volker, "Kritik am Kreuzzug Kaiser Heinrichs? Zu Hartmanns 3. Kreuzzugslied," in *Stauferzeit: Geschichte, Literatur und Kunst,* ed. Rüdiger Krahn, Bernd Timm, and Peter Wapnewski (Karlsruher Kulturwissenschaftliche Arbeiten, 1; Stuttgart, 1979), pp. 325-333.

Méry, Louis E., and F. Guindon, *Histoire analytique et chronologique des actes et des délibérations du corps et du conseil de la municipalité de Marseille depuis le Xe siècle jusqu'à nos jours* (8 vols., Marseilles, 1841-1873).

Meurer, Heribert, "Kreuzreliquiare aus Jerusalem," *Jahrbuch der Staatlichen Kunstsammlungen in Baden-Württemberg,* XIII (1976), 7-17.

Meurer, Heribert, "Zu den Staurotheken der Kreuzfahrer," *Zeitschrift für Kunstgeschichte,* XLVIII (1985), 65-76.

Meyvaert, Paul, "An Unknown Letter of Hulagu, Il-Khan of Persia, to King Louis IX of France," *Viator,* XI (1980), 245-259.

Miccoli, Giovanni, "La 'Crociata dei fanciulli' del 1212," *Studi medievali,* 3-II (1961), 407-443.

Michael, Emil, "Hat Papst Innocenz III. sich das [erzwingbare] Recht zuerkannt, auch die Laien zu Kreuzzugszwecken zu besteuern?," *Zeitschrift für katholische Theologie,* XIX (1895), 753-756.

Michaud, Joseph F., *Histoire des croisades,* 7th ed., ed. Jean L.A. Huillard-Bréholles (4 vols., Paris, 1857); tr. W. Robson as *Michaud's History of the Crusades* (3 vols., London, 1852; repr. New York, 1973).

Michel, Anton, *Humbert und Kerullarios* (Quellen und Forschungen aus dem Gebiete der Geschichte, ed. by the Görres-Gesellschaft, 21, 23; 2 vols., Paderborn, 1924-1930).

Michel, Anton, *Amalfi und Jerusalem im griechischen Kirchenstreit: Kardinal Humbert, Laycus von Amalfi, Niketas Stethatos, Symeon II. von Jerusalem und Bruno von Segni über die Azymen* (Orientalia christiana analecta, 121; Rome, 1939).

Michel, Anton, "Die byzantinische und römische Werbung um Symeon II. von Jerusalem," *Z Kirch.,* LXII (1943-1944), 164-177.

Michel, Anton, "Die Friedensbotschaft Grados an Antiocheia im Schisma des Kerullarios (1053-1054) und ihr Widerhall," *Studi Gregoriani,* II (1947), 163-188.

Michel, Anton, "Die römischen Angriffe auf Michael Kerullarios wegen Antiocheia (1053-1054)," *Byz. Z,* XLIV (1951), 419-427.

Michel, Anton, *Die Kaisermacht in der Ostkirche (813-1204)* (Darmstadt, 1959).

Mieli, Aldo, *La Science arabe et son rôle dans l'évolution scientifique mondiale* (Leyden, 1938).

Miller, Timothy, "The Knights of St. John and the Hospitals of the Latin West," *Speculum,* LIII (1978), 709-733.

Miller, William, *The Latins in the Levant: a History of Frankish Greece (1204-1566)* (London, 1908; repr. 1964; repr. New York, 1983).

Miller, William, *Essays on the Latin Orient* (Cambridge, Eng., 1921; repr. Chicago, 1967, New York, 1983).

Miller, William, *Trebizond, the Last Greek Empire* (London, 1926).

Millet, Gabriel, *Monuments byzantins de Mistra: matériaux pour l'étude de l'architecture et de la peinture en Grèce aux XIVe et XVe siècles* (Monuments de l'art byzantin, 2; Paris, 1910).

Minorsky, Vladimir F., *Studies in Caucasian History: 1. New Light on the Shaddādids of Ganja; 2. The Shaddādids of Ani; 3. Prehistory of Saladin* (Cambridge Oriental Series, 6; London, 1953).

Miret y Sans, Joaquín, *Itinerari de Jaume I "el Conqueridor"* (Barcelona, 1918).

Misbach, Henry L., *Genoese Trade and the Flow of Gold, 1154–1253* (Diss., Wisconsin, 1968; Ann Arbor, Mich., 1977).

Mogabgab, Theophilus A.H., ed. and tr., *Supplementary Excerpts on Cyprus, or Further Materials for a History of Cyprus* (3 parts, Nicosia, 1941–1944).

Möhring, Hannes, *Saladin und der Dritte Kreuzzug: Aiyubidische Strategie und Diplomatie im Vergleich vornehmlich der arabischen mit den lateinischen Quellen* (Frankfurter historische Abhandlungen, 21; Wiesbaden, 1980).

Mollat, Guillaume, *Les Papes d'Avignon (1305–1378),* 10th ed. (Bibliothèque de l'enseignement d'histoire ecclésiastique; Paris, 1964; 9th ed. tr. Janet Love (New York, 1965).

Mompherratos, Antonios, Διπλωματικαὶ ἐνέργειαι Μανουὴλ β'τοῦ Παλαιολόγου ἐν Εὐρώπῃ καὶ Ἀσίᾳ (Athens, 1913).

Monneret de Villard, Ugo, "La Vita, le opere e i viaggi di frate Ricoldo da Montecroce, O.P.," *O Chr. P,* X (1944), 227–274.

Monneret de Villard, Ugo, *Lo Studio dell' Islām in Europa nel XII e nel XIII secolo* (Studi e testi, 110; Vatican City, 1944).

Montalbán, Francisco J., *Manual de historia de las misiones,* 2nd ed. (Bilbao, 1952).

Monti, Gennaro M., *Da Carlo I a Roberto d'Angiò: ricerche e documenti* (Trani, 1936).

Monti, Gennaro M., *Nuovi studi angioini* (Reale deputazione di storia patria per le Puglie: Documenti e monografie, n.s., 21; Trani, 1937).

Monti, Gennaro M., *L'Italia e le crociate in Terra Santa* (Naples, 1941).

Monti, Gennaro M., *L'Espansione mediterranea del mezzogiorno d'Italia e della Sicilia* (Bologna, 1942).

Moore, E. A., *The Ancient Churches of Old Jerusalem: the Evidence of the Pilgrims* (London and Beirut, 1961).

Moranvillé, Henri, "Les Projets de Charles de Valois sur l'empire de Constantinople," *BÉ Char.,* LI (1890), 63–86.

Morgan, Jacques de, *Histoire du peuple arménien depuis les temps les plus reculés de ses annales jusqu'à nos jours* (Paris and Nancy, 1919).

Morgan, Margaret R., "The Meanings of Old French *polain,* Latin *pullanus,*" *Medium Aevum,* XLVIII (1979), 40–54.

Morghen, Raffaello, "L'Unità monarchica nell' Italia meridionale," *Questioni di storia medioevale, a cura di Ettore Rota* (Milan, 1946), pp. 275–302.

Morris, Colin, "Propaganda for War: the Dissemination of the Crusading Ideal in the Twelfth Century," in *The Church and War,* ed. W. J. Shiels (Studies in Church History, 20; Oxford, 1983), pp. 79–101.

Morris, Colin, "Policy and Visions: the Case of the Holy Lance at Antioch," *War and Government in the Middle Ages: Essays in Honour of J. O. Prestwich,* ed. John Gillingham and J. C. Holt (Woodbridge, 1984), pp. 33–45.

Moule, Arthur C., *Christians in China before 1550* (London, 1930).

Moutsopoulus, Nikolaos, "Le Monastère franc de Notre-Dame d'Isova (Gortynie)," *BC Hell.,* LXXX (1956), 76–94; addenda and corrigenda, p. 632.

Muir, William, *The Mameluke, or, Slave Dynasty of Egypt (1260-1517)* (London, 1896; repr. New York, 1973).

Muir, William, *The Caliphate, its Rise, Decline and Fall: from Original Sources* (New York, 1975).

Muldoon, James, *Popes, Lawyers and Infidels* (Liverpool, 1979).

Müller, Friedrich A., *Der Islam im Morgen- und Abendland* (2 vols., Berlin, 1885-1887).

Müller-Wiener, Wolfgang, *Castles of the Crusaders*, tr. J. Maxwell Brownjohn (London, 1966).

Munro, Dana C., "The Speech of Pope Urban II at Clermont, 1095," *Amer. HR*, XI (1905-1906), 231-242.

Munro, Dana C., "The Children's Crusade," *Amer. HR*, XIX (1913-1914), 516-524.

Munro, Dana C., *The Kingdom of the Crusaders* (New York, 1935).

Murphy-O'Connor, Jerome, *The Holy Land: an Archaeological Guide from the Earliest Times to 1700* (Oxford, 1980).

Musset, Lucien, *Les Peuples scandinaves au moyen âge* (Paris, 1951).

Musso, Gian G., *Navigazione e commercio genovese con il Levante* (Pubblicazioni degli Archivi di Stato, vol. 84; Rome, 1975).

Musso, Gian G., *I Genovesi e il Levante tra medioevo e età moderna: ricerche d'archivio* (Genoa, 1976).

Myers, Geoffrey M., *Les Chétifs* (The Old French Crusade Cycle, 5; University, Ala., 1981).

Nabe-von Schönberg, Uwe, *Die Westsyrische Kirche im Mittelalter (800-1150)* (Heidelberg, 1977).

Nada Patrone, Anna M., *La Quarta crociata e l'impero latino di Romania (1198-1261)* (Turin, 1972).

Nasrallah, Joseph, "Couvents de la Syrie du Nord portant le nom de Siméon," *Syria*, XLIX (1972), 127-159.

Nasrallah, Joseph, "Acre chrétienne du début de la prédication de l'Évangile aux croisades," *Proche-Orient chrétien*, XXIX (1979), 301-305.

Nataras, D., Ἱστορία περὶ τῶν ἐν Ἱεροσολύμοις πατριαρχευσάντων (Bucharest, 1717).

Negri, Teofilo O. de, *Storia di Genova* (Milan, 1968).

Nellmann, Eberhard, "Walthers unzeitgemässer Kreuzzugsappell: zur Funktion der Herkeiser-Strophen des Ottentons," *Zeitschrift für deutsche Philologie*, XCVIII (1979), Sonderheft, pp. 22-60.

Neumann, Carl, *Bernhard von Clairvaux und die Anfänge des zweiten Kreuzzuges* (Heidelberg, 1882).

Neumann, Carl, *Die Weltstellung des byzantinischen Reiches vor den Kreuzzügen* (Habilitationsschrift Heidelberg; Leipzig, 1894).

Nicholson, Robert L., *Tancred: a Study of his Career and Work in their Relation to the First Crusade and the Establishment of the Latin States in Syria and Palestine* (Thesis, Chicago, 1940; repr. New York, 1978).

Nicholson, Robert L., *Joscelyn I, Prince of Edessa* (Illinois Studies in the Social Sciences, 34-4; Urbana, 1954; repr. New York, 1983).

Nicholson, Robert L., "The Growth of the Latin States, 1118-1144," *H of C*, I (1955, 2nd ed. 1969), 410-447.

Nicholson, Robert L., *Joscelyn III and the Fall of the Crusader States, 1134-1199* (Leyden, 1973).

Nickerson, Mary E., "The Seigneury of Beirut in the Twelfth Century and the Brisebarre Family of Beirut-Blanchegarde," *Byzantion*, XIX (1949), 141–185. See also Hardwicke.

Nicol, Donald M., *The Despotate of Epiros* (Oxford, 1957).

Nicol, Donald M., "The Greeks and the Union of the Churches: the Preliminaries to the Second Council of Lyons, 1261–1274," in *Medieval Studies Presented to Aubrey Gwynn,* ed. John A. Watt, John B. Morrall, and Francis X. Martin (Dublin, 1961), pp. 454–480.

Nicol, Donald M., "Byzantium and the Papacy in the Eleventh Century," *Journal of Ecclesiastical History,* XIII (1962), 1–20.

Nicol, Donald M., *Refugees, Mixed Population and Local Patriotism in Epiros and Western Macedonia after the Fourth Crusade* (XVe Congrès international d'études byzantines: rapports et co-rapports: 1. Histoire; 2. Composition et mouvement de la population dans le monde byzantin; Athens, 1976).

Nicol, Donald M., "Symbiosis and Integration: Some Greco-Latin Families in Byzantium in the 11th to 13th Centuries," *Byz. F,* VII (1979), 113–135.

Nicol, Donald M., *The End of the Byzantine Empire* (Foundations of Medieval History; London, 1979).

Nix, Matthias, "Der Kreuzzugsaufruf Walthers im Ottenton und der Kreuzzugsplan Kaiser Ottos IV.," *Germanisch-Romanische Monatsschrift,* LXV (= n.s., XXXIV; 1984), 278–294.

Norden, Walter, *Der vierte Kreuzzug im Rahmen der Beziehungen des Abendlandes zu Byzanz* (Berlin, 1898).

Norden, Walter, *Das Papsttum und Byzanz: die Trennung der beiden Mächte und das Problem ihrer Wiedervereinigung bis zum Untergange des byzantinischen Reiches, 1453* (Berlin, 1903).

Norgate, Kate, *Richard the Lion Heart* (London, 1924).

Noth, Albrecht, *Heiliger Krieg und heiliger Kampf in Islam und Christentum: Beiträge zur Vorgeschichte und Geschichte der Kreuzzüge* (Bonner historische Forschungen, 28; Bonn, 1966).

Nowell, Charles E., "The Old Man of the Mountain," *Speculum,* XXII (1947), 497–519.

O'Callaghan, Joseph F., "The Affiliation of the Order of Calatrava with the Order of Cîteaux," *Analecta sacri ordinis Cisterciensis,* XV (1959), 163–193; XVI (1960), 3–59.

O'Callaghan, Joseph F., "The Foundation of the Order of Alcántara, 1176–1218," *Cath. HR,* XLVII (1961–1962), 471–486.

O'Callaghan, Joseph F., *A History of Medieval Spain* (Ithaca and London, 1975).

O'Callaghan, Joseph F., *The Spanish Military Order of Calatrava and its Affiliates* (Varior. Repr., CS, 37; London, 1975).

O'Neil, Bryan H. St.J., "Rhodes and the Origin of the Bastion," *Antiquaries Journal,* XXXIV (1954), 44–54.

Oeconomos, Lysimachos, *La Vie religieuse dans l'empire byzantin au temps des Comnènes et des Anges* (Paris, 1918).

Ohnsorge, Werner, "Ein Beitrag zur Geschichte Manuels I. von Byzanz," in *Festschrift Albert Brackmann dargebracht von Freunden, Kollegen und Schülern,* ed. Leo Santifaller (Weimar, 1931), pp. 371–393.

Ohnsorge, Werner, *Das Zweikaiserproblem im früheren Mittelalter: die Bedeutung des byzantinischen Reiches für die Entwicklung der Staatsidee in Europa* (Hildesheim, 1947).

Ohnsorge, Werner, *Abendland und Byzanz: Gesammelte Aufsätze zur Geschichte der byzantinisch-abendländischen Beziehungen und des Kaisertums* (Darmstadt, 1958).

Ohsson, Abraham C.M. d', *Histoire des Mongols depuis Tchinguiz-Khan jusqu'à Timur Bey ou Tamerlan* (4 vols., Amsterdam, 1852).

Oldenbourg, Zoë, *Les Croisades* (Geneva, 1977).

Olwer, Lluis N. d', *L'Expansió de Catalunya en la Mediterrània oriental* (Enciclopèdia Catalunya, 1; Barcelona, 1926).

Oman, Charles, *History of the Art of War in the Middle Ages*, 2nd ed. (2 vols., New York, 1924).

Opll, Ferdinand, *Das Itinerar Kaiser Friedrich Barbarossas (1152-1190)* (Forschungen zur Kaiser- und Papstgeschichte des Mittelalters: Beihefte zu J. F. Böhmer, *Regesta Imperii*, 1; Vienna, Cologne, and Graz, 1978).

Orfali, Gaudenzio, *Gethsémani, ou Notice sur l'église de l'Agonie ou de la Prière, d'après les fouilles récentes accomplies par la Custodie franciscaine de Terre Sainte (1909 et 1920)* (Paris, 1924).

Ormanian, Malachia, *L'Église arménienne: son histoire, sa doctrine, son régime, sa discipline, sa liturgie, son présent* (Paris, 1910).

Ostrogorski, Georgije (here, Georg Ostrogorsky), "Die ländliche Steuergemeinde des byzantinischen Reiches im 10. Jahrhundert," *VSWG*, XX (1928), 1-108.

Ostrogorski, Georgije (here, Georg Ostrogorsky), "Das Steuersystem im byzantinischen Altertum und Mittelalter," *Byzantion*, VI (1931), 229-240.

Ostrogorski, Georgije (here, Georges Ostrogorskij), *Pour l'histoire de la féodalité byzantine*, tr. Henri Grégoire and Paul Lemerle (Corpus Bruxellense historiae Byzantinae, Subsidia, 1; Brussels, 1954).

Ostrogorski, Georgije (here, Georges Ostrogorskij), *Quelques problèmes d'histoire de la paysannerie byzantine* (Corpus Bruxellense historiae Byzantinae, Subsidia, 2; Brussels, 1956).

Ostrogorski, Georgije (here, Georges Ostrogorskij), "Pour l'histoire de l'immunité à Byzance," *Byzantion*, XXVIII (1958), 165-254.

Ostrogorski, Georgije (here, Georg Ostrogorsky), *Geschichte des byzantinischen Staates* (Handbuch der Altertumswissenschaft, sect. 12. Byzantinisches Handbuch, parts 1, 2; 3rd ed., Munich, 1963); 2nd ed. tr. Joan M. Hussey as *History of the Byzantine State* (London, 1956); rev. ed. (Rutgers Byzantine Series; New Brunswick, N.J., 1969).

Oursel, Raymond, *Pèlerins du moyen âge: les hommes, les chemins, les sanctuaires* (Paris, 1978); Italian tr. as *Pellegrini del medioevo: gli uomini, le strade, i sanctuari* (Milan, 1979).

Outremer, see Kedar 1982 (2).

Ovadiah (here, Ovadiyah), Asher, "A Crusader Church in the Jewish Quarter of Jerusalem," *Eretz Israel*, XI (I. Dunayevsky Memorial Volume; 1973), 208-212 (in Hebrew, with an English summary on p. 29*).

Ovadiah, Asher, "A Restored Crusader Church in the Jewish Quarter," *Christian News from Israel*, XXV (1975), 150-153.

Paetow, Louis J., ed., *The Crusades and Other Historical Essays Presented to Dana C. Munro by his Former Students* (New York, 1928); includes Beaumont, Byrne, Duncalf, Gutsch, Joranson, Knappen, C5.

Painter, Sidney, "Western Europe on the Eve of the Crusades," *H of C*, I (1955, 2nd ed. 1969), 3-29.

Painter, Sidney, "The Third Crusade: Richard the Lionhearted and Philip Augustus,"

H of C, II (1962, 2nd ed. 1969), 45–85, and "The Crusade of Theobald of Champagne and Richard of Cornwall, 1239–1241," *ibid.,* 463–485.

Palacký, František, *Geschichte von Böhmen: Grösstentheils nach Urkunden und Handschriften* (5 vols. in 10, Prague, 1836–1867).

Pall, Francisc, "Ciriaco d'Ancona e la crociata contro i Turchi," *Bulletin de la Section historique de l'Académie roumaine,* XX (1938), 9–68.

Pall, Francisc, "Autour de la croisade de Varna: la question de la paix de Szeged et de sa rupture (1444)," *Bulletin de la Section historique de l'Académie roumaine,* XXII (1941), 144–158.

Pall, Francisc, "Les Croisades en Orient au bas moyen âge: observations critiques sur l'ouvrage de M. Atiya," *RHSEE,* XIX (1942), 527–583.

Pall, Francisc, "Un Moment décisif de l'histoire du sud-est européen: la croisade de Varna," *Balcania,* VII (1944), 102–120.

Panagopoulos, Beata K., *Cistercian and Mendicant Monasteries in Medieval Greece* (Chicago, 1979).

Papadopoulos, Chrysostomos, Ἱστορία τῆς ἐκκλησίας Ἱεροσολύμων (Alexandria, 1910; repr. Athens, 1970).

Papadopoulos, Chrysostomos, "Ἡ ἐκκλησία Ἀντιοχείας ἐπὶ τῆς κυριαρχίας τῶν Σελτζουκιδῶν καὶ τῶν Φράγκων ἐν Συρίᾳ," Θεολογία, XVI (1938), 97–117, 193–207.

Papadopoulos, Chrysostomos, Ἱστορία τῆς ἐκκλησίας Ἀντιοχείας (Alexandria, 1951).

Pappadopoulos, Jean B., *Théodore II Lascaris, empereur de Nicée* (Paris, 1908).

Parry, Vernon J., and Malcolm E. Yapp, eds., *War, Technology, and Society in the Middle East* (London, 1975).

Partington, James R., *History of Greek Fire and Gunpowder* (Cambridge, Eng., 1960).

Pattenden, Philip, "The Byzantine Early Warning System," *Byzantion,* LIII (1983), 258–299.

Peers, Edgar A., *Ramon Lull: a Biography* (London, 1929).

Peirce, Hayford, and Royall Tyler, *L'Art byzantin des origines au déclin: cinq volumes contenant mille phototypies* (5 vols., Paris, 1932–1934).

Pekař, Josef, *Žižka a jeho doba* (4 vols., Prague, 1927–1933).

Pellegrini, Lodovico, "Le Missioni franciscane sotto Alessandro IV (1254–1261)," *Studi francescani,* LXIV (1967), 91–118.

Pelliot, Paul, "Chrétiens d'Asie centrale et d'Extrême-Orient," *T'oung Pao,* XV (1914), 623–644.

Pelliot, Paul, "Les Mongols et la papauté," *RO Chr.,* XXIII (1922–1923), 3–30; XXIV (1924), 225–335; XXVIII (1931–1932), 3–84.

Pelliot, Paul, "Mélanges sur l'époque des croisades," *MAIBL,* XLIV (1960), 1–97 (separate ed., Paris, 1951).

Pelliot, Paul, *Recherches sur les Chrétiens d'Asie centrale et d'Extrême-Orient* (in *Oeuvres posthumes de Paul Pelliot,* ed. Jean Dauvillier and Louis Hambis, Paris, 1973).

Peres, Damião A., *Como nasceu Portugal,* 5th ed. (Porto, 1959).

Pernoud, Régine, *Essai sur l'histoire du port de Marseille des origines à la fin du XIIIe siècle* (Marseilles, 1935).

Pernoud, Régine, *Les Templiers* (Que sais-je, no. 1557; Paris, 1974).

Pernoud, Régine, *Les Hommes de la croisade* (Paris, 1977).

Pertusi, Agostino, ed., *Venezia e il Levante fino al secolo XV,* vol. I (Civiltà veneziana, Studi, 27; Florence, 1973); includes Prawer, Richard.

Pertusi, Agostino, *La Caduta di Costantinopoli: le testimonianze dei contemporanei* (Verona, 1976).

Pertusi, Agostino, "Venezia e Bizanzio: 1000-1204," *D Oaks P,* XXXIII (1979), 1-22.

Petech, Luciano, "Les Marchands italiens dans l'empire mongole," *JA,* CCL (1962), 549-574.

Pfeiffer, Erwin, "Die Cistercienser und der zweite Kreuzzug," *Cistercienser-Chronik* XLVII (1935), 8-10, 44-54, 78-81, 107-114, 145-150.

Pfeiffer, Wolfgang, "Acrische Gläser," *Journal of Glass Studies,* XII (1970), 67-69.

[Philippides], Chrysantos, [archbishop], Ἡ ἐκκλησία Τραπεζοῦντος (Ἀρχεῖον Ποντίου 4-5; Athens, 1933-1936).

Pillet, Maurice, "Notre-Dame de Tortose," *Syria,* X (1929), 40-51.

Piquet, Jules, *Des Banquiers au moyen âge: les Templiers: étude de leurs opérations financières* (Paris, 1939).

Pirenne, Henri, *Mahomet et Charlemagne,* 6th ed. by Jacques Pirenne and Fernand Vercauteren (Paris and Brussels, 1937).

Pirie-Gordon, Harry, "The Reigning Princes of Galilee," *Eng. HR,* XXVII (1912), 445-461.

Pissard, Hippolyte, *La Guerre sainte en pays chrétien: essai sur l'origine et le développement des théories canoniques* (Bibliothèque d'histoire religieuse, 10; Paris, 1912; repr. New York, 1980).

Pixton, Paul B., "Die Anwerbung des Heeres Christi: Prediger des fünften Kreuzzuges in Deutschland," *Deutsches Archiv,* XXXIV (1978), 166-191.

Pleehn, Chlodwig, *Kreuzritterburgen auf dem Peloponnes* (Munich and Zurich, 1977).

Poliak, Abraham N., *Feudalism in Egypt, Syria, Palestine and the Lebanon, 1250-1900* (Royal Asiatic Society Prize Publications Fund, 17; London, 1939).

Popper, William, *Egypt and Syria under the Circassian Sultans 1382-1468 A.D.: Systematic Notes to Ibn Taghrî Birdî's Chronicles of Egypt* (University of California Publications in Semitic Philology, 15-16; 2 vols., Berkeley, 1955-1957).

Porges, Walter, "The Clergy, the Poor and the Non-Combatants on the First Crusade," *Speculum,* XXI (1946), 1-23.

Porter, Arthur K., "Condrieu, Jerusalem and St. Gilles," *Art in America,* XIII (1924-1925), 117-129.

Powell, James M., *Anatomy of a Crusade, 1213-1221* (Philadelphia, 1986).

Powicke, Frederick M., *King Henry III and Lord Edward: the Community of the Realm in the Thirteenth Century* (2 vols., Oxford, 1947).

Powicke, Frederick M., *The Thirteenth Century, 1216-1307* (Oxford History of England, 4; Oxford, 1953).

Prawer, Joshua, "Colonization Activities in the Latin Kingdom of Jerusalem," *Revue belge de philologie et d'histoire,* XXIX (1951), 1063-1118.

Prawer, Joshua, "L'Établissement des coutumes du marché à St.-Jean d'Acre et la date de composition du Livre des Assises des Bourgeois," *RH Droit FÉ,* 4-XXIX (1951), 329-351.

Prawer, Joshua, "The *Assise de tenure* and the *Assise de vente:* a Study of Landed Property in the Latin Kingdom," *Economic History Review,* 2-IV (1951-1952), 77-87; rev. version in *Crusader Institutions,* pp. 343-357.

Prawer, Joshua, "Étude de quelques problèmes agraires et sociaux d'une seigneurie croisée au XIIIe siècle," *Byzantion,* XXII (1952), 5-61; XXIII (1953), 143-170; expanded and tr. as "Palestinian Agriculture and the Crusader Rural System," in *Crusader Institutions,* pp. 143-200.

Prawer, Joshua, "The Settlement of the Latins in Jerusalem," *Speculum,* XXVII (1952), 490–503; repr. in *Crusader Institutions,* pp. 85–101.

Prawer, Joshua, "Les Premiers temps de la féodalité dans le royaume latin de Jérusalem," *Tijdschrift voor rechtsgeschiedenis,* XXII (1954), 401–424; rev. tr. in *Crusader Institutions,* pp. 3–19.

Prawer, Joshua, "La Noblesse et le régime féodal du royaume latin de Jérusalem," *Le Moyen-âge,* LXV (4-XIV; 1959), 41–74; rev. tr. in *Crusader Institutions,* pp. 20–45.

Prawer, Joshua, "Étude sur le droit des *Assises de Jérusalem:* droit de confiscation et droit d'exhérédation," *RH Droit FÉ,* 4-XXXIX (1961), 520–551; 4-XL (1962), 29–42; expanded and tr. as "Roman Law and Crusader Legislation: the *Assises* on Confiscation and Disinheritance," in *Crusader Institutions,* pp. 430–468.

Prawer, Joshua, "La Bataille de Ḥaṭṭin," *Isr. Expl. J,* XIV (1964), 160–179.

Prawer, Joshua, *Estates, Communities and the Constitution of the Latin Kingdom* (Israel Academy of Sciences and Humanities: Proceedings, II, 6; Jerusalem, 1966).

Prawer, Joshua, "Jewish Resettlement in Crusader Jerusalem," *Ariel: a Review of Arts and Sciences in Israel,* no. 19 (1967), 60–66.

Prawer, Joshua, *Histoire du royaume latin de Jérusalem,* tr. Gerard Nahon and rev. by the author (2 vols., Paris, 1969–1970; 2nd ed., 1975).

Prawer, Joshua, *The Latin Kingdom of Jerusalem: European Colonialism in the Middle Ages* (London, 1972); published in New York (1972) as *The Crusaders' Kingdom.*

Prawer, Joshua, *The World of the Crusaders* (London, 1972).

Prawer, Joshua, "I Veneziani e le colonie veneziane nel regno latino de Gerusalemme," in *Venezia e il Levante fino al secolo XV,* ed. Agostino Pertusi, vol. I, part 2 (Civiltà veneziana, Studi, 27, Florence, 1973), pp. 625–656.

Prawer, Joshua, "A Crusader Tomb of 1290 from Acre and the Last Archbishops of Nazareth," *Isr. Expl. J,* XXIV (= Memorial M. Avi-Yonah; 1974), 241–251.

Prawer, Joshua, "The Armenians in Jerusalem under the Crusaders," in *Armenian and Biblical Studies,* ed. Michael E. Stone (Jerusalem, 1976).

Prawer, Joshua, "Crusader Cities," in *The Medieval City,* ed. Harry A. Miskimin, David Herlihy, and Abraham L. Udovitch (New Haven, 1977), pp. 179–199.

Prawer, Joshua, "The Autobiography of Obadyah the Norman, a Convert to Judaism at the Time of the First Crusade," in *Studies in Medieval Jewish History and Literature,* ed. Isadore Twersky (Harvard Judaic Monographs, 2; Cambridge, Mass., 1979), pp. 110–134.

Prawer, Joshua, *Crusader Institutions* (Oxford, 1980).

Prawer, Joshua, "Jerusalem in the Christian and Jewish Perspectives of the Early Middle Ages," in *Gli Ebrei nell' alto medioevo, Spoleto, 30 marzo–5 aprile 1978* (Settimane di studio del Centro italiano di studi sull' alto medioevo, 26; Spoleto, 1980), pp. 739–795.

Prawer, Joshua, "Military Orders and Crusader Politics in the Second Half of the XIIIth Century," in *Die geistlichen Ritterorden Europas,* ed. Josef Fleckenstein and Manfred Hellmann (Vorträge und Forschungen, 26; Sigmaringen, 1980), pp. 217–229.

Prawer, Joshua, "Social Classes in the Crusader States: the 'Minorities'," *H of C,* V (1985), 59–116, and "Social Classes in the Latin Kingdom: the Franks," *ibid.,* 117–192.

Preston, Helen G., *Rural Conditions in the Latin Kingdom of Jerusalem during the Twelfth and Thirteenth Centuries* (Thesis, University of Pennsylvania; Philadelphia, 1903).

Preto, Paolo, *Venezia e i Turchi* (Florence, 1975).

Pretzel, Ulrich, "Die Kreuzzugslieder Albrechts von Johansdorf," in *Festgabe für L. L. Hammerich, aus Anlass seines siebzigsten Geburtstages* (Copenhagen, 1962), pp. 229–244.

Primov, B., "Vtorijat krŭstonosen pochod prez bŭlgarskite zemi i Vizantija [The Second Crusade through the Balkans and Byzantium]," *Istoričeski pregled,* XXXIV-6 (1978), 37–57.

Pringle, R. Denys, "Some Approaches to the Study of Crusader Masonry Marks in Palestine," *Levant,* XIII (1981), 173–199.

Pringle, [R.] Denys, and Peter Leach, "Two Medieval Villages North of Jerusalem: Archaeological Investigations in al-Jib and ar-Ram," *Levant,* XV (1983), 141–177.

Pringle, [R.] Denys, "King Richard I and the Walls of Ascalon," *Palestine Exploration Quarterly,* CXVI (1984), 133–147.

Pringle, [R.] Denys, "Magna Mahumeria (al-Bīra): the Archaeology of a Frankish New Town in Palestine," in *Crusade and Settlement,* ed. Peter W. Edbury (Cardiff, 1985), pp. 147–168.

Pringle, [R.] Denys, *The Red Tower (al-Burj al-Ahmar): Settlement in the Plain of Sharon at the Time of the Crusaders and Mamluks A.D. 1099–1516* (British School of Archaeology in Jerusalem, Monograph Series, 1; London, 1986).

Pringle, [R.] Denys, "A Thirteenth-Century Hall at Montfort Castle in Western Galilee," *The Antiquaries Journal,* LXVI (1986), 52–81.

Pringle, [R.] Denys, "The Planning of Some Pilgrimage Churches in Crusader Palestine," *World Archaeology,* XVIII (1987), 341–362.

Prochaska, Antoni, *Król Wladyslaw Jagiello* (2 vols., Cracow, 1908).

Prutz, Hans, *Die Besitzungen des Deutschen Ordens im Heiligen Lande: ein Beitrag zur Culturgeschichte der Franken in Syrien* (Leipzig, 1877); cf. D64.

Prutz, Hans, *Kulturgeschichte der Kreuzzüge* (Berlin, 1883; repr. Hildesheim, 1964).

Prutz, Hans, *Entwicklung und Untergang des Tempelherrenordens* (Berlin, 1888).

Prutz, Hans, "Die Anfänge der Hospitaliter auf Rhodos 1310–1355," *Sitzungsberichte der Königlich Bayerischen Akademie der Wissenschaften, Philosophisch-philologische und historische Klasse,* Jahrgang 1908, 1. Abhandlung (1908), pp. 1–57.

Prutz, Hans, *Die geistlichen Ritterorden: ihre Stellung zur kirchlichen, politischen, gesellschaftlichen und wirtschaftlichen Entwicklung des Mittelalters* (Berlin, 1908).

Pryor, John H., "The Origins of the *Commenda* Contract," *Speculum,* LII (1977), 5–37.

Pryor, John H., "The Naval Architecture of Crusader Transport Ships: a Reconstruction of some Archetypes for Round-hulled Sailing Ships," *The Mariner's Mirror,* LXX (1984), 171–219, 275–292, 363–386.

Pryor, John H., "The Oaths of the Leaders of the First Crusade to Emperor Alexius I Comnenus: Fealty, Homage – πίστις, δουλεία," *Parergon: Bulletin of the Australian and New Zealand Association for Medieval and Renaissance Studies,* n.s., II (1984), 111–141.

Purcell, Maureen, *Papal Crusading Policy: the Chief Instruments of Papal Crusading Policy and Crusade to the Holy Land from the Final Loss of Jerusalem to the Fall of Acre 1244–1291* (Studies in the History of Christian Thought, 11; Leyden, 1975).

Quaresmius, Franciscus, *Historica, theologica et moralis Terrae Sanctae elucidatio* (2 vols., Antwerp, 1639).

Quatremère, Étienne M., "Notice historique sur les Ismaëliens," *Fundgruben des Orients,* IV (1914), 339–376; appendix by Josef von Hammer-Purgstall, IV, 376–379.

Queller, Donald E., and Susan J. Stratton, "A Century of Controversy on the Fourth Crusade," *Studies in Medieval and Renaissance History,* VI (1969), 233-277.

Queller, Donald E., and Joseph Gill, "Franks, Venetians and Pope Innocent III," *Studi veneziani,* XII (1970), 85-105.

Queller, Donald E., ed., *The Latin Conquest of Constantinople* (Major Issues in History; New York and London, 1971).

Queller, Donald E., Thomas K. Compton, and Donald A. Campbell, "The Fourth Crusade: the Neglected Majority," *Speculum,* XLIX (1974), 441-465.

Queller, Donald E., and Gerald W. Day, "Some Arguments in the Defense of the Venetians on the Fourth Crusade," *Amer. HR,* LXXXI (1976), 717-737.

Queller, Donald E., *The Fourth Crusade: the Conquest of Constantinople, 1201-1204* (Philadelphia, 1977; Leicester, 1978).

Queller, Donald E., *Medieval Diplomacy and the Fourth Crusade* (Varior. Repr., CS, 114; London, 1980).

Rabie, Hassanein, *The Financial System of Egypt A.H. 564-741/A.D. 1169-1341* (London Oriental Series, 25; London and New York, 1972).

Rachewiltz, Igor de, *Papal Envoys to the Great Khans* (Stanford, 1971).

Racine, Pierre, "Il Traffico dei Piacentini verso la Terra Santa (1268)," *Bollettino storico Piacentino,* LX (1965), 113-122.

Racine, Pierre, "Note sur le trafic vénéto-chypriote à la fin du moyen-âge," *Byz. F,* V (1977), 307-329.

Racine, Pierre, "L'Émigration italienne vers la Méditerranée orientale (2e moitié du XIIIe siècle)," *Byz. F,* VII (1979), 137-155.

Radonić, Jovan, *Zapadna Evropa i balkanski na vodi prema Turcima u pruoj polovini XV veka* [Western Europe and the Balkan Nations in their Relations with the Turks in the First Half of the Fifteenth Century] (Novi Sad, 1905).

Raedts, Peter, "The Children's Crusade of 1212," *J Med. H,* III (1977), 279-323.

Ragosta, Rosalba, ed., *Le Genti del Mare Mediterraneo,* vol. 1 (Biblioteca di storia economica, 5; Naples, 1981).

Rambert, Gaston, ed., *Histoire du commerce de Marseille* (3 vols., Marseilles, 1949-1951).

Rassow, Peter, "Die Kanzlei St. Bernhards von Clairvaux," *Studien und Mitteilungen aus dem Benediktiner- und Cisterciensorden,* XXXIV (= n.s., III; 1913), 63-103, 243-293.

Rassow, Peter, *Honor imperii: die neue Politik Friedrich Barbarossas 1152-1159* (Munich and Berlin, 1940).

Rassow, Peter, "Zum byzantinisch-normanischen Krieg 1147-1149," *MIÖG,* LXII (1954), 213-218.

Reinaud, Joseph T., "Histoire de la sixième croisade et de la prise de Damiette d'après les écrivains arabes," *JA,* VIII (1826), 18-40, 88-110, 149-169.

Revilla Vielva, Ramón, *Ordenes militares de Santiago, Alcántara, Calatrava y Montesa* (Madrid, 1927).

Rey, Emmanuel G., *Étude sur les monuments de l'architecture militaire des croisés en Syrie et dans l'île de Chypre* (CD inédits, 1st ser., Histoire politique; Paris, 1871).

Rey, Emmanuel G., *Les Colonies franques de Syrie au XIIe et XIIIe siècles* (Paris, 1883).

Rey, Emmanuel G., "Les Seigneurs de Giblet," *RO Latin,* III (1895), 398-422.

Rey, Emmanuel G., "Les Seigneurs de Barut," *RO Latin,* IV (1896), 12-18.

Rey, Emmanuel G., "Les Seigneurs de Montréal et de la Terre d'Outre le Jourdain," *RO Latin,* IV (1896), 19-24.

Rey, Emmanuel G., "Résumé chronologique de l'histoire des princes d'Antioche," *RO Latin,* IV (1896), 321–407.

Rey, Emmanuel G., "Les Dignitaires de la principauté d'Antioche, grand-officiers et patriarches (XIe–XIIIe siècle)," *RO Latin,* VIII (1900–1901), 116–157.

Riant, Paul E.D., *Expéditions et pèlerinages des Scandinaves en Terre Sainte au temps des croisades* (Thèse présentée à la Faculté des Lettres de Paris; Paris, 1865); tables (Paris, 1869).

Riant, Paul E.D., "Innocent III, Philippe de Souabe et Boniface de Montferrat: examen des causes qui modifièrent, au détriment de l'empire grec, le plan primitif de la quatrième croisade," *Rev. QH,* XVII (1875), 321–374; XVIII (1875), 5–75.

Riant, Paul E.D., "Un Dernier triomphe d'Urbain II," *Rev. QH,* XXXIV (1883), 247–255.

Riant, Paul E.D., "La Légende du martyre en Orient de Thiémon archévêque de Salzbourg (28 Septembre 1102)," *Rev. QH,* XXXIX (1886), 218–237.

Riant, Paul E.D., *Études sur l'histoire de l'église de Bethléem;* vol. 1 (Genoa, 1889). The materials prepared for vol. 2 were published after Riant's death by Charles Kohler as "Éclaircissements sur quelques points de l'histoire de l'église de Bethléem-Ascalon," *RO Latin,* I (1893), 141–160, 381–412, 475–525; II (1894), 35–72; publ. separately as vol. 2 of the *Études,* ed. Charles Kohler (Paris, 1896).

Richard, Jean, "La Papauté et les missions catholiques en Orient au moyen âge," *MÉF Rome,* LVIII (1941–1946), 248–266.

Richard, Jean, *Le Comté de Tripoli sous la dynastie toulousaine (1102–1187)* (Bibl. AH, 39; Paris, 1945; repr. New York, 1980).

Richard, Jean, "Note sur l'archidiocèse d'Apamée et les conquêtes de Raymond de Saint-Gilles en Syrie du Nord," *Syria,* XXV (1946–1948), 103–108.

Richard, Jean, "Le Casal de Psimolofo et la vie rurale en Chypre au XIVe siècle," *MÉF Rome,* LIX (1947), 121–153.

Richard, Jean, "Évêchés titulaires et missionaires dans le 'Provinciale Romanae Ecclesiae'," *MÉF Rome,* LXI (1949), 227–236.

Richard, Jean, "Le Début des relations entre la papauté et les Mongols de Perse," *JA,* CCXXXVII (1949), 291–297.

Richard, Jean, "Pairie d'Orient latin: les quatre baronnies des royaumes de Jérusalem et de Chypre," *RH Droit FÉ,* 4-XXVIII (1950), 67–88.

Richard, Jean, "Un Évêque d'Orient latin au XIVe siècle: Guy d'Ibelin, O.P., évêque de Limassol, et l'inventaire de ses biens (1367)," *BC Hell.,* LXXIV (1950), 98–133.

Richard, Jean, "La Révolution de 1369 dans le royaume de Chypre," *BÉ Char.,* CX (1952), 108–123.

Richard, Jean, "Colonies marchandes privilégiées et marché seigneurial: la fonde d'Acre et ses 'droitures'," *Le Moyen-âge,* LIX (= 4-VIII; 1953), 325–340.

Richard, Jean, *Le Royaume latin de Jérusalem* (Paris, 1953); rev. tr. by Janet Shirley, *The Latin Kingdom of Jerusalem* (Europe in the Middle Ages, Selected Studies, 11; 2 vols., Amsterdam, 1979).

Richard, Jean, "Les Listes de seigneuries dans le Livre de Jean d'Ibelin: recherches sur l'Assebèbe et Mimars," *RH Droit FÉ,* 4-XXXII (1954), 565–577.

Richard, Jean, "Quelques textes sur les premiers temps de l'église latine de Jérusalem," in *Recueil de travaux offerts à M. Clovis Brunel* (Mémoires et documents publiés par la Société de l'école des chartes, 12; 2 vols., Paris, 1955), II, 420–430.

Richard, Jean, "L'Extrême-Orient légendaire au moyen-âge: Roi David et Prêtre Jean," *Annales d'Ethiopie,* II (1957), 225–242.

Richard, Jean, "La Mission en Europe de Rabban Çauma et l'union des églises," in *Oriente ed Occidente nel medio evo: Convegno di scienze morali, storiche e filologiche 27 maggio — 1º giugno 1956* (Accademia nazionale dei Lincei, Fondazione Alessandro Volta, Atti dei convegni 12; Rome, 1957), pp. 162–167.

Richard, Jean, "Les Premiers missionnaires latins en Ethiopie (XIIe–XIVe siècles)," in *Atti del convegno internazionale di studi etiopici: Roma 2–4 aprile 1959* (Accademia nazionale dei Lincei, Anno 357: Problemi attuali di scienza e di cultura, Quaderno 48; Rome, 1959), pp. 323–329.

Richard, Jean, "Essor et déclin de l'église catholique de Chine au XIVe siècle," *Bulletin de la Société des missions étrangères de Paris,* 2nd ser., no. 134 (1960), 285–295.

Richard, Jean, "La Papauté et la direction de la première croisade," *Journal des Savants* (1960), pp. 49–58.

Richard, Jean, "Une Lettre concernant l'invasion mongole?," *BÉ Char.,* CXIX (1961), 243–245.

Richard, Jean, "La Fauconnerie de Jean de Francières et ses sources," *Le Moyen-âge,* LXIX (1963), 893–902.

Richard, Jean, "Le Royaume de Chypre et le Grand Schisme, à propos d'un document récemment découvert," *CRAIBL* (1965), pp. 498–507.

Richard, Jean, "Sur un passage du 'Pèlerinage de Charlemagne': le marché de Jérusalem," *Revue belge de philologie et d'histoire,* XLIII-2 (1965), 552–555.

Richard, Jean, "La Confrérie des 'Mosserins' d'Acre et les marchands de Mossoul au XIIIe siècle," *L'Orient syrien,* XI (1966), 451–460.

Richard, Jean, "La Vogue de l'Orient dans la littérature occidentale du moyen âge," in *Mélanges offerts à René Crozet à l'occasion de son soixante-dixième anniversaire,* ed. Pierre Gallais and Yves Jean Riou, vol. I (Poitiers, 1966), pp. 557–561.

Richard, Jean, "L'Ordonnance de décembre 1296 sur le prix du pain à Chypre," Ἐπετηρὶς τοῦ Κέντρου Ἐπιστημονικῶν Ἐρευνῶν, I (1967–1968), 45–51.

Richard, Jean, "L'Abbaye cistercienne de Jubin et le prieuré Saint-Blaise de Nicosie," Ἐπετηρὶς τοῦ Κέντρου Ἐπιστημονικῶν Ἐρευνῶν, III (1969–1970), 63–74.

Richard, Jean, "The Mongols and the Franks," *Journal of Asian History,* III (1969), 45–57.

Richard, Jean, "Isol le Pisan: un aventurier franc gouverneur d'une province mongole?," *Central Asiatic Journal,* XIV (1970), 186–194.

Richard, Jean, "Les Missionaires latins dans l'Inde au XIVe siècle," *Studi veneziani,* XII (1970), 231–242.

Richard, Jean, "Saint-Louis dans l'histoire des croisades," *Bulletin de la Société d'émulation de Bourbonnais* (1970), pp. 229–244.

Richard, Jean, "Chypre du protectorat à la domination vénitienne," in *Venezia e il Levante fino al secolo XV,* ed. Agostino Pertusi: vol. I, part 2 (Civiltà veneziana, Studi, 27; Florence, 1973), pp. 657–677.

Richard, Jean, "Ultimatums mongols et lettres apocryphes: l'Occident et les motifs de guerre des Tartares," *Central Asiatic Journal,* XVII (1973), 212–222.

Richard, Jean, "La Confrérie de la croisade: à propos d'un épisode de la première croisade," *Études de civilisation médiévale: Mélanges offerts à Edmond R. Labande* (Poitiers, 1974), pp. 617–622.

Richard, Jean, "L'Enseignement des langues orientales en Occident au moyen âge," *Revue des études islamiques,* XLIV (1976), 149–164.

Richard, Jean, "La Politique orientale de Saint Louis: la croisade de 1248," in *Sep-*

tième centenaire de la mort de Saint-Louis: Actes des colloques de Royaumont et de Paris (Paris, 1976), pp. 197–207.

Richard, Jean, *Le Droit et les institutions franques dans le royaume de Chypre* (XVe Congrès international d'études byzantines: rapports et co-rapports: 5. Chypre dans le monde byzantin: no. 3, Droit et institutions franques du royaume de Chypre; Athens, 1976).

Richard, Jean, *Orient et Occident au moyen âge: contacts et relations (XIIe–XVe s.)* (Varior. Repr., CS, 49; London, 1976).

Richard, Jean, *La Papauté et les missions d'Orient au moyen âge (XIIIe–XVe siècles)* (Collection de l'École française de Rome, 33; Rome, 1977).

Richard, Jean, "Les Mongols et l'Occident: deux siècles de contact," in *1274 année charnière: mutations et continuité* (Paris, 1977), pp. 377–423.

Richard, Jean, *Les Relations entre l'Orient et l'Occident au moyen âge* (Varior. Repr., CS, 69; London, 1977).

Richard, Jean, "Une Économie coloniale? Chypre et ses ressources agricoles au moyen-âge," *Byz. F,* V (1977), 331–352.

Richard, Jean, "Église latine et églises orientales dans les états des croisés: la destinée d'un prieuré de Josaphat," in *Mélanges offerts à Jean Dauvillier,* ed. Germain Sicard (Toulouse, 1979), pp. 743–752.

Richard, Jean, "Le Peuplement latin et syrien en Chypre au XIIIe siècle," *Byz. F,* VII (1979), 157–173.

Richard, Jean, "Une Ambassade mongole à Paris en 1262," *Journal des Savants* (1979), pp. 295–303.

Richard, Jean, "La Féodalité de l'Orient latin et le mouvement communal: un état des questions," in *Structures féodales et féodalisme dans l'Occident méditerranéen (Xe–XIIIe siècles)* (Collection de l'École française de Rome, 44; Rome, 1980), pp. 651–665.

Richard, Jean, "Louis de Bologne, patriarche d'Antioche, et la politique bourguignonne envers les états de la Méditerranée orientale," *Publication du Centre européen d'études burgundo-médianes,* XX (1980), 67–69.

Richard, Jean, "Une Famille de 'Vénitiens blancs' dans le royaume de Chypre au milieu du XVe siècle: les Audeth et la seigneurie du Marethasse," *Rivista di studi bizantini e slavi* (= Miscellanea Agostino Pertusi, 1; 1981), 89–129.

Richard, Jean, "Hospitals and Hospital Congregations in the Latin Kingdom during the First Period of the Frankish Conquest," in *Outremer* (1982), pp. 89–100.

Richard, Jean, *Croisés, missionnaires et voyageurs: perspectives orientales du monde latin médiéval* (Varior. Repr., CS, 182; London, 1983).

Richard, Jean, "Les Saint-Gilles et le comté de Tripoli," *Islam et Chrétiens du Midi (XIIe–XIVe siècle)* (Cahiers de Fanjeaux, 18; Toulouse, 1983), pp. 65–75.

Richard, Jean, *Saint Louis, roi de France féodale, soutien de la Terre Sainte* (Paris, 1983).

Richard, Jean, "Le Royaume de Chypre et l'embargo sur le commerce avec l'Égypte (fin XIIIe–début XIVe siècle)," *CRAIBL* (1984), pp. 120–134.

Richard, Jean, "Les Comtes de Tripoli et leurs vassaux sous la dynastie antiochienne," in *Crusade and Settlement,* ed. Peter W. Edbury (Cardiff, 1985), pp. 213–224.

Richard, Jean, "The Political and Ecclesiastical Organization of the Crusader States," *H of C,* V (1985), 193–250, and "Agricultural Conditions in the Crusader States," *ibid.,* 251–294.

Richard, Jean, "La Diplomatique royale dans les royaumes d'Arménie et de Chypre (XIIe–XVe siècles)," *BÉ Char.,* CXLIV (1986), 69–86.

Richard, Jean, "The Institutions of the Kingdom of Cyprus," *H of C,* VI (1989), 150–174.

Richmond, Ernest T., *The Dome of the Rock in Jerusalem: a Description of its Structure and Decoration* (Oxford, 1924).

Richmond, Ernest T., "Church of the Holy Sepulchre: Note on a Recent Discovery," *QDA Pal.,* I (1931–1932), 2.

Riezler, Sigmund O., "Der Kreuzzug Kaiser Friedrichs I.," *Forsch. DG,* X (1870), 1–150.

Riising, Anne, "The Fate of Henri Pirenne's Theses on the Consequences of the Islamic Expansion," *Classica et Mediaevalia,* XIII (1952), 87–130.

Riley-Smith, Jonathan, *The Knights of St. John in Jerusalem and Cyprus c. 1050–1310* (A History of the Order of the Hospital of St. John of Jerusalem, 1; London and New York, 1967).

Riley-Smith, Jonathan, "A Note on Confraternities in the Latin Kingdom of Jerusalem," *Bulletin of the Institute of Historical Research,* XLIV (1971), 301–308.

Riley-Smith, Jonathan, "The *Assise sur la Ligèce* and the Commune of Acre," *Traditio,* XXVII (1971), 179–204.

Riley-Smith, Jonathan, "Some Lesser Officials in Latin Syria," *Eng. HR,* LXXXVII (1972), 1–26.

Riley-Smith, Jonathan, "Government in Latin Syria and the Commercial Privileges of Foreign Merchants," in *Relations between East and West in the Middle Ages,* ed. Derek Baker (Edinburgh, 1973), pp. 109–132.

Riley-Smith, Jonathan, *The Feudal Nobility and the Kingdom of Jerusalem, 1174–1277* (London, 1973).

Riley-Smith, Jonathan, "The Survival in Latin Palestine of Muslim Administration," in *The Eastern Mediterranean Lands in the Period of the Crusades,* ed. Peter M. Holt (Warminster, 1977), pp. 9–22.

Riley-Smith, Jonathan, *What Were the Crusades?* (London, 1977).

Riley-Smith, Jonathan, "Latin Titular Bishops in Palestine and Syria, 1137–1291," *Cath. HR,* LXIV (1978), 1–15.

Riley-Smith, Jonathan, "Peace Never Established: the Case of the Kingdom of Jerusalem," *Transactions of the Royal Historical Society,* 5-XXVIII (1978), 87–102.

Riley-Smith, Jonathan, "The Title of Godfrey of Bouillon," *Bulletin of the Institute of Historical Research,* LII (1979), 83–86.

Riley-Smith, Jonathan, "Crusading as an Act of Love," *History,* LXV (1980), 177–192.

Riley-Smith, Jonathan, "The First Crusade and St. Peter," in *Outremer* (1982), pp. 41–63.

Riley-Smith, Jonathan, "The Motives of the Earliest Crusaders and the Settlement of Latin Palestine," *Eng. HR,* XCVIII (1983), 721–736.

Riley-Smith, Jonathan, "The First Crusade and the Persecution of the Jews," in *Persecution and Toleration,* ed. W. J. Shiels (Studies in Church History, 21; Oxford, 1984), pp. 51–72.

Riley-Smith, Jonathan, "Further Thoughts on Baldwin II's Établissement on the Confiscation of Fiefs," in *Crusade and Settlement,* ed. Peter W. Edbury (Cardiff, 1985), pp. 176–180.

Riley-Smith, Jonathan, *The First Crusade and the Idea of Crusading* (Philadelphia and London, 1986).

Riley-Smith, Jonathan, *The Crusades: a Short History* (London, 1987).

Ritchie, N., "Bohemund, Prince of Antioch: the Career of a Norman Crusader in

Italy, in Syria and in the Wars with the Byzantine Emperor," *History Today,* XXVIII (1978), 293-303.

Robbert, Louise Buenger, "The Venetian Money Market, 1150-1229," *Studi veneziani,* XIII (1971), 1-94.

Robbert, Louise Buenger, "Venice and the Crusades," *H of C,* V (1985), 379-451.

Roberg, Burkhard, "Die Tataren auf dem 2. Konzil von Lyon 1274," *Annuarium historiae conciliorum,* V (1973), 241-302.

Roberg, Burkhard, "Das 'Orientalische Problem' auf dem Lugdunense II," *Annuarium historiae conciliorum,* IX (1977), 43-66.

Roberg, Burkhard, "Subsidium Terrae Sanctae: Kreuzzug, Konzil und Steuern," *Annuarium historiae conciliorum,* XV (1983), 96-158.

Roberti, Melchiorre, "Ricerche intorno alla colonia veneziana in Costantinopoli nel secolo XII," in *Scritti storici in onore di Camillo Manfroni* (Padua, 1925), pp. 135-147.

Robinson, I. S., "Gregory VII and the Soldiers of Christ," *History,* LVIII (1973), 169-192.

Rodenberg, Carl, *Innocenz IV. und das Königreich Sizilien 1245-1254* (Halle, 1892).

Röhricht, Reinhold, *Beiträge zur Geschichte der Kreuzzüge* (2 vols., Berlin, 1874-1878).

Röhricht, Reinhold, "Die Pilgerfahrten nach dem Heiligen Lande vor den Kreuzzügen," *Raumers historisches Taschenbuch,* 5-V (1875), 321-396.

Röhricht, Reinhold, "Der Kinderkreuzzug von 1212," *Hist. Z,* XXXVI (1876), 1-8.

Röhricht, Reinhold, "Die Belagerung von 'Akkâ," *Forsch. DG,* XVI (1876), 483-524.

Röhricht, Reinhold, "Die Belagerung von Damiette (1218-1220): ein Beitrag zur Kriegsgeschichte des Mittelalters," *Raumers historisches Taschenbuch,* 5-VI (1876), 59-98.

Röhricht, Reinhold, "Die Kreuzzugsbewegung im Jahre 1217," *Forsch. DG,* XVI (1876), 137-158.

Röhricht, Reinhold, "Die Eroberung 'Akkâs durch die Muslimen," *Forsch. DG,* XX (1879), 93-126.

Röhricht, Reinhold, "Études sur les derniers temps du royaume de Jérusalem: A. La croisade du prince Édouard d'Angleterre (1270-74); B. Les Batailles de Hims (1281 et 1289); C. Les combats du sultan Bibars contre les Chrétiens en Syrie (1261-77)," *AO Latin,* I (1881), 617-652; II-1 (1884), 365-410.

Röhricht, Reinhold, "Die Kreuzpredigten gegen den Islam: ein Beitrag zur Geschichte der christlichen Predigt im 12. und 13. Jahrhundert," *Z Kirch.,* VI (1884), 550-572.

Röhricht, Reinhold, "Die Kreuzzüge des Grafen Theobald von Navarra und Richard von Cornwallis nach dem Heiligen Lande," *Forsch. DG,* XXVI (1886), 67-102.

Röhricht, Reinhold, "Syria sacra," *ZDPV,* X (1887), 1-48; "Nachträge," XI (1888), 139-142.

Röhricht, Reinhold, *Kleine Studien zur Geschichte der Kreuzzüge* (Wissenschaftliche Beilage zum Programm des Humboldt-Gymnasium zu Berlin; Berlin, 1890).

Röhricht, Reinhold, *Studien zur Geschichte des fünften Kreuzzuges* (Innsbruck, 1891).

Röhricht, Reinhold, *Die Deutschen im Heiligen Lande: ein chronologisches Verzeichnis derjenigen Deutschen, welche als Jerusalempilger und Kreuzfahrer sicher nachzuweisen oder wahrscheinlich anzusehen sind (ca. 650-1291)* (Innsbruck, 1894).

Röhricht, Reinhold, *Geschichte des Königreichs Jerusalem (1100 bis 1291)* (Innsbruck, 1898; repr. Amsterdam, 1967).

Röhricht, Reinhold, *Geschichte des ersten Kreuzzuges* (Innsbruck, 1901).

Romanin, Samuele, *Storia documentata di Venezia,* new ed. (10 vols., Venice, 1912–1921; repr. 1925, 1972–1975).

Roncaglia, Martiniano, "San Francesco d'Assisi in Oriente," *Studi francescani,* L (= 3-XXV; 1953), 97–106.

Roncaglia, Martiniano, *Storia della provincia di Terra Santa:* 1. *I Francescani in Oriente durante le crociate (secolo XIII)* (BTSOF, 4th ser., Studi, 1; Cairo, 1954); tr. Stephen A. Janto as *Saint Francis of Assisi and the Middle East* (Cairo, 1957).

Roncaglia, Martiniano, *Les Frères Mineurs et l'église grecque-orthodoxe au XIIIe siècle (1231–1274)* (BTSOF, 4th ser., Studi, 2; Cairo, 1954).

Rondelez, V., "Un Évêché en Asie centrale au XIVe siècle," *Neue Zeitschrift für Missionswissenschaft,* VI (1951), 1–17.

Rösch, Gerhard, "Der Kreuzzug Bohemunds gegen Dyrrhachion 1107–1108 in der lateinischen Tradition des 12. Jahrhunderts," *Römische historische Mitteilungen,* XXVI (1984), 181–190.

Roscher, Helmut, *Papst Innocenz III. und die Kreuzzüge* (Forschungen zur Kirchen- und Dogmengeschichte, 21; Göttingen, 1969).

Rosen-Ayalon, Myriam, "Une Mosaique médiévale du Saint-Sépulcre: contribution à l'histoire de l'art," *Revue biblique,* LXXXIII (1976), 237–253.

Rosetti, Radŭ, "Notes on the Battle of Nicopolis (1396)," *Slavonic and East European Review,* XV (1936–1937), 629–638.

Rossi, Ettore, *Storia della marina dell' ordine di San Giovanni di Gerusalemme, di Rodi e di Malta* (Rome and Milan, 1926).

Rossi, Ettore, "The Hospitallers at Rhodes, 1421–1523," *H of C,* III (1975), 314–339.

Rossi-Sabatini, Giuseppe, *L'Espansione di Pisa nel Mediterraneo fino alla Meloria* (Studi di lettere, storia e filosofia pubblicati dalla Scuola normale superiore di Pisa, 6; Florence, 1935).

Rottiers, Bernard E.A., *Description des monumens de Rhodes* (2 vols., text and atlas, Brussels, 1828–1830).

Rouillard, Germaine, "L'Epibolè au temps d'Alexis Ier Comnène," *Byzantion,* X (1935), 81–89.

Rouillard, Germaine, *La Vie rurale dans l'empire byzantin* (Paris, 1953).

Round, John H., "The Saladin Tithe," *Eng. HR,* XXXI (1916), 447–450.

Rousset, Paul, *Les Origines et les caractères de la première croisade* (Diss., Geneva; Neuchâtel, 1945; repr. New York, 1978).

Rousset, Paul, "L'Idée de croisade chez les chroniqueurs d'Occident," *Relazioni del X Congresso internazionale di scienze storiche, Roma 1955:* 3. *Storia del medio evo* (Florence, 1955), pp. 547–563.

Rousset, Paul, *Histoire des croisades* (Paris, 1957); Portuguese tr. by Roberto Cortes de Lacerda as *Historia das cruzadas* (Rio de Janeiro, 1980).

Rousset, Paul, "Étienne de Blois, croisé fuyard et martyr," *Genava,* n.s., XI (1963), 183–195.

Rousset, Paul, "L'Idéologie de croisade dans les guerres de religion au XVIe siècle," *Schweizerische Zeitschrift für Geschichte,* XXXI (1981), 174–184.

Rousset, Paul, *Histoire d'une idéologie: la croisade* (Lausanne, 1983).

Rowe, John G., "Paschal II and the Relation between the Spiritual and Temporal Powers in the Kingdom of Jerusalem," *Speculum,* XXXII (1957), 470–501.

Rowe, John G., "The Papacy and the Greeks (1122–1153)," *Church History,* XXVIII (1959), 115–130, 310–327.

Rowe, John G., "The Papacy and the Ecclesiastical Province of Tyre (1100–1187),"
Bulletin of the John Rylands Library, XLIII (1960), 160–189.

Rowe, John G., "Paschal II, Bohemund of Antioch and the Byzantine Empire," *Bulletin of the John Rylands Library,* XLIX (1966), 165–202.

Roy, Émile, "Les Poèmes français relatifs à la première croisade," *Romania,* LV (1929), 411–468.

Rubió y Lluch, Antoni, "La Lengua y la cultura catalanas en Grecia en el siglo XIV," *Homenaje à Menéndez y Pelayo,* II, ed. Juan Valera (Madrid, 1899), pp. 95–120.

Rubió y Lluch, Antoni, "Els Castells catalans de la Grècia continental," *Annuari de l'Institut d'estudis catalans,* II (1908), 364–425.

Rubió y Lluch, Antoni: On his very numerous writings concerning the Catalan expansion in the eastern Mediterranean see the bibliographical survey by Kenneth M. Setton, *Catalan Domination of Athens,* 2nd ed. (1975), pp. 286–291.

Rüdebusch, Dieter, *Der Anteil Niedersachsens an den Kreuzzügen und Heidenfahrten* (Quellen und Darstellungen zur Geschichte Niedersachsens, 80; Hildesheim, 1972).

Rüdt de (here, replaced by hyphen) Collenberg, Weyprecht H., *The Rupenides, Hethumides and Lusignans, the Structure of the Armeno-Cilician dynasties* (Calouste Gulbenkian Foundation Armenian Library; Paris, 1963).

Rüdt de Collenberg, Weyprecht H., "Les 'Raynouard', seigneurs de Nephin et de Maraclé en Terre Sainte, et leur parenté en Languedoc," *Cah. Civ. Méd.,* VII (1964), 289–311.

Rüdt de Collenberg, Weyprecht H., "Les Premiers Ibelins," *Le Moyen-âge,* LXXI (= 4-XX; 1965), 433–474.

Rüdt de Collenberg, Weyprecht H., "Les Grâces papales, autres que les dispenses matrimoniales, accordées à Chypre de 1305–1378," Ἐπετηρὶς τοῦ Κέντρου Ἐπιστημονικῶν Ἐρευνῶν, VIII (1975–1977), 187–252.

Rüdt de Collenberg, Weyprecht (here, Wipertus) H., "Les Dispenses matrimoniales accordées à l'Orient latin selon les registres du Vatican d'Honorius III à Clément VII (1233–1385)," *MÉF Rome, moyen âge – temps modernes,* LXXXIX (1977), 11–93.

Rüdt de Collenberg, Weyprecht H., "Les Ibelin aux XIIIe et XIVe siècles: généalogie compilée principalement selon les registres du Vatican," Ἐπετηρὶς τοῦ Κέντρου Ἐπιστημονικῶν Ἐρευνῶν, IX (1977–1979), 117–248; XI (1981–1982), 505–506.

Rüdt de Collenberg, Weyprecht (here, Wipertus) H., "État et origine du haut clergé de Chypre avant le Grand Schisme d'après les registres des papes du XIIIe et du XIVe siècle," *MÉF Rome, moyen âge – temps modernes,* XCI (1979), 197–332.

Rüdt de Collenberg, Weyprecht H., "Les Lusignan de Chypre: généalogie compilée principalement selon les registres de l'Archivio Segreto Vaticano et les manuscrits de la Biblioteca Vaticana," Ἐπετηρὶς τοῦ Κέντρου Ἐπιστημονικῶν Ἐρευνῶν, X (1979–1980), 85–319; XI (1981–1982), 507–512.

Rüdt de Collenberg, Weyprecht H. (here, Wipertus), "Le Royaume et l'église de Chypre face au Grand Schisme (1378–1417)," *MÉF Rome, moyen âge – temps modernes,* XCIV (1982), 621–701.

Rüdt de Collenberg, Weyprecht (here, Wipertus) H., "Les Cardinaux de Chypre Hugues et Lancelot de Lusignan," *Archivum historiae pontificiae,* XX (1982), 83–128.

Rüdt de Collenberg, Weyprecht H., *Familles de l'Orient latin, XIIe–XIVe siècles* (Varior. Repr., CS, 176; London, 1983).

Runciman, Steven, "The First Crusaders' Journey across the Balkan Peninsula," *Byzantion,* XIX (1949), 207–221.

Runciman, Steven, *A History of the Crusades* (3 vols., Cambridge, Eng., 1951–1954).

Runciman, Steven, "The Crusades of 1101," *Jahrbuch der österreichischen byzantinischen Gesellschaft,* I (1951), 3–12.

Runciman, Steven, "The Decline of the Crusading Idea," *Relazioni del X Congresso internazionale di scienze storiche, Roma 1955:* 3. *Storia del medio evo* (Florence, 1955), pp. 565–594.

Runciman, Steven, *The Eastern Schism: a Study of the Papacy and the Eastern Churches during the XIth and XIIth Centuries* (Oxford, 1955; repr. New York, 1983).

Runciman, Steven, "The Pilgrimages to Palestine before 1095," *H of C,* I (1955, 2nd ed. 1969), 68–78.

Runciman, Steven, "The First Crusade: Constantinople to Antioch," *H of C,* I (1955, 2nd ed. 1969), 280–304, and ". . . : Antioch to Ascalon," *ibid.,* 308–341.

Runciman, Steven, *The Sicilian Vespers: a History of the Mediterranean World in the Later 13th Century* (Cambridge, Eng., 1958; repr. Cambridge, 1982).

Runciman, Steven, *The Families of Outremer: the Feudal Nobility of the Crusader Kingdom of Jerusalem, 1099–1291* (The Creighton Lecture in History, 1959; London, 1960).

Runciman, Steven, "The Crusader States, 1243–1291," *H of C,* II (1962, 2nd ed. 1969), 557–598.

Runciman, Steven, *The Fall of Constantinople, 1453* (Cambridge, Eng., 1965).

Runciman, Steven, *The First Crusade* (Cambridge, Eng., 1980).

Runciman, Steven, "The Visit of King Amalric I to Constantinople in 1171," in *Outremer* (1982), pp. 153–158.

Russell, Frederick H., *The Just War in the Middle Ages* (Cambridge Studies in Medieval Life and Thought, 3rd ser., 8; Cambridge, Eng., and New York, 1975).

Russell, Josiah C., *Late Ancient and Medieval Population* (Transactions of the American Philosophical Society, n.s., 48, no. 3; Philadelphia, 1958).

Russell, Josiah C., *Medieval Regions and their Cities* (Newton Abbot, 1972).

Russell, Josiah C., "The Population of the Crusader States," *H of C,* V (1985), 295–314.

Russo, Francesco, "I Calabresi e la prima crociata," *Almanaco Calabrese* (1959), pp. 85–94.

Ryan, J. Joseph, "The Legatine Excommunication of Patriarch Michael Cerularius (1054) and a New Document from the First Crusade Epoch," *Studia Gratiana,* XIV (1967; = Collectanea Stephan Kuttner, 4), 13–49.

Ryan, James D., "Nicholas IV and the Evolution of the Eastern Missionary Effort," *Archivum historiae pontificiae,* XIX (1981), 79–95.

Saadé, Gabriel, "Histoire du Château de Saladin," *Studi medievali,* 3-IX (1968), 980–1016.

Sacy, Silvestre de, "Mémoire sur la dynastie des Assassins et sur l'étymologie de leur nom," *Histoire et mémoires de l'Institut royal de France, Classe d'histoire et de littérature ancienne,* IV (1818), Mémoires, 1–84.

Sacy, Silvestre de, "Mémoire sur le traité fait entre le roi de Tunis et Philippe-le-Hardi, en 1270, pour l'évacuation du territoire de Tunis par l'armée des croisés," *Histoire et mémoires de l'Institut royal de France, Académie des inscriptions et belles-lettres,* IX (1831), 448–477.

Sacy, Silvestre de, "Mémoire sur une correspondance de l'empereur de Maroc Yakoub, fils d'Abd-alhakk, avec Philippe-le-Hardi, conservée dans les archives du royaume," *Histoire et mémoires de l'Institut royal de France, Académie des inscriptions et belles-lettres,* IX (1831), 478–506.

Salamé-Sarkis, Hassan, *Contribution à l'histoire de Tripoli et de sa région à l'époque des croisades: problèmes d'histoire, d'architecture et de céramique* (Bibliothèque archéologique et historique, 106; Paris, 1980).

Salibi, Kamal S., "The Maronites of Lebanon under Frankish and Mamluk Rule (1099–1516)," *Arabica,* IV (1957), 288–303.

Salibi, Kamal S., "The Maronite Church in the Middle Ages and its Union with Rome," *Oriens christianus,* XLII (1958), 92–104.

Salibi, Kamal S., "The Buḥturids of the Ġarb: Mediaeval Lords of Beirut and of Southern Lebanon," *Arabica,* VIII (1961), 74–97.

Saller, Sylvester J., *Excavations at Bethany, 1949–1953* (Studium BF, 12; Jerusalem, 1957).

Sanaullah, Mawlawi F. (= Sanā-Allāh, Maulavī F.), *The Decline of the Saljūqid Empire* (Calcutta, 1938).

Sanchis Guillén, Vicente, *Expedición de Catalanes y Aragoneses al Oriente en el siglo XIV* (Madrid, 1890).

Santifaller, Leo, *Beiträge zur Geschichte des Lateinischen Patriarchats von Konstantinopel (1204–1261) und der venezianischen Urkunde* (Historisch-diplomatische Forschungen, 3; Weimar, 1938).

Saunders, John J., *Aspects of the Crusades* (University of Canterbury Publications, 3; Christchurch, N.Z., 1962).

Saunders, John J., *A History of Medieval Islam* (New York and London, 1965).

Saunders, John J., *Muslims and Mongols: Essays on Medieval Asia,* ed. G. W. Rice (University of Canterbury Publications, 24; Christchurch, N.Z., 1977).

Sauvaget, Jean, "La Citadelle de Damas," *Syria,* XI (1930), 59–90, 216–241.

Savage, Henry L., "Pilgrimages and Pilgrim Shrines in Palestine and Syria after 1095," *H of C,* IV (1977), 36–68.

Sayous, André E., "Les Méthodes commerciales de Barcelone au XIIIe siècle, d'après des documents inédits des archives de sa cathédrale," *Estudis universitaris catalans,* XVI (1931), 155–198.

Sayous, André E., "Les Méthodes commerciales de Barcelone au XIVe siècle, surtout d'après des protocoles inédits de ses archives notariales," *Estudis universitaris catalans,* XVIII (1933), 209–235.

Sayous, André E., "Le Capitalisme commercial et financier dans les pays chrétiens de la Méditerranée occidentale depuis la première croisade jusqu'à la fin du moyen âge," *VSWG,* XXIX (1936), 270–295.

Sayous, André E., "Les Méthodes commerciales de Barcelone au XVe siècle d'après des documents inédits de ses Archives: la bourse, le prêt et l'assurance maritimes, les sociétés commerciales, la lettre de change, une banque d'État," *RH Droit FÉ,* 4-XV (1936), 255–301.

Schadek, Hans, "Tunis oder Sizilien? Die Ziele der aragonischen Mittelmeerpolitik unter Peter III. von Aragon," *Gesammelte Aufsätze zur Kulturgeschichte Spaniens,* XXVIII (1975), 335–349.

Schaller, Hans M., "Die Kanzlei Friedrichs II., ihr Personal und ihr Sprachstil," *Archiv für Diplomatik,* III (1957), 207–286.

Schaller, Hans M., "Das Relief an der Kanzel der Kathedrale von Bitonto: ein Denkmal der Kaiseridee Friedrichs II.," *Archiv für Kulturgeschichte,* XLV (1963), 295–312.

Schaller, Hans M., "König Manfred und die Assassinen," *Deutsches Archiv,* XXI (1965), 173–193.

Schaube, Adolf, "Die Wechselbriefe König Ludwigs des Heiligen von seinem ersten Kreuzzug und ihre Rolle auf dem Geldmarkte von Genua," *Jahrbücher für Nationalökonomie und Statistik,* LXX (= 3-XV; 1898), 603–621, 730–748; LXXIII (= 3-XVIII; 1899), 145–184.

Schaube, Adolf, *Handelsgeschichte der romanischen Völker des Mittelmeergebiets bis zum Ende der Kreuzzüge* (Handbuch der mittelalterlichen und neueren Geschichte, Sect. 3, 5; Munich and Berlin, 1906).

Schein, Sylvia, "Gesta Dei per Mongolos 1300: the Genesis of a Non-Event," *Eng. HR,* XCIV (1979), 805–819.

Schein, Sylvia, "La Custodia Terrae Sanctae franciscaine et les Juifs de Jérusalem à la fin du moyen âge," *Revue des études juives,* CXLI (1982), 369–377.

Schein, Sylvia, "The Patriarchs of Jerusalem in the Late Thirteenth Century — seignors espiritueles et temporeles?," in *Outremer* (1982), pp. 297–305.

Schein, Sylvia, "The Future Regnum Hierusalem: a Chapter in Medieval State Planning," *J Med. H,* X (1984), 95–105.

Schein, Sylvia, "Philip IV and the Crusade: a Reconsideration," in *Crusade and Settlement,* ed. Peter W. Edbury (Cardiff, 1985), pp. 121–126.

Schlumberger, Gustave, *L'Épopée byzantine à la fin du Xe siècle* (3 vols., Paris, 1896–1905).

Schlumberger, Gustave, *Renaud de Châtillon* (Paris, 1898).

Schlumberger, Gustave, *Récits de Byzance et des croisades* (2 vols., Paris, 1916–1922).

Schlumberger, Gustave, *Byzance et les croisades* (Paris, 1927).

Schmandt, Raymond H., "The Fourth Crusade and the Just-War Theory," *Cath. HR,* LXI (1975), 191–221.

Schmeidler, Bernhard, *Der Dux und das Comune Venetiarum von 1141–1229: Beiträge zur Verfassungsgeschichte Venedigs vornehmlich im 12. Jahrhundert* (Hist. Stud., ed. Ebering, 35; Berlin, 1902).

Schmidt, Charles G.A., *Histoire et doctrine de la secte des Cathares ou Albigeois* (Paris, 1849; repr. New York, 1980).

Schmugge, Ludwig, "'Pilgerfahrt macht frei': eine These zur Bedeutung des mittelalterlichen Pilgerwesens," *Römische Quartalschrift,* LXXIV (1979), 16–31.

Schmugge, Ludwig, "Zisterzienser, Kreuzzug und Heidenkrieg," in *Die Zisterzienser,* ed. Kaspar Elm, R. Joerissen, and Hermann J. Roth (Aachen, 1980), pp. 57–68.

Schöber, Susanne, *Die altfranzösische Kreuzzugslyrik des 12. Jahrhunderts* (Diss. der Universität Salzburg, 7; Vienna, 1976).

Schollmeyer, Chrysologus, "Die missionarische Sendung des Frater Wilhelm von Rubruk," *Ostkirchliche Studien,* IV (1955), 138–146.

Schollmeyer, Chrysologus, "Die Missionsfahrt Bruder Wilhelms von Rubruk zu den Mongolen," *Zeitschrift für Missionskunde und Religionswissenschaft,* XL (1956), 200–205.

Schreiber, Georg, "Levantinische Wanderungen zum Westen," *Byz. Z,* XLIV (= Festschrift Franz Dölger; 1951), 517–523.

Schreiber, Ottomar, "Die Personal- und Amtsdaten der Hochmeister des Deutschen Ritterordens von seiner Gründung bis zum Jahre 1525," *Oberländische Geschichtsblätter,* III (Königsberg, 1909–1913), 615–762.

Schulz, Werner, *Andreaskreuz und Christusorden: Isabella von Portugal und der burgundische Kreuzzug* (Historische Schriften der Universität Freiburg, 1; Freiburg (Switzerland), 1976).

Schwerin, Ursula, *Die Aufrufe der Päpste zur Befreiung des Heiligen Landes von den*

Anfängen bis zum Ausgang Innozenz IV: ein Beitrag zur Geschichte der kurialen Kreuzzugspropaganda und der päpstlichen Epistolographie (Hist. Stud., ed. Ebering, 301; Berlin, 1937).

Seibt, Ferdinand, *Hussitica: zur Struktur einer Revolution* (Beihefte zum Archiv für Kulturgeschichte, 8; Cologne, Graz, and Weimar, 1965).

Seibt, Ferdinand, "Die Zeit der Luxemburger und der hussitischen Revolution," *Handbuch der Geschichte der böhmischen Länder,* ed. Karl Bosl: vol. I. *Die böhmischen Länder von der archäischen Zeit bis zum Ausgang der hussitischen Revolution* (Stuttgart, 1967), pp. 349–568.

Serjeant, Robert B., "Material for a History of Islamic Textiles up to the Mongol Conquest," *Ars Islamica,* IX (1942), 54–92; X (1943), 71–104; XI-XII (1946), 98–120; XIII-XIV (1948), 75–117; XV-XVI (1951), 29–85.

Serper, Arié, "La Prise de Nicée d'après la 'Chanson d'Antioche' de Richard le Pèlerin," *Byzantion,* XLVI (1976), 411–421.

Servatius, Carlo, *Paschalis II. (1099–1118): Studien zu seiner Person und seiner Politik* (Päpste und Papsttum, 14; Stuttgart, 1979).

Setton, Kenneth M., *Catalan Domination of Athens, 1311–1388* (Med. AA, Publ., 50; Cambridge, Mass., 1948; rev. ed., London, 1975).

Setton, Kenneth M., "On the Importance of Land Tenure and Agrarian Taxation in the Byzantine Empire from the 4th Century to the 4th Crusade," *American Journal of Philology,* LXXIV (1953), 225–259.

Setton, Kenneth M., general ed., *A History of the Crusades:* 1. *The First Hundred Years,* ed. Marshall W. Baldwin (Philadelphia, 1955; rev. ed., Madison, 1969); 2. *The Later Crusades, 1189–1311,* ed. Robert L. Wolff and Harry W. Hazard (Philadelphia, 1962; rev. ed., Madison, 1969); 3. *The Fourteenth and Fifteenth Centuries,* ed. Hazard (Madison, 1975); 4. *The Art and Architecture of the Crusader States,* ed. Hazard (Madison, 1977); 5. *The Impact of the Crusades on the Near East,* ed. Norman P. Zacour and Harry W. Hazard (Madison, 1985); 6. *The Impact of the Crusades on Europe,* ed. Hazard and Zacour (Madison, 1989).

Setton, Kenneth M., "The Archaeology of Medieval Athens," *Essays in Medieval Life and Thought Presented in Honor of Austin Patterson Evans,* ed. John H. Mundy, Richard W. Emery, and Benjamin N. Nelson (New York, 1955), pp. 227–258.

Setton, Kenneth M., "The Byzantine Background to the Italian Renaissance," *Proceedings of the American Philosophical Society,* C (1956), 1–76.

Setton, Kenneth M., "The Latins in Greece and the Aegean from the Fourth Crusade to the End of the Middle Ages," in *The Cambridge Medieval History,* IV-1, ed. Joan Hussey (Cambridge, Eng., 1966), 389–420, with bibliography pp. 908–938.

Setton, Kenneth M., *Europe and the Levant in the Middle Ages and the Renaissance* (Varior. Repr., CS, 29; London, 1974).

Setton, Kenneth M., "Catalan Society in Greece in the Fourteenth Century," in *Essays in Memory of Basil Laourdas,* ed. Louisa Laourdas (Thessalonica, 1975), pp. 241–284; repr. in his *Athens in the Middle Ages* (London, 1975).

Setton, Kenneth M., *Athens in the Middle Ages* (Varior. Repr., CS, 41; London, 1975).

Setton, Kenneth M., "The Catalans in Greece, 1311–1380," *H of C,* III (1975), 167–224, and "The Catalans and Florentines in Greece, 1380–1462," *ibid.,* 225–277.

Setton, Kenneth M., *The Papacy and the Levant (1204–1571)* (Memoirs of the American Philosophical Society, 114, 127, 161, 162; 4 vols., Philadelphia, 1976–1984).

Ševčenko, Ihor, "Intellectual Repercussions of the Council of Florence," *Church History,* XXIV (1955), 291–323.

Shahar, Shulamith, "Des Lépreux pas comme les autres: l'ordre de Saint-Lazare dans le royaume de Jérusalem," *Rev. hist.,* CCLXVII (1982), 19–41.

Siberry, Elizabeth, "Missionaries and Crusaders, 1095–1274: Opponents or Allies?," *Studies in Church History,* XX (1983), 103–110.

Siberry, Elizabeth, *Criticism of Crusading, 1095–1274* (New York and Oxford, 1985).

Siedschlag, Beatrice N., *English Participation in the Crusades, 1150–1220* (Ph.D. Thesis, Bryn Mawr, 1937; [Menasha, Wisc.], 1939).

Silberschmidt, Max, *Das orientalische Problem zur Zeit der Entstehung des türkischen Reiches nach venezianischen Quellen: ein Beitrag zur Geschichte der Beziehung Venedigs zu Sultan Bajezid I, zu Byzanz, Ungarn und Genua und zum Reiche von Kiptschak (1381–1400)* (Beiträge zur Kulturgeschichte des Mittelalters und der Renaissance, 27; Leipzig and Berlin, 1923).

Simonut, Noè, *Il Metodo di evangelizzazione dei Francescani tra Musulmani e Mongoli nei secoli XIII–XIV* (Milan, 1947).

Sinclair, Keith V., "The Hospital, Hospice and Church of the Healthy Belonging to the Knights of St. John of Jerusalem on Cyprus," *Medium Aevum,* XLIX (1980), 254–257.

Sinogowitz, Bernhard, "Über das byzantinische Kaisertum nach dem Vierten Kreuzzuge (1204–1205)," *Byz. Z,* XLV (1952), 345–355.

Sinor, Denis, "Un Voyageur du treizième siècle: le Dominicain Julien de Hongrie," *Bulletin of the School of Oriental and African Studies,* XIV (1952), 589–602.

Sinor, Denis, "Les Relations entre les Mongols et l'Europe jusqu'à la mort d'Arghoun et de Bela IV," *Cahiers d'histoire mondiale,* III (1956), 39–62.

Sinor, Denis, *Introduction à l'étude de l'Eurasie centrale* (Wiesbaden, 1963).

Sinor, Denis, "The Mongols and Western Europe," *H of C,* III (1975), 513–544.

Sivan, Emmanuel, "La Genèse de la contre-croisade: un traité damasquin du début de XIIe siècle," *JA,* CCLIV (1966), 197–224.

Sivan, Emmanuel, "Le Caractère sacré de Jérusalem dans l'Islam aux XIIe–XIIIe siècles," *Studia islamica,* XXVII (1967), 149–182.

Sivan, Emmanuel, "Notes sur la situation des Chrétiens à l'époque ayyūbide," *Revue de l'histoire des religions,* CLXXII (1967), 117–130.

Sivan, Emmanuel, "Réfugiés syro-palestiniens au temps des croisades," *Revue des études islamiques,* XXXV (1967), 135–147.

Sivan, Emmanuel, *L'Islam et la croisade: idéologie et propagande dans les réactions musulmanes aux croisades* (Paris, 1968).

Sivan, Emmanuel, "Saladin et le calife al-Nāṣir," *Scripta Hierosolymitana,* XXIII (1972), 126–145.

Slessarev, Vsevolod, *Prester John: the Letter and the Legend* (Minneapolis, 1959).

Slessarev, Vsevolod, "*Ecclesiae mercatorum* and the Rise of Merchant Colonies," *Business History Review,* XLI (1967), 181–197.

Smail, Raymond C., "Crusaders' Castles of the Twelfth Century," *Cambridge Historical Journal,* X (1950–1952), 133–149.

Smail, Raymond C., *Crusading Warfare, 1097–1193* (Cambridge Studies in Medieval Life and Thought, n.s., 3; Cambridge, Eng., 1956).

Smail, Raymond C., *The Crusaders in Syria and the Holy Land* (Ancient Peoples and Places, 82; London, 1973).

Smail, Raymond C., "Latin Syria and the West, 1149–1187," *Transactions of the Royal Historical Society,* 5-XIX (1969), 1–20.

Smail, Raymond C., "The International Status of the Latin Kingdom of Jerusalem,

1150–1192," in *The Eastern Mediterranean Lands in the Period of the Crusades,* ed. Peter M. Holt (Warminster, 1977), pp. 23–43.

Smail, Raymond C., "The Predicaments of Guy of Lusignan, 1183–87," in *Outremer* (1982), pp. 159–176.

Smedt, Charles de, "Les Sources de l'histoire de la croisade contre les Albigeois," *Rev. QH,* XVI (1874), 433–481.

Soldevila, Ferran, *Història de Catalunya,* 2nd ed. (3 vols., Barcelona, 1962).

Somerville, Robert, "The Council of Clermont and the First Crusade," *Studia Gratiana,* XX (1976 = Mélanges Gerard Fransen II), 323–337.

Soranzo, Giovanni, *Il Papato, l'Europa cristiana e i Tartari* (Pubblicazioni dell' Università cattolica del Sacro Cuore, 5th ser., 12; Milan, 1930).

Soteriou, Maria G., *Mistra: une ville byzantine morte* (Athens, 1935).

Sottas, Jules, *Les Messageries maritimes de Venise aux XIVe et XVe siècles* (Paris, 1938).

Sourdel, Dominique, *L'Islam médiéval* (Paris, 1979).

Sourdel-Thomine, Janine, "Les Conseils du šayḫ al-Harawī à un prince ayyūbide," *Bulletin d'études orientales de l'Institut français de Damas,* XVII (1961–1962), 205–266.

Southern, Richard W., *Western Views of Islam in the Middle Ages* (Cambridge, Mass., 1962).

Spence, R., "Gregory IX's Attempted Expedition to the Latin Empire of Constantinople: the Crusade for the Union of the Latin and Greek Churches," *Journal of Medieval Studies,* V (1979), 163–176.

Spreckelmeyer, Goswin, *Das Kreuzzugslied des lateinischen Mittelalters* (Münstersche Mittelalter-Schriften, 21; Munich, 1974).

Spuler, Bertold, *Die morgenländischen Kirchen* (Leyden, 1964).

Spuler, Bertold, *Die Goldene Horde: die Mongolen in Russland 1223–1502* (Das mongolische Weltreich: Quellen und Forschungen, 2; 2nd ed., Wiesbaden, 1965).

Spuler, Bertold, *Die Mongolen in Iran: Politik, Verwaltung und Kultur der Ilchanzeit 1220–1350* (Iranische Forschungen, 1; 2nd ed., Wiesbaden, 1965).

Starr, Joshua, *The Jews in the Byzantine Empire, 641–1204* (Texte und Forschungen zur byzantinisch-neugriechischen Philologie, 30; Athens, 1939).

Starr, Joshua, *Romania: the Jewries of the Levant after the Fourth Crusade* (Paris, 1949).

Stefano, Antonino de, *La Cultura in Sicilia nel periodo normanno* (Palermo, 1938).

Stern, Henri, "Les Représentations des conciles dans l'église de la Nativité à Bethléem," *Byzantion,* XI (1936), 101–152; XIII (1938), 415–459.

Sternfeld, Richard, *Karl von Anjou als Graf der Provence* (Historische Untersuchungen, 10; Berlin, 1888).

Sternfeld, Richard, *Ludwigs des Heiligen Kreuzzug nach Tunis 1270 und die Politik Karls I. von Sizilien* (Hist. Stud., ed. Ebering, 4; Berlin, 1896).

Sterns, Indrikis, "The Teutonic Knights in the Crusader States," *H of C,* V (1985), 315–378.

Stevenson, William B., *The Crusaders in the East: a Brief History of the Wars of Islam with the Latins in Syria during the 12th and 13th Centuries* (Cambridge, Eng., and New York, 1907).

Stickel, Erwin, *Der Fall von Akkon: Untersuchungen zum Abklingen des Kreuzzugsgedankens am Ende des 13. Jahrhunderts* (Geist und Werk der Zeiten, 45; Berne and Frankfurt, 1975).

Strayer, Joseph R., "The Crusade against Aragon," *Speculum,* XXVIII (1953), 102–113.

Strayer, Joseph R., "The Political Crusades of the Thirteenth Century," *H of C,* II (1962, 2nd ed. 1969), 343–375, and "The Crusades of Louis IX," *ibid.,* 487–518.

Streit, Ludwig, *Venedig und die Wendung des vierten Kreuzzuges gegen Konstantinopel* (Anklam, 1877).

Striker, Cecil L., and Y. Doğan Kuban, "Work at Kalenderhane Camii in Istanbul: Second Preliminary Report," *D Oaks P,* XXII (1968), 185–193; cf. "Fourth Report," *ibid.,* XXV (1971), 253–258.

Struck, Adolf, *Mistra, eine mittelalterliche Ruinenstadt: Streifblicke zur Geschichte und zu den Denkmälern des fränkisch-byzantinischen Zeitalters in Morea* (Vienna and Leipzig, 1910).

Struss, Lothar, *Epische Identität und historische Realität: der Albigenserkreuzzug und die Krise der Zeitgeschichtsdarstellung in der occitanischen, altfranzösischen und lateinischen Historiographie* (Theorie und Geschichte der Literatur und der schönen Künste, LI; Munich, 1980).

Strzygowski, Josef, "Ruins of Tombs of the Latin Kings on the Haram in Jerusalem," *Speculum,* XI (1936), 499–508.

Suárez Fernandes, Luis, *Juan II y la frontera de Granada* (Universidad de Valladolid, Consejo superior de investigaciones científicas: Estudios y documentos, Cuadernos de historia medieval, 2; Valladolid, 1954).

Sumberg, Lewis A.M., "The 'Tafurs' and the First Crusade," *Mediaeval Studies,* XXI (1959), 224–246.

Sumberg, Lewis A.M., *La Chanson d'Antioche: étude historique et littéraire: une chronique en vers français de la première croisade par le pèlerin Richard* (Paris, 1968).

Sumption, Jonathan, *The Albigensian Crusade* (London and Boston, 1978).

Sweeney, James R., "Hungary in the Crusades, 1169–1218," *International History Review,* III (1981), 467–481.

Sybel, Heinrich von, *Geschichte des ersten Kreuzzuges,* 2nd ed. (Leipzig, 1881).

Taeschner, Franz, "Futuwwa, eine gemeinschaftbildende Idee im mittelalterlichen Orient und ihre verschiedenen Erscheinungsformen," *Schweizerisches Archiv für Volkskunde,* LII (1956), 122–158.

Taeuber, Walter, *Geld und Kredit im Mittelalter* (Berlin, 1933).

Tamarati, Michel, *L'Église géorgienne des origines jusqu'à nos jours* (Rome, 1910).

Tatakis, Basile, *La Philosophie byzantine* (in Émile Bréhier, *Histoire de la philosophie,* fascicule supplémentaire, 2; Paris, 1949).

Ter-Grigorian Iskenderian, Galust, *Die Kreuzfahrer und ihre Beziehungen zu den armenischen Nachbarfürsten bis zum Untergange der Grafschaft Edessa* (Diss., Leipzig; Weida, 1915).

Ter-Mikelian, Arshak (here, Arshag Der Mikelian), *Die armenische Kirche in ihren Beziehungen zur byzantinischen vom IV. bis zum XIII. Jahrhundert* (Leipzig, 1892).

Terrasse, Henri, *L'Art hispano-mauresque des origines au XIIIe siècle* (Publication de l'Institut des hautes études marocaines, 25; Paris, 1932).

Terrasse, Henri, *Histoire du Maroc des origines à l'établissement du protectorat français* (2 vols., Casablanca, 1949–1950).

Tessier, Jules A., *Quatrième croisade: la diversion sur Zara et Constantinople* (Paris, 1884).

Thier, Ludger, *Kreuzzugsbemühungen unter Papst Clemens V. (1305–1314)* (Franziskanische Forschungen, 24; Werl, 1973).

Thiriet, Freddy, *La Romanie vénitienne au moyen-âge: le développement et l'exploitation du domaine colonial vénitien (XIIe–XVe siècles)* (BÉFAR, 193; Paris, 1959; rev. ed., Paris, 1975).

Thiriet, Freddy, *Études sur la Romanie gréco-vénitienne (Xe–XVe siècles)* (Varior. Repr., CS, 60; London, 1977).

Thiriet, Freddy, "La Crise des trafics vénitiens au Levant dans les premières années du XVe siècle," in *Studi in memoria di Federigo Melis,* ed. L. de Rosa (Naples, 1978), III, 59–72.

Thiriet, Freddy, "Recherches sur le nombre des 'Latins' immigrés en Romanie gréco-vénitienne aux XIIIe–XIVe siècles," in *Byzance et les Slaves: Mélanges Ivan Dujčev* (Paris, 1979), pp. 421–436.

Thomas, Antoninus H. "Les Statuts des chanoines du Saint-Sépulcre et leurs rapports avec les constitutions des Dominicains," *AF Praed.* XLVIII (1978), 5–22.

Thorau, Peter, *Sultan Baibars I. von Ägypten: ein Beitrag zur Geschichte des Vorderen Orients im 13. Jahrhundert* (Beihefte zum Tübinger Atlas des Vorderen Orients, Reihe B, Nr. 63; Wiesbaden, 1987).

Throop, Palmer A., *Criticism of the Crusade: a Study of Public Opinion and Crusade Propaganda* (Amsterdam, 1940).

Thuasne, Louis, *Djem-Sultan* (Paris, 1892).

Tisserant, Eugène, "La Légation en Orient du Franciscain Dominique d'Aragon (1245–47)," *RO Chr.,* XXIV (1924), 336–355.

Tolstov, Sergei P., *Auf den Spuren der altchoresmischen Kultur,* tr. Otto Mehlitz (Berlin, 1953).

Tomek, Václav V., *Dějepis města Prahy* (Nowočeská bibliothéka wydáwaná nákladem Musea králowstwí českého číslo XVIII; 12 vols., Prague, 1855–1901).

Tomek, Václav V., *Jan Žižka* (Prague, 1879).

Topping, Peter W., "The Morea, 1311–1364," *H of C,* III (1975), 104–140, and "The Morea, 1364–1460," *ibid.,* 141–166.

Topping, Peter W., *Studies on Latin Greece A.D. 1205–1715* (Varior. Repr., CS, 68; London, 1977).

Torre y del Cerro, Antonio de la, *Los Reyes Católicos y Granada* (Consejo superior de investigaciones científicas, Instituto Jerónimo Zurita; Madrid, 1946).

Toubert, Pierre, "Les Déviations de la croisade au milieu du XIIIe siècle: Alexandre IV contre Manfred," *Le Moyen-âge,* LXIX (1963), 391–401.

Tournebize, Henry F., *Histoire politique et religieuse de l'Arménie depuis les origines des Arméniens jusqu'à la mort de leur dernier roi (l'an 1393)* (Paris, 1910).

Tourtoulon, Charles de, *Don Jaime I el Conquistador, rey de Aragón, conde de Barcelona, señor de Montpeller, segun las crónicas y documentos inéditos,* 2nd rev. ed. tr. Teodoro Llorente y Olivares (2 vols., Valencia, 1874).

Tozer, Henry F., "The Franks in the Peloponnese," *Journal of Hellenic Studies,* IV (1883), 165–236.

Trabut-Cussac, Jean Paul, "Le Financement de la croisade anglaise de 1270," *BÉ Char.,* CXIX (1961), 113–140.

Tramontana, Salvatore, "Per la storia della 'Compagnia Catalana' in Oriente," *Nuova rivista storica,* XLVI (1962), 58–95.

Traquair, Ramsay, "Laconia: I, Mediaeval Fortresses," *ABS Athens,* XII (1905–1906), 259–276.

Traquair, Ramsay, "Mediaeval Fortresses of the North-Western Peloponnesus," *ABS Athens,* XIII (1906–1907), 268–281.

Traquair, Ramsay, "Frankish Architecture in Greece," *Journal of the Royal Institute of British Architects,* 3-XXXI (1923), 34–48, 73–83.

Treece, Henry, *The Crusades* (London, 1978).

Treitinger, Otto, *Die oströmische Kaiser- und Reichsidee nach ihrer Gestaltung im höfischen Zeremoniell* (Jena, 1938).

Treppo, Mario del, *I Mercanti catalani e l'espansione della Corona d'Aragona nel secolo XV* (Naples, 1972).

Tritton, Arthur S., *The Caliphs and their Non-Muslim Subjects: a Critical Study of the Covenant of 'Umar* (London, 1930).

Troll, Christian W., "Die Chinamission im Mittelalter," *Franziskanische Studien,* XLVII (1966), 109–150; XLIX (1967), 22–79.

Trudon des Ormes, Amédée L.A., "Listes des maisons et quelques dignitaires de l'ordre du Temple en Syrie, en Chypre et en France d'après les pièces de procès," *RO Latin,* V (1897), 389–459; VI (1898), 156–213; VII (1899), 223–274, 504–589.

Tuilier, André, "La Date exacte du chrysobulle d'Alexis Ier Comnène en faveur des Vénitiens et son contexte historique," *Rivista di studi bizantini e neoellenici,* n.s., IV (1967), 27–48.

Tumler, Marian, *Der Deutsche Orden im Werden, Wachsen und Wirken bis 1400 . . .* (Montreal and Vienna, 1955).

Turan, Osman, "Les Souverains seldjoukides et leurs sujets non musulmans," *Studia islamica,* I (1953), 65–100.

Tyan, Émile, *Institutions du droit public musulman* (2 vols., Paris, 1954–1957).

Tyan, Émile, *Histoire de l'organisation judiciaire en pays d'Islam* (Annales de l'Université de Lyon, 3rd ser.: Droit, fasc. 4; 2nd ed., Leyden, 1960).

Tyerman, Christopher J., "Marino Sanudo and the Lost Crusade: Lobbying in the Fourteenth Century," *Transactions of the Royal Historical Society,* 5-XXXII (1982), 57–73.

Tyerman, Christopher J., "Sed nihil fecit? The Last Capetians and the Recovery of the Holy Land," *War and Government in the Middle Ages: Essays in Honour of J. O. Prestwich,* ed. John Gillingham and J. C. Holt (Woodbridge, 1984), pp. 170–181.

Tyerman, Christopher J., "Philip VI and the Recovery of the Holy Land," *Eng. HR,* C (1985), 25–52.

Tyerman, Christopher J., "The Holy Land and the Crusades of the Thirteenth and Fourteenth Centuries," in *Crusade and Settlement,* ed. Peter W. Edbury (Cardiff, 1985), pp. 105–112.

Urban, William L., *The Prussian Crusade* (Washington, 1980).

Urban, William L., *The Livonian Crusade* (Washington, 1981).

Usseglio, Leopoldo, *I Marchesi di Monferrato in Italia ed in Oriente durante i secoli XII e XIII* (Biblioteca della Società storica subalpina, 100, 101, ed. posthumously by Carlo Patrucco; 2 vols., Casale Monferrato, 1926).

Uzunçarşili, Ismail H., *Osmanli devleti teşkilâtina medhal: Büyük Selçukîler, Anadolu Selçukîleri* (Introduction to the Administrative System of the Ottoman Empire: the Great Seljuks, the Seljuks of Rūm) (*Türk Tarih Kurumu yayînlarî,* 8, 10–10a; 2 vols., Istanbul, 1941, and Ankara, 1970).

Vacandard, Elphège, "Saint Bernard et la seconde croisade," *Rev. QH,* XXXVIII (1885), 398–457.

Vacandard, Elphège, *Vie de St.-Bernard, abbé de Clairvaux,* 4th ed. (2 vols., Paris, 1927).

Valentini, Giuseppe, "La Crociata da Eugenio IV a Callisto III (dai documenti d'archivio di Venezia)," *Archivum historiae pontificiae,* XII (1974), 91-123.

Valentini, Giuseppe, "La Crociata di Pio II sulla documentazione veneta d'archivio," *Archivum historiae pontificiae,* XIII (1975), 249-282.

Vallvé, Manuel, *Los Almogávares: la famosa expedición a Oriente de Catalanes y Aragoneses,* 2nd ed. (Barcelona, 1942).

Van Cleve, Thomas C., *Markward of Anweiler and the Sicilian Regency: a Study of Hohenstaufen Policy in Sicily during the Minority of Frederick II* (Oxford and Princeton, 1937).

Van Cleve, Thomas C., "The Fifth Crusade," *H of C,* II (1962, 2nd ed. 1969), 377-428, and "The Crusade of Frederick II," *ibid.,* 429-462.

Varagnac, André, "Croisade et marchandise: pourquoi Simon de Montfort s'en alla défaire les Albigeois," *Annales: Économies, sociétés, civilisations,* I (1946), 209-218.

Vasiliev, Alexander A., *Byzance et les Arabes,* tr. Henri Grégoire and Maurice Canard (2 vols., Brussels, 1935-1950).

Vasiliev, Alexander A., "The Foundation of the Empire of Trebizond (1204-1222)," *Speculum,* XI (1936), 3-37.

Vasiliev, Alexander A., *History of the Byzantine Empire 324-1453,* tr. Sarra M. Ragozin, 2nd ed. (Madison, 1952).

Vasilievsky, Vasil'y G., "Vizantija i Pečenegi," *Trudy V.G. Vasil'evskago* (= *Works*), I (St. Petersburg, 1908), pp. 1-175.

Vat, Odulphus van der, *Die Anfänge der Franziskanermissionen und ihre Weiterentwicklung im Nahen Orient und in den mohammedanischen Ländern während des 13. Jahrhunderts* (Missionswissenschaftliche Studien, n.s., 6; Werl, 1934).

Vazquez de Parga, Luis, José M. Lacarra, and Juan Uría Ríu, *Las Peregrinaciones a Santiago de Compostela* (3 vols., Madrid, 1948-1949).

Vehse, Otto, "Die Normannen im Mittelmeer," *Die Welt als Geschichte,* V (1939), 25-58, 233-276.

Vera Idoate, Gregorio, *Navarra y las cruzadas: ensayo histórico de las principales expediciones religioso-militares de Navarra desde fines del siglo VIII hasta mediados de XIV* (Pamplona, 1931).

Verlinden, Charles, *Les Empereurs belges de Constantinople* (Brussels, 1945).

Verlinden, Charles, *L'Esclavage dans l'Europe médiévale,* II (Ghent, 1977).

Vernadskiĭ, Georgiĭ V. (here, George Vernadsky), *The Mongols and Russia* (A History of Russia, 3; New Haven, 1953).

Vertôt, René A. de, abbé, *Histoire des chevaliers hospitaliers de St.-Jean de Jérusalem appelés depuis les chevaliers de Rhodes et aujourd'hui les chevaliers de Malte* (4 vols., Paris, 1726); tr. as *The History of the Knights Hospitallers of St. John of Jerusalem* ... (5 vols., Edinburgh, 1757; repr. London, 1775; repr. New York, 1981).

Viaud, Prosper, *Nazareth et ses deux églises de l'Annonciation et de Saint-Joseph d'après les fouilles récentes* (Paris, 1910).

Vic, Claude de (here, Devic), and Jean J. Vaissète, *Histoire générale de Languedoc avec des notes et les pièces justificatives,* ed. Édouard Dulaurier et al. (15 vols., Toulouse, 1872-1893); supplementary vol. by Ernest Roschach and Auguste Molinier, *Histoire graphique de l'ancienne province de Languedoc* (Toulouse, 1904).

Viller, Marcel, "La Question de l'union des églises entre Grecs et Latins depuis le concile de Lyon jusqu'à celui de Florence, 1274-1438," *Revue de l'histoire ecclésiastique,* XVII (1921), 260-305, 515-532; XVIII (1922), 20-60.

Villey, Michel, *La Croisade: essai sur la formation d'une théorie juridique* (L'église et l'état au moyen âge; Paris, 1942; repr. New York, 1980).

Vincent, Louis H., and Félix M. Abel, *Bethléem: le sanctuaire de la Nativité* (Paris, 1914).

Vincent, Louis H., and Ernest J.H. Mackay, with Félix M. Abel, *Hebron: le Ḥaram el-khalîl, sépulture des patriarches* (2 vols., text and album of plates, Paris, 1923).

Vincent, Louis H., and Félix M. Abel, *Emmaüs: sa basilique et son histoire* (Paris, 1932).

Vincent, Louis H., "Bethléem: le sanctuaire de la Nativité d'après les fouilles récentes," *Revue biblique,* XLV (1936), 544–574; XLVI (1937), 93–121.

Vincent, Louis H., "L'Éléona, sanctuaire primitif de l'Ascension," *Revue biblique,* LXIV (1957), 48–71.

Violante, Cinzio, *Economia, società, istituzioni a Pisa nel Medioevo: saggi e ricerche* (Bari, 1980).

Vitale, Vito, *Breviario della storia di Genova: lineamenti storici ed orientamenti bibliografici* (2 vols., Genoa, 1955).

Vliet, N. van der, *"Sainte Marie: où est elle née" et la piscine probatique* (Paris, 1938).

Voegelin, Eric, "The Mongol Orders of Submission to European Powers, 1245–1255," *Byzantion,* XV (1940–1941), 378–413.

Vogel, Cyrille, "Le Pèlerinage pénitentiel," in *Pellegrinaggi e culto dei santi in Europa fino alla Ia crociata* (Convegni del Centro di studi sulla spiritualità medievale, 4; Todi, 1963), pp. 37–94; also publ. in *Revue des sciences religieuses de l'Université de Strasbourg,* XXXVIII (1964), 113–153.

Vogüé, C.J. Melchior de, *Les Églises de la Terre Sainte* (Paris, 1860).

Vogüé, C.J. Melchior de, "Achard d'Arrouaise: poème sur le 'Templum Domini'," *AO Latin,* I (1881), 562–579.

Vollrath, Hanna, "Konrad III. und Byzanz," *Archiv für Kulturgeschichte,* LIX (1977), 321–365.

Vries, Wilhelm de, "Innocenz IV. (1243–1254) und der christliche Osten," *Ostkirchliche Studien,* XII (1963), 113–131.

Vries, Wilhelm de, "Die Päpste von Avignon und der christliche Osten," *O Chr. P,* XXX (1964), 85–128.

Vryonis, Speros, *The Decline of Medieval Hellenism in Asia Minor and the Process of Islamization from the Eleventh through the Fifteenth Century* (Berkeley, Los Angeles, and London, 1971).

Wace, Alan J.B., "Laconia: V, Frankish Sculptures at Parori and Geraki," *ABS Athens,* XI (1904–1905), 139–145.

Wakefield, Walter L., *Heresy, Crusade and Inquisition in Southern France, 1100–1250* (London, 1974).

Wal, Eugène J.W. de, *Histoire de l'ordre teutonique par un chevalier de l'ordre* (8 vols., Paris, 1784–1790).

Walker, Paul E., "The Crusade of John Tzimisces in the Light of New Arabic Evidence," *Byzantion,* XLVII (1977), 301–327.

Walsh, Richard J., "Charles the Bold and the Crusade: Politics and Propaganda," *J Med. H,* III (1977), 53–86.

Watt, W. Montgomery, *The Influence of Islam on Mediaeval Europe* (Edinburgh, 1970).

Weil, Gustav, *Geschichte der Chalifen* (5 vols., Mannheim, 1842–1862).

Weitzmann, Kurt, "Constantinopolitan Book Illumination in the Period of the Latin Conquest," *Gazette des beaux-arts,* 6-XXV (1944), 193–214.

Weitzmann, Kurt, "Thirteenth Century Crusader Icons on Mount Sinai," *Art Bulletin,* XLV (1963), 179–203.

Weitzmann, Kurt, "Icon Painting in the Crusader Kingdom," *D Oaks P,* XX (1966), 49–83.

Weitzmann, Kurt, "Four Icons on Mount Sinai: New Aspects in Crusader Art," *Jahrbuch der österreichischen Byzantinistik,* XXI (1972), 279–293.

Weitzmann, Kurt, "Three Painted Crosses at Sinai," *Kunsthistorische Forschungen: Otto Pächt zu seinem 70. Geburtstag,* ed. Artur Rosenauer and Gerold Weber (Salzburg, 1972), pp. 23–35.

Weitzmann, Kurt, *Illustrated Manuscripts at St. Catherine's Monastery on Mount Sinai* (Collegeville, Minn., 1973).

Weitzmann, Kurt, *The Monastery of Saint Catherine at Mount Sinai: the Icons:* 1. *From the Sixth to the Tenth Century,* photographs by John Galey (Princeton, 1976).

Weitzmann, Kurt, *Studies in the Arts at Sinai* (Princeton, 1982).

Wentzlaff-Eggebert, Friedrich, *Kreuzzugsdichtung des Mittelalters: Studien zu ihrer geschichtlichen und dichterischen Wirklichkeit* (Berlin, 1960).

Werveke, Hans van, *Filips van de Elzas en Willem van Tyrus: een episode uit de geschiedenis van de kruistochten* (Mededelingen van de Koninklijke Vlaamse Academie voor Wetenschappen, Letteren en Schone Kunsten van België, Klasse der Letteren, 33, no. 2; Brussels, 1971).

Werveke, Hans van, "La Contribution de la Flandre et du Hainaut à la troisième croisade," *Le Moyen-âge,* LXXVIII (1972), 55–90.

Wheeler, Benjamin W., "The Reconquest of Spain before 1095," *H of C,* I (1955, 2nd ed. 1969), 31–39.

Wieruszowski, Helene, "Politische Verschwörungen und Bündnisse König Peters von Aragon gegen Karl von Anjou am Vorabend der Sizilianischen Vesper," *QFIAB,* XXXVII (1957), 136–191.

Wieruszowski, Helene, "The Norman Kingdom of Sicily and the Crusades," *H of C,* II (1962, 2nd ed. 1969), 3–42.

Wiet, Gaston, *L'Égypte musulmane de la conquête arabe à la conquête ottomane 642–1517 de l'ère chrétienne,* 2nd ed. (Histoire de la nation égyptienne, 4; Paris, 1938).

Wilken, Friedrich, *Geschichte der Kreuzzüge nach morgenländischen und abendländischen Berichten* (7 vols., Leipzig, 1807–1832).

Willems, Eugène, "Cîteaux et la seconde croisade," *Revue d'histoire ecclésiastique,* XLIX (1954), 116–151.

Williams, David H., "Cistercian Settlement in the Lebanon," *Cîteaux,* XXV (1974), 61–74.

Williams, Patrick A., "The Assassination of Conrad of Montferrat: Another Suspect?," *Traditio,* XXVI (1970), 381–389.

Windecke, Eberhart, *Denkwürdigkeiten zur Geschichte des Zeitalters Kaiser Sigmunds* (Zum ersten Male vollständig herausg.), ed. Wilhelm Altmann (Berlin, 1893).

Winkelmann, Eduard, *Kaiser Friedrich II.* (Jahrbücher der deutschen Geschichte; 2 vols., Leipzig, 1889–1897).

Wisniewski, Roswitha, *Kreuzzugsdichtung: Idealität in der Wirklichkeit* (Impulse der Forschung, 44; Darmstadt, 1984).

Wittek, Paul, *Das Fürstentum Mentesche: Studien zur Geschichte Westkleinasiens im XIII.–XV. Jahrhundert* (Istanbuler Mitteilungen, 2; Istanbul, 1934).

Wittek, Paul, "De la Défaite d'Ankara à la prise de Constantinople," *Revue des études islamiques,* XII (1938), 1–34.

Wittek, Paul, *The Rise of the Ottoman Empire* (Royal Asiatic Society Monographs, 23; London, 1938).

Wolff, Robert L., "The Latin Empire of Constantinople and the Franciscans," *Traditio*, II (1944), 213-237.

Wolff, Robert L., "The Organisation of the Latin Patriarchate of Constantinople, 1204-1261: Social and Administrative Consequences of the Latin Conquest," *Traditio*, VI (1948), 33-60.

Wolff, Robert L., "Mortgage and Redemption of an Emperor's Son: Castile and the Latin Empire of Constantinople," *Speculum*, XXIX (1954), 45-84.

Wolff, Robert L., "Politics in the Latin Patriarchate of Constantinople 1204-1261," *D Oaks P,* VIII (1954), 225-303.

Wolff, Robert L., "The Latin Empire of Constantinople, 1204-1261," *H of C,* II (1962, 2nd ed. 1969), 187-233.

Wolff, Robert L., *Studies in the Latin Empire of Constantinople* (Varior. Repr., CS, 55; London, 1976).

Wolff, Theodor, *Die Bauernkreuzzüge des Jahres 1096: ein Beitrag zur Geschichte des ersten Kreuzzuges* (Tübingen, 1891).

Wollf, Alfred, *König Balduin I. von Jerusalem* (Königsberg, 1884).

Wormald, Francis, "The Pontifical of Apamea," *Nederlands kunsthistorisch Jaarboek*, V (1954), 271-279.

Yewdale, Ralph B., *Bohemond I, Prince of Antioch* (Princeton, 1924; repr. New York, 1980).

Youngs, G. R., "Three Cilician Castles," *Anatolian Studies*, XV (1965), 113-134.

Zaborov, Mikhail A., *Krestonoscy na vostoke* [The Crusaders in the East] (Moscow, 1980).

Zachariadou, Elizabeth A., *Trade and Crusade: Venetian Crete and the Emirates of Menteshe and Aydin (1300-1415)* (Library of the Hellenic Institute of Byzantine . . . Studies, 11; Venice, 1983).

Zachoder, Boris N., "Chorasan i obrazovanie gosudarstva Sel'džukov [Khorasan and the Formation of the State of the Seljuks]," *Voprosy istorii*, III-IV (1945), 119-141.

Zacour, Norman P., "The Children's Crusade," *H of C,* II (1962, 2nd ed. 1969), 325-342.

Zakythinos, Dionysios (here, Denis) A., *Le Despotat grec de Morée:* 1. *Histoire politique;* 2. *Vie et institutions* (2 vols., Paris and Athens, 1932-1953; rev. ed., London, 1975).

Zbinden, Nicolas, *Abendländische Ritter, Griechen und Türken im ersten Kreuzzug (Zur Problematik ihrer Begegnung)* (Texte und Forschungen zur byzantinisch-neugriechischen Philologie, 48; Athens, 1975).

Zepos, Pan J., *Droit et institutions franques du royaume de Chypre* (XVe Congrès international d'études byzantines: rapports et co-rapports: 5. Chypre dans le monde byzantin: no. 3. Droit et institutions franques du royaume de Chypre; Athens, 1976).

Zerbi, Pietro, *Papato, impero e respublica christiana dal 1197 al 1198* (Scienze storiche, 26; Milan, 1980).

Zerner-Chardavoine, Monique, *La Croisade albigeoise* (Collection archives, 75; Paris, 1979).

Zerner-Chardavoine, Monique, and Hélène Piéchon-Balloc, "La Croisade albigeoise, une revanche: des rapports entre la quatrième croisade et la croisade albigeoise," *Rev. hist.,* CCLXVII (1982), 3-18.

Ziada, Muhammad M., "The Mamluk Conquest of Cyprus in the Fifteenth Century," *Bulletin of the Faculty of Arts of the University of Egypt,* I-1 (1933), 90-113; II-1 (1934), 37-57.

Ziada, Mustafa M., "The Mamluk Sultans to 1293," *H of C,* II (1962, 2nd ed. 1969), 735–758.

Ziada, Mustafa M., "The Mamluk Sultans, 1291–1517," *H of C,* III (1975), 486–512.

Zimmert, Karl, "Der Friede von Adrianopel (Februar 1190)," *Byz. Z,* XI (1902), 303–320.

Zimmert, Karl, "Der deutsch-byzantinische Konflikt vom Juli 1189–Februar 1190," *Byz. Z,* XII (1903), 42–77.

Zöllner, Walter, *Geschichte der Kreuzzüge* (Berlin, 1977).

Zurita y Castro, Jeronimo de, ed., *Anales de la Corona de Aragón* (6 vols., Saragossa, 1610).

— British Committee on the Preservation and Restitution of Works of Art, Archives, and Other Material in Enemy Hands, *Works of Art in Greece, the Greek Islands and the Dodecanese: Losses and Survivals in the War* (London, 1946).

— *Il Regno normanno: Conferenze tenute in Palermo, per l'VIII centenario dell' incoronazione di Ruggero a re di Sicilia* (Biblioteca storica principato, 16; Messina and Milan, 1932).

— *La Reconquista española y la repoblación de pais* (Consejo superior de investigaciones científicas, Escuela de estudios medievales, Estudios, 25; Saragossa, 1951).

— *8 Centenario della morte di Ruggero II: Atti del Convegno internazionale di studi Ruggeriani (21–25 aprile 1954),* a cura del Comitato esecutivo (2 vols., Palermo, 1955).

— *Paix de Dieu et guerre sainte en Languedoc au XIIIe siècle* (Cahiers de Fanjeaux, 4; Toulouse, 1969).

— *1453–1953 Le cinq-centième anniversaire de la prise de Constantinople* (L'Hellénisme contemporain, 2-VII, Fascicule hors série; Athens, 1953).

— *Storia della cultura veneta* (Vicenza, 1976–).

Index of Topics for Secondary Works

CRUSADING THOUGHT

THE CRUSADES

EUROPE AND THE CRUSADES

THE CHRISTIAN EAST

Byzantium (general and to 1204)
    D. Baker, M. Beck 1978-1, Bon 1951, Brand 1968-2, Bréhier 1947, Bury 1930, Cahen
    1934, Chalandon 1900, Charanis 1952, 1955, Cognasso, Dagron, Daly, Danstrup,
    G. Day 1978, Diehl 1929, Dölger 1960, Friendley, Geanakoplos 1966, 1979, Grier-
    son, Guilland 1955, Hecht, Heisenberg, Hendrickx 1979, Hendy, Honigmann,
    Hussey 1950, 1962, 1966, Jurewicz, Kap-Herr, Karayannopulos 1956, 1958, Kindli-
    mann, Lamma, J. Laurent 1913, Leib 1924, Lemerle 1955, 1959, Lilie 1977, 1981,
    Neumann 1894, Nicol 1962, 1979-1, Ohnsorge 1931, 1947, 1958, Ostrogorski 1928,
    1931, 1954, 1956, 1958, 1963, Rouillard 1935, 1953, Schlumberger 1896, 1916, 1927,
    Setton 1953, Treitinger, Vasiliev 1935, 1952, Vasilievsky, Vollrath, Walker
The Greek states on the Adriatic and the Aegean 1204–1261
    Angold, Gardner, Loenertz 1973, Mompherratos, Nicol 1957, 1976, Pappadopou-
    los, Sinogowitz, Zakythinos
Byzantium 1261–1453
    Barker, Bosch, Chapman, Charanis 1951, Dade, Dennis 1960, 1982, Dölger 1934,
    Eszer, Geanakoplos 1959, 1975, Guilland 1953, Haussig, D. Jacoby 1981, Jugie
    1912, Laiou 1972, 1977, Nicol 1979-2, Pertusi 1976, Runciman 1965, *1453-1953*
Trebizond
    Bryer 1973, 1975, Fallmerayer, Janssens, W. Miller 1926, Vasiliev 1936
The Latin empire of Constantinople
    Balard 1978, Bernhard, Borsari 1966, Beyer 1976, Carile 1965, 1978-1,2, 1979, 1980,
    Dujčev 1979, Gerland 1905, Gjuzelev, Hendrickx 1969, 1970, 1971-1, 1976, 1977,
    Verlinden 1945, R. Wolff 1954-1, 1962, 1976
The Aegean islands
    Argenti 1958, 1979, Bury 1886, Fotheringham 1915, Hopf 1853, 1855, 1856, 1888,
    Loenertz 1962, 1965, 1975-2
Crete
    Borsari 1963, Cervellini, Gerland 1899, 1903, Jegerlehner 1903, 1904
Frankish Greece
    Bon 1949, 1953, 1969, Buchon 1840, 1843, 1845, Carile 1974, Cerone 1902, 1916,
    Cessi 1915, Cheetham, Gregorovius, Guardione, Hopf 1867, D. Jacoby 1963, 1967-1,
    1971, 1973, 1974, 1975-1,2, 1976, 1989, Kairophylas 1933, Lampros, Lemerle 1951,
    Loenertz 1943, 1970, Longnon 1942, 1946, 1949, 1950, 1962, 1965, Luttrell 1966-2,
    W. Miller 1908, 1921, Rösch, Setton 1966, 1974, 1975-2,3, Thiriet 1959, 1977, 1979,
    Topping 1975, 1977, Usseglio
The Catalan Company
    Banús y Comas, Burns 1954, Dujčev 1974, Giunta, Hillgarth 1975, D. Jacoby 1966,
    A. Lewis 1980, Olwer, Rubió y Lluch 1975, Sanchis Guillén, Setton 1948, 1975-1,
    Tramontana, Vallvé
Cyprus
    Banescu, Billioud, Edbury 1974, 1977-2, 1980, Furber, G. Hill, Iorga 1931, D. Ja-
    coby 1977-1, Luke, Mas Latrie 1844, 1852, 1879-1, Mogabgab, Richard 1947, 1952,
    1965-1, 1967, 1973-1, 1976-3, 1977-4, 1979-2, 1981, 1984, 1989, Rüdt de Collenberg
    1975, 1979-2, Zepos, Muhammad Ziada
Cilician Armenia
    Alishan 1888, 1893, Basmadjian, Boase 1978, Charanis 1963, Der Nersessian 1962,
    Dulaurier, Grousset 1947, Iorga 1930, V. Langlois, J. Laurent 1924-1, J. de Morgan,
    Richard 1986, Rüdt de Collenberg 1963, Tournebize

THE CHRISTIAN CHURCHES

PREACHING ORDERS AND MISSIONS

MILITARY ORDERS AND WARFARE

TRADE AND COMMERCE

Selective Index of Modern Co-authors, Editors, and Translators
and of Medieval Authors Not Listed in Alphabetical Position
in Sections H and J
(Z means name also appears in alphabetical position
in secondary section)

INDEX

COMPOSED BY METRICOMP, GRUNDY CENTER, IOWA, AND
CULTURA-WETTEREN, WETTEREN, BELGIUM
MANUFACTURED BY THOMSON-SHORE, INC., DEXTER, MICHIGAN
TEXT IS SET IN TIMES ROMAN, DISPLAY LINES IN GARAMOND

Library of Congress Cataloging-in-Publication Data
(Revised for v. 6)
Setton, Kenneth Meyer, 1914–
A history of the Crusades.
Includes bibliographical references and indexes.
Contents: v. 1. The first hundred years, edited by
M. W. Baldwin.—v. 2. The later Crusades, 1189–1311,
edited by R. L. Wolff and H. W. Hazard.—[etc.]—
v. 6. The impact of the crusades on Europe/edited
by Harry W. Hazard and Norman P. Zacour.
1. Crusades. I. Title.
D157.S482   940.1′8   68-9837
ISBN 0-299-10740-X (v. 6)